Account Number	Account Title

Liability Accounts

200	Accounts Payable
201	Notes Payable
202	Discount on Notes Payable
203	Loan Payable
204	Interest Payable
205	Vouchers Payable
206	Salaries Payable (or Wages Payable)
207	Sales Salaries Payable
208	Office Salaries Payable
209	Officers' Salaries Payable
210	Unearned Delivery Fees
211	Unearned Subscriptions
212	Unearned Ticket Fees
213	Unearned Laundry Fees
214	Unearned Management Fees
215	Unearned Rent
216	Unearned Service Fees
217	Unearned Commissions
218	Mortgage Note Payable
219	Travel Expenses Payable
220	Employees' Federal Income Taxes Payable
221	FICA Taxes Payable
222	Medical Insurance Premiums Payable
223	Employees' State Income Taxes Payable
224	Federal Unemployment Taxes Payable
225	State Unemployment Taxes Payable
226	Sales Tax Payable
227	Federal Excise Tax Payable
230	Estimated Product Warranty Payable
232	Estimated Property Taxes Payable
235	Other Liabilities
240	Commissions Payable

Stockholder's Equity Accounts

300	Capital Stock
310	Retained Earnings
320	Dividends

Revenue and Gain Accounts

400	Service Revenue
401	Ticket Revenue
402	Horse Boarding Fees Revenue
403	Concessions Revenue
404	Riding and Lesson Fees Revenue
405	Tennis Lesson Revenue
406	Campsite Rental Revenue
407	Rental Revenue

FINANCIAL ACCOUNTING

FINANCIAL ACCOUNTING

FIFTH EDITION

ROGER H. HERMANSON, PH.D., CPA
Regents Professor of Accounting
Ernst & Young–J. W. Holloway Memorial Professor
School of Accountancy
Georgia State University

JAMES DON EDWARDS, PH.D., CPA
J. M. Tull Professor of Accounting
J. M. Tull School of Accounting
University of Georgia

IRWIN

Homewood, IL 60430
Boston, MA 02116

Cover and part illustrations: Chris Sheban
Part opening photos: Kenji Kerins

© RICHARD D. IRWIN, INC., 1981, 1984, 1987, 1989, and 1992

Sponsoring editor: Ron M. Regis
Developmental editor: Diane M. Van Bakel
Special editing: Loretta Scholten
Project editor: Karen Smith
Production manager: Bette K. Ittersagen
Designer: Michael Warrell
Artist: Arcata Graphics
Compositor: Bi-Comp, Inc.
Color separator: Chapter One
Typeface: 10/12 Times Roman
Printer: Von Hoffmann Press

Library of Congress Cataloging-in-Publication Data

Hermanson, Roger H.
   Financial accounting / Roger H. Hermanson, James Don Edwards—
5th ed.
     p.   cm.
   Includes index.
   ISBN 0-256-08917-5   ISBN 0-256-11363-7 (Instructor's Edition)
   1. Accounting.   I. Edwards, James Don.   II. Title.
HF5635.H543   1992
657—dc20   91–23361

Printed in the United States of America
  2 3 4 5 6 7 8 9 0 VH 8 7 6 5 4 3 2

This Edition Is Dedicated to
RICHARD D. IRWIN
1905–1989
A Pioneer in Business Education

ABOUT THE AUTHORS

Professor Roger H. Hermanson, Ph.D., CPA, is Regents Professor of Accounting and Ernst & Young–J. W. Hollaway Memorial Professor at Georgia State University. He received his doctorate at Michigan State University in 1963 and is a CPA in Maryland and Georgia. Professor Hermanson taught and later served as chairperson of the Division of Accounting at the University of Maryland. He has authored or coauthored numerous articles for professional and scholarly journals and has coauthored numerous editions of several textbooks, including *Accounting Principles, Financial Accounting, Survey of Financial and Managerial Accounting, Auditing Theory and Practice,* and *Computerized Accounting with Peachtree Complete III.* He also has served on the editorial boards of the *Journal of Accounting Education, New Accountant, Accounting Horizons,* and *Management Accounting,* and currently serves as a reviewer for manuscripts submitted to *Accounting Horizons* and *Issues in Accounting Education.* Professor Hermanson is coeditor of the Trends in Accounting Education column for *Management Accounting.* He recently held the office of vice president of the American Accounting Association and served on its executive committee. He is also a member of the Institute of Management Accountants, the American Institute of Certified Public Accountants, and the Financial Executives Institute.

Professor Hermanson has been awarded two excellence in teaching awards, a doctoral fellow's award, and a Distinguished Alumni Professor award; and he was selected as the Outstanding Faculty Member for 1985 by the Federation of Schools of Accountancy. He has served as a consultant to many companies and organizations. He recently won the Literary Award given by the AWSCPA for his article, "Enforced Competition in the Accounting Profession: Does It Make Sense?" (published in *Accounting Horizons*). In 1990, Professor Hermanson was named Accounting Educator of the Year by the Georgia Society of CPAs.

Professor James Don Edwards, Ph.D., CPA, is the J. M. Tull Professor of Accounting at the University of Georgia. He is a graduate of Louisiana State University and has been inducted into the Louisiana State University Alumni Federation's Hall of Distinction. He received his M.B.A. from the University of Denver and his Ph.D. from the University of Texas and is a CPA in Texas and Georgia. He has served as a professor and chairman of the Department of Accounting and Financial Administration at Michigan State University, a professor and dean of the Graduate School of Business Administration at the University of Minnesota, and a Visiting Scholar at Oxford University in Oxford, England.

Professor Edwards is a past president of the American Accounting Association and a past national vice president and executive committee member of the Institute of Management Accountants. He has served on the board of directors of the American Institute of Certified Public Accountants and as chairman of the Georgia State Board of Accountancy. He was an original trustee of the Financial Accounting Foundation, the parent organization of the FASB, and a member of the Public Review Board of Arthur Andersen & Co.

He has published in *The Accounting Review, The Journal of Accountancy, The Journal of Accounting Research, Management Accounting,* and *The Harvard Business History Review.* He is also author of *History of Public Accounting in the United States.* He has served on various American Institute of Certified Public Accountants committees and boards, including the Objectives of Financial Statements Committee, Standards of Professional Conduct Committee, and the CPA Board of Examiners. He was the managing editor of the centennial issue of *The Journal of Accountancy.*

In 1974, Beta Alpha Psi, the National Accounting Fraternity, selected Professor Edwards for its first annual Outstanding Accountant of the Year award. This selection is made from industry, government, and educational leaders. In 1975, he was selected by the American Accounting Association as its "Outstanding Educator."

PREFACE

In April 1989 the major accounting firms issued a "white paper" calling for major changes in accounting education. The paper was entitled, *Perspectives on Education: Capabilities for Success in the Accounting Profession*." The firms made a five-year commitment of up to $4 million ". . . for the design and implementation of innovative curricula, new teaching methods, and supporting materials that will equip graduates with the capabilities for success in our profession."[1]

An Accounting Education Change Commission (AECC) was established under the leadership of the American Accounting Association to carry out the task of addressing necessary changes in accounting education. The AECC has made grants to several schools in support projects relating to the task.

Also, the Accounting Education Change Commission (AECC) has recommended some significant changes in higher education. The AECC stated:

The Accounting Education Change Commission (AECC) recommends a redirected focus for higher education—giving priority to teaching and curriculum and course development. The Commission urges accounting and business faculties to establish reward systems that reflect this priority. . . . [I]t is convinced that an increased emphasis on teaching and curriculum and course development is vital to the future of accounting education.[2]

The position of the AECC has been endorsed by the Executive Committee of the American Accounting Association, the American Institute of Certified Public Accountants, the Financial Executives Institute, the Institute of Management Accountants (formerly the National Association of Accountants), and the Federation of Schools of Accountancy.

In another of its publications, the AECC identified the capabilities needed by accounting graduates. Included among these capabilities were:

Ability to identify ethical issues and apply a value-based reasoning system to ethical questions.

Ability to apply accounting knowledge to solve real-world problems.[3]

The work of the AECC was influential in planning the Fifth Edition of our text. In keeping with recommendations of the AECC, we decided that the three major themes of this Fifth Edition of *Financial Accounting* should be **ethics, real world settings,** and **sound pedagogy.** Our goal is to help students apply sound accounting techniques ethically in real world settings. As in previous editions, we present the most modern accounting theory and practices. The text uses effective pedagogy by following a building-block approach in communicating this information. Later sections of this preface describe how we addressed this task.

This Fifth Edition is a major revision. In addition to a thorough updating of the content throughout the text, we have added new material, illustrations, real world information, and ethics cases. The production of the text is second to none, with its high-quality, four-color design, use of acetates for the work sheet in Chapter 4, photographs for part openers, and an expanded package of excellent supplements.

This text is for use in the first half of introductory accounting courses, whether conducted in colleges and universities or in business settings. *Financial Accounting* serves as a foundation for subsequent courses in accounting and business. We assume that students using this text have a limited understanding of business concepts. Thus, when new terms and concepts are introduced, they are defined, illustrated, and fully explained.

---

[1] Big-Eight Accounting Firms, *Perspectives on Education: Capabilities for Success in the Accounting Profession,* April 1989 (contained in Foreword).

[2] Accounting Education Change Commission, *Issues Statement No. 1,* "AECC Urges Priority for Teaching in Higher Education" (Bainbridge Island, WA, 1990), p. 1.

[3] Accounting Education Change Commission, *Position Statement No. One,* "Objectives of Education for Accountants" (Bainbridge Island, WA, 1990), pp. 7–8.

The two major reasons that the previous editions of *Financial Accounting* had such "staying power" with adopters were their readability and teachability. These two attributes combined to make it easy for students to learn from the text. In each revision, we continue to focus on improving these features even more. The result of our efforts is a text of which we are especially proud.

ORGANIZATION AND CONTENT

This section describes (1) the major changes in the organization of the text, (2) additions and changes in every chapter, and (3) significant additions and changes to specific chapters.

Major Changes in the Organization of the Text

☐ The topic of current liabilities was added to Chapter 9 to give more coverage of payables in that chapter.

☐ The "Plant Assets, Natural Resources; Intangibles" chapter was divided into two chapters (10 and 11) in this edition to improve the teachability of the important materials on these long-term assets.

☐ An important topic in accounting today, international accounting, now appears in an Appendix to Chapter 12. We believe that this coverage is the most complete of any introductory text. This Appendix will assist in meeting the accreditation standards of the American Assembly of Collegiate Schools of Business regarding internationalizing the curriculum.

☐ The chapter on "Measurement and Reporting of Stockholders' Equity—Paid-In Capital and Retained Earnings" was divided into two chapters (13 and 14) to improve their teachability. Many reviewers suggested this change.

☐ Chapter 17 of the previous edition, "Single Proprietorships and Partnerships," and Chapter 18 of the previous edition, "Payroll Accounting and Federal Income Taxes," were moved to Appendixes A and B, respectively, at the end of this text.

Additions and Changes Included in Every Chapter

In every chapter of the text, the following items were added: (1) "A Broader Perspective"—a boxed insert from current business literature, (2) "Ethics: A Closer Look"—a situation involving ethics, (3) "Self-Test"—true-false and multiple-choice questions with answers and explanations,

and (4) two or three new questions that relate to "A Broader Perspective" or to the financial statements in Appendix E at the end of the text.

Significant Additions and Changes to Specific Chapters

Changes were made in every chapter. However, several chapters deserve special mention.

In Chapter 2, "Recording Business Transactions," we added a new illustration to emphasize that transactions are entered in the journal before they are posted to the ledger. We also used a new format for recording each transaction: first show the journal entry; then show the posting to T-accounts; and finally, describe the effects of the transaction.

Chapter 4, "Completing the Accounting Cycle: Work Sheet, Closing Entries, and Classified Balance Sheet," now contains acetate overlays for the work sheet so students can better see the process of preparing a work sheet. We added a discussion of the operating cycle to help clarify the definitions of current assets and current liabilities.

In Chapter 6, "Measuring and Reporting Inventories," we expanded the description and illustrations of perpetual inventory procedure because of its increased use in practice.

Chapter 18, "Statement of Cash Flows," shows both the direct and indirect methods for determining "cash flows from operating activities," but the chapter emphasizes the indirect method as it did in the previous edition. We now present evidence that almost all companies use the indirect method. Also, the descriptions of items categorized as operating, financing, and investing activities have been substantially simplified (see Illustration 18.1).

KEY FEATURES

The key features of the text are described under the following headings: Ethics, Real World Emphasis, End-of-Chapter Material, and Pedagogy.

Ethics

Students have not been exposed to the variety of business situations in which ethical considerations exist. Throughout the text, we point out situations in which ethics should be a consideration and then hope students will "do the right thing" when those situations arise.

☐ A challenging and realistic case entitled "Ethics: A Closer Look" now appears in every chapter. In the previous edition, these cases were included in only seven chapters.

☐ Appendix F contains the codes of ethics of both the American Institute of Certified Public Accountants and the Institute of Management Accountants. We believe reading this appendix will help students understand the high standards of behavior expected of accountants.

Real World Emphasis

Without business experience, students sometimes lack a frame of reference in attempting to apply accounting concepts to business transactions. In this edition we sought to involve the student more in real world business applications as we introduced and explained the subject matter.

☐ Each chapter contains "A Broader Perspective." These situations, taken from articles in current business periodicals such as *Accounting Today, New Accountant, The Wall Street Journal, and Business Week,* relate to subject matter discussed in that chapter or present other useful information. These real world examples demonstrate the business relevance of accounting.

☐ New real world questions were added to most chapters. A new real world business decision case was added to some of the chapters.

☐ Appendix E at the end of the text includes excerpts from the annual reports of The Coca-Cola Company, Maytag Corporation, The Limited, Inc., and John H. Harland Company. Many of the real world questions, exercises, and business decision problems are based on these excerpts.

☐ Numerous illustrations adapted from *Accounting Trends & Techniques* show the frequency of use in business of various accounting techniques. Placed throughout the text, these illustrations give students real world data to consider while learning about different accounting techniques.

End-of-Chapter Material

We have included a vast amount of resource material for each chapter *within* the text from which the instructor may draw: (1) one of the largest selections of end-of-chapter questions, exercises, and problems available; (2) several comprehensive review problems that allow students to review all ma-

jor concepts covered to that point; and (3) from one to three business decision problems per chapter. Other key features regarding end-of-chapter material follow.

☐ A uniform chart of accounts appears on the inside covers of the text. This uniform chart of accounts is used consistently throughout the first 11 chapters. The use of general ledger applications software with this edition necessitated the creation of a uniform chart of accounts. We believe students will benefit from using the same chart of accounts for all homework problems in those chapters.

☐ Three comprehensive problems are included. Comprehensive review problems at the end of Chapters 4, 7, and 11 serve as "mini-practice sets" to test all material covered to that point.

☐ All end-of-chapter problem material (questions, exercises, problems, business decision problems, and comprehensive review problems) has been thoroughly revised. Each exercise and problem is identified with the learning objective(s) to which it relates.

☐ All end-of-chapter problem material has been traced back to the chapters to ensure that nothing is asked of a student that does not appear in the book. This feature was a strength of the previous edition, ensuring that instructors could confidently assign problems without having to check for applicability. Also, we took notes while teaching from the text and clarified problem and exercise instructions that seemed confusing to our students.

☐ Many of the problems, comprehensive review problems, and business decision problems in the text can be solved using newly developed software. Those problems that can be solved using *General Ledger Applications Software (GLAS),* developed by Jack E. Terry of Com-Source Associates, are identified in the margin with the symbol below.

This software package can also be used to solve the manual practice set.

Many other exercises, problems, and business decision problems can be solved using *Spreadsheet Applications Template Software (SPATS)* developed by Minta Berry. The exercises and problems solvable with *SPATS* are identified in the margin of the text with the following symbol:

Pedagogy

Students often come into financial accounting courses feeling anxious about learning the subject matter. Recognizing this apprehension, we studied ways to make learning easier and came up with some helpful ideas on how to make this edition work even better for students.

- Improvements in the text's organization reflect feedback from adopters, suggestions by reviewers, and a serious study of the learning process itself by the authors and editors. New subject matter is introduced only after the stage has been set by transitional paragraphs between topic headings. These paragraphs provide students with the reasons for proceeding to the new material and explain the progression of topics within the chapter.

- The Introduction now contains a section entitled "How to Study the Chapters in This Text," which should be very helpful to students.

- Each chapter has an "Understanding the Learning Objectives" section. These "summaries" enable the student to determine how well the Learning Objectives were accomplished. We were the first authors (1974) to ever include Learning Objectives in an accounting text. These objectives have been included at the beginning of the chapter, as marginal notes within the chapter, at the end of the chapter, and in supplements such as the Instructors' Resource Guide and the Study Guide. The objectives are also indicated in each exercise and problem.

- Demonstration problems and solutions are included for each chapter, and a different one appears for each chapter in the Study Guide. These demonstration problems help students to assess their own progress by showing them how problems that focus on the topic(s) covered in the chapter are worked before students do assigned homework problems.

- Key terms are printed in another color for emphasis. End-of-chapter glossaries contain the definition and the page number where the new term was first introduced and defined. Students can easily turn back to the original discussion and study the term's significance in context with the chapter material. A "New Terms Index"—an alphabetical list of all key terms in the text with page numbers—has been added at the end of the text.

- Each chapter includes a "Self-Test" consisting of true-false questions and multiple-choice questions. The answers and explanations appear at the end of the chapter.

- In the left-hand margin beside each exercise and problem, we have included a description of the requirements and the related Learning Objective(s). These descriptions let students know what they are expected to do in the problem.

- Throughout the text we use examples taken from everyday life to relate an accounting concept being introduced or discussed to students' experiences.

- Our research showed that for a financial accounting text today, an informal writing style and the active voice are more effective for learning than the formal style and passive voice. In this edition, we increased the use of informal style and the active voice.

- Wherever possible, we have added graphic illustrations to help explain accounting concepts to students. Learning is enhanced when a picture reinforces a verbal understanding of new material.

SUPPLEMENTS FOR THE INSTRUCTOR

A complete package of supplemental teaching aids contains all you need to efficiently and effectively teach the course.

The Instructor's Edition   This aid includes the text plus related material from the Instructor's Resource Guide. It is designed to help instructors prepare class assignments and lectures.

Instructor's Resource Guide   This guide now contains sample syllabi for both quarter- and semester-based courses. Revised for this edition, each chapter contains (1) a summary of major concepts; (2) learning objectives from the text; (3) space for the instructor's own notes; (4) an outline of the chapter with an indication of when each exercise can be worked; and (5) detailed lecture notes that also refer to specific end-of-chapter exercise and problem materials illustrating these concepts. Also included are (6) teaching transparencies masters and (7) a summary of the estimated completion time, learning objective(s), level of difficulty, and content of each exercise and problem that is useful in deciding which items to cover in class or to assign as homework.

Solutions Manual   The solutions manual contains suggested discussion points for each ethics case as well as detailed answers to questions, exercises, problems (Series A and B), business decision problems, and comprehensive review problems.

Solutions Transparencies   Acetate transparencies of solutions to all exercises and *all* problems with increased clarity are available free to adopters. These transparencies, while useful in many situations, are especially helpful when covering problems involving work sheets and in large classroom settings.

Teaching Transparencies   An expanded set of approximately 200 four-color acetates is available.

Achievement Tests, Series A, B, and C   Three series of achievement tests, prepared by Kenneth L. Coffey of Johnson County Community College, have been preprinted and are available in bulk to adopters. Series A and B consist of three one-hour exams, one one-hour midterm exam, and one two-hour final exam. Series C consists of a 20-minute exam for each chapter, one one-hour midterm exam, and one two-hour final exam.

Test Bank   The test bank, *expanded and revised significantly in this edition,* contains approximately 2,000 questions and problems to choose from in preparing examinations. This test bank contains true-false questions, multiple-choice questions, and short problems for each chapter. Questions and problems are generally arranged in the same sequence as the material in the text.

Computerized Testing Software   This improved microcomputer version of the Test Bank allows editing of questions; provides up to 99 different versions of each test; and allows question selection based on type of question or level of difficulty. The software is available on 5.25″ and 3.5″ disks.

Teletest   Teletest is an in-house testing service that will prepare your exams within 72 working hours after you phone the publisher.

Classroom Presentation Software   Computerized teaching transparencies are designed to support teaching the course using a computer, data display,

and an overhead projector. This software is available on 5.25″ and 3.5″ disks.

Videos   Videos may be used in the classroom or lab environment, as a check-out item in a video library, or for an on-campus closed-circuit television set-up.

The following items are intended for student use at the option of the instructor.

General Ledger Applications Software (GLAS)   Many problems, business decision problems, and comprehensive review problems (approximately 28) in the text can be solved using this newly developed software. GLAS is available on 5.25″ and 3.5″ disks and can be ordered with the text or as a separate item.

Spreadsheet Applications Template Software (SPATS)   Many additional exercises, problems, and business decision problems (approximately 85) can be solved using SPATS. It contains innovatively designed templates based on Lotus® 1-2-3® and includes a very effective tutorial for Lotus® 1-2-3®. SPATS is available on 5.25″ and 3.5″ disks. Upon adoption, this package is available to instructors for classroom or laboratory use.

Peachtree® Complete III™   This leading business accounting software is available for site license by contacting your Irwin representative. The version you will receive is the actual "full-featured" commercial software being sold to many U.S. companies.

Computerized Tutorials   These software packages, by Leland Mansuetti of Sierra College, include true-false questions and multiple-choice questions with explanations for both correct and incorrect answers by students. Upon adoption, these computerized tutorials are available to instructors for classroom or laboratory use. Tutorials are available on 5.25″ and 3.5″ disks.

SUPPLEMENTS FOR THE STUDENT

In addition to the text, the package of support items for the student includes the following:

Study Guide   Included for each chapter are learning objectives, a reference outline, a chapter review, and an additional demonstration problem and solution. Matching, true-false, and multiple-choice questions, completion questions and exercises, and solutions to all exercises and questions are also included.

Working Papers Working papers are available for completing assigned exercises, problems, business decision problems, and comprehensive review problems. In many instances, the working papers are partially filled in to reduce the "pencil pushing" required to solve the problems, yet the working papers are not so complete as to reduce the learning impact.

Check Figures A list of check figures gives key amounts for the A and B series problems, the business decision problems, and the comprehensive review problems in the text. Check figures are available in bulk, free to adopters.

Manual Practice Set *Rocky Mountain Clothes Company, Inc.*, revised by Frances H. Carpenter of the University of South Carolina, Columbia, illustrates special journals and includes a work sheet for a retailing company. This practice set can be used any time after Chapter 8.

Computer Supplements The following computer supplements are available:

☐ *Granite Bay Jet Ski, Inc., Level Two,* by Leland Mansuetti and Keith Weidkamp, both of Sierra College, is a computerized simulation that can be used with any Financial Accounting text using a corporate approach. Level Two is available on 5.25″ and 3.5″ disks and can be worked after Chapter 11.

☐ *It's Your Corporation,* by Donald V. Saftner of the University of Toledo, is a 3-month General Ledger practice set that takes the student through the accounting cycle each month. Additional transactions are added to increase the scope of coverage. This practice set may be used with problems from the text or to computerize manual practice sets. This practice set is available on 5.25″ and 3.5″ disks.

☐ *Electronic Spreadsheet Program (ESP),* a computerized spreadsheet package by John Wanlass of DeAnza College, can be used to solve many of the problems in the text and is also broad enough to be used in a separate computer accounting course. ESP is available on 5.25″ and 3.5″ disks.

We are indebted to many individuals for reviewing the manuscript of this edition. In addition to those listed on the acknowledgments page, we are especially indebted to colleagues and students at our respective universities for their helpful suggestions. Our families also provided needed support and showed great patience during the revision process.

Roger H. Hermanson
James Don Edwards

ACKNOWLEDGMENTS

Many instructors and students have made comments and suggestions that have helped us significantly in the preparation of this and all previous editions of this book. In particular we thank the following faculty who provided helpful suggestions for this edition:

Rubik Atamian, *The University of Texas, Pan American*

Martin E. Batross, *Franklin University*

Arnold Cirtin, *Ball State University*

David F. Fetyko, *Kent State University*

Jan Kraft, *Southwest State University*

Gorman W. Ledbetter, *East Carolina University*

Johanna D. Lyle, *Kansas State University*

Leo Ruggle, *Mankato State University*

Howard P. Sanders, *University of South Carolina, Columbia*

Ellen L. Sweatt, *DeKalb College*

Edwin D. Waters, *Tennessee Technological University*

Special thanks go to George T. Martin and members of the American Bankers Association for their helpful comments.

We also wish to thank the following individuals for their assistance: Ed Francisco, Thomas Gentry, Sally Stillwagon, Catherine Ware, and Patricia Wilson.

Special credit goes to Loretta Scholten for her outstanding editorial work on this and previous editions.

We would be remiss not to express a special thanks to the people in the Irwin editorial, production, and design departments: Lew Gossage, Loretta Haan, Bette Ittersagen, Nancy Lanum, Ron Regis, Karen Smith, Diane Van Bakel, and Michael Warrell. We also wish to thank task force members from the sales and marketing department: Jimmy Bartlett, Greg Bowman, Jeff Bubak, John Dorff, Diane Hilgers, Cindy Ledwith, Lynne Morrow, Rosalie Skears, Kurt Strand, and Scott Timian.

R.H.H.
J.D.E.

CONTENTS IN BRIEF

APPENDIXES

CONTENTS

PART I

THE BASIC ACCOUNTING MODEL
19

PART II

ACCOUNTING FOR ASSETS, LIABILITIES, AND STOCKHOLDERS' EQUITY
375

CHAPTER 14

CORPORATIONS: PAID-IN CAPITAL, RETAINED EARNINGS, DIVIDENDS, AND TREASURY STOCK 649

APPENDIXES

THE ACCOUNTING ENVIRONMENT

LEARNING OBJECTIVES

After studying this Introduction, you should be able to:

1. Define accounting.
2. Describe the functions performed by accountants.
3. Describe employment opportunities in accounting.
4. Differentiate between financial and managerial accounting.
5. Identify several organizations that have a role in the development of financial accounting standards.

You have embarked on the challenging and rewarding study of accounting—an old and time-honored discipline. History indicates that all developed societies require certain accounting records. Record-keeping in an accounting sense is thought to have begun about 4000 B.C.

The record-keeping, control, and verification problems of the ancient world had many characteristics similar to those we encounter today. For example, ancient governments also kept records of receipts and disbursements and used procedures that checked on the honesty and reliability of employees.

A study of the evolution of accounting suggests that accounting processes have developed primarily in response to business needs. Also, economic progress has affected the development of accounting processes. History shows that the higher the level of civilization, the more elaborate the accounting methods.

The emergence of double-entry bookkeeping was a crucial event in accounting history. In 1494, a Franciscan monk, Luca Pacioli, described the double-entry "Method of Venice" system in his text called *Summa de Arithmetica, Geometric, Proportion et Proportionalite* (Everything about Arithmetic, Geometry, and Proportion). Many consider Pacioli's *Summa* to be a reworked version of a manuscript that circulated among teachers and pupils of the Venetian school of commerce and arithmetic.

In accounting, the name "Luca Pacioli" will always be important for the contribution he made to accounting systems. At the age of 20, Pacioli became a tutor to three sons of a rich merchant. Later he lectured on mathematics and traveled throughout Italy. He also authored several books. Pacioli's friend Leonardo da Vinci helped prepare the drawings for one of Pacioli's books. Records indicate that Pacioli calculated the amount of bronze Leonardo needed for his large statue of the Duke. Thus, early civilizations recognized the accountant's special abilities in working with other professions to improve the overall quality of life.

Since Pacioli's days, the roles of accountants and professional accounting organizations have expanded in business and society. As professionals, accountants have a responsibility for performing public service above their commitment to personal economic gain. Complementing their obligation to society, accountants have analytical and evaluative skills needed in the solution of ever-growing world problems. The special abilities of accountants, their independence, and their ethical standards permit them to make a significant and unique contribution to business and areas of public interest.

You will probably find that of all the business knowledge you have acquired or will learn, the study of accounting will be the most useful. Your financial and economic decisions as a student and consumer involve accounting information. When you file income tax returns, accounting information will help determine your taxes payable. Understanding the discipline of accounting will also influence many of your future professional decisions. You cannot escape the effects of accounting information on your personal and professional life.

Every profit-seeking business organization that has economic resources, such as money, machinery, and buildings, uses accounting information. For this reason, accounting is called the *language of business*. Accounting also serves as the language providing financial information about not-for-profit organizations such as governments, churches, charities, fraternities, and hospitals. However, this text concentrates on the use of accounting as it relates to the business firm.

The accounting system of a profit-seeking business is an information system designed to provide relevant financial information on the resources of a business and the effects of the use of these resources. Information is relevant if it has some impact on a decision that must be made. Companies present this relevant information in their financial statements.[1] In preparing these statements, accountants consider the types of users of the information, such as owners and creditors, and decisions they make that require financial information.

As a background for studying accounting, this Introduction defines accounting and lists the functions accountants perform. You will learn about the employment opportunities in accounting and be able to differentiate between financial and managerial accounting. Accounting information must conform to certain standards. This Introduction discusses several prominent organizations contributing to these standards. As you continue your study of accounting in the chapters of this text, accounting—the language of business—will also become your language. You will also realize that you are constantly exposed to accounting information in your everyday life.

ACCOUNTING DEFINED

Objective 1

Define accounting

The American Accounting Association—one of the accounting organizations discussed later in this Introduction—defines accounting as **"the process of identifying, measuring, and communicating economic information to permit informed judgments and decisions by the users of the information."**[2] This information is primarily financial—stated in money terms. Accounting, then, is a measurement and communication process used to report on the activities of profit-seeking business organizations and not-for-profit organizations. As a measurement and communication process for business, accounting supplies information that permits informed judgments and decisions by users of the data.

The accounting process provides financial data for a broad range of individuals whose objectives in studying the data vary widely. Bank officials, for example, may study a company's financial statements to evaluate the company's ability to repay a loan. Prospective investors may compare accounting data from several companies to decide which company represents the best investment. Accounting also supplies management with significant financial data that are useful for decision making.

Reliable information is necessary before decision makers can make a sound decision involving the allocation of scarce resources. In decision making, you always have alternatives—even if one of the alternatives is to take no action or to delay action. Accounting information is valuable because decision makers can use it to evaluate the financial consequences of each alternative. Accountants eliminate the need for a "crystal ball" to estimate the future. They can reduce uncertainty by using professional judgment to quantify the future financial impact of various alternatives.

Although accounting information plays a significant role within the organization in reducing uncertainty, it also provides financial data for external purposes. To do this, accountants provide information about a company's financial resources and its performance. This information tells how a company's management has discharged its responsibility for protecting and managing the company's resources. Owners have the right to know how a company is managing their investments. In fulfilling this obligation, accountants prepare financial statements such

---

[1] When first studying any discipline, students encounter new terms. Usually these terms are set in boldface color and defined at their first occurrence. However, sometimes it is more feasible not to define a term at its first occurrence. This is true with the term *financial statements*. This term is defined later in the Introduction and set in boldface color. The boldface color terms are also listed and defined at the end of this Introduction, or in the case of the chapters, at the end of the chapter. After the definition of the term in the term list, a page number is given in italics indicating where the term is discussed in the chapter.

[2] American Accounting Association, *A Statement of Basic Accounting Theory* (Evanston, Ill., 1966), p. 1.

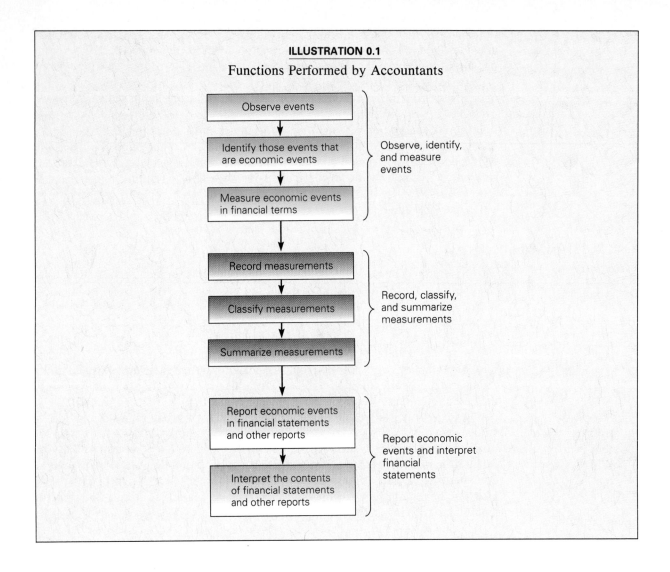

ILLUSTRATION 0.1

Functions Performed by Accountants

Observe events

Identify those events that are economic events

Measure economic events in financial terms

} Observe, identify, and measure events

Record measurements

Classify measurements

Summarize measurements

} Record, classify, and summarize measurements

Report economic events in financial statements and other reports

Interpret the contents of financial statements and other reports

} Report economic events and interpret financial statements

as an income statement, a statement of retained earnings, a balance sheet, and a statement of cash flows. In addition, they prepare tax returns for federal and state governments as well as fulfill other governmental filing requirements.

Accounting is often confused with bookkeeping. Bookkeeping is a mechanical process that records the routine economic activities of a business. Accounting includes bookkeeping but goes well beyond it in scope. Accountants analyze and interpret financial information, prepare financial statements, conduct audits, design accounting systems, prepare special business and financial studies, prepare forecasts and budgets, and provide tax services.

Specifically the accounting process consists of the following groups of functions (Illustration 0.1):

Objective 2
Describe the functions performed by accountants

1. Accountants **observe** many events (or activities) and **identify** and **measure** in financial terms (dollars) those events considered evidence of economic activity. (These three functions are often collectively referred to as *analyze*.) The purchase and sale of goods and services are examples of economic events.

2. Next, the economic events are **recorded, classified** into meaningful groups, and **summarized.**

3. Accountants **report** on economic events (or business activity) by preparing financial statements and special reports. Often accountants are asked to **interpret** these statements and reports for various groups such as management, investors, and creditors. Interpretation may involve determining how the business is performing compared to prior years and other similar businesses.

EMPLOYMENT OPPORTUNITIES IN ACCOUNTING

Objective 3
Describe employment opportunities in accounting

As stated earlier, accounting is an old profession. Business transactions have been recorded for centuries. However, only during the last half-century has accounting gained the same professional status as the medical and legal professions. Today, the accountants that practice their profession in the United States number well over a million. In addition, several million people hold accounting-related positions. Typically, accountants provide services in various branches of accounting. These branches include public accounting, management (industrial) accounting, governmental or other not-for-profit accounting, and higher education. The future for employment in accounting is very promising. You may want to consider accounting as a career.

Public Accounting

Public accounting firms offer professional accounting and related services for a fee to companies, other organizations, and individuals. An accountant may become a Certified Public Accountant (CPA). A CPA is a person who has passed an examination prepared and graded by the American Institute of Certified Public Accountants (AICPA). In addition, CPA candidates must meet other requirements, which include obtaining a state license. These requirements vary by state. A number of states require a CPA candidate to have completed certain accounting courses; worked a certain number of years in public accounting, industry, or government; and lived in that state a certain length of time before taking the CPA examination.

After a candidate passes the CPA examination, some states (called one-tier states) insist that the candidate meet all requirements before the state grants the CPA certificate and license to practice. Other states (called two-tier states) issue the CPA certificate immediately after the candidate passes the exam. However, these states issue the license to practice only after all other requirements have been met. CPAs who want to renew their license to practice must "stay current" by engaging in continuing professional education programs. They must also document this education to the state board of accountancy, the state CPA society, and (in the future) the American Institute of Certified Public Accountants. A person cannot claim to be a CPA and offer the services normally provided by a CPA unless that person holds an active license to practice.

Until recently, the public accounting profession in the United States consisted of the "Big-Eight" international CPA firms, several national firms, many regional firms, and numerous local firms. The Big-Eight firms included Arthur Andersen & Co.; Arthur Young & Co.; Coopers & Lybrand; Deloitte, Haskins & Sells; Ernst & Whinney; Peat Marwick Main & Co.; Price Waterhouse & Co.; and Touche Ross & Co. These public accounting firms provided auditing, tax, and management advisory (or consulting) services. Recently some of the Big-Eight firms have merged with non-Big-Eight firms or other Big-Eight firms to become the "Big-Six."

In 1987, KMG Main Hurdman and Peat Marwick Mitchell became the first major merger of CPA firms forming the world's largest accounting firm at that time. Perhaps it was the successful completion of this merger that persuaded other international firms to combine their practices. In 1989 Ernst & Whinney and

Arthur Young merged into Ernst & Young and moved ahead of KPMG Peat Marwick in size. Deloitte, Haskins & Sells and Touche Ross merged their two firms into a new firm called Deloitte & Touche. One of the primary motivations for those mergers was to be large enough to serve large international clients as the economy becomes more global.

Illustration 0.2 shows the ranking of the Big-Six CPA firms by approximate size of their U.S. revenues for 1990. As you can see in the illustration, the ranking would differ if the firms were ranked by number of offices, number of partners, or number of professionals.

Auditing A business seeking a loan or attempting to have its securities traded on a stock exchange usually must provide financial statements to support its request. Users of a company's financial statements are more confident that the company is presenting its statements fairly when a CPA has audited the statements. For this reason, companies hire CPA firms to conduct an examination (independent audit) of their accounting and related records. Independent auditors of the CPA firm check some of the company's records by contacting external sources. For example, the accountant may contact a bank to verify the cash balances of the client. After completing a company audit, independent auditors are able to give an independent auditor's opinion or report. (For an example of an auditor's opinion, see The Coca-Cola Company annual report in Appendix E at the end of the text.) This report states whether or not the company's financial statements fairly (equitably) report the economic performance and financial condition of the business. As you will learn in the section "Management (or Industrial) Accounting," auditors **within** a business also conduct audits. However, these audits are not independent audits.

Tax Services CPAs often provide expert advice on tax planning and the preparation of federal, state, and local tax returns. The objective in preparing tax returns is to use legal means to minimize the amount of taxes paid. Almost every major business decision has a tax impact. Tax planning helps clients know the tax effects of each financial decision.

Management Advisory (or Consulting) Services The management advisory services area is the fastest growing service area for most large CPA firms and for many smaller CPA firms. Management frequently identifies projects for which it decides to retain the services of a CPA. For example, management may seek help in selecting new computer hardware and software. Also, the auditing services provided by CPAs often result in suggestions to clients on how to improve their operations. For example, CPAs might suggest improvements in the design and installation of an accounting system, the electronic processing of accounting data, inventory control, budgeting, or financial planning. In addition, a relatively fast-growing service area provided by CPAs is financial planning, often for the executives of audit clients.

Management (or Industrial) Accounting

In contrast to public accountants, who provide accounting services for many clients, management accountants provide accounting services for a single business. Some companies employ only one management accountant, while other companies employ a large number. In a company with several management accountants, the person in charge of the accounting activity is often called the controller or chief financial officer.

Management accountants may or may not be CPAs. If these accountants pass an examination prepared and graded by the Institute of Certified Management

ILLUSTRATION 0.2

The Big-Six CPA Firms—Ranked by Approximate
1990 U.S. Revenues*

Firm Name	Location of Headquarters	Approximate U.S. Revenues	No. of Offices	No. of Partners	No. of Professionals
Ernst & Young	New York	$2,195,000,000	123	2,054	18,653
Arthur Andersen	Chicago	1,993,000,000	82	1,268	17,740
KPMG Peat Marwick	Montvale, N.J.	1,929,000,000	132	1,900	14,400
Deloitte & Touche	Wilton, Conn.	1,900,000,000	126	1,713	15,500
Coopers & Lybrand	New York	1,250,000,000	98	1,253	16,000
Price Waterhouse	New York	1,100,000,000	115	920	9,430

* This information is based on "An Annual Survey of America's Largest Accounting Firms" reported in *Accounting Today*. The revenues for Ernst & Young, Coopers & Lybrand, and Deloitte & Touche were estimated by *Accounting Today*. Reprinted by permission from *Accounting Today*, September 24, 1990, p. 56. Copyright Lebhar-Friedman, Inc., 475 Park Avenue, New York, NY 10022.

Accountants (ICMA) and meet certain other requirements, they become Certified Management Accountants (CMAs). The ICMA is an affiliate of the Institute of Management Accountants, an organization primarily consisting of management accountants employed in private industry.

Many management accountants specialize in one particular area of accounting. For example, some may specialize in measuring and controlling costs, others in budgeting—the development of plans for future operations—and still others in financial accounting and reporting. Many management accountants become specialists in the design and installation of computerized accounting systems. Other management accountants are internal auditors who conduct internal audits. Their job is to see that the company's divisions and departments follow the policies and procedures of management. This last group of management accountants may earn the designation of Certified Internal Auditor (CIA). The Institute of Internal Auditors (IIA) grants the CIA certificate to accountants after they have successfully completed an examination prepared and graded by the Institute and have met certain other requirements.

Governmental and Other Not-for-Profit Accounting

Many accountants, including CPAs, work in governmental and other not-for-profit accounting. They have essentially the same educational background and training as accountants in public accounting and management (or industrial) accounting.

Governmental agencies at the federal, state, and local levels employ governmental accountants. Often the duties of these accountants relate to tax revenues and expenditures. For example, Internal Revenue Service employees use their accounting background in reviewing tax returns and investigating tax fraud. Government agencies that regulate business activity, such as a state public service commission that regulates public utilities (e.g., telephone company, electric company, etc.) employ accountants. These agencies often employ governmental accountants who can review and evaluate the utilities' financial statements and rate increase requests. Also, FBI agents trained as accountants find their accounting background useful in investigating criminals involved in illegal business activities, such as drugs or gambling.

Not-for-profit organizations such as churches, charities, fraternities, and universities need accountants to record and account for funds received and disbursed. Even though these agencies do not have a profit motive, they should operate efficiently and use resources effectively.

A BROADER PERSPECTIVE

PROJECTION PUTS DEMAND FOR CPAs UP 40% BY 2000

Washington—Over the next decade, the demand for accountants and auditors will rise much faster than in the recent past, according to a government forecast.

The Bureau of Labor Statistics (BLS) report estimated total 1986 U.S. employment for accountants at 945,000. It concluded that an additional 376,000 accountants will be needed by the year 2000.

Although the BLS study also forecast strong growth for other disciplines, none match the 40 percent increase anticipated for accountants and auditors.

The demand for lawyers, for example, is expected to climb 36 percent. The need for physicians is projected to rise 38 percent; for engineers, 32 percent; for pharmacists, 24 percent; and for teachers, 19 percent.

"As the number of businesses increases, more accountants and auditors will be needed to set up books, prepare taxes, and provide management advice," the report said.

As a result of this upsurge in demand, BLS officials anticipate "favorable opportunities for those with a bachelor's or higher degree in accounting."

In sharp contrast to the bullish projections for accountants, BLS predicts very little growth ahead for "bookkeepers and accounting clerks."

The number of jobs in these occupations will rise only 4 percent, or 92,000, from the 2,116,000 such jobs that existed in 1986, the report said.

"Although the volume of business transactions is expected to grow rapidly, little change is expected in employment due to the increased use of computers," BLS said.

Nevertheless, the report concluded that opportunities for bookkeepers and accounting clerks "will remain numerous because the [occupational category] is large."

The government predicted that the demand for financial managers will climb 24 percent to 792,000 in 2000.

Professions On the Rise

The need for many professionals is expected to rise by the year 2000. This chart shows, in percent, the probable growth in demand for the following professions.

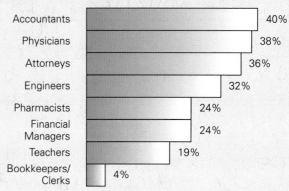

Source: U.S. Bureau of Labor Statistics

According to the government forecasters, "the need for sound financial data brought about by increasing competition, changing laws on taxes and other financial matters, growing emphasis on the accuracy of financial data, and the increasing variety and complexity of financial services should spur demand for financial managers."

Only average growth is expected in the number of these managers during the 1990s because the use of computers should make them more productive, BLS said.

Employment prospects "will be best for those familiar with a wide range of financial services," the study reported.

Reprinted by permission from *Accounting Today*, October 23, 1989, p. 14. Copyright Lebhar-Friedman, Inc., 425 Park Avenue, New York, NY 10022.

Higher Education   Approximately 10,000 accountants are employed in higher education. The activities of these academic accountants include teaching accounting courses, conducting scholarly and applied research and publishing the results, and performing service for the institution and the community. Faculty positions exist in two-year colleges, four-year colleges, and universities with graduate programs. A significant shortage of accounting faculty will probably develop due to the anticipated retirement in the late 1990s of many current faculty members. Starting salaries will continue to rise significantly because of the shortage. You may want to speak with some of your professors about the advantages and disadvantages of pursuing an accounting career in higher education.

FINANCIAL ACCOUNTING VERSUS MANAGERIAL ACCOUNTING

Objective 4

Differentiate between financial and managerial accounting

An accounting information system provides data to decision makers outside the business and inside the business. Decision makers **outside** the business **are affected in some way by the performance of the business.** Decision makers **inside** the business **are responsible for the performance of the business.** For this reason, accounting is divided into two categories: financial accounting and managerial accounting. This section discusses the distinction between financial and managerial accounting.

Financial Accounting

Financial accounting information is intended primarily for external use. Managerial accounting information is intended for internal use. Stockholders and creditors are examples of people outside a company who want and need financial accounting information. These outside persons decide on matters pertaining to the entire company, such as whether to extend credit to a company or to invest in a company. Consequently, financial accounting information relates to the company as a whole. Managerial accounting, on the other hand, serves the needs of those inside the company and focuses on the parts or segments of the company.

Financial statements convey financial accounting information to external users. Management accountants in a company prepare these financial statements. Thus, management accountants must be knowledgeable concerning financial accounting and reporting. The financial statements are the representations of management, not the CPA firm that performs the audit.

Several groups of individuals are external users of accounting information. Each group has different interests in the company and wants answers to certain questions. The groups and some of their possible questions are:

1. **Owners and prospective owners.** Has the company earned satisfactory income on its total investment? Should an investment be made in this company? Should the present investment be increased, decreased, or retained at the same level? Can the company install costly pollution control equipment and still be profitable?

2. **Creditors and lenders.** Should a loan be granted to the company? Will the company be able to pay its debts as they become due?

3. **Employees and their unions.** Does the company have the ability to pay increased wages? Is the company financially able to provide long-term employment for its work force?

4. **Customers.** Does the company offer useful products at fair prices? Will the company survive long enough to honor its product warranties?

5. **Governmental units.** Is the company (such as a local public utility) charging a fair rate for its services?

6. **General public.** Is the company providing useful products and gainful employment for citizens without causing serious environmental problems?

General-purpose financial statements provide much of the information needed by external users of financial accounting. These financial statements are formal reports providing information on a company's financial position, cash inflows and outflows, and the results of operations. Many companies publish these statements in an annual report. The annual report (see The Coca-Cola Company annual report in Appendix E at the end of the text) also contains the independent auditor's opinion as to the fairness of the financial statements, as well as information about the company's activities, products, and plans.

Financial accounting information is historical in nature, reporting on what has happened in the past. To facilitate comparisons between companies, this information must conform to certain accounting standards or principles called generally accepted accounting principles (GAAP). These generally accepted accounting principles for business or governmental organizations have been developed through accounting practice or have been established by an authoritative organization. You will learn about several of these authoritative organizations in the next major section of the chapter.

Managerial Accounting

Managerial accounting information is intended for internal use and provides special information for the managers of a company. The kind of information used by managers may range from broad, long-range planning data to detailed explanations of why actual costs varied from cost estimates.

Managerial accounting information should:

1. Relate to the part of the company for which the manager is responsible. For example, a production manager will want information on costs of production but not on advertising.
2. Involve planning for the future. For instance, a budget may be prepared that shows financial plans for the coming year.
3. Meet two tests: the accounting information must be useful (relevant) and must not cost more to gather and process than it is worth.

The purpose of managerial accounting is to generate information that a manager can use to make sound decisions. Internal management decisions can be classified into four major types:

1. **Financial decisions**—deciding what amounts of capital (funds) are needed to run the business and whether these funds are to be secured from owners or creditors. **Capital** used in this sense means **money** to be used by the company to purchase resources such as machinery and buildings and to pay expenses of conducting the business.
2. **Resource allocation decisions**—deciding how the total capital of a company is to be invested, such as the amount to be invested in machinery.
3. **Production decisions**—deciding what products are to be produced, by what means, and when.
4. **Marketing decisions**—setting selling prices and advertising budgets; determining the location of a company's markets and how to reach them.

DEVELOPMENT OF FINANCIAL ACCOUNTING STANDARDS

Objective 5

Identify several organizations that have a role in the development of financial accounting standards

Several organizations are influential in the establishment of generally accepted accounting principles (GAAP) for business or governmental organizations. These are the American Institute of Certified Public Accountants, the Financial Accounting Standards Board, the Governmental Accounting Standards Board, the Securities and Exchange Commission, the American Accounting Association, the Financial Executives Institute, and the Institute of Management Accountants. Each organization has contributed in a different way to the development of GAAP.

American Institute of Certified Public Accountants (AICPA)

The American Institute of Certified Public Accountants (AICPA) is a professional organization of CPAs. Many of these CPAs are in public accounting practice. Until recent years, the AICPA was the dominant organization in the development of accounting standards. In a 20-year period ending in 1959, the AICPA Committee on Accounting Procedure issued 51 *Accounting Research Bulletins* recommending certain principles or practices. From 1959 through 1973, the committee's successor, the Accounting Principles Board (APB), issued 31 numbered *Opinions* that CPAs generally are required to follow. Through its monthly magazine, the *Journal of Accountancy,* its research division, and its other divisions and committees, the AICPA continues to influence the development of accounting standards and practices. Two of its committees—the Accounting Standards Committee and the Auditing Standards Committee—are particularly influential in providing input to the Financial Accounting Standards Board (the current rule-making body) and to the Securities and Exchange Commission and other regulatory agencies.

Financial Accounting Standards Board (FASB)

In 1973, an independent, seven-member, full-time Financial Accounting Standards Board (FASB) replaced the **Accounting Principles Board (APB).** The FASB has issued numerous *Statements of Financial Accounting Standards.* The old *Accounting Research Bulletins* and *Accounting Principles Board Opinions* are still effective unless specifically superceded by a Financial Accounting Standards Board Statement. The FASB is the *private sector* organization now responsible for the development of new financial accounting standards.

The Emerging Issues Task Force of the FASB interprets official pronouncements for general application by accounting practitioners. The conclusions of this task force must also be followed in filings with the Securities and Exchange Commission.

Governmental Accounting Standards Board (GASB)

In 1984, the Governmental Accounting Standards Board (GASB) was established with a full-time chairperson and four part-time members. The GASB issues statements on accounting and financial reporting in the governmental area. This organization is the *private sector* organization now responsible for the development of new governmental accounting concepts and standards. The GASB also has the authority to issue interpretations of these standards.

Securities and Exchange Commission (SEC)

Created under the Securities and Exchange Act of 1934, the Securities and Exchange Commission (SEC) is a government agency that administers a number of important acts dealing with the interstate sale of securities (stocks and bonds). The SEC has the authority to prescribe accounting and reporting practices for companies under its jurisdiction. This includes virtually every major U.S. business corporation. Instead of exercising this power, the SEC has adopted a policy of working closely with the accounting profession, especially the FASB, in the development of accounting standards. The SEC indicates to the FASB the accounting topics it believes the FASB should address.

American Accounting Association (AAA)

Consisting largely of accounting educators, the American Accounting Association (AAA) has sought to encourage research and study at a theoretical level into the concepts, standards, and principles of accounting. One of its quarterly magazines, *The Accounting Review,* carries many articles reporting on scholarly accounting research. Another quarterly journal, *Accounting Horizons,* reports on more practical matters directly related to accounting practice. A third journal, *Issues in Accounting Education,* contains articles relating to accounting education matters. Students may join the AAA as associate members by contacting the American Accounting Association, 5717 Bessie Drive, Sarasota, Florida 34233.

Financial Executives Institute (FEI)

The Financial Executives Institute is an organization established in 1931 whose members are primarily financial policy-making executives. Slightly more than 13,000 financial officers, representing approximately 7,000 companies in the United States and Canada, comprise its membership. Through its Committee on

Corporate Reporting (CCR) and other means, the FEI is very effective in representing the views of the private financial sector to the FASB and to the Securities and Exchange Commission and other regulatory agencies.

Institute of Management Accountants (IMA)

The Institute of Management Accountants is an organization with approximately 75,000 members, consisting of management accountants in private industry and CPAs and academics who are interested in management accounting. The primary focus of the organization is on the use of management accounting information for internal decision making. However, management accountants prepare the financial statements for external users. Thus, through its Management Accounting Practices (MAP) Committee and other means, the IMA provides input on financial accounting standards to the Financial Accounting Standards Board and to the Securities and Exchange Commission and other regulatory agencies.

Other Organizations

Many other organizations such as the Financial Analysts Federation (comprised of investment advisors and investors), the Security Industry Associates (comprised of investment bankers), and CPA firms have committees or task forces that respond to Exposure Drafts of proposed FASB Statements issued by the FASB. Their reactions are in the form of written statements sent to the FASB and testimony given at FASB hearings. Many individuals also make their reactions known to the FASB in the same manner.

ETHICAL BEHAVIOR OF ACCOUNTANTS

Several accounting organizations have formulated codes of ethics that govern the behavior of their members. For instance, both the American Institute of Certified Public Accountants and the Institute of Management Accountants have formulated such codes. We have included the codes of ethics of these two organizations in Appendix F at the end of the text. By examining these codes, you will gain some understanding of the expectations that exist regarding the ethical behavior of accountants. Many business firms have also developed codes of ethics for their employees to follow.

Ethical behavior involves more than merely making sure you are not violating a code of ethics. Most of us sense what is right and wrong. Yet the "get rich quick" opportunities that arise tempt many of us. Almost any day, you can read in the newspaper about public officials and business leaders who did not "do the right thing." Greed ruled over their sense of right and wrong. These individuals followed slogans such as: "Get yours while the getting is good"; "Do unto others before they do unto you"; and "You have only done wrong if you get caught." More appropriate slogans might be: "If it seems too good to be true, it usually is"; "There are no free lunches"; and the golden rule, "Do unto others as you would have them do unto you."

An accountant's most valuable asset is his or her reputation. Those who take the *high road* of ethical behavior receive praise, honor, and are sought out for their advice and services. They also like themselves and what they represent. Occasionally, accountants do take the *low road* and suffer the consequences. They sometimes find their name in print in *The Wall Street Journal* in an unfavorable light, and former friends and colleagues look down on them. Occasionally, these individuals are removed from the profession. Fortunately, the accounting

ETHICS	Beth Stone is an accounting major at State University. She has a 3.8 grade-point average and is a member of Beta Alpha Psi, the national accounting fraternity. She has

ETHICS

A CLOSER LOOK

Beth Stone is an accounting major at State University. She has a 3.8 grade-point average and is a member of Beta Alpha Psi, the national accounting fraternity. She has decided to pursue a career in public accounting and has had her "heart set" on being employed by CPA Firm A after graduation because it has many clients in the high-tech industry. In a conversation with the head recruiter from Firm A, Beth was told that the firm had overhired the year before and probably would be unable to make her an offer at this time. Beth decided to interview with many other CPA firms and finally accepted a position with Firm B at a salary of $30,000 plus overtime pay. Although she had wanted to audit companies in the high-tech industry, Firm B has few clients in that industry. Firm B does have clients in the health care industry, which is Beth's second favorite industry.

Two months after Beth had accepted the offer from Firm B and before she had started working, she received an urgent call from the recruiter at Firm A. He was unaware that she had already accepted another offer and said the firm had recently experienced some unexpected turnover in its staff. As a result, he was in a position to make her an offer of $31,000 plus overtime pay. He could also guarantee that she would be able to specialize in the high-tech industry and would be working on interesting jobs with some talented people.

Required
a. What are Beth's options?
b. What should Beth do?

profession has many leaders who have taken the high road, gained the respect of friends and colleagues, and become role models for all of us to follow.

In each chapter in the text we have included an ethics case entitled, "A Closer Look." We think you will benefit from being exposed to the *situational ethics* contained in these cases.

HOW TO STUDY THE CHAPTERS IN THIS TEXT

The authors recommend that you proceed as follows in studying each chapter:

1. Begin each chapter by reading the Learning Objectives at the beginning of the chapter.
2. Read the section, "Understanding the Learning Objectives," at the end of the chapter for a preview of the chapter content.
3. Read the chapter content. Notice that the Learning Objectives appear in the margins at the appropriate places in the chapter. Each of the exercises at the end of each chapter identifies the learning objective(s) to which it pertains. If you learn best by reading about a concept and then working a short exercise that illustrates that concept, you will want to work the exercises as you read the chapter. Forms are provided in the Working Papers supplement for working these exercises.
4. Reread the section "Understanding the Learning Objectives" to determine if you have achieved each objective.
5. Study the New Terms to see if you understand each term. If you do not understand a certain term, refer back to the page indicated to read about the term in its original context.

6. Take the Self-Test and then check your answers with the correct answers at the end of the chapter.

7. Work the Demonstration Problem to further reinforce your understanding of the chapter content. Then compare your solution to the correct solution, which follows immediately.

8. Read ''A Closer Look,'' the ethics case, and think about how you would respond to the questions asked.

9. Look over the questions at the end of the chapter and think about an answer to each one. If you cannot answer a particular question, refer back into the chapter for the needed information.

10. Work at least some of the Exercises at the end of the chapter.

11. Work any of the Problems or Business Decision Problems assigned by your instructor, using the forms provided in the Working Papers supplement.

12. Work the Study Guide for the chapter. The Study Guide is a supplement that contains for each chapter Learning Objectives; Reference Outline; Chapter Review; Demonstration Problem and Solution (different than in the text); Matching, Completion, True-False, and Multiple-Choice Questions; and Solutions to all Questions and Exercises in the Study Guide.

If you perform each of the above steps for each chapter, you should do well in the course. A free computerized Tutorial is also available that can be used to further test your understanding. Ask your instructor about its availability at your school. A knowledge of accounting will serve you well regardless of the career you decide to pursue.

UNDERSTANDING THE LEARNING OBJECTIVES

1. Define accounting.
   □ Accounting is ''the process of identifying, measuring, and communicating economic information to permit informed judgments and decisions by the users of the information.''

2. Describe the functions performed by accountants.
   □ Accountants observe many events (or activities) and identify and measure in financial terms (dollars) those events considered evidence of economic activity.
   □ The economic events are recorded, classified into meaningful groups, and summarized.
   □ Accountants report on economic events (or business activity) by preparing financial statements and special reports. Often accountants are asked to interpret these statements and reports for various groups such as management, investors, and creditors.

3. Describe employment opportunities in accounting.
   □ An accountant may be employed in public accounting and specialize in auditing, tax, or management advisory (or consulting) services.
   □ Management accountants are employed by a single company and may specialize in measuring and controlling costs, budgeting, computerized accounting systems, internal auditing, or some other function.
   □ Other accountants are employed in government agencies or other not-for-profit organizations such as churches, charities, fraternities, and organizations.

□ Universities and colleges hire accountants (CPAs, CMAs, and CIAs who usually have a graduate degree) to teach accounting to students and conduct research on accounting issues.

4. Differentiate between financial and managerial accounting.

□ Financial accounting information is intended primarily for external use; it provides information for groups such as owners and prospective owners, creditors and lenders, employees and their unions, customers, governmental units, and the general public.

□ Managerial accounting information is intended for internal use; it provides special information for the managers of the company.

5. Identify several organizations that have a role in the development of financial accounting standards.

□ American Institute of Certified Public Accountants (AICPA)—made up of persons holding the CPA certificate. The Accounting Principles Board (APB) was under the AICPA.

□ Financial Accounting Standards Board (FASB)—issues FASB statements, which are the *rules* of financial accounting.

□ Governmental Accounting Standards Board (GASB)—issues GASB statements, which are the *rules* of governmental accounting.

□ Securities and Exchange Commission (SEC)—a government agency that has legislative authority over financial accounting standards. To date, the SEC has allowed the private sector to set the standards.

□ American Accounting Association (AAA)—an organization consisting largely of accountants who teach and engage in research.

□ Financial Executives Institute (FEI)—an organization whose members are primarily financial policy-making executives.

□ Institute of Management Accountants (IMA)—an organization consisting of management accountants in private industry and CPAs and academics who are interested in management accounting.

NEW TERMS

Academic accountants Accountants in the academic segment of the accounting profession who teach accounting courses, conduct scholarly and applied research and publish the results, and perform service for the institution and the community. *8*

Accounting "The process of identifying, measuring, and communicating economic information to permit informed judgments and decisions by the users of the information." *3*

Accounting Principles Board (APB) An organization created in 1959 by the AICPA and empowered to speak for it on matters of accounting principle; replaced in 1973 by the Financial Accounting Standards Board. *11*

American Accounting Association (AAA) A professional organization of accountants, many of whom are college or university professors of accounting. *11*

American Institute of Certified Public Accountants (AICPA) A professional organization of Certified

Public Accountants, most of whom are in public accounting practice. *10*

Annual report A pamphlet or document of varying length containing audited financial statements and other information about a company, distributed annually to its owners. *9*

Audit (independent) Performed by independent auditors to determine whether the financial statements of a business fairly reflect the economic performance of the business. *6*

Audit (internal) Performed by accounting employees of a company to determine if company policies and procedures are being followed. *7*

Certified Internal Auditor (CIA) An accountant who has passed an examination prepared and graded by the Institute of Internal Auditors (IIA) and who has met certain other requirements. *7*

Certified Management Accountants (CMA) Persons who have passed an examination prepared and graded by the Institute of Certified Management Accountants (ICMA), an affiliate of the Institute of Management Accountants, and who have met certain other requirements. *7*

Certified Public Accountant (CPA) A person who has passed an examination prepared and graded by the American Institute of Certified Public Accountants (AICPA) and has an active license to practice as a CPA. *5*

Controller or chief financial officer The executive officer in charge of a company's accounting activity. *6*

Financial accounting Relates to the company as a whole; the process of supplying financial information to parties external to the reporting entity. *9*

Financial Accounting Standards Board (FASB) A seven-member board of independent professionals that issues *Statements of Financial Accounting Standards*. The private sector organization now responsible for the development of new financial accounting standards. *11*

Financial Executives Institute (FEI) An organization whose members are primarily financial policy-making executives. *11*

Financial statements Formal reports providing information on a company's financial position, cash inflows and outflows, and the results of operations. *9*

Generally accepted accounting principles (GAAP) Accounting standards and principles that have been developed through accounting practice or have been established by an authoritative organization. *10*

Governmental Accounting Standards Board (GASB) The private sector organization now responsible for the development of new governmental accounting concepts and standards. *11*

Governmental or other not-for-profit accounting Governmental accountants are employed by government agencies at the federal, state, and local

levels. Other not-for-profit accountants record and account for receipts and disbursements for churches, charities, fraternities, and universities. *7*

Independent audit See Audit (independent).

Independent auditors Certified Public Accountants who perform an audit to determine whether or not a company's financial statements fairly (equitably) report the economic performance and financial condition of the company. *6*

Independent auditor's opinion or report The formal written statement by a Certified Public Accountant that states whether or not the company's financial statements fairly report the economic performance and financial condition of the company. *6*

Institute of Management Accountants (IMA) An organization consisting of management accountants in private industry and CPAs and academics who are interested in management accounting. *12*

Internal audit See Audit (internal).

Internal auditors Private accountants employed by a company to see that the policies and procedures established by the company are followed in its divisions and departments. *7*

Management accountants Accountants who provide accounting services for a single business and are employees of that business. *6*

Managerial accounting Relates to the process of supplying financial information for internal management use. *10*

Public accounting firms Offer professional accounting and related services for a fee to companies, other organizations, and individuals. *5*

Securities and Exchange Commission (SEC) A governmental agency created by Congress to administer acts dealing with interstate sales of securities and having the authority to prescribe the accounting and reporting practices of firms under its jurisdiction. *11*

QUESTIONS

1. Who was the author of the first book written on double-entry bookkeeping?

2. Why should almost everyone have some knowledge of accounting?

3. What does CPA stand for? How does one become a CPA? Do all CPAs work in public accounting?

4. How favorable do employment opportunities appear in accounting?

5. Identify what is meant by CPA, CMA, and CIA. What are some of the services provided by individuals with these designations?

6. What is the primary difference between internal auditors and independent auditors?

7. What is the role of accountants employed in government?

8. What activities are required of accountants employed in higher education?

9. Describe the basic difference between financial accounting and managerial accounting.

10. Name several organizations that have played or are playing an important role in the development of accounting standards. Describe each briefly.

11. What guides the ethical behavior of accountants?

12. *Real world question* In "A Broader Perspective" on page 8, how many new accountants will be required by the year 2000 and what percent increase does this amount represent?

The Coca-Cola Company

13. *Real world question*   Refer to the report of the independent auditors contained in The Coca-Cola Company annual report in Appendix E at the end of the text. Which CPA firm performed the audit? Whose responsibility are the financial statements—the company's or the auditor's?

The Coca-Cola Company

14. *Real world question*   Referring to the same report of the independent auditors mentioned in Question 13, did the auditors examine all the evidence supporting the amounts and disclosures in all of the financial statements?

The tools of accounting have changed in the twentieth century. The adding machine was used by accountants in summarizing accounting data for most of the century. The electronic calculator replaced the adding machine in performing this task only within the last several decades. The hand-written accounting "books" of old have been translated into files in a computer. Computerized accounting software packages are aiding the accountant in performing accounting tasks.

PART

I

THE BASIC ACCOUNTING MODEL

1

ACCOUNTING AND ITS USE IN BUSINESS DECISIONS

LEARNING OBJECTIVES

After studying this chapter, you should be able to:

1. Identify and describe the three basic forms of business organizations.
2. Distinguish among the three types of activities performed by business organizations.
3. Describe the content and purposes of the income statement, statement of retained earnings, and balance sheet.
4. State the basic accounting equation and describe its relationship to the balance sheet.
5. Using the underlying assumptions or concepts, analyze business transactions and determine their effects on items in the financial statements.
6. Prepare an income statement, a statement of retained earnings, and a balance sheet.

The Introduction to this text provided a background for your study of accounting. **(If you have not read the Introduction, you should do so before reading Chapter 1.)** You can now define accounting and explain the functions performed by accountants. After reading about the employment opportunities in accounting, you may have decided to consider a career in accounting. Even if you select another profession or occupation, accounting information will be useful throughout your lifetime.

Now you are ready to learn about the forms of business organizations and the types of business activities they perform. This chapter presents three of the financial statements used by businesses. In this chapter, you will also study the accounting process (or accounting cycle) that accountants use to prepare those financial statements. This accounting process uses financial data such as the records of sales made to customers and purchases made from suppliers. In a systematic manner, these data are analyzed, recorded, classified, summarized, and finally reported in the financial statements of businesses. As you study this chapter, you will begin to understand the unique, systematic nature of accounting—the language of business.

FORMS OF BUSINESS ORGANIZATIONS

Objective 1

Identify and describe the three basic forms of business organizations[1]

Accountants frequently refer to a business organization as an **accounting entity** or a **business entity.** A business entity is any business organization, such as a hardware store or grocery store, that exists as an economic unit. For accounting purposes, each business organization or entity has an existence separate from its owner(s), creditors, employees, customers, and other businesses. This separate existence of the business organization is known as the business entity concept. Thus, in the accounting records of the business entity, the activities of each business should be kept separate from the activities of other businesses and from the personal financial activities of the owner(s).

Assume, for example, that you own two businesses, a physical fitness center and a horse stable. According to the business entity concept, you would consider each business as an independent business unit. Thus, you would normally keep separate accounting records for each business. Now assume your physical fitness center is unprofitable because you are not charging enough for the use of your exercise equipment. You can determine this fact because you are treating your physical fitness center and horse stable as two separate business entities. You must also keep your personal financial activities separate from your two businesses. Therefore, you cannot include the car you drive only for personal use as a business activity of your physical fitness center or your horse stable. However, the use of your truck to pick up feed for your horse stable is a business activity of your horse stable.

As you will see in the discussion that follows on the three forms of business organizations—single proprietorships, partnerships, and corporations—the business entity concept applies to all forms of businesses. Thus, for accounting purposes, all three business forms are separate from other business entities and from their owners. You will learn that corporations are also **legally** separate from their owners, while this is not true for single proprietorships and partnerships. Single proprietorships are mentioned only briefly here and are discussed in detail in Appendix A at the end of the text.

---

[1] After reading a portion of text material that covers a certain learning objective, some students may want to work immediately an exercise that illustrates that material. The exercises at the end of each chapter are labeled with the learning objective to which they pertain. For instance, turn to pages 44–46 to see which learning objective(s) each exercise covers in Chapter 1.

**Single
Proprietorship**

A single proprietorship is an unincorporated business owned by an individual and often managed by that same individual. Single proprietors include physicians, lawyers, electricians, and other people who are "in business for themselves." Many small service-type businesses and retail establishments are single proprietorships. No legal formalities are necessary to organize such businesses, and usually business operations can begin with only a limited investment.

In a single proprietorship, the owner is solely responsible for all debts of the business. For accounting purposes, however, the business is a separate entity from the owner. Thus, single proprietors must keep the financial activities of the business, such as the receipt of fees from selling services to the public, separate from their personal financial activities. For example, owners of single proprietorships should not enter the cost of a personal house or car payment in the financial records of their business.

Partnership

A partnership is an unincorporated business owned by two or more persons associated as partners. Often the same persons who own the business also manage the business. Many small retail establishments and professional practices, such as dentists, physicians, attorneys, and many CPA firms, are partnerships.

Partnerships begin with a verbal or written agreement. A written agreement is preferable because it provides a permanent record of the terms of the partnership. These terms include the initial investment of each partner, the duties of each partner, the means of dividing profits or losses between the partners each year, and the settlement after the death or withdrawal of a partner. Each partner may be held liable for all the debts of the partnership and for the actions of each partner within the scope of the business. However, as with the single proprietorship, for accounting purposes, the partnership is a separate business entity.

Corporation

A corporation is a business incorporated under the laws of one of the states and owned by a few persons or by thousands of persons. Almost all large businesses and many small businesses are incorporated.

The corporation is unique in that it is a separate legal business entity. The owners of the corporation are called stockholders or shareholders. They buy shares of stock, which are units of ownership, in the corporation. Should the corporation fail, the owners would only lose the amount they paid for their stock. The corporate form of business protects the personal assets of the owners from the creditors of the corporation.[2]

The stockholders do not directly manage the corporation. They elect a board of directors to represent their interests. The board of directors selects the officers of the corporation, such as the president and vice presidents, who manage the corporation for the stockholders.

Accounting is necessary for all three forms of business organizations, and each company, regardless of business form, must follow generally accepted accounting principles (GAAP). Since corporations have such an important impact on our economy, we will use them in this text to illustrate the basic accounting principles and concepts. As stated earlier, accounting for single proprietorships and partnerships is discussed in Appendix A at the end of the text.

---

[2] When individuals seek a bank loan to finance the formation of a small corporation, the bank will often require those individuals to sign documents making them personally responsible for repaying the loan if the corporation cannot pay. In this instance, the individuals can lose their original investment plus the amount of the loan they are obligated to repay.

TYPES OF ACTIVITIES PERFORMED BY BUSINESS ORGANIZATIONS

Objective 2

Distinguish among the three types of activities performed by business organizations

The forms of business entities discussed in the previous section are classified according to the type of ownership of the business entity. Single proprietorships have one owner, partnerships have two or more owners, and corporations usually have many owners. Business entities can also be grouped by the type of business activities they perform—service companies, merchandising companies, and manufacturing companies. Any of these three types of activities can be performed by companies using any of the three forms of business organizations.

1. **Service companies.** Service companies perform services for a fee. This group includes companies such as accounting firms, law firms, dry cleaning establishments, and many others. Accounting for service companies is illustrated in the early chapters of this text.

2. **Merchandising companies.** Merchandising companies purchase goods that are ready for sale and then sell them to customers. Merchandising companies include such companies as auto dealerships, clothing stores, and supermarkets. Accounting for merchandising companies is first illustrated in Chapter 5.

3. **Manufacturing companies.** Manufacturing companies buy materials, convert them into products, and then sell the products to other companies or to final customers (consumers). Examples of manufacturing companies are steel mills, auto manufacturers, and clothing manufacturers.

All of these companies produce financial statements as the final end product of their accounting process. As stated in the Introduction, these financial statements provide relevant financial information both to those inside the company—management—and those outside the company—creditors, stockholders, and other interested parties. In the next section, you will learn about three common financial statements—the income statement, the statement of retained earnings, and the balance sheet. A fourth financial statement, the statement of cash flows, is discussed in Chapter 18.

FINANCIAL STATEMENTS OF BUSINESS ORGANIZATIONS

Objective 3

Describe the content and purposes of the income statement, statement of retained earnings, and balance sheet

Business entities may have many objectives and goals (for example, one of your objectives in owning a physical fitness center may be to improve *your* physical fitness). However, the two primary objectives of every business are profitability and solvency. Profitability is the ability to generate income. Unless a business can produce satisfactory income and pay its debts as they become due, the business will not survive to realize its other objectives. Solvency is the ability to pay debts as they become due.

The financial statement that reflects a company's profitability is the income statement. The statement of retained earnings shows the change in retained earnings between the beginning of a period (e.g., a month or a year) and the end of that period. The balance sheet reflects a company's solvency. The headings and elements of each statement are similar from company to company. You have probably noticed this similarity if you have seen financial statements of actual companies.

Chapter 18 thoroughly discusses and illustrates a fourth financial statement, the statement of cash flows. We only mention it now so you will know it exists. The statement of cash flows shows the cash inflows and outflows for a company over a period of time.

A BROADER PERSPECTIVE

THAT'S SHOW BIZ: PARAMOUNT SAYS $300M TAKE YIELDS ZIP

Movie studios, it seems, are good at special effects—on the big screen and in accounting ledgers.

A judge ruled Monday that Eddie Murphy's film *Coming to America* was based on humorist Art Buchwald's idea and that Buchwald is entitled to his slice of the film's net income. Paramount Pictures, the film's producer, says the movie's gross box-office sales have passed $300 million. But profit?

Paramount says the film hasn't made a cent. Buchwald jabbed, "If you believe that, then there's a wonderful S&L I'd like to sell you."

Yet movie industry insiders say the accounting is typical. "It's not startling to me," says Alex Ben Block, editor of the entertainment newsletter *Show Biz News*.

The film's contracts will be released by the court within a month. Here's a preview of what they might show:

Right off the top, movie theaters showing the film get 50% of gross box-office receipts. If *Coming to America* has made $300 million, theaters have cut Paramount's take to $150 million.

Paramount finances its own movies, and as Paramount lawyer Lon Sobel says, "This was no cheap movie. It had baby elephants running around and fabulously expensive sets and costumes." Lop off an estimated $40 million to make the film plus Murphy's $8 million salary, and you're down to $102 million.

Studios generally charge 15% of the cost of the movie to cover overhead—salaries for execs, fixed studio costs. Take off another $6 million, leaving $96 million. Take out the cost of prints of the movie and advertising. We're down to about $79 million.

Paramount didn't put up the money for those services for free. Take out $20 million for interest, calculated from the time the 1988 film began production a year earlier. That leaves $59 million. Murphy gets part of the studio gross—likely 10%. That's $15 million, leaving $44 million.

Paramount gets a distribution fee for getting the movie made. Standard is 35% of the studio's gross, in this case $52.5 million. That leaves the movie about $8.5 million short of having net income, though Paramount has made money off the film.

Buchwald might find himself out selling S&Ls after all.

Source: Pat Guy, *USA Today*, January 10, 1990, p. 2B. Copyright 1990, USA TODAY. Reprinted with permission.

The Income Statement

The income statement, sometimes called an *earnings statement,* reports the profitability of a business organization for a **stated period of time.** In accounting, profitability is measured for a period of time, such as a month or year, by comparing the revenues generated with the expenses incurred to produce these revenues. Revenues are the inflows of assets (such as cash) resulting from the sale of products or the rendering of services to customers. Revenues are measured by the prices agreed on in the exchanges in which a business delivers goods or renders services. Expenses are the costs incurred to produce revenues. Expenses are measured by the assets surrendered or consumed in serving customers. If the revenues of a period exceed the expenses of the same period, net income results. Thus,

$$\text{Net income} = \text{Revenues} - \text{Expenses}$$

Net income is often called the *earnings* of the company. If expenses exceed revenues, the business has a net loss, and it has operated unprofitably.

In Illustration 1.1, Part A shows the income statement of Bock Company for July 1994. Bock Company is a corporation that performs delivery services. Remember that an income statement is for a specified **period** of time.

Bock's income statement for the month ended July 31, 1994, shows that the revenues (or delivery fees) generated by serving customers for July totaled $5,700. Expenses for the month amounted to $3,600. As a result of these business activities, Bock's net income for July was $2,100. The **net income** amount is determined

---

ILLUSTRATION 1.1

A. Income Statement

BOCK COMPANY
Income Statement
For the Month Ended July 31, 1994

Revenues:		
Service revenue		$5,700
Expenses:		
Salaries expense	$2,600	
Rent expense	400	
Gas and oil expense	600	
Total expenses		3,600
Net income		$2,100

B. Statement of Retained Earnings

BOCK COMPANY
Statement of Retained Earnings
For the Month Ended July 31, 1994

Retained earnings, July 1	$ –0–
Add: Net income for July	2,100
Retained earnings, July 31	$2,100

C. Balance Sheet

BOCK COMPANY
Balance Sheet
July 31, 1994

Assets		Liabilities and Stockholders' Equity*	
Cash	$15,500	Liabilities:	
Accounts receivable	700	Accounts payable	$ 600
Trucks	20,000	Notes payable	6,000
Office equipment	2,500	Total liabilities	$ 6,600
		Stockholder's equity:	
		Capital stock	$30,000
		Retained earnings	2,100
		Total stockholders' equity	$32,100
Total assets	$38,700	Total liabilities and stockholders' equity	$38,700

* The liabilities and stockholders' equity portion of the balance sheet may be shown directly beneath the assets instead of to the right of them, as shown in the illustration. When liabilities and stockholders' equity are placed under the assets, the balance sheet is in the *vertical format* or *report form.* The vertical format is as acceptable as the *horizontal format* (or account form) used above. For an example of the vertical format, see the Solution to Demonstration Problem, page 41.

---

by subtracting the company's expenses of $3,600 from its revenues of $5,700. Corporations are taxable entities, but we ignore corporate income taxes at this point.

The Statement of Retained Earnings

One of the purposes of the *statement of retained earnings* is to connect the income statement and the balance sheet. The statement of retained earnings explains the changes in retained earnings that occurred between two balance sheet dates. These changes usually consist of the addition of net income (or deduction of net loss) and the deduction of dividends.

Dividends are the means by which a corporation rewards its stockholders (owners) for providing it with investment funds. A dividend is a payment (usually of cash) to the owners of the business; it is a distribution of income to owners rather than an expense of doing business. Since dividends are not an expense, they do not appear on the income statement.

The effect of a dividend is to reduce cash and retained earnings by the amount paid out. Then, the company no longer "retains" a portion of the income (earnings) but has passed it on to the stockholders (owners). Earning a return in the form of dividends is, of course, one of the primary reasons why people invest in corporations.

The statement of retained earnings for Bock Company for July 1994 is relatively simple (Part B of Illustration 1.1). Bock was organized on June 1 and did not earn any revenues or incur any expenses during June. So Bock's beginning retained earnings balance on July 1 is zero. Bock then adds its $2,100 net income for July. Since Bock paid no dividends in July, the $2,100 would be the ending balance.

In Illustration 1.1, Part B shows first that the beginning balance in retained earnings was $–0–. This balance is added to July's net income of $2,100 from the income statement (Part A) to arrive at the ending retained earnings balance of $2,100. Next, this ending balance is carried to the balance sheet (Part C). If there had been a net loss, it would have been deducted from the beginning balance on the statement of retained earnings.

Dividends could also have affected the Retained Earnings balance. To give a more realistic illustration, assume that (1) Bock Company's net income for August was $1,500 (revenues of $5,600 less expenses of $4,100) and (2) the company declared and paid dividends of $1,000. Then, Bock's statement of retained earnings for August would be:

BOCK COMPANY
Statement of Retained Earnings
For the Month Ended August 31, 1994

Retained earnings, July 31	$2,100
Add: Net income for August	1,500
Total	$3,600
Less: Dividends	1,000
Retained earnings, August 31	$2,600

The Balance Sheet

The balance sheet, sometimes called the *statement of financial position*, lists the company's assets, liabilities, and stockholders' equity (including dollar amounts) **as of a specific moment in time.** The specific moment of time is the close of business on the date appearing on the balance sheet. Notice how the heading of the balance sheet differs from the headings on the income statement and statement of retained earnings. A balance sheet is like a still photograph; it captures the financial position of a company at a particular **point** in time. The other two statements are for a **period** of time. As you study about the assets, liabilities, and stockholders' equity contained in a balance sheet, you will understand why this financial statement provides information about the solvency of the business.

Assets are things of value owned by the business. They are also called the **resources** of the business. Examples include cash, machines, and buildings. Assets have value because a business can use or exchange them to produce the services or products of the business. In Part C of Illustration 1.1, the assets of Bock Company, which performs delivery services, amount to $38,700. Bock's assets consist of cash, accounts receivable (amounts due from customers for services previously rendered or merchandise sold), delivery equipment, and office equipment.

Liabilities are the **debts** owed by a business. Typically, a business must pay its debts by certain dates. A business incurs many of its liabilities by purchasing an item on credit. Bock's liabilities consist of accounts payable (amounts owed to suppliers for previous purchases) and notes payable (written promises to pay a specific sum of money) totaling $6,600.[3]

Bock Company is a corporation. The owners' interest in a corporation is referred to as stockholders' equity. Bock's stockholders' equity consists of (1) $30,000 paid for shares of capital stock and (2) retained earnings of $2,100. Capital stock shows the amount of the owners' investment in the corporation. Retained earnings generally consists of the accumulated net income of the corporation minus dividends distributed to stockholders. These items will be discussed later in the text. At this point, you should simply note that the balance sheet heading includes the name of the organization and the title and date of the statement. Note also that the dollar amount of the total assets is equal to the claims on (or interest in) those assets. The balance sheet shows these claims under the heading "Liabilities and Stockholders' Equity."

The income statement, statement of retained earnings, and balance sheet of Bock Company are the end products of the accounting process, which we explain in the next section. These financial statements give a picture of the solvency and profitability of the company. The accounting process details how this picture was made.

THE FINANCIAL ACCOUNTING PROCESS

Objective 4
State the basic accounting equation and describe its relationship to the balance sheet

In this section, we explain first the accounting equation—the framework for the entire accounting process. Then, we show you how to recognize a business transaction and describe underlying assumptions that accountants use to record business transactions. Next, you will learn how to analyze and record business transactions. Bock Company will be your "tour guide" as you move from transaction to transaction. Accounting—the language of business—is now also becoming part of your language.

The Accounting Equation

In the balance sheet presented in Illustration 1.1 (Part C), the total assets of Bock Company were equal to its total liabilities and stockholders' equity. This equality shows that the assets of a business are equal to its equities; that is,

$$\text{Assets} = \text{Equities}$$

Assets were defined earlier as the things of value owned by the business, or the economic resources of the business. Equities are all claims to, or interests in, assets. For example, assume that you purchased a new company automobile for $5,000 by investing $400 in your own corporation and borrowing $4,600 in the name of the corporation from a bank. Your equity in the automobile is $400, and the bank's equity is $4,600. You can further describe the $4,600 as a liability because the corporation owes the bank $4,600. Also, you can describe your $400 equity as **stockholders' equity** or interest in the asset. Since the owners in a corporation are stockholders, the basic accounting equation becomes:

$$\text{Assets (A)} = \text{Liabilities (L)} + \text{Stockholders' Equity (SE)}$$

---

[3] Most notes bear interest, but in this chapter we assume that all notes bear no interest. Interest is an amount paid by the borrower to the lender (in addition to the amount of the loan) for use of the money over time.

From Bock Company's balance sheet in Illustration 1.1 (Part C), we can enter in the amount of its assets, liabilities, and stockholders' equity:

$$A = L + SE$$
$$\$38,700 = \$6,600 + \$32,100$$

Remember that someone must provide assets or resources—either a creditor or a stockholder. Therefore, this equation must always be in balance.

You can also look at the right side of the above equation in another manner. The liabilities and stockholders' equity show the sources of an existing group of assets. Thus, liabilities are not only claims against assets but also sources of assets.

Either creditors or owners provide all the assets in a corporation. As a business engages in economic activity, the **dollar amounts** and **composition** of its assets, liabilities, and stockholders' equity change. **However, the equality of the basic accounting equation always holds.**

Analysis of Transactions

Objective 5

Using the underlying assumptions or concepts, analyze business transactions and determine their effects on items in the financial statements

An accounting transaction is a business activity or event that must be recorded in the accounting records. For example, an exchange of cash for merchandise is evidence of a business event. An exchange takes place at an agreed price, and this price provides an objective measure of the economic activity that has occurred. For example, the objective measure of the exchange may be $5,000. These two factors—evidence and measurement—make possible the recording of a transaction. **Merely placing an order for goods is not a recordable transaction because no exchange has taken place.**

The evidence of the transaction is usually supported by a *source document*. A source document is any written or printed evidence of a business transaction that describes the essential facts of that transaction. Examples of source documents are receipts for cash paid or received, checks written or received, bills sent to customers for services performed or bills received from suppliers for items purchased, cash register tapes, sales tickets, and notes given or received. We handle source documents constantly in our everyday life. Each source document initiates the process of recording a transaction.

Underlying Assumptions or Concepts   In recording business transactions, accountants rely on certain underlying assumptions or concepts. Both preparers and users of financial statements must understand these assumptions.

1.   Business entity concept **(or accounting entity concept).** Data gathered in an accounting system relate to a specific business unit or entity. The business entity concept assumes that each business has an existence separate from its owners, creditors, employees, customers, other interested parties, and other businesses.

2.   Money measurement concept. Economic activity is initially recorded and reported in terms of a **common monetary unit of measure**—the dollar in the United States. This form of measurement is known as **money measurement.**

3.   Exchange-price (or cost) concept (principle). Most of the amounts entered in an accounting system are the objective money prices determined in the exchange process. As a result, most assets are recorded at their acquisition cost, measured in terms of money paid. Cost is the sacrifice made or the resources given up, measured in money terms, to acquire some desired thing, such as a new truck (asset).

4. **Going-concern (continuity) concept.** Unless strong evidence exists to the contrary, accountants assume that the business entity will continue operations into the indefinite future. Accountants call this assumption the **going-concern or continuity** concept. Assuming that the entity will continue indefinitely allows the accountant to value long-term assets, such as land, at cost on the balance sheet since they are to be used rather than sold. Market values of these assets would only be relevant if they were for sale. Thus, subsequent increases in value are not recorded. For instance, land recorded at its cost of $100,000 in 1988 is still shown at $100,000 on the December 31, 1994, balance sheet even though its market value has risen to $300,000.

5. **Periodicity (time periods) concept.** According to the **periodicity (time periods)** concept or assumption, an entity's life can be meaningfully subdivided into time periods (such as months or years) for purposes of reporting the results of its economic activities.

Now that you understand business transactions and the five basic accounting assumptions, you are ready to follow step by step some actual business transactions. The transactions of Bock Company serve as examples. These transactions are divided into two groups: (1) transactions affecting only the balance sheet in June, and (2) transactions affecting the income statement and/or the balance sheet in July. Then, a summary of the transactions is given.

Transactions Affecting Only the Balance Sheet   Since each transaction affecting a business entity must be recorded in the accounting records, the analysis of the transaction before the actual recording of the transaction is an important part of financial accounting. An error in transaction analysis will result in an incorrect picture given in the financial statements.

To illustrate the analysis of transactions and their effects on the basic accounting equation, the activities of Bock Company that led to the statements in Illustration 1.1 are presented below. The numbers 1a, 2a, and so on refer to the summary of transactions found later in Part B of Illustration 1.2. The first set of transactions (1a–5a) occurred in June 1994. The second set (1b–6b) occurred in July 1994.

*1a. **Owner Invested Cash***   When Bock Company was organized as a corporation on June 1, 1994, the company issued shares of capital stock for $30,000 cash to John Bock, his wife, and their son. This transaction increased assets (cash) of Bock by $30,000 and increased equities (the capital stock element of stockholders' equity) by $30,000. Consequently, the transaction yields the following basic accounting equation:

Trans-action	Explanation	Cash	Accounts Receiv-able	Assets Trucks	Office Equip-ment	=	Liabilities Accounts Payable	Notes Payable	+	Stockholders' Equity Capital Stock
	Beginning balances. . . .	$ –0–	$ –0–	$ –0–	$ –0–	=	$ –0–	$ –0–	+	$ –0–
1a	Owner invested cash. . . .	+30,000								+30,000
	Balances after transaction. .	$30,000				=				$30,000

Increased by $30,000

Increased by $30,000

2a. Borrowed Money   The company borrowed $6,000 from Bock's father. Bock signed the note for the company. The note bore no interest and promised to repay (recorded as a **note payable**) the amount borrowed within one year. After including the effects of this transaction, the basic equation is:

Trans-action	Explanation	Assets				=	Liabilities		+	Stockholders' Equity
		Cash	Accounts Receiv-able	Trucks	Office Equip-ment		Accounts Payable	Notes Payable		Capital Stock
	Balances before transaction .	$30,000				=				$30,000
2a	Borrowed money	+6,000						+6,000		
	Balances after transaction. .	$36,000				=		$6,000	+	$30,000

Increased by $6,000	Increased by $6,000

3a. Purchased Trucks and Office Equipment for Cash   Bock bought (by paying cash) three delivery trucks for $20,000 and office equipment for $1,500. Trucks and office equipment are assets because the company uses them to earn revenues in the future. **Note that this transaction does not change the totals in the basic equation but only changes the composition of the assets.** This transaction decreased cash and increased trucks and office equipment (assets) by the total amount of the cash decrease. Bock received two assets and gave up one asset of equal value. Total assets are still $36,000. The accounting equation now is:

Trans-action	Explanation	Assets				=	Liabilities		+	Stockholders' Equity
		Cash	Accounts Receiv-able	Trucks	Office Equip-ment		Accounts Payable	Notes Payable		Capital Stock
	Balances before transaction .	$36,000				=		$6,000	+	$30,000
3a	Purchased equipment for cash	−21,500		+20,000	+1,500					
	Balances after transaction. .	$14,500		$20,000	$1,500	=		$6,000	+	$30,000

Decreased by $21,500	Increased by $20,000	Increased by $1,500

4a. Purchased Office Equipment on Account (for Credit)   Bock purchased $1,000 of office equipment on account, agreeing to pay within 10 days after receiving the bill. (To purchase an item "on account" means to buy it on credit.) This transaction increased assets in the form of office equipment and liabilities in the form of **accounts payable** by $1,000. As stated earlier, accounts payable are amounts owed to suppliers for items purchased on credit. The $1,000 increase in the assets and the liabilities is shown as follows:

		Assets				=	Liabilities	+	Stockholders' Equity
Trans-action	Explanation	Cash	Accounts Receiv-able	Trucks	Office Equip-ment	Accounts Payable	Notes Payable		Capital Stock
	Balances before transaction .	$14,500		$20,000	$1,500 =		$6,000 +		$30,000
4a	Purchased office equipment on account				+1,000	+1,000			
	Balances after transaction . .	$14,500		$20,000	$2,500 =	$1,000	$6,000 +		$30,000

Increased by $1,000	Increased by $1,000

5a. Paid an Account Payable Eight days after receiving the bill, Bock paid $1,000 for the office equipment purchased on account (transaction 4a). This transaction reduced cash by $1,000 and reduced accounts payable by $1,000. Thus, the assets and liabilities both are reduced by $1,000, and the equation again balances as follows:

		Assets				=	Liabilities	+	Stockholders' Equity
Trans-action	Explanation	Cash	Accounts Receiv-able	Trucks	Office Equip-ment	Accounts Payable	Notes Payable		Capital Stock
	Balances before transaction .	$14,500		$20,000	$2,500 =	$1,000	$6,000 +		$30,000
5a	Paid an account payable . .	−1,000				−1,000			
	End-of-month balances . . .	$13,500	$ −0−	$20,000	$2,500 =	$ −0−	$6,000 +		$30,000

Decreased by $1,000	Decreased by $1,000

In Illustration 1.2, Part A shows a *summary of transactions* prepared in accounting equation form for November. A summary of transactions is a teaching tool used to show the effects of transactions on the accounting equation. Note that the stockholders' equity has remained at $30,000. This amount will change as the business begins to earn revenues or incur expenses. You can see how the totals at the bottom of Part A of Illustration 1.2 tie into the balance sheet shown in Part B. The date on the balance sheet is June 30, 1994. These totals become the beginning balances for July 1994.

Thus far, all transactions have consisted of exchanges or acquisitions of assets either by borrowing or by owner investment. This procedure was used so you could focus on the accounting equation as it relates to the balance sheet. However, people do not form a business only to **hold present assets.** Businesses are formed so **their assets can be used to generate greater amounts of assets.** Thus, a business increases its assets by providing goods or services to customers. The results of these activities are shown in the income statement. The section that follows shows more of the transactions of Bock Company as it begins its business of earning revenues and incurring expenses.

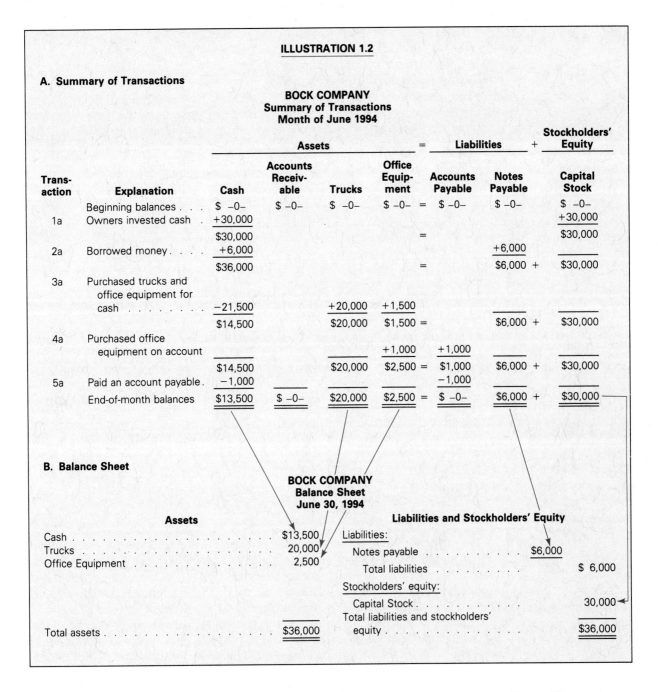

ILLUSTRATION 1.2

A. Summary of Transactions

BOCK COMPANY
Summary of Transactions
Month of June 1994

Trans-action	Explanation	Cash	Accounts Receiv-able	Trucks	Office Equip-ment	Accounts Payable	Notes Payable	Capital Stock
				Assets		= Liabilities	+	Stockholders' Equity
	Beginning balances . . .	$ –0–	$ –0–	$ –0–	$ –0– =	$ –0–	$ –0–	$ –0–
1a	Owners invested cash .	+30,000						+30,000
		$30,000			=			$30,000
2a	Borrowed money	+6,000					+6,000	
		$36,000			=		$6,000 +	$30,000
3a	Purchased trucks and office equipment for cash	–21,500		+20,000	+1,500			
		$14,500		$20,000	$1,500 =		$6,000 +	$30,000
4a	Purchased office equipment on account				+1,000	+1,000		
		$14,500		$20,000	$2,500 =	$1,000	$6,000 +	$30,000
5a	Paid an account payable.	–1,000				–1,000		
	End-of-month balances	$13,500	$ –0–	$20,000	$2,500 =	$ –0–	$6,000 +	$30,000

B. Balance Sheet

BOCK COMPANY
Balance Sheet
June 30, 1994

Assets		Liabilities and Stockholders' Equity	
Cash	$13,500	Liabilities:	
Trucks	20,000	Notes payable	$6,000
Office Equipment	2,500	Total liabilities	$ 6,000
		Stockholders' equity:	
		Capital Stock	30,000
Total assets	$36,000	Total liabilities and stockholders' equity	$36,000

Transactions Affecting the Income Statement and/or Balance Sheet To survive, a business must be profitable. This means that the revenues earned by providing goods and services to customers must exceed the expenses incurred.

In July 1994, Bock Company began selling services and incurring expenses. The explanations of transactions that follow will allow you to participate in this process and learn the necessary accounting procedures.

1b. Earned Service Revenue and Received Cash As its first transaction in July, Bock performed delivery services for customers and received $4,800 cash. This transaction increased the cash balance by $4,800. Stockholders' equity also increased by $4,800, and the accounting equation is in balance.

The $4,800 is a revenue earned by the business and, as such, increases stockholders' equity because owners prosper when the business earns profits. Likewise, the owners would sustain any losses. If the business continues to have losses, it may fail.

The amount of retained earnings is increased by revenues and decreased by expenses and dividends. In this first chapter, all of these items are shown as immediately affecting retained earnings. In later chapters, the revenues, expenses, and dividends are kept separate from retained earnings during the accounting period and transferred to retained earnings only at the end of an accounting period.

The effects of this $4,800 transaction on the financial status of Bock are:

Trans-action	Explanation	Cash	Assets: Accounts Receiv-able	Trucks	Office Equip-ment	=	Liabilities: Accounts Payable	Notes Payable	+	Capital Stock	Stockholders' Equity: Re-tained Earn-ings
	Beginning balances (Illustration 1.2)	$13,500	$–0–	$20,000	$2,500	=	$–0–	$6,000	+	$30,000	$ –0–
1b	Earned service revenue and received cash	+4,800									+4,800 (service revenue)
	Balances after transaction . .	$18,300		$20,000	$2,500	=		$6,000	+	$30,000	$4,800
		Increased by $4,800									*Increased by $4,800*

Note that the increase in stockholders' equity brought about by the revenue transaction is recorded as a separate item, "Retained earnings." We cannot record this increase as capital stock because the Capital Stock account is increased only when the company issues shares of stock. The expectation is that revenue transactions will exceed expenses and yield net income. If net income is not distributed to stockholders, it is in fact retained. As stated above, later chapters will show that because of complexities in handling large numbers of transactions, revenues will be shown as affecting retained earnings only at the end of an accounting period. The procedure presented above is a shortcut used to explain why the accounting equation remains in balance.

2b. Service Revenue Earned on Account (for Credit) Bock performed delivery services for a customer who agreed to pay $900 at a later date. The company granted credit rather than requiring the customer to pay cash immediately. This is called earning revenue *on account*. The transaction consists of an exchange of services for a promise by the customer to pay later. This transaction is similar to the preceding transaction in that stockholders' equity is increased because the company has earned revenues. However, the transaction differs because the company has not received cash. Instead, the company has received another asset, an *account receivable*. As noted earlier, an account receivable is the amount due from a customer for goods or services already provided. The company has a legal right to collect from the customer in the future. Accounting recognizes such claims as assets. The accounting equation, including this $900 item, is as follows:

Trans-action	Explanation	Assets				=	Liabilities		+	Stockholders' Equity	
		Cash	Accounts Receiv-able	Trucks	Office Equip-ment		Accounts Payable	Notes Payable		Capital Stock	Re-tained Earn-ings
	Balances before transaction . .	$18,300		$20,000	$2,500 =			$6,000	+	$30,000	$4,800
2b	Earned service revenue on account . . .		+900								+900 (service revenue)
	Balances after transaction . .	$18,300	$900	$20,000	$2,500 =			$6,000	+	$30,000	$5,700

Increased by $900

Increased by $900

3b. Collected Cash on Accounts Receivable   Bock collected $200 on account from the customer in transaction 2b. The customer will pay the remaining $700 later. This transaction affects only the balance sheet and consists of giving up a claim on a customer in exchange for cash. The effects of the transaction are to increase cash by $200 and to decrease accounts receivable by $200. **Note that this transaction consists solely of a change in the composition of the assets.** The revenue was recorded when the company performed the services. Therefore, the revenue is not recorded again when the cash is collected.

Trans-action	Explanation	Assets				=	Liabilities		+	Stockholders' Equity	
		Cash	Accounts Receiv-able	Trucks	Office Equip-ment		Accounts Payable	Notes Payable		Capital Stock	Re-tained Earn-ings
	Balances before transaction . .	$18,300	$900	$20,000	$2,500 =			$6,000	+	$30,000	$5,700
3b	Collected cash on account . .	+200	−200								
	Balances after transaction . .	$18,500	$700	$20,000	$2,500 =			$6,000	+	$30,000	$5,700

Increased by $200

Decreased by $200

4b. Paid Salaries   Bock paid employees $2,600 in salaries. This transaction is an exchange of cash for employee services. Typically, companies pay employees for their services after they perform their work. Salaries (or wages) are costs companies incur to produce revenues, and companies consider them an expense. Thus, the accountant treats the transaction as a decrease in an asset (cash) and a decrease in stockholders' equity because the company has incurred an expense. Expense transactions reduce net income. Since net income becomes a part of the retained earnings balance, expense transactions reduce the retained earnings.

Trans-action	Explanation	Cash	Accounts Receiv-able	Trucks	Office Equip-ment	Accounts Payable	Notes Payable	Capital Stock	Re-tained Earn-ings
						=		+	
	Balances before transaction . .	$18,500	$700	$20,000	$2,500 =		$6,000 +	$30,000	$5,700
4b	Paid salaries . .	−2,600							−2,600 (salaries expense)
	Balances after transaction . .	$15,900	$700	$20,000	$2,500 =		$6,000 +	$30,000	$3,100

Decreased by $2,600 (under Cash)   *Decreased by $2,600* (under Retained Earnings)

5b. Paid Rent In July, Bock paid $400 cash for office space rental. This transaction causes a decrease in cash of $400 and a decrease in the stockholders' equity of $400 because of the incurrence of rent expense.

Transaction 5b has the following effects on the amounts in the accounting equation:

Trans-action	Explanation	Cash	Accounts Receiv-able	Trucks	Office Equip-ment	Accounts Payable	Notes Payable	Capital Stock	Re-tained Earn-ings
						=		+	
	Balances before transaction . .	$15,900	$700	$20,000	$2,500 =		$6,000 +	$30,000	$3,100
5b	Paid rent	−400							−400 (rent expense)
	Balances after transaction . .	$15,500	$700	$20,000	$2,500 =		$6,000 +	$30,000	$2,700

Decreased by $400 (under Cash)   *Decreased by $400* (under Retained Earnings)

Paying cash for other expenses, such as advertising, gas and oil, and miscellaneous, would be recorded in the same way as transactions 4b and 5b.

6b. Received Bill for Gas and Oil Used At the end of the month, Bock received a $600 bill for gas and oil consumed during the month. This transaction involves an

ETHICS

A CLOSER LOOK

Jonathan Anders was taking an accounting course at State University. He was also engaged in helping companies find an accounting system that would fit their information needs. He advised one of his clients to acquire a software computer package that could be used to record the business transactions and would prepare the financial statements. The licensing agreement with the company that produced the software specified that the basic charge for one site is $4,000 and that $1,000 must be paid for each additional site at which the software is to be used.

Jonathan was pleased that his recommendation to acquire the software was followed. However, he was upset that the management of the company wanted him to install the software at eight other sites in the company and did not intend to pay the extra $8,000 due the software company. A member of management stated, "The software company will never know the difference and, besides, everyone else seems to be pirating software. If they do find out, we will pay the extra fee at that time. Our expenses are high enough without paying these unnecessary costs." Jonathan believed he might lose this client if he did not do as management instructed.

Required *a.* What would you do if you were Jonathan?

b. What do you think management will do if Jonathan refuses to install the program at the other sites?

increase in accounts payable (a liability) because Bock has not yet paid the bill and a decrease in retained earnings because Bock has incurred an expense. Bock's accounting equation now reads:

Trans-action	Explanation	Cash	Accounts Receiv-able	Trucks	Office Equip-ment	=	Accounts Payable	Notes Payable	+	Capital Stock	Re-tained Earn-ings	
				Assets		=	Liabilities		+	Stockholders' Equity		
	Balances before transaction . .	$15,500	$700	$20,000	$2,500	=		$6,000	+	$30,000	$2,700	
6b	Received bill for gas and oil used.						+600				−600	(gas and oil expense)
	End-of-month balances . . .	$15,500	$700	$20,000	$2,500	=	$600	$6,000	+	$30,000	$2,100	

Increased by $600

Decreased by $600

Summary of Balance Sheet and Income Statement Transactions   Part A of Illustration 1.3 summarizes the effects of all the preceding transactions on the assets, liabilities, and stockholders' equity of Bock Company in July. The beginning balances are those shown as ending balances in Part A of Illustration 1.2. The summary shows subtotals after each transaction; these subtotals are optional and may be omitted. Note how the accounting equation remains in balance after each transaction and at the end of the month.

ILLUSTRATION 1.3

A. Summary of Transactions

BOCK COMPANY
Summary of Transactions
Month of July 1994

			Assets			=	Liabilities		+	Stockholders' Equity	
Trans-action	Explanation	Cash	Accounts Receiv-able	Trucks	Office Equip-ment		Accounts Payable	Notes Payable		Capital Stock	Re-tained Earn-ings
	Beginning balances (Illustration 1.2)	$13,500	$–0–	$20,000	$2,500 =		$–0–	$6,000	+	$30,000	$ –0–
1b	Earned service revenue and received cash	+4,800									+4,800 (service revenue)
		$18,300		$20,000	$2,500 =			$6,000	+	$30,000	$4,800
2b	Earned service revenue on account . . .		+900								+900 (service revenue)
		$18,300	$900	$20,000	$2,500 =			$6,000	+	$30,000	$5,700
3b	Collected cash on account . .	+200	–200								
		$18,500	$700	$20,000	$2,500 =			$6,000	+	$30,000	$5,700
4b	Paid salaries . .	–2,600									–2,600 (salaries expense)
		$15,900	$700	$20,000	$2,500 =			$6,000	+	$30,000	$3,100
5b	Paid rent	–400									–400 (rent expense)
		$15,500	$700	$20,000	$2,500 =			$6,000	+	$30,000	$2,700
6b	Received bill for gas and oil used.						+600				–600 (gas and oil expense)
	End-of-month balances . . .	$15,500	$700	$20,000	$2,500 =		$600	$6,000	+	$30,000	$2,100

$38,700 $6,600 $32,100

B. Balance Sheet

BOCK COMPANY
Balance Sheet
July 31, 1994

Assets

Cash	$15,500
Accounts receivable . .	700
Trucks.	20,000
Office equipment. . . .	2,500
Total assets	$38,700

Liabilities and Stockholders' Equity

Liabilities:

Accounts payable. . .	$ 600
Notes payable	6,000
Total liabilities . . .	$ 6,600

Stockholders' equity:

Capital stock	$30,000
Retained earnings . .	2,100
Total stockholders' equity	$32,100
Total liabilities and stockholders' equity. .	$38,700

C. Income Statement

BOCK COMPANY
Income Statement
For the Month Ended July 31, 1994

Revenues:

Service revenue . . .	$5,700

Expenses:

Salaries expense . . .	$2,600
Rent expense	400
Gas and oil expense .	600
Total expenses . . .	3,600
Net income	$2,100

Objective 6

Prepare an income statement, a statement of retained earnings, and a balance sheet.

The ending balances in each of the columns in Part A of Illustration 1.3 are the dollar amounts in Part B and those reported earlier in the balance sheet in Part C of Illustration 1.1. The itemized data in the Retained Earnings column are the revenue and expense items in Part C of Illustration 1.3 and those reported earlier in the income statement in Part A of Illustration 1.1. The beginning balance in the Retained Earnings column ($–0–) plus net income for the month ($2,100) is equal to the ending balance in retained earnings ($2,100) shown earlier in Part B of Illustration 1.2.

Dividends Paid to Owners (Stockholders)   Stockholders' equity is (1) increased by capital contributed by stockholders and by revenues earned through operations and (2) decreased by expenses incurred in producing revenues. The payment of cash or other assets to stockholders in the form of dividends also reduces stockholders' equity. Thus, if the owners receive a dividend in the form of cash, the effect would be to reduce cash and stockholders' equity by that amount. This transaction would reduce the retained earnings part of stockholders' equity, and the amount of dividends is not an expense but rather a distribution of income.

Chapter 1 has introduced two important components of the accounting process—the accounting equation and the business transaction. In Chapter 2, you will learn about debits and credits and how accountants use them in recording transactions.

UNDERSTANDING THE LEARNING OBJECTIVES

1. Identify and describe the three basic forms of business organizations.
    □ A single proprietorship is an unincorporated business owned by an individual and often managed by that same individual.
    □ A partnership is an unincorporated business owned by two or more persons associated as partners and is often managed by those same persons.
    □ A corporation is a business incorporated under the laws of one of the states and owned by a few persons or by thousands of stockholders.

2. Distinguish among the three types of activities performed by business organizations.
    □ Service companies perform services for a fee.
    □ Merchandising companies purchase goods that are ready for sale and then sell them to customers.
    □ Manufacturing companies buy materials, convert them into products, and then sell the products to other companies or to final customers.

3. Describe the content and purposes of the income statement, statement of retained earnings, and balance sheet.
    □ The income statement reports the revenues and expenses of a company and shows the profitability of that business organization for a stated period of time
    □ The statement of retained earnings shows the change in retained earnings between the beginning of the period (e.g., a month) and the end of that period.
    □ The balance sheet lists the assets, liabilities, and stockholders' equity (including dollar amounts) of a business organization at a specific moment in time.

4. State the basic accounting equation and describe its relationship to the balance sheet.
   □ The accounting equation is: Assets = Liabilities + Stockholders' Equity.
   □ The left-hand side of the equation represents the left-hand side of the balance sheet and shows things of value owned by the business.
   □ The right-hand side of the equation represents the right-hand side of the balance sheet and shows who provided the funds to acquire the things of value (assets).

5. Using the underlying assumptions or concepts, analyze business transactions and determine their effects on items in the financial statements.
   □ Some transactions only affect balance sheet items: assets (such as cash, accounts receivable, and equipment), liabilities (such as accounts payable and notes payable), and stockholders' equity (Capital Stock and Retained Earnings accounts). Other transactions affect both balance sheet items and income statement items (revenues and expenses).
   □ Illustration 1.3 (Part A) shows the effects of business transactions on the accounting equation.

6. Prepare an income statement, a statement of retained earnings, and a balance sheet.
   □ The income statement is shown in Illustrations 1.1 (Part A) and 1.3 (Part C).
   □ The statement of retained earnings is shown in Illustration 1.1 (Part B).
   □ The balance sheet is shown in Illustration 1.1 (Part C) and 1.3 (Part B).

DEMONSTRATION PROBLEM

On June 1, 1994, Green Hills Riding Stable, Incorporated, was organized. The following transactions occurred during June:

June 1 Shares of capital stock were issued for $10,000 cash.
       4 A horse stable and riding equipment were rented (and paid for) for the month at a cost of $1,200.
       8 Horse feed for the month was purchased on credit, $800.
      15 Boarding fees of $3,000 for June were charged to those owning horses that were boarded at the stable. (This amount is due on July 10.)
      20 Miscellaneous expenses of $600 were paid.
      29 Land was purchased from a savings and loan association by borrowing $40,000 on a note from that association. The loan is due to be repaid in five years. Interest payments are due at the end of each month beginning July 31.
      30 Salaries of $700 for the month were paid.
      30 Riding and lesson fees were billed to customers in the amount of $2,400. (They are due on July 10.)

Required a. Prepare a summary of the above transactions. Use columns headed Cash, Accounts Receivable, Land, Accounts Payable, Notes Payable, Capital Stock, and Retained Earnings. Determine balances after each transaction to show that the basic equation is in balance.
          b. Prepare an income statement for June 1994.
          c. Prepare a statement of retained earnings for June 1994.
          d. Prepare a balance sheet as of June 30, 1994.

SOLUTION TO DEMONSTRATION PROBLEM

a.

GREEN HILLS RIDING STABLE, INCORPORATED
Summary of Transactions
Month of June 1994

		Assets			=	Liabilities		+	Stockholders' Equity	
Date	Explanation	Cash	Accounts Receivable	Land	=	Accounts Payable	Notes Payable	+	Capital Stock	Retained Earnings
June 1	Capital stock issued	$10,000			=				$10,000	
4	Rent expense.	−1,200								$−1,200
		$ 8,800			=				$10,000	$−1,200
8	Feed expense					$+800				−800
		$ 8,800			=	$ 800		+	$10,000	$−2,000
15	Boarding fees.		$+3,000							+3,000
		$ 8,800	$ 3,000		=	$ 800		+	$10,000	$ 1,000
20	Miscellaneous expenses . . .	−600								−600
		$ 8,200	$ 3,000		=	$ 800		+	$10,000	$ 400
29	Purchased land by borrowing			$+40,000			$+40,000			
		$ 8,200	$ 3,000	$ 40,000	=	$ 800	$ 40,000	+	$10,000	$ 400
30	Salaries paid	−700								−700
		$ 7,500	$ 3,000	$ 40,000	=	$ 800	$ 40,000	+	$10,000	$ −300
30	Riding and lesson fees billed		+2,400							+2,400
		$ 7,500	$ 5,400	$ 40,000	=	$ 800	$ 40,000	+	$10,000	$ 2,100

b.

GREEN HILLS RIDING STABLE, INCORPORATED
Income Statement
For the Month Ended June 30, 1994

Revenues:

Horse boarding fees revenue.	$3,000	
Riding and lesson fees revenue	2,400	
Total revenues		$5,400

Expenses:

Rent expense	$1,200	
Feed expense	800	
Salaries expense	700	
Miscellaneous expense	600	
Total expenses		3,300
Net Income		$2,100

c.

GREEN HILLS RIDING STABLE, INCORPORATED
Statement of Retained Earnings
For the Month Ended June 30, 1994

Retained earnings, June 1	$ –0–
Add: Net income for June	2,100
Total	$2,100
Less: Dividends	–0–
Retained earnings, June 30	$2,100

d.

GREEN HILLS RIDING STABLE, INCORPORATED
Balance Sheet
June 30, 1994
Assets

Cash	$ 7,500
Accounts receivable.	5,400
Land	40,000
Total assets	$52,900

Liabilities and Stockholders' Equity

Liabilities:

Accounts payable.		$ 800
Notes payable		40,000
Total liabilities		$40,800

Stockholders' equity:

Capital stock	$10,000	
Retained earnings	2,100	
Total stockholders' equity		12,100
Total liabilities and stockholders' equity . . .		$52,900

NEW TERMS

Accounting equation   Basically, Assets = Equities; in slightly expanded form for a corporation, Assets = Liabilities + Stockholders' Equity. *28*

Accounts payable   Amounts owed to suppliers for goods or services purchased on credit. *28*

Accounts receivable   Amounts due from customers for services already provided. *28*

Assets   Things of value owned by the business. Examples include cash, machines, and buildings. Assets possess service potential or utility to their owners that can be measured and expressed in money terms. *27*

Balance sheet   Financial statement that lists a company's assets, liabilities, and stockholders' equity (including dollar amounts) as of a specific moment in time. Also called *statement of financial position. 24, 27*

Business entity concept   The separate existence of the business organization. *22, 29*

Capital stock   The title given to an equity account showing the investment in a business corporation by its stockholders. *28*

Continuity   See Going concern.

Corporation   Business incorporated under the laws of one of the states and owned by a few persons or by thousands of persons. *23*

Cost   Sacrifice made or the resources given up, measured in money terms, to acquire some desired thing, such as a new truck (asset). *29*

Dividend   Payment (usually of cash) to the owners of the business; it is a distribution of income to owners rather than an expense of doing business. *27*

Entity   A unit that is deemed to have an existence separate and apart from its owners, creditors, employees, customers, other interested parties, and other businesses, and for which accounting records are maintained. *22, 29*

Equities   Broadly speaking, all claims to, or interests in, assets; includes liabilities and stockholders' equity. *28*

Exchange-price (or cost) concept (principle)   The objective money prices determined in the exchange process are used to record most assets. *29*

Expenses   Costs incurred to produce revenues, measured by the assets surrendered or consumed in serving customers. *25*

Going concern (continuity) concept   The assumption by the accountant that unless strong evidence exists to the contrary, a business entity will continue operations into the indefinite future. *30*

Income statement   Financial statement that shows the revenues and expenses and reports the profitability of a business organization for a stated period of time. Sometimes called an *earnings statement. 24, 25*

Liabilities   Debts owed by a business—or creditors' equity. Examples: notes payable, accounts payable. *28*

Manufacturing companies   Companies that buy materials, convert them into products, and then sell the products to other companies or to final customers. *24*

Merchandising companies   Companies that purchase goods that are ready for sale and then sell them to customers. *24*

Money measurement concept   Recording and reporting economic activity in terms of a common monetary unit of measure such as the dollar. *29*

Net income Amount by which the revenues of a period exceed the expenses of the same period. *25*

Net loss Amount by which the expenses of a period exceed the revenues of the same period. *25*

Notes payable Amounts owed to parties who loan the company money after the owner signs a written agreement (a note) for the company to repay each loan. *28*

Partnership An unincorporated business owned by two or more persons associated as partners. *23*

Periodicity (time periods concept) An assumption that an entity's life can be meaningfully subdivided into time periods (such as months or years) for purposes of reporting its economic activities. *30*

Profitability Ability to generate income. The income statement reflects a company's profitability. *24*

Retained earnings Accumulated net income less dividend distributions to stockholders. *28*

Revenues Inflows of assets (such as cash) resulting from the sale of products or the rendering of services to customers. *25*

Service companies Companies (such as accounting firms, law firms, or dry cleaning establishments) that perform services for a fee. *24*

Single proprietorship An unincorporated business owned by an individual and often managed by that same individual. *23*

Solvency Ability to pay debts as they become due. The balance sheet reflects a company's solvency. *24*

Source document Any written or printed evidence of a business transaction that describes the essential facts of that transaction, such as receipts for cash paid or received. *29*

Statement of cash flows Shows cash inflows and outflows for a company over a period of time. *24*

Statement of retained earnings Statement used to explain the changes in retained earnings that occurred between two balance sheet dates. *24, 26*

Stockholders' equity The owners' interest in a corporation. *28*

Stockholders or shareholders Owners of a corporation; they buy shares of stock, which are units of ownership, in the corporation. *23*

Summary of transactions Teaching tool used in chapter to show the effects of transactions on the accounting equation. *32*

Transaction A business activity or event that must be recorded in the accounting records. *29*

SELF-TEST

True-False

Indicate whether each of the following statements is true or false.

1. The three forms of business organizations are single proprietorship, partnership, and trust.

2. The three types of business activity are service, merchandising, and manufacturing.

3. The income statement shows the profitability of the company and is dated as of a particular date, such as December 31, 1994.

4. The statement of retained earnings shows both the net income for the period and the beginning and ending balances of retained earnings.

5. The balance sheet contains the same major headings as appear in the accounting equation.

Multiple-Choice

Select the best answer for each of the following questions.

1. The ending balance in retained earnings is shown in the:
   a. Income statement.
   b. Statement of retained earnings.
   c. Balance sheet.
   d. Both *(b)* and *(c)*.

2. Which of the following is *not* a correct form of the accounting equation?
   a. Assets = Equities.
   b. Assets = Liabilities + Stockholders' Equity.
   c. Assets − Liabilities = Stockholders' Equity.
   d. Assets + Stockholders' Equity = Liabilities.

3. Which of the following is *not* one of the five underlying assumptions or concepts mentioned in the chapter?
   a. Exchange-price concept.
   b. Inflation accounting concept.
   c. Business entity concept.
   d. Going-concern concept.

4. When the stockholders invest cash in the business, what is the effect?
   a. Liabilities increase and stockholders' equity increases.
   b. Both assets and liabilities increase.
   c. Both assets and stockholders' equity increase.
   d. None of the above.

5. When services are performed on account, what is the effect?
   a. Both cash and retained earnings decrease.
   b. Both cash and retained earnings increase.
   c. Both accounts receivable and retained earnings increase.
   d. Accounts payable increases and retained earnings decreases.

Now turn to page 53 to check your answers.

QUESTIONS

1. Accounting has often been called the language of business. In what respects would you agree with this description? How might you argue that this description is deficient?

2. Define asset, liability, and stockholders' equity.

3. How do liabilities and stockholders' equity differ? How are they similar?

4. How do accounts payable and notes payable differ? How are they similar?

5. Define revenues. How are revenues measured?

6. Define expenses. How are expenses measured?

7. What is a balance sheet? On what aspect of a business does the balance sheet provide information?

8. What is an income statement? On what aspect of a business does this statement provide information?

9. What information does the statement of retained earnings provide?

10. What is a transaction? What use does the accountant make of transactions? Why?

11. What is the accounting equation? Why must it always balance?

12. Give an example from your personal life that you believe illustrates your use of accounting information in reaching a decision.

13. You have been elected to the governing board of your church. At the first meeting you attend, mention is made of building a new church. What accounting information would the board need in deciding whether or not to go ahead?

14. A company purchased equipment for $1,000 cash. The vendor stated that the equipment was worth $1,200. At what amount should the equipment be recorded?

15. What is meant by money measurement?

16. Of what significance is the exchange-price (or cost) concept? How is the cost to acquire an asset determined?

17. What effect does the going-concern (continuity) concept have on amounts at which long-term assets are carried on the balance sheet?

18. Of what importance is the periodicity (time periods) concept to the preparation of financial statements?

19. Describe a transaction that would:
    a. Increase both an asset and the Capital Stock account.
    b. Increase both an asset and a liability.
    c. Increase one asset and decrease another asset.
    d. Decrease both a liability and an asset.
    e. Increase both an asset and the Retained Earnings account.
    f. Decrease both an asset and the Retained Earnings account.
    g. Increase a liability and decrease the Retained Earnings account.
    h. Increase the Dividends account and decrease an asset.

20. Identify the causes of increases and decreases in stockholders' equity.

21. *Real world question* Refer to "A Broader Perspective" on page 25. Do you believe that a movie that grossed $300 million made no profit? If you were to share in the profits of a movie, would you rather have a percentage of the gross revenues or a share of net income?

MAYTAG
CORPORATION

22. *Real world question* Refer to the financial statements of Maytag Corporation in Appendix E at the end of the text. What were the net income amounts in 1987, 1988, and 1989?

THE LIMITED, INC.

23. *Real world question* Referring to the financial statements of The Limited, Inc., in Appendix E at the end of the text, has net income increased or decreased over the period 1987–89?

EXERCISES

Exercise 1–1

Matching
(L.O. 1, 2)

Match the descriptions in Column B with the appropriate terms in Column A.

Column A		Column B
1. Corporation.	a.	An unincorporated business owned by an individual.
2. Merchandising company.	b.	The form of organization used by most large businesses.
3. Partnership.	c.	Buys raw materials and converts them into finished products.
4. Manufacturing company.	d.	Buys goods in their finished form and sells them to customers in that same form.
5. Service company.	e.	An unincorporated business with more than one owner.
6. Single proprietorship.	f.	Performs services for a fee.

Exercise 1–2

Compute net income and revenue

(L.O. 3)

Assume that retained earnings increased by $14,400 from June 30, 1993, to June 30, 1994. A cash dividend of $1,200 was declared and paid during the year.

a. Compute the net income for the year.

b. Assume expenses for the year were $36,000. Compute the revenue for the year.

Exercise 1–3

Compute retained earnings

(L.O. 3, 4)

On December 31, 1994, Buckley Company had assets of $135,000, liabilities of $97,500, and capital stock of $30,000. During 1994, Buckley earned revenues of $45,000 and incurred expenses of $33,750. Dividends declared and paid amounted to $3,000.

a. Compute the company's retained earnings on December 31, 1993.

b. Compute the company's retained earnings on December 31, 1994.

Exercise 1–4

Compute retained earnings and total assets at beginning of year

(L.O. 3, 4)

At the start of the year, a company had liabilities of $108,000 and capital stock of $300,000. At the end of the year, retained earnings amounted to $270,000. Net income for the year was $90,000, and $30,000 of dividends were declared and paid. Compute retained earnings and total assets at the beginning of the year.

Exercise 1–5

Analyze transactions

(L.O. 4, 5)

For each event below, determine if it has an effect on the basic elements of the accounting equation. For the events that do have an effect, present an analysis of the transaction showing its two sides or dual nature.

a. Purchased equipment for cash, $3,000.

b. Purchased a truck for $30,000, payment to be made later in the month.

c. Paid $600 for the current month's utilities.

d. Paid for the truck purchased in (b).

e. Employed Mary Childers as a salesperson at $1,500 per month. She is to start work next week.

f. Signed an agreement with a bank in which the bank agreed to lend the company up to $150,000 any time within the next two years.

Exercise 1–6

Indicate effect of transactions on items in the accounting equation

(L.O. 4, 5)

Mendez Company, engaged in a service business, completed the following selected transactions during July 1994:

a. Purchased office equipment on account.

b. Paid an account payable.

c. Earned service revenue on account.

d. Borrowed money by signing a note at the bank.

e. Paid salaries for month to employees.

f. Received cash on account from a charge customer.

g. Received gas and oil bill for month.

h. Purchased delivery truck for cash.

i. Declared and paid a cash dividend.

Using a tabular form similar to Illustration 1.3 (Part A), indicate the effect of each transaction on the accounting equation using (+) for increase and (−) for decrease. No dollar amounts are needed, and you need not fill in the Explanation column.

Exercise 1–7

Determine effect of transactions on stockholders' equity

(L.O. 5)

Indicate the immediate amount of change (if any) in the stockholders' equity balance based on each of the following transactions:

a. The owner invested $120,000 cash in the business by purchasing capital stock.

b. Land costing $20,000 was purchased by paying cash.

c. The company performed services for a customer who agreed to pay $32,000 in one month.

d. Paid salaries for the month, $28,800.

e. Paid $10,000 on an account payable.

Exercise 1–8
Analyze transactions
(L.O. 5)

Give examples of transactions that would have the following effects on the items in a firm's financial statements:

a. Increase cash; decrease some other asset.

b. Decrease cash; increase some other asset.

c. Increase an asset; increase a liability.

d. Increase an expense; decrease an asset.

e. Increase an asset other than cash; increase revenue.

f. Decrease an asset; decrease a liability.

Exercise 1–9
Identify transactions that increase expenses
(L.O. 5)

Which of the following transactions results in an increase in an expense? Why?

a. Employees were paid $40,000 for services received during the month.

b. $200,000 was paid to acquire land.

c. Paid a $20,000 note payable. No interest was involved.

d. Paid $100 as a refundable deposit when an additional telephone was installed.

Exercise 1–10
Compute net income
(L.O. 6)

Selected data for Freeman Company for 1994 are as follows (including all income statement data):

Revenue from services rendered on account	$264,000
Revenue from services rendered for cash	72,000
Cash collected from customers on account	201,600
Stockholders' equity, January 1, 1994	384,000
Expenses incurred on account	144,000
Expenses incurred for cash	96,000
Dividends declared and paid	24,000
Capital stock issued for cash	48,000
Stockholders' equity, December 31, 1994	504,000

Compute net income for 1994.

Exercise 1–11
Prepare income statement
(L.O. 6)

Assume that the following items were included in the Retained Earnings column in the summary of transactions for Glenn Company for July 1994:

Salaries expense	$120,000
Service revenue	240,000
Gas and oil expense	27,000
Rent expense	48,000
Dividends paid	30,000

Prepare an income statement for July 1994.

Exercise 1–12
Prepare statement of retained earnings
(L.O. 6)

Given the following facts, prepare a statement of retained earnings for King Company for August 1994:

Balance in retained earnings at end of July, $168,000.
Dividends paid in August, $57,600.
Net income for August, $72,000.

Exercise 1–13
Prepare balance sheet
(L.O. 6)

The column totals of a summary of transactions for Pullen Company as of December 31, 1994, were as follows (listed in alphabetical order):

Accounts payable	$ 30,000
Accounts receivable	60,000
Capital stock	100,000
Cash	40,000
Land	160,000
Notes payable	20,000
Retained earnings	?

Prepare a balance sheet.

PROBLEMS: SERIES A

Problem 1–1A

Prepare summary of
transactions
(L.O. 4, 5)

Ross Company, which provides financial advisory services, engaged in the following transactions during May 1994:

May 1 Received $200,000 cash for shares of capital stock issued when company was organized.
2 The company borrowed $32,000 from the bank on a note.
7 The company bought $182,400 of computer equipment for cash.
11 Cash received for services performed to date was $15,200.
14 Services performed for a customer who agreed to pay within a month were $10,000.
15 Employee services received in operating the business to date were paid, $13,200.
19 The company paid $14,000 on the note to the bank.
31 Interest paid to the bank for May was $140. (Interest is an expense, which reduces stockholders' equity.)
31 The customer of May 14 paid $3,200 of the amount owed the company.
31 An order was received from a customer for services to be rendered next week, which will be billed at $8,000.

Required

Prepare a summary of transactions (see Part A of Illustration 1.3). Use money columns headed Cash, Accounts Receivable, Equipment, Notes Payable, Capital Stock, and Retained Earnings. Determine balances after each transaction to show that the accounting equation balances.

Problem 1–2A

Prepare summary of
transactions and balance
sheet
(L.O. 4–6)

Santiago Company engaged in the following transactions in April 1994:

Apr. 1 The company was organized and received $192,000 cash from the owners in exchange for capital stock issued.
4 The company bought equipment for cash, $101,760.
9 The company bought additional equipment that cost $9,120 and agreed to pay for it in 30 days.
15 Cash received for services performed to date was $3,840.
16 Amount due from a customer for services performed totaled $5,280.
30 Of the receivable (see April 16), $3,072 was collected in cash.
30 Various operating costs of $6,240 were paid during the month.
30 An order was placed for equipment advertised at $28,800.

Required

a. Prepare a summary of transactions (see Part A of Illustration 1.3). Use money columns headed Cash, Accounts Receivable, Equipment, Accounts Payable, Capital Stock, and Retained Earnings. Determine balances after each transaction to show that the basic accounting equation balances.

b. Prepare a balance sheet as of April 30.

Problem 1–3A

Prepare income statement
(L.O. 6)

Following are the transactions for August 1994 of Ward Company, a theater:

Aug. 2 Paid current month's rent of building, $24,000.
7 Cash ticket revenue for the week was $14,400.
14 Cash ticket revenue for the week was $16,800.

Aug. 15   Paid cash dividends, $3,000.

  21   Cash ticket revenue for the week was $9,600.

  24   Paid month's advertising bill, $11,400.

  27   Paid miscellaneous expenses, $4,200.

  31   Paid rental on films shown during month, $30,000.

  31   Received $37,200 from operators of concessions for operating in theater during August.

  31   Cash ticket revenue for August 22–31 was $25,200.

  31   Paid salaries for the month, $39,600.

Required   Prepare an income statement for August 1994.

Problem 1–4A

Prepare income statement, statement of retained earnings, and balance sheet (L.O. 6)

Analysis of the transactions of the Moon Light Drive-In Theater for June 1994 disclosed the following:

Ticket revenue	$160,000
Rent of equipment	30,000
Film rental paid	53,400
Receipts from concessionaries	29,600
Advertising expense	18,600
Salaries expense	46,800
Utilities expense	14,100
Cash dividends	12,000

Balance sheet figures at June 30 include the following:

Cash	$228,000
Land	48,000
Accounts payable	62,400
Capital stock	114,000
Retained earnings as of June 1, 1994	84,900

Required   a.   Prepare an income statement for June 1994.

  b.   Prepare a statement of retained earnings for June 1994.

  c.   Prepare a balance sheet as of June 30, 1994.

Problem 1–5A

Prepare income statement, statement of retained earnings, and balance sheet (L.O. 4–6)

The following data are for Massey Service Company:

MASSEY SERVICE COMPANY
Balance Sheet
April 30, 1994
Assets

Cash		$ 56,000
Accounts receivable		80,000
Land		600,000
Total assets		$736,000

Liabilities and Stockholders' Equity

Liabilities:

Accounts payable		$ 64,000
Stockholders' equity:		
Capital stock	$400,000	
Retained earnings	272,000	672,000
Total liabilities and stockholders' equity		$736,000

The summarized transactions for May 1994 are as follows:

a. Issued additional capital stock for cash, $120,000.

b. Collected $80,000 on accounts receivable.

c. Paid $64,000 on accounts payable.

d. Services rendered to customers: for cash, $260,000; and on account, $120,000.

e. Employee services and other operating costs incurred: for cash, $60,000; and on account, $160,000.

f. Paid dividends of $16,000.

g. Purchased land for cash, $96,000.

h. Placed an order for new equipment expected to cost $320,000.

Required a. Prepare a summary of transactions (see Part A of Illustration 1.3) using column headings as given in the balance sheet. Determine balances after each transaction.

b. Prepare an income statement for May 1994.

c. Prepare a statement of retained earnings for May 1994.

d. Prepare a balance sheet as of May 31, 1994.

Problem 1–6A

State causes of balance sheet changes (L.O. 3, 6)

Given below are the balance sheets for April and May 1994, and the income statement for May, of Douglas Company (common practice is to show the most recent period first):

DOUGLAS COMPANY
Comparative Balance Sheets

	May 31, 1994	April 30, 1994
Assets		
Cash.	$ 86,400	$ 76,800
Accounts receivable	144,000	115,200
Land.	19,200	28,800
Total assets	$249,600	$220,800
Liabilities and Stockholders' Equity		
Accounts payable	$ 48,000	$ 57,600
Capital stock	144,000	144,000
Retained earnings.	57,600	19,200
Total liabilities and stockholders' equity	$249,600	$220,800

DOUGLAS COMPANY
Income Statement
For the Month Ended May 31, 1994

Revenues:		
Service revenue		$144,000
Expenses:		
Salaries expense	$96,000	
Rent expense	9,600	105,600
Net income		$ 38,400

All revenues earned are on account.

Required State the probable cause(s) of the change in each of the balance sheet accounts from April 30 to May 31, 1994.

PROBLEMS: SERIES B

Problem 1–1B

Prepare summary of
transactions
(L.O. 4, 5)

Harris Company completed the following transactions in September 1994:

Sept. 1 The company was organized and received $80,000 cash from the issuance of
capital stock.
5 The company bought equipment for cash at a cost of $21,600.
7 The company performed services for a customer who agreed to pay $8,000 in
one week.
14 The company received the $8,000 from the transaction of September 7.
20 Equipment that cost $3,200 was acquired today; payment was postponed until
September 28.
28 $2,400 was paid on the liability incurred on September 20.
30 Employee services for the month, $2,800, were paid.
30 Placed an order for new equipment advertised at $20,000.

Required   Prepare a summary of transactions (see Part A of Illustration 1.3) for the company for the
above transactions. Use money columns headed Cash, Accounts Receivable, Equipment,
Accounts Payable, Capital Stock, and Retained Earnings. Determine balances after each
transaction to show that the basic accounting equation balances.

Problem 1–2B

Prepare summary of
transactions and balance
sheet
(L.O. 4–6)

Hall Company completed the following transactions in June 1994:

June 1 The company was organized and received $60,000 cash from the issuance of
capital stock.
4 The company paid $48,000 cash for equipment.
7 The company borrowed $9,000 from its bank on a note.
9 Cash received for services performed to date was $4,500.
12 Costs of operating the business so far this month were paid in cash, $3,150.
18 Services performed for a customer who agreed to pay within a month amounted
to $5,400.
25 The company paid $4,065 on its loan from the bank, including $4,050 of principal
and $15 of interest. (The principal is the amount of the loan. Interest is an
expense, which reduces stockholders' equity.)
30 Costs of operating the business from June 13 to date were $3,825 and were paid in
cash.
30 An order was received from a customer for services to be performed tomorrow,
which will be billed at $3,000.

Required   a. Prepare a summary of transactions (see Part A of Illustration 1.3). Include money
columns for Cash, Accounts Receivable, Equipment, Notes Payable, Capital
Stock, and Retained Earnings. Determine balances after each transaction to show
that the basic accounting equation balances.
b. Prepare a balance sheet as of June 30, 1994.

Problem 1–3B

Prepare income statement
(L.O. 6)

The following transactions are for Cerda Company:

May 1 Paid May rent on the parking structure, $40,000.
8 Received cash for eight days' parking services, $19,360.
15 Received cash for a week's parking services, $24,160.
15 Salaries paid for first half of May, $9,600.
17 Received cash for shares of capital stock issued, $20,000.
19 Paid advertising expenses for May, $3,200.
22 Received cash for a week's parking services, $31,680.
31 Salaries paid for last half of May, $12,000.
31 Cash received for nine days' parking services, $28,160.
31 Purchased motorized sweeper to clean parking structure, $24,000 cash.

Required   Prepare an income statement for the month of May 1994.

Problem 1–4B

Prepare income statement
(L.O. 6)

Following are summarized transaction data for Foster Company for the year ending June 30, 1994. The company owns and operates an apartment building.

Rent revenue from building owned	$93,030
Building repairs	2,870
Building cleaning, labor cost	3,185
Property taxes on the building	3,605
Insurance on the building	1,225
Commissions paid to rental agent	5,250
Legal and accounting fees (for preparation of tenant leases)	1,260
Utilities expense	8,225
Cost of new awnings installed	2,800

Of the $93,030 of rent revenue above, $3,500 was not collected in cash until July 5, 1994.

Required

Prepare an income statement for the year ended June 30, 1994.

Problem 1–5B

Prepare summary of transactions, income statement, statement of retained earnings, and balance sheet
(L.O. 4–6)

The following data are for Evans Corporation:

EVANS CORPORATION
Balance Sheet
October 1, 1994
Assets

Cash	$204,000
Accounts receivable	18,000
Total assets	$222,000

Liabilities and Stockholders' Equity

Accounts payable	$ 54,000
Capital stock	132,000
Retained earnings	36,000
Total liabilities and stockholders' equity	$222,000

The summarized transactions for October 1994 are as follows:

Oct. 1 The accounts payable owed as of October 1 ($54,000) were paid.

1 The company paid rent for the premises for October, $19,200.

7 The company received cash of $4,200 for parking by daily customers during the week.

10 The company collected $14,400 of the accounts receivable in the balance sheet at October 1.

14 Cash receipts for the week from daily customers were $6,600.

15 Parking revenue earned but not yet collected from fleet customers was $3,000.

16 The company paid salaries of $2,400 for the period October 1–15.

19 The company paid advertising expenses of $1,200 for October.

21 Cash receipts for the week from daily customers were $7,200.

24 The company incurred miscellaneous expenses of $840, which will be due November 10.

31 Cash receipts for the last 10 days of the month from daily customers were $8,400.

31 The company paid salaries of $3,000 for the period October 16–31.

31 Billings to monthly customers totaled $21,600 for October.

31 Paid cash dividends of $24,000.

Required

a. Prepare a summary of transactions (see Part A of Illustration 1.3) using column headings as given in the above balance sheet. Determine balances after each transaction.

b. Prepare an income statement for October 1994.

c. Prepare a statement of retained earnings for October 1994.

d. Prepare a balance sheet as of October 31, 1994.

Problem 1–6B
State causes of balance sheet changes (L.O. 3, 6)

Given below are balance sheets for May and June 1994, and the income statement for June, of Doyle Company (common practice is to show the most recent period first):

DOYLE COMPANY
Comparative Balance Sheets

	June 30, 1994	May 31, 1994
Assets		
Cash	$ 42,000	$60,000
Accounts receivable	24,000	–0–
Land	36,000	36,000
Total assets	$102,000	$96,000
Liabilities and Stockholders' Equity		
Liabilities	$ 12,000	$24,000
Capital stock	60,000	60,000
Retained earnings	30,000	12,000
Total liabilities and stockholders' equity	$102,000	$96,000

DOYLE COMPANY
Income Statement
For the Month Ended June 30, 1994

Revenues:		
Service revenue		$96,000
Expenses:		
Salaries expense	$48,000	
Supplies bought and used	24,000	72,000
Net income		$24,000

A cash dividend of $6,000 was declared and paid in June.

Required   State the probable causes of the changes in each of the balance sheet accounts from May 31 to June 30, 1994.

BUSINESS DECISION PROBLEMS

Decision Problem 1–1
Identify information needed to make decision (L.O. 3)

Upon graduation from high school, Mark Bowman went to work for a builder of houses and small apartment buildings. During the next six years, Mark earned a reputation as an excellent employee—hardworking, dedicated, and dependable—in the light construction industry. He could handle almost any job requiring carpentry, electrical, or plumbing skills.

Mark then decided to go into business for himself under the name of Mark's Fix-It Shop, Inc. He invested cash, some power tools, and a used truck in his business. He completed many repair and remodeling jobs for both homeowners and apartment owners. The demand for his services was so large that he had more work than he could handle. He operated out of his garage, which he had converted into a shop, adding several new pieces of power woodworking equipment.

Now two years after going into business for himself, Mark is faced with a decision of whether to continue in his own business or to accept a position as construction supervisor for a home builder. He has been offered an annual salary of $40,000 and a package of "fringe benefits" (medical and hospitalization insurance, pension contribution, vacation and sick pay, and life insurance) worth approximately $7,500 per year. The offer is attractive to Mark. But he dislikes giving up his business since he has thoroughly enjoyed "being his own boss," even though it has led to an average workweek well in excess of the standard 40 hours.

Required Suppose Mark comes to you for assistance in gathering the information needed to help him make a decision. He brings along the accounting records that have been maintained for his business by an experienced accountant. Using logic and your own life experiences, indicate the nature of the information Mark needs if he is to make an informed decision. Pay particular attention to the information likely to be found in the accounting records for Mark's business that would be useful. Does the accounting information available enter directly into the decision? Explain.

Decision Problem 1–2
Prepare income statement and balance sheet; judge profitability of company (L.O. 6)

The Silvery Moon Drive-In Theater, Inc., opened for business on June 1, 1994. Analysis of the transactions for June 1994 discloses the following:

Ticket revenue	$71,000
Rent expense for premises and equipment	9,000
Film rental expense paid	17,800
Revenue received from operators of candy and popcorn concessions	10,000
Advertising expense	8,400
Salaries expense	15,600
Utilities expense	5,000

Asset and liability amounts as of June 30 that the accountant calculated include the following:

Cash	$100,000
Land	16,000
Accounts payable	20,800

The balance in the Capital Stock account on June 1 was $70,000.

Required
a. Prepare an income statement for June 1994.
b. Prepare a balance sheet as of June 30, 1994.
c. Did June seem to be a profitable month for this company?

ANSWERS TO SELF-TEST

True-False

1. *False.* Corporation, not trust, is the third form.
2. *True.* The accounting for all three of these will be covered in this text.
3. *False.* The income statement is dated using a period of time, such as "For the Year Ended December 31, 1994."
4. *True.* In addition, the statement of retained earnings shows dividends declared.
5. *True.* Both show assets, liabilities, and stockholders' equity.

Multiple-Choice

1. *d.* The ending balance in retained earnings is shown in both the statement of retained earnings and in the balance sheet.
2. *d.* This form of the equation would not balance.
3. *b.* The inflation accounting concept was not one of the ones discussed. The other two were the money measurement concept and the periodicity concept.
4. *c.* When the stockholders invest cash, assets and stockholders' equity increase.
5. *c.* The performance of services on account increases both accounts receivable and retained earnings.

2

RECORDING BUSINESS TRANSACTIONS

LEARNING OBJECTIVES

After studying this chapter, you should be able to:

1. Use the account as the basic classifying and storage unit for accounting information.
2. Express the effects of business transactions in terms of debits and credits to different types of accounts.
3. Record the effects of business transactions in a journal.
4. Post journal entries to the accounts in the ledger.
5. Prepare a trial balance to test the equality of debits and credits in the journalizing and posting process.

In Chapter 1, you learned that accountants classify business organizations according to the form of ownership of the business entity and by the type of business activities the business entity performs. The three forms of business organizations are single proprietorships, partnerships, and corporations. These organizations may perform three types of business activities—service, merchandising, and manufacturing. The three financial statements illustrated in Chapter 1 are the income statement, the statement of retained earnings, and the balance sheet. These statements are the end products of the financial accounting process (or cycle), which has the accounting equation as its foundation.

The raw data of accounting are the business transactions. The transactions in Chapter 1 were recorded as increases or decreases in the assets, liabilities, and stockholders' equity items of the accounting equation. This procedure showed you how the various transactions affected the items in the accounting equation. When working through these sample transactions, you probably noticed that listing all transactions as increases or decreases in the transactions summary columns would be too cumbersome in practice. Most businesses, even small ones, enter into many transactions every day. Chapter 2 teaches you how business transactions are actually recorded in the accounting process.

To understand the dual procedure of recording business transactions with debits and credits, you will use some new tools. You begin with the T-account, which classifies and summarizes the measurements of business activity. Then you learn how to use the journal and ledger. You will follow a company through its various business transactions using these tools. Like accountants, you will use a trial balance to check the equality of your recorded debits and credits. This is the double-entry accounting system that the Franciscan monk, Luca Pacioli, described centuries ago.

THE ACCOUNT AND RULES OF DEBIT AND CREDIT

A business may engage in thousands of transactions during a year. The data in these transactions must be classified and summarized before becoming useful information.

Steps in Recording Business Transactions

Illustration 2.1 shows the steps used in recording and posting the effects of a business transaction. Source documents provide the evidence that a business transaction occurred. These source documents include such items as bills received from suppliers for goods or services received, bills sent to customers for goods sold or services performed, and cash register tapes. The information in the source document serves as the basis for preparing a journal entry. Then that information is posted (transferred) to accounts in the ledger.

You can see from Illustration 2.1 that first the journal entry is prepared and then it is posted to the accounts in the ledger. However, before you can record the journal entry, you must understand the rules of debit and credit. To teach you these rules, we must temporarily skip the journal entry step and study the nature of an account.

The Account

Objective 1

Use the account as the basic classifying and storage unit for accounting information

Fortunately, most business transactions are repetitive in nature. This characteristic makes the task of accountants somewhat easier because they can classify the transactions into groups having common characteristics. For example, a company may have thousands of receipts or payments of cash during a year. As a result, a part of every cash transaction can be recorded and summarized in a single place called an *account*.

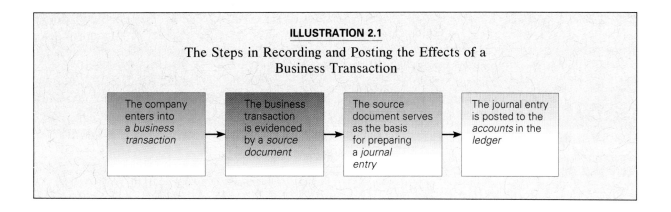

ILLUSTRATION 2.1

The Steps in Recording and Posting the Effects of a
Business Transaction

An account is a part of the accounting system used to classify and summarize the increases, decreases, and balances of each asset, liability, stockholders' equity item, revenue, and expense. Accounts are set up for each different type of business element, such as cash, accounts receivable, and accounts payable. Every business has a **Cash account** in its accounting system because knowledge of the amount of cash on hand is useful information.

Accountants may differ on the account title (or name) they give for the same item. For example, one accountant might name an account Notes Payable and another might call it Loans Payable. Both account titles refer to the amounts borrowed by the company. The account title should be logical to help the accountant group similar transactions into the same account. Once you give an account a title, you must use that same title for that account throughout the accounting records.

The number of accounts in a company's accounting system depends on the information needs of those interested in the business. **The main requirement is that each account provides useful information.** Thus, one account may be set up for all cash rather than having a separate account for each form of cash (coins on hand, currency on hand, and deposits in banks). The amount of cash is useful information; the form of cash often is not.

The T-Account

To understand how the increases and decreases in an account are recorded, texts use the T-account, which looks like a capital letter T. The title (name) of the item accounted for, such as cash, is written across the top of the T. Increases are recorded on one side of the vertical line of the T and decreases on the other side. A T-account appears as follows:

Title of Account

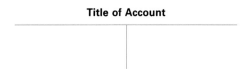

In Chapter 1, you saw that each business transaction affects at least two items. For example, if you—an owner—invest cash in your business, the company's assets increase and its stockholders' equity increases. This result was illustrated in the summary of transactions schedule in Chapter 1, Illustration 1.3. In the following sections, we will use debits and credits and the double-entry procedure to explain how to record the increases and decreases caused by business transactions.

Debits and Credits

Objective 2
Express the effects of
business transactions in
terms of debits and
credits to different types
of accounts

Accountants use the term debit instead of saying "place an entry on the left side of the T-account." They use the term credit for "place an entry on the right side of the T-account." **Debit** (abbreviated Dr.) simply means left side; **credit** (abbreviated Cr.) means right side.[1] Thus, a debit entry is an entry on the left side of an account, while a credit entry is an entry on the right side of an account. **For any account, the left side is the debit side, and the right side is the credit side, as shown below:**

Any Account

Left, or debit, side	Right, or credit, side

Double-Entry Procedure

Once a business event is recognized as a business transaction, it is analyzed to determine its increase or decrease effects on the assets, liabilities, stockholders' equity, revenues, or expenses of the business. These increase or decrease effects are then translated into debits and credits.

In each business transaction that is recorded, the total dollar amount of debits must equal the total dollar amount of credits. When we debit one account (or accounts) for $100, we must credit another account (or accounts) for a total of $100. The accounting requirement that each transaction be recorded by an entry that has equal debits and credits is called double-entry procedure, or duality. This double-entry procedure keeps the accounting equation in balance.

The dual recording process produces two sets of accounts—those with debit balances and those with credit balances. The totals of these two groups of accounts must be equal. Then, some assurance exists that the arithmetic part of the transaction recording process has been properly carried out. Now let us actually learn how to record business transactions in T-accounts using debits and credits.

Recording Changes in Assets, Liabilities, and Stockholders' Equity   From Chapter 1, you know that the foundation of the accounting process is the following basic accounting equation:

$$\text{Assets} = \text{Liabilities} + \text{Stockholders' Equity}$$

Recording transactions into the T-accounts is easier when you think first of the equal sign in the accounting equation. Then, remembering the equation, remember also that assets, which are on the left side of the equal sign, are increased on the left side of the T-accounts. Now, again remembering the equation, remember also that liabilities and stockholders' equity, to the right of the equal sign, are increased on the right side of the T-accounts. You already know that the left side of the T-account is the debit side and the right side is the credit side. So you should be able to fill in the rest of the rules of increases and decreases by deduction, such as:

Assets		=	**Liabilities**		+	**Stockholders' Equity**	
Debit for increases	Credit for decreases		Debit for decreases	Credit for increases		Debit for decreases	Credit for increases

---

[1] The abbreviations "Dr." and "Cr." are based on the Latin words "*debere*" and "*credere*." A synonym for *debit* an account is *charge* an account.

To summarize:

1. Assets are **increased** by debits (left side) of the T-account and **decreased** by credits (right side) of the T-account.
2. Liabilities and stockholders' equity are **decreased** by debits (left side) of the T-account and **increased** by credits (right side) of the T-account.

Applying these two rules keeps the accounting equation in balance. Now we will apply the debit and credit rules for assets, liabilities, and stockholders' equity to business transactions.

Assume a corporation issues shares of its capital stock for $10,000 (transaction 1). The company records the receipt of $10,000 as follows (the figure in parentheses refers to the number of the transaction and ties the two sides of the transaction together):

(Dr.)	Cash	(Cr.)	(Dr.)	Capital Stock	(Cr.)
(1)	10,000			(1)	10,000

The transaction involves first an increase in the asset, cash, which is recorded on the left side of the Cash account. Then, the transaction involves an increase in stockholders' equity, which is recorded on the right side of the Capital Stock account.

Assume the company borrowed $5,000 from a bank on a note (transaction 2). As explained in Chapter 1, a **note** is an unconditional written promise to pay to another party (in this case the bank) the amount owed either when demanded or at a specified date, usually with interest at a specified rate. We record this transaction as follows:

(Dr.)	Cash	(Cr.)	(Dr.)	Notes Payable	(Cr.)
(1)	10,000			(2)	5,000
(2)	5,000				

Note that liabilities, in this case Notes Payable, are increased by an entry on the right (credit) side of the account.

Recording Changes in Revenues and Expenses   In Chapter 1, we recorded the revenues and expenses directly in the Retained Earnings account. However, this procedure is not done in practice because of the volume of revenue and expense transactions. Instead, the expense accounts are treated as if they were subclassifications of the debit side of the Retained Earnings account, and the revenue accounts as if they were subclassifications of the credit side. Since the amounts of revenues and expenses are needed to prepare the income statement, a separate account is kept for each revenue and expense. The recording rules for revenues and expenses are:

a. Record increases in revenues on the right (credit) side of the T-account and decreases on the left (debit) side. The reasoning behind this rule is that revenues increase retained earnings, and, as explained earlier, increases in retained earnings are recorded on the right side.
b. Record increases in expenses on the left (debit) side of the T-account and decreases on the right (credit) side. The reasoning behind this rule is that expenses decrease retained earnings, and, as explained earlier, decreases in retained earnings are recorded on the left side.

To illustrate these rules, assume a company received $1,000 cash from a customer for services rendered (transaction 3). The Cash account, an asset, is increased on the left (debit) side of the T-account; and the Service Revenue account, an increase in retained earnings, is increased on the right (credit) side.

(Dr.)	Cash	(Cr.)	(Dr.)	Service Revenue	(Cr.)
(1)	10,000			(3)	1,000
(2)	5,000				
(3)	1,000				

Now assume a company paid $600 in salaries to employees (transaction 4). The Cash account, an asset, is decreased on the right (credit) side of the T-account; and the Salaries Expense account, a decrease in retained earnings, is increased on the left (debit) side.[2]

(Dr.)	Cash	(Cr.)		(Dr.)	Salaries Expense	(Cr.)
(1)	10,000	(4)	600	(4)	600	
(2)	5,000					
(3)	1,000					

Recording Changes in Dividends   Since dividends decrease retained earnings, increases are shown on the left side of the Dividends account and decreases on the right side. Thus, the payment of a $2,000 cash dividend is recorded (transaction 5) as follows:

(Dr.)	Cash	(Cr.)		(Dr.)	Dividends[3]	(Cr.)
(1)	10,000	(4)	600	(5)	2,000	
(2)	5,000	(5)	2,000			
(3)	1,000					

At the end of the accounting period, any balances in the expense, revenue, and Dividends accounts are transferred to the Retained Earnings account. This transfer occurs only after the information in the expense and revenue accounts has been used to prepare the income statement. This step is discussed and illustrated in Chapter 4.

Determining the Balance of an Account

To determine the balance of any T-account, total the debits to the account, total the credits to the account, and subtract the smaller sum from the larger. If the sum of the debits exceeds the sum of the credits, the account has a debit balance. For example, the Cash account shown below uses the information from the preceding transactions. The account has a debit balance of $13,400, computed as total debits of $16,000 less total credits of $2,600.

(Dr.)	Cash	(Cr.)	
(1)	10,000	(3)	600
(2)	5,000	(5)	2,000
(4)	1,000		
	16,000		2,600
Dr. bal.	13,400		

---

[2] Certain deductions are normally taken out of employees' pay for social security taxes, federal and state withholding, and so on. Those deductions will be ignored here.

[3] As we illustrate later in the text, dividends can be debited directly to the Retained Earnings account rather than to a Dividends account.

If, on the other hand, the sum of the credits exceeds the sum of the debits, the account will have a **credit balance.** For instance, assume that a company has an Accounts Payable account with a total of $10,000 in debits and $13,000 in credits. The account will have a credit balance of $3,000, as shown in the following T-account:

(Dr.)	**Accounts Payable**	(Cr.)
10,000		7,000
		6,000
10,000		13,000
	Cr. bal.	3,000

Normal Balances   Since asset, expense, and Dividend accounts are increased by debits, they **normally** have debit (or left-side) balances. Conversely, liability, capital stock, retained earnings, and revenue accounts are increased by credits and **normally** have credit (or right-side) balances.

The following diagram shows the normal balances of the seven types of accounts that we have used:

	Normal Balances	
Types of Accounts	**Debit**	**Credit**
Assets	X	
Liabilities		X
Stockholders' equity:		
Capital stock		X
Retained earnings		X
Dividends	X	
Expenses	X	
Revenues		X

Rules of Debit and Credit Summarized

At this point you are ready for a summary of the rules of debit and credit. At first, it may be necessary to memorize these rules. Later, as you proceed in your study of accounting, the rules will become automatic. Then, you will no longer ask yourself, "Is this increase or decrease a debit or credit?"

As stated earlier, asset accounts are increased on the debit side, while liability and stockholders' equity accounts are increased on the credit side. When the account balances are totaled, they will conform to the following two independent equations:

$$\text{Assets} = \text{Liabilities} + \text{Stockholders' Equity}$$

$$\text{Debits} = \text{Credits}$$

The arrangement of these two formulas gives the first three rules of debit and credit:

1. Increases in asset accounts are debits; decreases are credits.
2. Decreases in liability accounts are debits; increases are credits.
3. Decreases in stockholders' equity accounts are debits; increases are credits.

The debit and credit rules for expense and Dividends accounts and for revenue accounts follow logically if you remember that expenses and dividends are de-

ILLUSTRATION 2.2

Rules of Debit and Credit

Assets = Liabilities + Stockholders' Equity

Asset Accounts		=	Liability Accounts		+	Stockholders' Equity Account(s) (Capital Stock and Retained Earnings)	
Debit*	Credit		Debit	Credit*		Debit	Credit*
+ Debit for increase	– Credit for decrease		– Debit for decrease	+ Credit for increase		– Debit for decrease	+ Credit for increase

Debits	Credits
1. Increase assets.	1. Decrease assets.
2. Decrease liabilities.	2. Increase liabilities.
3. Decrease stock-holders' equity.	3. Increase stock-holders' equity.
4. Decrease revenues.	4. Increase revenues.
5. Increase expenses.	5. Decrease expenses.
6. Increase dividends.	6. Decrease dividends.

Expense Accounts and Dividends Account		Revenue Accounts	
Debit*	Credit	Debit	Credit*
+ Debit for increase	– Credit for decrease	– Debit for decrease	+ Credit for increase

* Normal balance.

creases in stockholders' equity and revenues are increases in stockholders' equity. Since stockholders' equity accounts decrease on the debit side, expense and Dividend accounts increase on the debit side. Since stockholders' equity accounts increase on the credit side, revenue accounts increase on the credit side. Debit and credit rules 4, 5, and 6 are:

4. Decreases in revenue accounts are debits; increases are credits.

5. Increases in expense accounts are debits; decreases are credits.

6. Increases in Dividends accounts are debits; decreases are credits.

Illustration 2.2 shows these six rules of debit and credit. Note first the treatment of expense and Dividends accounts as if they were subclassifications of the debit side of the Retained Earnings account. Then, note the treatment of the revenue accounts as if they were subclassifications of the credit side of the Retained Earnings account.

THE JOURNAL

Objective 3

Record the effects of business transactions in a journal

In explaining the rules of debit and credit, we recorded transactions directly in the accounts. Each ledger (general ledger) account shows only the increases and decreases in that account. Thus, all the effects of a single business transaction would not appear in any one account. For example, the Cash account contains only data on changes in cash and does not show how the cash was generated or how it was spent. To have a permanent record of an entire transaction, the accountant uses a book or record known as a *journal*.

A journal is a chronological (arranged in order of time) record of business transactions. A *journal entry* is the recording of a business transaction in the journal. A journal entry shows all the effects of a business transaction as expressed in terms of debit(s) and credit(s) and may include an explanation of the transaction. **A transaction is entered in a journal before it is entered in ledger accounts.** Because each transaction is initially recorded in a journal rather than directly in the ledger, a journal is called a **book of original entry.**

The General Journal

A business usually has more than one journal. Chapter 7 describes several special journals. In this chapter, we use the basic form of journal, which is the general journal. As shown in Illustration 2.3, a general journal contains the following columns:

1. **Date column.** The first column on each journal page is for the date. When entering the first journal entry on a page, this column is used for the year, month, and day (number). For all other journal entries on a page, only the day of the month is entered, until the month changes.

2. **Account Titles and Explanation column.** The first line of an entry shows the account debited. The second line shows the account credited. Notice that the credit account title is indented to the right. For instance, Illustration 2.3 first shows the debit to the Cash account and then shows the credit to the Capital Stock account. Any necessary explanation of a transaction appears on the line(s) below the credit entry and is indented halfway between the accounts debited and credited. A journal entry explanation should be complete enough to describe fully the transaction and prove the entry's accuracy, and yet be concise. If a journal entry is self-explanatory, the explanation may be omitted.

3. **Posting Reference column.** This column shows the account number of the debited or credited account. For instance, in Illustration 2.3, the number 100 in the first entry means that the Cash account number is 100. No number appears in this column until the information is posted to the appropriate ledger account. Posting is discussed later in the chapter.

4. **Debit column.** In the debit column, the amount of the debit is placed on the same line as the title of the account debited.

5. **Credit column.** In the credit column, the amount of the credit is placed on the same line as the title of the account credited.

Functions and Advantages of a Journal

A summary of the functions and advantages of using a journal follows.

The journal—
1. Records transactions in chronological order.
2. Shows the analysis of each transaction in terms of debit and credit.
3. Supplies an explanation of each transaction when necessary.
4. Serves as a source for future reference to accounting transactions.
5. Eliminates the need for lengthy explanations from the accounts.
6. Makes possible posting to the ledger at convenient times.
7. Assists in maintaining the ledger in balance because the debit(s) must always equal the credit(s) in each journal entry.
8. Aids in tracing errors when the ledger is not in balance.

ILLUSTRATION 2.3

General Journal

SPEEDY DELIVERY COMPANY
GENERAL JOURNAL   *Page 1*

Date		Account Titles and Explanation	Post. Ref.	Debit	Credit
1994 Nov.	28	Cash	100	5 0 0 0 0	
		Capital Stock	300		5 0 0 0 0
		Stockholders invested $50,000 cash in the business.			

THE LEDGER

A ledger (general ledger) is the complete collection of all the accounts of a company. The ledger may be in loose-leaf form, in a bound volume, or in a computer memory.

Accounts are classified into two general groups: (1) **balance sheet accounts** (assets, liabilities, and stockholders' equity) and (2) **income statement accounts** (revenues and expenses). The terms *real accounts* and *permanent accounts* also refer to balance sheet accounts. Balance sheet accounts are called real accounts because they are **not** subclassifications or subdivisions of any other account. They are called permanent accounts because their balances are not transferred (or closed) to any other account at the end of the accounting period. Income statement accounts and the Dividends account are also called nominal accounts because they are merely subclassifications of the stockholders' equity accounts. *Nominal* literally means "in name only." Nominal accounts are also called temporary accounts because they temporarily contain the revenue, expense, and dividend information that is transferred (or closed) to the Retained Earnings account at the end of the accounting period.

The chart of accounts is a complete listing of account titles and account numbers of all the accounts in the ledger. The chart of accounts can be compared to a table of contents. The groups of accounts usually appear in the following order: assets, liabilities, stockholders' equity, dividends, revenues, and expenses.

Individual accounts are arranged in sequence in the ledger. Each account typically has an identification number and a title to help locate accounts when recording data. For example, a company might number asset accounts 100–199; liability accounts, 200–299; stockholders' equity accounts and Dividends account, 300–399; revenue accounts, 400–499; and expense accounts, 500–599. We use this numbering system in this text. The uniform chart of accounts used in the first 11 chapters appears on the inside cover of the text. **Companies may use other numbering systems.** For instance, sometimes a company numbers its accounts in sequence starting with 1, 2, and so on. **The important idea is that companies use some numbering system.**

Now that you understand how to record debits and credits in an account and how all accounts together form a ledger, you are ready to study the accounting process in operation. To illustrate the accounting process, we use Speedy Delivery Company as our example.

THE ACCOUNTING PROCESS IN OPERATION

Speedy Delivery Company is a small corporation. The accounting process used by this company is similar to that of any small company. The ledger accounts used for the Speedy Delivery Company are:

	Acct. No.	Account Title	Description
Assets	100	Cash	Bank deposits and cash on hand.
	103	Accounts Receivable	Amounts owed to the company by customers.
	107	Supplies on Hand	Items such as paper, envelopes, writing materials, rope, and other materials used in performing services for customers or in doing administrative and clerical office work.
	108	Prepaid Insurance	Insurance policy premium paid in advance of the periods for which the insurance coverage applies.
	112	Prepaid Rent	Rent paid in advance of the periods for which the rent payment applies.
	150	Trucks	Trucks used to perform delivery services for customers.
Liabilities	200	Accounts Payable	Amounts owed to creditors for items purchased from them.
	210	Unearned Delivery Fees	Amounts received from customers before the services have been performed for the customers.
Stockholders' equity	300	Capital Stock	The stockholders' investment in the business.
	310	Retained Earnings	The earnings retained in the business.
Dividends	320	Dividends	The amount of dividends declared to stockholders.
Revenues	400	Service Revenue	Amounts earned by performing delivery services for customers.
Expenses	505	Advertising Expense	The cost of advertising incurred in the current period.
	506	Gas and Oil Expense	The cost of gas and oil used in trucks in the current period.
	507	Salaries Expense	The amount of salaries incurred in the current period.
	511	Utilities Expense	The cost of utilities incurred in the current period.

Notice that a gap is left between account numbers (100, 103, 107, etc.). These gaps provide flexibility in later adding new accounts between the existing accounts. Other Speedy Delivery Company accounts are introduced in the next chapter.

The Recording of Transactions and Their Effects on the Accounts

First, a transaction must be "journalized." Journalizing is the process of entering the effects of a transaction in a journal. Then, the information is transferred, or posted, to the proper accounts in the ledger. Posting is the process of recording in the ledger accounts the information contained in the journal. Posting is explained in more detail later in the chapter.

In the following example, notice that each business transaction affects two or more accounts in the ledger. Also note that the transaction date in both the general journal and the general ledger accounts is the same. In the ledger accounts, the date used is the date that the transaction was recorded in the general journal, even

---

ILLUSTRATION 2.4

Balance Sheet

SPEEDY DELIVERY COMPANY
Balance Sheet
November 30, 1994

Assets		Liabilities and Stockholders' Equity	
Cash	$50,000	Stockholders' equity:	
		Capital stock	$50,000
		Total liabilities and stock-	
Total assets	$50,000	holders' equity	$50,000

---

if the entry is not posted until several days later. Our example shows that the journal entries are posted to T-accounts. In practice, journal entries are normally posted to three-column ledger accounts, as you will see later in the chapter.

Accountants use the *accrual basis of accounting*. Under the accrual basis of accounting, revenues are recognized when the company makes a sale or performs a service, regardless of when the company receives the cash. Expenses are recognized as incurred, whether or not the company has paid out cash. Chapter 3 discusses the accrual basis of accounting in more detail.

In the Speedy Delivery Company example below, Transaction 1 increases (debits) Cash and increases (credits) Capital Stock by $50,000. First, the transaction is recorded in the general journal, then the entry is posted to the accounts in the general ledger.

Transaction 1:   Nov. 28, 1994   Stockholders invested $50,000 and formed Speedy Delivery Company.

General Journal

Date	Account Titles and Explanation	Post. Ref.	Debit	Credit
1994 Nov. 28	Cash	100	50000	
	Capital Stock	300		50000
	Stockholders invested $50,000 cash in the business.			

General Ledger

(Dr.)	**Cash**	Acct. No. 100 (Cr.)	(Dr.)	**Capital Stock**	Acct. No. 300 (Cr.)
1994 Nov. 28	50,000			1994 Nov. 28	50,000

No other transactions occurred in November. The company prepares financial statements at the end of each month. Illustration 2.4 shows the company's balance sheet at November 30, 1994.

The balance sheet reflects ledger account balances as of the close of business on November 30, 1994. These closing balances are the beginning balances on December 1, 1994. The ledger accounts show these closing balances as beginning balances (Beg. bal.).

Now assume that in December 1994, Speedy Delivery Company engages in the transactions given below. The proper recording of each transaction is shown in the journal and then in the ledger accounts (in T-account form), and the effects of each transaction are described.

Transaction 2:   Dec. 1   Paid cash for four small delivery trucks, $40,000.

General Journal

Date	Account Titles and Explanation	Post. Ref.	Debit	Credit
1994 Dec. 1	Trucks	150	4 0 0 0 0	
	Cash	100		4 0 0 0 0
	To record the purchase of four delivery trucks.			

General Ledger

Effects of Transaction

One asset, trucks, is increased (debited); and another asset, cash, is decreased (credited) by $40,000.

(Dr.)	**Trucks**	Acct. No. 150	(Cr.)
1994 Dec. 1	40,000		

(Dr.)	**Cash**	Acct. No. 100	(Cr.)
1994 Dec. 1 Beg. bal.	50,000	1994 Dec. 1	40,000

Transaction 3:   Dec. 1   Paid $2,400 cash for insurance on the trucks to cover a one-year period from this date.
General Journal

Date	Account Titles and Explanation	Post. Ref.	Debit	Credit
1994 Dec. 1	Prepaid Insurance	108	2 4 0 0	
	Cash	100		2 4 0 0
	Purchased truck insurance to cover a one-year period.			

General Ledger

(Dr.)	**Prepaid Insurance**	Acct. No. 108	(Cr.)
1994 Dec. 1	2,400		

(Dr.)	**Cash**	Acct. No. 100	(Cr.)
1994 Dec. 1 Beg. bal.	50,000	1994 Dec. 1	40,000
		1	2,400

Effects of Transaction

An asset, prepaid insurance, is increased (debited); and an asset, cash, is decreased (credited) by $2,400. The debit is to Prepaid Insurance rather than Insurance Expense because the policy covers more than the current accounting period of December (insurance policies are usually paid one year in advance). As you will see in Chapter 3, prepaid items are expensed as they are used. If this insurance policy was only written for December, the entire $2,400 debit would have been to Insurance Expense.

Transaction 4:   Dec. 1   Rented a building and paid $1,200 to cover a three-month period from this date.

General Journal

Date		Account Titles and Explanation	Post. Ref.	Debit	Credit
1994 Dec.	1	Prepaid Rent	112	1 2 0 0	
		Cash	100		1 2 0 0
		Paid three months' rent on a building.			

General Ledger

(Dr.)	**Prepaid Rent**	Acct. No. 112	(Cr.)
1994 Dec. 1	1,200		

(Dr.)		**Cash**	Acct. No. 100	(Cr.)
1994 Dec. 1	Beg. bal.	50,000	1994 Dec. 1	40,000
			1	2,400
			1	1,200

Effects of Transaction

An asset, prepaid rent, is increased (debited); and another asset, cash, is decreased (credited) by $1,200. The debit is to Prepaid Rent rather than Rent Expense because the payment covers more than the current month. If the payment had just been for December, the debit would have been to Rent Expense.

Transaction 5:   Dec. 4   Purchased $1,400 of supplies on account to be used over the next several months.

General Journal

Date		Account Titles and Explanation	Post. Ref.	Debit	Credit
1994 Dec.	4	Supplies on Hand	107	1 4 0 0	
		Accounts Payable	200		1 4 0 0
		To record the purchase of supplies for future use.			

General Ledger

(Dr.)	**Supplies on Hand**	Acct. No. 107	(Cr.)
1994 Dec. 4	1,400		

(Dr.)	**Accounts Payable**	Acct. No. 200	(Cr.)
		1994 Dec. 4	1,400

Effects of Transaction

An asset, supplies on hand, is increased (debited); and a liability, accounts payable, is increased (credited) by $1,400. The debit is to Supplies on Hand rather than Supplies Expense because the supplies are to be used over several accounting periods.

In each of the three preceding entries, an asset was debited rather than an expense. The reason for doing this was that the expenditure applies to (or benefits) more than just the current accounting period. Whenever a company will not fully use up an item such as insurance, rent, or supplies in the period when purchased, an asset should be debited. In practice, however, sometimes the expense is initially debited in these situations.

Companies sometimes buy items that they will fully use up within the current accounting period. For example, a company may buy supplies during the first part of the month that it intends to consume fully during that month. If the company will fully consume the supplies during the period of purchase, the best practice is to debit Supplies Expense at the time of purchase rather than Supplies on Hand. This same advice applies to insurance and rent. If a company purchases insurance that it will fully consume during the current period, the company should debit Insurance Expense at the time of purchase rather than Prepaid Insurance. Also, if a company pays rent that applies only to the current period, Rent Expense should be debited at the time of purchase rather than Prepaid Rent. As illustrated in Chapter 3, following this advice simplifies the procedures at the end of the accounting period.

Transaction 6:   Dec. 7   Received $4,500 from a customer in payment for future delivery services.

General Journal

Date		Account Titles and Explanation	Post. Ref.	Debit	Credit
1994 Dec.	7	Cash	100	4 5 0 0	
		Unearned Delivery Fees	210		4 5 0 0
		To record the receipt of cash from a customer in payment			
		for future delivery services.			

General Ledger

(Dr.)			**Cash**	Acct. No. 100	(Cr.)
1994				1994	
Dec. 1	Beg. bal.	50,000		Dec. 1	40,000
7		4,500		1	2,400
				1	1,200

(Dr.)	**Unearned Delivery Fees**	Acct. No. 210	(Cr.)
		1994	
		Dec. 7	4,500

Effects of Transaction

An asset, cash, is increased (debited); and a liability, unearned delivery revenue, is increased (credited) by $4,500. The credit is to Unearned Delivery Fees rather than Service Revenue because the $4,500 applies to more than just the current accounting period. Unearned Delivery Fees is a liability because, if the services are never performed, the $4,500 will have to be refunded. If the payment had been for services to be provided in December, the credit would have been to Service Revenue.

Transaction 7: Dec. 15 Performed delivery services for a customer for cash, $5,000.

General Journal

Date		Account Titles and Explanation	Post. Ref.	Debit	Credit
1994 Dec.	15	Cash	100	5 0 0 0	
		Service Revenue	400		5 0 0 0
		To record the receipt of cash for performing delivery			
		services for a customer.			

General Ledger

Effects of Transaction

An asset, cash, is increased (debited); and a revenue, service revenue, is increased (credited) by $5,000.

Acct. No.

(Dr.) **Cash** 100 *(Cr.)*

1994				1994		
Dec.	1	Beg. bal.	50,000	Dec.	1	40,000
	7		4,500		1	2,400
	15		5,000		1	1,200

Acct. No.

(Dr.) **Service Revenue** 400 *(Cr.)*

	1994	
	Dec. 15	5,000

Transaction 8: Dec. 17 Paid the $1,400 account payable resulting from the transaction of December 4.

General Journal

Date		Account Titles and Explanation	Post. Ref.	Debit	Credit
1994 Dec.	17	Accounts Payable	200	1 4 0 0	
		Cash	100		1 4 0 0
		Paid the account payable arising from the purchase of			
		supplies on December 4.			

General Ledger

Effects of Transaction

A liability, accounts payable, is decreased (debited); and an asset, cash, is decreased (credited) by $1,400.

Acct. No.

(Dr.) **Accounts Payable** 200 *(Cr.)*

1994		1994		
Dec. 17	1,400	Dec.	4	1,400

Acct. No.

(Dr.) **Cash** 100 *(Cr.)*

1994				1994		
Dec.	1	Beg. bal.	50,000	Dec.	1	40,000
	7		4,500		1	2,400
	15		5,000		1	1,200
					17	1,400

Transaction 9: Dec. 20 Billed a customer for delivery services performed, $5,700.

General Journal

Date		Account Titles and Explanation	Post. Ref.	Debit	Credit
1994 Dec.	20	Accounts Receivable	103	5 7 0 0	
		Service Revenue	400		5 7 0 0
		To record the performance of delivery services on account			
		for which a customer was billed.			

General Ledger

(Dr.)	**Accounts Receivable**	Acct. No. 103	(Cr.)
1994 Dec. 20	5,700		

(Dr.)	**Service Revenue**	Acct. No. 400	(Cr.)
		1994 Dec. 15	5,000
		20	5,700

Effects of Transaction

An asset, accounts receivable, is increased (debited); and a revenue, service revenue, is increased (credited) by $5,700.

Transaction 10: Dec. 24 Received a bill for advertising that appeared in a local newspaper in December, $50.

General Journal

Date		Account Titles and Explanation	Post. Ref.	Debit	Credit
1994 Dec.	24	Advertising Expense	505	5 0	
		Accounts Payable	200		5 0
		Received a bill for advertising for the month of December.			

General Ledger

(Dr.)	**Advertising Expense**	Acct. No. 505	(Cr.)
1994 Dec. 24	50		

(Dr.)	**Accounts Payable**	Acct. No. 200	(Cr.)
1994 Dec. 17	1,400	1994 Dec. 4	1,400
		24	50

Effects of Transaction

An expense, advertising expense, is increased (debited); and a liability, accounts payable, is increased (credited) by $50. The reason for debiting an expense rather than an asset is because all the cost pertains to the current accounting period, the month of December. Otherwise, Prepaid Advertising (an asset) would have been debited.

Transaction 11:   Dec. 26   Received $500 on accounts receivable from a customer.

General Journal

Date		Account Titles and Explanation	Post. Ref.	Debit	Credit
1994 Dec.	26	Cash	100	5 0 0	
		Accounts Receivable	103		5 0 0
		Received $500 from a customer on accounts receivable.			

General Ledger

Effects of Transaction

One asset, cash, is increased (debited); and another asset, accounts receivable, is decreased (credited) by $500.

				Acct. No.	
(Dr.)		**Cash**		100	*(Cr.)*

1994				1994	
Dec.	1	Beg. bal.	50,000	Dec. 1	40,000
	7		4,500	1	2,400
	15		5,000	1	1,200
	26		500	17	1,400

		Acct. No.	
(Dr.)	**Accounts Receivable**	103	*(Cr.)*

1994		1994	
Dec. 20	5,700	Dec. 26	500

Transaction 12:   Dec. 28   Paid salaries of $3,600 to truck drivers for the first four weeks of December. (Payroll and other deductions are to be ignored since they have not yet been discussed.)

General Journal

Date		Account Titles and Explanation	Post. Ref.	Debit	Credit
1994 Dec.	28	Salaries Expense	507	3 6 0 0	
		Cash	100		3 6 0 0
		Paid truck driver salaries for the first four weeks of December.			

General Ledger

Effects of Transaction

An expense, salaries expense, is increased (debited); and an asset, cash, is decreased (credited) by $3,600.

		Acct. No.	
(Dr.)	**Salaries Expense**	507	*(Cr.)*

1994	
Dec. 28	3,600

		Acct. No.	
(Dr.)	**Cash**	100	*(Cr.)*

1994				1994	
Dec.	1	Beg. bal.	50,000	Dec. 1	40,000
	7		4,500	1	2,400
	15		5,000	1	1,200
	26		500	17	1,400
				28	3,600

Transaction 13:   Dec. 29   Received and paid the utilities bill for December, $150.

General Journal

Date		Account Titles and Explanation	Post. Ref.	Debit	Credit
1994 Dec.	29	Utilities Expense	511	1 5 0	
		Cash	100		1 5 0
		Paid the utilities bill for December.			

General Ledger

Effects of Transaction

An expense, utilities expense, is increased (debited); and an asset, cash, is decreased (credited) by $150.

(Dr.)	**Utilities Expense**	Acct. No. 511	(Cr.)
1994 Dec. 29	150		

(Dr.)		**Cash**	Acct. No. 100	(Cr.)
1994 Dec. 1	Beg. bal.	50,000	1994 Dec. 1	40,000
7		4,500	1	2,400
15		5,000	1	1,200
26		500	17	1,400
			28	3,600
			29	150

Transaction 14:   Dec. 30   Received a bill for gas and oil used in the trucks for December, $680.

General Journal

Date		Account Titles and Explanation	Post. Ref.	Debit	Credit
1994 Dec.	30	Gas and Oil Expense	506	6 8 0	
		Accounts Payable	200		6 8 0
		Received a bill for gas and oil used in the trucks for December.			

General Ledger

Effects of Transaction

An expense, gas and oil expense, is increased (debited); and a liability, accounts payable, is increased (credited) by $680.

(Dr.)	**Gas and Oil Expense**	Acct. No. 506	(Cr.)
1994 Dec. 30	680		

(Dr.)	**Accounts Payable**	Acct. No. 200	(Cr.)
1994 Dec. 17	1,400	1994 Dec. 4	1,400
		24	50
		30	680

A BROADER PERSPECTIVE

WOMEN IN ACCOUNTING

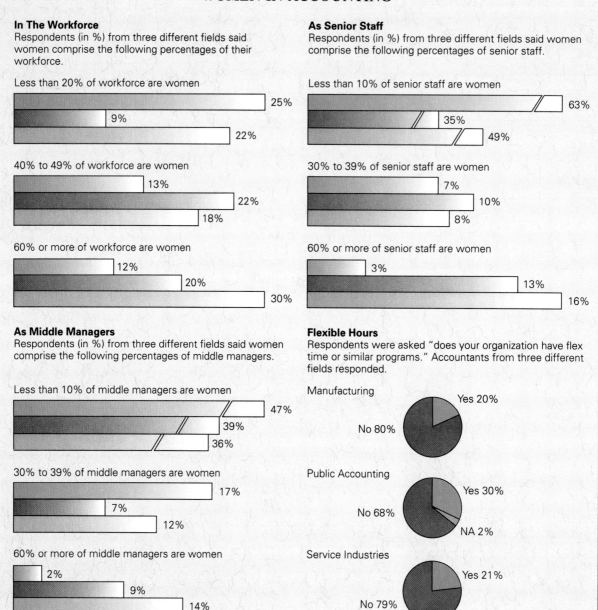

In The Workforce
Respondents (in %) from three different fields said women comprise the following percentages of their workforce.

Less than 20% of workforce are women
- 25%
- 9%
- 22%

40% to 49% of workforce are women
- 13%
- 22%
- 18%

60% or more of workforce are women
- 12%
- 20%
- 30%

As Senior Staff
Respondents (in %) from three different fields said women comprise the following percentages of senior staff.

Less than 10% of senior staff are women
- 63%
- 35%
- 49%

30% to 39% of senior staff are women
- 7%
- 10%
- 8%

60% or more of senior staff are women
- 3%
- 13%
- 16%

As Middle Managers
Respondents (in %) from three different fields said women comprise the following percentages of middle managers.

Less than 10% of middle managers are women
- 47%
- 39%
- 36%

30% to 39% of middle managers are women
- 17%
- 7%
- 12%

60% or more of middle managers are women
- 2%
- 9%
- 14%

Flexible Hours
Respondents were asked "does your organization have flex time or similar programs." Accountants from three different fields responded.

Manufacturing
- Yes 20%
- No 80%

Public Accounting
- Yes 30%
- No 68%
- NA 2%

Service Industries
- Yes 21%
- No 79%

Note: Forty-three percent of responding CPA firms report that women comprise more than half of their workforce.
Source: "For Women, Barriers Are Falling." Reprinted by permission from *Accounting Today*, March 5, 1990, p. S3. Copyright Lebhar-Friedman, Inc., 425 Park Avenue, New York, NY 10022.

Transaction 15:   Dec. 31   A dividend of $3,000 was paid to stockholders.

General Journal

Date		Account Titles and Explanation	Post. Ref.	Debit	Credit
1994 Dec.	31	Dividends	320	3 0 0 0	
		Cash	100		3 0 0 0
		Dividends were paid to stockholders.			

General Ledger	Effects of Transaction

General Ledger

(Dr.) **Dividends** Acct. No. 320 *(Cr.)*

1994 Dec. 31	3,000	

(Dr.) **Cash** Acct. No. 100 *(Cr.)*

1994 Dec. 1 Beg. bal.	50,000	1994 Dec. 1	40,000
7	4,500	1	2,400
15	5,000	1	1,200
26	500	17	1,400
		28	3,600
		29	150
		31	3,000

Effects of Transaction

The Dividends account is increased (debited); and an asset, cash, is decreased (credited) by $3,000.

Transaction 15 concludes the analysis of the Speedy Delivery Company transactions. The next section discusses and illustrates posting to three-column ledger accounts and cross-indexing.

THE USE OF THREE-COLUMN LEDGER ACCOUNTS

In practice, companies normally use three-column ledger accounts rather than T-accounts. The remainder of this chapter illustrates the use of three-column ledger accounts.

Posting to Three-Column Ledger Accounts

Objective 4

Post journal entries to the accounts in the ledger

A journal entry is like a set of instructions. The carrying out of these instructions is known as posting. As stated earlier, posting is recording in the ledger accounts the information contained in the journal. A journal entry directs the entry of a certain dollar amount as a debit in a specific ledger account and directs the entry of a certain dollar amount as a credit in a specific ledger account. Earlier, we posted the journal entries for the Speedy Delivery Company to T-accounts. In practice, however, these journal entries would be posted to three-column ledger accounts. First, we use a new example, Jenks Company, to illustrate the posting process to three-column ledger accounts. We will now show you how to post the Speedy Delivery Company journal entries to three-column ledger accounts.

In Illustration 2.5, the first journal entry for Jenks directs that $10,000 be posted in the ledger as a debit to the Cash account and as a credit to the Capital Stock account. The debit in the general ledger Cash account is posted by using the following procedure. The date, a short explanation, the journal designation, (''G'' for general journal) and the journal page number from which the debit is posted, and the $10,000 in the Debit column are entered in the Cash account. Then, the number of the account to which the debit is posted is entered in the Posting Reference column of the general journal. The credit is posted in a similar manner but as a credit to Account No. 300. The arrows in Illustration 2.5 show how these amounts were posted to the correct accounts.

Illustration 2.5 shows the three-column ledger account. In contrast to the two-sided T-account format shown so far, the three-column format has columns for debit, credit, and balance. The three-column form has the advantage that it shows the balance of the account after each item has been posted. In addition, in this chapter, we indicate whether each balance is a debit or a credit. In later chapters and in practice, the nature of the balance is usually not indicated since it is understood. Also, notice that we give an explanation for each item in the ledger accounts. Often accountants omit these explanations because each item can be traced back to the general journal for the explanation.

Posting is always from the journal to the ledger accounts. Postings can be made (1) at the time the transaction is journalized; (2) at the end of the day, week, or month; or (3) as each journal page is filled. The choice is a matter of personal taste. When posting the general journal, the date used in the ledger accounts is the date the transaction was recorded in the journal, not the date the journal entry was posted to the ledger accounts.

Cross-Indexing (Referencing)

Frequently, accountants must check and trace the origin of their transactions, so they provide for *cross-indexing*. Cross-indexing is the placing of (1) the account number of the ledger account in the general journal and (2) the general journal page number in the ledger account. As shown in Illustration 2.5, the account number of the ledger account to which the posting was made is placed in the Posting Reference column of the general journal. Note the arrow from Account No. 100 in the ledger to the 100 in the Posting Reference column beside the first debit in the general journal. The number of the general journal page **from** which the entry was posted is placed in the Posting Reference column of the ledger account. Note the arrow from page 1 in the general journal to G1 in the Posting Reference column of the Cash account in the general ledger. The notation ''G1'' means general journal, page 1. The date of the transaction is also shown in the general ledger. Note the arrows from the date in the general journal to the dates in the general ledger.

Cross-indexing aids the tracing of any recorded transaction, either from general journal to general ledger or from general ledger to general journal. Normally, cross-reference numbers are not placed in the Posting Reference column of the general journal until the entry is posted. If this practice is followed, the cross-reference numbers indicate that the entry has been posted.

An understanding of the posting and cross-indexing process can be obtained by tracing the entries from the general journal to the general ledger. The ledger accounts need not contain explanations of all the entries, since any needed explanations can be obtained from the general journal.

Compound Journal Entries

All the journal entries illustrated so far have involved one debit and one credit; these journal entries are called simple journal entries. Many business transactions, however, affect more than two accounts. The journal entry for these transactions will involve more than one debit and/or credit. Such journal entries are called compound journal entries.

ILLUSTRATION 2.5

General Journal and General Ledger; Posting and Cross-Indexing

JENKS COMPANY
GENERAL JOURNAL

Page 1

Date	Account Titles and Explanation	Post. Ref.	Debit	Credit
1994 Jan. 1	Cash	100	1 0 0 0 0	
	Capital Stock	300		1 0 0 0 0
	Stockholders invested $10,000 cash in the business.			
5	Cash	100	5 0 0 0	
	Notes Payable	201		5 0 0 0
	Borrowed $5,000 from the bank on a note.			

GENERAL LEDGER

Cash *Account No. 100*

Date	Explanation	Post. Ref.	Debit	Credit	Balance
1994 Jan. 1	Stockholder investment	G1	1 0 0 0 0		1 0 0 0 0 Dr.
5	Bank loan	G1	5 0 0 0		1 5 0 0 0 Dr.

Notes Payable *Account No. 201*

Date	Explanation	Post. Ref.	Debit	Credit	Balance
1994 Jan. 5	Borrowed cash	G1		5 0 0 0	5 0 0 0 Cr.

Capital Stock *Account No. 300*

Date	Explanation	Post. Ref.	Debit	Credit	Balance
1994 Jan. 1	Cash from stockholders	G1		1 0 0 0 0	1 0 0 0 0 Cr.

As an illustration of a compound journal entry, assume that on January 2, 1995, Speedy Delivery Company purchased $8,000 of machinery from Wilson Company. Speedy Delivery paid $2,000 cash with the balance due on March 3, 1995. The general journal entry for Speedy Delivery Company is:

				Debit	Credit
1995 Jan.	2	Machinery		8,000	
		Cash			2,000
		Accounts Payable			6,000
		Machinery purchased from Wilson Company.			

Note that two accounts, Cash and Accounts Payable, are credited in this one entry. However, the dollar totals of the debits and credits are equal.

Posting and Cross-Indexing— An Illustration

Illustration 2.6 shows how all the November and December transactions of Speedy Delivery Company presented on pages 66–75 would be journalized. As shown in Illustration 2.6, you skip a line between journal entries to show where one journal entry ends and another begins. This procedure is standard practice among accountants. Note that dollar signs are not used in journals or ledgers. When amounts are in even dollar amounts, the cents column may be left blank or zeros or a dash may be used. When lined accounting work papers are used, commas or a period are not needed to record an amount. When unlined paper is used, both commas and a period should be used.

Illustration 2.7 presents the three-column general ledger accounts of Speedy Delivery Company after the journal entries have been posted. Each ledger account would appear on a separate page in the ledger. You should trace the postings from the general journal to the general ledger to make sure you know how to post journal entries.

The Trial Balance

Objective 5

Prepare a trial balance to test the equality of debits and credits in the journalizing and posting process

Periodically, accountants use a *trial balance* to test the equality of their debits and credits. A trial balance is a listing of the ledger accounts and their debit or credit balances to determine that debits equal credits in the recording process. The accounts appear in the same order as in the general ledger and in the chart of accounts. Thus, they appear in the following order: assets, liabilities, stockholders' equity, dividends, revenues, and expenses. Within the assets category, the most liquid (closest to becoming cash) asset appears first and the least liquid appears last. Within the liabilities, those liabilities with the shortest ''maturities'' appear first. Illustration 2.8 shows the trial balance for Speedy Delivery Company. Note the listing of the account numbers and account titles on the left, the column for debit balances, the column for credit balances, and the equality of the two totals.

When the trial balance does not balance, the first thing to do is to retotal the two columns. If this step does not locate the error, divide the difference in the totals by 2 and then by 9. If the difference is divisible by 2, you may have transferred a debit-balanced account to the trial balance as a credit, or a credit-balanced account as a debit. If the difference is divisible by 2, look for an amount in the

ILLUSTRATION 2.6
General Journal (after posting)

SPEEDY DELIVERY COMPANY
GENERAL JOURNAL

Page 1

Date	Account Titles and Explanation	Post. Ref.	Debit	Credit
1994 Nov. 28	Cash	100*	5 0 0 0 0	
	Capital Stock	300		5 0 0 0 0
	Stockholders invested $50,000 cash in the business.			
Dec. 1	Trucks	150	4 0 0 0 0	
	Cash	100		4 0 0 0 0
	To record the purchase of four delivery trucks.			
1	Prepaid Insurance	108	2 4 0 0	
	Cash	100		2 4 0 0
	Purchased truck insurance to cover a one-year period.			
1	Prepaid Rent	112	1 2 0 0	
	Cash	100		1 2 0 0
	Paid three months' rent on a building.			
4	Supplies on Hand	107	1 4 0 0	
	Accounts Payable	200		1 4 0 0
	To record the purchase of supplies for future use.			
7	Cash	100	4 5 0 0	
	Unearned Delivery Fees	210		4 5 0 0
	To record the receipt of cash from a customer in payment for			
	future delivery services.			
15	Cash	100	5 0 0 0	
	Service Revenue	400		5 0 0 0
	To record the receipt of cash for performing delivery services			
	for a customer.			
17	Accounts Payable	200	1 4 0 0	
	Cash	100		1 4 0 0
	Paid the account payable arising from the purchase of supplies			
	on December 4.			

* These posting references would be inserted only after each amount has been posted.

ILLUSTRATION 2.6

(concluded)

GENERAL JOURNAL *(concluded)*   *Page 2*

Date		Account Titles and Explanation	Post. Ref.	Debit	Credit
1994 Dec.	20	Accounts Receivable	103	5 7 0 0	
		Service Revenue	400		5 7 0 0
		To record the performance of delivery services on account for			
		which a customer was billed.			
	24	Advertising Expense	505	5 0	
		Accounts Payable	200		5 0
		Received a bill for advertising for the month of December.			
	26	Cash	100	5 0 0	
		Accounts Receivable	103		5 0 0
		Received $500 from a customer on accounts receivable.			
	28	Salaries Expense	507	3 6 0 0	
		Cash	100		3 6 0 0
		Paid truck driver salaries for the first four weeks of December.			
	29	Utilities Expense	511	1 5 0	
		Cash	100		1 5 0
		Paid the utilities bill for December.			
	30	Gas and Oil Expense	506	6 8 0	
		Accounts Payable	200		6 8 0
		Received a bill for gas and oil used in the trucks for December.			
	31	Dividends	320	3 0 0 0	
		Cash	100		3 0 0 0
		Dividends were paid to stockholders.			

trial balance that is equal to one half of the difference. Thus, if the difference is $800, look for an account with a balance of $400 and see if it is in the wrong column.

If the difference is divisible by 9, you may have made a transposition error in transferring a balance to the trial balance or a slide error. A transposition error occurs when you have reversed two numbers in an amount (e.g., writing 753 as 573 or 110 as 101). A slide error occurs when you have placed the decimal point incorrectly (e.g., $1,500 recorded as $15.00). Thus, when a difference is divisible by 9, compare the trial balance amounts with the general ledger account balances to see if you made a transposition or slide error in transferring the amounts.

ILLUSTRATION 2.7
General Ledger—Extended Illustration

SPEEDY DELIVERY COMPANY
GENERAL LEDGER

Cash — *Account No. 100*

Date		Explanation	Post. Ref.	Debit	Credit	Balance
1994 Dec.	1	Beginning balance*				5 0 0 0 0 Dr.
	1	Trucks	G1		4 0 0 0 0	1 0 0 0 0 Dr.
	1	Prepaid insurance	G1		2 4 0 0	7 6 0 0 Dr.
	1	Prepaid rent	G1		1 2 0 0	6 4 0 0 Dr.
	7	Unearned service revenue	G1	4 5 0 0		1 0 9 0 0 Dr.
	15	Service revenue	G1	5 0 0 0		1 5 9 0 0 Dr.
	17	Paid account payable	G1		1 4 0 0	1 4 5 0 0 Dr.
	26	Collected account receivable	G2	5 0 0		1 5 0 0 0 Dr.
	28	Salaries	G2		3 6 0 0	1 1 4 0 0 Dr.
	29	Utilities	G2		1 5 0	1 1 2 5 0 Dr.
	31	Dividends	G2		3 0 0 0	8 2 5 0 Dr.

Accounts Receivable — *Account No. 103*

Date		Explanation	Post. Ref.	Debit	Credit	Balance
1994 Dec.	20	Service revenue	G2	5 7 0 0		5 7 0 0 Dr.
	26	Collections	G2		5 0 0	5 2 0 0 Dr.

Supplies on Hand — *Account No. 107*

Date		Explanation	Post. Ref.	Debit	Credit	Balance
1994 Dec.	4	Purchased on account	G1	1 4 0 0		1 4 0 0 Dr.

Prepaid Insurance — *Account No. 108*

Date		Explanation	Post. Ref.	Debit	Credit	Balance
1994 Dec.	1	One-year policy on trucks	G1	2 4 0 0		2 4 0 0 Dr.

* Beginning balances result from carrying forward a balance from a preceding page for this account. The Cash account, for example, is likely to use page after page over a period of time since so many transactions involve cash. This particular beginning balance came from the stockholders' investments in November.

ILLUSTRATION 2.7

(continued)

GENERAL LEDGER *(continued)*

Prepaid Rent   *Account No. 112*

Date		Explanation	Post. Ref.	Debit	Credit	Balance
1994 Dec.	1	Three-month payment	G1	1 2 0 0		1 2 0 0 Dr.

Trucks   *Account No. 150*

Date		Explanation	Post. Ref.	Debit	Credit	Balance
1994 Dec.	1	Paid cash	G1	4 0 0 0 0		4 0 0 0 0 Dr.

Accounts Payable   *Account No. 200*

Date		Explanation	Post. Ref.	Debit	Credit	Balance
1994 Dec.	4	Supplies	G1		1 4 0 0	1 4 0 0 Cr.
	17	Paid for supplies	G1	1 4 0 0		– 0 –
	24	Advertising	G2		5 0	5 0 Cr.
	30	Gas and oil	G2		6 8 0	7 3 0 Cr.

Unearned Delivery Fees   *Account No. 210*

Date		Explanation	Post. Ref.	Debit	Credit	Balance
1994 Dec.	7	Received cash	G1		4 5 0 0	4 5 0 0 Cr.

Capital Stock   *Account No. 300*

Date		Explanation	Post. Ref.	Debit	Credit	Balance
1994 Dec.	1	Beginning balance				5 0 0 0 0 Cr.

ILLUSTRATION 2.7

(concluded)

GENERAL LEDGER *(concluded)*

Dividends

Account No. 320

Date		Explanation	Post. Ref.	Debit	Credit	Balance
1994 Dec.	31	Cash	G2	3 0 0 0		3 0 0 0 Dr.

Service Revenue

Account No. 400

Date		Explanation	Post. Ref.	Debit	Credit	Balance
1994 Dec.	15	Cash	G1		5 0 0 0	5 0 0 0 Cr.
	20	On account	G2		5 7 0 0	1 0 7 0 0 Cr.

Advertising Expense

Account No. 505

Date		Explanation	Post. Ref.	Debit	Credit	Balance
1994 Dec.	24	On account	G2	5 0		5 0 Dr.

Gas and Oil Expense

Account No. 506

Date		Explanation	Post. Ref.	Debit	Credit	Balance
1994 Dec.	30	On account	G2	6 8 0		6 8 0 Dr.

Salaries Expense

Account No. 507

Date		Explanation	Post. Ref.	Debit	Credit	Balance
1994 Dec.	28	Cash paid	G2	3 6 0 0		3 6 0 0 Dr.

Utilities Expense

Account No. 511

Date		Explanation	Post. Ref.	Debit	Credit	Balance
1994 Dec.	29	Cash paid	G2	1 5 0		1 5 0 Dr.

ILLUSTRATION 2.8

Trial Balance

SPEEDY DELIVERY COMPANY
Trial Balance
December 31, 1994

Acct. No.	Account Title	Debits	Credits
100	Cash .	$ 8,250	
103	Accounts Receivable.	5,200	
107	Supplies on Hand .	1,400	
108	Prepaid Insurance .	2,400	
112	Prepaid Rent .	1,200	
150	Trucks .	40,000	
200	Accounts Payable .		$ 730
210	Unearned Delivery Fees		4,500
300	Capital Stock .		50,000
320	Dividends.	3,000	
400	Service Revenue .		10,700
505	Advertising Expense .	50	
506	Gas and Oil Expense.	680	
507	Salaries Expense .	3,600	
511	Utilities Expense .	150	
		$65,930	$65,930

If none of these steps locates the error, the error may be due to one of the following causes:

1. Failing to post part of a journal entry.
2. Posting a debit as a credit, or vice versa.
3. Incorrectly determining the balance of an account.
4. Recording the balance of an account incorrectly in the trial balance.
5. Omitting an account from the trial balance.
6. Making a transposition or slide error in the accounts or the journal.

Usually, you should work backward through the steps taken to prepare the trial balance. Assuming you have already retotaled the columns and traced the amounts appearing in the trial balance back to the general ledger account balances, use the following steps. Verify the balance of each general ledger account, verify postings to the general ledger, verify general journal entries, and then review the transactions and possibly the source documents.

The equality of the two totals in the trial balance does not necessarily mean that the accounting process has been error-free. Serious errors may have been made, such as failure to record a transaction, or posting a debit or credit to the wrong account. For instance, if a transaction involving payment of a $100 account payable is never recorded, the trial balance totals will still balance, but at an amount that is $100 too high. Both cash and accounts payable would be overstated by $100.

A trial balance can be compared at any time—at the end of a day, a week, a month, a quarter, or a year. Typically, a trial balance is prepared before preparing the financial statements. Dollar signs may be used but are not required.

Larry Robins was captain of the football team at Prestige University. He also earned a masters degree in business administration with a concentration in accounting.

Upon graduation, Larry accepted a position with Financial Deals, Inc., in the accounting and finance division. At first, things were going smoothly. Larry was tall, good looking, and had an outgoing personality. The president of the company took a liking to him. However, Larry was somewhat bothered when the president of the company started asking him to do some things that Larry recognized as being slightly unethical. When Larry mildly protested, the president said, "Come on, son, this is the way the business world works. You have great potential if you don't let things like this get in your way."

As time went on, the things Larry was asked to do became more unethical, and finally he was performing illegal acts. When he resisted doing some of these things, the president appealed to his "loyalty" and "being a team player" to gain his cooperation. The president also promised Larry great wealth sometime in the future. Finally, when Larry was told to falsify some financial statements by making improper adjusting entries and to sign some documents Larry knew to contain material errors, the president supported his "request" by stating, "You are in too deeply now to refuse to cooperate. If I go down, you are going with me." Through various company schemes, Larry had convinced some friends and relatives to invest about $10 million. Most of this would be lost if the various company schemes were discovered.

Larry could not sleep at night and began each day with a pain in his stomach and by becoming physically ill. He was under great strain and believed that he could lose his mind. He also heard that the president had a shady past and could become violent in retaliating against his enemies. If Larry "blows the whistle," he believes he will go to prison for his part in the schemes. (Note: This problem is based on an actual situation with some facts changed to protect the guilty.)

Required

a. What motivated Larry to go along with unethical and illegal actions?

b. What are Larry's options now?

c. What would you do if you were Larry?

d. What do you think the real "Larry" did?

What you have learned in this chapter is basic to your study of accounting. The entire process of accounting is based on the double-entry concept. In Chapter 3, you will learn that adjustments are usually needed to bring the accounts to their proper balances before accurate financial statements can be prepared.

UNDERSTANDING THE LEARNING OBJECTIVES

1. Use the account as the basic classifying and storage unit for information.
   - □ An account is a storage unit used to classify and summarize money measurements of business activities of a similar nature.
   - □ An account is set up whenever it is necessary to provide useful information about a particular business item to some party having a valid interest in the business.

2. Express the effects of business transactions in terms of debits and credits to different types of accounts.
   - □ A T-account resembles the letter T.
   - □ Debits are entries on the left-hand side of a T-account.

□ Credits are entries on the right-hand side of a T-account.

□ Asset, expense, and Dividends accounts are increased by debits.

□ Liability, stockholders' equity, and revenue accounts are increased by credits.

3. Record the effects of business transactions in a journal.

□ A journal contains a chronological record of the transactions of a business.

□ An example of a general journal is shown in Illustration 2.6.

□ Journalizing is the process of entering a transaction in a journal.

4. Post journal entries to the accounts in the ledger.

□ Posting is the process of transferring information recorded in the journal to the proper places in the ledger.

□ Cross-indexing is the placing of (1) the account number of the ledger account in the general journal and (2) the general journal page number in the ledger account.

□ An example of cross-indexing appears in Illustration 2.5.

5. Prepare a trial balance to test the equality of debits and credits in the journalizing and posting process.

□ A trial balance is a listing of the ledger accounts and their debit or credit balances.

□ If the trial balance does not balance, the accountant should work backward to discover the error.

□ A trial balance is shown in Illustration 2.8.

DEMONSTRATION PROBLEM

Green Hills Riding Stable, Incorporated, had the following balance sheet on June 30, 1994:

GREEN HILLS RIDING STABLE, INCORPORATED
Balance Sheet
June 30, 1994
Assets

Cash		$ 7,500
Accounts receivable		5,400
Land		40,000
Total assets		$52,900

Liabilities and Stockholders' Equity

Liabilities:		
Accounts payable		$ 800
Notes payable		40,000
Total liabilities		$40,800
Stockholders' equity:		
Capital stock	$10,000	
Retained earnings	2,100	
Total stockholders' equity		12,100
Total liabilities and stockholders' equity		$52,900

Transactions for July 1994 were as follows:

July   1   Additional shares of capital stock were issued for $25,000 cash.
     1   Paid for a prefabricated building constructed on the land at a cost of $24,000.
     8   Paid the accounts payable of $800.
    10   Collected the accounts receivable of $5,400.
    12   Horse feed to be used in July was purchased on credit for $1,100.
    15   Boarding fees for July were charged to customers in the amount of $4,500. (This amount is due on August 10.)
    24   Miscellaneous expenses of $800 for July were paid.
    31   Paid interest expense on the notes payable of $200.
    31   Salaries of $1,400 for the month were paid.
    31   Riding and lesson fees for July were billed to customers in the amount of $3,600. (They are due on August 10.)
    31   Paid a $1,000 dividend to the stockholders.

Required   *a.*   Prepare the journal entries to record the transactions for July 1994.

          b.   Post the journal entries to the ledger accounts after entering the beginning balances in those accounts. Insert cross-indexing references in the journal and ledger. Use the following chart of accounts:

100	Cash	310	Retained Earnings
103	Accounts Receivable	402	Horse Boarding Fees Revenue
130	Land	404	Riding and Lesson Fees Revenue
140	Buildings	507	Salaries Expense
200	Accounts Payable	513	Feed Expense
201	Notes Payable	540	Interest Expense
300	Capital Stock	568	Miscellaneous Expense

          c.   Prepare a trial balance.

SOLUTION TO DEMONSTRATION PROBLEM

a.

GREEN HILLS RIDING STABLE, INCORPORATED
GENERAL JOURNAL

Page 1

Date		Account Titles and Explanation	Post. Ref.	Debit	Credit
1994 July	1	Cash	100	2 5 0 0 0	
		Capital Stock	300		2 5 0 0 0
		Additional capital stock issued.			
	1	Buildings	140	2 4 0 0 0	
		Cash	100		2 4 0 0 0
		Paid for building.			
	8	Accounts Payable	200	8 0 0	
		Cash	100		8 0 0
		Paid accounts payable.			
	10	Cash	100	5 4 0 0	
		Accounts Receivable	103		5 4 0 0
		Collected accounts receivable.			
	12	Feed Expense	513	1 1 0 0	
		Accounts Payable	200		1 1 0 0
		Purchased feed on credit.			
	15	Accounts Receivable	103	4 5 0 0	
		Horse Boarding Fees Revenue	402		4 5 0 0
		Billed boarding fees for July.			
	24	Miscellaneous Expense	568	8 0 0	
		Cash	100		8 0 0
		Paid miscellaneous expense for July.			
	31	Interest Expense	540	2 0 0	
		Cash	100		2 0 0
		Paid interest.			
	31	Salaries Expense	507	1 4 0 0	
		Cash	100		1 4 0 0
		Paid salaries for July.			
	31	Accounts Receivable	103	3 6 0 0	
		Riding and Lesson Fees Revenue	404		3 6 0 0
		Billed riding and lesson fees for July.			
	31	Dividends	320	1 0 0 0	
		Cash	100		1 0 0 0
		Paid a dividend to stockholders.			

b.

GREEN HILLS RIDING STABLE, INCORPORATED
GENERAL LEDGER

Cash *Account No. 100*

Date		Explanation	Post. Ref.	Debit	Credit	Balance
1994 June	30	Balance				7 5 0 0 Dr.
July	1	Stockholders' investment	G1	2 5 0 0 0		3 2 5 0 0 Dr.
	1	Buildings	G1		2 4 0 0 0	8 5 0 0 Dr.
	8	Accounts payable	G1		8 0 0	7 7 0 0 Dr.
	10	Accounts receivable	G1	5 4 0 0		1 3 1 0 0 Dr.
	24	Miscellaneous expense	G1		8 0 0	1 2 3 0 0 Dr.
	31	Interest expense	G1		2 0 0	1 2 1 0 0 Dr.
	31	Salaries expense	G1		1 4 0 0	1 0 7 0 0 Dr.
	31	Dividends	G1		1 0 0 0	9 7 0 0 Dr.

Accounts Receivable *Account No. 103*

Date		Explanation	Post. Ref.	Debit	Credit	Balance
1994 June	30	Balance				5 4 0 0 Dr.
July	10	Cash	G1		5 4 0 0	– 0 –
	15	Riding and lesson fees	G1	4 5 0 0		4 5 0 0 Dr.
	31	Horse boarding fees	G1	3 6 0 0		8 1 0 0 Dr.

Land *Account No. 130*

Date		Explanation	Post. Ref.	Debit	Credit	Balance
1994 June	30	Balance				4 0 0 0 0 Dr.

Buildings *Account No. 140*

Date		Explanation	Post. Ref.	Debit	Credit	Balance
1994 July	1	Cash	G1	2 4 0 0 0		2 4 0 0 0 Dr.

GENERAL LEDGER *(continued)*

Accounts Payable — Account No. 200

Date		Explanation	Post. Ref.	Debit	Credit	Balance
1994 June	30	Balance				800 Cr.
July	8	Cash	G1	800		–0–
	12	Feed expense	G1		1100	1100 Cr.

Notes Payable — Account No. 201

Date		Explanation	Post. Ref.	Debit	Credit	Balance
1994 June	30	Balance				40000 Cr.

Capital Stock — Account No. 300

Date		Explanation	Post. Ref.	Debit	Credit	Balance
1994 June	30	Balance				10000 Cr.
July	1	Cash	G1		25000	35000 Cr.

Retained Earnings — Account No. 310

Date		Explanation	Post. Ref.	Debit	Credit	Balance
1994 June	30	Balance				2100 Cr.

Dividends — Account No. 320

Date		Explanation	Post. Ref.	Debit	Credit	Balance
1994 July	31	Cash	G1	1000		1000 Dr.

Horse Boarding Fees Revenue — Account No. 402

Date		Explanation	Post. Ref.	Debit	Credit	Balance
1994 July	15	Accounts receivable	G1		4500	4500 Cr.

GENERAL LEDGER *(concluded)*

Riding and Lesson Fees Revenue — *Account No. 404*

Date		Explanation	Post. Ref.	Debit	Credit	Balance
1994 July	31	Accounts receivable	G1		3 6 0 0	3 6 0 0 Cr.

Salaries Expense — *Account No. 507*

Date		Explanation	Post. Ref.	Debit	Credit	Balance
1994 July	31	Cash	G1	1 4 0 0		1 4 0 0 Dr.

Feed Expense — *Account No. 513*

Date		Explanation	Post. Ref.	Debit	Credit	Balance
1994 July	12	Accounts payable	G1	1 1 0 0		1 1 0 0 Dr.

Interest Expense — *Account No. 540*

Date		Explanation	Post. Ref.	Debit	Credit	Balance
1994 July	31	Cash	G1	2 0 0		2 0 0 Dr.

Miscellaneous Expense — *Account No. 568*

Date		Explanation	Post. Ref.	Debit	Credit	Balance
1994 July	24	Cash	G1	8 0 0		8 0 0 Dr.

c.

GREEN HILLS RIDING STABLE, INCORPORATED
Trial Balance
July 31, 1994

Acct. No.	Account Title	Debits	Credits
100	Cash	$ 9,700	
103	Accounts Receivable	8,100	
130	Land	40,000	
140	Buildings	24,000	
200	Accounts Payable		$ 1,100
201	Notes Payable		40,000
300	Capital Stock		35,000
310	Retained Earnings		2,100
320	Dividends	1,000	
402	Horse Boarding Fees Revenue		4,500
404	Riding and Lesson Fees Revenue		3,600
507	Salaries Expense	1,400	
513	Feed Expense	1,100	
540	Interest Expense	200	
568	Miscellaneous Expense	800	
		$86,300	$86,300

NEW TERMS

Account A part of the accounting system used to classify and summarize the increases, decreases, and balances of each asset, liability, stockholders' equity item, revenue, and expense. The three-column account is normally used. It contains columns for debit, credit, and balance. *57*

Accrual basis of accounting Recognizes revenues when sales are made or services are performed, regardless of when cash is received. Recognizes expenses as incurred, whether or not cash has been paid out. *66*

Chart of accounts The complete listing of the account titles and account numbers of all of the accounts in the ledger; somewhat comparable to a table of contents. *64*

Compound journal entry A journal entry with more than one debit and/or credit. *76*

Credit The right side of any account; when used as a verb, to enter a dollar amount on the right side of an account; credits increase liability, stockholders' equity, and revenue accounts and decrease asset, expense, and Dividends accounts. *58*

Credit balance The balance in an account when the sum of the credits to the account exceeds the sum of the debits to that account. *61*

Cross-indexing The placing of (1) the account number of the ledger account in the general journal and (2) the general journal page number in the ledger account. *76*

Debit The left side of any account; when used as a verb, to enter a dollar amount on the left side of an account; debits increase asset, expense, and Dividends accounts and decrease liability, stockholders' equity, and revenue accounts. *58*

Debit balance The balance in an account when the sum of the debits to the account exceeds the sum of the credits to that account. *60*

Double-entry procedure The accounting requirement that each transaction must be recorded by an entry that has equal debits and credits. *58*

Journal A chronological (arranged in order of time) record of business transactions; the simplest form of journal is the two-column general journal. *63*

Journal entry Shows all of the effects of a business transaction as expressed in terms of debit(s) and credit(s) and may include an explanation of the transaction. *63*

Journalizing A step in the accounting recording process that consists of entering the effects of a transaction in a journal. *65*

Ledger The complete collection of all of the accounts of a company; often referred to as the *general ledger. 64*

Nominal accounts Income statement accounts (revenues and expenses) and the Dividends account. *64*

Note An unconditional written promise to pay to another party the amount owed either when demanded or at a certain specified date. *59*

Permanent accounts Balance sheet accounts; their balances are not transferred (or closed) to any other account at the end of the accounting period. *64*

Posting Recording in the ledger accounts the information contained in the journal. *65, 75*

Real accounts Balance sheet accounts (assets, liabilities, and stockholders' equity). *64*

Simple journal entry An entry with one debit and one credit. *76*

T-account An account resembling the letter T, which is used for illustrative purposes only. Debits are entered on the left side of the account, and credits are entered on the right side of the account. *57*

Temporary accounts Nominal accounts; they temporarily contain the revenue, expense, and dividend information that is transferred (or closed) to the stockholders' equity account at the end of the accounting period. *64*

Trial balance A listing of the ledger accounts and their debit or credit balances to determine that debits equal credits in the recording process. *78*

SELF-TEST

True-False

Indicate whether each of the following statements is true or false.

1. A transaction must be journalized in the journal before it can be posted to the ledger accounts.
2. The left side of any account is the credit side.
3. Revenues, liabilities, and Capital Stock accounts are increased by debits.
4. The Dividends account is increased by debits.
5. If the trial balance has equal debit and credit totals, it cannot contain any errors.

Multiple-Choice

Select the best answer for each of the following questions.

1. When the stockholders invest cash in the business:
   a. Capital Stock is debited and Cash is credited.
   b. Cash is debited and Dividends is credited.
   c. Cash is debited and Capital Stock is credited.
   d. None of the above.

2. Assume that cash is paid for insurance to cover a three-year period. The recommended debit and credit are:
   a. Debit Insurance Expense, credit Cash.
   b. Debit Prepaid Insurance, credit Cash.
   c. Debit Cash, credit Insurance Expense.
   d. Debit Cash, credit Prepaid Insurance.

3. A company received cash from a customer in payment for future delivery services. The correct debit and credit are:
   a. Debit Cash, credit Unearned Delivery Fees.
   b. Debit Cash, credit Delivery Fee Revenue.
   c. Debit Accounts Receivable, credit Delivery Fee Revenue.
   d. None of the above.

4. A company performed delivery services for a customer for cash. The correct debit and credit are:
   a. Debit Cash, credit Unearned Delivery Fees.
   b. Debit Cash, credit Delivery Fee Revenue.
   c. Debit Accounts Receivable, credit Delivery Fee Revenue.
   d. None of the above.

5. A cash dividend of $500 was paid to stockholders. The correct journal entry is:

   a. Capital Stock. 500
      Cash   500

   b. Cash 500
      Dividends   500

   c. Dividends 500
      Cash   500

   d. Cash 500
      Capital Stock.   500

Now turn to page 105 to check your answers.

QUESTIONS

1. Describe the steps in recording and posting the effects of a business transaction.
2. Give some examples of source documents.
3. Define an account. What are the two basic forms (styles) of accounts illustrated in the chapter?
4. What is meant by the term double-entry procedure, or duality?
5. Describe how you would determine the balance of a T-account.
6. Define debit and credit. Name the types of accounts that are:
   a. Increased by a debit.
   b. Decreased by a debit.
   c. Increased by a credit.
   d. Decreased by a credit.

   Do you think this system makes sense? Can you conceive of other possible methods for recording changes in accounts?

7. Why are expense and revenue accounts used when all revenues and expenses could be shown directly in the Retained Earnings account?

8. What is the purpose of the Dividends account and how is it increased?

9. Are the following possibilities conceivable in an entry involving only one debit and one credit? Why?
   a. Increase a liability and increase an expense.
   b. Increase an asset and decrease a liability.
   c. Increase a revenue and decrease an expense.
   d. Decrease an asset and increase another asset.
   e. Decrease an asset and increase a liability.
   f. Decrease a revenue and decrease an asset.
   g. Decrease a liability and increase a revenue.

10. Describe the nature and purposes of the general journal. What does "journalizing" mean? Give an example of a compound entry in the general journal.

11. Describe a ledger and a chart of accounts. How do these two compare with a book and its table of contents?

12. Describe the act of posting. What difficulties could arise if no cross-indexing existed between the general journal and the ledger accounts?

13. Which of the following cash payments would involve the immediate recording of an expense? Why?
   a. Paid vendors for office supplies previously purchased on account.
   b. Paid an automobile dealer for a new company auto.
   c. Paid the current month's rent.
   d. Paid salaries for the last half of the current month.

14. What types of accounts appear in the unadjusted trial balance? What are the purposes of this trial balance?

15. You have found that the total of the Debits column of the trial balance of Burns Company is $200,000, while the total of the Credits column is $180,000. What are some possible causes of this difference? If the difference between the columns is divisible by 9, what types of errors are possible?

16. Store equipment was purchased for $2,000. Instead of debiting the Store Equipment account, the debit was made to Delivery Equipment. Of what help will the trial balance be in locating this error? Why?

17. A student remembered that the side toward the window in the classroom was the debit side of an account. The student took an examination in a room where the windows were on the other side of the room and became confused and consistently reversed debits and credits. Would the student's trial balance have equal debit and credit totals? If there were no existing balances in any of the accounts to begin with, would the error prevent the student from preparing correct financial statements? Why?

18. *Real world question* Refer to "A Broader Perspective" on page 74. Would you conclude that the opportunities for women are extremely limited in public accounting?

19. *Real world question* Refer to "A Broader Perspective" on page 74. What accommodations do CPA firms make to attract and retain female employees?

EXERCISES

Exercise 2–1
Indicate rules of debit and credit
(L.O. 1, 2)

Below is a diagram of the various types of accounts. Indicate where pluses (+) or minuses (−) should be inserted to indicate what effect debits and credits have on each account.

| Asset Accounts | = | Liability Accounts | + | Stockholders' Equity Accounts |
| Debit | Credit | Debit | Credit | Debit | Credit |

| Expense Accounts and Dividends Accounts | | Revenue Accounts | |
| Debit | Credit | Debit | Credit |

Exercise 2–2
Prepare journal entries
(L.O. 3)

Prepare the journal entry required for each of the following transactions:
a. Cash was received for services performed for customers, $4,800.
b. Services were performed for customers on account, $7,200.

Exercise 2–3

Prepare journal entries
(L.O. 3)

Prepare the journal entry required for each of the following transactions:

a. Capital stock was issued for $120,000.

b. Purchased machinery for cash, $60,000.

Exercise 2–4

Prepare journal entries
(L.O. 3)

Prepare the journal entry required for each of the following transactions:

a. Capital stock was issued for $100,000 cash.

b. A $60,000 loan was arranged with a bank. The bank increased the company's checking account by $60,000 after management of the company signed a written promise to return the $60,000 in 30 days.

c. Cash was received for services performed for customers, $1,600.

d. Services were performed for customers on account, $2,400.

Exercise 2–5

Prepare journal entries
(L.O. 3)

Prepare the journal entry (without dollar amounts) of a transaction that would involve the following combinations of types of accounts:

a. An asset and a liability.

b. An expense and an asset.

c. A liability and an expense.

d. Stockholders' equity and an asset.

e. Two asset accounts.

f. An asset and a revenue.

Exercise 2–6

Show entries using journal entries and T-accounts
(L.O. 3, 4)

For each of the unrelated transactions below first give the journal entry to record the transaction. Then show how the journal entry would be posted to T-accounts. You need not include explanations or account numbers.

a. Capital stock was issued for $96,000 cash.

b. Salaries for a period were paid to employees, $12,000.

c. Services were performed for customers on account, $19,200.

Exercise 2–7

Explain sets of debits and credits
(L.O. 1–4)

Explain each of the sets of debits and credits existing in the accounts below. There are 10 transactions to be explained. Each set is designated by the small letters to the left of the amount. For example, the first transaction is the issuance of capital stock for cash and is denoted by the letter *(a)*.

Cash					Service Revenue		
(a)	210,000	*(e)*	150,000			*(c)*	1,800
(d)	1,800	*(f)*	600			*(j)*	14,100
		(g)	3,600				
		(i)	30,000			Bal.	15,900
Bal.	27,600						

Accounts Receivable					Rent Expense	
(c)	1,800	*(d)*	1,800	*(f)*	600	
(j)	14,100					
Bal.	14,100					

Land				Delivery Expense	
(b)	150,000		*(h)*	1,200	
(i)	30,000				
Bal.	180,000				

Accounts Payable				Salaries Expense		
(e)	150,000	*(b)*	150,000	*(g)*	3,600	
		(h)	1,200			
		Bal.	1,200			

Capital Stock		
	(a)	210,000

Exercise 2–8

Prepare trial balance
(L.O. 5)

Assume the ledger accounts given in Exercise 2–7 are those of Beck Company as they appear at December 31, 1994. Prepare the trial balance as of that date.

Exercise 2–9

Prepare journal entries
(L.O. 3)

Prepare journal entries to record each of the following transactions for Lopez Company. Use the letter of the transaction in place of the date. Include an explanation for each entry.

a. Capital stock was issued for cash, $384,000.

b. Purchased trucks on account, $240,000.

c. Earned (but did not yet receive) service revenue, $4,800.

d. Collected the account receivable resulting from transaction *(c),* $4,800.

e. Paid the account payable for the delivery equipment purchased, $240,000.

f. Paid utilities for the month in the amount of $2,400.

g. Paid salaries for the month in the amount of $7,200.

h. Incurred delivery expenses in the amount of $1,920, but did not yet pay for them.

i. Purchased more trucks for cash, $48,000.

j. Performed delivery services on account, $24,000.

Exercise 2–10

Post journal entries to three-column ledger accounts
(L.O. 4)

Using the data in Exercise 2–9, post the entries to three-column ledger accounts. Write the letter of the transaction in the account before the dollar amount. Determine a balance for each account.

Exercise 2–11

Prepare trial balance
(L.O. 5)

Using your answer for Exercise 2–10, prepare a trial balance. Assume the date of the trial balance is March 31, 1994.

Exercise 2–12

Determine trial balance errors
(L.O. 5)

John Adams owns and manages a bowling center called Strike Lanes. He also maintains his own accounting records and was about to prepare financial statements for the year 1994. When he prepared the trial balance from the ledger accounts, the total of the debits column was $327,500, and the total of the credits column was $325,000. What are the possible reasons why the totals of the debits and credits are out of balance? How would you normally proceed to find an error if the two trial balance columns do not agree?

PROBLEMS: SERIES A

Problem 2–1A

Prepare journal entries
(L.O. 3)

Presented below are the transactions of Martino Company for March 1994:

Mar. 1 The company was organized and issued capital stock for $270,000 cash.
2 Paid $8,100 as the rent for March on a completely furnished building.
5 Paid cash for delivery trucks, $157,500.
6 Paid $3,360 as the rent for March on two forklift trucks.
9 Paid $1,800 for supplies received and used in March.
12 Performed delivery services for customers who promised to pay $67,500 at a later date.

Mar. 20 Collected cash of $54,000 from customers on account (see March 12 entry).
21 Received a bill for $1,350 for advertising in the local newspaper in March.
27 Paid cash for gas and oil consumed in March, $432.
31 Paid $6,300 to employees for services provided in March.
31 Received an order for services at $45,000. The services will be performed in April.
31 Paid cash dividend, $9,000.

Required Prepare the journal entries that would be required to record the above transactions in the general journal of the company.

Problem 2–2A

Record transactions in journal, post to T-accounts, and prepare trial balance (L.O. 3–5)

Chapman Company had the following transactions in August 1994:

Aug. 1 Issued capital stock for cash, $60,000.
3 Borrowed $20,000 from the bank on a note.
4 Purchased a truck for $21,200 cash.
6 Performed services for customers who promised to pay later, $14,400.
7 Paid employee salaries for first week, $2,800.
10 Collections were made for the services performed on August 6, $3,200.
14 Supplies were purchased for use this month, $2,000. They will be paid for next month.
17 A bill for $400 was received for gas and oil used to date.
25 Services were performed for customers who paid immediately, $18,000.
31 Paid employee salaries, $6,000.
31 Paid cash dividend, $1,600.

Required a. Prepare journal entries for the above transactions.

b. Post the journal entries to T-accounts. Enter the account number in the Posting Reference column of the journal as you post each amount. Use the following account numbers:

Acct. No.	Account Title
100	Cash
103	Accounts Receivable
150	Trucks
200	Accounts Payable
201	Notes Payable
300	Capital Stock
320	Dividends
400	Service Revenue
506	Gas and Oil Expense
507	Salaries Expense
518	Supplies Expense

c. Prepare a trial balance as of August 31, 1994.

Problem 2–3A

Record transactions in journal, post to T-accounts, and prepare trial balance (L.O. 3–5)

Crawford Company had the following transactions for July 1994:

July 2 Cash of $30,000 was received for capital stock issued to the owners.
3 The company paid rent for July, $1,500.
5 Office furniture was purchased for $18,000 cash.
9 A bill for $3,000 for advertising for July was received and paid.
14 Cash of $4,200 was received for services rendered to customers.
15 Salaries of $1,200 for the first half of July were paid.
20 The company performed services on account to Smith Company, $2,400. The account is to be paid August 10.
22 Office furniture was purchased on account from Martineze Company; the price was $2,400.
30 Cash of $13,500 was received for services rendered to customers.
31 Salaries of $1,200 for the second half of July were paid.

Required   *a.*   Prepare journal entries for the above transactions.

   b.   Post the journal entries to T-accounts. Enter the account number in the Posting Reference column of the journal as you post each amount. Use the following account numbers:

Acct. No.	Account Title
100	Cash
103	Accounts Receivable
160	Office Furniture
200	Accounts Payable
300	Capital Stock
400	Service Revenue
505	Advertising Expense
507	Salaries Expense
515	Rent Expense

   c.   Prepare a trial balance as of July 31, 1994.

Problem 2–4A

Prepare ledger accounts, journalize transactions, post to three-column ledger accounts, and prepare trial balance (L.O. 3–5)

Evans, Inc., is a company providing janitorial services and was organized July 1, 1994. The following account numbers and titles constitute the chart of accounts for the company:

Acct. No.	Account Title
100	Cash
103	Accounts Receivable
150	Trucks
160	Office Furniture
170	Equipment
200	Accounts Payable
201	Notes Payable
300	Capital Stock
310	Retained Earnings
320	Dividends
400	Service Revenue
506	Gas and Oil Expense
507	Salaries Expense
511	Utilities Expense
512	Insurance Expense
515	Rent Expense
518	Supplies Expense

Transactions for July are:

July 1 The company issued $288,000 of capital stock for cash.

     5 Office space was rented for July, and $5,760 was paid for the rental.

     8 Desks and chairs were purchased for the office on account, $28,800.

   10 Equipment was purchased for $40,320; a note was given, to be paid in 30 days.

   15 Purchased trucks for $172,800, paying $115,200 cash and giving a 60-day note to the dealer for $57,600.

   18 Paid for supplies received and already used, $2,880.

   23 Received $17,280 cash as service revenue.

   27 Insurance expense for July was paid, $4,320.

   30 Paid for gasoline and oil used by the truck in July, $576.

   31 Billed customers for services rendered, $40,320.

   31 Paid salaries for July, $51,840.

   31 Paid utilities bills for July, $5,280.

   31 Paid cash dividends, $9,600.

Required   a.   Prepare general ledger accounts for all of the above accounts except Retained Earnings. The Retained Earnings account has a beginning balance of zero and maintains this balance throughout the period.

b.   Journalize the transactions given for July 1994 in the general journal.

c.   Post the journal entries to three-column ledger accounts.

d.   Prepare a trial balance as of July 31, 1994.

Problem 2–5A

Prepare journal entries, post to three-column ledger accounts, and prepare trial balance (L.O. 3–5)

Wade Company is a lawn care company. Thus, the company earns its revenue from sending its trucks to customers' residences and certain commercial establishments to care for lawns and shrubbery. Wade Company's trial balance at the end of the first 11 months of the year is presented below.

WADE COMPANY
Trial Balance
November 30, 1994

Acct. No.	Account Title	Debits	Credits
100	Cash	$ 73,740	
103	Accounts Receivable	78,600	
150	Trucks	102,900	
160	Office Furniture	8,400	
200	Accounts Payable		$ 33,600
300	Capital Stock		30,000
310	Retained Earnings, January 1, 1994		30,540
400	Service Revenue		371,010
505	Advertising Expense	18,300	
506	Gas and Oil Expense	21,900	
507	Salaries Expense	65,850	
511	Utilities Expense	2,310	
515	Rent Expense	15,000	
518	Supplies Expense	75,600	
531	Entertainment Expense	2,550	
		$465,150	$465,150

Transactions for December are:

Dec. 2   Paid rent for December, $3,000.
5   Paid the accounts payable of $33,600.
8   Paid advertising for December, $1,200.
10   Purchased a new office desk on account, $1,050.
13   Purchased $240 of supplies on account for use in December.
15   Collected cash from customers on account, $70,800.
20   Paid for customer entertainment, $80.
24   Collected an additional $6,000 from customers on account.
26   Paid for gasoline used in the trucks in December, $270.
28   Billed customers for services rendered, $79,500.
30   Paid for more December supplies, $19,800.
31   Paid December salaries, $15,300.
31   Paid a $3,000 cash dividend. (The Dividends account is No. 320.)

Required   a.   Open three-column general ledger accounts for each of the accounts in the trial balance under the date of December 1, 1994. Place the word *Balance* in the explanation space of each account.

b.   Prepare entries in the general journal for the transactions given above for December 1994.

c.   Post the journal entries to three-column general ledger accounts.

d.   Prepare a trial balance as of December 31, 1994.

Problem 2–6A

Prepare corrected trial
balance
(L.O. 5)

Tom Gentry prepared the following trial balance from the ledger of the Fuller Company. The trial balance did not balance.

FULLER COMPANY
Trial Balance
December 31, 1994

Acct. No.	Account Title	Debits	Credits
100	Cash.	$ 59,200	
103	Accounts Receivable	40,800	
160	Office Furniture.	120,000	
172	Office Equipment.	48,000	
200	Accounts Payable.		$ 22,400
300	Capital Stock		160,000
310	Retained Earnings.		80,000
320	Dividends	28,800	
400	Service Revenue		360,000
507	Salaries Expense	280,000	
515	Rent Expense	40,000	
568	Miscellaneous Expense	7,200	
		$624,000	$622,400

The difference in totals in the trial balance caused Tom to carefully examine the company's accounting records. In searching back through the accounting records, Tom found that the following errors had been made.

1. One entire entry that included a $4,800 debit to Cash and a $4,800 credit to Accounts Receivable was never posted.

2. In computing the balance of the Accounts Payable account, a credit of $3,200 was omitted from the computation.

3. In preparing the trial balance, the Retained Earnings account balance was shown as $80,000. The ledger account has the balance as its correct amount of $83,200.

4. One debit of $2,400 to the Dividends account was posted as a credit to that account.

5. Office equipment of $8,000 was debited to Office Furniture when purchased.

Required Prepare a corrected trial balance for the Fuller Company as of December 31, 1994. Also, write a description of the effect(s) of each error.

PROBLEMS: SERIES B

Problem 2–1B

Prepare journal entries
(L.O. 3)

Hammond Laundry Company, Inc., entered into the following transactions in August 1994:

Aug. 1 Received cash for capital stock issued to owners, $384,000.

3 Paid rent for August on a building and laundry equipment rented, $6,720.

6 Performed laundry services for $57,600 cash.

8 Secured an order from a customer for laundry services of $48,000. The services are to be performed next month.

13 Performed laundry services for $76,800 on account to various customers.

15 Received and paid a bill for $840 for supplies used in operations.

23 Cash collected from customers on account, $52,800.

Aug. 31 Paid $25,920 to employees for services performed in August.
   31 Received the electric and gas bill for August, $720, but did not pay it at this time.
   31 Paid cash dividend, $7,200.

Required Prepare journal entries for the above transactions in the general journal.

Problem 2–2B

Record transactions in journal, post to T-accounts, and prepare trial balance (L.O. 3–5)

The transactions listed below are those of Hudson Company for April 1994:

Apr. 1 Cash of $480,000 was received for capital stock issued to the owners.
   3 Rent was paid for April, $3,200.
   6 Trucks were purchased for $56,000 cash.
   7 Office equipment was purchased on account from Wagner Company for $76,800.
   14 Salaries for first two weeks were paid, $11,200.
   15 $46,400 was received for services performed.
   18 An invoice was received from Roger's Gas Station for $400 for gas and oil used during April.
   23 A note was arranged with the bank for $80,000. The cash was received, and a note promising to return the $80,000 on May 30, 1994, was signed.
   29 Purchased trucks for $73,600 by signing a note.
   30 Salaries were paid, $14,400.

Required
a. Prepare journal entries for the above transactions.
b. Post the journal entries to T-accounts. Enter the account number in the Posting Reference column of the journal as you post each amount. Use the following account numbers:

Acct. No.	Account Title
100	Cash
150	Trucks
172	Office Equipment
200	Accounts Payable
201	Notes Payable
300	Capital Stock
400	Service Revenue
506	Gas and Oil Expense
507	Salaries Expense
515	Rent Expense

c. Prepare a trial balance as of April 30, 1994.

Problem 2–3B

Record transactions in journal, post to T-accounts, and prepare trial balance (L.O. 3–5)

The transactions below are those of Ruiz Company for the first week of April 1994.

Apr. 1 Ruiz Company was organized, and $320,000 of capital stock was issued for cash.
   1 The company borrowed $200,000 from its bank and issued its note payable to the bank.
   2 Paid $120,000 cash for land.
   2 Paid $380,000 cash for an office building located on the land purchased above.
   3 Purchased $48,000 of office equipment on account.
   4 Paid cash $3,200 for supplies to be consumed in April.
   5 Services performed on account were $2,000.
   6 Services performed for cash for the first week were $8,000.
   6 Paid salaries for the first week, $5,600.

Required
a. Prepare journal entries for the above transactions.
b. Post the journal entries to T-accounts. Enter the account number in the Posting Reference column of the journal as you post each amount. Use the following account numbers:

Acct. No.	Account Title
100	Cash
103	Accounts Receivable
130	Land
140	Buildings
172	Office Equipment
200	Accounts Payable
201	Notes Payable
300	Capital Stock
400	Service Revenue
507	Salaries Expense
518	Supplies Expense

c.   Prepare a trial balance as of April 6, 1994.

Problem 2–4B

Prepare ledger accounts, journalize transactions, post to three-column ledger accounts, and prepare trial balance (L.O. 3–5)

Joiner, Inc., was organized January 1, 1994. Its chart of accounts is as follows:

Acct. No.	Account Title
100	Cash
103	Accounts Receivable
150	Trucks
160	Office Furniture
172	Office Equipment
200	Accounts Payable
201	Notes Payable
300	Capital Stock
310	Retained Earnings
400	Service Revenue
506	Gas and Oil Expense
507	Salaries Expense
511	Utilities Expense
512	Insurance Expense
515	Rent Expense
530	Repairs Expense

Transactions for January are:

Jan. 1   The company received $480,000 cash and $240,000 of office furniture in exchange for $720,000 of capital stock.

2   Paid garage rent for January, $6,000.

4   Purchased office equipment on account, $13,200.

6   Purchased delivery trucks for $270,000; payment was made by giving cash of $150,000 and a 30-day note for the remainder.

12   Purchased insurance for January on the delivery trucks. The cost of the policy, $10,800, was paid in cash.

15   Received and paid January utilities bills, $960.

15   Paid salaries for first half of January, $3,600.

17   Cash received for delivery services to date amounted to $1,800.

20   Received bill for gasoline purchased and used in January, $180.

23   Purchased delivery trucks for cash, $108,000.

25   Cash sales of delivery services were $2,880.

27   Purchased an adding machine on account, $3,600.

31   Paid salaries for last half of January, $4,800.

31   Sales of delivery services on account amounted to $11,400.

31   Paid for repairs to a delivery truck, $1,120.

Required   *a.*   Prepare general ledger accounts for all the above accounts except Retained Earnings. The Retained Earnings account has a beginning balance of zero and maintains this balance throughout the period.

    b.   Journalize the transactions given for January 1994 in the general journal.

    c.   Post the journal entries to three-column ledger accounts.

    d.   Prepare a trial balance as of January 31, 1994.

Problem 2–5B

Prepare journal entries, post to three-column ledger accounts, and prepare trial balance (L.O. 3–5)

The trial balance of Langley Tennis Company at the end of the first 11 months of its fiscal year is given below.

LANGLEY COMPANY
Trial Balance
November 30, 1994

Acct. No.	Account Title	Debits	Credits
100	Cash	$ 81,180	
103	Accounts Receivable	81,750	
130	Land	60,000	
200	Accounts Payable		$ 18,750
201	Notes Payable		15,000
300	Capital Stock		60,000
310	Retained Earnings, January 1, 1994		53,700
413	Membership and Lesson Revenue		202,500
505	Advertising Expense	21,000	
507	Salaries Expense	66,000	
511	Utilities Expense	2,100	
515	Rent Expense	33,000	
518	Supplies Expense	2,250	
530	Repairs Expense	1,500	
531	Entertainment Expense	870	
540	Interest Expense	300	
		$349,950	$349,950

Transactions for December are:

Dec. 1   Paid building rent for December, $3,000.

     2   Paid vendors on account, $18,000.

     5   Purchased land for cash, $2,250.

     7   Sold memberships on account for December, $27,000.

   10   Paid the note payable of $15,000, plus interest of $150.

   13   Cash collections from customers on account, $36,000.

   19   Received a bill for repairs, $225.

   24   Paid the December utilities bill, $180.

   28   Received a bill for December advertising, $1,650.

   29   Paid the equipment repair bill received on the 19th, $225.

   30   Gave tennis lessons for cash, $4,500.

   30   Paid salaries, $6,000.

   30   Sales of memberships on account since December 7, $18,000 (for the month of December).

   30   Costs paid in entertaining customers in December, $255.

   30   Paid dividends of $1,500. (The Dividends account is No. 320.)

Required   *a.*   Open three-column general ledger accounts for each of the accounts in the trial balance. Place the word *Balance* in the explanation space and enter the date December 1, 1994, on this same line.

    b.   Prepare entries in the general journal for the transactions given above for December 1994.

c. Post the journal entries to three-column ledger accounts.

d. Prepare a trial balance as of December 31, 1994.

Problem 2–6B

Prepare corrected trial balance
(L.O. 5)

Darlene Martin prepared a trial balance for Parker Company that did not balance. The trial balance she prepared was as follows:

PARKER COMPANY
Trial Balance
December 31, 1994

Acct. No.	Account Title	Debits	Credits
100	Cash	$ 64,000	
103	Accounts Receivable	40,800	
170	Equipment	160,000	
200	Accounts Payable		$ 24,000
300	Capital Stock		120,000
310	Retained Earnings		40,000
320	Dividends	16,000	
400	Service Revenue		432,000
505	Advertising Expense	1,200	
507	Salaries Expense	176,000	
511	Utilities Expense	44,800	
515	Rent Expense	64,000	
		$566,800	$616,000

In trying to find out why the trial balance did not balance, Darlene discovered the following errors:

1. Cash was understated (too low) by $8,000 because of an error in addition in determining the balance of that account in the ledger.

2. A credit of $4,800 to Accounts Receivable in the journal was not posted to the ledger account at all.

3. A debit of $16,000 for a semiannual dividend was posted as a credit to the Capital Stock account.

4. The balance of $12,000 in the Advertising Expense account was entered as $1,200 in the trial balance.

5. Miscellaneous Expense (Account No. 568), with a balance of $3,200, was omitted from the trial balance.

Required   Prepare a correct trial balance as of December 31, 1994.

BUSINESS DECISION PROBLEM

Decision Problem 2–1

Prepare journal entries, post to T-accounts, and judge profitability
(L.O. 3, 4)

Jim Weaver lost his job as a carpenter with a contractor when a recession hit the construction industry. Jim had been making $50,000 per year. He decided to form his own company, Weaver Corporation, and do home repairs.

The following is a summary of the transactions of the business during the first three months of operations in 1993:

Jan. 15 Stockholders invested $20,000 in the business.

Feb. 25 Received payment of $4,400 for remodeling a basement into a recreation room. The homeowner purchased all of the building materials.

Mar. 5 Paid cash for an advertisement that appeared in the local newspaper, $110.

Apr. 10 Received $6,400 for converting a room over a garage into an office for a college professor. The professor purchased all of the materials for the job.

11 Paid gas and oil expenses for automobile, $700.

12 Miscellaneous business expenses were paid, $450.

15 Paid dividends of $4,000.

Required   *a.*   Prepare journal entries for the above transactions.

            b.   Post the journal entries to T-accounts.

            c.   How profitable is this new venture? Should Jim stay in this business?

ANSWERS TO SELF-TEST

True-False

1. *True.* The journal is the book of original entry. Any amounts appearing in a ledger account must have been posted from the journal.

2. *False.* The left side of any account is the *debit* side.

3. *False.* These accounts are all increased by credits.

4. *True.* Since drawings reduce stockholders' equity, the Dividends account is increased by debits.

5. *False.* An entire journal entry may not have been posted, or a debit or credit might have been posted to the wrong account.

Multiple-Choice

1. *c.* An asset, Cash, is increased by a debit, and the owner's Capital Stock account is increased by a credit.

2. *b.* Since the insurance covers more than the current accounting period, an asset is debited instead of an expense. The credit is to Cash.

3. *a.* The receipt of cash before services are performed creates a liability, Unearned Delivery Fees. To increase a liability, it is credited. Cash is debited to increase its balance.

4. *b.* Cash is increased by the debit, and Delivery Service Revenue is increased by the credit.

5. *c.* Dividends is increased by the debit, and Cash is decreased by the credit.

3

ADJUSTING THE ACCOUNTS

LEARNING OBJECTIVES

After studying this chapter, you should be able to:

1. Describe the basic characteristics of the cash basis and the accrual basis of accounting.
2. Identify the reasons why adjusting entries must be made.
3. Identify the classes and types of adjusting entries.
4. Prepare adjusting entries.
5. Determine the effects of failing to prepare adjusting entries.

Chapters 1 and 2 introduced the accounting process of analyzing, classifying, and summarizing business transactions into accounts. You learned how these transactions are entered into the journal and posted to the ledger accounts. You also know how the trial balance is used to test the equality of debits and credits in the journalizing and posting process. The purpose of the accounting process is to produce accurate financial statements. At this point in your study of accounting, you are concentrating on three financial statements—the income statement, the statement of retained earnings, and the balance sheet.

When you began to analyze business transactions in Chapter 1, you saw that the evidence of the transaction is usually a source document. A source document, you recall, is any written or printed evidence of a business transaction that describes the essential facts of that transaction. Examples of source documents are receipts for cash paid or received, checks written or received, bills sent to customers or bills received from suppliers, and so on. You should be familiar with some or all of these source documents by now. The giving, receiving, or creating of a source document triggered the journal entries made in Chapter 2. Source documents are used to prepare journal entries during an accounting period.

The journal entries we will discuss in this chapter are *adjusting entries*. The arrival of the end of the accounting period triggers adjusting entries. The purpose of adjusting entries is to bring the accounts to their proper balances before the financial statements are prepared. In this chapter, you will first learn the difference between the cash basis and accrual basis of accounting. Then you will learn about the classes and types of adjusting entries and how to prepare them.

CASH VERSUS ACCRUAL BASIS ACCOUNTING

Objective 1

Describe the basic characteristics of the cash basis and the accrual basis of accounting

Some relatively small businesses and professionals such as physicians and lawyers may account for their revenues and expenses on a cash basis. The cash basis of accounting recognizes revenues when cash is received and recognizes expenses when cash is paid out. For example, under the cash basis, a company would treat services rendered to clients in 1994 for which the company collected cash in 1995 as 1995 revenues. Similarly, under the cash basis, a company would treat expenses incurred in 1994 for which the company disbursed cash in 1995 as 1995 expenses.

Since the cash basis of accounting does not match ''efforts'' and ''accomplishments'' in terms of expenses incurred and revenues earned, it is generally considered theoretically unacceptable. The cash basis is acceptable in practice only under those circumstances when it approximates the results that a company could obtain under the accrual basis of accounting. Companies using the cash basis do not have to prepare any adjusting entries unless they discover they have made a mistake in preparing an entry during the accounting period. Under certain circumstances, companies may use the cash basis for income tax purposes.

Throughout the text we use the accrual basis of accounting because most companies use the accrual basis. The accrual basis of accounting recognizes revenues when sales are made or services are performed, regardless of when cash is received. Expenses are recognized as incurred, whether or not cash has been paid out. For instance, assume a company performs services for a customer on account. Although the company has received no cash, the revenue is recorded at the time the company performs the service. Later, when the company receives the cash, no revenue is recorded because the company has already recorded the revenue. Under the accrual basis, adjusting entries are needed to bring the accounts up to date for unrecorded economic activity that has taken place.

Illustration 3.1 shows when revenues and expenses are recognized under the cash basis and under the accrual basis.

ILLUSTRATION 3.1

Cash Basis and Accrual Basis of Accounting Compared

	Cash Basis	**Accrual Basis**
Revenues are recognized	As cash is received	As earned (goods are delivered or services are performed)
Expenses are recognized	As cash is paid	As incurred to produce revenues

An example of economic activity that would require an adjusting entry is the purchase and gradual use of office supplies. When a company purchases office supplies, the purchase is recorded in an asset account, Office Supplies on Hand. Even though the company uses the office supplies during the accounting period, their consumption is usually not recorded until the end of the period. The cost and nuisance of making an entry every time the company uses a small amount of office supplies outweighs the benefits of having accurate account balances during the period. Instead, an adjusting entry is made at the end of the period to bring the accounts to their proper balances before the financial statements are prepared.

THE NEED FOR ADJUSTING ENTRIES

Objective 2

Identify the reasons why adjusting entries must be made

The income statement of a business reports all revenues earned and all expenses incurred to generate those revenues during a given period. If the income statement does not report all revenues and expenses, it is incomplete, inaccurate, and possibly misleading. Similarly, a balance sheet that does not report all of an entity's assets, liabilities, and stockholders' equity at a specific point in time may be misleading. Each adjusting entry has a dual purpose: (1) to make the income statement report the proper revenue or expense and (2) to make the balance sheet report the proper asset or liability. Thus, every adjusting entry affects at least one income statement account and one balance sheet account.

Since those interested in the activities of a business need timely information, companies must prepare financial statements periodically. To prepare such statements, the accountant divides an entity's life into time periods. These time periods are usually equal in length and are called *accounting periods*. An accounting period may be one month, one quarter, or one year. An accounting year, or fiscal year, is an accounting period of one year. A fiscal year is any 12 consecutive months. The fiscal year may or may not coincide with the calendar year, which ends on December 31. Illustration 3.2 shows the fiscal year endings of a survey of 600 companies. More than half of the companies have a fiscal year that coincides with the calendar year. Companies in certain industries often have a fiscal year that differs from the calendar year. For instance, to avoid the Christmas holidays, many retail stores end their fiscal year on January 31. Other companies select a fiscal year ending at a time when inventories and business activity are lowest.

Periodic reporting and the matching principle necessitate the preparation of *adjusting entries*. Adjusting entries are journal entries made at the end of an accounting period or at any time financial statements are to be prepared to bring about a proper **matching** of revenues and expenses. The matching principle requires that expenses incurred in producing revenues be deducted from the revenues they generated during the accounting period. This matching of expenses and

SURVEY HOLDS SURPRISES FOR RECRUITING

Atlantic City, N.J.—Undergraduates' civic activities don't impress recruiters much when they're evaluating seniors for their firms.

"We were surprised," said Anthony T. Krzystofik, professor of accounting at the University of Massachusetts School of Management. He explained that recruiters look for indicators of leadership, not participation.

Krzystofik presented the results of his school's survey of recruiters and students to a personnel conference here sponsored by the Foundation for Accounting Education. The Foundation is the educational arm of the New York State Society of CPAs.

The UMass School of Management conducted separate surveys of the attitudes of recruiters and students.

In the survey of recruiters, there appeared to be a wide variance between the approaches taken by national and local firms.

Fully 75 percent of national-firm recruiters said they use definite interview techniques in approaching undergraduates, compared with a very small percent of local firm representatives.

Eighty-three percent of the national recruiters used their interviews to evaluate the candidates, compared with 31 percent of local-firms representatives. Three-quarters of the nationals said they used the interviews to sell the candidates on the firm, compared with 36 percent of the locals, Krzystofik reported.

Grade-point average ranked high in evaluation of the candidates, as did leadership, he said.

Highly detrimental to the candidates in the eyes of the recruiters, he said, were criminal convictions, low class rank, membership in fringe religious groups and a lack of involvement in extracurricular or social activities.

Candidates were also hurt by expressing an interest in investment banking, as were those who seemed not to fit a firm's culture or who lacked a professional image.

Factors that encouraged recruiters to invite students to visit their firms' offices included oral communication abilities, demonstrated leadership, self-confidence and an outgoing personality.

Richard Fein, director of placement at the UMass School of Management, said that his survey of students showed that fall recruiting is the biggest event in a student's life.

According to the survey, 84 percent of them spent three to eight hours a week getting ready for interviews. He said 85 percent thought the time was well spent even though more than 80 percent stated that their grades or their friendships suffered during the recruiting period.

Fein said that 98 percent of the students indicated that they did not feel recruiters misled them, and 86 percent were of the opinion that what the recruiters told them was reasonable.

The survey showed that 84 percent of the students rejected at least one invitation to visit a firm's offices.

As to why students declined office visits, Fein said that some have so many offers they can't accept them all. Another reason, he said, is that they may schedule office visits with firms that are their third or fourth choices. When they get a better offer, they cancel the least important invitations.

The benefits of office visits, according to the respondents, were to meet more people in a firm (95 percent), to see a firm's facilities (93 percent) and to ask more questions (82 percent).

Asked to rate various factors in the decisions to join a particular firm, 70 percent said the office interview was very important. Slightly more than half cited the training and education offered by a firm.

Forty-three percent were influenced by a firm's reputation. Rated last (31 percent) was salary and benefits.

Asked about the principal source of pressures to go into public accounting (rather than other areas of accounting), 47 percent said peer pressure was most influential and 40 percent said the heaviest pressure came from faculty.

Fein concluded that it would be helpful if students got a more substantive exposure to recruiters and their firms at the beginning of the process.

revenues is necessary for the income statement to present an accurate picture of the profitability of a business. Adjusting entries reflect unrecorded economic activity that has taken place but has not yet been recorded. Why has the company not recorded this activity by the end of the period? The reason is either (1) it is

ILLUSTRATION 3.2

Summary—Fiscal Year Endings by Month

	1989	1988	1987	1986
January	22	20	23	23
February	15	13	13	15
March	16	15	14	11
April	8	7	8	5
May	15	16	14	16
June	57	54	42	43
July	16	14	14	14
August	16	15	15	18
September	37	38	37	36
October	20	22	23	23
November	17	15	16	15
Subtotal	239	229	219	219
December	361	371	381	381
Total companies	600	600	600	600

Source: American Institute of Certified Public Accountants, *Accounting Trends & Techniques* (New York: AICPA, 1990), p. 23.

more convenient and economical to wait until the end of the period to record the activity, or (2) no source document concerning that activity has yet come to the accountant's attention.

Adjusting entries bring the amounts in the general ledger accounts to their proper balances before the company prepares its financial statements. That is, **adjusting entries convert the amounts that are actually in the general ledger accounts to the amounts that should be in the general ledger accounts for proper financial reporting.** To make this conversion, the accounts are analyzed to determine which accounts need adjustment. For example, assume a company purchased a three-year insurance policy costing $600 at the beginning of the year and debited $600 to Prepaid Insurance. At year-end, the company should remove $200 of the cost from the asset and record it as an expense. Failure to do so misstates assets and net income on the financial statements.

Companies **continuously** receive benefits from many assets such as prepaid expenses (e.g., prepaid insurance and prepaid rent). Thus, the expense relating to these items could also be recognized **continuously** as time elapses. An entry could be made frequently, even daily, to record the expense incurred. Typically, however, the entry is not made until financial statements are to be prepared. Therefore, if monthly financial statements are prepared, monthly adjusting entries are required. By custom, and in some instances by law, businesses report to their owners at least annually. Accordingly, adjusting entries will be required at least once a year. Remember, however, that the entry transferring an amount from an asset account to an expense account should transfer only the cost of the portion of the asset that has expired.

CLASSES AND TYPES OF ADJUSTING ENTRIES

Objective 3

Identify the classes and types of adjusting entries

Adjusting entries can be grouped into two broad classes: deferred (meaning to postpone or delay) items and accrued (meaning to grow or accumulate) items. Deferred items consist of adjusting entries involving data previously recorded in accounts. These entries involve the transfer of data already recorded in asset and liability accounts to expense and revenue accounts, respectively. Accrued items consist of adjusting entries relating to activity on which no data have been previously recorded in the accounts. These entries involve the initial, or first, recording of assets and liabilities and the related revenues and expenses (Illustration 3.3).

Deferred items consist of two types of adjusting entries: asset/expense adjustments and liability/revenue adjustments. For example, prepaid insurance and prepaid rent are shown as assets until they are used up; then they become expenses. Also, if a company receives cash for a service it has not yet rendered, the credit is to an unearned revenue (a liability account). However, as the company renders the service, the unearned revenue becomes earned revenue.

Accrued items also consist of two types of adjusting entries: asset/revenue adjustments and liability/expense adjustments. For example, assume a company performs a service for a customer but has not yet billed the customer. This transaction is recorded as an asset in the form of a receivable and as revenue because the company has earned a revenue. Also, assume a company owes its employees salaries that it has not yet paid. This transaction is recorded as a liability and an expense because the company has incurred an expense.

In this chapter, we use the Speedy Delivery Company example from Chapter 2 to illustrate each of the four types of adjusting entries: asset/expense, liability/revenue, asset/revenue, and liability/expense. Illustration 3.4 shows the trial balance of the Speedy Delivery Company at December 31, 1994. This trial balance is the same as the one shown in Chapter 2, Illustration 2.8. As you can see by looking at the trial balance, several accounts must be adjusted before accurate financial statements can be prepared. The adjustments for these accounts involve data that have already been recorded in the company's accounts.

In making adjustments for Speedy Delivery Company, we will need to add several additional accounts to the company's chart of accounts shown in Chapter 2 on page 65. These accounts are:

Type of Account	Acct. No.	Account Title	Description
Asset	121	Interest Receivable	The amount of interest earned but not yet received.
Contra asset*	151	Accumulated Depreciation— Trucks	The total depreciation cost taken on trucks. The balance of this account is deducted from that of Trucks on the balance sheet.
Liability	206	Salaries Payable	The amount of salaries earned by employees but not yet paid by the company.
Revenue	418	Interest Revenue	The amount of interest earned in the current period.
Expenses	512	Insurance Expense	The cost of insurance incurred in the current period.
	515	Rent Expense	The cost of rent incurred in the current period.
	518	Supplies Expense	The cost of supplies used in the current period.
	521	Depreciation Expense— Trucks	The portion of the cost of the trucks assigned to expense during the current period.

* The balance of a contra asset is deducted from the balance of an asset account on the balance sheet. The reasons for using a contra asset account are explained later in the chapter.

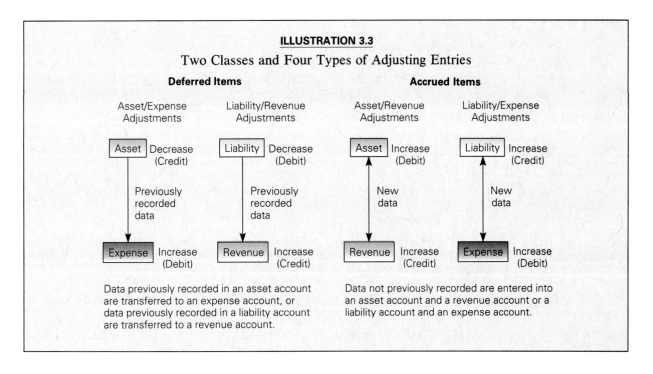

ILLUSTRATION 3.3

Two Classes and Four Types of Adjusting Entries

Deferred Items

Asset/Expense Adjustments

Liability/Revenue Adjustments

Asset | Decrease (Credit)

Previously recorded data

Expense | Increase (Debit)

Liability | Decrease (Debit)

Previously recorded data

Revenue | Increase (Credit)

Data previously recorded in an asset account are transferred to an expense account, or data previously recorded in a liability account are transferred to a revenue account.

Accrued Items

Asset/Revenue Adjustments

Liability/Expense Adjustments

Asset | Increase (Debit)

New data

Revenue | Increase (Credit)

Liability | Increase (Credit)

New data

Expense | Increase (Debit)

Data not previously recorded are entered into an asset account and a revenue account or a liability account and an expense account.

ILLUSTRATION 3.4

Trial Balance

SPEEDY DELIVERY COMPANY
Trial Balance
December 31, 1994

Acct. No.	Account Title	Debits	Credits
100	Cash	$ 8,250	
103	Accounts Receivable.	5,200	
107	Supplies on Hand	1,400	
108	Prepaid Insurance	2,400	
112	Prepaid Rent	1,200	
150	Trucks	40,000	
200	Accounts Payable		$ 730
210	Unearned Delivery Fees		4,500
300	Capital Stock		50,000
320	Dividends.	3,000	
400	Service Revenue		10,700
505	Advertising Expense	50	
506	Gas and Oil Expense.	680	
507	Salaries Expense	3,600	
511	Utilities Expense	150	
		$65,930	$65,930

Now you are ready to follow Speedy Delivery Company as it makes its adjustments for deferred items. If you find the process confusing, go back and study again the beginning of this chapter so you clearly understand the purpose of adjusting entries.

ADJUSTMENTS FOR DEFERRED ITEMS

This section discusses the two types of adjustments for deferred items: asset/expense adjustments and liability/revenue adjustments. In the asset/expense group, you will learn how to prepare adjusting entries for prepaid expenses and depreciation. In the liability/revenue group, you will learn how to prepare adjusting entries for unearned revenues.

Asset/Expense Adjustments— Prepaid Expenses and Depreciation

Speedy Delivery Company must make several asset/expense adjustments for prepaid expenses. A prepaid expense is an asset awaiting assignment to expense, such as prepaid insurance, prepaid rent, and supplies on hand. As you will see, the nature of these three adjustments is the same.

Prepaid Insurance When a company pays an insurance policy premium in advance, the purchase creates the asset, **prepaid insurance.** This advance payment is an asset because the company will receive insurance coverage in the future. With the passage of time, however, the asset gradually expires. The portion that has expired becomes an expense. To illustrate this point, recall that in Chapter 2, Speedy Delivery Company purchased on account an insurance policy on its trucks for the period December 1, 1994, to November 30, 1995. The journal entry made on December 1, 1994, to record the purchase of the policy was:

1994					
Dec.	1	Prepaid Insurance.		2,400	
		Accounts Payable.			2,400
		Purchased truck insurance to cover a one-year period.			

The two accounts relating to insurance are Prepaid Insurance (an asset) and Insurance Expense (an expense). After posting the above entry, the Prepaid Insurance account has a $2,400 debit balance on December 1, 1994. The Insurance Expense account has a zero balance on December 1, 1994, because no time has elapsed to use any of the policy's benefits.

(Dr.)	**Prepaid Insurance**	(Cr.)	(Dr.)	**Insurance Expense**	(Cr.)
1994			1994		
Dec. 1			Dec. 1		
Bal.	2,400		Bal.	–0–	

By December 31, 1994, one month of the period covered by the policy has expired. Therefore, part of the service potential (or benefits that can be obtained from the asset) has expired. The asset will now provide less future services or benefits than when the company acquired it. We must recognize this reduction of the asset's ability to provide future services by treating the cost of the services received from the asset as an expense. For the Speedy Delivery Company example, the service received was one month of insurance coverage. Since the policy provides the same services for every month of its one-year life, we assign an equal amount ($200) of cost to each month. Thus, Speedy Delivery charges $1/12$ of the annual premium to Insurance Expense on December 31, 1994. The adjusting journal entry is:

Adjustment 1—Insurance	1994 Dec.	31	Insurance Expense	200	
			Prepaid Insurance		200
			To record insurance expense for December.		

After posting the two journal entries above, the accounts in T-account format appear as follows:

(Dr.)	**Prepaid Insurance**	(Cr.)
1994 Dec. 1 Purchased on account 2,400	1994 Dec. 31 Adjustment 1 200	Decreased by $200
Bal. after adjustment 2,200		

(Dr.)	**Insurance Expense**	(Cr.)
Increased by $200 → 1994 Dec. 31 Adjustment 1 200		

In practice, accountants do not use T-accounts. Instead, they use three-column ledger accounts that have the advantage of showing a balance after each transaction. After posting the two entries above, the three-column ledger accounts appear as follows:

Prepaid Insurance   Account No. 108

Date	Explanation	Post. Ref.	Debit	Credit	Balance
1994 Dec. 1	Purchased on account	G1	2 4 0 0		2 4 0 0 Dr.
31	Adjustment	G3		2 0 0	2 2 0 0 Dr.

Insurance Expense   Account No. 512

Date	Explanation	Post. Ref.	Debit	Credit	Balance
1994 Dec. 31	Adjustment	G3	2 0 0		2 0 0 Dr.

Before the above adjusting entry was made, the entire $2,400 insurance payment that the company paid on December 1, 1994, was a prepaid expense for 12 months of protection. As explained earlier, a prepaid expense is an asset awaiting assignment to expense. So on December 31, 1994, one month of protection had passed, and an adjusting entry transferred $200 of the $2,400 ($2,400/12 = $200) to insurance expense. On the income statement for the year ended December 31, 1994, Speedy Delivery reports one month of insurance expense, $200, as one of the expenses it incurred in generating that year's revenues. The remaining amount of the prepaid expense, $2,200, is reported as an asset on the balance sheet. The $2,200 prepaid expense represents the cost of 11 months of insurance protection that remains as a future benefit.

In initially recording the $2,400 insurance purchase, an alternative procedure could have been followed. Instead of debiting Prepaid Insurance, the Insurance Expense could have been debited as follows:

1994				
Dec.	1	Insurance Expense	2,400	
		Cash		2,400
		Purchased truck insurance to cover a one-year period.		

If this had been done, the adjusting entry would have been a debit to Prepaid Insurance for $2,200, which would set up the asset in the books, and a credit to Insurance Expense for $2,200, reducing the period's expense. The result would be a $2,200 balance in the asset account and a $200 balance in the expense account, as shown in the T-accounts below. As you can see, the end result is the same either way, and either method is correct. The adjusting entry, however, will depend on which account the company originally debited for the prepayment. This is true of many of the other adjustments illustrated in this chapter.

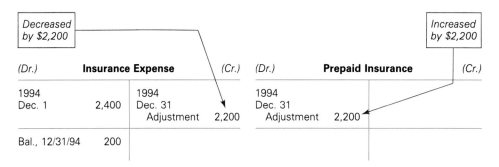

Prepaid Rent   Prepaid rent is another example of the gradual consumption of a previously recorded asset. Assume a company pays rent in advance to cover more than one accounting period. On the date it pays the rent, the company debits the prepayment to the Prepaid Rent account (an asset account). The company has not yet received benefits resulting from this expenditure. Thus, the expenditure creates an asset.

The measurement of rent expense is similar to insurance expense. Generally, the rental contract specifies the amount of rent per unit of time. If the prepayment covers a three-month rental, one third of this rental is charged to each month. The same amount is charged to each month even though some months have more days than other months.

For example, in Chapter 2, Speedy Delivery Company paid $1,200 rent in advance on December 1, 1994, to cover a three-month period beginning on that date. The journal entry made at that time was:

1994				
Dec.	1	Prepaid Rent	1,200	
		Cash		1,200
		Paid three months' rent on a building.		

Chapter 3 Adjusting the Accounts

The two accounts relating to rent are Prepaid Rent (an asset) and Rent Expense. After this entry is posted, the Prepaid Rent account has a $1,200 balance and the Rent Expense account has a zero balance because no part of the rent period has yet elapsed.

(Dr.)	**Prepaid Rent**	(Cr.)	(Dr.)	**Rent Expense**	(Cr.)
1994			1994		
Dec. 1			Dec. 1		
Bal. Cash paid	1,200		Bal.	–0–	

On December 31, 1994, an adjusting entry must be prepared. Since one third of the period covered by the prepaid rent has elapsed, one third of the $1,200 of prepaid rent is charged to expense. The required adjusting entry is:

Adjustment 2— *Rent*	1994 Dec.	31	Rent Expense . . . . Prepaid Rent . . . . To record rent expense for December.	400	400

After posting this adjusting entry, the T-accounts appear as follows:

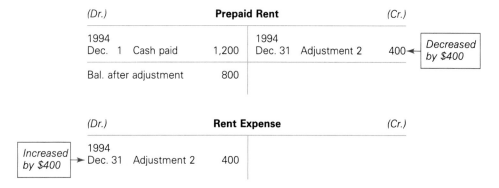

(Dr.)	**Prepaid Rent**		(Cr.)	
1994		1994		
Dec. 1 Cash paid	1,200	Dec. 31 Adjustment 2	400	*Decreased by $400*
Bal. after adjustment	800			

	(Dr.)	**Rent Expense**	(Cr.)
Increased by $400	1994 Dec. 31 Adjustment 2	400	

The $400 rent expense appears in the income statement for the year ended December 31, 1994. Speedy Delivery reports the remaining $800 of prepaid rent as an asset in the balance sheet on December 31, 1994. Thus, the adjusting entries have accomplished their purpose of maintaining the accuracy of the financial statements.

Supplies on Hand   Almost every business uses supplies in its operations. Supplies may be classified simply as supplies (to include all types of supplies), or more specifically as office supplies (paper, stationery, floppy diskettes, pencils), selling supplies (gummed tape, string, paper bags or cartons, wrapping paper), or, possibly, cleaning supplies (soap, disinfectants). Frequently, companies buy supplies in bulk. These supplies are an asset until the company uses them. This asset may be called **supplies on hand** or **supplies inventory.** Even though these terms indicate a prepaid expense, the asset does not use ''prepaid'' in its title.

On December 4, 1994, Speedy Delivery Company purchased supplies for $1,400 and recorded the transaction as follows:

1994					
Dec.	4	Supplies on Hand	1,400	
		Cash		1,400
		To record the purchase of supplies for future use.		

Speedy Delivery's two accounts relating to supplies are Supplies on Hand (an asset) and Supplies Expense. After the above entry is posted, the Supplies on Hand account shows a debit balance of $1,400 and the Supplies Expense account has a zero balance as shown in the following T-accounts:

(Dr.)	**Supplies on Hand**	(Cr.)	(Dr.)	**Supplies Expense**	(Cr.)
1994			1994		
Dec. 4			Dec. 4		
Bal. Cash paid 1,400			Bal. –0–		

An actual physical inventory (a count of the supplies on hand) at the end of the month showed that only $900 of supplies were on hand at that time. Thus, the company must have used $500 of supplies in December. An adjusting journal entry is required to bring the two accounts pertaining to supplies to their proper balances. The adjusting entry recognizes the reduction in the asset (Supplies on Hand) and the recording of an expense (Supplies Expense) by transferring $500 from the asset to the expense. From the information given, the asset balance should be $900 and the expense balance, $500. So the following adjusting entry is made:

Adjustment 3— Supplies

1994					
Dec.	31	Supplies Expense	500	
		Supplies on Hand		500
		To record supplies used during December.		

After posting this adjusting entry, the T-accounts appear as follows:

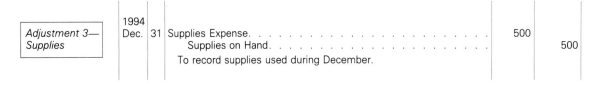

(Dr.)	**Supplies on Hand**		(Cr.)	
1994		1994		
Dec. 4 Cash paid	1,400	Dec. 31 Adjustment 3	500	*Decreased by $500*
Bal. after adjustment	900			

	(Dr.)	**Supplies Expense**		(Cr.)
Increased by $500	1994			
	Dec. 31 Adjustment 3	500		

The entry to record the use of supplies could be made when the supplies are issued from the storeroom. However, such careful accounting for small items each time they are issued is usually too costly a procedure.

Adjusting entries for supplies on hand, like for any other prepaid expense, are made before financial statements are prepared. Supplies expense appears in the income statement. Supplies on hand is an asset in the balance sheet.

Sometimes companies buy assets relating to insurance, rent, and supplies knowing that they will fully use them up before the end of the current accounting period (usually one month or one year). If so, an expense account is usually debited at the time of purchase rather than debiting an asset account. This procedure avoids having to make an adjusting entry at the end of the accounting period. As mentioned earlier, sometimes an expense is debited even though the asset will benefit more than the current period. Then, at the end of the accounting period, the adjusting entry must transfer some of the cost from the expense to the asset. For instance, assume that on January 1, a company paid $1,200 rent to cover a three-year period and debited the $1,200 to Rent Expense. At the end of the year, $800 must be transferred from Rent Expense to Prepaid Rent.

Depreciation   Just as prepaid insurance and prepaid rent indicate a gradual using up of a previously recorded asset, so does depreciation. However, the overall period of time involved in using up a depreciable asset (such as a building) is much longer and less definite than for prepaid expenses. Also, a prepaid expense generally involves a fairly small amount of money. Depreciable assets, however, usually involve larger sums of money.

A depreciable asset is a manufactured asset such as a building, machine, vehicle, or piece of equipment that provides service to a business. These assets in time lose their utility because of wear and tear from use or from obsolescence due to technological change. Since companies gradually use up these assets over time, depreciation expense is recorded on these assets. Depreciation expense is the amount of asset cost assigned as an expense to a particular time period. The process of recording depreciation expense is called depreciation accounting.

The three factors involved in computing depreciation expense are:

1. **Asset cost.** The asset cost is the amount that a company paid to purchase the depreciable asset.
2. **Estimated salvage value.** The estimated salvage value (scrap value) is the amount that the company can probably sell the asset for at the end of its estimated useful life.
3. **Estimated useful life.** The estimated useful life of an asset is the estimated number of time periods that a company can make use of the asset. Useful life is an estimate, not an exact measurement, that a company must make in advance. Unfortunately, individuals are unable to see 10 to 15 years into the future with precision.

The equation for determining the amount of depreciation expense for each time period is:

$$\text{Depreciation expense for each time period} = \frac{\text{Asset cost} - \text{Estimated salvage value}}{\text{Estimated number of time periods in asset's useful life}}$$

Accountants use different methods for recording depreciation. The method illustrated here is the **straight-line method.** We discuss other depreciation methods in Chapter 10. Straight-line depreciation assigns the same amount of depreciation expense to each accounting period over the life of the asset. The depreciation formula (straight-line) to compute straight-line depreciation for a one-year period is:

$$\text{Annual depreciation} = \frac{\text{Asset cost} - \text{Estimated salvage value}}{\text{Estimated number of years of useful life}}$$

To illustrate the use of this formula, recall that on December 1, Speedy Delivery Company purchased four small trucks at a cost of $40,000. The journal entry made at that time was:

1994				
Dec.	1	Trucks.	40,000	
		Cash		40,000
		To record the purchase of four delivery trucks.		

The estimated salvage value for each truck was $1,000, so Speedy Delivery estimated the total salvage value for all four trucks at $4,000. The company estimated the useful life of each truck to be four years. Using the straight-line depreciation formula, Speedy Delivery calculated the annual depreciation on the trucks as follows:

$$\text{Annual depreciation} = \frac{\$40,000 - \$4,000}{4 \text{ years}} = \$9,000$$

The amount of depreciation expense for one month would be $1/12$ of the annual amount. Thus, depreciation expense for December is $9,000 \div 12 = \$750$.

The difference between an asset's cost and its estimated salvage value is called an asset's **depreciable amount.** To satisfy the matching principle, the depreciable amount must be allocated as an expense to the various periods in the asset's useful life. This allocation is accomplished by debiting the amount of depreciation for a period to a depreciation expense account and crediting the amount to an accumulated depreciation account. Speedy Delivery's depreciation on its delivery trucks for December is $750. The company records the depreciation as follows:

Adjustment 4—Depreciation

1994				
Dec.	31	Depreciation Expense—Trucks.	750	
		Accumulated Depreciation—Trucks.		750
		To record depreciation expense for December.		

After posting the adjusting entry, the T-accounts appear as follows:

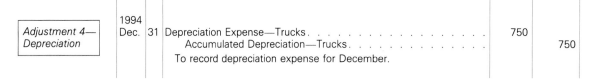

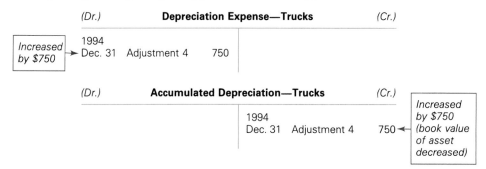

Depreciation expense is reported in the income statement. Accumulated depreciation is reported in the balance sheet as a deduction from the related asset.

The **accumulated depreciation account** is a contra asset account that shows the total of all depreciation recorded on the asset up through the balance sheet date. A **contra asset account** is a deduction from the asset to which it relates in the balance sheet. The purpose of a contra asset account is to reduce the original cost of the asset down to its remaining undepreciated cost or book value. The **undepreciated**

cost of the asset is the debit balance in the asset account (original cost) minus the credit balance in the accumulated depreciation contra account. Accountants also refer to an asset's cost less accumulated depreciation as the book value (or net book value) of the asset. Thus, book value is the cost not yet allocated to an expense. In the above example, the book value of the delivery equipment after the first month is:

Cost	$40,000
Less: Accumulated depreciation	750
Book value (or cost not yet allocated as an expense)	$39,250

The amount of the depreciation is credited to an accumulated depreciation account, which is a contra asset, rather than directly to the asset account. Contra accounts are used when it is desirable to show the statement reader the original amount of the account to which the contra account relates. For instance, for the asset Trucks, it is useful to know both the original cost of the asset and the total amount of depreciation that has been recorded on the asset. Therefore, the asset is used to show the original cost. The contra account, Accumulated Depreciation—Trucks, is used to show the total amount of recorded depreciation. By having both original cost and the accumulated depreciation amounts, a user can estimate the approximate percentage of the benefits embodied in the asset that the company has consumed. For instance, assume the accumulated depreciation amount is about three-fourths the cost of the asset. Then, the benefits would be approximately three-fourths consumed, and the company may have to replace the asset soon.

Thus, to provide more complete balance sheet information to users of financial statements, both the original acquisition cost and accumulated depreciation are shown. In the example described above for adjustment 4, the balance sheet at December 31, 1994, would show the asset and contra asset as follows:

Assets	
Trucks	$40,000
Less: Accumulated depreciation	750
	$39,250

As you may expect, the accumulated depreciation account balance increases each period by the amount of depreciation expense recorded until it finally reaches an amount equal to its depreciable cost.

Liability/Revenue Adjustments—Unearned Revenues

A liability/revenue adjustment involving unearned revenues covers situations in which a customer has transferred assets, usually cash, to the selling company before the receipt of merchandise or services. When assets are received before being earned, a liability called unearned revenue is created. Such receipts are debited to the asset account, Cash, and credited to a liability account. The liability account credited may be called Unearned Fees, Revenue Received in Advance, Advances by Customers, or some similar title. The seller must either provide the services or return the customer's money. By performing the services, the company earns revenue and cancels the liability.

Companies receive advance payments for many items, such as delivery services, tickets, and magazine or newspaper subscriptions. While we only illustrate and discuss advanced receipt of delivery fees, the other items are treated similarly.

Unearned Delivery Fees On December 7, Speedy Delivery Company received $4,500 from a customer in payment for future delivery services. The following journal entry was recorded:

1994				
Dec.	7	Cash	4,500	
		Unearned Delivery Fees		4,500
		To record the receipt of cash from a customer in payment for future delivery services.		

The two T-accounts relating to delivery fees are Unearned Delivery Fees (a liability) and Service Revenue. These accounts appear as follows on December 31, 1994 (before adjustment):

(Dr.)	**Unearned Delivery Fees**	*(Cr.)*
	1994	
	Dec. 7 Cash received in advance	4,500

(Dr.)	**Service Revenue**	*(Cr.)*
	1994	
	Bal. before adjustment	10,700*

* The $10,700 balance came from transactions discussed in Chapter 2.

The balance in the Unearned Delivery Fees liability account established when Speedy Delivery received the cash will be converted into revenue as the company performs the delivery services. Before Speedy Delivery prepares its financial statements, an adjusting entry must be made to transfer the amount of the services performed by the company from a liability account to a revenue account. If we assume that Speedy Delivery earned one third of the $4,500 in the Unearned Delivery Fees account by December 31, then the company will transfer $1,500 to the Service Revenue account as follows:

Adjustment 5— Revenue earned

1994				
Dec.	31	Unearned Delivery Fees.	1,500	
		Service Revenue		1,500
		To transfer a portion of delivery fees from the liability account to the revenue account.		

After posting the adjusting entry, the T-accounts would appear as follows:

(Dr.)	**Unearned Delivery Fees**	*(Cr.)*
Decreased by $1,500 →	1994	1994
	Dec. 31 Adjustment 5 1,500	Dec. 7 Cash received in advance 4,500
		Bal. after adjustment 3,000

(Dr.)	Service Revenue		(Cr.)
	1994		
	Bal. before adjustment	10,700	
	Dec. 31 Adjustment 5	1,500	Increased by $1,500
	Bal. after adjustment	12,200	

Speedy Delivery reports the service revenue in its income statement for 1994. The company reports the $3,000 balance in the Unearned Delivery Fees account as a liability in the balance sheet. In 1994, the company will likely earn the $3,000 and transfer it to a revenue account.

In initially recording the receipt of the $4,500 from a customer, an alternative procedure could have been followed. Instead of crediting Unearned Delivery Fees, the credit could have been to Service Revenue as follows:

1994				
Dec.	7	Cash	4,500	
		Service Revenue		4,500
		To record the receipt of cash from a customer in payment for future delivery services.		

If this alternative had been chosen, the adjusting entry would have been a debit to Service Revenue for $3,000 and a credit to Unearned Delivery Fees for $3,000. This adjustment would establish the liability for the unearned portion of the delivery fees and would reduce the revenue by that same $3,000 amount. The end result is the same as the original procedure, as shown in the following T-accounts after adjustment:

Service Revenue

1994			1994		
Dec. 31 Adjustment		3,000	Bal. before adjustment	10,700	
			Dec. 7 Cash received	4,500	
			Bal. after adjustment	12,200	

Unearned Delivery Fees

		1994	
		Dec. 31 Adjustment	3,000

Notice that the Service Revenue account has an ending balance of $12,200 and the Unearned Delivery Fees account has an ending balance of $3,000. These balances are the same as under the original procedure. The adjusting entry will depend on which account was originally credited for the receipt of $4,500 from the customer.

If Speedy Delivery does not perform the services, the company would have to refund the money to the delivery service customers. For instance, assume that for some reason, Speedy Delivery could not perform the remaining $3,000 of delivery services and would have to refund the money. Then, the company would make the following entry:

Unearned Delivery Fees		3,000	
Cash			3,000
To record the refund of unearned delivery fees.			

Thus, the company must either perform the services or refund the fees. This fact may serve to strengthen your understanding that unearned delivery fees and similar items are liabilities.

The adjusting entries for deferred items are made for data already recorded in a company's asset and liability accounts. Adjusting entries for accrued items, which we discuss in the next section, are made for business data not yet recorded in the accounting records. We will continue using Speedy Delivery Company for our example transactions.

ADJUSTMENTS FOR ACCRUED ITEMS

Accrued items require two types of adjusting entries: asset/revenue adjustments and liability/expense adjustments. The first group—asset/revenue adjustments—involves accrued assets; the second group—liability/expense adjustments—involves accrued liabilities.

Asset/Revenue Adjustments— Accrued Assets

Accrued assets are assets that exist at the end of an accounting period but have not yet been recorded. These assets represent rights to receive future payments that are not due at the balance sheet date. To present an accurate picture of the affairs of the business on the balance sheet, these rights must be recognized at the end of an accounting period by preparing an adjusting entry to correct the account balances. An example of this type of adjustment includes revenues earned but not billed. To indicate the dual nature of these adjustments, a related revenue is recorded in addition to the asset recorded. These adjustments may also be called accrued revenues because the revenues must also be recorded.

Interest Revenue   Interest received periodically on savings accounts is literally earned moment by moment. Rarely is payment of the interest made on the last day of the accounting period. Thus, the accounting records normally will not show the amount of interest revenue earned, which affects the amount of total assets owned by the investor, unless the company makes an adjusting entry. The adjusting entry needed at the end of the accounting period debits a receivable account (an asset) and credits a revenue account to record the interest earned and the asset owned.

For example, assume Speedy Delivery Company has some money in a savings account. The interest earned in December is $600. On December 31, 1994, the money earned one month's interest, although the company has received no money for the interest. An entry must be made to show the amount of interest earned by December 31, 1994, as well as the amount of the asset, interest receivable (the right to receive this interest). The entry to record the accrual of revenue is:

Adjustment 6— Interest revenue accrued	1994 Dec. 31	Interest Receivable	600	
		Interest Revenue		600
		To record one month's interest revenue.		

The T-accounts relating to interest would appear as follows:

(Dr.)	**Interest Receivable**		*(Cr.)*
Increased by $600 →	1994 Dec. 31 Adjustment 6	600	

(Dr.)   **Interest Revenue**   *(Cr.)*

	1994
	Dec. 31 Adjustment 6 600 ← *Increased by $600*

Speedy Delivery reports the $600 debit balance in Interest Receivable as an asset in the December 31, 1994, balance sheet. This asset accumulates gradually with the passage of time. The $600 credit balance in Interest Revenue is the interest earned during the month. You will recall that in **recording revenue under accrual basis accounting, it does not matter whether the company collects the actual cash during the year or not.** Regardless of whether the company receives the interest or not, the interest revenue earned is reported in the income statement for the year.

Unbilled Delivery Fees   A company may perform services for customers in one accounting period while it bills for the services in a different accounting period.

   Speedy Delivery Company performed $1,000 of delivery services on account for a client in the last few days of December. Since it takes time to do the paper work, Speedy Delivery will bill the client for the services in January. The necessary adjusting journal entry at December 31, 1994, is:

Adjustment 7— Unbilled revenues

1994			
Dec.	31	Accounts Receivable (or Delivery Fees Receivable)	1,000	
		Service Revenue		1,000
		To record unbilled delivery services performed in December.		

After posting the adjusting entry, the T-accounts will appear as follows:

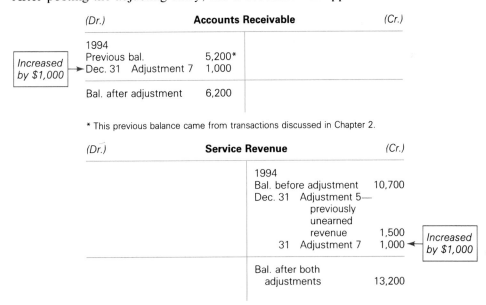

(Dr.)   **Accounts Receivable**   *(Cr.)*

1994		
Previous bal.	5,200*	
Increased by $1,000 → Dec. 31 Adjustment 7	1,000	
Bal. after adjustment	6,200	

* This previous balance came from transactions discussed in Chapter 2.

(Dr.)   **Service Revenue**   *(Cr.)*

	1994
	Bal. before adjustment 10,700
	Dec. 31 Adjustment 5—
	previously
	unearned
	revenue 1,500
	31 Adjustment 7 1,000 ← *Increased by $1,000*
	Bal. after both
	adjustments 13,200

The service revenue appears in the income statement, and the asset, accounts receivable, appears in the balance sheet.

Liability/Expense Adjustments— Accrued Liabilities

Accrued liabilities are liabilities that exist at the end of an accounting period but have not yet been recorded. They represent obligations to make payments not legally due at the balance sheet date, such as employee salaries. At the end of the accounting period, the company recognizes these obligations by preparing an adjusting entry including both a liability and an expense. For this reason, these obligations may also be called accrued expenses.

Salaries The recording of the payment of employee salaries usually involves a debit to an expense account and a credit to Cash. Unless a company pays salaries on the last day of the accounting period for a pay period ending on that date, it must make an adjusting entry to record any salaries incurred but not yet paid.

Speedy Delivery Company paid $3,600 of salaries on Friday, December 28, 1994, to cover the first four weeks of December. The entry made at that time was:

1994				
Dec.	28	Salaries Expense	3,600	
		Cash		3,600
		Paid truck driver salaries for the first four weeks of December.		

Assuming that the last day of December 1994 falls on a Monday, the above expense account does not show salaries earned by employees for the last day of the month. Nor does the account show the employer's obligation to pay these salaries. The T-accounts pertaining to salaries appear as follows before adjustment:

(Dr.)	**Salaries Expense**	(Cr.)	(Dr.)	**Salaries Payable**	(Cr.)
1994				1994	
Dec. 28 3,600				Dec. 28 Bal. –0–	

If salaries are $3,600 for four weeks, they are $900 per week. For a five-day workweek, daily salaries are $180. Speedy Delivery needs the following adjusting entry on December 31 to accrue salaries for one day:

Adjustment 8— Accrued salaries

1994				
Dec.	31	Salaries Expense	180	
		Salaries Payable		180
		To accrue one day's salaries that were earned but are unpaid.		

After adjustment, the two T-accounts involved appear as follows:

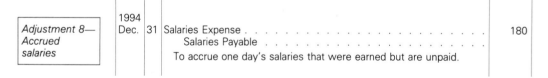

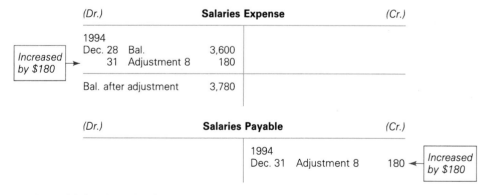

The debit in the adjusting journal entry brings the month's salaries expense up to its correct $3,780 amount for income statement purposes. The credit to Salaries Payable records the $180 salary liability to employees. The balance sheet shows salaries payable as a liability.

ETHICS

A CLOSER LOOK

Jim Hinson managed the Rapid Computer Repair Company for its owner, Barbara Taylor. Jim also kept the accounting records and was paid a bonus of 5% of net income for the year. Jim was having some financial difficulties and was really counting on a bonus of at least $5,000 this year.

Toward the end of December 1992, Jim decided to calculate the approximate amount of his bonus. He determined that net income for 1992 would only be about $80,000, giving him a bonus of $4,000.

To increase 1992 net income and increase his bonus, Jim decided to do several things, which he considered to be harmless. First, he decided that some supplies that he had just purchased would be recorded as assets instead of expenses and reported that way in the year-end financial statements even though they would be totally used up before the end of the year. Also, he decided to "leave the books open" and record some revenue from services performed in January 1993 as revenues of December 1992. He concluded that it really did not matter in which year revenues and expenses were reported as long as they were reported sometime. By taking these two actions, reported net income for 1992 would be $110,000, and Jim's bonus would be $5,500. He realized that his bonus for 1993 would be lower assuming he did not use this same method the following year.

Required

a. Is Jim's scheme harmless?

b. Will his method succeed in increasing his bonus if it goes undetected?

c. Do you think anything like this has ever happened?

d. What would you do if you were Barbara Taylor and discovered what was happening?

Another example of a liability/expense adjustment is when a company incurs interest on a note payable. The debit would be to Interest Expense, and the credit would be to Interest Payable. Examples of this adjustment are given in Chapter 9.

EFFECTS OF FAILING TO PREPARE ADJUSTING ENTRIES

Objective 5

Determine the effects of failing to prepare adjusting entries

Failure to prepare proper adjusting entries causes net income and the balance sheet to be in error. Illustration 3.5 shows the effect on net income and balance sheet items of failing to record each of the major types of adjusting entries.

Using Speedy Delivery Company as an example, this chapter has discussed and illustrated many of the typical entries that companies must make at the end of an accounting period. You will study other examples of adjusting entries in later chapters.

In the first three chapters of this text, you have learned several of the steps of the accounting process. These steps as a group are usually called the *accounting process* (or cycle). Chapter 4 will show the final steps in the accounting cycle.

UNDERSTANDING THE LEARNING OBJECTIVES

1. Describe the basic characteristics of the cash basis and the accrual basis of accounting.

☐ The cash basis of accounting recognizes revenues when cash is received and recognizes expenses when cash is paid out.

☐ The accrual basis of accounting recognizes revenues when sales are made or services are performed, regardless of when cash is received;

ILLUSTRATION 3.5

Effects of Failure to Recognize Adjustments

	Failure to Recognize	Effect on Net Income	Effect on Balance Sheet Items
1.	Consumption of the benefits of an asset (prepaid expense)	Overstates net income	Overstates assets Overstates retained earnings
2.	Earning of previously unearned revenues	Understates net income	Overstates liabilities Understates retained earnings
3.	Accrual of assets	Understates net income	Understates assets Understates retained earnings
4.	Accrual of liabilities	Overstates net income	Understates liabilities Overstates retained earnings

expenses are recognized as incurred, whether or not cash has been paid out.

☐ The accrual basis is more generally accepted than the cash basis because it provides a better matching of revenues and expenses.

2. Identify the reasons why adjusting entries must be made.

☐ Adjusting entries are needed to convert the amounts that are actually in the accounts to the amounts that should be in the accounts for proper periodic financial reporting.

☐ Adjusting entries reflect unrecorded economic activity that has taken place but has not yet been recorded.

3. Identify the classes and types of adjusting entries.

☐ Deferred items consist of adjusting entries involving data previously recorded in accounts. Adjusting entries in this class normally involve moving data from asset and liability accounts to expense and revenue accounts. The two types of adjustments within this deferred items class are asset/expense adjustments and liability/revenue adjustments.

☐ Accrued items consist of adjusting entries relating to activity on which no data have been previously recorded in the accounts. These entries involve the initial recording of assets and liabilities and the related revenues and expenses. The two types of adjustments within this accrued items class are asset/revenue adjustments and liability/expense adjustments.

4. Prepare adjusting entries.

☐ Entries for deferred items and accrued items are illustrated in the chapter.

5. Determine the effects of failing to prepare adjusting entries.

☐ Failure to prepare adjusting entries causes net income and the balance sheet to be in error.

DEMONSTRATION PROBLEM

The trial balance of Korman Company for December 31, 1994, includes, among other items, the following account balances:

	Debits	Credits
Supplies on Hand	$ 6,000	
Prepaid Rent.	25,200	
Buildings	200,000	
Accumulated Depreciation—Buildings		$33,250
Salaries Expense	124,000	
Unearned Delivery Fees.		4,000

Additional data

1. Some of the supplies represented by the $6,000 balance of the Supplies on Hand account have been consumed. An inventory count of the supplies actually on hand at December 31 totaled $2,400.

2. On May 1 of the current year, a rental payment of $25,200 was made for 12 months' rent; it was debited to Prepaid Rent.

3. The annual depreciation for the buildings is based on the cost shown in the Buildings account less an estimated salvage value of $10,000. The estimated useful lives of the buildings are 40 years each.

4. The salaries expense of $124,000 does not include $6,000 of unpaid salaries earned since the last payday.

5. The company has earned one fourth of the unearned delivery fees by December 31.

6. Delivery services of $600 were performed for a customer, but a bill has not yet been sent.

Required *a.* Prepare the adjusting journal entries for December 31, assuming adjusting entries are prepared only at year-end.

b. Based on the adjusted balance shown in the Accumulated Depreciation—Buildings account, how many years has Korman Company owned the building?

SOLUTION TO DEMONSTRATION PROBLEM

a.

KORMAN COMPANY
GENERAL JOURNAL

Date		Account Titles and Explanation	Post. Ref.	Debit	Credit
1994 Dec.	31	Supplies Expense		3 6 0 0	
		Supplies on Hand			3 6 0 0
		To record supplies expense ($6,000 − $2,400).			
	31	Rent Expense		1 6 8 0 0	
		Prepaid Rent			1 6 8 0 0
		To record rent expense ($25,200 × 8/12).			
	31	Depreciation Expense—Buildings		4 7 5 0	
		Accumulated Depreciation—Buildings			4 7 5 0
		To record depreciation [($200,000 − $10,000) ÷ 40 years].			
	31	Salaries Expense		6 0 0 0	
		Salaries Payable			6 0 0 0
		To record accrued salaries.			
	31	Unearned Delivery Fees		1 0 0 0	
		Service Revenue			1 0 0 0
		To record delivery fees earned.			
	31	Accounts Receivable		6 0 0	
		Service Revenue			6 0 0
		To record delivery fees earned.			

b. Eight years; computed as:

$$\frac{\text{Total accumulated depreciation}}{\text{Annual depreciation expense}} = \frac{\$33,250 + \$4,750}{\$4,750} = 8$$

NEW TERMS

Accounting period A time period normally of one month, one quarter, or one year into which an entity's life is arbitrarily divided for financial reporting purposes. *109*

Accounting year An accounting period of one year. The accounting year may or may not coincide with the calendar year. *109*

Accrual basis of accounting Recognizes revenues when sales are made or services are performed, regardless of when cash is received. Recognizes expenses as incurred, whether or not cash has been paid out. *108*

Accrued assets and liabilities Assets and liabilities that exist at the end of an accounting period but have not yet been recorded; they represent rights to receive, or obligations to make, payments that are not legally due at the balance sheet date. Examples are accrued fees receivable and salaries payable. *124, 125*

Accrued items See Accrued assets and liabilities.

Accrued revenues and expenses Other names for accrued assets and liabilities. *124, 126*

Accumulated depreciation account A contra asset account that shows the total of all depreciation recorded on the asset up through the balance sheet date. *120*

Adjusting entries Journal entries made at the end of an accounting period to bring about a proper matching of revenues and expenses; reflect economic activity that has taken place but has not yet been recorded.

Adjusting entries are made to bring the accounts to their proper balances before financial statements are prepared. *109*

Book value For depreciable assets, book value equals cost less accumulated depreciation. *121*

Calendar year The normal year, which ends on December 31. *109*

Cash basis of accounting Recognizes revenues when cash is received and recognizes expenses when cash is paid out. *108*

Contra asset account An account shown as a deduction from the asset to which it relates in the balance sheet; used to reduce the original cost of the asset down to its remaining undepreciated cost or book value. *120*

Deferred items Adjusting entries involving data previously recorded in the accounts. Data are transferred from asset and liability accounts to expense and revenue accounts. Examples are prepaid expenses, depreciation, and unearned revenues. *111*

Depreciable amount The difference between an asset's cost and its estimated salvage value. *120*

Depreciable asset A manufactured asset such as a building, machine, vehicle, or equipment on which depreciation expense is recorded. *119*

Depreciation accounting The process of recording depreciation expense. *119*

Depreciation expense The amount of asset cost assigned as an expense to a particular time period. *119*

Depreciation formula (straight-line) *119*

$$\text{Annual depreciation} = \frac{\text{Asset cost} - \text{Estimated salvage value}}{\text{Estimated number of years of useful life}}$$

Fiscal year An accounting year of any 12 consecutive months that may or may not coincide with the calendar year. For example, a company may have an accounting or fiscal year that runs from April 1 of one year to March 31 of the next. *109*

Matching principle An accounting principle requiring that expenses incurred in producing revenues be deducted from the revenues they generated during the accounting period. *109*

Prepaid expense An asset awaiting assignment to expense. An example is prepaid insurance. Assets such as cash and accounts receivable are not prepaid expenses. *114*

Salvage value (scrap value) The amount that the company can probably sell the asset for at the end of its estimated useful life. *119*

Service potential The benefits that can be obtained from assets. The future services that assets can render make assets "things of value" to a business. *114*

Unearned revenue Assets received from customers before services are performed for them. Since the revenue has not been earned, it is a liability, often called *revenue received in advance* or *advances by customers*. *121*

Useful life The estimated number of time periods that a company can make use of the asset. *119*

SELF-TEST

True-False

Indicate whether each of the following statements is true or false.

1. Every adjusting entry affects at least one income statement account and one balance sheet account.
2. All calendar years are also fiscal years, but not all fiscal years are calendar years.
3. The accumulated depreciation account is an asset account that shows the amount of depreciation for the current year only.
4. The Unearned Delivery Fees account is a revenue account.
5. If all of the adjusting entries are not made, the financial statements will be incorrect.

Multiple-Choice

Select the best answer for each of the following questions.

1. An insurance policy premium of $1,200 was paid on September 1, 1994, to cover a one-year period from that date. An asset was debited on that date. Adjusting entries are prepared once a year, at year-end. The necessary adjusting entry at the company's year-end, December 31, 1994, is:

   a. Prepaid Insurance 400
      Insurance Expense . . . 400

   b. Insurance Expense 800
      Prepaid Insurance . . . 800

   c. Prepaid Insurance 800
      Insurance Expense . . . 800

   d. Insurance Expense 400
      Prepaid Insurance . . . 400

2. Refer to the previous problem. If an expense had been debited when the premium was paid on September 1, 1994, which of the choices in (1) would

have been the correct adjusting entry on December 31, 1994?

3. The Supplies on Hand account has a balance of $1,500 at year-end. The actual amount of supplies on hand at the end of the period was $400. The necessary adjusting entry is:

a. Supplies Expense   1,100
      Supplies on Hand . . .   1,100

b. Supplies Expense   400
      Supplies on Hand . . .   400

c. Supplies on Hand   1,100
      Supplies Expense . . .   1,100

d. Supplies on Hand   400
      Supplies Expense . . .   400

4. A company purchased a truck for $20,000 on January 1, 1994. The truck has an estimated salvage value of $5,000 and is expected to last five years. Adjusting entries are prepared only at year-end. The necessary adjusting entry at December 31, 1994, the company's year-end, is:

a. Depreciation Expense—
      Trucks   4,000
      Accumulated Deprecia-
          tion—Trucks   4,000

b. Depreciation Expense—
      Trucks   3,000
      Trucks   3,000

c. Depreciation Expense—
      Trucks   3,000
      Accumulated Deprecia-
          tion—Trucks   3,000

d. Accumulated Depreciation—
      Trucks   3,000
      Depreciation Expense—
          Trucks   3,000

5. A company received cash of $24,000 on October 1, 1994, as subscriptions for a one-year period from that date. A liability account was credited when the cash was received. The magazine is to be published by the company and delivered to subscribers each month. The company prepares adjusting entries at the end of each month because it prepares financial statements each month. The adjusting entry the company would make at the end of each of the next 12 months would be:

a. Unearned Subscription Fees   6,000
      Subscription Fee Reve-
          nue.   6,000

b. Unearned Subscription Fees   2,000
      Subscription Fee Reve-
          nue.   2,000

c. Unearned Subscription Fees   18,000
      Subscription Fee Reve-
          nue.   18,000

d. Subscription Fee Revenue .   2,000
      Unearned Subscription
          Fees   2,000

6. When a company earns interest on a note receivable or on a bank account, the debit and credit are as follows:

	Debit	**Credit**
a.	Accounts Receivable	Interest Revenue
b.	Interest Receivable	Interest Revenue
c.	Interest Revenue	Accounts Receivable
d.	Interest Revenue	Interest Receivable

7. If $3,000 has been earned by a company's workers since the last payday in an accounting period, the necessary adjusting entry would be:
a. Debit an expense and credit a liability.
b. Debit an expense and credit an asset.
c. Debit a liability and credit an asset.
d. Debit a liability and credit an expense.

Now turn to page 143 to check your answers.

QUESTIONS

1. What events during an accounting period trigger the recording of "normal" journal entries? What event triggers the making of adjusting entries?

2. Describe the difference between the cash basis and accrual basis of accounting.

3. Why are adjusting entries necessary? Why not treat every cash disbursement as an expense and every cash receipt as a revenue when the cash changes hands?

4. "Adjusting entries would not be necessary if the cash basis of accounting were followed (assuming no mistakes were made in recording cash transactions as they occurred). Under the cash basis, receipts that are of a revenue nature are considered revenue when received, and expenditures that are of an expense nature are considered expenses when paid. It is the use of the accrual basis of accounting, where an effort is made to match expenses incurred against the revenues they create, that makes adjusting entries necessary." Do you agree with this statement? Why?

5. Why don't accountants keep all the accounts at their proper balances continuously throughout the

period so that adjusting entries would not have to be made before financial statements are prepared?

6. What is the fundamental difference between deferred items and accrued items?

7. Identify the types of adjusting entries that are included in each of the two major classes of adjusting entries.

8. Give an example of each of the following:
   a. Equal growth of an expense and a liability.
   b. Earning of revenue that was previously recorded as unearned revenue.
   c. Equal growth of an asset and a revenue.
   d. Equal growth of an expense and decrease in an asset.

9. A fellow student makes the following statement: "You can easily tell whether a company is using the cash or accrual basis of accounting. When an amount is paid for future rent or insurance services, a firm that is using the cash basis will debit an expense account while a firm that is using the accrual basis will debit an asset account." Is the student correct?

10. You notice that the Supplies on Hand account has a debit balance of $2,700 at the end of the accounting period. How would you determine the extent to which this account needs adjustment?

11. Some assets are converted into expenses as they expire and some liabilities become revenues as they are earned. Give examples of asset and liability accounts for which this statement is true. Give examples of asset and liability accounts to which the statement does not apply.

12. Give the depreciation formula to compute straight-line depreciation for a one-year period.

13. What does the term *accrued liability* mean?

14. What is meant by the term *service potential?*

15. When assets are received before they are earned,

what type of an account is credited? As the amounts are earned, what type of account is credited?

16. What does the word *accrued* mean? Is there a conceptual difference between interest payable and accrued interest payable?

17. Matching expenses incurred with revenues earned is more difficult than matching expenses paid with revenues received. Do you think the effort is worthwhile?

18. *Real world question*   Refer to "A Broader Perspective" on page 110 and then answer the following true or false questions:
   a. Grade-point average is important to recruiters, but leadership experience is not.
   b. A student's expressed interest in investment banking was viewed as a negative factor.
   c. Only rarely did any student reject an offer to visit a CPA firm's office.
   d. Salary and benefits were rated the most important factors in choosing between several offers.
   e. Both faculty and peers exerted heavy pressure on students to go into public accounting.

The Coca-Cola Company

19. *Real world question*   Refer to the accounting policies of The Coca-Cola Company described in its annual report in Appendix E at the end of the text. Approximately what percentage of the depreciable assets under property, plant, and equipment has been depreciated as of December 31, 1989?

MAYTAG CORPORATION

20. *Real world question*   Refer to the financial statements of Maytag Corporation in Appendix E. What percentage of depreciable property, plant, and equipment has been depreciated as of December 31, 1989? (Construction in progress is not a depreciable asset.)

EXERCISES

Exercise 3–1

Answer multiple-choice questions
(L.O. 1)

Select the correct response for each of the following multiple-choice questions:

1. The cash basis of accounting:
   a. Recognizes revenues when sales are made or services are rendered.
   b. Recognizes expenses as incurred.
   c. Is typically used by some relatively small businesses and professional persons.
   d. Recognizes revenues when cash is received and recognizes expenses when incurred.

2. The accrual basis of accounting:
   a. Recognizes revenues only when cash is received.
   b. Is used by almost all companies.
   c. Recognizes expenses only when cash is paid out.
   d. Recognizes revenues when sales are made or services are performed and recognizes expenses only when cash is paid out.

Exercise 3–2

Answer multiple-choice
questions
(L.O. 2)

Select the correct response for each of the following multiple-choice questions:

1. The least common accounting period among the following is:
   a. One month.
   b. Two months.
   c. Three months.
   d. Twelve months.

2. The need for adjusting entries is based on:
   a. The matching principle.
   b. Source documents.
   c. The cash basis of accounting.
   d. Activity that has already been recorded in the proper accounts.

Exercise 3–3

Answer multiple-choice
questions
(L.O. 3)

Select the correct response for each of the following multiple-choice questions:

1. Which of the following types of adjustments belongs to the "deferred items" class?
   a. Asset/revenue adjustments.
   b. Liability/expense adjustments.
   c. Asset/expense adjustments.
   d. Asset/liability adjustments.

2. Which of the following types of adjustments belongs to the "accrued items" class?
   a. Asset/expense adjustments.
   b. Liability/revenue adjustments.
   c. Asset/liability adjustments.
   d. Liability/expense adjustments.

Exercise 3–4

Prepare and post adjusting
entry for insurance under
two methods
(L.O. 4)

a. A one-year insurance policy was purchased on August 1 for $4,800, and the following entry was made at that time:

Prepaid Insurance	4,800	
Cash		4,800

What adjusting entry is necessary at December 31, the end of the accounting year?

b. Give the adjusting entry that would be necessary if the entry to record the purchase of the policy on August 1 had been:

Insurance Expense	4,800	
Cash		4,800

c. Show by the use of T-accounts that the end result is the same under either (a) or (b).

Exercise 3–5

Prepare adjusting entry for
rent
(L.O. 4)

Assume that rent of $57,600 was paid on September 1, 1994, to cover a one-year period from that date. Prepaid Rent was debited. If financial statements are prepared only on December 31 of each year, what adjusting entry is necessary on December 31, 1994, to bring the accounts involved to their proper balances?

Exercise 3–6

Prepare adjusting entry for
rent
(L.O. 4)

If in Exercise 3–5 Rent Expense had been debited on September 1, 1994, what adjusting entry would have been necessary on December 31, 1994?

Exercise 3–7

Determine date and entry for rent paid (L.O. 4)

At December 31, 1994, an adjusting entry was made as follows:

Rent Expense	6,000	
Prepaid Rent		6,000

You know that the gross amount of rent paid was $18,000, which was to cover a one-year period. Determine:

a.   The opening date of the year to which the $18,000 of rent applies.

b.   The entry that was made on the date the rent was paid.

Exercise 3–8

Prepare entries for purchase of supplies and adjustment at year-end (L.O. 4)

Supplies were purchased for cash on May 2, 1994, for $12,800. Show two ways in which this entry could be recorded; then show the adjusting entry that would be necessary for each, assuming that $3,200 of the supplies remained at the end of the year.

Exercise 3–9

Prepare adjusting entry for depreciation (L.O. 4)

Assume that a company acquires a building on January 1, 1994, at a cost of $500,000. The building has an estimated useful life of 40 years and an estimated salvage value of $100,000. What adjusting entry is needed on December 31, 1994, to record the depreciation for the entire year 1994?

Exercise 3–10

Determine salvage value of building (L.O. 4)

A building is being depreciated by an amount of $21,000 per year. You know that the building had an original cost of $232,500 and was expected to last 10 years. How was the $21,000 determined?

Exercise 3–11

Prepare entries for receipt of subscription fees and adjustment at year-end (L.O. 4)

On September 1, 1994, Bentley Company received a total of $480,000 as payment in advance for a number of one-year subscriptions to a monthly magazine. A liability account was credited to record this cash receipt. By the end of the year, one third of the magazines paid for in advance had been delivered. Give the entries to record the receipt of the subscription fees and to adjust the accounts at December 31, assuming annual financial statements are prepared at year-end.

Exercise 3–12

Prepare adjusting entry for accrued legal services (L.O. 4)

Haskell & Wells, a law firm, performed legal services in late December 1994 for clients. The $96,000 of services will be billed to the clients in January 1994. Give the adjusting entry that is necessary on December 31, 1994, if financial statements are prepared at the end of each month.

Exercise 3–13

Prepare adjusting entry for accrued salaries (L.O. 4)

Kroger Company incurs salaries at the rate of $3,000 per day. The last payday in January is Friday, January 27. Salaries for Monday and Tuesday of the next week have not been recorded or paid as of January 31. Financial statements are prepared monthly. Give the necessary adjusting entry on January 31.

Exercise 3–14

Prepare adjusting entry for accrued interest (L.O. 4)

A firm borrowed $80,000 on November 1. By December 31, $800 of interest had been incurred. Prepare the adjusting entry required on December 31.

Exercise 3–15

Determine effect on net income from failing to record adjusting entries (L.O. 5)

State the effect that each of the following would have on the amount of annual net income reported for 1994 and 1995.

a.   No adjustment was made for accrued salaries of $7,200 as of December 31, 1994.

b.   The collection of $6,400 for services yet unperformed as of December 31, 1994, was credited to a revenue account and not adjusted. The services are performed in 1995.

Exercise 3–16

Show the effects of failing to recognize indicated adjustments (L.O. 5)

In the following table, indicate the effects of failing to recognize each of the indicated adjustments by writing "O" for overstated and "U" for understated.

			Effect on Balance Sheet Items		
Failure to Recognize	Effect on Net Income	Assets	Liabilities	Stockholders' Equity	
1. Depreciation on a building					
2. Consumption of supplies on hand					
3. The earnings of ticket revenue received in advance					
4. The earning of interest on a bank account					
5. Salaries incurred but unpaid					

PROBLEMS: SERIES A

Problem 3–1A

Prepare adjusting entries, post to ledger accounts, and state the correct figures for the financial statements (L.O. 4)

The following data pertain to Santos Company:

	Account Title	Trial Balance Amount	Information for Adjustments
Item 1:	Buildings	$630,000	The estimated life of the asset is 50 years. Salvage value is estimated at $30,000.
	Accumulated Depreciation—Buildings	120,000	
Item 2:	Salaries Expense	73,500	Salaries earned by employees since last payday are $1,170.
Item 3:	Supplies on Hand	3,750	Of the office supplies purchased, only $1,350 remain at the end of the period.

Required

For each of the items:

a.   Prepare the annual year-end adjusting journal entry, dating it December 31, 1994.

b.   Set up partial ledger accounts showing only debit, credit, and balance. Enter balances as given, if any, and post the adjusting entries made in (a).

c.   State the correct figures for that item on the balance sheet. Show any related accounts for that item as they should appear on the balance sheet.

d.   State the correct figures for that item on the income statement.

Problem 3–2A

Prepare adjusting entries (L.O. 4)

The trial balance of Sund Company at December 31 of the current year includes, among other items, the following account balances:

	Debits
Prepaid Insurance	$48,000
Prepaid Rent	57,600
Supplies on Hand	11,200

Examination of the records shows that adjustments should be made for the following items:

a. Of the prepaid insurance in the trial balance, $20,000 is for coverage during the months after December 31 of the current year.

b. The balance in the Prepaid Rent account is for a 12-month period that started October 1 of the current year.

c. $600 of interest has been earned but not received.

d. Supplies used during the year amount to $7,200.

Required   Prepare the annual year-end adjusting journal entries at December 31.

Problem 3–3A

Prepare adjusting entries and post to ledger accounts (L.O. 4)

Sandy, Inc., has the following account balances, among others, in its trial balance at December 31 of the current year:

	Debits	Credits
Supplies on Hand	$ 14,880	
Prepaid Rent	28,800	
Service Revenue		$1,044,000
Salaries Expense	492,000	
Unearned Delivery Fees		54,000

Additional data

1. The inventory of supplies on hand at December 31 amounts to $1,080.

2. The balance in the Prepaid Rent account is for a one-year period starting October 1 of the current year.

3. One third of the $54,000 balance in Unearned Delivery Fees has been earned.

4. Since the last payday, the employees of the company have earned additional salaries in the amount of $21,720.

Required   *a.* Prepare the year-end adjusting journal entries at December 31. Assume page 22 of the general journal is used to record the journal entries.

b. Open ledger accounts for each of the accounts involved, enter the balances as shown in the trial balance, post the adjusting journal entries, and calculate year-end balances.

Problem 3–4A

Prepare adjusting entries (L.O. 4)

Dolphin Company adjusts and closes its books each December 31. You can assume the accounts for all prior years have been properly adjusted and closed. Given below are a number of the company's account balances prior to adjustment on December 31, 1994:

DOLPHIN COMPANY
Partial Trial Balance
December 31, 1994

	Debits	Credits
Prepaid Insurance	$ 7,875	
Supplies on Hand	6,450	
Buildings	255,000	
Accumulated Depreciation—Buildings		$ 96,000
Unearned Rent		2,700
Salaries Expense	69,000	
Service Revenue		277,500

Additional data

1. The Prepaid Insurance account balance represents the remaining cost of a four-year insurance policy dated June 30, 1992, having a total premium of $12,600.

2. The physical inventory of the office supply stockroom indicates that the supplies on hand cost $2,025.

3. The building was originally acquired on January 1, 1978, at which time management estimated that the building would last 40 years and have a salvage value of $15,000.

4. Salaries earned since the last payday but unpaid at December 31 amount to $2,625.

5. Interest earned but not collected on a savings account during the year amounts to $225.

6. The Unearned Rent account arose through the prepayment of rent by a tenant in the building for 12 months beginning October 1, 1994.

Required Prepare the annual year-end adjusting entries indicated by the additional data.

Problem 3–5A
Calculate correct net income
(L.O. 5)

The reported net income amounts for Lucia Company for calendar years 1994 and 1995 were $200,000 and $244,000, respectively. No annual adjusting entries were made at either year-end for any of the following transactions:

1. A fire insurance policy to cover a three-year period from the date of payment was purchased on March 1, 1994, for $7,200. The Prepaid Insurance account was debiteda at the date of purchase.

2. Subscriptions for magazines in the amount of $144,000 to cover an 18-month period from May 1, 1994, were received on April 15, 1994. The Unearned Subscriptions account was credited when the payments were received.

3. A building costing $360,000 and having an estimated useful life of 50 years and a salvage value of $60,000 was purchased and put into service on January 1, 1994.

4. On January 12, 1995, salaries of $19,200 were paid to employees. The account debited was Salaries Expense. One third of the amount paid was earned by employees in December of 1994.

Required Calculate the correct net income for 1994 and 1995. In your answer, start with the reported net income. Then show the effects of each correction (adjustment), using a plus or a minus to indicate whether reported income should be increased or decreased as a result of the correction. When the corrections are added to or deducted from the reported net income amounts, the result should be the correct net income amounts. The answer format should appear as follows:

Explanation of Corrections	1994	1995
Reported net income	$200,000	$244,000
To correct error in accounting for:		
a. Fire insurance policy premium:		
Correct expense in 1994	−2,000	
Correct expense in 1995		−2,400

Problem 3–6A
Prepare journal entries under cash basis and accrual basis and determine difference in net income
(L.O. 1, 4)

Stillwagon Publishing Company began operations on December 1, 1994. The company's bookkeeper intended to use the cash basis of accounting. Consequently, the bookkeeper recorded all cash receipts and disbursements for items relating to operations in revenue and expense accounts. No adjusting entries were made prior to preparing the financial statements for December.

Transactions

Dec. 1 Issued capital stock for $120,000 cash.
3 Received $144,000 for magazine subscriptions to run for two years from this date. The magazine is published monthly on the 23rd.
4 Paid for advertising to be run in a national periodical for six months (starting this month). The cost was $54,000.
7 Purchased an insurance policy to cover a two-year period beginning December 15, $43,200.
12 Paid the annual rent on the building, $72,000, effective through November 30, 1995.
15 Received $216,000 cash for two-year subscriptions starting with the December issue.

Dec. 15   Salaries for the period December 1–15 amounted to $48,000. Beginning as of this date, salaries will be paid on the 5th and 20th of each month for the preceding two-week period.

      20   Salaries for the period December 1–15 were paid.

      23   Supplies purchased for cash, $21,600. (Only $1,800 of these were subsequently used in 1994.)

      27   Printing costs applicable equally to the next six issues beginning with the December issue were paid in cash, $144,000.

      31   Cash sales of the December issue, $84,000.

      31   Unpaid salaries for the period December 16–31 amounted to $52,800.

      31   Sales on account of December issue, $36,000.

Required   *a.*   Prepare journal entries for the transactions as the bookkeeper prepared them.

           b.   Prepare journal entries as they would have been prepared under the accrual basis. Where the entry is the same as under the cash basis, merely indicate "same." Where possible, record the original transaction so that no adjusting entry will be necessary at the end of the month. Ignore explanations.

           c.   Compute the difference in net income between the cash and the accrual bases of accounting. Show the increase or decrease in each revenue and expense when the accrual basis is used instead of the cash basis.

PROBLEMS: SERIES B

Problem 3–1B

Prepare adjusting entries, post to ledger accounts, and state correct figures for financial statements (L.O. 4)

The following data pertain to Earth Company:

	Account Title	Trial Balance Amount	Information for Adjustments
Item 1:	Equipment	$480,000	The equipment has an estimated useful life of five years and an estimated salvage value of $120,000.
	Accumulated Depreciation— Equipment	72,000	
Item 2:	Salaries Expense	180,000	Salaries earned by employees but not yet paid, $2,400.
Item 3:	Prepaid Insurance	100,800	Of the prepaid insurance in the trial balance, only $26,400 is for additional protection after December 31.

Required   For each of the items:

           a.   Prepare the annual year-end adjusting journal entry, dating it December 31, 1994.

           b.   Set up partial ledger accounts showing only debit, credit, and balance. Enter balances as given, if any, and post the adjusting entries made in *(a)*.

           c.   State the correct figures for that item on the balance sheet. Show any related accounts for that item as they should appear on the balance sheet.

           d.   State the correct figures for that item on the income statement.

Problem 3–2B

Prepare adjusting entries (L.O. 4)

The trial balance of Orlando Company at December 31 of the current year includes, among other items, the following account balances:

	Debits	Credits
Prepaid Insurance	$ 14,592	
Buildings	316,000	
Accumulated Depreciation—Buildings		$63,200
Salaries Expense.	220,000	
Prepaid Rent	48,000	

Additional data

1. The balance in the Prepaid Insurance account is the advance premium for one year from September 1 of the current year.

2. The buildings are expected to last 25 years, with no salvage value expected.

3. Salaries incurred but not paid as of December 31 amount to $12,800.

4. The balance in Prepaid Rent is for a one-year period that started March 1 of the current year.

Required   Prepare the annual year-end adjusting journal entries at December 31.

Problem 3–3B
Prepare adjusting entries and post to ledger accounts
(L.O. 4)

Among the account balances shown in the trial balance of Green Company at December 31 of the current year are the following:

	Debits	Credits
Supplies on Hand	$ 13,920	
Prepaid Insurance	19,200	
Buildings	336,000	
Accumulated Depreciation—Buildings		$78,000

Additional data

1. The inventory of supplies on hand at December 31 amounts to $2,400.

2. The balance in the Prepaid Insurance account is for a two-year policy taken out June 1 of the current year.

3. Depreciation for the buildings is based on the cost shown in the Buildings account, less salvage value estimated at $36,000. When acquired, the lives of the buildings were estimated at 50 years each.

Required   a.   Prepare the year-end adjusting journal entries at December 31. Assume page 27 of the general journal is used to record the journal entries.

           b.   Open ledger accounts for each of the accounts involved, enter the balances as shown in the trial balance, post the adjusting journal entries, and calculate year-end balances.

Problem 3–4B
Prepare adjusting entries
(L.O. 4)

Ocean Blue Company occupies rented quarters on the main street of the city. To get this location, the company rented a store larger than needed, so a portion of the area is subleased (rented) to Ferris' Restaurant. The partial trial balance of Ocean Blue Company as of December 31, 1994, is as follows:

OCEAN BLUE COMPANY
Partial Trial Balance
December 31, 1994

	Debits	Credits
Cash.	$160,000	
Prepaid Insurance	22,800	
Store Fixtures.	176,000	
Accumulated Depreciation—Store Fixtures		$ 19,200
Notes Payable		40,000
Service Revenue		1,200,000
Supplies Expense	21,600	
Rent Expense.	28,800	
Salaries Expense	196,000	
Rental Revenue		8,800

Additional data

a.   Salaries of the store clerks amount to $720 per day and were last paid through Wednesday, December 27. December 31 is a Sunday. The store is closed Sundays.

b.   An analysis of the Store Fixtures account disclosed:

Balance, January 1, 1994	$128,000
Addition, July 1, 1994	48,000
Balance, December 31, 1994, per trial balance . . .	$176,000

The company estimates that all fixtures will last 20 years from the date they were acquired and that the salvage value will be zero.

c.   The store carries one combined insurance policy, which is taken out once a year effective August 1. The premium on the policy now in force amounts to $14,400 per year.

d.   Unused store supplies on hand at December 31, 1994, have a cost of $1,440.

e.   December's rent from Ferris' Restaurant has not yet been received, $800.

f.   Interest accrued on the note payable is $1,000.

Required   Prepare the annual year-end entries required by the statement of fact presented above.

Problem 3–5B

Calculate correct net income

(L.O. 5)

The reported net income amounts for Waste Control Company were: 1994, $96,000; and 1995, $114,000. *No* annual adjusting entries were made at either year-end for any of the transactions given below:

a.   A building was rented on April 1, 1994. Cash of $28,800 was paid on that date to cover a two-year period. Prepaid Rent was debited.

b.   The balance in the Office Supplies on Hand account on December 31, 1994, was $4,800. An inventory of the supplies on December 31, 1994, revealed that only $3,000 were actually on hand at that date. No new supplies were purchased during 1995. At December 31, 1995, an inventory of the supplies revealed that $600 were on hand.

c.   A building costing $600,000 and having an estimated useful life of 40 years and a salvage value of $120,000 was put into service on January 1, 1994.

d.   Services were performed for customers in December 1994. The $18,000 bill for these services was not sent until January 1995. The only transaction that was recorded was a debit to Cash and a credit to Service Revenue when payment was received in January.

Required   Calculate the correct net income for 1994 and 1995. In your answer, start with the reported net income amounts. Then show the effects of each correction (adjustment) using a plus or a minus to indicate whether reported income should be increased or decreased as a result of the correction. When the corrections are added to or deducted from the reported net income amounts, the result should be the correct net income amounts. The answer format should be as follows:

Explanation of Corrections	**1994**	**1995**
Reported net income	$96,000	$114,000
To correct error in accounting for:		
a. Prepaid rent:		
Correct expense in 1994	−10,800	
Correct expense in 1995		−14,400

Problem 3–6B

Prepare journal entries under cash basis and accrual basis and determine difference in net income

(L.O. 1, 4)

On June 1, 1994, Richard Crane opened a swimming pool cleaning and maintenance service business, Crane Company. He vaguely recalled the process of making journal entries and establishing ledger accounts from a high school bookkeeping course he had taken some years ago. At the end of June, he prepared an income statement for the month of June, but he had the feeling that he had not proceeded correctly. He contacted his brother, John, a recent college graduate with a major in accounting, for assistance. John immediately noted that his brother had kept his records on a cash basis.

Transactions

June 1 Received cash of $54,000 from various customers in exchange for service agreements to clean and maintain their pools for June, July, August, and September.

5 Paid rent for automotive and cleaning equipment to be used during the period June through September, $12,000. The payment covered the entire period.

8 Purchased a two-year liability insurance policy effective June 1 for $15,840 cash.

10 Received an advance of $15,000 from a Florida building contractor in exchange for an agreement to help service pools in his housing development during October through May.

16 Paid salaries for the first half of June, $16,800.

17 Paid $720 for advertising to be run in a local newspaper for two weeks in June and four weeks in July.

19 Paid the rent of $24,000 under a four-month lease on a building rented and occupied on June 1.

26 Purchased $10,800 of supplies for cash. (Only $1,800 of these supplies were used in June.)

29 Billed various customers for services rendered, $25,200.

30 Unpaid employee services received in the last half of June amounted to $15,600.

30 Received a bill for $1,200 for gas and oil used in June.

Required *a.* Prepare the entries for the transactions as Richard must have recorded them under the cash basis of accounting.

b. Prepare journal entries as they would have been prepared under the accrual basis. Where the entry is the same as under the cash basis, merely indicate "same." Where possible, record the original transaction so that no adjusting entry will be necessary at the end of the month. Ignore explanations.

c. Calculate the difference in the net income for June between the cash and the accrual bases of accounting. Show the increase or decrease in each revenue and expense when the accrual basis is used instead of the cash basis.

BUSINESS DECISION PROBLEMS

Decision Problem 3–1

Explain why adjusting entries are made and which accounts need adjustment (L.O. 2, 4)

You have just been hired by Hubble Company to help prepare adjusting entries at the end of an accounting period. It becomes obvious to you that management does not seem to have much of an understanding about the necessity for adjusting entries or which accounts might possibly need adjustment. The first step you take is to prepare the following unadjusted trial balance from the general ledger. Only those ledger accounts that had end-of-year balances are included in the trial balance.

	Debits	Credits
Cash	$ 60,000	
Accounts Receivable	18,000	
Supplies on Hand	3,000	
Prepaid Insurance	2,700	
Office Equipment	120,000	
Accumulated Depreciation—Office Equipment		$ 45,000
Buildings	360,000	
Accumulated Depreciation—Buildings		105,000
Accounts Payable		9,000
Loan Payable (Bank)		15,000
Unearned Commissions		30,000
Capital Stock		150,000
Retained Earnings		69,300
Commissions Revenue		270,000
Advertising Expense	6,000	
Salaries Expense	112,500	
Utilities Expense	7,500	
Miscellaneous Expense	3,600	
	$693,300	$693,300

Required   *a.*   Explain to management why adjusting entries in general are made.

b.   Explain to management why some of the specific accounts appearing in the trial balance may need adjustment and what the nature of each adjustment might be (do not worry about specific dollar amounts).

Decision Problem 3–2

Prepare an appraisal and an approximate income statement
(L.O. 1, 4)

A friend of yours, Jack Andrews, is quite excited over the opportunity he has to purchase the land and several miscellaneous assets of Harrison Bowling Lanes Company for $375,000. Marvin tells you that Mr. and Mrs. Harrison (the sole stockholders in the company) are moving due to Mr. Harrison's ill health. The annual rent on the building and equipment is $54,000.

Mr. Harrison reports that the business earned a profit of $75,000 in 1994 (last year). Jack believes an annual profit of $75,000 on an investment of $375,000 is a really good deal. But, before completing the deal, he asks you to look it over. You agree and discover the following:

1. Mr. Harrison has computed his annual profit for 1994 as the sum of his cash dividends plus the increase in the Cash account: Dividends of $45,000 + Increase in Cash account of $30,000 = $75,000 profit.

2. As buyer of the business, Jack will take over responsibility for repayment of a $300,000 loan (plus interest) on the land. The land was acquired at a cost of $624,000 seven years ago.

3. An analysis of the Cash account shows the following for 1994:

Rental revenues received		$420,000
Cash paid out in 1994 for—		
Salaries paid to employees in 1994	$240,000	
Utilities paid for 1994	18,000	
Advertising expenses paid	15,000	
Supplies purchased and used in 1994	24,000	
Interest paid on loan	18,000	
Loan principal paid	30,000	
Cash dividends	45,000	390,000
Increase in cash balance for the year		$ 30,000

4. You also find that the annual rent of $54,000, a December utility bill of $3,000, and an advertising bill of $4,500 have not been paid.

Required   *a.*   Prepare for Jack a written report giving your appraisal of Harrison Bowling Lanes Company as an investment. Comment on Mr. Harrison's method of computing the annual "profit" of the business.

b.   Include in your report an approximate income statement for 1994.

ANSWERS TO SELF-TEST

True-False

1. *True.* Every adjusting entry involves either moving previously recorded data from an asset account to an expense account or from a liability account to a revenue account (or in the opposite direction) or simultaneously entering new data in an asset account and a revenue account or in a liability account and an expense account.

2. *True.* A fiscal year is *any* 12 consecutive months, so all calendar years are also fiscal years. A calendar year, however, must end on December 31, so it does not include fiscal years that end on any date other than December 31 (such as June 30).

3. *False.* The accumulated depreciation account is a *contra asset* that shows the total of all depreciation recorded on an asset up through the balance sheet date.

4. *False.* The Unearned Delivery Fees account is a liability. As the fees are earned, the amount in that account will be transferred to a revenue account.

5. *True.* If an adjusting entry is overlooked and not made, at least one income statement account and one balance sheet account will be incorrect.

Multiple-Choice

1. *d.*   One third of the benefits have expired. Therefore, $400 must be moved from the asset to an expense.

2. *c.*   Two thirds of the benefits have not expired. Therefore, $800 would have to be transferred from the expense to an asset.

3. *a.* $1,100 of the supplies have been used, so that amount must be moved from the asset to an expense.

4. *c.*   The amount of annual depreciation is determined as ($20,000 − $5,000) divided by 5 =

$3,000. The debit is to depreciation expense, and the credit is to the accumulated depreciation account, a contra asset.

5. *b.*   Each month $2,000 would be transferred from the liability account, Unearned Subscription Fees, to a revenue account.

6. *b.*   An asset, Interest Receivable, is debited, and a revenue is credited.

7. *a.*   The debit would be to Salaries Expense, and the credit would be to Salaries Payable.

CHAPTER

4

COMPLETING THE ACCOUNTING CYCLE: WORK SHEET, CLOSING ENTRIES, AND CLASSIFIED BALANCE SHEET

LEARNING OBJECTIVES

After studying this chapter, you should be able to:

1. List the steps in the accounting cycle.

2. Prepare a work sheet for a service company.

3. Prepare an income statement, statement of retained earnings, and balance sheet using information contained in the work sheet.

4. Prepare adjusting and closing entries using information contained in the work sheet.

5. Prepare a post-closing trial balance.

6. Prepare a classified balance sheet.

7. Prepare reversing entries (Appendix 4-A).

8. Post adjusting and closing entries to three-column ledger accounts (Appendix 4-B).

145

This chapter organizes the steps you learned in Chapters 1 through 3 into what accountants call the *accounting cycle*. The accounting cycle is a series of steps performed during the accounting period to analyze, record, classify, summarize, and report useful financial information for the purpose of preparing financial statements. Chapter 4 presents all of the accounting cycle steps. In the beginning of the chapter, we show a diagram that correctly lists the order of the eight accounting steps and their relationship to each other.

As you study the accounting cycle, you will see two new steps—the preparation of the work sheet and closing entries. This chapter discusses these new steps. In addition, a classified balance sheet is presented. This balance sheet format more closely resembles actual company balance sheets that you may have seen. (Appendix E at the end of the text contains the classified balance sheets and other financial statements of four actual companies.) Chapter Appendix 4-A presents an optional step in the accounting cycle—preparing and posting reversing entries. This chapter continues using the Speedy Delivery Company example given in Chapters 2 and 3. After completing this chapter, you will have cleared the first hurdle in your study of accounting. That is, you will understand how accounting begins with source documents that serve as evidence of transactions of a business entity and ends with financial statements showing the solvency and profitability of that entity.

THE ACCOUNTING CYCLE SUMMARIZED

Objective 1
List the steps in the accounting cycle

Before you can visualize the eight steps in the accounting cycle, you must first be able to recognize a business transaction. Business transactions are measurable events that affect the financial condition of a business. For example, assume that the owner of a business spilled a pot of coffee in her office or broke her leg while skiing. These two events may briefly interrupt the operation of the business. However, they are not measurable in terms that will affect the solvency and profitability of the business.

Business transactions can be events involving the exchanges of goods for cash between the business and an external party, such as the sale of a book, or they can be other events, such as paying salaries to employees. These events have one fundamental criterion: They must have caused a measurable change in the amounts in the accounting equation, Assets = Liabilities + Stockholders' Equity. The evidence that a business event has occurred is a **source document** such as a sales ticket, check, and so on. Source documents are important because they are the ultimate proof of business transactions.

After you have determined that an event is a measurable business transaction and have adequate proof of this transaction, you must mentally analyze the transaction in terms of its effects on the accounting equation. You learned how to do this in Chapter 1. In Chapters 2 and 3, you performed other steps in the accounting cycle. The eight steps in the accounting cycle and the chapter(s) that discuss them are:

Performed throughout the accounting period
1. Analyze transactions by examining source documents (Chapters 1 and 2).
2. Journalize transactions in the journal (Chapter 2).
3. Post journal entries to the accounts in the ledger (Chapter 2).

Performed only at end of the accounting period
4. Prepare a trial balance of the accounts (Chapter 2) and complete the work sheet (Chapter 4). (This step includes adjusting entries from Chapter 3.)
5. Prepare financial statements (Chapter 4).
6. Journalize and post adjusting entries (Chapters 3 and 4).
7. Journalize and post closing entries (Chapter 4).
8. Prepare a post-closing trial balance (Chapter 4).

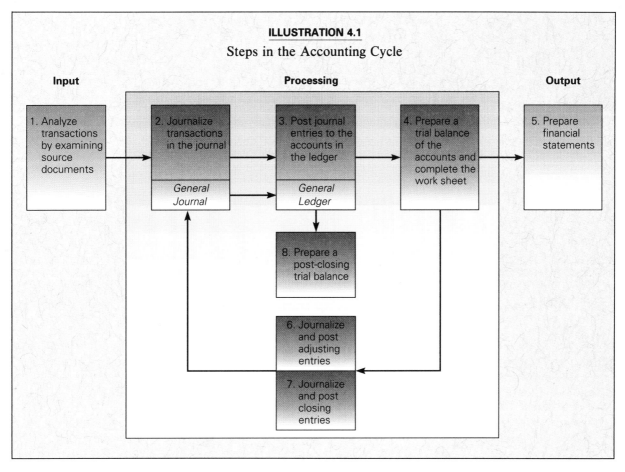

ILLUSTRATION 4.1

Steps in the Accounting Cycle

As indicated in the above list of accounting cycle steps, the first three steps are performed during the accounting period. The last five steps are performed at the end of the accounting period. Step 5 precedes steps 6 and 7 because management needs the financial statements at the earliest possible date. After the statements have been delivered to management, the adjusting and closing entries can be journalized and posted. Illustration 4.1 shows a diagram of the eight steps in the accounting cycle. The next section explains how to use the work sheet to facilitate the completion of the accounting cycle.

THE WORK SHEET

Objective 2

Prepare a work sheet for a service company

The work sheet is a columnar sheet of paper on which accountants summarize information needed to make the adjusting and closing entries and to prepare the financial statements. Work sheets are usually retained in the files to serve as documentation for these end-of-period entries. A work sheet is only an accounting tool and not part of the formal accounting records. Therefore, work sheets may vary in format and are often prepared in pencil so that errors can be easily corrected. Personal computers and spreadsheet software are frequently used to prepare work sheets. The Appendix to Chapter 7 describes the use of personal computers in accounting. Work sheets may be used each time financial statements are prepared—that is, monthly, quarterly, or at the end of the accounting year.

This chapter illustrates a 12-column work sheet that includes sets of columns for a trial balance (unadjusted), adjustments, adjusted trial balance, income statement, statement of retained earnings, and balance sheet. Each set of columns has a debit and credit column. Illustration 4.2 shows a work sheet for Speedy Delivery Company.

ILLUSTRATION 4.2
Work Sheet with Trial Balance Columns Filled In

SPEEDY DELIVERY COMPANY
Work Sheet
For the Month Ended December 31, 1994

Acct. No.	Account Titles	Trial Balance		Adjustments		Adjusted Trial Balance		Income Statement		Statement of Retained Earnings		Balance Sheet	
		Debit	Credit	Debit	Credit	Debit	Credit	Debit	Credit	Debit	Credit	Debit	Credit
100	Cash	8,250											
103	Accounts Receivable	5,200											
107	Supplies on Hand	1,400											
108	Prepaid Insurance	2,400											
112	Prepaid Rent	1,200											
150	Trucks	40,000											
200	Accounts Payable		730										
210	Unearned Delivery Fees		4,500										
300	Capital Stock		50,000										
310	Retained Earnings, 12/1/94		–0–										
320	Dividends	3,000											
400	Service Revenue		10,700										
505	Advertising Expense	50											
506	Gas and Oil Expense	680											
507	Salaries Expense	3,600											
508	Utilities Expense	150											
		65,930	65,930										

Include all accounts in the general ledger that have balances.

Column totals must be equal before proceeding.

The steps used to prepare a work sheet are listed below. The sections that follow describe these steps in greater detail.

1. Enter the titles and balances of ledger accounts in the Trial Balance columns.
2. Enter adjustments in the Adjustments columns.
3. Enter adjusted account balances in the Adjusted Trial Balance columns.
4. Extend adjusted balances of revenue and expense accounts from the Adjusted Trial Balance columns to the Income Statement columns.
5. Extend any balances in the Retained Earnings and Dividends accounts to the Statement of Retained Earnings columns.
6. Extend adjusted balances of asset, liability, and capital stock accounts from the Adjusted Trial Balance columns to the Balance Sheet columns.

In practice, accountants often work straight down from the first account appearing on the work sheet and continue down, sorting each item to the appropriate column of the work sheet. This procedure typically results in sorting the balance sheet accounts first.

The Trial Balance Columns

Instead of preparing a separate trial balance as was done in Chapter 2, the same trial balance can be entered in the work sheet. As shown in Illustration 4.2, the numbers and titles of the ledger accounts of Speedy Delivery Company are entered in the left-hand portion of the work sheet. Usually, only those accounts with balances as of the end of the accounting period are listed. (Alternatively, all the account titles in the chart of accounts could be listed, even those with zero balances.) The Retained Earnings account has been listed in the trial balance even though it has a zero balance (1) to show its relative position among the accounts and (2) to indicate that December 1994 is the first month of operations for this company. The balances of the ledger accounts are entered in the Trial Balance columns of the work sheet. The accounts are listed in the same order in which they appear in the general ledger: assets, liabilities, stockholders' equity, revenues, and expenses. Then, the columns are totaled. If the debit and credit column totals are not equal, an error exists that must be found and corrected before proceeding with the work sheet.

The Adjustments Columns

You learned in Chapter 3 that adjustments are required to bring the accounts up to date before preparing the income statement, statement of retained earnings (explained later in the chapter), and balance sheet. The Speedy Delivery Company adjustments discussed in Chapter 3 are entered in the Adjustments columns of the work sheet. Place Illustration 4.3 on top of Illustration 4.2. You can see that the debits and credits of the entries are cross-referenced by placing a key number to the left of each amount (letters could have been used). This key number facilitates the actual journalizing of the adjusting entries later without having to "rethink" the adjustments to record them. For example, the number *(1)* identifies the adjustment debiting Insurance Expense and crediting Prepaid Insurance. Note that in the Account Titles column, the Insurance Expense account title is written below the trial balance totals because the Insurance Expense account did not have a balance before the adjustment and, therefore, did not appear in the trial balance.

Brief explanations are often provided at the bottom of the work sheet for the keyed entries as in Illustration 4.3. Although these explanations are optional, they provide valuable information for other people who may later review the work sheet.

The adjustments for Speedy Delivery Company (explained in Chapter 3) are:

☐ Entry *(1)* records the expiration of $200 of prepaid insurance in December.

☐ Entry *(2)* records the expiration of $400 of prepaid rent in December.

☐ Entry *(3)* records the using up of $500 of supplies during the month.

☐ Entry *(4)* records $750 depreciation expense on the delivery truck for the month. Speedy Delivery acquired the truck at the beginning of December.

☐ Entry *(5)* records the earning of $1,500 of the $4,500 in the Unearned Delivery Fees account.

☐ Entry *(6)* records $600 of interest earned in December.

☐ Entry *(7)* records $1,000 of unbilled delivery services performed in December.

☐ Entry *(8)* records the $180 accrual of salaries expense at the end of the month.

Often it is difficult to discover all the adjusting entries that should be made. The following steps are helpful:

1. Examine adjusting entries made at the end of the preceding accounting period. The same types of entries often are necessary period after period.

2. Examine the account titles appearing in the trial balance. For example, if the company has an account titled Trucks, an entry must be made for depreciation.

3. Examine various business documents (such as bills for services received or rendered) to discover other assets, liabilities, revenues, and expenses that have not yet been recorded.

4. Ask the manager or other personnel specific questions regarding adjustments that may be necessary. For example, "Were any services performed during the month that have not yet been billed?"

After all the adjusting entries are entered in the Adjustments columns, the two columns are totaled. The totals of the two columns will be equal if all debits and credits are entered properly.

The Adjusted Trial Balance Columns

After the Speedy Delivery adjustments have been entered, the adjusted balance of each account is computed and entered in the Adjusted Trial Balance columns. Place Illustration 4.4 on top of Illustration 4.3. For example, Supplies on Hand (Account No. 107) had an unadjusted balance of $1,400. Adjusting entry *(3)* credited the account for $500, leaving a debit balance of $900. This amount is shown as a debit in the Adjusted Trial Balance columns.

All accounts having balances are extended to the Adjusted Trial Balance columns. Note carefully how the rules of debit and credit apply in determining whether an adjustment increases or decreases the account balance. For example, Salaries Expense (Account No. 507) has a $3,600 debit balance in the Trial Balance columns. This account is **increased** by a $180 debit adjustment, giving a $3,780 debit balance in the Adjusted Trial Balance columns.

Note also that some account balances remain the same because no adjustments have affected them. For example, the balance in Accounts Payable (Account No. 200) does not change. These account balances are simply extended to the Adjusted Trial Balance columns in the work sheet.

Next, the Adjusted Trial Balance debit and credit columns are totaled. The totals must be equal before taking the next step in completing the work sheet. If the Trial Balance columns and the Adjustments columns both balance but the Adjusted Trial Balance columns do not, the most probable cause is a math error or an error in extension. The Adjusted Trial Balance columns are not essential, but they make the next step of sorting the amounts to the Income Statement and the Balance Sheet columns much easier.

The Income Statement Columns

Now all Speedy Delivery's revenue and expense account balances in the Adjusted Trial Balance columns are extended to the Income Statement columns. Place Illustration 4.5 on top of Illustration 4.4. Since revenues carry credit balances, they are extended to the credit column. Expenses are extended to the debit column. Then, each column is subtotaled. The total expenses of Speedy Delivery are $6,510, and total revenues are $13,800. Thus, net income for the period is $7,290 ($13,800 − $6,510). This $7,290 amount is entered in the debit column to make the two column totals balance. A net loss is recorded in the opposite manner: expenses (debits) would have been larger than revenues (credits) so a net loss would be entered in the credit column to make the columns balance.

The Statement of Retained Earnings Columns

Next, the Statement of Retained Earnings columns are completed. Place Illustration 4.6 on top of Illustration 4.5. The $7,290 net income amount for December is entered in both the debit Income Statement column and the credit Statement of Retained Earnings column. Thus, this net income amount is the balancing figure for the Income Statement columns and is also shown in the **credit** Statement of Retained Earnings column. Net income is shown in the credit Statement of Retained Earnings column because it causes an increase in Retained Earnings. The $7,290 net income amount is then added to the beginning retained earnings balance of $–0–, and the dividends of $3,000 are deducted. As a result, the ending balance of the Retained Earnings account is $4,290.

The Balance Sheet Columns

Now the assets, liabilities, and capital stock accounts listed in the Adjusted Trial Balance columns are extended to the Balance Sheet columns. Assets are extended as debits, and liabilities and capital stock amounts are extended as credits.

Place Illustration 4.7 on top of Illustration 4.6. Note that the amount of ending retained earnings that was determined in the Statement of Earnings columns appears again in the Balance Sheet columns. The ending retained earnings amount is first shown as a debit in the Statement of Earnings columns to balance the Retained Earnings columns. Normally, the ending retained earnings is shown as a credit in the Balance Sheet columns because it increases stockholders' equity, and increases in stockholders' equity are accounted for as credits. Retained earnings will have a debit ending balance if losses and dividends have exceeded earnings. With the inclusion of the ending retained earnings amount, the Balance Sheet columns balance.

Locating Errors

If the Balance Sheet column totals do not agree on the first attempt, work backward through the process used in preparing the work sheet. Specifically, take the following steps until you discover the error:

1. Retotal the two Balance Sheet columns to see if you made an error in addition. If the column totals do not agree, check to see if you neglected to extend any balance sheet item or if you made an incorrect extension from the Adjusted Trial Balance columns.

2. Retotal the Statement of Retained Earnings columns and determine whether you entered the correct amount of retained earnings in the appropriate Statement of Retained Earnings and Balance Sheet columns.

ILLUSTRATION 4.8

Income Statement

SPEEDY DELIVERY COMPANY
Income Statement
For the Month Ended December 31, 1994

Revenues:

Service revenue		$13,200
Interest revenue		600
Total revenue		$13,800

Expenses:

Advertising expense	$ 50	
Gas and oil expense	680	
Salaries expense	3,780	
Utilities expense	150	
Insurance expense	200	
Rent expense	400	
Supplies expense	500	
Depreciation expense—trucks	750	
Total expenses		6,510
Net income		$ 7,290

---

3. Retotal the Income Statement columns and determine whether you entered the correct amount of net income or net loss for the period in the appropriate Income Statement and Statement of Retained Earnings columns.

PREPARING FINANCIAL STATEMENTS FROM THE WORK SHEET

Objective 3

Prepare an income statement, statement of retained earnings, and balance sheet using information contained in the work sheet

When the work sheet is completed, all the necessary information to prepare the income statement, statement of retained earnings, and balance sheet is readily available. Now, the information must only be recast into the appropriate financial statement format.

Income Statement

The information needed to prepare the income statement comes from the Income Statement columns in the work sheet. Thus, the income statement in Illustration 4.8 is prepared by using the information in the Income Statement columns in Illustration 4.7.

Statement of Retained Earnings

The statement of retained earnings is a financial statement that summarizes the transactions affecting the Retained Earnings account balance. The information needed to prepare this financial statement is taken from the Statement of Retained Earnings columns in the work sheet (Illustration 4.7).

Illustration 4.9 shows Speedy Delivery Company's statement of retained earnings for the month ended December 31, 1994. This statement was prepared by showing the beginning Retained Earnings account balance (Account No. 310), adding the net income (or deducting the net loss), and then subtracting the Dividends (Account No. 320). The ending Retained Earnings balance is then carried forward to the balance sheet. Remember that the **statement of retained earnings**

ILLUSTRATION 4.9

Statement of Retained Earnings

SPEEDY DELIVERY COMPANY
Statement of Retained Earnings
For the Month Ended December 31, 1994

Retained earnings, December 1, 1994	$ –0–
Net income for December	7,290
Total	$7,290
Less: Dividends	3,000
Retained earnings, December 31, 1994.	$4,290

ILLUSTRATION 4.10

Balance Sheet

SPEEDY DELIVERY COMPANY
Balance Sheet
December 31, 1994
Assets

Cash		$ 8,250
Accounts receivable.		6,200
Supplies on hand.		900
Prepaid insurance.		2,200
Prepaid rent		800
Interest receivable		600
Trucks.	$40,000	
Less: Accumulated depreciation	750	39,250
Total assets		$58,200

Liabilities and Stockholders' Equity

Liabilities:		
Accounts payable.		$ 730
Unearned delivery fees		3,000
Salaries payable		180
Total liabilities		$ 3,910
Stockholders' equity:		
Capital stock.	$50,000	
Retained earnings	4,290	
Total stockholders' equity		54,290
Total liabilities and stockholders' equity		$58,200

helps to relate income statement information to balance sheet information. The statement of retained earnings does this by indicating how net income, shown on the income statement, relates to the amount of retained earnings, shown on the balance sheet under stockholders' equity.

Balance Sheet

The information from the Balance Sheet columns of Speedy Delivery's work sheet (Illustration 4.7) is used to prepare Speedy Delivery's balance sheet. As stated above, the correct amount for the ending retained earnings is shown on the statement of retained earnings. Illustration 4.10 shows the completed balance sheet for Speedy Delivery.

JOURNALIZING ADJUSTING ENTRIES

Objective 4

Prepare adjusting and closing entries using information contained in the work sheet

Now that Speedy Delivery's financial statements have been completed from the work sheet, the adjusting entries must be entered in the general journal and posted to the appropriate ledger accounts. The process of preparing these adjusting entries is the same as that used in Chapter 3, except that the work sheet is now the source for making the entries. **The preparation of a work sheet does not eliminate the need to prepare and post adjusting entries because the work sheet is only an accounting tool and is not part of the formal accounting records.**

The numerical notations in the Adjustments columns and the adjustments explanations at the bottom of the work sheet identify each adjusting entry. The adjustment columns show each entry with its appropriate debit and credit. Speedy Delivery's adjusting entries as they would appear in the general journal after posting are:

SPEEDY DELIVERY COMPANY
GENERAL JOURNAL

Page 3

Date		Account Titles and Explanation	Post. Ref.	Debit	Credit
1994		**Adjusting Entries**			
Dec.	31	Insurance Expense	512	2 0 0	
		Prepaid Insurance	108		2 0 0
		To record insurance expense for December.			
	31	Rent Expense	515	4 0 0	
		Prepaid Rent	112		4 0 0
		To record rent expense for December.			
	31	Supplies Expense	518	5 0 0	
		Supplies on Hand	107		5 0 0
		To record supplies used during December.			
	31	Depreciation Expense—Trucks	521	7 5 0	
		Accumulated Depreciation—Trucks	151		7 5 0
		To record depreciation expense for December.			
	31	Unearned Delivery Fees	210	1 5 0 0	
		Service Revenue	400		1 5 0 0
		To transfer a portion of delivery fees from the liability account to			
		the revenue account.			
	31	Interest Receivable	121	6 0 0	
		Interest Revenue	418		6 0 0
		To record one month's interest revenue.			
	31	Accounts Receivable	103	1 0 0 0	
		Service Revenue	400		1 0 0 0
		To record unbilled delivery services performed in December.			
	31	Salaries Expense	507	1 8 0	
		Salaries Payable	206		1 8 0
		To accrue one day's salaries that were earned but are unpaid.			

THE CLOSING PROCESS

From Chapter 2, you learned that (1) revenue, expense, and Dividends accounts are **nominal (temporary) accounts** since they are merely subclassifications of a **real (permanent) account,** Retained Earnings; and (2) financial statements are prepared for certain accounting periods. The closing process is the act of transferring (1) the balances in the revenue and expense accounts to a clearing account called *Income Summary* and then to Retained Earnings, and (2) the balance in the Dividends account to the Retained Earnings account. Also, the closing process reduces revenue, expense, and Dividends account balances to zero so they will be ready to receive data for the next accounting period. The closing process may be performed monthly or annually.

The Income Summary account is a clearing account used only at the end of an accounting period to summarize revenues and expenses for the period. After all revenue and expense account balances are transferred to Income Summary, the balance in the Income Summary account represents the net income or net loss for the period. The balance in the Income Summary account is then closed, or transferred, to the Retained Earnings account. This action results in a zero balance in Income Summary.

The Dividends account is also closed at the end of the accounting period. This account shows the amount of dividends declared by the board of directors to the stockholders. The Dividends account is closed directly to the Retained Earnings account and not to Income Summary because dividends have no effect on income or loss for the period.

In accounting, the process of closing is often referred to as "closing the books." **Remember that only revenue, expense, and Dividend accounts are closed—not asset, liability, Capital Stock, or Retained Earnings accounts.**

The four basic steps in the closing process are:

1. **Closing the revenue account(s)**—transferring the balances in the revenue accounts to a clearing account called Income Summary.
2. **Closing the expense accounts**—transferring the balances in the expense accounts to a clearing account called Income Summary.
3. **Closing the Income Summary account**—transferring the balance of the Income Summary account to the Retained Earnings account.
4. **Closing the Dividends account**—transferring the balance of the Dividends account to the Retained Earnings account.

An explanation of each of these steps follows, using the closing process for the Speedy Delivery Company as an example.

Step 1: Closing the Revenue Account(s)

Revenues appear in the Income Statement credit column of the work sheet. Two revenue accounts appear in the Income Statement credit column for Speedy Delivery Company: delivery service revenue of $13,200 and interest revenue of $600 (Illustration 4.7). Since revenue accounts have credit balances, they must be debited for an equal amount to bring them to a zero balance. When Service Revenue and Interest Revenue are debited, Income Summary (Account No. 600) is credited. This entry is made in the general journal to close the Service Revenue and Interest Revenue accounts. The account numbers in the Posting Reference column are entered when the journal entry has been posted to the ledger. This statement is also true for the other closing journal entries illustrated.

SPEEDY DELIVERY COMPANY
GENERAL JOURNAL   *Page 4*

Date		Account Titles and Explanation	Post. Ref.	Debit	Credit
1994		**Closing Entries**			
Dec.	31	Service Revenue	400	1 3 2 0 0	
		Interest Revenue	418	6 0 0	
		Income Summary	600		1 3 8 0 0
		To close the revenue accounts in the Income Statement credit			
		column to Income Summary.			

After the closing entries have been posted, the Service Revenue and Interest Revenue accounts (in T-account format) of Speedy Delivery appear as shown below. Note that the accounts now have a zero balance.

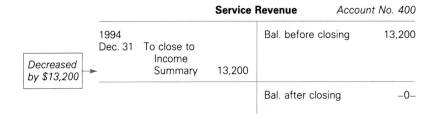

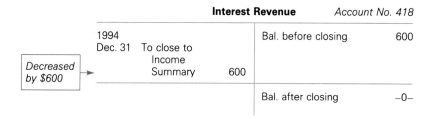

As a result of the above entry, the Income Summary account was credited for $13,800. The Income Summary account will be shown later.

Step 2: Closing the Expense Account(s)

Expenses appear in the Income Statement debit column of the work sheet. Speedy Delivery Company has eight expenses in the Income Statement debit column (Illustration 4.7). As shown by the column subtotal, these expenses add up to $6,510. Since expense accounts have debit balances, **each account** must be credited to bring it to a zero balance. Then, the debit in the closing entry is made to the Income Summary account for $6,510. Thus, to close the expense accounts, Speedy Delivery makes the following entry:

SPEEDY DELIVERY COMPANY
GENERAL JOURNAL   *Page 4*

Date	Account Titles and Explanation	Post. Ref.	Debit	Credit
1994				
Dec. 31	Income Summary	600	6 5 1 0	
	Advertising Expense	505		5 0
	Gas and Oil Expense	506		6 8 0
	Salaries Expense	507		3 7 8 0
	Utilities Expense	511		1 5 0
	Insurance Expense	512		2 0 0
	Rent Expense	515		4 0 0
	Supplies Expense	518		5 0 0
	Depreciation Expense—Trucks	521		7 5 0
	To close the expense accounts appearing in the Income Statement			
	debit column to Income Summary.			

The debit of $6,510 to the Income Summary account agrees with the Income Statement debit column subtotal in the work sheet. The comparison with the work sheet can serve as a check to make certain that all revenue and expense items have been listed and closed. If the debit in the above entry was made for a different amount than the column subtotal, the company would have an error in the closing entry for expenses.

Speedy Delivery's expense accounts appear as shown below after they have been closed. Note that each account has a zero balance after closing.

Advertising Expense   *Account No. 505*

Bal. before closing	50	1994		
		Dec. 31	To close to Income Summary	50
Bal. after closing	–0–			

Decreased by $50

Gas and Oil Expense   *Account No. 506*

Bal. before closing	680	1994		
		Dec. 31	To close to Income Summary	680
Bal. after closing	–0–			

Decreased by $680

Salaries Expense   *Account No. 507*

Bal. before closing	3,780	1994		
		Dec. 31	To close to Income Summary	3,780
Bal. after closing	–0–			

Decreased by $3,780

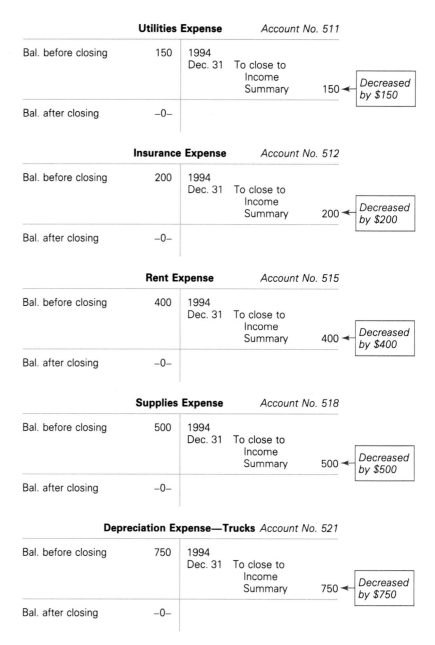

Remember that the expense accounts could be closed before the revenue accounts. The end result is the same either way.

After the revenues and expenses of Speedy Delivery have been closed, the total amounts that these accounts formerly carried are now carried in the Income Summary account.

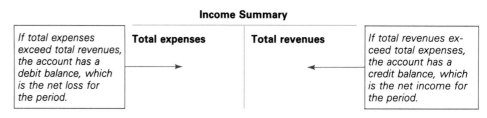

Speedy Delivery's Income Summary account appears as follows:

Income Summary   *Account No. 600*

1994			1994		
Dec. 31	From closing the expense accounts	6,510	Dec. 31	From closing the revenue account	13,800
				Bal. before closing this account (net income)	7,290

The credit balance of $7,290 is the company's net income for December.

Now Speedy Delivery's Income Summary account must be closed to its Retained Earnings account. The journal entry to do this is:

SPEEDY DELIVERY COMPANY
GENERAL JOURNAL   *Page 4*

Date		Account Titles and Explanation	Post. Ref.	Debit	Credit
1994					
Dec.	31	Income Summary	600	7 2 9 0	
		Retained Earnings	310		7 2 9 0
		To close the Income Summary account to the Retained Earnings account.			

After Speedy Delivery's Income Summary account is closed, the company's Income Summary and Retained Earnings accounts will appear as follows:

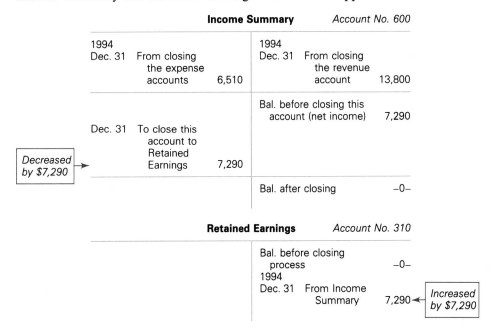

Income Summary   *Account No. 600*

1994			1994		
Dec. 31	From closing the expense accounts	6,510	Dec. 31	From closing the revenue account	13,800
				Bal. before closing this account (net income)	7,290
Dec. 31	To close this account to Retained Earnings	7,290			
				Bal. after closing	–0–

Decreased by $7,290

Retained Earnings   *Account No. 310*

	Bal. before closing process	–0–
1994		
Dec. 31	From Income Summary	7,290

Increased by $7,290

Step 4: Closing the Dividends Account

The last closing entry that must be made is to close Speedy Delivery's Dividends account. This account has a debit balance before closing. To close the account, the Dividends account is credited and the Retained Earnings account is debited.

Notice that the Dividends account is not closed to the Income Summary. The Dividends account is not an expense and does not enter into income determination.

The journal entry to close Speedy Delivery's Dividends account is:

SPEEDY DELIVERY COMPANY
GENERAL JOURNAL   *Page 4*

Date		Account Titles and Explanation	Post. Ref.	Debit	Credit
1994 Dec.	31	Retained Earnings	310	3000	
		Dividends	320		3000
		To close the Dividends account to the Retained Earnings account.			

After this closing entry is posted, the company's Dividends and Retained Earnings accounts appear as follows:

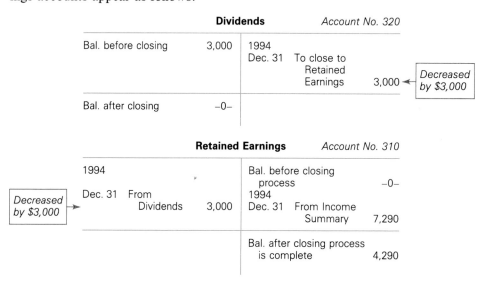

Dividends   *Account No. 320*

Bal. before closing   3,000 | 1994 Dec. 31   To close to Retained Earnings   3,000 ← *Decreased by $3,000*

Bal. after closing   –0–

Retained Earnings   *Account No. 310*

1994
Decreased by $3,000 → Dec. 31   From Dividends   3,000 | Bal. before closing process   –0–
1994
Dec. 31   From Income Summary   7,290

Bal. after closing process is complete   4,290

Closing Process Summarized

The closing process is the transferring of revenue and expense account balances to a clearing account called Income Summary and then transferring from Income Summary to Retained Earnings the amount of net income or net loss for the period. Closing also includes the elimination of the balance in the Dividends account by transferring that amount to Retained Earnings. A summary of the process used to close Speedy Delivery's accounts shown on the work sheet is as follows:

1. Each revenue account in the Income Statement credit column was debited and the Income Summary account was credited for the amount of total revenue earned for the period, $13,800. Note that the credit to Income Summary is equal to the subtotal of the Income Statement credit column of the work sheet. This relationship will be true no matter how many revenue accounts are closed.

2. Each expense account appearing in the Income Statement debit column was credited for its balance, and the Income Summary account was deb-

A BROADER PERSPECTIVE

SKILLS FOR THE LONG HAUL

The decision has been made: You've opted to start your career by joining an international accounting firm. But you can't help wondering if you have the right skills both for short- and long-term success in public accounting. . . .

Most students understand that accounting knowledge, organizational ability and interpersonal skills are critical to success in public accounting. But it is important for the beginner to realize that different skills are emphasized at different points in a public accountant's career. . . .

Let's examine the duties and skills needed at each level—Staff Accountant (years 1–2), Senior Accountant (years 3–4), Manager/Senior Manager (years 5–11) and Partner (years 11+).

Staff Accountant—Enthusiastic Learner Let's travel with Tracy as she begins her career at the staff level. At the outset, she works directly under a senior accountant on each of her audits and is responsible for completing audits and administrative tasks assigned to her. Her duties include documenting workpapers, interacting with client accounting staff, clerical tasks and discussing questions that arise with her senior. Tracy will work on different audit engagements during her first year and learn the firm's audit approach. She will be introduced to various industries and accounting systems.

The two most important traits to be demonstrated at the staff level are (1) a positive attitude and (2) the ability to learn quickly while adapting to unfamiliar situations. . . .

*****

Senior Accountant—Organizer and Teacher As a senior accountant, Tracy will be responsible for the day-to-day management of several audit engagements during the year. She will plan the audits, oversee the performance of interim audit testing and direct year-end field work. She will also perform much of the final wrap-up work, such as preparing checklists, writing the management letter and reviewing or drafting the financial statements. Throughout this process, Tracy will spend a substantial amount of time instructing and supervising staff accountants.

The two most critical skills needed at the senior level are (1) the ability to organize and control an audit and (2) the ability to teach staff accountants how to audit.

*****

Manager/Senior Manager—General Manager and Salesperson Upon promotion to manager, Tracy will begin the transformation from auditor to executive. She will manage several audits at one time and become active in billing clients as well as negotiating audit fees. She will handle many important client meetings and closing conferences. Tracy will also become more involved in the firm's administrative tasks. . . . Finally, outside of her client service and administrative duties, Tracy will be evaluated to a large extent on her community involvement and ability to assist the partners in generating new business for the firm.

The two skills most emphasized at the manager level are (1) general management ability and (2) sales and communication skills.

*****

Partner—Leader and Expert As a partner in the firm, Tracy will have many broad responsibilities. She will engage in high-level client service activities, business development, recruiting, strategic planning, office administration and counseling. Besides serving as the engagement partner on several audits, she will have ultimate responsibility for the quality of service provided to each of her clients. Although a certain industry or administrative function will become her specialty, she will often be called upon to perform a wide variety of audit and administrative duties when other partners have scheduling conflicts. She will be expected to serve as a positive example to those who work for her and will train others in her areas of expertise.

At the partnership level, what's looked for is leadership ability plus the ability to become an expert in a specific industry or administrative function.

*****

In the Meantime Those planning on a public accounting career should do more than just learn accounting. To develop the needed skills, a broad education background in business and nonbusiness courses is required plus participation in extracurricular activities, that promote leadership and communication skills. It is never too early to start building the skills for long-term success.

Source: Dana R. Hermanson and Heather M. Hermanson, *New Accountant*, January 1990, pp. 24–26, © 1990, New DuBois Corporation.

ited for the total amount of expenses incurred for the period, $6,510. Note that the debit to Income Summary is equal to the subtotal of the Income Statement debit column of the work sheet.

3. The balance of the Income Summary account, $7,290, was closed to the Retained Earnings account. Since the Income Summary account balance was a credit (indicating net income), it was closed by a debit to the Income Summary account and a credit to Retained Earnings. If a net loss had occurred, Income Summary would have had a debit balance. Closing would have been through a credit to Income Summary and a debit to Retained Earnings.

4. The balance in the Dividends account was closed to the Retained Earnings account by debiting the Retained Earnings account and crediting the Dividends account.

To explain the closing process, we used the T-account format to illustrate the adjusting and closing entries for Speedy Delivery Company. In Appendix 4-B, we show these same adjusting and closing entries in three-column ledger accounts.

Post-Closing Trial Balance

Objective 5
Prepare a post-closing trial balance

After closing has been completed, the only accounts in the general ledger that have not been closed are the balance sheet accounts (the permanent, or real, accounts). Since these accounts contain the opening balances for the coming accounting period, debit balance totals must equal credit balance totals. The preparation of a post-closing trial balance serves as a check on the accuracy of the closing process and ensures that the books are in balance at the start of the new accounting period. The post-closing trial balance differs from the adjusted trial balance in only two important respects: (1) it excludes all nominal (temporary) accounts since they have been closed, and (2) the Retained Earnings account has been updated to its proper ending balance.

A post-closing trial balance is a trial balance taken after the closing entries have been posted. The only accounts that should be open are assets, liabilities, capital stock, and Retained Earnings accounts. Account balances are listed in debit and credit columns and totaled to make sure debits and credits are equal.

Illustration 4.11 shows a post-closing trial balance for Speedy Delivery Company as of December 31, 1994. The amounts appearing in the post-closing trial balance are taken from the ledger after the closing entries have been posted. You can verify this by comparing the amounts in Illustration 4.11 with those appearing in the general ledger accounts for Speedy Delivery Company shown in chapter Appendix 4-B. This section concludes the Speedy Delivery Company illustration that we have used in Chapters 2, 3, and 4.

A CLASSIFIED BALANCE SHEET

Objective 6
Prepare a classified balance sheet

The balance sheets presented so far in this text have been unclassified balance sheets. An unclassified balance sheet has three major categories: assets, liabilities, and stockholders' equity. Illustration 4.10 (page 153) shows an unclassified balance sheet. A classified balance sheet contains the same three major categories but then subdivides them to provide useful information for interpretation and analysis by users of financial statements.

Illustration 4.12 shows an example of a classified balance sheet for Andrews Corporation. This new example is used so we can include items not contained in the Speedy Delivery Company balance sheet of Illustration 4.10. Note that the Andrews Corporation classified balance sheet is in a vertical format (assets ap-

ILLUSTRATION 4.11
Post-Closing Trial Balance

SPEEDY DELIVERY COMPANY
Post-Closing Trial Balance
December 31, 1994

Acct. No.	Account Title	Debits	Credits
100	Cash	$ 8,250	
103	Accounts Receivable	6,200	
107	Supplies on Hand	900	
108	Prepaid Insurance	2,200	
112	Prepaid Rent	800	
121	Interest Receivable	600	
150	Trucks	40,000	
151	Accumulated Depreciation—Trucks		$ 750
200	Accounts Payable		730
206	Salaries Payable		180
210	Unearned Delivery Fees		3,000
300	Capital Stock		50,000
310	Retained Earnings		4,290
		$58,950	$58,950

pearing above liabilities and stockholders' equity) rather than the horizontal format (assets on the left and liabilities and stockholders' equity on the right). The two formats are equally acceptable.

The Andrews Corporation classified balance sheet illustrated in this section has two of its three major categories subdivided. Andrews subdivides its assets into current assets; long-term investments; property, plant, and equipment; and intangible assets. The company subdivides its liabilities into current liabilities and long-term liabilities. Stockholders' equity is the same in a classified balance sheet as in an unclassified balance sheet. Later chapters will show further subdivisions of the stockholders' equity section.

You will study more about the individual items listed in the classified balance sheet in the remainder of the text. Our only purpose here is to give a brief description of some of the items that can be listed under each category.

Current Assets

Current assets are cash and other assets that a business will convert to cash or use up in a relatively short period of time—one year or one operating cycle, whichever is longer. An operating cycle is the time it takes to start with cash, buy necessary items to produce revenues (such as materials, supplies, labor, and/or finished goods), sell services or goods, and receive cash by collecting the resulting receivables. Companies in service industries and merchandising industries generally have operating cycles of much less than one year. However, companies in some manufacturing industries, such as distilling and lumber, have operating cycles of over one year. Common current assets in a service-type business include cash, marketable securities, accounts receivable, notes receivable, interest receivable, and prepaid expenses. Current assets are listed in order of liquidity (or how easily they are convertible into cash), from most liquid to least liquid.

Cash includes deposits in banks available for current operations at the balance sheet date plus cash on hand consisting of currency, undeposited checks, drafts, and money orders. Cash is the first current asset to appear on a balance sheet.

ILLUSTRATION 4.12

A Classified Balance Sheet

ANDREWS CORPORATION
Balance Sheet
June 30, 1994

Assets

Current assets:

Cash		$ 35,800
Marketable securities		4,000
Accounts receivable (due within one year)	$ 57,000	
Less: Allowance for uncollectible accounts	2,000	55,000
Notes receivable		15,000
Interest receivable		200
Prepaid insurance		2,000
Total current assets		$112,000

Long-term investments:

Bonds of Jones Corporation		50,000

Property, plant, and equipment:

Land		$ 30,000
Buildings	$300,000	
Less: Accumulated depreciation	100,000	200,000
Office furniture	$ 75,000	
Less: Accumulated depreciation	15,000	60,000
Office Equipment	$ 18,000	
Less: Accumulated depreciation	6,000	12,000
Total property, plant, and equipment		302,000

Intangible assets:

Patents		34,000
Total assets		$498,000

Liabilities and Stockholders' Equity

Current liabilities:

Accounts payable	$ 11,900	
Notes payable (due within one year)	6,000	
Taxes withheld from employees	800	
Salaries payable	1,100	
Interest payable	100	
Dividends payable	5,000	
Unearned subscriptions revenue	8,000	
Total current liabilities		$ 32,900

Long-term liabilities:

Notes payable, 10%, due in 2000	$ 50,000	
Bonds payable, 9%, due in 2010	100,000	150,000
Total liabilities		$182,900

Stockholders' equity:

Capital stock	$250,000	
Retained earnings	65,100	
Total stockholders' equity		315,100
Total liabilities and stockholders' equity		$498,000

Marketable securities are **temporary investments** that a company makes to earn a return on idle cash. The purpose of such investments is to earn additional money on cash that the business does not need at the present time but will probably need soon.

Accounts receivable (also called *trade accounts receivable*) are amounts owed to a business by customers. An account receivable arises when a company performs a service or sells merchandise on credit. Customers normally provide no written evidence of indebtedness on sales invoices or delivery tickets except their signatures. Notice the item "Allowance for uncollectible accounts" in the balance sheet of Andrews Corporation (Illustration 4.12). This is another contra asset account that allows a business entity to recognize in its balance sheet the possibility that the company will not collect some of its "on account" sales. The Allowance for Uncollectible Accounts account is discussed in Chapter 9.

A note is an unconditional written promise to pay another party the amount owed either when demanded or at a certain specified date, usually with interest (a charge made for use of the money) at a specified rate. A note is a **note receivable** on the balance sheet of the company to which the note is given. A note receivable arises *(a)* when a company makes a sale and receives a note from the customer, *(b)* when a customer gives a note for an amount due on an account receivable, or *(c)* when a company loans money and receives a note in return. Chapter 9 discusses notes at length.

Interest receivable arises when a company has earned but not collected interest by the balance sheet date. Usually, the amount is not due until later.

Prepaid expenses include items such as rent, insurance, and supplies that have been paid for but from which all the benefits have not yet been realized (or consumed). If prepaid expenses had not been paid for in advance, they would require the future disbursement of cash. Furthermore, prepaid expenses are considered assets because they have service potential.

Long-Term Assets   Long-term assets are assets that a business will have on hand or use for a relatively long period of time. Examples include long-term investments; plant, property, and equipment; and intangible assets.

Long-Term Investments   A long-term investment usually consists of securities of another company held with the intention of *(a)* obtaining control of another company, *(b)* securing a permanent source of income for the investor, or *(c)* establishing friendly business relations. The long-term investment classification in the balance sheet does **not** include those securities purchased for short-term purposes. For most businesses, long-term investments may take the form of capital stock or bonds of other corporations. Occasionally, long-term investments include funds accumulated for specific purposes, rental properties, and plant sites for future use.

Property, Plant, and Equipment   Property, plant, and equipment are assets with useful lives of over one year that a company acquired for use in the business rather than for resale. The terms **plant assets** or **fixed assets** are also used for property, plant, and equipment. To agree with the order in the heading, the items within property, plant, and equipment are listed in that order (property first, plant next, and equipment last). These items are *fixed assets* because the company uses them for long-term purposes. Several types of property, plant, and equipment are described below.

Land is ground the company uses for business operations. Land could include ground on which company locates its business buildings and that used for outside storage space or parking. Land owned for investment is not included as a plant asset; it is included in the "long-term investments" category.

Buildings are structures the company uses to carry on its business. Buildings that a company owns as investments are not included as plant assets.

Office furniture includes such items as file cabinets, desks, chairs, and shelves.

Office equipment includes items such as typewriters, computers, copiers, FAX machines, and phone answering machines.

Accumulated depreciation is a contra asset account to depreciable assets such as buildings, machinery, and equipment. This account shows the total depreciation taken for each related asset. On the balance sheet, companies deduct the accumulated depreciation (as a contra asset) from its related asset.

Intangible Assets   Intangible assets consist of the noncurrent, nonmonetary, non-physical assets of a business. Companies must charge the costs of intangible assets to expense over the period benefited up to a maximum period of 40 years. Among the intangible assets are rights granted by governmental bodies, such as patents and copyrights. Other intangible assets include leaseholds and goodwill.

A patent is a right granted by the federal government to the owner of an invention whereby he or she alone has the authority to manufacture a product or to use a process for a period of time.

A copyright is granted by the federal government and gives the owner the exclusive privilege of publication of written material for a period of time.

Leaseholds are rights to use rented properties, usually for several years.

Goodwill is an intangible value attached to a business evidenced by the ability to earn larger net income per dollar of investment than that earned by competitors in the same industry. The ability to produce superior profits is a valuable resource of a business. Normally, goodwill will be recorded only at the time of purchase and then only at the price paid for it.

Current Liabilities   Current liabilities are debts due within one year or one operating cycle, whichever is longer. The payment of current liabilities normally will require the use of current assets. Current liabilities are listed in the order of how soon they must be paid; the sooner a liability must be paid, the earlier it is listed. Examples of current liabilities follow.

Accounts payable are amounts owed to suppliers for goods or services purchased on credit. Accounts payable are generally due in 30 or 60 days and do not bear interest. In the balance sheet, accounts payable are shown in one amount that is the sum of the individual accounts payable.

Notes payable are unconditional written promises by the company to pay a certain sum of money at a certain or determinable future date. The notes may arise from borrowing money from a bank, from the purchase of assets, or from the giving of a note in settlement of an account payable. Generally, only notes payable due in one year or less are included as current liabilities.

Taxes withheld from employees are items such as federal income taxes, state income taxes, and social security taxes withheld from employees' paychecks. The company will pay these amounts to the proper governmental agencies within a short period.

Salaries payable are amounts owed to employees for services rendered. The company has not paid these salaries at the balance sheet date because they are not due until later.

Stuart Miller was taking his first accounting principles course and had just completed Chapter 4. He needed a job badly to help pay for his college expenses and was confident that he could keep a set of books for a small service company.

When Stuart asked his accounting instructor about part-time job opportunities, he was told that they were described on the bulletin board in the accounting department office. Among the job descriptions, he found the following:

Wanted, part-time bookkeeper to keep books for small dry cleaning company. Applicants should have completed at least one course in accounting with a grade of "B" or better. Some experience with personal computers and spreadsheet software is required. Person would be required to work 10 hours per week at a rate of $7.50 per hour. Hours are flexible. If qualified and interested call 651-4825 and ask for Mr. Finley.

Stuart knew that he did not meet the job qualifications, but thought he could do the job anyway. His grade on the first exam was a middle "C," and he had never used a personal computer. He decided to apply for the job.

When Mr. Finley asked about his qualifications, Stuart decided to tell "a little white lie." Stuart said that he was just about finished with his first course in accounting and that he was almost certain to earn a grade of "B." He also indicated that he had some experience with personal computers and spreadsheet software, but that he would have to "brush up a bit" because he had not worked with them for some time.

Required

a. What do you think of Stuart's ethical behavior?

b. If he got the job and was able to perform well, does this affect your assessment of his behavior?

c. What are some of the possible unfavorable consequences resulting from this situation?

Interest payable is interest that the company has accumulated on debts, such as notes or bonds. Usually, the company has not paid this accrued interest at the balance sheet date because the amount is not due until later.

Dividends payable are amounts the company has declared payable to stockholders; it represents a distribution of income. Since the corporation has not paid these declared dividends at the balance sheet date, they are a liability.

Unearned revenues (revenues received in advance) result when a company receives payment for goods or services before the company has earned the revenue, such as a subscription to a magazine. These unearned revenues represent a liability to perform the agreed services or other contractual requirements or to return the assets received.

Long-Term Liabilities

Long-term liabilities are debts such as a mortgage payable and bonds payable that are not due for a relatively long period of time, usually more than one year. Companies should show maturity dates in the balance sheet for all long-term liabilities. Normally, the liabilities with the earliest due dates are listed first.

Notes payable with maturity dates at lease one year beyond the balance sheet date are also long-term liabilities. **Bonds payable** are also long-term liabilities and are evidenced by formal printed certificates sometimes secured by liens (claims) on property, such as mortgages. Maturity dates should be shown in the balance sheet for all major long-term liabilities.

Stockholders'
Equity

Stockholders' equity shows the owners' interest (equity) in the business. This interest is equal to the amount contributed plus the income left in the business.

The two items under stockholders' equity in the Andrews Corporation balance sheet (Illustration 4.12) are capital stock and retained earnings. Capital stock shows the capital paid in to the company as the owners' investment. Retained earnings shows the cumulative income of the company less the amounts distributed to the owners in the form of dividends.

These first four chapters have concentrated on accounting for service companies. Although the basic accounting principles and the accounting process apply to all companies, accounting for merchandising companies involves some special accounting practices and procedures. In the next chapter, you will study accounting as it pertains to merchandising companies. A classified income statement will also be presented.

UNDERSTANDING THE LEARNING OBJECTIVES

1. List the steps in the accounting cycle.
    - ☐ Analyze transactions by examining source documents.
    - ☐ Journalize transactions in the journal.
    - ☐ Post journal entries to the accounts in the ledger.
    - ☐ Prepare a trial balance of the accounts and complete the work sheet.
    - ☐ Prepare financial statements.
    - ☐ Journalize and post adjusting entries.
    - ☐ Journalize and post closing entries.
    - ☐ Prepare a post-closing trial balance.

2. Prepare a work sheet for a service company.
    - ☐ The work sheet is a columnar sheet of paper on which accountants summarize information needed to make the adjusting and closing entries and to prepare the financial statements.
    - ☐ Work sheets may vary in format. The work sheet illustrated in the chapter has 12 columns—two each for trial balance, adjustments, adjusted trial balance, income statement, statement of retained earnings, and balance sheet.

3. Prepare an income statement, statement of retained earnings, and balance sheet using information contained in the work sheet.
    - ☐ The information needed to prepare the income statement is in the Income Statement columns of the work sheet. Net income for the period is the amount needed to balance the two Income Statement columns in the work sheet.
    - ☐ The information needed to prepare the statement of retained earnings is in the Statement of Retained Earnings columns of the work sheet. The ending Retained Earnings balance is carried forward to the balance sheet.
    - ☐ The information needed to prepare the balance sheet is in the Balance Sheet columns of the work sheet.

4. Prepare adjusting and closing entries using information contained in the work sheet.
    - ☐ Adjusting entries were explained in Chapter 3. They are necessary to bring the accounts to their proper balances before preparing the financial statements.

 ☐ Closing entries are necessary to reduce the balances of revenue, expense, and Dividends accounts to zero so they will be ready to receive data for the next accounting period.
 ☐ Revenue account(s) are closed by debiting them and crediting the Income Summary account.
 ☐ Expense account(s) are closed by crediting them and debiting the Income Summary account.
 ☐ The balance in the Income Summary account represents the net income or net loss for the period.
 ☐ To close the Income Summary account, the balance is transferred to the Retained Earnings account.
 ☐ To close the Dividends account, the balance is transferred to the Retained Earnings account.

5. Prepare a post-closing trial balance.
 ☐ Only the balance sheet accounts have balances and appear on the post-closing trial balance.
 ☐ All revenue, expense, and Dividends accounts have zero balances and are not included in the post-closing trial balance.

6. Prepare a classified balance sheet.
 ☐ A classified balance sheet subdivides the major categories on the balance sheet into subcategories. For instance, a classified balance sheet subdivides assets into current assets; long-term investments; property, plant, and equipment; and intangible assets. It subdivides liabilities into current liabilities and long-term liabilities. Stockholders' equity is no different in a classified balance sheet than in an unclassified balance sheet. Later chapters will show further subdivisions of the stockholders' equity section. Liabilities are subdivided into current liabilities and long-term liabilities.

7. Prepare reversing entries (Appendix 4-A).
 ☐ Reversing entries reverse the effects of the adjusting entries to which they relate. They are prepared on the first day of the next accounting period following the period in which the adjusting entries were made.
 ☐ Adjusting entries that increase assets or liabilities may be reversed, while those that decrease assets or liabilities may not be reversed.
 ☐ The purpose of a reversing entry is to simplify the first entry relating to that same item in the next accounting period. Reversing entries are completely optional.

8. Post adjusting and closing entries to three-column ledger accounts (Appendix 4-B).

APPENDIX 4-A: REVERSING ENTRIES

Objective 7
Prepare reversing entries

For certain types of adjusting entries, reversing entries may be prepared as of the first day of the next accounting period. **Reversing entries** are so named because they reverse the effects of the adjusting entries to which they relate. The purpose of a reversing entry is to simplify the first entry relating to that same item in the next accounting period.

 If reversing entries are used, not all adjusting entries need to be reversed on the first day of the next accounting period. Ideal entries for reversal are those relating to situations where a company is going to pay or receive cash in the following period for an item that accrues and has resulted in an adjusting entry. Examples of such items would include accrued salaries and unbilled fees. Adjustments for items that will **not** result in a subsequent receipt or payment of cash, such as the adjustment for depreciation, are not reversed. **A general rule to follow is that you may reverse all adjusting journal entries that increase assets or liabilities, but you do not reverse those adjusting journal entries that decrease assets or liabilities.** Thus, adjusting entries that involve accruals of assets (accrued receivables) and liabilities (accrued payables) may be reversed.

To illustrate, assume that a company made an adjusting entry on December 31, 1993, to recognize $180 of accrued salaries payable. The company pays salaries every four weeks. Thus, the next payday is Friday, January 25, 1994. Below we illustrate the entries from December 31, 1993, through January 25, 1994, assuming (1) the company uses no reversing entry and (2) the company uses a reversing entry.

(1) Entries when no reversing entry is used.	(2) Entries when a reversing entry is used.

1993
Dec. 31
 	
The adjusting entry made on December 31, 1993
 	
Salaries Expense 180
  Salaries Payable. 180
To record one day's salaries that were earned but are unpaid.
	1993
	Dec. 31
	
	The adjusting entry made on December 31, 1993
	
	Salaries Expense 180
	  Salaries Payable. 180
	To record one day's salaries that were earned but are unpaid.

1994 **Jan. 1** No reversing entry.	**1994** **Jan. 1** *The reversing entry made on January 1, 1994* Salaries Payable. . . . . 180 Salaries Expense . . . . . 180 To reverse the adjusting entry made on December 31, 1993.

1994
Jan. 25
 	
The entry to record the payment of salaries on January 25, 1994
 	
Salaries Payable. 180
Salaries Expense 3,420
  Cash. 3,600
Paid salaries for four weeks ending January 25.
	1994
	Jan. 25
	
	The entry to record the payment of salaries on January 25, 1994
	
	Salaries Expense 3,600
	  Cash. 3,600
	Paid salaries for four weeks ending January 25.

Whether or not the company uses a reversing entry, the adjusting entry as of December 31, 1993, is the same. The reversing entry dated January 1, 1994, shown in the second column above, is the exact reverse of the debit and credit used in the adjusting entry. Use of the reversing entry simplifies the entry made on January 25 because it is not necessary to remember that accrued salaries payable of $180 have been recorded. When the company makes the $3,600 payment, the entry is simply a debit to Salaries Expense and a credit to Cash for $3,600.

Another reason for using reversing entries is that when the company maintains its accounts on a computer, the computer may have been programmed to debit Salaries Expense and credit Cash every time the company pays salaries. The use of a reversing entry on January 1 permits the January 25 entry to be recorded in this manner.

The end result in the accounts is the same whether or not a reversing entry is used. To prove this, the accounts as they would appear are shown below. The beginning balance in Salaries Payable results from the adjusting entry made on December 31, 1993. Adjusting entries from 1993 are not shown since they were the same under either method.

---

1. T-accounts when no reversing entry is used.

2. T-accounts when reversing entry is used.

Cash			**Cash**		
	1994 Jan. 25	3,600		1994 Jan. 25	3,600

Salaries Payable			**Salaries Payable**		
1994 Jan. 25	180	1994 Beg. bal.	180	1994 Jan. 1 Reversing entry	180	1994 Beg. bal.	180

Salaries Expense			**Salaries Expense**		
1994 Jan. 25	3,420		1994 Jan. 25	3,600	1994 Jan. 1 Reversing entry	180
			Bal.	3,420	

Reversing entries are optional and relate to bookkeeping technique. They have no effect on the financial statements. Students may encounter the use of reversing entries in more advanced accounting courses or in practice. An understanding of reversing entries is not essential to understanding the remainder of this text since we will not use them.

APPENDIX 4-B: LEDGER ACCOUNTS AFTER CLOSING PROCESS COMPLETED

Objective 8

Post adjusting and closing entries to three-column ledger accounts

The ledger accounts for Speedy Delivery Company after the adjusting and closing entries have been posted are shown below. Assume that all adjusting entries were made on page 3 of the general journal and that all closing entries were entered on page 4. The initial December 31 balances in the ledger accounts below are before the adjusting and closing entries have been posted. The balances are labeled as a debit or a credit to assist you in understanding the example. Normally, these labels are not included in the ledger since an experienced accountant knows whether each balance is a debit or credit.

SPEEDY DELIVERY COMPANY
GENERAL LEDGER

Cash   *Account No. 100*

Date		Explanation	Post. Ref.	Debit	Credit	Balance
1994 Dec.	31	Balance				8250 Dr.

Accounts Receivable   *Account No. 103*

Date		Explanation	Post. Ref.	Debit	Credit	Balance
1994 Dec.	31	Balance				5200 Dr.
	31	Adjustment	G3	1000		6200 Dr.

Supplies on Hand   *Account No. 107*

Date		Explanation	Post. Ref.	Debit	Credit	Balance
1994 Dec.	31	Balance				1400 Dr.
	31	Adjustment	G3		500	900 Dr.

Prepaid Insurance   *Account No. 108*

Date		Explanation	Post. Ref.	Debit	Credit	Balance
1994 Dec.	31	Balance				2400 Dr.
	31	Adjustment	G3		200	2200 Dr.

Prepaid Rent   *Account No. 112*

Date		Explanation	Post. Ref.	Debit	Credit	Balance
1994 Dec.	31	Balance				1200 Dr.
	31	Adjustment	G3		400	800 Dr.

GENERAL LEDGER *(continued)*

Interest Receivable

Account No. 121

Date		Explanation	Post. Ref.	Debit	Credit	Balance
1994 Dec.	31	Balance				– 0 –
	31	Adjustment	G3	6 0 0		6 0 0 Dr.

Trucks

Account No. 150

Date		Explanation	Post. Ref.	Debit	Credit	Balance
1994 Dec.	31	Balance				4 0 0 0 0 Dr.

Accumulated Depreciation—Trucks

Account No. 151

Date		Explanation	Post. Ref.	Debit	Credit	Balance
1994 Dec.	31	Balance				– 0 –
	31	Adjustment	G3		7 5 0	7 5 0 Cr.

Accounts Payable

Account No. 200

Date		Explanation	Post. Ref.	Debit	Credit	Balance
1994 Dec.	31	Balance				7 3 0 Cr.

Salaries Payable

Account No. 206

Date		Explanation	Post. Ref.	Debit	Credit	Balance
1994 Dec.	31	Balance				– 0 –
	31	Adjustment	G3		1 8 0	1 8 0 Cr.

Unearned Delivery Fees

Account No. 210

Date		Explanation	Post. Ref.	Debit	Credit	Balance
1994 Dec.	31	Balance				4 5 0 0 Cr.
	31	Adjustment	G3	1 5 0 0		3 0 0 0 Cr.

GENERAL LEDGER *(continued)*

Capital Stock   *Account No. 300*

Date		Explanation	Post. Ref.	Debit	Credit	Balance
1994 Dec.	31	Balance				5 0 0 0 0 Cr.

Retained Earnings   *Account No. 310*

Date		Explanation	Post. Ref.	Debit	Credit	Balance
1994 Dec.	31	Balance				– 0 –
	31	Net income	G4		7 2 9 0	7 2 9 0 Cr.
	31	Dividends	G4	3 0 0 0		4 2 9 0 Cr.

Dividends   *Account No. 320*

Date		Explanation	Post. Ref.	Debit	Credit	Balance
1994 Dec.	31	Balance				3 0 0 0 Dr.
	31	To close	G4		3 0 0 0	– 0 –

Service Revenue   *Account No. 400*

Date		Explanation	Post. Ref.	Debit	Credit	Balance
1994 Dec.	31	Balance				1 0 7 0 0 Cr.
	31	Adjustment	G3		1 5 0 0	1 2 2 0 0 Cr.
	31	Adjustment	G3		1 0 0 0	1 3 2 0 0 Cr.
	31	To close	G4	1 3 2 0 0		– 0 –

Interest Revenue   *Account No. 418*

Date		Explanation	Post. Ref.	Debit	Credit	Balance
1994 Dec.	31	Balance				– 0 –
	31	Adjustment	G3		6 0 0	6 0 0 Cr.
	31	To close	G4	6 0 0		– 0 –

GENERAL LEDGER *(continued)*

Advertising Expense   *Account No. 505*

Date		Explanation	Post. Ref.	Debit	Credit	Balance
1994 Dec.	31	Balance				5 0 Dr.
	31	To close	G4		5 0	– 0 –

Gas and Oil Expense   *Account No. 506*

Date		Explanation	Post. Ref.	Debit	Credit	Balance
1994 Dec.	31	Balance				6 8 0 Dr.
	31	To close	G4		6 8 0	– 0 –

Salaries Expense   *Account No. 507*

Date		Explanation	Post. Ref.	Debit	Credit	Balance
1994 Dec.	31	Balance				3 6 0 0 Dr.
	31	Adjustment	G3	1 8 0		3 7 8 0 Dr.
	31	To close	G4		3 7 8 0	– 0 –

Utilities Expense   *Account No. 511*

Date		Explanation	Post. Ref.	Debit	Credit	Balance
1994 Dec.	31	Balance				1 5 0 Dr.
	31	To close	G4		1 5 0	– 0 –

Insurance Expense   *Account No. 512*

Date		Explanation	Post. Ref.	Debit	Credit	Balance
1994 Dec.	31	Balance				– 0 –
	31	Adjustment	G3	2 0 0		2 0 0 Dr.
	31	To close	G4		2 0 0	– 0 –

GENERAL LEDGER *(concluded)*

Rent Expense   *Account No. 515*

Date		Explanation	Post. Ref.	Debit	Credit	Balance
1994 Dec.	31	Balance				– 0 –
	31	Adjustment	G3	4 0 0		4 0 0 Dr.
	31	To close	G4		4 0 0	– 0 –

Supplies Expense   *Account No. 518*

Date		Explanation	Post. Ref.	Debit	Credit	Balance
1994 Dec.	31	Balance				– 0 –
	31	Adjustment	G3	5 0 0		5 0 0 Dr.
	31	To close	G4		5 0 0	– 0 –

Depreciation Expense—Trucks   *Account No. 521*

Date		Explanation	Post. Ref.	Debit	Credit	Balance
1994 Dec.	31	Balance				– 0 –
	31	Adjustment	G3	7 5 0		7 5 0 Dr.
	31	To close	G4		7 5 0	– 0 –

Income Summary   *Account No. 600*

Date		Explanation	Post. Ref.	Debit	Credit	Balance
1994 Dec.	31	Balance				– 0 –
	31	Revenue	G4		1 3 8 0 0	1 3 8 0 0 Cr.
	31	Expenses	G4	6 5 1 0		7 2 9 0 Cr.
	31	To close	G4	7 2 9 0		– 0 –

As each of Speedy Delivery's expense and revenue accounts is closed, its balance is reduced to zero. The balances formerly in those accounts are transferred to the Income Summary account. Note that the Income Summary account shows clearly the net income for the period—the final amount transferred, or closed, to the Retained Earnings account. Then, the Dividends account is closed to Retained Earnings. The balance in the Retained Earnings account of $4,290 is the amount of retained earnings shown in the balance sheet for December 31, 1994.

DEMONSTRATION PROBLEM

The demonstration problems for Chapters 1 and 2 used information for Green Hills Riding Stable, Incorporated, to illustrate concepts. Financial statements were prepared without benefit of a work sheet. This problem illustrates the use of a work sheet for Green Hills Riding Stable for the month ended July 31, 1994. The closing process is also illustrated. The trial balance for Green Hills Riding Stable, Incorporated, as of July 31, 1994, was as follows:

GREEN HILLS RIDING STABLE, INCORPORATED
Trial Balance
July 31, 1994

Acct. No.	Account Title	Debits	Credits
100	Cash	$ 9,700	
103	Accounts Receivable.	8,100	
130	Land	40,000	
140	Buildings	24,000	
200	Accounts Payable		$ 1,100
201	Notes Payable.		40,000
300	Capital Stock		35,000
310	Retained Earnings, July 1.		2,100
320	Dividends.	1,000	
402	Horse Boarding Fees Revenue		4,500
404	Riding and Lesson Fees Revenue		3,600
507	Salaries Expense	1,400	
513	Feed Expense.	1,100	
540	Interest Expense	200	
568	Miscellaneous Expense	800	
		$86,300	$86,300

Additional data

Depreciation expense for the month is $200. Accrued salaries on July 31 are $300.

Required   *a.*   Prepare a 12-column work sheet for the month ended July 31, 1994.

                 b.   Journalize the adjusting entries.

                 c.   Journalize the closing entries.

SOLUTION TO DEMONSTRATION PROBLEM

      a.   See the work sheet on page 178.

GREEN HILLS RIDING STABLE, INCORPORATED
Work Sheet
For the Month Ended July 31, 1994

Acct. No.	Account Titles	Trial Balance Debit	Trial Balance Credit	Adjustments Debit	Adjustments Credit	Adjusted Trial Balance Debit	Adjusted Trial Balance Credit	Income Statement Debit	Income Statement Credit	Statement of Retained Earnings Debit	Statement of Retained Earnings Credit	Balance Sheet Debit	Balance Sheet Credit
100	Cash	10,700				10,700						10,700	
103	Accounts Receivable	8,100				8,100						8,100	
130	Land	40,000				40,000						40,000	
140	Buildings	24,000				24,000						24,000	
200	Accounts Payable		1,100				1,100						1,100
201	Notes Payable		40,000				40,000						40,000
300	Capital Stock		35,000				35,000						35,000
310	Retained Earnings, July 1, 1994		3,100				3,100				3,100		
320	Dividends	1,000				1,000				1,000			
402	Horse Boarding Fees Revenue		4,500				4,500		4,500				
404	Riding and Lesson Fees Revenue		3,600				3,600		3,600				
507	Salaries Expense	1,400		(2) 300		1,700		1,700					
513	Feed Expense	1,100				1,100		1,100					
540	Interest Expense	200				200		200					
568	Miscellaneous Expense	800				800		800					
		87,300	87,300										
520	Depreciation Expense—Buildings			(1) 200		200		200					
141	Accumulated Depreciation—Buildings				(1) 200		200						200
206	Salaries Payable				(2) 300		300						300
				500	500	87,800	87,800						
								4,000	8,100			82,800	76,600
	Net Income							4,100			4,100		
								8,100	8,100	1,000	7,200		6,200
	Retained Earnings, July 31, 1994									6,200			
										7,200	7,200	82,800	82,800

Adjustments:
(1) To record depreciation of building for July.
(2) To record accrued salaries of $300.

b.

GREEN HILLS RIDING STABLE, INCORPORATED
GENERAL JOURNAL

Page 4

Date		Account Titles and Explanation	Post. Ref.	Debit	Credit
1994		**Adjusting Entries**			
July	31	Depreciation Expense—Buildings	520	2 0 0	
		Accumulated Depreciation—Buildings	141		2 0 0
		To record depreciation expense.			
	31	Salaries Expense	507	3 0 0	
		Salaries Payable	206		3 0 0
		To record accrued salaries.			

c.

GREEN HILLS RIDING STABLE, INCORPORATED
GENERAL JOURNAL

Page 4

Date		Account Titles and Explanation	Post. Ref.	Debit	Credit
1994		**Closing Entries**			
July	31	Horse Boarding Fees Revenue	402	4 5 0 0	
		Riding and Lesson Fees Revenue	404	3 6 0 0	
		Income Summary	600		8 1 0 0
		To close revenue accounts.			
	31	Income Summary	600	4 0 0 0	
		Salaries Expense	507		1 7 0 0
		Feed Expense	513		1 1 0 0
		Interest Expense	540		2 0 0
		Miscellaneous Expense	568		8 0 0
		Depreciation Expense—Buildings	520		2 0 0
		To close expense accounts.			
	31	Income Summary	600	4 1 0 0	
		Retained Earnings	310		4 1 0 0
		To close Income Summary account.			
	31	Retained Earnings	300	1 0 0 0	
		Dividends	320		1 0 0 0
		To close Dividends account.			

NEW TERMS*

Accounting cycle Series of steps performed during the accounting period to analyze, record, classify, summarize, and report useful financial information for the purpose of preparing financial statements. The steps include analyzing transactions, journalizing transactions, posting journal entries, taking a trial balance and completing the work sheet, preparing financial statements, journalizing and posting adjusting entries, journalizing and posting closing entries, and taking a post-closing trial balance. *146*

Accounts payable Amounts owed to suppliers for goods or services purchased on credit. *166*

Accounts receivable Amounts due from customers for services performed or merchandise sold on credit. *165*

Bonds payable Written promises to pay a definite sum at a certain date as evidenced by formal printed certificates that are sometimes secured by liens on property, such as mortgages. *167*

Buildings Structures used to carry on the business. *166*

Capital stock Shows the capital paid in to the company as the owners' investment. *168*

Cash Includes deposits in banks available for current operations at the balance sheet date plus cash on hand consisting of currency, undeposited checks, drafts, and money orders. *163*

Classified balance sheet Subdivides the three major balance sheet categories (assets, liabilities, and stockholders' equity) to provide more information for users of financial statements. Assets may be divided into current assets; long-term investments; property, plant, and equipment; and intangible assets. Liabilities may be divided into current liabilities and long-term liabilities. *162*

Closing process The act of transferring the balances in the revenue and expense accounts to a clearing account called *Income Summary* and then to the Retained Earnings account. The balance in the Dividends account is also transferred to the Retained Earnings account. *155*

Copyright Grants the owner the exclusive privilege of publication of written material for a period of time. *166*

Current assets Cash and other assets that a business will convert into cash or use up in a relatively short period of time, one year or one operating cycle, whichever is longer. *163*

Current liabilities Debts due within one year or one operating cycle, whichever is longer. The payment of current liabilities normally will require the use of current assets. *166*

Dividends payable Amounts declared payable to stockholders and that represent a distribution of income. *167*

Goodwill An intangible value attached to a business evidenced by the ability to earn larger net income per dollar of investment than that earned by competitors in the same industry. *166*

Income Summary account A clearing account used only at the end of an accounting period to summarize revenues and expenses for the period. *155*

Intangible assets Noncurrent, nonmonetary, nonphysical assets of a business. *166*

Interest payable Interest that has accumulated on debts, such as notes or bonds. This accrued interest has not yet been paid at the balance sheet date because the amount is not due until later. *167*

Interest receivable Arises when interest has been earned but not collected at the balance sheet date. *165*

Land Ground the company uses for business operations. Land could include ground on which the company locates its business buildings and that used for outside storage space or a parking lot. *166*

Leaseholds Rights to use rented properties. *166*

Long-term assets Assets that will be on hand or will be used by a business for a relatively long period of time. Examples include long-term investments; property, plant, and equipment, and intangible assets. *165*

Long-term investment Usually securities of another company held with the intention of (*a*) obtaining control of another company, (*b*) securing a permanent source of income for the investor, or (*c*) establishing friendly business relations. *165*

Long-term liabilities Debts such as a mortgage payable and bonds payable that are not due for a relatively long period of time, usually more than one year. *167*

Marketable securities Temporary investments that a company makes to earn a return on idle cash. *165*

Note An unconditional written promise to pay to another party the amount owed either when demanded or at a certain date. *165*

Notes payable Unconditional written promises by a company to pay a certain sum of money at a certain or determinable future date. *166*

Office equipment Includes items such as typewriters, computers, copiers, FAX machines, and phone answering machines. *166*

Operating cycle The time it takes to start with cash, buy necessary items to produce revenues (such as materials, supplies, labor, and/or inventories), sell services or goods, and receive cash by collecting the resulting receivables. *163*

Patent A right granted by the federal government to the owner of an invention whereby he or she alone has the authority to manufacture a product or to use a process for a period of time. *166*

Post-closing trial balance A trial balance taken after the closing entries have been posted. *162*

---

* Some of these terms have been defined in earlier chapters but are included here for your convenience.

Prepaid expenses   Assets awaiting assignment to expense. Items such as rent, insurance, and supplies that have been paid for but from which all of the benefits have not yet been realized (or consumed). Prepaid expenses are classified as current assets. *165*

Property, plant, and equipment   Assets with useful lives of over one year that a company acquired for use in a business rather than for resale; also called *plant assets* or *fixed assets*. *165*

Retained earnings   Shows the cumulative income of the company less the amounts distributed to the owners in the form of dividends. *168*

Reversing entries   Reverse the effects of the adjusting entries to which they relate. They are made on the first day of the next accounting period. Their purpose is to simplify the recording of subsequent transactions relating to those same items. Reversing entries may only be used for certain types of adjusting entries—usually those accruals where cash is to be paid or received in the next accounting period. *169*

Salaries payable   Amounts owed to employees for services rendered. *166*

Statement of retained earnings   A financial statement that summarizes the transactions affecting the Retained Earnings account balance. *152*

Stockholders' equity   Shows the owners' interest (equity) in the business. *168*

Taxes withheld from employees   Items such as federal income taxes, state income taxes, and social security taxes withheld from employees' paychecks. *166*

Unclassified balance sheet   A balance sheet showing only three major categories: assets, liabilities, and stockholders' equity. *162*

Unearned revenues (revenues received in advance)   Result when payment is received for goods or services before revenue has been earned. *167*

Work sheet   A columnar sheet of paper on which accountants have summarized information needed to make the adjusting and closing entries and to prepare the financial statements. *147*

SELF-TEST

True-False

Indicate whether each of the following statements is true or false.

1. All of the steps in the accounting cycle are performed only at the end of the accounting period.
2. At the end of the accounting period, three trial balances are prepared.
3. The amounts in the Adjustments columns are always added to the amounts in the Trial Balance columns to determine the amounts in the Adjusted Trial Balance columns.
4. If a net loss occurs, it appears in the Income Statement credit column and Statement of Retained Earnings debit column.
5. After the closing process is complete, no balance can exist in any revenue, expense, Dividends, or Income Summary account.
6. The post-closing trial balance may contain revenue and expense accounts.

Multiple-Choice

Select the best answer for each of the following questions.

1. Which of the following accounts is *least* likely to be adjusted on the work sheet?
   a. Supplies on Hand.
   b. Cash.
   c. Prepaid Rent.
   d. Unearned Delivery Fees.
2. If the Balance Sheet columns do not balance, the error is most likely to exist in the:
   a. General journal.
   b. General ledger.
   c. Last six columns of the work sheet.
   d. First six columns of the work sheet.
3. Net income for a period will appear in all but which one of the following?
   a. Income Statement debit column of the work sheet.
   b. Statement of Retained Earnings credit column of the work sheet.
   c. Statement of retained earnings.
   d. Balance sheet.
4. Which of the following statements is *false* regarding the closing process?
   a. The Dividends account is closed to Income Summary.
   b. The closing of expense accounts results in a debit to Income Summary.
   c. The closing of revenues results in a credit to Income Summary.
   d. The Income Summary account is closed to the Retained Earnings account.
5. Which of the following statements is *true* regarding the classified balance sheet?
   a. Current assets include cash, accounts receivable, and equipment.
   b. "Plant, property, and equipment" is one category of long-term assets.
   c. Current liabilities include accounts payable, salaries payable, and notes receivable.
   d. Stockholders' equity is subdivided into current and long-term categories.

Now turn to page 196 to check your answers.

QUESTIONS

1. Which of the steps in the accounting cycle are performed throughout the accounting period?

2. Which of the steps in the accounting cycle are performed only at the end of the accounting period?

3. At what stage of the accounting cycle is a work sheet usually prepared?

4. Why are the financial statements prepared before the adjusting and closing entries are journalized and posted?

5. Describe the purposes for which the work sheet is prepared.

6. You have taken over a set of accounting books for a small business as a part-time job. At the end of the first accounting period, you have partially completed the work sheet by entering the proper ledger accounts and balances in the Trial Balance columns. You turn to the manager and ask, "Where is the list of additional information I can use in entering the adjusting entries?" The manager indicates there is no such list. (In all the text problems you have done, you have always been given this information.) How would you obtain the information for this real-life situation? What are the consequences of not making all of the required adjustments at the end of the accounting period?

7. How are the amounts in the Adjusted Trial Balance columns of a work sheet determined?

8. The work sheet for Bridges Company contains only the following four adjustments in its Adjustments columns:

   1. Expiration of insurance, $1,200.
   2. Depreciation of equipment, $4,000.
   3. Depreciation of building, $10,000.
   4. Salaries accrued, $3,000.

   The Trial Balance columns show totals of $1,600,000. What are the totals of the Adjusted Trial Balance columns?

9. After the Adjusted Trial Balance columns of a work sheet have been totaled, which account balances are extended to the Income Statement columns, which account balances are extended to the Retained Earnings columns, and which account balances are extended to the Balance Sheet columns?

10. How is the statement of retained earnings prepared?

11. What is the purpose of closing entries? What accounts are not affected by closing entries?

12. A company has net income of $5,000 for the year. In which columns of the work sheet would net income appear?

13. Is it possible to prepare monthly financial statements without journalizing and posting adjusting and closing entries? How?

14. What is the purpose of a post-closing trial balance?

15. How is a classified balance sheet different than an unclassified balance sheet?

16. *(Based on Appendix 4–A)*   To what kind of entries do reversing entries relate? On what date are reversing entries made?

17. *Real world question*   Refer to "A Broader Perspective" on page 161. Then answer the following true-false questions.
    a. The same skills are needed at each level in a CPA firm.
    b. The two most important traits at the staff accountant level are a positive attitude and the ability to learn quickly while adapting to unfamiliar situations.
    c. The senior accountant needs management skills in addition to technical skills.
    d. Partners become increasingly involved in technical matters and have less and less interaction with people.

18. *Real world question*   Referring to Appendix E at the end of the text, identify the classifications (or categories) of assets used by The Coca-Cola Company, Maytag Corporation, The Limited, Inc., and John H. Harland Company in their respective balance sheets.

19. *Real world question*   Referring to Appendix E at the end of the text, identify the classifications (or categories) of liabilities used by The Coca-Cola Company, Maytag Corporation, The Limited, Inc., and John H. Harland Company in their respective balance sheets.

EXERCISES

Exercise 4–1

Identify the steps in the accounting cycle
(L.O. 1)

List the steps in the accounting cycle. Would the system still work if any of the steps were performed "out of order"?

Exercise 4–2

Determine where items would appear in work sheet

(L.O. 2)

Three of the major column headings on a work sheet are Trial Balance, Income Statement, and Balance Sheet. For each of the following items, determine under which major column heading it would appear and whether it would be a debit or credit. (For example, Cash would appear under the debit side of the Trial Balance Sheet columns.)

	Trial Balance		Income Statement		Balance Sheet	
	Debit	Credit	Debit	Credit	Debit	Credit
a. Accounts Receivable						
b. Accounts Payable						
c. Interest Revenue						
d. Advertising Expense						
e. Capital Stock						
f. Fees Earned						
g. Net income for the month						

Exercise 4–3

Determine where items would appear in work sheet (L.O. 2)

Assume a beginning balance in Retained Earnings of $42,000 and net income for the year of $18,000. Illustrate how these would appear in the Statement of Retained Earnings columns and Balance Sheet columns in the work sheet.

Exercise 4–4

Determine where items would appear in work sheet (L.O. 2)

In Exercise 4–3, if there were a debit balance of $108,000 in the Retained Earnings account as of the beginning of the year and a net loss of $96,000 for the year, show how these would be treated in the work sheet.

Exercise 4–5

Find cause of Balance Sheet columns not in balance (L.O. 2)

Richard Kelley was preparing the work sheet for Hayes Company. He calculated the net income to be $26,000. When he totaled the Balance Sheet columns, the column totals were debit, $241,800; and credit, $189,800. What was the probable cause of this difference? If this was not the cause, what should he do to find the error?

Exercise 4–6

Prepare work sheet (L.O. 2)

The Trial Balance of the Higgins Company at December 31, 1994, contains the following account balances (the accounts are listed in alphabetical order to increase your skill in sorting amounts to the proper work sheet columns).

HIGGINS COMPANY
Trial Balance Account Balances
December 31, 1994

Accounts Payable.	$ 21,000
Accounts Receivable	92,000
Accumulated Depreciation—Buildings.	25,000
Accumulated Depreciation—Equipment	9,000
Buildings	140,000
Capital Stock.	65,000
Cash	30,000
Equipment.	36,000
Prepaid Insurance	3,600
Retained Earnings	4,800
Salaries Expense	96,000
Service Revenue	280,000
Supplies on Hand.	4,000
Utilities Expense	3,200

Using the account balances given above and the additional information presented below, prepare a work sheet for Higgins Company. Arrange the accounts in their approximate usual order.

Additional data

1. Supplies on hand at December 31, 1994, have a cost of $1,200.
2. The balance in the Prepaid Insurance account represents the cost of a two-year insurance policy covering the period from January 1, 1994, through December 31, 1995.
3. Estimated lives of depreciable assets are buildings, 40 years; and equipment, 20 years. No salvage values are anticipated.

Exercise 4–7

Prepare statement of retained earnings (L.O. 3)

Cambry Corporation had a January 1, 1994, balance in its Retained Earnings account of $40,000. During 1994, net income was $25,000 and dividends paid were $12,000. Prepare a statement of retained earnings for the year ended December 31, 1994.

Exercise 4–8

Prepare adjusting and closing entries (L.O. 4)

Refer to the work sheet prepared in Exercise 4–6. Prepare the adjusting and closing journal entries.

Exercise 4–9

Prepare adjusting entries and determine correct net income (L.O. 4)

Rinaldo Company reports net income of $200,000 for the current year. Examination of the work sheet and supporting data indicates that the following items were ignored:

1. Accrued salaries were $12,000 at December 31.
2. Depreciation on equipment acquired on July 1 amounted to $16,000.

Based on the above information, *(a)* what adjusting journal entries should have been made at December 31, and *(b)* what is the correct net income?

Exercise 4–10

Post to Income Summary account from Income Statement column totals (L.O. 4)

The Income Statement column totals on a work sheet prepared at December 31, 1994, are debit, $640,000; and credit, $800,000. In T-account format, show how the postings to the Income Summary account would appear as a result of the closing process. Identify what each posting represents.

Exercise 4–11

Show how closing entries would be posted to T-accounts (L.O. 4)

After adjustment, selected account balances of Misty Campground are:

	Debits	Credits
Retained Earnings		$320,000
Rental Revenue		480,000
Salaries Expense	$168,000	
Depreciation Expense—Buildings	32,000	
Utilities Expense	104,000	
Dividends	16,000	

In T-account format, show how journal entries to close the books for the period would be posted. You do not need to show the closing journal entries. Enter the above balances in the accounts before doing so. Key the postings from the first closing entry with the number (1), the second with the number (2), and so on.

Exercise 4–12

Prepare closing journal entries (L.O. 4)

After adjustment, selected account balances of Keller Corporation are:

	Debits	Credits
Service Revenue		$160,000
Commissions Expense	$84,000	
Advertising Expense	16,000	
Salaries Expense	52,000	

Give the journal entries required to close the books for the period.

Exercise 4–13

Prepare closing journal entries

(L.O. 4)

The following account balances appeared in the Income Statement columns of the work sheet prepared for Knox Company for the year ended December 31, 1994:

	Income Statement	
	Debit	Credit
Service Revenue		337,500
Advertising Expense.	1,350	
Salaries Expense	123,750	
Utilities Expense	2,250	
Insurance Expense	900	
Rent Expense	6,750	
Supplies Expense	2,250	
Depreciation Expense—Equipment	4,500	
Interest Expense	562	
Interest Revenue		1,125
	142,312	338,625
Net Income	196,313	
	338,625	338,625

Prepare the closing journal entries.

Exercise 4–14

Identify accounts in post-closing trial balance

(L.O. 5)

Which of the following accounts are likely to appear in the post-closing trial balance for the Blake Company?

1. Accounts Receivable.
2. Cash.
3. Service Revenue.
4. Buildings.
5. Salaries Expense.
6. Capital Stock.
7. Dividends.
8. Accounts Payable.
9. Income Summary.
10. Unearned Subscriptions Revenue.

Exercise 4–15

Classify items for balance sheet

(L.O. 6)

Using the legend at the right, determine the category (number) into which each item below would be placed.

Item	Legend
_____ *a.* Land.	1. Current assets.
_____ *b.* Marketable securities.	2. Long-term investments.
_____ *c.* Notes payable, due in three years.	3. Property, plant, and equipment.
_____ *d.* Taxes withheld from employees.	4. Intangible assets.
_____ *e.* Patents.	5. Current liabilities.
_____ *f.* Retained earnings.	6. Long-term liabilities.
_____ *g.* Unearned subscriptions revenue.	7. Stockholders' equity.
_____ *h.* Bonds of another corporation (an investment).	
_____ *i.* Notes payable, due in six months.	
_____ *j.* Accumulated depreciation.	

Exercise 4–16

Show entries for salaries if (1) no reversing entry is used and (2) reversing entry is used (L.O. 7)

(Based on Appendix 4–A)   Assume that an adjusting entry made on December 31, 1993, was as follows:

1993				
Dec.	31	Salaries Expense	9,600	
		Salaries Payable		9,600
		To accrue salaries for last four days of December.		

Show how a January 2, 1994, payment of $14,400 of salaries would be recorded, assuming (1) no reversing entry is used and (2) a reversing entry is used on January 1, 1994 (show this entry also). Then show by the use of T-accounts that the end result is the same whether or not a reversing entry is used.

PROBLEMS: SERIES A

Problem 4–1A

Prepare closing entries (L.O. 4)

Given below is the adjusted trial balance of Kwik Repair Company:

KWIK REPAIR COMPANY
Adjusted Trial Balance
June 30, 1994

	Debits	Credits
Cash.	$ 13,000	
Accounts Receivable	42,000	
Office Equipment	110,000	
Accumulated Depreciation—Office Equipment		$ 30,000
Accounts Payable		10,800
Notes Payable		20,000
Capital Stock		50,000
Retained Earnings, June 30, 1993.		5,500
Dividends	10,000	
Service Revenue		180,000
Rent Expense	12,000	
Advertising Expense.	5,000	
Salaries Expense	90,000	
Supplies Expense	1,500	
Insurance Expense	1,200	
Depreciation Expense—Office Equipment	10,000	
Interest Expense	1,000	
Miscellaneous Expense	600	
	$296,300	$296,300

Required   Prepare the closing journal entries at the end of the fiscal year, June 30, 1994.

Problem 4–2A

Prepare income
statement, statement of
retained earnings,
classified balance sheet,
closing entries, and
post-closing trial balance
(L.O. 3–6)

The adjusted trial balance for Cepeda Company follows.

CEPEDA COMPANY
Adjusted Trial Balance
December 31, 1994

	Debits	Credits
Cash.	$ 30,000	
Accounts Receivable	20,000	
Interest Receivable	200	
Notes Receivable	4,000	
Prepaid Insurance	960	
Prepaid Rent	2,400	
Supplies on Hand	600	
Equipment	60,000	
Accumulated Depreciation—Equipment		$ 12,500
Buildings	140,000	
Accumulated Depreciation—Buildings		15,000
Land	56,240	
Accounts Payable		60,000
Notes Payable		10,000
Interest Payable		750
Salaries Payable		7,000
Capital Stock		100,000
Retained Earnings, January 1, 1994		20,200
Dividends	40,000	
Service Revenue		300,000
Insurance Expense	1,920	
Rent Expense	9,600	
Advertising Expense	1,200	
Depreciation Expense—Equipment	2,500	
Depreciation Expense—Buildings	3,000	
Supplies Expense	2,280	
Salaries Expense	150,000	
Interest Expense	750	
Interest Revenue		200
	$525,650	$525,650

Required

a. Prepare an income statement.

b. Prepare a statement of retained earnings.

c. Prepare a classified balance sheet.

d. Prepare the closing journal entries.

e. Prepare a post-closing trial balance.

Problem 4–3A

Prepare work sheet, adjusting entries, and closing entries (L.O. 2, 4)

The following trial balance and additional data are for Lynch Realty Company:

LYNCH REALTY COMPANY
Trial Balance
December 31, 1994

	Debits	Credits
Cash.	$ 52,800	
Accounts Receivable	117,120	
Prepaid Rent	46,080	
Equipment	173,760	
Accumulated Depreciation—Equipment		$ 21,120
Accounts Payable		62,400
Capital Stock		96,000
Retained Earnings, January 1, 1994		49,920
Dividends	46,080	
Commissions Revenue		643,200
Salaries Expense	321,600	
Travel Expense	96,480	
Miscellaneous Expense	18,720	
	$872,640	$872,640

Additional data

1. The prepaid rent is for the period July 1, 1994, to June 30, 1995.
2. The equipment has an expected life of 10 years with no salvage value.
3. Accrued salaries are $11,520.
4. Travel expenses accrued but unreimbursed at December 31 were $17,280.

Required

a. Prepare a 12-column work sheet for the year ended December 31, 1994. You need not include account numbers or explanations of adjustments.

b. Prepare adjusting journal entries.

c. Prepare closing journal entries.

Problem 4–4A

Prepare work sheet, adjusting entries, and closing entries (L.O. 2, 4)

The following trial balance and additional data are for Martin Company:

MARTIN COMPANY
Trial Balance
December 31, 1994

	Debits	Credits
Cash.	$ 75,000	
Accounts Receivable	120,000	
Notes Receivable	15,000	
Prepaid Insurance	9,000	
Supplies on Hand	6,000	
Buildings	240,000	
Accumulated Depreciation—Buildings		$120,000
Equipment	90,000	
Accumulated Depreciation—Equipment		60,000
Accounts Payable		30,000
Capital Stock		90,000
Retained Earnings, January 1, 1994		31,500
Dividends	54,000	
Service Revenue		480,000
Salaries Expense	180,000	
Advertising Expense	8,400	
Utilities Expense	12,000	
Miscellaneous Expense	2,100	
	$811,500	$811,500

Additional data

1. Accrued interest on notes receivable is $752.
2. Insurance expense for the year is $7,200.
3. A physical inventory shows that supplies costing $1,200 are on hand at December 31, 1994.
4. The building has an expected life of 10 years with no salvage value.
5. The equipment has an expected life of 12 years with no salvage value.
6. Accrued salaries are $12,000.

Required *a.* Prepare a 12-column work sheet for the year ended December 31, 1994. You need not include account numbers or explanations of adjustments.

b. Prepare adjusting journal entries.

c. Prepare closing journal entries.

Problem 4–5A

Prepare work sheet and closing entries
(L.O. 2, 4)

The following trial balance and additional data are for Miles Company:

MILES COMPANY
Trial Balance
December 31, 1994

	Debits	Credits
Cash.	$109,050	
Accounts Receivable	123,750	
Notes Receivable	11,250	
Land.	90,000	
Buildings.	165,000	
Accumulated Depreciation—Buildings		$ 49,500
Store Fixtures	83,400	
Accumulated Depreciation—Store Fixtures.		16,680
Accounts Payable.		56,850
Notes Payable		75,000
Capital Stock.		240,000
Retained Earnings, January 1, 1994.		47,820
Dividends	30,000	
Service Revenue		358,350
Salaries Expense	96,000	
Advertising Expense.	18,000	
Travel Expense.	111,000	
Insurance Expense	4,350	
Interest Revenue		600
Interest Expense	3,000	
	$844,800	$844,800

The company consistently followed the policy of initially debiting all prepaid items to expense accounts.

Additional data

1. The buildings have an expected life of 50 years with no salvage value.
2. The store fixtures have an expected life of 10 years with no salvage value.
3. Accrued interest on notes receivable is $450.
4. Accrued interest on the notes payable is $750.
5. Accrued salaries are $2,100.
6. Prepaid insurance is $600.
7. Prepaid advertising is $1,500.

Required *a.* Prepare a 12-column work sheet for the year ended December 31, 1994. You need not include account numbers. Briefly explain the entries in the Adjustments columns at the bottom of the work sheet, as was done in Illustration 4.3.

b. Prepare the required closing entries.

Problem 4–6A
Prepare work sheet,
income statement,
statement of retained
earnings, classified
balance sheet, and
adjusting and closing
entries
(L.O. 2–6)

The following trial balance and additional data are for Time-Share Property Management Company:

TIME-SHARE PROPERTY MANAGEMENT COMPANY
Trial Balance
December 31, 1994

	Debits	Credits
Cash	$304,000	
Prepaid Rent	28,800	
Prepaid Insurance	7,680	
Office Equipment	24,000	
Accumulated Depreciation—Office Equipment		$ 5,760
Automobiles	64,000	
Accumulated Depreciation—Automobiles		16,000
Accounts Payable		2,880
Unearned Management Fees		12,480
Capital Stock		320,000
Retained Earnings		20,640
Dividends	28,000	
Commissions Revenue		240,000
Management Fee Revenue		19,200
Salaries Expense	159,840	
Advertising Expense	2,400	
Gas and Oil Expense	14,240	
Supplies Expense	2,400	
Miscellaneous Expense	1,600	
	$636,960	$636,960

Additional data

1. Insurance expense for the year, $3,840.
2. Rent expense for the year, $19,200.
3. Depreciation expense: office equipment, $2,880; and automobiles, $12,800.
4. Salaries earned but unpaid at December 31, $26,640.
5. Supplies on hand at December 31, $800.
6. The unearned management fees were received and recorded on November 1, 1994. The advance payment covered six months' management of an apartment building.

Required a. Prepare a 12-column work sheet for the year ended December 31, 1994. You need not include account numbers or explanations of adjustments.
b. Prepare an income statement.
c. Prepare a statement of retained earnings.
d. Prepare a classified balance sheet.
e. Prepare adjusting and closing entries.

PROBLEMS: SERIES B

Problem 4–1B

Prepare closing entries
(L.O. 4)

Given below is the adjusted trial balance of Moore Company:

MOORE COMPANY
Adjusted Trial Balance
June 30, 1994

	Debits	Credits
Cash.	$ 48,000	
Accounts Receivable	40,000	
Office Equipment	35,000	
Accumulated Depreciation—Office Equipment		$ 14,000
Automobiles	40,000	
Accumulated Depreciation—Automobiles		20,000
Accounts Payable		53,000
Capital Stock		75,000
Retained Earnings, June 30, 1993.		14,700
Dividends	5,000	
Commissions Revenue		130,000
Salaries Expense	25,000	
Commissions Expense.	90,000	
Gas and Oil Expense	4,000	
Rent Expense	4,800	
Supplies Expense	1,400	
Utilities Expense	2,000	
Depreciation Expense—Office Equipment	3,500	
Depreciation Expense—Automobiles	8,000	
	$306,700	$306,700

Required   Prepare the closing journal entries at the end of the fiscal year, June 30, 1994.

Problem 4–2B

Prepare income
statement, statement of
retained earnings,
classified balance sheet,
closing entries, and
post-closing trial balance
(L.O. 3–6)

The adjusted trial balance for Murphy Company follows:

MURPHY COMPANY
Adjusted Trial Balance
December 31, 1994

	Debits	Credits
Cash	$117,200	
Accounts Receivable	48,000	
Interest Receivable	400	
Notes Receivable	20,000	
Prepaid Insurance	2,400	
Supplies on Hand	1,800	
Land	32,000	
Buildings	190,000	
Accumulated Depreciation—Buildings		$ 40,000
Office Equipment	28,000	
Accumulated Depreciation—Office Equipment		8,000
Accounts Payable		38,000
Salaries Payable		8,500
Interest Payable		900
Notes Payable (due 1995)		64,000
Capital Stock		120,000
Retained Earnings, January 1, 1994		42,800
Dividends	40,000	
Commissions Revenue		372,520
Advertising Expense	14,000	
Commissions Expense	75,440	
Travel Expense	12,880	
Depreciation Expense—Buildings	8,500	
Salaries Expense	88,400	
Depreciation Expense—Office Equipment	2,800	
Supplies Expense	3,800	
Insurance Expense	3,600	
Repairs Expense	1,900	
Utilities Expense	3,400	
Interest Expense	1,800	
Interest Revenue		1,600
	$696,320	$696,320

Required *a.* Prepare an income statement for the year ended December 31, 1994.

b. Prepare a statement of retained earnings.

c. Prepare a classified balance sheet.

d. Prepare the closing journal entries.

e. Prepare a post-closing trial balance.

Problem 4–3B

Prepare work sheet, adjusting entries, and closing entries (L.O. 2, 4)

The following trial balance and additional data are for Ortiz Company:

ORTIZ COMPANY
Trial Balance
December 31, 1994

	Debits	Credits
Cash.	$ 56,000	
Accounts Receivable	88,000	
Prepaid Rent	7,200	
Prepaid Insurance.	2,400	
Equipment	80,000	
Accumulated Depreciation—Equipment		$ 40,000
Accounts Payable.		30,000
Capital Stock		100,000
Retained Earnings, January 1, 1994		35,600
Dividends	24,000	
Service Revenue		350,000
Commissions Expense.	250,000	
Travel Expense	36,000	
Miscellaneous Expense	12,000	
	$555,600	$555,600

Additional data

1. The prepaid rent is for the period January 1, 1994, to December 31, 1995.
2. The equipment is expected to last 10 years with no salvage value.
3. The prepaid insurance was for the period April 1, 1994, to March 31, 1995.
4. Accrued commissions payable total $3,000 at December 31.

Required *a.* Prepare a 12-column work sheet for the year ended December 31, 1994. You need not include account numbers or explanations of adjustments.

b. Prepare the adjusting journal entries.

c. Prepare the closing journal entries.

Problem 4–4B

Prepare work sheet, adjusting entries, and closing entries (L.O. 2, 4)

The following trial balance and additional data are for Same-Day Cleaning Service:

SAME-DAY CLEANING SERVICE
Trial Balance
December 31, 1994

	Debits	Credits
Cash.	$ 56,000	
Accounts Receivable	50,000	
Prepaid Insurance.	9,600	
Prepaid Rent	18,000	
Office Furniture.	20,000	
Accumulated Depreciation—Office Furniture		$ 7,000
Equipment	60,000	
Accumulated Depreciation—Equipment		17,500
Trucks.	150,000	
Accumulated Depreciation—Trucks		46,876
Accounts Payable.		24,000
Notes Payable		10,000
Capital Stock.		80,000
Retained Earnings, January 1, 1994		13,724
Dividends	60,000	
Service Revenue		480,000
Salaries Expense	220,000	
Gas and Oil Expense	6,000	
Supplies Expense	23,000	
Utilities Expense	6,000	
Interest Expense	500	
	$679,100	$679,100

Additional data

1. The balance in the Prepaid Insurance account represents the remaining cost of five-year insurance policy purchased on January 2, 1993. The account was last adjusted on December 31, 1993.

2. The balance in the Prepaid Rent account represents the amount paid on January 2, 1994, to cover rent for the period from January 1, 1994, through June 30, 1995.

3. The plant assets are being depreciated at the following annual amounts: office furniture, $2,000; equipment, $5,000; and trucks, $18,750.

4. Accrued interest on the note payable is $200.

5. Accrued salaries at December 31, 1994, are $6,000.

6. A physical inventory shows that $4,000 of supplies are on hand at December 31, 1994.

Required   *a.*   Prepare a 12-column work sheet for the year ended December 31, 1994. You need not include account numbers or explanations of adjustments.

b.   Prepare adjusting journal entries.

c.   Prepare closing journal entries.

Problem 4–5B

Prepare work sheet and closing entries
(L.O. 2, 4)

The following trial balance and additional data are for Powers Company:

POWERS COMPANY
Trial Balance
December 31, 1994

	Debits	Credits
Cash.	$ 26,490	
Accounts Receivable	54,390	
Notes Receivable	75,000	
Supplies on Hand	900	
Equipment	33,000	
Accumulated Depreciation—Equipment		$ 6,600
Accounts Payable		29,550
Notes Payable		9,000
Capital Stock		150,000
Retained Earnings, January 1, 1994		20,685
Service Revenue		179,010
Interest Revenue		375
Interest Expense	225	
Salaries Expense	142,200	
Advertising Expense.	29,250	
Supplies Expense	1,110	
Miscellaneous Expense	3,705	
Insurance Expense	1,800	
Legal and Accounting Expense	3,750	
Utilities Expense	1,800	
Rent Expense	21,600	
	$395,220	$395,220

The company consistently followed the policy of initially debiting all prepaid items to expense accounts.

Additional data

1. Prepaid fire insurance is $525.

2. Supplies on hand are $638.

3. Prepaid rent expense is $2,625.

4. The equipment is expected to last 10 years with no salvage value.

5. Accrued salaries are $2,625.

Required   *a.*   Prepare a 12-column work sheet for the year ended December 31, 1994. You need not include account numbers. Briefly explain the entries in the Adjustments columns at the bottom of the work sheet, as was done in Illustration 4.3.

b.   Prepare the December 31, 1994, closing entries.

Problem 4–6B

Prepare work sheet, income statement, statement of retained earnings, classified balance sheet, and adjusting and closing entries
(L.O. 2–6)

The following trial balance and additional data are for Rhodes Company:

RHODES COMPANY
Trial Balance
December 31, 1994

	Debits	Credits
Cash.	$ 55,400	
Accounts Receivable	61,600	
Supplies on Hand	4,000	
Prepaid Rent	12,240	
Prepaid Advertising	2,880	
Prepaid Insurance	4,400	
Office Equipment	7,600	
Accumulated Depreciation—Office Equipment		$ 2,760
Office Furniture	29,200	
Accumulated Depreciation—Office Furniture		8,280
Accounts Payable		25,200
Notes Payable (due 1995)		4,000
Capital Stock		80,000
Retained Earnings, January 1, 1994		22,400
Dividends	42,520	
Service Revenue		200,000
Salaries Expense	98,800	
Utilities Expense	20,000	
Miscellaneous Expense	4,000	
	$342,640	$342,640

Additional data

1. Supplies on hand at December 31, 1994, are $1,000.
2. Rent expense for 1994 is $10,608.
3. Advertising expense for 1994 is $2,304.
4. Insurance expense for 1994 is $2,400.
5. Depreciation expense is: office equipment, $912; and office furniture, $2,920.
6. Accrued interest on notes payable is $150.
7. Accrued salaries are $4,200.

Required   *a.*   Prepare a 12-column work sheet for the year ended December 31, 1994. You need not include account numbers or explanations of adjustments.

b.   Prepare an income statement.

c.   Prepare a statement of retained earnings.

d.   Prepare a classified balance sheet.

e.   Prepare adjusting and closing entries.

BUSINESS DECISION PROBLEM

Decision Problem 4–1

Prepare report on profitability of business
(L.O. 3)

Jane and Ronald Ryder met while both were employed in the interior trim and upholstery department of an auto manufacturer. After their marriage, they decided to earn some extra income by doing small jobs involving canvas, vinyl, and upholstered products. Their work was considered excellent, and at the urging of their customers, they decided to go into business for themselves, operating out of the basement of the house they owned. To do this, they invested $60,000 cash in their business. They spent $42,000 for a sewing machine (expected life is 10 years) and $6,000 for other miscellaneous tools and equipment (expected life is 5 years). They undertook only custom work, with the customers purchasing the required materials, so as to avoid stocking any inventory other than supplies. An advance deposit was generally required on all jobs.

The business seemed successful from the start, as the Ryders received orders from many customers. But they felt something was wrong. They worked hard and charged competitive prices. Yet there seemed to be barely enough cash available for withdrawal from the business to cover immediate personal needs. Summarized, the checkbook of the business for 1994, their second year of operations, shows:

Balance, January 1, 1994		$ 9,600
Cash received from customers:		
For work done in 1993	$ 18,000	
For work done in 1994	160,000	
For work to be done in 1995	24,000	202,000
		$211,600
Cash paid out:		
Two-year insurance policy dated January 1, 1994	$ 9,600	
Utilities	24,000	
Supplies	72,000	
Other expenses	36,000	
Taxes, including sales taxes	13,200	
Dividends	50,000	204,800
Balance, December 31, 1994		$ 6,800

The Ryders feel, considering how much they worked, that they should have earned more than the $50,000 they withdrew as dividends from their business. This is $15,000 less than their combined income when they were employed by the auto manufacturer. They are seriously considering giving up their business and going back to work for the auto manufacturer. They turn to you for advice. You discover the following:

1. Of the supplies purchased in 1994, $12,000 were used on jobs billed to customers in 1994; no supplies were used for any other work.

2. Work completed in 1994 and billed to customers for which cash had not yet been received by year-end amounted to $54,000.

Required   Prepare a written report for the Ryders, responding to their belief that their business is not sufficiently profitable. (Hint: Prepare an income statement for 1994 and include it in your report.)

ANSWERS TO SELF-TEST

True-False

1. *False.* Only the last five steps are performed at the end of the period. The first three steps are performed throughout the accounting period.

2. *True.* The three trial balances are: the (unadjusted) trial balance, the adjusted trial balance, and the post-closing trial balance. The first two trial balances appear on the work sheet.

3. *False.* If a debit-balance account (such as Prepaid Rent) is credited in the adjustment, the amount in the Adjustments columns is deducted from the amount in the Trial Balance columns to determine the amount for that item in the Adjusted Trial Balance columns.

4. *True.* The net loss appears in the Income Statement credit column to balance the Income Statement columns. Then the loss appears in the Statement of Retained Earnings debit column because it will reduce Retained Earnings.

5. *True.* All of these accounts are closed, or reduced to zero balances, as a result of the closing process.

6. *False.* All revenue and expense accounts have zero balances after closing.

Multiple-Choice

1. *b.* The other accounts are very likely to be adjusted. The Cash account would be adjusted only if an error has been made involving that account.

2. *c.* The Adjusted Trial Balance columns should balance before items are spread to the Income Statement, Statement of Retained Earnings, and Balance Sheet columns. Therefore, if the Balance Sheet columns do not balance, the error is likely to exist in the last six columns of the work sheet.

3. *d.* The net income for the period does not appear in the balance sheet. It does appear in all of the other places listed.

4. *a.* The dividends account is closed to the Retained Earnings account rather than to the Income Summary account.

5. *b.* "Plant, property, and equipment" is one of the long-term asset categories. Response *(a)* should not include equipment. Response *(c)* should not include notes receivable. Stockholders' equity is not subdivided into current and long-term categories.

COMPREHENSIVE REVIEW PROBLEM

Problem covers all steps in the accounting cycle covered in Chapters 1–4. Open ledger accounts and enter beginning balances. Journalize transactions and post to ledger accounts. Prepare work sheet, income statement, statement of retained earnings, classified balance sheet, adjusting and closing entries, and post-closing trial balance.

Taylor Delivery Service Company has the following chart of accounts:

Acct. No.	Account Title	Acct. No.	Account Title
100	Cash	310	Retained Earnings
103	Accounts Receivable	320	Dividends
107	Supplies on Hand	400	Service Revenue
108	Prepaid Insurance	507	Salaries Expense
112	Prepaid Rent	511	Utilities Expense
140	Buildings	512	Insurance Expense
141	Accumulated Depreciation—Buildings	515	Rent Expense
150	Trucks	518	Supplies Expense
151	Accumulated Depreciation—Trucks	520	Depreciation Expense—Buildings
200	Accounts Payable	521	Depreciation Expense—Trucks
206	Salaries Payable	568	Miscellaneous Expense
300	Capital Stock	600	Income Summary

The post-closing trial balance as of May 31, 1994, was as follows:

TAYLOR DELIVERY SERVICE COMPANY
Post-Closing Trial Balance
May 31, 1994

Acct. No.	Account Title	Debits	Credits
100	Cash	$ 20,000	
103	Accounts Receivable	30,000	
107	Supplies on Hand	14,000	
108	Prepaid Insurance	4,800	
112	Prepaid Rent	12,000	
140	Buildings	320,000	
141	Accumulated Depreciation—Buildings		$ 36,000
150	Trucks	80,000	
151	Accumulated Depreciation—Trucks		30,000
200	Accounts Payable		24,000
300	Capital Stock		300,000
310	Retained Earnings		90,800
		$480,800	$480,800

The transactions for June 1994 were as follows:

June 1 Performed delivery services for customers on account, $40,000.

       3 Paid dividends, $10,000.

       4 Purchased a $20,000 truck on account.

       7 Collected $22,000 of the accounts receivable.

       8 Paid $16,000 of the accounts payable.

     11 Purchased $4,000 of supplies on account. The asset account for supplies was debited.

     17 Performed delivery services for cash, $32,000.

     20 Paid the utilities bills for June, $1,200.

     23 Paid miscellaneous expenses for June, $600.

     28 Paid salaries of $28,000 for June.

Additional data

1. Depreciation expense on the buildings for June is $800.

2. Depreciation expense on the trucks for June is $400.

3. Accrued salaries at June 30 are $2,000.

4. A physical count showed that there are $12,000 of supplies on hand on June 30.

5. The prepaid insurance balance of $4,800 applies to a two-year period beginning June 1, 1994.

6. The prepaid rent of $12,000 applies to a one-year period beginning June 1, 1994.

7. Performed $12,000 of delivery services for customers as of June 30 that will not be billed to those customers until July.

Required *a.* Open three-column ledger accounts for the accounts listed in the chart of accounts.

b. Enter the May 31, 1994, account balances in the accounts.

c. Journalize the transactions for June 1994.

d. Post the June journal entries and include cross-references (assume all journal entries appear on page 10 of the journal).

e. Prepare a 12-column work sheet as of June 30, 1994.

f. Prepare an income statement, a statement of retained earnings, and a classified balance sheet.

g. Prepare and post the adjusting entries (assume they appear on page 11 of the general journal).

h. Prepare and post the closing entries (assume they appear on page 12 of the general journal).

i. Prepare a post-closing trial balance.

5

MERCHANDISING TRANSACTIONS, INTRODUCTION TO INVENTORIES, AND CLASSIFIED INCOME STATEMENT

After studying this chapter, you should be able to:

1. Record journal entries for sales transactions involving merchandise.
2. Describe briefly cost of goods sold and the distinction between perpetual and periodic inventory procedures.
3. Record journal entries for purchase transactions involving merchandise.
4. Describe the freight terms and record transportation costs.
5. Determine cost of goods sold.
6. Prepare a classified income statement.
7. Prepare a work sheet and closing entries for a merchandising company.

In the first four chapters, you learned about the accounting process and how it begins with the recording of business transactions and results in the preparation of financial statements. As you studied the accounting process, you followed step by step the business transactions of a service company—Speedy Delivery Company. This company provided a delivery service to customers in return for a fee. Your study of accounting began with service companies as examples because they are the least complicated type of business. You are now ready to apply the accounting process to a more complex type of business—a merchandising company. The fundamental accounting concepts for service-type businesses also apply to merchandising businesses, but some additional accounts and techniques are needed to account for purchases and sales.

The normal flow of goods from manufacturer to final customer is as follows:

Merchandising Companies

Manufacturers produce goods from raw materials and normally sell them to wholesalers. After performing certain functions, such as packaging or labeling, wholesalers normally sell the goods to retailers. Retailers sell the goods to final customers. The two middle boxes in the diagram above represent merchandising companies. These companies buy goods in finished form for resale.

In this chapter, you will see a comparison of the income statements of a service company and a merchandising company. Then, you will study how to record merchandise-related transactions. Finally, you will become familiar with the work sheet and the closing process for a merchandising company.

TWO INCOME STATEMENTS COMPARED—SERVICE COMPANY AND MERCHANDISING COMPANY

Illustration 5.1 compares the main divisions of an income statement of a service company with those of a merchandising company. To determine profitability or net income for a service company, total expenses incurred are deducted from revenues earned. A merchandising company is a more complex type of business and, therefore, has a more complex income statement.

As shown in Illustration 5.1, merchandising companies first must deduct from revenues the cost of the goods they sell to customers. Then, they deduct other expenses. The income statement of a merchandising company has three main divisions: (1) sales revenues, (2) cost of goods sold, and (3) expenses. Sales revenues result from the sale of goods by the company; cost of goods sold indicates how much the company paid for the goods that were sold; and expenses are the company's expenses in running the business.

The next two sections of the chapter discuss the first two main divisions of the income statement of a merchandising company. The third division (expenses) is similar to expenses for a service company and has been illustrated in preceding chapters. As you study these chapter sections, keep in mind how the divisions of the merchandising income statement are related to each other and produce the final figure—net income or net loss—which indicates the profitability of the company.

ILLUSTRATION 5.1

Condensed Income Statements of a Service Company and a Merchandising Company Compared

SERVICE COMPANY Income Statement For the Year Ended December 31, 1994		MERCHANDISING COMPANY Income Statement For the Year Ended December 31, 1994	
Service revenues	$13,200	Sales revenues	$262,000
		Cost of goods sold	159,000
		Gross margin	$103,000
Expenses.	6,510	Expenses.	74,900
Net income	$ 6,690	Net income	$ 28,100

SALES REVENUES

Objective 1

Record journal entries for sales transactions involving merchandise

The sale of goods occurs between two parties. The seller of the goods transfers them to the buyer in exchange for cash or a promise to pay later. This exchange is a relatively simple business transaction.

Sellers make sales to create revenues. As you recall, revenue is the inflow of assets resulting from the rendering of services or the sale of goods to customers. Illustration 5.1 showed a condensed income statement to emphasize its major divisions. Now the more complete income statement actually prepared by accountants is described. The merchandising company that we will use to illustrate the income statement is Hanson Retail Food Store. This section first explains how to record sales revenues, including the effect of trade discounts. Next, you will learn how to record the two deductions from sales revenues—sales discounts and sales returns and allowances (Illustration 5.2). The amount that remains is net sales. The formula, then, for determining net sales is:

Net sales = Gross sales − (Sales discounts + Sales returns and allowances)

Recording Gross Sales

In a sales transaction, the seller transfers the legal ownership (title) of the goods to the buyer. Usually, the physical delivery of the goods occurs at the same time as the sale of the goods. A business document called an *invoice* (called a *sales invoice* by the seller and a *purchase invoice* by the buyer) is used as a basis for recording the sale.

An invoice is a document, prepared by the seller of merchandise and sent to the buyer, that contains the details of a sale, such as the number of units sold, unit price, total price billed, terms of sale, and manner of shipment. A retail company prepares the invoice at the point of sale. A wholesale company, which supplies goods to retailers, prepares the invoice after the shipping department notifies the accounting department that it shipped the goods to the retailer. Illustration 5.3 shows an invoice prepared by a wholesale company for goods sold to a retail company.

Using the invoice as the source document, a wholesale company records the revenue from the sale at the time of the sale for the following reasons:

1. The seller has passed **legal title** of the goods to the buyer, and the goods are now the responsibility and property of the buyer.

2. The seller has established the selling price of the goods.

ILLUSTRATION 5.2

Partial Income Statement of Merchandising Company

HANSON RETAIL FOOD STORE
Partial Income Statement
For the Year Ended December 31, 1994

Operating revenues:

Gross sales		$282,000
Less: Sales discounts	$ 5,000	
Sales returns and allowances . . .	15,000	20,000
Net sales		$262,000

ILLUSTRATION 5.3

Invoice

BRYAN WHOLESALE CO.   **Invoice No.:** 1258
476 Mason Street   **Date:** Dec. 19, 1994
Detroit, Michigan 48823

Customer's Order No.: 218
Sold to: Baier Company
Address: 2255 Hannon Street
              Big Rapids, Michigan   48106   **Date Shipped:** Dec. 19, 1994
Terms: Net 30, FOB Destination   **Shipped by:** Nagel Trucking Co.

Description	Item Number	Quantity	Price per Unit	Total Amount
True-tone stereo radios	Model No. 5868-24393	200	$100	$20,000
		Total		$20,000

---

3. The seller has completed its obligation.

4. The seller has exchanged the goods for another asset, such as cash or accounts receivable.

5. The seller can determine the costs incurred in selling the goods.

Each time a company makes a sale, the company earns revenue. This revenue increases a revenue account called *Sales*. Recall from Chapter 2 that revenues are increased by credits. Therefore, the Sales account is credited for the amount of the sale.

Usually sales are for cash or on account. When a sale is for cash, the credit to the Sales account is accompanied by a debit to Cash; when a sale is on account, the Sales account credit is accompanied by a debit to Accounts Receivable. For example, a $20,000 sale for cash is recorded as follows:

Cash	20,000	
Sales		20,000
To record the sale of merchandise for cash.		

A $20,000 sale on account is recorded as follows:

Accounts Receivable	20,000	
Sales		20,000
To record the sale of merchandise on account.		

A seller usually quotes the gross selling price, also called the invoice price, of goods to the buyer, but sometimes a seller quotes a list price of goods along with trade discounts that are available. In this latter situation, the buyer must calculate the gross selling price. The list price less all trade discounts is the **gross selling price.** Merchandising companies use the gross selling price to determine the actual selling price to the customer.

Determining Gross Selling Price when Companies Offer Trade Discounts

A **trade discount** is a percentage deduction, or discount, from the specified list price or catalog price of merchandise. Trade discounts are used to:

1. Reduce the cost of catalog publication. A seller can use a catalog for a longer period of time when it prints list prices in the catalog and gives separate discount sheets to salespersons whenever prices change.
2. Grant quantity discounts.
3. Allow quotation of different prices to different types of customers, such as retailers and wholesalers.

The seller's invoice may show trade discounts. However, trade discounts are not recorded in the seller's accounting records because they are only used to calculate the gross selling price. Nor are trade discounts recorded on the books of the purchaser. To illustrate, assume an invoice contains the following data:

List price, 200 swimsuits at $24.	$4,800
Less: Trade discount, 30%	1,440
Gross selling price (invoice price)	$3,360

The seller records a sale of $3,360. The purchaser records a purchase of $3,360. **Thus, list prices and their trade discounts are not entered on the books of either the seller or the purchaser.**

Sometimes the list price of a product is subject to several trade discounts; this series of discounts is called a **chain discount.** Chain discounts exist, for example, when a wholesaler receives two trade discounts because of certain services performed, such as packaging and distributing. When more than one discount is given, each discount is applied to the declining balance successively. If a product has a list price of $100 and is subject to trade discounts of 20% and 10%, the gross selling price (invoice price) would be $100 - 0.2(\$100) = \$80; \$80 - 0.1(\$80) = \$72$, computed as follows:

List price	$100
Less 20%	− 20
	$ 80
Less 10%	− 8
Gross selling price (invoice price)	$ 72

The same results can be obtained by multiplying the list price by the complements of the trade discounts allowed. The complement of 20% is 80% because 20% + 80% = 100%. The complement of 10% is 90% because 10% + 90% = 100%. Thus, the gross selling price is $100 × 0.8 × 0.9 = $72.

Recording Deductions from Gross Sales

Two common deductions from gross sales are (1) sales discounts and (2) sales returns and allowances. These deductions are recorded in contra revenue accounts to the Sales account. Contra accounts have normal balances that are opposite the balance of the account they reduce. For example, since the Sales account normally has a credit balance, the Sales Discounts account and Sales Returns and Allowances account will have debit balances. The methods used to record these contra revenue accounts are explained in the paragraphs that follow.

Sales Discounts   Whenever a company sells goods on account, it clearly specifies terms of payment on the invoice. For example, the invoice in Illustration 5.3 states the terms of payment as "net 30."

"Net 30" is sometimes written as "n/30." This "n/30" term means that the buyer may not take a discount and must pay the entire amount of the invoice ($20,000) on or before 30 days after December 19, 1994 (invoice date)—on or before January 18, 1995. In Illustration 5.3, if the terms had read "n/10/EOM" (EOM means end of month), the buyer could not take a discount, and the invoice would be due on the 10th day of the month following the month of sale—or January 10, 1995. Credit terms vary from industry to industry.

In some industries, credit terms include a *cash discount* of 1% to 3% to induce early payment of an amount due. A cash discount is a deduction from the invoice price that can be taken only if the invoice is paid within a specified period of time. A cash discount differs from a trade discount in that a cash discount is a deduction from the gross sales price for the prompt payment of an invoice, while a trade discount is a deduction from the list price to determine the gross selling price (or invoice price). A cash discount is called a sales discount by the seller and a purchase discount by the buyer.

Companies often state cash discount terms as follows:

- 2/10, n/30—means a buyer may deduct a discount of 2% of the invoice price of the merchandise if the buyer pays within 10 days following the invoice date. If payment is not made within the discount period, the entire invoice price is due 30 days from the invoice date.
- 2/EOM, n/60—means a buyer may deduct a 2% discount from the invoice price if the buyer pays the invoice by the end of the month. If payment is not made within the discount period, the entire invoice price is due 60 days from the invoice date.
- 2/10/EOM, n/60—means a buyer may deduct a 2% discount from the invoice price if the buyer pays the invoice by the 10th day of the month following the month of sale. If payment is not made within the discount period, the entire invoice price is due 60 days from the invoice date.

Sellers cannot record the sales discount before they receive payment since they do not know before that time when the buyer will pay the invoice. A cash discount taken by the buyer reduces the amount of cash that the seller actually collects from the sale of the goods, so the seller must indicate this fact in the accounting records of the company. The following illustration shows how to record a sale and a subsequent sales discount.

Assume that on July 12, a business sold merchandise for $2,000 on account; terms are 2/10, n/30. On July 21 (nine days after invoice date), the business received a $1,960 check in payment of the account. The required journal entries for the seller are:

July	12	Accounts Receivable	2,000	
		Sales		2,000
		To record sale on account; terms 2/10, n/30.		
	21	Cash	1,960	
		Sales Discounts	40	
		Accounts Receivable		2,000
		To record collection on account, less discount.		

The Sales Discounts account is a contra revenue account to the Sales account. In the income statement, this contra revenue account is deducted from gross sales. The Sales Discounts account is used (rather than directly reducing the Sales account) so the managers can examine the sales discounts figure to evaluate the company's sales discount policy. Note that the Sales Discounts account is not an expense incurred in generating revenue. Rather, the purpose of the account is to reduce recorded revenue to the amount actually realized from the sale.

Sales Returns and Allowances   Merchandising companies usually allow a customer to return goods that are defective or unsatisfactory for a variety of reasons, such as wrong color, wrong size, wrong style, wrong amounts, or inferior quality. In fact, when the seller's policy is "satisfaction guaranteed," some companies allow customers to return goods simply because the customer does not like the merchandise. A sales return is merchandise returned by a buyer. Sellers and buyers regard a sales return as a cancellation of a sale. Sometimes the customer keeps the unsatisfactory goods, and the seller gives the customer an allowance off the original price. A sales allowance is a deduction from the original invoiced sales price granted to a customer when the customer keeps the merchandise but is dissatisfied for any of a number of reasons, including inferior quality, damage, or deterioration in transit. In such cases, if a seller agrees to the sales return or sales allowance, the seller communicates with the buyer by sending a credit memorandum indicating that the seller is reducing (crediting) the account receivable with that buyer. A credit memorandum is a document that provides space for the name and address of the concerned parties and contains the preprinted words, "WE CREDIT YOUR ACCOUNT," followed by a space for the reason for the credit and the amount to be credited. A credit memorandum is used as the basis for recording a sales return or a sales allowance.

In theory, both sales returns and sales allowances could be recorded as debits to the Sales account because they cancel part of the recorded selling price. However, the amount of sales returns and sales allowances is useful information to managers and, therefore, should be shown separately. The amount of returns and allowances in relation to goods sold can be an indication of the quality of the goods (high-return percentage, low quality) or of pressure applied by salespersons (high-pressure sales, high returns). Thus, sales returns and sales allowances are recorded in a separate *Sales Returns and Allowances account*. The Sales Returns and Allowances account is a contra revenue account (to Sales) used to record the selling price of merchandise returned by buyers or reductions in selling prices granted. (Some companies use separate accounts for sales returns and for sales allowances, but this text does not.)

Following are two examples illustrating the recording of sales returns in the Sales Returns and Allowances account:

1. Assume that a customer returns $300 of goods sold on account. If payment has not yet been received, the required entry is:

```
Sales Returns and Allowances . . . . . . . . . . . . . . . .    300
    Accounts Receivable  . . . . . . . . . . . . . . . . . .            300
    To record a sales return from a customer.
```

2. Assume that the customer has already paid the account and the seller gives the customer a cash refund. Now, the credit is to Cash rather than to Accounts Receivable. If the customer has taken a 2% discount when paying the account, the company would return to the customer the sales price less the sales discount amount. For example, if a customer returns goods that sold for $300, on which a 2% discount was taken, the following entry would be made:

```
Sales Returns and Allowances . . . . . . . . . . . . . . . .    300
    Cash  . . . . . . . . . . . . . . . . . . . . . . . . . .            294
    Sales Discounts. . . . . . . . . . . . . . . . . . . . . .              6
    To record a sales return from a customer who had taken a dis-
    count and was sent a cash refund.
```

The debit to the Sales Returns and Allowances account is for the full selling price of the purchase. The credit to Sales Discounts reduces the balance of that account.

Now we will illustrate the recording of a sales allowance in the Sales Returns and Allowances account. Assume that a company grants a $400 allowance to a customer for damage resulting from improperly packed merchandise. If the customer has not yet paid the account, the required entry would be:

```
Sales Returns and Allowances . . . . . . . . . . . . . . . .    400
    Accounts Receivable  . . . . . . . . . . . . . . . . . .            400
    To record sales allowance granted for damaged merchandise.
```

If the customer has already paid the account, the credit is to Cash instead of Accounts Receivable. If the customer took a 2% discount when paying the account, the company would refund only the net amount ($392). Sales Discounts would be credited for $8. The entry would be:

```
Sales Returns and Allowances . . . . . . . . . . . . . . . .    400
    Cash  . . . . . . . . . . . . . . . . . . . . . . . . . .            392
    Sales Discounts  . . . . . . . . . . . . . . . . . . . . .              8
    To record sales allowance when a customer has paid and taken a 2%
    discount.
```

ILLUSTRATION 5.4

Partial Income Statement*

HANSON RETAIL FOOD STORE
Partial Income Statement
For the Year Ended December 31, 1994

Operating revenues:

Gross sales.		$282,000
Less: Sales discounts	$ 5,000	
Sales returns and allowances	15,000	20,000
Net sales.		$262,000

* This illustration is the same as Illustration 5.2, repeated here for your convenience.

Reporting Net Sales in the Income Statement

Illustration 5.4 contains a partial income statement showing how a company would report sales, sales discounts, and sales returns and allowances. However, many times the income statement published in a company's annual report begins with "Net sales" because the details of this computation are not important to financial statement users outside the company.

COST OF GOODS SOLD

Objective 2
Describe briefly cost of goods sold and the distinction between perpetual and periodic inventory procedures

The second main division of an income statement for a merchandising business is cost of goods sold. Cost of goods sold is the cost to the seller of the goods sold to customers. For a merchandising company, the cost of goods sold can be relatively large. All merchandising companies have a quantity of goods on hand to sell to customers that is called *merchandise inventory*. Merchandise inventory (or inventory) is the quantity of goods on hand and available for sale at any given time. Cost of goods sold is determined by computing the cost of (1) the beginning inventory, (2) the net cost of goods purchased, and (3) the ending inventory.

Illustration 5.5 gives the cost of goods sold section of Hanson Retail Food Store's income statement. The merchandise inventory on January 1, 1994, was $24,000. The net cost of purchases for the year was $166,000. Thus, Hanson had $190,000 of merchandise available for sale during 1994. On December 31, 1994, the merchandise inventory was $31,000, meaning this amount was left unsold. Subtracting the unsold amount of inventory (the ending inventory), $31,000, from the amount Hanson had available for sale during the year, $190,000, gives the cost of goods sold for the year of $159,000. Understanding this relationship, as shown on Hanson Retail Food Store's partial income statement in Illustration 5.5, gives you the necessary background to determine the cost of goods sold as presented in this section. This illustration is repeated at the end of the following discussion.

Two Procedures for Accounting for Inventories

To determine the cost of goods sold, accountants must have accurate merchandise inventory figures. Accountants use two basic methods for determining the amount of merchandise inventory—perpetual inventory procedure and periodic inventory procedure. Perpetual inventory procedure is only mentioned briefly in this chapter. Periodic inventory procedure is used extensively in this chapter. In the next chapter, we emphasize perpetual inventory procedure and further compare it with periodic inventory procedure.

ILLUSTRATION 5.5

Determination of Cost of Goods Sold for Hanson Retail Food Store

Cost of goods sold:

Merchandise inventory, January 1, 1994			$ 24,000
Purchases		$167,000	
Less: Purchase discounts.	$3,000		
Purchase returns and allowances	8,000	11,000	
Net purchases.		$156,000	
Add: Transportation-in		10,000	
Net cost of purchases			166,000
Cost of goods available for sale			$190,000
Less: Merchandise inventory, December 31, 1994			31,000
Cost of goods sold.			$159,000

When discussing inventory, we need to clarify whether we are referring to the physical goods on hand or the Merchandise Inventory account, which is the financial representation of the physical goods on hand. The difference between perpetual and periodic inventory procedures is the frequency with which the Merchandise Inventory account is updated to reflect what is physically on hand. Under perpetual inventory procedure, the Merchandise Inventory account is continuously updated to reflect items on hand. For example, your supermarket uses a scanner to ring up your purchases. When your box of Rice Krispies crosses the scanner, the Merchandise Inventory account is adjusted to show that one less box of Rice Krispies is on hand. Hence, the name *perpetual inventory procedure*.

Under periodic inventory procedure, the Merchandise Inventory account is updated only periodically—after a physical count has been made. Hence, the name *periodic inventory procedure*. Usually, the physical count will only take place immediately before the preparation of financial statements.

Perpetual Inventory Procedure Companies use **perpetual inventory procedure** in a variety of business settings. Historically, companies that sold merchandise with a high individual unit value, such as automobiles, furniture, and appliances, used perpetual inventory procedure. Today, computerized cash registers and accounting software programs can be designed to automatically keep track of inflows and outflows of each type of inventory item. This computerization makes it economical for many retail stores to use perpetual inventory procedure even for goods of low unit value, such as groceries.

Under perpetual inventory procedure, the Merchandise Inventory account provides close control over the actual goods on hand by showing the cost of the goods that are supposed to be on hand at any particular point in time. The Merchandise Inventory account is debited for each purchase and credited for each sale so that the current balance is shown in the account at all times. Also, the company usually maintains detailed unit records showing the quantities of each type of goods that should be on hand at any time. At the end of the accounting period, company personnel take a physical inventory by actually counting the number of units of inventory on hand. This physical count can be compared with the records showing the number of units that should be on hand. Chapter 6 describes perpetual inventory procedure in more detail.

Periodic Inventory Procedure   Merchandising companies selling low unit value merchandise (such as nuts and bolts, nails, Christmas cards, or pencils) often find that if they have not computerized their inventory systems, the extra costs of record-keeping under perpetual inventory procedure more than outweigh the benefits. Close control of such items is not economically feasible. These merchandising companies often use periodic inventory procedure.

Under **periodic inventory procedure,** companies do not use the Merchandise Inventory account to record each purchase and sale of merchandise as under perpetual inventory procedure. Instead, a company makes adjustments to the Merchandise Inventory account only at the end of the accounting period to bring the account to its proper balance. Also, the company usually does not maintain other unit records that show the exact number of units that should be on hand. Thus, the use of periodic inventory procedure reduces record-keeping considerably, but it also reduces the control over inventory items.

As stated above, companies using periodic inventory procedure make no entries to the Merchandise Inventory account to record purchases or sales during the accounting period, nor do they usually maintain unit records. Thus, these companies have no up-to-date balance against which to check the physical inventory count at the end of the accounting period. Also, these companies make no attempt to determine the cost of goods sold at the time of each sale. Instead, the cost of all the goods sold during the accounting period is determined at the **end** of the period. The determination of cost of goods sold requires the knowledge of these three items:

1. Beginning inventory (cost of goods on hand at the beginning of the period).

2. Net cost of purchases during the period.

3. Ending inventory (cost of unsold goods on hand at the end of the period).

This information would be shown as follows:

Beginning inventory	$ 24,000
Add: Net cost of purchases during the period	140,000
Cost of goods available for sale during the period	$164,000
Deduct: Ending inventory	20,000
Cost of goods sold during the period	$144,000

From the above schedule you see that the company began the accounting period with $24,000 of merchandise and purchased an additional $140,000, making a total of $164,000 of goods that could have been sold during the period. Then, a physical inventory showed that $20,000 remained unsold at the end of the period, which implies that $144,000 was the cost of goods sold during the period. Of course, the $144,000 is not necessarily the precise amount of goods sold during the period because no actual record was made of the dollar amount of goods sold. Periodic inventory procedure basically assumes that everything not on hand at the end of the period has been sold. This method disregards problems such as theft or breakage because the Merchandise Inventory account contains no up-to-date balance at the end of the accounting period against which the physical count can be compared.

The main emphasis of this chapter will be on periodic inventory procedure. You are now ready for an in-depth discussion of the accounts and journal entries used under periodic inventory procedure.

**Purchases of
Merchandise**

Under periodic inventory procedure, a merchandising company uses the Purchases account to record the cost of merchandise bought for resale during the
current accounting period. The Purchases account is increased by debits and
appears with the income statement accounts in the chart of accounts.

Objective 3

Record journal entries for
purchase transactions
involving merchandise

To illustrate entries affecting the Purchases account, assume that Hanson Retail Food Store made two purchases of merchandise from Smith Wholesale Company. Hanson purchased $30,000 of merchandise on credit (on account) on May 4
and on May 21 purchased $20,000 of merchandise for cash. The required journal
entries for Hanson are:

May	4	Purchases	30,000	
		Accounts Payable.		30,000
		To record purchase of merchandise on account.		
	21	Purchases	20,000	
		Cash		20,000
		To record purchase of merchandise for cash.		

**Deductions from
Purchases**

On the buyer's books, purchase discounts and purchase returns and allowances
are deducted from purchases to arrive at net purchases. These items are recorded
in contra accounts to the Purchases account.

Purchase Discounts   Often companies purchase merchandise under credit terms
that permit the buyer to deduct a stated cash discount if the buyer pays the invoice
within a specifed time period. Assume that credit terms for Hanson's May 4
purchase are 2/10, n/30. If Hanson pays for the merchandise by May 14, the store
may take a 2% discount. Thus, Hanson must pay only $29,400 to settle the $30,000
account payable. The entry to record the payment of the invoice on May 14 is:

May	14	Accounts Payable.	30,000	
		Cash		29,400
		Purchase Discounts		600
		To record payment on account within discount period.		

The purchase discount is recorded only when the invoice is paid within the discount period and the discount is taken. The Purchase Discounts account is a contra
account to Purchases that reduces the recorded invoice price of the goods purchased to the price actually paid. Purchase discounts are reported in the income
statement as a deduction from purchases.

Note that the May 4 purchase was recorded at the invoice price. This method is
called the gross price method. An alternative is to record purchases net of the
purchase discounts. This latter alternative is described below.

Companies base purchase discounts on the invoice price of goods. If an invoice
shows purchase returns or allowances, they must be deducted from the invoice
price before calculating purchase discounts. For example, in the transaction
above, the invoice price of goods purchased was $30,000. If Hanson returns
$2,000 of the goods, the purchase discount is calculated on $28,000.

Net Price Method   Most well-managed companies take advantage of all the discounts made available to them by their suppliers. Effective internal control over
cash disbursements makes certain that the company takes these discounts. A

company should consider borrowing cash to pay invoices within the discount period.

For example, assume a company purchases goods for $10,000 under terms 2/10, n/30. The buyer is unable to pay at the end of 10 days but expects to be able to pay at the end of 30 days. To take the $200 discount offered, the buyer needs a $9,800 loan for 20 days, beginning on the last day of the 10-day discount period. The buyer would benefit if the interest cost of such a loan is less than $200.

Some companies prefer to use the net price method because (1) the accounting theory behind the method is superior, and (2) the method strengthens internal control.

Under the net price method, a purchase is recorded in Purchases and Accounts Payable net of the discount. Thus, the discount is **deducted** from the invoice price **before** entering the transaction in the accounts. To illustrate, assume a company makes a $1,500 purchase on May 14 under terms 2/10, n/30. The company pays the invoice on May 24 and takes the discount. The entries comparing the net price method and the gross price method are:

			Net Price Method		Gross Price Method	
May	14	Purchases	1,470		1,500	
		Accounts Payable.		1,470		1,500
		Purchased goods under terms 2/10, n/30.				
	24	Accounts Payable.	1,470		1,500	
		Cash		1,470		1,470
		Purchase Discounts*				30
		Paid account within discount period.				

* This account would not appear in the net price entry.

Theoretically, the net price method is preferred over the gross price method because it records the goods at their actual cost. Thus, the cost principle of accounting is applied, and goods are recorded at the total amount of resources given up to acquire them. Also, the liability is shown in the Accounts Payable account at the amount for which it could be settled. In spite of these factors, many companies continue to use the gross price method.

Note that in the above net price example, the company did not show the discounts taken. However, if the company had not paid the invoice within 10 days, an entry would have been made to the Discounts Lost account. For example, assume that the invoice in the above example was paid on May 28 instead of May 24. Then, the entries for the payment comparing the net price and gross price methods are:

			Net Price Method		Gross Price Method	
May	28	Accounts Payable.	1,470		1,500	
		Discounts Lost*	30			
		Cash		1,500		1,500
		Paid account after discount had expired.				

* This account would not appear in the gross price entry.

Under the net price method, the only time discounts appear is when the company has lost them. When discounts of 2% or more are available, effective cash management calls for internal control procedures ensuring that the company pays all invoices within the discount period. The failure to take a discount highlights a deviation from company policy and directs management's attention to this fact. Calling management's attention to deviations is sometimes called "management by exception." Losses resulting from inefficiency are contained in the Discounts Lost account, which is reported among nonoperating expenses near the bottom of the income statement. Some companies prefer the net price method because it strengthens internal control over cash disbursements.

Interest Rate Implied in Cash Discounts   To decide whether you should take advantage of discounts by using your cash or borrowing, you can make this simple analysis. Assume that you must pay $10,000 within 30 days or $9,800 within 10 days to settle a $10,000 invoice with terms of 2/10, n/30. By advancing payment 20 days from the final due date, you can secure a discount of $200. The interest expense incurred to borrow $9,800 at 12% per year for 20 days is $65.33. In this case, you would save $134.67 ($200 − $65.33) by borrowing the money and paying the invoice within the discount period.

In terms of an annual rate of interest, the 2% rate of discount for 20 days is equivalent to a 36% annual rate: $(360 \div 20) \times 2\%$. The formula is:

$$\text{Equivalent annual rate of interest} = \frac{\text{The number of days in a year (assumed to be 360)}}{\text{The number of days from the end of the discount period until the final due date}} \times \text{The percentage rate of discount}$$

All cash discount terms can be converted into their approximate annual interest rate equivalents by use of this formula. Thus, a company could afford to pay up to 36% $[(360 \div 20) \times 2\%]$ on borrowed funds to take advantage of discount terms of 2/10, n/30. The company could pay 18% on terms of 1/10, n/30.

Purchase Returns and Allowances   A purchase return occurs when a buyer returns merchandise to a seller. When a buyer receives an allowance (or reduction in the price of goods shipped), a purchase allowance results. In such cases, the buyer commonly uses a debit memorandum to notify the seller that the account payable with the seller is being reduced (Accounts Payable is debited). A debit memorandum is similar to a credit memorandum except for the preprinted words, "WE DEBIT YOUR ACCOUNT." The buyer may use a copy of a debit memorandum to record the returns or allowances or may wait for confirmation, usually in the form of a credit memorandum, from the seller.

Both returns and allowances serve to reduce the buyer's debt to the seller and to reduce the cost of the goods purchased. The buyer may want to know the amount of returns and allowances as the first step in controlling the costs incurred in returning unsatisfactory merchandise or negotiating purchase allowances. For this reason, purchase returns and allowances are recorded in a separate Purchase Returns and Allowances account. If Hanson returned $350 of merchandise to Smith Wholesale before paying for the goods, the following journal entry would be made:

Accounts Payable.	350	
Purchase Returns and Allowances		350
To record return of damaged merchandise to supplier.		

The entry would have been the same to record a $350 allowance. Only the explanation would change.

If Hanson had already paid the account, the debit would be to Cash instead of Accounts Payable, since Hanson would receive a refund of cash. If the company took a discount at the time it paid the account, then only the net amount would be refunded. For instance, if a 2% discount had been taken, Hanson's journal entry for the return would be:

Cash	343	
Purchase Discounts	7	
Purchase Returns and Allowances		350
To record return of damaged merchandise to supplier and record receipt of cash.		

Purchase Returns and Allowances is a contra account to the Purchases account, and the income statement shows it as a deduction from purchases. Assuming that a company records purchases under the gross price method, when both purchase discounts and purchase returns and allowances are deducted from purchases, the result is net purchases.

Transportation Costs

Objective 4
Describe the freight terms and record transportation costs

Transportation costs are an important part of cost of goods sold. To understand how to account for transportation costs, you must know the meaning of the following terms:

□ **FOB shipping point:** The term FOB shipping point means "free on board at shipping point"; that is, the buyer incurs all transportation costs after the merchandise has been loaded on a railroad car or truck at the point of shipment. Thus, the buyer is responsible for ultimately paying the freight charges.

□ **FOB destination:** The term FOB destination means "free on board at destination"; that is, the seller ships the goods to their destination without charge to the buyer. Thus, the seller is ultimately responsible for paying the freight charges.

□ **Passage of title:** Passage of title is a legal term used to indicate transfer of legal ownership of goods. Title to the goods normally passes from seller to buyer at the FOB point. Thus, when goods are shipped FOB shipping point, title usually passes to the buyer at the shipping point. When goods are shipped FOB destination, title usually passes at destination.

□ **Freight prepaid:** When the **seller** must initially pay the freight at the time of shipment, companies use the term freight prepaid.

□ **Freight collect:** When the **buyer** must initially pay the freight bill on the arrival of the goods, companies use the term freight collect.

To illustrate the use of these terms, assume that a company ships certain goods FOB shipping point, freight collect. Title passes at the shipping point. The buyer is responsible for paying the $100 freight costs and does so. No entry for freight charges is made on the seller's books. The entry on the **buyer's books** is:

Transportation-In (or Freight-In)	100	
Cash		100
To record payment of freight bill on goods purchased.		

The Transportation-In account is used to record inward freight costs incurred in the acquisition of merchandise. Transportation-In is an adjunct account in that it is added to net purchases to arrive at net cost of purchases. An adjunct account is closely related to another account (Purchases, in this instance), and its balance is added to the balance of the related account in the financial statements. Recall that a contra account is just the opposite of an adjunct account. A contra account, such as accumulated depreciation, is **deducted** from the related account in the financial statements.

If the seller ships the goods FOB destination, freight prepaid, the seller is responsible for and pays the freight bill. The seller does not bill a separate freight cost to the buyer, so the buyer shows no entry for freight on its books. The seller, however, has undoubtedly considered the freight cost in setting selling prices. The following entry is required on the **seller's books:**

Delivery Expense (or Transportation-Out Expense)	100	
Cash		100
To record freight cost on goods sold.		

When the terms are FOB destination, the seller records the freight costs as deliv-ery expense, which is a selling expense shown on the income statement with other selling expenses.

FOB terms are especially important at the end of an accounting period. Goods that are in transit at the end of an accounting period belong to either the seller or the buyer, and one of these parties must include these goods in its ending inventory. Goods shipped FOB destination belong to the seller while in transit, and the seller should include these goods in its ending inventory. Goods shipped FOB shipping point belong to the buyer while in transit, and the buyer should record these goods as a purchase and include them in its ending inventory. For example, assume that a seller ships goods on December 30, 1993, and they arrive at their destination on January 5, 1994. If terms are FOB destination, the seller includes the goods in its December 31, 1993, inventory, and neither seller nor buyer re-cords the exchange transaction until January 5, 1994. If terms are FOB shipping point, the buyer includes the goods in its December 31, 1993, inventory, and both parties record the exchange transaction as of December 30, 1993.

Sometimes the seller initially prepays the freight as a convenience to the buyer, even though the buyer is ultimately responsible for paying it. In such cases, the buyer merely reimburses the seller for the amount of freight paid. For example, assume that Wood Company sold merchandise to Loud Company with terms of FOB shipping point, freight prepaid. The freight charges were $100. The following entries are necessary on the books of the buyer and the seller:

Buyer—Loud Company		**Seller—Wood Company**	
Transportation-In 100		Accounts Receivable. . . . 100	
Accounts Payable . . .	100	Cash	100

Such entries are necessary because Wood initially paid the freight charges when the company was not required to ultimately do so. Therefore, Loud Company must reimburse Wood for the charges. If the buyer pays freight for the seller (e.g., FOB destination, freight collect), the buyer merely deducts the freight paid from the amount owed to the seller. The following entries are necessary on the books of the buyer and the seller:

Buyer—Loud Company		**Seller—Wood Company**	
Accounts Payable 100		Delivery Expense 100	
Cash	100	Accounts Receivable. .	100

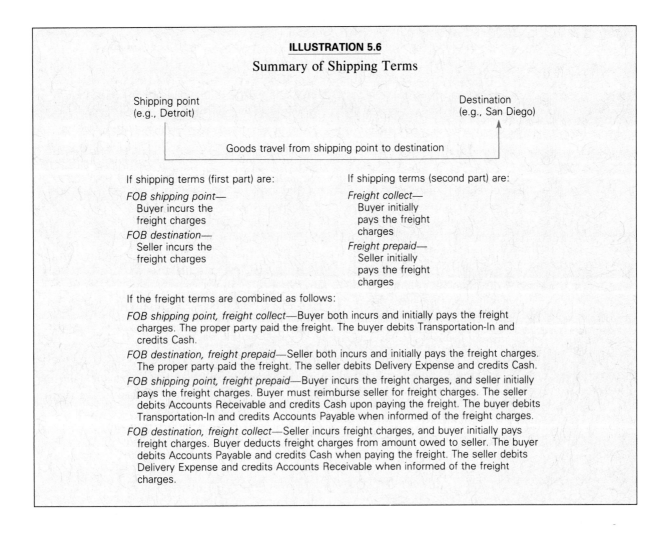

ILLUSTRATION 5.6

Summary of Shipping Terms

Shipping point   Destination
(e.g., Detroit)   (e.g., San Diego)

Goods travel from shipping point to destination

If shipping terms (first part) are: If shipping terms (second part) are:

FOB shipping point—   *Freight collect—*
   Buyer incurs the   Buyer initially
   freight charges   pays the freight
                                                        charges
FOB destination—   *Freight prepaid—*
   Seller incurs the   Seller initially
   freight charges   pays the freight
                                                        charges

If the freight terms are combined as follows:

FOB shipping point, freight collect—Buyer both incurs and initially pays the freight
   charges. The proper party paid the freight. The buyer debits Transportation-In and
   credits Cash.

FOB destination, freight prepaid—Seller both incurs and initially pays the freight charges.
   The proper party paid the freight. The seller debits Delivery Expense and credits Cash.

FOB shipping point, freight prepaid—Buyer incurs the freight charges, and seller initially
   pays the freight charges. Buyer must reimburse seller for freight charges. The seller
   debits Accounts Receivable and credits Cash upon paying the freight. The buyer debits
   Transportation-In and credits Accounts Payable when informed of the freight charges.

FOB destination, freight collect—Seller incurs freight charges, and buyer initially pays
   freight charges. Buyer deducts freight charges from amount owed to seller. The buyer
   debits Accounts Payable and credits Cash when paying the freight. The seller debits
   Delivery Expense and credits Accounts Receivable when informed of the freight
   charges.

Purchase discounts may only be taken on the purchase price of goods. Therefore, if a buyer owes the seller for freight charges, the buyer cannot take a discount on the freight charges owed, even if the buyer makes payment within the discount period.

Illustration 5.6 summarizes the discussion of freight terms and the resulting journal entries to record the freight changes.

Merchandise Inventories

Merchandise inventory is the cost of goods on hand and available for sale at any given time. For the management of a company to determine the cost of goods sold in any accounting period, it needs inventory information. Management must know its cost of goods on hand at the start of the period (beginning inventory), the net cost of purchases made during the period, and the cost of goods on hand at the close of the period (ending inventory). Since the ending inventory of the preceding period is the beginning inventory for the current period, management already knows the cost of the beginning inventory. Companies record purchases, purchase discounts, purchase returns and allowances, and transportation-in throughout the period. Therefore, management needs to determine only the cost of the ending inventory at the end of the period.

Taking a Physical Inventory   Under periodic inventory procedure, company personnel determine ending inventory cost by taking a *physical inventory*. Taking a physical inventory consists of counting physical units of each type of merchandise on hand. To calculate inventory cost, multiply the number of units of each kind of merchandise by its unit cost. Then combine the total costs of the various kinds of merchandise to provide the total ending inventory cost.

In taking a physical inventory, company personnel must be careful to ensure that they count all goods owned, regardless of where they are located, and include them in the inventory. Thus, companies should not record goods shipped to potential customers "on approval" as sold but should include these goods in their inventory. Similarly, companies should not record consigned goods (goods delivered to another party who will attempt to sell the goods for the owner at a commission) as sold goods. These goods remain the property of the owner (consignor) until sold by the consignee and must be included in the owner's inventory.

Merchandise in transit is merchandise in the hands of a freight company on the date of a physical inventory. Buyers must record merchandise in transit at the end of the accounting period as a purchase if the goods were shipped FOB shipping point and they have received title to the merchandise. In general, the goods belong to the party who must ultimately bear the transportation charges.

Determining Cost of Goods Sold

Objective 5

Determine cost of goods sold

When accounting personnel know the beginning and ending inventories and the various items making up the net cost of purchases, they can determine the cost of goods sold.

To illustrate, assume the following account balances for Hanson Retail Food Store as of December 31, 1994:

Merchandise Inventory, January 1, 1994	$ 24,000 Dr.
Purchases	167,000 Dr.
Purchase Discounts	3,000 Cr.
Purchase Returns and Allowances	8,000 Cr.
Transportation-In	10,000 Dr.

By taking a physical inventory, Hanson determined the December 31, 1994, merchandise inventory to be $31,000. Hanson then calculated its cost of goods sold as shown in Illustration 5.7. This computation appears in a section of the income statement directly below the calculation of net sales.

In Illustration 5.7, Hanson's beginning inventory ($24,000) plus net cost of purchases ($166,000) is equal to cost of goods available for sale ($190,000). Ending inventory cost ($31,000) is deducted from cost of goods available for sale to arrive at cost of goods sold ($159,000). The following diagram shows the relationship between these items:

Beginning inventory	+	Net cost of purchases	=	Cost of goods available for sale
$24,000		**$166,000**		**$190,000**

Cost of goods available for sale	−	Ending inventory	=	Cost of goods sold
$190,000		**$31,000**		**$159,000**

ILLUSTRATION 5.7

Determination of Cost of Goods Sold for Hanson Retail Food Store*

Cost of goods sold:

Merchandise inventory, January 1, 1994		$ 24,000
Purchases	$167,000	
Less: Purchase discounts. $3,000		
Purchase returns and allowances 8,000	11,000	
Net purchases.	$156,000	
Add: Transportation-in	10,000	
Net cost of purchases		166,000
Cost of goods available for sale		$190,000
Less: Merchandise inventory, December 31, 1994		31,000
Cost of goods sold.		$159,000

* This illustration is the same as Illustration 5.5, repeated here for your convenience.

Another way of looking at this relationship is shown in the following diagram:

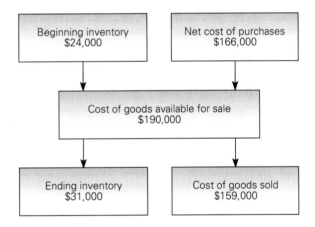

Beginning inventory and net cost of purchases combine to form cost of goods available for sale. The cost of goods available for sale is divided into ending inventory (which is the cost of goods not sold) and cost of goods sold.

To continue the calculation appearing in Illustration 5.7, net cost of purchases ($166,000) is equal to purchases ($167,000), **less** purchase discounts ($3,000) and purchase returns and allowances ($8,000), **plus** transportation-in ($10,000).

As shown in Illustration 5.7, ending inventory cost appears in the income statement as a deduction from cost of goods available for sale to compute cost of goods sold. Ending inventory cost (merchandise inventory) is also reported as a current asset in the end-of-period balance sheet.

Lack of Control under Periodic Inventory Procedure

Companies use periodic inventory procedure because of its simplicity and relatively low cost. However, as mentioned earlier, periodic inventory procedure provides for little control over inventory. Any items not included in the physical count of inventory at the end of the period are assumed to have been sold. Thus, even if the items have been stolen, they are assumed to have been sold, and their cost would be included in cost of goods sold.

To illustrate, assume that the cost of goods available for sale was $200,000 and ending inventory was $60,000. These figures suggest that the cost of goods sold was $140,000. Now assume that $2,000 of goods were actually shoplifted during the year. If such goods had not been stolen, the ending inventory would have been $62,000 and the cost of goods sold only $138,000. Thus, the $140,000 cost of goods sold calculated under periodic inventory procedure includes both the cost of the merchandise delivered to customers and the cost of merchandise stolen (if any).

CLASSIFIED INCOME STATEMENT

Objective 6

Prepare a classified income statement

In preceding chapters, we illustrated the unclassified (or single-step) income statement. An unclassified income statement has only two categories of items—revenues and expenses. In contrast, a classified income statement divides both revenues and expenses into operating and nonoperating items. The statement also separates operating expenses into selling and administrative expenses. A classified income statement, also called a multiple-step income statement, is introduced in this section.

Illustration 5.8 presents a classified income statement for Hanson Retail Food Store. This statement uses the previously presented data on sales (Illustration 5.4) and cost of goods sold (Illustration 5.7), together with additional assumed data on operating expenses and other expenses and revenues. Note in Illustration 5.8 that a classified income statement has the following four major sections:

1. Operating revenues.
2. Cost of goods sold.
3. Operating expenses.
4. Nonoperating revenues and expenses (other revenues and other expenses).

The classified income statement shows important relationships that help in analyzing how well the company is performing. For example, by deducting cost of goods sold from operating revenues, you can determine by what amount sales revenues exceed the cost of items being sold. If this margin, called gross margin, is inadequate, a company may need to increase its selling prices or decrease its cost of goods sold. The classified income statement subdivides operating expenses into selling and administrative expenses. Thus the statement users can see how much expense is being incurred in selling the product and how much in administering the business. Statement users can also make comparisons with other years' data for the same business and with other businesses. Nonoperating revenues and expenses appear at the bottom of the income statement because they are less significant in assessing the profitability of the business.

In the paragraphs that follow, we explain the major headings of the classified income statement shown in Illustration 5.8. The terms in some of these headings are already familiar to you.

1. Operating revenues are the revenues generated by the major activities of the business—usually the sale of products or services or both.

2. Cost of goods sold is the major expense in merchandising companies. Illustration 5.7 showed the cost of goods sold section of the classified income statement. This chapter has already discussed the items used in calculating cost of goods sold. The amount by which sales revenues exceed the cost of goods sold is usually shown in the top part of the income statement. The excess of net sales over cost of goods sold is the gross margin or gross profit. Gross margin may also be expressed as a percentage rate, computed by dividing gross margin by net sales. In Illustration 5.8, the gross margin rate is approximately 39.3% ($103,000/

ILLUSTRATION 5.8

Classified Income Statement for a Merchandising Company

HANSON RETAIL FOOD STORE
Income Statement
For the Year Ended December 31, 1994

Operating revenues:

Gross sales			$282,000
Less: Sales discounts		$ 5,000	
Sales returns and allowances		15,000	20,000
Net sales			$262,000

Cost of goods sold:

Merchandise inventory, January 1, 1994		$ 24,000	
Purchases	$167,000		
Less: Purchase discounts	$3,000		
Purchase returns and allowances	8,000	11,000	
Net purchases	$156,000		
Add: Transportation-in	10,000		
Net cost of purchases		166,000	
Cost of goods available for sale		$190,000	
Less: Merchandise inventory, December 31, 1994		31,000	
Cost of goods sold			159,000
Gross margin			$103,000

Operating expenses:

Miscellaneous selling expenses:

Sales salaries and commissions expense	$ 26,000	
Salespersons' travel expense	3,000	
Delivery expense	2,000	
Advertising expense	4,000	
Rent expense—store building	2,500	
Supplies expense	1,000	
Utilities expense	1,800	
Depreciation expense—store equipment	700	
Other selling expenses	400	$ 41,400

Miscellaneous administrative expenses:

Salaries expense, executive	$ 29,000	
Rent expense—administrative building	1,600	
Insurance expense	1,500	
Supplies expense	800	
Depreciation expense—office equipment	1,100	
Other administrative expenses	300	34,300
Total operating expenses		75,700
Income from operations		$ 27,300

Nonoperating revenues and expenses:

Nonoperating revenues:		
Interest revenue		1,400
		$ 28,700
Nonoperating expenses:		
Interest expense		600
Net income		$ 28,100

$262,000). The gross margin rate indicates that out of each sales dollar, approximately 39 cents is available to cover other expenses and produce income. Business owners watch the gross margin rate closely since a small percentage fluctuation can cause a large dollar change in net income. Also, a downward trend in the gross margin rate may indicate a problem, such as theft of merchandise.

3. Operating expenses for a merchandising company are those expenses, other than cost of goods sold, incurred in the normal business functions of a company. Usually, operating expenses are classified as either selling expenses or administrative expenses. Selling expenses are expenses a company incurs in selling and marketing efforts. Examples include salaries and commissions of salespersons, expenses for salespersons' travel, delivery, advertising, rent and utilities on a sales building, sales supplies used, and depreciation on delivery equipment used in sales. Administrative expenses are expenses a company incurs in the overall management of a business. Examples include administrative salaries, rent and utilities on an administrative building, insurance expense, administrative supplies used, and depreciation on office equipment.

Certain operating expenses may be related partly to the selling function and partly to the administrative function. For example, a company might incur rent, taxes, and insurance on a building for both sales and administrative purposes. Expenses covering both the selling and administrative functions must be analyzed and prorated between the two functions on the income statement. For instance, if $1,000 of depreciation expense relates 60% to selling and 40% to administrative based on the square footage or number of employees, the income statement would show $600 as a selling expense and $400 as an administrative expense.

4. Nonoperating revenues (other revenues) are revenues not related to the sale of products or services regularly offered for sale by a business. An example of a nonoperating revenue is interest that a business earns on notes receivable. Nonoperating expenses (other expenses) are expenses not related to the acquisition and sale of the products or services regularly offered for sale. An example of a nonoperating expense is interest incurred on money borrowed by the company.

Important Relationships in the Income Statement

The more important relationships in the income statement of a merchandising firm can be summarized in equation form, as follows:

1. Net sales = Gross sales − (Sales discounts + Sales returns and allowances).

2. Net purchases = Purchases − (Purchase discounts + Purchase returns and allowances).

3. Net cost of purchases = Net purchases + Transportation-in.

4. Cost of goods sold = Beginning inventory + Net cost of purchases − Ending inventory.

5. Gross margin = Net sales − Cost of goods sold.

6. Income from operations = Gross margin − Operating (selling and administrative) expenses.

7. Net income = Income from operations + Nonoperating revenues − Nonoperating expenses.

Each relationship is important because of the way it relates to an overall measure of business profitability. For example, a company may produce a high gross margin on sales. However, because of large sales commissions and delivery expenses, the owner may realize only a very small percentage of the gross margin as profit. The classifications in the income statement allow a user to focus on the whole picture as well as on how net income was derived (statement relationships).

Future illustrations may vary somewhat in form, but the basic organization of the classified income statement described above will be retained.

THE WORK SHEET FOR A MERCHANDISING COMPANY

Objective 7

Prepare a work sheet and closing entries for a merchandising company

Illustration 5.9 shows a work sheet for a merchandising company. To keep the illustration simple, a different retail company will be introduced. Lyons Company is a small sporting goods corporation. The illustration for Lyons Company focuses on the merchandise-related accounts. The fixed assets (land, building, and equipment) are not shown. Except for the merchandise-related accounts, the work sheet for a merchandising company is the same as for a service company. Recall that use of a work sheet assists in the preparation of the adjusting and closing entries. The work sheet also contains all the information needed for the preparation of the financial statements.

To further simplify this illustration, assume Lyons needs no adjusting entries at month-end. The trial balance is taken from the ledger accounts at December 31, 1994. The $7,000 merchandise inventory in the trial balance is the beginning inventory. The sales and sales-related accounts and the purchases and purchases-related accounts summarize the merchandising activity for December 1994.

Completing the Work Sheet

Any revenue accounts (Sales) and contra purchases accounts (Purchase Discounts, Purchase Returns and Allowances) that appear in the Adjusted Trial Balance credit columns of the work sheet are carried to the Income Statement credit column. Beginning inventory, contra revenue accounts (Sales Discounts, Sales Returns and Allowances), Purchases, Transportation-In, and expense accounts (Selling Expenses, Administrative Expenses) shown in the Adjusted Trial Balance debit column are carried to the Income Statement debit column.

Note that the amount of ending merchandise inventory, $8,000, is entered in the Income Statement credit column because it is deducted from cost of goods available for sale (beginning inventory plus net cost of purchases) in determining cost of goods sold. The ending inventory is also entered in the Balance Sheet debit column to establish the proper balance in the Merchandise Inventory account. The reason both beginning and ending inventories are brought to the Income Statement columns is because both are used to calculate cost of goods sold in the income statement. Net income or net loss for the period will balance the Income Statement columns as it did in previous work sheets. Net income/loss is carried to the Statement of Retained Earnings credit/debit column. For Lyons Company, the net income is $5,843 for the month of December and is carried to the Retained Earnings credit column.

The beginning balance in Retained Earnings is carried to the Statement of Retained Earnings credit column. The Dividends balance is carried to the Statement of Retained Earnings debit column. All other assets (Cash and Accounts Receivable) are carried to the Balance Sheet debit column. The liability (Accounts Payable), Capital Stock, and ending Retained Earnings balance are carried to the Balance Sheet credit column.

Financial Statements for a Merchandising Company

Once the work sheet has been completed, the financial statements are prepared. Next, any adjusting and closing entries are entered in the journal and posted to the ledger. This process clears the accounting records for the next accounting period. Finally, a post-closing trial balance is prepared.

Income Statement Illustration 5.10 shows the income statement Lyons prepared from its work sheet in Illustration 5.9. The focus in this income statement is on the determination of the cost of goods sold.

ILLUSTRATION 5.9

Work Sheet for a Merchandising Company

LYONS COMPANY
Work Sheet
For the Month Ended December 31, 1994

Acct. No.	Account Titles	Trial Balance Debit	Trial Balance Credit	Adjustments Debit	Adjustments Credit	Adjusted Trial Balance Debit	Adjusted Trial Balance Credit	Income Statement Debit	Income Statement Credit	Statement of Retained Earnings Debit	Statement of Retained Earnings Credit	Balance Sheet Debit	Balance Sheet Credit
100	Cash	19,663				19,663						19,663	
103	Accounts Receivable	1,880				1,880						1,880	
105	Merchandise Inventory, December 1	7,000				7,000		7,000	8,000			8,000	
200	Accounts Payable		700				700						700
300	Capital Stock		10,000				10,000						10,000
310	Retained Earnings, December 1		15,000				15,000				15,000		
320	Dividends	2,000				2,000				2,000			
410	Sales		14,600				14,600		14,600				
411	Sales Discounts	44				44		44					
412	Sales Returns and Allowances	20				20		20					
500	Purchases	6,000				6,000		6,000					
501	Purchase Discounts		82				82		82				
502	Purchase Returns and Allowances		100				100		100				
503	Transportation-In	75				75		75					
557	Miscellaneous Selling Expenses	2,650				2,650		2,650					
567	Miscellaneous Administrative Expenses	1,150				1,150		1,150					
		40,482	40,482			40,482	40,482	16,939	22,782			29,543	10,700
	Net Income							5,843			5,843		
								22,782	22,782	2,000	20,843		
	Retained Earnings, December 31									18,843			18,843
										20,843	20,843	29,543	29,543

ILLUSTRATION 5.10

Income Statement for a Merchandising Company

LYONS COMPANY
Income Statement
For the Month Ended December 31, 1994

Operating revenues:			
Gross sales.			$14,600
Less: Sales discounts		$ 44	
Sales returns and allowances		20	64
Net sales.			$14,536
Cost of goods sold:			
Merchandise inventory, December 1, 1994.		$ 7,000	
Purchases	$6,000		
Less: Purchase discounts	$ 82		
Purchase returns and allowances	100	182	
Net purchases	$5,818		
Add: Transportation-in	75		
Net cost of purchases		5,893	
Cost of goods available for sale.		$12,893	
Less: Merchandise inventory, December 31, 1994		8,000	
Cost of goods sold			4,893
Gross margin			$ 9,643
Operating expenses:			
Miscellaneous selling expenses.		$ 2,650	
Miscellaneous administrative expenses		1,150	
Total operating expenses.			3,800
Net income.			$ 5,843

ILLUSTRATION 5.11

Statement of Retained Earnings

LYONS COMPANY
Statement of Retained Earnings
For the Month Ended December 31, 1994

Retained earnings, December 1, 1994	$15,000
Add: Net income for the month.	5,843
Total.	$20,843
Deduct: Dividends.	2,000
Retained earnings, December 31, 1994	$18,843

Statement of Retained Earnings The statement of retained earnings, as you recall, is a financial statement that summarizes the transactions affecting the Retained Earnings account balance. In Illustration 5.11, the statement of retained earnings shows the increase in equity resulting from net income and the decrease in equity resulting from dividends.

ILLUSTRATION 5.12

Balance Sheet for a Merchandising Company

LYONS COMPANY
Balance Sheet
December 31, 1994
Assets

Current assets:

Cash.		$19,663
Accounts receivable.		1,880
Merchandise inventory.		8,000
Total assets		$29,543

Liabilities and Stockholders' Equity

Current liabilities:

Accounts payable.		$ 700

Stockholders' equity:

Capital stock	$10,000	
Retained earnings.	18,843	
Total stockholders' equity		28,843
Total liabilities and stockholders' equity		$29,543

Balance Sheet   The balance sheet, Illustration 5.12, contains the assets, liabilities, and stockholders' equity items taken from the work sheet. Note the $8,000 ending inventory is shown as a current asset. The Retained Earnings account balance comes from the statement of retained earnings.

Closing Entries

Recall from Chapter 4 that the closing process normally takes place after the accountant has prepared the financial statements for the period. The closing process closes revenue and expense accounts by transferring their balances to a clearing account called Income Summary and then to Retained Earnings. The closing process reduces the revenue and expense account balances to zero so that information for each accounting period may be accumulated separately from any previous period.

Closing entries may be prepared directly from the work sheet in Illustration 5.9 using the same procedure as presented in Chapter 4. The closing entries for Lyons Company are given below.

The first journal entry **debits** all items appearing in the Income Statement credit column of the work sheet and **credits** Income Summary for the total of the column, $22,782.

1st entry	1994 Dec.	31	Merchandise Inventory (ending)	8,000	
			Sales	14,600	
			Purchase Discounts.	82	
			Purchase Returns and Allowances	100	
			Income Summary.		22,782
			To close accounts with a credit balance in the Income Statement columns and to establish ending merchandise inventory.		

The second entry **credits** all items appearing in the Income Statement debit column and **debits** Income Summary for the total of that column, $16,939.[1]

2nd entry	Dec.	31	Income Summary.	16,939
			Merchandise Inventory (beginning)		7,000
			Sales Discounts		44
			Sales Returns and Allowances		20
			Purchases		6,000
			Transportation-In		75
			Miscellaneous Selling Expenses		2,650
			Miscellaneous Administrative Expenses.		1,150
			To close accounts with a debit balance in the Income Statement columns.		

In the third entry, the credit balance in the Income Summary account of $5,843 is closed to the Retained Earnings account.

3rd entry	Dec.	31	Income Summary.	5,843
			Retained Earnings		5,843
			To close the Income Summary account to the Retained Earnings account.		

In the fourth entry, the Dividends account balance of $2,000 is closed to the Retained Earnings account by debiting Retained Earnings and crediting Dividends.

4th entry	Dec.	31	Retained Earnings	2,000
			Dividends		2,000
			To close the Dividends account to the Retained Earnings account.		

Note how the first three closing entries tie into the totals shown in the Income Statement columns of the work sheet in Illustration 5.9. In the first closing journal entry, the credit to the Income Summary account is equal to the total of the Income Statement credit column. In the second entry, the debit to the Income Summary account is equal to the subtotal of the Income Statement debit column. The difference between the totals of the two Income Statement columns ($5,843) represents net income and is the amount of the third closing entry.

The effects of these closing entries are shown in the following T-accounts:

Merchandise Inventory

Bal. before closing		7,000	1994 Dec. 31	To close to Income Summary	7,000
1994 Dec. 31	To establish actual ending inventory balance	8,000			

---

[1] You may close debit balanced accounts (in the Income Statement) before credit balanced accounts. This practice does not affect the balance of the Income Summary account or the amount of net income.

Sales

1994 Dec. 31 To close to Income Summary	14,600	Bal. before closing	14,600
		Bal. after closing	–0–

Sales Discounts

Bal. before closing	44	1994 Dec. 31 To close to Income Summary	44
Bal. after closing	–0–		

Sales Returns and Allowances

Bal. before closing	20	1994 Dec. 31 To close to Income Summary	20
Bal. after closing	–0–		

Purchases

Bal. before closing	6,000	1994 Dec. 31 To close to Income Summary	6,000
Bal. after closing	–0–		

Purchase Discounts

1994 Dec. 31 To close to Income Summary	82	Bal. before closing	82
		Bal. after closing	–0–

Purchase Returns and Allowances

1994 Dec. 31 To close to Income Summary	100	Bal. before closing	100
		Bal. after closing	–0–

Transportation-In

Bal. before closing	75	1994 Dec. 31 To close to Income Summary	75
Bal. after closing	–0–		

Miscellaneous Selling Expenses

Bal. before closing	2,650	1994 Dec. 31 To close to Income Summary	2,650
Bal. after closing	–0–		

A BROADER PERSPECTIVE

SOVIETS READY NEW CHART OF ACCOUNTS

New York—The United Nations is stepping in to help the Soviet Union modernize its accounting system.

According to Karl Sauvant, acting director of the U.N. Center for Transnational Corporations (UNCTC), a new Soviet chart of accounts will be ready in the first half of 1991.

Sauvant said the new chart will comply with international standards, including the definition of relevant concepts, the provision of explanations and the drafting of instructions.

A task force created by the Soviet Ministry of Finance and the UNCTC expects to present a first draft of the new chart to the Soviet Ministry of Finance in September.

According to Sauvant, the Ministry of Finance will present the draft to all 15 Soviet republics for approval. It must then be approved by the Methodological Council and finally the Council of Ministers.

Alexander Antonov, deputy minister of finance and chairman of Inaudit, the government agency which until recently had a monopoly on accounting in the Soviet Union, is optimistic about the modernized chart.

"By next year we expect to be working with an accounting system that complies with international standards to a greater extent than the systems of most other countries do," said Antonov. "We fully recognize the need for a system that provides the information that foreign investors expect from accounting reports."

The current chart of accounts of the USSR is a detailed 200-page document that serves as the manual for the country's 2 million to 3 million bookkeepers who function as rudimentary accountants, Sauvant said. Those bookkeepers are not, however, professionals trained to provide financial or managerial accounting analyses.

At its September meeting the task force will also consider a blueprint for the organization of a true accounting profession in the Soviet Union. The task force will address such issues as the need for an institute of chartered accountants, education requirements and an ethics code.

Source: Glen Alan Cheney, *Accounting Today*. Reprinted by permission from *Accounting Today*, August 27, 1990, p. 13. Copyright Lebhar-Friedman, Inc., 425 Park Avenue, New York, NY 10022.

Miscellaneous Administrative Expenses

Bal. before closing	1,150	1994 Dec. 31 To close to Income Summary	1,150
Bal. after closing	–0–		

Income Summary

1994 Dec. 31 From closing accounts appearing in Income Statement debit column of work sheet	16,939	1994 Dec. 31 From closing accounts appearing in Income Statement credit column of work sheet	22,782
1994 Dec. 31 To close to Retained Earnings account	5,843	Bal. (net income) before closing this account	5,843
		Bal. after closing	–0–

ETHICS	John Bentley is the chief financial officer for World Auto Parts Corporation. The company buys approximately $500 million of auto parts each year from small suppliers from all over the world and resells them to auto repair shops in the United States.
A CLOSER LOOK	Most of the suppliers have cash discount terms of 2/10, n/30. Mr. Bentley has instructed his personnel who are in charge of paying invoices to pay on the 30th day but to take the 2% discount even though they are not entitled to do so. If any supplier complains about this practice, Mr. Bentley instructs his purchasing agent to find another supplier who will go along with the practice. When some of his own employees questioned the practice, Mr. Bentley responded as follows:

This practice really does no harm. These small suppliers are much better off to "go along" and have our business than to not go along and lose it. For most of them, we are their largest customer. Besides, if they are willing to sell to others at a 2% discount, why should they not be willing to sell to us at that same discount even though we pay a little later? The benefit to our company is very significant. Last year our profits were $100 million. A total of $10 million of the profits was attributable to this practice. Do you really want me to change this practice and give up 10% of our profits?

Required
a. Do you agree that the total impact of this practice could be as much as $10 million?

b. Are the small suppliers probably "better off" to go along with the practice?

c. Is this practice ethical?

Retained Earnings

1994			1994		
Dec. 31	From closing Dividends account	2,000	Dec. 31	Beg. bal.	15,000
				From closing Income Summary account	5,843
				End. bal.	18,843

Dividends

			1994		
Bal. before closing		2,000	Dec. 31	To close to Retained Earnings account	2,000
Bal. after closing		–0–			

After the entries have been posted to the ledger, only the balance sheet accounts have balances. The revenue, expense, and dividends accounts have zero balances. Lyons would now prepare a post-closing trial balance similar to the one illustrated for Speedy Delivery Company in Chapter 4. The chapter appendix illustrates an alternative closing procedure.

UNDERSTANDING THE LEARNING OBJECTIVES

1. Record journal entries for sales transactions involving merchandise.
   - In a sales transaction, the seller transfers the legal ownership (title) of the goods to the buyer.
   - An invoice is a document, prepared by the seller of merchandise and sent to the buyer, that contains the details of a sale, such as the num-

ber of units sold, unit price, total price, terms of sale, and manner of shipment.

☐ Usually sales are for cash or on account. When a sale is for cash, the debit is to Cash, and the credit is to Sales. When a sale is on account, the debit is to Accounts Receivable, and the credit is to Sales.

☐ When companies offer trade discounts, the gross selling price (gross invoice price) at which the sale is recorded is equal to the list price minus any trade discounts.

☐ Two common deductions from gross sales are (1) sales discounts and (2) sales returns and allowances. These deductions are recorded in contra revenue accounts to the Sales account. Both the Sales Discounts account and the Sales Returns and Allowances account normally have debit balances. Net sales = Sales − (Sales discounts + Sales returns and allowances).

☐ Sales discounts arise when the seller offers the buyer a cash discount of 1% to 3% to induce early payment of an amount due.

☐ Sales returns result from merchandise being returned by a buyer because the goods are considered unsatisfactory or have been damaged. A sales allowance is a deduction from the original invoiced sales price granted to a customer when the customer keeps the merchandise but is dissatisfied.

2. Describe briefly cost of goods sold and the distinction between perpetual and periodic inventory procedures.

☐ Cost of goods sold = Beginning inventory + Net cost of purchases − Ending inventory. Net cost of purchases = Purchases − (Purchase discounts + Purchase returns and allowances) + Transportation-in.

☐ Two methods of accounting for inventory are perpetual inventory procedure and periodic inventory procedure. Under perpetual inventory procedure, the inventory account is continuously updated during the accounting period. Under periodic inventory procedure, the inventory account is updated only periodically—after a physical count has been made.

3. Record journal entries for purchase transactions involving merchandise.

☐ Purchases of merchandise are recorded by debiting Purchases and crediting Cash (for cash purchases) or crediting Accounts Payable (for purchases on account).

☐ When the net price method is used, a purchase is recorded in Purchases and Accounts Payable *net* of the discount.

☐ If a discount is missed, the Discounts Lost account is debited. This procedure focuses management's attention on discounts missed rather than on discounts taken.

☐ Two common deductions from purchases are shown in (1) purchase discounts and (2) purchase returns and allowances. In the general ledger, both of these items normally carry credit balances. From the buyer's side of the transactions, cash discounts are purchase discounts, and merchandise returns and allowances are purchase returns and allowances.

4. Describe the freight terms and record transportation costs.

☐ FOB shipping point means "free on board at shipping point"—the buyer incurs the freight.

□ FOB destination means "free on board at destination"—the seller incurs the freight.

□ Passage of title is a legal term used to indicate transfer of legal ownership of goods.

□ Freight prepaid is when the seller must initially pay the freight at the time of shipment.

□ Freight collect is when the buyer must initially pay the freight on the arrival of the goods.

5. Determine cost of goods sold.

□ Expansion and application of the relationship introduced in Learning Objective 2. Beginning inventory + Net cost of purchases = Cost of goods available for sale − Ending inventory = Cost of goods sold.

6. Prepare a classified income statement.

□ A classified income statement has four major sections—operating revenues, cost of goods sold, operating expenses, and nonoperating revenues and expenses.

□ Operating revenues are the revenues generated by the major activities of the business—usually the sale of products or services or both.

□ Cost of goods sold is the major expense in merchandising companies.

□ Operating expenses for a merchandising company are those expenses other than cost of goods sold incurred in the normal business functions of a company. Usually, operating expenses are classified as either selling expenses or administrative expenses.

□ Nonoperating revenues and expenses are revenues and expenses not related to the sale of products or services regularly offered for sale by a business.

7. Prepare a work sheet and closing entries for a merchandising company.

□ Except for the merchandise-related accounts, the work sheet for a merchandising company is the same as for a service company.

□ Any revenue accounts and contra purchases accounts that appear in the Adjusted Trial Balance credit column of the work sheet are carried to the Income Statement credit column.

□ Beginning inventory, contra revenue accounts, Purchases, Transportation-In, and expense accounts shown in the Adjusted Trial Balance debit column are carried to the Income Statement debit column.

□ Ending merchandise inventory is entered in the Income Statement credit column and in the Balance Sheet debit column.

□ Closing entries may be prepared directly from the work sheet. The first journal entry debits all items appearing in the Income Statement credit column and credits Income Summary. The second entry credits all items appearing in the Income Statement debit column and debits Income Summary. The third entry debits Income Summary and credits the Retained Earnings account (assuming positive net income). The fourth entry debits the Retained Earnings account and credits the Dividends account.

APPENDIX: ALTERNATIVE CLOSING PROCEDURE

Many of the users of this text prefer the closing process illustrated in the chapter because it is easy to perform. If you are satisfied with that approach, you need not read this appendix. Some users, however, prefer an alternative procedure that they believe communicates more effectively the purposes behind the closing process. Since the end result of both methods is the same, both are correct. The procedure used depends on personal preference.

This appendix illustrates the alternative closing procedure. Under this alternative procedure, the beginning inventory balance and balances in all purchase-related accounts are transferred into the Cost of Goods Sold account in an **adjusting entry.** In a separate **adjusting entry,** the ending inventory is established by debiting Merchandise Inventory and crediting Cost of Goods Sold.

Using the same data from Illustration 5.9, the required adjusting entries for inventory and cost of goods sold under this alternative procedure are as shown below.

The first adjusting entry transfers into the Cost of Goods Sold account the net cost of all the goods available for sale during the year. At this point the Cost of Goods Sold account contains the cost of goods available for sale. The second adjusting entry then removes from the Cost of Goods Sold account the cost of goods unsold at year-end and establishes this amount as the ending inventory.

1994				
Dec.	31	Cost of Goods Sold.	12,893	
		Purchase Discounts.	82	
		Purchase Returns and Allowances	100	
		Merchandise Inventory (beginning)		7,000
		Purchases		6,000
		Transportation-In		75
		To transfer the beginning inventory and the accounts comprising net purchases to the Cost of Goods Sold account.		
	31	Merchandise Inventory (ending)	8,000	
		Cost of Goods Sold		8,000
		To set up ending inventory and reduce Cost of Goods Sold by the cost of goods not sold.		

The result of these two entries is that the Cost of Goods Sold account contains the amount of expense incurred during the year for merchandise delivered to customers. The Cost of Goods Sold account is closed as follows:

1994				
Dec.	31	Income Summary.	4,893	
		Cost of Goods Sold		4,893
		To close Cost of Goods Sold to Income Summary.		

This final entry would generally be included in the compound closing entry for all expenses closed at the end of the period rather than being journalized separately. A difference between the two alternatives is that the method in the chapter does not set up a ledger account for Cost of Goods Sold, while this method does.

Illustration 5.13 shows how a work sheet is prepared using this alternative procedure and focuses on the merchandise-related accounts.

ILLUSTRATION 5.13

Work Sheet Using Alternative Procedure

LYONS COMPANY
Work Sheet
For the Month Ended December 31, 1994

Acct. No.	Account Titles	Trial Balance Debit	Trial Balance Credit	Adjustments Debit	Adjustments Credit	Adjusted Trial Balance Debit	Adjusted Trial Balance Credit	Income Statement Debit	Income Statement Credit	Statement of Retained Earnings Debit	Statement of Retained Earnings Credit	Balance Sheet Debit	Balance Sheet Credit
100	Cash	19,663				19,663						19,663	
103	Accounts Receivable	1,880				1,880						1,880	
105	Merchandise Inventory, December 1	7,000			(1) 7,000								
200	Accounts Payable		700				700						700
300	Capital Stock		10,000				10,000						10,000
310	Retained Earnings, December 1		15,000				15,000				15,000		
320	Dividends	2,000				2,000				2,000			
410	Sales		14,600				14,600		14,600				
411	Sales Discounts	44				44		44					
412	Sales Returns and Allowances	20				20		20					
500	Purchases	6,000			(1) 6,000								
501	Purchase Discounts		82	(1) 82									
502	Purchase Returns and Allowances		100	(1) 100									
503	Transportation-In	75			(1) 75								
557	Miscellaneous Selling Expenses	2,650				2,650		2,650					
567	Miscellaneous Administrative Expenses	1,150				1,150		1,150					
		40,482	40,482										
504	Cost of Goods Sold			(1) 12,893	(2) 8,000	4,893		4,893					
105	Merchandise Inventory, December 31*			(2) 8,000		8,000						8,000	
				21,075	21,075	40,300	40,300	8,757	14,600			29,543	10,700
	Net Income							5,843			5,843		
								14,600	14,600		20,843		
	Retained Earnings, December 31									18,843			18,843
										20,843	20,843	29,543	29,543

Adjustments:
(1) To transfer the beginning inventory and the accounts comprising net purchases to the Cost of Goods Sold account.
(2) To set up ending inventory and reduce Cost of Goods Sold by the cost of goods not sold.
* If desired, the $8,000 in the Adjustments debit column and in the Balance Sheet debit column may be placed on the same line as the $7,000 beginning inventory figure.

Trial Balance Columns   The Trial Balance columns have the same data as shown in Illustration 5.9 in this chapter.

Adjusted Trial Balance Columns   Note that under this method the net balance in Cost of Goods Sold ($4,893) is shown in the Adjusted Trial Balance debit column. Also, the $8,000 ending inventory appears in this same column.

Income Statement Columns   The only purchase-related item that appears in the Income Statement columns is the cost of goods sold ($4,893).

Balance Sheet Columns   The Balance Sheet columns have the same data as shown in Illustration 5.9 in this chapter.

Closing Entries   The closing entries under this alternative procedure are as follows:

1994				
Dec.	31	Sales	14,600	
		Income Summary.		14,600
		To close accounts with a balance in the Income Statement credit column.		
	31	Income Summary.	8,757	
		Sales Discounts		44
		Sales Returns and Allowances		20
		Miscellaneous Selling Expenses		2,650
		Miscellaneous Administrative Expenses		1,150
		Cost of Goods Sold		4,893
		To close accounts with a balance in the Income Statement debit column.		
	31	Income Summary.	5,843	
		Retained Earnings		5,843
		To close the Income Summary account to the Retained Earnings account.		
	31	Retained Earnings	2,000	
		Dividends		2,000
		To close the Dividends account to the Retained Earnings account.		

DEMONSTRATION PROBLEM 5–A

The following transactions occurred between Companies X and Y in June of 1994:

June 10   Company X purchased merchandise from Company Y for $80,000; terms 2/10/EOM, n/60, FOB destination.

11   Company Y paid freight of $1,200.

14   Company X received an allowance of $4,000 from the gross invoice price because of damaged goods.

23   Company X returned $8,000 of goods purchased because they were not the quality ordered.

30   Company Y received payment in full from Company X.

Required   *a.*   Journalize the transactions for Company X using the gross price method.

b.   Journalize the transactions for Company Y.

SOLUTION TO DEMONSTRATION PROBLEM 5–A

a.

GENERAL JOURNAL

Date		Account Titles and Explanation	Post. Ref.	Debit	Credit
		Company X			
1994 June	10	Purchases		8 0 0 0 0	
		Accounts Payable			8 0 0 0 0
		Purchased merchandise from Company Y; terms 2/10/EOM, n/60.			
	14	Accounts Payable		4 0 0 0	
		Purchase Returns and Allowances			4 0 0 0
		Received an allowance from Company Y for damaged goods.			
	23	Accounts Payable		8 0 0 0	
		Purchase Returns and Allowances			8 0 0 0
		Returned merchandise to Company Y because of improper quality.			
	30	Accounts Payable ($80,000 − $4,000 − $8,000)		6 8 0 0 0	
		Purchase Discounts ($68,000 × 0.02)			1 3 6 0
		Cash ($68,000 − $1,360)			6 6 6 4 0
		Paid the amount due to Company Y.			

b.

GENERAL JOURNAL

Date		Account Titles and Explanation	Post. Ref.	Debit	Credit
		Company Y			
1994 June	10	Accounts Receivable		8 0 0 0 0	
		Sales			8 0 0 0 0
		Sold merchandise to Company X; terms 2/10/EOM, n/60.			
	11	Delivery Expense		1 2 0 0	
		Cash			1 2 0 0
		Paid freight on sale of merchandise shipped FOB destination.			
	14	Sales Returns and Allowances		4 0 0 0	
		Accounts Receivable			4 0 0 0
		Granted an allowance to Company X for damaged goods.			
	23	Sales Returns and Allowances		8 0 0 0	
		Accounts Receivable			8 0 0 0
		Merchandise returned from Company X due to improper quality.			
	30	Cash ($68,000 − $1,360)		6 6 6 4 0	
		Sales Discounts ($68,000 × 0.02)		1 3 6 0	
		Accounts Receivable ($80,000 − $4,000 − $8,000)			6 8 0 0 0
		Received the amount due from Company X.			

DEMONSTRATION PROBLEM 5-B

TWIN'S MUSIC STORE
Trial Balance
July 31, 1994

Acct. No.	Account Title	Debits	Credits
100	Cash	$ 93,560	
103	Accounts Receivable	9,200	
105	Merchandise Inventory, August 1, 1993	62,800	
108	Prepaid Insurance	1,440	
112	Prepaid Rent	9,600	
172	Office Equipment	24,000	
173	Accumulated Depreciation—Office Equipment		$ 9,000
200	Accounts Payable		16,000
300	Capital Stock		20,000
310	Retained Earnings, August 1, 1993		24,000
320	Dividends	16,000	
410	Sales		600,000
412	Sales Returns and Allowances	2,000	
500	Purchases	388,000	
502	Purchase Returns and Allowances		2,800
503	Transportation-In	10,400	
505	Advertising Expense	2,000	
507	Salaries Expense	46,400	
511	Utilities Expense	2,800	
518	Supplies Expense	3,600	
		$671,800	$671,800

Clay Twin has prepared the above trial balance for Twin's Music Store. The following information will be used to prepare the work sheet.

1. A 12-month fire insurance policy was purchased for $1,440 on April 1, 1994, the date on which insurance coverage began.

2. On February 1, 1994, Twin paid $9,600 for the next 12 months' rent. The payment was recorded in the Prepaid Rent account.

3. Depreciation expense on the office equipment is $3,000.

4. Merchandise inventory at July 31, 1994, was $52,800.

Required   *a.* Prepare a 12-column work sheet for Twin's Music Store for the fiscal year ended July 31, 1994. Use the chart of accounts on the inside covers of the text to assign additional account numbers as needed.

b. Prepare a classified income statement for the fiscal year ended July 31, 1994. Do not separate operating expenses into selling and administrative categories.

c. Prepare a statement of retained earnings for the fiscal year ended July 31, 1994.

d. Prepare a classified balance sheet for July 31, 1994.

e. Prepare closing entries.

SOLUTION TO DEMONSTRATION PROBLEM 5-B

a. See the work sheet on following page.

TWIN'S MUSIC STORE
Work Sheet
For the Year Ended July 31, 1994

Acct. No.	Account Titles	Trial Balance Debit	Trial Balance Credit	Adjustments Debit	Adjustments Credit	Adjusted Trial Balance Debit	Adjusted Trial Balance Credit	Income Statement Debit	Income Statement Credit	Statement of Retained Earnings Debit	Statement of Retained Earnings Credit	Balance Sheet Debit	Balance Sheet Credit
100	Cash	93,560				93,560						93,560	
103	Accounts Receivable	9,200				9,200						9,200	
105	Merchandise Inventory	62,800				62,800		62,800	52,800			52,800	
108	Prepaid Insurance	1,440			(1) 480	960						960	
112	Prepaid Rent	9,600			(2) 4,800	4,800						4,800	
172	Office Equipment	24,000				24,000						24,000	
173	Accumulated Depreciation—Office Equipment		9,000		(3) 3,000		12,000						12,000
200	Accounts Payable		16,000				16,000						16,000
300	Capital Stock		20,000				20,000						20,000
310	Retained Earnings, August 1, 1993		24,000				24,000				24,000		
320	Dividends	16,000				16,000				16,000			
410	Sales		600,000				600,000		600,000				
412	Sales Returns and Allowances	2,000				2,000		2,000					
500	Purchases	388,000				388,000		388,000					
502	Purchase Returns and Allowances		2,800				2,800		2,800				
503	Transportation-In	10,400				10,400		10,400					
505	Advertising Expense	2,000				2,000		2,000					
507	Salaries Expense	46,400				46,400		46,400					
511	Utilities Expense	2,800				2,800		2,800					
518	Supplies Expense	3,600				3,600		3,600					
		671,800	671,800										
512	Insurance Expense			(1) 480		480		480					
515	Rent Expense			(2) 4,800		4,800		4,800					
525	Depreciation Expense—Office Equipment			(3) 3,000		3,000		3,000					
				8,280	8,280	674,800	674,800	526,280	655,600				
	Net Income							129,320			129,320		
								655,600	655,600	16,000	153,320	185,320	48,000
	Retained Earnings, August 31, 1994									137,320			137,320
										153,320	153,320	185,320	185,320

Adjustments:
(1) Expiration of prepaid insurance ($1,440 × $\frac{4}{12}$).
(2) Expiration of prepaid rent ($9,600 × $\frac{6}{12}$).
(3) Depreciation expense on office equipment for the fiscal year ended July 31, 1994.

b.

TWIN'S MUSIC STORE
Income Statement
For the Year Ended July 31, 1994

Operating revenues:

Gross sales			$600,000
Less: Sales returns and allowances			2,000
Net sales			$598,000

Cost of goods sold:

Merchandise inventory, August 1, 1993		$ 62,800	
Purchases	$388,000		
Less: Purchase returns and allowances	2,800		
Net purchases	$385,200		
Add: Transportation-in	10,400		
Net cost of purchases		395,600	
Cost of goods available for sale		$458,400	
Merchandise inventory, July 31, 1994		52,800	
Cost of goods sold			405,600
Gross margin			$192,400

Operating expenses:

Selling expenses:

Advertising expense		$ 2,000	

Administrative expenses:

Supplies expense	$ 3,600		
Salaries expense	46,400		
Utilities expense	2,800		
Insurance expense	480		
Rent expense	4,800		
Depreciation expense—office equipment	3,000	61,080	
Total operating expenses			63,080
Net income			$129,320

---

c.

TWIN'S MUSIC STORE
Statement of Retained Earnings
For the Year Ended July 31, 1994

Retained earnings, August 1, 1993	$ 24,000
Net income for the year	129,320
Total	$153,320
Less: Dividends	16,000
Retained earnings, July 31, 1994	$137,320

---

d.

TWIN'S MUSIC STORE
Balance Sheet
July 31, 1994
Assets

Current assets:

Cash	$ 93,560	
Accounts receivable	9,200	
Merchandise inventory	52,800	
Prepaid insurance	960	
Prepaid rent	4,800	
Total current assets		$161,320

Property, plant, and equipment:

Office equipment	$ 24,000	
Less: Accumulated depreciation	12,000	
Total property, plant, and equipment		12,000
Total assets		$173,320

Liabilities and Stockholders' Equity

Liabilities:

Accounts payable		$ 16,000

Stockholders' equity:

Capital stock	$ 20,000	
Retained earnings	137,320	
Total stockholders' equity		157,320
Total liabilities and stockholders' equity		$173,320

e. Closing entries:

1994				
July	31	Merchandise Inventory	52,800	
		Sales	600,000	
		Purchase Returns and Allowances	2,800	
		Income Summary		655,600
		To close accounts with credit balances in the Income Statement columns and to set up the ending merchandise inventory.		
	31	Income Summary	526,280	
		Merchandise Inventory		62,800
		Sales Returns and Allowances		2,000
		Purchases		388,000
		Transportation-In		10,400
		Advertising Expense		2,000
		Salaries Expense		46,400
		Utilities Expense		2,800
		Supplies Expense		3,600
		Insurance Expense		480
		Rent Expense		4,800
		Depreciation Expense—Office Equipment		3,000
		To close accounts with debit balances in the Income Statement columns.		
	31	Income Summary	129,320	
		Retained Earnings		129,320
		To close the Income Summary account to the Retained Earnings account.		
	31	Retained Earnings	16,000	
		Dividends		16,000
		To close Dividends account.		

NEW TERMS

Adjunct account Closely related to another account; its balance is added to the balance of the related account in the financial statements. *215*

Administrative expenses Expenses a company incurs in the overall management of a business. *222*

Cash discount A deduction from the gross invoice price that can be taken only if the invoice is paid within a specified period of time: to the seller, it is a sales discount; to the buyer, it is a purchase discount. *206*

Chain discount Occurs when the list price of a product is subject to a series of trade discounts. *205*

Classified income statement Divides both revenues and expenses into operating and nonoperating items. The statement also separates operating expenses into selling and administrative expenses. Also called the multiple-step income statement. *220*

Consigned goods Goods delivered to another party who will attempt to sell the goods for the owner at a commission. *218*

Cost of goods available for sale Equal to beginning inventory plus net cost of purchases. *218*

Cost of goods sold Shows the cost to the seller of the goods sold to customers; under periodic inventory procedure, cost of goods sold is computed as Beginning inventory + Net cost of purchases − Ending inventory. *209, 220, 222*

Delivery expense A selling expense recorded by the seller for freight costs incurred when terms are FOB destination. *216*

Discounts Lost account The account used to show the amount of discounts not taken when purchased merchandise is recorded using the net price method. *213*

FOB destination Means "free on board at destination"; goods are shipped to their destination without charge to the buyer; the seller is responsible for paying the freight charges. *215*

FOB shipping point Means "free on board at shipping point"; buyer incurs all transportation costs after the merchandise is loaded on a railroad car or truck at the point of shipment. *215*

Freight collect Terms that require the buyer to pay the freight bill on arrival of the goods. *215*

Freight prepaid Terms that indicate the seller has paid the freight bill at the time of shipment. *215*

Gross margin or gross profit Net sales − Cost of goods sold; identifies the number of dollars available to cover expenses other than cost of goods sold; may be expressed as a percentage rate. *220, 222*

Gross selling price The list price less all trade discounts. *205*

Income from operations Gross margin − Operating (selling and administrative) expenses. *222*

Inventory See Merchandise inventory.

Invoice A document, prepared by the seller of merchandise and sent to the buyer, that contains the details of a sale, such as the number of units sold, unit price, total price billed, terms of sale, and manner of shipment; a purchase invoice from the buyer's point of view and a sales invoice from the seller's point of view. *203*

Manufacturers Companies that produce goods from raw materials and normally sell them to wholesalers. *202*

Merchandise in transit Merchandise in the hands of a freight company on the date of a physical inventory. *218*

Merchandise inventory The quantity of goods on hand and available for sale at any given time. *209, 217*

Net cost of purchases Net purchases + Transportation-in. *215, 222*

Net income Income from operations + Nonoperating revenues − Nonoperating expenses. *222*

Net price method An accounting procedure in which purchases and accounts payable are initially recorded at gross price less discount offered for prompt payment. Records discounts lost rather than discounts taken. *213*

Net purchases Purchases − (Purchase discounts + Purchase returns and allowances). *215, 222*

Net sales Gross sales − (Sales discounts + Sales returns and allowances). *203, 222*

Nonoperating expenses (other expenses) Expenses incurred by a business that are not related to the acquisition and sale of the products or services regularly offered for sale. *222*

Nonoperating revenues (other revenues) Revenues not related to the sale of products or services regularly offered for sale by a business. *222*

Operating expenses Those expenses other than cost of goods sold incurred in the normal business functions of a company. *222*

Operating revenues Those revenues generated by the major activities of a business. *220*

Passage of title A legal term used to indicate transfer of legal ownership of goods. *215*

Periodic inventory procedure A method of accounting for merchandise acquired for sale to customers wherein the cost of merchandise sold and the cost of merchandise on hand are determined only at the end of the accounting period by taking a physical inventory. *210*

Perpetual inventory procedure A method of accounting for merchandise acquired for sale to customers wherein the Merchandise Inventory account is continuously updated to reflect items on hand; this account is debited for each purchase and credited for each sale so that the current balance is shown in the account at all times. *210*

Physical inventory Consists of counting physical units of each type of merchandise on hand. *218*

Purchase discount See Cash discount.

Purchase Discounts account A contra account to Purchases that reduces the recorded gross invoice cost of the purchase to the price actually paid. *212*

Purchase Returns and Allowances account An account used under periodic inventory procedure to record the cost of merchandise returned to a seller and to record reductions in selling prices granted by a seller because merchandise was not satisfactory to a buyer; viewed as a reduction in the recorded cost of purchases. *214*

Purchases account An account used under periodic inventory procedure to record the cost of goods or merchandise bought for resale during the current accounting period. *212*

Retailers Companies that sell goods to final consumers. *202*

Sales allowance A deduction from original invoiced sales price granted to a customer when the customer keeps the merchandise but is dissatisfied for any of a number of reasons, including inferior quality or damage or deterioration in transit. *207*

Sales discount See Cash discount.

Sales Discounts account A contra revenue account to Sales; it is shown as a deduction from gross sales in the income statement. *207*

Sales return From the seller's point of view, merchandise returned by a buyer for any of a variety of reasons; to the buyer, a purchase return. *207*

Sales Returns and Allowances account A contra revenue account to Sales used to record the selling price of merchandise returned by buyers or reductions in selling prices granted. *207*

Selling expenses Expenses a company incurs in selling and marketing efforts. *222*

Trade discount A percentage deduction, or discount, from the specified list price or catalog price of merchandise to arrive at the gross invoice price; granted to particular categories of customers (e.g., retailers and wholesalers). Also see Chain discount. *205*

Transportation-In account An account used under periodic inventory procedure to record inward freight costs incurred in the acquisition of merchandise; a part of cost of goods sold. *215*

Unclassified income statement Shows only major categories for revenues and expenses. Also called the single-step income statement. *220*

Wholesalers Companies that sell goods to other companies (retailers) for resale. *202*

SELF-TEST

True-False

Indicate whether each of the following statements is true or false.

1. Sales discounts and sales returns and allowances are deducted from gross sales to determine net sales.

2. Under periodic inventory procedure, the cost of goods sold is reflected in the balance of the Purchases account.

3. Transportation costs on goods shipped FOB destination are added to net purchases to arrive at net cost of purchases.

4. An income statement that separates revenues and expenses into operating and nonoperating items is called a classified income statement.

5. The merchandise inventory amount in the Balance Sheet debit column of the work sheet is the ending inventory.

Multiple-Choice

Select the best answer for each of the following questions.

1. The entry on the books of the seller to record the return of merchandise sold on account for which no payment has been received is:
   a. Accounts Receivable (Dr.); Sales Returns and Allowances (Cr.).
   b. Sales (Dr.); Accounts Receivable (Cr.).
   c. Sales Returns and Allowances (Dr.); Accounts Receivable (Cr.).
   d. None of the above.

2. Cost of goods sold refers to:
   a. Cost of goods available for sale less ending inventory.
   b. Cost prices that are identified with the items that were sold during the period.
   c. Net cost of purchases plus beginning inventory.
   d. Net sales less gross margin.
   e. All of the above except *(c)*.

3. An account payable of $400 is subject to a 2% discount if paid within the 10-day discount period. Part of the entry to record this payment would be:
   a. A credit to Accounts Payable of $392.
   b. A debit to Accounts Payable of $400.
   c. A credit to Accounts Payable of $400.
   d. A credit to Cash of $400.
   e. A debit to Purchase Discounts of $8.

4. In the income statement:
   a. The amount shown as "Net sales" includes all cash sales plus only those charge sales for which cash has been received.
   b. Expenses are subtracted from revenues to determine the balance of the Retained Earnings account.
   c. Operating expenses are usually classified as either "Selling expenses" or "Administrative expenses."
   d. Ending inventory is added to the net cost of purchases to determine goods available for sale.
   e. "Net income from operations" and "Net income" are synonymous.

5. The closing entries for merchandise-related accounts include:
   a. A credit to Merchandise Inventory for the cost of the beginning inventory.
   b. A debit to Purchase Discounts.
   c. A credit to Purchases.
   d. A debit to Merchandise Inventory for the ending inventory.
   e. All of the above.

QUESTIONS

1. Which account titles are likely to appear in the accounting system of a merchandising company that do not appear in the system employed by a service enterprise?

2. Explain the difference between trade discounts and cash discounts. What are chain discounts and purchase discounts?

3. Sales discounts and sales returns and allowances are deducted from sales on the income statement to arrive at net sales. Why not deduct these amounts directly from the Sales account by debiting Sales each time a sales discount, return, or allowance occurs?

4. How is cost of goods sold determined under periodic inventory procedure?

5. You find yourself in a conversation with a business executive who uses perpetual (rather than periodic) inventory procedure. The executive says, "Sure, it's cumbersome to keep perpetual inventory records, but it's much easier than performing a physical count of your inventory at the end of every year as must be done under periodic procedure." What would be your response?

6. Is it possible for a firm to use perpetual procedure for some of the products it sells and periodic procedure for others? Explain.

7. Perpetual inventory procedure is said to afford control over inventory. Explain exactly what this control consists of and how it is provided.

8. Periodic inventory procedure is said to afford little control over inventory. Explain why.

9. What useful purpose does the Purchases account serve?

10. How should purchase discounts lost be shown in the income statement?

11. Explain how use of the net price method of accounting for purchases can improve internal control.

12. A financial manager is explaining a firm's policy to you and states, "Our firm is in a tight financial position. No one will lend us money to take advantage of our discounts. Even though we can't pay within the discount period, I do the next best thing. I pay each bill as soon as I can thereafter." Do you agree that this is the next best approach? Why?

13. What do the letters *FOB* stand for? When terms are *FOB destination,* who incurs the freight? Who owns the goods until they arrive at their destination?

14. What type of an expense is delivery expense? Where is this expense reported in the income statement?

15. What are some of the problems encountered in taking a physical inventory? How does the accountant solve these problems?

16. What is gross margin? Why might management be interested in the percentage of gross margin to sales?

17. What is a contra account? Why is it used? What are some examples of contra accounts?

18. What are the four major sections in a classified income statement for a merchandising company, and in what order do these sections appear?

19. If the cost of goods available for sale and the cost of the ending inventory are known, what other amount appearing on the income statement can be calculated?

20. After closing entries are posted to the ledger, which types of accounts have balances? Why?

MAYTAG
CORPORATION

21. *Real world question* Based on the financial statements of Maytag Corporation contained in Appendix E, what were the 1989 selling, general, and administrative expenses?

THE LIMITED, INC.

22. *Real world question* Based on the financial statements of The Limited, Inc., contained in Appendix E, what were the 1989 cost of goods sold, occupancy, and buying costs?

HARLAND

23. *Real world question* Based on the financial statements of John H. Harland Company contained in Appendix E, what was the 1989 employees' profit sharing expense?

EXERCISES

Exercise 5–1

Apply rules of debit and credit for merchandise-related accounts (L.O. 1, 3)

In the following table, indicate how (debit or credit) each account shown is increased and decreased, and indicate the normal balance (debit or credit).

Title of Account	Increased by (debit or credit)	Decreased by (debit or credit)	Normal Balance (debit or credit)
Sales			
Sales Returns and Allowances			
Sales Discounts			
Accounts Receivable			
Purchases			
Purchase Returns and Allowances			
Purchase Discounts			
Discounts Lost			
Accounts Payable			
Transportation-In			

Exercise 5–2

Prepare entries for merchandise return and allowance on both buyer's and seller's books (L.O. 1, 3)

a. Rankin Company purchased merchandise from Weeks Company on account. Before paying the account, Rankin returned damaged merchandise with an invoice price of $12,600. Assuming use of periodic inventory procedure, prepare entries on both firms' books to record the return.

b. Prepare the required entries assuming that Weeks Company granted an allowance of $4,200 on the damaged goods instead of accepting the return.

Exercise 5–3

Determine end of discount period and prepare entry to record payment (L.O. 1, 3)

What is the last payment date on which the cash discount can be taken on goods sold on March 5 for $256,000; terms 3/10/EOM, n/60? Assume that the bill is paid on this date and prepare the correct entry on both the seller's and buyer's books to record the payment.

Exercise 5–4

Calculate effect of trade and cash discounts on payment (L.O. 1, 3)

You have purchased merchandise with a list price of $16,000. Because you are a wholesaler, you are granted trade discounts of 30%, 20%, and 10%. The cash discount terms are 2/EOM, n/60. How much will you remit if you pay by the end of the month of purchase? How much will you remit if you do not pay until the following month?

Exercise 5–5

Determine equivalent rate of interest in a discount (L.O. 3)

Merchandise with a gross selling price of $15,000 was purchased by you under terms of 3/10, n/60, on January 2, 1994. You believe that by March 3, 1994, you could pay a loan taken out to take advantage of the discount. What is the highest annual rate of interest you could afford to pay on the loan and be as well off as if you had taken the discount? Use the formula in the text.

Exercise 5–6

Determine cost of goods sold (L.O. 2, 5)

Quality Company uses periodic inventory procedure. Determine the cost of goods sold for the company, assuming purchases during the period were $48,000; transportation-in was $360; purchases returns and allowances were $1,200; beginning inventory was $30,000; purchase discounts were $2,400; and ending inventory was $15,600.

Exercise 5–7

Prepare entries for purchase, transportation-in, purchase discount, and payment (L.O. 3, 4)

Knight Company purchased goods for $36,800 on June 14 under the following terms: 3/10, n/30; FOB shipping point, freight collect. The bill for the freight amounted to $1,200. Assume the invoice was paid within the discount period, and prepare all entries required on Knight's books using gross price procedure.

Exercise 5–8

Prepare entry for payment (L.O. 3)

Refer to the data in Exercise 5–7 and assume that the invoice was paid on July 11. Prepare the entry to record the payment made on that date.

Exercise 5–9

Record purchases using net price method (L.O. 3)

Cracker Company uses the net price method for handling purchase discounts. Prepare the journal entries necessary to record the following 1994 transactions:

Oct. 6 Purchased $3,000 of merchandise; terms 2/10, n/30.
   7 Purchased $10,000 of merchandise; terms 2/10, n/30.
   17 Paid the invoice for the October 7 purchase.
   31 Paid the invoice for the October 6 purchase.

Exercise 5–10

Supply missing terms in formulas showing income statement relationships (L.O. 5, 6)

In each of the following equations, supply the missing term(s):

a. Net sales = Gross sales − _____ _____ − Sales returns and allowances.

b. Cost of goods sold = Beginning inventory + Net cost of purchases − _____ _____ .

c. Gross margin = _____ _____ − Cost of goods sold.

d. Net income from operations = _____ _____ − Operating expenses.

e. Net income = Net income from operations + _____ _____ − _____ _____ .

Exercise 5–11

Supply missing amounts in the income statement (L.O. 2, 5, 6)

In each case below, use the information provided to calculate the missing information:

	Case 1	Case 2	Case 3
Gross sales	$800,000	$?	$?
Sales discounts	?	32,000	24,000
Sales returns and allowances	24,000	56,000	40,000
Net sales	760,000	1,512,000	?
Merchandise inventory, January 1	320,000	?	480,000
Purchases	480,000	960,000	?
Purchase discounts	9,600	16,800	16,000
Purchase returns and allowances	30,400	39,200	40,000
Net purchases.	440,000	?	840,000
Transportation-in.	32,000	48,000	40,000
Net cost of purchases	472,000	952,000	?
Cost of goods available for sale	?	1,352,000	1,360,000
Merchandise inventory, December 31	?	480,000	560,000
Cost of goods sold.	400,000	?	800,000
Gross margin	?	640,000	400,000

Exercise 5–12

Prepare partial work sheet using merchandise-related accounts (L.O. 7)

Given the balances shown in the partial trial balance below, indicate where else the balances would appear in the work sheet. The ending inventory is $256. The amounts are unusually small for ease in writing the numbers.

Account Title	Trial Balance		Adjustments		Adjusted Trial Balance		Income Statement		Statement of Retained Earnings		Balance Sheet	
	Debit	Credit	Debit	Credit	Debit	Credit	Debit	Credit	Debit	Credit	Debit	Credit
Merchandise Inventory	320											
Sales		2,240										
Sales Discounts	48											
Sales Returns and Allowances	128											
Purchases	1,600											
Purchase Discounts		32										
Purchase Returns and Allowances		64										
Transportation-In	96											

Exercise 5–13

Prepare closing entries
(L.O. 7)

Using the data in Exercise 5–12, prepare closing entries for the accounts shown above.

PROBLEMS: SERIES A

Problem 5–1A

Journalize merchandise transactions on buyer's books
(L.O. 1–4)

On July 2, 1994, Worrill Company purchased merchandise with a list price of $73,600 from Mitchell Company. The terms were 3/EOM, n/60; FOB shipping point, freight collect. Trade discounts of 15%, 10%, and 5% were granted by Mitchell Company. Worrill Company paid the freight bill of $1,920 on July 5. On July 5, it was discovered that merchandise with a list price of $6,400 had been seriously damaged in transit; these items were returned for full credit.

Required   Assume that Worrill Company makes payment on the last day of the discount period and prepare all the necessary entries for both companies. Assume the buyer uses periodic inventory procedure and gross price procedure.

Problem 5–2A

Journalize merchandise transactions on buyer's and seller's books
(L.O. 1–3)

The transactions for Jennifer Company and Joiner Company follow. Assume the buyer uses periodic inventory procedure and gross price procedure.

May 18   Jennifer Company sold to Joiner Company merchandise with a sales price of $48,000; terms 2/10/EOM.

29   Joiner Company returned $6,000 of the merchandise to Jennifer Company.

June 3   Joiner Company requested a gross allowance of $4,000 from Jennifer Company due to defective merchandise. Jennifer Company issued a credit memo granting the allowance.

7   Joiner Company paid the net amount due.

Required   a.   Journalize the transactions for Jennifer Company.

b.   Journalize the transactions for Joiner Company.

Problem 5–3A

Compute approximate annual rate of interest in discount terms
(L.O. 3)

Compute the approximate annual rate of interest being charged in each of the following terms if the discount is not taken and the invoice is paid when due.

a.   2/10, n/30.

b.   1/10, n/45.

c.   3/EOM, n/90, goods purchased on July 16.

In view of your computations, comment on the desirability of borrowing to take advantage of discounts.

Problem 5–4A

Journalize merchandise
transactions after
determining lowest bidder
(L.O. 3, 4)

The following are events and transactions of Shadow Company during April 1994.

Apr. 1 The planning department requested the purchasing department to order 1,000 units of a given material.

3 The purchasing department sent out requests for quotations to companies J, M, and A.

7 Quotations received are as follows:

J—List price: $25.20 each, less 30% and 20%. On all orders for more than 500 units, an additional 10% discount is allowed on the total order. Terms: 3/10, n/30, FOB destination, freight prepaid.

M—List price: $28.80 each, less 35% and 30%. Terms: 2/10, n/30, FOB shipping point.

A—List price: $12.60 each. Terms: n/30, FOB destination, freight prepaid.

The shipping cost under each bid is determined to be $300, $120, and $180, respectively.

Apr. 8 Placed order with lowest bidder. The company takes advantage of all cash discounts.

15 Invoice received covering above merchandise.

16 Receiving department report stated that merchandise is as ordered. Invoice is checked and found to be correct. (Record invoice at its gross amount.)

24 Invoice is paid.

Required   Prepare dated journal entries for the above, where appropriate, including computations showing the actual cost of each bid, assuming that Shadow Company uses periodic inventory procedure and gross price procedure.

Problem 5–5A

Journalize merchandise
transactions on buyer's
and seller's books
(L.O. 1–4)

Davenport Company purchased merchandise on March 1, 1994, from McConnell Company at a list price of $30,000, FOB shipping point. Trade discounts of 30%, 25%, and 5% were granted. Cash discount terms were 2/EOM, n/60. The buyer paid the freight of $744 on March 4, 1994. The buyer notified the seller that a $3,600 credit net of trade discounts should be granted against the amount due because of damaged merchandise. The seller agreed and sent the buyer a credit memorandum on March 25, 1994. Payment was made on March 26.

Required   Record all entries on the books of both buyer and seller, assuming that the buyer uses periodic inventory procedure and net price procedure.

Problem 5–6A

Prepare and post journal
entries; prepare classified
income statement,
statement of retained
earnings, and classified
balance sheet
(L.O. 1–6)

The transactions and data given below are for Recall Company (which uses periodic inventory procedure and gross price procedure):

May 1 Recall Company was organized as a corporation. John Recall invested the following assets in the business for stock: $210,000 cash; $80,000 of merchandise; and $50,000 of land.

5 The company purchased and paid cash for merchandise having a gross cost of $90,000, from which a 2% cash discount was granted.

8 Cash of $2,100 was paid to a trucking company for delivery of the merchandise purchased May 5. The goods were sold FOB shipping point.

14 The company sold merchandise on account, $150,000; terms 2/10, n/30.

16 Of the merchandise sold May 14, $6,600 was returned for credit.

19 Salaries for services received were paid as follows: to office employees, $6,600; and to salespersons, $17,400.

23 The company collected the amount due on $60,000 of the accounts receivable arising from the sales of May 14.

25 The company purchased and paid cash for merchandise costing $72,000 gross, less a 2% cash discount.

27 Of the merchandise purchased May 25, $12,000 gross was returned to the vendor, who gave Recall Company a check for the proper amount.

May 28 A trucking company was paid $1,500 for delivery to Recall Company of the goods purchased May 25. The goods were sold FOB shipping point.

29 The company sold merchandise on account, $7,200; terms 2/10, n/30.

30 Cash sales were $36,000 gross, less a 2% cash discount.

30 Cash of $48,000 was received from the sales of May 14.

31 Paid store rent for May, $9,000.

Additional data

The inventory on hand at the close of business on May 31 was $139,400 at cost.

Required *a.* Prepare journal entries for the transactions.

b. Post the journal entries to the proper ledger accounts.

c. Prepare a classified income statement and a statement of retained earnings for the month ended May 31, 1994.

d. Prepare a classified balance sheet as of May 31, 1994.

Problem 5–7A

Prepare journal entries, classified income statement, statement of retained earnings, and classified balance sheet (L.O. 1–6)

The following information is for Cholly Company.

A suggestion: You may want to set up T-accounts and enter the December 31, 1993, balances given below and post your journal entries to arrive at ending balances.

CHOLLY COMPANY
Post-Closing Trial Balance
December 31, 1993

	Debits	Credits
Cash	$190,000	
Accounts Receivable	330,000	
Merchandise Inventory	280,000	
Accounts Payable		$210,000
Capital Stock		400,000
Retained Earnings		190,000
	$800,000	$800,000

Summarized transactions for 1994

1. Cash sales, $670,000.
2. Sales on account at gross invoice prices, $1,480,000.
3. Purchases on account at gross invoice prices, $1,600,000.
4. Accounts receivable collected $1,375,000 (after taking cash discounts of $120,000).
5. Sales returns (from sales on account), $45,000.
6. Purchase returns (from purchases on account), $22,000.
7. Accounts payable paid $1,290,000 (after taking cash discounts of $24,000).
8. Miscellaneous selling expenses incurred and paid, $196,000.
9. Miscellaneous administrative expenses incurred and paid, $182,000.
10. Land purchased for $540,000 (cash, $330,000; long-term mortgage note, $210,000).
11. Interest expense incurred and paid, $12,000.

Additional data

The merchandise inventory at December 31, 1994, was $344,000. The company uses periodic inventory procedure and gross price procedure.

Required *a.* Prepare journal entries for the summarized transactions for 1994.

b. Prepare a classified income statement and a statement of retained earnings for the year ended December 31, 1994.

c. Prepare a classified balance sheet as of December 31, 1994.

Problem 5–8A

Prepare work sheet and closing entries (L.O. 7)

The trial balance and additional data given below are for Nova Company.

NOVA COMPANY
Trial Balance
December 31, 1994

	Debits	Credits
Cash	$ 50,640	
Accounts Receivable	145,040	
Notes Receivable	20,000	
Merchandise Inventory, January 1, 1994	85,200	
Supplies on Hand	2,400	
Store Fixtures	88,000	
Accumulated Depreciation—Store Fixtures		$ 17,600
Accounts Payable		78,800
Notes Payable		24,000
Capital Stock		200,000
Retained Earnings		225,160
Dividends	20,000	
Sales		922,360
Sales Returns and Allowances	5,160	
Interest Revenue		1,000
Interest Expense	600	
Purchases	500,840	
Purchase Returns and Allowances		4,040
Transportation-In	7,840	
Sales Salaries Expense	138,400	
Advertising Expense	78,000	
Supplies Expense	2,960	
Miscellaneous Administrative Expenses	9,880	
Insurance Expense	4,800	
Office Salaries Expense	80,800	
Officers' Salaries Expense	160,000	
Legal and Accounting Expense	10,000	
Utilities Expense	4,800	
Rent Expense	57,600	
	$1,472,960	$1,472,960

The company consistently followed the policy of initially debiting all prepaid items to expense accounts.

Additional data

1. Prepaid insurance amounted to $1,400.
2. Supplies on hand, $1,700.
3. Prepaid rent expense (store only), $7,000.
4. Store fixtures have an expected life of 10 years with no salvage value.
5. Accrued sales salaries, $4,000.
6. Accrued office salaries, $3,000.
7. Merchandise inventory was $150,000 on December 31, 1994. (This latter information does not require an adjusting entry.)

Required Prepare:

a. A 12-column work sheet for the year ended December 31, 1994. You do not have to show account numbers.
b. The December 31, 1994, closing entries.

PROBLEMS: SERIES B

Problem 5–1B

Journalize merchandise transactions on buyer's and seller's books (L.O. 1, 3, 4)

Tony Brown Company purchased merchandise with a list price of $120,000, FOB destination, freight prepaid, from Mexican Company on August 15, 1994. Trade discounts of 20% and 10% were allowed, and credit terms were 2/10, n/30. Mexican Company paid the freight charges of $3,000 on August 16. On August 17, Tony Brown Company requested a purchase allowance of $5,640 because some of the merchandise had been damaged in transit. On August 20, it received a credit memorandum from Mexican Company granting the allowance.

Required

Record all the entries required on the books of both the buyer and the seller, assuming that the buyer uses periodic inventory procedure and gross price procedure. Also assume that payment is made on the last day of the discount period.

Problem 5–2B

Journalize merchandise transactions on buyer's and seller's books (L.O. 1–3)

The transactions for Tanner Company and Stillwell Company are as follows:

Mar. 12 Tanner Company purchased merchandise from Stillwell Company, $108,000, terms 2/10/EOM, n/60.

20 Tanner Company returned $36,000 of the merchandise to Stillwell Company.

Apr. 7 Stillwell Company received proper payment in full from Tanner Company.

16 Tanner Company had requested, and on this date received, a credit memorandum granting a gross allowance of $6,400 from Stillwell Company due to improper quality of merchandise purchased on March 12.

Both companies use periodic inventory procedure.

Required

a. Journalize the transactions for Tanner Company and use gross price procedure for invoices.

b. Journalize the transactions for Stillwell Company.

Problem 5–3B

Compute approximate annual rate of interest in discount terms (L.O. 3)

Compute the approximate annual rate of interest being charged in each of the following terms under the assumption that the discount is not taken and the invoice is paid when due:

a. 3/10, n/60.

b. 1/10, n/30.

c. 2/EOM, n/60, goods purchased on January 15.

In view of your computations, comment on the desirability of borrowing to take advantage of discounts.

Problem 5–4B

Prepare schedule showing determination of lowest bid (L.O. 3, 4)

The purchasing department of Tamara Company asked for and received the following price quotations on 2,800 units of a given product that it wished to buy:

Mitchell, Inc.—List price: $30.40 each, less 15%. Terms: 2/10, n/30, FOB shipping point. (Transportation charges are determined to be $2,880.)

Jordan Corp.—List price: $27.20 each. Terms: n/30, FOB destination. (Transportation charges are determined to be $700.)

Sims Corp.—List price: $44 each, less 20%, 15%, and 10% trade discounts. Terms: 3/10, n/45, FOB destination. (Transportation charges are determined to be $1,060.)

Worthy Co.—List price: $34.80, less 15% and 10%. Terms: n/30, FOB shipping point. (Transportation charges are determined to be $4,000.)

Required

Decide which bid should be accepted and support your conclusion with a schedule showing the net cost of each bid. Assume the company's policy is to take advantage of all cash discounts.

Problem 5–5B

Journalize merchandise transactions on buyer's and seller's books (L.O. 1–4)

On August 1, 1994, Speedy Company sold merchandise to Mac Company, $36,000 list price, FOB destination. (The seller prepaid the freight of $480 on August 1, 1994.) Other terms were trade discounts of 30% and 10%, and a cash discount of 2/10/EOM, n/60. On August 8, 1994, Mac Company returned $6,000 (at list price) of the merchandise. The balance due was paid on September 9, 1994.

Required

Journalize all entries required on the books of both the buyer and the seller, assuming the buyer uses periodic inventory procedure and net price procedure.

Problem 5–6B

Prepare and post journal entries; prepare classified income statement, statement of retained earnings, and classified balance sheet
(L.O. 1–6)

The data given below are for Bolden Company (which uses periodic inventory procedure and gross price procedure):

BOLDEN COMPANY
Balance Sheet
December 31, 1994
Assets

Cash	$ 45,600
Accounts receivable	79,200
Merchandise inventory	67,200
Total assets	$192,000

Liabilities and Stockholders' Equity

Accounts payable	$ 50,400
Capital stock.	24,000
Retained earnings	117,600
Total liabilities and stockholders' equity	$192,000

Summarized transactions for 1995

1. Sales for cash, $160,800.
2. Sales on account, $355,200.
3. Purchases on account (gross), $384,000.
4. Collected $330,000 on accounts receivable of $334,800. Sales discounts were $4,800.
5. Sales returns (charge sales), $10,800.
6. Purchase returns, $5,280.
7. Cash payments on accounts payable were $309,600 after taking purchase discounts of $5,760.
8. Land purchased (gave one half in cash and long-term note for one half), $148,800.
9. Selling expenses incurred and paid for, $47,040.
10. Administrative expenses incurred and paid for, $43,680.
11. Interest expense on long-term note on land incurred and paid for, $2,880.

Additional data

Merchandise inventory at December 31, 1995, per physical count was $82,560.

Required

a. Prepare journal entries for the summarized transactions.

b. Post the journal entries to the proper ledger accounts (after entering the balances as of December 31, 1994).

c. Prepare a classified income statement and a statement of retained earnings for the year ended December 31, 1995.

d. Prepare a classified balance sheet as of December 31, 1995.

Problem 5–7B

Journalize and post transactions; prepare trial balance and partial income statement
(L.O. 1–6)

The following transactions are for Hall Supply Company:

May 1 Sherry Hoffman invested $400,000 in her new business for all the stock of the corporation.

1 Purchased merchandise on account from Cook Company, $26,000; terms n/10/EOM, FOB shipping point.

3 Sold merchandise for cash, $16,000.

6 Paid transportation charges on May 1 purchase, $400 cash.

7 Returned $2,000 of merchandise to Cook Company due to improper size.

10 Requested and was granted an allowance of $1,000 by Cook Company for improper quality of certain items.

14 Sold goods on account to Henry Company, $10,000; terms 2/20, n/30.

May 16 Cash refunded on returns of sales made on May 3, $100.

18 Purchased goods on account from Turner Company invoiced at $16,200, including $200 of transportation charges prepaid by Turner; terms 2/15, n/30, FOB shipping point.

19 Henry Company returned $200 of merchandise purchased on May 14.

24 Returned $1,600 of defective merchandise to Turner Company.

28 Henry Company remitted balance due on sale of May 14.

31 Paid Turner Company for the purchase of May 18 after adjusting for transaction of May 24.

Additional data

The company was organized as a corporation on May 1 and uses periodic inventory procedure. The May 31 inventory was $28,000.

Required

a. Journalize the transactions in the records of Hall Supply Company, using gross price procedure.

b. Post the entries to the proper ledger accounts.

c. Prepare a trial balance as of May 31.

d. Prepare a partial income statement for May, through the gross margin figure.

Problem 5–8B

Prepare work sheet and closing entries (L.O. 7)

The following trial balance and additional data are for Gibson Company.

GIBSON COMPANY
Trial Balance
December 31, 1994

	Debits	Credits
Cash	$ 51,750	
Accounts Receivable	247,500	
Notes Receivable	22,500	
Merchandise Inventory, January 1, 1994	124,800	
Land	150,000	
Buildings	330,000	
Accumulated Depreciation—Buildings		$ 99,000
Store Fixtures	166,800	
Accumulated Depreciation—Store Fixtures		33,360
Accounts Payable		113,700
Notes Payable		150,000
Capital Stock		60,000
Retained Earnings		455,790
Dividends	30,000	
Sales		1,654,500
Sales Returns and Allowances	6,000	
Sales Discounts	11,100	
Purchases	938,700	
Purchase Returns and Allowances		4,200
Purchase Discounts		7,800
Transportation-In	21,900	
Sales Salaries	192,000	
Advertising Expense	36,000	
Delivery Expense	13,800	
Officers' Salaries	222,000	
Insurance Expense	8,700	
Interest Revenue		1,200
Interest Expense	6,000	
	$2,579,550	$2,579,550

The company consistently followed the policy of initially debiting all prepaid items to expense accounts.

Additional data

1. The building has an expected life of 50 years with no salvage value.

2. The store fixtures have an expected life of 10 years with no salvage value.

3. Accrued interest on notes receivable is $900.

4. Accrued interest on the mortgage note is $1,500.

5. Accrued sales salaries are $4,200.

6. Prepaid insurance is $1,200.

7. Prepaid advertising is $3,000.

8. Cost of merchandise inventory on hand December 31, 1994, is $166,500. (This latter information does not require an adjusting entry.)

Required   *a.* Prepare a 12-column work sheet for the year ended December 31, 1994. You do not have to show account numbers.

           b. Prepare the required closing entries.

BUSINESS DECISION PROBLEMS

Decision Problem 5–1

Compute approximate annual rate of interest in discount terms and amount saved if borrowed funds to take discounts; advise company regarding cash discounts (L.O. 3)

Olan Company received invoices for the following merchandise purchases at the specified sales terms during the current year.

Invoice No.	Amount of Purchase	Terms of Sale
1	$180,000	1/10, n/30
2	300,000	2/10, n/30
3	450,000	3/20, n/60
4	360,000	2/15, n/60
5	300,000	2/10, n/30

The company did not take advantage of the cash discounts. Each invoice was paid at the end of the allowable credit period. The company could have borrowed money at 8% interest from a local bank.

Required   *a.* Compute the approximate equivalent annual rate of interest incurred on each of the invoices by not taking advantage of cash discounts.

           b. Compute the net dollar amount that Olan Company could have saved if it had borrowed money at 8% and paid the invoices on the last day of the discount period.

           c. What recommendation would you make to the company concerning the company's policy on cash discounts?

Decision Problem 5–2

Prepare classified income statement and schedules to explain changes in balance sheet accounts (L.O. 5, 6)

Louis Penn decided to open a men's clothing store called The Men's Shop. On January 2, 1994, Penn invested the following assets in his business for all the stock in the company: $24,000 of cash; $60,000 of merchandise inventory; and $72,000 of store equipment. During 1994, Penn made the following cash disbursements:

$360,000 for merchandise purchases
240,000 for operating expenses

On December 31, 1994, Penn prepared the following balance sheet:

THE MEN'S SHOP
Balance Sheet
December 31, 1994
Assets

Current assets:

Cash	$312,000	
Accounts receivable.	96,000	
Merchandise inventory	90,000	
Total current assets		$498,000

Property, plant, and equipment:

Equipment	$ 72,000	
Less: Accumulated depreciation	12,000	
Total property, plant, and equipment		60,000
Total assets		$558,000

Liabilities and Stockholders' Equity

Current liabilities:

Accounts payable (merchandise purchases)	$ 60,000	
Salaries payable	12,000	
Total liabilities		$ 72,000

Stockholders' equity:

Capital stock	$156,000	
Retained earnings.	330,000	
Total stockholders' equity		486,000
Total liabilities and stockholders' equity		$558,000

Required   *a.*   Using the information given above, prepare a classified income statement for the year ended December 31, 1994. Show how each of the following items is determined: net income, cost of goods sold, operating expenses, and sales.

b.   Prepare schedules to explain the change in each of the balance sheet account balances.

Decision Problem 5–3

Prepare income statement and balance sheet (L.O. 5, 6)

Willie Alloway taught physical education classes at Cason High School for 20 years. In 1993, Willie's uncle died and left him $600,000. Willie quit his teaching job in December 1993 and opened a hardware store in January 1994. On January 2, 1994, Willie deposited $360,000 in a checking account opened in the store's name, Alloway's Hardware Store, for all the stock in the company. During the first week of January, Willie rented a building and paid the first year's rent of $28,800 in advance. Also during that week, he purchased the following assets for cash:

Delivery truck costing $60,000.
Store equipment costing $30,000.
Office equipment costing $18,000.
Merchandise inventory costing $60,000.

During the remainder of the first six months of 1994, Willie received cash of $420,000 from customers and disbursed cash of $192,000 for additional merchandise purchases and $90,000 for operating expenses.

Willie had never had an accounting course, but he had heard the term *net income*. He decided to compute his net income for the first six months of 1994 and prepared the following schedule:

Cash receipts		$420,000
Cash disbursements:		
Delivery truck	$ 60,000	
Store equipment	30,000	
Office equipment	18,000	
Prepaid rent	28,800	
Merchandise purchases	252,000	
Operating expenses	90,000	(478,800)
Net loss		$ (58,800)

Required   *a.*   Do you agree with Willie Alloway's statement that his hardware store suffered a net loss of $58,800 for the six months ended June 30, 1994? If not, show how you would determine the net income (or net loss).

Assume that the annual depreciation amounts are as follows:

Delivery truck, $6,000
Store equipment, $1,500
Office equipment, $1,128

Also assume that you obtain the following information:

Alloway owes $48,000 to creditors for merchandise purchases.
Customers owe Alloway $60,000.
Merchandise costing $36,000 is on hand.

   b.   Can Alloway prepare a balance sheet on June 30, 1994, or does he have to wait until December 31, 1994, to prepare a balance sheet? If a balance sheet can be prepared on June 30, 1994, prepare one.

Decision Problem 5–4

Classify income statement items
(L.O. 6)

From the consolidated statements of income of The Coca-Cola Company shown in Appendix E, identify the 1989 net operating revenues; cost of goods sold; gross profit; selling, administrative, and general expenses; and operating income. Do the results of 1989 compare favorably with those of 1988?

ANSWERS TO SELF-TEST

True-False

1. *True.* To compute net sales, sales discounts and sales returns and allowances are deducted from gross sales.

2. *False.* The Purchases account balance shows the cost of merchandise acquired; cost of goods sold is determined by subtracting ending inventory from the total cost of goods available for sale.

3. *False.* FOB shipping point, not FOB destination, results in freight charges being added to purchases.

4. *True.* This type of income statement is a classified or multiple-step income statement.

5. *True.* The Balance Sheet columns of the work sheet show the ending balance of each real account.

Multiple-Choice

1. *c.* Sales returns and allowances are debited to the Sales Returns and Allowances account when incurred.

2. *e.* Net cost of purchases plus beginning inventory is cost of goods available for sale.

3. *b.* The entire entry for this transaction is:

Accounts Payable.	400	
Purchase Discounts.		8
Cash		392

4. *c.* A classified income statement consists of major sections, such as operating revenues, cost of goods sold, operating expenses, and nonoperating revenues and expenses. Operating expenses are further divided into selling expenses and administrative expenses.

5. *e.* All of the entries mentioned in (*a–d*) are included in closing the merchandise-related accounts.

6

MEASURING AND REPORTING INVENTORIES

LEARNING OBJECTIVES

After studying this chapter, you should be able to:

1. Explain and calculate the effects of inventory errors on certain financial statement items.
2. Indicate which costs are properly included in inventory.
3. Calculate cost of ending inventory and cost of goods sold under the four major inventory costing methods using perpetual and periodic inventory procedures.
4. Explain the advantages and disadvantages of the four major inventory costing methods.
5. Record merchandise transactions under perpetual inventory procedure.
6. Apply net realizable value and the lower-of-cost-or-market method to inventory.
7. Estimate cost of ending inventory using the gross margin and retail inventory methods.

You may have been to a "pre-inventory sale" at your favorite retail store and witnessed the bargain prices designed to reduce the merchandise inventory on hand and to minimize the time and expense of "taking the inventory." A smaller inventory enhances the probability of taking an accurate inventory since the store has less merchandise to count. From Chapter 5 you know that companies use inventory amounts to determine the cost of goods sold, which is a major expense of a merchandising company that affects the company's net income. In this chapter, you will learn how important inventories are in preparing an accurate income statement, statement of retained earnings, and balance sheet.

This chapter discusses merchandise inventory carried by merchandising companies—retailers and wholesalers. **Merchandise inventory** is the quantity of goods held by a merchandising company for resale to customers.

The merchandise inventory figure used by accountants depends on the quantity of inventory items and the cost of the items. Merchandising companies determine the quantity of inventory items by a physical count. This chapter discusses four accepted methods of costing the items: (1) specific identification; (2) first-in, first-out (FIFO); (3) last-in, first-out (LIFO); and (4) weighted-average. Each method has advantages and disadvantages.

In studying this chapter, you should be impressed by the importance of having accurate inventory figures and the serious consequences of using inaccurate inventory figures. Then, you will understand why your favorite retail store is closing early to "take inventory" or why its employees are working late to "take inventory." You will connect this taking of inventory with the cost of goods sold figure on the store's income statement, the inventory figure and the retained earnings amount on the store's balance sheet, and the retained earnings amount shown on the statement of retained earnings.

INVENTORIES AND COST OF GOODS SOLD

Inventory is often the largest and most important asset owned by a merchandising business. The inventory of some companies, like car dealerships or jewelry stores, may cost several times more than any other asset the company owns. As an asset, the inventory figure has a direct impact on reporting the solvency of the company in the balance sheet. As a factor in determining cost of goods sold, the inventory figure has a direct impact on reported profitability of the company's operations as shown in the income statement. Thus, the importance of the inventory figure should not be underestimated.

Importance of Proper Inventory Valuation

Objective 1

Explain and calculate the effects of inventory errors on certain financial statement items

A merchandising company can prepare accurate income statements, statements of retained earnings, and balance sheets only if the company has correctly valued its inventory. On the income statement, inventory is used to determine the cost of goods sold. Since the cost of goods sold figure affects the company's net income, it also affects the retained earnings balance, which is shown in the statement of retained earnings. On the balance sheet, incorrect inventory amounts affect both the reported ending inventory and retained earnings. Inventories appear on the balance sheet under the heading "Current Assets," which reports current assets in a descending order of liquidity. Since inventories will be consumed or converted into cash within a year or one operating cycle, whichever is longer, the order of liquidity usually shows inventories following cash and receivables on the balance sheet.

You will recall that the cost of goods sold figure is determined by adding the beginning inventory to the net cost of purchases and deducting the ending inventory. In each accounting period, the appropriate expenses must be matched with the revenues of that period to determine the net income. Applied to inventory, matching involves determining (1) how much of the cost of goods available for sale during the period should be deducted from current revenues and (2) how much should be allocated to goods on hand and thus carried forward as an asset (merchandise inventory) in the balance sheet to be matched against future revenues. Cost of goods sold is determined by deducting the ending inventory from the cost of goods available for sale. As a result, a highly significant relationship exists: **net income for an accounting period depends directly on the valuation of ending inventory.** This relationship involves three items.

First, a merchandising company must be sure that it has properly valued its ending inventory. If the ending inventory is overstated, cost of goods sold will be understated, resulting in an overstatement of gross margin and net income. Also, overstatement of ending inventory will cause current assets, total assets, retained earnings, and stockholders' equity to be overstated. Thus, any change in the calculation of ending inventory will be reflected, dollar for dollar (ignoring any income tax effects), in net income, current assets, total assets, retained earnings, and stockholders' equity.

Second, when a company misstates its ending inventory in the current year, the company carries forward that misstatement into the next year. This misstatement occurs because **the ending inventory amount of the current year is the beginning inventory amount for the next year.**

Third, an error in one period's ending inventory automatically causes an error in the opposite direction in the next period. After two years, however, the error will "wash out," and assets and stockholders' equity will be properly stated.

Illustrations 6.1 and 6.2 prove that net income for an accounting period depends directly on the valuation of the inventory. Taylor Company's income statements and the statements of retained earnings for years 1993 and 1994 show this relationship.

In Illustration 6.1, the correctly stated ending inventory for the year 1993 is $70,000. As a result, Taylor has a gross margin of $270,000 and net income of $100,000. The statement of retained earnings shows a beginning retained earnings balance of $240,000 and an ending retained earnings balance of $340,000. When the ending inventory is overstated by $10,000, as shown on the right in Illustration 6.1, the gross margin is $280,000, and net income is $110,000. The statement of retained earnings then has an ending retained earnings of $350,000. The ending inventory overstatement of $10,000 causes a $10,000 overstatement of net income and a $10,000 overstatement of retained earnings. The balance sheet would show both an overstated inventory and retained earnings. Due to the error in ending inventory, both management and creditors may overestimate the profitability of the business.

Illustration 6.2 is a continuation of Illustration 6.1 and gives Taylor's operations for the year ended December 31, 1994. Note that the ending inventory in Illustration 6.1 now becomes the beginning inventory of Illustration 6.2. However, Taylor's inventory at December 31, 1994, is now an accurate inventory of $90,000. As a result, the gross margin in the income statement with the beginning inventory correctly stated is $290,000, and Taylor has net income of $183,000 and an ending retained earnings of $523,000. In the income statement at the right, in which the beginning inventory is overstated by $10,000, the gross margin is $280,000 and net income is $173,000, with the ending retained earnings also at $523,000.

Thus, in contrast to an overstated ending inventory, which results in an overstatement of net income, an overstated beginning inventory results in an understatement of net income. If the beginning inventory is overstated, then cost of goods available for sale and cost of goods sold will also be overstated. Conse-

ILLUSTRATION 6.1

Effects of an Overstated Ending Inventory

TAYLOR COMPANY

For Year Ended December 31, 1993

	Ending Inventory Correctly Stated		Ending Inventory Overstated by $10,000	
Income Statement				
Sales		$800,000		$800,000
Cost of goods available for sale.	$600,000		$600,000	
Ending inventory	70,000		80,000	
Cost of goods sold		530,000		520,000
Gross margin		$270,000		$280,000
Other expenses.		170,000		170,000
Net income.		$100,000		$110,000
Statement of Retained Earnings				
Beginning retained earnings		$240,000		$240,000
Net income.		100,000		110,000
Ending retained earnings.		$340,000		$350,000

ILLUSTRATION 6.2

Effects of an Overstated Beginning Inventory

TAYLOR COMPANY

For Year Ended December 31, 1994

	Beginning Inventory Correctly Stated		Beginning Inventory Overstated by $10,000	
Income Statement				
Sales		$850,000		$850,000
Beginning inventory	$ 70,000		$ 80,000	
Purchases	580,000		580,000	
Cost of goods available for sale.	$650,000		$660,000	
Ending inventory	90,000		90,000	
Cost of goods sold		560,000		570,000
Gross margin		$290,000		$280,000
Other expenses.		107,000		107,000
Net income.		$183,000		$173,000
Statement of Retained Earnings				
Beginning retained earnings		$340,000		$350,000
Net income.		183,000		173,000
Ending retained earnings.		$523,000		$523,000

quently, gross margin and net income will be understated. Note, however, that when net income in the second year is closed to retained earnings, the Retained Earnings account will be stated at its proper amount. The overstatement of net income in the first year is offset by the understatement of net income in the second year. For the two years combined, then, the net income is correct. At the end of the second year, the balance sheet contains the correct amounts for both inventory and retained earnings.

The effects of errors in inventory valuation are summarized as follows:

	Ending Inventory		Beginning Inventory	
	Understated	**Overstated**	**Understated**	**Overstated**
Cost of goods sold	Overstated	Understated	Understated	Overstated
Net income.	Understated	Overstated	Overstated	Understated

DETERMINING INVENTORY COST

To place the proper valuation on inventory, a business must answer the question: Which costs should be included in inventory cost? Then, when the business purchases identical goods at different costs, it must answer the question: Which cost should be assigned to the items sold? In this section, you will learn how accountants answer these questions.

The costs included in inventory depend on two variables: quantity and price. To arrive at a current inventory figure, companies must begin with an accurate physical count of inventory items. The quantity of inventory is multiplied by the unit cost to compute the cost of ending inventory. This section first discusses the taking of a physical inventory and then the methods of costing the physical inventory under both perpetual and periodic inventory procedure. The remainder of the chapter discusses departures from the cost basis of inventory measurement.

Objective 2
Indicate which costs are properly included in inventory

Taking a Physical Inventory

As briefly described in Chapter 5, to take a physical inventory, a company must count, weigh, measure, or estimate the physical quantities of the goods on hand. For example, a clothing store may count its suits; a hardware store may weigh such items as bolts, washers, and nails; a gasoline company may measure gasoline in storage tanks; and a lumberyard may estimate such items as quantities of lumber, coal, or other bulky materials. Throughout the taking of a physical inventory, the goal should be accuracy.

Taking a physical inventory may disrupt the normal operations of a business. Thus, the count should be administered as quickly and as efficiently as possible. The actual taking of the inventory is not considered an accounting function; however, accountants often plan and coordinate the count. Proper forms are required to record accurate counts and determine totals. Identification names or symbols must be chosen, and those persons who count, weigh, or measure the inventory items must know these symbols.

Taking a physical inventory often involves the use of inventory tags, such as the tag shown in Illustration 6.3. These tags are consecutively numbered for control purposes. A tag usually consists of a stub and a detachable duplicate section. The duplicate section facilitates checking in case of discrepancies. The format of the tags can vary. However, the tag usually provides space for (1) a detailed description and identification of inventory items by product, class, and model; (2) location of items; (3) quantity of items on hand; and (4) initials of the counters and checkers.

ILLUSTRATION 6.3

Inventory Tag

Inventory Tag
JMA Corp.

Inventory Tag No. _281_   Date _____
Description _____
　　　　　　　_____
Location _____
Quantity Counted _____
Counted by _____
Checked by _____

- -

Duplicate Inventory Tag

Inventory Tag No. _281_   Date _____
Description _____
　　　　　　　_____
Location _____
Quantity Counted _____
Counted by _____
Checked by _____

After the descriptive information is entered on the tags, these tags may be attached to the bins, shelves, or racks that contain the goods. The counters usually work in pairs and record their counts on the detachable sections of the tags and turn them in. Discrepancies between counts of the same items by different teams are reconciled by supervisors, and the correct counts are assembled on intermediate inventory sheets. When the inventory counts are completed and checked, the final sheets are sent to the accounting department for pricing and extensions (quantity × price). The tabulated result is the dollar amount of the physical inventory. Later in the chapter you will study the different methods accountants use to cost inventory.

Costs Included in Inventory Cost

Usually, inventory cost includes all the necessary outlays to obtain the goods, get the goods ready to sell, and have the goods in the desired location for sale to customers. Thus, inventory cost includes:

1. Seller's invoice price less any purchase discount.
2. Cost of the buyer's insurance to cover the goods while in transit.
3. Transportation charges when borne by the buyer.
4. Handling costs, such as the cost of pressing clothes wrinkled during shipment.

In theory, the cost of *each* unit of inventory should include its net invoice price plus its share of other costs incurred in shipment. The 1986 Tax Reform Act requires companies to make assignments of these costs to inventory for tax purposes. For accounting purposes, these cost assignments are recommended but not required.

Practical difficulties arise in allocating some of these costs to inventory items. Assume, for example, that the freight bill on a shipment of clothes does not state separately the cost of shipping one shirt. Also, assume that the company wants to include the freight cost as part of the inventory cost of the shirt. Then, the freight cost would have to be *allocated* in some manner to each unit because it cannot be measured directly. In practice, allocations of freight, insurance, and handling costs to the individual units of inventory purchased are often not worth the additional cost incurred to perform the allocations. Consequently, many companies do not assign the costs of freight, insurance, and handling to inventory. Instead, they expense these costs as incurred. When companies omit these costs from both beginning and ending inventories, the omission minimizes the effect on net income of expensing these costs.

Even if a cost is derived for each unit in inventory, the inventory valuation problem is not solved. Two other aspects of the problem must be considered.

1. If goods were purchased at varying unit costs, how should cost of goods available for sale be allocated between the units sold and those that remain in inventory? For example, assume that Hi Fi Buys, Inc., purchased two identical VCRs for resale. One was purchased for $450 and the other for $400. If one recorder was sold during the period, should Hi Fi Buys assign it a cost of $450, $400, or an average cost of $425?

2. Does the fact that current replacement costs are less than the costs of some units in inventory have any bearing on the amount at which inventory should be carried? Using the same example as above, if Hi Fi Buys can currently buy all VCRs at a price of $400, is it reasonable to carry some units in inventory at $450 rather than $400?

These questions are answered in the next section.

Inventory Valuation under Changing Prices

Inventories generally should be accounted for at historical cost, which is the cost at which the items were purchased. However, this rule does not indicate how to assign costs to ending inventory and to cost of goods sold when the goods have been purchased at different unit costs. For example, suppose that a retailer has three units of a given product on hand. One unit was bought for $20, another for $22, and a third for $24. If the retailer sells two of the units for $30 each, what is the cost of the two units sold?

Methods of Determining Inventory Cost

Four inventory costing methods have been developed to solve this type of problem. They are: (1) specific identification; (2) first-in, first-out (FIFO); (3) last-in, first-out (LIFO); and (4) weighted-average. These costing methods are explained below. Illustration 6.4 shows the frequency of use of these methods in a sample of 600 companies for the years 1986–89. Obviously, some companies use one method for certain inventory items and another method for other inventory items.

Objective 3

Calculate cost of ending inventory and cost of goods sold under the four major inventory costing methods using perpetual and periodic inventory procedures (applies to each method separately)

Before presenting the inventory costing methods, we present a brief introduction to perpetual inventory procedure and a comparison of periodic and perpetual inventory procedures.

Perpetual Inventory Procedure

In Chapter 5, the emphasis was on periodic inventory procedure. Under periodic inventory procedure, the Purchases account is debited when goods are acquired; other accounts, such as Purchase Discounts, Purchase Returns and Allowances, and Transportation-In, are used for purchase-related transactions. Cost of goods sold is determined only at the end of the period as the difference between cost of

ILLUSTRATION 6.4

Frequency of Use of Inventory Methods

	Number of Companies			
	1989	**1988**	**1987**	**1986**
Methods:				
First-in, first-out (FIFO)	401	396	392	383
Last-in, first-out (LIFO)	366	379	393	393
Average cost.	200	213	216	223
Other	48	50	49	53
	1015	1038	1050	1052
Use of LIFO:				
All inventories	26	20	18	23
50% or more of inventories	191	207	221	229
Less than 50% of inventories	99	90	86	74
Not determinable	50	62	68	67
Companies using LIFO	366	379	393	393

Source: American Institute of Certified Public Accountants, *Accounting Trends & Techniques* (New York: AICPA, 1990), p. 105.

goods available for sale and ending inventory. No records are kept of the cost of items as they are sold, and no information is provided on possible inventory shortages. Any goods not in ending inventory are assumed to have been sold.

The recent development of inventory management software packages is causing more and more businesses to change from periodic to perpetual inventory procedure. Under perpetual inventory procedure, companies have no purchases and purchase-related accounts. Instead, all entries involving merchandise purchased for sale to customers are entered directly in the Merchandise Inventory account. Thus, **Merchandise Inventory is debited or credited in place of debiting or crediting Purchases, Purchase Discounts, Purchase Returns and Allowances, and Transportation-In. At the time of each sale, two entries are made. The first debits Accounts Receivable or Cash and credits Sales at the retail selling price. The second debits Cost of Goods Sold and credits Merchandise Inventory at cost.** Therefore, Merchandise Inventory at the end of the period will show the cost of the goods that should be on hand. Comparison of this amount with the cost obtained by taking and pricing a physical inventory will reveal inventory shortages. Thus, perpetual inventory procedure is an important element in providing internal control over goods in inventory.

Perpetual Inventory Records   Even though companies can apply perpetual inventory procedure manually, the tracking of units and dollars in and out of inventory is much easier using a computer. With either manual or computer processing, a record will be maintained for each item in inventory. Illustration 6.5 gives an example of an inventory record for Entertainment World, a firm that sells many different brands of television sets. The inventory record in Illustration 6.5 shows the information on one particular brand and model of television set carried in inventory. Other information given on the record includes (1) the maximum and minimum number of units the company wishes to stock at any time, (2) when and how many units were acquired and at what cost, and (3) when and how many units were sold and what cost was assigned to cost of goods sold. The number of units on hand and their cost are readily available also. Entertainment World assumes

ILLUSTRATION 6.5

Perpetual Inventory Record (FIFO method)

Item _____TV-96874_____ Maximum _____26_____

Location _____ Minimum _____6_____

1993 Date	Purchased			Sold			Balance		
	Units	Unit Cost	Total	Units	Unit Cost	Total	Units	Unit Cost	Total
July 1							8	$300	$2,400
5	10	$300	$3,000				18	300	5,400
7				12	$300	$3,600	6	300	1,800
12	10	315	3,150				{ 6	300	1,800
							{ 10	315	3,150
22				{ 6	300	1,800			
				{ 2	315	630	8	315	2,520
24	8	320	2,560				{ 8	315	2,520
							{ 8	320	2,560

that the first units acquired are the first units sold. This assumption is referred to as the first-in, first-out (FIFO) method of inventory costing and is discussed in detail later.

Comparing Journal Entries under Periodic and Perpetual Inventory Procedures

As stated in the preceding section, several differences exist between accounting for inventories under periodic procedure and under perpetual procedure. These differences will be illustrated by using some of the data from Illustration 6.5 and making some additional assumptions. Later, some additional journal entries under perpetual inventory procedure will be illustrated.

The purchase on July 5 would be recorded as follows under each of the methods:

Periodic Procedure		
Purchases	3,000	
Accounts Payable. . . .		3,000

Perpetual Procedure		
Merchandise Inventory. . . .	3,000	
Accounts Payable		3,000

Assuming the merchandise sold on July 7 was priced at $4,800, the sale would be recorded as follows:

Periodic Procedure		
Accounts Receivable	4,800	
Sales		4,800

Perpetual Procedure		
Accounts Receivable.	4,800	
Sales		4,800
Cost of Goods Sold	3,600	
Merchandise Inventory. .		3,600

Several other types of transactions that were not included in Illustration 6.5 could occur. A sample of these transactions follows:

1. Assume that two of the units purchased on July 5 were returned to the supplier because they were defective. The entries would be:

Periodic Procedure   **Perpetual Procedure**

Accounts Payable	600			Accounts Payable	600	
Purchase Returns and				Merchandise		
Allowances		600		Inventory	.	600

2. Assume instead that the supplier granted an allowance of $600 to the company because of the defective merchandise. The entries would be:

Periodic Procedure   **Perpetual Procedure**

Accounts Payable	600			Accounts Payable	600	
Purchase Returns and				Merchandise		
Allowances		600		Inventory		600

3. Assume that the company incurred and paid freight charges of $100 on the purchase of July 5. The entries would be:

Periodic Procedure   **Perpetual Procedure**

Transportation-In	100			Merchandise Inventory . .	100	
Cash		100		Cash		100

Notice in the entries above that, under perpetual inventory procedure, the Merchandise Inventory account is used to record purchases, purchase returns and allowances, purchase discounts, and transportation-in. Also, when goods are sold, Cost of Goods Sold is debited (increased) and Merchandise Inventory is credited (reduced).

At the end of the accounting period, under perpetual procedure, the only merchandise-related expense account to be closed is Cost of Goods Sold. The Purchases, Purchase Returns and Allowances, Purchase Discounts, and Transportation-In accounts do not even exist.

An Extended Illustration of Four Inventory Methods under Perpetual and Periodic Inventory Procedures

The data for purchases, sales, and beginning inventory given in Illustration 6.6 will be used to illustrate each of the four inventory costing methods. Except for the specific identification method, each method is presented using, first, perpetual inventory procedure and, then, periodic inventory procedure. Total goods available for sale consist of 80 units with a total cost of $690. A physical inventory determined that 20 units are on hand at the end of the period. Sales revenue for the 60 units sold was $780. The questions to be answered are: What is the cost of the 20 units in inventory? What is the cost of the 60 units sold?

Specific Identification The specific identification method of inventory costing attaches the actual cost to an identifiable unit of product. This method is easily applied when large inventory items (such as autos) are purchased and sold. Under the specific identification method, each unit in inventory, unless it is unique, must be identified with a serial number plate or identification tag.

To illustrate, assume that the company in Illustration 6.6 can identify the 20 units on hand at year-end as 10 units from the August 12 purchase and 10 units from the December 21 purchase. The ending inventory is computed as shown in Illustration 6.7, where the **$181 ending inventory cost is subtracted from the $690 cost of goods available for sale to obtain the $509 cost of goods sold.** Note that you

ILLUSTRATION 6.6

Beginning Inventory, Purchases, and Sales

Beginning Inventory and Purchases					Sales			
Date	Units	Unit Cost	Total Cost		Date	Units	Price	Total
Beginning inventory	10	$8.00	$ 80		March 10	10	$12.00	$120
March 2	10	8.50	85		July 14	20	12.00	240
May 28	20	8.40	168		September 7	10	14.00	140
August 12.	10	9.00	90		November 22	20	14.00	280
October 12	20	8.80	176					
December 21	10	9.10	91					
	80		$690			60		$780

Ending inventory = 20 units, determined by taking a physical inventory.

ILLUSTRATION 6.7

Determining Ending Inventory under Specific Identification

	Units	Unit Cost	Total Cost
Ending inventory composed of purchases made on:			
August 12	10	$9.00	$ 90
December 21	10	9.10	91
Ending inventory	20		$181
Cost of goods sold composed of:			
Beginning inventory.	10	8.00	$ 80
Purchases made on:			
March 2	10	8.50	85
May 28	20	8.40	168
October 12	20	8.80	176
			$509
Cost of goods available for sale			$690
Ending inventory.			181
Cost of goods sold.			$509

can also determine the cost of goods sold for the year by recording the cost of each unit sold. The $509 cost of goods sold is reported as an expense on the income statement, and the $181 ending inventory is a current asset on the balance sheet.

The specific identification costing method attaches cost to an identifiable unit of inventory. The method does not involve any assumptions about the flow of the costs as in the other inventory costing methods. Conceptually, the method matches the cost to the physical flow of the inventory, thus eliminating the emphasis on the timing of the cost determination. Therefore, periodic and perpetual inventory procedures will produce the same results for the specific identification method.

Objective 4

Explain the advantages and disadvantages of the four major inventory costing methods (applies to each method separately)

Advantages and Disadvantages of Specific Identification Companies that use the specific identification method of inventory costing state their cost of goods sold and ending inventory at the actual cost of specific units sold and on hand. Some accountants argue that this method provides the most precise matching of costs and revenues and is, therefore, the most theoretically sound method. This statement is true for some one-of-a-kind items, such as autos or real estate. For these items, use of any other method would seem completely illogical.

One disadvantage of the specific identification method is that it permits the manipulation of income. For example, assume that a company bought three identical units of a given product at different prices. One unit cost $2,000, the second cost $2,100, and the third cost $2,200. The company sold one unit for $2,800. The units are alike, so the customer does not care which of the identical units the company ships. However, the gross margin on the sale could be either $800, $700, or $600, depending on which unit the company ships.

FIFO (First-In, First-Out) Sometimes companies use a method that involves a cost flow assumption rather than using specific identification. For instance, the FIFO (first-in, first-out) method of inventory costing assumes that the costs of the first goods purchased are the first costs charged to cost of goods sold when the company actually sells the goods. Thus, the first goods purchased are assumed to be the first goods sold. In some companies, the first units "in" (bought) must be the first units "out" (sold) to avoid large losses from spoilage. Such items as fresh dairy products, fruits, and vegetables should be sold on a FIFO basis. In these cases, an assumed first-in, first-out flow corresponds with the actual physical flow of goods.

Since a company using FIFO assumes the older units to be the first units sold and the newer units to be still on hand, the ending inventory consists of the most recent purchases. Under perpetual inventory procedure, the ending balance in the Merchandise Inventory account will reflect these most recent purchases as a result of making the required entries during the period. Also, the cost of goods sold will already have been recorded in the Cost of Goods Sold account. Under periodic inventory procedure, to determine the cost of the ending inventory at the end of the period under FIFO, you would begin by listing the cost of the most recent purchase. If the ending inventory contains more units than acquired in the most recent purchase, it will also include units from the next-to-the-latest purchase at the unit cost incurred, and so on. You would list these units from the latest purchases until the number of units agrees with the number of units in the ending inventory.

Illustration 6.8 shows how you would determine the cost of ending inventory under FIFO using perpetual inventory procedure. This illustration uses the same format as the perpetual inventory record shown earlier. The company keeps a record of the balance in the inventory account as it makes purchases and sells items from inventory. Notice in Illustration 6.8 that each time a sale occurs, the items sold are assumed to be the oldest items on hand. Thus, after each transaction, you can readily determine the balance in the Merchandise Inventory account from the perpetual inventory record. The balance after the December 21 purchase represents the 20 units from the most recent purchases. The total cost of ending inventory is $179, which the company reports as a current asset on the balance sheet. During the accounting period, a total of $511 would have been debited to Cost of Goods Sold as sales occurred. Adding this $511 to the ending inventory of $179 accounts for all of the $690 cost of goods available for sale.

Illustration 6.9 shows how you can determine the cost of ending inventory under FIFO using periodic inventory procedure. The company assumes that 20 units in inventory consist of 10 units purchased December 21 and 10 units pur-

ILLUSTRATION 6.8

Determining FIFO Cost of Ending Inventory under Perpetual Inventory Procedure

Date	Purchased Units	Purchased Unit Cost	Purchased Total	Sold Units	Sold Unit Cost	Sold Total	Balance Units	Balance Unit Cost	Balance Total	
Beg. inv.							10	$8.00	$ 80	
Mar. 2	10	$8.50	$ 85				10 10	8.00 8.50	80 85	*Sales are assumed to be from the oldest units on hand.*
Mar. 10				10	$8.00	$80	10	8.50	85	
May 28	20	8.40	168				10 20	8.50 8.40	85 168	
July 14				10 10	8.50 8.40	85 84	10	8.40	84	
Aug. 12	10	9.00	90				10 10	8.40 9.00	84 90	
Sept. 7				10	8.40	84	10	9.00	90	*Total of $179 would agree with balance already existing in Merchandise Inventory account.*
Oct. 12	20	8.80	176				10 20	9.00 8.80	90 176	
Nov. 22				10 10	9.00 8.80	90 88	10	8.80	88	
Dec. 21	10	9.10	91				10 10	8.80 9.10	88 ⎱ 91 ⎰	

Total cost of ending inventory = $179

ILLUSTRATION 6.9

Determining FIFO Cost of Ending Inventory under Periodic Procedure

	Units	Unit Cost	Total Cost	
Ending inventory composed of purchases made on:				
December 21	10	$9.10	$ 91	
October 12	10	8.80	88	
Ending inventory	20		$179	
Cost of goods sold composed of:				
Beginning inventory.	10	8.00	$ 80	
Purchases made on:				
March 2	10	8.50	85	
May 28	20	8.40	168	
August 12	10	9.00	90	*Used to establish the ending balance in the Merchandise Inventory account*
October 12	10	8.80	88	
			$511	
Cost of goods available for sale			$690	
Ending inventory			179	
Cost of goods sold			$511	

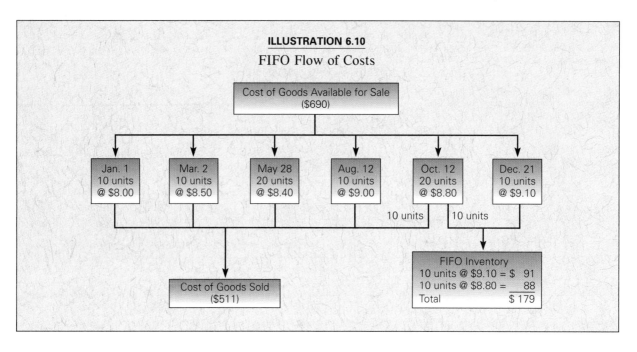

ILLUSTRATION 6.10

FIFO Flow of Costs

chased October 12. As with the perpetual inventory procedure, the total cost of ending inventory is $179, and the cost of goods sold is $511. **Under FIFO, the use of perpetual and periodic inventory procedures will result in the same total costs for ending inventory and cost of goods sold.**

Illustration 6.10 shows the relationship between the cost of goods sold and the cost of ending inventory under FIFO using periodic inventory procedure. The cost of goods available for sale of 80 units for the period consists of the beginning inventory and all of the purchases during the period. Under FIFO, the ending inventory of 20 units is composed of the most recent purchases—10 units of December 21 purchase and 10 units of October 12 purchase—costing $179. Beginning inventory and other earlier purchases are assumed to have been sold during the period, representing the cost of goods sold of $511.

Advantages and Disadvantages of FIFO   The FIFO method has four major advantages: (1) it is easy to apply, (2) the assumed flow of costs corresponds with the normal physical flow of goods, (3) **no manipulation of income is possible,** and (4) the balance sheet amount for inventory is likely to approximate the current market value. All the advantages of FIFO occur because when a company sells goods, the first costs it removes from inventory are the oldest unit costs. A company cannot manipulate income by choosing which unit to ship because the cost of a unit sold is not determined by a serial number. Instead, the cost attached to the unit sold is always the oldest cost. Thus, under FIFO, purchases made at the end of the period have no effect on cost of goods sold or net income.

The disadvantages of FIFO include (1) the recognition of ''paper'' profits and (2) a heavier tax burden if used for tax purposes in periods of inflation. These disadvantages are discussed later as advantages of LIFO.

LIFO (Last-In, First-Out)   The LIFO (last-in, first-out) method of inventory costing assumes that the costs of the most recent purchases are the first costs charged to cost of goods sold when the company actually sells the goods. **The results can differ under perpetual and periodic inventory procedure.**

Illustration 6.11 shows the LIFO method using perpetual inventory procedure. Under perpetual inventory procedure, the inventory composition and balance are

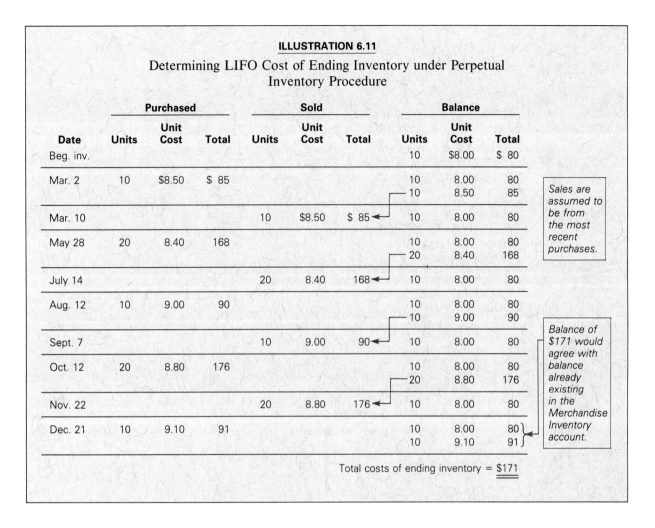

ILLUSTRATION 6.11

Determining LIFO Cost of Ending Inventory under Perpetual
Inventory Procedure

Date	Purchased			Sold			Balance		
	Units	Unit Cost	Total	Units	Unit Cost	Total	Units	Unit Cost	Total
Beg. inv.							10	$8.00	$ 80
Mar. 2	10	$8.50	$ 85				10	8.00	80
							10	8.50	85
Mar. 10				10	$8.50	$ 85	10	8.00	80
May 28	20	8.40	168				10	8.00	80
							20	8.40	168
July 14				20	8.40	168	10	8.00	80
Aug. 12	10	9.00	90				10	8.00	80
							10	9.00	90
Sept. 7				10	9.00	90	10	8.00	80
Oct. 12	20	8.80	176				10	8.00	80
							20	8.80	176
Nov. 22				20	8.80	176	10	8.00	80
Dec. 21	10	9.10	91				10	8.00	80
							10	9.10	91

Sales are assumed to be from the most recent purchases.

Balance of $171 would agree with balance already existing in the Merchandise Inventory account.

Total costs of ending inventory = $171

updated with each purchase and sale. Notice in Illustration 6.11 that each time a
sale occurs, the items sold are assumed to be the most recent ones acquired.
Despite the numerous purchases and sales during the year, the ending inventory
still includes the 10 units from beginning inventory in our example. The remainder
of the ending inventory consists of the last purchase because no sale occurred
after the December 21 purchase. The total cost of the 20 units in ending inventory
is $171; the cost of goods sold is $519.

Illustration 6.12 shows the use of LIFO under periodic inventory procedure.
Under periodic procedure, since the company charges the latest costs to cost of
goods sold, the ending inventory consists of the oldest costs. Therefore, when
determining the cost of inventory under periodic inventory procedure, the oldest
units and their costs are listed first. Thus, the first units listed are those in beginning inventory, then the first purchase, and so on, until the number of units listed
agrees with the number of units in ending inventory. Thus, ending inventory in
Illustration 6.12 is composed of the 10 units from beginning inventory and the 10
units purchased on March 2. The total cost of these 20 units, $165, is the ending
inventory cost; the cost of goods sold is $525.

Applying LIFO on a perpetual basis during the accounting period as shown in
Illustration 6.11 results in different ending inventory and cost of goods sold figures
than applying LIFO only at year-end using periodic inventory procedure. (Compare Illustrations 6.11 and 6.12 to verify that ending inventory and cost of goods
sold are different under the two procedures.) For this reason, if LIFO is applied on

ILLUSTRATION 6.12

Determining LIFO Cost of Ending Inventory under
Periodic Inventory Procedure

	Units	Unit Cost	Total Cost
Ending inventory composed of:			
Beginning inventory	10	$8.00	$ 80
March 2 purchase	10	8.50	85
Ending inventory	20		$165
Cost of goods sold composed of purchases made on:			
December 21	10	9.10	$ 91
October 12	20	8.80	176
August 12	10	9.00	90
May 28	20	8.40	168
			$525
Cost of goods available for sale			$690
Ending inventory			165
Cost of goods sold			$525

a perpetual basis during the period, special adjustments are sometimes necessary at year-end to take full advantage of using LIFO for tax purposes. Complicated applications of LIFO perpetual that require such adjustments are beyond the scope of this text and are not illustrated here.

Illustrations 6.13 and 6.14 show the flow of inventory costs under LIFO using both the perpetual and periodic inventory procedures. Note that ending inventory and cost of goods sold are different under the two procedures.

Advantages and Disadvantages of LIFO The advantages of the LIFO method are directly related to the fact that prices have risen almost constantly for decades. LIFO supporters claim that this upward trend in prices leads to inventory, or "paper," profits if the FIFO method is used. Inventory, or "paper," profits are equal to the current replacement cost to purchase a unit of inventory at time of sale minus the unit's historical cost.

For example, assume a company has three units of a product on hand, each purchased at a different cost: $12, $15, and $20 (the most recent cost). The sales price of the unit normally will rise because the unit's replacement cost is rising. Assume that the company sells one unit for $30. FIFO gross margin would be $18 ($30 − $12), while LIFO would show a gross margin of $10 ($30 − $20). LIFO supporters would say that the extra $8 gross margin shown under FIFO represents inventory profit because that "profit" is merely the additional amount that the company must spend over cost of goods sold to purchase another unit of inventory ($8 + $12 = $20). Thus, the profit is not real; it exists only on paper. The company cannot distribute the $8 to owners, but must retain it in the company if the company is to continue handling that particular product. LIFO shows the actual profits that the company can distribute to the owners while still replenishing inventory.

During periods of inflation, LIFO shows the largest cost of goods sold of any of the costing methods because the newest costs charged to cost of goods sold are also the highest costs. The larger the cost of goods sold, the smaller the net

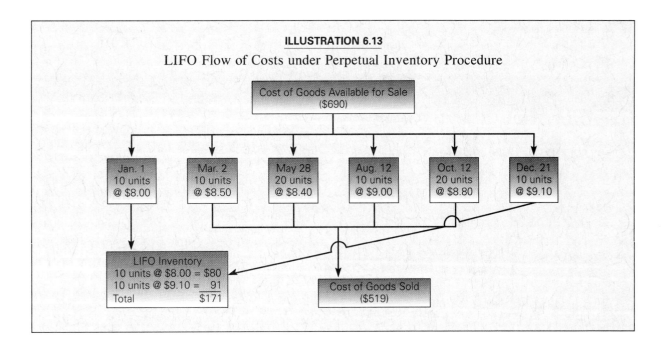

ILLUSTRATION 6.13

LIFO Flow of Costs under Perpetual Inventory Procedure

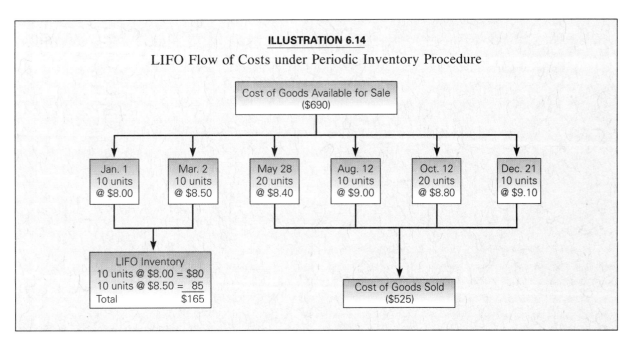

ILLUSTRATION 6.14

LIFO Flow of Costs under Periodic Inventory Procedure

income. If a company uses LIFO for income tax purposes, the resulting lower taxable income means lower income taxes. Companies may only use LIFO for tax purposes if they use it for financial statement purposes. Many companies use LIFO for financial statement purposes for this reason (Illustration 6.4, page 266).

To further illustrate the appeal of LIFO, assume that Company B has one unit of product Y on hand that cost $20. The company sold the unit for $30; other selling expenses totaled $7. Assume that the income tax rate is 50%. The company purchases an identical unit for $22 before the end of the accounting period. Using FIFO, Company B computes its net income as follows:

Net sales	$30.00
Cost of goods sold	20.00
Gross margin.	$10.00
Expenses	7.00
Net operating margin	$ 3.00
Federal income taxes (50% rate)	1.50
Net income	$ 1.50

According to the above schedule, the company is selling product Y at a price that is high enough to produce net income. However, consider the following:

Cash secured from sale	$30.00
Expenses and taxes paid ($7.00 + $1.50)	8.50
Cash available for replacement of inventory	$21.50
Cost to replace inventory	22.00
Additional cash required to replace inventory	$ 0.50

Thus, Company B is reporting net income of $1.50, but it cannot replace its inventory unless it obtains more cash.

Note how the results differ when Company B uses LIFO to measure inventory:

Net sales	$30.00
Cost of goods sold	22.00
Gross margin.	$ 8.00
Expenses	7.00
Net operating margin	$ 1.00
Federal income taxes (50% rate)	0.50
Net income	$ 0.50
Cash secured from sale	$30.00
Expenses and taxes paid ($7.00 + $0.50)	7.50
Cash available for replacement of inventory	$22.50
Cost to replace inventory	22.00
Cash available after replacement of inventory . . .	$ 0.50

In this case, inventory profits are $2, the difference between the original cost of the inventory ($20) and its replacement cost at the time the company sold the inventory ($22). Note that the tax savings under LIFO are equal to the tax rate times the inventory profits (0.5 × $2 = $1).

Those who favor LIFO argue that its use leads to a better matching of costs and revenues than the other methods. When a company uses LIFO, the income statement reports both sales revenue and cost of goods sold in current dollars. The resulting gross margin is a better indicator of management's ability to generate income than gross margin computed using FIFO, which may include substantial inventory profits.

Supporters of FIFO argue that LIFO (1) matches the cost of goods **not** sold against revenues, (2) grossly understates inventory, and (3) permits income manipulation.

The first criticism—that LIFO matches the cost of goods **not** sold against revenues—is an extension of the debate over whether the assumed flow of costs should agree with the physical flow of goods. LIFO supporters contend that it makes more sense to match current costs against current revenues than to worry about matching costs for the physical flow of goods.

The second criticism—that LIFO grossly understates inventory—is valid. A company may report LIFO inventory at a fraction of its current replacement cost, especially if the historical costs included are from several decades ago. LIFO supporters contend that the increased usefulness of the income statement more than offsets the negative effect of this undervaluation of inventory on the balance sheet.

The third criticism—that LIFO permits income manipulation—is also valid. Income manipulation is possible under LIFO. For example, assume that management wishes to reduce income. The company could purchase an abnormal amount of goods at current high prices near the end of the current period with the purpose of selling the goods in the next period. Under LIFO, these higher costs will be charged to cost of goods sold in the current period, resulting in a substantial decline in reported net income. To obtain higher income, management could delay making the normal amount of purchases until the next period and thus include some of the older, lower costs in cost of goods sold.

Weighted-Average   The weighted-average method of inventory costing is a means of costing ending inventory using a weighted-average unit cost. Companies most often use the weighted-average method to determine a unit cost for units that are basically the same, such as identical games in a toy store or identical electrical tools in a hardware store. Since the units are alike, they can be assigned the same unit cost.

Under perpetual inventory procedure, **a new weighted-average unit cost is computed after each purchase by dividing total cost of goods available for sale by total units available for sale.** The unit cost is referred to as a moving weighted-average because it changes after each purchase. Illustration 6.15 shows how the moving weighted-average is computed using perpetual inventory procedure. The new weighted-average unit cost computed after each purchase is used as the unit cost for inventory items sold until a new purchase is made. The 20 units in ending inventory are valued at a unit cost of $8.929 for a total inventory cost of $178.58. Cost of goods sold under this procedure is $690 minus the $178.58, or $511.42.

Under periodic inventory procedure, a company determines the average cost by dividing the total number of units purchased during the entire period plus those in beginning inventory into total cost of goods available for sale for the period. The ending inventory is carried at this per unit cost. Illustration 6.16 shows how a company uses the weighted-average method to determine inventory costs using periodic inventory procedure. Weighted-average cost per unit is computed by dividing the cost of units available for sale, $690, by the total number of units available for sale, 80. Thus, the weighted-average cost per unit is $8.625, meaning that each unit sold or remaining in inventory is valued at $8.625.

Advantages and Disadvantages of Weighted-Average   When a company uses the weighted-average method and prices are rising, cost of goods sold is less than that obtained under LIFO, but more than that obtained under FIFO. Inventory is not as badly understated as under LIFO, but it is not as up to date as under FIFO. Weighted-average costing takes a "middle-of-the-road" approach. A company can manipulate income under the weighted-average costing method by buying or failing to buy goods near year-end. However, the effects of buying or not buying are reduced due to the averaging process.

ILLUSTRATION 6.15

Determining Ending Inventory under Weighted-Average Method Using
Perpetual Inventory Procedure

	Purchased			Sold			Balance			
Date	Units	Unit Cost	Total	Units	Unit Cost	Total	Units	Unit Cost	Total	
Beg. inv.							10	$8.00	$ 80.00	A new unit cost is calculated after each purchase.
Mar. 2	10	$8.50	$ 85				20	8.25 ᵃ	165.00	
Mar. 10				10	$8.25	$ 82.50	10	8.25	82.50	
May 28	20	8.40	168				30	8.35 ᵇ	250.50	The unit cost of sales is the most recently calculated unit cost.
July 14				20	8.35	167.00	10	8.35	83.50	
Aug. 12	10	9.00	90				20	8.675ᶜ	173.50	
Sept. 7				10	8.675	86.75	10	8.675	86.75	
Oct. 12	20	8.80	176				30	8.758ᵈ	262.75	
Nov. 22				20	8.758	175.17*	10	8.758	87.58	Balance of $178.58 would agree with balance already existing in the Merchandise Inventory account.
Dec. 21	10	9.10	91				20	$8.929ᵉ	$178.58	

ᵃ $165.00/20 = $8.25.
ᵇ $250.50/30 = $8.35.
ᶜ $173.50/20 = $8.675.
ᵈ $262.75/30 = $8.758.
ᵉ $178.58/20 = $8.929.
* Rounding difference

Differences in Costing Methods Summarized

The four inventory costing methods—specific identification, FIFO, LIFO, and weighted-average—involve assumptions about how costs flow through a business. In some instances, assumed cost flows may correspond with the actual physical flow of goods. For example, fresh meats and dairy products must flow in a FIFO manner to avoid spoilage losses. In contrast, lumber or coal stacked in a pile will be used in a LIFO manner because the newest units purchased will be unloaded on top of the pile and sold first. Gasoline held in a tank is a good example of an inventory that has an average physical flow. As the tank is refilled, the new gasoline is mixed with the old. Thus, any amount used will consist of a blend of the old gas with the new.

Although physical flows are sometimes cited as support for an inventory method, accountants now recognize that an inventory method's assumed cost flows need not necessarily correspond with the actual physical flow of the goods. In fact, good reasons exist for simply ignoring physical flows and choosing an inventory method based on more significant criteria.

Illustrations 6.17 and 6.18 use the data from Illustration 6.6 to show the cost of goods sold, inventory cost, and gross margin for each of the four basic costing methods using perpetual and periodic inventory procedures, respectively.

The differences shown for the four methods occur because the company paid different prices for goods purchased. No differences would occur if purchase prices were constant. Since a company's purchase prices are seldom constant, the inventory costing method used by the company affects cost of goods sold,

---

ILLUSTRATION 6.16

Determining Ending Inventory under Weighted-Average Method

	Units	Unit Cost	Total Cost
Beginning inventory	10	$8.00	$ 80.00
Purchases			
March 2	10	8.50	85.00
May 28.	20	8.40	168.00
August 12	10	9.00	90.00
October 12	20	8.80	176.00
December 21	10	9.10	91.00
Total	80		$690.00

Weighted-average unit cost is
$690 ÷ 80, or $8.625.
Ending inventory then is $8.625 × 20 . . . .   172.50

Cost of goods sold:
$8.625 × 60 . . . . $517.50

ILLUSTRATION 6.17

Summary of Effects of Employing Different Inventory Costing Methods with Same Basic Data—Use of Perpetual Inventory Procedure

	Specific Identification	FIFO	LIFO	Weighted-Average
Sales	$780.00	$780.00	$780.00	$780.00
Cost of goods sold:				
Beginning inventory	$ 80.00	$ 80.00	$ 80.00	$ 80.00
Purchases	610.00	610.00	610.00	610.00
Cost of goods available for sale	$690.00	$690.00	$690.00	$690.00
Ending inventory	181.00	179.00	171.00	178.58
Cost of goods sold	$509.00	$511.00	$519.00	$511.42
Gross margin	$271.00	$269.00	$261.00	$268.58

ILLUSTRATION 6.18

Summary of Effects of Employing Different Inventory Costing Methods with Same Basic Data—Use of Periodic Inventory Procedure

	Specific Identification	FIFO	LIFO	Weighted-Average
Sales	$780.00	$780.00	$780.00	$780.00
Cost of goods sold:				
Beginning inventory	$ 80.00	$ 80.00	$ 80.00	$ 80.00
Purchases	610.00	610.00	610.00	610.00
Cost of goods available for sale	$690.00	$690.00	$690.00	$690.00
Ending inventory	181.00	179.00	165.00	172.50
Cost of goods sold	$509.00	$511.00	$525.00	$517.50
Gross margin	$271.00	$269.00	$255.00	$262.50

inventory cost, gross margin, and net income. Therefore, companies must disclose on their financial statements which inventory costing method(s) was (were) used.

Which Is the "Correct" Method   All four methods of inventory costing are acceptable; no single method is the only correct method. Different methods are attractive under different conditions.

If a company wants to match sales revenue with current cost of goods sold, it would use LIFO. If a company seeks to reduce its income taxes in a period of rising prices, it would also use LIFO. On the other hand, LIFO often charges against revenues the cost of goods not actually sold, and LIFO may allow the company to manipulate net income by changing the time when the company makes additional purchases.

The FIFO and specific identification methods result in a more precise matching of historical cost with revenue. However, FIFO can give rise to "paper" profits, while specific identification can give rise to income manipulation. The weighted-average method also allows manipulation of income. Only under FIFO is the manipulation of net income not possible.

Changing Inventory Methods

Generally, companies may use the inventory method that best fits their individual circumstances. However, this freedom of choice does not include changing inventory methods every year or so, especially if the goal is to report higher income. Continuous switching of methods violates the **accounting principle of consistency,** which requires the repeated use of the same accounting methods in preparing financial statements. Consistency of methods in preparing financial statements enables financial statement users to compare statements from period to period and determine trends.

Companies may sometimes make a change in inventory method in spite of the principle of consistency. Improved financial reporting is the only justification for a change in inventory method. If a company changes its inventory method, the company must make a full disclosure of the change. Usually, the company makes a full disclosure in a footnote to the financial statements. The footnote consists of a complete description of the change, the reasons why the change was made, and, if possible, the effect of the change on net income.

For example, when J. M. Tull Industries, Inc., changed from lower of average cost or market to LIFO, the following footnote appeared in its annual report:

Note B. Change in accounting method for inventory. Effective with the year ending December 31, 1975, the company changed its method of determining inventory cost from the lower of average cost or market method to the last-in, first-out (LIFO) method for substantially all inventory. This change was made because management believes LIFO more clearly reflects income by providing a closer matching of current cost against current revenue.

Journal Entries under Perpetual Inventory Procedure

Objective 5

Record merchandise transactions under perpetual inventory procedure.

Now we illustrate in more detail the journal entries made when using perpetual inventory procedure. Data from Illustration 6.8 serve as the basis for some of the entries.

The Merchandise Inventory account is debited to record the increases in the asset due to purchase costs and transportation-in costs. Merchandise Inventory is credited to record the decreases in the asset brought about by purchase returns and allowances, purchase discounts, and cost of goods sold to customers. The balance in the account is the cost of the inventory that should be on hand at any date.

You would record the purchase of 10 units on March 2 in Illustration 6.8 as follows:

Mar.	2	Merchandise Inventory	85	
		Accounts Payable.		85
		To record purchase of 10 units at $8.50 on account.		

The 10 units purchased must also be recorded on the perpetual inventory record, as shown in Illustration 6.8.

The use of perpetual inventory procedure requires that two journal entries be made for each sale. One entry is at selling price—a debit to Accounts Receivable (or Cash) and a credit to Sales. The other entry is at cost—a debit to Cost of Goods Sold and a credit to Merchandise Inventory. Assuming that the 10 units sold on March 10 in Illustration 6.8 had a retail price of $13 each, you would record the following entries:

Mar.	10	Accounts Receivable	130	
		Sales		130
		To record 10 units sold at $13 each on account.		
	10	Cost of Goods Sold	80	
		Merchandise Inventory		80
		To record cost of $8 on each of the 10 units sold.		

When a company sells merchandise to customers, the company transfers the cost of the merchandise from an asset account (Merchandise Inventory) to an expense account (Cost of Goods Sold). The company makes this transfer because the sale reduces the asset, and the cost of the goods sold is one of the expenses of making the sale. Thus, the Cost of Goods Sold account accumulates the cost of all the merchandise that the company sells during a period.

A sales return also requires two entries, one at selling price and one at cost.

Assume that a customer returned merchandise that cost $20 and was sold originally for $32. The entry to reduce the accounts receivable and to record the sales return of $32 is as follows:

Mar.	17	Sales Returns and Allowances	32	
		Accounts Receivable		32
		To record the reduction in amount owed by a customer upon return of goods.		

The Merchandise Inventory account should be increased and the Cost of Goods Sold account should be decreased by $20 as follows:

Mar.	17	Merchandise Inventory	20	
		Cost of Goods Sold		20
		To record replacement of goods returned to inventory.		

Sales returns affect both revenues and cost of goods sold because the goods charged to cost of goods sold are actually returned to the seller. However, sales allowances granted customers affect revenues only because the customers have returned no goods. Thus, if the company had granted a sales allowance of $32 on March 17, only the first entry would be required.

The balance of the Merchandise Inventory account is the cost of the inventory which should be on hand. This is one of the major reasons why some companies choose to use perpetual inventory procedure. The cost of inventory that should be on hand is readily available. Periodically, usually at year-end, a physical inventory is taken to determine the accuracy of the balance shown. Management may wish to investigate any major discrepancies between the balance shown in the account and the cost based on the physical count. Greater control over inventory is thereby achieved. If a shortage is discovered, an adjusting entry is required. The entry, assuming that a $15 shortage (at cost) is discovered, is:

Dec.	31	Loss from Inventory Shortage	15	
		Merchandise Inventory		15
		To record inventory shortage.		

Assume that the Cost of Goods Sold account had a balance of $200,000 by year-end. At the end of the year, the Cost of Goods Sold account is closed to Income Summary. There are no other purchase-related accounts to be closed.

Dec.	31	Income Summary.	200,000	
		Cost of Goods Sold		200,000
		To close Cost of Goods Sold account to Income Summary at the end of the year.		

DEPARTURES FROM COST BASIS OF INVENTORY MEASUREMENT

As stated earlier, historical cost should generally be used to value inventories and cost of goods sold. However, in some circumstances, departures from historical cost are justified. One of these circumstances is when the utility or value of inventory items is less than the cost of those items. A decline in the selling price of the goods or in their replacement cost may indicate such a loss of utility. This section explains how accountants account for some of these departures from the cost basis of inventory measurement.

Net Realizable Value

Objective 6

Apply net realizable value and the lower-of-cost-or-market method to inventory

Companies should not carry goods in inventory at more than their net realizable value. Net realizable value is the estimated selling price of an item less the estimated costs that the company will incur in preparing the item for sale and selling it. Damaged, obsolete, or shopworn goods often have a net realizable value that is lower than their historical cost and must be written down to their net realizable value. The goods do not have to be damaged, obsolete, or shopworn for this situation to occur. Technological changes and increased competition have caused significant reductions in selling prices for such products as computers, VCRs, calculators, and microwave ovens.

To illustrate a necessary write-down in the cost of inventory, assume that an automobile dealer has a demonstrator on hand. The dealer acquired the auto at a cost of $8,000. The auto had an original selling price of $9,600. Since the dealer used the auto as a demonstrator and the new models are coming in, the auto now has an estimated selling price of only $8,100. However, the dealer can get the $8,100 only if the demonstrator receives some scheduled maintenance, including a tune-up and some paint damage repairs. This work and the sales commission will cost $300. The net realizable value of the demonstrator, then, is $7,800 (selling price of $8,100 less costs of $300). For inventory purposes, the required journal entry is:

Loss Due to Decline in Market Value of Inventory   200
    Merchandise Inventory   200

To write down inventory to net realizable value ($8,000 − $7,800).

This entry treats the $200 inventory decline as a loss in the period in which the decline in utility occurred. Such an entry is necessary only when the net realizable value is less than cost. If net realizable value declines but still exceeds cost, the dealer would continue to carry the item at cost.

Lower-of-Cost-or-Market Method

The lower-of-cost-or-market (LCM) method is an inventory costing method that values inventory at the lower of its historical cost or its current market (replacement) cost. The term *cost* refers to historical cost of inventory as determined under the specific identification, FIFO, LIFO, or weighted-average inventory method. *Market* generally refers to a merchandise item's replacement cost in the quantity usually purchased. The basic assumption of the LCM method is that if the purchase price of an item has fallen, its selling price also has fallen or will fall. The LCM method has long been accepted in accounting.

Under LCM, inventory items are written down to market value when the market value is less than the cost of the items. For example, assume that the market value of the inventory is $39,600 and its cost is $40,000. Then, the company would record a $400 loss because the inventory has lost some of its revenue-generating ability. The company must recognize the loss in the period the loss occurred. On the other hand, if ending inventory has a market value of $45,000 and a cost of $40,000, the company would not recognize this increase in value. To do so would recognize revenue before the time of sale.

LCM Applied   A company may apply LCM to each inventory item (such as Trivial Pursuit), each inventory class (such as games), or total inventory. Illustration 6.19 shows an application of the method to individual items and total inventory.

If LCM is applied on an item-by-item basis, ending inventory would be $5,000. The company would deduct the $5,000 ending inventory from cost of goods available for sale on the income statement and would report this inventory in the current assets section of the balance sheet. Under the class method, a company applies LCM to the total cost and total market for each class of items compared. One class might be games; another might be toys. Then, the company values each class at the lower of its cost or market amount. If LCM is applied on a total inventory basis, ending inventory would be $5,100, since total cost of $5,100 is lower than total market of $5,150.

The annual report of Du Pont contains an actual example of applying LCM. The report states that "substantially all inventories are valued at cost as determined by the last-in, first-out (LIFO) method; in the aggregate, such valuations are not in excess of market." The term *in the aggregate* means that Du Pont applied LCM to total inventory.

ILLUSTRATION 6.19

Application of Lower-of-Cost-or-Market Method

Item	Quantity	Unit Cost	Unit Market	Total Cost	Total Market	LCM on Item-by-Item Basis
1	100 units	$10	$9.00	$1,000	$ 900	$ 900
2	200 units	8	8.75	1,600	1,750	1,600
3	500 units	5	5.00	2,500	2,500	2,500
				$5,100	$5,150	$5,000

Estimating Inventory

Objective 7
Estimate cost of ending inventory using the gross margin and retail inventory methods

A company using periodic inventory procedure may wish to estimate its inventory for any of the following reasons:

1. To obtain an inventory cost for use in monthly or quarterly financial statements without taking a physical inventory. The effort of taking a physical inventory can be very expensive and disrupts normal business operations; once a year is often enough.
2. To compare with physical inventories to determine whether shortages exist.
3. To determine the amount recoverable from an insurance company when fire has destroyed inventory or the inventory has been stolen.

The paragraphs that follow discuss two recognized methods of estimating the cost of ending inventory—the gross margin method and the retail inventory method.

Gross Margin Method   The gross margin method is one method of estimating an inventory when a company has not taken a physical inventory. The steps in calculating ending inventory under the gross margin method are:

1. Estimate gross margin (based on net sales) using the same gross margin rate experienced in prior accounting periods.
2. Determine estimated cost of goods sold by deducting estimated gross margin from net sales.
3. Determine estimated ending inventory by deducting estimated cost of goods sold from cost of goods available for sale.

Thus, the gross margin method estimates ending inventory by deducting estimated cost of goods sold from cost of goods available for sale.

The gross margin method assumes that a fairly stable relationship exists between gross margin and net sales. In other words, gross margin has been a fairly constant percentage of net sales, and this relationship is assumed to have continued into the current period. If this percentage relationship has changed, the gross margin method will not yield satisfactory results.

To illustrate the gross margin method of computing inventory, assume that Field Company has for several years maintained a rate of gross margin on net sales of 30%. The following data for 1993 are available: the January 1 inventory was $40,000; net cost of purchases of merchandise was $480,000; and net sales of merchandise were $700,000. As shown in Illustration 6.20, the inventory for December 31, 1993, can be estimated by deducting the estimated cost of goods sold from the actual cost of goods available for sale.

A BROADER PERSPECTIVE

The item at the right illustrates the type of disclosure regarding inventories that is presented in the footnotes to the financial statements. Notice that the company discloses the inventory costing methods used, as well as the bases for cost and market.

PREMIER INDUSTRIAL CORPORATION
Partial Balance Sheet
As of May 31, 1988, and 1987
(in thousands)

	1988	1987
Current assets:		
Cash (including temporary investments of $125,365 and $109,659 in 1988 and 1987, respectively)	$130,188	$117,272
Receivables (less allowance for doubtful accounts of $1,339 and $1,552 in 1988 and 1987, respectively)	78,309	71,252
Inventories (note 2)	79,008	70,197
Prepaid expenses	5,195	5,251
Total current assets	$292,700	$263,972

Notes to Financial Statements

1 (In part): Summary of Significant Accounting Policies
(d) Inventories
Inventories are stated at the lower of cost or market, cost being determined on the basis of either the first-in, first-out (FIFO) method or on the last-in, first-out (LIFO) method and market on the basis of lower of replacement cost or net realizable value.

(2) Inventories
The current cost of inventories valued under the LIFO method (approximately 16% and 17% of total inventory at current cost at May 31, 1988 and 1987) exceeded their LIFO carrying values by $6,591,000 and $5,718,000 at May 31, 1988 and 1987, respectively. Because the cost of certain inventories is determined on the LIFO method, it is not practical to present separately the components (raw materials, work-in-process, and finished goods) of inventory.

ILLUSTRATION 6.20

Inventory Estimation Using Gross Margin Method

Merchandise inventory, January 1, 1993		$ 40,000
Net cost of purchases		480,000
Cost of goods available for sale		$520,000
Less estimated cost of goods sold:		
Net sales	$700,000	
Gross margin (30% of $700,000)	210,000	
Estimated cost of goods sold		490,000
Estimated inventory, December 31, 1993		$ 30,000

An alternative format for calculating estimated ending inventory is to use the standard income statement format and solve for the one unknown (ending inventory):

Net sales.		$700,000
Less cost of goods sold:		
Merchandise inventory, January 1, 1993	$ 40,000	
Net cost of purchases	480,000	
Cost of goods available for sale.	$520,000	
Less estimated inventory, December 31, 1993	?	
Estimated cost of goods sold.		490,000 (70% of net sales)
Estimated gross margin		$210,000 (30% of net sales)

We know that:

$$\begin{matrix} \text{Cost of goods} \\ \text{available for sale} \end{matrix} - \begin{matrix} \text{Ending} \\ \text{inventory} \end{matrix} = \begin{matrix} \text{Cost of} \\ \text{goods sold} \end{matrix}$$

Therefore (let X = Ending inventory):

$$\$520,000 - X = \$490,000$$
$$X = \$30,000$$

The gross margin method is not precise enough to be used for year-end financial statements. At year-end, a physical inventory must be taken and valued by the use of either the specific identification, FIFO, LIFO, or weighted-average methods.

Retail Inventory Method Retail stores frequently use the retail inventory method (hence, the name *retail inventory*) to estimate ending inventory when taking a physical inventory during an accounting period (such as monthly or quarterly) is too time consuming and significantly interferes with business operations. The retail inventory method estimates the cost of the ending inventory by applying a cost/retail price ratio to ending inventory stated at retail prices. The advantage of this method is that companies can estimate ending inventory (at cost) without taking a physical inventory. Thus, the use of this estimate permits the preparation of interim financial statements (monthly or quarterly) without taking a physical inventory.

The retail inventory method works as follows:

1. Accounting records must show the beginning inventory and the amount of goods purchased during the period at both cost and retail prices.
2. The cost/retail price ratio is found by dividing the cost of goods available for sale by the retail price of the goods available for sale.
3. Retail sales are then deducted from the retail price of the goods available for sale to determine ending inventory at retail.
4. The cost/retail price ratio or percentage is multiplied by the ending inventory at retail prices to reduce it to the ending inventory at cost.

Illustration 6.21 shows an example of the retail method. In the illustration, the cost ($22,000) and retail ($40,000) amounts for beginning inventory are available from the preceding period's computation. The amounts for purchases, purchase

ILLUSTRATION 6.21

Inventory Estimation Using Retail Inventory Method

	Cost	Retail
Merchandise inventory, January 1, 1993	$ 22,000	$ 40,000
Purchases	182,000	303,000
Purchase returns and allowances	(2,000)	(3,000)
Purchase discounts	(3,000)	
Transportation-in	5,000	
Goods available for sale	$204,000	$340,000
Cost/retail price ratio:		
$204,000/$340,000 = 60%		
Sales		280,000
Ending inventory at retail prices		$ 60,000
Times cost/retail price ratio		×60%
Ending inventory at cost, December 31, 1993	36,000	

returns and allowances, purchase discounts, and transportation-in are obtained from the accounting records. The amounts for purchase discounts and transportation-in only appear in the cost column, as shown. The sales amount ($280,000) is obtained from the Sales account and is, of course, stated at retail (sales) prices. The difference between what was available for sale at retail prices and what was sold at retail prices (which, of course, is sales) equals what should be on hand (ending inventory of $60,000) expressed in retail prices. The retail price of the ending inventory needs to be converted into cost for use in the financial statements by multiplying it times the cost/retail price ratio. In the example, the cost/retail price ratio is 60%, which means that on the average, 60 cents of each sales dollar is cost of goods sold. Ending inventory at retail ($60,000) is multiplied by 60% to find inventory at cost ($36,000).

Once ending inventory has been estimated at cost ($36,000), the cost of ending inventory can be deducted from cost of goods available for sale ($204,000) to determine cost of goods sold ($168,000). Cost of goods sold can also be found by multiplying the cost/retail price ratio of 60% by sales of $280,000.

In 1994, the $36,000 and $60,000 amounts will appear on the schedule as beginning inventory at cost and retail, respectively. Other 1994 data regarding purchases, purchase returns and allowances, purchase discounts, and transportation-in will be included to determine goods available for sale at cost and at retail. From these amounts, a new cost/retail price ratio for 1994 will be computed.

At the end of each year, a physical inventory usually is taken at retail prices. Since the retail prices are marked on the individual items (while the cost is not), taking an inventory at retail prices is more convenient than taking an inventory at cost. The results of the physical inventory can then be compared to the calculation of inventory at retail under the retail inventory method to determine whether a shortage exists.

Both the gross margin and the retail methods can be used to detect inventory shortages. To illustrate how shortages can be determined using the retail inventory method example given above, assume that a physical inventory taken on December 31, 1993, shows only $56,000 of retail-priced goods in the store. Comparing this amount to the $60,000 of goods that should be on hand (shown in

ETHICS	Jack Gardner started a small hardware store two years ago and was struggling to make it

ETHICS

A CLOSER LOOK

Jack Gardner started a small hardware store two years ago and was struggling to make it successful. The first year of operations resulted in a substantial loss, and in the second year a small net income was realized. Jack's initial cash investment was almost depleted because he had to withdraw money for living expenses. The current year of operations had looked much better. The customer base was growing and seemed to be loyal. To increase sales, however, Jack had to invest his remaining funds and the proceeds of a $50,000 bank loan into doubling the size of his inventory and purchasing some new display shelves and a new truck.

At the end of the third year, Jack's accountant asked him for his ending inventory figure and later told him that initial estimates indicated that net income (and taxable income) for the year would be approximately $100,000. Jack was delighted until he was told that the amount of federal income taxes on that income would be about $20,000. Jack told the accountant that he did not have $20,000 and could not even borrow it, since he already had an outstanding loan at the bank.

Jack asked the accountant for a copy of the income statement figures so that he could see if any items had been overlooked that might reduce his net income. He noticed that ending inventory of $200,000 had been deducted from cost of goods available for sale of $800,000 to arrive at cost of goods sold of $600,000. Net sales of $900,000 and expenses of $200,000 could not be changed. But Jack hit upon a scheme to reduce his net income. The next day he told his accountant that he had made an error in determining ending inventory and that its correct amount was $150,000. This lower inventory amount would increase cost of goods sold by $50,000 and reduce net income by that same amount. The resulting income taxes would be about $7,000. Even paying this amount of taxes would be difficult, but Jack thought it could be done.

To justify his action in his own mind, Jack used the following arguments: (1) federal taxes are too high, and the federal government seems to be taxing the "little guy" out of existence; (2) no harm is really done because, when the business becomes more profitable, I will use correct inventory amounts, and this "loan" from the government will be paid back; (3) since I am the only one who knows the correct ending inventory, I will not get caught; and (4) I'll bet a lot of other people do this same thing.

Required

a. Do you believe that Jack's scheme will work?

b. What would you do if you were Jack's accountant?

c. Comment on each of Jack's points of justification.

Illustration 6.21) indicates a $4,000 inventory shortage at retail. The $4,000 will be converted to $2,400 of cost ($4,000 × 0.60) and reported as a "Loss from inventory shortage" in the income statement. Knowledge of such shortages may lead to management action to reduce or prevent them, such as increasing security or improving the training of employees.

You should now understand the importance of taking an accurate ending inventory and knowing how to value this inventory. Chapter 7 takes you back to the accounting process (or cycle) and builds on the knowledge you have already acquired as you study accounting systems and special journals.

UNDERSTANDING THE LEARNING OBJECTIVES

1. Explain and calculate the effects of inventory errors on certain financial statement items.

   □ Net income for an accounting period depends directly on the valuation of ending inventory.

☐ If ending inventory is overstated, cost of goods sold will be understated, resulting in an overstatement of gross margin, net income, and retained earnings.

☐ When ending inventory is misstated in the current year, that misstatement is carried forward into the next year.

☐ An error in the net income of one year caused by misstated ending inventory automatically causes an error in net income in the opposite direction in the next period (e.g., misstated beginning inventory).

2. Indicate which costs are properly included in inventory.

☐ Inventory cost includes all necessary outlays to obtain the goods, get the goods ready to sell, and have the goods in the desired location for sale to customers.

☐ Inventory cost includes:

1. Seller's gross invoice price less purchase discount.

2. Cost of insurance on the goods while in transit.

3. Transportation charges when borne by the buyer.

4. Handling costs, such as the cost of pressing clothes wrinkled during shipment.

3. Calculate cost of ending inventory and cost of goods sold under the four major inventory costing methods using perpetual and periodic inventory procedures.

☐ **Specific identification:** Attaches actual cost of each unit of product to units in ending inventory and cost of goods sold. Specific identification creates precise matching in determining net income.

☐ **FIFO (first-in, first-out):** Ending inventory consists of the most recent purchases. FIFO assumes that the costs of the first goods purchased are the first costs charged to cost of goods sold when the goods are actually sold. FIFO usually creates higher net income since the costs charged to cost of goods sold are lower.

☐ **LIFO (last-in, first-out):** Ending inventory consists of the oldest costs. LIFO assumes that the costs of the most recent purchases are the first costs charged to cost of goods sold. Net income is usually lower under LIFO since the costs charged to cost of goods sold are higher due to inflation. The ending inventory may differ between perpetual and periodic inventory procedures.

☐ **Weighted-average:** Ending inventory is priced using a weighted-average unit cost. Under perpetual procedure, a new weighted average is determined after each purchase. Under periodic procedure the average is determined by dividing the total number of units purchased plus those in beginning inventory into total cost of goods available for sale. In determining cost of goods sold, this average unit cost is applied to each item. Under the weighted-average method, net income is usually higher than income under LIFO and lower than income under FIFO.

4. Explain the advantages and disadvantages of the four major inventory costing methods.

☐ **Specific identification:**
Advantages: (1) States cost of goods sold and ending inventory at the actual cost of specific units sold and on hand, and (2) it provides the most precise matching of costs and revenues.
Disadvantage: Income manipulation is possible.

☐ **FIFO:**

Advantages: (1) Easy to apply, (2) the assumed flow of costs often corresponds with the normal physical flow of goods, (3) no manipulation of income is possible, and (4) the balance sheet amount for inventory is likely to approximate the current market value.

Disadvantages: (1) Recognizes ''paper'' profits, and (2) tax burden is heavier if used for tax purposes.

☐ **LIFO:**

Advantages: (1) Both sales revenue and cost of goods sold are reported in current dollars, and (2) lower income taxes result if used for tax purposes when prices are rising.

Disadvantages: (1) Matches the cost of goods *not* sold against revenues, (2) grossly understates inventory, and (3) permits income manipulation.

☐ **Weighted-average:**

Advantages: Due to the averaging process, the effects of year-end buying or not buying are lessened.

Disadvantages: Manipulation of income is possible.

5. Record merchandise transactions under perpetual inventory procedure.

☐ Perpetual inventory procedure requires an entry to Merchandise Inventory whenever goods are purchased, returned, sold, or otherwise adjusted, so that inventory records reflect actual units on hand at all times. Thus, an entry is required to record cost of goods sold for each sale.

6. Apply net realizable value and the lower-of-cost-or-market method to inventory.

☐ Inventory items are written down to market value when the market value is less than the cost of the items. If market value is greater than cost, the increase in value is not recognized.

☐ LCM may be applied to each inventory item, each inventory class, or total inventory.

7. Estimate cost of ending inventory using the gross margin and retail inventory methods.

☐ The steps in calculating ending inventory under the gross margin methods are:

1. Gross margin is estimated (based on net sales) using the same gross margin rate experienced in prior accounting periods.

2. Estimated cost of goods sold is determined by deducting estimated gross margin from net sales.

3. Estimated ending inventory is determined by deducting estimated cost of goods sold from cost of goods available for sale.

☐ The retail inventory method estimates the cost of the ending inventory by applying a cost/retail price ratio to ending inventory stated at retail prices. The cost/retail price ratio is found by dividing the cost of goods available for sale by the retail price of the goods available for sale.

DEMONSTRATION PROBLEM 6–A

Following are data related to System Company's beginning inventory, purchases, and sales of a given item of product for the year 1994:

Beginning Inventory and Purchases				Sales	
	Units		**Unit Cost**		**Units**
Beginning inventory	6,250	@	$5.00	February 3	5,250
March 15	5,000	@	5.20	May 4	4,500
May 10	8,750	@	5.50	September 16	8,000
August 12	6,250	@	5.80	October 9	7,250
November 20	3,750	@	6.20		
	30,000				25,000

Required *a.* Compute the ending inventory under each of the following methods:
1. Specific identification (assume that ending inventory consists of equal amounts from the August 12 and November 20 purchases).
2. FIFO: *(a)* Assume use of perpetual inventory procedure.
   (b) Assume use of periodic inventory procedure.
3. LIFO: *(a)* Assume use of perpetual inventory procedure.
   (b) Assume use of periodic inventory procedure.
4. Weighted-average: *(a)* Assume use of perpetual inventory procedure.
   (b) Assume use of periodic inventory procedure.
   (Carry unit cost to four decimal places and round total cost to nearest dollar.)

b. Give the journal entries to record the individual purchases and sales (Cost of Goods Sold entry only) under the LIFO method and perpetual procedure.

SOLUTION TO DEMONSTRATION PROBLEM 6–A

a. The ending inventory consists of:

	Units
Beginning inventory	6,250
Purchases.	23,750
Goods available	30,000
Sales	25,000
Ending inventory.	5,000

1. Ending inventory under specific identification:

Purchased	**Units**	**Unit Cost**	**Total Cost**
November 20	2,500	$6.20	$15,500
August 12	2,500	5.80	14,500
			$30,000

2. Ending inventory under FIFO:
    (a) Perpetual:

Date	Purchased Units	Purchased Unit Cost	Sold Units	Sold Unit Cost	Balance Units	Balance Unit Cost	Balance Total Cost
Beg. inv.					6,250	$5.00	$31,250
Feb. 3			5,250	$5.00	1,000	5.00	5,000
Mar. 15	5,000	$5.20			1,000	5.00	5,000
					5,000	5.20	26,000
May 4			1,000	5.00			
			3,500	5.20	1,500	5.20	7.800
May 10	8,750	5.50			1,500	5.20	7,800
					8,750	5.50	48,125
Aug. 12	6,250	5.80			1,500	5.20	7,800
					8,750	5.50	48,125
					6,250	5.80	36,250
Sept. 16			1,500	5.20			
			6,500	5.50	2,250	5.50	12,375
					6,250	5.80	36,250
Oct. 9			2,250	5.50			
			5,000	5.80	1,250	5.80	7.250
Nov. 20	3,750	6.20			1,250	5.80	7,250
					3,750	6.20	23,250

Ending inventory = (1,250 × $5.80) + (3,750 × $6.20) = $30,500

(b) Periodic:

Purchased	Units	Unit Cost	Total Cost
November 20	3,750	$6.20	$23,250
August 12	1,250	5.80	7,250
	5,000		$30,500*

* Note that the cost of ending inventory is the same as under perpetual.

3. Ending inventory under LIFO:
   (a) Perpetual:

Date	Purchased Units	Purchased Unit Cost	Sold Units	Sold Unit Cost	Balance Units	Balance Unit Cost	Balance Total Cost
Beg. inv.					6,250	$5.00	$31,250
Feb. 3			5,250	$5.00	1,000	5.00	5,000
Mar. 15	5,000	$5.20			1,000	5.00	5,000
					5,000	5.20	26,000
May 4			4,500	5.20	1,000	5.00	5,000
					500	5.20	2,600
May 10	8,750	5.50			1,000	5.00	5,000
					500	5.20	2,600
					8,750	5.50	48,125
Aug. 12	6,250	5.80			1,000	5.00	5,000
					500	5.20	2,600
					8,750	5.50	48,125
					6,250	5.80	36,250
Sept. 16			6,250	5.80			
			1,750	5.50	1,000	5.00	5,000
					500	5.20	2,600
					7,000	5.50	38,500
Oct. 9			7,000	5.50			
			250	5.20	1,000	5.00	5,000
					250	5.20	1,300
Nov. 20	3,750	6.20			1,000	5.00	5,000
					250	5.20	1,300
					3,750	6.20	23,250

Ending inventory = (1,000 × $5.00) + (250 × $5.20) + (3,750 × $6.20) = $29,550

(b) Periodic:

	Units	Unit Cost	Total Cost
Merchandise inventory, January 1	5,000	$5.00	$25,000

4. Ending inventory under weighted-average:
    (a) Perpetual:

Date	Purchased Units	Purchased Unit Cost	Sold Units	Sold Unit Cost	Balance Units	Balance Unit Cost	Balance Total Cost
Beg. inv.					6,250	$5.0000	$31,250
Feb. 3			5,250	$5.00	1,000	5.0000	5,000
Mar. 15	5,000	$5.20			6,000	5.1667[a]	31,000
May 4			4,500	5.1667	1,500	5.1667	7,750
May 10	8,750	5.50			10,250	5.4512[b]	55,875
Aug. 12	6,250	5.80			16,500	5.5833[c]	92,125
Sept. 16			8,000	5.5833	8,500	5.5833	47,459*
Oct. 9			7,250	5.5833	1,250	5.5833	6,980*
Nov. 20	3,750	6.20			5,000	6.0460[d]	30,230

Ending inventory = (5,000 × $6.0460) = $30,230

[a] $\frac{\$31,000}{6,000} = \$5.1667.$ [b] $\frac{\$55,875}{10,250} = \$5.4512.$ [c] $\frac{\$92,125}{16,500} = \$5.5833.$ [d] $\frac{\$30,230}{5,000} = \$6.0460.$

* Rounding difference.

(b) Periodic:

Purchased	Units	Unit Cost	Total Cost
Merchandise inventory, January 1	6,250	$5.00	$ 31,250
March 15	5,000	5.20	26,000
May 10	8,750	5.50	48,125
August 12	6,250	5.80	36,250
November 20	3,750	6.20	23,250
	30,000		$164,875

Weighted-average unit cost = $164,875 ÷ 30,000 = $5.4958
Ending inventory cost = $5.4958 × 5,000 = $27,479

b.   Journal entries under LIFO perpetual:

Feb.	3	Cost of Goods Sold . . . .
		     Merchandise Inventory.
		     To record cost of $5 on 5,250 units sold.
			26,250	26,250

Mar.	15	Merchandise Inventory. . . . .
		     Accounts Payable . . . .
		     To record purchase of 5,000 units at $5.20 on account.
			26,000	26,000

May	4	Cost of Goods Sold . . . .
		     Merchandise Inventory.
		     To record cost of $5.20 on 4,500 units sold.
			23,400	23,400

	10	Merchandise Inventory. . . . .
		     Accounts Payable . . . .
		     To record purchase of 8,750 units at $5.50 on account.
			48,125	48,125

Aug.	12	Merchandise Inventory. . . . .
		     Accounts Payable . . . .
		     To record purchase of 6,250 units at $5.80 on account.
			36,250	36,250

Sept.	16	Cost of Goods Sold . . . .
		     Merchandise Inventory.
		     To record cost of $5.80 and $5.50 on 6,250 units and 1,750
		     units sold, respectively.
			45,875	45,875

Oct.	9	Cost of Goods Sold . . . .
		     Merchandise Inventory.
		     To record cost of $5.50 and $5.20 on 7,000 units and 250
		     units sold, respectively.
			39,800	39,800

Nov.	20	Merchandise Inventory. . . . .
		     Accounts Payable . . . .
		     To record purchase of 3,750 units at $6.20 on account.
			23,250	23,250

DEMONSTRATION PROBLEM 6–B

a.   The following information is available for Mortgage Company for 1993.

Merchandise inventory, January 1, 1993	$ 160,000
Net cost of purchases	1,920,000
Merchandise sales	2,800,000

Mortgage Company has for several years maintained a rate of gross margin on sales of 30%. Estimate the ending inventory for December 31, 1993.

b.   The following information is available for Aiken Company for 1993.

	Cost	Retail Price
Beginning inventory	$ 94,400	$ 160,000
Purchases, net	721,600	1,200,000
Goods available for sale	$816,000	$1,360,000
Sales.		1,120,000

Ending inventory at retail on December 31, 1993, was $240,000. Calculate ending inventory at cost and cost of goods sold.

SOLUTION TO DEMONSTRATION PROBLEM 6–B

a.

Merchandise inventory, January 1, 1993	$ 160,000
Net cost of purchases	1,920,000
Goods available for sale.	$2,080,000
Less estimated cost of goods sold:	
Sales $2,800,000	
Gross margin (30% of $2,800,000) 840,000	
Estimated cost of goods sold	1,960,000
Estimated inventory, December 31, 1993	$ 120,000

b. Cost/retail price ratio: $816,000/$1,360,000 = 60%.

	Cost	Retail Price
Goods available for sale	$816,000	$1,360,000
Sales		1,120,000
Ending inventory at retail prices.		$ 240,000
Times cost/retail price ratio		×60%
Ending inventory at cost, December 31, 1993	144,000	
Cost of goods sold	$672,000	

NEW TERMS

FIFO (first-in, first-out)   A method of costing inventory that assumes the costs of the first goods purchased are the first costs charged to cost of goods sold when the company actually sells the goods. *270*

Gross margin method   A procedure for estimating inventory cost in which estimated cost of goods sold (determined using an estimated gross margin) is deducted from the cost of goods available for sale to determine estimated ending inventory. The estimated gross margin is calculated using gross margin rates (in relation to net sales) of prior periods. *284*

Inventory, or "paper," profits   Equal to the current replacement cost to purchase a unit of inventory at time of sale minus the unit's historical cost. *274*

LIFO (last-in, first-out)   A method of costing inventory that assumes the costs of the most recent purchases are the first costs charged to cost of goods sold when the company actually sells the goods. *272*

Lower-of-cost-or-market (LCM) method   An inventory costing method that values inventory at the lower of its historical cost or its current market (replacement) cost. *283*

Merchandise inventory   The quantity of goods held by a merchandising company for resale to customers. *260*

Net realizable value   Estimated selling price of an item less the estimated costs that will be incurred in preparing the item for sale and selling it. *282*

Retail inventory method   A procedure for estimating the cost of the ending inventory by applying a cost/retail price ratio to ending inventory stated at retail prices. *286*

Specific identification   An inventory costing method that attaches the actual cost to an identifiable unit of product. *268*

Weighted-average method   A method of costing ending inventory using a weighted-average unit cost. Under perpetual inventory procedure, a new weighted average is calculated after each purchase. Under periodic procedure, the weighted average is determined by dividing the total number of units purchased plus those in beginning inventory into total cost of goods available for sale. Units in the ending inventory are carried at this per unit cost. *277*

SELF-TEST

True-False

Indicate whether each of the following statements is true or false.

1. In a period of rising prices, FIFO will result in a lower net income figure than that resulting from LIFO.

2. An understatement of the beginning inventory will result in an overstatement of the net income for the period.

3. Inventory cost methods should be changed at will to control reported net income.

4. In a period of rising prices, LIFO yields the highest cost of goods sold.

5. The net realizable value of an inventory item cannot be greater than its expected selling price.

Multiple-Choice

Select the best answer for each of the following questions.

On January 1, 1994, Davison Company's inventory of product J consisted of 2,000 units at $15 each. During the period, the company purchased 8,000 units of product J at $18 each and sold 7,800 units. Assume the use of periodic inventory procedure for Questions 1–6.

1. Cost of goods sold using weighted-average is:
   a. $140,400.
   b. $135,280.
   c. $135,720.
   d. $138,000.
   e. None of the above.

2. Cost of ending inventory using weighted-average is:
   a. $32,280.
   b. $33,600.
   c. $38,720.
   d. $36,000.
   e. None of the above.

3. Cost of goods sold using FIFO is:
   a. $117,000.
   b. $134,400.
   c. $140,400.
   d. None of the above.

4. Cost of ending inventory using FIFO is:
   a. $39,600.
   b. $33,600.
   c. $57,000.
   d. None of the above.

5. Cost of goods sold using LIFO is:
   a. $117,000.
   b. $123,000.
   c. $134,400.
   d. $140,400.
   e. None of the above.

6. Cost of ending inventory using LIFO is:
   a. $33,600.
   b. $51,000.
   c. $39,600.
   d. $57,000.
   e. None of the above.

7. During a period of rising prices, which inventory pricing method might be expected to give the highest valuation for inventory on the balance sheet?
   a. FIFO.
   b. LIFO.
   c. Weighted-average.
   d. Specific identification.

Now turn to page 308 to check your answers.

QUESTIONS

1. Why does an understated ending inventory understate net income for the period by the same amount?

2. Why does an error in ending inventory affect two accounting periods?

3. Why is proper inventory valuation so important?

4. What cost elements are included in inventory?

5. What does it mean to "take a physical inventory"?

6. What is the cost flow assumption? What is meant by the physical flow of goods? Does a relationship between cost flows and the physical flow of goods exist, or should such a relationship exist?

7. What are the main advantages of using FIFO and LIFO?

8. Why are ending inventory and cost of goods sold the same under FIFO perpetual and FIFO periodic?

9. Indicate how a company can manipulate the amount of net income it reports if it uses the LIFO method of inventory measurement. Why is the same manipulation not possible under FIFO?

10. Would you agree with the following statement? Reducing the amount of taxes payable currently is a valid objective of business management and, since LIFO results in such a reduction, all businesses should use LIFO.

11. Why is perpetual inventory procedure being used increasingly in business?

12. What is net realizable value, and how is it used?

13. Why is it considered acceptable accounting practice to recognize a loss by writing down an item of merchandise in inventory to market, but unacceptable to recognize a gain by writing up an item of merchandise in inventory?

14. Under what operating conditions will the gross margin method of computing inventory cost produce approximately correct amounts?

15. Should a company rely exclusively on the gross margin method to determine the ending inventory and cost of goods sold for the end-of-year financial statements?

16. What are three reasons why a company would want to estimate its inventory?

17. How can the retail method be used to estimate inventory?

MAYTAG
CORPORATION

18. *Real world question* Based on the financial statements of Maytag Corporation contained in Appendix E, what was the 1989 beginning inventory?

THE LIMITED, INC.

19. *Real world question* Based on the financial statements of The Limited, Inc., contained in Appendix E, what was the 1989 ending inventory?

HARLAND

20. *Real world question* Based on the financial statements of John H. Harland Company contained in Appendix E, what was the 1989 beginning inventory?

EXERCISES

Exercise 6–1
Determine effects of inventory errors
(L.O. 1)

In the following table, enter the word *over* if the item would be overstated and the word *under* if the item would be understated for each of the independent situations. Enter *no* if there would be no effect.

| | For the Current Year | | | |
	Beginning Inventory	Ending Inventory	Net Income	Retained Earnings
a. Ending inventory for current year overstated.				
b. Ending inventory for current year understated.				
c. Ending inventory for prior year overstated.				
d. Ending inventory for prior year understated.				

Exercise 6–2
Maximize and minimize net income using the specific identification method
(L.O. 3)

Burell Company inventory records show a July 1, 1993, inventory for one of its products of four units at $1,600 each and the following purchases.

	Units	Unit Cost
July 12	5	@ $1,804
August 23	10	@ $1,872
September 29	6	@ $1,892
November 18	8	@ $1,916
February 16	12	@ $1,848
May 4	7	@ $1,936

The June 30, 1994, inventory consisted of 11 units. Using the specific identification method of costing inventory, prepare a schedule showing the ending inventory that will:

a. Maximize net income.

b. Minimize net income.

Exercise 6–3

Prepare journal entries using FIFO perpetual inventory procedure (L.O. 3, 5)

Dawson Company had the following transactions during February:

1. Purchased 270 units at $130.
2. Sold 216 units at $180.
3. Purchased 340 units at $150.
4. Sold 245 units at $190.
5. Sold 135 units at $200.

The beginning inventory consisted of 135 units purchased at a cost of $110.

Prepare the journal entries relating to inventory for the five transactions above, assuming inventory is accounted for using perpetual procedure and the FIFO inventory method. Do not record the entry for sales.

Exercise 6–4

Prepare journal entries using LIFO perpetual inventory procedure (L.O. 3, 5)

Repeat Exercise 6–3 using the LIFO inventory method.

Exercise 6–5

Compute ending inventory using weighted-average perpetual procedure (L.O. 3)

Duke Company had a beginning inventory of 80 units at $6 (total = $480) and the following inventory transactions during 1993:

1. January 8, sold 20 units.
2. January 11, purchased 40 units at $7.50.
3. January 15, purchased 40 units at $8.00.
4. January 22, sold 40 units.

Using the information above, price the ending inventory at its weighted-average cost, assuming perpetual inventory procedure.

Exercise 6–6

Compute ending inventory using FIFO and LIFO periodic inventory procedure (L.O. 3)

Nance Company inventory records show a January 1 inventory of 400 units at $16 (total, $6,400) and the following purchases:

	Units	Unit Cost	Total Cost
February 14	140 @	$14.60	$2,044
March 18	400 @	14.40	5,760
July 21	300 @	15.20	4,560
September 27	300 @	14.60	4,380
November 27.	100 @	15.60	1,560

The December 31 inventory is 700 units.

a. Present a short schedule showing the measurement of the ending inventory using the FIFO method, assuming periodic procedure.
b. Do the same using the LIFO method.

Exercise 6–7

Prepare journal entries and compute cost of goods sold (L.O. 3)

Using the information given in Exercise 6–6, give the journal entries to record purchases (total all purchases in one entry), and compute cost of goods sold for both FIFO and LIFO, assuming periodic inventory procedure.

Exercise 6–8

Determine effects on net income of LIFO versus FIFO (L.O. 3, 4)

Welch Company's inventory of a certain product was 6,000 units with a cost of $20 each on January 1, 1993. During 1993, numerous units of this product were purchased and sold. Also during 1993, the purchase price of this product fell steadily until at year-end it was $16. The inventory at year-end was 10,000 units. State which of the two methods of inventory measurement, LIFO or FIFO, would have resulted in higher reported net income and explain briefly.

Exercise 6–9

Compute carrying cost of inventory item
(L.O. 6)

Passmore Company has a camper it has used as a demonstration model. At the time the camper was put into use, it carried a sticker price of $19,000 and cost Passmore $16,400. The newer camper models are expected to be received shortly, so Passmore has decided to sell the demonstrator. Before it can be sold, $350 in cleanup costs and $700 for tires are expected to be incurred. After the camper has been cleaned and tires installed, it can be sold for $17,000. Salespeople earn a 5% commission on each camper they sell.

a. Compute the amount at which the camper should be carried in inventory.

b. Give the journal entry to record the write-down.

Exercise 6–10

Compute value of ending inventory using LCM applied on an item-by-item basis
(L.O. 6)

Your assistant has compiled the following schedule to assist you in determining the decline in inventory from cost to LCM, item by item:

	Item			
	A	B	C	D
Units	220	220	620	1,020
Unit cost	$38	$18	$14	$22.40
Unit market	$36	$20	$14	$22.80

Compute the cost of the ending inventory using the LCM method applied to individual items.

Exercise 6–11

Compute value of ending inventory using LCM
(L.O. 6)

Using the information given in Exercise 6–10, compute the amount of ending inventory using the LCM method applied to total inventory.

Exercise 6–12

Determine insurance settlement using gross margin method
(L.O. 7)

Fiel Company follows the practice of taking a physical inventory at the end of each calendar-year accounting period to establish the ending inventory amount for financial statement purposes. Its financial statements for the past few years indicate a normal gross margin of 30%. On July 18, a fire destroyed the entire store building and contents. The records were in a fireproof vault and are intact. These records, through July 17, show:

Merchandise inventory, January 1	$ 80,000
Merchandise purchases	1,680,000
Purchase returns	32,000
Transportation-in	100,000
Sales	2,560,000
Sales returns	80,000

The company was fully covered by insurance and asks you to determine the amount of its claim for loss of merchandise.

PROBLEMS: SERIES A

Problem 6–1A

Determine effects of inventory errors
(L.O. 1)

Tucker Company reported net income in 1993 of $274,160, in 1994 of $296,240, and in 1995 of $249,780. Analysis of its inventories shows that certain clerical errors were made so that inventory figures were as follows:

	Incorrect	Correct
December 31, 1993	$55,660	$65,320
December 31, 1994	64,400	53,820

Required   *a.* Compute the amount of net income for each of the three years, assuming the clerical errors in computing the inventory had not been made.

b. Determine the total net income for the three years with the use of the incorrect inventories and compare this with the total net income determined when correct inventories are used.

Problem 6–2A

Determine effects of inventory errors and comment on the implications (L.O. 1)

As of December 31, 1995, the financial records of Hawkins Company were examined for the years ended December 31, 1992, 1993, 1994, and 1995. With regard to merchandise inventory, the examination disclosed the following:

1. December 31, 1992: Inventory of $60,000 was included twice.
2. December 31, 1993: Inventory was overstated by $30,000.
3. December 31, 1994: Inventory of $66,000 was omitted.
4. December 31, 1995: Inventory was correct.

The reported net income for each year was as follows:

1992	$115,200
1993	163,200
1994	201,000
1995	253,800

Required

a. What is the correct net income for 1992, 1993, 1994, and 1995?
b. What is (are) the error(s) in each December 31 balance sheet?
c. Comment on the implications of the corrected net income as contrasted with reported net income.

Problem 6–3A

Compute cost of goods sold and gross margin after determining correct inventory cost (L.O. 2)

Rivera Company, a newly organized business, embarked on an extensive purchasing program in November 1993. It opened its doors for business on December 15, 1993. The company decided to use a calendar-year accounting period, and as of December 31, 1993, its accounts showed the following:

Sales.	$ 46,200
Purchases	495,000
Transportation-in	56,100
Purchase discounts	9,900

All purchases were subject to discount terms of 2/10, n/30. The cost of the inventory on December 31, 1993, at vendors' gross invoice prices was $462,000.

Required

Present a partial income statement showing the computation of cost of goods sold and the gross margin for the period ending December 31, 1993, assuming that all of the purchase discounts were taken. (Hint: You need to determine the correct inventory cost by adding the appropriate amount of transportation costs and deducting the appropriate amount of discounts.)

Problem 6–4A

Compute ending inventory under specific identification, FIFO, LIFO, and weighted-average, using periodic and perpetual inventory procedures (L.O. 3)

The purchases and sales of a certain product for Burdette Company for April 1993 are shown below. There was no inventory on April 1.

	Purchases			Sales	
	Units	**Unit Cost**			**Units**
April 3	2,900 @	$7.20	April 4		1,740
April 10	2,320 @	7.40	April 11		1,450
April 22	4,640 @	6.80	April 16		1,450
April 28	2,610 @	7.00	April 26		1,160
			April 30		1,740

Required   *a.* Compute the ending inventory of the above product as of April 30 under each of the following methods using perpetual inventory procedure: (1) specific identification (maximize net income), (2) FIFO, (3) LIFO, and (4) weighted-average.

                b. Compute the ending inventory of the above product as of April 30 under each of the following methods using periodic inventory procedure: (1) FIFO, (2) LIFO, and (3) weighted-average.

Problem 6–5A

Record the journal entries under FIFO and LIFO using perpetual and periodic inventory procedures (L.O. 5)

Refer to the information in Problem 6–4A.

Required

a. Give the journal entries to record the purchases and the cost of goods sold (but not for sales) for the month using both FIFO and LIFO methods under perpetual procedure.

b. Give the journal entry to record the purchases and prepare the appropriate closing entries under both FIFO and LIFO methods applied under periodic procedure for the month of April.

Problem 6–6A

Compute ending inventory and cost of goods sold under FIFO and LIFO using perpetual and periodic inventory procedures (L.O. 3)

Listed below are the purchases and sales of a certain product made by Shannon Company during 1993. The company had 20,000 units of this product on hand at January 1, 1993, with a cost of $8 per unit.

	Purchases			Sales	
	Units	Unit Cost		Units	Sales Price
February 20	4,000 @	$8.00	February 2.	6,000 @	$12.00
April 18	10,000 @	7.80	April 23	8,000 @	10.00
August 28.	10,000 @	7.60	September 3.	8,000 @	9.60
December 22	8,000 @	7.68	December 24	7,000 @	9.80

Complete the following requirements under both the perpetual and periodic inventory procedures.

Required   *a.* Compute the cost of the ending inventory and cost of goods sold assuming the use of the FIFO method of inventory measurement.

                b. Repeat *(a)* above, assuming the use of LIFO.

                c. Comment on the difference in cost of goods sold under FIFO and LIFO.

Problem 6–7A

Compute ending inventory using LCM on an item-by-item basis and compare to LCM on total basis (L.O. 6)

The accountant for Rose Company prepared the following schedule of the company's inventory at December 31, 1993, and used the lower of the total cost or total market value basis.

		Cost	Market Value	Total Value	
Item	Quantity	per Unit	per Unit	Cost	Market
A	2,000	$3.20	$3.20		
B	800	2.40	2.24		
C	2,800	1.60	1.44		
D	2,400	1.20	1.28		

Required   *a.* State whether this method is an acceptable method of inventory measurement and determine the appropriate amounts.

                b. Compute the amount of the ending inventory using the LCM method on an individual item basis.

c. State the effect on net income in 1993 if the method in *(b)* was used rather than the method in *(a)*.

Problem 6–8A
Prepare income statements by estimating cost of goods sold using gross margin method
(L.O. 7)

As part of a loan agreement with a local bank, Brant Company must present quarterly and cumulative income statements for the year 1994. The company uses periodic inventory procedure and marks its merchandise to sell at a price that will yield a gross margin of 35%. Selected data for the first six months of 1994 were as follows:

	First Quarter	Second Quarter
Sales	$294,500	$299,250
Purchases	190,000	213,750
Purchase returns and allowances	11,400	12,350
Purchase discounts	3,610	3,700
Sales returns and allowances	9,500	4,750
Transportation-in	8,360	4,750
Miscellaneous selling expenses	29,450	28,500
Miscellaneous administrative expenses	19,950	18,050

The cost of the physical inventory taken December 31, 1993, was $36,100.

Required

a. Indicate how the income statements may be prepared without taking a physical inventory at the end of each of the first two quarters of 1994.

b. Prepare income statements for the first quarter, the second quarter, and the first six months of 1994.

Problem 6–9A
Estimate ending inventory using retail inventory method
(L.O. 7)

The following data pertain to Victory Department Store for the fiscal year ended June 30, 1994.

	Cost	Retail
Merchandise inventory, July 1, 1993	$ 105,000	$ 155,400
Purchases, net	1,323,000	1,944,600
Sales		2,016,000

Required   Use the retail method to estimate the cost of the inventory on June 30, 1994.

PROBLEMS: SERIES B

Problem 6–1B
Determine effects of inventory errors
(L.O. 1)

Scott Company reported net income in 1993 of $598,000, in 1994 of $621,000, and in 1995 of $667,000. Analysis of its inventories shows that certain clerical errors were made so that inventory figures were as follows:

	Incorrect	Correct
December 31, 1993	$184,000	$207,000
December 31, 1994	174,800	161,000

Required

a. Compute the amount of net income for each of the three years, assuming that the clerical errors in computing the inventory had not been made.

b. Determine the total net income for each of the three years with the use of the incorrect inventories and compare this amount with the total net income determined when correct inventories are used.

Problem 6–2B

Determine effects of inventory errors
(L.O. 1)

An examination of the records of Hollis Company on December 31, 1995, disclosed the following with regard to merchandise inventory for 1995 and prior years:

1. December 31, 1992: Inventory was understated $49,200.
2. December 31, 1993: Inventory of $34,440 was included twice.
3. December 31, 1994: Inventory of $30,750 was omitted.
4. December 31, 1995: Inventory was correct.

The reported net income for each year was as follows:

1992	$289,050
1993	349,320
1994	377,610
1995	345,630

Required

a. What is the correct net income for 1992, 1993, 1994, and 1995?
b. What is (are) the error(s) in each December 31 balance sheet?
c. Comment on the implications of the corrected net income compared with reported net income.

Problem 6–3B

Compute ending inventory and cost of goods sold under specific identification, FIFO, LIFO, and weighted-average methods using perpetual and periodic inventory procedures
(L.O. 3)

Following are data relating to the beginning inventory, purchases, and sales of a given item of product of Jan Company for the year 1993:

Purchases			Sales	
	Units	**Unit Cost**		**Units**
Merchandise inventory, January 1	1,260 @	$5.00	March 20	1,000
February 2	900 @	5.50	May 4	1,840
April 5	1,800 @	6.00	July 28	1,550
June 15	1,080 @	6.20	October 22	1,550
September 30	1,260 @	6.50		
November 28	1,620 @	6.70		

Required

Compute the ending inventory and cost of goods sold under each of the following methods using perpetual and periodic inventory procedures:

a. Specific identification (the ending inventory should maximize net income).
b. FIFO.
c. LIFO.
d. Weighted-average (moving average); round unit costs to four decimal places and total costs to the nearest dollar.

Problem 6–4B

Compute cost of ending inventory and cost of goods sold under FIFO, LIFO, and weighted-average using perpetual and periodic inventory procedures
(L.O. 3)

In 1993, McCoy Toy Company made the following purchases and sales of one of its products, the Race Car.

Purchases			Sales	
	Units	**Unit Cost**		**Units**
February 18	1,950 @	$12.24	January 31	1,950
March 22	3,250 @	12.64	April 12	650
July 12	3,250 @	12.80	August 15	1,300
November 18	2,600 @	13.52	December 5	5,850

The December 31, 1992, inventory of the Race Car was 1,950 units at a cost of $11.52.

Complete the following requirements, first using perpetual inventory procedure, and then using periodic inventory procedure.

Required

a. Compute the cost of ending inventory and cost of goods sold for the year, assuming the FIFO method of inventory measurement.

b. Repeat (a) above, assuming the use of LIFO.

c. Repeat (a) above, assuming the use of the weighted-average method. Round unit costs to four digits and round total cost to nearest dollar.

Problem 6–5B

Prepare journal entries under FIFO and LIFO using both perpetual and periodic inventory procedures (L.O. 5)

The purchases and sales of Adams Corporation for July 1993 are shown below. Inventory consisted of 580 units on July 1 purchased for $7.60 each.

	Purchases			Sales	
	Units	**Unit Cost**			**Units**
July 7	200	@ $7.00	July 2		400
July 10	500	@ 7.60	July 8		260
July 19	350	@ 8.00	July 12		320
July 26	220	@ 7.80	July 20		130
July 29	200	@ 8.20	July 27		550

Required

a. Give the journal entries to record the purchases and the cost of goods sold for the month under both FIFO and LIFO methods using perpetual procedure. Also, prepare the appropriate closing entries using both FIFO and LIFO methods under perpetual procedure for July.

b. Give the journal entry to record the purchases and prepare the appropriate closing entries under both FIFO and LIFO methods using periodic procedure for July.

Problem 6–6B

Compute gross margin using FIFO and LIFO (L.O. 3)

Russell Company was organized on January 1, 1993. Selected data for 1993–95 are as follows:

Year Ended December 31	Inventory		Annual Data	
	FIFO	**LIFO**	**Purchases**	**Sales**
1993	.$3,600	$2,700	$16,200	$18,300
1994	4,500	3,150	13,500	21,450
1995	7,500	4,500	16,650	18,450

Required

Compute the gross margin using partial income statements for each of the three years under FIFO and under LIFO.

Problem 6–7B

Compute value of ending inventory using LCM applied on a total basis and on an item-by-item basis (L.O. 6)

The data below relate to the ending inventory of Oates Company at December 31, 1993.

Item	Quantity	Unit Cost	Unit Market
1	4,200	$1.40	$1.34
2	8,400	1.12	1.26
3	2,800	1.06	1.12
4	7,000	1.96	1.76
5	5,600	1.76	1.82
6	1,400	1.26	1.12

Required

a. Compute the ending inventory, applying the LCM method to the total inventory.

b. Repeat (a) above, applying the method to individual items.

c. State the effect on net income in 1993 if the method in (b) were used rather than the method in (a).

Problem 6–8B

Explain estimating
inventory and determine
how much insurance is
needed to fully insure the
inventory
(L.O. 7)

Taylor Company employs a fiscal year ending September 30. At this time, inventories are usually at a very low level because of reduced activity. The management of the company wishes to maintain full insurance coverage on its inventory at all times. Management is confident that the calculation of the estimated inventory is accurate and is willing to rely on the calculation to determine the company's insurance needs. The company has earned around 40% gross margin on net sales over the last few years. Given below are data for the seven months ending April 30, 1993.

Sales	$780,000
Sales returns	78,000
Sales discounts	19,500
Inventory, October 1, 1992	58,500
Purchases	594,750
Purchase returns	44,850
Purchase discounts	13,650
Transportation-in	29,250
Miscellaneous selling expenses	68,250
Miscellaneous administrative expenses	58,500

Required

a. Indicate, in general, how the company can estimate its inventory at any given date.

b. Assuming the inventory is at its highest level on April 30, for how much should the company insure the inventory if it is to be fully insured?

Problem 6–9B

Explain estimating
inventory and estimate
inventory using gross
margin method
(L.O. 7)

The sales and cost of goods sold for Bruce Company for the past five years were as follows:

Year	Sales (net)	Cost of Goods Sold
1990	$ 832,080	$557,494
1991	899,520	602,678
1992	1,028,880	679,060
1993	984,720	669,610
1994	1,062,720	712,022

For the seven months ended July 31, 1995, the following information is available from the accounting records of the company:

Sales	$774,816
Purchases	458,880
Purchase returns	2,880
Sales returns	17,376
Merchandise inventory, January 1, 1995	94,800

In requesting the extension of credit by a new supplier, Bruce Company has been asked to present current financial statements. It does not want to take a complete physical inventory at July 31, 1995.

Required

a. Indicate how financial statements can be prepared without taking a complete physical inventory.

b. From the data given, estimate the inventory at July 31, 1995.

Problem 6–10B

Estimate ending inventory using retail inventory method
(L.O. 7)

The following data pertain to a certain department of First Department Store for the year ended December 31, 1993.

	Cost	Retail
Merchandise inventory, January 1, 1993	$ 44,000	$ 66,000
Purchases, net	484,000	814,000
Sales		792,000

Required — Use the retail method to estimate the cost of the inventory on December 31, 1993.

BUSINESS DECISION PROBLEMS

Decision Problem 6–1

Determine insurance settlement using gross margin method
(L.O. 7)

J. B. Bies owns and operates a sporting goods store. On February 2, 1993, the store suffered extensive fire damage, and all of the inventory was destroyed. Mr. Bies uses periodic inventory procedure and has the following information in his accounting records, which luckily were not damaged by the fire.

Merchandise inventory, January 1	$160,000
Purchases:	
January 8	64,000
January 20	96,000
January 30	128,000
Sales:	
During January	480,000
February 1	32,000

Mr. Bies also knows that his gross margin rate has been 40% for the last three years.

The insurance company has offered to pay $112,000 to settle Mr. Bies' inventory loss unless he can adequately prove that he suffered a greater loss.

Required — Should Mr. Bies settle for $112,000? If not, how can he prove to the insurance company that he suffered a greater loss? What is the estimated amount of this loss?

Decision Problem 6–2

Minimize income taxes and compute cost of goods sold and cost of ending inventory
(L.O. 3, 4)

Roadhouse Company, which began operations on January 2, sells a single product, product J. The following data relate to the purchases of product J for the year:

	Units	Unit Cost
January 2	250 @	$2.00
February 15	400 @	2.00
April 8	500 @	2.16
June 6	200 @	2.26
August 19	400 @	2.30
October 5	300 @	2.50
November 22	250 @	2.80

Periodic inventory procedure is used. On December 31, a physical inventory of product J showed that 400 units were on hand.

Mr. Roadhouse is trying to decide which of the following inventory costing methods he should adopt: weighted-average, FIFO, or LIFO. Since Mr. Roadhouse is short of cash, he wants to minimize the amount of income taxes payable.

Required   In this case, which of the three inventory costing methods will minimize the amount of income taxes payable? What will be the cost of goods sold and the cost of ending inventory under this method?

Decision Problem 6–3
Determine lower of cost
or market
(L.O. 6)

In the financial statements of Premier Industrial Corporation located in "A Broader Perspective," inventories are stated at LCM. Determine the current cost of inventories for 1987 and 1988 and state whether they are being carried at cost or market value.

ANSWERS TO SELF-TEST

True-False

1. *False*. FIFO will result in a higher net income figure than LIFO in a period of rising prices because the cost of goods sold is composed of the earliest costs.
2. *True*. The understatement of beginning inventory will cause cost of goods sold to be understated and net income to be overstated.
3. *False*. The accounting principle of consistency requires the repeated use of the same accounting

methods in preparing financial statements. However, a company may switch from one inventory method to another, but only if it can justify the switch as an improvement in financial reporting.

4. *True*. In a period of rising prices, LIFO results in the highest cost of goods sold because the latest purchases are assumed to be sold.
5. *True*. Net realizable value is equal to selling price less costs incurred to sell.

Multiple-Choice

1. *c*. The cost of goods sold using weighted-average is computed:

$$\text{Cost of goods available for sale} = (2,000 \times \$15) + (8,000 \times \$18)$$
$$= \$174,000$$

$$\text{Unit cost} = \$174,000 \div 10,000$$
$$= \$17.40$$

$$\text{Cost of goods sold} = \$17.40 \times 7,800$$
$$= \$135,720$$

2. *a*. Cost of ending inventory = $174,000 − $135,720 = $38,280
3. *b*. 2,000 units of beginning inventory and 5,800 units at $18 are assumed to be sold under FIFO:

$$\text{Cost of goods sold} = (2,000 \times \$15) + (5,800 \times \$18)$$
$$= \$134,400$$

4. *a*. $$\text{Cost of ending inventory} = \$174,000 - \$134,400$$
$$= \$39,600$$

5. *d*. Under LIFO, the inventory purchased during the period is assumed to be sold:

$$\text{Cost of goods sold} = 7,800 \times \$18 = \$140,400$$

6. *a*. $$\text{Cost of ending inventory} = \$174,000 - \$140,400$$
$$= \$33,600$$

7. *a*. During a period of rising prices, FIFO results in the lowest cost of goods sold, thus the highest valuation for inventory on the balance sheet (ending inventory).

7

ACCOUNTING SYSTEMS AND SPECIAL JOURNALS

After studying this chapter, you should be able to:

1. Describe the relationship between subsidiary accounts in subsidiary ledgers and control accounts in the general ledger.
2. Describe the relationship between special journals and the general journal.
3. Record transactions in special journals.
4. Post special journals.
5. Describe alternative methods of processing data.
6. Describe microcomputer applications in accounting (Appendix 7-A).
7. Describe basic computer concepts (Appendix 7-B).

In Chapters 1 through 6, you learned how to produce financial statements by processing the raw data of business transactions through the steps of the accounting cycle. The process of analyzing, recording, classifying, summarizing, and reporting business transactions is the same for all businesses. However, the speed and efficiency of the processing depends on the accounting system used.

For example, assume you decide to drive home after your accounting class. You can either go home the "long way" by using the side roads or "make time" by using the superhighway. Whichever route you take, your destination is going to be the same—home. The process of going home is the same whether you take the side roads or the superhighway—you are driving your car. However, the system you use to get to your destination—the side roads or the superhighway—is different. You probably decide to take the superhighway because it is faster. The accounting process also can be accomplished faster and more efficiently by using one particular accounting system. This chapter identifies various accounting systems and describes their features.

So far in this text you have used the manual accounting system with one general journal and one general ledger. Now you will be introduced to two additions to that manual system—subsidiary ledgers and special journals. Then, you will proceed to a discussion of other systems used in accounting, ending with computerized accounting systems. This chapter enables you to process business transactions in a more efficient manner.

THE PROCESSING OF DATA—MANUAL SYSTEM

The masses of raw data generated by even a small business are not useful until processed. Businesses must routinely process these data in an orderly and efficient manner to accomplish the following:

1. Determine and report on a timely basis the results of operations (income statement) and financial position (balance sheet) of the firm.
2. Pay bills when due.
3. Send correct quantities and items of inventory to customers.
4. Conduct other aspects of business, such as sending invoices to customers and ordering merchandise, in an orderly and purposeful manner.
5. Efficiently prepare reports required by the government or regulatory agencies.

Businesses accomplish this orderly and efficient processing of accounting data by using the accounting system that best fits their needs. The basic accounting system is the manual system with one general journal and one general ledger. Usually, very small businesses use this basic system. Given an unlimited amount of time, all businesses could process their business transactions through this manual system. However, as a business grows, its number of business transactions also grows, and the company looks for ways to speed up the accounting process by streamlining its accounting system.

An accounting system can be defined as a set of records (journals, ledgers, work sheets, trial balances, and reports) plus the procedures and equipment regularly used to process business transactions. To be effective, accounting systems should:

1. Provide for the efficient processing of data at the least possible cost. (The cost of the system should be less than the value of the benefits received.)
2. Ensure a high degree of accuracy.
3. Provide for internal control to prevent theft or fraud.
4. Provide for the growth of a business.

In this chapter, you will learn first how a business begins to expand its accounting system by using control accounts in the general ledger and adding subsidiary ledgers that show the details of these control accounts. Then, you will learn about other journals (called special journals) that companies use along with the general journal.

CONTROL ACCOUNTS AND SUBSIDIARY LEDGERS

Objective 1

Describe the relationship between subsidiary accounts in subsidiary ledgers and control accounts in the general ledger

To process information efficiently, a business must adapt its accounting system to the type and quantity of information it needs. When a business has only a few customers and suppliers, it can set up a separate account for each customer and supplier in the general ledger. However, when a business has many customers and suppliers, it establishes a control account for accounts receivable and a control account for accounts payable in the general ledger. Also, the business adds subsidiary ledgers for receivables and payables to the accounting system to show the balances for individual customers and suppliers.

A control account is an account in the general ledger that shows the total balance of all the subsidiary accounts related to it. An example of a control account is the general ledger **Accounts Receivable** control account. This account summarizes all the amounts owed to the company. Since this account is a summary account, it would be impossible to send out individual customer statements showing a summary of each customer's purchases, payments, and balance due based on the summary data provided in this account.

Subsidiary ledger accounts show the details supporting the related general ledger control account balance. Companies may use the subsidiary ledger accounts for **receivables** to send out customer statements. They may use the subsidiary ledger accounts for **payables** to determine the amount payable to each supplier. Usually, companies alphabetize these accounts by the name of the customer or supplier rather than numbering the accounts. At the time a company prepares its financial statements, the sum of the balances in the subsidiary accounts in a subsidiary ledger should agree with the balance in the related general ledger control account.

A subsidiary ledger, then, is a group of related accounts showing the details of the balance of a general ledger control account. **Subsidiary ledgers are in a separate book or computer file from the general ledger.** Having separate subsidiary ledgers shortens the general ledger trial balance. Also, having separate subsidiary ledgers promotes a division of labor.

In T-account form, the relationship between a control account and subsidiary accounts is as follows:

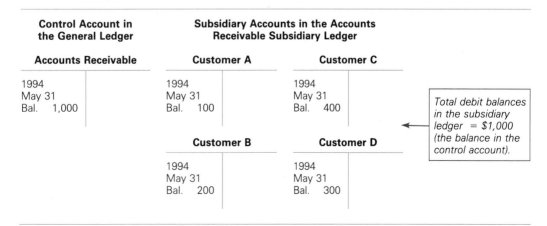

Note that the sum of all balances in the subsidiary accounts ($100 + $200 + $400 + $300) on May 31, 1994, is equal to the balance on that same date in the control account ($1,000).

When a transaction occurs that affects a control account, the transaction also affects at least one of the accounts in the subsidiary ledger. A transaction is entered in the journal before it is entered in the ledger accounts. Thus, the journal entry must indicate the subsidiary ledger account(s) affected by the transaction. Then, posting will be made to both the control account (indicated by the account number) and the subsidiary ledger account (indicated by the √). For example, if a company makes a $400 sale on July 10 to Debby Kahan on account, the journal entry would be:

July	10	Accounts Receivable—D. Kahan.	103/√	400	
		Sales.	410		400
		To record sale of merchandise on account.			

The amount of the sale ($400) would be posted as a debit to both the Accounts Receivable control account (103) in the general ledger and D. Kahan's account in the subsidiary ledger (indicated by the √) and as a credit to the Sales account (410) in the general ledger.

Detailed subsidiary ledgers may exist for other accounts in the general ledger in addition to the Accounts Receivable account. Some examples of accounts that frequently have detailed subsidiary ledgers are:

General Ledger Control Account	Subsidiary Ledger
Accounts Receivable ←⟶	Accounts receivable subsidiary ledger (account for each customer)
Accounts Payable ←⟶	Accounts payable subsidiary ledger (account for each creditor)
Office Equipment, Trucks, Store Fixtures, etc. ←⟶	Equipment subsidiary ledger (account for each item of equipment)

The number of subsidiary ledgers maintained by a company varies according to the company's information requirements. Companies generally set up control accounts and subsidiary ledgers whenever they have many transactions in a given account and they need detailed information about these transactions on a continuing basis. This chapter focuses on the use of an accounts receivable subsidiary ledger and an accounts payable subsidiary ledger.

In the next section, you will learn about special journals. You should remember that companies may use control accounts and subsidiary ledgers even if they do not use special journals. Companies are likely to use both subsidiary ledgers and special journals when they have numerous similar transactions.

SPECIAL JOURNALS

Objective 2
Describe the relationship between special journals and the general journal

Until now, only one book of original entry, the general journal, has been used to record transactions. As the transactions of a company increase, the first step in altering the manual accounting system is usually to use special journals along with the original general journal. Each special journal is a book of original entry that records one particular type of transaction, such as sales on account, cash receipts, purchases on account, or cash disbursements.

The advantages of using special journals are:

1. **Saves time in journalizing.** Each transaction takes only one line; a full description is usually not necessary. Special journals reduce the amount of writing because it is not necessary to repeat the account titles printed at the top of the special column or columns.
2. **Saves time in posting.** Many amounts are posted as column totals rather than individually.
3. **Eliminates detail from the general ledger.** Column totals are posted to the general ledger. The details remain in the special journals.
4. **Promotes division of labor.** Several persons can work simultaneously on the accounting records. This specialization and division of labor pinpoints responsibility and allows for more rapid location of errors.
5. **Aids in management analysis.** The journals themselves can be useful to management in analyzing classes of transactions, such as credit sales, because all similar transactions are in one place.

Special journals, then, systematize the original recording of major recurring types of transactions. The number and format of the special journals used in a company depend primarily on the nature of the company's business transactions. The special journals illustrated in this chapter are the sales, cash receipts, purchases, and cash disbursements journals.

☐ The sales journal records all sales of merchandise on account (on credit).

☐ The cash receipts journal records all inflows of cash into the business.

☐ The purchases journal records all purchases of merchandise on account (on credit). Merchandise refers to items of inventory that are available for sale to customers.

☐ The cash disbursements journal records all payments (or outflows) of cash by the business.

The use of special journals does **not** eliminate the general journal. The general journal records all transactions that cannot be entered in one of the special journals, such as adjusting entries and closing entries. All five of these journals are books of original entry. If a transaction is recorded in any one of the journals, that transaction will be posted and become part of the accounting records. Therefore, a transaction recorded in a special journal should **not** also be recorded in the general journal because the entry would then be recorded twice.

The Posting Reference column in the ledger should indicate the source of the posting. The abbreviations used in this text for the five journals are:

	Journal	Transaction	Abbreviation
Special Journals	Sales journal	Merchandise sold on account	S
	Cash receipts journal	Cash receipts from all sources	CR
	Purchases journal	Merchandise purchased on account	P
	Cash disbursements journal	Cash payments for all purposes	CD
	General journal	Any transactions not included in the special journals are recorded in the general journal	G

The sections that follow will show you how to use each of the four special journals. We place you in the position of "keeping the books." In other words, you are the "bookkeeper," or accounting clerk, for John Mason Company, a corporation. As you study these journals, you will realize how effective they are in facilitating the recording process.

Sales Journal

Objective 3
Record transactions in special journals

Companies normally make sales either for cash or on account (on credit). They use the sales journal for sales on account and the cash receipts journal for cash sales. The simplest form of sales journal has only one money column (labeled Accounts Receivable Dr. and Sales Cr.) because every sale on account is journalized by this same debit and credit. The headings in this form of sales journal might appear as follows:

Date	Customer	Invoice No.	Accounts Receivable Dr. Sales Cr.	
			Amount	√

Variations in the sales journal will depend on the information needs of the business. For example, a company could use a separate Sales Cr. column for each department. If a company does this, it will need a separate column for Accounts Receivable Dr. because the debit will always be to Accounts Receivable regardless of which department sold the goods. The headings in a sales journal with separate columns for each department might appear as follows:

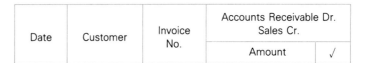

Accounts Receivable Dr.		Date	Customer	Invoice No.	Sales Cr.		
Amount	√				Dept. A	Dept. B	Dept. C

In either format, the customer's name is necessary to know which subsidiary ledger account is affected by the sales transaction. The invoice number simply provides documentation that a sale actually occurred. The column with the check mark is similar to a Posting Reference column. A check mark in that column indicates that the amount of the transaction has been posted to the customer's accounts receivable subsidiary ledger account. The column heading indicates which account(s) should be debited or credited for the column total.

Illustration 7.1 on page 315 shows a sales journal with only one money column for John Mason Company, a retail clothing store. In Illustration 7.1, five credit sales transactions occurred in April. Each sale is backed up by an invoice showing the customer name and address, a description of the items sold, dollar amount, and credit terms. The invoice number for each sale is listed in the sales journal.

Objective 4
Post special journals

Posting the Sales Journal As John Mason's bookkeeper, you would post the individual amounts in the money column daily to each individual customer's account in the subsidiary ledger. The daily posting shows the amount currently due from the customer. As you post each individual amount, you place a check mark, √, in the column headed √ opposite the amount. This check mark shows that you have posted the amount. You should also enter the posting reference of S1 (sales journal, page 1) in the accounts receivable subsidiary ledger accounts as each amount is posted. At the end of the month, you would post the total of the money column, $290, in the general ledger as a debit to the Accounts Receivable control account and as a credit to the Sales account. Then, you would enter the posting reference of S1 (sales journal, page 1) in the Accounts Receivable control account and the Sales account. Next, you would write the account numbers, 103 for Accounts Receivable and 410 for Sales, in the sales journal under the total of the money column to show that you posted $290 to these accounts.

As shown in Illustration 7.1, when you have completed the posting of accounts receivable, the Accounts Receivable control account in the general ledger will show a balance of $290. This $290 is equal to the sum of the balances in the

ILLUSTRATION 7.1

Sales Journal

**JOHN MASON COMPANY
SALES JOURNAL**   *Page 1*

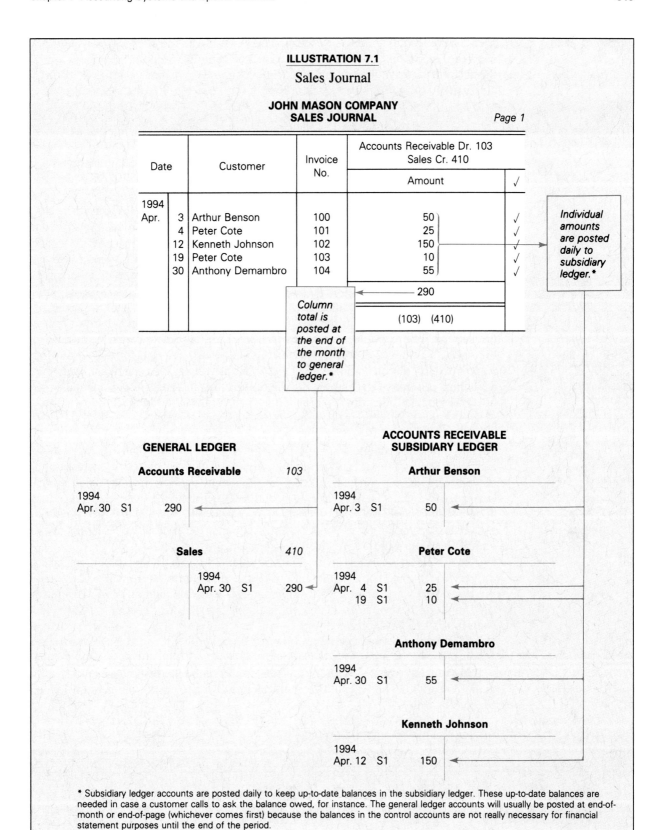

Date	Customer	Invoice No.	Accounts Receivable Dr. 103 Sales Cr. 410	
			Amount	✓
1994 Apr. 3	Arthur Benson	100	50	✓
4	Peter Cote	101	25	✓
12	Kenneth Johnson	102	150	✓
19	Peter Cote	103	10	✓
30	Anthony Demambro	104	55	✓
			290	
			(103) (410)	

Individual amounts are posted daily to subsidiary ledger.*

Column total is posted at the end of the month to general ledger.*

GENERAL LEDGER

Accounts Receivable   *103*

1994
Apr. 30   S1   290   ⟵

Sales   *410*

                        1994
                        Apr. 30   S1   290   ⟵

ACCOUNTS RECEIVABLE SUBSIDIARY LEDGER

Arthur Benson

1994
Apr. 3   S1   50   ⟵

Peter Cote

1994
Apr. 4   S1   25   ⟵
    19   S1   10   ⟵

Anthony Demambro

1994
Apr. 30   S1   55   ⟵

Kenneth Johnson

1994
Apr. 12   S1   150   ⟵

* Subsidiary ledger accounts are posted daily to keep up-to-date balances in the subsidiary ledger. These up-to-date balances are needed in case a customer calls to ask the balance owed, for instance. The general ledger accounts will usually be posted at end-of-month or end-of-page (whichever comes first) because the balances in the control accounts are not really necessary for financial statement purposes until the end of the period.

accounts receivable subsidiary ledger accounts, assuming no previous balances were in the control account or the subsidiary accounts. Since the composition of the accounts receivable subsidiary ledger accounts is constantly changing, companies usually do not number these accounts but keep them in alphabetical order.

Cash Receipts Journal

Companies use the cash receipts journal for all transactions involving the receipt of cash. The most frequent types of cash receipts transactions are cash sales and collections on accounts receivable. Therefore, separate credit columns appear for those items in the cash receipts journal shown in Illustration 7.2 on page 318. Notice that three of the transactions recorded in the cash receipts journal were collections of accounts receivable that were recorded in the sales journal.

Many other types of transactions may result in the receipt of cash by the business, but these transactions involve various accounts as the credits. Since these other accounts do not occur with enough frequency to warrant special columns, they appear in the **Other Accounts Cr.** column of the cash receipts journal. However, if after several months or periods, a certain transaction appears regularly in the Other Accounts Cr. column, the company might want to revise its format of the cash receipts journal to provide a special column for that type of transaction. For example, a company that has several rental properties may wish to provide a column for Rental Revenue Cr. in the cash receipts journal. An Other Accounts Dr. column could be included to handle transactions such as the sale of a machine (discussed in Chapter 10) where the company has a debit to at least one other account besides the Cash account. The total of the debit columns should equal the total of the credit columns in every special journal.

Posting the Cash Receipts Journal   You would post the individual amounts in the Accounts Receivable Cr. column daily to the customers' accounts in the accounts receivable subsidiary ledger to keep the customer balances current. You would also post the items in the Other Accounts Cr. column daily to the individual accounts indicated (Accounts 130 and 420). You would post the totals of the Cash Dr., Sales Discounts Dr., Sales Cr., and Accounts Receivable Cr. columns at the end of the month to their respective general ledger accounts.

The amounts appearing in the Other Accounts Cr. column normally pertain to different accounts. Thus, you would not post the column total. You would place the letter "X" in parentheses (X) immediately below the column total. This letter "X" in parentheses indicates that you have not posted the amount shown as the column total to any account.

The ledger accounts in Illustration 7.2 show only the postings of the cash receipts journal of John Mason Company.

After you have posted John Mason's sales and cash receipts journals in Illustrations 7.1 and 7.2, the Accounts Receivable control account in the general ledger appears as follows:

		Accounts Receivable					Account No. 103
Date		Explanation	Post. Ref.	Debit	Credit	Balance	
1994 Apr.	30		S1	2 9 0		2 9 0	Dr.
	30		CR5		2 2 5	6 5	Dr.

Illustration 7.3 on page 320 shows the subsidiary accounts at the same point in time.

You would prepare a schedule of accounts receivable at the end of the period to ensure that the total of the balances in the accounts receivable subsidiary ledger agrees with the control account. This schedule is merely a listing of open account balances. An example of this schedule for John Mason Company follows:

JOHN MASON COMPANY
Schedule of Accounts Receivable
As of April 30, 1994

Peter Cote.	$10
Anthony Demambro	55
Balance in the control account	$65

Purchases Journal

Companies use the purchases journal to record all purchases of merchandise made on account. Several formats can be used for the purchases journal. One common format has only one money column headed Purchases Dr. and Accounts Payable Cr. The headings in a purchases journal with one money column might be as follows:

Date	Creditor	Terms	Invoice No.	Purchases Dr. Accounts Payable Cr.	
				Amount	√

Note that the above purchases journal has a Terms column. The sales journal discussed in the previous section did not have a Terms column because a company's terms are generally the same for each customer. However, the purchases journal uses a Terms column because various creditors often differ in the terms they offer a company. Persons responsible for paying the company's bills must know the terms offered on purchased merchandise so they can pay for the merchandise within the discount period. Cash discount terms are based on the date of the invoice. We assume that the date of purchase and the date of the invoice are the same.

Often companies make purchases for several departments. When management wants to keep the purchases of each department separate, a purchases journal could provide a separate column for the purchases of each department and a separate column headed Accounts Payable Cr. The headings in such a purchases journal might appear as follows:

Purchases Dr.			Date	Creditor	Terms	Invoice No.	Accounts Payable Cr.	
Dept. A	Dept. B	Dept. C					Amount	√

Illustration 7.4 on page 322 shows the John Mason Company purchases journal with one money column. Note that John Mason made eight purchases of merchandise on account during the month.

Posting the Purchases Journal You would post the individual amounts in the money column daily to the accounts payable subsidiary ledger so that the subsidiary account balances will be current at all times. Then, at the end of the month, you would post the money column total to the general ledger Purchases account as a debit and to the general ledger Accounts Payable control account as a credit.

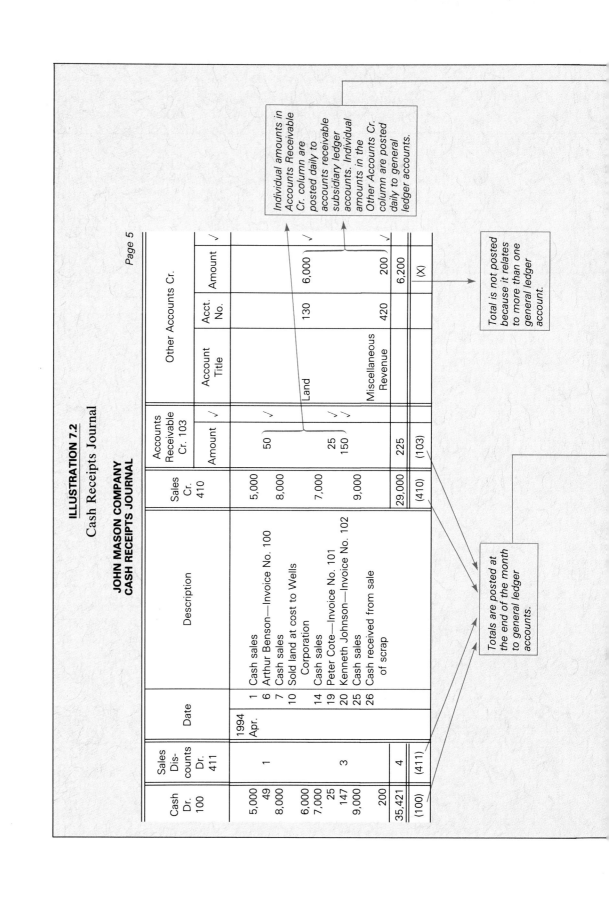

ILLUSTRATION 7.2
Cash Receipts Journal

JOHN MASON COMPANY
CASH RECEIPTS JOURNAL

Page 5

Cash Dr. 100	Sales Discounts Dr. 411	Date	Description	Sales Cr. 410	Accounts Receivable Cr. 103 Amount	√	Other Accounts Cr. Account Title	Acct. No.	Amount	√
		1994 Apr.								
5,000		1	Cash sales	5,000						√
49	1	6	Arthur Benson—Invoice No. 100		50	√				
8,000		7	Cash sales	8,000						
6,000		10	Sold land at cost to Wells Corporation				Land	130	6,000	√
7,000		14	Cash sales	7,000						
25		19	Peter Cote—Invoice No. 101		25	√				
147	3	20	Kenneth Johnson—Invoice No. 102		150	√				
9,000		25	Cash sales	9,000						
200		26	Cash received from sale of scrap				Miscellaneous Revenue	420	200	√
35,421	4			29,000	225				6,200	
(100)	(411)			(410)	(103)				(X)	

Individual amounts in Accounts Receivable Cr. column are posted daily to accounts receivable subsidiary ledger accounts. Individual amounts in the Other Accounts Cr. column are posted daily to general ledger accounts.

Total is not posted because it relates to more than one general ledger account.

Totals are posted at the end of the month to general ledger accounts.

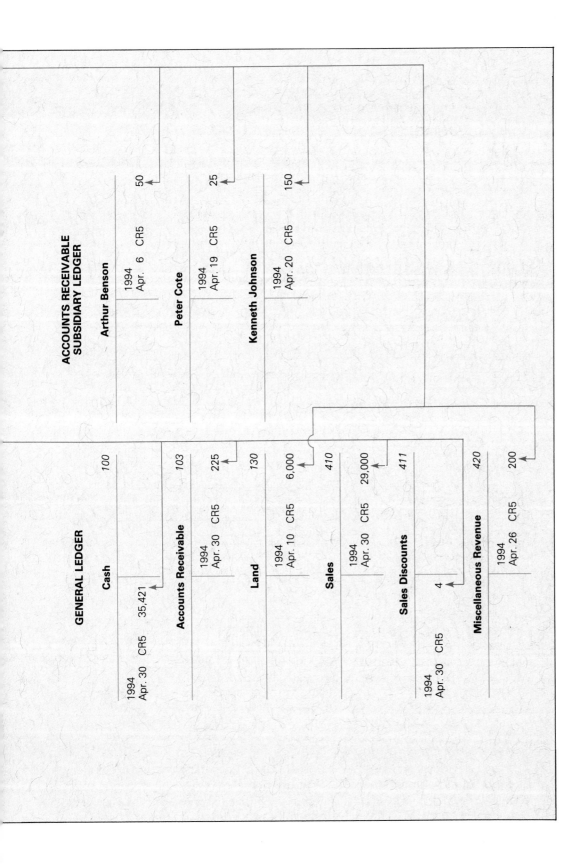

ACCOUNTS RECEIVABLE
SUBSIDIARY LEDGER

Arthur Benson

1994
Apr. 6   CR5   50

Peter Cote

1994
Apr. 19 CR5   25

Kenneth Johnson

1994
Apr. 20 CR5   150

GENERAL LEDGER

Cash   100

1994
Apr. 30 CR5 35,421

Accounts Receivable   103

1994
Apr. 30 CR5   225

Land   130

1994
Apr. 10 CR5   6,000

Sales   410

1994
Apr. 30 CR5   29,000

Sales Discounts   411

1994
Apr. 30 CR5   4

Miscellaneous Revenue   420

1994
Apr. 26 CR5   200

319

ILLUSTRATION 7.3
Accounts Receivable Subsidiary Ledger

JOHN MASON COMPANY
ACCOUNTS RECEIVABLE SUBSIDIARY LEDGER
Arthur Benson

Date		Explanation	Post. Ref.	Debit	Credit	Balance
1994 Apr.	3		S1	5 0		5 0 Dr.
	6		CR5		5 0	– 0 –

Peter Cote

Date		Explanation	Post. Ref.	Debit	Credit	Balance
1994 Apr.	4		S1	2 5		2 5 Dr.
	19		S1	1 0		3 5 Dr.
	19		CR5		2 5	1 0 Dr.

Anthony Demambro

Date		Explanation	Post. Ref.	Debit	Credit	Balance
1994 Apr.	30		S1	5 5		5 5 Dr.

Kenneth Johnson

Date		Explanation	Post. Ref.	Debit	Credit	Balance
1994 Apr.	12		S1	1 5 0		1 5 0 Dr.
	20		CR5		1 5 0	– 0 –

Cash Disbursements Journal

The cash disbursements journal records all transactions that involve the payment of cash. To have an acceptable level of control over cash disbursements, most companies pay all bills by check. Therefore, the cash disbursements journal (Illustration 7.5 on page 324) contains a column in which to record the number of the check written for each disbursement.

Payments on accounts payable constitute a major type of cash disbursement transaction. These accounts payable were initially recorded in the purchases journal when the purchases on account were made. Therefore, the cash disbursements journal provides a separate column entitled Accounts Payable Dr. Many payments on account involve a purchase discount, so this journal provides a separate column for discounts (Purchase Discounts Cr.). John Mason Company frequently purchases numerous supplies by writing a check, so its cash disbursements journal has a separate column for Supplies Expense (Supplies Expense Dr.). As with other special journals, companies adapt the cash disbursements journal to their individual needs. For instance, a company could add an Other Accounts Cr. column to record transactions such as the purchase of land by paying cash and giving a note, since the company must credit an additional account besides Cash.

Posting the Cash Disbursements Journal   As shown in Illustration 7.5, you would post individual items in the Accounts Payable Dr. column daily to accounts in the accounts payable subsidiary ledger. You would post individual items in the Other Accounts Dr. column daily to the appropriate accounts in the general ledger. Then, you would post the column totals for Accounts Payable Dr., Supplies Expense Dr., Cash Cr., and Purchase Discounts Cr. at the end of the month to accounts in the general ledger. However, you would not post the total of the Other Accounts Dr. column. Illustration 7.5 shows only the amounts in the accounts from the posting of the cash disbursements journal to make it easier to trace the postings.

After you have posted both the purchases journal and cash disbursements journal, the general ledger Accounts Payable control account appears as follows:

Accounts Payable   *Account No. 200*

Date	Explanation	Post. Ref.	Debit	Credit	Balance
1994 Apr. 30		P10		2 4 1 0 0	2 4 1 0 0 Cr.
30		CD7	1 8 3 0 0		5 8 0 0 Cr.

Illustration 7.6 on page 326 shows the accounts payable subsidiary ledger of John Mason Company after the posting of the purchases journal and the cash disbursements journal.

At the end of the period, a schedule of accounts payable is prepared to make certain that the total of the balances in the accounts payable subsidiary ledger accounts agrees with the balance in the Accounts Payable control account. The schedule for John Mason Company appears below.

JOHN MASON COMPANY
Schedule of Accounts Payable
As of April 30, 1994

Booth Corporation	$1,500
Mertz Company	300
Nelson Company	4,000
Balance in the control account	$5,800

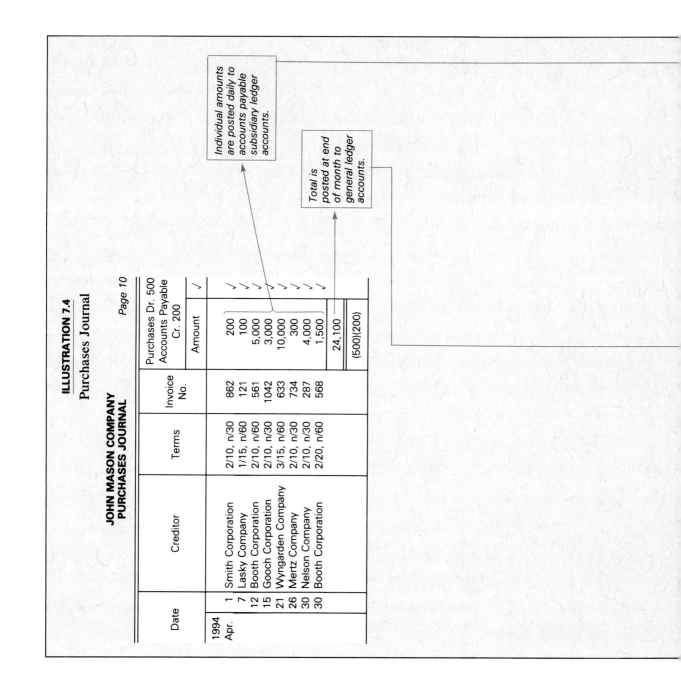

ILLUSTRATION 7.4
Purchases Journal

JOHN MASON COMPANY
PURCHASES JOURNAL
Page 10

Date		Creditor	Terms	Invoice No.	Purchases Dr. 500 Accounts Payable Cr. 200	
					Amount	√
1994 Apr.	1	Smith Corporation	2/10, n/30	862	200	√
	7	Lasky Company	1/15, n/60	121	100	√
	12	Booth Corporation	2/10, n/60	561	5,000	√
	15	Gooch Corporation	2/10, n/30	1042	3,000	√
	21	Wyngarden Company	3/15, n/60	633	10,000	√
	26	Mertz Company	2/10, n/30	734	300	√
	30	Nelson Company	2/10, n/30	287	4,000	√
	30	Booth Corporation	2/20, n/60	568	1,500	√
					24,100	
					(500)(200)	

Individual amounts are posted daily to accounts payable subsidiary ledger accounts.

Total is posted at end of month to general ledger accounts.

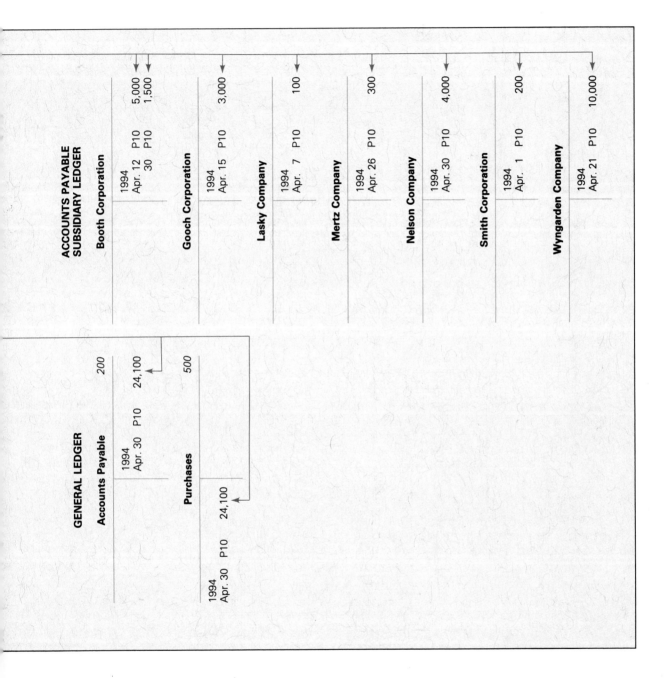

ACCOUNTS PAYABLE SUBSIDIARY LEDGER

Booth Corporation

1994			
Apr. 12	P10	5,000
30	P10	1,500

Gooch Corporation

1994		
Apr. 15	P10	3,000

Lasky Company

1994		
Apr. 7	P10	100

Mertz Company

1994		
Apr. 26	P10	300

Nelson Company

1994		
Apr. 30	P10	4,000

Smith Corporation

1994		
Apr. 1	P10	200

Wyngarden Company

1994		
Apr. 21	P10	10,000

GENERAL LEDGER

Accounts Payable

			200
1994			
Apr. 30	P10	24,100

Purchases

			500
1994			
Apr. 30	P10	24,100

323

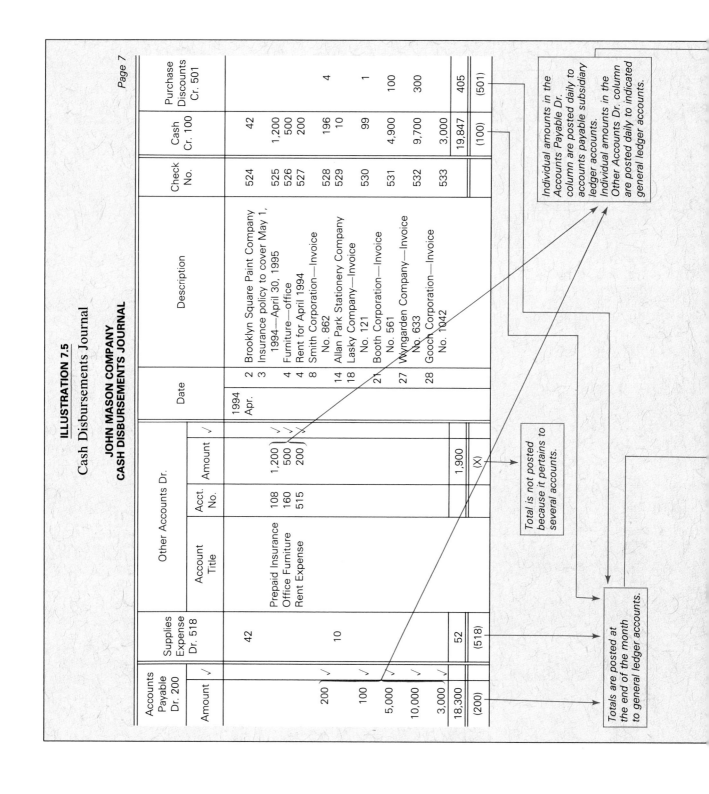

ILLUSTRATION 7.5

Cash Disbursements Journal

JOHN MASON COMPANY
CASH DISBURSEMENTS JOURNAL

Page 7

Date		Other Accounts Dr.				Accounts Payable Dr. 200		Supplies Expense Dr. 518	Description	Check No.	Cash Cr. 100	Purchase Discounts Cr. 501
		Account Title	Acct. No.	Amount	√	Amount	√					
1994 Apr.	2							42	Brooklyn Square Paint Company	524	42	
	3	Prepaid Insurance	108	1,200	√				Insurance policy to cover May 1, 1994—April 30, 1995	525	1,200	
	4	Office Furniture	160	500	√				Furniture—office	526	500	
	4	Rent Expense	515	200	√				Rent for April 1994	527	200	
	8					200	√		Smith Corporation—Invoice No. 862	528	196	4
	14							10	Allan Park Stationery Company	529	10	
	18					100	√		Lasky Company—Invoice No. 121	530	99	1
	21					5,000	√		Booth Corporation—Invoice No. 561	531	4,900	100
	27					10,000	√		Wyngarden Company—Invoice No. 633	532	9,700	300
	28					3,000	√		Gooch Corporation—Invoice No. 1042	533	3,000	
				1,900		18,300		52			19,847	405
				(X)		(200)		(518)			(100)	(501)

Total is not posted because it pertains to several accounts.

Totals are posted at the end of the month to general ledger accounts.

Individual amounts in the Accounts Payable Dr. column are posted daily to accounts payable subsidiary ledger accounts.

Individual amounts in the Other Accounts Dr. column are posted daily to indicated general ledger accounts.

324

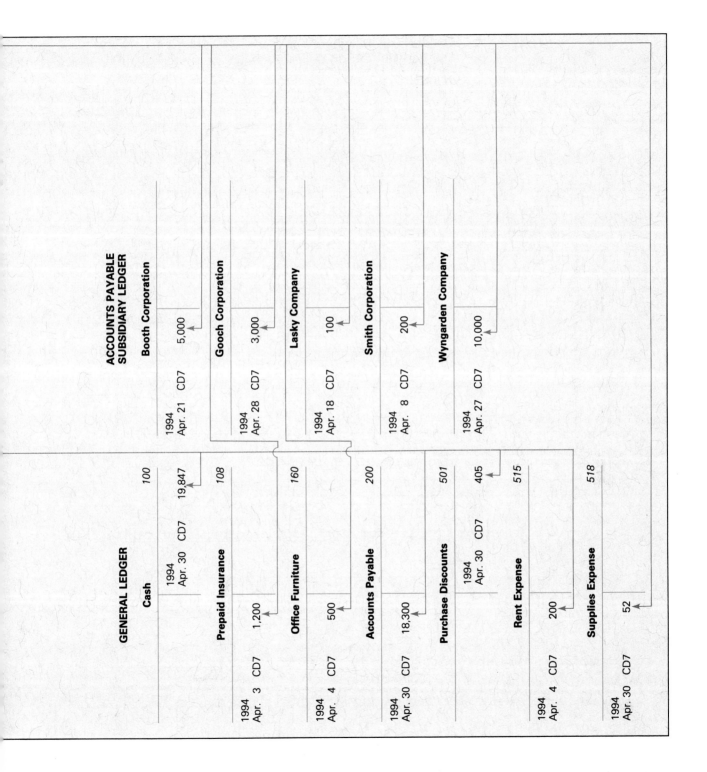

GENERAL LEDGER

Cash 100

1994			
Apr. 30	CD7		19,847

Prepaid Insurance 108

1994			
Apr. 3	CD7	1,200	

Office Furniture 160

1994			
Apr. 4	CD7	500	

Accounts Payable 200

1994			
Apr. 30	CD7	18,300	

Purchase Discounts 501

1994			
Apr. 30	CD7		405

Rent Expense 515

1994			
Apr. 4	CD7	200	

Supplies Expense 518

1994			
Apr. 30	CD7	52	

ACCOUNTS PAYABLE SUBSIDIARY LEDGER

Booth Corporation

1994			
Apr. 21	CD7		5,000

Gooch Corporation

1994			
Apr. 28	CD7		3,000

Lasky Company

1994			
Apr. 18	CD7		100

Smith Corporation

1994			
Apr. 8	CD7		200

Wyngarden Company

1994			
Apr. 27	CD7		10,000

ILLUSTRATION 7.6

Accounts Payable Subsidiary Ledger

JOHN MASON COMPANY
ACCOUNTS PAYABLE SUBSIDIARY LEDGER
Booth Corporation

Date		Explanation	Post. Ref.	Debit	Credit	Balance
1994 Apr.	12		P10		5000	5000 Cr.
	21		CD7	5000		–0–
	30		P10		1500	1500 Cr.

Gooch Corporation

Date		Explanation	Post. Ref.	Debit	Credit	Balance
1994 Apr.	15		P10		3000	3000 Cr.
	28		CD7	3000		–0–

Lasky Company

Date		Explanation	Post. Ref.	Debit	Credit	Balance
1994 Apr.	7		P10		100	100 Cr.
	18		CD7	100		–0–

Mertz Company

Date		Explanation	Post. Ref.	Debit	Credit	Balance
1994 Apr.	26		P10		300	300 Cr.

Nelson Company

Date		Explanation	Post. Ref.	Debit	Credit	Balance
1994 Apr.	30		P10		4000	4000 Cr.

ILLUSTRATION 7.6

(concluded)

ACCOUNTS PAYABLE SUBSIDIARY LEDGER *(concluded)*
Smith Corporation

Date		Explanation	Post. Ref.	Debit	Credit	Balance
1994 Apr.	1		P10		200	200 Cr.
	8		CD7	200		–0–

Wyngarden Company

Date		Explanation	Post. Ref.	Debit	Credit	Balance
1994 Apr.	21		P10		10000	10000 Cr.
	27		CD7	10000		–0–

General Ledger Illustrated

After you have posted all four special journals, the general ledger appears as shown in Illustration 7.7, pages 328–30.

General Journal

As stated earlier in the chapter, each transaction that does not fit in a special journal would appear in the general journal. For example, a company could use the general journal to record the receipt of a note from a customer in settlement of an account receivable. A note would allow the company to begin earning interest on the amount due. Note the following example of such an entry:

Notes Receivable	120	2,000	
Accounts Receivable—A. Smith.	103/√		2,000
To record the receipt of a 60-day, 12% note from Alex Smith in settlement of his account receivable.			

The √ shows that the credit has also been posted to the accounts receivable subsidiary ledger account.

Other types of transactions that would appear in the general journal include the purchase of equipment or some other asset by giving a note, the payment of an account payable by giving a note, sales returns and allowances, and purchase returns and allowances. For instance, the entry to record a sales allowance of $100 granted to John Burke for damaged merchandise is:

Sales Returns and Allowances	412	100	
Accounts Receivable—J. Burke.	103/√		100
To record a sales allowance of $100 to John Burke for damaged merchandise.			

ILLUSTRATION 7.7

General Ledger

JOHN MASON COMPANY
GENERAL LEDGER
Cash   *Account No. 100*

Date		Explanation	Post. Ref.	Debit	Credit	Balance
1994 Apr.	1	Beginning balance (assumed)				1 0 0 0 0 Dr.
	30		CR5	3 5 4 2 1		4 5 4 2 1 Dr.
	30		CD7		1 9 8 4 7	2 5 5 7 4 Dr.

Accounts Receivable   *Account No. 103*

Date		Explanation	Post. Ref.	Debit	Credit	Balance
1994 Apr.	30		S1	2 9 0		2 9 0 Dr.
	30		CR5		2 2 5	6 5 Dr.

Prepaid Insurance   *Account No. 108*

Date		Explanation	Post. Ref.	Debit	Credit	Balance
1994 Apr.	3		CD7	1 2 0 0		1 2 0 0 Dr.

Land   *Account No. 130*

Date		Explanation	Post. Ref.	Debit	Credit	Balance
1994 Apr.	1	Beginning balance (assumed)				1 8 0 0 0 Dr.
	10		CR5		6 0 0 0	1 2 0 0 0 Dr.

Office Furniture   *Account No. 160*

Date		Explanation	Post. Ref.	Debit	Credit	Balance
1994 Apr.	4		CD7	5 0 0		5 0 0 Dr.

ILLUSTRATION 7.7
(continued)

GENERAL LEDGER *(continued)*
Accounts Payable   *Account No. 200*

Date		Explanation	Post. Ref.	Debit	Credit	Balance
1994 Apr.	30		P10		2 4 1 0 0	2 4 1 0 0 Cr.
	30		CD7	1 8 3 0 0		5 8 0 0 Cr.

Capital Stock   *Account No. 300*

Date		Explanation	Post. Ref.	Debit	Credit	Balance
1994 Apr.	1	Beginning balance (assumed)				1 0 0 0 0 Cr.

Retained Earnings   *Account No. 310*

Date		Explanation	Post. Ref.	Debit	Credit	Balance
1994 Apr.	1	Beginning balance (assumed)				1 8 0 0 0 Cr.

Sales   *Account No. 410*

Date		Explanation	Post. Ref.	Debit	Credit	Balance
1994 Apr.	30		S1		2 9 0	2 9 0 Cr.
	30		CR5		2 9 0 0 0	2 9 2 9 0 Cr.

Sales Discounts   *Account No. 411*

Date		Explanation	Post. Ref.	Debit	Credit	Balance
1994 Apr.	30		CR5	4		4 Dr.

ILLUSTRATION 7.7

(concluded)

GENERAL LEDGER *(concluded)*
Miscellaneous Revenue   *Account No. 420*

Date	Explanation	Post. Ref.	Debit	Credit	Balance
1994 Apr. 26		CR5		2 0 0	2 0 0 Cr.

Purchases   *Account No. 500*

Date	Explanation	Post. Ref.	Debit	Credit	Balance
1994 Apr. 30		P10	2 4 1 0 0		2 4 1 0 0 Dr.

Purchase Discounts   *Account No. 501*

Date	Explanation	Post. Ref.	Debit	Credit	Balance
1994 Apr. 30		CD7		4 0 5	4 0 5 Cr.

Rent Expense   *Account No. 515*

Date	Explanation	Post. Ref.	Debit	Credit	Balance
1994 Apr. 4		CD7	2 0 0		2 0 0 Dr.

Supplies Expense   *Account No. 518*

Date	Explanation	Post. Ref.	Debit	Credit	Balance
1994 Apr. 30		CD7	5 2		5 2 Dr.

All adjusting and closing entries would appear in the general journal. For instance, the general journal would be used to record an adjusting entry for depreciation expense of $1,500 on an office building as follows:

Depreciation Expense—Buildings	520	1,500	
Accumulated Depreciation—Buildings	141		1,500
To record depreciation expense.			

ALTERNATIVE METHODS OF PROCESSING DATA

Objective 5
Describe alternative methods of processing data

The variety of equipment used in an accounting system is extensive, ranging from the hand-posted special journals of a manual system to large computers. Regardless of the accounting system a company selects, all companies use the basic steps of the accounting cycle to process their data. Also, the end result—financial statements—is the same for all companies. The selection that a company makes of one system over another depends on the company's individual situation, such as the volume of transactions, types of transactions, need for speed, resources of the company, and other cost-benefit considerations. In this section, you will study some of the alternative accounting systems available to companies.

Manual System

So far in this text, you have used the manual system. The manual system is the typical system used by some of today's smaller businesses that have one accountant and possibly one or two accounting clerks to handle their accounting function. In the manual system, accounting clerks record all accounting entries by hand. Then, they summarize the journals and post to the general ledger. Textbooks use the manual system to teach accounting because all other systems are based on it. In this chapter, you learned about the advantages of adding subsidiary ledgers and special journals to the manual system.

Manual systems called "one write" or "pegboard" systems were developed decades ago to assist small businesses to streamline their accounting tasks. By creating one document and aligning other records under it (using a pegboard), companies can record transactions more efficiently. For instance, these systems permit the writing of a check and the simultaneous recording of the check in the cash disbursements journal. Some of these systems are still in use today, but eventually computers will probably replace most of them.

During the 1950s, companies also used bookkeeping machines to supplement manual systems. These machines recorded recurring transactions such as sales on account. They posted transactions to the general ledger and subsidiary ledger accounts and computed new balances. However, with the development of computers, bookkeeping machines became obsolete. They were quite expensive, and computers easily outperformed them.

Microcomputers and Minicomputers

In this age of fast-developing computer technology with the continued lowering of computer prices, many small and medium-size businesses are turning to computers and off-the-shelf software to maintain their accounting records. Large businesses may use mainframe computers (described later), while small businesses might use microcomputers and/or minicomputers. Microcomputers are smaller than minicomputers and accommodate one person, while several persons can use a minicomputer at the same time. The distinction between microcomputers and minicomputers is more one of price rather than quality or capacity.

If greed, fraud, and financial excess were themes of the 1980s, contrition, repentance, and prudence may be the watchwords for the 1990s.

Some of the best-known offenders of the past decade are hanging their heads and apologizing, even detailing their illegal deeds as lessons for ethical betterment.

Ethics has become a popular subject in the world of high finance.

The nation's two largest commodity markets, the Mercantile Exchange and Board of Trade in Chicago, are insisting their members attend classes in ethics. The Mercantile Exchange was a hotbed of illegal trading practices that were uncovered by the FBI and led to 45 indictments.

Business schools, Harvard being a key example, are emphasizing ethics courses as never before. Many such programs are receiving substantial financial support from outside donors including $20 million pledged by former Securities and Exchange Commission Chairman John Shad.

As the classroom and counseling programs grow, the fallen angels of Wall Street have become object lessons in how not to behave in the new environment of purity and honesty.

Michael Milken's tearful guilty plea in late April, a frank admission by the king of junk bonds that he really was a crook who is ashamed of what he did, could be a symbol of the change in attitude.

But several years before Milken's fall from grace, Dennis Levine set in motion the collapse of the big-time illegal inside traders when he was caught and sent to jail. Levine had made nearly $12 million in three years of stock transactions emanating from the inside knowledge he gained as a mergers and acquisitions specialist on Wall Street.

Released after fewer than three years in a minimum security federal prison, Levine now is trying to atone for his sins by telling his story in classrooms at Columbia University, New York University, and the prestigious Wharton School of Business and Finance at the University of Pennsylvania.

He told it in more detail in the most recent issue of *Fortune* magazine.

"I have been addressing students, hoping to steer them away from the mistakes I made," Levine wrote. "They are conscious of ethical issues—all the way from misappropriating office supplies to out-and-out felonies like inside trading or illegal dumping of toxic wastes.

". . . my former life was destroyed because I figured the odds were 1,000 to 1 against my getting caught. It would comfort me if I could help even one person avoid throwing away a lifetime on a foolish gamble like that."

Microcomputers cost from a few hundred dollars to about $10,000. Minicomputers generally cost between $10,000 and $100,000. Microcomputers can fit on top of a desk; minicomputers are larger—about the size of a six-foot refrigerator. Divisions of large companies may use minicomputers since they can have several terminals connected to them. Companies use microcomputers for word processing, graphics, database management, and preparing spreadsheets for planning and decision making as well as for processing business transactions. Microcomputers can be networked (linked) into a system as powerful as a minicomputer. Many business executives have microcomputers on their desks and use them daily. As the price of computers continues to decline, more businesses will use computer systems. Appendix 7-A at the end of this chapter describes in more detail the use of the microcomputer in accounting.

Confessing all with the stated intention of warning others is a catharsis for some financial and business professionals who strayed from the straight and narrow and were caught.

José Gomez did it in the wake of the 1985 ESM Government Securities scandal in Fort Lauderdale. As an executive with the outside auditing firm hired to police ESM's financial records, Gomez discovered the fraud—which grew into a $300 million scam—but covered [it] up. He had borrowed $200,000 from ESM to enhance an upwardly mobile life style, a clear conflict of interest.

Repentant, Gomez told me his story shortly before he began serving a 12-year prison term in March 1987. He will be eligible for parole early next year.

"I betrayed my own principles," he said. "The lessons are don't let ambition get in the way of your principles, don't spend more than you make, and don't take the easy way out like I did."

* * * * *

A big accounting firm polled business leaders two years ago for their attitudes on ethical problems and solutions. They generally blamed the ethical crisis on business concentration on short-term results and the decay of American cultural and social institutions.

Legislation, the respondents said, offers the least effective way to encourage ethical behavior. Shad, the man who pledged to raise $20 million for Harvard students to study ethics, summed up his views succinctly:

"Ethics pays. It's smart to be ethical."

* * * * *

Required a. Do you believe that the individuals mentioned in this article took one "big leap" into dishonesty or do you think they did some "little unethical things" first? What motivates these individuals to perform illegal acts?

b. Do you agree that the outlook for the future is a more ethical business climate?

c. Do you agree that ethics pays?

Source: James Russell, "Back to Basics: Ethics and Prudence," *The Miami Herald*, May 13, 1990, pp. 1G, 2G.

Service Bureaus

Some businesses still find it economical to send certain data (e.g., payroll, inventory, and accounts receivable) to a local service bureau for processing. A service bureau is a large computer facility that takes data from a client, enters the data into its computer, produces required statements or reports, and returns this output to the client. Client personnel do not have to interact with the computer. Service bureaus can usually meet the specific output requirements of a business if the company does some advance planning.

Time-Sharing Terminals

Significant advances have been made in the field of computer time sharing. Time sharing occurs when several users utilize the same host computer to process data. In a time-sharing arrangement, client personnel interact with a computer through a remote terminal located in the client's building. The users literally share time on the host computer through remote terminals and the use of modems and telephone lines or the use of radio waves. A company employee operating a remote terminal can call up the host computer. Typical applications of time sharing enable clients to process large amounts of transactions data (e.g., printing and summarizing sales invoices, and updating inventory, accounts receivable, and accounts payable records).

Mainframe In-House Computer

Many business firms purchase their own mainframe computer to process data. The cost of these computers can be several hundred thousand dollars. Where the volume of transactions is very large, the decision to purchase a large computer is often justified. Terminals may exist throughout the company for employees to use to communicate with the mainframe computer. Appendix 7-B contains more information about basic concepts regarding computers.

This chapter described how the recording and classifying functions in accounting could be made more efficient. An understanding of a manual accounting system also helps you understand how computerized accounting systems operate.

In the next chapter, you will learn the general principles of internal control and how to control cash. Cash is one of a company's most important assets; however, it is also the company's most mobile asset. As you study the subject of controlling cash, you will realize that, to be successful, a company must attempt to hire and retain competent and trustworthy employees and must also establish an effective system of internal control.

UNDERSTANDING THE LEARNING OBJECTIVES

1. Describe the relationship between subsidiary accounts in subsidiary ledgers and control accounts in the general ledger.
   - □ A control account is an account, such as accounts receivable, in the general ledger that shows the total balance of all the subsidiary accounts related to it.
   - □ Subsidiary ledger accounts, such as individual customer accounts, show the details supporting the related general ledger account balance.

2. Describe the relationship between special journals and the general journal.
   - □ Each special journal is a book of original entry that records one particular type of transaction, such as sales on account, cash receipts, purchases on account, or cash disbursement.
   - □ The general journal is used to record all transactions that cannot be entered in one of the special journals.

3. Record transactions in special journals.
   - □ The dollar amounts of journal entries are entered in columns established in the special journals. Each of the special journals has its unique sets of columns.

4. Post special journals.
   - □ For certain columns in the special journals, only the column total is posted to the general ledger.
   - □ For some columns in the special journals, the column total is posted to the general ledger, and the individual amounts in the column are posted to subsidiary ledger accounts.
   - □ For a few columns in the special journals, the column total is not posted, but the individual amounts in the column are posted to general ledger accounts.

5. Describe alternative methods of processing data.
   - ☐ Manual systems are still in use in some small businesses. The use of special journals and/or "one write" systems can make them more efficient. Bookkeeping machines were once in use, but they have been replaced by computers.
   - ☐ Microcomputers and minicomputers are taking over a larger and larger share of the task of processing data as the cost of computers declines and the speed and ease of use increase.
   - ☐ Some companies still use service bureaus and time-sharing terminals for special accounting tasks such as payroll.
   - ☐ Mainframe computers are used by many medium to large companies to handle accounting and other tasks.

6. Describe microcomputer applications in accounting (Appendix 7-A).
   - ☐ Currently, numerous accounting system packages for microcomputers are available on the market. These packages allow companies to gather information and produce financial statements much more efficiently than with manual systems.
   - ☐ The modules normally include: General Ledger, Accounts Receivable, Accounts Payable, Inventory Management, Payroll, and Invoicing.
   - ☐ Another type of computer program is the electronic spreadsheet. Spreadsheets are ideal for creating large schedules and performing great volumes of calculations.
   - ☐ Database management software is used to develop integrated accounting systems and to help solve problems by accessing needed data from the database files.
   - ☐ Microcomputers are used increasingly in audit, tax, and management consulting activities of public accounting firms.
   - ☐ Future applications of the computer in public accounting will involve the use of "expert systems" and artificial intelligence.

7. Describe basic computer concepts (Appendix 7-B).
   - ☐ The storage unit is the computer's internal memory system.
   - ☐ The arithmetic unit of a computer performs simple computations and comparisons.
   - ☐ The control unit of a computer interprets the program, assigns storage space, and alters the sequence of operations if so instructed by the program.
   - ☐ Peripheral equipment can be attached to the computer and used mainly for input and output of information.

APPENDIX 7-A: THE USE OF THE MICROCOMPUTER IN ACCOUNTING*

Objective 6

Describe microcomputer applications in accounting

The use of the microcomputer in American business has greatly increased in recent years due to decreasing computer prices and significant technological advances in both computer hardware and software. Microcomputers now frequently cost under $5,000 and have as much power as computers that would have cost millions of dollars and filled several large rooms only a short time ago. The

---

* Written by Gary Fayard, Partner in the Atlanta Office of Ernst & Young, and Dana R. Hermanson, formerly Senior Accountant in the Atlanta Office of Ernst & Young, and now a doctoral student at the University of Wisconsin.

microcomputer is especially useful in accounting because of the great need for fast and accurate information processing when dealing with large volumes of financial data. To further your understanding of the microcomputer and its use in accounting, we will discuss the following topics: computerized accounting systems, computer spreadsheets, database management systems, and the use of microcomputers in public accounting.

COMPUTERIZED ACCOUNTING SYSTEMS

Numerous accounting system packages for microcomputers are currently available on the market, and most of them cost from just under $100 to $2,500. Two of the most popular accounting software packages are Peachtree Complete Accounting III® and DacEasy Accounting 4.1.® Software companies have designed these packages for small businesses, and the packages can provide many advantages over manual accounting systems. Companies can greatly reduce the clerical work performed by their accounting staff. In addition, companies can also substantially reduce clerical errors in the financial data by changing from a manual to a computerized accounting system. Computerized systems also allow companies to gather information and produce reports much more efficiently than is possible with manual systems. The proper implementation of one of these accounting system packages can result in a company having a computerized accounting system that is both more efficient and less expensive than a manual system.

Now that you understand the potential advantages of using an accounting system package, let us examine the typical characteristics of a package on the market today. One basic characteristic of all effective systems is that some type of control exists over who can use the computer to make journal entries. Many packages have a password that a person must use to get into the accounting system. The importance of this control cannot be overstated.

Another common characteristic of most accounting packages today is that they are menu driven. The term "menu driven" means that the program user selects an option listed on the screen to access the part of the accounting system that he or she wishes to use. For example, when the user first turns on the computer and enters the proper password, a screen similar to this may appear:

```
                    XYZ Company
            1> General Ledger
            2> Accounts Receivable
            3> Accounts Payable
            4> Inventory Management
            5> Payroll
            6> Invoicing
            7> End Session
```

Assume the user wanted to access the Accounts Payable section of the program. Then, he or she would type a "3" into the computer and hit "ENTER." The user would now have access to the Accounts Payable section, and another menu would appear that would provide the user with several options within that section. The menu system makes accounting packages much more "user friendly."

The final characteristic to be discussed is the typical organization or format of a computerized accounting package. Most packages are divided into the modules shown on the screen above—General Ledger, Accounts Receivable, Accounts Payable, Inventory Management, Payroll, and Invoicing. Let us now briefly discuss the function of each module.

The General Ledger module contains all of a company's accounts and their balances. General journal entries are made in this module. These entries include all entries not made in one of the other system modules. For example, an entry relating to accounts receivable would be made in the Accounts Receivable module. However, an entry to record the borrowing of cash from a bank does not fit into any of the specific modules and would be made in the General Ledger module as a general journal entry. Adjusting entries would also be entered in the General Ledger module. One other function performed in the General Ledger module is the printing of a company's financial statements. Most accounting packages will automatically make all the necessary closing entries before printing out the financial statements.

The Accounts Receivable module is used to record sales on credit to various customers and amounts received from customers. The file of customers in this module serves as the accounts receivable subsidiary ledger. The Accounts Receivable control account in the General Ledger module is usually automatically updated when entries are made in the Accounts Receivable module.

The Accounts Payable module is used to record credit purchases of merchandise from various vendors and payments the company made to those vendors. The file of suppliers in this module serves as the accounts payable subsidiary ledger. The Accounts Payable control account in the General Ledger module is usually automatically updated when entries are made in the Accounts Payable module.

The Inventory Management module maintains the perpetual inventory. This module reflects all purchases and sales of inventory. The Inventory Management module interfaces with the Accounts Receivable and Accounts Payable modules to keep track of the receivables and payables resulting from sales and purchases.

The Payroll module is used to record all the payroll entries. The totals from the Payroll module are often automatically posted to the appropriate General Ledger accounts, although this automatic posting is not always available.

The Invoicing module is simply used to print the sales invoices that are sent to customers. Sometimes this Invoicing module is combined with the Accounts Receivable module into one module.

ELECTRONIC SPREADSHEETS

Another type of computer program that has become extremely popular during the last decade is the electronic spreadsheet. Two of the most popular spreadsheet programs are LOTUS 1-2-3® and Microsoft Excel®. These programs have numerous applications in business and specifically in accounting. Spreadsheets are ideal for creating large schedules and performing large volumes of calculations. Their specific uses in accounting range from performing depreciation calculations to creating trial balances and other schedules. Other specific uses of spreadsheets will be discussed in the section on the use of the microcomputer in public accounting.

Let us now examine the basics of the electronic spreadsheet. An electronic spreadsheet is simply a large blank ''page'' on the computer screen that contains rows and columns. The spreadsheet is so large that a user can see only a very small percentage of the sheet on the screen at one time. The blocks created by the intersection of the rows and columns are called cells, and each cell can hold one or more words, a number, or the product of a mathematical formula. A typical blank spreadsheet appears as follows:

```
          A   B   C   D   E   F   G

    1

    2   ▨  (Cursor)

    3

    4              □  (Cell C4)

    5

    6

    7

    8

    9

   10

  A2>  (Type appears here)

  (Cursor location)
```

The cursor indicates the cell on the screen in which the user can enter information at a given time. For example, on the above screen, the user can now enter one or more words, a number, or a formula into cell A2. Note that the information will appear at the bottom (on some programs, at the top) of the screen next to the cursor location until the user presses the ENTER key to transfer the information to its cell. The user can move the cursor around the screen by pressing different cursor control keys.

By going through the following example you can gain a better understanding of how the electronic spreadsheet actually works. Assume you are an accountant in Burke Company and wish to create an income statement for 1993 and a projected income statement for 1994 like those shown below:

	A	B	C	D
1	▨	BURKE CO.		
2		INCOME STATEMENT	PROJECTED	
3		YEAR ENDED 12/31/93	12/31/94	
4				
5	Sales	1,000,000	1,100,000	
6	Cost of Goods Sold	600,000	660,000	
7	Gross Profit	400,000	440,000	
8	Other Expenses	100,000	110,000	
9	Net Income	300,000	330,000	
10				

A1>

Your first step in creating these statements is to set up the proper headings. In cell B1 you would enter BURKE CO. by moving the cursor to B1, typing in the words BURKE CO., and pressing the ENTER key to transfer the words to cell B1. Likewise, you would enter the appropriate headings into cells B2, B3, C2, and C3. Your second step is to enter the income statement items in column A. You would place these items in cells A5 through A9 in the same way that you entered the other headings.

Now that you have entered all of the headings and titles, you can begin to enter the financial figures into the 1993 Income Statement. Cell B5 will contain the Sales figure of $1,000,000, and B6 will hold the $600,000 Cost of Goods Sold figure. You will enter these numbers in the same manner that you entered the headings and titles. Cell B7 will not hold a specific word or number; however, it will contain the result of a mathematical formula (B5 − B6). By moving the cursor to B7, typing +B5 − B6, and pressing the ENTER key, you enter the result of this formula into B7. Finally, you enter $100,000 in cell B8. You will enter the result of +B7 − B8 in cell B9.

The final step in constructing this spreadsheet is to complete cells C5 through C9, which will show the projected Income Statement figures for 1994. Assuming that Sales, Cost of Goods Sold, and Other Expenses will increase by 10% from 1993 to 1994, you can enter the following formulas for cells C5, C6, and C8. Cell C5 will contain the number resulting from the formula +B5*1.1. Cells C6 and C8 will show the results of +B6*1.1 and +B8*1.1, respectively. Finally, C7 and C9 will hold the results of +C5 − C6 and +C7 − C8, respectively. Your spreadsheet is now complete, as it presents the 1993 Income Statement for Burke Company and a projected Income Statement for 1994.

You have only used a few of the columns and rows available in a typical spreadsheet. Most spreadsheets contain many columns and rows. For instance, a recent version of LOTUS 1-2-3 contains 256 columns and 8,192 rows.

While the Income Statement you just constructed is a simple example of spreadsheet use, you should note several more advanced functions that spreadsheets can perform. First, when showing a current schedule and projections of that schedule far into the future, the user can play "what if" games by changing various numbers or formulas in the spreadsheet. Then, the program will recalculate all of the schedules based on the changes made. Second, many spreadsheet programs allow the user to construct various types of graphs showing the data contained in spreadsheet schedules. Finally, the user can print out on paper the schedules that appear on the computer screen for use by other people.

The computerized spreadsheet is a powerful tool, but the potential for inefficient use of spreadsheets is great. To promote better use of spreadsheets, Ernst & Young has developed the following tips for its staff:

1. Spend time on planning. Planning how to design, organize, and construct your spreadsheet can ensure that the spreadsheet meets your requirements. This planning reduces errors and makes the spreadsheet easier to use.

2. Keep the overall design simple. Spreadsheet design should aim at producing clear and concise analyses. Quality is more important than quantity.

3. Organize the spreadsheet to make it easy to understand. Separate data input areas from reports. Include instructions and a table of contents to make the spreadsheet understandable to other people.

4. Use simple formulas to make your printed output more understandable and to make errors easier to detect.

5. Use validation tests to alert you if errors occur.

6. Test the spreadsheet before use. Always check spreadsheet calculations before using the results.

7. Use graphics to highlight patterns or trends in your data and to make your spreadsheets more interesting and understandable.

8. Document the spreadsheet. Both users and reviewers need adequate documentation of spreadsheet logic and design. Proper headings and descriptions, as well as other documentation, are important for a well-designed spreadsheet.

9. Use the "protect" command to safeguard the spreadsheet and identify where data should be entered.

10. Make regular backups. Maintain up-to-date copies of spreadsheet files to avoid losing important data and development work.

DATABASE MANAGEMENT SYSTEMS

In many accounting systems, various applications of the same data have been developed independently. As a result, although inventory, purchasing, sales, and production all use part numbers to identify inventory items, the computer would have to store each piece of information in each file for each application. The same data stored in separate files could vary as far as accuracy and timeliness. Inefficiencies (data redundancy) and inaccuracies (data inconsistency) can result. A database management system helps solve these problems by storing related data together independent of the application. Many of today's accounting systems have integrated applications through the use of a database management system. Thus, in the above example, the computer stores the inventory part number in only one file but all the applications use it.

Companies use database management software frequently on microcomputers. Two of the most popular microcomputer database management systems are dBASE IV® and rBASE®. Companies can use these systems to develop integrated accounting systems. These systems are also useful for many single applications. With database software, you can easily enter data into a microcomputer and then analyze, sort, and print the information using English-like commands. The advantage of using the database management system for a single application over writing the application in a programming language (i.e., BASIC, PASCAL) is that the database management system takes care of data file access for you.

Now we will look at an example of a database application. The database file can be any organized collection of related information, such as monthly sales information. The information is kept in records, with each record consisting of a series of fields. A field is the part of a record that holds a particular item of information. An example of a record might be all information related to a salesperson. The fields in the record might include the salesperson's name, address, and ZIP code.

Suppose you are a sales manager and must maintain information about your salespersons, your customers, and your company's product. You could use a database management system to help you keep up with this information. In this case, you would probably have three database files—one for salespersons, one for customers, and one for products. However, the database management system can be instructed to match the salespersons to the customers, the customers to the products, and so on. Once you have defined this information to the database management system, you can use English-like commands to help answer such questions as: Which products have been sold? Who are the customers? What are the amounts of sales by salespersons? You would also be able to print a customer list sorted by ZIP code, alphabetical order, or salesperson.

USE OF MICROCOMPUTERS IN PUBLIC ACCOUNTING

Microcomputers are having far-reaching effects in all areas of accounting. The following discussion explains some of the uses of microcomputers in public accounting.

Auditing

Auditing involves performing an examination of the financial statements of a company to enable the Certified Public Accountant to express an opinion on the financial statements. The examination of the financial statements involves many different types of tests. Many times auditors use statistical sampling techniques to test the details of account balances. The microcomputer is very useful in helping both to plan and select the sample and to evaluate the results of the sample.

A typical example of microcomputer-based statistical sampling is the selection of random numbers for a test of cash disbursements. You do this by entering the sequences of the checks written during the year. Then, the statistical sampling package selects a random sample of the checks to be tested. After the checks have been tested for accuracy and source document support, the findings are entered in the statistical package to evaluate the results of the sample and to form conclusions about the entire population of cash disbursements.

The microcomputer has had a tremendous impact on the auditing profession in the areas of analytical review and trial balance/financial statement preparation. Microcomputer packages are available that enable the auditor to enter the client's general ledger information and post adjusting journal entries. These packages will print analytical review information, such as percentage changes in expense accounts as compared with the prior year. Also, such packages are useful in calculating financial ratios. They will also consolidate the financial statements of several related companies and print consolidated financial statements. Another benefit of some of these packages is that they will print the financial information in a way to facilitate income tax return preparation.

Other uses of the microcomputer in auditing are calculations of present/future values, amortization schedules for debt, depreciation schedules for fixed assets, and flowcharting of accounting systems.

Auditors use computer spreadsheets extensively both for their ease of use and the capability quickly to change and recalculate computations. Use of a computer spreadsheet to calculate the income tax provision is a typical example. This calculation can be a complicated computation, and it is subject to change if the company makes adjustments to the financial statements as a result of the audit. The use of a computer spreadsheet allows the auditor to quickly reflect the adjusted amounts and recalculate the income tax provision.

Tax

The microcomputer has also had a dramatic impact on the tax practice of public accounting firms. Microcomputers are used to prepare tax returns, and they are used extensively in income tax and estate tax planning. In tax planning, both specialized tax programs and computer spreadsheets are used. Use of the microcomputer allows the tax professional to ask ''what if'' questions and quickly see the results of different tax strategies.

Another important use of the microcomputer is in the area of tax research. By using a modem, companies can access research databases over phone lines. These databases have current tax law, tax cases, and revenue rulings that can be quickly searched and the information found downloaded to the microcomputer for review and printing.

A BROADER PERSPECTIVE

MORE FIRMS ARE RECOMMENDING PACKAGES

The number of accounting firms recommending that their clients install some software packages continues to grow annually.

In 1989, four out of 10 computerized accounting firms recommended that their clients install a general ledger or data base management package, but in 1990 this jumped to nearly six out of every 10 (59 percent) firms recommending installation to their clients.

* * * * *

According to *Accounting Today*'s 1990 Computerization in Accounting Firms survey, the single most often mentioned software package in the data base file management category that accounting firms recommended to their clients was Lotus 1-2-3 with a 35 percent mention. In the 1989 survey, Lotus 1-2-3 was also the top package, but not by the significant margin it was in 1990. Although not strictly a data base management package, perhaps the versatility of the spreadsheet in addition to its file management functions made it the package of choice.

* * * * *

Ashton-Tate dBase II/dBase III + was the No. 2 software brand recommended in both 1989 and 1990, although it dropped from 11 percent in 1989 to 9 percent in 1990.

Next came Borland (Paradox) which dropped from 4 percent in 1989 to 3 percent in 1990, followed by in-house developed programs, which dropped from 4 percent in 1989 to 2 percent in 1990. Lotus (Symphony) went from 6 percent in 1989 to 4 percent in 1990.

* * * * *

In the general ledger category, Peachtree Complete Accounting was the most recommended software package in 1990 with 29 percent, followed by MAS Master Accounting with 17 percent.

Other mentions were AccPac Plus, 12 percent; DAC Easy, 11 percent; AccPac BPI, 9 percent; Great Plains Accounting Series, 9 percent; Real World Accounting System, 9 percent; Solomon III, 9 percent; CYMA Professional Accounting Series, 7 percent; and Open Systems Accounting, 7 percent.

Also, One Write Plus, 6 percent; Harmony, 4 percent; Cougar Mountain, 3 percent; Ready To Run With Lotus, 3 percent; SBT Database, 3 percent; IBM's Platinum, 3 percent; DK, 2 percent; AccPac Bedford, 2 percent; Macola Accounting Systems, 2 percent; and Prentice Hall Software, 2 percent.

* * * * *

Source: *Accounting Today,* May 28, 1990, pp. S13, 19. Reprinted with permission.

Management Consulting Services

Management consultants, as the name implies, work with clients in a variety of areas. These areas include advising on acquisitions of computer hardware and software, implementing accounting systems, analyzing staffing needs, reviewing manufacturing procedures and cost systems, and performing financial modeling tasks.

Financial modeling is the process of taking historical financial information and projecting the results based on various scenarios. Accountants can perform financial modeling by use of a computer spreadsheet. However, accountants often use microcomputer financial modeling packages to develop most large, complicated models.

The following are examples of the uses of financial modeling.

1.   A manufacturer needs help in overcoming a seasonal cash shortage. The nature of the manufacturer's business involves the annual buildup of large inventories. This buildup results in dramatic increases in payables. Using a financial model, the company is able to anticipate its cash requirements and avert an annual cash crisis.

2.   A manufacturer wants to expand its business by acquiring the manufacturing capabilities of existing companies. Using a financial model, the com-

pany can develop a series of projections of the anticipated results of various acquisitions and the impact on the company's debt service and borrowing capabilities.

3. A privately held company has plans to go public. A key ingredient to a successful public offering is a well-conceived business plan that allows underwriters to make an objective initial assessment of the company's current situation and future potential. The company can use a financial model to prepare projections of its financial statements. The company would include these projected financial statements in its business plan to allow the underwriters to assess the company's future potential.

YOUR FUTURE AND THE MICROCOMPUTER

The microcomputer is now firmly established as a valuable tool in accounting. As computer technology continues to progress, accountants will find more and more ways in which to use these powerful machines.

Future applications of the computer in public accounting will involve the use of "expert systems" and artificial intelligence. Expert systems are software programs designed to duplicate the decisions of an "expert," given certain facts and circumstances. For instance, the program might be able to predict whether or not a client is a going concern with the same success rate as could an expert on this topic. These programs are extremely expensive and time consuming to develop.

Artificial intelligence is a much broader concept than expert systems. The field of artificial intelligence is devoted to making the computer think like a human being by being able to interact with humans and adapt to unstructured situations. In the distant future we may have computers that think and respond like humans.

Your success as an accountant in the future may depend greatly on your ability to use microcomputers efficiently and effectively. We hope this appendix has alerted you to the need for an understanding of the uses of the microcomputer in accounting.

APPENDIX 7-B: THE COMPUTER—BASIC CONCEPTS

Objective 7
Describe basic computer concepts

The basic concepts discussed in this appendix are the computer, computer components, and the applications of electronic data processing to accounting. This appendix is for those who have little understanding of computers.

THE COMPUTER

The search for greater speed, accuracy, and storage capacity in an accounting system has presented a persistent challenge to both the accounting profession and the designers of information systems. This challenge has been met over the years by the increasing use of more sophisticated devices. The most recent sophisticated device has been the computer. The computer has permitted human participation in the processing of data to be limited to the preparation of the input (transaction) data and the program, or set of instructions, telling the computer how to process these data. If properly programmed, the computer is capable of journalizing and posting transactions with great speed and a high degree of accuracy.

The distinguishing features of a computer are its abilities to accept instructions on the processing of transaction data, store these instructions, and execute them any number of times precisely in the desired sequence. The computer uses elementary logic to alter the sequence of instructions by observing the outcome of a numeric or alphabetic comparison. For example, accountants can instruct the computer to test whether the cash balance is zero before each transaction and to continue processing cash disbursements only if the balance is greater than zero. Use of such techniques allows the computer to perform functions that are most time consuming when performed manually.

The advantages of a computerized accounting system are many. Computers remain exceedingly accurate at high calculating speeds. Since users can give sets of operating instructions to the computer at the outset, the computer conserves human effort. Computers can take over the performance of repetitive tasks, routine numerical decision making, and certain types of logical decision making. The time has come when almost every business should consider using a computerized system of accounting.

COMPUTER COMPONENTS

A computer consists of three basic components: storage unit, arithmetic unit, and control unit.

The storage unit (sometimes called core storage) of a computer is its internal **memory** system. Storage units record and retain data until they are required by and transferred to other areas of the computer. This unit is the most expensive component of the computer. To determine the optimum size of the storage unit, users must consider speed and cost factors. Generally, the greater the speed and storage required, the greater the cost. Users can add storage space to the computer by utilizing peripheral devices such as disks, drums, or tape units for temporary external storage.

The arithmetic unit of a computer performs simple computations and comparisons. Arithmetic units handle mathematical operations such as addition, subtraction, multiplication, and division. These units are also the logic unit of the computer.

The control unit of a computer is the unit that interprets the program (the set of instructions submitted to the computer that specifies the operations to be performed and the correct sequence of operations), assigns storage space, and alters the sequence of operations if so instructed by the program. If the unit encounters a situation for which no explicit instructions are given, it will instruct the computer to halt operations. The computer operator can then find and correct the problem situation and restart the processing by means of a console. The **console** allows the operator to exercise control over the computer when necessary.

Users can attach peripheral equipment to the computer to feed unprocessed information into the computer and receive the output of processed information. Examples of peripheral equipment are tape drives and printers. The manner in which the user connects and controls this peripheral equipment varies from computer to computer.

Illustration 7.8 shows a schematic design of a simple computer system. The control unit controls operation of the system. The peripheral equipment is not part of the computer but it transmits data into and out of the computer as directed by the control unit. The control unit sends the data to the storage unit until time is available to process the data. At that time, the data are recalled from storage and transferred to the arithmetic unit, where the required arithmetic operations are performed. On completion, the control unit sends the processed data either to the peripheral equipment or, if more processing is necessary using the data, back to storage. The peripheral equipment will display the processed output in a predefined format.

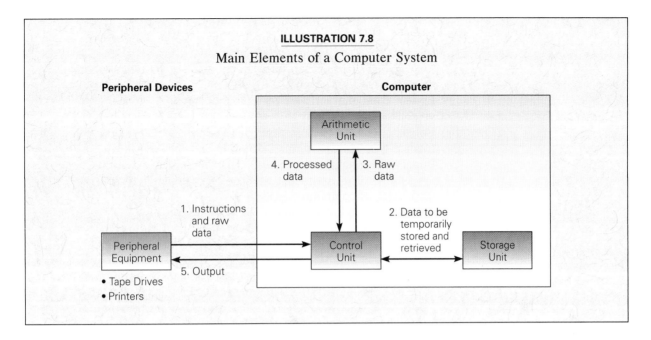

ILLUSTRATION 7.8

Main Elements of a Computer System

APPLICATIONS OF ELECTRONIC DATA PROCESSING TO ACCOUNTING

Early electronic data processing applications in accounting were in the areas of payroll, accounts receivable, accounts payable, and inventory. Now programs exist for all phases of accounting, including manufacturing operations and total integration of other accounting programs with the general ledger. Nearly all applications of data processing, and particularly those that involve the accounting process, have made considerable use of files.

A file is a grouping of records arranged in some order. For example, the accounts receivable subsidiary ledger is a file. The records are the individual customer accounts. Files also exist for accounts payable and inventory. Developments in the hardware and software areas will have a significant impact on how accounting tasks will be performed in the future.

DEMONSTRATION PROBLEM

The Discount Softwarehouse uses special journals for sales, cash receipts, purchases, and cash disbursements, as well as a general journal. These journals follow the same design as those illustrated in this chapter, except that the column for Supplies Expense Dr. is omitted from the cash disbursements journal.

Transactions

May 1 Sold Baxter Company $12,000 of computer software on account; terms 2/10, n/30; Invoice No. 94-128.

4 Bought computer software on account from the Ace Company; Invoice No. 152; terms n/10, $8,400.

7 Cash sales, $38,000.

10 Rental revenue received, $1,600.

11 Received amount due from Baxter Company for sale of May 1. The discount was taken.

12 Paid for office equipment received today, $4,800 (Check No. 260). The equipment was for the company's own use.

May 14   Paid Ace Company for purchase of May 3 (Check No. 261).

14   Sold $8,000 of computer software on account to Mosley Company; Invoice No. 94-129; terms 2/10, n/30.

15   Sold $2,800 of computer software on account to Wilks Company; Invoice No. 94-130; terms 2/10, n/30.

15   Bought computer software on account from Ace Company, $3,960; Invoice No. 224; terms n/10.

16   Bought computer merchandise on account from Carr Company, $6,000; Invoice No. 324-CD; terms 2/10, n/30.

17   Bought office equipment today for $3,800 and gave a 30-day, 14% note in payment. The equipment was for the company's own use.

20   Cash sales of computer supplies, $7,200.

20   Collected $3,080 on account from Thomas Gibson.

22   Cash sales of computer software, $4,480.

23   Cash sales of computer software, $1,200.

24   Collected net amount due from Mosley Company on sale of August 14.

25   Collected net amount due from Wilks Company on sale of August 15.

25   Paid Ace Company on invoice of August 15 (Check No. 262).

26   Paid Carr Company on invoice of August 16 (Check No. 263).

27   Paid delivery expense in cash, $1,600 (Check No. 264).

27   Paid advertising expense in cash, $3,200 (Check No. 265).

28   Sold ten laser printers for $14,800 on account to Wilks Company; Invoice No. 94-131; terms 2/10, n/30.

29   Sold five microcomputers for $19,600 on account to Mosley Company; Invoice No. 94-132; terms 2/10, n/30.

31   Bought computer software on account from the Ace Company, $3,560; Invoice No. 468; terms n/10.

Required   *a.*   Enter the transactions for May 1994 in the proper journals. All journal pages are to be numbered page 10.

b.   Post the individual accounts receivable and accounts payable transactions to the subsidiary ledgers. Only one customer, Thomas Gibson, owed the company a balance of $7,000 at the beginning of May. The company had one account payable to Carr Company for $4,000 at the beginning of the month. Andrews will not pay this $4,000 until a dispute over damaged merchandise is settled.

c.   Post the entries to the general ledger accounts shown below.

On May 1, 1994, the following accounts had balances:

Cash	$20,000
Accounts Receivable	7,000
Merchandise Inventory	20,000
Capital Stock.	30,000
Retained Earnings	13,000

d. Prepare a trial balance as of the end of the period. General ledger accounts are:

100	Cash	407	Rental Revenue
103	Accounts Receivable	410	Sales
105	Merchandise Inventory	411	Sales Discounts
172	Office Equipment	500	Purchases
200	Accounts Payable	501	Purchase Discounts
201	Notes Payable	505	Advertising Expense
300	Capital Stock	519	Delivery Expense
310	Retained Earnings		

SOLUTION TO DEMONSTRATION PROBLEM

a.

DISCOUNT SOFTWAREHOUSE
SALES JOURNAL   *Page 10*

Date		Customer	Invoice No.	Accounts Receivable Dr. 103 Sales Cr. 410	
				Amount	√
1994					
May	1	Baxter Company	94-128	12,000	√
	14	Mosley Company	94-129	8,000	√
	15	Wilks Company	94-130	2,800	√
	28	Wilks Company	94-131	14,800	√
	29	Mosley Company	94-132	19,600	√
				57,200	
				(103) (410)	

DISCOUNT SOFTWAREHOUSE
CASH RECEIPTS JOURNAL   *Page 10*

Cash Dr. 100	Sales Discounts Dr. 411	Date		Description	Sales Cr. 410	Accounts Receivable Cr. 103		Other Accounts Cr.			
						Amount	√	Account Title	Acct. No.	Amount	√
		1994									
38,000		May	7	Cash sales	38,000						
1,600			10	Rental revenue				Rental Revenue	407	1,600	√
11,760	240		11	Baxter Company—Invoice 94-128		12,000	√				
7,200			20	Cash sales	7,200						
3,080			20	Thomas Gibson		3,080	√				
4,480			22	Cash sales	4,480						
1,200			23	Cash sales	1,200						
7,840	160		24	Mosley Company—Invoice 94-129		8,000	√				
2,744	56		25	Wilks Company—Invoice 94-130		2,800	√				
77,904	456				50,880	25,880				1,600	
(100)	(411)				(410)	(103)				(X)	

**DISCOUNT SOFTWAREHOUSE
PURCHASES JOURNAL**

Page 10

Date		Creditor	Terms	Invoice No.	Purchases, Dr. 500 Accounts Payable Cr. 200	
					Amount	√
1994 May	4	Ace Company	n/10	152	8,400	√
	15	Ace Company	n/10	224	3,960	√
	16	Carr Company	2/10, n/30	324-CD	6,000	√
	31	Ace Company	n/10	468	3,560	√
					21,920	
					(500) (200)	

**DISCOUNT SOFTWAREHOUSE
CASH DISBURSEMENTS JOURNAL**

Page 10

Accounts Payable Dr. 200		Other Accounts Dr.				Date	Description	Check No.	Cash Cr. 100	Purchase Discounts Cr. 501
Amount	√	Account Title	Acct. No.	Amount	√					
						1994				
		Office Equipment	172	4,800	√	May 12	Office equipment	260	4,800	
8,400	√					14	Ace Company—Invoice 152	261	8,400	
3,960	√					25	Ace Company—Invoice 224	262	3,960	
6,000	√					26	Carr Company—Invoice 324-CD	263	5,880	120
		Delivery Expense	519	1,600	√	27	Delivery expense	264	1,600	
		Advertising Expense	505	3,200	√	27	Advertising expense	265	3,200	
18,360				9,600					27,840	120
(200)				(X)					(100)	(501)

**DISCOUNT SOFTWAREHOUSE
GENERAL JOURNAL**

Page 10

Date		Account Titles and Explanation	Post. Ref.	Debit	Credit
1994 May	17	Office Equipment	172	3800	
		Notes Payable	201		3800
		Terms of note, 30 days, 14%.			

b.

DISCOUNT SOFTWAREHOUSE
ACCOUNTS RECEIVABLE SUBSIDIARY LEDGER

Baxter Company

Date		Explanation	Post. Ref.	Debit	Credit	Balance
1994 May	1		S10	1 2 0 0 0		1 2 0 0 0
	11		CR10		1 2 0 0 0	– 0 –

Thomas Gibson

Date		Explanation	Post. Ref.	Debit	Credit	Balance
1994 May	1	Beginning balance				7 0 0 0
	20		CR10		3 0 8 0	3 9 2 0

Mosley Company

Date		Explanation	Post. Ref.	Debit	Credit	Balance
1994 May	14		S10	8 0 0 0		8 0 0 0
	24		CR10		8 0 0 0	– 0 –
	29		S10	1 9 6 0 0		1 9 6 0 0

Wilks Company

Date		Explanation	Post. Ref.	Debit	Credit	Balance
1994 May	15		S10	2 8 0 0		2 8 0 0
	25		CR10		2 8 0 0	– 0 –
	28		S10	1 4 8 0 0		1 4 8 0 0

DISCOUNT SOFTWAREHOUSE
ACCOUNTS PAYABLE SUBSIDIARY LEDGER

Ace Company

Date		Explanation	Post. Ref.	Debit	Credit	Balance
1994 May	4		P10		8 4 0 0	8 4 0 0
	14		CD10	8 4 0 0		– 0 –
	15		P10		3 9 6 0	3 9 6 0
	25		CD10	3 9 6 0		– 0 –
	31		P10		3 5 6 0	3 5 6 0

Carr Company

Date		Explanation	Post. Ref.	Debit	Credit	Balance
1994 May	1	Beginning balance				4000
	16		P10		6000	10000
	26		CD10	6000		4000

c.

DISCOUNT SOFTWAREHOUSE
GENERAL LEDGER

Cash   *Account No. 100*

Date		Explanation	Post. Ref.	Debit	Credit	Balance
1994 May	1	Beginning balance				20000
	31		CR10	77904		97904
	31		CD10		27840	70064

Accounts Receivable   *Account No. 103*

Date		Explanation	Post. Ref.	Debit	Credit	Balance
1994 May	1	Beginning balance				7000
	31		S10	57200		64200
	31		CR10		25880	38320

Merchandise Inventory   *Account No. 105*

Date		Explanation	Post. Ref.	Debit	Credit	Balance
1994 May	1	Beginning balance				20000

Office Equipment   *Account No. 172*

Date		Explanation	Post. Ref.	Debit	Credit	Balance
1994 May	11		CD10	4800		4800
	17		G10	3800		8600

Accounts Payable   *Account No. 200*

Date		Explanation	Post. Ref.	Debit	Credit	Balance
1994 May	1	Beginning balance				4 0 0 0
	31		P10		2 1 9 2 0	2 5 9 2 0
	31		CD10	1 8 3 6 0		7 5 6 0

Notes Payable   *Account No. 201*

Date		Explanation	Post. Ref.	Debit	Credit	Balance
1994 May	17		G10		3 8 0 0	3 8 0 0

Capital Stock   *Account No. 300*

Date		Explanation	Post. Ref.	Debit	Credit	Balance
1994 May	1	Beginning balance				3 0 0 0 0

Retained Earnings   *Account No. 310*

Date		Explanation	Post. Ref.	Debit	Credit	Balance
1994 May	1	Beginning balance				1 3 0 0 0

Rental Revenue   *Account No. 407*

Date		Explanation	Post. Ref.	Debit	Credit	Balance
1994 May	10		CR10		1 6 0 0	1 6 0 0

Sales   *Account No. 410*

Date		Explanation	Post. Ref.	Debit	Credit	Balance
1994 May	31		S10		5 7 2 0 0	5 7 2 0 0
	31		CR10		5 0 8 8 0	1 0 8 0 8 0

GENERAL LEDGER (concluded)

Sales Discounts   *Account No. 411*

Date		Explanation	Post. Ref.	Debit	Credit	Balance
1994 May	31		CR10	4 5 6		4 5 6

Purchases   *Account No. 500*

Date		Explanation	Post. Ref.	Debit	Credit	Balance
1994 May	31		P10	2 1 9 2 0		2 1 9 2 0

Purchase Discounts   *Account No. 501*

Date		Explanation	Post. Ref.	Debit	Credit	Balance
1994 May	31		CD10		1 2 0	1 2 0

Advertising Expense   *Account No. 505*

Date		Explanation	Post. Ref.	Debit	Credit	Balance
1994 May	27		CD10	3 2 0 0		3 2 0 0

Delivery Expense   *Account No. 519*

Date		Explanation	Post. Ref.	Debit	Credit	Balance
1994 May	27		CD10	1 6 0 0		1 6 0 0

d.

DISCOUNT SOFTWAREHOUSE
Trial Balance
May 31, 1994

Acct. No.	Account Title	Debits	Credits
100	Cash	$ 70,064	
103	Accounts Receivable.	38,320	
105	Merchandise Inventory.	20,000	
172	Office Equipment	8,600	
200	Accounts Payable		$ 7,560
201	Notes Payable.		3,800
300	Capital Stock		30,000
310	Retained Earnings		13,000
407	Rental Revenue		1,600
410	Sales.		108,080
411	Sales Discounts	456	
500	Purchases	21,920	
501	Purchase Discounts		120
505	Advertising Expense	3,200	
519	Delivery Expense	1,600	
		$164,160	$164,160

NEW TERMS

Arithmetic unit A central component of a computer that performs simple computations and comparisons. *344*

Cash disbursements journal A special journal used for all payments (or outflows) of cash by the company. *313*

Cash receipts journal A special journal used for all transactions involving inflows of cash into the company. *313*

Console The component of an electronic computer system that enables an operator to communicate manually with the system and start, stop, or alter operations. *344*

Control account An account in the general ledger that shows the total balance of all the subsidiary accounts related to it. *311*

Control unit The unit of a computer that interprets the program, assigns storage space, and alters the sequence of operations if so instructed by the program. *344*

File A grouping of similar data arranged in an identifiable order. *345*

General journal A general-purpose journal used to record all transactions that cannot be entered in one of the special journals. *313*

Instructions Coded information that causes the computer's control unit to perform specified operations. *344*

Microcomputers Desktop computers that can be used for word processing, graphics, database management, and spreadsheets; and to maintain the accounting records for a small business; designed for use by one person. *331*

Minicomputers Medium-sized computers that can be used to maintain the accounting records for a small or medium-sized business; designed for use by several persons. *331*

Other accounts Miscellaneous accounts. *316*

Peripheral equipment Can be attached to a computer and used mainly to feed unprocessed information into the computer and receive the output of processed information. *344*

Program The set of instructions submitted to the computer that specifies the operations to be performed and the correct sequence. *344*

Purchases journal A special journal used to record all purchases of merchandise on account (on credit). *313*

Sales journal A special journal used to record all sales of merchandise on account (on credit). *313*

Schedule of accounts payable Prepared at the end of the period to make certain that the total of the balances in the accounts payable subsidiary ledger accounts agrees with the balance in the Accounts Payable control account balance. *321*

Schedule of accounts receivable Prepared at the end of the period to ensure that the total of the balances in the accounts receivable subsidiary ledger accounts agrees with the Accounts Receivable control account balance. *317*

Service bureau A large computer facility that takes data from a client, enters the data into its computer, produces required statements or reports, and returns this output to the client. *333*

Special journal A book of original entry that records

one particular type of transaction, such as sales on account, cash receipts, purchases on account, or cash disbursements. *312*

Storage unit   A computer's internal memory system; it serves to record and retain data until they are required by and transferred to other areas of the computer. *344*

Subsidiary ledger   A group of related accounts showing the details of the balance of a general ledger control account. *311*

Subsidiary ledger accounts   Accounts in a subsidiary ledger that show the details supporting the related general ledger control account balance. *311*

Time sharing   A system whereby several users utilize the same host computer to process data. *333*

SELF-TEST

True-False

Indicate whether each of the following statements is true or false.

1. An accounting system is a set of records plus the procedures and equipment regularly used to process business transactions.

2. Subsidiary ledgers can only be established for accounts receivable and accounts payable.

3. When special journals are in use, there is no need for a general journal.

4. The sales journal should only be used for sales of merchandise on account, and the purchases journal should only be used for purchases of merchandise on account.

5. All of the column totals in the cash receipts and cash disbursements journals should be posted to general ledger accounts at the end of the period.

6. All companies should use computers to process their data.

Multiple-Choice

Select the best answer for each of the following questions.

1. The orderly and efficient processing of data is necessary so that (select the *false* answer):
   a. Results of operations and financial position of the firm are reported on a timely basis.
   b. Bills are paid when due.
   c. Proper quantities and items of inventory are sent to customers.
   d. Special journals can be used.

2. Which of the following statements is true regarding control accounts and subsidiary ledgers?
   a. Subsidiary ledger accounts should be posted daily, but control accounts do not need to be posted daily.
   b. Both subsidiary ledger accounts and control accounts should be posted daily.
   c. Neither subsidiary ledger accounts nor control accounts need to be posted daily.
   d. Subsidiary ledger accounts and control accounts can only be used when special journals are used.

3. Which of the following is true regarding the sales journal?
   a. It can only have one money column.

b. It should be used for all sales of merchandise.
   c. Usually only the column total(s) is (are) posted.
   d. It can be used even when there are many departments for which sales need to be recorded separately.

4. When special journals are used, the general journal would be used for all of the following journal entries *except:*
   a. Adjusting entries.
   b. Closing entries.
   c. Purchase allowances.
   d. Purchase discounts.

5. Which of the following statements is *true* regarding alternative methods of processing data?
   a. "One write" or "pegboard" systems are no longer in use.
   b. Bookkeeping machines are no longer in general use.
   c. Minicomputers have almost completely replaced microcomputers and mainframe computers in performing accounting tasks.
   d. Service bureaus and time-sharing terminals are no longer in use.

Now turn to page 369 to check your answers.

QUESTIONS

1. The processing of data is usually very costly. Why bother with this task?

2. Is the balance of a control account equal to the total of its subsidiary accounts at all times? Explain.

3. In a manual system, the subsidiary accounts receivable and accounts payable accounts usually do not have account numbers. Why?

4. What is the definition of a special journal?

5. Describe the purpose of each of the following

journals by giving the types of entries that would be recorded in each: sales, purchases, cash receipts, cash disbursements, and general.

6. Why might a sales journal or a purchases journal have more than one money column?

7. Why are some column totals in special journals posted while others are not?

8. Why does the purchases journal have a Terms column while the sales journal does not?

9. How can you tell whether a special journal has been completely posted? Describe the posting marks.

10. What is the purpose in preparing a schedule of accounts receivable and a schedule of accounts payable?

11. Of what use is the general journal when special journals are used?

12. Identify the alternative methods of processing data. What factors should a company consider in deciding which alternative to select?

13. *(Based on Appendix 7–A)* Describe the nature of computerized accounting systems designed for the microcomputer.

14. *(Based on Appendix 4–A)* Describe how information is entered into an electronic spreadsheet.

15. *(Based on Appendix 4–A)* For what purposes are microcomputers used in public accounting practice?

16. *(Based on Appendix 4–B)* What are the three basic components of a computer and what is the function of each?

17. *Real world question* Refer to "A Broader Perspective" on page 342. What are some of the software packages that are most frequently recommended by CPA firms to their clients? What functions do these highly recommended packages perform?

The Coca-Cola Company

18. *Real world question* Refer to Note 18 in The Coca-Cola Company annual report in Appendix E at the end of the text. If you were creating the accounting system, into what lines of business would you segregate revenues and expenses?

EXERCISES

Exercise 7–1

Prepare T-accounts to show Accounts Receivable control and subsidiary accounts (L.O. 1)

The correct accounts receivable subsidiary ledger account balances for a company are as follows at the end of an accounting period:

Dobbins.	$3,600
Grant	4,800
Nickel.	7,200
Walters	6,000

Using T-accounts, show how these accounts would appear and what the balance on this same date would be in the Accounts Receivable control account in the general ledger. If the balance in the control account is $24,000, what should be done?

Exercise 7–2

Match transactions with journals in which they would be recorded (L.O. 2, 3)

Match each transaction in column A with the appropriate journal in column B in which it would be recorded. Assume each journal listed is used as a book of original entry and is designed as illustrated in the chapter.

Column A	Column B
1. Purchased merchandise on account.	a. Sales journal.
2. Recorded depreciation expense.	b. Cash receipts journal.
3. Sold merchandise on account.	c. Purchases journal.
4. Sold merchandise for cash.	d. Cash disbursements journal.
5. Collected cash on account.	e. General journal.
6. Gave a note to a trade creditor.	
7. Received cash for services performed.	
8. Granted a sales allowance to a customer.	
9. Paid rent for the month.	
10. Received notice of a purchase allowance from a trade creditor.	
11. Paid a trade creditor.	
12. Recorded closing entries at the end of the period.	

Exercise 7–3

Design sales journal for company with three selling departments (L.O. 3, 4)

You are employed by a company that has three selling departments. You are asked to design a sales journal that will provide a departmental breakdown of credit sales. Give the column headings you would use and describe how postings would be made.

Exercise 7–4

Post data from cash receipts journal to T-accounts (L.O. 4)

The column totals of a cash receipts journal are as follows:

Cash Dr..	$78,800
Sales Discounts Dr..	400
Sales Cr.	40,000
Accounts Receivable Cr..	20,000
Other Accounts Cr. (sold land at cost for $18,000 and sold scrap for $1,200.	19,200

Using T-accounts, post the amounts that appear in the cash receipts journal. When would the individual amounts in the Accounts Receivable Cr. column be posted? When would the information in the Other Accounts Cr. column be posted?

Exercise 7–5

Determine postings to general ledger (L.O. 4)

Which of the following amounts would be posted to the general ledger?

a. The Cash Cr. column total in the cash disbursements journal.
b. The Other Accounts Dr. column total in the cash disbursements journal.
c. The individual items in the purchases journal.
d. The individual items in the sales journal.
e. The column total in the sales journal.

Exercise 7–6

Indicate how special journal columns should be posted (L.O. 4)

Using the following legend, indicate how the data in each special journal column should be posted:

1—Do not post the individual amounts in the column, but post the column total to general ledger account(s) at the end of the accounting period.
2—Post the individual amounts in the column to subsidiary ledger accounts during the accounting period, and post the column total to general ledger account(s) at the end of the accounting period.
3—Post the individual amounts in the column to general ledger accounts during the accounting period and do not post the column total.

Special journals:
Sales journal:
  Accounts Receivable Dr., Sales Cr.. 2

Cash receipts journal:
  Cash Dr. . . . . ____
  Sales Discounts Dr. . . . ____
  Sales Cr. . . . ____
  Accounts Receivable Cr. . . . ____
  Other Accounts Cr.. . . ____

Purchases journal:
  Purchases Dr., Accounts Payable Cr. . . . ____

Cash disbursements journal:
  Accounts Payable Dr.. . . ____
  Supplies Expense Dr.. . . ____
  Other Accounts Dr.. . . ____
  Cash Cr. . . . ____
  Purchase Discounts Cr.. . . ____

Exercise 7–7

Answer multiple-choice questions
(L.O. 1, 3, 5)

For each of the following questions, select the best answer.

1. Select the **true** statement regarding control accounts and subsidiary accounts.
   a. A control account must equal the total of the related subsidiary accounts at all times during the accounting period.
   b. The only subsidiary accounts are those for accounts receivable and accounts payable.
   c. Both control and subsidiary accounts appear in the general ledger.
   d. A company has fewer control accounts than subsidiary accounts.

2. The sales journal is:
   a. Used only to record sales on credit.
   b. Used to record all sales.
   c. Used only to record cash sales.
   d. None of the above.

3. The cash receipts journal:
   a. Cannot be used to record cash sales.
   b. Is used to record amounts received on accounts receivable and all other cash receipts.
   c. Cannot be used to record the sale of a plant asset for cash.
   d. Usually has only one money column.

4. The cash disbursements journal:
   a. Cannot be used to record purchases on account.
   b. Is used only to record the payment of accounts payable.
   c. Cannot be used to record the purchase of a plant asset for cash.
   d. Usually has only one money column.

5. Which of the following statements is **true?**
   a. The end result (financial statements) is different depending on which method of processing is used.
   b. One method of processing data is the best for all companies.
   c. Microcomputers can be used to maintain the accounting records of a small company.
   d. The purchase of a mainframe in-house computer is almost never justified.

Exercise 7–8

Answer multiple-choice questions (based on Appendix 7–A)
(L.O. 6)

Answer the following multiple-choice questions regarding the use of microcomputers in accounting. Select the best answer.

1. Characteristics of microcomputer accounting system packages include (select the **false** statement):
   a. Many packages have a password that must be used to get into the accounting system.
   b. These packages are usually menu driven.
   c. These packages usually cost in excess of $2,500.
   d. Modules in the packages generally include: General Ledger, Accounts Receivable, Accounts Payable, Inventory Management, Payroll, and Invoicing.

2. All but which one of the following is a characteristic of computer spreadsheets?
   a. The user can play "what if" games by changing various numbers or formulas in the spreadsheet, and the program will recalculate all of the schedules automatically.
   b. Many spreadsheet programs allow the user to construct various types of graphs showing the data contained in the spreadsheet schedules.
   c. The schedules that appear on the user's computer screen can be printed out on paper for use by other people.
   d. Because the spreadsheet packages are so well designed, it is virtually impossible to use them inefficiently.

3. A database management system (select the **true** statement):
   a. Stores related data together independent of any one application.

b. Enables one item of information to be stored in only one file but to be used by all the applications.

c. Uses English-like commands.

d. All of the above.

4. Which of the following statements is **false**?

a. Artificial intelligence is a much narrower concept than expert systems.

b. The microcomputer is helpful in selecting statistical samples and in evaluating the results.

c. Microcomputers are used to prepare tax returns and are used extensively in income and estate tax planning.

d. Complicated financial modeling can be performed on microcomputers.

Exercise 7–9

Answer matching question regarding computer terminology (based on Appendixes 7–A and 7–B) (L.O. 7)

Match each description in column A with the appropriate term in column B.

Column A	Column B
1. A computer's internal memory system.	a. Program.
2. Equipment that is attached to the computer.	b. Arithmetic unit.
3. A part of the computer that interprets the program.	c. Service bureau.
4. Any grouping of similar items of data arranged in some identifiable order.	d. Peripheral equipment.
	e. Microcomputer
5. A part of a computer that does the computing.	f. File.
6. A set of instructions submitted to a computer that specifies the operations to be performed and their correct sequence.	g. Storage unit.
	h. Control unit.
7. A large computer facility that rents out time for data processing.	
8. A small computer that can be used to maintain the accounting records for a small company.	

PROBLEMS: SERIES A

Problem 7–1A

Record transactions in sales and purchases journals; post to T-accounts in general and subsidiary ledgers (L.O. 1, 3, 4)

a. Camp Stereo Store sold merchandise on account to the following customers on the dates indicated:

Date	Customer	Invoice No.	Amount
1994			
Dec. 2	Susan Moore	300	$ 400
8	Margaret Allen	301	4,800
14	Barbara Malloy	302	3,600
21	Janet Gibson	303	2,400
31	Susan Miller	304	1,800

Required

Record the transactions on page 5 of a sales journal. Using T-accounts, post the data to accounts in the general ledger and accounts receivable subsidiary ledger. The general ledger account numbers are:

Accounts Receivable	103
Sales	410

b. Emery Appliance Store purchased merchandise on account from the following companies on the dates indicated:

Date	Creditor	Terms	Invoice No.	Amount
1994				
Sept. 2	Baker Company	2/20, n/60	642	$15,000
7	Dexter Company	2/10, n/30	441	18,000
15	Hanley Corporation	2/EOM	543	6,000
23	Stanton Company	1/15, n/30	286	13,500
28	Welker Corporation	2/10, n/30	324	22,500

Required   Record the transactions on page 20 of a purchases journal. Using T-accounts, post the data to accounts in the general ledger and accounts payable subsidiary ledger. The general ledger account numbers are:

Accounts Payable 200
Purchases. 500

Problem 7–2A

Journalize transactions in appropriate journal; post to accounts in general and accounts receivable subsidiary ledgers; prepare schedule of accounts receivable (L.O. 1–4)

On June 30, 1994, the Accounts Receivable control account balance on the books of Ricardo's Wholesale Shoe Company was equal to the total balances of the accounts in the accounts receivable subsidiary ledger. The balances were as follows: Accounts Receivable control account (Account No. 103), $68,720; Billings, Inc., $26,400, Haygood Products, Inc., $12,320; and Johnson Company, $30,000.

Transactions (ignore the fact that usually the terms to all customers are the same)

July 1   Sales of merchandise on account to Johnson Company, $4,800; Invoice No. 306; terms n/30.

3   Cash sales, $13,800.

5   Received cash for land sold at its original cost of $20,000.

5   Received $18,000 cash as partial collection of amount due today from Billings, Inc. No discount was allowed.

9   Sold merchandise on account to Glasco Company, $3,600; Invoice No. 307; terms 3/10, n/30.

11   Received $12,073.60 from Haygood Products, Inc. A discount of 2% of the account receivable balance was granted.

16   Sold merchandise on account to Wilson Company, $4,000; Invoice No. 308; terms n/30.

18   Sold merchandise on account to Haygood Products, Inc., $7,200; Invoice No. 309; terms n/30.

20   Allowed Haygood Products, Inc., credit for $1,000 on goods returned to Ricardo's on Invoice No. 309.

22   Sold $4,800 of merchandise to Billings, Inc.; Invoice No. 310; terms n/10.

23   Received $16,000 cash on balance due today from Johnson Company. No discount was taken.

25   Sold $6,000 of merchandise on account to Billings, Inc.; Invoice No. 311; terms n/10.

27   Allowed Billings, Inc., credit of $400 on goods sold July 25 and damaged in transit due to faulty packing by Ricardo's.

31   Sold $5,200 of merchandise on account to May Company; Invoice No. 312; terms 2/10, n/30.

31   Cash sales, $82,400.

Required   Prepare a sales journal (Illustration 7.1) and cash receipts journal (Illustration 7.2). Also set up a general journal. Then, using the above information:

a.   Completely journalize each transaction in the appropriate journal.

b.   Post only the amounts pertaining to accounts receivable to the subsidiary accounts and to the control account. You will have to set up some additional subsidiary accounts. Keep all subsidiary accounts in alphabetical order. You will need additional accounts for Glasco Company, May Company, and Wilson Company.

c.   Prepare a schedule of accounts receivable at July 31, 1994, and compare it with the balance of the control account at the same date.

Problem 7–3A

Journalize transactions in appropriate journal; post to general and subsidiary ledger accounts; prepare schedule of accounts payable
(L.O. 1–4)

On June 30, 1994, the Accounts Payable control account on the books of Ricardo's Wholesale Shoe Company was equal to the total of the accounts in the accounts payable subsidiary ledger. The balances were as follows: Accounts Payable control account (Account No. 200), $62,000; Gate Company, $28,200; Jones Corporation, $9,800; and White Company, $24,000.

Transactions

July 1   Purchased merchandise on account costing $20,000 from Hall Company; Invoice No. 562; terms 2/10, n/30.
      2   Paid Gate Company $20,000 on account with Check No. 101. No discount was available when the purchase was originally made.
      3   Paid rent for the month of July with Check No. 102, $2,400.
      5   Gave Jones Corporation a 60-day, 12% note for the amount owed.
      6   Purchased merchandise on account costing $10,000 from Gate Company; Invoice No. 261; terms 2/10, n/30.
      9   Paid $19,600 to Hall Company on the July 1 purchase with Check No. 103.
     11   Paid $8,000 for a life insurance policy on top executives to cover the period from August 1, 1994, to July 31, 1995. Used Check No. 104.
     17   Purchased merchandise on account costing $16,000 from Hall Company; Invoice No. 581; terms 2/10, n/30.
     21   Received credit from White Company for $4,000 on merchandise returned to it. No discount was available as of the date of purchase.
     23   Purchased merchandise on account costing $6,000 from Andrews Corporation; Invoice No. 1031; terms n/30.
     25   Paid $12,000 to White Company with Check No. 105. No discount was allowed as of the date of purchase.
     27   Purchased merchandise on account costing $14,000 from Sand Corporation; Invoice No. 328; terms 2/10, n/30.
     29   Paid Hall Company $8,000 on the purchase of July 17, Check No. 106.
     31   Purchased merchandise on account costing $16,000 from Dodge Company; Invoice No. 168; terms 2/20, n/60.

Required   Prepare a purchases journal (Illustration 7.4) and a cash disbursements journal (Illustration 7.5). The Supplies Expense Dr. column is not needed in the cash disbursements journal. Also set up a general journal. Then, using the above information:

a.   Completely journalize each transaction in the appropriate journal.

b.   Post only the amounts pertaining to accounts payable to the subsidiary accounts and to the control account. You should arrange all subsidiary accounts in alphabetical order. You will need additional accounts for Andrews Corporation, Hall Company, Dodge Company, and Sand Corporation.

c.   Prepare a schedule of accounts payable at July 31, 1994, and compare it with the balance of the control account at the same date.

Problem 7–4A

Post data from journals to ledger accounts after entering beginning balances in the accounts; prepare trial balance (L.O. 4)

The post-closing trial balance of Lansing Department Store as of November 30, 1994, was as follows:

LANSING DEPARTMENT STORE
Post-Closing Trial Balance
November 30, 1994

	Debits	Credits
Cash	$ 17,500	
Accounts Receivable	13,750	
Notes Receivable	1,250	
Merchandise Inventory—Men's Clothing	3,750	
Merchandise Inventory—Women's Clothing	4,500	
Merchandise Inventory—Appliances	3,000	
Merchandise Inventory—Furniture	7,000	
Merchandise Inventory—Bargain Basement	1,750	
Merchandise Inventory—Other Departments	1,250	
Office Equipment	5,000	
Accumulated Depreciation—Office Equipment		$ 2,000
Buildings	70,000	
Accumulated Depreciation—Buildings		13,750
Accounts Payable		10,876
Capital Stock		50,000
Retained Earnings		52,124
	$128,750	$128,750

The company has five major selling departments and several minor ones. Separate general ledger accounts are maintained for sales and purchases for each of the major departments. Sales and purchases for the minor departments are grouped under Sales—Other Departments and Purchases—Other Departments.

The December transactions were recorded in the company's five journals: sales journal, cash receipts journal, purchases journal, cash disbursements journal, and general journal. At December 31, 1994, the column totals in the sales journal were as follows:

Accounts Receivable Dr.	Sales— Men's Clothing Cr.	Sales— Women's Clothing Cr.	Sales— Appliances Cr.	Sales— Furniture Cr.	Sales— Bargain Basement Cr.	Sales— Other Departments Cr.
112,750	20,000	22,500	17,500	30,000	15,000	7,750

The column totals of the cash receipts journal were as follows:

Cash Dr.	Sales Discounts Dr.	Sales— Men's Clothing Cr.	Sales— Women's Clothing Cr.	Sales— Appliances Cr.	Sales— Furniture Cr.	Sales— Bargain Basement Cr.	Sales— Other Departments Cr.	Accounts Receivable Cr.	Other Accounts Cr.
166,500	1,538	11,250	12,500	10,000	16,250	6,000	6,750	96,412	8,876

The entries in the Other Accounts Cr. column resulted from the collection of $6,500 of rental revenue (December 8) and $2,376 of miscellaneous revenue from the sale of scrap (December 14).

The column totals in the purchases journal were as follows:

Purchases— Men's Clothing Dr.	Purchases— Women's Clothing Dr.	Purchases— Appliances Dr.	Purchases— Furniture Dr.	Purchases— Bargain Basement Dr.	Purchases— Other Departments Dr.	Accounts Payable Cr.
26,250	27,000	13,750	25,500	18,750	10,874	122,124

The column totals of the cash disbursements journal were:

Accounts Payable Dr.	Supplies Expense Dr.	Other Accounts Dr.	Cash Cr.	Purchase Discounts Cr.
96,500	13,750	11,388	120,888	750

The entries in the Other Accounts Dr. column result from the payment of $638 for ordinary repairs to the buildings (December 15) and $10,750 for the purchase of a small storage building (December 22).

The general journal includes the following entry at the date indicated:

Dec.	18	Office Equipment	2,000	
		Notes Payable		2,000

Required The beginning balances should be entered in the general ledger accounts. These balances are given in the November 30, 1994, trial balance. Then, post the data from the journals. After posting, prepare a trial balance as of December 31, 1994.

Problem 7–5A
Journalize transactions; post to general ledger accounts; prepare trial balance
(L.O. 3, 4)

Middleton Wholesale Food Company uses special journals for sales, cash receipts, purchases, and cash disbursements, as well as a general journal. These journals follow the same general design as those illustrated in this chapter.

Transactions

Dec. 1 Purchased merchandise on account from Wemberton Company, $22,400; Invoice No. C1109; terms 2/10, n/30.

   2 Purchased merchandise on account from Ray Company, $12,800; Invoice No. 1888Z; terms n/10.

   3 Bought office equipment from Dynasty Company, $31,040; Invoice No. 854. Gave a 30-day, 12% note in payment.

   5 Purchased merchandise on account from Cain Company, $17,600; Invoice No. X9784; terms 2/10, n/30.

   6 Cash sales, $22,720.

   7 Collected rent revenue for December, $30,400.

   8 Sold $16,000 of merchandise on account to Jonathan, Inc.; Invoice No. 3345; terms 2/10, n/30.

   10 Sold $22,400 of merchandise on account to Zips Company; Invoice No. 3346; terms 2/10, n/30.

   11 Sold $25,600 of merchandise on account to Timber Company; Invoice No. 3347; terms 2/10, n/30.

Dec. 12 Paid Wemberton Company for purchase of December 1 with Check No. 201.

12 Paid Ray Company for purchase of December 2 with Check No. 202.

14 Paid Cain Company for purchase of December 5 with Check No. 203.

16 Cash sales, $63,040.

18 Collected amount due on sale of December 8 to Jonathan, Inc.

20 Collected amount due on sale of December 10 to Zips Company.

21 Collected amount due on sale of December 11 to Timber Company.

23 Cash sales, $40,000.

24 Paid *The Courier News* for advertising expense, $2,400 (Check No. 204).

26 Sold $19,200 of merchandise on account to Timber Company; Invoice No. 3348; terms 2/10, n/30.

26 Sold $44,800 of merchandise on account to Trustee Company; Invoice No. 3349; terms 2/10, n/30.

27 Sold $95,040 of merchandise on account to Clean Company; Invoice No. 3350; terms 2/10, n/30.

28 Purchased merchandise from Ray Company, $7,500; Invoice No. 19272; terms n/10.

30 Purchased merchandise on account from Cain Company, $8,000; Invoice No. X9924; terms 2/10, n/30.

Required a. Enter the transactions for December 1994 in the proper journals. All journals are to be numbered page 40.

b. Post individual receivables and payables to the accounts receivable subsidiary ledger and the accounts payable subsidiary ledger, respectively.

c. Post the entries to the general ledger accounts. The Cash account and the Capital Stock account each have a beginning balance of $80,000. The Retained Earnings account has no beginning balance because the business was organized at the end of November.

d. Prepare a trial balance as of the end of the period. General ledger accounts are:

Acct. No.	Account Title	Acct. No.	Account Title
100	Cash	407	Rental Revenue
103	Accounts Receivable	410	Sales
172	Office Equipment	411	Sales Discounts
200	Accounts Payable	500	Purchases
201	Notes Payable	501	Purchase Discounts
300	Capital Stock	505	Advertising Expense
310	Retained Earnings		

PROBLEMS: SERIES B

Problem 7–1B

Record transactions in sales and purchases journals; post to T-accounts in general and subsidiary ledgers

(L.O. 1, 3, 4)

a. Sports Clothing Store sold goods on account to the following customers on the dates indicated:

Date	Customer	Invoice No.	Amount
1994			
June 1	Simon Walls	200	$1,800
4	Mark White	201	1,200
12	Cassey Hanson	202	2,400
18	Marianne Burke	203	3,600
29	Roger Jones	204	3,000

Required   Record the transactions on page 1 of a sales journal. Then, using T-accounts, post the data to accounts in the general ledger and accounts receivable subsidiary ledger.
The general ledger account numbers are:

Accounts Receivable 103
Sales 410

b.   Pender's Book Store purchased merchandise on account from the following companies on the dates indicated:

Date	Creditor	Terms	Invoice No.	Amount
1994				
July 3	Able Press	2/10, n/30	240	$ 750
5	Decker, Inc.	1/15, n/30	360	375
14	Gifts & More, Inc.	2/20, n/30	142	1,500
22	Stanton Publishers, Inc.	2/20, n/60	58	1,875
30	Wells Company	2/10, n/30	410	2,625

Required   Record the transactions on page 10 of a purchases journal. Then, using T-accounts, post the data to accounts in the general ledger and accounts payable subsidiary ledger.
The general ledger account numbers are:

Accounts Payable. 200
Purchases 500

Problem 7–2B

Journalize transactions in appropriate journals; post to accounts in general ledger and accounts receivable subsidiary ledger; prepare schedule of accounts receivable (L.O. 1–4)

On August 31, 1994, the Accounts Receivable control account on the books of Reynolds Wholesale Furniture Store was equal to the total of the accounts in the accounts receivable subsidiary ledger. The balances were as follows: Accounts Receivable control account (Account No. 103), $90,000; Battle Corporation, $36,000; East Corporation, 24,000; and Ferguson Company, $30,000.

Transactions (ignore the fact that normally the terms to all customers are the same)

Sept. 1   Received $13,720 from Ferguson Company. A discount of $280 had been taken.
2   On this date, merchandise was sold on account for $22,000 to Olivia Company; Invoice No. 501; terms 2/20, n/30.
4   Cash sales, $50,000.
7   Received $18,000 on account from Battle Corporation. No discount was taken.
8   Received $40,000 cash for land sold at its original cost.
12   Sold merchandise on account to Ferguson Company, $18,000; Invoice No. 502; terms n/30.
15   Received payment for $10,000 of the merchandise purchased on September 2 by Olivia Company. The discount was taken on this payment.
18   Sold merchandise on account to the Miles Corporation, $68,000; Invoice No. 503; terms n/30.
21   Cash sales, $114,000.
23   Allowed $2,000 credit to Miles Corporation for goods returned.
26   Sold merchandise on account to Newton Company, $20,000; Invoice No. 504; terms 2/20, n/30.
29   Received $20,000 cash from Miles Corporation to apply against the amount due on Invoice No. 503.
30   Cash sales were $78,000.

Required   Prepare a sales journal (Illustration 7.1) and a cash receipts journal (Illustration 7.2). Also set up a general journal. Then, using the above information:

a. Completely journalize the transactions in the appropriate journals.

b. Post only the amounts pertaining to accounts receivable to the subsidiary accounts and to the control account. You will have to prepare additional subsidiary accounts and should keep them all in alphabetical order. You will need additional accounts for Miles Corporation, Newton Company, and Olivia Company.

c. Prepare a schedule of accounts receivable at September 30, 1994, and compare it with the balance of the control account at the same date.

Problem 7–3B

Journalize transactions in appropriate journal; post to general ledger and subsidiary ledger accounts; prepare schedule of accounts payable (L.O. 1–4)

On August 31, 1994, the Accounts Payable control account on the books of Reynolds Wholesale Furniture Store was equal to the total of the accounts in the accounts payable subsidiary ledger. The balances were as follows: Accounts Payable control account (Account No. 200), $72,000; Bond Corporation, $16,000; Heizburg Company, $32,000; and Zales Corporation, $24,000.

Transactions

Sept. 1 Purchased merchandise on account costing $30,000 from Worling Company; Invoice No. 542; terms 2/10, n/30.

3 Paid Bond Corporation $16,000 with Check No. 451. The original discount of 2% was not taken because the discount period had expired.

4 Paid rent for the month of September, $1,000, with Check No. 452.

5 Paid Heizburg Company $18,000 on account with Check No. 453. No discount was offered.

6 Gave Heizburg Company a $14,000, 30-day, 12% note for the balance due.

7 Purchased merchandise on account costing $16,000 from York Corporation; Invoice No. 982; terms 2/10, n/30.

8 Purchased merchandise on account costing $18,000 from Bond Corporation; Invoice No. 1522; terms 2/10, n/30.

9 Received credit from York Corporation for returning $2,000 of the $16,000 of merchandise purchased.

12 Paid Worling Company the amount due on the purchase of September 1 with Check No. 454.

15 Purchased merchandise on account costing $24,000 from New Point Corporation; Invoice No. 841; terms n/30.

17 Paid Bond Corporation the amount due on the purchase of September 8 with Check No. 455.

20 Purchased merchandise on account costing $26,000 from Bond Corporation; Invoice No. 1566; terms 2/10, n/30.

22 Purchased merchandise on account costing $14,000 from Quarter Company; Invoice No. 1910; terms n/30.

25 Paid $16,000 on account to New Point Corporation on the purchase of September 15 with Check No. 456.

29 Received $6,000 credit from Bond Corporation for returning part of the merchandise purchased on September 20.

30 Purchased merchandise on account having a cost of $10,000 from Jane Company; Invoice No. 2125; terms n/60.

Required Prepare a purchases journal (Illustration 7.4) and cash disbursements journal (Illustration 7.5). The Supplies Expense column is not needed in the cash disbursements journal. Also set up a general journal. Then, using the above information:

a. Completely journalize each transaction in the appropriate journals.

b. Post only the amounts pertaining to accounts payable to the subsidiary accounts and to the control account. You will have to create some additional subsidiary accounts. You should arrange all subsidiary accounts in alphabetical order. You will need additional accounts for Jane Company, New Point Corporation, Quarter Company, Worling Company, and York Corporation.

c. Prepare a schedule of accounts payable at September 30, 1994, and compare it with the balance of the control account at the same date.

Problem 7–4B

Post data from journals to ledger accounts after entering beginning balances in the accounts; prepare trial balance (L.O. 4)

A post-closing trial balance of Sanchez Department Store as of November 30, 1994, was as follows:

SANCHEZ DEPARTMENT STORE
Post-Closing Trial Balance
November 30, 1994

	Debits	Credits
Cash	$140,000	
Accounts Receivable	96,000	
Merchandise Inventory—Men's Clothing	48,000	
Merchandise Inventory—Women's Clothing	80,000	
Merchandise Inventory—Shoes	8,000	
Merchandise Inventory—Cosmetics and Jewelry . . .	32,000	
Merchandise Inventory—Sporting Goods	44,000	
Merchandise Inventory—Miscellaneous	10,400	
Office Equipment	40,000	
Accumulated Depreciation—Office Equipment		$ 13,600
Land	25,280	
Buildings	320,000	
Accumulated Depreciation—Buildings		77,600
Accounts Payable		80,800
Notes Payable		8,000
Capital Stock		400,000
Retained Earnings		263,680
	$843,680	$843,680

The company has five major selling departments and several minor ones. Separate general ledger accounts are maintained for sales and purchases for each of the major departments. Sales and purchases for the minor departments are grouped under Sales—Miscellaneous and Purchases—Miscellaneous.

The December transactions were recorded in the company's five journals: sales journal, cash receipts journal, purchases journal, cash disbursements journal, and general journal. At December 31, 1994, the column totals in the sales journal were as follows:

Accounts Receivable Dr.	Sales— Men's Clothing Cr.	Sales— Women's Clothing Cr.	Sales— Shoes Cr.	Sales— Cosmetics and Jewelry Cr.	Sales— Sporting Goods Cr.	Sales— Miscellaneous Cr.
324,000	80,000	100,000	33,600	32,000	62,400	16,000

The column totals of the cash receipts journal were as follows:

Cash Dr.	Sales Discounts Dr.	Sales— Men's Clothing Cr.	Sales— Women's Clothing Cr.	Sales— Shoes Cr.	Sales— Cosmetics and Jewelry Cr.	Sales— Sporting Goods Cr.	Sales— Miscel- laneous Cr.	Accounts Receivable Cr.	Other Accounts Cr.
560,800	4,480	48,000	64,000	26,400	48,000	25,600	32,000	288,000	33,280

The entries in the Other Accounts Cr. column resulted from the sale of land at cost of $25,280 (December 4) and $8,000 of revenue from the operation of a delivery service for other companies (December 31).

The column totals in the purchases journal were as follows:

Purchases— Men's Clothing Dr.	Purchases— Women's Clothing Dr.	Purchases— Shoes Dr.	Purchases— Cosmetics and Jewelry Dr.	Purchases— Sporting Goods Dr.	Purchases— Miscellaneous Dr.	Accounts Payable Cr.
112,000	152,000	48,000	60,000	111,200	32,000	515,200

The column totals of the cash disbursements journal were as follows:

Accounts Payable Dr.	Supplies Expense Dr.	Other Accounts Dr.	Cash Cr.	Purchase Discounts Cr.
468,000	77,600	63,200	597,600	11,200

The entries in the Other Accounts Dr. column resulted from the payment of $7,680 for a delivery truck (December 7) and $55,520 for the purchase of a garage (December 15).

The general journal includes the following entry at the date indicated:

Dec.	21	Buildings.	69,600	
		Notes Payable		69,600

Required The beginning balances should be entered in the general ledger accounts. These balances are given in the November 31, 1994, trial balance. Then, post the data from the journals. Prepare a trial balance as of December 31, 1994.

Problem 7–5B
Journalize transactions; post to general ledger accounts; prepare trial balance
(L.O. 3, 4)

Arizona Microcomputer Store uses special journals for sales, cash receipts, purchases, and cash disbursements, as well as a general journal. These journals follow the same general design as those illustrated in this chapter.

Transactions

Aug. 1 Sold Marlin, Inc., a $24,000 computer on account; terms 2/10, n/30; Invoice No. WI-A1.

3 Bought computer merchandise on account from Quark Company; Invoice No. 33-NP; terms n/10, $16,800.

5 Cash sales, $76,000.

9 Rent revenue received, $3,200.

11 Received amount due from Marlin, Inc., for sale of August 1. The discount was taken.

11 Paid for office equipment received today, $9,600 (Check No. 132). The equipment was for the company's own use.

12 Paid Quark Company for purchase of August 3 (Check No. 133).

14 Sold a $16,000 computer on account to Evans, Inc.; Invoice No. WI-A2; terms 2/10, n/30.

15 Sold a $5,600 computer on account to Brunsby Company; Invoice No. WI-A3; terms 2/10, n/30.

15 Bought computer merchandise on account from Quark Company, $7,920; Invoice No. 34-NP; terms n/10.

17 Bought computer merchandise on account from Southern Company, $12,000; Invoice No. 98-VX; terms 2/10, n/30.

Aug. 18 Bought office equipment today for $7,600 and gave a 30-day, 12% note in payment. The equipment was for the company's own use.

19 Cash sales of computer software, $14,400.

21 Cash sales of computer software, $8,960.

22 Cash sales of computer software, $2,400.

23 Collected net amount due from Evans, Inc., on sale of August 14.

24 Collected net amount due from Brunsby Company on sale of August 15.

25 Paid Quark Company on invoice of August 15 (Check No. 134).

26 Paid Southern Company on invoice of August 17 (Check No. 135).

27 Bought computer merchandise on account from Southern Company, $14,000; Invoice No. 120-VX; terms 2/10, n/30.

28 Paid delivery expense in cash, $3,200 (Check No. 136).

28 Paid advertising expense in cash, $6,400 (Check No. 137).

29 Sold two computers for $29,600 on account to Brunsby Company; Invoice No. WI-A4; terms 2/10, n/30.

30 Sold three computers for $39,200 on account to Evans, Inc.; Invoice No. WI-A5; terms 2/10, n/30.

31 Bought computer merchandise on account from Quark Company, $7,120; Invoice No. 137-NP; terms n/10.

Required *a.* Enter the transactions for August 1994 in the proper journals. All journal pages are to be numbered page 5.

b. Post individual receivables and payables to the accounts receivable subsidiary ledger and accounts payable subsidiary ledger, respectively.

c. Post the entries to the general ledger accounts shown below. The following account balances existed on August 1, 1994: Cash, $40,000; Inventory, $120,000; Capital Stock, $60,000; Retained Earnings, $100,000.

d. Prepare a trial balance as of the end of the period. General ledger accounts are:

Acct. No.	Account Title	Acct. No.	Account Title
100	Cash	407	Rental Revenue
103	Accounts Receivable	410	Sales
105	Merchandise Inventory	411	Sales Discounts
172	Office Equipment	500	Purchases
200	Accounts Payable	501	Purchase Discounts
201	Notes Payable	505	Advertising Expense
300	Capital Stock	519	Delivery Expense
310	Retained Earnings		

BUSINESS DECISION PROBLEMS

Decision Problem 7–1

Describe and discuss special journals (L.O. 2–4)

Ernest Hicks, the golf professional at the Deep Valley Country Club, has been using a general journal to record all business transactions. The volume of business has been increasing, and now he seeks your assistance in devising some special journals. He wants his wife to keep track of all receipts, disbursements, and adjusting entries in her office at home. He and his assistant are to record all credit sales and purchases at the golf shop.

Sales are classified as follows: Golf Equipment, Golf Supplies, Apparel, Lessons, Cart Rental, and Miscellaneous Services. Sales are made both for cash and on account. No sales discounts are offered.

Purchases are made from many different suppliers. Items purchased include apparel, golf supplies, and golf equipment. Periodic inventory procedure is used.

Required *a.* Determine which special journals should be used.

b. Show the column headings that could be used in each of the special journals. Illustrate the use of each special journal by journalizing enough assumed transactions for 1994 so that at least one number appears in each of the columns you have designed.

c. Describe the posting of each special journal you have designed.

Decision Problem 7–2

Describe important factors in deciding how to process data
(L.O. 5)

Cite some of the factors that would be important in deciding whether a company should utilize a manual accounting system, a time-sharing facility, a service bureau, or a computer system installed at the firm.

ANSWERS TO SELF-TEST

True-False

1. *True.* This description of an accounting system is correct.

2. *False.* Subsidiary ledgers can be established for any account in the general ledger for which detailed information is needed. Accounts receivable and accounts payable are likely candidates.

3. *False.* A general journal is still needed to record adjusting entries, closing entries, and any other entries that will not fit a special journal.

4. *True.* Only sales of merchandise on account are recorded in the sales journal, and only purchases on account are recorded in the purchases journal.

5. *False.* For instance, the "Other Accounts" column totals are not posted at all because they consist of entries to different accounts.

6. *False.* The costs and benefits of each alternative need to be compared. Some small businesses still do very well with a manual system.

Multiple-Choice

1. *d.* Special journals are not a result of orderly and efficient processing of data; they can lead to the orderly and efficient processing of data.

2. *a.* Subsidiary ledger accounts need to be posted daily so that a company knows the details behind the control account. For instance, in case customers call and ask how much they owe on their accounts, this information needs to be up to date. The control account balance, however, is usually only needed when financial statements are to be prepared. Thus, daily posting to control accounts is not necessary and may not even be possible, since many of the postings to these accounts are

monthly column totals from columns in special journals.

3. *d.* The sales journal can have one Sales column for each department. If so, it will need an Accounts Receivable debit column also.

4. *d.* Adjusting entries, closing entries, and purchase allowances would have to be recorded in the general journal because they do not fit the other journals. Purchase discounts can be recorded in the cash disbursements journal when payments of the invoices are recorded.

5. *b.* Bookkeeping machines became obsolete because computers could be purchased that cost less and would do more.

COMPREHENSIVE REVIEW PROBLEM

Problem reviews concepts covered in Chapters 1–7; enter beginning balances in general ledger accounts; journalize transactions; post journal data to general ledger and subsidiary ledger accounts; prepare work sheet, classified income statement, and classified balance sheet; journalize and post adjusting and closing entries; prepare post-closing trial balance and schedules of accounts receivable and accounts payable

This problem is based on the materials in Chapters 1 through 7.

Fitness Store sells sporting equipment, clothes, and shoes for use in sports such as tennis, golf, skiing, jogging, racquetball, and so on. The company has been in business for about five years. Most sales are for cash, but some are on credit. Financial statements are prepared at the end of each month. The post-closing trial balance as of November 30, 1994, appears as follows:

FITNESS STORE
Post-Closing Trial Balance
November 30, 1994

Acct. No.	Account Title	Debits	Credits
100	Cash	$144,000	
103	Accounts Receivable	40,000	
105	Merchandise Inventory	200,000	
107	Supplies on Hand	9,600	
108	Prepaid Insurance	5,600	
160	Office Furniture	32,000	
161	Accumulated Depreciation—Office Furniture		$ 14,160
170	Equipment	80,000	
171	Accumulated Depreciation—Equipment		37,760
200	Accounts Payable		36,000
300	Common Stock		240,000
310	Retained Earnings		183,280
		$511,200	$511,200

The chart of accounts for Fitness Store is as follows:

Acct. No.	Account Title	Acct. No.	Account Title
100	Cash	411	Sales Discounts
103	Accounts Receivable	412	Sales Returns and Allowances
105	Merchandise Inventory	420	Miscellaneous Revenue
107	Supplies on Hand	500	Purchases
108	Prepaid Insurance	501	Purchase Discounts
160	Office Furniture	502	Purchase Returns and Allowances
161	Accumulated Depreciation—Office Furniture	503	Transportation-In
		512	Insurance Expense
170	Equipment	515	Rent Expense
171	Accumulated Depreciation—Equipment	518	Supplies Expense
200	Accounts Payable	523	Depreciation Expense—Office Furniture
300	Common Stock		
310	Retained Earnings	524	Depreciation Expense—Equipment
410	Sales	600	Income Summary

Schedules of accounts receivable and accounts payable prepared at November 30, 1994, are as follows:

FITNESS STORE
Schedule of Accounts Receivable
As of November 30, 1994

Bill Bradley.	$ 6,400
Manny Croon.	7,200
Bill Dirdon	6,000
Gil Giles	8,800
Pete Noon	8,000
J. R. Tone	3,600
	$40,000

FITNESS STORE
Schedule of Accounts Payable
As of November 30, 1994

Athletic Shoe Corporation	$ 7,200
Rackets, Inc.	12,000
Sports Clothes, Inc.	16,800
	$36,000

The company uses a sales journal, cash receipts journal, purchases journal, cash disbursements journal, and general journal. All purchases are to be recorded at the gross amount. Notice that recording purchases at the gross amount causes the cash disbursements journal to have a Purchase Discounts Cr. column rather than a Discount Lost Dr. column.

Transactions

Dec. 1 Paid rent for use of the sales building for the month of December, $12,800; Check No. 200.

2 Cash sales were $33,600.

4 Sold merchandise on account to Bill Bradley, $2,000; Invoice No. 512; terms 2/10, n/30.

5 Received payment on account from the following customers:

Name	Gross Amount	Discount Taken	Net Amount Received
Manny Croon	$7,200	$144	$7,056
Bill Dirdon	6,000	120	5,880
Gil Giles	8,800	176	8,624
Pete Noon	8,000	160	7,840

7 Paid Rackets, Inc., $12,000 on account; deducted a 2% discount from that amount; Check No. 201.

8 Paid Sports Clothes, Inc., $16,800 owed on account; deducted a 2% discount from that amount; Check No. 202.

10 Cash sales were $57,600.

12 Granted a sales allowance to Bill Bradley for $800 because of damaged merchandise.

14 Received payment from Bill Bradley, $5,600. No discount was taken.

15 Paid Athletic Shoe Corporation, $7,200; Check No. 203. No discount was involved.

17 Purchased $22,400 of sports equipment on account from Rackets, Inc.; Invoice No. 210; terms 2/10, n/30, FOB destination.

Dec. 19   Cash sales were $52,800.

20   Purchased $13,600 of sports clothing on account from Sports Clothes, Inc.; Invoice No. 620; terms n/30, FOB shipping point.

20   Paid freight charge of $480 to Rapid Delivery Company on today's purchase from Sports Clothes, Inc.; Check No. 204.

22   Received payment on account from J. R. Tone, $3,600. No discount was taken.

23   Purchased $8,000 of sports shoes on account from Athletic Shoe Corporation; Invoice No. 125; terms n/30, FOB destination.

24   Sold merchandise on account to Gil Giles, $6,800; Invoice No. 513; terms 2/10, n/30.

26   Paid the invoice for the purchase on December 17 after taking the discount; Check No. 205.

26   Sold merchandise to Pete Noon, $7,200; Invoice No. 514; terms 2/10, n/30.

27   Cash sales were $36,000.

28   Sold merchandise on account to Louise Ward, $7,280; Invoice No. 515; terms 2/10, n/30.

29   Purchased $19,200 of clothing on account from Sports Clothes, Inc.; Invoice No. 1006; terms n/30, FOB shipping point.

29   Paid freight of $320 to Rapid Delivery Company for today's purchase from Sports Clothes, Inc.; Check No. 206.

30   Sold merchandise on account to Jan Young, $9,600; Invoice No. 516; terms 2/10, n/30.

31   Received a $1,600 allowance on the purchase of December 29 because some of the merchandise was damaged.

31   Cash sales were $16,800.

31   Received $800 from the sale of scrap materials located on the premises.

Additional data

1.   Of the prepaid insurance, $1,200 expired in December.

2.   The supplies on hand at December 31 were $7,200.

3.   Depreciation expense on the office furniture for December was $240.

4.   Depreciation expense on the equipment for December was $640. The equipment was used in the store.

5.   The merchandise inventory on December 31 was $160,000.

Required   a.   Enter the beginning balances for December 1994 into the general ledger accounts, the subsidiary accounts receivable ledger accounts, and the subsidiary accounts payable ledger accounts.

b.   Journalize in the appropriate journal the transactions given below for the month of December. All special journal pages should be identified as Page No. 6.

c.   Post the data in the journals to the appropriate general ledger and subsidiary ledger accounts.

d.   Prepare a work sheet as of December 31, 1994. Use the additional data given above to prepare the necessary adjustments on the work sheet.

e.   Prepare a classified income statement and balance sheet. Rent expense, depreciation expense—equipment, and supplies expense are the only selling expenses.

f.   Journalize in the general journal the adjusting entries and closing entries. The adjusting entries are entered on page 6 of the general journal, and the closing entries are entered on page 7 of the general journal.

g.   Post the adjusting entries and closing entries to the general ledger accounts.

h.   Prepare a post-closing trial balance.

i.   Prepare a schedule of accounts receivable and a schedule of accounts payable at December 31.

Assets are things of value owned by a business. They consist of various items such as cash, automobiles, equipment, investments, buildings, ore deposits, and any other items that can be measured and expressed in money terms and have service potential or utility to their owner.

Liabilities are debts owed by a business. They consist of amounts owed to suppliers, credit card balances, and any other financial obligation.

II

ACCOUNTING FOR ASSETS, LIABILITIES, AND STOCKHOLDERS' EQUITY

CHAPTER 13

CORPORATIONS: FORMATION, ADMINISTRATION, AND CLASSES OF CAPITAL STOCK

CHAPTER 14

CORPORATIONS: PAID-IN CAPITAL, RETAINED EARNINGS, DIVIDENDS, AND TREASURY STOCK

CHAPTER 15

BONDS PAYABLE AND BOND INVESTMENTS

CHAPTER 16

STOCK INVESTMENTS—COST, EQUITY, AND CONSOLIDATIONS

8

CONTROL OF CASH

LEARNING OBJECTIVES

After studying this chapter, you should be able to:

1. Describe the necessity for and features of internal control.
2. Define cash and list the objectives sought by management in handling a company's cash.
3. Identify procedures for controlling cash receipts and disbursements.
4. Prepare a bank reconciliation and make necessary journal entries based on that schedule.
5. Explain why a petty cash fund is used, describe its operations, and make the necessary journal entries.
6. Describe the operation of the voucher system and make entries in its special journals—the voucher register and the check register.

So far in this text you have studied examples of small corporations. When a corporation is small, the president can make all the important decisions and usually maintain a close watch over the affairs of the business. Often the president personally signs the checks. However, as the business grows and the need arises for additional employees, including other officers and managers, the president begins to lose absolute control and must trust employees to take over some of the affairs of the business. At this point, the president realizes that precautions must be taken to protect the company's interests. As a result, the president establishes an internal control structure.

The internal control structure of a company is defined as "the policies and procedures established to provide reasonable assurance that specific entity objectives will be achieved."[1] The three elements of an internal control structure are the control environment, the accounting system, and the control procedures.

The control environment reflects the overall attitude, awareness, and actions of the board of directors, management, and owners. The accounting system consists of the methods and records established to identify, assemble, analyze, classify, record, and report an entity's transactions to provide complete, accurate, and timely financial information. The control procedures of a company are those policies and procedures, in addition to the control environment and the accounting system, that management has established to provide reasonable assurance that the company will achieve its specific objectives. These control procedures may involve procedures pertaining to proper authorization, segregation of duties, design and use of adequate documents and records, adequate safeguards over access to assets, and independent checks on performance.

You may think that the sole purpose of internal control is to prevent theft and fraud. However, internal control serves many purposes. Company policies must be implemented, especially those policies that require compliance with federal law. Personnel must perform their assigned duties to promote efficiency of operations. Correct accounting records must be maintained so that accurate and reliable information is presented in the accounting reports.

This chapter discusses the internal control structure that a company establishes to protect its assets and promote the accuracy of its accounting records. You will learn how internal control is established through control of cash receipts and cash disbursements, proper use of the bank checking account, preparation of the bank reconciliation, protection of petty cash funds, and usage of the voucher system. The internal control structure is enhanced by hiring competent and trustworthy employees.

INTERNAL CONTROL

Objective 1

Describe the necessity for and features of internal control

An effective internal control structure of a company includes its plan of organization and all the procedures and actions taken by the company to:

1. Protect its assets against theft and waste.
2. Ensure compliance with company policies and federal law.
3. Evaluate the performance of all personnel in the company so as to promote efficiency of operations.
4. Ensure accurate and reliable operating data and accounting reports.

[1] AICPA, *Statement on Auditing Standards No. 55*, "Consideration of the Internal Control Structure in a Financial Statement Audit" (New York, 1988), p. 4. The fifth edition of this text adopts the terminology (internal control structure) of the AICPA. Previous editions have referred to the "internal control system."

As you study the basic procedures and actions of an effective internal control structure, you will realize that even small corporations can benefit from using some internal control measures. Preventing theft and waste is only a part of internal control.

In general terms, the purpose of internal control is to ensure the efficient operations of a business, thus enabling the business to effectively reach its goals. Since additional control procedures are necessary in a computer environment, a discussion of these controls concludes this section on internal control.

Protection of Assets

Assets can be protected by (1) segregation of employee duties, (2) assignment of specific duties to each employee, (3) rotation of employee job assignments, and (4) use of mechanical devices.

Segregation of Employee Duties To accomplish segregation of duties, the employee responsible for safeguarding an asset must be someone other than the employee who maintains the accounting records for that asset. Also, responsibility for related transactions should be divided among employees so that one employee's work serves as a check on the work of other employees.

When a company segregates the duties of employees, then collusion between at least two employees is necessary to steal assets and cover up the theft in the accounting records. For example, an employee could not steal cash from a company and have the theft go undetected unless someone changes the cash records to cover the shortage. To change the records, the employee stealing the cash must also maintain the cash records or be in collusion with the employee who maintains the cash records.

Assigning Specific Duties to Each Employee When the responsibility for a particular work function is assigned to one employee, that employee is accountable for specific tasks. Then, if a problem occurs, the employee responsible can be quickly identified.

When a company gives each of its employees specific duties, it can easily trace lost documents or determine how a particular transaction is recorded. Also, the employee responsible for a given task is the person best able to provide information about that task. In addition, being responsible for specific duties gives people a sense of pride and importance that usually makes them want to perform to the best of their ability.

Rotation of Employees' Job Assignments Some companies rotate job assignments where feasible. This policy discourages employees from engaging in long-term schemes to steal from the company. Employees realize that if they steal from the company, the next employee assigned to that position may discover the theft.

Frequently, companies have the policy that all employees must take an annual vacation. This policy also discourages theft because many dishonest schemes collapse when the employee does not attend to the scheme on a daily basis.

Mechanical Devices Companies can use mechanical devices to help protect their assets. Devices such as check protectors (machines that perforate the check amount into the check), cash registers, and time clocks make it impossible for employees to alter certain company documents and records.

Compliance with Company Policies and Federal Law

Internal control policies are effective only when the employees of a company follow those policies. To ensure that employees carry out its internal control policies, a company must hire competent and trustworthy employees. Thus, the execution of effective internal control begins with the time and effort a company expends in hiring employees. Once the company hires the employees, it must train those employees and clearly communicate to them company policies, such as obtaining proper authorization before making a cash disbursement. Frequently, written job descriptions are effective in establishing the responsibilities and duties of employees. The initial training of employees should be such that they know what their duties are and how to perform them.

In publicly held corporations, the company's internal control structure must satisfy the requirements of federal law. In December 1977, Congress enacted the Foreign Corrupt Practices Act (FCPA). This law requires publicly held corporations to devise and maintain an effective system of internal control and to keep accurate accounting records. The passage of this law came about partly because of the cover-ups in company accounting records of bribes and kickbacks made to foreign governments or government officials. The FCPA made this specific type of bribery illegal.

Evaluation of Personnel Performance

To evaluate how well company employees are doing their jobs, many companies use an internal auditing staff. Internal auditing consists of investigating and evaluating employees' compliance with the company's policies and procedures. Companies employ internal auditors to perform these audits. These individuals are trained in company policies and internal auditing duties. For instance, internal auditors might periodically test the effectiveness of controls and procedures involving cash receipts and cash disbursements.

Internal auditors should encourage operating efficiency throughout the company and be constantly alert for breakdowns in the company's internal control structure. In addition, internal auditors make recommendations for the improvement of the company's internal control structure when necessary. All companies and nonprofit organizations can benefit from internal auditing. However, internal auditing is especially necessary in large organizations because the owner(s) cannot be personally involved with all aspects of the business.

Accuracy of Accounting Records

Companies should maintain complete and accurate accounting records. The best method to ensure that such accounting records are kept is to hire and train competent and honest individuals. Periodically, supervisors should evaluate an employee's performance to make sure the employee is following company policies. Inaccurate or inadequate accounting records serve as an invitation to theft by dishonest employees because the theft can be easily concealed.

Most accounting transactions are supported by one or more business documents. These source documents are an integral part of the internal control structure. For optimal control, source documents should be serially numbered. (Transaction documentation and related aspects of internal control will be presented throughout the text.)

Since source documents serve as documentation of business transactions, from time to time the validity of these documents should be checked. For example, to review a merchandise transaction, the documents used to record the transaction should be checked against the proper accounting records. When the accounting department records a merchandise transaction, it should receive copies of the following four documents:

1. **Purchase requisition.** A purchase requisition (Illustration 8.1) is a written request from an employee inside the company to the purchasing department to purchase certain items.

ILLUSTRATION 8.1

Purchase Requisition

PURCHASE REQUISITION   No. _____2416_____

BRYAN WHOLESALE COMPANY

From: _Automotive Supplies Department_   **Date:** _November 20, 1994_

To: _Purchasing Department_

Suggested supplier: _Wilkes Radio Company_

Please purchase the following items:

Description	Item Number	Quantity	Estimated Price
True-tone stereo radios	_Model No. 5868-24393_	_200_	_$50 per unit_

Reason for request:

Customer order
Baier Company

To be filled in by purchasing department:

Date ordered _11/21/94_

Purchase order number _N-145_

Approved _R.S.T._

2. **Purchase order.** A **purchase order** (Illustration 8.2) is a document sent from the purchasing department to a supplier requesting that merchandise or other items be shipped to the purchaser.

3. **Invoice.** An **invoice** (Illustration 8.3) is the statement sent by the supplier to the purchaser requesting payment for the merchandise shipped.

4. **Receiving report.** A **receiving report** is a document prepared by the receiving department showing the descriptions and quantities of all items received from a supplier in a particular shipment. A copy of the purchase order can serve as a receiving report if the quantity ordered is omitted. Then, the receiving department personnel will not know what quantity to expect and probably will count the quantity received more accurately.

These four documents together serve as authorization to pay for merchandise and should be checked against the accounting records. Without these documents, a company might fail to pay a legitimate invoice, pay fictitious invoices, or pay an invoice more than once. Companies can accomplish proper internal control only by periodically checking the source documents of business transactions with the accounting records of those transactions. Illustration 8.4 shows the flow of documents and goods in a merchandise transaction.

Unfortunately, even if a company implements all of the above features in its internal control structure, theft may still occur. If employees are dishonest, they can usually figure out a way to steal from a company, thus circumventing even the most effective internal control structure. Therefore, companies should carry adequate casualty insurance on assets. This insurance will reimburse the company for loss of a nonmonetary asset such as specialized equipment. Companies should also have **fidelity bonds** on employees handling cash and other negotiable instruments. These bonds will ensure that a company is reimbursed for losses due to theft of cash and other monetary assets. With both casualty insurance on assets and fidelity bonds on employees, a company can recover at least a portion of any loss that occurs.

ILLUSTRATION 8.2

Purchase Order

PURCHASE ORDER	No. _N-145_

BRYAN WHOLESALE COMPANY
476 Mason Street
Detroit, Michigan 48823

To: _Wilkes Radio Company_
2515 West Peachtree Street
Atlanta, Georgia 30303

Ship to: _Above address_

Date: _November 21, 1994_
Ship by: _December 20, 1994_
FOB terms requested: _Destination_
Discount terms requested: _2/10, n/30_

Please send the following items:

Description	Item Number	Quantity	Price per Unit	Total Amount
True-tone stereo radios	5868-24393	200	$50	$10,000

Ordered by: _Jane Knight_

Please include order number on all invoices and shipments.

ILLUSTRATION 8.3

Invoice

INVOICE	Invoice No.: _1574_
	Date: _Dec. 15, 1994_

WILKES RADIO COMPANY
2515 West Peachtree Street
Atlanta, Georgia 30303

Customer's Order No.: _N-145_
Sold to: _Bryan Wholesale Co._
Address: _476 Mason Street_
Detroit, Michigan 48823
Terms: _2/10, n/30, FOB destination_

Date shipped: _Dec. 15, 1994_
Shipped by: _Nagel Trucking Co._

Description	Item Number	Quantity	Price per Unit	Total Amount
True-tone stereo radios	Model No. 5868-24393	200	$50	$10,000
		Total		$10,000

Internal Control in a Computer Environment

The use of computers to maintain financial records necessitates the use of the same internal control principles of separation of duties and control over access that are used in a manual accounting system. The exact control steps taken depend on whether a company is using mainframe computers and minicomputers or microcomputers.

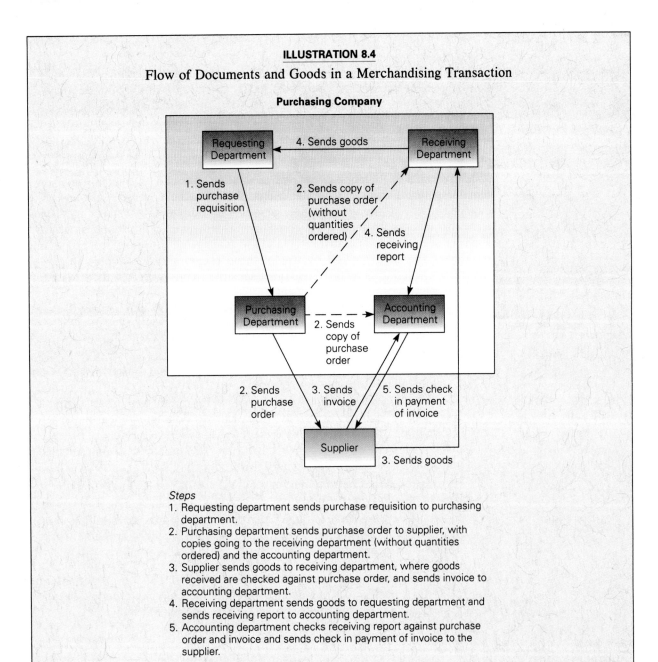

ILLUSTRATION 8.4

Flow of Documents and Goods in a Merchandising Transaction

Purchasing Company

Steps
1. Requesting department sends purchase requisition to purchasing department.
2. Purchasing department sends purchase order to supplier, with copies going to the receiving department (without quantities ordered) and the accounting department.
3. Supplier sends goods to receiving department, where goods received are checked against purchase order, and sends invoice to accounting department.
4. Receiving department sends goods to requesting department and sends receiving report to accounting department.
5. Accounting department checks receiving report against purchase order and invoice and sends check in payment of invoice to the supplier.

Mainframe computers and minicomputers are used in the accounting environments of large corporations. Because of the size and complexity of these computers, specially trained persons are needed to keep these computer systems operating. Systems specialists operate the computer system itself, while programmers develop the programs that direct the computer to perform specific tasks. In a mainframe or minicomputer environment, internal control should include the following:

1. Computer access should be controlled by placing the computer in an easily secured room, and only persons authorized to operate the computer should be allowed to enter the room.

2. Systems specialists who operate the computer should not have access to programming, and programmers should not have access to the computer.

This policy prevents a person from making unauthorized changes to programs.

3. Some programs, such as ones used to print monthly accounts receivable statements to send to credit customers, should be run only during an authorized time period. If programs and data are stored on magnetic tape, the tapes should be stored under lock and key and under the control of a "librarian." The librarian should be independent of the computer systems and programming functions.

Many smaller companies use microcomputers instead of a mainframe or a minicomputer. The use of microcomputers causes the control environment to change somewhat. Small companies generally do not employ systems specialists and programmers. Instead, these companies usually use "off the shelf programs" such as accounting, spreadsheet, database management, and word processing packages. The data created by use of these programs are valuable (e.g., the company's accounting records) and often sensitive. Thus, controls are also important in a microcomputer environment.

In a microcomputer environment, the following controls can be useful:

1. The microcomputer should be kept under lock and key, and only persons authorized to use the computer should have a key.

2. Each computer user should have tight control over his or her diskettes on which programs and data are stored. Just as one person maintains custody over a certain set of records in a manual system, in a computer system a single person maintains custody over diskettes containing a certain type of information (such as the accounts receivable subsidiary ledger). These diskettes should be locked up at night, and backup copies should be made and retained in a different secured location.

3. Passwords should be required (and kept secret) to gain entry into data files maintained on the hard disk.

4. In situations where a local area network (LAN) is present that links the microcomputers into one system, only certain computers in the network should have access to some data files (e.g., the accounting records).

The use of computers in accounting does not lessen the need for internal control. In fact, access to a computer by an unauthorized person could result in significant theft in a shorter span of time than in a manual system.

Controlling Cash

Objective 2

Define cash and list the objectives sought by management in handling a company's cash

In the preceding section, you learned about some of the general principles of internal control. This section focuses specifically on the control of cash. Since cash is the most liquid of all assets, a business cannot survive and prosper if it does not have adequate control over its cash.

In accounting, cash includes coins; currency; certain undeposited negotiable instruments such as checks, bank drafts, and money orders; amounts in checking and savings accounts; and demand certificates of deposit. A certificate of deposit (CD) is an interest-bearing deposit in a bank that can be withdrawn at will (demand CD) or at a fixed maturity date (time CD). Cash only includes demand CDs that may be withdrawn at any time without prior notice or penalty. Cash does not include postage stamps, IOUs, time CDs, or notes receivable.

In the general ledger, usually two cash accounts are maintained—Cash (bank checking and savings account balances) and Petty Cash. The balances of these two accounts are combined into one amount and reported as "Cash" on the company's balance sheet.

Since many business transactions involve cash, it is a vital factor in the operation of a business. Of all the company's assets, cash is the most easily mishandled either through theft or carelessness. To control and manage its cash, a company should:

1. Account for all cash transactions accurately so that correct information will be available regarding cash flows and balances.
2. Make certain that enough cash is available to pay bills as they come due.
3. Avoid holding too much idle cash because excess cash could be invested to generate income, such as interest.
4. Prevent loss of cash due to theft or fraud.

The need to control cash is clearly evident. Although you might think first about how to protect cash from the greedy hands of a dishonest employee, as you can see from the list above, the control of cash has many aspects. Without the proper timing of cash flows and the protection of idle cash, a business cannot survive. This section discusses cash receipts and cash disbursements. Later in the chapter, you will learn about the importance of preparing a bank reconciliation for each bank checking account and controlling the petty cash fund. The voucher system is also described.

Controlling Cash Receipts

Objective 3

Identify procedures for controlling cash receipts and disbursements

When a merchandising company sells its merchandise, it may receive cash immediately or several days or weeks later. The cash received immediately *over the counter* is usually recorded and placed in a cash register. The presence of the customer as the sale is *rung up* usually ensures that the cashier enters the correct amount of the sale in the cash register. At the end of each day, the cash in each cash register should be reconciled with the cash register tape or computer printout for that register. When payment is received later, it is almost always in the form of checks. A record of the checks received should be prepared as soon as they are received. Some merchandising companies receive all their cash receipts on a delayed basis in the form of payments on accounts receivable (see the cash receipts cycle for merchandise transactions in Illustration 8.5).

Although businesses vary their specific procedures for controlling cash receipts, they usually observe the following principles:

1. A record of all cash receipts should be prepared as soon as cash is received. Most thefts of cash occur before a record is made of the receipt. Once a record is made, it is easier to trace a theft.
2. All cash receipts should be deposited as soon as feasible, preferably on the day they are received or on the next business day. Undeposited cash is more susceptible to misappropriation.
3. The employee who handles cash receipts should not also be the employee who records the receipts in the accounting records. This control feature follows the general principle of *segregation of duties* given earlier in the chapter, as does item 4 below.
4. If possible, the employee who receives the cash should not also be the employee who disburses the cash. This control measure is possible in all but the smallest companies.

Controlling Cash Disbursements

Controls are also needed over cash disbursements. Since a company spends most of its cash by check, many of the internal controls for cash disbursements deal with checks and authorizations for cash payments. The basic principle of segregation of duties is also applied in controlling cash disbursements. Following are some basic control procedures for cash disbursements:

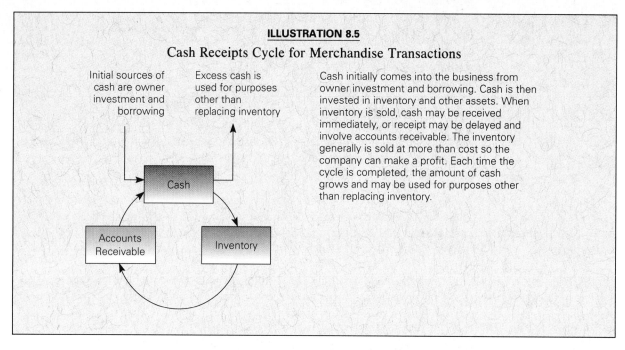

ILLUSTRATION 8.5

Cash Receipts Cycle for Merchandise Transactions

Initial sources of cash are owner investment and borrowing

Excess cash is used for purposes other than replacing inventory

Cash initially comes into the business from owner investment and borrowing. Cash is then invested in inventory and other assets. When inventory is sold, cash may be received immediately, or receipt may be delayed and involve accounts receivable. The inventory generally is sold at more than cost so the company can make a profit. Each time the cycle is completed, the amount of cash grows and may be used for purposes other than replacing inventory.

Cash

Accounts Receivable

Inventory

1. All disbursements should be made by check or from petty cash. Proper approval for all disbursements should be obtained, and a permanent record of each disbursement should be created. In many retail stores, refunds for returned merchandise are made from the cash register. If this practice is followed, refund tickets should be prepared and approved by a supervisor before cash is refunded.

2. All checks should be serially numbered, and access to checks should be limited to employees authorized to write checks.

3. Preferably, two signatures should be required on each check so that one person alone cannot withdraw funds from the bank account.

4. If possible, the employee who authorizes payment of a bill should not be allowed to sign checks. Otherwise, the checks could be written to "friends" in payment of fictitious invoices.

5. Approved documents should be required to support all checks issued.

6. The employee authorizing cash disbursements should make certain that payment is for a legitimate purpose and is made out for the exact amount and to the proper party.

7. When liabilities are paid, the supporting documents should be stamped "paid," and the date and number of the check issued should be indicated. These procedures lessen the chance of paying the same debt more than once.

8. Those employees who sign checks should not have access to canceled checks and should not prepare the bank reconciliation. This policy makes it more difficult for an employee to conceal a theft.

9. The bank reconciliation should be prepared each month, preferably by an employee who has no other cash duties, so that errors and shortages will be quickly discovered.

10. All checks incorrectly prepared should be voided. These checks should be physically marked "void" and retained to prevent their unauthorized use.

11. Large companies may need a voucher system (described later) for close control of cash disbursements.

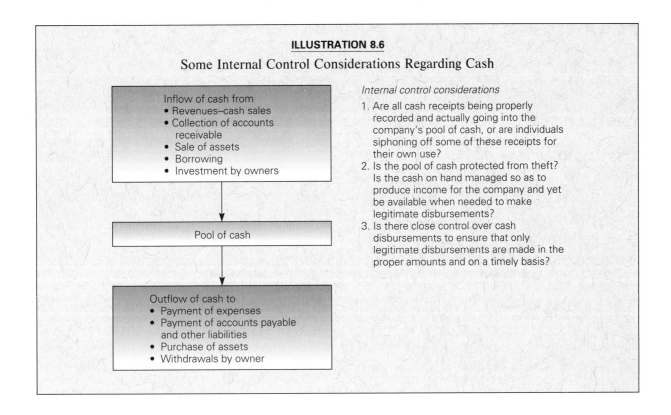

ILLUSTRATION 8.6

Some Internal Control Considerations Regarding Cash

Inflow of cash from
• Revenues–cash sales
• Collection of accounts receivable
• Sale of assets
• Borrowing
• Investment by owners

Pool of cash

Outflow of cash to
• Payment of expenses
• Payment of accounts payable and other liabilities
• Purchase of assets
• Withdrawals by owner

Internal control considerations

1. Are all cash receipts being properly recorded and actually going into the company's pool of cash, or are individuals siphoning off some of these receipts for their own use?
2. Is the pool of cash protected from theft? Is the cash on hand managed so as to produce income for the company and yet be available when needed to make legitimate disbursements?
3. Is there close control over cash disbursements to ensure that only legitimate disbursements are made in the proper amounts and on a timely basis?

12. Use of the net price method of recording purchases (described in Chapter 5) helps avoid loss of purchase discounts by calling attention to discounts missed.

Illustration 8.6 shows an overview of some of the internal control considerations relating to cash.

Most companies use checking accounts to handle their cash transactions. The company deposits its cash receipts in a bank checking account and writes checks to pay its bills. The bank sends the company a statement each month. The company checks this statement against its records to determine if it must make any corrections or adjustments in either the company's balance or the bank's balance. You will learn how to do this later in the chapter when the bank reconciliation is discussed. In the next section, you will learn about the bank checking account. If you have a personal checking account, some of this information will be familiar to you.

THE BANK CHECKING ACCOUNT

Banks seek to earn income by providing a variety of services to individuals, businesses, and other entities such as churches or libraries. One of these services is the checking account. A **checking account** is a money balance maintained in the bank that is subject to withdrawal by the depositor, or owner of the money, on demand. To provide depositors with an accurate record of depositor funds received and disbursed, a bank uses the business documents discussed in this section.[2]

---

[2] Due to relaxed federal regulations, institutions other than banks—such as savings and loan associations and credit unions—now offer checking account services. All of these institutions function somewhat similarly; but, for simplicity's sake, only banks will be discussed here.

The Signature Card A bank requires a new depositor to complete a signature card, which provides the signatures of persons authorized to sign checks drawn on an account. The bank retains the card and uses it to identify signatures on checks paid by the bank. The bank does not compare every check with this signature card. Usually, it makes a comparison only when the depositor disputes the validity of a check paid by the bank or when a check for an unusually large sum is presented for payment.

Deposit Ticket When depositors make a bank deposit, they prepare a deposit ticket or slip. A deposit ticket is a form that shows the date and the items that make up the deposit (Illustration 8.7). The ticket is often preprinted to show the depositor's name, address, and account number. Items comprising the deposit—cash and a list of checks—are entered on the ticket when the deposit is made. After making the deposit, the depositor is given a receipt showing the date of the deposit and the amount deposited.

Check A check is a written order on a bank to pay a specific sum of money to the party designated as the payee by the party issuing the check. Thus, every check transaction involves three parties: the **bank,** the payee (party to whom the check is made payable), and the drawer (depositor). Most depositors use serially numbered checks that are preprinted with information about the depositor, such as name, address, and telephone number. Often a business check will have an attached remittance advice. A remittance advice informs the payee why the drawer (or maker) of the check is making this payment. Before the check is cashed or deposited, the payee detaches the remittance advice from the check (Illustration 8.8).

Bank Statement A **bank statement** is a statement issued (usually monthly) by a bank describing the activities in a depositor's checking account during the period. Illustration 8.9 shows a bank statement that includes the following data:

1. Deposits made to the checking account during the period.
2. Checks paid out of the depositor's checking account by the bank during the period. These checks have *cleared* the bank and are *canceled*.
3. Other deductions from the checking account for such items as service charges, NSF (nonsufficient funds) checks, safe-deposit box rent, and check printing fees. Banks assess service charges on the depositor to cover the cost of handling the checking account, such as check clearing charges. An NSF check is a customer's check returned from the customer's bank to the depositor's bank because the funds in the customer's checking account balance were insufficient to cover the check. The depositor's bank deducts the amount of the returned check from the depositor's checking account. Since the customer still owes the depositor money, the depositor will restore the amount of the NSF check to the account receivable for that customer in the company's books.
4. Other additions to the checking account for items such as proceeds of a note collected by the bank for the depositor and interest earned on the account.

In addition to the data shown in the bank statement in Illustration 8.9, bank statements also can show nonroutine deposits made to the depositor's checking account. Such deposits are not made directly by the depositor but by a third party. For example, the bank may have received a wire transfer of funds for the depositor.

ILLUSTRATION 8.7
Deposit Ticket

CURRENCY	150	—
COIN	45	50

NAME ___M. MILLER COMPANY___

ACCT. NO. ___10-03-38-3___

DATE ___July 7___ 19 _94_

CHECKS AND OTHER ITEMS ARE RECEIVED FOR DEPOSIT SUBJECT TO THE TERMS AND CONDITIONS OF THIS FINANCIAL INSTITUTION'S ACCOUNT AGREEMENT. **DEPOSITS MAY NOT BE AVAILABLE FOR IMMEDIATE WITHDRAWAL.**

© HARLAND 1989

SIGN HERE **ONLY** IF CASH RECEIVED FROM DEPOSIT

GEORGIA NATIONAL
BANK
ATHENS, GA 30601

⑃061103768⑃

CHECKS	LIST CHECKS SINGLY		
	Williams	100	—
	Sloans	200	—
TOTAL FROM OTHER SIDE			
SUB-TOTAL		495	50
TOTAL ITEMS	LESS CASH RECEIVED		
TOTAL DEPOSIT		495	50

64-376/611

DEPOSIT TICKET
PLEASE ITEMIZE ADDITIONAL CHECKS ON REVERSE SIDE

ILLUSTRATION 8.8
Check with Attached Remittance Advice

M. MILLER COMPANY
1216 Dawson Rd.
Albany, Ga. 30605

GEORGIA NATIONAL
BANK
ATHENS, GA 30601

N̲O̲ 2897

64-376
611

EXPENSE CHECK

___July 8,___ 19_94_

PAY ___Five hundred sixty and no/100--------------------___ DOLLARS $560.00

TO THE ORDER OF ___K.F. Frazer Co.___

M. Miller

⑃002897⑃ ⑃061103768⑃ 01⑃00⑃024⑃

M · W · V · HARLAND NO·805

DETACH AND RETAIN THIS STATEMENT
THE ATTACHED CHECK IS IN PAYMENT OF ITEMS DESCRIBED BELOW. IF NOT CORRECT PLEASE NOTIFY US PROMPTLY. NO RECEIPT DESIRED.
GEORGIA NATIONAL BANK

DATE	DESCRIPTION	AMOUNT
7/8/94	P.O. No. R2130--Payment of your invoice #4501	$560.00

ILLUSTRATION 8.9

Bank Statement

THE

GEORGIA NATIONAL
B A N K

P. O. BOX 1684
ATHENS, GEORGIA 30603

DIRECT INQUIRIES TO THE ABOVE ADDRESS OR CALL (404) 548-5511

CHECKING STATEMENT

H   R. L. LEE COMPANY
        1021 ROY LANE
        ATHENS, GA 30603   01 45 65 2

ACCOUNT NUMBER	STATEMENT DATE	
01-45-65-2	5/31/94	21 ENCLOSURES

BEGINNING BALANCE	ADDITIONS	SUBTRACTIONS	ENDING BALANCE
$2,248.00	$12,358.00	$11,354.00	$3,252.00

SUBTRACT 22 ITEMS

CHECKS	AMOUNT	DATE PAID	CHECKS	AMOUNT	DATE PAID	CHECKS	AMOUNT	DATE PAID
9515*	351.00	5/3	9531	1,250.00	5/8	9537	111.00	5/22
9519*	154.00	5/3	9532	800.00	5/15	9538	2,071.00	5/23
9527	208.00	5/7	9533	925.00	5/15	9539	413.00	5/25
9528	467.00	5/7	9534	417.00	5/18	9540	1,093.00	5/25
9529	125.00	5/7	9535	230.00	5/17	9541	1,005.00	5/25
9530	411.00	5/8	9536	169.00	5/21	9542	818.00	5/29
						9543	211.00	5/29

NSF CHECK   102.00 5/30
SERVICE CHARGE   8.00 5/31
SAFE DEPOSIT BOX RENT   15.00 5/31
*PRECEDING CHECK(S) NOT PAID DURING THIS PERIOD

ADD 23 ITEMS

AMOUNT	DATE	AMOUNT	DATE	AMOUNT	DATE
624.00	5/1	514.00	5/10	333.00	5/22
776.00	5/2	401.00	5/11	407.00	5/23
526.00	5/3	702.00	5/14	371.00	5/24
474.00	5/4	303.00	5/15	331.00	5/25
631.00	5/7	471.00	5/16	507.00	5/28
608.00	5/8	653.00	5/17	601.00	5/29
1,225.00**	5/8	414.00	5/18	400.00	5/30
667.00	5/9	419.00	5/21		

**NOTE COLLECTED FROM A CUSTOMER

ENDING BALANCE FOR EACH DAY YOUR ACCOUNT HAD ACTIVITY

BALANCE	DATE	BALANCE	DATE	BALANCE	DATE
2,248.00	4/30	5,327.00	5/10	6,371.00	5/22
2,872.00	5/1	5,728.00	5/11	4,707.00	5/23
3,648.00	5/2	6,430.00	5/14	5,078.00	5/24
3,669.00	5/3	5,008.00	5/15	2,898.00	5/25
4,143.00	5/4	5,479.00	5/16	3,405.00	5/28
3,974.00	5/7	5,902.00	5/17	2,977.00	5/29
4,146.00	5/8	5,899.00	5/18	3,275.00	5/30
4,813.00	5/9	6,149.00	5/21	3,252.00	5/31

A **wire transfer of funds** is an interbank transfer of funds by telephone. Companies that operate in many widely scattered locations and therefore have checking accounts with several different local banks often use an interbank transfer of funds. These companies may set up special procedures to avoid accumulating too much idle cash in local bank accounts. One such procedure involves the use of special-instruction bank accounts. For example, **transfer bank accounts** may be set up so local banks automatically transfer to a central bank (by wire or bank

ILLUSTRATION 8.10

Debit Memorandum (top) and Credit Memorandum (bottom)

GENERAL LEDGER **DEBIT** ACCT. TITLE	R. L. Lee Company 1021 Roy Lane Athens, GA 30603	Acct. No. 01 45 65 2 DATE May 31, 1994

DESCRIPTION	AMOUNT
Safe Deposit Box Rental	
CONTRA ENTRY	
DRAWN BY CWT CENTER APPROVED BY MRC TOTAL	15 00

BANKERS SYSTEMS, INC., ST. CLOUD, MN 56301

⑈037600800⑈

GENERAL LEDGER **CREDIT** ACCT. TITLE	R. L. Lee Company 1021 Roy Lane Athens, GA 30603	Acct. No. 01 45 65 2 DATE 5/8/94

DESCRIPTION	AMOUNT
Collection of note for the Lee Company from X Company	
CONTRA ENTRY	
DRAWN BY CWT CENTER APPROVED BY MRC TOTAL	1,225 00

BANKERS SYSTEMS, INC., ST. CLOUD, MN 56301

⑈037600208⑈

draft) all amounts on deposit in excess of a stated amount. In this way, funds not needed for local operations are sent quickly to company headquarters, where the company can use the funds or invest them.

Frequently, the bank returns canceled checks and original deposit tickets with the bank statement. Since it is expensive to sort, handle, and mail these items, some banks no longer return them to the depositor. These banks usually store the documents on microfilm, with photocopies available if needed. Most depositors need only a detailed bank statement, as shown in Illustration 8.9, and not the original documents to show what transactions occurred during a given period.

When banks debit or credit a depositor's checking account, they prepare debit and credit memos. These memos may also be returned with the bank statement. A debit memo is a form used by a bank to explain a deduction from the depositor's account; a credit memo explains an addition to the depositor's account. The terms *debit memo* and *credit memo* may seem reversed, but remember that the depositor's checking account is a liability—an account payable—of the bank. So, when the bank seeks to reduce a depositor's balance, a debit memo is prepared. To increase the balance, a credit memo is prepared. Illustration 8.10 shows examples of debit and credit memos. Some banks no longer mail these documents to the depositor and rely instead on explanations in the bank statement.

Information that the depositor did not know before receiving the bank statement (items 3 and 4 on page 388) requires new journal entries on the company's books. After the entries have been made to record the new information, the balance in the Cash account is the actual cash available to the company. When the depositor has already received notice of NSF checks and other bank charges or credits, the needed journal entries may have been made earlier. In this chapter, we assume no entries have been made for these items unless stated otherwise.

When a company receives its bank statement, it must reconcile the balance shown by the bank with the cash balance shown in the company's books. If you have a personal checking account, you also should reconcile your bank statement with your checkbook. You can use the reconciliation form on the back of the bank statement to list your checks that have not yet been paid by the bank and your deposits not yet shown on the bank statement. Some small businesses may also use this form. However, they may instead prepare a separate bank reconciliation, which you will learn how to prepare in the next section.

BANK RECONCILIATION

Objective 4

Prepare a bank reconciliation and make necessary journal entries based on that schedule

A bank reconciliation, often called a **bank reconciliation statement** or **schedule,** is a schedule the company (depositor) prepares to *reconcile,* or explain, the difference between the cash balance shown on the bank statement and the cash balance on the company's books. The bank reconciliation is prepared to determine the company's actual cash balance. Illustration 8.11 shows an example of a bank reconciliation.

The bank reconciliation is divided into two main sections. One section, at the top in Illustration 8.11, begins with the balance shown on the bank statement. The second section, at the bottom in Illustration 8.11, begins with the company's balance as shown on the company's books. Adjustments are made to both the *bank* and *book* balances; after these adjustments, both adjusted balances should be the same.

The steps in preparing a bank reconciliation are as follows:

a. **Deposits.** Compare the deposits listed on the bank statement with the deposits on the company's books. This comparison can be made by placing check marks in the bank statement and in the company's books by the deposits that agree. Then determine the deposits in transit. A deposit in transit is typically a day's cash receipts recorded in the depositor's books in one period but recorded as a deposit by the bank in the succeeding period. The most common deposit in transit is the deposit of the cash receipts of the last business day of the month. Normally, deposits in transit occur only near the end of the period covered by the bank statement. For example, a deposit made in a bank's night depository on May 31 would be recorded by the company on May 31 and by the bank on June 1. Thus, the deposit will not appear on a bank statement for the month ended May 31. The deposits in transit listed in last month's bank reconciliation should also be checked against the bank statement. Any deposit made during the month that is missing from the bank statement (unless it involves a deposit made at the end of the period) should be investigated immediately.

b. **Paid checks.** If canceled checks are returned with the bank statement, first compare them to the bank statement to be sure the amounts on the statement agree with the checks. Then, sort the checks in numerical order. Next, determine which checks are outstanding. Outstanding checks are checks issued by a depositor that have not yet been paid by the bank on which they are drawn. The party receiving the check may not deposit it immediately. Once deposited, checks may take several days to clear the

---

ILLUSTRATION 8.11

Bank Reconciliation

R. L. LEE COMPANY
Bank Reconciliation
May 31, 1994

① Balance per bank statement, May 31, 1994 . . . . $3,252
② Add: Deposit in transit   452
                                                              $3,704

③ Less: Outstanding checks:
    No. 9544 . . . . $322
    No. 9545   168
    No. 9546   223   713
Adjusted balance, May 31, 1994 . . . . $2,991

① Balance per ledger, May 31, 1994 . . . . $1,891
④ Add: Note collected (including interest of $25)   1,225
                                                              $3,116

⑤ Less: NSF check (R. Johnson) $102
⑥   Safe-deposit box rent   15
⑥   Service charges.   8   125
Adjusted balance, May 31, 1994 . . . . $2,991

---

banking system. The outstanding checks are determined by a process of elimination. The check numbers that have cleared the bank are compared with a list of the check numbers issued by the company. Check marks are used in the company's record of checks issued to identify those checks returned by the bank. Checks issued that have not yet been returned by the bank are the outstanding checks. If the bank does not return checks but provides only a listing of the cleared checks on the bank statement, the outstanding checks are determined by comparing this list with the company's record of checks issued.

Sometimes checks written long ago will still be outstanding. Checks outstanding as of the beginning of the month will appear on the prior month's bank reconciliation. Most of these will have cleared during the current month; those that have not cleared should be listed as still outstanding on the current month's reconciliation.

c. **Bank debit and credit memos.** Verify all debit and credit memos on the bank statement. Debit memos reflect deductions for such items as service charges, NSF checks, safe-deposit box rent, and notes paid by the bank for the depositor. Credit memos reflect additions for such items as wire transfers of funds from another bank in which the company has funds to the home office bank and notes collected for the depositor by the bank. Check the bank debit and credit memos with the depositor's books to see if they have already been recorded. Journal entries should be made for any such items not already recorded in the company's books.

d. **Errors.** List any errors found. A common error is that the depositor records a check in the accounting records at an amount that differs from the actual amount on the check. For example, a $47 check may be recorded at $74. The check will clear the bank at the amount written on the check ($47), but the depositor frequently does not catch the error until the bank statement or canceled checks are reviewed.

Deposits in transit, outstanding checks, and bank service charges usually account for the difference between the company's Cash account balance and the bank balance. (These same items can cause a difference between your personal checkbook balance and the bank balance shown on your bank statement.) Remember that **all items shown on the bank reconciliation as adjustments of the book (ledger) balance require journal entries to adjust the Cash account** (items 4, 5, and 6 in Illustration 8.11 and in the following example); **items appearing on the bank balance side do not require entries by the depositor** (items 2 and 3). Any bank errors, of course, should be called to the bank's attention.

To illustrate the preparation of the bank reconciliation shown in Illustration 8.11, assume the following (these items are keyed by number into that illustration):

1. On May 31, 1994, R. L. Lee Company showed a balance in its Cash account of $1,891. On June 2, Lee received its bank statement for the month ended May 31, which showed an ending balance of $3,252.

2. A matching of debits to the Cash account on the books with deposits on the bank statement showed that the $452 receipts of May 31 were included in Cash but not included as a deposit on the bank statement. This deposit was in the bank's night deposit chute on May 31.

3. A comparison of checks issued with checks that had cleared the bank showed three checks outstanding:

No. 9544	$322
No. 9545	168
No. 9546	223
Total	$713

4. Included with the bank statement was a credit memo for $1,225 (principal of $1,200 + interest of $25) for collection of a note owed to Lee by Shipley Company.

5. Included with the bank statement was a $102 debit memo for an NSF check written by R. Johnson and deposited by Lee.

6. Charges made to Lee's account include $15 for safe-deposit box rent and $8 for service charges.

After reconciling the book and bank balances, Lee Company finds that its actual cash balance is $2,991. The following entries are needed to record information from the bank reconciliation:

④	Cash	1,225	
	Notes Receivable—Shipley Company.		1,200
	Interest Revenue.		25
	To record note collected from Shipley Company.		
⑤	Accounts Receivable—R. Johnson*	102	
	Cash		102
	To charge NSF check back to customer, R. Johnson.		
⑥	Bank Service Charge Expense (or Miscellaneous Expense)	23	
	Cash		23
	To record bank service charges.		

* This debit would be posted to the Accounts Receivable control account in the general ledger and to R. Johnson's account in the accounts receivable subsidiary ledger.

The income statement for the period ending May 31, 1994, would include the $23 bank service charge as an expense. The May 31 balance sheet would show $2,991 cash, the actual cash balance.

The three entries above could be combined into one compound entry as follows:

Cash	1,100	
Bank Service Charge Expense	23	
Accounts Receivable—R. Johnson	102	
Notes Receivable		1,200
Interest Revenue		25
To correct the accounts for needed changes identified in the bank reconciliaton.		

The deposit in transit and the outstanding checks have already been recorded in the depositor's books and will be handled routinely when they reach the bank. Since these items appear on the bank balance side of the reconciliation, they require no entry in the company's books. These items will be processed by the bank in the subsequent period.

When a company maintains more than one checking account, it must reconcile each account separately with the balance on the bank statement for that account. The depositor should also check carefully to see that the bank did not make an error in keeping the transactions of the two accounts separate.

Certified and Cashier's Checks

To make sure a check will not *bounce* and become an NSF check, a payee may demand a certified or cashier's check from the maker. Both certified checks and cashier's checks are liabilities of the issuing bank rather than the depositor. As a result, these checks are usually accepted without question.

☐ A certified check is a check written, or drawn, by a **depositor** and taken to the depositor's bank for certification. The bank will stamp *certified* across the face of the check and insert the name of the bank and the date; the certification will be signed by a bank official. The bank will certify a check only when the depositor's balance is large enough to cover the check. The bank deducts the amount of the check from the depositor's account at the time it certifies the check.

☐ A cashier's check is a check drawn by a **bank** made out to either the depositor or a third party after deducting the amount of the check from the depositor's account or receiving cash from the depositor.

In this section, you learned that all cash receipts should be deposited in the bank and all cash disbursements should be made by check. However, the next section explains the convenience of having small amounts of cash (petty cash) available for minor expenditures.

PETTY CASH FUNDS

Objective 5

Explain why a petty cash fund is used, describe its operations, and make the necessary journal entries

At times, every business finds it convenient to have small amounts of cash available for immediate payment of items such as delivery charges, postage stamps, taxi fares, supper money for employees working overtime, and other small items. To permit these disbursements to be made in cash and still maintain adequate control over cash, companies frequently establish a petty cash fund of a round figure such as $100 or $500.

A BROADER PERSPECTIVE

HOW THE FDIC WORKS

Every two days on average, somewhere in the country, a bank fails. The federal government repeatedly assures depositors that their $2.7 trillion in savings are safe, backed by the full faith and credit of [the] government.

But how safe are deposits? Is the government prepared for the possibility of a deepening bank crisis?

The Federal Deposit Insurance Corp. backs deposits with $13.2 billion in its insurance fund.

But critics point out that reserves are less than 1% of insured deposits—just 70 cents for every $100, the lowest level since the fund was established in the early 1930s. Last year the figure was 80 cents. A preferred level, experts say, is $1.25.

Robert Litan of the Brookings Institution, newly hired by the House Banking Committee to examine the FDIC's strength, warns that reserves could be further depleted, because "there are still a lot of banks out there that are broke."

The FDIC was chartered in 1933 to stabilize a banking industry stunned by the Depression. With the failure of 9,000 banks from 1929 to 1933, the FDIC helped calm depositors by insuring every deposit up to $2,500. The limit was gradually raised to $40,000 in 1974, then to its current level of $100,000 in 1980.

The Federal Savings and Loan Insurance Corp. was created for savings and loans. When the S&L debacle mushroomed out of control, FSLIC became insolvent and FDIC assumed its function in 1989. The bill for cleaning up the S&L mess, now estimated at $400 billion, goes to the Resolution Trust Corp. and will be paid primarily by taxpayers.

The FDIC builds reserves by charging annual assessments to member banks across the USA and investing the premiums. Then it draws on those funds to pay off depositors when a bank fails.

But in 1988, weakened by large bank failures, mainly in the Southwest, the insurance fund suffered its first annual drop—$4.3 billion. More money was paid out because of bank failures than came in from assessments.

Last year, the fund declined by another $851 million, up to three times as much as initially predicted by the FDIC. And though the FDIC estimates it will show a surplus this year—barring any major bank failures—the Office of Management and Budget says it will decline by $2.2 billion, a calculation the FDIC disputes.

From the FDIC's inception through last year, federally insured banks paid FDIC an assessment of 8.3 cents for every $100 in deposits. These premiums generated $1.9 billion for FDIC last year. In the face of the FDIC's heavy payouts, however, this year the rate was raised to 12 cents per $100. That's expected to generate $3 billion in assessments for the reserve fund for 1990. In 1991, the rate increases again to 15 cents—an expected $3.9 billion for the reserves next year.

Usually one individual, called the *petty cash custodian* or *cashier,* is responsible for the operation of the fund, which includes control of the petty cash fund and documenting the disbursements made from the fund. By assigning the responsibility for the fund to one individual, the company has internal control over the cash in the fund. In this section, you will learn how to both establish and operate a petty cash fund.

Establishing the Fund

The petty cash fund is established by writing a check for, say, $100. The amount of a petty cash fund should be large enough to make disbursements for a reasonable period, such as a month.

For example, assume a $100 petty cash fund is to be established. A check in that amount is drawn, payable to cash or the petty cash custodian. The following entry is required:

Rep. Henry Gonzalez, chairman of the House Banking Committee, thinks the $100,000 limit on insured deposits is too high. The original intent of deposit insurance, Gonzalez says, was to protect the small depositor. Instead, a $100,000 guarantee favors the big money managers. "Individuals can have $10 million in separate accounts. That wasn't the intent," Gonzalez says. High deposit insurance also promotes excessive risk taking, because bankers and depositors know the government has assumed the risks of lending.

President Bush opposes lowering the limit on deposit insurance.

Federal regulators assure anxious depositors that if reserves were depleted, FDIC would borrow from the Treasury. "No insured depositor has ever lost a penny because of a bank closing," says FDIC's David Barr.

"The government is standing behind insured deposits, so the individual depositor should not worry about the size of the FDIC's fund," says George Pennacchi, assistant professor of finance at Wharton School. "In no one's imagination would FDIC default on an insured deposit."

When a Bank Collapses What happens when a bank fails?

First, the FDIC tries to find a buyer for the entire institution. If no buyer materializes, FDIC looks for a healthy local bank to assume insured deposits. Deposits in all accounts up to $100,000 are federally in-

sured. As a last resort, FDIC takes over and pays off insured depositors, a process that takes two or three days.

Only 10 banks failed in 1980, but so many have collapsed since then—1,110—that FDIC has the closing routine down to a science. Many customers don't even realize their bank has failed until they get a monthly statement with the institution's new name.

It used to take a whole weekend to shut down a bank. Now, the federal team generally goes in on Thursday armed with computers, works furiously into the night, and reopens the bank under new management on Friday with no interruption in service. The team reviews the books and counts every chair and framed picture, while curious locals peer into windows.

"The primary goal anytime a bank fails is to make sure consumer business is not disturbed," says Mary-Liz Meany of the American Bankers Association.

Sometimes the deposits alone are transferred to a healthy local bank—called an agent bank. Depositors may keep accounts in the bank picked by FDIC or move them to a bank of their choice.

For those with deposits over the $100,000 limit, FDIC first verifies the amount that's uninsured, then pays depositors what's available after the failed bank's assets are liquidated. Depositors seldom recover all the uninsured funds.

Source: Denise Kalette, *USA Today*, May 20, 1990, p. 3B.

Petty Cash	100	
Cash		100
To establish a petty cash fund.		

The check is cashed, and the money is turned over to the petty cash custodian, who normally places the money in a small box that can be locked. The fund is now ready to be disbursed as needed.

Operating the Fund One of the conveniences of the petty cash fund is that payments from the fund require no journal entries at the time of payment. Thus, using a petty cash fund avoids the need for making many entries for small amounts. Only when the fund is reimbursed, or the end of the accounting period arrives, will an entry be made in the journal.

When cash is disbursed from the fund, the petty cash custodian prepares a petty cash voucher, which should be signed by the person receiving the funds. A petty cash voucher (Illustration 8.12) is a document or form that shows the amount of and reason for a petty cash disbursement. A voucher should be prepared for each disbursement from the fund. If an invoice for the expenditure is provided, the invoice should be stapled to the petty cash voucher. The employee responsible for petty cash is at all times accountable for having cash and petty cash vouchers equal to the total amount of the fund.

Replenishing the Fund

The petty cash fund should be replenished at the end of the accounting period, or sooner if it becomes low. The reason for replenishing the fund at the end of the accounting period is that no record of the fund expenditure is in the accounts until the check is written and a journal entry is made. (The fund is sometimes referred to as an **imprest** fund since it is replenished when it becomes low.) The petty cash vouchers are presented to the employee having authority to order that the fund be reimbursed. The vouchers are examined by that employee; and if all is in order, a check is drawn to restore the fund to its original amount.

To determine which accounts to debit, the petty cash vouchers are summarized according to the reasons for expenditure. The petty cash vouchers are then stamped or defaced to prevent reuse. The journal entry to record replenishing the fund would debit the various accounts indicated by the summary and credit Cash.

For example, assume the $100 petty cash fund currently has a money balance of $7.40. A summary of the vouchers shows payments of $22.75 for transportation-in, $50.80 for stamps, and $19.05 for an advance to an employee; these payments total $92.60. After the vouchers have been examined and approved, a check is drawn for $92.60 which, when cashed, restores the cash in the fund to its $100 balance. The journal entry to record replenishment is:

Transportation-In	22.75	
Postage Expense	50.80	
Advances to Employees	19.05	
Cash		92.60
To replenish petty cash fund.		

Note that the entry to record replenishing the fund does not credit the Petty Cash account. Entries are made to the Petty Cash account only when the fund is established, when the end of the accounting period arrives and the fund is not replenished, or when the size of the fund is changed.

At the end of an accounting period, any petty cash disbursements for which the fund has **not** yet been replenished must be recorded. Since the fund has not been replenished, **the credit would be to Petty Cash rather than Cash.** Failure to make an entry at the end of an accounting period would cause errors in both the income statement and balance sheet. The easiest way to record these disbursements is to replenish the fund. Replenishing the fund at the end of an accounting period is handled exactly as at any other time.

If, after a period of time, the petty cash custodian finds that the petty cash fund is larger than needed, the excess petty cash should be deposited in the company's checking account. **The required entry to record a decrease in the size of the fund debits Cash and credits Petty Cash for the amount returned and deposited.** On the other hand, a petty cash fund may be too small, requiring replenishment every few days. **The entry to record an increase in the size of the fund debits Petty Cash and credits Cash for the amount of the increase.**

ILLUSTRATION 8.12

Petty Cash Voucher

PETTY CASH VOUCHER NO. __359__

To __Local Cartage, Inc.__   Date __June 29,__ __1994__

EXPLANATION	ACCT. NO.	AMOUNT
Freight on parts	27	12 57

APPROVED BY__ a.e.s.__   RECEIVED PAYMENT __Ken Black__

To illustrate, the entry to **decrease** the size of the petty cash fund by $50 would be:

```
Cash . . . . . . . . . . . . . . . . . . . . . . . . . . . . . . . . .   50
     Petty Cash. . . . . . . . . . . . . . . . . . . . . . . . . . .        50
        To decrease the size of the petty cash fund by $50.
```

The entry to **increase** the size of the petty cash fund by $600 would be:

```
Petty Cash. . . . . . . . . . . . . . . . . . . . . . . . . . . . .  600
     Cash . . . . . . . . . . . . . . . . . . . . . . . . . . . . .        600
        To increase the size of the petty cash fund by $600.
```

Cash Short and Over

Errors can be made in making change from the petty cash fund. These errors cause the amount of cash in the fund to be more or less than the amount of the fund less the total vouchers. When the fund is restored to its original amount, the credit to Cash is for the difference between the established amount and the actual cash in the fund. Debits are made for all vouchered items. Any discrepancy should be debited or credited to an account called *Cash Short and Over*. The Cash Short and Over account is an expense or a revenue, depending on whether it has a debit or credit balance.

To illustrate, assume in the preceding example that the balance in the fund was only $6.10 instead of $7.40. To restore the fund to $100, a check for $93.90 is needed. Since the petty cash vouchers total only $92.60, the fund is short $1.30. In this case, the entry for replenishment is:

```
Transportation-In . . . . . . . . . . . . . . . . . . . . . . . . .  22.75
Postage Expense . . . . . . . . . . . . . . . . . . . . . . . . . .  50.80
Advances to Employees. . . . . . . . . . . . . . . . . . . . . . .  19.05
Cash Short and Over . . . . . . . . . . . . . . . . . . . . . . . .   1.30
     Cash . . . . . . . . . . . . . . . . . . . . . . . . . . . . .        93.90
        To replenish petty cash fund.
```

Entries in the Cash Short and Over account may be entered from other change-making activities. For example, assume that a clerk accidentally shortchanges a customer $1 and that total cash sales for the day are $740.50. At the end of the day, actual cash will be $1 over the sum of the sales tickets or the total of the cash register tape. The journal entry to record the day's cash sales is:

Cash	741.50	
Sales		740.50
Cash Short and Over		1.00
To record cash sales for the day.		

THE VOUCHER SYSTEM

Objective 6

Describe the operation of the voucher system and make entries in its special journals—the voucher register and the check register

Companies often suffer substantial losses from the embezzlement of cash. Frequently, the embezzlement results from the paying of fictitious invoices. Thus, every business must make sure that its cash payments are proper and timely. In small companies, such a problem often does not exist because the owner usually has personal knowledge of all transactions and personally signs all checks. However, in larger companies, the owners and high-level officers may have no direct part in the payment process. These companies can effectively control cash disbursements by using the voucher system.

The use of a voucher system can be expensive. Only those companies with the size and need for a voucher system should consider installing one.

The **voucher system** is a set of procedures, special journals, and authorization forms designed to provide control over cash payments. The special journals used in the voucher system are the voucher register and the check register. These journals are defined later in this section. (Other special journals, such as the sales journal and cash receipts journal, would still be used.)

When a company uses the voucher system, each transaction that involves a cash payment is entered on a voucher (Illustration 8.13) and recorded in the voucher register before payment. A **voucher** is a form with spaces provided for data about a liability that must be paid. The data include items such as a creditor's name and address, description of the goods or services received, invoice number, terms of payment, due date, and amount due, and often show the ledger accounts and amounts to be debited. The voucher also has spaces for signatures of those approving the payment.

An invoice or other business document is the basis for making a journal entry in the voucher register. The voucher usually forms a *jacket* for the invoice, purchase order, and receiving report. Each voucher should undergo careful examination and receive either approval or disapproval for payment. By the time a voucher is approved for payment, several employees have confirmed that the claim being paid is proper and accurate, thus reducing the chances of embezzlement.

Procedures for Preparing a Voucher

The preparation of a voucher begins with the receipt of an invoice from a creditor or with approved evidence that a liability has been incurred and cash should be disbursed. Then, the procedures are as follows:

1. Basic data are entered on the voucher from the invoice.
2. The invoice, voucher, and receiving report are sent to the employees responsible for verifying the correctness of the description of the goods as to quantity and quality, dollar amounts, and other details. Each employee initials the voucher when satisfied as to its correctness.

ILLUSTRATION 8.13

A Voucher

ATWELL SUPPLY COMPANY

Atwell Plaza

Atwell, Texas 78712

VOUCHER

VOUCHER NO. ____141____
OUR P.O. NO. ____2514____
VENDOR'S INVOICE ____416____
PAID BY CHECK NO. ____587____
DATE PAID ____7/18/94____

Payable To: Gregory Corporation
48 Cadillac Square
Detroit, Michigan 48226

DATE		ACCT. NO.	DESCRIPTION	QUANTITY	UNIT PRICE	TOTAL
July	14	126	X-16 Transistors	100	$2.00	$200.00
			TOTAL			$200.00
			DISCOUNT	2%		4.00
			NET PAYABLE			$196.00

TERMS 2/10, n/30
EXPLANATIONS: *Due date is August 13, 1994*

AUDITED AS TO CORRECTNESS *a.T.*	APPROVED FOR PAYMENT *L.S.W.*	ENTERED IN VOUCHER REGISTER *R.E.L.*	DATE ENTERED 7/14/94

---

3. When the voucher and accompanying documents are returned to the accounting department, a notation is made on the voucher as to the proper accounts to be debited and credited.

4. After a final review by an authorized employee, the proper entry is made in the voucher register, and the voucher is filed in the unpaid voucher file.

The name **voucher system** comes from the fact that **every check issued is authorized by a voucher.** A voucher really can be any written form that serves as a receipt or evidence of authority to act. However, as applied to the voucher system, a voucher is a form that confirms a liability and, as such, serves as the basis for an accounting entry.

In some businesses, the discount and payment terms run from the invoice date. Then, a voucher should be prepared for each invoice (Illustration 8.13). The voucher should be filed according to the date on which the discount period terminates or payment is due. However, when the discount and payment terms are computed from the end of the month, the voucher may be modified, reducing the number of vouchers prepared and the entries made in the voucher register. Then, all invoices received from a particular creditor are accumulated and listed on one

ILLUSTRATION 8.14

A Voucher Register

**JACKSON COMPANY
VOUCHER REGISTER**

Line No.	Voucher Date 1994		Voucher No.	Payee	Explanation	Terms	Date Paid*		Check No.*	Vouchers Payable Cr. 205
1	May	2	223	Hanley Company	Ring binders	2/10, n/30	May	12	1350	980.00
2		4	224	Moore Transport	Transportation, binders			5	1347	13.00
3		6	225	White Stationery Company	Office supplies	2/10, n/30		12	1351	102.00
4		8	226	Specialty Advertisers	Advertising			8	1348	1,200.00
5		10	227	Blanch Company	Office equipment and supplies			10	1349	1,010.00
6										
7		14	228	Swanson Company	Filler paper	2/10, n/30		26	1356	3,920.00
8		16	229	Rizzo Company	Office desk	n/30		25	1355	640.00
9		18	230	Warren Company	Spiral binders	2/10, n/30		28	1357	4,900.00
10		20	231	First National Bank	Mortgage payment			20	1353	154.00
11		22	232	Falconer Company	Books	n/30				10,000.00
12		24	233	Petty cash	Reimbursement			24	1354	132.00
13		26	234	Swanson Company	Discount lost (No. 228)			26	1356	80.00
14		28	235	Celoron Company	Drawing sets	2/20, n/30				9,800.00
15		31	236	Payroll account	Salaries and wages			31	1358	24,000.00
16										56,931.00
										(205)

* Added later when paid.

voucher at the end of the month. One check is written on the due date to pay for all invoices listed on the voucher. These vouchers are filed according to their individual due dates.

Special Journals Used

When a voucher system is used, the voucher register replaces the purchases journal, and the check register replaces the cash disbursements journal. Illustration 8.14 shows a voucher register, and Illustration 8.15 shows a check register for Jackson Company, assuming the journals have been posted.

Voucher Register A voucher register is a multicolumn special journal containing a record of all vouchers prepared, listed chronologically by date and voucher number. A brief explanation of each transaction may also be included. Since each entry in the voucher register includes a credit to an account called the *Vouchers Payable account*, a column titled *Vouchers Payable Cr.* is included in the voucher

Discounts Lost Dr. 543	Merchandise Purchases Dr. 500	Transportation-In Dr. 503	Salaries Expense Dr. 507	Supplies Expense Dr. 518	Advertising Expense Dr. 505	Other Accounts Dr.			
						Account Name	Acct. No.	Amount Dr.	✓
	980.00								
		13.00							
				102.00					
					1,200.00				
						Office Equipment	172	1,000.00	✓
						Supplies on Hand	107	10.00	✓
	3,920.00								
						Office Equipment	172	640.00	✓
	4,860.00	40.00							
						Mortgage Note Payable	218	44.00	✓
						Interest Expense	540	110.00	✓
	10,000.00								
		31.88		60.12	40.00				
80.00									
	9,800.00								
			24,000.00						
80.00	29,560.00	84.88	24,000.00	162.12	1,240.00			1,804.00	
(543)	(500)	(503)	(507)	(518)	(505)			(x)	

register (Illustration 8.14). In addition to this credit column, the voucher register has debit columns for the accounts most frequently debited when a liability is incurred, as well as a column to enter the other accounts debited (Other Accounts Dr. column).

At the end of each month, the Vouchers Payable Cr. column total is posted to the general ledger control account, Vouchers Payable. In Illustration 8.14, a voucher is prepared for each invoice. Note that the vouchers in this illustration are recorded net of purchase discounts allowed. If a discount is missed, another voucher is prepared for the discount lost (Illustration 8.14, line 13). (As described below, the voucher system can also be used when purchases are recorded at the gross amount.) The total of each of the specifically titled columns is posted to the designated account. The debits in the Other Accounts Dr. column are posted individually to the accounts named, usually on a daily basis. The total of the Other Accounts column is not posted because each of the amounts it includes affects a different account.

ILLUSTRATION 8.15

Check Register

JACKSON COMPANY						**Page No.:** *24*
CHECK REGISTER						**Month:** *May 1994*

Line No.	Date 1994		Payee	Voucher No.	Check No.	Vouchers Payable Dr. 205, Cash Cr. 100
1	May	5	Moore Transport	224	1347	13.00
2		8	Specialty Advertisers	226	1348	1,200.00
3		10	Blanch Company	227	1349	1,010.00
4		12	Hanley Company	223	1350	980.00
5		12	White Stationery Company	225	1351	102.00
6		20	VOID		1352	
7		20	First National Bank	231	1353	154.00
8		24	Petty cash	233	1354	132.00
9		25	Rizzo Company	229	1355	640.00
10		26	Swanson Company	228] 234]	1356	4,000.00
11		28	Warren Company	230	1357	4,900.00
12		31	Payroll account	236	1358	24,000.00
						37,131.00
						(205)(100)

Check Register A check register is a special journal showing all checks issued, listed chronologically by date and by check number. One line is allotted to each check. No check may be issued unless authorized by an approved voucher.

The check register in Illustration 8.15 shows the entry and procedure when a check is issued in payment of a voucher. Note that Check No. 1352 is marked *void*. This notation usually means that a mistake was made in writing the check, and another check had to be prepared.

The net price method was used in Illustration 8.15, so the check register has only one money column. The column total is posted in the general ledger as a debit to Vouchers Payable and a credit to Cash. If the gross price method is used, invoices are entered gross (before discount deductions) in the voucher register, and a Purchase Discounts Cr. column should be included in the check register. Separate columns would be needed for the debit to Vouchers Payable and the credit to Cash, since the dollar amounts posted to these two accounts would differ by the amount of the discount taken (see Demonstration Problem 8-C for an example).

In a voucher system, the voucher register and the check register are the two primary journals from which postings are made to the Vouchers Payable control account in the general ledger. When a company uses a voucher system, these two journals replace the traditional purchases and cash disbursements journals. However, a sales journal, cash receipts journal, and general journal would still be used.

Procedures for Paying a Voucher

When a voucher is due for payment, it is removed from the unpaid voucher file in the accounting department. A check is prepared for the amount payable. The check, voucher, and supporting documents are then typically sent to the person

---

ILLUSTRATION 8.16

Vouchers Payable Account

GENERAL LEDGER

	Vouchers Payable					*Account No. 205*
Date	Explanation	Post. Ref.	Debit	Credit	Balance
1994 May 1	Beginning balance				– 0 –
31	From voucher register			5 6 9 3 1	5 6 9 3 1
31	From check register		3 7 1 3 1		1 9 8 0 0

---

authorized to sign checks, usually the treasurer. The treasurer examines the documents. If they are in order, the treasurer initials the voucher to show that final approval has been given and signs the check. The check is mailed to the creditor, usually with a remittance advice attached. The voucher is then returned to the accounting department.

On receipt of the paid voucher, the accounting department makes an entry in the check register showing the date paid, check number, voucher number, and amount paid. The check number and date paid are also inserted in the voucher register and on the voucher itself. The voucher then is filed in the paid voucher file.

Files Maintained in a Voucher System

Two files are maintained in a voucher system—unpaid voucher file and paid voucher file.

The **unpaid voucher file** contains all vouchers that have been prepared and approved as proper liabilities but have not yet been paid. These vouchers are filed according to their due dates. The unpaid voucher file takes the place of the accounts payable subsidiary ledger. The total of the vouchers in the unpaid voucher file should equal the total of the *open* items (those items not paid) in the voucher register and also should equal the balance in the Vouchers Payable control account in the general ledger.

The **paid voucher file** contains all vouchers that have been paid. These vouchers are often filed by voucher number in numerical order, but they can be filed by vendor name. Vouchers become a permanent and convenient reference for anyone who wants to check the details of past cash disbursements.

Unpaid Vouchers at the End of the Period

At the end of the accounting period, the total of unpaid vouchers is shown in three places. First, the individual unpaid vouchers are shown in the voucher register, consisting of the vouchers for which no data appear in the Date Paid and Check No. columns (Illustration 8.14, lines 11 and 14). Second, the total is shown as the ending balance in the Vouchers Payable account, shown in Illustration 8.16 for Jackson Company. Third, the total is shown in a schedule prepared at the end of the period—the schedule of unpaid vouchers. Illustration 8.17 shows the schedule

ETHICS

A CLOSER LOOK

The City Club Restaurant is a member-owned entity in Carson City. The manager, John Blue, has managed the restaurant for 20 years and has received only minimal salary increases over that period. He believes he is grossly underpaid in view of the significant inflation that has occurred. A few years ago he began supplementing his income by placing phony "peanut" invoices in the petty cash box, writing a petty cash voucher for the amount of each invoice, withdrawing an amount of cash equal to the amount of each invoice for his personal use, and later approving the vouchers for reimbursement. Through this mechanism, John was able to increase his income by about $12,000 per year, an amount that he considered fair. No one else knows what is happening, and the manager feels fully justified in supplementing his income in this way.

Required   Discuss the ethics of this situation.

ILLUSTRATION 8.17
Schedule of Unpaid Vouchers

JACKSON COMPANY
Schedule of Unpaid Vouchers
May 31, 1994

Voucher No.	Name	Amount
232	Falconer Company	$10,000
235	Celoron Company.	9,800
		$19,800

of unpaid vouchers for Jackson Company. In a balance sheet prepared at the end of an accounting period, the total of unpaid vouchers would normally be labeled as "Accounts payable" rather than "Vouchers payable."

Now that you have learned how to control a company's most liquid asset, cash, you are ready to study about receivables and payables. You probably already realize that the backbone of our economy is credit. In all probability the automobile you bought or plan to buy will be financed. Companies are anxious to offer credit to worthy customers and prospective customers. The many offers of credit from oil companies and banks that you will probably receive are evidence of the importance companies place on credit as a method of expanding their business.

UNDERSTANDING THE LEARNING OBJECTIVES

1. Describe the necessity for and features of internal control.
   □ The internal control structure of a company includes its plan of organization and all the procedures and actions taken by the company to protect its assets against theft and waste, ensure compliance with company policies and federal law, evaluate the performance of all personnel in the company so as to promote efficiency of operations, and ensure accurate and reliable operating data and accounting records.

☐ The purpose of internal control is to ensure the efficient operations of a business.

2. Define cash and list the objectives sought by management in handling a company's cash.

☐ Cash includes coins; currency; undeposited negotiable instruments such as checks, bank drafts, and money orders; amounts in checking and saving accounts; and demand certificates of deposit.

☐ To protect their cash, companies should account for all cash transactions accurately, make certain enough cash is available to pay bills as they come due, avoid holding too much idle cash, and prevent loss of cash due to theft or fraud.

3. Identify procedures for controlling cash receipts and disbursements.

☐ Procedures for controlling cash receipts include such basic principles as recording all cash receipts as soon as cash is received; depositing all cash receipts as soon as feasible, preferably on the day they are received or on the next business day; and preventing the employee who handles cash receipts from also recording the receipts in the accounting records or from disbursing cash.

☐ Procedures for controlling cash disbursements include, among others, making all disbursements by check or from petty cash, using checks that are serially numbered, requiring two signatures on each check, and having a different person authorize payment of a bill than the person allowed to sign checks.

4. Prepare a bank reconciliation and make necessary journal entries based on that schedule.

☐ A bank reconciliation is prepared to *reconcile,* or explain, the difference between the cash balance shown on the bank statement and the cash balance shown on the company's books.

☐ A bank reconciliation is shown in Illustration 8.11.

☐ Journal entries are needed for all items that appear in the bank reconciliation as adjustments to the balance per ledger to arrive at the adjusted cash balance.

5. Explain why a petty cash fund is used, describe its operations, and make the necessary journal entries.

☐ Companies establish a petty cash fund to permit minor disbursements to be made in cash and still maintain adequate control over cash.

☐ When the cash in the petty cash fund becomes low, the fund should be replenished. A journal entry is necessary to record the replenishment.

6. Describe the operation of the voucher system and make entries in its special journals—the voucher register and the check register.

☐ The voucher system is a set of procedures, special journals, and authorization forms designed to provide control over cash payments.

☐ A voucher is a form with spaces provided for data about a liability that must be paid.

☐ A voucher register is a multicolumn special journal containing a record of all vouchers prepared, listed chronologically by date and voucher number.

☐ A check register is a special journal showing all checks issued, listed chronologically by date and check number.

DEMONSTRATION PROBLEM 8–A

You are the manager of a restaurant that has a magazine store as a separate unit. Your accountant comes in once a year to prepare financial statements and the tax return. In the current year, you have a feeling that even though business seems good, net income is going to be lower. You ask the accountant to prepare condensed statements on a monthly basis. All sales are priced to yield an estimated gross margin of 40%. You, your accountant, and several of the accountant's assistants take physical inventories at the end of each of the four months indicated below. The resulting sales, cost of goods sold, and gross margins are:

	March		April		May		June	
	Restau-rant	Magazine Store	Restau-rant	Magazine Store	Restau-rant	Magazine Store	Restau-rant	Magazine Store
Sales	$145,200	$212,000	$156,200	$171,000	$152,400	$156,000	$165,000	$142,000
Cost of goods sold . . .	93,100	126,000	95,200	124,000	91,900	123,000	102,000	124,500
Gross margin	$ 52,100	$ 86,000	$ 61,000	$ 47,000	$ 60,500	$ 33,000	$ 63,000	$ 17,500

Required What would you suspect after analyzing these reports? What sales control procedures would you recommend to correct the situation? All of the points covered in this problem were not specifically covered in the chapter, although the principles were. Use logic, common sense, and knowledge gained elsewhere in coming up with some of the control procedures.

SOLUTION TO DEMONSTRATION PROBLEM 8–A

The gross margin percentages are as follows:

	March	April	May	June
Restaurant	35.88%	39.05%	39.70%	38.18%
Magazine store	40.57	27.49	21.15	12.32

Either cash or inventory is being stolen or given away in the magazine store. Several things could be done to improve the sales control procedures:

1. The manager could hire an investigator to come in and watch the employees in action. If cash is being pocketed, the employees could be fired.

2. The prices of magazines could be changed to odd amounts so that employees would not be as able to make change without going to the cash register. Also, the "No Sale" lever could be removed from the cash register.

3. The customers could be encouraged to ask for their cash register receipts by having a monthly drawing (for some prize) by cash register receipt number.

4. The cash register should be placed in a prominent position so that each customer could see the amount recorded for each sale. The customer is not going to be willing to pay 65 cents when the employee rings up 50 cents.

5. The cash register tapes should be inaccessible to the employees. The manager (and possibly assistant manager) should have the only keys to the cash registers.

6. Mention to the employees that you have an effective control structure. They don't have to know what the structure is.
7. Pay the employees a competitive wage.
8. Require that all sales be rung up immediately after the sale.
9. The manager or assistant manager should reconcile the cash register tapes at the end of each day.

DEMONSTRATION PROBLEM 8–B

The following data pertain to Arthur Company:

1. Balance per bank statement, dated March 31, 1994, is $17,800.
2. Balance of the Cash account on the company's books as of March 31, 1994, is $17,836.
3. The $5,200 deposit of March 31 was not shown on the bank statement.
4. Of the checks recorded as cash disbursements in March, some checks, totaling $4,200, have not yet cleared the bank.
5. Service and collection charges for the month were $40.
6. The bank erroneously charged the Arthur Company account for the $800 check of another company. The check was included with the canceled checks returned with the bank statement.
7. The bank credited the company's account with the $4,000 proceeds of a noninterest-bearing note that it collected for the company.
8. A customer's $300 check marked NSF was returned with the bank statement.
9. As directed, the bank paid and charged to the company's account a $2,030 noninterest-bearing note of Arthur Company. This payment has not been recorded by the company.
10. An examination of the cash receipts and the deposit tickets revealed that the bookkeeper erroneously recorded a customer's check of $382 as $328.
11. The bank credited the company for $80 of interest earned on the company's checking account.

Required *a.* Prepare a bank reconciliation as of March 31, 1994.
    b. Prepare the necessary journal entry or entries to adjust the Cash account.

SOLUTION TO DEMONSTRATION PROBLEM 8–B

a.

ARTHUR COMPANY
Bank Reconciliation
March 31, 1994

Balance per bank statement, March 31, 1994		$17,800
Add: Deposit in transit	$5,200	
Check charged in error.	800	6,000
		$23,800
Less: Outstanding checks.		4,200
Adjusted balance, March 31, 1994		$19,600
Balance per ledger, March 31, 1994		$17,836
Add: Note collected	$4,000	
Interest earned on checking account	80	
Error in recording customer's check	54	4,134
		$21,970
Less: Service and collection charges	$ 40	
NSF check.	300	
Arthur Company note charged against account.	2,030	2,370
Adjusted balance, March 31, 1994		$19,600

b.

1994					
Mar.	31	Cash.	1,764	
		Bank Service Charge Expense	40	
		Accounts Receivable.	300	
		Notes Payable	2,030	
		Notes Receivable		4,000
		Interest Revenue		80
		Accounts Receivable.		54
		To record adjustments to Cash account.		

Alternatively:

1994				
Mar.	31	Cash.	4,134	
		Notes Receivable		4,000
		Interest Revenue		80
		Accounts Receivable.		54
		To record additions to Cash account.		
	31	Bank Service Charge Expense	40	
		Accounts Receivable.	300	
		Notes Payable	2,030	
		Cash.		2,370
		To record deductions from Cash account.		

DEMONSTRATION PROBLEM 8–C

Alarm Company uses a voucher system to control cash disbursements. Purchases are recorded at gross invoice prices. As of April 30, 1994, two vouchers are unpaid: Voucher No. 404 payable to Soul Company for $1,700 and Voucher No. 405 payable to Alcantar Company for $100.

Alarm Company engaged in the following transactions affecting vouchers payable:

May 1 Prepared Voucher No. 406 payable to Lake Company for merchandise purchased; price on invoice dated April 30 is $800. Terms are 2/10, n/30, FOB destination.

2 Issued Check No. 385 in payment of Voucher No. 405; no discount was offered on this purchase.

4 Received a credit memo for $200 for merchandise returned to Soul Company. Purchase was originally recorded in Voucher No. 404. (Record in general journal with notation of return on Voucher No. 404.)

5 Prepared Voucher No. 407 payable to Martin Brothers for merchandise with an invoice price of $1,900 on invoice dated May 3; terms are 2/10, n/30, FOB shipping point, freight prepaid. Supplier paid $100 freight bill and added $100 to the invoice for a total billing of $2,000.

6 Prepared Voucher No. 408 payable to UGA, Inc., for cost incurred to deliver merchandise sold, $240; terms n/10.

8 Issued Check No. 386 to pay Voucher No. 404, less return and less a 2% discount.

9 Issued Check No. 387 to pay Voucher No. 406.

12 Prepared Voucher No. 409 payable to Holt Insurance Company for $600, the three-year premium on an insurance policy. Issued Check No. 388 to pay Voucher No. 409.

13 Issued Check No. 389 to pay Voucher No. 407.

15 Prepare Voucher No. 410 payable to Cash for salaries of $4,000 for the first half of May. Issued Check No. 390 in payment of Voucher No. 410. Cashed the check and paid employees in cash.

16 Issued Check No. 391 to pay Voucher No. 408.

23 Prepared Voucher No. 411 payable to Strait Company for merchandise with an invoice price of $600 on invoice dated May 22; terms are 2/10, n/30, FOB shipping point, freight collect.

24 Prepared Voucher No. 412 payable to Trail-Lines, Inc., for $100 freight on merchandise purchased on May 23.

26 Prepared Voucher No. 413 payable to Tell Telephone Company for $250 for monthly telephone service.

28 Prepared Voucher No. 414 payable to Flowers, Inc., for costs incurred to deliver merchandise sold, $160; terms n/30.

31 Prepared Voucher No. 415 payable to Cash for salaries for the last half of May, $4,400. Issued Check No. 392 in payment of Voucher No. 415. Cashed the check and paid employees in cash.

Required a. Record the transactions above using a voucher register, check register, and a general journal. You need not include account numbers.

b. Prepare a Vouchers Payable account and post the portions of the entries that affect this account.

c. Prepare a schedule (list) of unpaid vouchers to prove the accuracy of the balance in the Vouchers Payable account.

SOLUTION TO DEMONSTRATION PROBLEM 8–C

a. The voucher register is on the following page; the check register and the general journal are on page 413.

a.

ALARM COMPANY
VOUCHER REGISTER

Voucher Date 1994	Voucher No.	Payee	Terms	Date Paid	Check No.	Vouchers Payable Cr.	Purchases Dr.	Transportation-In Dr.	Delivery Expense Dr.	Salaries Expense Dr.	Other Accounts Dr. Account Name	Other Accounts Dr. Post. Ref.	Other Accounts Dr. Amount Dr.
May 1	406	Lake Company	2/10, n/30	May 9	387	800	800						
5	407	Martin Brothers	2/10, n/30	13	389	2,000	1,900	100					
6	408	UGA, Inc.	n/10	16	391	240			240				
12	409	Holt Insurance Company		12	388	600					Prepaid Insurance		600
15	410	Cash		15	390	4,000				4,000			
23	411	Strait Company	2/10, n/30			600	600						
24	412	Trail-Lines, Inc.				100		100					
26	413	Tell Telephone Company				250					Utilities Expense		250
28	414	Flowers, Inc.	n/30			160			160				
31	415	Cash		31	392	4,400				4,400			
						13,150	3,300	200	400	8,400			850

a. (concluded)

ALARM COMPANY
CHECK REGISTER

Page 5

Date 1994		Payee	Voucher No.	Check No.	Vouchers Payable Dr.	Purchase Discounts Cr.	Cash Cr.
May	2	Alcantar Company	405	385	100		100
	8	Soul Company	404	386	1,500	30	1,470
	9	Lake Company	406	387	800	16	784
	12	Holt Insurance Company	409	388	600		600
	13	Martin Brothers	407	389	2,000	38	1,962
	15	Cash	410	390	4,000		4,000
	16	UGA, Inc.	408	391	240		240
	31	Cash	415	392	4,400		4,400
					13,640	84	13,556

ALARM COMPANY
GENERAL JOURNAL

Page 17

Date	Account Titles and Explanation	Post. Ref.	Debit	Credit
1994 May 4	Vouchers Payable		200	
	Purchase Returns and Allowances			200
	To record receipt of credit memo for merchandise returned;			
	Voucher No. 404.			

b.

ALARM COMPANY
GENERAL LEDGER

Vouchers Payable

Account No. 205

Date	Explanation	Post. Ref.	Debit	Credit	Balance
1994 Apr. 30	Beginning balance				1 800 Cr.
May 4	Credit memo; Voucher No. 404	G17	200		1 600 Cr.
31		VR12		13 150	14 750 Cr.
31		CR5	13 640		1 110 Cr.

c.

ALARM COMPANY
Schedule of Unpaid Vouchers
May 31, 1994

Voucher No.	Name	Amount
411	Strait Company	$ 600
412	Trail-Lines, Inc.	100
413	Tell Telephone Company	250
414	Flowers, Inc.	160
		$1,110

NEW TERMS

Accounting system Methods and records established to identify, assemble, analyze, classify, record, and report an entity's transactions to provide complete, accurate, and timely financial information. *378*

Bank reconciliation A schedule the company (depositor) prepares to *reconcile,* or explain, the difference between the cash balance shown on the bank statement and the cash balance on the company's books; often called a *bank reconciliation statement* or *schedule. 392*

Bank statement A statement issued (usually monthly) by a bank describing the activities in a depositor's checking account during the period. *388*

Cash Includes coins; currency; certain undeposited negotiable instruments such as checks, bank drafts, and money orders; amounts in checking and savings accounts; and demand certificates of deposit. *384*

Cashier's check A check drawn by a bank made out to either the depositor or a third party after deducting the amount of the check from the depositor's account or receiving cash from the depositor. *395*

Certificate of deposit (CD) An interest-bearing deposit in a bank that can be withdrawn at will (demand CD) or at a fixed maturity date (time CD). *384*

Certified check A check written, or drawn, by a depositor and taken to the depositor's bank for certification. The check is deducted from the depositor's balance immediately and becomes a liability of the bank. Thus, the check will usually be accepted without question. *395*

Check A written order on a bank to pay a specific sum of money to the party designated as the payee by the party issuing the check. *388*

Check register A special journal showing all checks issued, listed chronologically by date and by check number. *404*

Checking account A money balance maintained in the bank that is subject to withdrawal by the depositor, or owner of the money, on demand. *387*

Control environment Reflects the overall attitude, awareness, and actions of the board of directors, management, and owners. *378*

Control procedures Policies and procedures, in addition to the control environment and the accounting system, that management has established to provide reasonable assurance that the company will achieve its specific objectives. *378*

Credit memo A form used by a bank to explain an addition to the depositor's account. *391*

Debit memo A form used by a bank to explain a deduction from the depositor's account. *391*

Deposit in transit Typically, a day's cash receipts recorded in the depositor's books in one period but recorded as a deposit by the bank in the succeeding period. *392*

Deposit ticket A form that shows the date and the items that make up the deposit. *388*

Drawer The party (depositor) writing a check. *388*

Fidelity bonds Ensure that a company is reimbursed for losses due to theft of cash and other monetary assets. *381*

Internal auditing Consists of investigating and evaluating employees' compliance with the company's policies and procedures. Internal auditing is performed by company personnel. *380*

Internal auditors Auditors employed by the company to perform internal audits. These auditors are trained in company policies and in internal auditing duties such as testing effectiveness of controls and procedures involving cash receipts and cash disbursements. *380*

Internal control structure Policies and procedures established to provide reasonable assurance that specific entity objectives will be achieved. *378*

Invoice Statement sent by the supplier to the purchaser requesting payment for the merchandise shipped. *381*

NSF check A customer's check returned from the customer's bank to the depositor's bank because the funds in the customer's checking account balance were insufficient to cover the check. *388*

Outstanding checks Checks issued by a depositor that have not yet been paid by the bank on which they are drawn. *392*

Paid voucher file A permanent file used in a voucher system where paid vouchers are filed in numerical sequence. *405*

Payee The party to whom a check is made payable. *388*

Petty cash fund A nominal sum of money established as a separate fund from which minor cash disbursements for valid business purposes are made. The cash in the fund plus the vouchers covering disbursements must always equal the balance at which the fund was established and at which it is carried in the Petty Cash account. *395*

Petty cash voucher A document or form that shows the amount of, and reason for, a petty cash disbursement. *398*

Purchase order A document sent from the purchasing department to a supplier requesting that merchandise or other items be shipped to the purchaser. *381*

Purchase requisition A written request from an employee inside the company to the purchasing department to purchase certain items. *380*

Receiving report A document prepared by the receiving department showing the descriptions and quantities of all items received from a supplier in a particular shipment. *381*

Remittance advice Informs the payee why the drawer (or maker) of the check is making this payment. *388*

Segregation of duties Having the employee responsible for safeguarding an asset be someone other than the employee who maintains the accounting records for that asset. *379*

Service charges Charges assessed by the bank on the depositor to cover the cost of handling the checking account. *388*

Signature card Provides the signatures of persons authorized to sign checks drawn on an account. *388*

Transfer bank accounts A bank account set up so that local banks automatically transfer to a central bank (by wire or written bank draft) all amounts on deposit in excess of a stated amount. *390*

Unpaid voucher file Contains all vouchers that have been prepared and approved as proper liabilities but have not yet been paid. Serves as an accounts payable subsidiary ledger under a voucher system; unpaid vouchers are filed according to their due dates. *405*

Voucher A form with spaces provided for data about a liability that must be paid. The data include items such as creditor's name and address, description of the goods or services received, invoice number, terms of payment, due date, and amount due, and often show the ledger accounts and amounts to be debited. The voucher also has spaces for signatures of those approving the liability for payment. *400*

Voucher register A multicolumn special journal used in a voucher system; the voucher register contains a record of all vouchers prepared, listed in order by date and voucher number. A brief explanation of each transaction also may be included. In addition to a credit column for Vouchers Payable, a voucher register normally has various debit columns for accounts such as Purchases, Salaries, and Transportation-In. *402*

Voucher system A set of procedures, special journals, and authorization forms designed to provide control over cash payments. *400*

Wire transfer of funds Interbank transfer of funds by telephone. *390*

SELF-TEST

True-False

Indicate whether each of the following statements is true or false.

1. Cash includes certain negotiable instruments, demand certificates of deposit, and postdated checks, among other items.

2. While a company must make certain it has enough cash to pay bills, it should avoid holding excess cash.

3. All cash receipts should be deposited intact in the bank, and cash disbursements should not be made directly from cash receipts.

4. In a bank reconciliation, outstanding checks are deducted from the cash balance per books.

5. The Petty Cash account is debited for the establishment of the fund but is not credited for expenditures from the fund.

6. In a voucher system, the unpaid voucher file replaces the accounts payable subsidiary ledger.

Multiple-Choice

Select the best answer for each of the following questions.

1. Which of the following is the objective of an effective internal control structure?

a. Protect the company's assets against theft and waste.

b. Promote efficiency of operations by evaluating personnel performance.

c. Ensure compliance with company policies and federal law.

d. Enhance accurate and reliable operating data and accounting reports.

e. All of the above.

Use the following information to answer Questions 2–4.

Balance per bank statement	$3,983.98
Deposits in transit	1,236.00
Outstanding checks	1,931.24
Balance per ledger	3,488.74
Bank service charges	15.00
NSF checks issued by a customer	185.00

2. The adjusted cash balance is:
  a. $2,593.50.
  b. $3,288.74.
  c. $4,524.74.
  d. $4,624.74.
  e. $3,783.98.

3. In the bank reconciliation, outstanding checks should be:
  a. Deducted from the balance per bank statement.
  b. Deducted from the balance per ledger.
  c. Added to the balance per bank statement.
  d. Added to the balance per books.
  e. Disregarded in the bank reconciliation.

4. In the entry to record NSF checks, the credit should be to:
  a. Cash Short and Over.
  b. Accounts Receivable.
  c. Cash.
  d. Petty Cash.
  e. None of the above.

5. The $200 petty cash fund currently has cash of $42.20. A summary of the petty cash vouchers shows payments of $50.45 for office supplies, $58.05 for an advance to an employee, and $49.30 for transportation-in. The entry to replenish the petty cash fund would include:
  a. A debit to Advances to Employees for $58.05.
  b. A credit to Cash for $157.80.
  c. A debit to Office Supplies for $50.45.
  d. A debit to Transportation-In for $49.30.
  e. All of these.

6. In a voucher system, a company no longer has need for:
  a. A petty cash fund.
  b. A sales journal.
  c. An accounts payable subsidiary ledger.
  d. A general journal.
  e. A check register.

Now turn to page 432 to check your answers.

QUESTIONS

1. Why should a company establish an internal control structure?

2. Identify some features that if present would strengthen an internal control structure.

3. Name several control documents that are used in merchandise transactions.

4. What are the four objectives sought in effective cash management?

5. List four essential features of internal control over cash receipts.

6. Why is it so important that a company have segregation of employee duties?

7. The bookkeeper of a given company was stealing cash received from customers in payment of their accounts. To conceal the theft, the bookkeeper made out false credit memos indicating returns and allowances made by or granted to customers. What feature of internal control would have prevented the thefts?

8. List six essential features of internal control over cash disbursements.

9. "The difference between a company's Cash account balance and the balance on its bank statement is usually a matter of timing." Do you agree or disagree? Why?

10. Explain how transfer bank accounts can help bring about effective cash management.

11. Where does a bank service charge belong on the bank reconciliation?

12. Describe the operation of a petty cash fund and its advantages. Indicate how control is maintained over petty cash transactions.

13. What should the petty cash custodian do with the excess cash if the petty cash fund is too large? What entry would be made to reduce the size of the fund?

14. What can be accomplished with a voucher system that is not accomplished through use of a purchases journal and a cash disbursements journal?

15. What should be the relationship between the balance in the Vouchers Payable account, the *open* items in the voucher register, and the total of all vouchers in the unpaid vouchers file?

16. You are the chief accountant of Reedcot Company. An invoice has just been received from Sunray Company in the amount of $4,000, with credit terms of 2/10, n/30. List the procedures you would follow in processing this invoice through the point of filing it in the unpaid vouchers file.

17. Refer to the situation described in Question 16.

Assume that the time for payment of the voucher has arrived and the payment is to be made within the discount period. List the actions that would be taken if the company uses the net price method.

18. What would be the procedures if the discount period had elapsed before payment was made in Question 17?

19. List the posting steps that would be used to post the data shown in Illustration 8.14. How many amounts would actually be posted?

The Coca-Cola Company

20. *Real world question* From the consolidated balance sheet of The Coca-Cola Company in Appendix E, identify the total 1989 cash and marketable securities. Explain the definition of cash equivalents and marketable securities in accordance with the footnotes.

MAYTAG CORPORATION

21. *Real world question* Based on the financial statements of Maytag Corporation contained in Appendix E, what was the 1989 ending cash and cash equivalents balance?

THE LIMITED, INC.

22. *Real world question* Based on the financial statements of The Limited, Inc., in Appendix E, what was the 1989 beginning cash and cash equivalents balance?

HARLAND

23. *Real world question* Based on the financial statements of John H. Harland Company contained in Appendix E, what was the 1989 ending short-term investments balance?

EXERCISES

Exercise 8–1
Answer true-false questions about internal control
(L.O. 1)

State whether each of the following statements about internal control is **true** or **false**:

a. Those employees responsible for safeguarding an asset should maintain the accounting records for that asset.

b. Complete, accurate, and up-to-date accounting records should be maintained.

c. Whenever possible, responsibilities should be assigned and duties subdivided in such a way that only one employee is responsible for a given function.

d. Employees should be assigned to one job and should remain in that job so that skill levels will be as high as possible.

e. The use of check protectors, check registers, and time clocks is recommended.

f. An internal auditing function should not be implemented because it leads the employees to believe that management does not trust them.

g. One of the best protections against theft is to hire honest, competent employees.

h. A foolproof internal control structure can be devised if management puts forth the effort.

Exercise 8–2
Answer multiple-choice question about internal control
(L.O. 1)

Concerning internal control, which one of the following statements is correct? Explain.

a. Broadly speaking, internal control is only necessary in large organizations.

b. The purposes of internal control are to check the accuracy of accounting data, safeguard assets against theft, promote efficiency of operations, and ensure that management's policies are being followed.

c. Once an internal control structure has been established, it should be effective as long as the formal organization remains unchanged.

d. An example of internal control is having one individual count the day's cash receipts and compare the total with the total of the cash register tapes.

Exercise 8–3
Determine available cash balance from bank statement and Cash account data
(L.O. 4)

The bank statement for House Company at the end of August showed a balance of $37,200. Checks outstanding totaled $42,000, and deposits in transit were $63,900. If these amounts are the only pertinent data available to you, what was the available balance of cash at the end of August?

Exercise 8–4

Prepare bank reconciliation and specify cash available
(L.O. 4)

From the following data, prepare a bank reconciliation and determine the correct available cash balance for Big, Inc., as of October 31, 1994.

Balance per bank statement, October 31, 1994	$37,264
Ledger account balance, October 31, 1994	21,568
Note collected by bank not yet entered into ledger	16,000
Bank service charges not yet entered by Big, Inc.	48
Deposit in transit	4,480
Outstanding checks:	
No. 327	1,744
No. 328	768
No. 329	1,040
No. 331	672

Exercise 8–5

Record necessary journal entry or entries to correct cash balance
(L.O. 4)

The following is a bank reconciliation for Massey Company as of August 31, 1994.

Balance per bank statement, August 31, 1994		$ 7,470
Add: Deposit in transit		5,676
		$13,146
Less: Outstanding checks		6,024
Adjusted balance, August 31, 1994		$ 7,122
Balance per ledger, August 31, 1994		$ 7,248
Add: Error correction		54*
		$ 7,302
Less: NSF checks	$150	
Service charges	30	180
Adjusted balance, August 31, 1994		$ 7,122

* The error occurred when the bookkeeper debited Accounts Payable and credited Cash for $160, instead of the correct amount, $106.

Prepare the journal entry or entries needed to adjust or correct the Cash account.

Exercise 8–6

Determine checks outstanding
(L.O. 4)

On March 1 of the current year, Parkway Company had outstanding checks of $120,000. During March, the company issued an additional $456,000 of checks. As of March 31, the bank statement showed $384,000 of checks had cleared the bank during the month. What is the amount of outstanding checks on March 31?

Exercise 8–7

Determine deposits in transit
(L.O. 4)

Fuller Company's bank statement as of August 31, 1994, shows total deposits into the company's account of $77,010 and a total of 14 separate deposits. On July 31, deposits of $4,050 and $3,150 were in transit. The total cash receipts for August were $98,760, and the company's records show 13 deposits made in August. What is the amount of deposits in transit at August 31?

Exercise 8–8

Prepare bank reconciliation and necessary journal entry or entries
(L.O. 4)

Packard Company deposits all cash receipts intact each day and makes all payments by check. On October 31, after all posting was completed, its Cash account had a debit balance of $27,680. The bank statement for the month ended on October 31 showed a balance of $25,520. Other data are:

1. Outstanding checks total $2,720.
2. October 31 cash receipts of $5,360 were placed in the bank's night depository and do not appear on the bank statement.
3. Bank service charges for October are $96.
4. Check No. 772 for store supplies on hand was entered at $2,592, but paid by the bank at its actual amount of $2,016.

Prepare a bank reconciliation for Packard as of October 31. Also prepare any needed journal entries.

Exercise 8–9
Record reimbursement of petty cash fund
(L.O. 5)

On August 31, 1994, Mason Company's petty cash fund contained coins and currency of $329.60, an IOU from an employee of $40, and vouchers showing expenditures of $160 for postage, $68 for taxi fare, and $184 to entertain a customer. The Petty Cash account shows a balance of $800. The fund is replenished on August 31 because financial statements are to be prepared. What journal entry is required on August 31?

Exercise 8–10
Record reimbursement of petty cash fund
(L.O. 5)

Use the data in Exercise 8–9. What entry would have been required if the amount of coin and currency had been $348? Which of the accounts debited would not appear in the income statement?

Exercise 8–11
Prepare journal entries regarding petty cash
(L.O. 5)

Bunting Company has a $600 petty cash fund. The following transactions occurred in December:

Dec. 2 The petty cash fund was increased to $900.
     8 Petty Cash Voucher No. 318 for $16.14 delivery expense was prepared and paid. The fund was not replenished at this time.
   20 The company decided that the fund was too large and reduced it to $750.

Prepare any necessary journal entries for the above transactions.

Exercise 8–12
Determine vouchers payable balance; compute current month's vouchers paid
(L.O. 6)

Refer to Illustration 8.14.

a. Assuming that all vouchers written before May 1, 1994, have been paid, what is the balance in the Vouchers Payable account on May 31, 1994?

b. All checks written in May were in payment of May vouchers. What is the total dollar amount of vouchers paid in May?

c. Explain how it is possible to determine the cash paid out in May to pay May's vouchers without looking at the check register.

Exercise 8–13
Prepare general journal entries to record selected transactions and indicate whether recorded in voucher or check register
(L.O. 6)

Daniel Company uses a voucher system. Recently, the company had the following transactions:

a. Prepared Voucher No. 801 for purchase of merchandise from Columbia Company, $2,500.

b. Issued Check No. 723 to pay Voucher No. 801.

c. Prepared Voucher No. 802 to set up a petty cash fund, $750.

d. Issued Check No. 724 to pay Voucher No. 802.

e. Prepared Voucher No. 804 for $100 freight on merchandise in Voucher No. 801.

f. Prepared Voucher No. 805 to replenish petty cash when it contained cash of $140 and receipts for postage, $330; supplies, $170; and miscellaneous expense, $100.

g. Issued Check No. 725 to pay Voucher No. 805.

Prepare entries in general journal form to record the above transactions. Identify the journal or book of original entry in which each transaction would normally appear.

Exercise 8–14
Describe what amounts and information would appear in a voucher system to record payment for purchase under net price procedure when discount is lost
(L.O. 6)

Assume that Walker Company uses a voucher register and a check register exactly like Illustration 8.14 and Illustration 8.15. On May 1, Walker Company purchased merchandise from Alex Company, $6,000; terms 2/10, n/30. Walker prepared Voucher No. 567 for $5,880. On May 29, Walker paid for the merchandise purchased from Alex Company and missed the discount (Check No. 489).

State what information should be entered in the voucher register and the check register to record the payment of May 29. Assume that the last voucher used was No. 598.

PROBLEMS: SERIES A

Problem 8–1A

Prepare bank
reconciliation with
necessary journal entry or
entries
(L.O. 4)

The bank statement for Metro Company's account with First National Bank for the month ended April 30, 1994, showed a balance of $65,316. On this date, the company's Cash account balance was $57,162. Returned with the bank statement were (1) a debit memo for service charges of $60; (2) a debit memo for a customer's NSF check of $600; and (3) a credit memo for a $13,200 wire transfer of funds on April 30 from Security Bank, the local bank used by the company's branch office. Further investigation revealed that outstanding checks amounted to $7,800; the cash receipts of April 30 of $9,726 did not appear as a deposit on the bank statement; and the canceled checks included a check for $2,460 (drawn by the president of the company to cover travel expenses on a recent trip), which the company has yet to record.

Required   *a.*   Prepare a bank reconciliation for the month ended April 30, 1994.

               b.   Prepare any necessary journal entry or entries.

Problem 8–2A

Prepare bank
reconciliation with
necessary journal entry or
entries
(L.O. 4)

The following information pertains to Western Company. The June 30, 1994, bank reconciliation was as follows:

	Cash Account	Bank Statement
Balance on June 30	$204,195.84	$205,955.84
Add: Deposit not credited by bank (credited to company by bank on July 1)		2,971.20
Total		$208,927.04
Deduct: Outstanding checks:		
No. 732 . . . . $ 196.80		
No. 894 . . . . 160.00		
No. 904 . . . . 1,531.20		
No. 905 . . . . 2,001.60		
No. 906 . . . . 841.60		4,731.20
Adjusted cash balance, June 30	$204,195.84	$204,195.84

The July bank statement was as follows:

Balance on July 1	$205,955.84	
Deposits during July	50,964.16	$256,920.00
Canceled checks returned:		
No. 732 . . . . $ 196.80		
No. 904 . . . . 1,531.20		
No. 905 . . . . 2,001.60		
No. 906 . . . . 841.60		
No. 907 . . . . 201.12		
No. 908 . . . . 15,312.00		
No. 910 . . . . 10,100.48		
No. 912 . . . . 469.44	$ 30,654.24	
NSF check of Horace Company	556.32	
Service charge	20.00	31,230.56
Bank statement balance, July 31		$225,689.44

The cash receipts deposited in July, including receipts of July 31, amounted to $63,235.20. Checks written in July:

No. 907	. . . . . .	$ 201.12
No. 908	. . . . . .	15,312.00
No. 909	. . . . . .	296.00
No. 910	. . . . . .	10,100.48
No. 911	. . . . . .	636.80
No. 912	. . . . . .	469.44
No. 913	. . . . . .	11,664.00
No. 914	. . . . . .	160.00

The cash balance per the ledger on July 31, 1994, was $228,591.20.

Required Prepare a bank reconciliation and any necessary journal entry or entries.

Problem 8–3A

Prepare bank reconciliation with necessary journal entry or entries (L.O. 4)

The following information is taken from the books and records of Taeko Company.

Balance per ledger, July 31, 1994.	$92,968
Collections received on the last day of July and debited to Cash in Bank on books but not entered by bank until August.	21,248
Debit memo for customer's check returned unpaid (uncollectible check is on hand, but no entry for the return has been made on the books)	2,000
Debit memo for bank service charge for July.	60
Checks issued but not paid by bank.	20,136
Credit memo for proceeds of a note receivable that was left at the bank for collection but has not been recorded on the books as collected.	3,200
Check for an account payable entered on books as $1,920 but issued and paid by the bank in the correct amount of $3,360	
Balance per bank statement, July 31, 1994	91,556

Required Prepare a bank reconciliation and the necessary journal entry or entries to adjust the accounts.

Problem 8–4A

Prepare bank reconciliation with necessary journal entry or entries; comment on control of cash receipts (L.O. 2, 4)

The following data for March 1994 are summarized from the accounts of Brothers Company. The accountant who prepares the monthly bank reconciliation also acts as cashier.

Cash Receipts			Cash Disbursements		
			Check No.		
Mar. 2	. . . . . .	$ 8,800	811	. . . .	$ 7,072
4	. . . . . .	25,600	812	. . . .	9,808
5	. . . . . .	10,400	813	. . . .	11,664
11	. . . . . .	22,400	814	. . . .	7,104
13	. . . . . .	28,000	815	. . . .	12,912
14	. . . . . .	33,600	816	. . . .	19,200
19	. . . . . .	8,000	817	. . . .	30,400
20	. . . . . .	6,400	818	. . . .	21,600
27	. . . . . .	480	819	. . . .	6,000
29	. . . . . .	2,560	820	. . . .	5,600

At March 1 the checks outstanding were:

Check No.		
109	. . . . . .	$ 720
692	. . . . . .	12,800
696	. . . . . .	4,464
810	. . . . . .	10,096

There were no deposits in transit. The balance of the Cash in Bank account per books was $122,800 at March 31. The bank statement for March is as follows:

	BANK STATEMENT		
Date	**Checks**	**Deposits**	**Balance**
Mar. 1			136,000
3		8,800	144,800
4	7,072		
4	9,808		127,920
6		36,000	163,920
9	12,912		
9	7,104		143,904
16		84,000	227,904
19	19,200		
19	21,600		187,104
24		14,400	201,504
25	4,464		
25	10,096		186,944
26	30,400		
26	8,000 NSF		148,544
27	8,000 DM		140,544
29		3,040	143,584
31	32 DM		143,552

The debit memoranda (DM) are for the payment of a company note and for the monthly service charge.

Required

a. Prepare a bank reconciliation as of March 31, 1994.

b. Prepare the journal entry or entries necessary to correct the books.

c. Comment on the company's control of cash receipts.

Problem 8–5A

Prepare bank reconciliation with necessary journal entry or entries
(L.O. 4)

The following information pertains to the bank reconciliation to be prepared for Penland Company as of May 31, 1994:

1. Balance per bank statement as of May 31, 1994, was $21,960.

2. Balance per Penland Company's Cash account at May 31, 1994, was $23,812.

3. A late deposit on May 31 did not appear on the bank statement, $1,900.

4. Outstanding checks as of May 31 totaled $2,200.

5. During May, the bank credited Penland Company with the proceeds, $3,020, of a note that it had collected for the company.

6. Service and collection charges for the month amount to $8.

7. Comparison of the canceled checks with copies of these checks reveals that one check in the amount of $468 had been recorded in the books at $684. The check had been issued in payment of an account payable.

8. A review of the deposit slips with the bank statement showed that a deposit of $1,000 of Pendler and Company has been credited to the Penland Company account.

9. A $120 check received from a customer, Diane Barba, was returned with the bank statement marked NSF.

10. During May, the bank paid a $6,060 note of Penland Company and charged it to the company's account per instructions received. Penland Company had not recorded the payment of this note.

11. An examination of the cash receipts and the deposit tickets revealed that the bookkeeper erroneously recorded a customer's check of $648 as $848.

Required   *a.*   Prepare a bank reconciliation as of May 31, 1994.

b.   Prepare the journal entry or entries necessary to adjust the accounts as of May 31, 1994.

Problem 8–6A

Compute Cash account balance, amount of receipts not deposited, and amount of unrecorded check; prepare bank reconciliation with necessary journal entry or entries
(L.O. 4)

The bank reconciliation for Telecom Company for April 30, 1994, was as follows:

	Cash Account	Bank Statement
Balance as of April 30, 1994	$130,504	$214,848
Deposit in transit		5,800
		$220,648
Outstanding checks		104,800
Service charges.	$ 96	
Note paid on demand	14,560	14,656
Adjusted balance on April 30, 1994	$115,848	$115,848

The bank statement for May shows:

Balance, May 1, 1994		$214,848
Deposits		282,896
		$497,744
Checks cleared	$487,600	
Service charges	120	487,720
Balance, May 31, 1994.		$ 10,024

The total cash receipts for May amount to $281,672. The total checks drawn amount to $310,000. This total does not include one check drawn and signed by and payable to the treasurer of the company, who has disappeared. No record of this check appears anywhere in the company's records. Checks outstanding on May 31 total $73,200.

Required   *a.*   Compute the balance in the Cash account as shown by the company's records, excluding the check drawn payable to the treasurer.

b.   Compute the amount of receipts for May not deposited, if any.

c.   Compute the amount of the check drawn payable to the treasurer.

d.   Prepare a bank reconciliation as of May 31, 1994.

e.   Prepare any required journal entry or entries.

f.   Describe a procedure that, if followed, might have prevented the theft of funds by the treasurer.

Problem 8–7A

Prepare journal entries to record establishment and reimbursement of petty cash fund
(L.O. 5)

The following transactions pertain to the petty cash fund of Prince Company:

Nov.   2   An $800 check is drawn, cashed, and the cash placed in the care of the assistant office manager to be used as a petty cash fund.

Dec. 17   The fund is replenished. An analysis of the fund shows:

Coins and currency	$196.54
Petty cash vouchers for:	
Delivery expenses	231.30
Transportation-in	348.16
Postage stamps purchased	20.00

Dec. 31 The end of the accounting period falls on this date. The fund was not replenished. Its contents on this date consist of—

Coins and currency	$669.40
Petty cash vouchers for:	
Delivery expenses	42.20
Postage stamps	48.40
Advance to employee.	40.00

Required   Present journal entries to record the above transactions. Use the Cash Short and Over account for any shortage or overage in the fund.

Problem 8–8A

Prepare entries in voucher and check registers using net price method for purchase discounts (L.O. 6)

Notecard Company was organized January 1 of the current year, 1994. It uses a voucher register and a check register with the same column headings as in Illustrations 8.14 and 8.15, except there are only four debit columns headed Discounts Lost, Merchandise Purchases, Transportation-In, and Other Accounts.

Transactions

Jan. 2 Received merchandise from Washington Company on terms of 2/10, n/30. The invoice received was in the amount of $20,800.

3 Paid transportation charges to Mack Trucking Company on purchase of January 2, $348.

6 Paid Billboard Display Company $13,200 for billboard advertising for a three-month period beginning February 1, 1994.

15 Paid Washington Company for the purchase of January 2.

17 Received merchandise from Turner Company on terms of 2/10, n/30. The invoice received was for $16,800.

18 Received merchandise from Printer Company on terms of 2/10, n/30. The invoice received was for $72,800. Paid net amount today to establish a good credit rating.

23 Received invoice for $7,200 from Wake, Inc., for office equipment recently received. Terms are 2/10, n/30.

30 Recorded the discount lost on the Turner Company invoice of January 17.

Required   Enter the above approved transactions for January in these registers and total the registers. Start with Voucher No. 1 and Check No. 1. Vouchers are prepared for the net amount of the invoice. For discounts lost, a new voucher is prepared for the amount of the discount. You need not include account numbers.

Problem 8–9A

Prepare entries in voucher and check registers using net price method for purchase discounts; confirm balance in Vouchers Payable (L.O. 6)

Jones Company has been conducting business for several years and uses a voucher register and a check register with the same column headings as in Illustrations 8.14 and 8.15, except there are only four debit columns headed Discounts Lost, Merchandise Purchases, Transportation-In, and Other Accounts. The last voucher used was No. 443, and the last check issued was No. A727. As of December 31, 1994, the following three vouchers were in the unpaid voucher file:

Voucher No. 399	$ 5,760
Voucher No. 412	11,200
Voucher No. 442	3,280
	$20,240

The total of the unpaid voucher file agreed with the credit balance in the Vouchers Payable control account. The following transactions occurred during January 1995. Vouchers are prepared for the net amount of the invoice. For discounts lost, a new voucher is prepared for the amount of the discount.

Jan. 2 An invoice in the amount of $5,600 was received from Chaps Company for office equipment already received. Terms were 2/10, n/30, FOB shipping point.

3 Paid a $3,200 note that matured this date plus $64 interest. Payee: Federal Bank.

Jan. 4 Received an invoice for $4,000 from Keene Company for merchandise recently received. Terms were 2/10, n/30.

5 Paid Voucher No. 399 to Guapo Company, $5,760. This information should only be recorded in the check register.

7 Paid $560 to Friendly Service for transportation. Of this amount, $160 was properly chargeable to the purchase from Keene Company, and the balance applied to the purchase of office equipment from Chaps Company. Freight on office equipment should be debited to Office Equipment.

11 Paid Chaps Company for the purchase of office equipment on January 2.

14 Paid Voucher No. 442 to Bugle Company, $3,280. This information should only be recorded in the check register.

15 Paid $880 to Varn Company for advertising services received in January.

20 Paid Keene Company for the purchase of January 4.

22 Received an invoice for $12,000 from Keene Company for merchandise; terms, 2/10, n/30.

31 Paid Radcliff Company $70,400. This amount included $1,408 chargeable to Transportation-In. The balance paid was the net cost of merchandise received today. Terms were 2/10, n/30.

Required   Set up a voucher register and a check register as described and enter the above transactions. You need not include account numbers. Total the registers at January 31. List the unpaid vouchers at January 31 and compare the total with the balance in the Vouchers Payable account (Account No. 205) at that date, after posting has been completed. The Vouchers Payable control account should be set up in general ledger format.

PROBLEMS: SERIES B

Problem 8–1B

Prepare bank reconciliation with necessary journal entry or entries (L.O. 4)

The bank statement for Brown Company's general checking account with First National Bank for the month ended August 31, 1994, showed an ending balance of $106,180; service charges of $200, an NSF check returned of $4,200; and the collection of a $20,200 note. Further investigation revealed that a wire transfer of $36,000 from the bank account maintained by a branch office of the company had not been recorded by the company as having been deposited in the First National Bank account. In addition, a comparison of deposits with receipts showed a deposit in transit of $42,000. Checks outstanding amounted to $30,120, while the cash ledger balance was $66,260.

Required

a. Prepare a bank reconciliation for the Brown Company account for August 31, 1994.

b. Prepare the necessary journal entry or entries.

Problem 8–2B

Prepare bank reconciliation with necessary journal entry or entries (L.O. 4)

The following data pertain to Dennis Company:

1. Balance per the bank statement dated June 30, 1994, is $81,520.

2. Balance of the Cash account on the company books as of June 30, 1994, is $25,220.

3. Outstanding checks as of June 30, 1994, are $40,000.

4. The bank deposit of June 30 for $6,280 was not included in the deposits per the bank statement. The deposit will be credited to the company's account by the bank on July 31.

5. The bank had collected $60,300 that it credited to the Dennis Company account. The bank charged the company a collection fee of $40 on the above note.

6. The bank erroneously charged the Dennis Company account for a $28,000 check of Dennis Company. The check was found among the canceled checks returned with the bank statement.

7. Bank service charges for June, exclusive of the collection fee, amounted to $200.

8. Among the canceled checks was one for $1,380 given in payment of an account. The bookkeeper had recorded the check at $1,740 in the company records.

9. A check of Aaron, a customer, for $8,400, deposited on June 20, was returned by the bank marked NSF. No entry has been made to reflect the returned check on the company records.

10. A check for $1,920 of Joines, a customer, which has been deposited in the bank, was erroneously recorded by the bookkeeper as $3,360.

Required   Prepare a bank reconciliation as of June 30, 1994. Also prepare any necessary journal entry or entries.

Problem 8–3B
Prepare bank
reconciliation with
necessary journal entry or
entries
(L.O. 4)

The following data pertain to Table Company. The bank reconciliation as of June 30, 1994, showed a deposit in transit of $5,400 (which was credited to the company's account by the bank in July) and three checks outstanding:

No. 760	$2,400
No. 770	4,400
No. 771	3,200

During July, the following checks were written and entered in the Cash account:

No. 781	$3,000
No. 782	3,300
No. 783	5,620
No. 784	2,540
No. 785	5,052
No. 786	3,380
No. 787	4,600
No. 788	5,640
No. 789	720
No. 790	9,708
No. 791	9,600
No. 792	3,696

As of July 31, all the checks that were written, except No. 787, were mailed to the payees. Check No. 787 was kept in the vault pending receipt of a statement from the payee. Four deposits were made at the bank:

July 7	$30,000
14	38,400
21	22,800
28	27,600

The bank statement which was received on August 2, correctly included all deposits and showed a balance as of July 31 of $101,040. The following checks were returned: Nos. 770, 771, 781, 782, 783, 784, 785, 786, 789, and 790. With the paid checks were three debit memoranda for—

1. Fee of $16 for the collection of a note on July 30.
2. Monthly service charge of $20.
3. Payment of $3,000 noninterest-bearing note of Table Company.

The bank included a credit for $12,000 dated July 29. The bank telephoned the company on the morning of August 3 to explain that this credit was in error because it represented a transaction between the bank and Tablet Company.

Another credit memorandum showed the bank collected a $4,400 noninterest-bearing note for Table Company.

The balance in the Cash account on the books of Table Company as of July 31 was $61,740.

Required Prepare a bank reconciliation for Table Company as of July 31, 1994. Also prepare any necessary journal entries.

Problem 8–4B

Compute unadjusted Cash account balance; prepare bank reconciliation with necessary journal entry or entries
(L.O. 4)

Parks Company's bank reconciliation of July 31, 1994, included the following information:

Balance per bank statement, July 31, 1994		$41,700
Balance per ledger, July 31, 1994		38,490
Less: Outstanding checks:		
No. 672	$ 700	
No. 674	2,450	
No. 679	2,800	
No. 691	3,010	8,960
Add: Deposit in transit*		5,750

* Credited to the company's account by the bank in August.

Parks Company's records show the following receipts and disbursements for the month ended August 31, 1994:

Cash Receipts			Cash Disbursements	
			Check No.	
Aug. 4	$ 4,700		692	$3,500
6	7,000		693	4,200
20	14,000		694	3,150
31	10,500		695	3,000
			696	3,500

The bank statement covering the month ended August 31 showed:

Balance, July 31, 1994		$41,700
Deposits (4)		31,450
		$73,150
Checks deducted (6)	$17,010	
Service charges	14	17,024
Balance, August 31, 1994		$56,126

The checks returned by the bank were Nos. 672, 674, 691, 692, 693, and 694.

Required
a. Compute the unadjusted cash balance per books as of August 31, 1994.
b. Prepare a bank reconciliation as of August 31, 1994.
c. Prepare any necessary journal entry or entries as of the same date.

Problem 8–5B

Prepare bank reconciliation; determine cash receipts and checks drawn; prepare necessary journal entry or entries
(L.O. 4)

The bank statement of Texas Company's checking account with First National Bank shows:

Balance, June 30, 1994		$295,320
Deposits		436,800
		$732,120
Less: Checks deducted	$432,000	
Service charges	120	432,120
Balance, July 31, 1994		$300,000

The following additional data are available:

1. A credit memorandum included with the canceled checks returned indicates the collection of a note by the bank for Texas Company, $24,000.
2. An NSF check in the amount of $11,040 was returned by the bank and included in the total of checks deducted on the bank statement.
3. Deposits in transit as of July 31, $60,000, and as of June 30, $28,800.
4. Checks outstanding as of June 30, all of which cleared the bank in July, $40,800; checks outstanding as of July 31, $98,400.
5. Balance per ledger account as of July 31, $229,128.
6. Deposits of Teksize Company credited to Texas Company account by bank, $24,000.
7. Check of Teksize Company charged against Texas Company account by bank, $4,800.
8. Deposit of July 21 recorded by the company as $7,644, and by the bank at actual amount of $8,076. The receipts for the day were from collections on account.

Required

a. Prepare a bank reconciliation as of July 31, 1994, for Texas Company.
b. Determine the amount of cash receipts for July shown by Texas Company's accounts prior to adjustment.
c. Determine the amount of checks drawn by Texas in July.
d. Prepare any journal entry or entries needed at July 31, 1994.

Problem 8–6B

Compute correct cash balance, unadjusted cash balance per books, undeposited receipts, and unrecorded check; prepare bank reconciliation with necessary journal entry or entries; state how theft could have been prevented
(L.O. 2, 4)

The treasurer of Grey Company prepared the following correct bank reconciliation as of April 30, 1994:

Balance per bank statement, April 30		$470,360
Add: Deposit in transit		29,360
		$499,720
Deduct: Outstanding checks		144,800
Adjusted balance		$354,920
Balance per ledger, April 30		$363,040
Less: NSF check	$8,000	
Service charges	120	8,120
Adjusted balance		$354,920

The bank statement for May shows:

Balance, May 1, 1994		$ 470,360
Deposits		883,200
		$1,353,560
Checks cleared	$1,320,320	
Service charges	280	1,320,600
Balance, May 31, 1994		$ 32,960

The Grey Company deposits shown on the bank statement include the proceeds of a $240,000 note payable drawn by the treasurer of Grey Company payable to the bank in 60 days. No entry was made for the note in the company's books. The total cash receipts as shown by Grey Company records amount to $654,400, and the total checks recorded amount to $613,120. This latter total does not include one check drawn and signed by the treasurer payable to himself. The treasurer has disappeared. No record of this check appears anywhere in the company's records. Checks outstanding on May 31, 1994, total $133,600.

Required   *a.*   Compute the unadjusted cash balance as of May 31 shown by the company's record.

b.   Compute the amount of the undeposited receipts, if any, as of May 31.

c.   Compute the amount of the check drawn payable to the treasurer.

d.   Prepare a bank reconciliation as of May 31.

e.   Prepare any necessary journal entry or entries.

f.   State the particular feature of a good system of internal control that is designed to prevent theft of funds such as illustrated here.

Problem 8–7B

Prepare journal entries to record establishment and reimbursement of petty cash fund
(L.O. 5)

Following are selected transactions of Keith Company during 1994.

Mar. 1   Established a petty cash fund of $1,000 that will be under the control of the assistant office manager.

Apr. 3   Fund is replenished on this date. Prior to replenishment, the fund consisted of the following:

Coin and currency	$625.12
Petty cash vouchers indicating disbursements for:	
Postage stamps	140.00
Supper money for office employees working overtime	48.00
Office supplies	43.60
Window-washing service	80.00
Flowers for wedding of employee	28.00
Flowers for hospitalized employee	12.00
Advance to employee	20.00

The employee's IOU is to be deducted from the employee's next paycheck.

Required   Present journal entries for the above transactions. Use the Cash Short and Over account for any shortage or overage in the fund.

Problem 8–8B

Prepare entries in voucher and check registers using net price method for purchase discounts
(L.O. 6)

Count Company was organized January 1 of the current year. The company uses a voucher register and a check register with the same column headings as in Illustrations 8.14 and 8.15, except there are only four debit columns headed Discounts Lost, Merchandise Purchases, Transportation-In, and Other Accounts.

Transactions

Jan. 1   Received an invoice from Leslie Company in the amount of $4,800 for office equipment. Terms were 2/10, n/30, FOB shipping point.

3   Received an invoice from Murray Company for merchandise in the amount of $8,400. Terms were 2/10, n/30.

5   Received an invoice from Slowe Company for merchandise in the amount of $5,400. Terms were 2/10, n/30.

7   Paid $720 to Holt Services Company for advertising services received in January.

10   Paid $540 of freight charges to Chapala Company. Of this, $120 was properly chargeable to the office equipment (you should debit Office Equipment) received on January 1 and the rest to merchandise received from Murray Company.

14   Paid Slowe Company the amount due.

20   Paid Murray Company the correct amount due.

31   Paid Streer Company the net amount of $48,420 for merchandise received today.

31   The January 1 Leslie Company voucher was misfiled and had not been paid as of the end of the month. Recognize the lost discount.

Required   Enter the approved transactions for the month of January in these registers. Total the
registers. Start with Voucher No. 1 and Check No. 1. Vouchers are prepared for the net
amount of the invoice. For discounts lost, a new voucher is prepared for the amount of the
discount. You need not include account numbers.

Problem 8–9B

Prepare entries in voucher
and check registers using
net price procedure for
purchase discounts;
confirm balance in
Vouchers Payable
(L.O. 6)

Taza Company has been organized for several years and uses a voucher register and a
check register with the same column headings as in Illustrations 8.14 and 8.15, except there
are only four debit columns headed Discounts Lost, Merchandise Purchases, Transportation-In, and Other Accounts. The last voucher number used was No. 8743, and the last
check issued was No. 1096. As of August 31, 1994, the following three vouchers were in the
unpaid voucher file:

Voucher No. 8696	$ 5,280
Voucher No. 8741	10,640
Voucher No. 8742	4,560
	$20,480

The total of the unpaid voucher file agreed with the credit balance in the Vouchers Payable
control account.

The following transactions occurred during September 1994. Vouchers are prepared for
the net amount of the invoice. For any discounts lost, a new voucher is prepared for the
amount of the discount.

Sept. 3   Paid a $4,800 note that matured this date plus $80 interest to Hudson Bank.
       5   Received an invoice for $5,600 from Lampley Company for merchandise. Terms
           were 2/10, n/30.
       6   Paid Voucher No. 8696 to Auburn Company, $5,280. This information should
           only be recorded in the check register.
      10   Received an invoice for $2,352 from Thompson Company for merchandise.
           Terms were 2/10, n/30.
      15   Paid Lampley Company the amount owed on its invoice of September 5.
      17   Paid $1,040 to Watch Company for advertising placed in September.
      30   Paid $71,200 to Asa Company. This included $1,424 chargeable to the Transpor-
           tation-In account. The balance paid was the net cost of merchandise received
           today. Terms were 2/10, n/30.
      30   Paid Thompson Company the amount due on the purchase of September 10.

Required   Enter these transactions in the voucher register and the check register. You need not
include account numbers. Total the registers as of September 30. List the unpaid vouchers
at September 30 and compare the total with the balance in the Vouchers Payable control
account (Account No. 205) at that date after posting the proper amounts thereto. The
Vouchers Payable control account should be set up in general ledger format.

BUSINESS DECISION PROBLEMS

Decision Problem 8–1

List procedures that
would have prevented
theft of cash
(L.O. 1, 3)

Cecil Kent was set up in business by his father, who purchased the business of an elderly
acquaintance wishing to retire. One of the few changes in personnel made by Cecil was to
install a college classmate as the office manager-bookkeeper-cashier-sales manager.

During the course of the year, Cecil had to borrow money from the bank (with his father
as co-signer) because, although the business seemed profitable, it was continually short of
cash. The investment in inventories and receivables grew substantially during the year.
Finally, after a year had elapsed, Cecil's father employed a Certified Public Accountant to
audit the records of Cecil's business. The CPA reported that the office manager-bookkeeper-cashier-sales manager had been stealing funds and had been using a variety of
schemes to cover his actions. More specifically, he had—

1. Pocketed cash receipts from sales and understated the cash register readings at the end of the day or altered the copies of the sales tickets retained.

2. Stolen checks mailed to the company in payment of accounts receivable, credited the proper accounts, and then created fictitious receivables to keep the records in balance.

3. Issued checks to fictitious suppliers and deposited them in accounts bearing their names with himself as signer of checks drawn on these accounts; the books were kept in balance by charging the purchases to the inventory account.

4. Stolen petty cash funds by drawing false vouchers purporting to cover a variety of expenses incurred.

5. Prepared false sales returns vouchers indicating the return of cash sales to cover further thefts of cash receipts.

Required
For each of the above items, indicate at least one feature of effective internal control that would have prevented the losses due to dishonesty.

Decision Problem 8–2

Describe method used to steal cash; determine amount stolen; prepare correct bank reconciliation; describe internal control procedures that would have prevented such theft (L.O. 1, 3, 4)

The outstanding checks of Penney Company at November 30, 1994, were:

No. 237.	$3,000.00
No. 271.	3,267.00
No. 3686.	2,037.00
No. 3687.	2,412.00
No. 3688.	4,206.00

During the month, checks numbered 3689–3728 were issued, and all of these checks cleared the bank except Nos. 3727 and 3728 for $2,889.00 and $2,178.00, respectively. Check Nos. 3686, 3687, and 3688 also cleared the bank.

The bank statement on December 31 showed a balance of $71,832. Service charges amounted to $60, and two checks were returned by the bank, one marked NSF in the amount of $342 and the other marked "No account" in the amount of $6,000.

Harrell recently retired as the office manager-cashier-bookkeeper for the company and was replaced by Kozart. Kozart noted the absence of an internal control structure but was momentarily deterred from embezzling for lack of a scheme of concealment. Finally, Kozart hit on several schemes. The $6,000 check marked "No account" by the bank is the product of one scheme. Kozart took cash receipts and replaced them with a check drawn on a nonexistent account to make it appear that a customer had given the company a worthless check.

The other scheme was more subtle. Kozart pocketed cash receipts to bring them down to an amount sufficient to prepare the following reconciliation statement:

Balance per bank statement, December 31, 1994		$71,832.00
Add: Deposit in transit		8,513.40
		$80,345.40
Deduct: Outstanding checks:		
No. 3727	$2,889.00	
No. 3728	2,178.00	5,067.00
Adjusted balance, December 31, 1994		$75,278.40
Balance, Cash account, December 31, 1994.		$81,680.40
Deduct:		
Worthless check.	$6,000.00	
NSF check	342.00	
Service charges	60.00	6,402.00
Adjusted balance, December 31, 1994		$75,278.40

Required   *a.* State the nature of the second scheme used by Kozart. What is the total amount Kozart appears to have stolen by use of the two schemes together?

           b. Prepare a correct bank reconciliation as of December 31, 1994.

           c. Suggest procedures that would have defeated the attempts of Kozart to steal funds and conceal these actions.

Decision Problem 8–3

Cite weaknesses in control over petty cash; explain how internal control over petty cash can be improved
(L.O. 1, 5)

Theresa Hargrave recently acquired an importing business from a friend. The business employs 10 salesclerks and 4 office employees. A petty cash fund of $500 has been established. All 14 employees are allowed to make disbursements from the fund. Vouchers are not used, and no one keeps a record of the disbursements. The petty cash is kept in a large shoe box in the office.

Required

Discuss the operation of the petty cash fund from an internal control point of view. Indicate the weaknesses that currently exist, and suggest how the internal control system can be improved.

Decision Problem 8–4

Discuss steps to prevent theft
(L.O. 1, 3)

During the Persian Gulf War (Desert Storm), a managerial accountant in the United States was called back to active duty with the Army. An acquaintance of the accountant forged papers and assumed the identity of the accountant. He obtained a position in a small firm as the only accountant. Eventually he took over (from the manager) the functions of approving bills for payment, preparing and signing checks, and almost all other financial duties. On one weekend, he traveled to some neighboring cities and prepared and mailed invoices made out to the company he worked for. On Monday morning he returned to work and began receiving, approving, and paying the invoices he had prepared. The following weekend he returned to the neighboring cities and cashed and deposited the checks in bank accounts under his own signature card. After continuing this practice for several months, he withdrew all the funds and never was heard from again.

Required   Discuss some of the steps that could have been taken to prevent this theft. Remember that the company is a small firm with limited financial resources.

ANSWERS TO SELF-TEST

True-False

1. *False.*   Postdated checks are not included as cash.

2. *True.*   A company should avoid holding too much idle cash because excess cash could be invested to yield income such as interest.

3. *True.*   For control purposes, a company should deposit all cash receipts intact in the bank.

4. *False.*   Outstanding checks are ones that have already been correctly recorded as credits to the Cash accounts of the depositor. Outstanding

checks should be deducted from the balance per bank.

5. *True.*   Expenditures from the fund are debited to the related expenses or assets and Cash is credited when the petty cash fund is replenished.

6. *True.*   The unpaid voucher file takes the place of the accounts payable subisidary ledger, and thus should be equal to the balance in the Accounts (Vouchers) Payable control account in the general ledger.

Multiple-Choice

1. *e.* An effective internal control structure helps a company achieve all the objectives mentioned in answers *(a)–(d)*.

2. *b.* The adjusted cash balance is computed either way:

Balance per bank statement.	$3,983.98
Add: Deposits in transit	1,236.00
Deduct: Outstanding checks	(1,931.24)
Adjusted balance	$3,288.74
Balance per ledger	$3,488.74
Less: Bank service charges	(15.00)
NSF checks	(185.00)
Adjusted balance	$3,288.74

3. *a.* Outstanding checks have been recorded in the company's accounting records, but have not been recorded in the bank's records.

4. *c.* The entry to record NSF checks is:

Accounts Receivable	185	
Cash		185

5. *e.* The entry to replenish the petty cash fund is:

Office Supplies	50.45	
Advances to Employees	58.05	
Transportation-In	49.30	
Cash		157.80

When the petty cash fund is reimbursed, there is no change in the Petty Cash account.

6. *c.* In a voucher system, the unpaid vouchers file replaces an accounts payable subsidiary ledger.

9

RECEIVABLES AND PAYABLES

LEARNING OBJECTIVES

After studying this chapter, you should be able to:

1. Account for uncollectible accounts receivable under the allowance method.
2. Account for uncollectible accounts receivable under the direct write-off method.
3. Record credit card sales and collections.
4. Define liabilities, current liabilities, and long-term liabilities.
5. Define clearly determinable, estimated, and contingent liabilities.
6. Account for clearly determinable, estimated, and contingent liabilities.
7. Account for notes receivable and payable, including calculation of interest.
8. Record the discounting of notes receivable.
9. Account for borrowing money using an interest-bearing note versus a noninterest-bearing note.

Much of the growth of business in recent years is due to the immense expansion of credit. Managers of companies have learned that by granting customers the privilege of *charging* their purchases, sales and profits increase. Not only is the use of credit a convenient way to make purchases, but most people could not own high-priced items such as automobiles without credit.

In this chapter, you will study receivables and payables. For a company, a receivable is any sum of money due to be paid to that company from any party for any reason. Similarly, a payable describes any sum of money to be paid by that company to any party for any reason.

The receivables you will learn about are primarily receivables arising from the sale of goods and services. This chapter discusses two types of receivables: accounts receivable, which companies offer for short-term credit with no interest charge; and notes receivable, which companies sometimes extend for both short- and long-term credit with an interest charge. Particular attention is given to accounting for uncollectible receivables.

Companies, like customers, also use credit. To a company, this credit is shown as accounts payable or notes payable. Accounts payable normally result from the purchase of goods or services and do not carry an interest charge. Accounts payable have already been discussed in earlier chapters. Short-term notes payable carry an interest charge and may arise from the same transactions as accounts payable, but they can also result from borrowing money from a bank or other institution. Chapter 4 identified accounts payable and short-term notes payable as current liabilities. A company also incurs other current liabilities, including payables such as sales tax payable and estimated product warranty payable, and certain liabilities that are contingent on the occurrence of future events. Long-term notes payable usually result from borrowing money from a bank or other institution to finance the acquisition of plant assets. As you study this chapter and learn how important credit is to our economy, you will realize that credit in some form will probably always be with us—including our national debt.

ACCOUNTS RECEIVABLE

In Chapter 3, you learned that revenues and expenses may be recorded on the cash basis or the accrual basis of accounting. The cash basis recognizes revenues when cash is received and expenses when cash is paid out. The accrual basis recognizes revenues when sales are made or services are performed and expenses when they are incurred. Most companies use the accrual basis of accounting since it better reflects the actual results of the operations of a business.

Under the accrual basis, merchandising companies that extend credit record revenue when they make a sale because at this time the company has earned and realized the revenue. The company has earned the revenue because it has completed the seller's part of the sales contract by delivering the goods. The company has realized the revenue because it has received the customer's promise to pay in exchange for the goods. This promise to pay by the customer is an account receivable to the seller. Accounts receivable, then, are amounts that customers owe a company for goods sold and services rendered on account. Frequently, these receivables resulting from credit sales of goods and services are called trade receivables.

When a company sells goods on open account, customers do not sign formal, written promises to pay, but they agree to abide by the company's customary credit terms. However, customers may sign a sales invoice to acknowledge purchase of goods. Payment terms for open account sales typically run from 30 to 60 days. Companies usually do not charge interest on amounts owed, except on some past-due amounts.

Unfortunately, customers do not always keep their promises to pay, and companies must make provision for these uncollectible accounts in their records. Companies use two methods for handling uncollectible accounts: the allowance method, which provides in advance for uncollectible accounts; and the direct write-off method, which recognizes bad accounts as an expense when judged uncollectible. The following two sections discuss these methods. Since the allowance method is the preferred method to record uncollectible accounts for financial accounting purposes, we discuss it in greater detail. However, the federal tax law now requires the use of the direct write-off method.

The Allowance Method for Recording Uncollectible Accounts

Objective 1

Account for uncollectible accounts receivable under the allowance method

The careful screening of credit customers by companies does not eliminate all uncollectible accounts. Companies can expect some of their accounts to become uncollectible. The matching principle requires that expenses incurred in producing revenues be deducted from those revenues during the accounting period. The allowance method of recording uncollectible accounts adheres to this principle by recognizing the uncollectible accounts expense in advance of the time when the *specific accounts* are identified as being uncollectible. The required entry has some similarity to the depreciation entry in Chapter 3 because it debits an expense and credits an allowance (contra asset). The purpose of the entry is to make the income statement fairly present the proper expense and the balance sheet fairly present the asset. Uncollectible accounts expense (also called **doubtful accounts expense** or **bad debts expense**) is an operating expense that a business incurs when it sells on credit. We are inclined to classify uncollectible accounts expense as a selling expense because it results from credit sales. Other accountants might classify it as an administrative expense because the credit department has an important role in setting credit terms.

To adhere to the matching principle, the uncollectible accounts expense must be matched against the revenues it generates. Thus, an uncollectible account arising from a sale made in 1994 must be treated as a 1994 expense even though this treatment requires the use of estimates. Estimates are necessary because the company cannot determine until 1995 or later which customer accounts existing at year-end 1994 will become uncollectible.

Recording the Uncollectible Account Adjustment   When a company estimates uncollectible accounts, it makes an adjusting entry at the end of each accounting period. Uncollectible Accounts Expense is debited, thus recording the operating expense in the proper period. The credit is to an account called *Allowance for Uncollectible Accounts*.

As a contra account to the Accounts Receivable account, the Allowance for Uncollectible Accounts (also called **Allowance for Doubtful Accounts** or **Allowance for Bad Debts**) reduces accounts receivable to their net realizable value. Net realizable value is the amount the company expects to collect from accounts receivable. The specific uncollectible accounts are unknown when the uncollectible accounts adjusting entry is made. Thus, the company cannot enter credits in either the Accounts Receivable control account or the customers' accounts receivable subsidiary ledger accounts. If only one or the other were credited, the Accounts Receivable control account balance would not agree with the total of the balances in the accounts receivable subsidiary ledger. Without crediting the Accounts Receivable control account, the allowance account lets the company show that some of its accounts receivable probably will not be collected.

To illustrate the adjusting entry for uncollectible accounts, assume a company has $100,000 of accounts receivable and estimates its uncollectible accounts expense for a given year at $4,000. The required year-end adjusting entry is:

Dec.	31	Uncollectible Accounts Expense	4,000	
		Allowance for Uncollectible Accounts		4,000
		To record estimated uncollectible accounts.		

The debit to Uncollectible Accounts Expense brings about the desired matching of expenses and revenues on the income statement since uncollectible accounts expense is matched against the revenues of the accounting period. The credit to Allowance for Uncollectible Accounts reduces accounts receivable to their net realizable value on the balance sheet. When the books are closed, Uncollectible Accounts Expense is closed to Income Summary. The allowance is reported on the balance sheet as a deduction from accounts receivable as follows:

BRICE COMPANY
Balance Sheet
December 31, 1994
Assets

Current assets:		
Cash		$21,200
Accounts receivable	$100,000	
Less: Allowance for uncollectible accounts	4,000	96,000

Now the question is: How do companies estimate their uncollectible accounts? The next section answers this question.

Estimating Uncollectible Accounts   Accountants use two basic methods to estimate uncollectible accounts for a period. The first method—percentage-of-sales method—focuses on the income statement and the relationship of uncollectible accounts to sales. The second method—percentage-of-receivables method—focuses on the balance sheet and the relationship of the allowance for uncollectible accounts to accounts receivable. Either of these two estimation methods is acceptable, and over time the results obtained under both methods are likely to be similar. However, some accountants prefer the percentage-of-sales method because they claim it does a better job of matching expenses with revenues.

Percentage-of-Sales Method   The percentage-of-sales method estimates uncollectible accounts from the credit sales of a given period. In theory, the method is based on an average percentage of prior years' actual uncollectible accounts to prior years' credit sales. **If cash sales are small or make up a fairly constant percentage of total sales, the calculation can be based on total net sales.** Since at least one of these conditions is usually met, companies commonly use total net sales rather than credit sales. The formula is:

$$\text{Amount of journal entry for uncollectible accounts} = \frac{\text{Sales}}{\text{(total or credit)}} \times \frac{\text{Percentage estimated as uncollectible}}{}$$

To illustrate, assume that Rankin Company's uncollectible accounts from 1992 sales were 1.1% of total net sales. A similar calculation for 1993 showed an uncollectible account percentage of 0.9%. The average for the two years is 1% [(1.1 + 0.9) ÷ 2]. Rankin does not expect 1994 to differ from the previous two years. Total net sales for 1994 were $500,000; receivables at year-end were $100,000; and the Allowance for Uncollectible Accounts had a zero balance. Rankin would make the following adjusting entry for 1994:

Dec.	31	Uncollectible Accounts Expense	5,000	
		Allowance for Uncollectible Accounts		5,000
		To record estimated uncollectible accounts ($500,000 × 0.01).		

Using T-accounts, Rankin would show:

Uncollectible Accounts Expense		**Allowance for Uncollectible Accounts**	
Dec. 31 Adjustment 5,000			Bal. before adjustment –0– Dec. 31 Adjustment 5,000
			Bal. after adjustment 5,000

Uncollectible Accounts Expense is closed to Income Summary. The accounts receivable less the allowance is reported among current assets in the balance sheet as follows:

Accounts receivable	$100,000	
Less: Allowance for uncollectible accounts	5,000	$95,000

Rankin could instead present this information in a balance sheet as follows:

Accounts receivable (less estimated uncollectible accounts, $5,000).	$95,000

On the income statement, the uncollectible accounts expense is matched against revenues in the period in which the sales occur. We believe the expense should be classified as a selling expense, since it is a normal consequence of selling on credit.

The Allowance for Uncollectible Accounts account usually has either a debit or credit balance before the year-end adjustment. **Under the percentage-of-sales method, the company ignores any existing balance in the allowance when calculating the amount of the year-end adjustment.**

For example, assume that in the situation above, Rankin's allowance had a $300 credit balance before adjustment. The adjusting entry would still be for $5,000. However, the balance sheet would show $100,000 accounts receivable less a $5,300 allowance for uncollectible accounts, resulting in net receivables of $94,700. Uncollectible Accounts Expense would still appear on the income statement as 1% of total net sales, or $5,000.

In applying the percentage-of-sales method, companies annually review the percentage of uncollectible accounts to the previous year's sales. If the percentage rate is still valid, the company makes no change. However, if the situation has changed significantly, the company increases or decreases the percentage rate to reflect the changed condition. For example, in periods of inflation and high interest rates, the percentage rate may have to be increased to reflect decreased customer ability to pay. However, if the company adopts a more stringent credit policy, the percentage rate may have to be decreased because the company expects fewer uncollectible accounts.

Percentage-of-Receivables Method   The percentage-of-receivables method estimates uncollectible accounts by determining the desired size of the Allowance for Uncollectible Accounts. The ending balance in Accounts Receivable is multiplied by a rate (or rates) based on experience regarding uncollectible accounts. In the percentage-of-receivables method, the company may use either an overall rate or a different rate for each age category of receivables.

The amount of the entry for uncollectible accounts under the percentage-of-receivables method using an overall rate is calculated as follows:

$$
\begin{pmatrix} \text{Amount of} \\ \text{entry for} \\ \text{uncollectible} \\ \text{accounts} \end{pmatrix} = \begin{pmatrix} \text{Accounts} \\ \text{Receivable} \\ \text{ending} \\ \text{balance} \end{pmatrix} \times \begin{pmatrix} \text{Percentage} \\ \text{estimated as} \\ \text{uncollectible} \end{pmatrix} - \begin{pmatrix} \text{Existing credit} \\ \text{balance in} \\ \text{Allowance for} \\ \text{Uncollectible} \\ \text{Accounts or} \end{pmatrix} + \begin{pmatrix} \text{Existing debit} \\ \text{balance in} \\ \text{Allowance for} \\ \text{Uncollectible} \\ \text{Accounts} \end{pmatrix}
$$

Using the same information as before, Rankin will make an estimate of uncollectible accounts at the end of 1994. The balance of accounts receivable is $100,000, and the allowance account has no balance. If Rankin estimates that 6% of the receivables will be uncollectible, the adjusting entry would be:

Dec.	31	Uncollectible Accounts Expense	6,000	
		Allowance for Uncollectible Accounts		6,000
		To record estimated uncollectible accounts		
		($100,000 × 0.06).		

Using T-accounts, Rankin would show:

Uncollectible Accounts Expense		Allowance for Uncollectible Accounts	
Dec. 31 Adjustment 6,000		Bal. before adjustment –0– Dec. 31 Adjustment 6,000	
		Bal. after adjustment 6,000	

If Rankin had a $300 credit balance in the allowance account, the entry would be the same as the one just given, except that the amount would be $5,700. The difference in amounts arises because management wants the allowance account to contain a credit balance equal to 6% of the outstanding receivables when the two accounts are presented on the balance sheet. The calculation of the necessary adjustment is [($100,000 × 0.06) − $300] = $5,700. **Thus, under the percentage-of-receivables method, any balance in the allowance account must be considered when adjusting for uncollectible accounts.**

Using T-accounts, Rankin would show:

Uncollectible Accounts Expense		Allowance for Uncollectible Accounts	
Dec. 31 Adjustment 5,700		Bal. before adjustment 300 Dec. 31 Adjustment 5,700	
		Bal. after adjustment 6,000	

As another example, suppose that Rankin had a $300 debit balance in the allowance account before adjustment. Then, a credit of $6,300 would be necessary to get the balance to the required $6,000 credit balance. The calculation of the necessary adjustment is [($100,000 × 0.06) + $300] = $6,300.

Using T-accounts, Rankin would show:

Uncollectible Accounts Expense		Allowance for Uncollectible Accounts	
Dec. 31 Adjustment 6,300		Bal. before adjustment 300	Dec. 31 Adjustment 6,300
			Bal. after adjustment 6,000

No matter what the preadjustment allowance balance is, when Rankin uses the percentage-of-receivables method, the Allowance for Uncollectible Accounts is adjusted so that it has a credit balance of $6,000—which is equal to 6% of its $100,000 in Accounts Receivable. The desired $6,000 ending credit balance in the Allowance for Uncollectible Accounts serves as a "target" in making the adjustment.

The method just illustrated used one uncollectibility rate for all accounts receivable, regardless of their age. However, a different percentage can be used for each age category of accounts receivable. When accountants decide to use a **different rate** for each age category of receivables, they prepare an aging schedule. An aging schedule classifies accounts receivable according to their age (how long they have been outstanding) and uses a different uncollectibility percentage rate for each age category. Companies base these percentages on experience. Illustration 9.1 presents an aging schedule. This schedule shows that the older the receivable, the less likely the company will collect the receivable.

Classifying accounts receivable according to age gives the company a better basis for estimating the total amount of uncollectible accounts. For example, based on experience, a company can expect only 1% of the accounts not yet due (sales made less than 30 days before the end of the accounting period) to be uncollectible. At the other extreme, a company can expect 50% of all accounts over 90 days past due to be uncollectible. For each age category, the accounts receivable are multiplied by the percentage estimated as uncollectible to find the estimated amount uncollectible. The sum of the estimated amounts uncollectible for all categories yields the total estimated amount uncollectible and is the desired credit balance (the target) in the Allowance for Uncollectible Accounts.

Since the aging schedule approach is an alternative under the percentage-of-receivables method, the balance in the allowance account before adjustment affects the year-end adjusting entry amount recorded for uncollectible accounts. For example, Illustration 9.1 shows that $24,400 is needed as the ending credit balance in the allowance account. If the allowance account currently has a $5,000 credit balance, the adjustment will be for $19,400.

The information contained in an aging schedule may be useful to management for purposes other than estimating uncollectible accounts. Visible information on collection patterns of accounts receivable may suggest the need for changes in credit policies or for added financing. For example, if the age of many customer balances has increased, thus placing these accounts in the 61–90 days past-due category, collection efforts may have to be strengthened, or the company may have to find other sources of cash to pay its debts within the discount period.

The process of estimating the amount of a company's uncollectible accounts establishes the Allowance for Uncollectible Accounts, which is a contra account

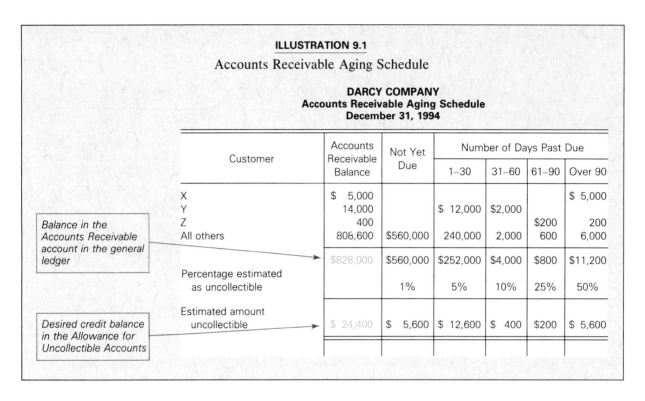

ILLUSTRATION 9.1
Accounts Receivable Aging Schedule

DARCY COMPANY
Accounts Receivable Aging Schedule
December 31, 1994

Customer	Accounts Receivable Balance	Not Yet Due	Number of Days Past Due			
			1–30	31–60	61–90	Over 90
X	$ 5,000					$ 5,000
Y	14,000		$ 12,000	$2,000		
Z	400				$200	200
All others	808,600	$560,000	240,000	2,000	600	6,000
	$828,000	$560,000	$252,000	$4,000	$800	$11,200
Percentage estimated as uncollectible		1%	5%	10%	25%	50%
Estimated amount uncollectible	$ 24,400	$ 5,600	$ 12,600	$ 400	$200	$ 5,600

Balance in the Accounts Receivable account in the general ledger

Desired credit balance in the Allowance for Uncollectible Accounts

to Accounts Receivable. As time passes and it becomes evident that certain customer accounts cannot be collected, they must be written off. In the next section, you will learn how accountants write off uncollectible accounts.

Write-Off of Receivables   When a specific customer's account is considered uncollectible, that account is written off. The Allowance for Uncollectible Accounts is debited. The credit is to the Accounts Receivable control account in the general ledger and to the customer's subsidiary ledger account in the accounts receivable subsidiary ledger. For example, assume Smith's $750 account has been determined to be uncollectible. The entry to write off this account is:

Allowance for Uncollectible Accounts	750	
Accounts Receivable—Smith		750
To write off Smith's account as uncollectible.		

The credit balance in Allowance for Uncollectible Accounts before making the above entry represented **potential** uncollectible accounts that had not yet been specifically identified. Debiting the allowance account and crediting Accounts Receivable shows that the particular account of Smith has now been **identified** as uncollectible. Notice that the debit in the entry to write-off an account receivable **does not involve recording an expense.** The uncollectible accounts expense was recognized in the same accounting period as the sale. If Smith's $750 uncollectible account is recorded in Uncollectible Accounts Expense again, it would be "double counted" as an expense.

The net realizable value of accounts receivable is not affected by a write-off. For example, suppose that Amos Company has total accounts receivable of $50,000 and an allowance of $3,000 before the above entry; the net realizable value of the accounts receivable is $47,000, as shown below. After posting the above entry, accounts receivable are $49,250, and the allowance is $2,250; net realizable value is still $47,000.

A BROADER PERSPECTIVE

ALLOWANCE FOR LOSSES ON FINANCING RECEIVABLES

GE Capital maintains an allowance for losses on financing receivables at an amount that it believes is sufficient to provide adequate protection against future losses in the portfolio. For small-balance and certain large-balance receivables, the allowance for losses is determined principally on the basis of actual experience during the preceding three years. Further allowances also are provided to reflect management's judgment of additional loss potential. For other receivables, principally the larger loans and leases, the allowance for losses is determined primarily on the basis of management's judgment of net loss potential, including specific allowances for known troubled accounts.

All accounts or portions thereof deemed to be uncollectible or to require an excessive collection cost are written off to the allowance for losses. Small-balance accounts are progressively written down (from 10% when more than three months delinquent to 100% when more than 12 months delinquent) to record the balances at estimated realizable value. However, if at any time during that period an account is judged to be uncollectible, such as in the case of a bankruptcy, the remaining balance is written off. Larger-balance accounts are reviewed at least quarterly, and those accounts that are more than three months delinquent are written down, if necessary, to record the balances at estimated realizable value.

Source: General Electric Company, *1989 Annual Report*, p. 48.

	Before Write-Off	Entry for Write-Off	After Write-Off
Accounts receivable	$50,000 Dr.	$750 Cr.	$49,250 Dr.
Allowance for uncollectible accounts	3,000 Cr.	750 Dr.	2,250 Cr.
Net realizable value	$47,000		$47,000

If the Allowance for Uncollectible Accounts is adjusted only at year-end, it may have developed a debit balance before adjustment as a result of writing off uncollectible accounts during the year. One reason for this debit balance is that companies do not often carry accounts receivable in their records that are more than one year old. Consequently, by the end of 1994, all accounts from 1993 sales either will have been collected or written off. If the estimates were exact, the allowance resulting from 1993 would have a zero balance. However, if estimates were less than actual write-offs, the allowance account may have developed a debit balance. Also, some accounts from 1994 sales probably have been charged off during 1994. Yet the company has not yet made the year-end uncollectible accounts adjusting entry for 1994. The result is very likely to be a debit balance in the allowance account before the annual adjustment.

After a company has used the allowance method for several years, the balance in the allowance account consists of the net amount of inadequate or excessive estimates of uncollectible accounts of prior years. Errors in estimating preceding years' uncollectibles are corrected by increasing or decreasing the current year's estimate.

Uncollectible Accounts Recovered   Sometimes companies collect accounts considered to be uncollectible after the accounts have been written off. A company usually learns that an account has been written off erroneously when it receives payment. Then, the company reverses the original write-off entry and reinstates the account by debiting Accounts Receivable and crediting Allowance for Uncollectible Accounts for the amount received. The debit is posted to both the general ledger account and to the customer's accounts receivable subsidiary ledger account. The amount received is also recorded as a debit to Cash and a credit to Accounts Receivable. The credit is posted to both the general ledger and to the customer's accounts receivable subsidiary ledger account.

To illustrate, assume that on May 17 a company received a $750 check from Smith in payment of the account that was previously written off. The two required journal entries are:

May	17	Accounts Receivable—Smith	750	
		Allowance for Uncollectible Accounts		750
		To reverse original write-off of Smith's account.		
	17	Cash	750	
		Accounts Receivable—Smith		750
		To record collection of account.		

If a company only collects part of a previously written off account, the usual procedure is to reinstate only that portion of the account actually collected, unless evidence indicates that the amount will be collected in full. If full payment is expected, the entire amount of the account may be reinstated.

The Direct Write-Off Method for Recording Uncollectible Accounts

Objective 2

Account for uncollectible accounts receivable under the direct write-off method

In contrast to the allowance method of writing off uncollectible accounts, the direct write-off method directly charges the identified uncollectible accounts receivable to an expense account, Uncollectible Accounts Expense. No year-end adjusting entry is made to record estimated uncollectible accounts. Some companies use this method for small, immaterial accounts receivable and uncollectible accounts. When these amounts are material (relatively large), the direct write-off method is unacceptable for accounting purposes because it might not match uncollectible accounts expense against the sales that created them.

To illustrate the direct write-off method, assume a company considers a $200 account for Robert Hill uncollectible. Under this method, the journal entry to write off the account is:

Uncollectible Accounts Expense	200	
Accounts Receivable—Robert Hill		200
To write off Robert Hill's account.		

Assume that several months later, $125 is received on Robert Hill's account. The company does not expect to collect the remaining $75. The required journal entries are:

Accounts Receivable—Robert Hill	125	
Uncollectible Accounts Expense		125
To reinstate portion of account written off.		
Cash	125	
Accounts Receivable—Robert Hill		125
To record collection on account.		

Although companies must use the direct write-off method for income tax purposes, this method is usually not acceptable for financial accounting because (1) it does not properly match expenses and revenues, and (2) it overstates accounts receivable on the balance sheet since the allowance account is not used.

Because of the uncollectible accounts that may arise when a company offers customers credit, many companies now allow customers to use bank or external credit cards. As you will see, this policy relieves the company of the headaches involved in trying to collect overdue accounts.

Credit Cards

Objective 3
Record credit card sales
and collections

Credit cards are either nonbank (American Express and Diners Club) or bank (VISA and MasterCard) charge cards that customers use to charge purchases of goods and services. For some businesses, uncollectible accounts losses and other costs of extending credit are a burden. By paying a service charge of 2% to 8%, businesses can pass these costs on to banks and other credit agencies issuing national credit cards. The banks and credit card agencies then absorb the uncollectible accounts and costs of extending credit and maintaining records.

Usually, banks and credit card agencies issue credit cards to approved credit applicants for an annual fee. When a business agrees to honor these credit cards, the business also agrees to pay the percentage fee charged to the business by the bank or credit agency.

When making a credit card sale, the seller checks the customer's card against a list of canceled cards and calls the credit agency for approval if the sale exceeds a prescribed amount, such as $50. This procedure allows the seller to avoid accepting a lost, stolen, or canceled card. Also, this policy protects the credit agency from a sale causing the customer to exceed an established credit limit.

The accounting procedures used by the seller for credit card sales differ depending on whether the business accepts a nonbank or a bank credit card. The difference in accounting procedures is shown by the illustrations that follow.

To illustrate the entries for the use of **nonbank** credit cards (such as American Express or Diners Club), assume that a restaurant has Diners Club invoices amounting to $1,400 at the end of a day. The Diners Club charges the restaurant a 5% service charge. The restaurant uses the Credit Card Expense account to record the credit card agency's service charge and makes the following entry:

Accounts Receivable—Diners Club	1,330	
Credit Card Expense.	70	
Sales		1,400
To record credit card sales.		

The restaurant mails the invoices to Diners Club. Sometime later, the restaurant receives payment from Diners Club and makes the following entry:

Cash.	1,330	
Accounts Receivable—Diners Club		1,330
To record remittance from Diners Club.		

To illustrate the accounting entries for the use of **bank** credit cards (such as VISA or MasterCard), assume that a retailer has made sales of $1,000 for which VISA cards were accepted and the VISA service charge is $50 (which is 5% of sales). VISA sales are treated as cash sales because the receipt of cash is certain.

The credit card sales invoices are deposited in a VISA checking account in a bank in the name of the company just as checks are deposited in a regular checking account. The entry to record this deposit is:

Cash.	950	
Credit Card Expense.	50	
Sales		1,000
To record VISA credit card sales.		

Just as every company must have current assets such as cash and accounts receivable to operate, every company incurs current liabilities in conducting its operations. Corporations (IBM and General Motors), partnerships (CPA firms), and single proprietorships (corner grocery stores) all have one thing in common—they have liabilities. The next section discusses some of the current liabilities companies incur.

CURRENT LIABILITIES

Objective 4

Define liabilities, current liabilities, and long-term liabilities

Liabilities result from some **past transaction** and are obligations to pay cash, provide services, or deliver goods at some time in the **future.** Each of the liabilities discussed in previous chapters and the new liabilities presented in this chapter meet this definition. On the balance sheet, liabilities are divided into current liabilities and long-term liabilities. Current liabilities are obligations that are (1) payable within one year or one operating cycle, whichever is longer, or (2) will be paid out of current assets or result in the creation of other current liabilities. Long-term liabilities are obligations that do not qualify as current liabilities. This chapter focuses on current liabilities. Long-term liabilities are covered in Chapter 15.

Since the definition of a current liability uses the term *operating cycle,* you must know what that term means. As mentioned in Chapter 4, an operating cycle (or cash cycle) is the time it takes to begin with cash, buy necessary items to produce revenues (such as materials, supplies, labor, and/or finished goods), sell goods or services, and receive cash by collecting the resulting receivables. For most companies, this period is no longer than a few months. Service companies generally have the shortest operating cycle, since they do not have cash tied up in inventory. Manufacturing companies generally have the longest cycle, since their cash is tied up in several inventory accounts and then in accounts receivable before coming back as cash. Even for manufacturing companies, the cycle is generally less than one year. Thus, as a practical matter, current liabilities are those due in one year or less, and long-term liabilities are those due after one year from the balance sheet date.

The operating cycle for various types of businesses can be depicted as follows:

Type of Business	Operating Cycle
Service company selling for cash only	Instantaneous
Service company selling on credit	Cash → Accounts receivable → Cash
Merchandising company selling for cash	Cash → Inventory → Cash
Merchandising company selling on credit	Cash → Inventory → Accounts receivable → Cash
Manufacturing company selling on credit	Cash → Materials inventory → Work in process inventory → Finished goods inventory → Accounts receivable → Cash

Current liabilities can be divided into the following three groups:

Objective 5
Define clearly
determinable, estimated,
and contingent liabilities

1. **Clearly determinable liabilities.** The existence of the liability and its amount are certain. Examples include most of the liabilities discussed previously, such as accounts payable, notes payable, interest payable, unearned delivery fees, and wages payable. Sales tax payable, federal excise tax payable, and current portions of long-term debt are other examples. Also, most of the payroll liabilities introduced in Appendix B at the end of the text are clearly determinable liabilities.

2. **Estimated liabilities.** The existence of the liability is certain, but its amount can only be **estimated.** An example is estimated product warranty payable.

3. **Contingent liabilities.** The existence of the liability is uncertain and usually the amount is uncertain because contingent liabilities depend (or are **contingent**) on some future event occurring or not occurring. Examples include liabilities arising from lawsuits, discounted notes receivable, income tax disputes, penalties that may be assessed because of some past action, and failure of another party to pay a debt that a company has guaranteed.

The following table identifies the characteristics of these types of current liabilities:

Type of Liability	Is the Existence Certain?	Is the Amount Certain?
Clearly determinable liabilities	Yes	Yes
Estimated liabilities	Yes	No
Contingent liabilities	No	No

Clearly Determinable Liabilities

Objective 6
Account for clearly
determinable, estimated,
and contingent liabilities

Clearly determinable liabilities also have a clearly determinable amount. Other sections of this chapter discuss clearly determinable liabilities such as notes payable. In this section, we discuss the following additional liabilities that are clearly determinable—sales tax payable, federal excise tax payable, and current portions of long-term debt.

Sales Tax Payable Many states have a state sales tax on items purchased by consumers. The company selling the product to the customer is responsible for collecting the sales tax from the customer. When the company collects the taxes, the debit is to Cash and the credit is to Sales Tax Payable. Periodically, the company pays the sales taxes collected to the state. At that time, the debit is to Sales Tax Payable and the credit is to Cash.

To illustrate, assume that a company sells merchandise in a state that has a 6% sales tax. If goods with a sales price of $1,000 are sold on credit, the following entry is made:

Accounts Receivable.	1,060	
Sales		1,000
Sales Tax Payable		60
To record sales and sales tax payable.		

Now assume that sales for the entire period are $100,000 and that $6,000 is in the Sales Tax Payable account when the company remits the funds to the state taxing agency. The following entry shows the payment to the state:

Sales Tax Payable	6,000	
Cash		6,000
To record the payment to the state for sales taxes collected from customers.		

An alternative method of recording sales taxes payable is to include these taxes in the credit to Sales. For instance, in the above situation the sales could have been recorded as follows:

Accounts Receivable	1,060	
Sales		1,060

When sales taxes are recorded in the same account as sales revenue, the sales tax must be separated from sales revenue at the end of the accounting period. To make this separation, we add the sales tax rate to 100% and divide this percentage into recorded sales revenue. For instance, assume that total recorded sales revenues for an accounting period are $10,600, and the sales tax rate is 6%. To find the sales revenue, the following formula is used:

$$\text{Sales} = \frac{\text{Amount recorded in Sales account}}{100\% + \text{Sales tax rate}}$$

$$= \frac{\$10,600}{106\%} = \$10,000$$

The answer of $10,000 gives sales revenue for the period. Sales tax is equal to recorded sales revenue of $10,600 less actual sales revenue of $10,000, or $600.

Federal Excise Tax Payable   Some goods, such as alcoholic beverages, tobacco, gasoline, cosmetics, tires, luxury automobiles, boats, airplanes, cameras, radios, television sets, and jewelry, are subject to federal excise tax. The 1990 federal budget compromise increased the amount of tax on many of these items. The entries a company makes when selling these goods are similar to those made for sales taxes payable. For example, assume that the Dixon Jewelry Store sells a diamond ring to a young couple for $2,000. The sale is subject to a 6% sales tax and a 10% federal excise tax. The entry to record the sale is:

Accounts Receivable	2,320	
Sales		2,000
Sales Tax Payable		120
Federal Excise Tax Payable		200
To record the sale of a diamond ring.		

The company records the remittance of the taxes to the federal taxing agency by debiting Federal Excise Tax Payable and crediting Cash.

Current Portions of Long-Term Debt   Any portion of long-term debt that will become due within the next year is moved to the current liability section of the balance sheet. For instance, assume a company signed a series of 10 individual notes payable for $10,000 each that come due (one each year) in the 6th year through the 15th year. Each year, beginning in the fifth year, another $10,000 would be moved from the long-term liability category to the current liability category on the balance sheet. The current portion would then be paid within one year.

Payroll Liabilities   Several current liabilities arise from payroll accounting. Appendix B at the end of the text discusses payroll accounting and related liabilities.

Estimated Liabilities

Managers of companies that have estimated liabilities know these liabilities exist but can only estimate the amount. The primary accounting problem is to arrive at a reasonable estimate of the amount of the liability as of the balance sheet date. An example of an estimated liability is product warranty payable.

Estimated Product Warranty Payable   When companies sell products, such as computers, they must often guarantee against defects by placing a warranty on their products. When defects occur, the company is obligated to reimburse the customer or repair the product. For many products, the number of defects that will occur can be predicted based on experience. To provide for a proper matching of revenues and expenses, the accountant estimates the amount of warranty expense that will result from an accounting period's sales. Product Warranty Expense is debited and Estimated Product Warranty Payable is credited for that amount.

To illustrate, assume that a company sells personal computers and warrants all parts for a one-year period. The average price per computer is $1,500, and the company sells 1,000 computers in 1994. The company expects 10% of the computers to develop defective parts within one year of sale. By the end of 1994, 40 computers sold in 1994 have already been returned for repairs. The estimated average cost of warranty repairs per defective computer is $150. To arrive at a reasonable estimate of the amount of the entry to be made at the end of the accounting period, the accountant makes the following calculation:

Number of computers sold.	1,000
Percent estimated to develop defects.	× 10%
Total estimated defective computers	100
Deduct computers defective to date	40
Estimated additional number to become defective during warranty period.	60
Estimated warranty repair cost per computer.	×$ 150
Estimated product warranty payable.	$9,000

The entry made at the end of the accounting period is:

Product Warranty Expense	9,000	
Estimated Product Warranty Payable		9,000
To record estimated product warranty expense.		

When a customer returns one of the computers purchased in 1994 for repair work in 1995 (during the warranty period), the cost of the repairs is debited to

Estimated Product Warranty Payable. For instance, assume that Mr. Holman returns his computer for repairs within the warranty period. The repair cost includes parts, $40, and labor, $160. The following entry is made:

Estimated Product Warranty Payable	200	
Repair Parts Inventory		40
Wages Payable		160
To record replacement of parts under warranty.		

Other Estimated Liabilities   Another estimated liability that is (unfortunately) becoming quite common relates to clean-up costs for industrial pollution. One company had the following note in its 1986 financial statements:

In the past, the Company treated hazardous waste at its chemical facilities. Testing of the ground waters in the areas of the treatment impoundments at these facilities disclosed the presence of certain contaminants. In compliance with environmental regulations, the Company developed a plan that will prevent further contamination, provide for remedial action to remove the present contaminants and establish a monitoring program to monitor ground water conditions in the future. A similar plan has been developed for a site previously used as a metal pickling facility. Estimated future costs of $2,860,000 have been accrued in the accompanying financial statements for 1986 to complete the procedures required under these plans.

Contingent Liabilities

When liabilities are contingent, the company is not sure that the liability exists and is usually uncertain about the amount of the liability. *FASB Statement No. 5* defines a contingency as "an existing condition, situation, or set of circumstances involving uncertainty as to possible gain or loss to an enterprise that will ultimately be resolved when one or more future events occur or fail to occur."[1]

According to *FASB Statement No. 5,* if the liability is probable and the amount can be reasonably estimated, contingent liabilities may be recorded in the accounts. However, since most contingent liabilities may not occur and the amount often cannot be reasonably estimated, the accountant usually does not record them in the accounts. Instead, these contingent liabilities are disclosed in notes to the financial statements.

Many contingent liabilities arise as the result of lawsuits. In fact, 379 of the 600 companies that were included in the annual survey of accounting practices conducted by the AICPA reported contingent liabilities resulting from litigation.[2]

The following two examples taken from annual reports are typical of the disclosures made in notes to the financial statements. Be aware that just because a suit is brought, the company being sued is not necessarily guilty.

One company included the following note in its annual report to describe its contingent liability regarding various lawsuits against the company.

Contingent Liabilities

Various lawsuits and claims, including those involving ordinary routine litigation incidental to its business, to which the Company is a party, are pending, or have been asserted, against the Company. In addition, the Company was advised in 1985 that the United States Environmental Protection Agency had determined the existence of PCBs in a river and harbor near Sheboygan, Wisconsin, and that the Company, as well as others, allegedly

---

[1] FASB, *Statement of Financial Accounting Standards No. 5,* "Accounting for Contingencies" (Stamford, Conn., 1975). Copyright © by Financial Accounting Standards Board, High Ridge Park, Stamford, Connecticut 06905, U.S.A.

[2] AICPA, *Accounting Trends & Techniques* (New York, 1990), p. 53.

contributed to that contamination. It is not presently possible to determine with certainty what corrective action, if any, will be required, what portion of any costs thereof will be attributable to the Company, or whether all or any portion of such costs will be covered by insurance or will be recoverable from others. Although the outcome of these matters cannot be predicted with certainty, and some of them may be disposed of unfavorably to the Company, management has no reason to believe that their disposition will have a materially adverse effect on the consolidated financial position of the Company.

Another company dismissed a former employee of the company and included the following note to disclose the contingent liability resulting from the ensuing litigation:

Contingencies

In May 1988, a jury awarded $5.2 million to a former employee of the Company for an alleged breach of contract and wrongful termination of employment. The Company has appealed the judgment on the basis of errors in the judge's instructions to the jury and insufficiency of evidence to support the amount of the jury's award. The Company is vigorously pursuing the appeal.

The Company and its subsidiaries are also involved in various other litigation arising in the ordinary course of business.

Since it presently is not possible to determine the outcome of these matters, no provision has been made in the financial statements for their ultimate resolution. The resolution of the appeal of the jury award could have a significant effect on the Company's earnings in the year that a determination is made; however, in management's opinion, the final resolution of all legal matters will not have a material adverse effect on the Company's financial position.

Contingent liabilities may also arise from discounted notes receivable, income tax disputes, penalties that may be assessed because of some past action, and failure of another party to pay a debt that a company has guaranteed.

The remainder of this chapter discusses notes receivable and notes payable. Business transactions often involve one party giving another party a note.

NOTES RECEIVABLE AND NOTES PAYABLE

Objective 7
Account for notes receivable and payable, including calculation of interest

In Chapter 4, you learned that a note (also called a promissory note) is an unconditional written promise by a borrower (maker) to pay a definite sum of money to the lender (payee) on demand or on a specific date. On the balance sheet of the lender (payee), a note is a receivable; on the balance sheet of the borrower (maker), a note is a payable. Since the note is usually negotiable, the payee may transfer it to another party, who then receives payment from the maker. An example of a promissory note is shown in Illustration 9.2.

A customer may give a note to a business for an amount due on an account receivable or for the sale of a large item such as a refrigerator. Also, a business may give a note to a supplier in exchange for merchandise to sell or to a bank or an individual for a loan. Thus, a company may have notes receivable or notes payable arising from transactions with customers, suppliers, banks, or individuals.

Companies usually do not establish a subsidiary ledger for notes. Instead, they maintain a file of the actual notes receivable and copies of notes payable.

Interest Calculation

Most promissory notes have an explicit interest charge. Interest is the fee charged for use of money over a period of time. To the maker of the note, or borrower, interest is an expense; to the payee of the note, or lender, interest is a revenue. A borrower incurs interest expense; a lender earns interest revenue. For convenience, interest is sometimes calculated on the basis of a 360-day year, and we will calculate it on that basis in this text. (Some companies use a 365-day year.)

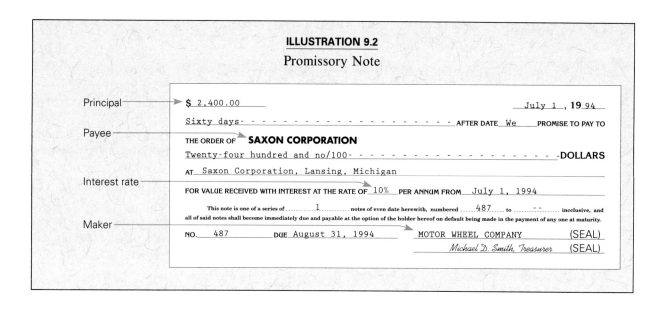

ILLUSTRATION 9.2

Promissory Note

Principal → $ 2,400.00   July 1 , 19 94

Sixty days- AFTER DATE We   PROMISE TO PAY TO

Payee → THE ORDER OF **SAXON CORPORATION**

Twenty-four hundred and no/100- - - - - - - - - - - - - - - - - - - -DOLLARS

AT Saxon Corporation, Lansing, Michigan

Interest rate → FOR VALUE RECEIVED WITH INTEREST AT THE RATE OF 10% PER ANNUM FROM July 1, 1994

This note is one of a series of ....1............ notes of even date herewith, numbered ......487...... to ....- -...... inclusive, and
all of said notes shall become immediately due and payable at the option of the holder hereof on default being made in the payment of any one at maturity.

Maker → NO.___487___ DUE August 31, 1994   MOTOR WHEEL COMPANY   (SEAL)

                                                 Michael D. Smith, Treasurer   (SEAL)

The basic formula for computing interest is:

Interest = Principal × Rate × Time, or I = P × R × T

Principal is the face value of the note. The **rate** is the stated interest rate on the note; interest rates are generally stated on an annual basis. **Time,** which is the amount of time the note is to run, can be expressed in either days or months.

To show how interest is calculated, assume a company borrowed $20,000 from a bank. The note has a principal (face value) of $20,000, an annual interest rate of 10%, and a life of 90 days. The interest calculation is:

$$\text{Interest} = \$20,000 \times 0.10 \times 90/360$$
$$\text{Interest} = \$500$$

Note that in this calculation the time period is expressed as a fraction of a 360-day year because the interest rate is expressed on an annual basis.

Determination of Maturity Date

The **maturity date** is the date on which a note becomes due and must be paid. Sometimes notes require monthly installments (or payments) but usually all of the principal and interest must be paid at the same time as in Illustration 9.2. The wording used in the note expresses the maturity date and determines when the note is to be paid. Examples of the maturity date wording are:

1. *On demand.* "On demand, I promise to pay. . . ." When the maturity date is "on demand," it is at the option of the holder and cannot be computed. The holder is the payee, or another person who legally acquired the note from the payee.

2. *On a stated date.* "On July 18, 1994, I promise to pay. . . ." When the maturity date is designated, computing the maturity date is not necessary.

3. *At the end of a stated period.*
    a. "One year after date, I promise to pay. . . ." When the maturity is expressed in years, the note matures on the same day of the same month as the date of the note in the year of maturity.
    b. "Four months after date, I promise to pay. . . ." When the maturity is expressed in months, the note will mature on the same date in the

month of maturity. For example, one month from July 18, 1994, is August 18, 1994, and two months from July 18, 1994, is September 18, 1994. If a note is issued on the last day of a month and the month of maturity has fewer days than the month of issuance, the note matures on the last day of the month of maturity. A one-month note dated January 31, 1994, matures on February 28, 1994.

c. "Ninety days after date, I promise to pay. . . ." When the maturity is expressed in days, the exact number of days must be counted. The first day (date of origin) is omitted, and the last day (maturity date) is included in the count. For example, a 90-day note dated October 19, 1994, matures on January 17, 1995, as shown below:

Life of note (days)		90 days
Days remaining in October not counting date of origin of note:		
Days to count in October (31 − 19)	12	
Total days in November	30	
Total days in December	31	73
Maturity date in January		17 days

A note falling due on a Sunday or a holiday is due on the next business day.

Accounting for Notes in Normal Business Transactions

Sometimes a company receives a note when it sells high-priced merchandise, but often a note results from the conversion of an overdue open account. When a customer does not pay an account receivable when due, the company (creditor) may insist that the customer (debtor) give a note in place of the account receivable. This action allows the customer more time to pay the balance of the account, and the company earns interest on the balance until paid. Also, the company may be able to sell the note to a bank or other financial institution, as you will learn later.

To illustrate the conversion of an open account to a note, assume that Price Company (maker) had purchased $18,000 of merchandise on August 1 from Cooper Company (payee) on open account. The normal credit period has elapsed, and Price cannot pay the invoice. Cooper agrees to accept Price's $18,000, 15%, 90-day note dated September 1 to settle Price's open account. Assuming Price paid the note at maturity and both Cooper and Price have a December 31 year-end, the entries on the books of the payee and the books of the maker are:

Cooper Company, Payee

Aug.	1	Accounts Receivable—Price Company	18,000	
		Sales		18,000
		To record sale of merchandise on account.		
Sept.	1	Notes Receivable	18,000	
		Accounts Receivable—Price Company		18,000
		To record exchange of note from Price Company for open account.		
Nov.	30	Cash	18,675	
		Notes Receivable		18,000
		Interest Revenue ($18,000 × 0.15 × 90/360)		675
		To record receipt of Price Company note principal and interest.		

Price Company, Maker

Aug.	1	Purchases		18,000	
		Accounts Payable—Cooper Company			18,000
		To record purchase of merchandise on account.			
Sept.	1	Accounts Payable—Cooper Company		18,000	
		Notes Payable			18,000
		To record exchange of note to Cooper Company for open account.			
Nov.	30	Notes Payable		18,000	
		Interest Expense ($18,000 × 0.15 × $\frac{90}{360}$)		675	
		Cash			18,675
		To record payment of note principal and interest.			

The $18,675 paid by Price to Cooper is called the *maturity value of the note.* Maturity value is the amount that the maker must pay on a note on its maturity date; typically, it includes principal and accrued interest, if any.

Sometimes the maker of a note does not pay the note when it becomes due. In the next section, you will learn how to record the fact that a note has not been paid at maturity.

Dishonored Notes

A dishonored note is a note that the maker failed to pay at maturity. Since the note has matured, the holder or payee should remove the note from Notes Receivable and record the amount due in Accounts Receivable. The debit to Accounts Receivable is posted to the general ledger and to the maker's accounts receivable subsidiary ledger account.

At the maturity date of a note, the maker is obligated to pay the principal plus interest. If the interest has not been accrued on the maker's books, the maker of a dishonored note should record interest expense for the life of the note by debiting Interest Expense and crediting Interest Payable. The payee should record the interest earned and remove the note from its Notes Receivable account. Thus, the payee of the note should debit Accounts Receivable for the maturity value of the note and credit Notes Receivable for the note's face value and Interest Revenue for the interest. After these entries have been posted, the full liability on the note—principal plus interest—is included in the records of both parties. Interest will continue to accrue on the note until it is paid, replaced by a new note, or written off as uncollectible.

To illustrate, assume that Price did not pay the note at maturity. The entries on each party's books are:

Cooper Company, Payee

Nov.	30	Accounts Receivable—Price Company		18,675	
		Notes Receivable			18,000
		Interest Revenue			675
		To record dishonor of Price Company note.			

Price Company, Maker

Nov.	30	Interest Expense		675	
		Interest Payable			675
		To record interest on note payable.			

When the maker of a note is unable to pay at maturity, sometimes the maker pays the interest on the original note or includes the interest in the face value of a new note given to replace the old note. The new note is accounted for in the same manner as the old note. However, if it later becomes clear that the maker of a dishonored note will never pay, the payee should write off the account with a debit to Uncollectible Accounts Expense (or to an account with a title such as Loss on Dishonored Notes) and a credit to Accounts Receivable. The debit should be to the Allowance for Uncollectible Accounts if annual provision was made for uncollectible notes receivable.

Renewal of Notes

As stated above, notes are frequently renewed rather than paid at their maturity date. Sometimes the interest on the old note is paid at the maturity date and sometimes it is included in the face value of the new note.

Assume that Price Company pays the interest at the maturity date and then issues a new 15%, 90-day note for $18,000. The entries on both sets of books would be:

Cooper Company, Payee			**Price Company, Maker**		
Cash	675		Interest Expense	675	
Interest Revenue . .		675	Cash		675
To record the receipt of interest on Price Company note.			To record the payment of interest on note to Cooper Company.		
(Optional entry)			(Optional entry)		
Notes Receivable	18,000		Notes Payable	18,000	
Notes Receivable . .		18,000	Notes Payable . . .		18,000
To replace old 15%, 90-day note from Price Company with new 15%, 90-day note.			To replace old 15%, 90-day note to Cooper Company with new 15%, 90-day note.		

Although the second entry on each set of books has no effect on the existing account balances, it sometimes is made to indicate that the old note was renewed (or replaced). The new note, or a copy, is substituted for the old note in a file of notes.

Now assume that Price Company does not pay the interest at the maturity date but instead includes the interest in the face value of the new note. The entries on both sets of books would be:

Cooper Company, Payee			**Price Company, Maker**		
Notes Receivable	18,675		Interest Expense	675	
Interest Revenue . .		675	Notes Payable	18,000	
Notes Receivable . .		18,000	Notes Payable . . .		18,675
To record the replacement of the old Price Company $18,000, 15%, 90-day note with a new $18,675, 15%, 90-day note.			To record the replacement of the old $18,000, 15%, 90-day note to Cooper Company with a new $18,675, 15%, 90-day note.		

Accruing Interest

On an interest-bearing note, interest accrues, or accumulates, on a day-to-day basis but usually is only recorded at the note's maturity date. If, however, the note is outstanding at the end of an accounting period, then the time period of the interest overlaps the end of the accounting period, and an adjusting entry is needed. Both the payee and maker of the note must make an adjusting entry to record the accrued interest so that the proper assets and revenues for the payee and the proper liabilities and expenses for the maker are reported. Failure to record accrued interest understates the payee's assets and revenues by the amount of the interest earned but not collected and understates the maker's expenses and liabilities by the interest expense incurred but not yet paid.

The paragraphs that follow show you how to record accrued interest on the payee's books and the maker's books. You will also see how to record the entry in the succeeding period when the interest is received or paid.

Payee's Books   To illustrate how to record accrued interest on the payee's books, assume that the payee, Cooper Company (in the above example), has a fiscal year ending on October 31 instead of a December 31 year-end. On October 31, Cooper would make the following adjusting entry relating to the Price Company note:

Oct.	31	Interest Receivable	450	
		Interest Revenue ($18,000 × 0.15 × $60/360$)		450
		To record interest earned on Price Company note for the period September 1 through October 31.		

The Interest Receivable account shows the interest earned but not yet collected. Interest receivable is reported as a current asset in the balance sheet because the interest will be collected in 30 days. The interest revenue will be reported in the income statement.

When Price pays the note on November 30, Cooper makes the following entry to record the collection of the note's principal and interest.

Nov.	30	Cash.	18,675	
		Notes Receivable		18,000
		Interest Receivable		450
		Interest Revenue		225
		To record collection of Price Company note and interest.		

Note that the entry credits the Interest Receivable account for the $450 interest accrued from September 1 through October 31, which was debited to the account in the previous entry, and credits Interest Revenue for the $225 interest earned in November.

Maker's Books   Assume Price Company's accounting year also ends on October 31 instead of December 31. Price's accounting records would be incomplete unless the company makes an adjusting entry to record the liability owed for the accrued interest on the note it gave to Cooper Company. The entry is:

Oct.	31	Interest Expense ($18,000 × 0.15 × $60/360$)	450	
		Interest Payable.		450
		To record accrued interest on note to Cooper Company for the period September 1 through October 31.		

The **Interest Payable account,** which shows the interest expense incurred but not yet paid, is reported as a current liability in the balance sheet because the interest will be paid in 30 days. Interest expense will be reported in the income statement.

When the note is paid, Price will make the following entry:

Nov.	30	Notes Payable	18,000	
		Interest Payable.	450	
		Interest Expense	225	
		Cash.		18,675
		To record payment of principal and interest on note to Cooper Company.		

In this illustration, Cooper's financial position made it possible for the company to *carry* the Price note to the maturity date. Sometimes a company needs money immediately and must "sell" a note receivable. The next section discusses the procedure companies use to sell a note.

Discounting (Selling) Notes Receivable

Objective 8
Record the discounting of notes receivable

When a company finds it must sell a note, the company usually takes the note to a bank or finance company. After endorsing the note, the company receives cash in return for the note. Three parties are now involved—the party that writes the note (the maker), the company that accepts the note and sells it to the bank (the payee), and the bank that buys the note. Since a note is a negotiable instrument (may be transferred legally to another party), it must be paid regardless of who holds the note at maturity. As long as the holder obtained the note legally, the maturity value will be paid to the holder of the note. Illustration 9.3 shows the actions that occur between the three parties.

Discounting a note receivable is the act of selling a note receivable with recourse to a bank.[3] *Discounting* means that the bank deducts the interest from the maturity value of the note immediately and gives the seller of the note only the net proceeds; and **with recourse** means that if the maker does not pay the bank at maturity, the bank can collect the maturity value from the company that discounted the note at the bank. Selling a note with recourse really changes the transaction from an outright selling transaction to a borrowing transaction. Thus, in recording the transaction, the company discounting the note records interest expense or interest revenue rather than a loss or gain on the sale. A note may be sold without recourse, but this situation is rare.

When the note is sold with recourse, the party discounting the note has a contingent liability (or is said to be "contingently liable") on the note. As noted earlier, a **contingent liability** is a liability that may become an actual liability if a future event does or does not occur. If the maker of the note does not pay on the maturity date, the contingent liability becomes an actual liability of the company that discounted the note.

The rate of interest the bank charges on the discounted note is called the **discount rate.** The bank may charge a different rate of interest than is stated on the note receivable. The bank uses the discount rate to compute the bank discount

---

[3] Actually, the term *discounting* has two meanings in accounting. The first meaning is to deduct interest in advance. The second meaning is to sell a note to a bank. We will use the term *discounting* to mean the act of a company selling a note to a bank, which then deducts the interest in advance. Thus, we refer to a company discounting a note receivable in this broader sense of the term.

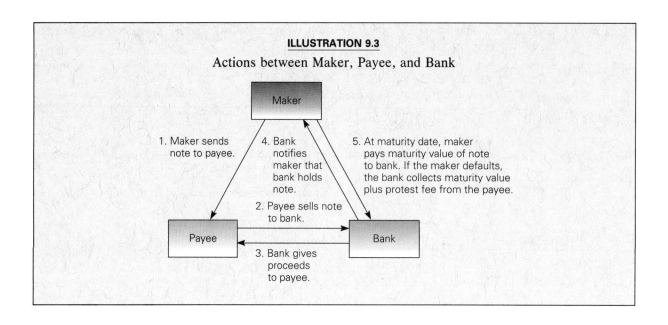

ILLUSTRATION 9.3

Actions between Maker, Payee, and Bank

amount on the note's maturity value. For example, the payee of the note may have been satisfied with a 9% rate, while the bank now seeks a 10% discount rate. The bank discount will be computed using the 10% discount rate. The cash proceeds received by the seller are equal to the maturity value of the note less the bank discount. The cash proceeds are computed as follows:

1. Determine the maturity value of the note (face value plus interest), since this value is the amount on which the bank discount is calculated.

$$\text{Maturity value} = \text{Face value} + \left(\text{Face value} \times \text{Rate of interest on note} \times \frac{\text{Life of note}}{360}\right)$$

2. Determine the discount period. Count the exact number of days from the date of sale (discounting) to the maturity date. Exclude the date of sale, but include the maturity date in the count. Another way of calculating the discount period is to calculate the number of days the payee held the note and deduct this total from the life of the note.

3. Using the bank's discount rate, compute the bank discount on the maturity value for the discount period.

$$\text{Bank discount} = \text{Maturity value} \times \text{Discount rate charged by bank} \times \frac{\text{Discount period}}{360}$$

4. Deduct the bank discount from the maturity value to determine the cash proceeds.

$$\text{Cash proceeds} = \text{Maturity value} - \text{Bank discount}$$

To help you understand the recording of a discounted note receivable, the following section gives an example of recording a discounted note.

Example of Recording a Discounted Note   Assume that on May 4, 1994, Clark Company received from Kent Company a $10,000, 9%, 60-day note, dated May 4, 1994. The maturity date of the note is determined as follows:

Life of note	60 days
Days remaining in May not counting date of note (31 − 4) 27	
Total days in June 30	57
Maturity date in July	3 days

Thus, the maturity date of the note is July 3, 1994.

On May 14, 1994, Clark sold the note to Michigan National Bank, which charged a discount rate of 10%. Using the steps listed above, the discount and the cash proceeds are determined as follows:

1. Determining maturity value:

Face value of note	$10,000.00
Add interest at 9% for 60 days:	
Face value × Interest rate on note × (Life of note ÷ 360)	
($10,000 × 0.09 × 60/360)	150.00
Maturity value of note	$10,150.00

2. Determining discount period:

Days in May	31
Less date of discounting	14
Days of discount period in May	17
Days in June	30
Days of discount period in July (maturity date is July 3)	3
Total discount period	50

3. Computing bank discount:

Maturity value × Rate of interest charged by bank × (Discount period ÷ 360)	
($10,150 × 0.10 × 50/360) . .	$ 140.97

4. Computing cash proceeds:

Maturity value	$10,150.00
Less: Bank discount	140.97
Cash proceeds	$10,009.03

Illustration 9.4 shows the relationship between face value, maturity value, and cash proceeds (follow the arrows). The journal entry Clark Company would make to record this transaction is:

May	14	Cash	10,009.03	
		Notes Receivable		10,000.00
		Interest Revenue		9.03
		To record sale of note receivable.		

When a company discounts a note, the proceeds received are rarely, if ever, exactly equal to the face value. The difference between the proceeds and face value of the note is recorded as interest expense or interest revenue. If the proceeds are less than the face value, interest expense is recorded; if the proceeds are greater than the face value, interest revenue is recorded.

Balance Sheet Presentation of Notes Receivable Discounted In the Clark Company example above (assume a June 30 accounting year-end), Clark should show a contingent liability of $10,000 for notes receivable discounted in its June 30, 1994,

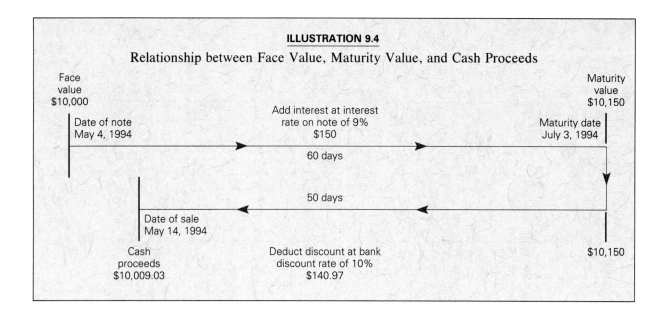

ILLUSTRATION 9.4

Relationship between Face Value, Maturity Value, and Cash Proceeds

balance sheet. If we assume that the total of all Clark's notes receivable that have not been discounted is $60,000, an acceptable method of presenting this information in the balance sheet is:

Assets

Current assets:

Cash	$xx,xxx
Accounts receivable	xx,xxx
Notes receivable (Note 1)	60,000

Notes to Financial Statements:
Note 1: At June 30, 1994, the company is contingently liable for a customer's $10,000 note receivable that it has endorsed and discounted at the local bank. This note is not included in the $60,000 of notes shown.

Discounted Notes Receivable Paid by Maker When a discounted note receivable matures, it is usually the duty of the holder (the bank in the above illustration) to present the note to the maker for payment. If the maker pays the holder at maturity, the endorser (the company that discounted the note) is thereby relieved of its contingent liability.

Assume that in the above example, Kent Company pays the $10,000 note plus interest of $150 to Michigan National Bank on July 3, 1994, the note's maturity date. Clark Company, which discounted the note at the bank, is no longer liable for the note. No entry is necessary on Clark's books.

Discounted Notes Receivable Not Paid by Maker In the above illustration, the maker paid the bank when the note matured. However, if the note is not paid at maturity and is written with recourse, the holder can collect from the endorser, who, in turn, can try to collect from the maker.

Assume that Kent Company dishonors its note. Michigan National Bank will collect the principal ($10,000), interest ($150), and a protest fee ($10) from Clark Company. Clark must make the following entry:

July	3	Accounts Receivable—Kent Company	10,160	
		Cash.		10,160
		To record cash paid to bank for Kent Company's dishonored note.		

Clark, of course, will now try to collect $10,160 from Kent. However, if this attempt is unsuccessful, the $10,160 will be removed from Accounts Receivable and treated as an uncollectible account or a loss on dishonored notes.

Short-Term Financing through Notes Payable

Objective 9

Account for borrowing money using interest-bearing note versus noninterest-bearing note

A company sometimes needs short-term financing. This situation may occur when (1) the company's cash receipts are delayed because of lenient credit terms granted customers, or (2) the company needs cash to finance the buildup of seasonal inventories, such as before Christmas. Short-term financing may be secured by issuing interest-bearing notes or by issuing noninterest-bearing notes.

Interest-Bearing Notes To receive short-term financing from a bank, a company may issue an interest-bearing note to the bank. An interest-bearing note specifies the interest rate that will be charged on the principal borrowed. The company receives from the bank the principal borrowed; when the note matures, the company pays the bank the principal plus the interest.

Accounting for an interest-bearing note is simple. For example, assume the company's accounting year ends on December 31. Needham Company issued a $10,000, 90-day, 9% note on December 1, 1993. The following entries would be made to record the loan, the accrual of interest on December 31, 1993, and its payment on March 1, 1994:

1993 Dec.	1	Cash.	10,000	
		Notes Payable		10,000
		To record 90-day bank loan.		
	31	Interest Expense	75	
		Interest Payable.		75
		To record accrued interest on a note payable at year-end ($10,000 $\times$ 0.09 $\times$ $^{30}/_{360}$).		
1994 Mar.	1	Notes Payable	10,000	
		Interest Expense	150	
		Interest Payable.	75	
		Cash.		10,225
		To record principal and interest paid on bank loan.		

Noninterest-Bearing Notes (Discounting Notes Payable) A company may also issue a noninterest-bearing note to receive short-term financing from a bank. A noninterest-bearing note does not have a stated interest rate applied to the face value of the note. Instead, the note is drawn for a maturity amount from which a bank discount is deducted, and the proceeds are given to the borrower. **Bank discount** is the difference between the maturity value of the note and the cash proceeds given to the borrower. The **cash proceeds,** as defined earlier, are equal to the maturity amount of a note less the bank discount. This entire process is called discounting a note payable. The purpose of this process is to introduce interest into what appears to be a noninterest-bearing note. The meaning of *discounting* here is to deduct interest in advance.

Because interest is related to time, the bank discount is not interest on the date the loan is made; however, it becomes interest expense to the company and interest revenue to the bank as time passes. To illustrate, assume that on December 1, 1993, Needham Company presented its $10,000, 90-day, noninterest-bearing note to the bank, which discounted the note at 9%. The discount is $225 ($10,000 × 0.09 × 90/360), and the proceeds to Needham are $9,775. The entry required on the date of the note's issue is:

1993				
Dec.	1	Cash.	9,775	
		Discount on Notes Payable.	225	
		Notes Payable		10,000
		Issued 90-day note to bank.		

Notes Payable is credited for the face value of the note. Discount on Notes Payable is a contra account used to reduce Notes Payable from face value to the net amount of the debt. The balance in the Discount on Notes Payable account is reported on the balance sheet as a deduction from the balance in the Notes Payable account.

Over time, the discount becomes interest expense. If the note in the example above was paid before the end of the fiscal year, the entire $225 of discount would be charged to Interest Expense and credited to Discount on Notes Payable when the note was paid. However, if Needham's fiscal year ended on December 31, an adjusting entry would be required as follows:

1993				
Dec.	31	Interest Expense	75	
		Discount on Notes Payable.		75
		To record accrued interest on a note payable at year-end.		

This entry records the interest expense incurred by Needham for the 30 days the note has been outstanding. The expense can be calculated as $10,000 × 0.09 × 30/360, or 30/90 × $225. Notice that for entries involving discounted notes payable, no separate Interest Payable account is needed. The Notes Payable account already contains the total liability that will be paid at **maturity,** $10,000. From the date the proceeds are given to the borrower to the maturity date, the liability grows by reducing the balance in the Discount on Notes Payable contra account. Thus, the current liability section of the December 31, 1993, balance sheet would show:

Current liabilities:		
Notes payable.	$10,000	
Less: Discount on notes payable	150	$9,850

The $9,850 is the amount that would have to be paid to the bank if the company wishes to repay the loan on December 31 rather than at the maturity date (if the interest rate has not changed). The original amount borrowed, $9,775, plus the accrued interest for 30 days, $75, equals $9,850.

ETHICS

A CLOSER LOOK

The Landers Chemical Company manufactures and sells various types of chemicals. The company is being sued for alleged damages caused by one of its chemicals, dioxenole. The claim in the suit is that the chemical causes severe lung damage when inhaled, and that the company did not warn users of this hazard or inform users that the product should only be used in a well-ventilated area. Several users of the product have joined in a class action suit against the company claiming the product has caused them severe lung damage when following the instructions on the container.

The company's lawyers have privately advised management of the company that its defense is weak and the case will probably be lost. If the case is lost, damages are estimated at about $20,000,000. Product liability insurance would cover approximately $15,000,000 of the damages. The total assets of the company are now $11,567,273.

The management of the company realizes that this situation creates a contingent liability that must be disclosed in notes to the financial statements. Management prepared the following note to be included with the financial statements.

The company is being sued in a class action suit alleging that dioxenole has caused lung damage to certain individuals. The suit seeks $20,000,000 in damages. Management asserts that these persons did not take common sense precautions in using the product. Management believes the suit is without merit and that the outcome of this matter will not materially affect the company's financial position.

When challenged on the misleading wording of this note, one member of management confidentially stated, "We will probably lose the suit. But if we state that fact in the note, we would be admitting guilt before the case is tried and would have no chance of winning in court. The lawyer for the other side could use the note against us in the case. The wording we have used is very common in instances such as this."

Required

a. Do you agree with management that admitting liability in the note would result in certain loss of the case?

b. Do you believe that management's actions are ethical?

c. How would you change the last sentence of the note to reflect the situation more accurately?

When the note is paid at maturity, the entry is:

1994				
Mar.	1	Notes Payable	10,000	
		Interest Expense	150	
		Cash.		10,000
		Discount on Notes Payable.		150
		To record note payment and interest expense.		

The T-accounts for Discount on Notes Payable and for Interest Expense appear as follows:

Discount on Notes Payable					**Interest Expense**			
1993		1993			1993		1993	
Dec. 1	225	Dec. 31	75		Dec. 31	75	Dec. 31 To close 75	
Dec. 31 Balance 150		1994			1994			
		Mar. 1	150		Mar. 1	150		

ILLUSTRATION 9.5

Comparison between Interest-Bearing Notes and Noninterest-Bearing Notes

Interest-Bearing Notes	Noninterest-Bearing Notes

1993 Dec.	1	Cash	10,000			1993 Dec.	1	Cash	9,775	
		Notes Payable		10,000				Discount on Notes		
		To record 90-day bank loan.						Payable	225	
								Notes Payable		10,000
								To record 90-day bank loan.		
	31	Interest Expense	75				31	Interest Expense	75	
		Interest Payable		75				Discount on Notes		
		To record accrued interest on a note payable at year-end.						Payable		75
								To record accrued interest on a note payable at year-end.		
1994 Mar.	1	Notes Payable	10,000			1994 Mar.	1	Notes Payable	10,000	
		Interest Expense	150					Interest Expense	150	
		Interest Payable	75					Cash		10,000
		Cash		10,225				Discount on Notes		
		To record note principal and interest payment.						Payable		150
								To record note payment and interest expense.		

Illustration 9.5 shows the comparison of journal entries between interest-bearing notes and noninterest-bearing notes used by Needham Company.

After studying receivables and payables in this chapter, you will study plant assets in the next chapter. These long-term assets include land and depreciable assets such as buildings, machinery, and equipment.

UNDERSTANDING THE LEARNING OBJECTIVES

1. Account for uncollectible accounts receivable under the allowance method.
   □ Companies use two methods to account for uncollectible accounts: the allowance method, which provides in advance for uncollectible accounts; and the direct write-off method, which recognizes uncollectible accounts as an expense when judged to be uncollectible. The allowance method is the preferred method.
   □ The two basic methods for estimating uncollectible accounts under the allowance method are the percentage-of-sales method and the percentage-of-receivables method.
   □ The percentage-of-sales method focuses attention on the income statement and the relationship of uncollectible accounts to sales. The debit to Uncollectible Accounts Expense is a certain percent of credit sales or total net sales.
   □ The percentage-of-receivables method focuses attention on the balance sheet and the relationship of the allowance for uncollectible accounts to

accounts receivable. The credit to the Allowance for Uncollectible Accounts is the amount necessary to bring that account up to a certain percentage of the Accounts Receivable balance.

2. Account for uncollectible accounts receivable under the direct write-off method.
   □ Under the direct write-off method, Uncollectible Accounts Expense is debited only when particular accounts are identified as being uncollectible.

3. Record credit card sales and collections.
   □ Credit cards are charge cards used by customers to charge purchases of goods and services. These cards are of two types—nonbank credit cards (such as American Express) and bank credit cards (such as VISA).
   □ The sale is recorded at the gross amount of the sale, and the cash or receivable is recorded at the net amount the company will receive.

4. Define liabilities, current liabilities, and long-term liabilities.
   □ Liabilities result from some past transaction and are obligations to pay cash, provide services, or deliver goods at some time in the future.
   □ Current liabilities are obligations that are (1) payable within one year or one operating cycle, whichever is longer, or (2) will be paid out of current assets or result in the creation of other current liabilities.
   □ Long-term liabilities are obligations that do not qualify as current liabilities.

5. Define clearly determinable, estimated, and contingent liabilities.
   □ Clearly determinable liabilities are those for which the existence of the liability and its amount are certain.
   □ Estimated liabilities are those for which the existence of the liability is certain, but its amount can only be estimated.
   □ Contingent liabilities are those for which the existence, and usually the amount, are uncertain because these liabilities depend (or are contingent) on some future event occurring or not occurring.

6. Account for clearly determinable, estimated, and contingent liabilities.
   □ Clearly determinable liabilities, such as accounts payable, notes payable, interest payable, unearned delivery fees, and sales tax payable, are relatively easy to account for because both their existence and amount are known. For instance, when sales taxes are collected, they are credited to Sales Tax Payable. When the taxes are remitted, that account is debited.
   □ When an estimated liability exists, such as estimated product warranty payable, the amount is unclear. Thus, the accountant estimates the amount of expense that should be matched against revenues of the accounting period. For instance, Product Warranty Expense is debited and Product Warranty Payable is credited for estimated product warranty costs. When the company makes repairs under warranty, the accountant debits Estimated Product Warranty Payable instead of an expense.
   □ Contingent liabilities, such as those arising from lawsuits, discounted notes receivable, income tax disputes, penalties, or guarantees, are recorded in the accounts only if they are likely to occur and their

amount can be reasonably estimated. Very few of these liabilities meet these criteria. Therefore, most contingent liabilities are described in notes to the financial statements rather than recorded in the accounts.

7. Account for notes receivable and payable, including calculation of interest.

□ A promissory note is an unconditional written promise by a borrower (maker) to pay the lender (payee) or someone else who legally acquired the note a certain sum of money on demand or at a definite time.

□ Interest is the fee charged for the use of money through time. Interest = Principal × Rate of interest × Time.

8. Record the discounting of notes receivable.

□ The cash proceeds are computed by determining the maturity value of the note, the discount period, and the amount of the discount charged by the bank. The bank discount is deducted from the maturity value to find the cash proceeds.

9. Account for borrowing money using an interest-bearing note versus a non-interest-bearing note.

□ Companies sometimes need short-term financing. Short-term financing may be secured by issuing interest-bearing notes or by issuing noninterest-bearing notes.

□ An interest-bearing note specifies the interest rate that will be charged on the principal borrowed.

□ A noninterest-bearing note does not have a stated interest rate applied to the face value of the note.

DEMONSTRATION PROBLEM 9–A

a. Post Company estimates its uncollectible accounts expense to be 1% of sales. Sales in 1994 were $1,125,000.

Required   Prepare the journal entries for the following transactions:

1. The company prepared the adjusting entry for uncollectible accounts for 1994.

2. On January 15, 1995, the company decided that the account for John Nunn in the amount of $750 was uncollectible.

3. On February 12, 1995, John Nunn's check for $750 arrived.

b. A $22,500, 90-day, 12% note dated June 15, 1994, was received by Lyle Company from Stone Company in payment of its account.

Required   Prepare the journal entries in the records of Lyle Company for each of the following:

1. Lyle Company received the note on June 15, 1994.

2. Lyle Company discounted the note on July 15, 1994, at 10% at Citizens National Bank.

3. Stone Company paid the note at maturity.

4. Assume that Stone Company did not pay the note at maturity. Citizens National Bank charged the note to Lyle Company and charged a protest fee of $30. Lyle Company decided that the note was uncollectible.

SOLUTION TO DEMONSTRATION PROBLEM 9–A

a.

1.	1994 Dec.	31	Uncollectible Accounts Expense . . . . Allowance for Uncollectible Accounts . . . . To record estimated uncollectible accounts for the year.	11,250	11,250
2.	1995 Jan.	15	Allowance for Uncollectible Accounts . . . . Accounts Receivable—John Nunn . . . . To write off the account of John Nunn as uncollectible.	750	750
3.	Feb.	12	Accounts Receivable—John Nunn . . . . Allowance for Uncollectible Accounts . . . . To correct the write-off of John Nunn's account on January 15.	750	750
		12	Cash . . . . Accounts Receivable—John Nunn . . . . To record the collection of John Nunn's account receivable.	750	750

b.

1.	1994 June	15	Notes Receivable. . . . . Accounts Receivable—Stone Company . . . . To record receipt of a note from Stone Company.	22,500.00	22,500.00

2.	July	15	Cash . . . .
			    Notes Receivable. . . . .
			    Interest Revenue. . . . .
			To record the discounting of the Stone Company note.
				22,788.75	22,500.00
					288.75

			Computation of cash proceeds:
			Maturity value
			  $[\$22,500 + (\$22,500 \times 0.12 \times {}^{90}\!/_{360})]$ 23,175.00
			Discount = $\$23,175 \times 10\% \times {}^{60}\!/_{360}$ . . . 386.25
			    Proceeds . . . . $\underline{\$22,788.75}$		

3.			No entry.		
4.	Sept.	13	Accounts Receivable—Stone Company . . . . Cash . . . . To record the charge made against Lyle Company account for the Stone Company note of $22,500, interest of $675, and protest fee of $30.	23,205.00	23,205.00
		13	Allowance for Uncollectible Accounts* . . . . Accounts Receivable—Stone Company . . . . To write off the Stone Company note as uncollectible.	23,205.00	23,205.00

* This debit assumes that notes receivable were taken into consideration when an allowance was
established. If not, the debit should be to Loss from Dishonored Notes Receivable.

DEMONSTRATION PROBLEM 9–B

a.   Prepare the entries on the books of Cromwell Company assuming the company borrowed $10,000 at 7% from First National Bank and signed a 60-day noninterest-bearing note payable on December 1, 1993, accrued interest on December 31, 1993, and paid the debt on the maturity date.

b.   Prepare the entries on the books of Cromwell Company assuming it purchased equipment from Jones Company for $5,000 and signed a 30-day, 9% interest-bearing note payable on February 24, 1994. The note was paid on its maturity date.

SOLUTION TO DEMONSTRATION PROBLEM 9–B

a.

1993				
Dec.	1	Cash.	9,883.33	
		Bank Discount	116.67	
		Notes Payable		10,000.00
	31	Interest Expense	58.33	
		Bank Discount		58.33
		($10,000 × 0.07 × 30/360.)		
1994				
Jan.	30	Notes Payable	10,000.00	
		Interest Expense	58.34	
		Bank Discount		58.34
		Cash.		10,000.00

b.

1994				
Feb.	24	Purchases	5,000.00	
		Notes Payable		5,000.00
Mar.	26	Notes Payable	5,000.00	
		Interest Expense	37.50	
		Cash.		5,037.50
		($5,000 × 0.09 × 30/360) = $37.50		

NEW TERMS

Aging schedule   A means of classifying accounts receivable according to their age; used to determine the necessary balance in an Allowance for Uncollectible Accounts. A different uncollectibility percentage rate is used for each age category. *441*

Allowance for Uncollectible Accounts   A contra-asset account to the Accounts Receivable account; it reduces accounts receivable to their net realizable value. Also called *Allowance for Doubtful Accounts* or *Allowance for Bad Debts*. *437*

Bad debts expense   See Uncollectible accounts expense.

Bank discount   The difference between maturity value of a note and the actual amount—the note's proceeds—given to the borrower. *461*

Cash proceeds   The maturity amount of a note less the bank discount. *458*

Clearly determinable liabilities   Liabilities for which both their existence and amount are certain. Examples include accounts payable, notes payable, interest payable, unearned delivery fees, wages payable, sales tax payable, federal excise tax payable, current portions of long-term debt, and various payroll liabilities. *447*

Contingent liabilities Liabilities for which their existence is uncertain. Their amount is also usually uncertain. Both their existence and amount depend on some future event occurring or not occurring. Examples include liabilities arising from lawsuits, discounted notes receivable, income tax disputes, penalties that may be assessed because of some past action, and failure of another party to pay a debt that this company has guaranteed. *447, 450*

Credit Card Expense account Used to record credit card agency's service charge for services rendered in processing credit card sales. *445*

Credit cards Nonbank charge cards (American Express and Diners Club) and bank charge cards (VISA and MasterCard) that customers use to charge their purchases of goods and services. *445*

Current liabilities Obligations that (1) are payable within one year or one operating cycle, whichever is longer, or (2) will be paid out of current assets or result in the creation of other current liabilities. *446*

Direct write-off method A way of accounting for uncollectible accounts receivable in which identified uncollectible amounts are charged directly to an expense account. *444*

Discount on Notes Payable A contra account used to reduce Notes Payable from face value to the net amount of the debt. *462*

Discount rate The rate of interest the bank charges on a discounted note. *457*

Discounting a note payable The act of borrowing on a noninterest-bearing note drawn for a maturity amount, from which a bank discount is deducted, and the proceeds are given to the borrower. *462*

Discounting a note receivable The act of selling a note receivable with recourse to a bank. *Discounting* means that the bank deducts the interest from the maturity value of the note immediately and gives the seller of the note only the proceeds. *With recourse* means that if the maker does not pay the bank at maturity, the bank can collect the maturity value from the company that discounted the note at the bank. *457*

Dishonored note A note that the maker failed to pay at maturity. *454*

Estimated liabilities Liabilities for which their existence is certain, but their amount can only be estimated. An example is estimated product warranty payable. *447*

Interest The fee charged for use of money over a period of time (I = P × R × T). *451*

Interest Payable account An account showing the interest expense incurred but not yet paid; reported as a current liability in the balance sheet. *457*

Interest Receivable account An account showing the interest earned but not yet collected; reported as a current asset in the balance sheet. *456*

Liabilities Obligations that result from some past transaction and are obligations to pay cash, perform services, or deliver goods at some time in the future. *446*

Long-term liabilities Obligations that do not qualify as current liabilities. *446*

Maker (of a note) The party who prepares a note and is responsible for paying the note at maturity. *451*

Maturity date The date on which a note becomes due and must be paid. *452*

Maturity value The amount that the maker must pay on the note on its maturity date. *454*

Net realizable value The amount the company expects to collect from accounts receivable. *437*

Operating cycle The time it takes to start with cash, buy necessary items to produce revenues (such as materials, supplies, labor, and/or finished goods), sell goods or services, and receive cash by collecting the resulting receivables. *446*

Payable Any sum of money due to be paid by a company to any party for any reason. *436*

Payee (of a note) The party who receives a note and will be paid cash at maturity. *451*

Percentage-of-receivables method A method for determining the desired size of the Allowance for Uncollectible Accounts by basing the calculation on the Accounts Receivable balance at the end of the period. *440*

Percentage-of-sales method A method of estimating the uncollectible accounts from the sales of a given period's total net sales or credit sales. *438*

Principal (of a note) The face value of a note. *452*

Promissory note An unconditional written promise by a borrower (maker) to pay a definite sum of money to the lender (payee) on demand or at a specific date. *451*

Rate (of a note) The stated interest rate on the note. *452*

Receivable Any sum of money due to be paid to a company from any party for any reason. *436*

Time (of a note) The amount of time the note is to run; can be expressed in days or months. *452*

Trade receivables Amounts customers owe a company for goods sold or services rendered on account. Also called *accounts receivable* or *trade accounts receivable*. *436*

Uncollectible accounts expense An operating expense that a business incurs when it sells on credit; also called *doubtful accounts expense* or *bad debts expense*. *437*

With recourse A legal term meaning that if the maker does not pay the bank at maturity, the bank can collect the amount due from the company that sold the note to the bank. *457*

SELF-TEST

True-False

Indicate whether each of the following statements is true or false.

1. The percentage-of-sales method estimates the uncollectible accounts from the ending balance in Accounts Receivable.

2. Under the allowance method, uncollectible accounts expense is recognized when a specific customer's account is written off.

3. Bank credit card sales are treated as cash sales because the receipt of cash is certain.

Multiple-Choice

Select the best answer for each of the following questions.

1. Which of the following statements is false?
   a. Any existing balance in the Allowance for Uncollectible Accounts is ignored in calculating the uncollectible accounts expense under the percentage-of-sales method.
   b. The percentage-of-receivables method may use either an overall rate or a different rate for each age category.
   c. The Allowance for Uncollectible Accounts reduces accounts receivable to the net realizable value.
   d. The direct write-off method is unacceptable in any circumstance.
   e. None of the above.

2. Hunt Company estimates uncollectible accounts using the percentage-of-receivables method and expects that 5% of outstanding receivables will be uncollectible for 1994. The balance in Accounts Receivable is $200,000, and the allowance account has a $3,000 credit balance at year-end. The uncollectible accounts expense for 1994 will be:
   a. $7,000.
   b. $10,000.
   c. $13,000.
   d. $9,850.
   e. None of the above.

3. Which type of company typically has the longest operating cycle?
   a. Service company.
   b. Merchandising company.
   c. Manufacturing company.
   d. All equal.

4. Maxwell Company records its sales taxes in the same account as sales revenues. The sales tax rate is 6%. At the end of the current period, the Sales account has a balance of $265,000. The amount of sales tax payable is:
   a. $12,000.
   b. $15,000.

4. Liabilities result from some future transaction.

5. Current liabilities are classified as clearly determinable, estimated, and contingent.

6. A dishonored note is removed from Notes Receivable and the total amount due is recorded in Accounts Receivable.

7. When an interest-bearing note is issued to a bank, the difference between the cash proceeds and the maturity amount is debited to Discount on Notes Payable.

   c. $15,900.
   d. $18,000.

5. Dawson Company sells FAX machines. During 1994, the company sold 2,000 FAX machines. The company estimates that 5% of the machines will require repairs under warranty. To date, 30 machines have been repaired. The estimated cost of warranty repairs per defective FAX machine is $200. The required amount of the adjusting entry to record estimated product warranty payable is:
   a. $400,000.
   b. $6,000.
   c. $14,000.
   d. $–0–.

6. To compute interest on a promissory note, all of the following elements must be known except:
   a. The face value of the note.
   b. The stated interest rate.
   c. The name of the payee.
   d. The life of the note.
   e. None of the above.

7. When a note receivable is discounted with recourse at a bank, which of the following would be false?
   a. The net proceeds to the seller are equal to the maturity value less bank discount.
   b. The seller must pay the maturity value to the bank if the note is dishonored.
   c. The party discounting the note should disclose a contingent liability on the note.
   d. Interest expense or interest revenue may be recorded depending on the difference between the proceeds and maturity value of the note.

8. Keats Company issued its own $10,000, 90-day, noninterest-bearing note to a bank. If the note is discounted at 10%, the proceeds to Keats are:
   a. $10,000.
   b. $9,000.
   c. $9,750.
   d. $10,250.
   e. None of the above.

Now turn to page 478 to check your answers.

QUESTIONS

1. In view of the difficulty in estimating future events, would you recommend that accountants wait until collections are made from customers before recording sales revenue? Should they wait until known accounts prove to be uncollectible before charging an expense account?

2. The credit manager of a company has established a policy of seeking to completely eliminate all losses from uncollectible accounts. Is this policy a desirable objective for a company? Explain.

3. What are the two major purposes to be accomplished in establishing an allowance for uncollectible accounts?

4. In view of the fact that it is impossible to estimate the exact amount of uncollectible accounts receivable for any one year in advance, what exactly does the Allowance for Uncollectible Accounts account contain after a number of years?

5. What must be considered before adjusting the allowance for uncollectible accounts under the percentage-of-receivables method?

6. How might information in an aging schedule prove useful to management for purposes other than estimating the size of the required allowance for uncollectible accounts?

7. For a company using the allowance method of accounting for uncollectible accounts, which of the following directly affects its reported net income: (1) the establishment of the allowance, (2) the writing off of a specific account, or (3) the recovery of an account previously written off as uncollectible?

8. Explain why the direct write-off method of accounting for uncollectible accounts is generally unacceptable.

9. Why might a retailer agree to sell by credit card when such a substantial discount is taken by the credit card agency in paying the retailer?

10. Define liabilities, current liabilities, and long-term liabilities.

11. What is an operating cycle? Which type of company is likely to have the shortest operating cycle, and which is likely to have the longest operating cycle? Why?

12. Describe the differences between clearly determinable, estimated, and contingent liabilities. Give one or more examples of each type.

13. In what instances might a company acquire notes receivable?

14. How is the maturity value of a note calculated?

15. How do a dishonored note receivable and a discounted note receivable differ? How is each reported in the balance sheet?

16. Under what circumstances does the account Discount on Notes Payable arise? How is it reported in the financial statements? Explain why.

17. *Real world question* Refer to "A Broader Perspective" on page 443. What factors are taken into account by the General Electric Company in determining the adjusting entry to establish the desired balance in the Allowance for Uncollectible Accounts?

18. *Real world question* Refer to "A Broader Perspective" on page 443. Explain how the General Electric Company writes off uncollectible accounts.

19. *Real world question* Refer to the four annual reports in Appendix E at the end of the text. Where possible, determine the percentage of accounts receivable existing on December 31, 1989, that each of the companies estimates will be uncollectible (round to the nearest whole percent).

EXERCISES

Exercise 9–1
Prepare journal entries to record uncollectible accounts expense
(L.O. 1)

The accounts of Hopkins Company as of December 31, 1994, show Accounts Receivable, $165,000; Allowance for Uncollectible Accounts, $1,050 (credit balance); Sales, $1,087,500; and Sales Returns and Allowances, $19,500. Prepare journal entries to adjust for possible uncollectible accounts under each of the following assumptions:

a. Uncollectible accounts are estimated at 1% of net sales.
b. The allowance is to be increased to 3% of accounts receivable.

Exercise 9–2
Record write-off and subsequent recovery of account
(L.O. 1)

On April 1, 1993, Parker Company, which uses the allowance method of accounting for uncollectible accounts, wrote off Bob Dyer's $198 account. On December 14, 1993, the company received a check in that amount from Dyer marked "in full payment of account." Prepare the necessary entries for all of the above.

Exercise 9–3
Use aging schedule to estimate Allowance for Uncollectible Accounts (L.O. 1)

Compute the required balance of the Allowance for Uncollectible Accounts for the following receivables:

Accounts Receivable	Age (months)	Probability of Collection
$165,000	Less than 1	95%
82,500	1–3	85
39,000	3–6	75
10,500	6–9	35
2,250	9–12	10

Exercise 9–4
Prepare journal entries for write-off and subsequent collection of account under direct write-off method (L.O. 2)

Because its credit sales are immaterial in amount, Peach Tree Company accounts for its uncollectible accounts using the direct write-off method. During 1993, the following accounts were written off as uncollectible:

Apr. 10	J. Fox	$375
July 17	B. Cobb	720
Oct. 11	L. Willis	510

On December 10, payment in full is received from J. Fox. Prepare journal entries for the above.

Exercise 9–5
Record use of bank and nonbank credit cards (L.O. 3)

Skyway, Inc., sold $99,000 of goods in May to customers who used their Carte Blanche credit cards. Such sales are subject to a 3% discount by Carte Blanche.

a. Prepare journal entries to record the sales and the subsequent receipt of cash from the credit card company.

b. Do the same as requirement *(a)*, but assume the credit cards used were Visa cards.

Exercise 9–6
Answer questions regarding note in financial statements (L.O. 4, 5)

Assume the following note appeared in the annual report of a company:

In 1990, two small retail customers filed separate suits against the company alleging misrepresentation, breach of contract, conspiracy to violate federal laws and state antitrust violations arising out of their purchase of retail grocery stores through the company from a third party. Damages sought range up to $22.5 million in each suit for actual and treble damages and punitive damages of $2.5 million in one suit and $22.5 million in the other. The company is vigorously defending the actions and management believes there will be no adverse financial effect.

What kind of liability is being reported? Why is it classified this way? Do you think it is possible to calculate a dollar amount for this obligation? How much would the company have to pay if it lost the suit and had to pay the full amount?

Exercise 9–7
Determine sales revenue and sales tax payable (L.O. 6)

The Ricardo Company sells merchandise in a state that has a 5% sales tax. Rather than record sales taxes collected in a separate account, the company records both the sales revenue and the sales taxes in the Sales account. At the end of the first quarter of operations, when it is time to remit the sales taxes to the state taxing agency, the company has $472,500 in the Sales account. Determine the correct amount of sales revenue and the amount of sales tax payable.

Exercise 9–8
Determine maturity dates on several notes (L.O. 7)

Determine the maturity date for each of the following notes:

Issue Date	Life
January 13, 1993	30 days
January 31, 1993	90 days
June 4, 1993	1 year
December 2, 1993	1 month

Exercise 9-9

Prepare entries for a note
(L.O. 7)

John gave a $90,000, 120-day, 12% note to Steve in exchange for merchandise. John uses periodic inventory procedure. Prepare journal entries needed to record the issuance of the note and the entries needed at maturity for both parties, assuming payment is made.

Exercise 9-10

Prepare entries when maker defaults
(L.O. 7)

Prepare the entries that John and Steve (Exercise 9-9) would make at maturity date, assuming John defaults.

Exercise 9-11

Prepare entries at date of discounting of note
(L.O. 8)

On May 7, 1993, Axle Company gave a 180-day, $45,000, 14% note to Spoke Company. On August 20, Spoke Company discounted the note at 15%. Prepare the entries each company would make on the discounting date.

Exercise 9-12

Prepare entries at maturity date
(L.O. 8)

Using the information in Exercise 9-11 prepare the entries that would be recorded on the books of each company, assuming Axle Company (a) fails to pay the note at maturity and (b) pays the note at maturity.

Exercise 9-13

Prepare entries for noninterest-bearing note and interest-bearing note
(L.O. 9)

Bob Katz is negotiating a bank loan of $7,500 for 90 days. The bank's current interest rate is 16%. Prepare Katz's entries to record the loan under each of the following assumptions:

a. Katz signs a note for $7,500. Interest is deducted in calculating the proceeds turned over to him.

b. Katz signs a note for $7,500 and receives that amount. Interest is to be paid at maturity.

Exercise 9-14

Prepare entries at maturity date
(L.O. 9)

Prepare the entry or entries that would be made at maturity date for each alternative in Exercise 9-13, assuming the loan is paid before the end of the accounting period.

PROBLEMS: SERIES A

Problem 9-1A

Write off uncollectible account, record expense under alternative methods of estimation
(L.O. 1)

As of December 31, 1993, Flint Company's accounts prior to adjustment show:

Accounts receivable	$ 42,000
Allowance for uncollectible accounts (credit balance)	1,500
Sales.	450,000

Flint Company follows a practice of estimating uncollectible accounts at 1% of sales.

On February 23, 1994, the account of Dan Hall in the amount of $600 was considered uncollectible and written off. On August 12, 1994, Hall remitted $375 and indicated that he intends to pay the balance due as soon as possible. By December 31, 1994, no further remittance had been received from Hall and no further remittance was expected.

Required *a.* Prepare journal entries to record all of the above transactions and adjusting entries.

b. Give the entry necessary as of December 31, 1993, if Flint Company estimated its uncollectible accounts at 8% of outstanding receivables rather than at 1% of sales.

Problem 9-2A

Record use of bank and nonbank credit cards
(L.O. 3)

At the close of business on a certain date, Jack's Restaurant had credit card sales of $7,200. Of this amount, $4,800 were VISA sales invoices, which can be deposited in a bank for immediate credit, less a discount of 3%. The balance of $2,400 consisted of American Express charges, subject to a 3% service charge. These invoices were mailed to American Express. Shortly thereafter, a check was received.

Required Prepare journal entries for all of the above.

Problem 9–3A

Prepare journal entries for sales and excise taxes (L.O. 6)

Santiago Company sells merchandise in a state that has a 5% sales tax. On January 2, 1994, goods with a sales price of $40,000 were sold on credit. Sales taxes collected are recorded in a separate account. Assume that sales for the entire month were $900,000. On January 31, 1994, the company remitted the sales taxes collected to the state taxing agency.

Required

a. Prepare the general journal entries to record the January 2 sales revenue. Also prepare the entry to show the remittance of the taxes on January 31.

b. Now assume that the merchandise sold is also subject to federal excise taxes of 12%. The federal excise taxes collected are also remitted to the proper agency on January 31. Show the entries on January 1 and January 31.

Problem 9–4A

Prepare journal entries for product warranty (L.O. 6)

Richards Company sells used cars and warrants all parts for a one-year period. The average price per car is $14,000, and the company sold 600 in 1993. The company expects 30% of the cars to develop defective parts within one year of sale. The estimated average cost of warranty repairs per defective car is $500. By the end of the year, 100 cars sold that year had been returned and repaired under warranty. On January 4, 1994, a customer returned a car purchased in 1993 for repairs under warranty. The repairs were made on January 8. The cost of the repairs included parts, $360, and labor, $240.

Required

a. Calculate the amount of the estimated product warranty payable.

b. Prepare the entry to record the estimated product warranty payable on December 31, 1993.

c. Prepare the entry to record the repairs made on January 8, 1994.

Problem 9–5A

Account for discounted note receivable (L.O. 8)

On June 1, 1993, Lenardo Company received a $36,000, 120-day, 8% note from Shore Company dated June 1, 1993. On August 15, 1993, the note was discounted at the bank. The rate of discount was 12%.

Required   Determine:

a. The maturity value of the note.

b. The number of days from the discount date to the maturity date.

c. The dollar amount of the discount.

d. The cash proceeds received by the company.

e. The proper entry to record the receipt of proceeds at the date of discount.

Problem 9–6A

Prepare entries to record a number of note transactions, discounting of a note receivable, adjusting entries for interest, and entries for payment of notes (L.O. 7–9)

Prop Company is in the power boat manufacturing business. As of September 1, the balance in its Notes Receivable account is $96,000. The balance in Dishonored Notes Receivable is $30,330. A schedule of the notes (including the dishonored note) is as follows:

Face Amount	Maker	Date of Note	Life	Interest Rate	Comments
$ 60,000	C. Glass Co.	6/1/93	120 days	12%	
36,000	A. Lamp Co.	6/15/93	90	8	
42,000	C. Wall Co.	7/1/93	90	10	Discounted 8/16/93 at 6%
30,000	N. Case Co.	7/1/93	60	6	Dishonored, interest, $300; protest fee, $30.
$168,000					

Following are Prop Company's transactions for September:

Sept.   5   The C. Glass Company note was discounted at Ridge County Bank. The discount rate is 10%.

     10   Received $18,330 from N. Case Company as full settlement of the amount due from it. The company does not charge losses on notes to the Allowance for Uncollectible Accounts account.

     ?   The A. Lamp Company note was collected when due.

     ?   The C. Glass Company note was not paid at maturity. The bank deducted the balance from Prop Company's bank balance. A protest fee of $24 was also deducted.

Sept. ?   C. Wall Company paid its note at maturity.

    30   Received a new 60-day, 12% note from C. Glass Company for the total balance due on the dishonored note. The note was dated as of the maturity date of the dishonored note. Prop Company accepted the note in good faith.

Required   Prepare dated journal entries for the above transactions.

Problem 9–7A

Account for discounted note payable
(L.O. 9)

Falls Company discounted its own $45,000, noninterest-bearing, 180-day note on November 16, 1993, at Niagara County Bank at a discount rate of 12%.

Required   Prepare dated journal entries for:

a.   The original discounting on November 16.

b.   The adjustment required at the end of the company's calendar-year accounting period.

c.   Payment at maturity.

Problem 9–8A

Prepare entries to record a number of note transactions, discounting of a note (customer's and own), adjusting entries for interest, and payment of notes
(L.O. 7–9)

Following are selected transactions of Raft Company:

Oct. 31   Discounted its own 30-day, $22,500, noninterest-bearing note at Peach State Bank at 12%.

Nov. 8   Received a $6,750, 30-day, 9% note from Oar Company in settlement of an account receivable. The note is dated November 8.

    15   Purchased merchandise by issuing its own 90-day note for $9,000. The note is dated November 15 and bears interest at 12%.

    20   Discounted the Oar Company note at 12% at Peach State Bank.

    30   Peach State Bank notified Raft Company that it had charged the note of October 31 against the company's checking account.

Required   Assume all notes falling due after November 30 were paid in full on their due dates by the respective makers. Prepare dated journal entries for Raft Company for all of the above transactions (including the payment of the notes after November 30) and all necessary adjusting entries, assuming a fiscal year accounting period ending on November 30.

PROBLEMS: SERIES B

Problem 9–1B

Write off uncollectible account, record expense under alternative methods of estimation (L.O. 1)

Presented below are selected accounts of ABC Company as of December 31, 1993. Prior to closing the accounts and making allowance for uncollectible accounts entries, the $1,500 account of Golf Company is to be written off (this was a credit sale of February 12, 1993).

Accounts receivable	$120,000
Allowance for uncollectible accounts.	2,000
Sales.	560,000
Sales returns and allowances	10,000

Required   a.   Prepare journal entries to record all of the above transactions and the uncollectible accounts expense for the period. Assume the estimated expense is 2% of net sales.

b.   Give the entry to record the estimated expense for the period if the allowance is to be adjusted to 5% of outstanding receivables instead of as in (a) above.

Problem 9–2B

Record use of bank and nonbank credit cards
(L.O. 3)

The cash register at Dan's Place at the close of business on a certain date showed cash sales of $5,400 and credit card sales of $6,600 ($3,600 VISA and $3,000 American Express). The VISA invoices were discounted 5% when they were deposited. The American Express charges were mailed to the company and are subject to a 5% service charge. A few days later, a check was received for the net amount of the charges.

Required   Prepare journal entries for all of the above transactions.

Problem 9–3B

Prepare journal entries for sales and excise taxes (L.O. 6)

Trask Company sells merchandise in a state that has a 6% sales tax. On July 1, 1994, goods with a sales price of $20,000 were sold on credit. Sales taxes collected are recorded in a separate account. Assume that sales for the entire month were $600,000. On July 31, 1994, the company remitted the sales taxes collected to the state taxing agency.

Required

a. Prepare the general journal entries to record the July 1 sales revenue and sales tax payable. Also prepare the entry to show the remittance of the taxes on July 31.

b. Now assume that the merchandise sold is also subject to federal excise taxes of 10% in addition to the 6% sales tax. The federal excise taxes collected are also remitted to the proper agency on July 31. Show the entries on July 1 and July 31.

Problem 9–4B

Prepare journal entries for product warranty (L.O. 6)

Crown Company sells racing bicycles and warrants all parts for a one-year period. The average price per bicycle is $300, and the company sold 5,000 in 1993. The company expects 20% of the bicycles to develop defective parts within one year of sale. The estimated average cost of warranty repairs per defective bicycle is $25. By the end of the year, 700 bicycles sold that year had been returned and repaired under warranty. On January 2, 1994, a customer returned a bicycle purchased in 1993 for repairs under warranty. The repairs were made on January 3. The cost of the repairs included parts, $30, and labor, $5.

Required

a. Calculate the amount of the estimated product warranty payable.

b. Prepare the entry to record the estimated product warranty payable on December 31, 1993.

c. Prepare the entry to record the repairs made on January 3, 1994.

Problem 9–5B

Account for discounted note receivable (L.O. 8)

Bull Company received on July 24, 1993, a note from Steer Company with the following description:

Face amount	$240,000
Life of note	45 days
Date of note	7/24/93
Interest rate on note	10%
Date of discounting note at the bank.	8/23/93
Rate of discount charged by the bank	12%

Required   Determine:

a. The maturity date of the note.

b. The maturity value of the note.

c. The number of days from the discount date to the maturity date.

d. The dollar amount of the discount.

e. The cash proceeds received by the company.

f. The entry to record the receipt of the proceeds at the date of discount.

Problem 9–6B

Prepare entries to record a number of note transactions, discounting of a note (customer's and own), adjusting entries for interest, and payment of notes (L.O. 7–9)

Sterling Company has an accounting period of one year, ending on July 31. On July 1, 1993, the balances of certain ledger accounts are Notes Receivable, $1,920,000; and Notes Payable, $4,500,000. A schedule of the notes receivable (including the discounted note) is as follows:

Face Amount	Maker	Date of Note	Life	Interest Rate	Date Discounted	Discount Rate
$1,350,000	Rage Co.	5/15/93	60 days	12%	6/1/93	12%
600,000	Dot Co.	5/31/93	60	12	—	—
1,320,000	Fixx Co.	6/15/93	30	10	—	—
$3,270,000						

The note payable is a 60-day bank loan dated May 20, 1993. Notes Payable—Discount was debited for the discount of $30,000.

Following are the company's transactions during July:

July 1 Sterling Company discounted its own $900,000, 60-day, noninterest-bearing note at Key Bank. The discount rate is 10%, and the note was dated today.

3 Received a 20-day, 12% note, dated today, from Sox Company in settlement of an account receivable of $180,000.

6 Purchased merchandise from Junk Company, $1,440,000, and issued a 60-day, 12% note, dated today, for the purchase.

8 Sold merchandise to Fan Company, $1,800,000. A 30-day, 12% note, dated today, is received to cover the sale.

14 The $1,350,000 note discounted on June 1, 1993, is paid by Rage Company directly to the holder in due course.

15 Fixx Company sent a $600,000, 30-day, 12% note, dated today, and a check to cover the part of the old note not covered by the new note, *plus* all interest expense incurred on the prior note.

18 The Fan Company note of July 8 is discounted at Key Bank for the remaining life of the note. The discount rate is 12%.

19 The note payable dated May 20, 1993, was paid in full.

23 Sox Company dishonored its note of July 3 and sent a check for the interest on the dishonored note and a new 30-day, 12% note dated July 23, 1993.

30 The Dot Company note dated May 31, 1993, was paid with interest in full.

Required Prepare dated journal entries for the above transactions and necessary July 31 adjustments.

Problem 9–7B

Account for discounted note payable

(L.O. 9)

On November 1, 1993, Lotus Company discounted its own $150,000, 180-day, noninterest-bearing note at its bank at 18%. The note was paid on its maturity date. Lotus Company uses a calendar-year accounting period.

Required Prepare dated journal entries to record (a) the discounting of the note, (b) the year-end adjustment, and (c) the payment of the note.

Problem 9–8B

Prepare entries to record a number of note transactions, discounting of a note (customer's and own), adjusting entries for interest, and payment of notes

(L.O. 7–9)

House Company engaged in the following transactions in 1993:

May 31 Discounted its own 30-day, $48,000, noninterest-bearing note at Second National Bank at 12%.

June 8 Received a $8,000, 90-day, 9% note from Star Company in settlement of its account balance. The note is dated June 8.

15 Issued a $33,600, 120-day, 10% note, dated today, to purchase merchandise. House Company uses periodic inventory procedure.

20 Discounted the Star Company note at 12% at Second National Bank.

30 The bank notified House Company that it had charged the note of May 31 against the company's checking account balance.

Required Assume all notes falling due after June 30 were paid in full on their due dates by the respective makers. Prepare dated journal entries for House Company for all of the above transactions (including the payment of the notes after June 30) and all necessary adjusting entries, assuming a fiscal year accounting period ending on June 30.

BUSINESS DECISION PROBLEMS

Decision Problem 9-1

Compare costs of maintaining own accounts receivable with costs of allowing the use of credit cards; identify other factors to consider (L.O. 1, 3)

Alice Lyle runs a hardware store, selling items for both cash and on account. During 1993, which seemed to be a typical year, some of her operating data and other data were as follows:

Sales:	
For cash	$ 600,000
On credit	1,200,000
Cost of obtaining credit reports on customers	1,800
Cost incurred in paying a part-time bookkeeper to keep the accounts receivable subsidiary ledger up to date	6,000
Cost associated with preparing and mailing invoices to customers and other collection activities	9,000
Uncollectible accounts expense	22,500
Average outstanding accounts receivable balance (on which Alice estimates she could have earned 10% if it had been invested in other assets)	90,000

A national credit card agency has approached Alice and tried to convince her that, instead of carrying her own accounts receivable, she should only accept the agency's credit card for sales on credit. The agency would pay Alice within two days after she submits sales charges, deducting 6% from the amount and paying her 94%.

Required

a. Using the data given, prepare an analysis showing whether or not Alice would benefit from switching to the credit card method of selling on credit.

b. What other factors should be taken into consideration?

Decision Problem 9-2

Evaluate alternative means of making sales (L.O. 3, 4)

Jim Hayes operates a large fruit and vegetable stand on the outskirts of a city. In a typical year he sells $750,000 of goods to regular customers. His sales are 40% for cash and 60% on credit. He carries all of the credit himself. Only after a customer has a total of $300 unpaid balance on which no payments have been made for two months does he refuse that customer credit for future purchases. His income before taxes is approximately $92,000. The total of uncollectible accounts for a given year is about 10% of credit sales, or $45,000.

You are one of Jim's regular customers. He knows that you are taking a college course in accounting and has asked you to tell him your opinion of several alternatives recommended to him to reduce or eliminate the $45,000 per year uncollectible accounts expense. The alternatives are as follows:

1. Do not sell on credit.
2. Sell on credit by national credit card only.
3. Allow customers to charge only until their account balance reaches $37.50.
4. Allow a bill collector to "go after" uncollectible accounts. He would keep half of what he collects.
5. Require all credit customers to sign a note so that Jim can discount these at the local bank.

Required

Give Jim your opinion as to the advisability of following any of these alternatives.

ANSWERS TO SELF-TEST

True-False

1. *False.* The percentage-of-sales method estimates the uncollectible accounts from the credit sales of a given period.

2. *False.* Under the direct write-off method, uncollectible accounts expense is recognized when a specific customer's account is written off.

3. *True*. Nonbank credit card sales are treated as credit sales.

4. *False*. Liabilities do result from a past transaction.

5. *True*. Current liabilities are classified into those three categories.

Multiple-Choice

1. *d.* The direct write-off method may be used if accounts receivable and uncollectible amounts are immaterial. Also, this method must be used for tax purposes.

2. *a.* The uncollectible accounts expense for 1994 is computed as follows:

Allowance balance after adjustment ($200,000 × 0.05)	$10,000
Balance before adjustment	(3,000)
Uncollectible accounts expense	$ 7,000

3. *c.* Manufacturing companies tend to have the longest operating cycle. They must invest cash in raw materials, convert these raw materials into finished goods, sell the items on account, and then collect the accounts receivable.

6. *True*. The note has passed its maturity date and should be removed from the Notes Receivable account. The maturity value plus any protest fee should be debited to Accounts Receivable.

7. *False*. Discount on Notes Payable is recorded when a noninterest-bearing note is issued.

4. *b.* $265,000 divided by 1.06 = $250,000; $265,000 − $250,000 = $15,000.

5. *c.* 2,000 × 5% = 100 machines expected to be defective. 100 − 30 already returned = 70 more expected to be returned. 70 × $200 = $14,000 estimated product warranty payable.

6. *c.* The name of the payee is not needed to compute interest expense on a promissory note.

7. *d.* Interest expense or interest revenue is the difference between the proceeds and the *face* value of the note.

8. *c.* The proceeds from a bank are computed as follows:

$$\text{Discount amount} = \$10,000 \times 0.10 \times \tfrac{90}{360}$$
$$= \$250$$
$$\text{Proceeds} = \$10,000 - \$250 = \$9,750$$

10

PROPERTY, PLANT, AND EQUIPMENT

LEARNING OBJECTIVES

After studying this chapter, you should be able to:

1. List the characteristics of plant assets and identify the costs of acquiring plant assets.
2. List the four major factors affecting depreciation expense.
3. Describe the various methods of calculating depreciation expense.
4. Distinguish between capital and revenue expenditures for plant assets.
5. Describe the subsidiary records used to control plant assets.

In Chapter 4, you were introduced to the classified balance sheet. The asset section of a classified balance sheet is divided into (1) current assets and (2) property, plant, and equipment. Current assets were discussed in previous chapters. This chapter begins a discussion of property, plant, and equipment, which are often called plant and equipment or simply **plant assets.**

Plant assets are long-lived assets because their useful lives are expected to last for more than one year. Long-lived assets consist of tangible assets and intangible assets. **Tangible assets** have physical characteristics that we can see and touch. These tangible assets include (1) plant assets such as buildings, machinery, vehicles, and furniture, which are discussed in this chapter; and (2) natural resources such as gas and oil, which are discussed in Chapter 11. **Intangible assets** (also discussed in Chapter 11) have no physical characteristics that we can see and touch but represent exclusive privileges and rights to their owners.

You should be aware that a difference exists between the physical life of an asset and its economic life. For example, on TV you may have seen a demolition crew setting off explosives in a huge building and wondered why a decision was made to destroy what looked like a perfectly good building. The reason the building was destroyed was because the building had "lived" its economic life. The land on which the building stood could be put to better use, possibly by constructing a new building.

NATURE OF PLANT ASSETS

Objective 1

List the characteristics of plant assets and identify the costs of acquiring plant assets

To be classified as a **plant asset,** an asset must (1) be tangible, that is, capable of being seen and touched; (2) have a useful service life of more than one year; and (3) be used in business operations rather than held for resale. Common plant assets are buildings, machines, tools, and office equipment. On the balance sheet, you will find these assets included under the heading "Property, plant, and equipment."

Plant assets include all long-lived tangible assets that are used to generate the principal revenues of the business. Inventory is a tangible asset but not a plant asset because inventory is usually not long-lived and it is held for sale rather than for use. What represents a plant asset to one company may be inventory to another. For example, a business such as a retail appliance store may classify a delivery truck as a plant asset because the truck is used to deliver merchandise, but a business such as a truck dealership would classify the same delivery truck as inventory because the truck is held for sale. Also, land held for speculation or not yet put into service is a long-term investment rather than a plant asset because the land is not being used by the business. However, standby equipment that is used only in peak or emergency periods is classified as a plant asset because the equipment is used in the operations of the business.

Accountants view plant assets as a collection of **service potentials** that are consumed over a long period of time. For example, over several years, a delivery truck may provide 100,000 miles of delivery services to an appliance business. A new building may provide 40 years of shelter, while a machine may perform a particular operation on 400,000 parts. In each instance, purchase of the plant asset actually represents the advance payment or prepayment of expected services. Plant asset costs are a **form of prepaid expense.** As was the case with short-term prepayments, the accountant must allocate the cost of these services to the accounting periods benefited.

Accounting for plant assets presents the following four challenges:

1. Record the acquisition cost of the asset.
2. Record the allocation of the asset's original cost to periods of its useful life through depreciation.

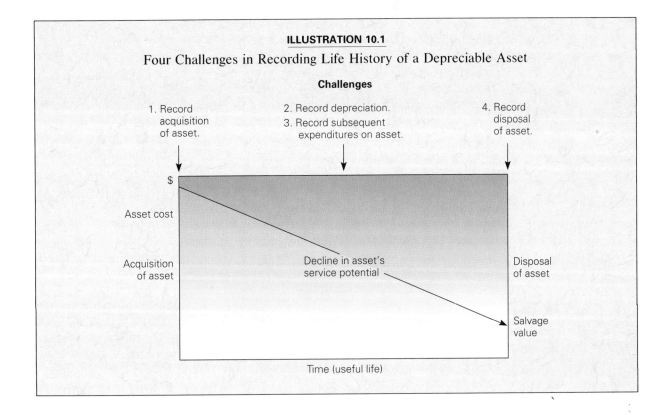

ILLUSTRATION 10.1

Four Challenges in Recording Life History of a Depreciable Asset

Challenges

1. Record acquisition of asset.

2. Record depreciation.
3. Record subsequent expenditures on asset.

4. Record disposal of asset.

$

Asset cost

Acquisition of asset

Decline in asset's service potential

Disposal of asset

Salvage value

Time (useful life)

3. Record subsequent expenditures on the asset.
4. Account for the disposal of the asset.

These four accounting challenges are shown in Illustration 10.1. Note how the asset's life begins with its procurement and the recording of its acquisition cost, which is usually in the form of a dollar purchase; then, as the asset provides services through time, accountants must record the asset's depreciation and any subsequent expenditures related to the asset; and, finally, accountants must record the disposal of the asset. The first three challenges are discussed in this chapter; the disposal of an asset is discussed in Chapter 11. The last section in this chapter explains how accountants use subsidiary ledgers to control assets.

Remember that in recording the life history of an asset, accountants seek to match expenses related to the asset with the revenues generated by the asset. Since the measurement of periodic expense associated with plant assets affects net income, accounting for property, plant, and equipment is important to financial statement users.

INITIAL RECORDING OF PLANT ASSETS

When a company acquires a plant asset, accountants record the asset at the cost of acquisition (historical cost) because this cost is objective, verifiable, and the best measure of an asset's fair value at the time of purchase. Even if the market value of the asset changes over time, the acquisition cost continues to be the amount reported in the asset account in subsequent accounting periods.

The acquisition cost **of a plant asset is the amount of cash/or cash equivalents given up to acquire that asset and place it in operating condition at its proper location.** Thus, cost includes all normal, reasonable, and necessary expenditures to obtain the asset and get it ready for use. Acquisition cost also includes the repair and reconditioning costs for used or damaged assets. Unnecessary costs (such as traffic tickets or fines) that must be paid as a result of hauling machinery to a new plant are not part of the acquisition cost of the asset.

In this section, you will learn which costs are capitalized for (1) land and land improvements, (2) buildings, (3) group purchases of assets, (4) machinery and other equipment, (5) self-constructed assets, (6) noncash acquisitions, and (7) gifts of plant assets.

Land and Land Improvements

The cost of land includes its purchase price and other costs such as option cost, if any; real estate commissions; title search and title transfer fees; title insurance premiums; existing mortgage note assumed; unpaid taxes (back taxes) assumed by purchaser; cost of surveying, clearing, and grading; and local assessments for sidewalks, streets, sewers, and water mains. **When land purchased as a building site contains an unusable building that must be removed, the entire purchase price should be debited to Land, including the cost of removing the building less any cash received from the sale of salvaged items,** such as crops or fruit on the land, that occurs while the land is being readied for use.

To illustrate, assume that Spivey Company purchased an old farm on the outskirts of San Diego, California, as a factory site. The company paid $225,000 for the property. In addition, the company agreed to pay unpaid property taxes from previous periods (called *back taxes*) of $12,000. Attorneys' fees and other legal costs relating to the purchase of the farm totaled $1,800. The farm buildings were demolished at a cost of $18,000. Some of the structural pieces of the building were salvageable and were sold for $3,000. The purpose of the demolition was to construct a new building at the site. Since new construction was to take place, the city assessed Spivey Company $9,000 for water mains, sewers, and street paving. The cost of the land is computed as follows:

	Land
Cost of factory site	$225,000
Back taxes	12,000
Attorneys' fees and other legal costs	1,800
Demolition	18,000
Sale of salvaged parts	(3,000)
City assessment	9,000
	$262,800

All costs relating to the farm purchase and razing of the old buildings are assignable to the Land account because the old buildings purchased with the land were not usable. The real goal was to purchase the land, but the land was not available without the buildings.

Land is considered to have an unlimited life and is therefore not depreciable. However, land improvements, including driveways, temporary landscaping, parking lots, fences, lighting systems, and sprinkler systems, are attachments to the land that have limited lives and therefore are depreciable. Depreciable land improvements should be recorded in a separate account called Land Improvements. The cost of permanent landscaping, including leveling and grading, should be recorded in the Land account.

Buildings

When an existing building is purchased, its cost includes purchase price, repair and remodeling costs, unpaid taxes assumed by the purchaser, legal costs, and real estate commissions paid.

The cost of constructing new buildings is often more difficult to determine. Usually this cost includes architect's fees; building permits; payments to contractors; **cost of digging the foundation;** labor and materials to build the building; salaries of officers supervising the construction; and insurance, taxes, and **interest during the construction period. Any miscellaneous amounts earned from the building during construction reduce the cost of the building.** For example, if a small completed portion of the building is rented out during construction of the remainder of the building, the rental proceeds are credited to the Buildings account.

Group Purchases of Assets

Sometimes land and other assets are purchased for a lump sum. When land and buildings are purchased together and both are to be used, the total cost should be divided so that separate ledger accounts may be established for land and for buildings. This division of cost is necessary to establish the proper balances in the appropriate accounts, which is especially important later because reported income will be affected by the depreciation recorded on the buildings.

Returning to our example of Spivey Company, suppose one of the existing buildings was going to be remodeled for use by the company. Then, Spivey would have to determine what portion of the purchase price of the farm, back taxes, and legal fees ($225,000 + $12,000 + $1,800 = $238,800) it could assign to the buildings and what portion it could assign to the land. (The net cost of demolition would not be incurred, and the city assessment would be incurred at a later time.) Spivey would assign the $238,800 to the land and the buildings on the basis of their appraised values. For example, assume that the land itself was appraised at $162,000 and the buildings were appraised at $108,000. The cost assignable to each of these plant assets would be determined as follows:

Asset	Appraised Value	Percent of Total Value
Land	$162,000	60% (162/270)
Buildings . . .	108,000	40 (108/270)
	$270,000	100% (270/270)

	Percent of Total Value	×	Purchase Price	=	Cost Assigned
Land	60%	×	$238,800*	=	$143,280
Buildings. . . .	40	×	238,800	=	95,520
					$238,800

* The purchase price is the sum of the cash price, back taxes, and legal fees.

The journal entry to record the purchase of the land and buildings would be:

Land	143,280	
Buildings	95,520	
Cash		238,800
To record purchase of land and buildings.		

When the city eventually assesses the charges for the water mains, sewers, and street paving, these costs will still be debited to the Land account as they were in the previous example.

**Machinery and
Other Equipment**

When machinery or other equipment (such as delivery or office equipment) is purchased, its cost includes the seller's **net** invoice price (whether the discount is taken or not), transportation charges, insurance in transit, cost of installation, costs of accessories, testing and break-in costs, and other costs needed to put the machine or equipment in operating condition in its intended location for use. **The cost of machinery does not include costs of removing and disposing of a replaced, old machine that has been used in operations.** Such costs are part of the gain or loss on disposal of the old machine, as discussed in Chapter 11.

To illustrate, assume that Clark Company purchases new equipment to replace old equipment that it has used in operations for five years. The company pays a net purchase price of $150,000, brokerage fees of $5,000, legal fees of $2,000, and freight and insurance in transit of $3,000. In addition, the company pays $1,500 to remove old equipment and $2,000 to install new equipment. The cost of new equipment is computed as follows:

Net purchase price.	$150,000
Brokerage fees	5,000
Legal fees	2,000
Freight and insurance in transit	3,000
Installation costs.	2,000
Total cost	$162,000

**Self-Constructed
Assets**

If a company builds a plant asset for its own use, the cost would include cost of materials and labor directly traceable to construction of the asset. Also included in the cost of the asset are indirect costs, such as interest costs related to the asset, and amounts paid for utilities (such as heat, light, and power) and for supplies used during construction. To determine how much of these indirect costs should be capitalized, the company compares utility and supply costs during the construction period with utility and supply costs paid in a period when no construction occurred. The increase is recorded as part of the asset's cost. For example, assume a company normally incurred a $600 utility bill for June. This year a machine was constructed during June, and the utility bill was $975. The $375 increase would be recorded as part of the machine's cost.

To illustrate further, assume that Tanner Company needed a new die-casting machine and received a quote from Smith Company for $23,000, plus $1,000 freight costs. Tanner decided to build the machine rather than buy it. The company incurred the following costs to build the machine: materials, $4,000; labor, $13,000; and indirect services of heat, power, and supplies, $3,000. The machine should be recorded at its cost of $20,000 ($4,000 + $13,000 + $3,000) rather than $24,000, the price that would have been paid if the machine had been purchased. The $20,000 is the cost of the resources given up to construct the machine. Also, recording the machine at $24,000 would require Tanner to recognize a gain on construction of the assets. Accountants generally do not subscribe to the idea that a business can earn revenue (or realize a gain), and therefore net income, by dealing with itself.

The general guidelines discussed and illustrated above can be applied to other plant assets, such as furniture and fixtures. The accounting methods are the same.

**Noncash
Acquisitions**

When a plant asset is purchased for cash, its acquisition cost is simply the agreed cash price. However, when plant assets are acquired in exchange for other non-cash assets (shares of stock, a customer's note, or tract of land) or as gifts, a cash price is more difficult to establish. Three possible asset valuation bases are discussed in this section.

Fair Market Value   Fair market value is the price that would be received for an item being sold in the normal course of business (not at a forced liquidation sale). Accountants seek to record noncash exchange transactions at fair market value.

The general rule on noncash exchanges is that **the noncash asset received is valued at its fair market value or the fair market value of what was given up, whichever is more clearly evident.** The reason for not using the book value of the old asset to value the new asset is that the asset being given up is often carried in the accounting records at historical cost or book value. Neither amount may adequately represent the actual fair market value of either the old or the new asset. Therefore, if the fair market value of one of the assets is clearly evident, this amount is more representative of the value that should be recorded for the new asset in the accounting records at the time of the exchange.

Appraised Value   Exchanges of items, neither of which has a fair market value, may be recorded at their appraised values as determined by a professional appraiser. Appraised value is an expert's opinion as to what an item's fair market price would be if the item were sold. Appraisals are often used to value works of art, rare books, and antiques.

Book Value   The book value of an asset is its recorded cost less accumulated depreciation. An old asset's book value is usually not a valid indication of the new asset's fair market value. The book value of an asset given up is an acceptable basis for measuring the value of the new asset received only if a better basis is not available.

Gifts of Plant Assets

Occasionally, a company will receive an asset without giving up anything for it. For example, to attract industry to an area and provide jobs for local residents, a city may give a tract of land to a company on which to build a factory. Although such a gift costs the recipient company nothing, the asset (land) is usually recorded at its fair market value. Gifts of plant assets are recorded at fair market value because accounting seeks to provide information on all assets owned by the company. Omitting some assets may make information provided misleading. Assets received as gifts are credited to Paid-In Capital—Donations.

DEPRECIATION OF PLANT ASSETS

Depreciation is recorded on all plant assets except land. Since the amount of depreciation may be relatively large, depreciation expense is often a significant factor in determining net income. For this reason, most financial statement users are interested in the amount of, and the methods used to compute, a company's depreciation expense.

Depreciation is the amount of plant asset cost allocated to each accounting period benefiting from the plant asset's use and is a **process of allocation, not valuation.** Since eventually all assets except land wear out or become so inadequate or outmoded that they are sold or discarded, depreciation must be recorded on every plant asset except land. Depreciation is recorded even when the market value of a plant asset temporarily rises above its original cost because eventually the asset will no longer be useful.

Major causes of depreciation are (1) physical deterioration, (2) inadequacy for future needs, and (3) obsolescence. Physical deterioration results from the use of the asset—wear and tear—and the action of the elements. For example, an automobile may have to be replaced after a time because its body rusted out. The inadequacy of a plant asset is its inability to produce enough products or provide enough services to meet current demands. For example, an airline cannot provide air service for 125 passengers on a flight serviced by a plane with a seating capacity of 90. The obsolescence of an asset is its decline in usefulness brought about by inventions and technological progress. For example, the development of the xerographic process of reproducing printed matter rendered almost all previous methods of duplication obsolete.

The use of a plant asset in business operations transforms a plant asset cost into an operating expense. Depreciation, then, is an operating expense resulting from the use of a depreciable plant asset.

Because depreciation does not require a current cash outlay, it is often called a *noncash expense*. Cash was given up in the period when the asset was acquired, not during the periods when depreciation expense is recorded.

Factors Affecting Depreciation

Objective 2
List the four major factors affecting depreciation expense

To compute depreciation expense, accountants consider four major factors:

1. Cost of the asset.

2. Estimated salvage value of the asset. Salvage value (or **scrap value**) is the amount of money the company expects to recover, less disposal costs, on the date a plant asset is scrapped, sold, or traded in.

3. Estimated useful life of the asset. Useful life refers to the length of time the company owning the asset intends to use it; useful life is not necessarily the same time period as either economic life or physical life. The economic life of a car may be 7 years and its physical life may be 10 years, but if a company has a policy of trading cars every 3 years, the useful life for depreciation purposes is 3 years. Useful life may be expressed in years, months, working hours, or units of production. Obsolescence may also affect useful life. For example, a machine may be capable of producing units for 20 years, but it is expected to be obsolete in 6 years. Thus, its estimated useful life is 6 years—not 20.

4. Depreciation method to be used in depreciating the asset. The four common depreciation methods are discussed in the next section.

Illustration 10.2 shows the relationship among these factors. Assume Ace Company purchased an office building for a cost of $100,000. The building has an estimated salvage value of $15,000 and a useful life of 20 years. The depreciable cost of the building is $85,000 (cost less estimated salvage value), and this depreciable base is allocated over the useful life of the building using a proper depreciation method under the circumstances.

Now you know the nature of plant assets and how to initially record them. Next, you are ready to study the various plant asset depreciation methods accountants use. You may have read about some of these depreciation methods in the business section of your daily newspaper.

Depreciation Methods[1]

Objective 3
Describe the various methods of calculating depreciation expense

Today, many different methods are available for calculating depreciation on assets. This section discusses and illustrates the most common methods—straight-line, units-of-production, and two accelerated depreciation methods (sum-of-the-years'-digits and double-declining-balance).

As is true for inventory methods, a company is normally free to adopt the method(s) of depreciation it believes most appropriate for its business operations.

---

[1] Because depreciation expense is an estimate, calculations may be rounded to the nearest dollar.

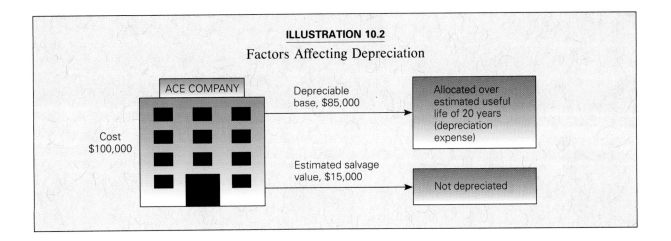

ILLUSTRATION 10.2

Factors Affecting Depreciation

The theoretical guideline is to use a depreciation method that reflects most closely the underlying economic circumstances. Thus, companies should adopt the depreciation method that allocates plant asset cost to accounting periods according to the benefits received from the use of the asset. Illustration 10.3 shows the frequency of use of these methods for a sample of 600 companies. You can see that most companies use the straight-line method for financial reporting purposes. Also, some companies use one method for certain assets and another method for other assets.

In practice, the measurement of benefits from the use of a plant asset is impractical and often not possible. As a result, a depreciation method must meet only one standard: The depreciation method **must** allocate plant asset cost to accounting periods in a systematic and rational manner. The four methods discussed in this section meet this requirement.

Regardless of the method or methods chosen, the company must disclose its depreciation method(s) in the footnotes to its financial statements. This information is included in the first footnote, which contains a summary of significant accounting policies.

The disclosure is generally straightforward: Sears, Roebuck and Co.'s Annual Report states simply that "depreciation is provided principally by the straight-line method." Companies may use different depreciation methods for different assets. General Electric uses an accelerated method for most of its property, plant, and equipment; however, some assets are depreciated on a straight-line basis, while the company's mining properties are depreciated under the units-of-production method.

The illustrations of the four depreciation methods given below are based on the following data: On January 1, 1994, a machine was purchased for $54,000 with an estimated useful life of 10 years, or 50,000 units of output, and an estimated salvage value of $4,000.

Straight-Line Method   The straight-line depreciation method has been the most widely used depreciation method in the United States for many years because it is easily applied. To apply the straight-line method, an equal amount of plant asset cost is charged to each accounting period. The formula for calculating depreciation under the straight-line method is:

$$\frac{\text{Depreciation}}{\text{per period}} = \frac{\text{Asset cost} - \text{Estimated salvage value}}{\begin{array}{c}\text{Number of accounting periods}\\ \text{in estimated useful life}\end{array}}$$

ILLUSTRATION 10.3

Depreciation Methods Used

Method	Number of Companies			
	1989	1988	1987	1986
Straight-line	562	563	559	561
Declining-balance	40	44	44	49
Sum-of-the-years'-digits	16	11	12	14
Accelerated method—not specified	69	70	76	77
Units-of-production	50	53	51	48
Other	8	9	12	12

Source: American Institute of Certified Public Accountants, *Accounting Trends & Techniques* (New York: AICPA, 1990), p. 261.

ILLUSTRATION 10.4

Straight-Line Depreciation Schedule

End of Year	Depreciation Expense Dr.; Accumulated Depreciation Cr.	Total Accumulated Depreciation	Book Value
			$54,000
1	$ 5,000	$ 5,000	49,000
2	5,000	10,000	44,000
3	5,000	15,000	39,000
4	5,000	20,000	34,000
5	5,000	25,000	29,000
6	5,000	30,000	24,000
7	5,000	35,000	19,000
8	5,000	40,000	14,000
9	5,000	45,000	9,000
10	5,000	50,000	4,000*
	$50,000		

* Estimated salvage value.

Using our example of a machine purchased for $54,000, the depreciation is:

$$\frac{\$54,000 - \$4,000}{10 \text{ years}} = \$5,000 \text{ per year}$$

Illustration 10.4 presents a schedule of annual depreciation entries, cumulative balances in the accumulated depreciation account, and the book (or carrying) values of the $54,000 machine.

Use of the straight-line method is appropriate for assets where (1) time rather than obsolescence is the major factor limiting the asset's life and (2) relatively constant amounts of periodic services are received from the asset. Assets that possess these features include pipelines, fencing, and storage tanks.

Units-of-Production (Output) Method The units-of-production depreciation method assigns an equal amount of depreciation to each unit of product manufactured or service rendered by an asset. Since this method of depreciation is based on physical output, it is applied in situations where usage rather than obsolescence is the main factor leading to the demise of the asset. Under this method, first the depreciation charge per unit of output is computed; then this figure is multiplied by the number of units of goods or services produced during the accounting period to find the period's depreciation expense. The formula is:

$$\frac{\text{Depreciation}}{\text{per unit}} = \frac{\text{Asset cost} - \text{Estimated salvage value}}{\substack{\text{Estimated total units of production} \\ \text{(or service) during useful life of asset}}}$$

$$\frac{\text{Depreciation}}{\text{per period}} = \frac{\text{Depreciation}}{\text{per unit}} \times \frac{\text{Number of units of goods}}{\text{or services produced}}$$

The depreciation charge for the $54,000 machine is determined as follows:

$$\frac{\$54,000 - \$4,000}{50,000 \text{ units}} = \$1 \text{ per unit}$$

If the machine produced 1,000 units in 1994 and 2,500 units in 1995, depreciation expense for those years would be $1,000 and $2,500, respectively.

Accelerated Depreciation Methods Accelerated depreciation methods record higher amounts of depreciation during the early years of an asset's life and lower amounts in the asset's later years. A business might choose an accelerated depreciation method for the following reasons:

1. The value of the benefits received from the asset decline with age (for example, office buildings).
2. The asset is a high-technology asset subject to rapid obsolescence (for example, computers).
3. Repairs increase substantially in the asset's later years, and under this method the depreciation and repairs together remain fairly constant over the asset's life (for example, automobiles).

The two most common accelerated methods of depreciation are the *sum-of-the-years'-digits (SOYD)* method and the *double-declining-balance (DDB)* method.

Sum-of-the-Years'-Digits Method The sum-of-the-years'-digits (SOYD) method is so called because the consecutive digits for each year of an asset's estimated life are added together and used as the denominator of a fraction. The numerator is the number of years of useful life remaining at the **beginning** of the accounting period. To compute that period's depreciation expense, this fraction is then multiplied by the acquisition cost of the asset less the estimated salvage value. The formula is:

$$\frac{\text{Depreciation}}{\text{per period}} = \frac{\substack{\text{Number of years of useful} \\ \text{life remaining at beginning} \\ \text{of accounting period}}}{\text{SOYD}} \times \left(\substack{\text{Asset} \\ \text{cost}} - \substack{\text{Estimated} \\ \text{salvage value}} \right)$$

The years are totaled to find SOYD. For an asset with a 10-year useful life, SOYD = $10 + 9 + 8 + 7 + 6 + 5 + 4 + 3 + 2 + 1 = 55$. Alternatively, rather than adding the digits for all years together, the following formula can be used to find the SOYD for any given number of periods:

$$\text{SOYD} = \frac{n(n+1)}{2}$$

ILLUSTRATION 10.5

Sum-of-the-Years'-Digits Depreciation Schedule

End of Year	Depreciation Expense Dr.; Accumulated Depreciation Cr.	Total Accumulated Depreciation	Book Value
			$54,000
1. $50,000* × 10/55	$ 9,091	$ 9,091	44,909
2. $50,000 × 9/55	8,182	17,273	36,727
3. $50,000 × 8/55	7,273	24,546	29,454
4. $50,000 × 7/55	6,364	30,910	23,090
5. $50,000 × 6/55	5,455	36,365	17,635
6. $50,000 × 5/55	4,545	40,910	13,090
7. $50,000 × 4/55	3,636	44,546	9,454
8. $50,000 × 3/55	2,727	47,273	6,727
9. $50,000 × 2/55	1,818	49,091	4,909
10. $50,000 × 1/55	909	50,000	4,000
	$50,000		

* $54,000 cost − $4,000 salvage value.

where n is the number of periods in the asset's useful life. Thus, SOYD for an asset with a 10-year useful life is:

$$SOYD = \frac{10(10 + 1)}{2} = 55$$

The SOYD method is applied to the data given earlier for the $54,000 machine as follows. First, determine that at the beginning of year 1 (1994), the machine has 10 years of useful life remaining. Then, using the formula above, compute the first year's depreciation as 10/55 times $50,000 (the $54,000 cost less the $4,000 salvage value). The depreciation for the first year is $9,091, as shown in Illustration 10.5. Note that the fraction gets smaller every year, resulting in a declining depreciation charge for each successive year.

Double-Declining-Balance Method   The double-declining-balance (DDB) method of computing periodic depreciation charges is applied by first calculating the straight-line depreciation rate. The straight-line rate is calculated by dividing 100% by the number of years of useful life of the asset. Then multiply this rate by 2. The resulting double-declining rate is applied to the declining book value of the asset. **Salvage value is ignored in making the calculations.** However, at the point where book value is equal to the salvage value, no more depreciation is taken. The formula for DDB depreciation is:

$$\text{Depreciation per period} = \left(2 \times \text{Straight-line rate}\right) \times \left(\text{Asset cost} - \text{Accumulated depreciation}\right)$$

The calculations for the $54,000 machine using the DDB method are shown in Illustration 10.6. The straight-line rate is 10% (100%/10 years), which, when doubled, yields a DDB rate of 20%. (Expressed as a fraction, the straight-line rate is 1/10, and the DDB rate is 2/10.) Since at the beginning of year 1 no accumulated depreciation has been recorded, the calculation is based on cost. In each of the following years, the calculation is based on book value at the beginning of the year.

In the 10th year, depreciation could be increased to $3,247 if the asset is to be retired and its salvage value is still $4,000. This higher depreciation amount for the

ILLUSTRATION 10.6

Double-Declining-Balance (DDB) Depreciation Schedule

End of Year	Depreciation Expense Dr.; Accumulated Depreciation Cr.	Total Accumulated Depreciation	Book Value
			$54,000
1. (20% of $54,000)	$10,800	$10,800	43,200
2. (20% of $43,200)	8,640	19,440	34,560
3. (20% of $34,560)	6,912	26,352	27,648
4. (20% of $27,648)	5,530	31,882	22,118
5. (20% of $22,118)	4,424	36,306	17,694
6. (20% of $17,694)	3,539	39,845	14,155
7. (20% of $14,155)	2,831	42,676	11,324
8. (20% of $11,324)	2,265	44,941	9,059
9. (20% of $9,059)	1,812	46,753	7,247
10. (20% of $7,247)	1,449*	48,202	5,798

* This amount could be $3,247 so as to reduce the book value to the estimated salvage value of $4,000. Accumulated depreciation would be $50,000.

ILLUSTRATION 10.7

Summary of Depreciation Methods

Method	Base	Calculation
Straight-line	Asset cost − Estimated salvage value	Base ÷ Number of accounting periods in estimated useful life
Units-of-production	Asset cost − Estimated salvage value	(Base ÷ Estimated total units of production) × Units produced this period
Sum-of-the-years'-digits	Asset cost − Estimated salvage value	Base × (Number of years of useful life remaining at beginning of accounting period) / SOYD
Double-declining-balance	Asset cost − Accumulated depreciation	Base × (2 × Straight-line rate)

last year ($3,247) would reduce the book value of $7,247 down to the salvage value of $4,000. If an asset is continued in service, depreciation should only be recorded until the asset's book value equals its estimated salvage value.

Illustration 10.7 summarizes the four depreciation methods.

Illustration 10.8 compares three depreciation methods discussed above—straight-line, sum-of-the-years'-digits, and double-declining-balance—using the same example of a machine purchased on January 1, 1994, for $54,000. The machine has an estimated useful life of 10 years and an estimated salvage value of $4,000.

Partial-Year Depreciation

So far we have assumed that the assets were put into service at the beginning of an accounting period and have ignored the fact that assets are often put into service **during** an accounting period. When assets are acquired sometime during an accounting period, the first recording of depreciation is usually for a partial year. The depreciation for the partial year is normally calculated to the nearest full month the asset was in service. For example, an asset purchased on or before the

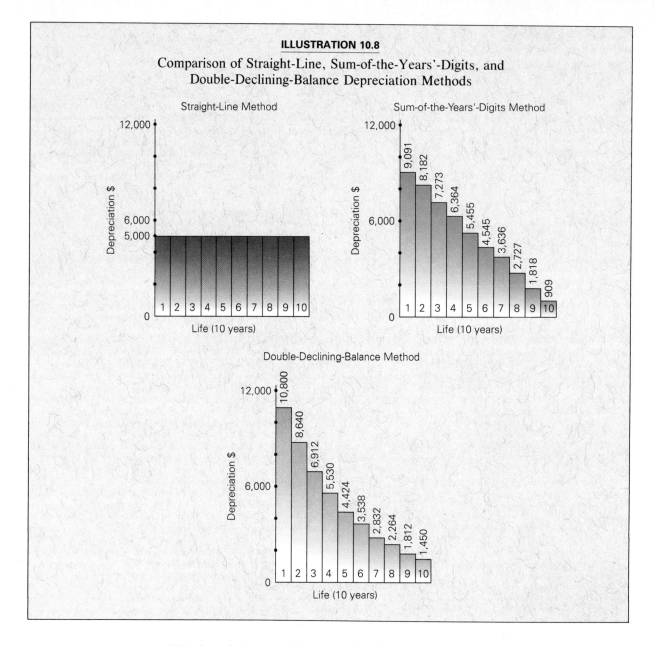

ILLUSTRATION 10.8

Comparison of Straight-Line, Sum-of-the-Years'-Digits, and Double-Declining-Balance Depreciation Methods

15th day of the month is treated as if it were purchased on the 1st day of the month; an asset purchased after the 15th of the month is treated as if it were acquired on the 1st day of the following month.

In this section, you will learn how to calculate partial-year depreciation for each of the four depreciation methods—straight-line, units-of-production, sum-of-the-years'-digits, and double-declining-balance. The example used is a machine purchased for $7,600 on September 1, 1994, with an estimated salvage value of $400 and an estimated useful life of five years.

Straight-Line Method   Partial-year depreciation calculations for the straight-line depreciation method are relatively easy. First, find the 12-month charge by the normal computation explained earlier. Then, multiply this annual amount by the fraction of the year for which the asset was in use. For example, for the $7,600 machine purchased September 1, 1994 (estimated salvage value, $400; and estimated useful life, five years), the annual straight-line depreciation is [($7,600 −

$400)/5 years] = $1,440. The machine will be used four months prior to the end of the accounting year, December 31, or one third of a year. The 1994 depreciation is ($1,440/3) = $480.

Units-of-Production Method   The units-of-production method requires no unusual computations to record depreciation for a partial year. The partial-year depreciation is still computed by multiplying the depreciation charge per unit by the number of units produced. The charge for a partial year will probably be less than for a full year because fewer units of goods or services are produced.

Sum-of-the-Years'-Digits Method   Under the SOYD method, the computation of partial-year depreciation is more complex. Problems occur because the 12 months for which depreciation is computed using the SOYD fraction do not correspond with the 12 months for which the financial statements are being prepared. For example, the depreciation recorded in 1994 on the $7,600 asset is for the last four months of 1994, which is the first one third of the first year of the asset's life. The depreciation for the four months of 1994 is computed as ($7,600 − $400) × $5/15$ × $1/3$; thus, depreciation is $800. In 1995, the depreciation recorded is $2,240, computed as follows:

For the first two thirds of the year:	($7,200 × $5/15$ × $2/3$) = $1,600
For the last one third of the year:	($7,200 × $4/15$ × $1/3$) = 640
Total depreciation expense for 1995	$2,240

With the SOYD method, annual depreciation charges will have to be computed in this same way throughout the asset's life as follows:

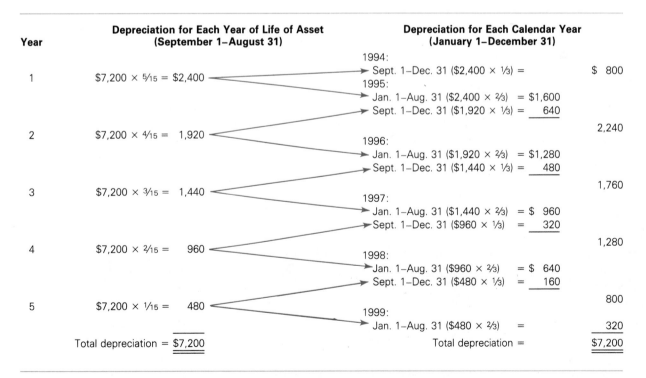

Year	Depreciation for Each Year of Life of Asset (September 1–August 31)	Depreciation for Each Calendar Year (January 1–December 31)	
		1994:	
		Sept. 1–Dec. 31 ($2,400 × $1/3$) =	$ 800
1	$7,200 × $5/15$ = $2,400	**1995:**	
		Jan. 1–Aug. 31 ($2,400 × $2/3$) = $1,600	
		Sept. 1–Dec. 31 ($1,920 × $1/3$) = 640	
2	$7,200 × $4/15$ = 1,920		2,240
		1996:	
		Jan. 1–Aug. 31 ($1,920 × $2/3$) = $1,280	
		Sept. 1–Dec. 31 ($1,440 × $1/3$) = 480	
3	$7,200 × $3/15$ = 1,440		1,760
		1997:	
		Jan. 1–Aug. 31 ($1,440 × $2/3$) = $ 960	
		Sept. 1–Dec. 31 ($960 × $1/3$) = 320	
4	$7,200 × $2/15$ = 960		1,280
		1998:	
		Jan. 1–Aug. 31 ($960 × $2/3$) = $ 640	
		Sept. 1–Dec. 31 ($480 × $1/3$) = 160	
5	$7,200 × $1/15$ = 480		800
		1999:	
		Jan. 1–Aug. 31 ($480 × $2/3$) =	320
	Total depreciation = $7,200	Total depreciation =	$7,200

Double-Declining-Balance Method   Under the double-declining-balance method, it is relatively easy to determine depreciation for a partial year and then for subsequent full years. For the partial year, simply multiply the fixed rate times the cost of the asset times the fraction of the partial year. For example, DDB depreciation on the $7,600 asset for 1994 is ($7,600 × 0.4 × ⅓) = $1,013. For subsequent years, the depreciation is computed using the regular procedure of multiplying the book value at the beginning of the period by the fixed rate. In this case, the 1995 depreciation would be [($7,600 − $1,013) × 0.4] = $2,635.

Changes in Estimates

After an asset is depreciated down to its estimated salvage value, no more depreciation is recorded on the asset even if it continues to be used. However, when the estimated useful life of an asset or its salvage value is found to be incorrect **before** the asset is depreciated down to its estimated salvage value, revised depreciation charges are computed. These revised charges do not correct **past** depreciation taken; **they merely compensate for past incorrect charges through changed expense amounts in current and future periods.** The new depreciation charge per period is computed by dividing the book value less the newly estimated salvage value by the estimated periods of useful life remaining.

For example, assume that a machine cost $30,000, has an estimated salvage value of $3,000, and originally had an estimated useful life of eight years. At the end of the fourth year of the machine's life, the balance in its accumulated depreciation account (assuming use of the straight-line method) was ($30,000 − $3,000) × ⁴⁄₈ = $13,500. Now assume that at the beginning of the fifth year it is estimated that the asset will last six more years. The newly estimated salvage value is $2,700. The revised depreciation per period is determined as follows:

Original cost	$30,000
Less: Accumulated depreciation at the end of the year	13,500
Book value at the beginning of 5th year	$16,500
Revised salvage value	2,700
Remaining depreciable base	$13,800
Revised depreciation per period: $13,800/6	$ 2,300

Had the units-of-production method been in use, a revision of the life estimate would be in the form of units. Thus, to determine depreciation expense, a new per unit depreciation charge must be computed by dividing book value less salvage value by the estimated remaining units of production. This per unit charge is then multiplied by the periodic production to determine depreciation expense.

Continuing the above machine example and using the double-declining-balance method, the book value at the beginning of year 5 would be $9,492.19 (cost of $30,000 less accumulated depreciation of $20,507.81). Depreciation expense for year 5 would be calculated as twice the new straight-line rate times book value. The straight-line rate is 100%/6 = 16.67%. So twice the straight-line rate is 33.33%, or ⅓. Thus, ⅓ × $9,492.19 = $3,164.06.

Under the sum-of-the-years'-digits method, a new fraction must be calculated. The sum-of-the-years'-digits is now 6 + 5 + 4 + 3 + 2 + 1 = 21. The fraction for year 5 is ⁶⁄₂₁. Depreciation under the sum-of-the-years'-digits method would be computed as follows:

Book value at the beginning of 5th year.	$10,500.00
Revised salvage value	2,700.00
Remaining depreciable base.	$ 7,800.00
Depreciation expense for year 5: $7,800 × ⁶⁄₂₁	$ 2,228.57

Depreciation for Tax Purposes

Tax depreciation is substantially different than depreciation used for accounting purposes. In accounting, depreciation methods are designed to match the expense of a capital investment against the revenue the investment produces. The depreciable period or useful life used for tax purposes is based on law and has no relationship to the useful life of the asset; thus, no attempt is made to match revenues and expenses.

Before 1981, several depreciation methods were available for tax purposes, including methods described in this chapter. The Economic Recovery Tax Act of 1981 introduced a new depreciation system known as the **Accelerated Cost Recovery System (ACRS).** However, the Tax Reform Act of 1986 substantially modified the ACRS rules. For purposes of discussion, we shall refer to these rules as **modified ACRS.**

The assets are grouped into one of eight different classes (see the table below). Each class has an assigned life over which costs of the assets (not reduced by salvage) are depreciated.

Assets in the 3-, 5-, 7-, and 10-year classes may be depreciated by using the 200% declining-balance method, earlier referred to as the double-declining-balance method. Assets in the 15- and 20-year classes may be depreciated by using the 150% declining-balance method. Assets in the 27.5- and 31.5-year classes must be depreciated by using straight-line depreciation. The declining-balance methods result in faster write-offs in the first few years of an investment's life. Cash saved from reduced taxes in the early years of life of the assets can be invested in new productive assets or can be applied to the replacement of the old assets when they become obsolete or worn out.

Class of Investment	Kinds of Assets
3 years	Investment in some short-lived assets.
5 years	Automobiles, light-duty trucks, and machinery and equipment used in research and development.
7 years	All other machinery and equipment, such as dies, drills, or presses, furniture, and fixtures.
10 years	Some longer-lived equipment.
15 years	Sewage treatment plants and telephone distribution plants.
20 years	Sewer pipes and very long-lived equipment.
27.5 years	Residential rental property.
31.5 years	Nonresidential real estate.

Tax depreciation methods are not generally acceptable for financial reporting purposes because they have little relation to the actual useful life of the asset and do not necessarily match revenues and expenses. Thus, tax depreciation methods only apply to the preparation of income tax returns.

Depreciation and Financial Reporting

APB Opinion No. 12 requires that the methods of depreciation used and the amount of depreciation expense for the period be separately disclosed in the body of the income statement or in the notes to the financial statements. Major classes of plant assets and their related accumulated depreciation amounts are to be reported as shown in Illustration 10.9 (using assumed data).

The presentation of cost less accumulated depreciation in the balance sheet gives the statement user a better understanding of the percentages of a company's plant assets that have been used up than if the balance sheet presented only the book value (remaining undepreciated cost) of the assets. For example, reporting

---

ILLUSTRATION 10.9

Partial Balance Sheet

REED COMPANY
Partial Balance Sheet
June 30, 1994

Property, plant, and equipment:

Land		$30,000
Buildings.	$75,000	
Less: Accumulated depreciation	45,000	30,000
Equipment.	$ 9,000	
Less: Accumulated depreciation	1,500	7,500
Total property, plant, and equipment		$67,500

---

buildings of $75,000 less $45,000 of accumulated depreciation, resulting in a net amount of $30,000, is quite different from merely reporting $30,000 of buildings. In the first case, the statement user can see that the assets are about 60% used up. In the latter case, the statement user has no way of knowing whether the assets are new or old.

A Misconception   Some financial statement users mistakenly believe that the amount of accumulated depreciation represents funds available for replacing old plant assets with new assets. **However, the accumulated depreciation account balance does not represent cash; accumulated depreciation shows simply how much of an asset's cost has been charged to expense.** The plant asset and its contra account, accumulated depreciation, are used so that data on the total original acquisition cost and accumulated depreciation are readily available to meet reporting requirements.

Costs or Market Values in the Balance Sheet   Plant assets are reported in the balance sheet at **original** cost less accumulated depreciation. One of the justifications for reporting the remaining undepreciated costs of the asset rather than market values is the going-concern concept. As you recall from Chapter 1, the going-concern concept assumes that the company will remain in business indefinitely, which implies the company will use its plant assets rather than sell them. Market values generally are not considered relevant for use in the primary financial statements, although they may be reported in supplemental statements (as described in Appendix C at the end of the text).

Furthermore, an asset cannot be written up to a market value above its cost merely because its value has increased. Neither can an asset be written down below its cost if future revenues from the asset are expected to exceed its cost.

RECORD SUBSEQUENT EXPENDITURES (CAPITAL AND REVENUE) ON ASSETS

Objective 4

Distinguish between capital and revenue expenditures for plant assets

Companies often make expenditures on plant assets after these assets have been in use for some time. These expenditures are debited to (1) an asset account, (2) an accumulated depreciation account, or (3) an expense account.

Expenditures debited to an asset account or to an accumulated depreciation account are called capital expenditures. Capital expenditures increase the book value of plant assets. Revenue expenditures, on the other hand, do not qualify as

A BROADER PERSPECTIVE

FLEETWOOD ENTERPRISES, INC.

Partial Balance Sheet **($000)**				**Amounts in thousands**	**1988**	**1987**
	1988	**1987**		Land.	$ 7,360	$ 6,077
				Buildings and improvements . . .	94,875	83,341
Total current assets.	$360,077	$353,928		Machinery and equipment	46,048	41,658
Investments in and Advances to				Idle facilities, net of accumulated		
Unconsolidated Subsidiaries . . .	50,897	38,298		depreciation	12,197	10,064
Property, Plant and Equipment. . .	103,001	89,979			$160,480	$141,140
	$513,975	$482,205		Less accumulated depreciation . .	(57,479)	(51,161)
					$103,001	$ 89,979

NOTES TO CONSOLIDATED FINANCIAL
STATEMENTS

1. (In part): Summary of Significant Accounting
Policies

Depreciation: Depreciation is provided using straight-line or accelerated methods based on the following estimated useful lives:

Buildings and improvements . . . . 10–30 years
Machinery and equipment . . . . . 3–10 years

4. Property, Plant, and Equipment

Property, plant, and equipment is stated at cost and consists of the following [shown in the right column]:

Idle facilities include closed plants and certain other properties which are not in current use by the Company and are not being depreciated. There were 13 idle plant facilities at the end of 1988 and 12 in 1987. The Company has no immediate plans to reopen any of these facilities and most are being offered for sale.

The carrying value of idle facilities was $12,197,000 at April 24, 1988, and $10,064,000 at April 26, 1987, net of accumulated depreciation of $4,274,000 and $3,147,000, respectively. In the opinion of management, the carrying values of idle facilities are not in excess of net realizable value.

Source: Based on American Institute of Certified Public Accountants, *Accounting Trends & Techniques* (New York: AICPA, 1989), p. 135.

capital expenditures because they help to generate the current period's revenues rather than future periods' revenues. As a result, revenue expenditures are expensed immediately and are reported in the income statement as expenses.

Expenditures Capitalized in Asset Accounts

Betterments or improvements to existing plant assets are capital expenditures because they increase the **quality** of services obtained from the asset. Because betterments or improvements add to the service-rendering ability of assets, they are charged to the asset accounts. For example, installing an air conditioner in an automobile that did not previously have one is a betterment. Such an expenditure is debited to the asset account, Automobiles.

Expenditures Capitalized as Charges to Accumulated Depreciation

Occasionally, expenditures made on plant assets extend the **quantity** of services **beyond the original estimate** but do not improve the quality of the services. Since these expenditures will benefit an increased number of future periods, they are capitalized rather than expensed. However, since there is no visible, tangible addition to, or improvement in, the quality of services, the expenditures are charged to the accumulated depreciation account. Such expenditures are viewed as canceling a part of the existing accumulated depreciation and are often called **extraordinary repairs.**

To illustrate, assume that after operating a press for four years, a company spent $5,000 to recondition the press. The effect of the reconditioning is to increase the machine's life to 14 years instead of the original estimate of 10 years. The journal entry to record the extraordinary repair is:

Accumulated Depreciation—Machinery.	5,000	
Cash (or Accounts Payable)		5,000
To record the cost of reconditioning a press.		

When the press was acquired, it cost $40,000. The press had an estimated useful life of 10 years and no salvage value. At the end of the fourth year, the balance in its accumulated depreciation account under the straight-line method is $[(\$40,000 \div 10) \times 4] = \$16,000$. After the $5,000 spent to recondition the press is debited to the accumulated depreciation account, the balances in the asset account and its related accumulated depreciation account are as follows:

	Before Extraordinary Repair	After Extraordinary Repair
Press	$40,000	$40,000
Accumulated depreciation	16,000	11,000
Book value (end of four years)	$24,000	$29,000

The effect of the expenditure, then, is to increase the carrying amount (book value) of the asset by reducing its contra account, accumulated depreciation. Under the straight-line method, the new book value of the press, $29,000, is divided equally among the 10 remaining years in amounts of $2,900 per year.

As a practical matter, expenditures for major repairs not extending the asset's life are also sometimes charged to accumulated depreciation to avoid distortion of net income that might result if these expenditures were expensed in the year incurred. Then, a revised depreciation expense must be calculated, and the cost of major repairs is spread over a number of years. This treatment is not theoretically correct.

To illustrate, assume the same facts as in the above example except that the $5,000 expenditure did not extend the life of the asset. However, because of the size of this expenditure, it is still charged to accumulated depreciation. Now the $29,000 remaining book value would be spread over the remaining six years of the life of the press. Under the straight-line method, annual depreciation would then be $(\$29,000 \div 6) = \$4,833$.

Expenditures Charged to Expense

Recurring and/or minor expenditures that neither add to the asset's quality of service-rendering ability nor extend its quantity of services beyond the asset's original estimated useful life are treated as expenses. Thus, regular maintenance (lubricating a machine) and ordinary repairs (replacing a broken fan belt on an automobile) are expensed immediately as revenue expenditures. For example, if the company mentioned previously spends $190 to repair the press after using it for some time, this amount should be debited to Maintenance Expense or Repairs Expense.

In many companies, any expenditure below an arbitrary minimum, such as $100, is charged to expense regardless of its impact on the asset's useful life. This practice is followed to avoid calculating and preparing adjusting entries for depreciation for such a nominal cost.

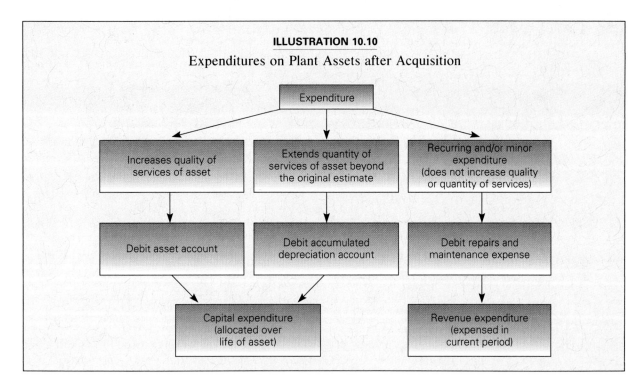

ILLUSTRATION 10.10

Expenditures on Plant Assets after Acquisition

Low-Cost Items   Most businesses purchase low-cost items that provide years of service at a relatively low unit cost, such as paperweights, hammers, wrenches, and drills. Because of the small dollar amounts involved, it is impractical to use the ordinary depreciation methods for such assets, and it is often costly to maintain records of individual items. Also, the effect of the costs of such items on the financial statements is not significant. Accordingly, it is more efficient to record the items as expenses when they are purchased. This practice of accounting for such low unit cost items as expenses is an example of the modifying convention of materiality that we will discuss in Chapter 12.

Illustration 10.10 shows a graphical summary of these expenditures on plant assets after acquisition.

Errors in Classification

In practice, it is often difficult to distinguish between an expenditure that should be debited to the asset account and an expenditure that should be debited to the accumulated depreciation account. For example, some expenditures seem to affect both the quality and quantity of services. Even if the wrong account is debited for the expenditure, the book value of the plant asset at that point will be the same amount it would have been if the correct account had been debited. A difference will arise in the carrying value of the asset for financial statement purposes for the remaining useful life of the asset. Both the asset and accumulated depreciation accounts will be misstated.

As an example of the effect of misstated asset and accumulated depreciation accounts, assume Watson Company had an asset that had originally cost $15,000 and had been depreciated to a book value of $6,000 at the beginning of 1994. At that time, the equipment was estimated to have a remaining useful life of two years. The company spent $4,000 in early January 1994 to install a new motor in the equipment. This motor was expected to extend the useful life of the asset four years beyond the original estimate. Since the expenditure served to extend the life, it should be capitalized by a debit to the accumulated depreciation account.

ILLUSTRATION 10.11

Expenditure Extending Plant Asset Life

	December 31, 1993	After Expenditure Entry Correct	After Expenditure Entry Incorrect
Cost	$15,000	$15,000	$19,000†
Accumulated depreciation	9,000	5,000*	9,000
Book value	$ 6,000	$10,000	$10,000
Remaining life.	2 years	6 years	6 years
Depreciation expense per year	$ 3,000	$1,667	$ 1,667

* ($9,000 − $4,000).
† ($15,000 + $4,000).

The calculations for depreciation expense if the entry were made correctly and if the expenditure had been improperly charged (debited) to the asset account are shown in Illustration 10.11.

If an expenditure that should be expensed is capitalized, the effects are more significant. Assume now that $6,000 in repairs expense is incurred for a plant asset that originally cost $40,000 and had a useful life of four years and no estimated salvage value. This asset had been depreciated using the straight-line method for one year and had a book value of $30,000 ($40,000 cost − $10,000 first-year depreciation) at the beginning of 1994. The $6,000 that should have been charged to repairs expense in 1994 was capitalized instead. The charge for depreciation should have remained at $10,000 for each of the next three years. With the incorrect entry, however, depreciation increases.

Regardless of whether the repair was debited to the asset account or the accumulated depreciation account, the depreciation expense amount will be changed to $12,000 for each of the next three years [($30,000 book value + $6,000 repairs expense) ÷ 3 more years of useful life]. As a result, net income for the year 1994 will be overstated $4,000 due to the effects of these two errors: (1) repairs expense is understated by $6,000, causing income to be overstated by $6,000; and (2) depreciation expense is overstated by $2,000, causing income to be understated by $2,000. In 1995, depreciation will again be overstated by $2,000, causing 1995 income to be understated by $2,000.

You should realize that the $6,000 recording error affects more than just the expense accounts and net income. Plant asset and retained earnings accounts on the balance sheet will also reflect the impact of this error. Illustration 10.12 shows the effect of incorrectly capitalizing the $6,000 rather than correctly expensing it.

SUBSIDIARY RECORDS USED TO CONTROL PLANT ASSETS

Objective 5

Describe the subsidiary records used to control plant assets

Most companies maintain formal records (ranging from handwritten documents to computer tapes) to ensure control over their plant assets. These records include an asset account and a related accumulated depreciation account in the general ledger for **each** major class of depreciable plant assets, such as buildings, factory machinery, office equipment, delivery equipment, and store equipment.

Since the general ledger account frequently cannot contain detailed information about each item in a major class of depreciable plant assets, many companies use plant asset subsidiary ledgers. For example, the general ledger account for office equipment may contain entries for such items as microcomputers, FAX machines, copying machines, calculators, dictating equipment, and filing cabinets, but it

ILLUSTRATION 10.12

Effect of Revenue Expenditure Treated as Capital Expenditure

	For 1994 under Correctly Expensing	For 1994 under Incorrectly Capitalizing
1994 depreciation expense.	$10,000	$12,000
1994 repair expense	6,000	–0–
1994 net income overstated by $4,000, which affects retained earnings.	$16,000	$12,000
Asset cost.	$40,000	$46,000
Accumulated depreciation	20,000	22,000
Book value.	$20,000	$24,000

	For 1995 under Correctly Expensing	For 1995 under Incorrectly Capitalizing
1995 depreciation expense.	$10,000	$12,000
1995 repair expense	–0–	–0–
1995 net income understated by $2,000, which affects retained earnings.	$10,000	$12,000
Asset cost.	$40,000	$46,000
Accumulated depreciation	30,000	34,000
Book value.	$10,000	$12,000

cannot contain detailed information about these items. Plant asset subsidiary ledgers and detailed records provide more information and make it possible for the company to maintain better control over plant and equipment.

When subsidiary ledgers are kept for each major class of plant and equipment, there may be a subsidiary ledger for factory machinery, office equipment, and other classes of depreciable plant assets. Then there may be an additional subsidiary ledger for each type of asset within each category. For example, the subsidiary office equipment ledger may contain accounts for microcomputers, typewriters, copying machines, calculators, and so on. (The subsidiary ledger concept was discussed and illustrated in Chapter 7.) Also, a detailed record will normally exist for each item represented in a subsidiary ledger account. For example, if there is a subsidiary ledger account for microcomputers, there may be a separate detailed record for each microcomputer represented in the subsidiary microcomputer ledger account. Each detailed record should include information such as the following: a description of the asset, identification or serial number, location of the asset, date of acquisition, cost, estimated salvage value, estimated useful life, annual depreciation, accumulated depreciation, insurance coverage, repairs, and gain or loss on final disposal of the asset. Illustration 10.13 shows how the detailed record for one particular microcomputer might appear as of December 31, 1992.

To enhance control over plant and equipment, the identification or serial number for each asset should be stenciled on or otherwise attached to the asset. Periodically, a physical inventory should be taken to determine whether all items shown in the accounting records actually exist, whether they are located where they should be, and whether they are still being used. A company that does not use detailed records and identification numbers or take physical inventories may find it difficult to determine whether assets have been discarded or stolen.

ETHICS	The Speare Steel Company has been using the sum-of-the-years'-digits depreciation method for its fixed assets acquired five years ago. The resulting pattern of depreciation seemed to match well with the pattern of revenues that would result from use of the assets. The estimated useful life of the assets is 25 years. During the current year, the industry has been severely affected by foreign competition and was operating at only 60% of capacity. Prices were falling, and the company would have to start reporting losses unless some way could be found to reduce expenses. Management discovered that by switching to the straight-line method, expenses could be reduced enough to report a small profit this year and probably over the next five years. They considered this a relatively painless way of solving the problem.
A CLOSER LOOK	
	Reporting income is important to management since their executive bonuses are tied to net income. As far as management could determine, the straight-line method is acceptable. In fact, they discovered that more companies use straight-line for book purposes than any other method.
Required	Do you see anything wrong with the company switching to the straight-line method?

ILLUSTRATION 10.13

Detailed Record of a Specific Plant Asset

Item IBM PS/2, 50Z

Id. No. Z-43806

Location Rm. 403, Adm. bldg.

Date acquired Jan. 1, 1991

Cost $3,000

Estimated salvage value $200

Estimated useful life 4 yrs.

Depreciation per year $700

Accumulated depreciation:
  12/31/91 $ 700
  12/31/92 1,400
  12/31/93 _____
  12/31/94 _____

Insurance coverage:
  United Ins. Co.
  Pol. No. 0052-61481-24
  Amt. $3,000

Repairs:
  6/13/92 $140
  _____   _____
  _____   _____

Disposal date _____

Gain or loss _____

The general ledger control account balance for each major class of plant and equipment should equal the total of the amounts shown in the subsidiary ledger accounts for that class of plant assets. Also, the totals shown in the detailed records for a specific subsidiary ledger account (such as microcomputers) should equal the balance of that account. Each time a plant asset is acquired, exchanged, or disposed of, an entry should be posted to both a general ledger control account and the appropriate subsidiary ledger account. The detailed record for the item(s) affected also should be updated.

In this chapter, you learned how to account for the acquisition of plant assets and depreciation. The next chapter discusses how to record the disposal of plant assets and how to account for natural resources and intangible assets.

UNDERSTANDING THE LEARNING OBJECTIVES

1. **List the characteristics of plant assets and identify the costs of acquiring plant assets.**
   - ☐ To be classified as a plant asset, an asset must (1) be tangible, (2) have a useful service life of more than one year, and (3) be used in business operations rather than held for resale.
   - ☐ In accounting for plant assets, accountants must:
     1. Record the acquisition cost of the asset.
     2. Record the allocation of the asset's original cost to periods of its useful life through depreciation.
     3. Record subsequent expenditures on the asset.
     4. Account for the disposal of the asset.

2. **List the four major factors affecting depreciation expense.**
   - ☐ Accountants consider four major factors in computing depreciation: (1) cost of the asset, (2) estimated salvage value of the asset, (3) estimated useful life of the asset, and (4) depreciation method to use in depreciating the asset.

3. **Describe the various methods of calculating depreciation expense.**
   - ☐ **Straight-line method:**
     Assigns an equal amount of depreciation to each period. The formula for calculating straight-line depreciation is:

   $$\frac{\text{Depreciation}}{\text{per period}} = \frac{\text{Asset cost} - \text{Estimated salvage value}}{\begin{array}{c}\text{Number of accounting periods}\\ \text{in estimated useful life}\end{array}}$$

   - ☐ **Units-of-production method:**
     Assigns an equal amount of depreciation to each unit of product manufactured by an asset. The units-of-production depreciation formulas are:

   $$\frac{\text{Depreciation}}{\text{per unit}} = \frac{\text{Asset cost} - \text{Estimated salvage value}}{\begin{array}{c}\text{Estimated total units of production (or service)}\\ \text{during useful life of asset}\end{array}}$$

   $$\frac{\text{Depreciation}}{\text{per period}} = \frac{\text{Depreciation}}{\text{per unit}} \times \frac{\text{Number of units of goods}}{\text{or services produced}}$$

   - ☐ **Sum-of-the-years'-digits (SOYD) method:**
     SOYD is an accelerated depreciation method. The SOYD depreciation formulas are:

   $$\frac{\text{Depreciation}}{\text{per period}} = \frac{\begin{array}{c}\text{Number of years}\\ \text{of useful life}\\ \text{remaining at beginning}\\ \text{of accounting period}\end{array}}{\text{SOYD}} \times \left(\begin{array}{c}\text{Asset} \\ \text{cost}\end{array} - \begin{array}{c}\text{Estimated} \\ \text{salvage value}\end{array}\right)$$

   $$\text{Sum-of-the-years'-digits (SOYD)} = \frac{n(n + 1)}{2}$$

   - ☐ **Double-declining-balance method:**
     DDB is an accelerated depreciation method. Salvage value is ignored in making annual calculations. The formula for DDB depreciation is:

   $$\frac{\text{Depreciation}}{\text{per period}} = (2 \times \text{Straight-line rate}) \times \left(\begin{array}{c}\text{Asset} \\ \text{cost}\end{array} - \begin{array}{c}\text{Accumulated} \\ \text{depreciation}\end{array}\right)$$

4. Distinguish between capital and revenue expenditures for plant assets.
   □ Capital expenditures are debited to an asset account or an accumulated depreciation account and increase the book value of plant assets. Expenditures that increase the quality of services or extend the quantity of services beyond the original estimate are considered to be capital expenditures.
   □ Revenue expenditures are expensed immediately and reported in the income statement as expenses. Recurring and/or minor expenditures that neither add to the asset's quality of service-rendering abilities nor extend its quantity of services beyond the asset's original estimated useful life are treated as expenses.

5. Describe the subsidiary records used to control plant assets.
   □ Plant asset subsidiary ledgers contain detailed information about each item in a major class of depreciable plant assets that cannot be maintained in the general ledger account.
   □ Control over plant and equipment is enhanced by plant asset subsidiary ledgers and other detailed records. Information in a detailed record may include a description of the asset, identification or serial number, location of the asset, date of acquisition, cost, estimated salvage value, estimated useful life, annual depreciation, accumulated depreciation, insurance coverage, repairs, and gain or loss on final disposal of the asset. A periodic physical inventory should be taken to determine whether items in accounting records actually exist.

DEMONSTRATION PROBLEM 10–A

Chicago Company purchased a 2-square-mile farm under the following terms: cash paid, $486,000; mortgage note assumed, $240,000, and accrued interest on mortgage note assumed, $6,000. The company paid $55,200 for brokerage and legal services to acquire the property and secure clear title. Chicago planned to subdivide the property into residential lots and to construct homes on these lots. Clearing and leveling costs of $21,600 were paid. Crops on the land were sold for $14,400. A house on the land, to be moved by the buyer of the house, was sold for $5,040. The other buildings were torn down at a cost of $9,600, and salvaged material was sold for $10,080.

Approximately 6 acres of the land were deeded to the township for roads, and another 10 acres were deeded to the local school district as the site for a future school. After the subdivision was completed, this land would have an approximate value of $7,680 per acre. The company secured a total of 1,200 saleable lots from the remaining land.

Required Present a schedule showing in detail the composition of the cost of the 1,200 salable lots.

SOLUTION TO DEMONSTRATION PROBLEM 10–A

CHICAGO COMPANY
Schedule of Cost of 1,200 Residential Lots

Costs incurred:		
Cash paid.	$486,000	
Mortgage note assumed	240,000	
Interest accrued on mortgage note assumed	6,000	
Broker and legal services.	55,200	
Clearing and leveling costs	21,600	
Tearing down costs	9,600	$818,400
Less proceeds from sale of:		
Crops	$ 14,400	
House	5,040	
Salvaged materials.	10,080	29,520
Net cost of land to be subdivided into 1,200 lots		$788,880

DEMONSTRATION PROBLEM 10–B

Christin Company acquired and put into use a machine on January 1, 1994, at a total cost of $45,000. The machine was estimated to have a useful life of 10 years and a scrap value of $5,000. It was also estimated that the machine would produce one million units of product during its life. The machine produced 90,000 units in 1994 and 125,000 units in 1995.

Required Compute the amounts of depreciation to be recorded in 1994 and 1995 under each of the following:

a. Straight-line method.
b. Units-of-production method.
c. Sum-of-the-years'-digits method.
d. Double-declining-balance method.
e. Assume 30,000 units were produced in the first quarter of 1996. Compute depreciation for this quarter under each of the four methods.

SOLUTION TO DEMONSTRATION PROBLEM 10–B

a. Straight-line method:

1994: ($45,000 − $5,000)/10 = $4,000

1995: ($45,000 − $5,000)/10 = $4,000

b. Units-of-production method:

1994: [($45,000 − $5,000)/1,000,000] × 90,000 = $3,600

1995: [($45,000 − $5,000)/1,000,000] × 125,000 = $5,000

c. Sum-of-the-years'-digits method:

1994: ($45,000 − $5,000) × $10/55$ = $7,272.73

1995: ($45,000 − $5,000) × $9/55$ = $6,545.45

    d.   Double-declining-balance method:

       1994: $45,000 \times 20\% = \underline{\underline{\$9,000}}$

       1995: ($45,000 - \$9,000) \times 20\% = \underline{\underline{\$7,200}}$

    e.   Straight-line: ($45,000 - \$5,000)/10 \times \frac{1}{4} = \underline{\underline{\$1,000}}$

       Units-of-production: ($30,000 \times \$0.04) = \underline{\underline{\$1,200}}$

       Sum-of-the-year's-digits: ($45,000 - \$5,000) \times \frac{8}{55} \times \frac{1}{4} = \underline{\underline{\$1,454.55}}$

       Double-declining-balance:
       ($45,000 - \$9,000 - \$7,200) \times 0.2 \times \frac{1}{4} = \underline{\underline{\$1,440}}$

NEW TERMS

Accelerated depreciation methods Record higher amounts of depreciation during the early years of an asset's life and lower amounts in later years. *491*

Acquisition cost Amount of cash and/or cash equivalents given up to acquire a plant asset and place it in operating condition at its proper location. *483*

Appraised value An expert's opinion as to what an item's market price would be if the item were sold. *487*

Betterments (improvements) Capital expenditures that are properly charged to asset accounts because they add to the service-rendering ability of the assets; they increase the quality of services that can be obtained from an asset. *499*

Book value An asset's recorded cost less its accumulated depreciation. *487*

Capital expenditures Expenditures that are debited to an asset account or to an accumulated depreciation account. *498*

Depreciation The amount of plant asset cost allocated to each accounting period benefiting from the plant asset's use *(487)*. The **straight-line-depreciation** method charges an equal amount of plant asset cost to each period *(489)*. The **units-of-production depreciation** method assigns an equal amount of depreciation for each unit of product manufactured or service rendered by an asset *(490)*. The **sum-of-the-years'-digits (SOYD)** *(491)* and the **double-declining-balance (DDB)** *(492)* methods assign decreasing amounts of depreciation to successive periods of time.

Double-declining-balance depreciation (DDB) See Depreciation.

Extraordinary repairs Expenditures that are viewed as canceling a part of the existing accumulated depreciation because they increase the quantity of services expected from an asset. *499*

Fair market value The price that would be received for an item being sold in the normal course of business (not at a forced liquidation sale). *487*

Inadequacy The inability of a plant asset to produce enough products or provide enough services to meet current demands. *488*

Land improvements Attachments to land, such as driveways, landscaping, parking lots, fences, lighting systems, and sprinkler systems, that have limited lives and therefore are depreciable. *484*

Low-cost items Items that provide years of services at a relatively low unit cost, such as hammers, paperweights, and drills. *501*

Modified ACRS A tax method of depreciation that assigns assets into particular groups that have specified lives for depreciation purposes. The 1986 Tax Reform Act modified the Accelerated Cost Recovery System. *497*

Obsolescence Decline in usefulness of an asset brought about by inventions and technological progress. *488*

Physical deterioration Results from use of the asset—wear and tear—and the action of the elements. *487*

Plant and equipment A shorter title for property, plant, and equipment; also called *plant assets*. Included are land and manufactured or constructed assets such as buildings, machinery, vehicles, and furniture. *482*

Revenue expenditures Expenditures (on a plant asset) that are immediately expensed. *498*

Salvage value The amount of money the company expects to recover, less disposal costs, on the date a plant asset is scrapped, sold, or traded in. Also called *scrap or residual value*. *488*

Straight-line-depreciation See Depreciation.

Sum-of-the-year's-digits depreciation (SOYD) See Depreciation.

Units-of-production depreciation See Depreciation.

Useful life Refers to the length of time the company owning the asset intends to use it. *488*

SELF-TEST

True-False

Indicate whether each of the following statements is true or false.

1. The cost of machinery includes its purchase price, transportation charges, installation costs, and cost of removing old machine.

2. Depreciation is the process of valuation of an asset to arrive at its market value.

3. The book value of a plant asset represents its market value.

4. Expenditures made on plant assets that increase the quality of services are debited to the asset account.

5. Plant asset subsidiary ledgers provide detailed information that the general ledger account can not provide.

Multiple-Choice

Select the best answer for each of the following questions.

1. On July 1, 1994, Chapman Company purchased equipment for $100,000 and paid installation and testing costs of $10,000. The equipment has a useful life of 10 years and an estimated salvage value of $10,000. If Chapman uses the straight-line depreciation method, the depreciation expense for the year ended June 30, 1995, is:
   a. $9,000.
   b. $10,000.
   c. $11,000.
   d. $20,000.
   e. $22,000.

2. In Question 1, if the equipment were purchased on January 1, 1995, and Chapman used the double-declining-balance method, the depreciation expense for the year ended June 30, 1995, would be:
   a. $22,000.
   b. $18,000.
   c. $9,000.
   d. $11,000.
   e. $10,000.

3. In Question 1, if Chapman uses the sum-of-the-years'-digits method, the depreciation expense for the year ended June 30, 1995, is:

   a. $18,182.
   b. $20,000.
   c. $16,364.
   d. $1,818.
   e. $2,000.

4. Allen Company purchased a computer on January 3, 1994, for $10,000. The computer had an estimated salvage value of $3,000 and a useful life of five years. At the beginning of 1996, the estimated salvage value changed to $1,000, and the computer is expected to have a remaining useful life of two years. Using the straight-line method, the depreciation expense for 1996 is:
   a. $1,400.
   b. $1,750.
   c. $2,250.
   d. $1,800.
   e. $3,100.

5. The result of recording a capital expenditure as a revenue expenditure is an:
   a. Understatement of current year's expense.
   b. Overstatement of current year's expense.
   c. Overstatement of current year's net income.
   d. Understatement of subsequent year's net income.
   e. None of the above.

Now turn to page 517 to check your answers.

QUESTIONS

1. What is the main distinction between inventory and a plant asset?

2. Which of the following items are properly classifiable as plant assets on the balance sheet?
   a. Advertising to inform the public about new energy-saving programs at a manufacturing plant.
   b. A truck acquired by a manufacturing company to be used to deliver the company's products to wholesalers.
   c. An automobile acquired by an insurance company to be used by one of its salespersons.

   d. Adding machines acquired by an office supply company to be sold to customers.
   e. The cost of constructing and paving a driveway that has a useful life of 10 years.

3. In general terms, what does the cost of a plant asset include?

4. In what way does the purchase of a plant asset resemble the prepayment of an expense?

5. Britt Company purchased an old farm with a vacant building as a factory site for $520,000. Britt decided to use the building in its operations. How

should Britt allocate the purchase price between the land and the building? How should this purchase be handled if the building is to be torn down in order to build a new one?

6. Describe how a company may determine the cost of a self-constructed asset.

7. In any exchange of noncash assets, the accountant's task is to find the most appropriate valuation for the asset received. What is the general rule for determining the most appropriate valuation in such a situation?

8. Why should periodic depreciation be recorded on all plant assets except land?

9. Define the terms *inadequacy* and *obsolescence* as used in accounting for plant and equipment.

10. What four factors must be known to compute depreciation on a plant asset? How *objective* is the calculation of depreciation?

11. A friend, Sara Jones, tells you her car depreciated $2,500 last year. Explain whether her concept of depreciation is the same as the accountant's concept.

12. What does the term *accelerated depreciation* mean? Give an example showing how depreciation is accelerated.

13. Provide a theoretical reason to support using an accelerated depreciation method.

14. If a machine has an estimated useful life of nine years, what will be the total digits to use in calculating depreciation under the sum-of-the-years'-digits method? How is this figure used in the depreciation calculation?

15. Emily Company purchased a machine that originally had an estimated eight years of useful life. At the end of the third year, Emily determined that the machine would last only three more years. Does this revision affect past depreciation taken?

16. What does the balance in the accumulated depreciation account represent? Does this balance represent cash that can be used to replace the related plant asset when it is completely depreciated?

17. What is the justification for reporting plant assets on the balance sheet at undepreciated cost (book value) rather than market value?

18. Distinguish between *capital expenditures* and *revenue expenditures*.

19. For each of the following, state whether the expenditure made should be charged to an expense, an asset, or an accumulated depreciation account:
    a. Cost of installing air-conditioning equipment in a building that was not air conditioned.
    b. Painting of an owned factory building every other year.
    c. Cost of replacing the roof on a 10-year-old building that was purchased new and has an estimated total life of 40 years. The expenditure did not extend the life of the asset beyond the original estimate.
    d. Cost of repairing an electric motor. The expenditure extended the estimated useful life beyond the original estimate.

20. Indicate which type of account (asset, accumulated depreciation, or expense) would be debited for each of the following expenditures:
    a. Painting an office building at a cost of $400. The building is painted every year.
    b. Adding on a new plant wing at a cost of $10,000.
    c. Expanding a paved parking lot at a cost of $60,000.
    d. Replacing a stairway with an escalator at a cost of $6,000.
    e. Replacing the transmission in an automobile at a cost of $600, thus extending its useful life two years beyond the original estimate.
    f. Replacing a broken fan belt at a cost of $150.

21. How do subsidiary records provide control over a company's plant assets?

22. What advantages can accrue to a company that maintains plant asset subsidiary records?

23. *Real world question* In the financial statements of Fleetwood Enterprises, Inc., in "A Broader Perspective" (page 499), determine the total historical cost and total accumulated depreciation on *all* property, plant, and equipment. Note the difference between your computation and the total historical cost and total accumulated depreciation disclosed in footnote (4). Explain this difference. Which set of numbers is more appropriate?

The Coca-Cola Company

24. *Real world question* From the consolidated balance sheet of The Coca-Cola Company in Appendix E, identify the 1989 gross property, plant, and equipment and the net property, plant, and equipment. What percentage of the depreciable assets have been depreciated?

MAYTAG CORPORATION

25. *Real world question* Based on the financial statements of Maytag Corporation contained in Appendix E, what was the 1989 ending balance in the Land account?

THE LIMITED, INC.

26. *Real world question* Based on the financial statements of The Limited, Inc., contained in Appendix E, what was the 1989 ending net property and equipment balance?

HARLAND

27. *Real world question* Based on the financial statements of John H. Harland Company contained in Appendix E, what was the 1989 ending balance of accumulated depreciation and amortization?

EXERCISES

Exercise 10–1
Determine cost of land
(L.O. 1)

Brown Company paid $200,000 cash for a tract of land on which it plans to erect a new warehouse, and paid $2,500 in legal fees related to the purchase. Brown also agreed to assume responsibility for $8,000 of unpaid taxes on the property. The company incurred a cost of $9,000 to remove an old apartment building from the land.

Prepare a schedule showing the cost of the land acquired.

Exercise 10–2
Determine cost of land
and building when
acquired together
(L.O. 1)

Drake Company paid $350,000 cash for real property consisting of a tract of land and a building. The company intended to remodel and use the old building. To allocate the cost of the property acquired, Drake had the property appraised. The appraised values were as follows: land, $240,000; and office building, $160,000. The cost of clearing the land was $7,500. The building was remodeled at a cost of $32,000. The cost of a new identical office building was estimated to be $180,000.

Prepare a schedule showing the cost of the assets acquired.

Exercise 10–3
Determine cost of
machine
(L.O. 1)

Lark Company purchased a heavy machine to be used in its factory for $150,000, less a 2% cash discount. The company paid a fine of $750 because an employee hauled the machine over city streets without securing the required permits. The machine was installed at a cost of $4,500, and testing costs of $1,500 were incurred to place the machine in operation.

Prepare a schedule showing the recorded cost of the machine.

Exercise 10–4
Record cost of office
equipment, depreciation,
and maintenance expense
(L.O. 1, 3, 4)

Ace Company purchased some office equipment for $6,200 cash on March 1, 1993. Cash of $100 was paid for freight costs incurred. The furniture is being depreciated over four years under the straight-line method, assuming a salvage value of $300. The company employs a calendar-year accounting period. On July 1, 1994, $40 was spent to refinish the furniture.

Prepare journal entries for the Ace Company to record all of the above data, including the annual depreciation adjustments through 1994.

Exercise 10–5
Determine cost of
machine in noncash
acquisition (L.O. 1)

A machine is acquired in exchange for 50 shares of Jobe Corporation capital stock. The stock recently traded at $160 per share. The machine cost $12,000 three years ago. At what amount should the machine be recorded?

Exercise 10–6
Compute annual
depreciation for two years
under each of four
different depreciation
methods (L.O. 3)

On January 2, 1993, a new machine was acquired for $360,000. The machine has an estimated salvage value of $30,000 and an estimated useful life of 10 years. The machine is expected to produce a total of 500,000 units of product throughout its useful life. Compute depreciation for 1993 and 1994 using each of the following methods:

a. Straight-line.
b. Units-of-production (assume 30,000 and 60,000 units were produced in 1993 and 1994, respectively).
c. Sum-of-the-years'-digits.
d. Double-declining-balance.

Exercise 10–7
Determine information
concerning machinery
(L.O. 3)

Drake Company finds its company records are incomplete concerning a piece of machinery used in its plant. According to the company records, the machinery has a useful life of 10 years and a salvage value of $5,000. $2,500 has been depreciated each year using the straight-line method. If the Accumulated Depreciation account shows a balance of $15,000, what is the original cost of the machinery and how many years remain to be depreciated?

Exercise 10–8
Compute depreciation
under SOYD and DDB
methods (L.O. 3)

Wilson Company purchased a machine on April 1, 1993, for $30,000. The machine has an estimated useful life of five years with no expected salvage value. The company's accounting year ends on December 31.

Compute the depreciation expense for 1994 under (*a*) the sum-of-the-years'-digits method and (*b*) the double-declining-balance method.

Exercise 10–9
Compute DDB
depreciation
(L.O. 3)

Farmer Company purchased a machine for $400 and incurred installation costs of $100. The machine's estimated salvage value is $25, and it has an estimated useful life of four years. Compute the annual depreciation charges for this machine under the double-declining-balance method.

Exercise 10–10
Compute depreciation before and after revision of expected life and salvage value (L.O. 3)

Spring Company acquired a delivery truck on January 2, 1993, for $33,500. The truck had an estimated salvage value of $1,500 and an estimated useful life of eight years. At the beginning of 1996, a revised estimate shows that the truck has a remaining useful life of six years. The estimated salvage value changed to $500.

Compute the depreciation charge for 1993 and the revised depreciation charge for 1996 using the straight-line method.

Exercise 10–11
Allocate periodic depreciation to building and to expense (L.O. 3)

Assume that the truck described in Exercise 10–10 was used 40% of the time in 1994 to haul materials used in the construction of a building by Spring Company for its own use. (Remember that 1994 is before the revision was made on estimated life.) During the remaining time, the truck was used to deliver merchandise sold by Spring to its customers.

Prepare the journal entry to record straight-line depreciation on the truck for 1994.

Exercise 10–12
Compute straight-line depreciation given reduced estimated life and salvage value (L.O. 3)

Lapp Company purchased a computer for $25,000 and placed it in operation on January 2, 1992. Depreciation was recorded for 1992 and 1993 using the straight-line method, a six-year life, and an expected salvage value of $1,000. The introduction of a new model of this computer caused the company in 1994 to revise its estimate of useful life to a total of four years and to reduce the estimated salvage value to zero.

Compute the depreciation expense on the computer for 1994.

Exercise 10–13
Compute straight-line depreciation after major overhaul (L.O. 3, 4)

On January 2, 1993, a company purchased and placed in operation a new machine at a total cost of $12,000. Depreciation was recorded on the machine for 1993 and 1994 under the straight-line method using an estimated useful life of five years and no expected salvage value. Early in 1995, the machine was overhauled at a cost of $4,000. The useful life of the machine was revised upward to a total of seven years.

Compute the depreciation expense on the machine for 1995.

Exercise 10–14
Compute error in net income when installation and freight costs are expensed (L.O. 4)

Grant Company purchased a machine on January 3, 1993, at a cost of $30,000. Freight and installation charges of $6,000 were incurred and debited to Repairs Expense. Straight-line depreciation was recorded on the machine in 1993 and 1994 using an estimated life of 10 years and no expected salvage value.

Compute the amount of the error in net income for 1993 and 1994, and state whether net income is understated or overstated.

Exercise 10–15
Determine the effect of an error in classification (L.O. 4)

Jolly Company owns a plant asset that originally cost $50,000 in 1990. The asset has been depreciated for three years assuming an 8-year useful life and no salvage value. During 1993, Jolly incorrectly capitalized $25,000 in repairs on the plant asset rather than expensing them. Describe the impact of this error on the asset's cost and Jolly's net income over the next five years.

PROBLEMS: SERIES A

Problem 10–1A
Determine cost of land (L.O. 1)

Ralph Company paid a local realtor $1,000 to find a suitable site for its new factory. When the site was found, Ralph agreed to pay the owner $15,000 cash, to assume responsibility for a $5,000 mortgage note on the property and $100 of accrued interest on the note, and to pay back taxes of $250 on the property. Ralph also paid legal fees of $125 and a $150 title insurance premium in acquiring the property. A local lumberyard paid Ralph $200 for some walnut trees that it removed from the property. Ralph also paid the city $1,750 to widen the street in front of the property and received $500 for a narrow strip of land deeded to the city in order to widen the street. Grading and leveling costs of $750 were also incurred by Ralph.

Required   Prepare a schedule showing the amount to be recorded as the cost of the land.

Problem 10–2A
Determine cost of machine (L.O. 1)

Walton Company purchased a machine for use in its operations that had a gross invoice price of $80,000 excluding sales tax. A 4% sales tax was levied on the sale. The company paid freight costs of $2,000. Special electrical connections were run to the machine at a cost of $2,800, and a special reinforced base for the machine was built at a cost of $3,600. The machine was dropped and damaged while being mounted on this base. Repairs cost $800. Raw materials with a cost of $200 were consumed in testing the machine. Safety guards were installed on the machine at a cost of $280, and the machine was placed in operation. In addition, $100 of costs were incurred in removing an old machine.

Required   Prepare a schedule showing the amount at which the machine should be recorded in Walton Company's account.

Problem 10–3A

Determine cost of land (L.O. 1)

Tolbert Company purchased 2 square miles of farmland under the following terms: $605,000 cash; and liability assumed on mortgage note of $200,000 and interest accrued on mortgage note assumed, $8,000. The company paid $42,000 of legal and brokerage fees and also paid $2,000 for a title search on the property.

The company planned to use the land as a site for a new office building and a new factory. Clearing and leveling costs of $18,000 were paid. Crops on the land were sold for $4,600, and one of the houses on the property was sold for $12,000. The other buildings were torn down at a cost of $9,000; sale of salvaged materials yielded cash proceeds of $8,500. Approximately 1% of the land acquired was deeded to the county for roads. The cost of excavating a basement for the office building amounted to $5,700.

Required   Prepare a schedule showing the amount at which the land should be carried on Tolbert Company's books.

Problem 10–4A

Determine cost of truck; prepare entry for depreciation under DDB and for straight-line depreciation assuming change in estimated life and salvage value (L.O. 1, 3)

Brambley Company purchased a used panel truck for $9,000 cash. The next day the company's name and business were painted on the truck at a total cost of $465. The truck was then given a minor overhaul at a cost of $60, and new tires were mounted on the truck at a cost of $600, less a trade-in allowance of $75 for the old tires. The truck was placed in service on April 1, 1993, at which time it had an estimated useful life of five years and a salvage value of $1,050.

Required

a.   Prepare a schedule showing the cost to be recorded for the truck.

b.   Prepare the journal entry needed to record depreciation at the end of the calendar-year accounting period, December 31, 1993. Use the double-declining-balance method.

c.   Assume that the straight-line depreciation method has been used. At the beginning of 1996 it is estimated the truck will last another four years. The estimated salvage value changed to $600. Prepare the entry to record depreciation for 1996.

Problem 10–5A

Compute cost of land, land improvements, building, and machinery; prepare entry to correct the accounts (L.O. 1, 4)

You are the new controller for Blake Company, which began operations on October 1, 1993, after a "start-up" period that ran from the middle of 1992. While reviewing the accounts, you find an account entitled "Fixed Assets," which contains the following items:

Cash paid to previous owner of land and old building	$ 80,000
Cash given to construction company as partial payment for the new building	30,000
Legal and title search fees	1,000
Real estate commission	6,000
Cost of demolishing old building	7,000
Cost of leveling and grading	4,000
Architect's fee (90% building and 10% improvements)	15,000
Cost of excavating basement for new building	9,000
Cash paid to construction company for new building	120,000
Repair damage done by vandals	3,000
Sprinkler system for lawn	13,000
Lighting system for parking lot	17,000
Paving of parking lot	25,000
Net invoice price of machinery	480,000
Freight cost incurred on machinery	21,000
Installation and testing of machinery	8,000
Medical bill paid for employee injured in installing machinery	1,500
Landscaping (permanent)	16,000
Repair damage to building in installation of machinery	2,000
Special assessment paid to city for water mains and sewer line	19,000
Account balance	$877,500

In addition to the above, you discover that cash receipts of $500 from selling materials salvaged from the old building were credited to Miscellaneous Revenues in 1993. Digging deeper, you find that the plant manager spent all of his time for the first nine months of 1993 supervising installation of land improvements (10%), building construction (40%), and installation of machinery (50%). The plant manager's nine-month salary of $45,000 was debited to Officers' Salaries Expense.

Required

a. List the above items on a form containing columns for Land, Land Improvements, Building, and Machinery. Sort the items into the appropriate columns, omitting those items not properly included as an element of asset cost. Show negative amounts in parentheses. Total your columns.

b. Prepare one compound journal entry to reclassify and adjust the accounts and to eliminate the Fixed Assets account. Do not attempt to record depreciation for the partial year.

Problem 10–6A

Compute depreciation for first year under each of four different depreciation methods (L.O. 3)

Vincent Company acquired and put into use a machine on January 1, 1993, at a cash cost of $24,000 and immediately spent $1,000 to install it. The machine was estimated to have a useful life of eight years and a scrap value of $5,000 at the end of this time. It was further estimated that the machine would produce 500,000 units of product during its life. In the first year, the machine produced 100,000 units.

Required

Prepare journal entries to record depreciation for 1993 using:

a. Straight-line method.

b. Units-of-production method.

c. Sum-of-the-years'-digits method.

d. Double-declining-balance method.

Problem 10–7A

Compute depreciation for two years using three depreciation methods; partial-year depreciation used first year (L.O. 3)

Connors Company paid $24,000 for a machine on April 1, 1993, and placed it in use on that same date. The machine has an estimated life of 10 years and an estimated salvage value of $4,000.

Required

Compute the amount of depreciation to the nearest dollar the company should record on this asset for the years ending December 31, 1993, and 1994, under each of the following methods:

a. Straight-line.

b. Sum-of-the-years'-digits.

c. Double-declining-balance.

PROBLEMS: SERIES B

Problem 10–1B

Determine cost of land (L.O. 1)

In seeking a site for its new home office building, Short Company paid a local realtor $3,000 to find the appropriate location. Short agreed to pay the owner of the site $50,000 cash, to assume responsibility for a $20,000 mortgage note on the property and $300 of accrued interest on the note, and to pay back taxes of $800 on the property. Short also paid legal fees of $400 and a $500 title insurance premium in acquiring the property. A local salvage company paid Short $9,000 for a building that it moved from the property. In addition, Short paid the city $8,000 to extend water mains and sewer lines to the property.

Required

Prepare a schedule showing the amount to be recorded as the cost of the land.

Problem 10–2B

Determine cost of machine (L.O. 1)

Zorn Company purchased a machine for use in its operations that had a gross invoice price of $10,000 excluding sales tax. A 4% sales tax was levied on the sale. The company estimated the total cost of hauling the machine from the dealer's warehouse to the company's plant at $700, which did not include a fine of $200 for failure to secure the necessary permits to use city streets in transporting the machine. In delivering the machine to its plant, a Zorn employee damaged the truck used; repairs cost $450. The machine was also slightly damaged with repair costs amounting to $200.

Zorn incurred installation costs of $4,000 that included the $500 cost of shoring up the floor under the machine. Testing costs amounted to $300. Safety guards were installed on the machine at a cost of $80, and the machine was placed in operation.

Required   Prepare a schedule showing the amount at which the machine should be recorded in Zorn's accounts.

Problem 10–3B

Determine cost of land and building
(L.O. 1)

Greene Company planned to erect a new factory building and a new office building in Atlanta, Georgia. A report on a suitable site showed an appraised value of $75,000 for land and orchard and $50,000 for a building.

After considerable negotiation, the company and the owner reached the following agreement. Greene Company was to pay $90,000 in cash, assume a $37,500 mortgage note on the property, assume the interest of $800 accrued on the mortgage note, and assume unpaid property taxes of $5,500. Greene Company paid $7,500 cash for brokerage and legal services in acquiring the property.

Shortly after acquisition of the property, Greene Company sold the fruit on the trees for $1,100, remodeled the building into an office building at a cost of $16,000, and removed the trees from the land at a cost of $3,750. Construction of the factory building was to begin in a week.

Required   Prepare schedules showing the proper valuation of the assets acquired by Greene Company.

Problem 10–4B

Prepare entry for acquisition of machine, for depreciation under DDB, and for straight-line depreciation assuming change in estimated life
(L.O. 1, 3)

York Company acquired and placed into use a heavy factory machine on October 1, 1993. The machine had an invoice price of $288,000, but the company received a 3% cash discount by paying the bill on the date of acquisition. An employee of York Company hauled the machine down a city street without a permit. As a result, the company had to pay a $1,200 fine. Installation and testing costs totaled $28,640. The machine is estimated to have a $28,000 salvage value and a seven-year useful life. (A fraction should be used for the double-declining-balance calculation rather than a percentage.)

Required   *a.* Prepare the journal entry to record the acquisition of the machine.

b. Prepare the journal entry to record depreciation for 1993 under the double-declining-balance method.

c. Assume that the straight-line depreciation method has been used. At the beginning of 1996 it is estimated the machine will last another six years. Prepare the journal entry to record depreciation for 1996. The estimated salvage value will not change.

Problem 10–5B

Compute cost of land, land improvements, building, and machinery; prepare entry to correct the accounts
(L.O. 1, 4)

Spartan Company has the following entries in its Building account:

Debits		
1993		
May 5	Cost of land and building purchased	$125,000
5	Broker fees incident to purchase of land and building	7,500
1994		
Jan. 3	Contract price of new wing added to south end	52,500
15	Cost of new machinery, estimated life 10 years	100,000
June 10	Real estate taxes for six months ended 6/30/94	2,250
Aug. 10	Cost of building parking lot for employees in back of building	3,100
Sept. 6	Replacement of windows broken in August	100
Oct. 10	Repairs due to regular usage	1,400
Credits		
1993		
May 24	Transfer to Land account, per allocation of purchase cost authorized in minutes of board of directors	$ 20,000
1994		
Jan. 5	Proceeds from lease of second floor for six months ended 12/31/93	5,000

The original property was acquired on May 5, 1993. Spartan Company immediately engaged a contractor to construct a new wing on the south end of the building. While the new wing was being constructed, the company leased the second floor as temporary warehouse space to Charles Company. During this period (July 1 to December 31, 1993), the company installed new machinery costing $100,000 on the first floor of the building. Regular operations began on January 2, 1994.

Required
a. Compute the correct balance for the Buildings account as of December 31, 1994. The company employs a calendar-year accounting period.

b. Prepare the necessary journal entries to correct the records of Spartan Company at December 31, 1994. No depreciation entries are required.

Problem 10–6B

Compute depreciation for first year under each of four different depreciation methods (L.O. 3)

Noel Company acquired and placed into use equipment on January 2, 1993, at a cash cost of $748,000. Transportation charges amounted to $6,000, and installation and testing costs totaled $44,000.

The equipment was estimated to have a useful life of nine years and a salvage value of $30,000 at the end of its life. It was further estimated that the equipment would be used in the production of 1,920,000 units of product during its life. During 1993, 426,000 units of product were produced.

Required

Compute the depreciation for the year ended December 31, 1993, using:

a. Straight-line method.
b. Units-of-production method.
c. Sum-of-the-years'-digits method.
d. Double-declining-balance method (use a fraction rather than a percentage).

Problem 10–7B

Compute depreciation for two years using three depreciation methods; partial-year depreciation used first year (L.O. 3)

Alton Company purchased a machine on October 1, 1993, for $40,000. The machine has an estimated salvage value of $12,000 and an estimated useful life of eight years.

Required

Compute the amount of depreciation to the nearest dollar Alton should record on the machine for the years ending December 31, 1993, and 1994, under each of the following methods:

a. Straight-line.
b. Sum-of-the-years'-digits.
c. Double-declining-balance.

BUSINESS DECISION PROBLEMS

Decision Problem 10–1

Compute correct cost of land, building, and land improvements; compute depreciation; prepare entry to correct the accounts
(L.O. 1, 3)

Martin Company has the following entries in its Buildings account:

		Debits	
1993			
Jan.	2	Cost of land and old buildings purchased	$450,000
	2	Legal fees incident to purchase	6,000
	2	Fee for title search	750
	12	Cost of demolishing old buildings on land	12,000
June	16	Cost of insurance during construction of new building	3,000
July	30	Payment to contractor on completion of new building	675,000
Aug.	5	Architect's fees for design of new building	30,000
Sept.	15	City assessment for sewers and sidewalks (considered permanent)	10,500
Oct.	6	Cost of landscaping (considered permanent).	6,000
Nov.	1	Cost of driveways and parking lots	37,500
		Credit	
Jan.	15	Proceeds received upon sale of salvaged materials from old buildings	3,000

You are in charge of auditing Martin Company's Buildings account. In addition to the entries in the account, you are given the following information:

1. The company began using the new building on September 1, 1993. The building is estimated to have a 40-year useful life and no salvage value.
2. The company began using the driveways and parking lots on November 1, 1993. The driveways and parking lots are estimated to have a 10-year useful life and no salvage value.
3. The straight-line depreciation method is used to depreciate all of the company's plant assets.

Required
a. Prepare a schedule that shows separately the cost of land, buildings, and land improvements.
b. Compute the amount of depreciation expense for 1993.
c. What journal entries are required to correct the accounts at December 31, 1993? Assume that closing entries have not been made.

Decision Problem 10–2

Compute partial-year depreciation under each of four different methods; cite circumstances in which each of the different methods seems most appropriate (L.O. 2, 3)

On October 1, 1994, Gordon Company acquired and placed into use new equipment costing $210,000. The equipment has a useful life of five years and an estimated salvage value of $10,000. It is estimated that the equipment will produce 2,000,000 units of product during its life. In the last quarter of 1994, the equipment produced 120,000 units of product.

Required
a. Compute the depreciation for the last quarter of 1994, using each of the following methods:

1. Straight-line.
2. Units-of-production.
3. Sum-of-the-years'-digits.
4. Double-declining-balance.

b. Describe the conditions in which each of the above four methods would be most appropriate.

Decision Problem 10–3

Determine the number of depreciation methods used; cite the advantages of each method (L.O. 3)

The following footnote excerpted from the 1989 annual report of John H. Harland Company describes the company's accounting policies for property, plant, and equipment:

Property, plant, and equipment are carried at cost. Depreciation of buildings is computed primarily by the declining balance method. Depreciation of equipment, furniture and fixtures is calculated by the straight-line or sum-of-the-years'-digits methods. Accelerated methods are used for income tax purposes for all property where it is allowed.

Required
a. How many different depreciation methods are used by John H. Harland Company? Does this practice conform with generally accepted accounting principles?
b. Discuss why each of these methods might be selected by management to depreciate their depreciable plant assets.

ANSWERS TO SELF-TEST

True-False

1. *False*. The cost of removing the old machine is not included in the cost of new machine.
2. *False*. Depreciation is a process of allocation, not valuation, and the book value of an asset has nothing to do with its market value.
3. *False*. See the explanation for answer 2.
4. *True*. Expenditures that improve the quality of services are charged to the asset account.
5. *True*. Plant asset subsidiary ledgers enhance control over plant assets by providing detailed information.

Multiple-Choice

1. *b.* The depreciation expense using the straight-line method is computed as follows:

$$(\$110,000 - \$10,000)/10 = \$10,000$$

2. *d.*

Double-declining-balance rate $= 2 \times (100\%/10)$

$= 20\%$

Depreciation expense $= (20\% \times \$110,000) \times \frac{6}{12}$

$= \$11,000$

3. *a.*

$$\text{SOYD} = \frac{10(10 + 1)}{2} = 55$$

Depreciation expense $= \frac{10}{55} \times (\$110,000 - \$10,000)$

$= \$18,182$

4. *e.* At the beginning of 1996, the balance of accumulated depreciation is $2,800 (annual depreciation of $1,400 × 2) and book value is $7,200 ($10,000 − $2,800). The revised annual depreciation expense is $3,100 [($7,200 − $1,000)/2].

5. *a.* The error in recording a capital expenditure as a revenue expenditure results in an overstatement of current year's expense, as well as an understatement of current year's net income.

11

PLANT ASSET DISPOSALS, NATURAL RESOURCES, AND INTANGIBLE ASSETS

LEARNING OBJECTIVES

After studying this chapter, you should be able to:

1. Calculate and prepare entries for the sale, retirement, and destruction of plant assets.

2. Describe and record exchanges of dissimilar and similar plant assets.

3. Discuss the differences between accounting principles and tax rules in the treatment of gains and losses from the exchange of plant assets.

4. Determine the periodic depletion cost of a natural resource and calculate depreciation of plant assets located on extractive industry property.

5. Prepare entries for the acquisition and amortization of intangible assets.

The study of long-term assets, which includes plant assets, natural resources, and intangible assets, began in Chapter 10. Discussion in that chapter focused on determining plant asset cost, computing depreciation, and distinguishing between capital and revenue expenditures. This chapter begins by discussing the disposal of plant assets. The next topic is accounting for natural resources such as ores, minerals, oil and gas, and timber. The final topic is accounting for intangible assets such as patents, copyrights, franchises, trademarks and trade names, leases, and goodwill.

Although several long-term assets are discussed in this chapter, you will see that accounting for all long-term assets is basically the same. When a company purchases a long-term asset, the asset is recorded at cost. As the company receives benefits from the asset and the future service potential is reduced, the cost is transferred from an asset account to an expense account. Finally, the asset is sold, retired, or traded in on a new asset. Since the lives of long-term assets can extend for many years, the methods accountants use in reporting such assets can have a dramatic effect on the financial statements of many accounting periods.

DISPOSAL OF PLANT ASSETS

All plant assets except land eventually wear out or become inadequate or obsolete and must be sold, retired, or traded for new assets. **When a plant asset is disposed of, both the asset's cost and accumulated depreciation must be removed from the accounts.** Overall, then, all asset disposals have the following in common:

1. The asset's depreciation must be brought up to date.
2. To record the disposal, you must:
   a. Write off the asset's cost.
   b. Write off the accumulated depreciation.
   c. Record any consideration (usually cash) received or paid or to be received or paid.
   d. Record gain or loss, if any.

As you study this section, remember these common procedures used by accountants to record the disposal of plant assets. In the paragraphs that follow, we discuss accounting for the (1) sale of plant assets, (2) retirement of plant assets without sale, (3) destruction of plant assets, (4) exchange of plant assets, and (5) cost of dismantling and removing plant assets.

Sale of Plant Assets

Objective 1
Calculate and prepare entries for the sale, retirement, and destruction of plant assets

Companies frequently dispose of plant assets by selling them. By comparing an asset's book value (cost less accumulated depreciation) with its selling price (or net amount realized if there are selling expenses), the company may show either a gain or loss. If the sales price is greater than the asset's book value, the company will show a gain. If the sales price is less than the asset's book value, the company will show a loss. Of course, if the sales price is equal to the asset's book value, no gain or loss occurs.

To illustrate accounting for the sale of a plant asset, assume that equipment costing $45,000 with accumulated depreciation of $14,000 is sold for $35,000. A gain of $4,000 is realized as computed below.

Equipment cost	$45,000
Accumulated depreciation	14,000
Book value	$31,000
Sales price	35,000
Gain realized	$ 4,000

The journal entry to record the sale is:

Cash.	35,000	
Accumulated Depreciation—Equipment	14,000	
Equipment		45,000
Gain on Disposal of Plant Assets		4,000
To record sale of equipment at a price greater than book value.		

If on the other hand, the equipment is sold for $28,000, a loss of $3,000 ($31,000 book value − $28,000 sales price) is realized. The journal entry to record the sale is:

Cash.	28,000	
Accumulated Depreciation—Equipment	14,000	
Loss from Disposal of Plant Assets	3,000	
Equipment		45,000
To record sale of equipment at a price less than book value.		

If the equipment is sold for $31,000, no gain or loss occurs. The journal entry to record the sale is:

Cash.	31,000	
Accumulated Depreciation—Equipment	14,000	
Equipment		45,000
To record sale of equipment at a price equal to book value.		

Accounting for Depreciation to Date of Disposal When a plant asset is sold or otherwise disposed of, it is important to record the depreciation up to the date of sale or disposal. For example, if an asset is sold on April 1 and depreciation was last recorded on December 31, depreciation for three months (January 1–April 1) should be recorded. If depreciation is not recorded for the three months, operating expenses for that period will be understated, and the gain on the sale of the asset will be understated or the loss overstated.

To illustrate, assume that on August 1, 1995, Ray Company sold a machine for $1,500. When the machine was purchased on January 2, 1987, it cost $12,000 and was being depreciated at the straight-line rate of 10% per year. As of December 31, 1994, after closing entries were made, the machine's accumulated depreciation account had a balance of $9,600. Before a gain or loss can be determined and before an entry can be made to record the sale, the following entry must be made to record depreciation for the seven months ended July 31, 1995:

July	31	Depreciation Expense—Machinery	700	
		Accumulated Depreciation—Machinery		700
		To record depreciation for seven months		
		($12,000 × 0.10 × 7/12).		

The $200 loss on the sale is computed as shown below:

Machine cost	$12,000
Accumulated depreciation ($9,600 + $700)	10,300
Book value.	$ 1,700
Sales price.	1,500
Loss realized	$ 200

The journal entry to record the sale is:

Cash	1,500	
Accumulated Depreciation—Machinery	10,300	
Loss from Disposal of Plant Assets	200	
Machinery		12,000
To record sale of machinery at a price less than book value.		

Retirement of Plant Assets without Sale

When a plant asset is retired from service, the asset's cost and accumulated depreciation must be removed from the plant asset accounts. For example, Hayes Company would make the following journal entry when it retired a fully depreciated machine that cost $15,000 and had no salvage value:

Accumulated Depreciation—Machinery	15,000	
Machinery		15,000
To record the retirement of a fully depreciated machine.		

Occasionally, a company continues to use a plant asset after it has been fully depreciated. In such a case, the asset's cost and accumulated depreciation should **not** be removed from the accounts until the asset is sold, traded, or retired from service. Of course, no more depreciation may be recorded on a fully depreciated asset because total depreciation expense taken on an asset may not exceed its cost.

Sometimes a plant asset is retired from service or discarded before it is fully depreciated. If the asset is to be sold as scrap (even if not immediately), its cost and accumulated depreciation should be removed from the asset and accumulated depreciation accounts. In addition, its estimated salvage value should be recorded in a Salvaged Materials account, and a gain or loss on disposal should be recognized. To illustrate, assume that a machine with a $10,000 original cost and $7,500 of accumulated depreciation is retired. If the machine's estimated salvage value is $500, the following entry is required:

Salvaged Materials	500	
Accumulated Depreciation—Machinery	7,500	
Loss from Disposal of Plant Assets	2,000	
Machinery		10,000
To record retirement of machinery, which will be sold for scrap at a later time.		

Destruction of Plant Assets

Plant assets are sometimes wrecked in accidents or destroyed by fire, flood, storm, or other causes. Losses are normally incurred in such situations. For example, assume that an **uninsured** building costing $40,000 with accumulated depreciation of $12,000 was completely destroyed by a fire. The journal entry is:

Fire Loss.	28,000	
Accumulated Depreciation—Buildings	12,000	
Buildings.		40,000
To record fire loss.		

If the building was **insured,** only the amount of the fire loss exceeding the amount to be recovered from the insurance company would be debited to the Fire Loss account. To illustrate, assume that in the example above, the building was partially insured and that $22,000 is recoverable from the insurance company. The journal entry is:

Receivable from Insurance Company	22,000	
Fire Loss.	6,000	
Accumulated Depreciation—Buildings	12,000	
Buildings.		40,000
To record fire loss and amount recovered from insurance company.		

Exchanges of Plant Assets (Nonmonetary Assets)

Nonmonetary assets are those items whose price may change over time, such as inventories, property, plant, and equipment. In accounting for the exchange of nonmonetary assets, ordinarily the recorded amount should be based on the fair value of the asset given up or the fair value of the asset received, whichever is more clearly evident. If a gain or loss results from the exchange, the loss is always recognized; the gain may or may not be recognized, depending on whether the asset exchanged is similar or dissimilar to the asset received.

Similar assets are those of the same general type, that perform the same function, or that are employed in the same line of business. Examples of the exchange of similar assets include exchanging a building for another building, a delivery truck for another delivery truck, and equipment for other equipment. Conversely, examples of the exchange of dissimilar assets include exchanging a building for land, and equipment for inventory.

In general, losses on nonmonetary assets are recognized, regardless of whether the assets are similar or dissimilar in nature. Gains are recognized if the assets are dissimilar in nature because the earnings process related to those assets is considered to be completed. With one exception, gains are deferred on the exchange of similar nonmonetary assets. The exception occurs when monetary consideration is received in addition to the similar asset. In this case, a partial gain may be recognized when cash is received along with an asset. Because the specific details of monetary consideration are reserved for an intermediate accounting text, assume in the examples given that cash has been paid, not received. Both gains and losses on the disposal of nonmonetary assets are computed by comparing the book value of the asset given up with the fair value of the asset given up.

The proper accounting for exchanges of dissimilar and similar plant assets is illustrated below.

Objective 2

Describe and record
exchanges of dissimilar
and similar plant assets

Exchanges of Dissimilar Plant Assets   Sometimes a machine is traded for a dissimilar plant asset such as a truck. Exchanges of dissimilar plant assets are accounted for by recording the new asset at the fair market value of the asset received or the asset(s) given up, whichever is more clearly evident.[1] The cash price of the new asset may be stated; if so, the cash price should be used to record the new asset. If the cash price is not stated, the fair market value of the old asset plus any cash paid is assumed to be the cash price and is used to record the new asset. Thus, the asset received would normally be recorded at either (1) the stated cash price of the new asset or (2) a known fair value of the asset given up plus any cash paid.

The book value of the old asset is removed from the accounts by debiting accumulated depreciation and crediting the old asset. The Cash account is credited for any amount paid. If the amount at which the new asset is recorded exceeds the book value of the old asset plus any cash paid, a gain is recorded to balance the journal entry. If the situation is vice versa, a loss is recorded to balance the journal entry.

To illustrate such an exchange, assume that an old factory machine is exchanged for a new delivery truck. The machine cost $45,000 and had an accumulated depreciation balance of $38,000. The truck had a $55,000 cash price and was acquired by trading in a machine with a fair value of $3,000 and paying $52,000 cash. The journal entry to record the exchange is:

Trucks	55,000	
Accumulated Depreciation—Machinery	38,000	
Loss from Disposal of Plant Assets	4,000	
Machinery		45,000
Cash		52,000
To record loss on exchange of dissimilar plant assets.		

The $4,000 loss on the exchange can also be computed as the book value of the old asset less the fair market value of the old asset. The calculation is as follows:

Machine cost	$45,000
Accumulated depreciation	38,000
Book value	$ 7,000
Fair market value of old asset	
(trade-in allowance)	3,000
Loss realized	$ 4,000

To illustrate the recognition of a gain from an exchange of dissimilar plant assets, assume that the fair market value of the above machine was $9,000 instead of $3,000, and that $46,000 was paid in cash. The gain would be $2,000 ($9,000 fair market value less $7,000 book value). The journal entry to record the exchange would be:

[1] APB, *APB Opinion No. 29,* "Accounting for Nonmonetary Transactions" (New York: AICPA, May 1973), par. 16.

Trucks		55,000	
Accumulated Depreciation—Machinery		38,000	
Machinery			45,000
Cash.			46,000
Gain on Disposal of Plant Assets			2,000
To record gain on exchange of dissimilar plant assets.			

The gain of $2,000 on the exchange can also be computed as the fair market value of the old asset less the book value of the old asset. The calculation is as follows:

Machine cost	$45,000
Accumulated depreciation	38,000
Book value	$ 7,000
Fair market value of old asset	
(trade-in allowance)	9,000
Gain realized	$ 2,000

Remember, both gains and losses are always recognized on exchanges of dissimilar plant assets. As shown below, gains on exchanges of similar plant assets should not be recognized.

Exchanges of Similar Plant Assets   Plant assets such as automobiles, trucks, and office equipment are often exchanged by trading the old asset for a similar new one. When such an exchange occurs, the company usually receives a trade-in allowance for the old asset,[2] and the balance is paid in cash. The cash price of the new asset is often stated. If not, the cash price is assumed to be the fair market value of the old asset plus the cash paid.

When similar assets are exchanged, the general rule that new assets are recorded at the fair market value of what is given up or received is modified slightly. **The new asset is recorded at (1) the cash price of the asset received or (2) the book value of the old asset plus the cash paid, whichever is lower.** When this rule is applied to exchanges of similar assets, **losses are recognized, but gains are not.**

To illustrate the accounting for exchanges of similar plant assets, assume that $50,000 cash and delivery truck No. 1—which cost $45,000, had $38,000 accumulated depreciation, and had a $5,000 fair market value—were exchanged for delivery truck No. 2. The new truck has a cash price (fair market value) of $55,000. A loss of $2,000 is realized on the exchange.

Cost of delivery truck No. 1	$45,000
Accumulated depreciation	38,000
Book value	$ 7,000
Fair market value of old asset	
(trade-in allowance)	5,000
Loss on exchange of plant assets	$ 2,000

---

[2] Trade-in allowance is sometimes expressed as the difference between *list* price and cash paid, but we choose to define it as the difference between *cash* price and cash paid because this latter definition seems to agree with current practice for exchange transactions.

The journal entry to record the exchange is:

Trucks (cost of No. 2)	55,000	
Accumulated Depreciation—Trucks	38,000	
Loss from Disposal of Plant Assets	2,000	
Trucks (cost of No. 1)		45,000
Cash		50,000
To record loss on exchange of similar plant assets.		

Note that exchanges of similar plant assets are recorded just like exchanges of dissimilar plant assets when a *loss* occurs from the exchange.

Accounting for any gain resulting from exchanges of similar plant assets is handled differently than a gain resulting from exchanges of dissimilar plant assets. To illustrate, assume that in the preceding example, delivery truck No. 1 (now with a fair market value of $9,000) and $46,000 cash were given in exchange for delivery truck No. 2. A gain of $2,000 is indicated on the exchange:

Cost of delivery truck No. 1	$45,000
Accumulated depreciation	38,000
Book value	$ 7,000
Fair market value of old asset	
(trade-in allowance)	9,000
Gain indicated	$ 2,000

The journal entry to record the exchange is:

Trucks (cost of No. 2)	53,000	
Accumulated Depreciation—Trucks	38,000	
Trucks (cost of No. 1)		45,000
Cash		46,000
To record exchange of similar plant assets.		

When similar assets are exchanged, a gain is not recognized. The new asset is recorded at book value of the old asset ($7,000) plus cash paid ($46,000). The gain is deducted from the cost of the new asset ($55,000). Thus, the cost basis of the new delivery truck is equal to $55,000 less the $2,000 gain, or $53,000. This $53,000 cost basis is used in recording depreciation on the truck and determining any gain or loss on its disposal.

Book value of old truck (No. 1)	$ 7,000	
Cash paid	46,000	
Cost of new truck (No. 2)	$53,000	
Fair market value of new truck (No. 2)	$55,000	(equal)
Less: Gain indicated	2,000	
Cost of new truck (No. 2)	$53,000	

The justification used by the Accounting Principles Board for not recognizing gains on exchanges of similar plant assets is that "revenue should not be recognized merely because one productive asset is substituted for a similar productive asset but rather should be considered to flow from the production and sale of the goods or services to which the substituted productive asset is committed.''[3] In effect, the gain on an exchange of similar plant assets is realized in future accounting periods in the form of increased net income resulting from smaller depreciation charges on the newly acquired asset. In the preceding example, annual depreciation expense is less if it is based on the truck's $53,000 cost basis than if it is based on the truck's $55,000 cash price. Thus, future net income per year will be larger.

Objective 3

Discuss the differences between accounting principles and tax rules in the treatment of gains and losses from the exchange of plant assets

Tax Rules and Plant Asset Exchanges   The Internal Revenue Code does not allow recognition of **gains or losses** for income tax purposes when similar productive assets are exchanged. For income tax purposes, the cost basis of the new asset is the book value of the old asset plus any additional cash (called boot) paid.

Accounting principles and income tax laws agree on the treatment of gains, but they disagree on the treatment of losses. Thus, in the previous example involving a $2,000 loss on the exchange of delivery trucks, the loss should not be recognized for income tax purposes. In this case, the loss is treated as an adjustment of the cost of the new asset. The transaction would be recorded as follows for income tax purposes:

Trucks (cost of No. 2) ($7,000 + $50,000)	57,000	
Accumulated Depreciation—Trucks	38,000	
Trucks (cost of No. 1)		45,000
Cash.		50,000
To record exchange of similar plant assets using tax method.		

The new asset is recorded at the $7,000 book value of the old asset plus the cash payment of $50,000. The unrecognized loss of $2,000 is added to the cost basis of the new asset. This $57,000 cost basis is used in recording depreciation on the truck and determining any gain or loss on its disposal. The cost basis of the new asset is computed as follows:

Book value of old truck (No. 1)	$ 7,000
Cash paid	50,000
Cost of new truck (No. 2)	$57,000
Fair market value of new truck (No. 2).	$55,000 (equal)
Add: Unrecognized loss	2,000
Cost of new truck (No. 2)	$57,000

Illustration 11.1 summarizes the rules for recording exchanges of plant assets for accounting and income tax purposes. Studying this illustration may help you remember how to record exchange transactions.

Because of differences between accounting principles and income tax laws, two sets of depreciation records must be kept if a **material** (relatively large) **loss** occurs on an exchange of similar plant assets. One set of depreciation records is based on the accounting valuation of the new asset (cash price of new asset or fair market value of old asset plus cash paid) and is used to determine net income for financial reporting purposes; the second set is based on the tax valuation of the new asset (book value of old asset plus cash paid).

---

[3] *APB Opinion No. 29*, par. 16.

ILLUSTRATION 11.1

Summary of Rules for Recording Exchanges of Plant Assets

	Dissimilar Assets	Similar Assets	
	For Both Accounting and Tax Purposes	**For Accounting Purposes**	**For Tax Purposes**
Recognize Gains?	Yes	No	No
Recognize Losses?	Yes	Yes	No
Record New Asset at:	Cash price of new asset **or** fair market value of old asset plus cash paid	**If loss:** Cash price of new asset **or** fair market value of old asset plus cash paid **If gain:** Book value of old asset plus cash paid	Book value of old asset plus cash paid

If the loss is immaterial, some companies follow the tax method in their books to account for a loss from an exchange of similar plant assets to avoid keeping two sets of accounting records. For example, assume a company that earns approximately $1,000,000 per year suffers a $25 loss on an exchange of plant assets. In relation to $1,000,000, $25 is immaterial, and the company need only keep one set of accounting records regarding the exchange and not show the loss.

Removal Costs   Removal costs are incurred to dismantle and remove a company's old plant asset. These costs are deducted from salvage proceeds to determine the asset's net salvage value. Removal costs are associated with the old asset, not the new asset acquired as a replacement.

The next section discusses natural resources. Again, you will note the underlying accounting principle of matching expenses of an accounting period with the revenues earned in that **same** accounting period.

NATURAL RESOURCES

Resources supplied by nature, such as ore deposits, mineral deposits, oil reserves, gas deposits, and timber stands, are known as **natural resources** or **wasting assets.** Natural resources represent inventories of raw materials that can be consumed (exhausted) through extraction or removal from their natural setting (e.g., removing oil from the ground).

On the balance sheet, natural resources are classified as a separate group among noncurrent assets under headings such as "Timber stands" and "Oil reserves." Natural resources are typically recorded at their cost of acquisition plus exploration and development cost; they are reported on the balance sheet at total cost less accumulated depletion. (Accumulated depletion is similar to the accumulated depreciation used for plant assets.) When analyzing the financial condition of companies owning natural resources, caution must be exercised because the historical costs reported for the natural resources may only be a small fraction of their current value.

Depletion

Depletion is the exhaustion of a natural resource that results from the physical removal of a part of the resource. In each accounting period, the depletion recognized is an estimate of the cost of the natural resource that was removed from its natural setting during the period. **Depletion is recorded by debiting a depletion expense account and crediting an accumulated depletion account, which is a contra account to the natural resource asset account.**

By crediting the accumulated depletion account instead of the asset account, the original cost of the entire natural resource continues to be reported on the financial statements, and statement users can see the percentage of the resource that has been removed. This depletion cost is combined with other extraction, mining, or removal costs to determine the total cost of the resource available. This total cost is assigned to either the cost of natural resources sold or the inventory of the natural resource still on hand. Thus, it is possible that all, some, or none of the depletion and removal costs recognized in an accounting period will be expensed in that period, depending on the portion sold. If all of the resource is sold, all of the depletion and removal costs are expensed. The cost of any portion not yet sold will be part of the cost of inventory.

Objective 4

Determine the periodic depletion cost of a natural resource and calculate depreciation of plant assets located on extractive industry property

Computing Periodic Depletion Cost   Depletion charges usually are computed by the units-of-production method. Total cost is divided by the estimated number of units—tons, barrels, or board feet—**that can be economically extracted** from the property. This calculation provides a per unit depletion cost. For example, assume that in 1994 a company paid $650,000 for a tract of land containing ore deposits. The company spent $100,000 in exploration costs. The results indicated that approximately 900,000 tons of ore can be economically removed from the land, after which the land will be worth $50,000. Costs of $200,000 were incurred to develop the site, including the cost of running power lines and building roads. Total cost subject to depletion is the net cost assignable to the natural resource plus the exploration and development costs. When the property is purchased, a journal entry is made to assign the purchase price to the two assets purchased— the natural resource and the land. The entry would be:

Land	50,000	
Ore Deposits	600,000	
Cash		650,000
To record purchase of land and mine.		

After the purchase, all other costs mentioned above are debited to the natural resource account. The entry would be:

Ore Deposits ($100,000 + $200,000)	300,000	
Cash		300,000
To record costs of exploration and development.		

The formula for finding depletion cost per unit is:

$$\frac{\text{Depletion cost}}{\text{per unit}} = \frac{\frac{\text{Cost of}}{\text{site}} - \frac{\text{Residual value}}{\text{of land}} + \frac{\text{Costs to}}{\text{develop site}}}{\frac{\text{Number of units that can be}}{\text{economically extracted}}}$$

In some instances, companies buy only the right to extract the natural resource from someone else's land. When the land is not purchased, its residual value is irrelevant and should be ignored. If there is an obligation to restore the land to a usable condition, these estimated restoration costs should be added to the costs to develop the site.

In the above example where the land was purchased, the total costs of the mineral deposits is equal to the cost of the site ($650,000) minus the residual value of land ($50,000) plus costs to develop the site ($300,000), or a total of $900,000. The unit (per ton) depletion charge is $1 ($900,000/900,000 tons).

The formula to compute the depletion cost of a period is:

$$\frac{\text{Depletion cost}}{\text{of a period}} = \frac{\text{Depletion cost}}{\text{per unit}} \times \frac{\text{Number of units extracted}}{\text{during period}}$$

In this example, if 100,000 tons are mined in 1994, the entry to record the depletion cost of $100,000 ($1 × 100,000) for the period is:

Depletion.	100,000	
Accumulated Depletion—Ore Deposits[4]		100,000
To record depletion for 1994.		

The Depletion account contains the "in the ground" cost of the ore or natural resource mined. This cost is combined with other extractive costs to determine the total cost of the ore mined. To illustrate, assume that in addition to the $100,000 depletion cost, mining labor costs totaled $320,000, and other mining costs, such as depreciation, property taxes, power, and supplies, totaled $60,000. If 80,000 tons were sold and 20,000 remained on hand at the end of the period, the total cost of $480,000 would be allocated as follows:

Depletion cost	$100,000
Mining labor cost	320,000
Other mining costs	60,000
Total cost of 100,000 tons mined ($4.80 per ton)	$480,000
Less: Ore inventory (20,000 tons at $4.80)	96,000
Cost of ore sold	$384,000

Note that the average cost per ton to mine 100,000 tons was $4.80 ($480,000/100,000). The income statement would show cost of ore sold of $384,000. Depletion would not be reported separately as an expense because depletion is included in cost of ore sold. The balance sheet would show inventory of ore on hand (a

[4] Instead of crediting the accumulated depletion account, the Ore Deposits account could have been credited directly. But for reasons indicated earlier, the credit is usually to an accumulated depletion account.

current asset) at $96,000 ($4.80 × 20,000). The balance sheet would also report the cost less accumulated depletion of the natural resource as follows:

Ore deposits.	$900,000	
Less: Accumulated depletion	100,000	$800,000

Another method of calculating depletion cost is the percentage of revenue method. This method, used only for income tax purposes and not for financial statements, is not discussed in this text.

Depreciation of Plant Assets Located on Extractive Industry Property   Depreciable plant assets erected on extractive industry property are depreciated in the same manner as other depreciable assets. **If such assets will be abandoned when the natural resource is exhausted, they should be depreciated over the shorter of the (a) physical life of the asset or (b) life of the natural resource.** In some cases, periodic depreciation charges are computed using the units-of-production method. Using this method matches the life of the plant asset with the life of the natural resource. This method is recommended where the **physical** life of the plant asset equals or exceeds the life of the natural resource but its **useful** life is limited to the life of the natural resource.

Assume mining property is acquired and a building on the site is purchased for exclusive use in the mining operations. Also assume that the units-of-production method is used for computing building depreciation. Relevant facts are:

Building cost	$310,000
Estimated physical life of building	20 years
Estimated salvage value of building (after mine exhausted)	$ 10,000
Capacity of mine	1,000,000 tons
Expected life of mine	10 years

Since the life of the mine (10 years or 1,000,000 tons) is shorter than the life of the building (20 years), the building should be depreciated over the life of the mine. In this case, the depreciation charge should be based on tons of ore rather than years because the mine's "life" could be longer or shorter than 10 years, depending on how rapidly the ore is removed from the mine.

Suppose that during the first year of operations, 150,000 tons of ore are extracted. Building depreciation for the first year is $45,000, computed as follows:

$$\text{Depreciation per unit} = \frac{\text{Asset cost} - \text{Estimated salvage value}}{\text{Total tons of ore in mine that can be economically extracted}}$$

$$= \frac{\$310,000 - \$10,000}{1,000,000 \text{ tons}} = \$0.30 \text{ per ton}$$

$$\text{Depreciation for year} = \text{Depreciation per unit} \times \text{Units extracted}$$

$$= \$0.30 \text{ per ton} \times 150,000 \text{ tons} = \$45,000$$

Depreciation on the building would be included on the income statement as part of the cost of ore that was sold and would be carried as part of inventory cost for

A BROADER PERSPECTIVE

E. I. DU PONT DE NEMOURS AND COMPANY
Partial Balance Sheet
($ millions)

	December	
	1988	**1987**
Total Current Assets	$10,238	$ 9,953
Property, Plant and Equipment		
(Note 11)	$36,879	$33,400
Less: Accumulated Depreciation,		
Depletion and Amortization	19,658	17,546
	$17,221	$15,854

Summary of Significant Accounting Policies

Property, Plant and Equipment

Property, plant and equipment (PP&E) is carried at cost, and, except for petroleum and coal PP&E, is generally classified in depreciable groups and depreciated by an accelerated method that produces results similar to the sum-of-the-years' digits method. Depreciation rates range from 4 percent to 12 percent per annum on direct manufacturing facilities and from 2 percent to 10 percent per annum on other facilities; in some instances appropriately higher or lower rates are used.

Petroleum and coal PP&E, other than that described below, is depreciated on the straight-line method at various rates calculated to extinguish carrying values over estimated useful lives.

Generally, the gross carrying value of PP&E (including petroleum and coal) surrendered, retired, sold, or otherwise disposed of is charged to accumulated depreciation, depletion and amortization; any salvage or other recovery therefrom is credited to accumulated depreciation, depletion and amortization. Maintenance and repairs are charged to operations; replacements and betterments are capitalized.

Oil and Gas Properties

The company's exploration and production activities are accounted for under the successful efforts method. Costs of acquiring unproved properties are capitalized, and impairment of those properties, which are individually insignificant, is provided for by amortizing the cost thereof based on past experience and the estimated holding period. Geological, geophysical and delay rental costs are expensed as incurred. Costs of exploratory dry holes are expensed as the wells are determined to be dry. Costs of productive properties, production and support equipment, and development costs are capitalized and amortized on a unit-of-production basis.

Coal Properties

Costs of undeveloped properties and development costs applicable to the opening of new coal mines are capitalized and amortized on a unit-of-production basis. Costs of additional mine facilities required to maintain production after a mine reaches the production stage, generally referred to as "receding face costs," are expensed as incurred; however, costs of additional air shafts and new portals are capitalized and amortized.

Notes to Financial Statements

Dollars in millions, except per share.

Note 11. Property, Plant, and Equipment

December 31	1988	1987
Agricultural and Industrial Chemicals .	$ 4,720	$ 4,198
Biomedical Products	1,149	1,051
Coal	3,006	2,911
Fibers.	7,505	6,805
Industrial and Consumer Products . .	2,462	2,401
Petroleum Exploration and Production	9,405	8,277
Petroleum Refining, Marketing and		
Transportation	2,863	2,509
Polymer Products	4,457	4,059
Corporate	1,312	1,189
	$36,879	$33,400

Property, Plant and Equipment includes gross assets acquired under capital leases of $144 and $157 at December 31, 1988 and 1987; related amounts included in accumulated depreciation, depletion and amortization were $89 and $79 at December 31, 1988 and 1987.

Maintenance and repairs expense was $1,569 in 1988, $1,484 in 1987 and $1,440 in 1986.

Source: Based on American Institute of Certified Public Accountants, *Accounting Trends & Techniques* (New York: AICPA, 1989), p. 138.

those tons of ore that were not sold during the period. Accumulated depreciation on the building would be reported on the balance sheet with the related asset account.

Plant assets and natural resources are tangible assets used by a company to produce revenues. A company may also acquire intangible assets to assist in producing revenues.

INTANGIBLE ASSETS

Intangible assets have no physical characteristics but are of value because of the advantages or exclusive privileges and rights they provide to a business. Intangible assets generally arise from two sources: (1) exclusive privileges granted by governmental authority or by legal contract, such as patents, copyrights, franchises, trademarks and trade names, and leases; and (2) superior entrepreneurial capacity or management know-how and customer loyalty, which is called *goodwill*.

All intangible assets are nonphysical, but not all nonphysical assets are classified as intangibles. For example, accounts receivable and prepaid expenses are nonphysical, but they are classified as current assets rather than intangible assets. Intangible assets are generally both nonphysical and noncurrent; they are reported in a separate long-term section of the balance sheet entitled "Intangible assets."

Acquisition of Intangible Assets

Objective 5
Prepare entries for the acquisition and amortization of intangible assets

Like most other assets, intangible assets are recorded initially at cost. However, computing an intangible asset's acquisition cost differs from computing a plant asset's acquisition cost. **Only outright purchase costs are included in the acquisition cost of an intangible asset;** the acquisition cost does **not** include cost of internal development or self-creation of the asset. If an intangible asset is internally generated in its entirety, none of its costs will be capitalized. Therefore, some companies have extremely valuable assets that may not even be recorded in their asset accounts. The reasons for this practice can be understood by studying the history of accounting for research and development costs.

Research and development (R&D) **costs** are costs incurred in a planned search for new knowledge and in translating such knowledge into new products or processes. Prior to 1975, research and development costs were often capitalized as intangible assets when future benefits were expected from their incurrence. Since it was often difficult to determine the costs applicable to future benefits, many companies expensed all such costs as they were incurred. Other companies capitalized those costs that related to proven products and expensed the rest as incurred.

As a result of these varied accounting practices, the Financial Accounting Standards Board in *Statement No. 2* in 1974 ruled that all research and development costs, other than those directly reimbursable by government agencies and others, must be expensed when incurred. Immediate expensing is justified on the grounds that (1) the amount of costs applicable to the future cannot be measured with any high degree of precision; (2) doubt exists as to whether any future benefits will be received; and (3) even if benefits are expected, they cannot be measured. Thus, research and development costs no longer appear as intangible assets on the balance sheet. The same line of reasoning is applied to other costs associated with internally generated intangible assets, such as the internal costs of developing a patent.

**Amortization of
Intangible Assets**

Amortization is the systematic write-off of the cost of an intangible asset to expense. A portion of an intangible asset's cost is allocated to each accounting period in the economic (useful) life of the asset. All intangible assets are subject to amortization, which is similar to plant asset depreciation. Generally, amortization is recorded by debiting Amortization Expense and crediting the intangible asset account. An accumulated amortization account could be used to record amortization. However, usually the information gained from such accounting would not be significant because intangibles do not normally account for as significant an amount of total asset dollars as do plant assets.

Intangibles should be amortized over the shorter of (1) their economic life, (2) their legal life, or (3) 40 years. The 40-year limitation was established by the Accounting Principles Board. *APB Opinion No. 17* requires an intangible asset acquired after October 31, 1970, to be amortized over a period not to exceed 40 years. Straight-line amortization must be used unless another method of amortization (such as units-of-production) can be shown to be superior. Straight-line amortization is calculated in the same way as straight-line depreciation for plant assets.

Patents

A patent is a right granted by the federal government giving the owner the exclusive right to manufacture, sell, lease, or otherwise benefit from an invention for a limited period of time. The value of a patent lies in its ability to produce revenue. Patents have a legal life of 17 years. Protection for the patent owner begins at the time of patent application and lasts for 17 years from the date the patent is granted.

The purchase of a patent should be recorded in the Patents account at cost. The Patents account should also be debited for the cost of the **first** successful defense of the patent in lawsuits (assuming an outside law firm was hired rather than using internal legal staff). Also, the cost of any competing patents that were purchased to ensure revenue-generating capability of the purchased patent should be debited to the Patents account.

The cost of a purchased patent should be amortized over the shorter of 17 years (or remaining legal life) or its estimated useful life. If a patent cost $40,000 and has a useful life of 10 years, the journal entries to record the patent and periodic amortization are:

Patents	40,000	
Cash		40,000
To record purchase of patent.		
Patent Amortization Expense	4,000	
Patents		4,000
To record patent amortization.		

If the patent becomes worthless before it is fully amortized, the unamortized balance in the Patents account should be charged to expense.

As noted on page 533 in the discussion on research and development costs, all R&D costs incurred in the internal development of a product, process, or idea that is later patented must be expensed, rather than capitalized. In the above example, the cost of the purchased patent was amortized over its useful life of 10 years. If the patent had been the result of an internally generated product or process, its cost of $40,000 would have been expensed as incurred, in accordance with *Statement No. 2* of the Financial Accounting Standards Board.

Copyrights

A copyright is an exclusive right granted by the federal government giving the owner protection against the illegal reproduction by others of the owner's written works, designs, and literary productions. The copyright period is for the life of the creator plus 50 years. Since most publications have a limited life, the cost of the copyright may appropriately be charged to expense on a straight-line basis over the life of the first edition published or based on projections of the number of copies to be sold per year.

Franchises

A franchise is a contract between two parties granting the franchisee (the purchaser of the franchise) certain rights and privileges ranging from name identification to complete monopoly of service. In many instances, both parties are private businesses. For example, an individual who wishes to open a hamburger restaurant may purchase a McDonald's franchise; the two parties involved are the individual business owner and McDonald's Corporation. This franchise would allow the business owner to use the McDonald's golden arch, and would provide the owner with advertising and many other benefits. The legal life of a franchise may be limited by contract.

The parties involved in a franchise arrangement are not always private businesses. A franchise may also be granted to a private company by a government agency. A city may give a franchise to a utility company, giving the utility company the exclusive right to provide service to a particular area.

In addition to providing benefits, a franchise usually places certain restrictions on the franchisee. These restrictions are generally related to rates or prices charged; they may also be in regard to product quality or to the particular supplier from whom supplies and inventory items must be purchased.

If periodic payments to the grantor of the franchise are required, they should be debited to a Franchise Expense account. If a lump-sum payment is made to obtain the franchise, the cost should be recorded in an asset account entitled Franchise and amortized over the shorter of the legal life (if limited by contract), the economic life of the franchise, or 40 years.

Trademarks; Trade Names

A trademark is a symbol, design, or logo that is used in conjunction with a particular product or company. A trade name is a brand name under which a product is sold or a company does business. Often trademarks and trade names are extremely valuable to a company, but if they have been internally developed, they will have no recorded asset cost. However, if such items are purchased by a business from an external source, they are recorded at cost and amortized over their economic life or 40 years, whichever is shorter.

Leases

A lease is a contract to rent property. The owner of the property is the grantor of the lease and is called the **lessor.** The person or company obtaining rights to possess and use the property is called the **lessee.** The rights granted under the lease are called a leasehold. The accounting for a lease depends on whether it is a capital lease or an operating lease.

Capital Leases A capital lease transfers to the lessee virtually all rewards and risks that accompany ownership of property. A lease is a capital lease if, among other provisions, it (1) transfers ownership of the leased property to the lessee at the end of the lease term or (2) contains a bargain purchase option that permits the lessee to buy the property at a price significantly below fair value at the end of the lease term.

A capital lease is a means of financing property acquisitions and has the same economic impact as a purchase made on an installment plan. Thus, the lessee in a capital lease must record the leased property as an asset and the lease obligation as a liability. Because a capital lease is an asset, the leased property is depreciated over its useful life to the lessee. A part of each lease payment is recorded as interest expense, with the balance viewed as a payment on the lease liability.

The proper accounting for capital leases for both lessees and lessors has been an extremely difficult problem. Further discussion of capital leases is left for an intermediate accounting text.

Operating Leases If a lease does not qualify as a capital lease, it is an operating lease. A one-year lease on an apartment and a week's rental of an automobile are examples of operating leases. Such leases make no attempt to transfer any of the rewards and risks of ownership to the lessee. As a result, there may be no record-able transaction when a lease is signed.

In some situations, the lease may call for an immediate cash payment that must be recorded. Assume, for example, that a business signed a lease that required the immediate payment of the annual rent of $15,000 for each of the first and fifth years of a five-year lease. The lessee would record the payment as follows:

Prepaid Rent	15,000	
Leasehold	15,000	
Cash		30,000
To record first and fifth years' rent on a five-year lease.		

Since the Leasehold account is actually a long-term prepaid rent account for the fifth year's annual rent, it is classified as an intangible asset until the beginning of the fifth year. Then the Leasehold account is reclassified as a current asset. Accounting for the balance in the Leasehold account depends on the terms of the lease. In the above example, the $15,000 in the Leasehold account will be charged to expense over the fifth year only. The balance in Prepaid Rent will be charged to expense in the first year. Thus, assuming the lease year and fiscal year coincide, the entry for the first year is:

Rent Expense	15,000	
Prepaid Rent		15,000
To record rent expense.		

The entry in the fifth year is:

Rent Expense	15,000	
Leasehold		15,000
To record rent expense.		

The accounting for the second, third, and fourth years will be the same as for the first year. The rent will be recorded in Prepaid Rent when paid in advance for the year and then expensed. The amount in the Leasehold account may be transferred to Prepaid Rent at the beginning of the fifth year by debiting Prepaid Rent and crediting Leasehold. If this entry was made, the credit in the above entry would have been to Prepaid Rent.

In some cases, when a lease is signed, a lump-sum payment is paid that does not cover a specific year's rent. This payment is debited to the Leasehold account and amortized over the life of the lease. The straight-line method is required unless another method can be shown to be superior. Assume the $15,000 rent for the fifth year in the above example was, instead, a lump-sum payment on the lease in addition to the annual rent payments. An annual adjusting entry to amortize the $15,000 over five years is required. The entry would read:

Rent Expense.	3,000	
Leasehold		3,000
To amortize leasehold.		

In this example, the annual rental expense is $18,000: $15,000 annual cash rent plus $3,000 amortization of leasehold ($15,000/5).

Periodic rent may be based on current-year sales or usage rather than being a constant amount. For example, if a lease called for rent equal to 5% of current-year sales and sales were $400,000 in 1994, the rent for 1994 would be $20,000. The rent would either be paid or adjusted to the correct amount at the end of the year.

Leasehold Improvements

A leasehold improvement is any physical alteration made by the lessee to the leased property in which benefits are expected beyond the current accounting period. Leasehold improvements made by a lessee usually become the property of the lessor after the lease has expired. However, since leasehold improvements are an asset of the lessee during the lease period, they should be debited to a Leasehold Improvements account. Leasehold improvements are then amortized to expense over the period of time benefited by the improvements. The amortization period for leasehold improvements should be the shorter of the life of the improvements or the life of the lease. If the lease can (and probably will) be renewed at the option of the lessee, the option period should be included in the life of the lease.

As an illustration, assume that on January 2, 1994, Wolf Company leases a building for 20 years under a nonrenewable lease at an annual rental of $20,000, payable on each December 31. Wolf immediately incurs a cost of $80,000 for improvements to the building, such as interior walls for office separation, ceiling fans, and recessed lighting. The improvements have an estimated life of 30 years. The $80,000 should be amortized over the 20-year lease period, since that period is shorter than the life of the improvements, and Wolf will not be able to use the improvements beyond the life of the lease. If only annual financial statements are prepared, the following journal entry will properly record the rental expense for the year ended December 31, 1994:

Rent Expense (or Leasehold Improvement Expense)	4,000	
Leasehold Improvements		4,000
To record amortization of leasehold improvement.		
Rent Expense.	20,000	
Cash.		20,000
To record annual rent.		

Thus, the total cost to rent the building each year equals the $20,000 cash rent plus the amortization of the leasehold improvements.

Although leaseholds are intangible assets, leaseholds and leasehold improvements are sometimes shown in the property, plant, and equipment section of the balance sheet.

Goodwill   In accounting, goodwill is an intangible value attached to a company resulting mainly from the company's management skill or know-how and a favorable reputation with customers. A company's value may be greater than the total of the fair market value of its tangible and identifiable intangible assets. This greater value means that the company is able to generate an above-average income on each dollar invested in the business. Thus, proof of the existence of goodwill for a company can be found only in its ability to generate superior earnings or income.

A Goodwill account will appear in the accounting records only if goodwill has been purchased. Goodwill cannot be purchased by itself; an entire business or a part of a business must be purchased to obtain the accompanying intangible asset, goodwill.

To illustrate, assume that Lenox Company purchased all of Martin Company's assets for $700,000. Lenox also agrees to assume responsibility for a $350,000 mortgage note payable owed by Martin. Goodwill is determined as the difference between the amount paid for the business including the debt assumed ($700,000 + $350,000 = $1,050,000) and the **fair market value** of the assets purchased. Notice that fair market value of the assets rather than book value is used to determine the amount of goodwill. The following shows the computation for the amount of goodwill purchased by Lenox:

Cash paid		$ 700,000
Mortgage note payable assumed		350,000
Total price paid		$1,050,000
Less fair market values of individually identifiable assets:		
Accounts receivable	$ 95,000	
Merchandise inventory	100,000	
Land	240,000	
Buildings	275,000	
Equipment	200,000	
Patents	65,000	975,000
Goodwill		$ 75,000

The $75,000 is the amount of goodwill to be recorded as an intangible asset on the books of Lenox Company; **all the other assets will be recorded at their fair market value,** and the liability will be recorded at the amount due. Specific reasons for the existence of goodwill in a company might include good reputation, customer loyalty, superior product design, unrecorded intangible assets (because they were developed internally), and superior human resources. Since these positive factors are not individually quantifiable, they are all grouped together and referred to as *goodwill*. The journal entry to record this purchase is:

Accounts Receivable.	95,000	
Merchandise inventory.	100,000	
Land	240,000	
Buildings	275,000	
Equipment	200,000	
Patents	65,000	
Goodwill	75,000	
Cash.		700,000
Mortgage Note Payable		350,000
To record the purchase of Martin Company's assets and assumption of mortgage note payable.		

ETHICS

A CLOSER LOOK

The ABC Corporation acquired the XYZ Company for $10,000,000 cash. The following assets were acquired:

Accounts receivable		$80,000

	Old Book Value	Fair Market Value
Merchandise inventory	$ 200,000	$ 300,000
Buildings	3,000,000	4,000,000
Land	1,000,000	3,000,000
Equipment	500,000	700,000

The fair market values of the assets were established by an experienced appraiser with an excellent reputation. ABC also assumed the liability for paying XYZ's $50,000 of accounts payable.

John Gilbert, the company's accountant, prepared the following journal entry to record the purchase:

Accounts Receivable	80,000	
Merchandise Inventory	300,000	
Buildings	4,000,000	
Land	3,000,000	
Equipment	700,000	
Goodwill	1,970,000	
Accounts Payable		50,000
Cash		10,000,000
To record the purchase of XYZ Company.		

In explaining the entry to the president, John informed him that the assets had to be recorded at their fair market values. He also stated that the goodwill had to be amortized over a period not to exceed 40 years for accounting purposes, but that the goodwill could not be amortized for tax purposes.

The president reacted with, "It's not fair that we are prohibited from amortizing goodwill for tax purposes when it is a part of the cost of the purchase. Besides, appraisals are very inexact, and maybe some of our other assets are worth more than the one appraiser indicated. I want you to reduce goodwill down to $470,000 and assign the other $1,500,000 to the buildings and equipment. Then, we can benefit from the depreciation on these assets. If I need to find an appraiser who will support the new allocations, I will." When John protested, the president stated, "If you are going to have a future with us, you need to be a team player. We just can't afford to lose those tax deductions."

John feared that if he did not "go along," he would soon be unemployed.

Required

a. What are the possible consequences for John in this situation depending on his actions?

b. Assuming that the president cannot find another appraiser to support the new allocations, what would you do if you were John?

c. If the president can find a reputable appraiser to support these new allocations, what would you do if you were John?

ILLUSTRATION 11.2

Intangible Assets Held by Sample of 600 Companies

Assets Being Amortized	Number of Companies			
	1989	**1988**	**1987**	**1986**
Goodwill recognized in a business combination . . .	367	340	338	312
Patents, patent rights.	62	67	59	63
Trademarks, brand names, copyrights	38	41	34	39
Software	27	23	27	18
Licenses, franchises, memberships	19	22	26	23
Other—described	52	47	20	27
Intangible assets (not otherwise described)	56	37	37	35

Source: American Institute of Certified Public Accountants, *Accounting Trends & Techniques* (New York: AICPA, 1990), p. 133.

Goodwill, like all other intangibles, must be amortized. No legal life exists for goodwill, and the useful life of goodwill usually cannot be reasonably estimated. If, for example, the new owner made substantial changes in the method of doing business, goodwill that existed at the purchase date could rapidly disappear. Therefore, current accounting practice requires the amortization of goodwill over a period not to exceed 40 years. This requirement is necessary because the value of purchased goodwill will eventually disappear. Other goodwill may be generated in its place, but the organization cannot record its internally created goodwill any more than it can record other internally generated intangible assets.

The entry to amortize the $75,000 goodwill over a 40-year period is:

Goodwill Amortization Expense	1,875	
Goodwill		1,875
To amortize goodwill ($75,000/40 years).		

Reporting Amortization

Illustration 11.2 shows the frequencies of intangible assets being amortized by a sample of 600 companies for the years 1986–89.

Amortization expense for most intangible assets discussed in this chapter appears among the operating expenses on the income statement. The account titles used are all of this type: "Amortization of Goodwill (or Patents, Copyrights, Franchises, Leaseholds) Expense." Periodic amortization of leaseholds and leasehold improvements is often reported as rent expense. The amortization of goodwill is an expense in determining accounting income but is not a deductible expense in determining taxable income.

Illustration 11.3 summarizes the amortization rules for intangible assets.

Balance Sheet Presentation

Illustration 11.4 shows the extended balance sheet for Reed Company in Illustration 10.9. Unlike plant assets or natural resources, intangible assets are usually presented at a net amount in the balance sheet.

This chapter concludes your study of accounting for long-term assets. In Chapter 12, you will learn about accounting theory and international accounting. With the developing global economy, international accounting takes on increased importance.

ILLUSTRATION 11.3

Rules for Amortization of Intangible Assets

		Amortized over Shorter of	
Intangible Asset	**Useful Life**	**Legal Life**	**Maximum Life (years)**
Patents	?	17 years	40
Copyrights	?	Life of author plus 50 years	40
Franchises	?	No limit (unless limited by contract)	40
Trademarks; trade names	?	No limit	40
Leasehold improvements	?	Life of lease	40
Goodwill	?	No limit	40

ILLUSTRATION 11.4

Partial Balance Sheet

REED COMPANY
Partial Balance Sheet
June 30, 1994

Property, plant, and equipment:		
Land		$ 30,000
Buildings.	$ 75,000	
Less: Accumulated depreciation	45,000	30,000
Equipment	$ 9,000	
Less: Accumulated depreciation	1,500	7,500
Total property, plant, and equipment . . .		$ 67,500
Natural resources:		
Mineral deposits	$300,000	
Less: Accumulated depletion	100,000	$200,000
Total natural resources		$200,000
Intangible assets:		
Patents		$ 10,000
Goodwill		20,000
Total intangible assets.		$ 30,000

UNDERSTANDING THE LEARNING OBJECTIVES

1. Calculate and prepare entries for the sale, retirement, and destruction of plant assets.

    □ By comparing an asset's book value (cost less accumulated depreciation) with its sales price, the company will show either a gain or a loss. If sales price is greater than book value, the company will show a gain. If sales price is less than book value, the company will show a loss.

    □ When a plant asset is retired from service, the asset's cost and accumulated depreciation must be removed from the plant asset accounts.

    □ Plant assets are sometimes wrecked in accidents or destroyed by fire, flood, storm, and other causes. Losses are normally incurred in such situations. If the asset was insured, only the amount of the loss exceeding the amount to be recovered from the insurance company would be debited to the loss account.

2. Describe and record exchanges of dissimilar and similar plant assets.
   □ In exchanges of dissimilar assets, the asset received is recorded at either (1) the stated cash price of the new asset or (2) the known fair value of the asset given up plus any cash paid.
   □ In exchanges of similar assets, the new asset is recorded at (1) the cash price of the asset received or (2) the book value of the old asset plus the cash paid, whichever is lower.

3. Discuss the differences between accounting principles and tax rules in the treatment of gains and losses from the exchange of plant assets.
   □ When dissimilar assets are exchanged, gains and losses are recognized for both accounting and tax purposes.
   □ When similar assets are exchanged, losses are recognized for accounting purposes, but gains are not. For income tax purposes, neither gains nor losses are recognized; the new asset is recorded at the book value of the old asset plus any cash paid.

4. Determine the periodic depletion cost of a natural resource and calculate depreciation of plant assets located on extractive industry property.
   □ Depletion charges usually are computed by the units-of-production method. Total cost is divided by the estimated number of units that are economically extractable from the property. This calculation provides a per unit depletion cost that is multiplied by the units extracted each year to obtain the depletion cost for that year.
   □ Depreciable assets located on extractive industry property should be depreciated over the shorter of the (a) physical life of the asset or (b) life of the natural resource. The periodic depreciation charges usually are computed using the units-of-production method. Using this method matches the life of the plant asset with the life of the natural resource.

5. Prepare entries for the acquisition and amortization of intangible assets.
   □ Only outright purchase costs are included in the acquisition cost of an intangible asset. If an intangible asset is internally generated, it is immediately expensed.
   □ Intangibles should be amortized over the shorter of (1) their economic life, (2) their legal life, or (3) 40 years. Straight-line amortization must be used unless another method can be shown to be superior.

DEMONSTRATION PROBLEM 11-A

On January 2, 1991, Datron Company purchased a machine for $36,000 cash. The machine has an estimated useful life of six years and an estimated salvage value of $1,800. The straight-line method of depreciation is being used.

Required   a. Compute the book value of the machine as of July 1, 1994.

b. Assume the machine was disposed of on July 1, 1994. Prepare the journal entries to record the disposal of the machine under each of the following unrelated assumptions:
   1. The machine was sold for $12,000 cash.
   2. The machine was sold for $18,000 cash.

3. The machine and $24,000 cash were exchanged for a new machine that had a cash price of $39,000. Use the accounting method rather than the income tax method.

4. The machine was completely destroyed by fire. Cash of $10,800 is expected to be recovered from the insurance company.

SOLUTION TO DEMONSTRATION PROBLEM 11–A

a.

DATRON COMPANY
Schedule to Compute Book Value
July 1, 1994

Cost $36,000

Less accumulated depreciation:

$$\frac{\$36,000 - \$1,800}{6 \text{ years}} = \$5,700 \text{ per year}$$

$5,700 × 3½ years = $19,950 19,950

Book value $16,050

b.

1. Cash 12,000
    Accumulated Depreciation—Machinery 19,950
    Loss from Disposal of Plant Assets. 4,050
        Machinery. 36,000
    To record sale of machinery at a loss.

2. Cash 18,000
    Accumulated Depreciation—Machinery 19,950
        Machinery. 36,000
        Gain on Disposal of Plant Assets. 1,950
    To record sale of machinery at a gain.

3. Machinery (new) 39,000
    Accumulated Depreciation—Machinery 19,950
    Loss from Disposal of Plant Assets. 1,050
        Machinery (old). 36,000
        Cash 24,000
    To record exchange of machines.

4. Receivable from Insurance Company 10,800
    Accumulated Depreciation—Machinery 19,950
    Fire Loss 5,250
        Machinery. 36,000
    To record loss of machinery.

DEMONSTRATION PROBLEM 11–B

Hewlett Company acquired on January 1, 1994, a tract of property containing timber at a cost of $8,000,000. After the timber is removed, the land will be worth about $3,200,000 and will be sold to another party. Costs of developing the site were $800,000. A building was erected at a cost of $160,000. The building had an estimated physical life of 20 years and will have an estimated salvage value of $80,000 when the timber is gone. It was expected that 50,000,000 board feet of timber can be economically cut. During the first year, 16,000,000 board feet were cut. The units-of-production basis is used to depreciate the building.

Required   Prepare the entries to record:

    a. The acquisition of the property.

    b. The development costs.

    c. Depletion costs for the first year.

    d. Depreciation on the building for the first year.

SOLUTION TO DEMONSTRATION PROBLEM 11–B

a.	Land	3,200,000	
	Timber Stands	4,800,000	
	Cash		8,000,000
	To record purchase of land and timber.		
b.	Timber Stands	800,000	
	Cash		800,000
	To record costs of development of the site.		
c.	Depletion	1,792,000	
	Accumulated Depreciation—Timber Stands		1,792,000
	To record depletion for 1994:		
	($4,800,000 + $800,000)/50,000,000 = $0.112 per board foot.		
	$0.112 × 16,000,000 = $1,792,000.		
d.	Depreciation Expense—Buildings	25,600	
	Accumulated Depreciation—Buildings		25,600
	To record depreciation expense:		

$$\frac{\$160,000 - \$80,000}{50,000,000 \text{ board feet}} = \$0.0016 \text{ per board foot.}$$

$$\$0.0016 \times 16,000,000 = \$25,600$$

DEMONSTRATION PROBLEM 11–C

On January 2, 1994, Beresford Company purchased a 10-year sublease on a warehouse for $30,000. Beresford will also pay annual rent of $6,000. Beresford immediately incurred costs of $20,000 for improvements to the warehouse, such as lighting fixtures, replacement of a ceiling, heating system, and loading dock. The improvements have an estimated life of 12 years and no residual value.

Required   Prepare the entries to record:

    a. The payment for the sublease on a warehouse.

    b. The rent payment for the first year.

    c. The payment for the improvements.

    d. Amortization of the leasehold for the first year.

    e. Amortization of the leasehold improvements for the first year.

SOLUTION TO DEMONSTRATION PROBLEM 11–C

a. Leasehold 30,000
      Cash 30,000
    To record purchase of sublease on warehouse.

b. Rent Expense 6,000
      Cash 6,000
    To record annual rent.

c. Leasehold Improvements 20,000
      Cash 20,000
    To record payment for leasehold improvement.

d. Rent Expense 3,000
      Leasehold 3,000
    To record leasehold amortization for 1994:

$$\text{Annual amortization} = \frac{\$30,000}{10 \text{ years}}$$
$$= \$3,000$$

e. Rent Expense 2,000
      Leasehold Improvements 2,000
    To amortize leasehold improvement:

$$\text{Annual amortization} = \frac{\$20,000}{10 \text{ years}}$$
$$= \$2,000$$

NEW TERMS

Amortization The term used to describe the systematic write-off of the cost of an intangible asset to expense. *534*

Boot The additional cash outlay made when one asset is exchanged for a similar one. *527*

Capital lease A lease that transfers to the lessee virtually all of the rewards and risks that accompany ownership of property. *535*

Copyright An exclusive right granted by the federal government giving the owner protection against the illegal reproduction by others of the owner's written works, designs, and literary productions. *535*

Depletion The exhaustion of a natural resource; an estimate of the cost of the resource that was removed from its natural setting during the period. *529*

Franchise A contract between two parties granting the franchisee (the purchaser of the franchise) certain rights and privileges ranging from name identification to complete monopoly of service. *535*

Goodwill An intangible value attached to a company resulting mainly from the company's management skill or know-how and a favorable reputation with customers. Evidenced by the ability to generate an above-average rate of income on each dollar invested in the business. *538*

Intangible assets Items that have no physical characteristics but are of value because of the advantages or exclusive privileges and rights they provide to a business. *533*

Lease A contract to rent property. Grantor of the lease is the **lessor;** the party obtaining the rights to possess and use property is the **lessee.** *535*

Leasehold The rights granted under a lease. *535*

Leasehold improvement Any physical alteration made by the lessee to the leased property in which benefits are expected beyond the current accounting period. *537*

Natural resources Ore deposits, mineral deposits, oil reserves, gas deposits, and timber stands supplied by nature. *528*

Operating lease A lease that does not qualify as a capital lease. *536*

Patent A right granted by the federal government giving the owner the exclusive right to manufacture, sell, lease, or otherwise benefit from an invention for a limited period of time. *534*

Research and development (R&D) costs Costs incurred in a planned search for new knowledge and in translating such knowledge into a new product or process. *533*

Trademark A symbol, design, or logo that is used in conjunction with a particular product or company. *535*

Trade name A brand name under which a product is sold or a company does business. *535*

Wasting assets See Natural resources.

SELF-TEST

True-False

Indicate whether each of the following statements is true or false.

1. When a plant asset is sold or otherwise disposed of, depreciation should be recorded up to the date of sale or disposal.

2. In an exchange of similar assets, the new asset is recorded at the cash price of the asset received or the book value of the old asset plus the cash paid, whichever is lower.

3. A gain resulting from an exchange of similar assets is recognized for accounting purposes, but not for income tax purposes.

4. Depletion is recorded by directly crediting a natural resource asset.

5. Recorded goodwill may have been purchased by itself or developed internally like other intangible assets.

Multiple-Choice

Select the best answer for each of the following questions.

1. When a plant asset is used after it has been fully depreciated:
   a. Depreciation can be taken in excess of its cost.
   b. Part of the depreciation should be reserved.
   c. The cost and accumulated depreciation should remain in the ledger and no more depreciation should be taken.
   d. The cost should be adjusted to market value.
   e. The cost and accumulated depreciation should be removed from the books.

2. A computer costing $3,000 and having an estimated salvage value of $300 and an original life of five years is exchanged for a new computer. The cash price of the new computer is $4,000, and a trade-in allowance of $1,000 is received. The old computer has been depreciated for three years using the straight-line method. The new computer would be recorded at:
   a. $4,380.
   b. $2,380.
   c. $3,000.
   d. $4,000.
   e. None of the above.

3. In Question 2, the gain or loss on the exchange under income tax rules would be:
   a. Loss of $380.
   b. Gain of $1,620.
   c. Gain of $1,000.
   d. Gain of $380.
   e. None of the above.

4. Land containing a mine having an estimated 2,000,000 tons of economically extractable ore is purchased for $500,000. After the ore deposit is removed, the land will be worth $100,000. If 200,000 tons of ore are mined and sold during the first year, the depletion cost charged to expense for the year is:
   a. $400,000.
   b. $50,000.
   c. $40,000.
   d. $500,000.
   e. None of the above.

5. Austin Company purchased a patent for $36,000. The patent is expected to have value for 8 years even though its legal life is 17 years. The amortization for the first year is:
   a. $36,000.
   b. $4,500.
   c. $2,118.
   d. $4,050.
   e. None of the above.

Now turn to page 555 to check your answers.

QUESTIONS

1. When depreciable plant assets are sold for cash, how is the gain or loss measured?

2. A plant asset that cost $15,000 and has a related accumulated depreciation account balance of $15,000 is still being used in business operations. Would it be appropriate to continue recording depreciation on this asset? Explain. When should the asset's cost and accumulated depreciation be removed from the accounting records?

3. A machine and $10,000 cash were exchanged for a delivery truck. How should the cost basis of the delivery truck be measured?

4. What circumstance requires that two sets of depreciation records be kept, one for accounting purposes and one for income tax purposes?

5. A plant asset was exchanged for a new asset of a similar type. How is the cost of the new asset determined for (a) accounting purposes and (b) income tax purposes?

6. When similar assets are exchanged, a resulting gain is not recognized. Justify this.

7. a. Distinguish between depreciation, depletion, and amortization. Name two assets that are subject to depreciation, to depletion, and to amortization.
   b. Distinguish between tangible and intangible assets, and classify the above-named assets in part (a) accordingly.

8. A building with an estimated physical life of 40 years was constructed at the site of a coal mine. The coal mine is expected to be completely exhausted within 20 years. Over what length of time should the building be depreciated, assuming the building will be abandoned after all the coal has been extracted?

9. What is the proper accounting treatment for the costs of removing or dismantling a company's old plant assets?

10. What are the characteristics of intangible assets? Give an example of an asset that has no physical existence but is not classified as an intangible asset.

11. What reasons justify the immediate expensing of most research and development costs?

12. Over what length of time should intangible assets be amortized?

13. If a franchise has an unlimited economic life, over what period should it be amortized?

14. Describe the typical accounting for a patent.

15. During 1994, Almay Company incurred $82,000 of research and development costs in its laboratory to develop a patent that was granted on December 29, 1994. Legal fees (outside counsel) and other costs associated with registration of the patent totaled $15,200. What amount should be recorded as a patent on December 29, 1994?

16. What is a capital lease? What features may characterize a capital lease?

17. What is the difference between a leasehold (under an operating lease contract) and a leasehold improvement? Is there any difference in the accounting procedures applicable to each?

18. Brush Company leased a tract of land for 40 years at an agreed annual rental fee of $10,000. The effective date of the lease was July 1, 1993. During the last six months of 1993, Brush constructed a building on the land at a cost of $250,000. The building was placed in operation on January 2, 1994, at which time it was estimated to have a physical life of 50 years. Over what period of time should the building be depreciated? Why?

19. You note that a certain store seems to have a steady stream of regular customers, a favorable location, courteous employees, high-quality merchandise, and a reputation for fairness in dealing with customers, employees, and suppliers. Does it follow automatically that this business should have goodwill recorded as an asset? Explain.

The Coca-Cola Company

20. *Real world question* From the consolidated balance sheet of The Coca-Cola Company in Appendix E, identify the 1989 intangible assets ending balance. What percentage increase does this amount represent over the 1988 ending balance and what percentage did the intangible assets balance represent of the 1988 and 1989 total assets?

MAYTAG CORPORATION

21. *Real world question* Based on the financial statements of Maytag Corporation contained in Appendix E, what was the 1989 allowance for amortization of intangibles?

EXERCISES

Exercise 11–1
Record sale of equipment; account for removal costs (L.O. 1)

Plant equipment originally costing $9,000, on which $6,000 of depreciation has been accumulated, was sold for $2,250.

a. Prepare the journal entry to record the sale.
b. Prepare the entry to record the sale of the equipment if $25 of removal costs were incurred to allow the equipment to be moved.

Exercise 11–2
Update depreciation and record sale of truck (L.O. 1)

On August 31, 1993, Drew Company sold a truck for $2,300 cash. The truck was acquired on January 1, 1990, at a cost of $5,800. Depreciation of $3,600 on the truck has been recorded through December 31, 1992, using the straight-line method, four-year expected useful life, and an expected salvage value of $1,000.

Prepare the journal entries to update the depreciation on the truck on August 31, 1993, and to record the sale of the truck.

Exercise 11–3

Record destruction of machinery by fire—uninsured and insured asset (L.O. 1)

A machine costing $32,000, on which $24,000 of depreciation has been accumulated, was completely destroyed by fire. What journal entry should be made to record the machine's destruction and the resulting fire loss under each of the following unrelated assumptions?

a.   The machine was *not* insured.

b.   The machine was insured, and it is estimated that $6,000 will be recovered from the insurance company.

Exercise 11–4

Record exchange of automobiles (L.O. 2)

Spivey Company owned an automobile acquired on January 1, 1991, at a cash cost of $18,720; at that time, the automobile was estimated to have a useful life of four years and a $1,440 salvage value. Depreciation has been recorded through December 31, 1993, on a straight-line basis. On January 1, 1994, the automobile was traded for a new automobile. The old automobile had a fair market value (trade-in allowance) of $3,600. Cash of $16,560 was paid. Prepare the journal entry to record the trade-in under generally accepted accounting principles.

Exercise 11–5

Record variety of cases involving sale, retirement, or exchange of equipment (L.O. 1–3)

Equipment costing $88,000, on which $60,000 of accumulated depreciation has been recorded, was disposed of on January 2, 1993. What journal entries are required to record the equipment's disposal under each of the following unrelated assumptions?

a.   The equipment was sold for $32,000 cash.

b.   The equipment was sold for $23,200 cash.

c.   The equipment was retired and hauled to the junkyard. No material was salvaged.

d.   The equipment was exchanged for similar equipment having a cash price of $120,000. A trade-in allowance of $40,000 from the cash price was received, and the balance was paid in cash.

e.   The equipment was exchanged for similar equipment having a cash price of $120,000. A trade-in allowance of $20,000 was received, and the balance was paid in cash. (Record this transaction twice—first for tax purposes, and second for financial reporting purposes.)

Exercise 11–6

Determine depletion cost and expense (L.O. 4)

Brown Company paid $2,000,000 for the right to extract all of the mineral-bearing ore, estimated at 5 million tons, that can be economically extracted from a certain tract of land. During the first year, Brown Company extracted 500,000 tons of the ore and sold 400,000 tons. What part of the $2,000,000 should be charged to expense during the first year?

Exercise 11–7

Compute periodic depletion cost per unit (L.O. 4)

College Mining Company purchased a tract of land containing ore for $350,000. After spending $50,000 in exploration costs, the company determined that 600,000 tons of ore existed on the tract but only 500,000 tons could be economically removed. No other costs were incurred. When the company finishes with the tract, it estimates the land will be worth $100,000. Determine the depletion cost per unit.

Exercise 11–8

Compute depreciation charge on plant asset (L.O. 4)

The Milano Mining Company acquired a tract of land for mining purposes and erected a building on-site at a cost of $300,000 and no salvage value. Though the building has a useful life of 10 years, the mining operations are expected to last only 6 years. The company has determined that 800,000 tons of ore exist on the tract but only 600,000 tons can be economically removed. If 100,000 tons of ore are extracted in the first year of operations, what is the appropriate depreciation charge, using the units-of-production method?

Exercise 11–9

Determine patent cost and periodic amortization (L.O. 5)

Mulkey Company purchased a patent on January 1, 1979, at a total cost of $17,000. In January 1990, the company hired an outside law firm and successfully defended the patent in a lawsuit. The legal fees amounted to $3,750. What will be the amount of patent cost amortized in 1993? (The useful life of the patent is the same as its legal life—17 years.)

Exercise 11–10

Record franchise; record accrued franchise fees and franchise amortization (L.O. 5)

Bob Martin paid Hungry Hank's Hamburgers $30,000 for the right to operate a fast-food restaurant in Gordonville under the Hungry Hank's name. Bob also agreed to pay an operating fee of 0.5% of sales for advertising and other services rendered by Hungry Hank's. Bob began operations on January 2, 1993. Sales for 1993 amounted to $300,000.

Give the entries needed to record the payment of the $30,000 and to record expenses incurred relating to the right to use the Hungry Hank's name.

Exercise 11–11

Record leasehold; record rent accrued and leasehold amortization (L.O. 5)

Pratt Company leased the first three floors in a building under an operating lease contract for a 10-year period beginning January 1, 1993. The company paid $64,000 in cash (not representing a specific period's rent) and agreed to make annual payments equal to 1% of the first $400,000 of sales and 0.5% of all sales over $400,000. Sales for 1993 amounted to $1,200,000. Payment of the annual amount will be made in January 1994.

Prepare journal entries to record the cash payment of January 1, 1993, and the proper expense to be recognized for the use of the space in the leased building for 1993.

Exercise 11–12

Determine amount of goodwill (L.O. 5)

Lark Company purchased all of the assets of Edson Company for $500,000. Lark Company also agreed to assume responsibility for Edson Company's liabilities of $50,000. The fair market value of the assets acquired was $450,000. How much goodwill should be recorded in this transaction?

PROBLEMS: SERIES A

Problem 11–1A

Update depreciation and record sale of typewriter (L.O. 1)

On January 1, 1991, Barrett Company purchased an electronic typewriter for $14,100 cash. The typewriter has a useful life of five years and an expected salvage value of $600; it is being depreciated annually under the straight-line method. The company spent $360 to clean and adjust the typewriter on February 2, 1994, and sold the typewriter on August 1, 1994, for $3,000.

Required

Prepare journal entries to record the above data for 1994, assuming Barrett Company has a calendar-year accounting period.

Problem 11–2A

Update depreciation and record exchange of automobiles under GAAP (L.O. 1, 2)

Rice, Inc., purchased a new 1994 model automobile on December 31, 1994. The cash price of the new automobile was $7,800, from which Rice received a trade-in allowance of $1,200 for a 1992 model traded in. The 1992 model had been acquired on January 1, 1992, at a cost of $5,750. Depreciation has been recorded on the 1992 model through December 31, 1993, using the straight-line method, an expected four-year useful life, and an expected salvage value of $750.

Required

a. Record depreciation expense for 1994.

b. Prepare the journal entries needed to record the exchange of automobiles using the method required under generally accepted accounting principles.

Problem 11–3A

Update depreciation and record six cases of asset disposal (L.O. 1, 2)

On January 1, 1991, Kent Company purchased a truck for $24,000 cash. The truck has an estimated useful life of six years and an expected salvage value of $3,000. Depreciation on the truck was computed using the straight-line method.

Required

a. Prepare a schedule showing the computation of the book value of the truck on December 31, 1993.

b. Prepare the journal entry to record depreciation for the six months ended June 30, 1994.

c. Prepare journal entries to record the disposal of the truck on June 30, 1994, under each of the following unrelated assumptions:

 1. The truck was sold for $2,000 cash.
 2. The truck was sold for $14,000 cash.
 3. The truck was scrapped. Used parts valued at $3,700 were salvaged.
 4. The truck (which has a fair market value of $6,000) and $18,000 of cash were exchanged for a used back hoe that did not have a known market value.
 5. The truck and $16,500 cash were exchanged for another truck that had a cash price of $28,500.
 6. The truck was stolen July 1, and insurance proceeds of $4,200 were expected.

Problem 11–4A

Update depreciation and record exchange of plant asset for similar asset (L.O. 2, 3)

Roberts Company purchased a new Model II computer on October 1, 1993. Cash price of the new computer was $66,560; Roberts received a trade-in allowance of $24,800 from the cash price for a Model I computer. The old computer was acquired on January 1, 1991, at a cost of $61,440. Depreciation has been recorded through December 31, 1992, on a straight-line basis, with an estimated useful life of four years and $10,240 expected salvage value.

Required *a.* Prepare the journal entries needed to record the exchange using the income tax method.

b. Repeat part *(a)* applying generally accepted accounting principles.

Problem 11–5A
Record leasehold amortization; record depreciation and trade-in (L.O. 2, 5)

On July 1, 1993, Rivers Company had the following balances in its plant asset and accumulated depreciation accounts:

	Asset	Accumulated Depreciation
Land	$ 560,000	
Leasehold	210,000	
Buildings	2,626,400	$308,140
Equipment	1,142,400	364,000
Trucks	198,800	59,710

Additional data

1. The leasehold covers a plot of ground leased on July 1, 1988, for a period of 25 years under an operating lease.

2. The office building is on the leased land and was completed on July 1, 1989, at a cost of $806,400; its physical life is set at 40 years. The factory building is on the owned land and was completed on July 1, 1988, at a cost of $1,820,000; its life is also set at 40 years with no expected salvage value.

3. The equipment has a 15-year useful life with no expected salvage value.

4. The company owns three trucks—A, B, and C. Truck A, purchased on July 1, 1991, at a cost of $44,800, had an expected useful life of three years and a salvage value of $2,800. Truck B, purchased on January 2, 1992, at a cost of $70,000, had an expected life of four years and a salvage value of $5,600. Truck C, purchased on January 2, 1993, at a cost of $84,000, had an expected life of five years and a salvage value of $8,400.

The following transactions occurred in the fiscal year ended June 30, 1994:

1993
July 1 Rent for July 1, 1993, through June 30, 1994, on leased land was paid, $26,600.
Oct. 1 Truck A was traded in on truck D. Cash price of the new truck was $89,600. Cash of $75,600 was paid. Truck D has an expected life of four years and a salvage value of $4,900.

1994
Feb. 2 Truck B was sold for $39,200 cash.
June 1 Truck C was completely demolished in an accident. The truck was not insured.

Required Prepare journal entries to record the above transactions and the necessary June 30, 1994, adjusting entries. Use the straight-line depreciation method.

Problem 11–6A
Determine depletion for period and depreciation on building and mining equipment; compute average cost per ton of ore mined (L.O. 4)

In December 1992, Tanner Company acquired a mine for $1,125,000. The mine contained an estimated 5 million tons of ore. It was also estimated that the land would have a value of $100,000 when the mine was exhausted and that only 2 million tons of ore could be economically extracted. A building was erected on the property at a cost of $150,000. The building had an estimated useful life of 35 years and no salvage value. Specialized mining equipment was installed at a cost of $206,250. This equipment had an estimated useful life of seven years and an estimated $13,750 salvage value. The company began operating on January 1, 1993, and put all of its assets into use on that date. During the year ended December 31, 1993, 200,000 tons of ore were extracted. The company decided to use the units-of-production method to record depreciation on the building and the straight-line method to record depreciation on the equipment.

Required Prepare journal entries to record the depletion and depreciation charges for the year ended December 31, 1993. Show calculations.

Problem 11–7A

Record cost and amortization of patent
(L.O. 5)

Houston Company purchased a patent for $90,000 on January 2, 1993. The patent was estimated to have a useful life of 10 years. The $90,000 cost was properly charged to an asset account and amortized in 1993. On January 1, 1994, the company incurred legal and court costs of $27,000 in a successful defense of the patent in a lawsuit. The legal work was performed by an outside law firm.

Required

a. Compute the patent amortization expense for 1993 and give the entry to record it.

b. Compute the patent amortization expense for 1994 and give the entry to record it.

Problem 11–8A

Record amortization expense for a variety of intangible assets
(L.O. 5)

Given below are selected transactions and other data for Davis Company:

a. The company purchased a patent in early January 1990 for $60,000 and began amortizing it over 10 years. In 1992, the company hired an outside law firm and successfully defended the patent in an infringement suit at a cost of $16,000.

b. Research and development costs incurred in 1992 of $18,000 were expected to provide benefits over the three succeeding years.

c. On January 2, 1993, the company rented space in a warehouse for five years at an annual fee of $4,000. Rent for the first and last years was paid in advance.

d. A total of $40,000 was spent uniformly throughout 1993 by the company in promoting its lesser known trademark, which is expected to have an indefinite life.

e. In January 1991, the company purchased all of the assets and assumed all of the liabilities of another company, paying $80,000 more than the fair market value of all identifiable assets acquired, less the liabilities assumed. The company expects the benefits for which it paid the $80,000 to last 10 years.

Required

For each of the unrelated transactions given above, prepare journal entries to record only those entries required for 1993. Note any items that do not require an entry in 1993.

PROBLEMS: SERIES B

Problem 11–1B

Update depreciation and record sale of truck
(L.O. 1)

On July 31, 1993, Krane Company sold a truck for $3,920 cash. The truck was acquired on January 1, 1990, at a cost of $18,560; depreciation has been recorded on the truck through December 31, 1992, using the straight-line method, a four-year useful life, and $3,200 expected salvage value.

Required

Prepare all entries needed to record the above information for the year 1993.

Problem 11–2B

Record exchange of automobiles under GAAP and tax regulations
(L.O. 2)

Ray Company traded in an automobile that cost $18,000 and on which $15,000 of depreciation has been recorded for a new automobile with a cash price of $34,500. The company received a trade-in allowance (its fair value) for the old automobile of $2,100 and paid the balance in cash.

Required

a. Record the exchange of the automobiles applying generally accepted accounting principles.

b. Record the exchange of the automobiles applying federal income tax regulations.

Problem 11–3B

Update depreciation and record six cases of asset disposal
(L.O. 1, 2)

On January 2, 1991, Blake Company purchased a delivery truck for $105,000 cash. The truck has an estimated useful life of six years and an estimated salvage value of $9,000. The straight-line method of depreciation is being used.

Required

a. Prepare a schedule showing the computation of the book value of the truck on December 31, 1993.

b. Assume the truck is to be disposed of on July 1, 1994. What journal entry is required to record depreciation for the six months ended June 30, 1994?

c. Prepare the journal entries to record the disposal of the truck on July 1, 1994, under each of the following unrelated assumptions:
1. The truck was sold for $35,000 cash.
2. The truck was sold for $64,000 cash.

3. The truck was retired from service, and it is expected that $27,500 will be received from the sale of salvaged materials.
4. The truck and $80,000 cash were exchanged for office equipment that had a cash price of $140,000.
5. The truck and $90,000 cash were exchanged for a new delivery truck that had a cash price of $150,000.
6. The truck was completely destroyed in an accident. Cash of $34,000 is expected to be recovered from the insurance company.

Problem 11–4B

Update depreciation and record exchange of plant asset for similar asset (L.O. 2)

Blount Moving Company purchased a new moving van on October 1, 1993. The cash price of the new van was $27,000, and the company received a trade-in allowance of $4,000 for a 1991 model. The balance was paid in cash. The 1991 model had been acquired on January 1, 1991, at a cost of $18,000. Depreciation has been recorded through December 31, 1992, on a straight-line basis, with three years of expected useful life and no expected salvage value.

Required

Prepare journal entries to record the exchange of the moving vans using the method required by generally accepted accounting principles.

Problem 11–5B

Record leasehold amortization; record depreciation and trade-in (L.O. 2, 5)

On January 1, 1993, Morton Company had the following balance in its plant asset and accumulated depreciation accounts:

	Asset	Accumulated Depreciation
Land	$ 208,000	
Leasehold.	260,000	
Buildings	1,141,920	$ 95,550
Equipment	998,400	463,320
Trucks	149,760	52,930

Additional data

1. The leasehold covers a plot of ground leased on January 1, 1989, for a period of 20 years.
2. Building No. 1 is on the owned land and was completed on July 1, 1992, at a cost of $655,200; its life is set at 40 years with no salvage value. Building No. 2 is on the leased land and was completed on July 1, 1989, at a cost of $486,720; its life is also set at 40 years with no expected salvage value.
3. The equipment had an expected useful life of eight years with no estimated salvage value.
4. Truck A, purchased on January 1, 1991, at a cost of $49,920, had an expected life of 2½ years and a salvage value of $3,120. Truck B, purchased on July 1, 1991, at a cost of $43,680, had an expected life of two years and a salvage value of $7,280. Truck C, purchased on July 1, 1992, at a cost of $56,160, had an expected life of three years and a salvage value of $7,020.

The following transactions occurred in 1993:

Jan. 2   Rent for 1993 on leased land was paid, $29,120.
April 1   Truck B was traded in for truck D. The cash price of the new truck was $49,920. A trade-in allowance of $9,360 was granted from the cash price. The balance was paid in cash. Truck D has an expected life of 2½ years and a salvage value of $3,120. (Use GAAP method.)
      1   Truck A was sold for $9,360 cash.

Required

Prepare journal entries to record the 1993 transactions and the necessary December 31, 1993, adjusting entries, assuming a calendar-year accounting period. Use the straight-line depreciation method.

Problem 11–6B

Determine depletion for
period and depreciation on
mining equipment;
compute average cost per
ton of ore mined
(L.O. 4)

On January 2, 1993, Mitchell Mining Company acquired land with ore deposits at a cash
cost of $500,000. Exploration and development costs amounted to $50,000. The residual
value of the land is expected to be $100,000. The ore deposits contain an estimated 3
million tons. Present technology will allow the economical extraction of only 85% of the
total deposit. Machinery, equipment, and temporary sheds were installed at a cost of
$75,000. The assets will have no further value to the company when the ore body is
exhausted; they have a physical life of 12 years. In 1993, 100,000 tons of ore were extracted. The company expects the mine to be exhausted in 10 years, with sharp variations
in annual production.

Required

a.   Compute the depletion charge for 1993. Round to the nearest cent.

b.   Compute the depreciation charge for 1993 under the units-of-production method.

c.   If all other mining costs, except depletion, amounted to $350,000, what was the
       average cost per ton mined in 1993? (The depreciation calculated in (*b*) is included
       in the $350,000.)

Problem 11–7B

Record cost and
amortization of patent
(L.O. 5)

Stone Company spent $133,280 to purchase a patent on January 2, 1993. Management
assumes that the patent will be useful during its full legal life. In January 1994, the company
hired an outside law firm and successfully defended the patent in a lawsuit at a cost of
$25,600. Also, in January 1994, the company paid $38,400 to obtain patents that could, if
used by competitors, make the earlier Stone patent useless. The purchased patents will
never be used.

Required   Give the entries for 1993 and 1994 to record the information relating to the patents.

Problem 11–8B

Record amortization
expense for a variety of
intangible assets
(L.O. 5)

Following are selected transactions and other data relating to Floyd Company for the year
ended December 31, 1993.

a.   The company rented the second floor of a building for five years on January 2,
       1993, and paid the annual rent of $5,000 for the first and fifth years in advance.

b.   In 1992, the company incurred legal fees of $15,000 in applying for a patent and
       paid a fee of $5,000 to a former employee who conceived of a device that
       substantially reduced the cost of manufacturing one of the company's products.
       The patent on the device has a market value of $150,000 and is expected to be
       useful for 10 years.

c.   In 1992, the company entered into a 10-year operating lease on several floors of a
       building, paying $10,000 in cash immediately and agreeing to pay $5,000 at the end
       of each of the 10 years of life in the lease. The company then incurred costs of
       $20,000 to install partitions, shelving, and fixtures. These items would normally
       last 25 years.

d.   The company spent $6,000 promoting a trademark in a manner that it believed
       enhanced the value of the trademark considerably. The trademark has an indefinite
       life.

e.   The company incurred costs amounting to $50,000 in 1992 and $65,000 in 1993 for
       research and development of new products that are expected to enhance the
       company's revenues for at least five years.

f.   The company paid $50,000 to the author of a book that the company published on
       July 2, 1993. Sales of the book are expected to be made over a two-year period
       from that date.

Required   For each of the situations described above, prepare only the journal entries to record the
           expense applicable to 1993.

BUSINESS DECISION PROBLEMS

Decision Problem 11–1

Record exchange of similar assets; adjust accounts for errors in accounting for depreciable assets

(L.O. 2, 3)

Paige Company acquired machine A for $50,000 on January 2, 1991. Machine A had an estimated useful life of four years and no salvage value. The machine was depreciated on the straight-line basis. On January 2, 1993, machine A was exchanged for machine B. Machine B had a cash price of $60,000. In addition to machine A, cash of $50,000 was given up in the exchange. The company recorded the exchange in accordance with income tax regulations instead of in accordance with generally accepted accounting principles. Machine B has an estimated useful life of five years and no salvage value. The machine is being depreciated using the straight-line method.

Required

a. What journal entry did the Paige Company make when it recorded the exchange of machines? (Show computations.)

b. What journal entry should the Paige Company have made to record the exchange of machines in accordance with generally accepted accounting principles?

c. Assume the error is discovered on December 31, 1994, before adjusting journal entries have been made. What journal entries should be made to correct the accounting records? What adjusting journal entry should be made to record depreciation for 1994? (Ignore income taxes.)

d. What effect did the error have on reported net income for 1993? (Ignore income taxes.)

e. How should machine B be reported on the December 31, 1994, balance sheet?

Decision Problem 11–2

Record purchase of two businesses and explain differences between the two; advise client as to which company should be purchased

(L.O. 5)

Jack Barkley is trying to decide whether to buy Company A or Company B. Both Company A and Company B have assets with the following book values and fair market values:

	Book Value	Fair Market Value
Accounts receivable	$120,000	$120,000
Inventories	360,000	600,000
Land	300,000	540,000
Buildings	360,000	840,000
Equipment	144,000	240,000
Patents	96,000	120,000

Liabilities that would be assumed on the purchase of either company include accounts payable, $240,000, and notes payable, $60,000.

The only difference between Company A and Company B is that Company A has net income that is about average for the industry, while Company B has net income that is greatly above average for the industry.

Required

a. Assume Barkley can buy Company A for $2,160,000 or Company B for $2,760,000. Prepare the journal entries to record the acquisition of (1) Company A and (2) Company B. What accounts for the difference between the purchase price of the two companies?

b. Assume Barkley can buy either company for $2,160,000. Which company would you advise Barkley to buy? Why?

Decision Problem 11–3

Determine the amount of depreciation, depletion, and amortization applicable to particular categories of assets

(L.O. 5)

In the financial statements of E. I. Du Pont and Company in "A Broader Perspective," note (11) discloses the components of property, plant, and equipment which total to the $36,879,000 contained on the 1988 balance sheet. Accumulated depreciation, depletion, and amortization have not been similarly broken down.

From the information contained in note (11), assume that agricultural and industrial chemicals, biomedical products, and fibers are assets subject to amortization; that coal and petroleum exploration and production are assets subject to depletion; and that the remaining assets are subject to depreciation.

Required   Break down the 1988 accumulated depreciation, depletion, and amortization amount of $19,658,000, assuming the amounts are directly proportional to the percentages of the assets subject to depreciation, depletion, and amortization, respectively.

ANSWERS TO SELF-TEST

True-False

1. *True.* It is important to record the depreciation up to the date of sale or disposal when a plant asset is sold or disposed of.

2. *True.* This rule avoids recording gains or losses on exchanges of similar assets.

3. *False.* A gain on an exchange of similar assets is not recognized for either accounting or income tax purposes.

4. *False.* Depletion is recorded by crediting the Accumulated Depletion account, which is a contra asset account to the natural resource asset account.

5. *False.* Goodwill cannot be purchased by itself, nor can it be recorded if developed internally.

Multiple-Choice

1. *c.* The cost and accumulated depreciation should not be removed from the asset's account until the disposal of the asset.

2. *d.* On the date of exchange, the book value of the old computer is $1,380 ($3,000 minus accumulated depreciation of $1,620). The new computer is recorded at the fair market value of the asset ($4,000) or the book value of the old asset plus cash paid ($1,380 + $3,000), whichever is lower. Thus, the cost of the new computer would be fair market value of $4,000.

3. *a.* The loss is computed by subtracting the trade-in allowance of $1,000 from the book value of the old computer of $1,380.

4. *c.* The depletion charge for the first year is computed as follows:

$$\text{Depletion charge per ton} = (\$500,000 - \$100,000)/2,000,000$$
$$= \$0.20$$

$$\text{Depletion charge for the year} = \$0.20 \times 200,000$$
$$= \$40,000$$

Since all of the ore extracted was sold, all of the $40,000 is expensed as cost of ore sold.

5. *b.* The patent is amortized over eight years:

$$\text{Annual amortization charge} = \$36,000/8$$
$$= \$4,500$$

COMPREHENSIVE REVIEW PROBLEM

Problem reviews concepts covered in Chapters 1–11; journalize transactions; post journal data to general ledger; prepare work sheet, classified income statement, statement of retained earnings, and classified balance sheet; journalize and post adjusting and closing entries; prepare post-closing trial balance

(Notice to Students Certain payroll entries are included in this problem that are discussed and illustrated in Appendix B at the end of the book. These entries were included to make the problem more realistic. While these entries are relatively easy to make and we do give you some hints as to how to record them, you may want to glance at Appendix B if you have difficulty making the payroll entries.)

The Denver Office Equipment Company began operations on January 1, 1989. The company sells FAX machines, copiers, telephones, and related supplies. The company uses perpetual inventory procedure and prepares financial statements each month. The general journal is the only journal used. All purchases are made from a state that has no sales tax and are recorded at the gross purchase price. All sales are subject to a 4% sales tax. Credit terms on all sales are 2/10, n/30. While the company does maintain subsidiary ledgers for accounts receivable and accounts payable, you do not need to do so. (The comprehensive review problem at the end of Chapter 7 illustrated the use of subsidiary ledgers.) The post-closing trial balance at November 30, 1994, was as follows:

DENVER OFFICE EQUIPMENT COMPANY
Post-Closing Trial Balance
November 30, 1994

Acct. No.	Account Title	Debits	Credits
100	Cash.	$ 35,240	
101	Petty Cash	300	
103	Accounts Receivable.	29,120	
104	Allowance for Uncollectible Accounts		$ 1,800
105	Merchandise Inventory.	60,500	
106	Repair Parts Inventory	7,200	
107	Supplies on Hand	5,600	
108	Prepaid Insurance	14,400	
120	Notes Receivable	30,000	
121	Interest Receivable	1,400	
130	Land.	250,000	
140	Buildings	700,000	
141	Accumulated Depreciation—Buildings		88,750
150	Trucks	105,000	
151	Accumulated Depreciation—Trucks		85,794
172	Office Equipment	63,000	
173	Accumulated Depreciation—Office Equipment		44,583
199	Goodwill	10,000	
200	Accounts Payable.		20,000
201	Notes Payable		10,000
202	Discount on Notes Payable.	400	
204	Interest Payable.		1,100
226	Sales Tax Payable		29,080
230	Estimated Product Warranty Payable		34,000
300	Capital Stock		500,000
310	Retained Earnings		497,053
		$1,312,160	$1,312,160

Other accounts in the chart of accounts are:

Acct. No.	Account
220	Employees' Federal Income Taxes Payable
221	FICA Taxes Payable
222	Medical Insurance Premiums Payable
223	Employees' State Income Taxes Payable
320	Dividends
410	Sales
411	Sales Discounts
412	Sales Returns and Allowances
418	Interest Revenue
504	Cost of Goods Sold
507	Salaries Expense
512	Insurance Expense
518	Supplies Expense
520	Depreciation Expense—Buildings
521	Depreciation Expense—Trucks
525	Depreciation Expense—Office Equipment
534	Uncollectible Accounts Expense
535	Product Warranty Expense
538	Payroll Tax Expense
540	Interest Expense
551	Goodwill Amortization Expense
557	Miscellaneous Selling Expenses
567	Miscellaneous Administrative Expenses
600	Income Summary

Transactions for December were as follows:

Dec. 1 Products with an original cost of $15,000 were sold to various customers on account for $25,000. A 4% sales tax was charged.

2 Accounts receivable with an invoice price of $28,000 and 4% sales tax were collected. All of the customers took the 2% discount that was available on the amount of the invoice price.

3 Accounts payable with an invoice price of $20,000 were paid. A 2% cash discount was taken on each one. (The discount was taken on the full amount since no sales tax was involved.)

3 Merchandise was purchased on account from Apex Company for $20,000; terms 2/10, n/30, FOB shipping point, freight collect. The goods and the invoice were received on this date. Paid freight of $750 on the purchase. (Round amounts to the nearest dollar.)

4 A 90-day note receivable from Carlin Company for $10,000, dated November 4, 1994, with an interest rate of 10%, was discounted at the Last National Bank at 14%.

5 Products with a cost of $30,000 were sold to various customers on account for $50,000. A 4% sales tax was charged.

6 Goods with an original cost of $1,000 and a selling price of $1,500 were returned by a customer, Shelby Company, because they were the wrong goods. The 4% sales tax was canceled. The customer had not yet paid for the goods.

7 The company granted an allowance to a customer of $800 plus the applicable 4% sales tax because goods were damaged during shipment. An $832 check was sent to reimburse the customer because the customer had already paid for $800 of the goods and had not taken the cash discount.

8 The company returned goods with an invoice price of $2,000 to the Apex Company (relating to the December 3 purchase) because they were the wrong goods.

9 The company received a $300 allowance from the Apex Company (relating to the December 3 purchase) because of some damaged goods that the company will keep and sell at a discount.

10 Products with a cost of $20,000 were sold to various customers on account for $32,000. A 4% sales tax was charged.

Dec. 10 Collected accounts receivable with an invoice price of $23,500 and a 4% sales tax. All of the customers took the 2% cash discount.

13 Paid the amount due to Apex Company on the purchase of December 3.

15 Incurred salaries expense of $20,000. The amounts withheld from employees' paychecks were: federal withholding, $4,400; FICA tax, $1,502; medical insurance premiums, $1,600; and state withholding, $1,200. All of the amounts withheld should be credited to liability accounts. Paid $11,298 as the net amount due to employees.

15 Collected accounts receivable with an invoice price of $50,000 and a 4% sales tax. All of the customers took the 2% cash discount.

16 The company discounted its own noninterest-bearing $5,000, 30-day note payable at the Last National Bank. The discount rate charged by the bank is 14%. (Round amounts to the nearest dollar.)

17 Merchandise with an invoice price of $35,000 was purchased on account from Apex Company. Terms were 2/10, n/30, FOB shipping point, freight collect. The goods and the invoice were received on this date. Freight of $760 was paid.

20 Accounts receivable with an invoice price of $32,000 and sales tax of 4% were collected. All of the customers took the 2% cash discount.

22 Products with a cost of $20,000 were sold to various customers on account for $55,000. A 4% sales tax was charged.

23 Merchandise with an invoice price of $45,000 was purchased on account from Apex Company. Terms were 2/10, n/30, FOB shipping point, freight collect. The goods and the invoice were received on this date. Freight of $150 was paid.

26 A customer came in with a product that had a broken part. The product was under warranty, and an employee handed the customer a repair part that cost the company $50. No labor cost was involved.

27 Paid the Apex Company the amount due on the purchase of December 17.

30 Products with a cost of $10,000 were sold to various customers on account for $15,000. A 4% sales tax was charged.

30 An account receivable of $500 from James Beckett was determined to be uncollectible and was written off.

31 Incurred salaries expense of $20,000. The amounts withheld from employees' paychecks were: federal withholding, $4,400; FICA tax, $1,502; medical insurance premiums, $1,600; and state withholding, $1,200. All of the amounts withheld should be credited to liability accounts. Paid $11,298 as the net amount due to employees.

31 The company paid dividends of $5,000.

31 Paid miscellaneous selling expenses of $4,000 and miscellaneous administrative expenses of $3,000.

Additional data

1. Estimated uncollectible accounts are 1% of net sales (round to the nearest dollar).

2. Prepaid insurance expires at the rate of $2,400 per month.

3. An inventory of supplies shows that $1,800 of supplies are on hand at the end of the month.

4. A physical inventory shows that $60,000 of inventory is on hand at the end of the month.

5. All of the plant assets were acquired on January 1, 1989. Information regarding each plant asset is as follows:

	Estimated Useful Life	Estimated Salvage Value	Depreciation Method
Buildings	40 years	$100,000	Straight-line
Trucks	8 years	15,000	Double-declining-balance
Office equipment	10 years	8,000	Sum-of-the-years'-digits

One twelfth of the annual depreciation is taken each month on these assets (round to the nearest dollar).

6. The note payable existing at the beginning of the month is a 60-day note dated November 30, 1994, and carries an interest rate of 12%. Remember that a new note payable was signed this month.

7. An examination of the petty cash box showed the following (debit all expenses to Miscellaneous Expense):

Coin and currency	$158.00
Vouchers for:	
Postage stamps	25.00
Taxi fares	58.00
Other miscellaneous items	54.00

The fund was not reimbursed at this time.

8. The bank statement and the accounting records as of December 31 revealed the following:

Balance per bank	$106,619
Outstanding checks	6,000
Bank service charges	150
Note collected by the bank:	
Principal	10,000
Interest	250

9. The remaining $10,000 note receivable is a 90-day, 10%, note dated November 30, 1994 (round interest to the nearest dollar).

10. The employer's portion of FICA taxes for the month was $3,004. The debit should be to Payroll Taxes Expense. No state or federal unemployment taxes were incurred.

11. Product warranty expense for the month is estimated to be $4,000.

12. The remaining goodwill is being amortized at $200 per month.

Required a. Journalize the December transactions in the general journal. The November 30, 1994, balances already appear in the ledger accounts. (Round all amounts to the nearest dollar.)

b. Post the journal entries to the general ledger. Assume that these postings are made from page 20 of the general journal.

c. Prepare a work sheet.

d. Prepare a classified income statement, a statement of retained earnings, and a classified balance sheet. On the classified income statement, you need not divide operating expenses into selling and administrative categories.

e. Journalize and post the adjusting and closing entries. Assume that all these postings are from page 21 of the general journal.

f. Prepare a post-closing trial balance.

12

ACCOUNTING THEORY AND INTERNATIONAL ACCOUNTING

LEARNING OBJECTIVES

After studying this chapter, you should be able to:

1. Identify and discuss the underlying assumptions or concepts of accounting.
2. Identify and discuss the major principles of accounting.
3. Identify and discuss the modifying conventions (or constraints) of accounting.
4. Describe the Conceptual Framework Project of the Financial Accounting Standards Board.
5. Discuss the differences in international accounting among nations (Appendix).

In the preceding chapters, you learned how accountants use the accounting process (or cycle) to account for the activities of a business. Chapter 1 made a brief mention of the body of theory underlying accounting procedures. Other chapters have also mentioned theoretical concepts. In this chapter, we discuss accounting theory in greater depth. Now that you have learned some accounting procedures, you are better able to relate these theoretical concepts to accounting practice. Accounting theory is "a set of basic concepts and assumptions and related principles that explain and guide the accountant's actions in identifying, measuring, and communicating economic information."[1]

To some people, the word *theory* has the connotation of being abstract and "out of reach." In accounting, understanding the theory behind the accounting process helps one make decisions in diverse accounting situations. Accounting theory provides a logical framework for accounting practice.

The first part of the chapter describes underlying accounting assumptions or concepts, the measurement process used in accounting, major accounting principles, and modifying conventions or constraints. This body of accounting theory has developed over the years and is contained in authoritative accounting literature and textbooks. The second part of the chapter describes the results of a major effort by the Financial Accounting Standards Board to construct a conceptual framework for accounting. This conceptual framework builds on the accounting theory that has developed over time and serves as a basis for formulating accounting standards in the future. By presenting the traditional body of theory first and the conceptual framework second, we give you a sense of the historical development of accounting theory. While there is some overlap between the two parts of the chapter, we reemphasize the fact that the conceptual framework builds on traditional theory rather than replacing it.

The chapter Appendix discusses international accounting. As businesses expand their operations across international borders, accountants must become aware of the accounting challenges this expansion presents.

TRADITIONAL ACCOUNTING THEORY

Traditional accounting theory consists of underlying assumptions, rules of measurement, accounting principles, and modifying conventions (or constraints). The following sections describe each of these important aspects of accounting theory that have a great influence on accounting practice.

UNDERLYING ASSUMPTIONS OR CONCEPTS

Objective 1

Identify and discuss the underlying assumptions or concepts of accounting

The major underlying assumptions or concepts of accounting are (1) business entity, (2) going concern (continuity), (3) money measurement, (4) stable dollar, and (5) periodicity. This section discusses the effects of these assumptions on the accounting process.

Business Entity

Data gathered in an accounting system are assumed to relate to a specific business unit or entity. The business entity concept assumes that each business has an existence separate from its owners, creditors, employees, customers, other interested parties, and other businesses. For each business (such as a horse stable or a fitness center), the business, not the business owner, is the accounting entity.

[1] American Accounting Association, *A Statement of Basic Accounting Theory* (Sarasota, Fla., 1966), pp. 1–2.

Financial statements must be identified as belonging to a particular business entity. The content of the financial statements must be limited to reporting the activities, resources, and obligations of that entity.

A business entity may be made up of several different **legal** entities. For instance, a large business (such as General Motors Corporation) may consist of several separate corporations, each of which is a separate legal entity. For reporting purposes, however, the corporations may be considered as one business entity because they have a common ownership. Chapter 17 illustrates this concept.

Going Concern (Continuity)

Accountants record business transactions for an entity assuming the entity is a ''going concern.'' The going-concern (continuity) assumption states that an entity will continue to operate indefinitely unless strong evidence exists that the entity will terminate. The termination of an entity occurs when a company ceases business operations and sells its assets. The process of termination is called liquidation. If liquidation appears likely, the going-concern assumption is no longer valid.

The going-concern assumption is often cited to justify the use of historical costs rather than market values in measuring assets. Market values are thought to be of little or no significance to an entity intending to use its assets rather than sell them. On the other hand, if an entity is to be liquidated, liquidation values should be used to report assets.

The going-concern assumption permits the accountant to record certain items as assets. For example, printed advertising matter may be on hand to promote a special sale next month. This advertising material may have little, if any, value to anyone but its owner. However, since the owner expects to continue operating long enough to benefit from the advertising, the accountant classifies the expenditure as an asset, prepaid advertising, and not an expense.

Money Measurement

The economic activity of a business is normally recorded and reported in money terms. Money measurement is the use of a monetary unit of measurement, such as the dollar, instead of physical or other units of measurement. The use of a particular monetary unit provides accountants with a common unit of measurement to report economic activity. Without a monetary unit, it would be impossible to add such items as buildings, equipment, and inventory on a balance sheet.

Financial statements identify their unit of measure (the dollar in the United States) so the statement user can make valid comparisons of amounts. For example, it would be difficult to compare relative asset amounts or profitability of a company reporting in U.S. dollars with a company reporting in Japanese yen.

Stable Dollar

In the United States, accountants make another assumption regarding money measurement—the stable dollar assumption. Under the stable dollar assumption, the dollar is accepted as a **reasonably stable** unit of measurement. Thus, accountants make no adjustments in the primary financial statements for the changing value of the dollar.

A difficulty with following the stable dollar assumption occurs in depreciation accounting. Assume, for example, that a company acquired a building in 1964 and computed the 30-year depreciation on the building without adjusting for any changes in the value of the dollar. Thus, the depreciation deducted in 1994 is the same as the depreciation deducted in 1964. The company makes no adjustments for the difference between the values of the 1964 dollar and the 1994 dollar. Both dollars are treated as **equal monetary units** of measurement even though substantial price inflation has occurred over the 30-year period. Accountants and business executives have expressed concern over this inflation problem, especially since 1970. Appendix C at the end of the text discusses inflation accounting in more detail.

Periodicity (Time Periods)

According to the periodicity (time periods) assumption, an entity's life can be divided into time periods (such as months or years) for purposes of reporting its economic activities. After accountants divide an entity's life into time periods, they attempt to prepare accurate reports on the entity's activities for these periods. Although these time-period reports provide useful and timely financial information for investors and creditors, they may be inaccurate for some of these time periods because accountants use estimates, such as depreciation expense and other adjusting entries.

Accounting reports cover relatively short periods of time. The time periods are usually of equal length so that statement users can make valid comparisons of a company's performance from period to period. The length of the accounting period must be stated in the financial statements. For instance, so far in this text, the income statements were for either a one-month or a one-year period. Companies that publish their financial statements, such as publicly held corporations, generally prepare monthly statements for internal management and publish financial statements quarterly and annually for statement users outside the company.

Accrual Basis and Periodicity   In Chapter 3, you learned that financial statements more accurately reflect the financial status and operations of a company when prepared under the accrual basis of accounting rather than the cash basis. Under the cash basis of accounting, revenues are recorded when cash is received, and expenses are recorded when cash is paid. Under the accrual basis, however, revenues are recorded when services are rendered or products are sold, and expenses are recorded when incurred.

The periodicity assumption makes necessary the adjusting entries prepared under the accrual basis. Without the periodicity assumption, a business would have only one time period running from the inception of the business to its termination. Then, the concepts of cash basis and accrual basis accounting would be irrelevant because all revenues and all expenses would be recorded in that one time period and would not have to be assigned to artificially short time periods of one year or less.

Approximation and Judgment because of Periodicity   To provide periodic financial information, accountants must often make estimates of such things as expected uncollectible accounts and useful lives of depreciable assets. Uncertainty about future events prevents precise measurement and makes estimates necessary in accounting. However, the estimates are often reasonably accurate.

OTHER BASIC CONCEPTS

Other basic accounting concepts that affect the accounting for entities are (1) general-purpose financial statements, (2) substance over form, (3) consistency, (4) double entry, and (5) articulation. A discussion of these basic accounting concepts follows.

General-Purpose Financial Statements

As you know, financial statements present the results of the financial accounting process. Accountants prepare these general-purpose financial statements at regular intervals to meet many of the information needs of external parties and top-level internal managers. In contrast, accountants can gather special-purpose financial information for a specific decision, usually on a one-time basis. For example, management may need specific information to decide whether or not to purchase a new computer. Since special-purpose financial information must be specific, this information is best obtained from the detailed accounting records rather than from the financial statements.

Substance over Form

In some business transactions, the economic substance of the transaction may conflict with its legal form. For example, a contract that is legally a lease may, in fact, be equivalent to a purchase. A company may have a three-year contract to lease (rent) an automobile at a stated monthly rental fee. At the end of the lease period, the company will receive title to the auto after paying a nominal sum (say, $1). The economic substance of this transaction is a purchase rather than a lease of the auto. Thus, under the substance-over-form concept, the auto is shown as an asset on the balance sheet and is depreciated instead of showing rent expense on the income statement. Accountants should record the **economic substance** of a transaction rather than be guided by the **legal form** of the transaction.

Consistency

When discussing inventories in Chapter 6, we introduced the consistency concept. Consistency generally requires that a company use the same accounting principles and reporting practices through time. This concept prohibits indiscriminate switching of principles or methods, such as changing inventory methods every year. However, consistency does not prohibit a change in accounting principles if the information needs of financial statement users are better served by the change. When a company makes a change in principles, it must make the following disclosures in the financial statements: (1) nature of the change; (2) reasons for the change; (3) effect of the change on current net income, if significant; and (4) cumulative effect of the change on past income.

Double Entry

Chapter 2 introduced the basic accounting concept of the double-entry method of recording transactions. Under the double-entry approach, every transaction has a two-sided effect on **each** party engaging in the transaction. Thus, to record a transaction, each party debits at least one account and credits at least one account. The total debits equal the total credits in each journal entry.

Articulation

When learning how to prepare work sheets in Chapter 4, you also learned that financial statements are fundamentally related and **articulate** (interact) with each other. For example, the amount of net income is carried from the income statement to the statement of retained earnings. The ending balance on the statement of retained earnings is carried to the balance sheet to bring total assets and total equities into balance.

Illustration 12.1 is a summary of the underlying assumptions or concepts. The next section discusses the measurement process used in accounting.

MEASUREMENT IN ACCOUNTING

In the introduction to this text, accounting was defined as "the process of identifying, measuring, and communicating economic information to permit informed judgments and decisions by the users of the information."[2] In this section, we focus on the **measurement** process of accounting.

---

[2] Ibid., p. 1.

ILLUSTRATION 12.1

The Underlying Assumptions or Concepts

Assumption or Concept	Description	Importance
Business entity	Each business has an existence separate from its owners, creditors, employees, customers, other interested parties, and other businesses.	Defines scope of the business. Identifies which transactions should be recorded on the company's books. Examples in Chapter 1 were horse stable and physical fitness center.
Going concern (continuity)	An entity will continue to operate indefinitely unless strong evidence exists that the entity will terminate.	Allows a company to continue carrying plant assets at their historical costs in spite of a change in their market values.
Money measurement	The use of a monetary unit of measurement, such as the dollar, instead of physical or other units of measurement.	Provides accountants with a common unit of measure to report economic activity. This concept permits us to add and subtract items on the financial statements.
Stable dollar	The dollar is accepted as a reasonably stable unit of measure.	Permits us to make no adjustments in the financial statements for the changing value of the dollar. This assumption works fairly well in the United States because of our relatively low rate of inflation.
Periodicity (time periods)	An entity's life can be subdivided into time periods (such as months or years) for purposes of reporting its economic activities.	Permits us to prepare financial statements that cover periods shorter than the entire life of a business. Thus, we have an idea as to how well a business is performing before it terminates its operations. The need for adjusting entries arises because of this concept and the use of accrual accounting.
General-purpose financial statements	Only one set of financial statements is prepared to serve the needs of all types of users.	Allows companies to prepare only one set of financial statements instead of a separate set for each potential user of those statements. The financial statements should be free of bias so they do not favor the interests of any one type of user.

Accountants measure a business entity's assets, liabilities, and stockholders' equity, and any changes that occur in them. The effects of these changes are assigned to particular time periods (periodicity) to find the net income or net loss of the accounting entity.

Measuring Assets and Liabilities

Accounting measures the various assets of a business in different ways. Cash is measured at its specified amount. Claims to cash, such as notes and accounts receivable, are measured at their expected cash inflows, taking into consideration possible uncollectibles. Inventories, prepaid expenses, plant assets, and intangibles are measured at their historical costs (actual amounts paid). Some items, such as inventory, are later carried at the lower-of-cost-or-market value. Plant assets and intangibles are later carried at original cost less accumulated depreciation or amortization. Liabilities are measured in terms of the cash that will be paid or the value of services that will be performed to satisfy the liabilities.

Measuring Changes in Assets and Liabilities

From the previous chapters, you have learned that accountants can easily measure some changes in assets and liabilities, such as the exchange of one asset for another of equal value, acquisition of an asset on credit, and payment of a liability.

Assumption or Concept	Description	Importance
Substance over form	Accountants should record economic substance of a transaction rather than its legal form.	Encourages the accountant to record the true nature of a transaction rather than its apparent nature. This approach is the accounting equivalent of "tell it like it is." If an apparent lease transaction has all the characteristics of a purchase, it should be recorded as a purchase.
Consistency	Generally requires that a company use the same accounting principles and reporting practices every accounting period.	Prevents a company from changing accounting methods whenever it likes to present a "better picture" or to manipulate income. The inventory and depreciation chapters both mentioned the importance of this concept.
Double entry	Every transaction has a two-sided effect on each company or party engaging in the transaction.	Uses a system of checks and balances to help identify whether or not errors have been made in recording transactions. When the debits do not equal the credits, this inequality immediately signals us to stop and find the error.
Articulation	Financial statements are fundamentally related and articulate (interact) with each other.	Changes in account balances that occur during an accounting period are reflected in financial statements that are related to one another. For instance, earning revenue increases net income on the income statement, retained earnings on the statement of retained earnings, and assets and retained earnings on the balance sheet. The statement of retained earnings ties the income statement and balance sheet together.

Other changes in assets and liabilities, such as those recorded in adjusting entries, are more difficult to measure because they often involve estimates and/or calculations. The accountant must determine when a change has taken place and the amount of the change. These decisions involve matching revenues and expenses and are guided by the principles discussed below.

THE MAJOR PRINCIPLES

Objective 2

Identify and discuss the major principles of accounting

As stated in the introduction to this text, generally accepted accounting principles (GAAP) set forth standards or methods for presenting financial accounting information. A standardized presentation format enables users to compare the financial information of different companies more easily. Generally accepted accounting principles have been either developed through accounting practice or established by authoritative organizations. Major authoritative organizations that have contributed to the development of the principles are the American Institute of Certified Public Accountants (AICPA), the Financial Accounting Standards Board (FASB), the Securities and Exchange Commission (SEC), the American Accounting Association (AAA), the Financial Executives Institute (FEI), and the Institute of Management Accountants (IMA).

In this section, you will study the following principles:

1. Exchange-price (or cost) principle.
2. Matching principle.
3. Revenue recognition principle.
4. Expense recognition principle.
5. Gain and loss recognition principle.
6. Full disclosure principle.

Exchange-Price (or Cost) Principle

When a transfer of resources takes place between two parties, such as buying merchandise on account, the accountant must follow the exchange-price (or cost) principle when presenting that information. The exchange-price (or cost) principle requires transfers of resources to be recorded at prices agreed on by the parties to the exchange at the time of exchange. This principle sets forth (1) what goes into the accounting system—transaction data; (2) when it is recorded—at the time of exchange; and (3) the amounts—exchange prices—at which assets, liabilities, stockholders' equity, revenues, and expenses are recorded.

As applied to most assets, this principle is often called the cost principle, meaning that purchased or self-constructed assets are initially recorded at historical cost. Historical cost is the amount paid, or the fair value of the liability incurred or other resources surrendered, to acquire an asset and place it in a condition and position for its intended use. For instance, when the cost of a plant asset (such as a machine) was recorded in Chapter 10, its cost included the net purchase price plus any costs of reconditioning, testing, transporting, and placing the asset in the location for its intended use. The term **exchange-price principle** is preferred to **cost principle** because it seems inappropriate to refer to liabilities, stockholders' equity, and such assets as cash and accounts receivable as being measured in terms of cost.

Matching Principle

Using the matching principle, net income of a period is determined by associating or relating revenues earned in a period with expenses incurred to generate those revenues. The logic underlying this principle is that whenever economic resources are used, someone will want to know what was accomplished and at what cost. Every evaluation of economic activity will involve matching benefit with sacrifice. The application of the matching principle is discussed and illustrated below.

Revenue Recognition Principle

Revenue is not difficult to define or measure; it is the inflow of assets from the sale of goods and services to customers, measured by the amount of cash expected to be received from customers. However, the crucial question for the accountant is **when** to record a revenue. Under the revenue recognition principle, revenues should be **earned** and **realized** before they are recognized (recorded).

Earning of Revenue All economic activities undertaken by a company to create revenues are part of the earning process. The actual receipt of cash from a customer may have been preceded by many activities, including (1) placing advertisements, (2) calling on the customer several times, (3) submitting samples, (4) acquiring or manufacturing goods, and (5) selling and delivering goods. Costs are incurred by the company for these activities. Although revenue was actually being earned by these activities, in most instances accountants do not recognize revenue until the time of sale because of the requirement that revenue be **substantially** earned before it is recognized (recorded). This requirement is called the earning principle.

Realization of Revenue Under the realization principle, the accountant does not recognize (record) revenue until the seller acquires the right to receive payment from the buyer. The seller acquires the right to receive payment from the buyer at the time of sale for merchandise transactions or when services have been performed in service transactions. Legally, a sale of merchandise occurs when title to the goods passes to the buyer. When title passes depends on the shipping terms—FOB shipping point or FOB destination (as discussed in Chapter 5). As a practical matter, accountants generally record revenue when goods are delivered.

The advantages of recognizing revenue at the time of sale are that (1) the actual transaction—delivery of goods—is an observable event; (2) revenue is easily measured; (3) risk of loss due to price decline or destruction of the goods has passed to the buyer; (4) revenue has been earned, or substantially so; and (5) because the revenue has been earned, expenses and net income can be determined. As discussed below, the disadvantage of recognizing revenue at the time of sale is that the revenue might not be recorded in the period during which most of the activity creating it occurred.

Exceptions to the Realization Principle The following examples illustrate instances when practical considerations may cause accountants to vary the point of revenue recognition from the time of sale. These examples illustrate the effect that the business environment has on the development of accounting principles and standards.

Cash Collection as Point of Revenue Recognition Some small companies record revenues and expenses at the time of cash collection and payment, which may not occur at the time of sale. This procedure is known as the **cash basis** of accounting. The cash basis is acceptable primarily in service enterprises that do not have substantial credit transactions or inventories, as is the case with doctors or dentists.

Installment Basis of Revenue Recognition When a company is going to collect the selling price of goods sold in installments (such as monthly or annually) and considerable doubt exists as to collectibility, the company may use the installment basis of accounting. Companies make these sales in spite of the doubtful collectibility of the account because their margin of profit is high and the goods can be repossessed if the payments are not received. Under the installment basis, the percentage of total gross margin (selling price of a good minus its cost) recognized in a period is equal to the percentage of total cash from a sale that is received in that period. Thus, the gross margin recognized in a period is equal to the amount of cash received times the gross margin percentage (gross margin divided by selling price). The formula to recognize gross margin on cash collections made on installment sales of a certain year is:

$$\text{Cash collections} \times \frac{\text{Gross margin}}{\text{percentage}} = \frac{\text{Gross margin}}{\text{recognized}}$$

To be more precise, we expand the descriptions in the formula as follows:

$$\begin{array}{c}\text{Cash collections} \\ \text{this year resulting} \\ \text{from installment} \\ \text{sales made in a} \\ \text{certain year}\end{array} \times \begin{array}{c}\text{Gross margin} \\ \text{percentage} \\ \text{for the year} \\ \text{of sale}\end{array} = \begin{array}{c}\text{Gross margin} \\ \text{recognized this year} \\ \text{on cash collections} \\ \text{this year from} \\ \text{installment sales made} \\ \text{in a certain year}\end{array}$$

To illustrate, assume a company sold a stereo set. The facts of the sale are:

Date of Sale	Selling Price	Cost	Gross Margin (Selling price − Cost)	Gross Margin Percentage (Gross margin ÷ Selling price)
October 1, 1994	$500	$300	($500 − $300) = $200	($200 ÷ $500) = 40%

The buyer makes 10 equal monthly installment payments of $50 each to pay for the set (10 × $50 = $500). If the company receives three monthly payments in 1994, the total amount of cash received in 1994 is $150 (3 × $50).

The gross margin to recognize in **1994** is:

1994 cash collections from 1994 installment sales	×	Gross margin percentage on 1994 installment sales	=	1994 gross margin recognized on 1994 cash collections from 1994 installment sales
$150	×	**40%**	=	**$60**

The company collects the other installments when due so it receives a total of $350 in 1995 from 1994 installment sales. The gross margin to recognize in **1995** on these cash collections is shown below.

1995 cash collections from 1994 installment sales	×	Gross margin percentage on 1994 installment sales	=	1995 gross margin recognized on 1995 cash collections from 1994 installment sales
$350	×	**40%**	=	**$140**

In summary, the total receipts and gross margin recognized in the two years are as follows:

Year	Total Amount of Cash Received	Gross Margin Recognized
1994	$150 (30%)	$ 60 (30%)
1995	350 (70%)	140 (70%)
Total	$500 100%	$200 100%

The installment basis of revenue recognition may be used for tax purposes only in very limited circumstances. **Since the installment basis delays revenue recognition beyond the time of sale, it is acceptable for accounting purposes only when considerable doubt exists as to collectibility of the installments.**

Revenue Recognition on Long-Term Construction Projects   Revenue from a long-term construction project can be recognized under two different methods: (1) the completed-contract method or (2) the percentage-of-completion method. The completed-contract method does not recognize any revenue until the period in which the project is completed. At that point, all revenue is recognized even though the contract may have required three years to complete. Thus, the **completed-contract method recognizes revenues at the time of sale,** as is true for most sales transactions. Costs incurred on the project are carried forward in an inventory account (Construction in Process) and are charged to expense in the period in which the revenue is recognized.

Some accountants argue that waiting so long to recognize any revenue is unreasonable. Revenue-producing activities have been performed during each year of construction, and revenue should be recognized in each year of construction even if estimates are needed. The percentage-of-completion method is a method of recognizing revenue based on the estimated stage of completion of a long-term project. The stage of completion is measured by comparing actual costs incurred in a period with the total estimated costs to be incurred on the project. The percentage-of-completion method is preferable when dependable estimates of costs can be obtained, both estimated and incurred.

To illustrate, assume that a company has a contract to build a dam for $44 million. The estimated construction cost is $40 million. Estimated gross margin is calculated as follows:

Sales Price of Dam	Estimated Costs to Construct Dam	Estimated Gross Margin (Sales price − Estimated costs)
$44 million	$40 million	($44 million − $40 million) = $4 million

The $4 million gross margin is recognized in the financial statements by recording the correct amount of revenue for the year and then deducting actual costs incurred that year.

The formula to recognize revenue is:

$$\left(\begin{array}{c}\text{Construction costs} \\ \text{incurred during} \\ \text{the period}\end{array} \div \begin{array}{c}\text{Total estimated} \\ \text{construction costs}\end{array}\right) \times \begin{array}{c}\text{Total} \\ \text{sales} \\ \text{price}\end{array} = \begin{array}{c}\text{Revenue} \\ \text{recognized} \\ \text{for period}\end{array}$$

Suppose that by the end of the first year (1994), the company had incurred **actual** construction costs of $30 million. The $30 million of construction costs is 75% of the total estimated construction costs ($30 million ÷ $40 million = 75%). Under the percentage-of-completion method, the 75% figure would be used to **assign** revenue to the first year. In 1995, another $6 million of construction costs is incurred. In 1996, the final $4 million of construction costs is incurred. The amount of revenue to assign to each year is determined as follows:

Year	Ratio of Actual Construction Costs to Total Estimated Construction Costs	× Agreed Price of Dam	= Amount of Revenue to Recognize
1994	($30 million ÷ $40 million) = 75% 75%	× $44 million	= $33 million
1995	($6 million ÷ $40 million) = 15% 15%	× $44 million	= $6.6 million
1996	($4 million ÷ $40 million) = 10% 10%	× $44 million	= $4.4 million

The amount of gross margin to recognize in each year is as follows:

Year	Revenues	− Construction Costs	= Gross Margin
1994	$33.0 million	− $30.0 million	= $3.0 million
1995	6.6	− 6.0	= 0.6
1996	4.4	− 4.0	= 0.4
Total	$44.0 million	− $40.0 million	= $4.0 million

ILLUSTRATION 12.2

Methods of Accounting for Long-Term Contracts

	Number of Companies			
	1989	1988	1987	1986
Percentage-of-completion	92	86	89	90
Units-of-delivery	33	37	35	36
Completed contract	6	8	6	9
Not determinable	2	3	2	4

Source: American Institute of Certified Public Accountants, *Accounting Trends & Techniques* (New York: AICPA, 1990), p. 285.

Period costs, such as general and administrative expenses, would be deducted from gross margin to determine net income. For instance, assuming general and administrative expenses were $100,000 in 1995, net income would be ($600,000 − $100,000) = $500,000.

Illustration 12.2 shows the frequencies of references to the methods of accounting for long-term contracts in the financial statements of a sample of 600 companies for the years 1986–89. The percentage-of-completion method seems to be the most widely used.

Revenue Recognition at Completion of Production   Recognizing revenue at the time of completion of production or extraction is called the production basis. The production basis is considered acceptable procedure when accounting for many farm products (wheat, corn, and soybeans) and for certain precious metals (gold). Accountants justify recognizing revenue before the sale of these products because (1) the products are homogeneous in nature, (2) they can usually be sold at their market prices, and (3) unit production costs for these products are often difficult to determine.

Recognizing revenue on completion of production or extraction is accomplished by debiting inventory (an asset) and crediting a revenue account for the expected selling price of the goods. All costs incurred in the period can then be treated as expenses. For example, assume that 1,000 ounces of gold are mined at a time when gold sells for $400 per ounce. The entry to record the extraction of 1,000 ounces of gold would be:

Inventory of Gold	400,000	
Revenue from Extraction of Gold		400,000
To record extraction of 1,000 ounces of gold. Selling price is $400 per ounce.		

If the gold is later sold at $400 per ounce, Cash is debited and Inventory of Gold is credited for $400,000 as follows:

Cash	400,000	
Inventory of Gold		400,000
To record sale of 1,000 ounces of gold at $400 per ounce.		

If expenses in producing the gold amounted to $300,000, net income on the gold mined would be $100,000.

Expense Recognition Principle

Expense recognition is closely related to, and sometimes discussed as part of, the revenue recognition principle. The expense recognition principle states that expenses should be recognized (recorded) as they are incurred to produce revenues. An **expense** is the outflow or using up of assets in the generation of revenue. An expense is incurred **voluntarily** to produce a revenue. For instance, the cost of a television set delivered by a dealer to a customer in exchange for cash is an asset "consumed" to produce revenue. Similarly, the cost of such services as labor are voluntarily incurred to produce revenue.

The Measurement of Expense   Most assets used in operating a business are measured in terms of their historical costs. Therefore, expenses, such as depreciation, resulting from the consumption of those assets in producing revenues are measured in terms of the historical costs of those assets. Other expenses, such as wages, are paid for currently and are measured in terms of their current costs.

The Timing of Expense Recognition   The matching principle implies that a relationship exists between expenses and revenues. For certain expenses, such as cost of goods sold, this relationship is easily seen. However, when a direct relationship cannot be seen, the costs of assets with limited lives may be charged to expense in the periods benefited on a systematic and rational allocation basis. Depreciation of plant assets is an example.

Product costs are costs incurred in the acquisition or manufacture of goods. Included as product costs for purchased goods are invoice, freight, and insurance-in-transit costs. For manufacturing companies, product costs include all costs of materials, labor, and factory operations necessary to produce the goods. Product costs are assumed to attach to the goods purchased or produced and are carried in inventory accounts as long as the goods are on hand. Product costs are charged to expense when the goods are sold. The result is a precise matching of cost of goods sold expense to its related revenue.

Period costs are costs that cannot be traced to specific products and are expensed in the period in which incurred. Selling and administrative costs are examples of period costs.

Gain and Loss Recognition Principle

The gain and loss recognition principle states that gains may be recorded only when realized, but losses should be recorded when they first become evident. Thus, losses are recognized at an earlier point than are gains. This principle is related to the conservatism concept.

Gains typically result from the sale of long-term assets for more than their book value, as was illustrated in Chapter 11. Gains should not be recognized until they are realized through sale or exchange. Recognizing potential gains before they are actually realized is forbidden in accounting.

Losses consume assets, as do expenses. However, unlike expenses, they do not produce revenues. Losses are usually *involuntary,* such as the loss suffered from destruction by fire of an uninsured building. A loss on the sale of a building may be "voluntary" if management decided to sell the building even though it meant incurring a loss. Losses should be recorded when they first become evident, as in Chapter 6 when we applied the lower-of-cost-or-market method and recorded the loss from market decline of inventory before we actually sold the inventory.

ILLUSTRATION 12.3

The Major Principles

Principle	Description	Importance
Exchange-price (or cost) principle	Requires transfers of resources to be recorded at prices agreed on by the parties to the exchange at the time of the exchange.	Tells the accountant to record a transfer of resources at an objectively determinable amount at the time of the exchange. Also, self-constructed assets are recorded at their actual cost rather than at some estimate of what they would have cost if they had been purchased. Chapter 10 relies heavily on this principle in recording the acquisition of plant assets.
Matching principle	Net income of a period is determined by associating or relating revenues earned in a period with expenses incurred to generate those revenues.	Identifies how to calculate net income under the accrual concept of income. Chapter 3 first illustrated the matching principle, but all chapters reinforce the importance of this fundamental principle.
Revenue recognition principle	Revenues should be earned and realized before they are recognized (recorded).	Informs accountant that revenues generally should be recognized when services are performed or goods are sold. Exceptions are made for installment sales, long-term construction projects, certain farm products, and precious metals.
Expense recognition principle	Expenses should be recognized (recorded) as they are incurred to produce revenues.	Indicates that expenses are to be recorded as soon as they are incurred rather than waiting until some future time.
Gain and loss recognition principle	Gains may only be recorded when realized, but losses should be recorded when they first become evident.	Tells the accountant to be conservative when recognizing gains and losses. Gains can only be recognized when they have been realized through sale (or exchange). Losses should be recognized as soon as they become evident. Thus, potential losses can be recorded, but only gains that have actually been realized can be recorded.
Full disclosure principle	Information important enough to influence the decisions of an informed user of the financial statements should be disclosed.	Requires the accountant to disclose everything that is important. A good rule to follow is—if in doubt, disclose. Another good rule is—if use of accounting methods is not consistent, disclose all the facts and the effect on income.

Full Disclosure Principle

The full disclosure principle states that information important enough to influence the decisions of an informed user of the financial statements should be disclosed. Depending on its nature, this information should be disclosed either in the financial statements, in notes to the financial statements, or in supplemental statements. For instance, Appendix E at the end of this text illustrates how The Coca Cola Company discloses information in notes to its financial statements. In judging whether or not to disclose information, it is better to err on the side of too much disclosure rather than too little. Many lawsuits against CPAs and their clients have resulted from inadequate or misleading disclosure of the underlying facts.

Illustration 12.3 summarizes the major principles and describes the importance of each one.

MODIFYING CONVENTIONS (OR CONSTRAINTS)

Objective 3

Identify and discuss the modifying conventions (or constraints) of accounting

In certain instances, accounting principles are not strictly applied because of modifying conventions (or constraints). Modifying conventions are customs emerging from accounting practice that alter the results that would be obtained from a strict application of accounting principles. Three such modifying conventions are cost-benefit, materiality, and conservatism.

Cost-Benefit The cost-benefit consideration involves deciding whether the benefits of including optional information in financial statements exceed the costs of providing the information. Users tend to think information is cost free since they incur none of the costs of providing the information. Preparers realize that providing information is costly. The benefits of using information should exceed the costs of providing it. The measurement of benefits is nebulous and inexact, which makes application of this modifying convention difficult in practice.

Materiality Materiality is a modifying convention that allows the accountant to deal with immaterial (unimportant) items in an expedient but theoretically incorrect manner. The fundamental question the accountant must ask in judging the materiality of an item is whether a knowledgeable user's decisions would be different if the information were presented in the theoretically correct manner. If not, the item is immaterial and may be reported in a theoretically incorrect but expedient manner. For instance, since small dollar amount items (such as the cost of calculators) often do not make a difference in a statement user's decision to invest in the company, they are considered **immaterial** (unimportant) and may be expensed when purchased. However, because large dollar amount items (such as the cost of mainframe computers) usually do make a difference in such a decision, they are considered **material** (important) and should be recorded as assets and depreciated. The accountant should record all material items in a theoretically correct manner. **Immaterial items may be recorded in a theoretically incorrect manner simply because it is more convenient and less expensive to do so.** For example, the purchase of a wastebasket may be debited to an expense account rather than an asset account even though the wastebasket has an expected useful life of 30 years. It simply is not worth the cost of recording depreciation expense on such a small item over its life.

Materiality has been defined by the FASB as "the magnitude of an omission or misstatement of accounting information that, in the light of surrounding circumstances, makes it probable that the judgment of a reasonable person relying on the information would have been changed or influenced by the omission or misstatement."[3] The term **magnitude** in this definition suggests that the materiality of an item may be assessed by looking at its **relative** size. A $10,000 error in an expense in a company with earnings of $30,000 is material. The same error in a company earning $30,000,000 may not be material.

Materiality involves more than the relative size of dollar amounts. Often the nature of the item may make it material. For example, it may be quite significant to know that a company is paying bribes or making illegal political contributions, even if the dollar amounts of such items are relatively small.

Conservatism Conservatism means being cautious or prudent and making sure that net assets and net income are not overstated. Such overstatement can mis-

---

[3] FASB, *Statement of Financial Accounting Concepts No. 2*, "Qualitative Characteristics of Accounting Information" (Stamford, Conn., 1980), p. xv. Copyright © by the Financial Accounting Standards Board, High Ridge Park, Stamford, Connecticut 06905, U.S.A. Quoted (or excerpted) with permission. Copies of the complete documents are available from the FASB.

ILLUSTRATION 12.4

Modifying Conventions

Modifying Convention	Description	Importance
Cost-benefit	Optional information should only be included in financial statements if the benefits of providing it exceed its costs.	Lets the accountant know that information that is not required should not be made available if the costs exceed its benefits. An example may be companies going to the expense of providing information on the effects of inflation when users do not seem to benefit significantly from the information.
Materiality	Only items that would affect a knowledgeable user's decision are considered to be material (important) and must be reported in a theoretically correct way.	Allows accountant to treat immaterial (relatively small dollar amount) information in a theoretically incorrect but expedient manner. For instance, a wastebasket can be expensed rather than capitalized and depreciated even though it may last for 30 years.
Conservatism	Transactions should be recorded in such a manner that net assets and net income are not overstated.	Warns the accountant that net assets and net income are not to be overstated. "Anticipate (and record) all possible losses and do not anticipate (or record) any possible gains" is common advice under this constraint. Also, conservative application of the matching principle involves making sure that adjustments for expenses for such items as uncollectible accounts, warranties, and depreciation are adequate.

lead potential investors and creditors regarding making an investment in the company or a loan to the company. You saw conservatism applied when (1) the lower-of-cost-or-market rule was used for inventory in Chapter 6 and (2) when a gain could not be recognized on a trade-in of similar assets in Chapter 11. Accountants must realize a fine line exists between conservative and incorrect accounting.

The remainder of this chapter discusses the Conceptual Framework Project of the Financial Accounting Standards Board. The Conceptual Framework Project is designed to resolve some disagreements as to the proper theoretical foundation for accounting. Only the portions of the project relevant to this text are presented.

Illustration 12.4 is a summary of the modifying conventions and the importance of each one.

THE FINANCIAL ACCOUNTING STANDARDS BOARD'S CONCEPTUAL FRAMEWORK PROJECT

Objective 4

Describe the Conceptual Framework Project of the Financial Accounting Standards Board

The exact nature of the basic concepts and related principles composing accounting theory has been debated for years. The debate continues today even though numerous references can be found to "generally accepted accounting principles" (GAAP). To date, all attempts to present a concise statement of GAAP have received only limited acceptance.

Due to this limited success, many accountants suggest that the starting point in reaching a concise statement of GAAP is to seek agreement on the objectives of financial accounting and reporting. The belief is that if a person (1) carefully studies the environment, (2) knows what objectives are sought, (3) can identify certain qualitative traits of accounting information, and (4) can define the basic elements of financial statements, that person can discover the principles and standards that will lead to the attainment of the stated objectives. The FASB has taken the first three steps in "Objectives of Financial Reporting by Business Enterprises" and in "Qualitative Characteristics of Accounting Information."[4] The fourth step is represented by two concepts statements entitled "Elements of Financial Statements of Business Enterprises" and "Elements of Financial Statements."[5]

OBJECTIVES OF FINANCIAL REPORTING

Financial reporting objectives are the broad overriding goals sought by accountants engaging in financial reporting. According to the FASB, the first objective of financial reporting is to:

provide information that is useful to present and potential investors and creditors and other users in making rational investment, credit, and similar decisions. The information should be comprehensible to those who have a reasonable understanding of business and economic activities and are willing to study the information with reasonable diligence.[6]

The term *other users* is interpreted broadly and includes employees, security analysts, brokers, and lawyers. Financial reporting should provide information to all who are willing to learn to use it properly.

The second objective of financial reporting is to:

provide information to help present and potential investors and creditors and other users in assessing the amounts, timing, and uncertainty of prospective cash receipts from dividends [owner withdrawals] or interest and the proceeds from the sale, redemption, or maturity of securities or loans. Since investors' and creditors' cash flows are related to enterprise cash flows, financial reporting should provide information to help investors, creditors, and others assess the amounts, timing, and uncertainty of prospective net cash inflows to the related enterprise.[7]

This objective ties the cash flows of investors (owners) and creditors to the cash flows of the enterprise, a tie-in that appears entirely logical. Enterprise cash inflows are the source of cash for dividends (owner withdrawals), interest, and redemption of maturing debt.

Third, financial reporting should:

provide information about the economic resources of an enterprise, the claims to those resources (obligations of the enterprise to transfer resources to other entities and owners' equity), and the effects of transactions, events, and circumstances that change its resources and claims to those resources.[8]

A number of conclusions can be drawn from these three objectives and from a study of the environment in which financial reporting is carried out. For example, financial reporting should:

---

[4] FASB, *Statement of Financial Accounting Concepts No. 1*, "Objectives of Financial Reporting by Business Enterprises" (Stamford, Conn., 1978); and *Statement of Financial Accounting Concepts No. 2*, "Qualitative Characteristics of Accounting Information" (Stamford, Conn., 1980). Copyright © by the Financial Accounting Standards Board, High Ridge Park, Stamford, Connecticut 06905, U.S.A. Quoted (or excerpted) with permission. Copies of the complete documents are available from the FASB.

[5] FASB, *Statement of Financial Accounting Concepts No. 3*, "Elements of Financial Statements of Business Enterprises" (Stamford, Conn., 1980); and *Statement of Financial Accounting Concepts No. 6*, "Elements of Financial Statements" (Stamford, Conn., 1985). Copyright © by the Financial Accounting Standards Board, High Ridge Park, Stamford, Connecticut 06905, U.S.A. Quoted (or excerpted) with permission. Copies of the complete documents are available from the FASB.

[6] FASB, *Statement of Financial Accounting Concepts No. 1*, p. viii.

[7] Ibid.

[8] Ibid.

1. Provide information about an enterprise's past performance because such information is used as a basis for prediction of future enterprise performance.

2. Focus on earnings and its components, despite the emphasis in the objectives on cash flows. (Earnings computed under the accrual basis provide a better indicator of ability to generate favorable cash flows than do statements prepared under the cash basis.)

On the other hand, financial reporting does not seek to:

1. Measure the value of an enterprise but rather provides information that may be useful in determining its value.

2. Evaluate management's performance, predict earnings, assess risk, or estimate earning power but rather provides information to persons who wish to make these evaluations.

These conclusions are some of those reached in *Statement of Financial Accounting Concepts No. 1.* As the Board stated, these statements "are intended to establish the objectives and concepts that the Financial Accounting Standards Board will use in developing standards of financial accounting and reporting."[9] How successful the Board will be in the approach adopted remains to be seen.

QUALITATIVE CHARACTERISTICS

Qualitative characteristics are those characteristics that accounting information should possess to be useful in decision making. This criterion is difficult to apply. The usefulness of accounting information in a given instance depends not only on information characteristics but also on the capabilities of the decision makers and their professional advisers, if any. Accountants cannot specify who the decision makers are, their characteristics, the decisions to be made, or the methods chosen to make the decisions; therefore, attention is directed to characteristics of accounting information. The FASB's graphic summarization of the problems faced is presented in Illustration 12.5.[10]

Relevance

For information to have relevance, it must be pertinent to or affect a decision. The information must "make a difference" to someone who does not already have the information. Relevant information is capable of making a difference in a decision either by affecting user predictions of outcomes of past, present, or future events or by confirming or correcting expectations. Note that information need not be a prediction to be useful in developing, confirming, or altering expectations. Expectations are commonly based on the present or past. For example, any attempt to predict future earnings of a company would quite likely start with a review of present and past earnings. Also, information that merely confirms prior expectations may be less useful, but this information is still relevant because it reduces uncertainty.

Certain types of accounting information have been criticized because of an alleged lack of relevance. For example, some would argue that a cost of $1 million paid for a tract of land 40 years ago and reported in the current balance sheet at that amount is irrelevant (except for possible tax implications) to users for decision making today. Such criticism has encouraged research into the types of information relevant to users. Suggestions have been made that a different valuation basis, such as current cost, be used in reporting such assets.

---

[9] Ibid., p. i.

[10] FASB, *Statement of Financial Accounting Concepts No. 2*, p. 15.

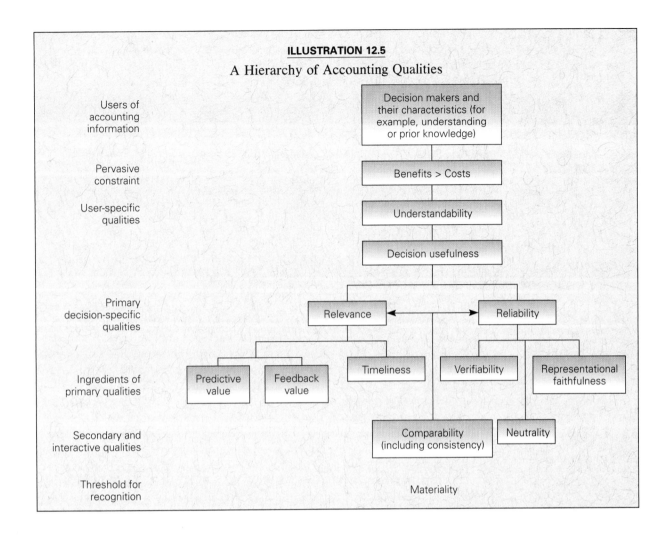

ILLUSTRATION 12.5

A Hierarchy of Accounting Qualities

Users of accounting information — Decision makers and their characteristics (for example, understanding or prior knowledge)

Pervasive constraint — Benefits > Costs

User-specific qualities — Understandability

Decision usefulness

Primary decision-specific qualities — Relevance ↔ Reliability

Ingredients of primary qualities — Predictive value, Feedback value, Timeliness, Verifiability, Representational faithfulness

Secondary and interactive qualities — Comparability (including consistency), Neutrality

Threshold for recognition — Materiality

Predictive Value and Feedback Value Since actions taken now can affect only future events, information is obviously relevant when it possesses predictive value, or improves users' abilities to predict outcomes of events. Information that reveals the relative success of users in predicting outcomes possesses feedback value. Feedback reports on past activities and can make a difference in decision making by (1) reducing uncertainty in a situation, (2) refuting or confirming prior expectations, and (3) providing a basis for further predictions. For example, a report on the first quarter's earnings of a company reduces the uncertainty surrounding the amount of such earnings, confirms or refutes the predicted amount of such earnings, and provides a possible basis on which to predict earnings for the full year. You should remember that although accounting information may possess predictive value, it does not consist of predictions. Making predictions is a function performed by the decision maker, not the accountant.

Timeliness Timeliness requires that accounting information be provided at a time when it may be considered in reaching a decision. Utility of information decreases with age—to know what the net income for 1993 was in early 1994 is much more useful than to receive this information a year later. If information is to be of any value in decision making, it must be available **before** the decision is made. If not, the information is of little value. In determining what constitutes timely information, consideration must be given to the other qualitative characteristics and to the cost of gathering information. For example, a timely estimated amount for uncollectible accounts may be more valuable than a later, verified actual amount. Timeliness alone cannot make information relevant, but otherwise relevant information might be rendered irrelevant by a lack of timeliness.

Reliability

In addition to being relevant, information must be reliable to be useful. Information has reliability when it faithfully depicts for users what it purports to represent. Thus, accounting information is reliable if users can depend on it to reflect the underlying economic activities of the organization. The reliability of information depends on its representational faithfulness, verifiability, and neutrality. The information must also be complete and free of bias.

Representational Faithfulness   Insight into this quality may be gained by considering a map. A map possesses representational faithfulness when it shows roads and bridges (among other things) where roads and bridges actually exist. A correspondence exists between what is shown on the map and what is present physically. Similarly, representational faithfulness exists when accounting statements on economic activity correspond to the actual underlying activity. Where no correspondence exists, the cause may be (1) bias or (2) lack of completeness.

1. **Effects of bias.**   Accounting measurements are biased if they are consistently too high or too low. Bias in accounting measurements may exist due to the choice of measurement method or to bias introduced either deliberately or through lack of skill by the measurer.

2. **Completeness.**   To be free from bias, information must be sufficiently complete to ensure that it validly represents underlying events and conditions. Completeness means that all significant information must be disclosed in a way that aids understanding and does not mislead. Relevance of information also may be reduced if information that would make a difference to a user is omitted. Currently, full disclosure generally requires presentation of a balance sheet, an income statement, a statement of cash flows, and necessary notes to the financial statements and supporting schedules. A statement of changes in stockholders' (or owners') equity is also required in annual reports of corporations. Such statements must be complete, with items properly classified and segregated (such as reporting sales revenue separately from other revenues). Required disclosures may be made in (1) the body of the financial statements, (2) the notes to such statements, (3) special communications, and/or (4) the president's letter or other management reports in the annual report.

Another aspect of completeness is that full disclosure must be made of all changes in accounting principles and their effects.[11] Disclosure should also be made of unusual activities (loans to officers), changes in expectations (losses on inventory), depreciation expense for the period, long-term obligations entered into that are not recorded by the accountant (a 20-year lease on a building), new arrangements with certain groups (pension and profit-sharing plans for employees), and significant events that occur after the date of the statements (loss of a major customer). Accounting policies (major principles and their manner of application) followed in preparing the financial statements should also be disclosed.[12] Because of its emphasis on disclosure, this aspect of reliability is often called the *full disclosure principle*.

---

[11] APB, *APB Opinion No. 20,* "Accounting Changes" (New York: AICPA, July 1971).

[12] APB, *APB Opinion No. 22,* "Disclosure of Accounting Policies" (New York: AICPA, April 1972).

Verifiability   Financial information has verifiability when it can be substantially duplicated by independent measurers using the same measurement methods. Verifiability is directed toward eliminating measurer bias, rather than measurement method bias. The requirement that financial information be based on objective evidence is based on demonstrated needs of users for reliable, unbiased financial information. Unbiased information is especially needed when parties with opposing interests (credit seekers and credit grantors) rely on the same information. Reliability of information is enhanced if the information is verifiable.

Financial information will never be free of subjective opinion and judgment; it will always possess varying degrees of verifiability. Some measurements can be supported by canceled checks and invoices. Other measurements, such as periodic depreciation charges, can never be verified because of their very nature. Thus, financial information in many instances is verifiable only in that it represents a consensus as to what would be reported if the same procedures had been followed by other accountants.

Neutrality   Neutrality in accounting information means that the information should be free of measurement method bias. The primary concern should be relevance and reliability of the information that result from application of the principle, not the effect that the principle may have on a particular interest. Nonneutral accounting information is designed to favor one set of interested parties over others. For example, a particular form of measurement might favor owners over creditors, or vice versa. "To be neutral, accounting information must report economic activity as faithfully as possible, without coloring the image it communicates for the purpose of influencing behavior in *some particular direction*."[13] Accounting standards should not be developed and used like certain tax regulations that deliberately seek to foster or restrain certain types of activity. Verifiability seeks to eliminate measurer bias; neutrality seeks to eliminate measurement method bias.

Comparability (and Consistency)   When comparability in financial information exists, reported differences and similarities in information are real and are not the result of differing accounting treatments. Comparable information will reveal relative strengths and weaknesses in a single company through time and between two or more companies at the same point in time.

Consistency requires that a company use the same accounting principles and reporting practices through time. Consistency leads to comparability of financial information for a single company through time. Comparability between companies is more difficult to achieve because the same activities may be accounted for in different ways. For example, Company B may use one method of depreciation, while Company C accounts for an identical asset in similar circumstances using another method. A high degree of intercompany comparability in accounting information will not exist unless accountants are required to account for the same activities in the same manner across companies and through time.

Pervasive Constraints   As Illustration 12.5 shows, two pervasive constraints must be considered in providing useful information. First, the benefits secured from the information must be greater than the costs of providing that information. Second, only material items

---

[13] FASB, *Statement of Financial Accounting Concepts No. 2*, par. 100.

need be disclosed and accounted for strictly in accordance with generally accepted accounting principles (GAAP). Both cost-benefit and materiality were discussed earlier in the chapter.

THE BASIC ELEMENTS OF FINANCIAL STATEMENTS

Thus far we have discussed objectives of financial reporting and qualitative characteristics of accounting information. A third important task in developing a conceptual framework for any discipline is that of identifying and defining its basic elements. The FASB identified and defined the basic elements of financial statements in *Concepts Statement No. 3*. Later, some of the definitions were revised in *Concepts Statement No. 6*. Most of the terms were defined earlier in this text in a less technical way to convey a general understanding of the terms. The more technical definitions are listed below. (These items are not repeated in this chapter's New Terms.)

Assets are probable future economic benefits obtained or controlled by a particular entity as a result of past transactions or events.

Liabilities are probable future sacrifices of economic benefits arising from present obligations of a particular entity to transfer assets or provide services to other entities in the future as a result of past transactions or events.

Equity or net assets is the residual interest in the assets of an entity that remains after deducting its liabilities. In a business enterprise, the equity is the ownership interest. In a not-for-profit organization, which has no ownership interest in the same sense as a business enterprise, net assets is divided into three classes based on the presence or absence of donor-imposed restrictions—permanently restricted, temporarily restricted, and unrestricted net assets.

Comprehensive income is the change in equity of a business enterprise during a period from transactions and other events and circumstances from nonowner sources. It includes all changes in equity during a period except those resulting from investments by owners and distributions to owners.

Revenues are inflows or other enhancements of assets of any entity or settlements of its liabilities (or a combination of both) from delivering or producing goods, rendering services, or other activities that constitute the entity's ongoing major or central operations.

Expenses are outflows or other using up of assets or incurrences of liabilities (or a combination of both) from delivering or producing goods, rendering services, or carrying out other activities that constitute the entity's ongoing major or central operations.

Gains are increases in equity (net assets) from peripheral or incidental transactions of an entity and from all other transactions and other events and circumstances affecting the entity except those that result from revenues or investments by owners.

Losses are decreases in equity (net assets) from peripheral or incidental transactions of an entity and from all other transactions and other events and circumstances affecting the entity except those that result from expenses or distributions to owners.

Investments by owners are increases in equity of a particular business enterprise resulting from transfers to it from other entities of something valuable to obtain or increase ownership interests (or equity) in it. Assets are most commonly received as investments by owners, but that which is received may also include services or satisfaction or conversion of liabilities of the enterprise.

Distributions to owners are decreases in equity of a particular business enterprise resulting from transferring assets, rendering services, or incurring liabilities by the enterprise to owners. Distributions to owners decrease ownership interest (or equity) in an enterprise.[14]

---

[14] FASB, *Statement of Financial Accounting Concepts No. 6*, "Elements of Financial Statements" (a replacement of *FASB Concepts Statement No. 3*) (Stamford, Conn., 1985).

ETHICS	Maplehurst Company manufactures large spinning machines for use in the textile indus-

ETHICS

A CLOSER LOOK

Maplehurst Company manufactures large spinning machines for use in the textile industry. The company had purchased $100,000 of small hand tools to use in its business. The company's accountant recorded the tools in an asset account and was going to write them off over a period of 20 years. Management wanted to write these tools off as an expense of this year because revenues this year had been abnormally high and were expected to be at lower levels in the future. Management's goal was to ''smooth out'' income rather than showing sharp increases and decreases. When told by the accountant that $100,000 was a material item that must be accounted for in a theoretically correct manner, management decided to consider the tools as consisting of 10 groups each having a cost of $10,000. Since amounts under $20,000 are considered to be immaterial for this company, all of the tools could then be charged to expense this year.

The accountant is concerned about this treatment. She believes that management's position could not be successfully defended if the auditors challenge the expensing of these items.

Required

a. Is management being ethical in this situation?

b. Is the accountant correct in believing that management's position could not be successfully defended?

c. What would you do if you were the accountant?

Note that the requirement that assets and liabilities be based on past transactions normally rules out the recording of contracts that are mutual promises to do something, such as entering into an employment contract with an officer. For a similar reason, the accountant refuses to record an asset and a liability when a contract is signed whereby the entity agrees to purchase a certain number of units of a product over a future period of time.

RECOGNITION AND MEASUREMENT IN FINANCIAL STATEMENTS

In December 1984, the FASB issued *Statement of Financial Accounting Concepts No. 5,* ''Recognition and Measurement in Financial Statements of Business Enterprises,''[15] describing recognition criteria and providing guidance as to the timing and nature of information to be included in financial statements. The recognition criteria established in the *Statement* are fairly consistent with those used in current practice. The *Statement* indicates, however, that when information that is more useful than currently reported information is available at a reasonable cost, it should be included in financial statements.

A slightly modified income statement format is recommended. The income statement may become a statement of earnings and comprehensive income. ''Earnings'' would generally be computed in the same way as income after extraordinary items (covered in Chapter 14) is presently calculated. Then, cumula-

---

[15] FASB, *Statement of Financial Accounting Concepts No. 5,* ''Recognition and Measurement in Financial Statements of Business Enterprises'' (Stamford, Conn., 1984). Copyright © by the Financial Accounting Standards Board, High Ridge Park, Stamford, Connecticut 06905, U.S.A. Copies of the complete document are available from the FASB. (In case you are wondering why we do not mention *Statement of Financial Accounting Concepts No. 4,* it pertains to accounting for not-for-profit organizations and is, therefore, not relevant to this text.)

tive account adjustments (such as changes in accounting principle) and other nonowner changes in equity would be added or deducted in arriving at "comprehensive income." The lower part of the statement would appear as follows:

Earnings	xx
+ or − Cumulative account adjustments (e.g., cumulative effect of changes in accounting principle)	xx
+ or − Other nonowner changes in equity (e.g., gains or losses on market changes in noncurrent marketable equity securities*)	xx
Comprehensive income	xx

* This item is discussed in Chapter 16.

The *Statement* also indicates that a balance sheet does not show the value of a business, but when used in combination with other information and other financial statements, the balance sheet is helpful in estimating the value of a business. The importance of cash flow information (covered in Chapter 18) is also mentioned.

UNDERSTANDING THE LEARNING OBJECTIVES

1. Identify and discuss the underlying assumptions or concepts of accounting.
   - ☐ The major underlying assumptions or concepts of accounting are (1) business entity, (2) going concern (continuity), (3) money measurement, (4) stable dollar, and (5) periodicity.
   - ☐ Other basic accounting concepts that affect the accounting for entities are (1) general-purpose financial statements, (2) substance over form, (3) consistency, (4) double entry, and (5) articulation.

2. Identify and discuss the major principles of accounting.
   - ☐ The major principles include exchange-price (or cost), matching, revenue recognition, expense and loss recognition, and full disclosure. Major exceptions to the realization principle include cash collection as point of revenue recognition, installment basis of revenue recognition, the percentage-of-completion method of recognizing revenue on long-term construction projects, and revenue recognition at completion of production.

3. Identify and discuss the modifying conventions (or constraints) of accounting.
   - ☐ Modifying conventions include cost-benefit, materiality, and conservatism.

4. Describe the Conceptual Framework Project of the Financial Accounting Standards Board.
   - ☐ The FASB has defined the objectives of financial reporting, qualitative characteristics of accounting information, and elements of financial statements.
   - ☐ Financial reporting objectives are the broad overriding goals sought by accountants engaging in financial reporting.
   - ☐ Qualitative characteristics are those characteristics that accounting information should possess to be useful in decision making. The two primary qualitative characteristics are relevance and reliability. Another qualitative characteristic is comparability.

      □ Pervasive constraints include cost-benefit analysis and materiality.

      □ The basic elements of financial statements have been identified and defined by the FASB.

      □ The FASB has also described revenue recognition criteria and provided guidance as to the timing and nature of information to be included in financial statements.

5. Discuss the differences in international accounting among nations (Appendix).

      □ Accounting principles differ among nations because they were developed independently.

      □ There have been attempts at harmonizing accounting principles throughout the world.

      □ Various differences in accounting principles that exist between nations are described.

APPENDIX: INTERNATIONAL ACCOUNTING*

WHY ACCOUNTING PRINCIPLES AND PRACTICES DIFFER AMONG NATIONS

Objective 5

Discuss the differences in international accounting among nations

In today's world, we do not find it surprising to discover a British bank in Atlanta, Coca-Cola in Paris, and French airplanes in Zaire. German automobile parts are assembled in Spain and sold in the United States. Japan buys oil from Saudi Arabia and sells cameras in Italy. Soviet livestock eat American grain, and the British sip tea from Sri Lanka and China. Business has become truly international, but accounting, often described as the language of business, does not cross borders so easily. Accounting principles and reporting practices differ from country to country, and international decision making is made more difficult by the lack of a common communication system. However, since business is practiced at an international level, accounting must find a way to provide its services at that level.

The problem is that accounting reflects the national economic and social environment in which it is practiced, and this environment is not the same in Bangkok as in Boston. Some economies, for example, are mainly agricultural. Others are based on manufacturing, trade, or service industries. Still others export natural resources, such as oil or gold, while a few derive most of their income from tourism. Accounting for inventories and natural resources, cost accounting techniques, and methods of foreign currency translation have a different orientation, emphasis, and degree of refinement in these different economies.

Other accounting differences stem from the various legal or political systems of nations. In centrally controlled economies (of which there are a declining number), for instance, the state owns all or most of the property. It makes little sense to prescribe full disclosure of accounting procedures to protect investors when little or no private ownership of property exists. In these nations with centrally controlled economies, an accounting profession is virtually nonexistent. One of the great challenges for Western nations over the next few decades is to assist the nations of Eastern Europe and the independent republics of the Soviet Union to build an accounting profession within those nations to serve the companies that will evolve under their new market-oriented economies. Some of these countries standardize their accounting methods and incorporate them into law.

---

* The authors wish to express their appreciation to William P. Hauworth II, Partner, Arthur Andersen & Co., Chicago, Illinois, for updating this appendix.

In most market-oriented economies, the development of accounting principles and reporting practices is left mainly to the private sector. Where uniformity exists, it occurs more by general agreement or consensus of interested parties than by governmental decree. In countries where business firms are predominately family owned, disclosure practices usually are less complete than in countries where large, publicly held corporations dominate. The requirement in many countries that the financial statements must conform to the tax return contributes to diversity in accounting practices among countries.

The degree of development of the accounting profession and the general level of education of a country also influence accounting practices and procedures. Nations that lack a well-organized accounting profession may adopt, almost in total, the accounting methods of other countries. Commonwealth countries, for example, tend to follow British accounting standards; the former French colonies of Africa use French systems; Bermuda follows Canadian pronouncements; and the influence of the United States is widespread. At the same time, levels of expertise vary. In countries that have little knowledge or understanding of statistics, nothing is gained by advocating statistical accounting and auditing techniques. Accounting systems designed for electronic data processing are not helpful in countries where few or no businesses use computers.

Even in advanced countries, genuine differences of opinion exist regarding accounting theory and appropriate accounting methods. American standards, for example, require the periodic amortization of goodwill to expense, but British and Dutch standards do not. The lack of agreement on the objectives of financial statements and the lack of any effort in most countries to articulate objectives also contribute to diversity. Accounting methods also differ within nations. Most countries, including the United States, permit several depreciation methods and two or more inventory costing methods.

ATTEMPTED HARMONIZATION OF ACCOUNTING PRACTICES

The question arises as to whether financial statements that reflect the economic and social environment of, say, France can also be useful to a potential American investor. Can some of the differences between French and American accounting be eliminated or at least explained so that French and American investors will understand each other's reports and find them useful when they make decisions?

Several organizations are working to achieve greater understanding and harmonization of different accounting practices. These organizations include the Organization for Economic Cooperation and Development (OECD), the European Community (EC), the International Accounting Standards Committee (IASC), and the International Federation of Accountants (IFAC). These organizations study the information needs and accounting and reporting practices of different nations, and some of them issue pronouncements recommending specific practices and procedures for adoption by all members.

The IASC is making a significant contribution to the development of international accounting standards. It was founded in London in 1973 by the professional accountancy bodies of 10 countries: Australia, Canada, France, Germany, Ireland, Japan, Mexico, the Netherlands, the United Kingdom, and the United States. The IASC selects a topic for study from lists of problems submitted by the profession all over the world. After research and discussion by special committees, the IASC issues an exposure draft of a proposed standard for consideration by the profession and the business and financial communities. After about six months' further study of the topic in light of the comments received, the IASC issues the final international accounting standard. To date, 26 standards have been issued on topics as varied as *Disclosure of Accounting Policies* (IAS 1), *Deprecia-*

tion Accounting (IAS 4), *Statement of Changes in Financial Position* (IAS 7), and *Revenue Recognition* (IAS 18). Setting international standards is not easy. If the standards are too detailed or rigid, the flexibility needed to reflect different national environments will be lost. On the other hand, if pronouncements are vague and allow too many alternative methods, there is little point in setting international standards.

One major problem is obtaining compliance with these standards. There is no organization, nor is there likely to be an organization, to ensure compliance with international standards. Adoption is left to national standard-setting bodies or legislatures, which may or may not adopt a recommended international standard. Generally, members commit themselves to support the objectives of the international body. The members promise to use their best endeavors to see that international standards are formally adopted by local professional accountancy bodies, by government departments or other authorities that control the securities markets, and by the industrial, business, and financial communities of their respective countries.

The American Institute of Certified Public Accountants (AICPA), for example, issued a revised statement in 1975 reaffirming its support for the implementation of international standards adopted by the IASC. The AICPA's position is that international accounting standards must be specifically adopted by the Financial Accounting Standards Board (FASB), which is not a member of the IASC, to achieve acceptance in the United States. However, if no significant difference exists between an international standard and U.S. practice, compliance with U.S. generally accepted accounting principles (GAAP) constitutes compliance with the international standard. Where a significant difference exists, the AICPA publishes the IASC standard together with comments on how it differs from GAAP in the United States and undertakes to urge the FASB to give early consideration to harmonizing the differences.[16] Significant support for IASC standards has also resulted from a resolution adopted by the World Federation of Stock Exchanges in 1975. The resolution binds members to require conformance with IASC standards in securities listing agreements.[17]

Although these developments are important for the international harmonization of accounting, the success of international pronouncements ultimately depends on the willingness of the members to support them. In some cases, national legislation is required and may be slow or difficult to pass. The EC, for example, issues "Directives" that must be accepted as compulsory objectives by the 12 member states (Belgium, Denmark, France, Germany, Greece, Ireland, Italy, Luxembourg, the Netherlands, Portugal, Spain, and the United Kingdom) but are translated into national legislation at the discretion of each member state. The EC's important *Fourth Directive* was adopted in 1978 to regulate the preparation, content, presentation, audit, and publication of the accounts and reports of companies. It applies to all limited-liability companies (corporations) registered in the EC, except banks and insurance companies. Under the directive, member states were to introduce legislation by July 1980 so that accounts in all EC countries would conform to the directive as of the fiscal year beginning January 1, 1982.

The general movement toward international harmonization of accounting standards is increasing in other areas of society. The accounting profession, national standard-setting bodies, universities, academic societies, and multinational corporations have all shown an increased interest in international accounting problems in recent years. The AICPA has an International Practice Division as a formal part

---

[16] American Institute of Certified Public Accountants, *CPA Letter*, August 1975.

[17] *CA Magazine*, January 1975, p. 52.

A BROADER PERSPECTIVE

RED REVOLUTION JOSTLES WORLD RULE MAKERS

Chicago—The leisurely world of writing international accounting standards is being revved up to high speed by political changes in the Communist world.

The standards-writers must now deal with the urgent needs of East Bloc nations that have to adopt internationally acceptable accounting and reporting standards to do business with the West.

Arthur Wyatt, incoming chairman of the International Association of Accounting Standards (IASC) and a senior partner of Arthur Andersen, Chicago, reported that IASC has received inquiries from representatives of East Bloc nations interested in improving business relations with the West.

"Most recently, Hungary has appealed for help in arranging accounting rules that would pave the way for joint ventures with Western companies," he said.

"Sessions were held for that same purpose in Moscow last June," he added.

A companion organization, the International Federation of Accountants (IFAC) reported that Poland also has appealed for help.

The World Bank has been prodding the Polish leadership to install adequate accounting standards before it grants funds needed to develop the nation's economy.

IFAC is a worldwide organization that represents 104 national professional accounting bodies in 78 countries.

* * * * *

Members of IFAC are automatically inducted into IASC, and the two bodies cooperate closely. IFAC concerns itself with the needs of the accounting profession. IASC focuses on seeking harmony in accounting and reporting standards of individual countries.

Bringing consistency to international accounting poses problems that challenge the best efforts of IFAC and IASC. To get new standards, Wyatt said, IASC and other accounting bodies tend to permit variations that protect ingrained ways of accounting.

But that may change. "Securities regulators in many countries are focusing on these alternatives and pressure may be brought to eliminate as many of them as is practical," Wyatt said.

* * * * *

Drastic changes are sweeping across Europe, said Wyatt: "Finding ways to integrate underdeveloped nations into the Western economies will not be easy."

None of these countries has qualified for membership in the international accounting organizations. Politics is not the reason. Eastern European countries lack an organized accounting profession, essential for dealing with private enterprise in the West. Besides that, they are not profit-oriented, which makes their approach to business an odd fit for western companies.

Wyatt hopes that in time his organization can encourage them to develop an accounting profession similar to that of the West.

* * * * *

Said Wyatt, "One thing that won't work for the U.S. is to say 'you have to do things our way.' We must be prepared to accept some changes as we go forward with international standards-setting."

Source: Bradford E. Smith, *Accounting Today*, January 22, 1990, p. 12. Reprinted with permission.

of its organization. The American Accounting Association officially established an International Accounting section in 1976 and has approximately one dozen international accounting organizations as Associate Members. The University of Lancaster (England) and the University of Illinois have international accounting research centers that support research studies and conduct international conferences and seminars. Georgia State University received a Touche Ross & Co. grant to internationalize its accounting curriculum. Many universities currently offer courses in international business and accounting.

All this activity helps increase the flow of information and our understanding of the accounting and reporting practices in other parts of the world. Greater understanding improves the likelihood that unnecessary differences will be eliminated and enhances the general acceptance of international standards.

The difficulty of achieving harmonization was illustrated in a recent effort to gain international agreement on the treatment of goodwill.[18] The International Accounting Standards Committee issued an exposure draft, known as E32, that included a provision that goodwill be recorded as an asset and amortized against earnings over a period of five years. If a company wanted to use a longer period, it would have to justify and explain its position in the financial statements.

Currently, the United Kingdom and the Netherlands write off goodwill immediately against "reserves" (a part of stockholders' equity) and bypass the income statement. This method gives them an advantage when making acquisitions because future earnings are not reduced by the amortization of goodwill. Some countries record goodwill as an asset but have amortization periods that exceed five years. For instance, in the United States goodwill can be written off over a period not to exceed 40 years. Other countries, such as Holland, permit either approach.

Companies in the United Kingdom generally oppose the change because it would reduce reported earnings and would remove their advantage in making acquisitions. However, they might be willing to support a change if the write-off period were longer, say, 20 years. The Dutch seem to be opposed to any change in their current accounting for goodwill. The French generally agreed with the proposal but would like a longer write-off period. Arthur Wyatt, the U.S. delegate to the IASC, felt that executives of U.S. companies might oppose a five-year write-off period because it would reduce income and affect their compensation plans that are often tied to income. If harmonization is to be achieved regarding accounting for goodwill, compromise will be necessary.

The remainder of this appendix gives examples of the accounting methods used in different countries and of the concepts that underlie these methods to illustrate the difficulty of achieving international harmonization.

FOREIGN CURRENCY TRANSLATION

Foreign currency translation is probably the most common problem in an international business environment. Foreign currency translation has two main components: accounting for transactions in a foreign currency and translating the financial statements of foreign enterprises into a different, common currency. This topic is presented here to give you an idea of the complexity of the harmonization effort.

Accounting for Transactions in a Foreign Currency

Suppose an American automobile dealership imports vehicles from Japan and promises to pay for them in yen 90 days after receiving them. If no change in the dollar-yen exchange rate occurs between the date the goods are received and the date the invoice is paid, no problem exists. Both the purchase and the payment will be recorded at the same dollar value. But if the yen appreciates against the dollar during the 90-day period, the importer must pay more dollars for the yen needed on the settlement date.[19] Which exchange rate should the importer use to record the purchase of the vehicles—the rate in effect on the purchase date or on the payment date?

One approach to the problem is to regard the purchase of the automobiles and settlement of the invoice as two separate transactions and record them at two

---

[18] This discussion is based on an article by Anne O'Carroll, "IASC's Goodwill Proposal Draws Much Negative Criticism," *Corporate Accounting International*, no. 1 (November 1989), pp 8–9.

[19] This example ignores the possibility that the importer might obtain a forward exchange contract, a discussion of which is beyond the scope of this text.

different exchange rates. The difference between the amount recorded in Accounts Payable on the purchase date and the amount of cash paid on the settlement date is considered an exchange gain or loss. This approach, known as the "time-of-transaction" method, was the prescribed or predominant practice in 61 of 64 countries surveyed in 1979,[20] including the United States.[21] The time-of-transaction method is also the method recommended in the IASC's Statement No. 21, *Accounting for the Effects of Changes in Foreign Exchange Rates,* issued in July 1983.

Another approach, known as the "time-of-settlement" method, regards the transaction and its settlement as a single event. If this method is used, the amount recorded on the purchase date is regarded as an estimate of the settlement amount. Any fluctuations in the exchange rate between the purchase date and the settlement date are accounted for as part of the transaction and are not treated as a separate gain or loss. Consequently, the effect on earnings is not recognized until the purchased items are sold.

Although the time-of-transaction method is widely used, the treatment of resulting exchange gains and losses is not uniform. If the gains or losses are realized (that is, if settlement is made within the same accounting period as the purchase), most countries recognize the gains and losses in the income statement for that period. If the exchange gains or losses are unrealized—that is, if they result from translating accounts payable (or accounts receivable for the vendor) at the balance sheet date—the treatment varies. Recording unrealized losses was the prescribed or predominant practice in 54 countries in 1979. Only 40 countries, however, similarly recognized exchange gains in income, the remaining nations preferring to defer them until settlement. In the United States, under the provisions of FASB *Statement No. 52,* both realized and unrealized transaction gains and losses are recognized in earnings of the period in which the exchange rate changes.

Translating Financial Statements

Financial statements of foreign subsidiaries are translated into a single common unit of measurement, such as the dollar, for purposes of consolidation. Considerable argument has arisen in recent years regarding the correct way to make this translation; that is, which exchange rate should be used to translate items in the balance sheet and income statement, and what treatment is appropriate for any resulting exchange gains and losses? Items translated at the historical rate cannot result in exchange gains or losses. However, items translated at the exchange rate in effect on the balance sheet date (the current rate) can result in exchange gains and losses if the current rate differs from the rate in effect when those items were recorded (the historical rate). If the current rate is used, a related question arises: Should the resulting exchange gains or losses be recognized immediately in income or deferred in some way?

The methods used to translate financial statements fall basically into two groups: translation of all items at the current rate and translation of some items at the current rate and others at the historical rates. The two groups are based on different concepts of both consolidation and international business.

---

[20] Price Waterhouse International, *International Survey.* Data on the different methods used and on the number of countries using each method described in these examples are derived substantially from this publication.

[21] FASB, *Statement of Financial Accounting Standards No. 8,* "Accounting for the Translation of Foreign Currency Transactions and Foreign Currency Financial Statements" (Stamford, Conn., 1975). The "time-of-transaction" method is also prescribed by FASB *Statement No. 52,* "Foreign Currency Translation" (Stamford, Conn., 1981), which supersedes FASB *Statement No. 8.*

The Current-Rate Approach   The current-rate or closing-rate approach translates all assets and liabilities at the current rate, the exchange rate in effect on the balance sheet date. The main advantage of this method is its simplicity; it treats all items uniformly. The approach is based on the view that a foreign subsidiary is a separate unit from the domestic parent company. The subsidiary's assets are viewed as being acquired largely out of local borrowing. Multinational groups, therefore, consist of entities that operate independently but contribute to a central fund of resources. Consequently, in consolidation it is believed that stockholders of the parent company are interested primarily in the parent company's net investment in the foreign subsidiary.

The Current/Historical-Rates Approach   The current/historical-rates approach regards the parent company and its foreign subsidiaries as a single business undertaking. Assets owned by a foreign subsidiary are viewed as indistinguishable from assets owned by the parent company. Foreign assets should, therefore, be reflected in consolidated statements in the same way that similar assets of the parent company are reported, that is, at historical cost in the parent company's currency.

Three translation methods are commonly used under this approach. The current-noncurrent method translates current assets and current liabilities at the current rate—the rate in effect on the balance sheet date—while noncurrent items are translated at their respective historical rates. The historical rate is the rate in effect when an asset or liability is originally recorded. Under the monetary-nonmonetary method, the current rate is used for monetary assets and liabilities—that is, for those that have a fixed, nominal value in terms of the foreign currency—while historical rates are applied to nonmonetary items. The temporal method is a variation of the monetary-nonmonetary method. Cash, receivables and payables, and other assets and liabilities carried at current prices (for example, marketable securities carried at current market value) are translated at the current rate of exchange. All other assets and liabilities are translated at historical rates.

Disagreement over the appropriate translation method seems likely to continue because of the different concepts of parent-subsidiary relations on which they are founded. In 1979, only six countries prescribed a single method. The temporal method was required in Austria, Canada, Bermuda, Jamaica, and the United States (under FASB *Statement No. 8*), while Uruguay required the current-rate method. Since that time the United States and Canada have changed to the current-rate method (FASB *Statement No. 52*). Apart from these 6 nations, 24 countries, including most of Europe, Japan, and Australia, predominantly followed the current-rate approach, while in 25 countries, including Germany, South Africa, and most of Central and South America, some variation of the current/historical-rates approach was common practice.

The treatment of exchange gains and losses produced by translating items at the current rate varies and is not strictly related to the translation method used. In 1979, the predominant practice in 42 nations, including much of Europe, Latin America, Japan, and the United States, was to recognize all gains and losses immediately in income. Eighteen of these countries used the current-rate translation method, and 23 followed one of the current/historical-rates methods. Alternative treatments of translation gains and losses included recording them directly in stockholders' equity (Australia), recognizing some of them immediately in income and deferring others (United Kingdom), and recognizing some in income and deferring and amortizing others over the remaining life of the items concerned (Canada and Bermuda).

Since the issuance of FASB *Statement No. 52,* the immediate recognition of translation gains and losses in income is not permitted in the United States. Instead, they are reported separately and accumulated in a separate component of stockholders' equity until the parent company's investment in the foreign subsidiary is sold or liquidated, at which time they are reported as part of the gain or loss on sale or liquidation of the investment.

INVENTORIES

Variations in accounting for inventories relate principally to the basis for determining cost and whether cost, once determined, should be increased or decreased to reflect the market value of the inventories.

Determination of Cost

Although other methods are occasionally used in some countries, this text discusses three principal bases for determining inventory cost: first-in, first-out (FIFO); last-in, first-out (LIFO); and average cost.

The most frequently used methods in 1979 were FIFO and average cost. Each of these methods was predominant in 31 countries, although no country required the use of one method to the exclusion of the other. FIFO was more common in Europe, although Austria, France, Greece, and Portugal used an average method. FIFO also predominated in Australia, Canada, South Africa, and the United States. The average method was generally followed in Latin America, Japan, and much of Africa. LIFO was the principal method in only one country—Italy—although it was a common minority method in Japan, the United States, most of Latin America, and several European countries. LIFO was considered an unacceptable method in Australia, Brazil, France, Ireland, Malawi, Norway, Peru, and the United Kingdom. IASC's Statement No. 2, *Valuation and Presentation of Inventories in the Context of the Historical Cost System,* supports the preference of the majority of countries and recommends the use of FIFO or average cost.

Market Value of Inventories

Only seven countries in 1979 did not require or predominantly follow the principle that inventories should be carried at the lower-of-cost-or-market value. Five of these countries, including Japan, used cost, even when cost exceeded market value. In the other two countries—Portugal and Switzerland—most enterprises wrote down inventories to amounts below both cost and market value, a practice permitted by law.

The main difference in the countries that did use the lower-of-cost-or-market approach was in the interpretation of "market value." Forty-eight countries equated market value with net realizable value, meaning estimated selling price in the ordinary course of business less costs of completion and necessary selling expenses. This view was essentially required in 22 countries, including Australia, France, Ireland, South Africa, and the United Kingdom. IASC Statement No. 2 also requires this interpretation. Austria, Greece, Italy, and Venezuela interpreted market value as replacement cost—the current cost of replacing the inventories in their present condition and location.

The United States defines market value as replacement cost, with the stipulation that it cannot exceed net realizable value or fall below net realizable value reduced by the normal profit margin. In 1979, Chile, the Dominican Republic, Mexico, Panama, and the Philippines also used this interpretation of market value.

ACCOUNTING FOR THE EFFECTS OF CHANGING PRICES

The final example of international differences illustrates an opportunity for international harmonization that is almost unique. Accounting for the effects of changing prices is a relatively recent development, so it may be possible to achieve a general international approach to the problem before national practices become too varied and too entrenched.

In Appendix B at the end of the text, two approaches to accounting for the effects of changing prices on business enterprises are discussed: general price-level (constant-dollar) accounting and current-cost accounting. The FASB, in *Statement No. 33,* required both methods.[22] However, *Statement No. 82* eliminated the requirements to use the first of these methods.[23] The first approach attempts to reflect the effects of changes in general purchasing power on historical-cost financial statements, while the second is concerned with the impact of specific price changes. FASB *Statement No. 89* made reporting the effects of inflation completely optional.[24]

A number of countries are concerned about the loss of relevance of historical-cost financial reporting in inflationary environments, and several have adopted one of the two standard approaches—constant dollar or current cost. Some countries, usually those with the longest history of severe inflation, have issued standards that are mandatory for all enterprises, or at least for large or publicly held entities. In other countries, the accounting profession recommends, but does not prescribe, a form of inflation-adjusted statements, usually as supplementary information. Few countries, however, are prepared to abandon the present system based on historical cost and nominal units of currency for their primary financial statements, at least until decision makers have had sufficient experience with inflation accounting to give an opinion on its utility. Exceptions to this view are Argentina, Brazil, and Chile, which now require incorporation of general price-level accounting in the primary financial statements of all enterprises.

The United Kingdom's standard, until it was withdrawn, prescribed the provision of current-cost information either in the primary financial statements or as supplementary statements or additional information. New Zealand requires a supplementary income statement and balance sheet on a current-cost basis. Australia and South Africa recommend, but do not yet require, similar supplementary current-cost statements. Germany recommends the incorporation of current-cost information in notes to the historical-cost financial statements; while in the Netherlands, some companies prepare the primary statements on a current-cost basis, and some provide only supplementary information.

The fact that the accountancy bodies of various nations are adopting neither a uniform approach nor a uniform application of any approach, even with something as relatively new as accounting for changing prices, highlights the difficulty of achieving international harmonization of accounting standards. Adoption of different approaches to accounting for changing prices by different countries will make the preparation of consolidated financial statements by multinational corporations especially difficult, while at the same time comparability of the financial reports of companies in different nations will be further reduced. However, even

---

[22] FASB, *Statement of Financial Accounting Standards No. 33,* "Financial Reporting and Changing Prices" (Stamford, Conn., 1979).

[23] FASB, *Statement of Financial Accounting Standards No. 82,* "Financial Reporting and Changing Prices: Elimination of Certain Disclosures" (Stamford, Conn., 1984).

[24] FASB, *Statement of Financial Accounting Standards No. 89,* "Financial Reporting and Changing Prices" (Stamford, Conn., 1987).

if all countries adopted a similar approach, a major barrier to comparability would still remain: the price indexes used in each country to compute adjustments for price changes are not comparable in composition, accuracy, frequency of publication, or timeliness.

Many accountants are reluctant to see current-cost-adjusted statements replace historical-cost financial statements because they believe historical cost is the most objective basis of valuation. However, business entities may be more likely to favor inflation accounting, once they become accustomed to it, because of its tax implications—assuming the tax law will permit the method. Since inflation accounting generally leads to lower profit figures than those computed on the historical-cost basis, companies have a strong incentive to adopt inflation accounting in those countries where computation of the tax liability is based on reported net income. Governments, on the other hand, could then decide to prohibit the use of inflation accounting for tax purposes when a decline in tax revenues becomes apparent.

The current trend in the use of approaches to accounting for changing prices appears to be toward current-cost accounting and away from general price-level accounting. It has been suggested that, of the two approaches, governments prefer current-cost accounting, and this preference may influence the decisions of the accounting profession in some countries. As one British writer has pointed out:

No government wants to have the effects of its currency debasement measured by anyone—certainly not by every business enterprise in the country. Much better to point the finger at all those individual prices moving around because of the machinations of big business, big labour and big aliens.[25]

Whether current-cost accounting will become common practice or whether some combination of current-cost and general price-level accounting will gain favor should depend on the usefulness to decision makers of the information provided by each approach. One thing is clear: As inflation again becomes a problem, more countries will adopt some form of inflation accounting. The opportunity to achieve a higher level of international harmonization while national standards are still at the development stage should not be missed.

We have attempted in these few pages to provide a broad and general picture of the variety of accounting principles and reporting practices that exist across the world. Articulation among countries is a challenging problem—and one that will receive increasing attention in the years to come.

SELECTED BIBLIOGRAPHY

The sources listed below will provide you with additional information about international accounting.

Arthur Andersen & Co. (London). *European Review*, nos. 1–5 (January 1981–May 1982).

Choi, Frederick D. S., and Gerhard G. Mueller. *An Introduction to Multinational Accounting*. Englewood Cliffs, N.J.: Prentice-Hall, 1984.

Gandy, Lisa A. "German and Japanese Annual Reports Lack Sufficient Information." *Corporate Accounting International*, no. 1 (November 1989), pp. 14–15.

Hauworth, William P., II. "A Comparison of Various International Proposals on Inflation Accounting: A Practitioner's View." Monograph, 1980.

Hobson, D. "International Harmonization." *Public Finance and Accountancy* (May 1983), pp. 34–36.

---

[25] P. H. Lyons, "Farewell to Historical Costs?" *CA Magazine*, February 1976, p. 23.

Horner, Lawrence D. "Efficient Markets and Universal Standards." *Chief Executive* (Winter 1985), p. 38.

International Financial Reporting Standards: Problems and Prospects. ICRA Occasional Paper No. 13. Lancaster, England: International Centre for Research in Accounting, University of Lancaster, 1977.

London, David Aron. "Soviets Begin to Westernize Accounting Standards with East-West Joint Ventures." *Corporate Accounting International,* no. 1 (November 1989), pp. 6–7.

O'Carroll, Anne. "IASC's Goodwill Proposal Draws Much Negative Criticism." *Corporate Accounting International,* no. 1 (November 1989), pp. 8–9.

Price Waterhouse International. *International Survey of Accounting Principles and Reporting Practices,* 1979.

Stamp, Edward. *The Future of Accounting and Auditing Standards. ICRA Occasional Paper No. 18*. Lancaster, England: International Centre for Research in Accounting, University of Lancaster, 1979.

Stamp, Edward, and Maurice Moonitz. "International Auditing Standards—Parts I and II." *The CPA Journal* LII, nos. 6 and 7 (June–July 1982).

DEMONSTRATION PROBLEM

For each of the transactions or circumstances described below and the entries made, state which, if any, of the assumptions, concepts, principles, or modifying conventions of accounting have been violated. For each violation, give the entry to correct the improper accounting assuming the books have not been closed.

During the year, Dorsey Company did the following:

1. Had its buildings appraised. They were found to have a market value of $410,000, although their book value was only $380,000. The accountant debited the Buildings and Accumulated Depreciation—Buildings accounts for $15,000 each and credited Capital from Appreciation. No separate mention was made of this action in the financial statements.

2. Purchased a number of new electric pencil sharpeners for its offices at a total cost of $60. These pencil sharpeners were recorded as assets and are being depreciated over five years.

3. Produced a number of agricultural products at a cost of $26,000. These costs were charged to expense when the products were harvested. The products were set up in inventory at their net market value of $35,000, and the Farm Revenues Earned account was credited for $35,000.

SOLUTION TO DEMONSTRATION PROBLEM

1. The realization principle and the modifying convention of conservatism may have been violated. Such write-ups simply are not looked on with favor in accounting. To correct the situation, the entry made needs to be reversed:

Capital from Appreciation	30,000	
Buildings		15,000
Accumulated Depreciation—Buildings		15,000

2. Theoretically, no violations occurred, but the cost of compiling insignificant information could be considered a violation of acceptable accounting practice. As a practical matter, the $60 could have been expensed on materiality grounds.

3. No violations occurred. The procedures followed are considered acceptable for farm products that are interchangeable and readily marketable. No correcting entry is needed, provided due allowance has been made for the costs to be incurred in delivering the products to the market.

NEW TERMS

Accounting theory ''A set of basic concepts and assumptions and related principles that explain and guide the accountant's actions in identifying, measuring, and communicating economic information.'' *562*

Business entity concept The specific unit for which accounting information is gathered. Business entities have a separate existence from owners, creditors, employees, customers, other interested parties, and other businesses. *562*

Comparability A qualitative characteristic of accounting information; when information is comparable, it reveals differences and similarities that are real and are not the result of differing accounting treatments. *581*

Completed-contract method A method of recognizing revenue on long-term projects under which no revenue is recognized until the period in which the project is completed; similar to recognizing revenue upon the completion of a sale. *570*

Completeness A qualitative characteristic of accounting information; requires disclosure of all significant information in a way that aids understanding and does not mislead; sometimes called the *full disclosure principle*. *580*

Conservatism Being cautious or prudent and making sure that net assets and net income are not overstated. *575*

Consistency Requires a company to use the same accounting principles and reporting practices through time. *565*

Cost-benefit consideration Determining whether benefits of including information in financial statements exceed costs. *575*

Cost principle See Exchange-price principle.

Current/historical-rates approach Regards the parent company and its foreign subsidiaries as a single business undertaking. All assets are shown at historical cost in the parent company's currency. *591*

Current-noncurrent method Translates current assets and current liabilities at the current rate. *591*

Current rate Exchange rate in effect on the balance sheet date. *590*

Current-rate or closing-rate approach The current-rate or closing-rate method translates all assets and liabilities at current rate, the exchange rate in effect on the balance sheet date. *591*

Earning principle The requirement that revenue be substantially earned before it is recognized (recorded). *568*

Exchange gains or losses (time-of-transaction method) The difference between the amount recorded in Accounts Payable on the purchase date and amount of cash paid on the settlement date. *590*

Exchange-price (or cost) principle Transfers of resources are recorded at prices agreed on by the parties to the exchange at the time of the exchange. *568*

Expense recognition principle Expenses should be recognized as they are incurred to produce revenues. *573*

Feedback value A qualitative characteristic that information has when it reveals the relative success of users in predicting outcomes. *579*

Financial reporting objectives The broad overriding goals sought by accountants engaging in financial reporting. *577*

Full disclosure principle Information important enough to influence the decisions of an informed user of the financial statements should be disclosed. *574*

Gain and loss recognition principle Gains may be recorded only when realized, but losses should be recorded when they first become evident. *573*

Gains Typically result from the sale of long-term assets for more than their book value. *573*

Going concern (continuity) assumption The assumption that an entity will continue to operate indefinitely unless strong evidence exists that it will terminate. *563*

Historical cost The amount paid, or the fair value of a liability incurred or other resources surrendered, to acquire an asset and place it in a condition and position for its intended use. *568*

Historical rate The exchange rate in effect when an asset or liability is originally recorded. *591*

Installment basis A revenue recognition procedure in which the percentage of total gross margin recognized in a period on an installment sale is equal to the percentage of total cash from the sale that is received in that period. *569*

Liquidation Terminating a business by ceasing business operations and selling off its assets. *563*

Losses Asset expirations that are usually involuntary and do not create revenues. *573*

Matching principle The principle that net income of a period is determined by associating or relating revenues earned in a period with expenses incurred to generate those revenues. *568*

Materiality A modifying convention that allows the accountant to deal with immaterial (unimportant) items in an expedient but theoretically incorrect manner; also a qualitative characteristic specifying that financial accounting report only information significant enough to influence decisions or evaluations. *575*

Modifying conventions Customs emerging from accounting practice that alter the results that would be obtained from a strict application of accounting principles; conservatism is an example. *575*

Monetary-nonmonetary method The current exchange rate is used in translating monetary assets and liabilities, while the historical rate is applied to nonmonetary items. *591*

Money measurement Use of a monetary unit of measurement, such as the dollar, instead of physical or other units of measurement—feet, inches, grams, and so on. *563*

Neutrality A qualitative characteristic that requires accounting information to be free of measurement method bias. *581*

Percentage-of-completion method A method of recognizing revenue based on the estimated stage of completion of a long-term project. The stage of completion is measured by comparing actual costs incurred in a period with total estimated costs to be incurred in all periods. *571*

Period costs Costs that cannot be traced to specific products and are expensed in the period in which incurred. *573*

Periodicity (time periods) assumption An assumption of the accountant that an entity's life can be divided into time periods for purposes of reporting its economic activities. *564*

Predictive value A qualitative characteristic that information has when it improves users' abilities to predict outcomes of events. *579*

Product costs Costs incurred in the acquisition or manufacture of goods. Product costs are accounted for as if they were attached to the goods, with the result that they are charged to expense when the goods are sold. *573*

Production basis A method of revenue recognition used in limited circumstances that recognizes revenue at the time of completion of production or extraction. *572*

Qualitative characteristics Characteristics that accounting information should possess to be useful in decision making. *578*

Realization principle A principle that directs that revenue is recognized only after the seller acquires the right to receive payment from the buyer. *569*

Relevance A qualitative characteristic requiring that information be pertinent to or affect a decision. *578*

Reliability A qualitative characteristic requiring that information faithfully depict for users what it purports to represent. *580*

Representational faithfulness A qualitative characteristic requiring that accounting statements on economic activity correspond to the actual underlying activity. *580*

Revenue recognition principle The principle that revenues should be earned and realized before they are recognized (recorded). *568*

Stable dollar assumption An assumption that the dollar is a reasonably stable unit of measurement. *563*

Temporal method Cash, receivables and payables, and other assets and liabilities carried at current prices are translated at the current rate of exchange. All other assets and liabilities are translated at historical rates. *591*

Timeliness A qualitative characteristic requiring that accounting information be provided at a time when it may be considered before making a decision. *579*

Verifiability A qualitative characteristic of accounting information; information is verifiable when it can be substantially duplicated by independent measurers using the same measurement methods. *581*

SELF-TEST

True-False

Indicate whether each of the following statements is true or false.

1. The business entity concept assumes that each business has an existence separate from all parties except its owners.

2. When the substance of a transaction differs from its legal form, the accountant should record the economic substance.

3. The matching principle is fundamental to the accrual basis of accounting.

4. Exceptions to the realization principle include the installment basis of revenue recognition for sales revenue and the completed-contract method for long-term construction projects.

5. Immaterial items do not have to be recorded at all.

6. The Conceptual Framework Project resulted in identifying two primary qualitative characteristics that accounting information should possess— relevance and reliability.

7. *(Based on Appendix)* Pronouncements issued by the International Accounting Standards Committee (IASC) must be followed by member nations.

Multiple-Choice

Select the best answer for each of the following questions.

1. The underlying assumptions of accounting include all the following except:
   a. Business entity.
   b. Going concern.
   c. Matching.
   d. Money measurement and periodicity.

2. The concept that requires that all companies use the same accounting practices and reporting practices through time is:
   a. Substance over form.
   b. Consistency.
   c. Articulation.
   d. None of the above.

3. Which of the following statements is false regarding the revenue recognition principle?
   a. Revenue must be substantially earned before it is recognized.
   b. The accountant usually recognizes revenue before the seller acquires the right to receive payment from the buyer.
   c. Some small companies use the cash basis of accounting.
   d. Under the installment basis, the gross margin recognized in a period is equal to the amount of cash received from installment sales times the gross margin percentage for the year of sale.

4. Assume the following facts regarding the construction of a bridge:

Construction costs this period	$ 3,000,000
Total estimated construction costs . . .	10,000,000
Total sales price	15,000,000

The revenue that should be recognized this period is:
   a. $3,000,000.
   b. $4,500,000.
   c. $5,000,000.
   d. $6,500,000.

5. Modifying conventions include all of the following except:
   a. Periodicity.
   b. Cost-benefit.
   c. Materiality.
   d. Conservatism.

6. Which of the following is not part of the Conceptual Framework Project?
   a. Objectives of financial reporting.
   b. Quanitative characteristics.
   c. Qualitative characteristics.
   d. Basic elements of financial statements.

7. *(Based on Appendix)* Which of the following statements is true regarding the environment of international accounting?
   a. More and more nations are switching to a market-oriented economy.
   b. The accounting practices around the world are almost completely harmonized.
   c. The other nations of the world are willing to accept accounting methods used in the United States as the best methods to use in their own country.
   d. The topic of international accounting is becoming less and less relevant over time.

Now turn to page 606 to check your answers.

QUESTIONS

1. Name the assumptions underlying generally accepted accounting principles. Comment on the validity of the stable unit of measurement assumption during periods of high inflation.

2. Why does the accountant use the business entity concept?

3. When is the going-concern assumption not to be used?

4. What is meant by the term *accrual basis of accounting?* What is its alternative?

5. What does it mean to say that accountants record substance rather than form?

6. If a company changes an accounting principle because the change better meets the information needs of users, what disclosures must be made?

7. What is the exchange-price (or cost) principle? What is the significance of adhering to this principle?

8. What two requirements generally must be met before revenue will be recognized in a period?

9. Under what circumstances, if any, is the receipt of cash an acceptable time to recognize revenue?

10. What two methods may be used in recognizing revenues on long-term construction contracts?

11. Define expense. What principles guide the recognition of expense?

12. How does an expense differ from a loss?

13. What is the full disclosure principle?

14. What role does cost-benefit play in financial reporting?

15. What is meant by the accounting term *conservatism?* How does it affect the amounts reported in the financial statements?

16. Does materiality relate only to the relative size of dollar amounts?

17. Identify the three major parts of the conceptual framework project that are included in the text.

18. What are the two primary qualitative characteristics?

19. *(Based on Appendix)* Why do differences exist in accounting standards and practices from nation to nation?

20. *(Based on Appendix)* How successful have efforts at harmonization been to date?

21. *Real world question* Refer to "A Broader Perspective" on page 588. Why do East Bloc nations have to develop internationally acceptable accounting and reporting standards? What is the present status of the accounting profession in these nations?

22. *Real world question* The 1988 annual report of the American Ship Building Company stated:

Revenues, costs, and profits applicable to construction and conversion contracts are included in the consolidated statements of operations using the . . . percentage-of-completion accounting method. . . . The completed contract method was used for income tax reporting in the years this method was allowed.

Why might the management of a company want to use two different methods for accounting and tax purposes?

23. *Real world question* Chevron Corporation's 1988 Annual Report states:

Environmental expenditures that relate to current or future revenues are expensed or capitalized as appropriate. Expenditures that relate to an existing condition caused by past operations, and do not contribute to current or future revenue generation, are expensed.

What principle of accounting is being followed by this policy?

EXERCISES

Exercise 12–1

Match theory terms with definitions
(L.O. 1–3)

Match the items in Column A with the proper descriptions in Column B.

Column A	Column B
1. Going concern (continuity).	a. An assumption relied on in the preparation of the primary financial statements that would be unreasonable when the inflation rate is high.
2. Consistency.	
3. Disclosure.	
4. Periodicity.	b. Concerned with relative dollar amounts.
5. Conservatism.	c. The usual basis for the recording of assets.
6. Stable dollar.	d. Required if the accounting treatment differs from that previously used for a particular item.
7. Matching.	
8. Materiality.	e. An assumption that would be unreasonable to use in reporting on a firm that had become insolvent.
9. Exchange-price.	
10. Business entity.	f. None of these.
	g. Requires a company to use the same accounting procedures and practices through time.
	h. An assumption that the life of an entity can be subdivided into time periods for reporting purposes.
	i. Discourages undue optimism in measuring and reporting net assets and net income.
	j. Requires separation of personal from business activities in the recording and reporting processes.

Exercise 12–2

Compute net income under accrual basis and under installment method
(L.O. 2)

Hendricks Company sells its products on an installment sales basis. Data for 1993 and 1994 follow:

	1993	1994
Installment sales	$200,000	$240,000
Cost of goods sold on installment sales	140,000	180,000
Other expenses	30,000	40,000
Cash collected from 1993 sales	120,000	60,000
Cash collected from 1994 sales		160,000

a.   Compute the net income for 1994, assuming use of the accrual (sales) basis of revenue recognition.

b.   Compute the net income for 1994, assuming use of the installment method of recognizing gross margin.

Exercise 12–3

Recognize revenue under percentage-of-completion method (L.O. 2)

A company has a contract to build a ship at a price of $500 million and an estimated cost of $400 million. In 1994, costs of $100 million were incurred. Under the percentage-of-completion method, how much revenue would be recognized in 1994?

Exercise 12–4

Compute effect on financial statements of incorrectly expensing an asset
(L.O. 2)

A company follows a practice of expensing the premium on its fire insurance policy when the policy is paid. In 1994, the company charged to expense the $5,760 premium paid on a three-year policy covering the period July 1, 1994, to June 30, 1997. In 1991, a premium of $5,280 was charged to expense on the same policy for the period July 1, 1991, to June 30, 1994.

a.   State the principle of accounting that was violated by this practice.

b.   Compute the effects of this violation on the financial statements for the calendar year 1994.

c.   State the basis on which the company's practice might be justified.

Exercise 12–5

Compute gross margin under GAAP and then as production is completed
(L.O. 2)

Boston Company produces a product at a cost of $30 per unit that it sells for $45. The company has been very successful and is able to sell all of the units it can produce. During 1994, the company manufactured 50,000 units, but because of a transportation strike, it was able to sell and deliver only 40,000 units.

a.   Compute the gross margin for 1994 following generally accepted accounting principles. The cost of the units sold should be entitled "cost of goods sold" and treated as an expense.

b.   Compute the gross margin for 1994, assuming the realization principle is ignored and revenue is recognized as production is completed.

Exercise 12–6

Match accounting qualities with proper descriptions
(L.O. 4)

Match the accounting qualities in Column B with the proper descriptions in Column A. Some descriptions will be used more than once.

Column A: Descriptions	Column B: Accounting Qualities
a. Users of accounting information.	1. Relevance.
b. Pervasive constraint.	2. Feedback value.
c. User-specific qualities.	3. Decision makers.
d. Primary decision-specific qualities.	4. Representational faithfulness.
e. Ingredients of primary qualities.	5. Reliability.
f. Secondary and interactive qualities.	6. Comparability.
g. Threshold for recognition.	7. Benefits exceed costs.
	8. Predictive value.
	9. Timeliness.
	10. Decision usefulness.
	11. Verifiability.
	12. Understandability.
	13. Neutrality.
	14. Materiality.

PROBLEMS: SERIES A

Problem 12–1A

Compute net income assuming revenues are recognized at time of sale and then assuming installment method is used
(L.O. 2)

Gerhardt Real Estate Sales Company sells lots in its development in Dry Creek Canyon under terms calling for small cash down payments with monthly installment payments spread over a few years. Following are data on the company's operations for its first three years:

	1992	1993	1994
Gross margin rate	45%	48%	50%
Cash collected in 1994 from sales of lots made in.	$320,000	$400,000	$480,000

The total selling price of the lots sold in 1994 was $1,600,000, while general and administrative expenses (which are not included in the costs used to determine gross margin) were $400,000.

Required

a. Compute net income for 1994 assuming revenue is recognized on the sale of a lot.

b. Compute net income for 1994 assuming use of the installment method of accounting for sales and gross margin.

Problem 12–2A

Compute net income under completed-contract and percentage-of-completion methods
(L.O. 2)

Given below are the contract prices and costs relating to all of Orlando Company's long-term construction projects (in millions of dollars):

		Costs Incurred		
	Contract Price	Prior to 1994	In 1994	Costs to Be Incurred in Future Years
On projects completed in 1994 . . .	$23	$ 2	$18	$–0–
On incomplete projects	72	12	24	24

General and administrative expenses for 1994 amounted to $900,000. Assume that the general and administrative expenses are not to be treated as a part of the construction cost.

Required

a. Compute net income for 1994 using the completed-contract method.

b. Compute net income for 1994 using the percentage-of-completion method.

Problem 12–3A

Indicate agreement or disagreement with accounting practices followed and comment
(L.O. 1–3)

In each of the circumstances described below, the accounting practices followed may be questioned. You are to indicate whether you agree or disagree with the accounting practice employed and to state the assumptions, concepts, or principles that justify your position.

1. The cost of certain improvements to leased property having a life of five years was charged to expense because the improvements would revert to the lessor when the lease expires in three years.

2. The salaries paid to the top officers of the company were charged to expense in the period in which they were incurred even though the officers spent over half of their time planning next year's activities.

3. A company spent over $4.8 million in developing a new product and then spent an additional $5.4 million promoting it. All of these costs were incurred and charged to expense this year even though future years would also benefit.

4. No entry was made to record the belief that the market value of the land owned (carried in the accounts at $278,400) had increased.

5. No entry was made to record the fact that costs of $240,000 were expected to be incurred in fulfilling warranty provisions on products sold this year. The revenue from products sold was recognized this year.

6. The acquisition of a tract of land was recorded at the price paid for it of $518,400, even though the company would have been willing to pay $600,000.

7. A truck acquired at the beginning of the year was reported at year-end at 80% of its acquisition price even though its market value then was only 65% of its original acquisition price.

Problem 12–4A

Answer multiple-choice questions regarding the Conceptual Framework Project
(L.O. 4)

Select the best answer to each of the following questions:

1. In the Conceptual Framework Project, how many financial reporting objectives were identified by the FASB?
   a. One.
   b. Two.
   c. Three.
   d. Four.

2. The two primary qualitative characteristics are:
   a. Prediction value and feedback value.
   b. Timeliness and verifiability.
   c. Comparability and neutrality.
   d. Relevance and reliability.

3. A pervasive constraint of accounting information is that:
   a. Benefits must exceed costs.
   b. The information must be timely.
   c. The information must be neutral.
   d. The information must be verifiable.

4. To be reliable, information must (identify the *incorrect* quality):
   a. Be verifiable.
   b. Be timely.
   c. Have representational faithfulness.
   d. Be neutral.

5. The *basic elements* of financial statements consist of:
   a. Terms and their definitions.
   b. The objectives of financial reporting.
   c. The qualitative characteristics.
   d. The new income statement format.

Problem 12–5A

Answer fill-in-the-blank questions regarding international accounting (based on Appendix)
(L.O. 5)

Supply the missing word(s) in the following statements:

a. Accounting must reflect the national _____ and _____ environment in which it is practiced.

b. Other accounting differences among nations stem from the legal or _____ differences.

c. Commonwealth nations tend to adopt _____ accounting standards.

d. Several organizations are working to achieve greater understanding and _____ of accounting principles.

e. Ultimately, the success of international pronouncements depends on the willingness of the nations to _____ them.

f. _____ _____ translation is probably the most common problem in an international business environment.

PROBLEMS: SERIES B

Problem 12–1B

Compute income assuming revenues are recognized at time of sale and then assuming installment method is used
(L.O. 2)

Cortez Video, Inc., sells video recorders under terms calling for a small down payment and monthly payments spread over three years. Following are data for the first three years of the company's operations:

	1992	1993	1994
Sales.	$720,000	$1,080,000	$1,440,000
Cost of video sets sold.	504,000	648,000	720,000
Gross margin	$216,000	$ 432,000	$ 720,000
Gross margin as a percentage of sales.	30%	40%	50%
Cash collected in 1994:			
From 1992 sales			$216,000
From 1993 sales			288,000
From 1994 sales			468,000

General and selling expenses amounted to $432,000 in 1994.

Required

a. Compute net income for 1994, assuming revenues are recognized at the time of sale.

b. Compute net income for 1994, using the installment method of accounting for sales and gross margin.

Problem 12–2B

Compute income under completed-contract and percentage-of-completion methods
(L.O. 2)

The following data relate to Jackson Construction Company's long-term construction projects for the year 1994:

	Completed Projects	Incomplete Projects
Contract price.	$18,000,000	$96,000,000
Costs incurred prior to 1994	3,700,000	16,000,000
Costs incurred in 1994	11,100,000	32,000,000
Estimated costs to be incurred in future years.	–0–	32,000,000

General and administrative expenses incurred in 1994 amounted to $2 million, none of which is to be considered a construction cost.

Required

a. Compute net income for 1994 under the completed-contract method.

b. Compute net income for 1994 under the percentage-of-completion method.

Problem 12–3B

Match principles, assumptions, or concepts with certain accounting procedures followed
(L.O. 1–3)

For each of the numbered items listed below, state the letter or letters of the principle(s), assumption(s), or concept(s) used to justify the accounting procedure followed. The accounting procedures are all correct.

A—Business entity.
B—Conservatism.
C—Earning principle of revenue recognition.
D—Going concern (continuity).
E—Exchange-price principle.
F—Matching principle.
G—Period cost (or principle of immediate recognition of expense).
H—Realization principle.
 I—Stable dollar assumption.

1. The estimated liability for federal income taxes was increased by $28,000 over the amount reported on the tax return to cover possible differences found by the Internal Revenue Service in determining the amount of income taxes payable.

2. A truck purchased in January was reported at 80% of its cost even though its market value at year-end was only 70% of its cost.

3. The collection of $56,000 of cash for services to be performed next year was reported as a current liability.

4. The president's salary was treated as an expense of the year even though he spent most of his time planning the next two years' activities.

5. No entry was made to record the company's receipt of an offer of $560,000 for land carried in its accounts at $336,000.

6. A stock of printed stationery, checks, and invoices with a cost of $11,200 was treated as a current asset at year-end even though it had no value to others.

7. A tract of land acquired for $196,000 was recorded at that price even though it was appraised at $224,000, and the company would have been willing to pay that amount.

8. The company paid and charged to expense the $8,400 paid to Craig Nelson for rent of a truck owned by him. Craig Nelson is owner of the company.

9. $67,200 of interest collected on $560,000 of 12% bonds was recorded as interest revenue even though the general level of prices increased 16% during the year.

Problem 12–4B

Answer matching question regarding the Conceptual Framework Project (L.O. 4)

Match the descriptions in Column B with the proper terms in Column A.

Column A		Column B
1. Financial reporting objectives.	a.	Information is free of measurement method bias.
	b.	The benefits exceed the costs.
2. Qualitative characteristics.	c.	Relatively large items must be accounted for in a theoretically correct way.
3. Relevance.	d.	The information can be substantially duplicated by independent measurers using the same measurement methods.
4. Predictive value.		
5. Feedback value.	e.	When information improves users' ability to predict outcomes of events.
6. Timeliness.		
7. Reliability.	f.	Broad overriding goals sought by accountants engaging in financial reporting.
8. Representational faithfulness.		
	g.	When information is pertinent or bears on a decision.
9. Verifiability.	h.	The characteristics that accounting information should possess to be useful in decision making.
10. Neutrality.		
11. Comparability.	i.	Information that reveals the relative success of users in predicting outcomes.
12. Consistency.		
13. Cost-benefit.	j.	When accounting statements on economic activity correspond to the actual underlying activity.
14. Materiality.		
	k.	When information is provided soon enough that it may be considered in decision making.
	l.	When information faithfully depicts for users what it purports to represent.
	m.	Requires a company to use the same accounting principles and reporting practices through time.
	n.	When reported differences and similarities in information are real and not the result of differing accounting treatments.

Problem 12–5B

Answer multiple-choice questions regarding international accounting (based on Appendix) (L.O. 5)

Select the best answer to each of the following questions:

1. Methods used to account for transactions between companies in different nations when goods are received on one date and the invoice is paid on another date include:
   a. Time-of-transaction method.
   b. Time-of-settlement method.
   c. Current-rate method.
   d. Both (a) and (b) are correct.

2. Which of the following statements is *false* regarding translating financial statements of foreign subsidiaries?

    a. Under the *current-rate approach,* all assets and liabilities are translated at the exchange rate in effect on the balance sheet date.

    b. Under the *current-noncurrent method,* current assets and current liabilities are translated at the current rate, and noncurrent items are translated at their historical rates.

    c. Under the *monetary-nonmonetary method,* nonmonetary assets and liabilities are translated at their historical rate.

    d. The nations of the world now have settled on the current-rate method.

3. Variations between nations in accounting for inventories include all *except* which of the following?

    a. The basis for determining cost.

    b. Whether "cost" should be increased or decreased to reflect changes in market value.

    c. Whether inventories should be written down to an amount below both cost and market.

    d. Whether standard costs should be used.

4. In accounting for the effects of inflation, the approach that seems to be favored by most nations that have adopted an approach is:

    a. Current-cost.

    b. Constant-dollar (general price-level adjusted statements).

    c. A combination of *(a)* and *(b)* in one set of financial statements.

    d. Both *(a)* and *(b)* as two sets of financial statements.

BUSINESS DECISION PROBLEM

Decision Problem 12–1

Indicate agreement or disagreement with accounting practices followed; comment (L.O. 1–3)

Jeff Jacobs recently received his accounting degree from State University and went to work for a Big-Six CPA firm. After he had been with the firm for about six months, he was sent to the Franklin Clothing Company to work on the audit. He was not very confident of his knowledge at this early point in his career. He noticed, however, that some of the company's transactions and events were recorded in a way that might be in violation of accounting theory and generally accepted accounting principles.

Required

Study each of the following facts and see if you believe that the auditors should challenge the financial accounting practices used or the intentions of management. Give the reasoning behind your conclusions. (Some of the situations covered relate to other chapters you have studied in this text.)

1. The company recorded purchases of merchandise at the net invoice price rather than the gross invoice price.

2. Goods shipped to the company from a supplier, FOB destination, were debited to Purchases. The goods were not included in ending inventory because the goods had not yet arrived.

3. The company held the books open at the end of 1994 in order to record some early 1995 sales as 1994 revenue. The justification for this procedure was that 1994 was not a good year in terms of profits.

4. The company counted some items twice in taking the physical inventory at the end of the year. The employee taking the inventory said he had forgotten to include some items in last year's physical inventory, and counting some items twice now would make up for the items missed last year so that net income this year would be "about correct."

5. The company switched from FIFO to LIFO in accounting for inventories. The preceding year it had switched from the weighted-average method to FIFO. The reason given for the most recent change was that federal income taxes would be lower. No indication of this switch was to appear in the financial statements.

6. Since things were pretty hectic at year-end, the accountant made no effort to reconcile the bank account. His reason was that the bank probably had not made any errors. The bank balance was lower than the book balance, so the accountant debited Miscellaneous Expense and credited Cash for the difference.

7. When a customer failed to pay the amount due, the accountant debited Bad Debts Expense and credited Accounts Receivable. The amount of accounts written off in this manner was huge. When the company later collects an account that has already been written off, Cash is debited and Miscellaneous Revenue is credited.

8. The company's buildings were appraised for insurance purposes. The appraised values were $5 million higher than the book value. The accountant debited Buildings and credited Capital from Appreciation for the difference.

9. A machine was completely depreciated and was still being used. The accountant stopped recording depreciation on the machine and did not go back and correct earlier years and reduce accumulated depreciation.

10. One of the senior members of management stated the company planned to replace all of the furniture next year. He said that the cash in the Accumulated Depreciation account would be used to pay for the furniture.

11. The accountant stated that even though research and development costs incurred to develop a new product would benefit future periods, these costs must be expensed as incurred. This year $100,000 of these costs were charged to expense.

12. An old truck was traded for a new truck. Since the trade-in value of the old truck was higher than its book value, a gain was recorded on the transaction.

13. The company paid for a franchise giving it the exclusive right to operate in a given geographical area for 60 years. The accountant is amortizing the asset over 60 years.

14. The company leases a building and has a nonrenewable lease that expires in 15 years. The company made some improvements to the building. Since the improvements will last 30 years, they are being written off over 30 years.

ANSWERS TO SELF-TEST

True-False

1. *False.* The business entity concept assumes that each business has an existence separate from its owners, creditors, employees, customers, other interested parties, and other businesses.

2. *True.* Accountants should be guided by the economic substance of a transaction rather than its legal form.

3. *True.* The accrual basis of accounting seeks to match effort and accomplishment by matching expenses against the revenues they created.

4. *False.* Exceptions include the installment basis for sales and the percentage-of-completion method for long-term construction projects.

5. *False.* Immaterial items do have to be recorded, but they can be recorded in an incorrect way (e.g., expensing a wastebasket that will last many years).

6. *True.* Relevance and reliability are the two primary characteristics.

7. *False.* The IASC can only recommend specific practices and procedures for adoption by member nations.

Multiple-Choice

1. *c.* The matching concept is one of the major principles of accounting rather than an assumption.

2. *d.* If you answered *(b)*, you should note that the consistency concept requires that a given company (not all companies) use the same accounting principles and reporting practices through time.

3. *b.* Usually, the accountant does not recognize revenue until the seller acquires the right to receive payment from the buyer.

4. *b.* $3,000,000/$10,000,000 \times $15,000,000 = $4,500,000.

5. *a.* Periodicity is an underlying assumption rather than a modifying convention.

6. *b.* The category, quantitative characteristics, is not part of the Conceptual Framework Project.

7. *a.* The move from communism toward democracy is causing East European nations, Soviet republics, and certain other nations to pursue a market-oriented economy.

13

CORPORATIONS: FORMATION, ADMINISTRATION, AND CLASSES OF CAPITAL STOCK

LEARNING OBJECTIVES

After studying this chapter, you should be able to:

1. State the advantages and disadvantages of the corporate form of business.

2. List the values commonly associated with capital stock and give their definitions.

3. List the various kinds of stock and describe the differences between them.

4. Present in proper form the stockholders' equity section of a balance sheet.

5. Account for the issuances of stock for cash, by subscription, and for other assets.

6. Determine book values of both preferred and common stock.

In this chapter, you begin your study of the corporate form of business organization. Although corporations are fewer in number than single proprietorships and partnerships, corporations possess the bulk of our business capital and currently supply us with most of our goods and services.

This chapter discusses the advantages and disadvantages of the corporation, how to form and direct a corporation, and some of the unique situations encountered in accounting for and reporting on the different classes of corporate stock.

THE CORPORATION

A corporation is an entity recognized by law as possessing an existence separate and distinct from its owners; that is, it is a separate legal entity. Endowed with many of the rights and obligations possessed by a person, a corporation can, for example, enter into contracts in its own name; buy, sell, or hold property; borrow money; hire and fire employees; and sue and be sued.

Corporations have proved to be remarkably well-suited vehicles for obtaining the huge amounts of capital necessary for large-scale business operations. Corporations acquire their capital by issuing shares of stock, which are the units into which the ownership of a corporation is divided. Investors buy shares of stock in a corporation for two basic reasons. First, investors expect the value of their shares to increase over time so that the stock may be sold in the future at a profit. Also, while investors hold stock, they expect the corporation to pay them dividends (usually in cash) in return for using their money. Chapter 14 discusses the various kinds of dividends and their accounting treatment.

Advantages of the Corporate Form of Business

Objective 1
State the advantages and disadvantages of the corporate form of business

Corporations have many advantages compared to single proprietorships and partnerships. The major advantages of a corporation over a single proprietorship are the same advantages a partnership has over a single proprietorship. Although corporations usually have more owners than partnerships, both have a broader base for investment, risk, responsibilities, and talent than do single proprietorships. Since corporations are more comparable to partnerships than to single proprietorships, the discussion of advantages that follows contrasts the partnership with the corporation.

1. **Easy transfer of ownership.** In a partnership, a partner cannot transfer ownership in the business to another person if the other partners do not want the new person involved in the partnership. In a publicly held (owned by many stockholders) corporation, shares of stock are traded on a stock exchange between unknown parties; one owner usually cannot dictate to whom shares can or cannot be sold by another owner.

2. **Limited liability.** Each partner in a partnership is personally responsible for all the debts of the business. In a corporation, the stockholders are not personally responsible for the corporation's debts; the maximum amount a stockholder can lose is the amount of his or her investment. However, when a small, closely held corporation (owned by only a few stockholders) borrows money, banks and lending institutions often require an officer of the small corporation to sign the loan agreement. Then, the officer will have to repay the loan if the corporation does not.

3. **Continuous existence of the entity.** In a partnership, many circumstances, such as the death of a partner, can cause the termination of the business entity. These same circumstances have no effect on a corporation because it is a legal entity, separate and distinct from its owners.

4. **Easy capital generation.** The easy transfer of ownership and the limited liability of stockholders are attractive features to potential investors. Thus, it is relatively easy for a corporation to raise capital by issuing shares of stock to many investors. Corporations with thousands of stockholders are not uncommon.

5. **Professional management.** Generally, the partners in a partnership are also the managers of that business, but they may or may not have the necessary expertise to manage a business. In a publicly held corporation, most of the owners (stockholders) do not participate in the day-to-day operations and management of the entity. Usually, professionals are hired to run the business on a daily basis.

6. **Separation of owners and entity.** Since the corporation is considered a separate legal entity, the owners do not have the power to bind the corporation to business contracts. This feature eliminates the potential problem of mutual agency that exists between partners in a partnership. In a corporation, one stockholder cannot jeopardize other stockholders through poor decision making.

Disadvantages of the Corporate Form of Business

The corporate form of business has its disadvantages. These disadvantages include the following:

1. **Double taxation.** Because a corporation is a separate legal entity, its net income is subject to double taxation. The corporation pays a tax on its income, and stockholders pay a tax on corporate income received as dividends.

2. **Government regulation.** Because corporations are created by law, they are subject to greater regulation and control than are single proprietorships and partnerships.

3. **Entrenched, inefficient management.** A corporation may be burdened with an inefficient management that remains in control because it can use corporate funds to solicit the needed stockholder votes to back its positions. Stockholders scattered across the country, who individually own only small portions of a corporation's stock, usually find it difficult to organize themselves and oppose existing management.

4. **Limited ability to raise creditor capital.** The limited liability of stockholders makes a corporation an attractive means for accumulating stockholder capital. At the same time, this limited liability feature limits the amount of creditor capital a corporation can amass because **creditors cannot look to the personal assets of stockholders for satisfaction of the debts of a corporation if the corporation cannot pay.** Thus, beyond a certain point, creditors will not lend some corporations money without the personal guarantee of a stockholder or officer of the corporation to repay the loan if the corporation does not.

Incorporating

Corporations are chartered by the state. Each state has a corporation act that permits the formation of corporations by qualified persons. Incorporators are persons seeking to bring a corporation into existence. Most state corporation laws require a minimum of three incorporators, each of whom must be of legal age, and a majority of whom must be citizens of the United States.

The laws of each state view a corporation organized in that state as a domestic corporation and a corporation organized in any other state as a foreign corporation. If a corporation intends to conduct business solely within one state, it normally seeks incorporation in that state because most state laws are not as severe for domestic corporations as for foreign corporations. Corporations conducting interstate business usually incorporate in the state that has laws most advantageous to the corporation being formed. Important considerations in choosing a state are the powers granted to the corporation, the taxes levied, the defenses permitted against hostile takeover attempts by other companies or individuals, and the reports required by the state.

Articles of Incorporation

Once incorporators agree on the state in which to incorporate, they apply for a corporate charter. A corporate charter is a contract between the state and the incorporators of a corporation, and their successors, granting the corporation its legal existence. The application for the corporation's charter is called the articles of incorporation.

After the information requested in the incorporation application form is supplied, the articles of incorporation are filed with the proper office in the state of incorporation. Each state requires different information in the articles of incorporation, but most states ask for the following information:

1. Name of corporation.
2. Location of principal offices.
3. Purposes of business.
4. Number of shares of stock authorized, class or classes of shares, and voting and dividend rights of each class of shares.
5. Value of assets paid in by the original **subscribers** (persons who contract to acquire shares).
6. Limitations on authority of the management and owners of the corporation.

On approval by the state office (which is frequently the secretary of state's office), the charter is granted, and the corporation is created.

Bylaws

As soon as the corporation obtains the charter, it is authorized to operate its business. The incorporators call the first meeting of the stockholders. Two of the purposes of this meeting are to elect a board of directors and to adopt the bylaws of the corporation.

The bylaws are a set of rules or regulations adopted by the board of directors of a corporation to govern the conduct of corporate affairs. The bylaws must be in agreement with the laws of the state and the policies and purposes in the corporate charter. The bylaws contain, along with other information, provisions for the following: (1) the place, date, and manner of calling the annual stockholders' meeting; (2) the number of directors and the method for electing them; (3) the duties and powers of the directors; and (4) the method for selecting officers of the corporation.

Organization Costs

Organization costs are costs of organizing a corporation, such as state incorporation fees and legal fees applicable to incorporation. These costs should be debited to an account called *Organization Costs*. The Organization Costs account is an asset since the costs yield benefits over the life of the corporation; if the fees had not been paid, no corporate entity would exist. Since the account is classified on the balance sheet as an intangible asset, it is amortized over a period not to exceed

40 years. Most organization costs are written off fairly rapidly because they are small in amount, and rapid amortization of no less than five years is allowed for tax purposes.

As an illustration, assume that De-Leed Corporation pays state incorporation fees of $10,000 and attorney's fees of $5,000 for services rendered related to the acquisition of a charter with the state. The entry to record these costs is:

Organization Costs	15,000	
Cash		15,000
To record costs incurred in organizing corporation.		

If the corporation amortizes the organization costs over a 10-year period, the entry to record amortization at the end of the year is:

Amortization Expense—Organization Costs	1,500	
Organization Costs		1,500
To record organization costs amortization expense		
($15,000/10 years = $1,500).		

Directing the Corporation

The corporation is managed through the delegation of authority in a line from the stockholders to the directors to the officers, as shown in the organization chart in Illustration 13.1. The stockholders elect the board of directors. The board of directors formulates the broad policies of the company and selects the principal officers, who execute the policies.

Stockholders Stockholders do not have the right to participate actively in the management of the business unless they serve as directors and/or officers. However, stockholders do have certain basic rights, including the right to (1) dispose of their shares, (2) buy additional newly issued shares in a proportion equal to the percentage of shares they already own (called the preemptive right), (3) share in dividends when declared, (4) share in assets in case of liquidation, and (5) participate in management indirectly by voting at the stockholders' meeting.

The preemptive right is important to stockholders because it allows them to maintain their percentage of ownership in a corporation when additional shares are issued. For example, assume Joe Thornton owns 10% of the outstanding shares of Corporation X. When Corporation X decides to issue 1,000 additional shares of stock, Joe Thornton has the right to buy 100 (10%) of the new shares. Should he decide to do so, he will maintain his 10% interest in the corporation. If he does not wish to exercise his preemptive right, the corporation may sell the shares to others.[1]

Normally, stockholders' meetings are held annually. At the annual stockholders' meeting, stockholders indirectly share in management by voting on such questions as changing the charter, increasing the number of authorized shares of stock to be issued, approving pension plans, selecting the independent auditor, and other related matters.

---

[1] The preemptive right has been eliminated by some corporations because its existence makes it difficult to issue large blocks of stock to the stockholders of another corporation to acquire that corporation.

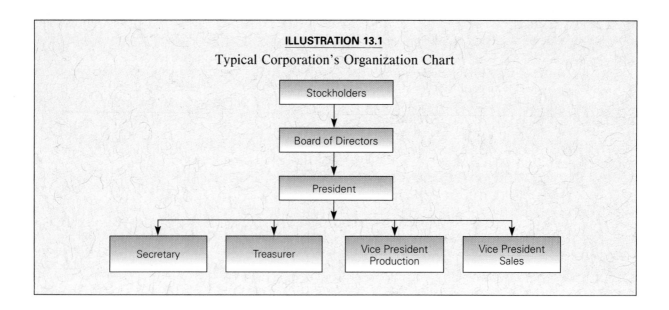

ILLUSTRATION 13.1
Typical Corporation's Organization Chart

At stockholders' meetings, each stockholder is entitled to one vote for each share of voting stock held. Stockholders who do not personally attend the stockholders' meeting may vote by proxy. A proxy is a legal document signed by a stockholder, giving a designated person the authority to vote the stockholder's shares at a stockholders' meeting.

Board of Directors The board of directors is elected by the stockholders and is primarily responsible for formulating policies for the corporation. The board appoints administrative officers and delegates to them the execution of the policies established by the board. The board also has more specific duties including (1) authorizing contracts, (2) declaring dividends, (3) establishing executive salaries, and (4) granting authorization to borrow money. The decisions of the board are recorded in the minutes of its meetings. These minutes are an important source of information to the independent auditor, since they may serve as notice to record transactions (such as a dividend declaration) or to recognize that certain transactions may be taking place in the near future (such as a large loan).

Corporate Officers Officers of a corporation usually are specified in the corporation's bylaws. The number of officers and their exact titles vary from corporation to corporation, but most have a president, several vice presidents, a secretary, a treasurer, and a controller.

The president is the chief executive officer of the corporation. He or she is empowered by the bylaws to hire all necessary employees except those appointed by the board of directors.

Most corporations have more than one vice president. Each vice president is usually responsible for one particular corporate operation, such as sales, engineering, or production. The corporate secretary is responsible for maintaining the official records of the company and records the proceedings of meetings of stockholders and directors. The treasurer is accountable for corporate funds and may be charged with the general supervision of the accounting function within the company. A controller is usually directly charged with carrying out the accounting function. The controller usually reports to the treasurer of the corporation.

DOCUMENTS, BOOKS, AND RECORDS RELATING TO CAPITAL STOCK

Capital stock consists of transferable units of ownership in a corporation. Each unit of ownership is called a *share of stock*. Typically, between 100 and 400 million shares of corporate capital stock are traded every business day on stock exchanges such as the New York Stock Exchange and the American Stock Exchange, and on the over-the-counter market. These sales (or *trades*) seldom involve the corporation issuing the stock as a party to the exchange, but rather are made by existing stockholders to other individual or institutional investors. These trades are followed by the physical transfer of the stock certificates.

A stock certificate is a printed or engraved document serving as evidence that the holder owns a certain number of shares of capital stock. When a stockholder sells shares of stock, the stockholder signs over the stock certificate to the new owner, who presents it to the issuing corporation. When the old certificate arrives at the issuing corporation, the certificate is canceled and attached to its corresponding stub in the stock certificate book. A new certificate is prepared for the new owner. The number of shares of stock outstanding at any time can be determined by summing the shares shown on the open stubs (stubs without certificates attached) in the stock certificate book.

Stockholders' Ledger

Among the more important records maintained by a corporation is the stockholders' ledger. The stockholders' ledger contains a group of subsidiary accounts showing the number of shares of stock currently held by each stockholder. Since the ledger contains an account for **each** stockholder, in a large corporation this ledger may have more than a million individual accounts. Each stockholder's account shows the number of shares currently or previously owned, their certificate numbers, and the dates on which shares were acquired or sold. Entries are made in terms of the number of shares rather than in dollars.

The stockholders' ledger and the stock certificate book contain the same information, but the stockholders' ledger summarizes it alphabetically by stockholder. Since a stockholder may own a dozen or more certificates, each representing a number of shares, this summary enables a corporation to (1) determine the number of shares a stockholder is entitled to vote at a stockholders' meeting and (2) prepare one dividend check per stockholder rather than one per stock certificate.

Many large corporations with actively traded shares turn the task of maintaining reliable stock records over to an outside *stock-transfer agent* and a *stock registrar*. The stock-transfer agent, usually a bank or trust company, is employed by a corporation to transfer stock between buyers and sellers. The stock-transfer agent cancels the certificates covering shares sold, issues new stock certificates, and makes appropriate entries in the stockholders' ledger. New certificates are then sent to the stock registrar, typically another bank, that maintains separate records of the shares outstanding. This control system makes it difficult for a corporate employee to issue stock certificates fraudulently and steal the proceeds.

The Minutes Book

The minutes book, kept by the secretary of the corporation, is (1) a record book in which actions taken at stockholders' and board of directors' meetings are recorded and (2) the written authorization for many actions taken by corporate officers. Remember that all actions taken by the board of directors and the stockholders must be in accordance with the provisions contained in the corporate charter and the bylaws. The minutes book contains a variety of data, including:

1. A copy of the corporate charter.
2. A copy of the bylaws.

   3. Dividends declared by the board of directors.
   4. Authorization for the acquisition of major assets.
   5. Authorization for borrowing.
   6. Authorization for increases or decreases in capital stock.

PAR VALUE AND NO-PAR CAPITAL STOCK

Par Value Stock

Objective 2
List the values commonly associated with capital stock and give their definitions

Many times, par value stock is issued. Par value is an arbitrary amount assigned to each share of a given class of stock and printed on the stock certificate. **Par value per share is no indication of the amount for which the stock will sell; it is simply the amount per share that is credited to the capital stock account for each share issued.** Also, the total par value of all issued stock constitutes the legal capital of the corporation. The concept of legal capital exists to help protect creditors from losses. Legal capital, or **stated capital,** is an amount prescribed by law below which a corporation may not reduce stockholders' equity through declaration of dividends or other payments to stockholders. Legal capital does not guarantee that a company will be able to pay its debts, but it does serve to keep a company from compensating owners to the detriment of creditors.

No-Par Stock

Laws permitting the issuance of no-par stock **(stock without par value)** were first enacted in the state of New York in 1912. Similar, but not uniform, legislation has since been passed in many other states.

A corporation might issue no-par stock for two reasons. One reason is to avoid confusion. The use of a par value may confuse some investors because the par value usually does not conform to market value. When stock has no par value, this source of confusion is avoided.

A second reason is related to state laws regarding the original issue price per share. A discount on capital stock is the amount by which the par value of shares issued exceeds their issue price. Thus, if stock with a par value of $100 is issued at $80, the discount is $20. Most states will not permit the original issuance of stock at a discount. Only a few states (e.g., Maryland and California) allow its issuance. The original purchasers of the shares are contingently liable for the discount unless they have transferred (by contract) the discount liability to subsequent holders. If the contingent liability has been transferred, the present stockholders are contingently liable to creditors for the difference between par value and issue price. Although this contingent liability seldom becomes an actual liability, the issuance of no-par stock avoids such a possibility.

No-Par Stock with a Stated Value

The board of directors of a corporation issuing no-par stock may assign a stated value to each share of capital stock. Stated value is an arbitrary amount assigned by the board of directors to each share of a given class of no-par stock. This stated value, like par value, may be set at any amount by the board, although some state statutes specify a minimum amount, such as $5 per share. Stated value may be established either before or after the shares are issued, if not specified by applicable state law.

OTHER VALUES COMMONLY ASSOCIATED WITH CAPITAL STOCK

Market Value

Market value is the price at which shares of capital stock are bought and sold by investors in the market; it is generally the value of greatest interest to investors. Market price is directly affected by (1) all the factors that influence general economic conditions, (2) investors' expectations concerning the corporation, and (3) the corporation's earnings.

Book Value	Book value per share is the amount per share that each stockholder would receive if the corporation were liquidated without incurring any further expenses and if assets were sold and liabilities liquidated at their recorded amounts. A later section discusses book value per share in greater detail.
Liquidation Value	Liquidation value is the amount a stockholder would receive if a corporation discontinued operations and liquidated by selling its assets, paying its liabilities, and distributing the remaining cash among the stockholders. Since the assets might be sold for more or less than the amounts at which they are recorded in the corporation's accounts, liquidation value may be more or less than book value. If only one class of capital stock is outstanding, each stockholder would receive, per share, the amount obtained by dividing the remaining cash by the number of shares of stock outstanding. If two or more classes of stock are outstanding, liquidation value depends on the rights of the various classes.
Redemption Value	Certain capital stock may be issued with the stipulation that the corporation has the right to redeem it. Redemption value is the price per share at which a corporation may call in (or redeem) its capital stock for retirement.

CAPITAL STOCK AUTHORIZED AND OUTSTANDING

Objective 3

List the various kinds of stock and describe the differences between them

The corporate charter states the number of shares and the par value, if any, per share of each class of stock that the corporation is permitted to issue. Capital stock authorized is the number of shares of stock that a corporation is entitled to issue as designated in its charter. Par value is an arbitrary amount printed on each stock certificate that may be assigned to each share of a given class of stock, usually at the time of incorporation.

A corporation might not issue all of its authorized stock immediately; some stock might be held for future issuance when additional funds are needed. If all authorized stock has been issued and more funds are needed, the consent of the state of incorporation will be required to increase the number of authorized shares.

The authorization to issue stock is not a transaction that results in a journal entry with a debit and credit. Instead, the authorization is noted in the capital stock account in the ledger (and often in the general journal) as a reminder of the number of shares authorized. Capital stock issued is the number of shares of stock that have been sold and issued to stockholders.

Capital stock outstanding is the number of authorized shares of stock that have been issued and that are currently held by stockholders. The total ownership of a corporation rests with the holders of the capital stock outstanding. If, for example, a corporation is authorized to issue 10,000 shares of capital stock but has issued only 8,000 shares, the holders of the 8,000 shares own 100% of the corporation.

Each outstanding share of stock of a given class is identical to any other outstanding share of that class with respect to the rights and privileges possessed. Shares authorized but not yet issued are referred to as unissued shares (the above example has 2,000 unissued shares). No rights or privileges attach to these shares until they are issued; they are not, for example, entitled to dividends, nor can they be voted at stockholders' meetings.

The number of shares issued and the number of shares outstanding may be different. Issued stock includes shares that have been issued at some point in time, while outstanding shares are those shares that are currently held by stockholders. All outstanding stock is issued stock, but the reverse is not necessarily true. The difference is due to shares, called *treasury stock,* that have been returned to the corporation by stockholders. Chapter 14 discusses treasury stock.

CLASSES OF CAPITAL STOCK

A corporation may issue two classes of capital stock—common and preferred. These classes are discussed in the following sections.

Common Stock

If a corporation issues only one class of stock, this stock is known as *common stock.* The rights of the stockholder are enjoyed equally by all the holders of common shares. Common stock is usually referred to as the **residual equity** in the corporation. This term means that all other claims against the corporation rank ahead of the claims of the common stockholder.

Preferred Stock

Preferred stock is capital stock that carries certain features or rights not carried by common stock. Different classes of preferred stock may exist, each with slightly different characteristics.

Companies issue preferred stock for the following reasons: (1) to avoid the use of bonds that have fixed interest charges that must be paid regardless of the amount of net income; (2) to avoid issuing so many additional shares of common stock that earnings per share will be less in the current year than in prior years; and (3) to avoid diluting the common stockholders' control of the corporation, since preferred stockholders generally have no voting rights.

Unlike common stock, which has no set maximum or minimum dividend, the dividend return on preferred stock is usually stated at an amount per share or as a percentage of par value. Therefore, the amount of the dividend per share is usually fixed.

Illustration 13.2 shows the various classes and combinations of capital stock outstanding for a sample of 600 companies.

TYPES OF PREFERRED STOCK

When a corporation issues both preferred and common stock, the preferred stock may be:

1. Preferred as to dividends. If it is, it may be:
   a. Noncumulative or cumulative.
   b. Participating or nonparticipating.
2. Preferred as to assets in the event of liquidation.
3. Convertible or nonconvertible.
4. Callable.

Stock Preferred as to Dividends

A dividend is a distribution of assets (usually cash) that represents a withdrawal of earnings by the owners. Dividends are similar in nature to withdrawals by single proprietors and partners.

Stock preferred as to dividends means that the preferred stockholders are entitled to receive a specified dividend per share before any dividend on common stock is paid. A dividend on preferred stock is the amount paid to preferred stockholders as a return for the use of their money. For no-par preferred stock, the dividend is stated as a specific dollar amount per share per year, such as $4.40.

ILLUSTRATION 13.2

Capital Structures

	1989	1988	1987	1986
Common stock with:				
No preferred stock	438	440	430	427
One class of preferred stock	117	117	128	117
Two classes of preferred stock	36	38	36	48
Three or more classes of preferred stock	9	5	6	8
Total companies	600	600	600	600
Companies included above with two or more classes of common stock	58	60	52	43

Source: American Institute of Certified Public Accountants, *Accounting Trends & Techniques* (New York: AICPA, 1990), p. 186.

For par value preferred stock, the dividend is usually stated as a percentage of the par value, such as 8% of par value, although the dividend can also be stated as a specific dollar amount per share. Most preferred stock has a par value.

Dividends on preferred stock usually are paid quarterly. A dividend—in full or in part—can be paid on preferred stock only if it is declared by the board of directors. In some states, preferred stock dividends can be declared only if the corporation has retained earnings (income that has been retained in the business) at least equal in dollar amount to the dividend declared.

Noncumulative Preferred Stock   Noncumulative preferred stock is preferred stock on which the right to receive a dividend expires if the dividend is not declared. When noncumulative preferred stock is outstanding, a dividend omitted or not paid in any one year need not be paid in any future year. Because omitted dividends are usually lost forever, noncumulative preferred stocks are not attractive to investors and rarely are issued.

Cumulative Preferred Stock   Cumulative preferred stock is preferred stock for which the right to receive a basic dividend, usually each quarter, accumulates if the dividend is not paid. Unpaid cumulative preferred dividends must be paid before any dividends can be paid on the common stock. For example, assume a company has cumulative, $10 par value, 10% preferred stock outstanding of $100,000, common stock outstanding of $100,000, and retained earnings of $30,000. No dividends have been paid for two years. The preferred stockholders are entitled to dividends of $20,000 ($10,000 per year times two years) before any dividends can be paid to the common stockholders.

Dividends in arrears are cumulative unpaid dividends, including the quarterly dividends not declared for the current year. Dividends in arrears are never shown as a liability of the corporation since they are not a legal liability until declared by the board of directors. However, since the amount of dividends in arrears may influence the decisions of users of a corporation's financial statements, such dividends should be, and usually are, disclosed in a footnote. An appropriate footnote might read: "Dividends in the amount of $20,000, representing two years' dividends on the company's 10%, cumulative preferred stock, were in arrears as of December 31, 1994."

Participating Preferred Stock Participating preferred stock allows the preferred stockholders to receive dividends above the stated preference dividend rate under certain conditions that are specified in the preferred stock contract. The participation feature can work in many ways. For example, assume that the preferred stock contract states that when the total dividend distributed to stockholders in a given year exceeds $8 per share to preferred stockholders and $8 per share to common stockholders, the remaining amount will be distributed in an equal amount per share to all stockholders. If there are 2,000 shares of preferred stock and 4,000 shares of common stock outstanding, a distribution of $108,000 would be shared as follows:

		Preferred	Common
1. Preferred stockholders are paid their dividends (2,000 shares × $8)		$16,000	
2. Common stockholders are paid an amount equal to the preferred dividend per share (4,000 shares × $8)			$32,000
3. The remainder of the dividend is divided so as to pay the same amount per share:			

	Shares	Ratio		
Preferred	2,000	(²⁄₆ × $60,000)	20,000	
Common	4,000	(⁴⁄₆ × $60,000)		40,000
Total	6,000			
Total dividend			$36,000	$72,000

The preferred stockholders receive the first $16,000 of the current year's dividends. The common stockholders receive the next $32,000 of dividends. Any dividends over $48,000 per year are paid in an equal amount per share. In years when dividends are not sufficient to pay at least $48,000 of dividends, the distribution would be as follows:

Amount of Dividends to Be Paid	Split between	
	Preferred	Common
$ 8,000	$ 8,000	$ –0–
16,000	16,000	–0–
24,000	16,000	8,000
32,000	16,000	16,000
40,000	16,000	24,000

The participation also may be based on the relative total par values of the outstanding shares instead of the number of shares outstanding.

Nonparticipating Preferred Stock Participating preferred stock was popular in the early 1900s but has seldom been issued since that time. Most preferred stock is nonparticipating. Nonparticipating preferred stock is preferred stock that is entitled to its cumulative stated dividend only, regardless of the size of the dividend paid on common stock.

Stock Preferred as to Assets

Most preferred stocks are preferred as to assets in the event of dissolution and liquidation of the corporation. Stock preferred as to assets is preferred stock that receives special treatment in case of liquidation. Preferred stockholders are entitled to receive the par value (or a larger stipulated liquidation value) per share before any assets may be distributed to common stockholders. If the corporation has cumulative preferred dividends in arrears at liquidation, they usually are payable even if there are not enough accumulated earnings to cover the dividends. Also, the cumulative dividend for the current year is payable. Stock may be preferred as to assets, dividends, or both.

Convertible Preferred Stock

Convertible preferred stock is preferred stock that is convertible into common stock of the issuing corporation. Many preferred stocks do not carry this special feature; they are nonconvertible. Holders of convertible preferred stock shares may exchange them, at their option, for a certain number of shares of common stock of the same corporation.

Investors find convertible preferred stock attractive because of the greater probability that the dividends on the preferred stock will be paid (as compared to dividends on common shares) and because the conversion privilege may be the source of substantial price appreciation. To illustrate this latter feature, assume that Olsen Company issued 1,000 shares of 6%, $100 par value convertible preferred stock at $100 per share. The stock is convertible at any time into four shares of Olsen $10 par value common stock, which has a current market value of $20 per share. In the next several years, the company reported much higher net income and increased the dividend on the common stock from $1 to $2 per share. Assume that the common stock now sells at $40 per share. The preferred stockholders can (1) convert each share of preferred stock into four shares of common stock and increase the annual dividend they receive from $6 to $8; (2) sell their preferred stock at a substantial gain, since it will sell in the market at approximately $160 per share, the market value of the four shares of common stock into which it is convertible; or (3) continue to hold their preferred shares in the expectation of realizing an even larger gain at a later date.

If all 1,000 shares of $100 par value Olsen Company preferred stock are converted into 4,000 shares of $10 par value common stock, the entry is:

Preferred Stock	100,000	
Common Stock		40,000
Paid-In Capital in Excess of Par Value—Common		60,000
To record the conversion of preferred stock into common stock.		

Callable Preferred Stock

Most preferred stocks are callable at the option of the issuing corporation. Callable preferred stock means that the corporation can inform nonconvertible preferred stockholders that they must surrender their stock to the company and convertible preferred stockholders that they must either surrender their stock or convert it to common shares.

Preferred shares are usually callable at par value plus a small premium of 3% or 4% of the par value of the stock. This call premium is the difference between the amount at which a corporation calls its preferred stock for redemption and the par value of the stock.

An issuing corporation may force conversion of **convertible** preferred stock by calling in the preferred stock for redemption. If these stockholders do not want to surrender their stock, they will have to convert it to common shares. When preferred stockholders surrender their stock, the corporation pays these stockholders par value plus the call premium, any dividends in arrears from past years, and a prorated portion of the current period's dividend. If the market value of common shares is higher than the amount the stockholders would receive in redemption, they should convert their preferred shares to common shares. For instance, assume that a stockholder owns 1,000 shares of convertible preferred stock. Each share is callable at $104 per share, convertible to two common shares (currently selling at $62 per share), and entitled to $10 of unpaid dividends. If the issuing corporation calls in its preferred stock, the stockholder would receive either (1) $114,000 [($104 + $10) × 1,000] if the shares are surrendered or (2) common shares worth $124,000 ($62 × 2,000) if the shares are converted. Obviously, the stockholder should convert these preferred shares to common shares.

You may wonder why a corporation would call in its preferred stock. Corporations call in preferred stock for many reasons: (1) the outstanding preferred stock may require, for example, a 12% annual dividend at a time when the company can secure capital to retire the stock by issuing a new 8% preferred stock; (2) the issuing company may have been sufficiently profitable to enable it to retire the preferred stock out of earnings; or (3) the company may wish to force conversion of its convertible preferred stock because the cash dividend on the equivalent common shares will be less than the dividend on the preferred shares.

BALANCE SHEET PRESENTATION OF STOCK

Objective 4

Present in proper form the stockholders' equity section of a balance sheet

At this point, it may be helpful to see how capital stock is reported in the balance sheet. The stockholders' equity section of a corporation's balance sheet contains two main elements: paid-in capital and retained earnings. Paid-in capital is the part of stockholders' equity that normally results from cash or other assets invested by owners. Paid-in capital may result from services performed for the corporation in exchange for capital stock and from certain other transactions to be discussed in Chapter 14. As stated earlier, retained earnings is the part of stockholders' equity resulting from accumulated net income, reduced by dividends and net losses. The Retained Earnings account is increased **periodically** by net income earned and decreased by net losses. In addition, Retained Earnings is **decreased** by **dividends** declared to stockholders. Since Retained Earnings is a capital account and represents accumulated net income retained by the company, it normally has a **credit** balance. Retained earnings is discussed in more detail in Chapter 14.

The illustration below shows the proper financial reporting for preferred and common stock. Assume that a corporation is authorized to issue 10,000 shares of $100 par value, 6%, cumulative, convertible preferred stock, all of which have been issued and are outstanding; and 200,000 shares of $10 par value common stock, of which 80,000 shares are issued and outstanding. The stockholders' equity section of the balance sheet (assuming $450,000 of retained earnings) is:

Stockholders' equity:

Paid-in capital:

Preferred stock—$100 par value, 6%, cumulative, convertible (5 common for 1 preferred); authorized, issued, and outstanding, 10,000 shares.	$1,000,000	
Common stock—$10 par value; authorized, 200,000 shares; issued and outstanding, 80,000 shares	800,000	
Total paid-in capital		$1,800,000
Retained earnings.		450,000
Total stockholders' equity		$2,250,000

Notice that the balance sheet lists preferred stock before common stock (because the preferred stock is preferred as to dividends, assets, or both). The conversion rate may be disclosed in a parenthetical note within the description of preferred stock or in a footnote.

A BROADER PERSPECTIVE

THE COCA-COLA COMPANY
Partial Balance Sheet
($000)

	1988	1987
Shareholders' Equity		
Preferred stock, $1 par value—Authorized: 100,000,000 shares; 3,000 shares of cumulative money market preferred stock issued and outstanding in 1988, stated at aggregate liquidation preference	$ 300,000	$ —
Common stock, $1 par value—Authorized: 700,000,000 shares; Issued: 417,394,567 shares in 1988; 415,977,479 shares in 1987	417,395	415,977
Additional paid-in capital	380,264	338,594
Reinvested earnings	4,385,142	3,783,625
Unearned restricted stock issued for future services	(51,467)	(37,414)
Foreign currency translation adjustment	(17,010)	(4,247)
	$5,414,324	$4,496,535
Less treasury stock, at cost (62,606,056 common shares in 1988; 43,621,336 common shares in 1987)	2,069,022	1,309,361
	$3,345,302	$3,187,174

Notes to Consolidated Financial Statements

8. Preferred Stock

On September 7, 1988, the Company issued four series of non-voting cumulative money market preferred stock (MMP), consisting of 750 shares each. All shares were issued at a price of $100,000 per share. Dividends, which are cumulative, are generally determined every 49 days through auction procedures. Weighted average dividend rates (per annum) were as follows:

Series	Weighted Average Dividend Rate Year Ended December 31, 1988
A	6.52%
B	6.51%
C	6.77%
D	6.81%

The shares of MMP of each series are redeemable on the second business day preceding any dividend payment date at the option of the Company, as a whole or in part, at $100,000 per share plus accrued dividends.

9. Common Stock

The number of common stock shares outstanding and related changes for the three years ended December 31, 1988, are as follows (in $000):

	1988	1987	1986
Stock outstanding at January 1,	372,356	385,011	385,982
Sales to employees exercising stock options (net of treasury shares)	906	1,339	1,213
Treasury stock issued in connection with an acquisition	—	—	485
Stock issued under Restricted Stock Award Plan	512	178	210
Treasury stock purchased	(18,985)	(14,172)	(2,879)
Stock outstanding at December 31,	354,789	372,356	385,011

Source: American Institute of Certified Public Accountants, *Trends & Techniques* (New York: AICPA, 1989), pp. 208–9.

STOCK ISSUANCES FOR CASH

Issuance of Par Value Stock for Cash

Objective 5
Account for the issuances of stock for cash, by subscription, and for other assets

Each share of capital stock (common or preferred) is either with par value or without par value, depending on the terms of the corporation's charter. The par value, if any, is stated in the charter and printed on the stock certificates issued. Par value may be any amount—1 cent, 10 cents, 16⅔ cents, $1, $5, or $100. Low par values of $10 or less are common in our economy.

As previously mentioned, par value gives no clue as to the stock's market value. Shares with a par value of $5 have sold in the market for well over $600, and many $100 par value preferred stocks have sold for considerably less than par. Par value is not even a reliable indicator of the price at which shares can be issued. Even in new corporations, shares are often issued at prices well in excess of par value and may even be issued for less than par value if state laws permit. However, par value does give the accountant a constant amount at which to record capital stock issuances in the capital stock accounts. Also, as stated earlier, the total par value of all outstanding shares is generally the legal capital of the corporation.

To illustrate the issuance of stock for cash, assume that 10,000 authorized shares of $20 par value common stock are issued at $22 per share. The following entry is made:

Cash	220,000	
Common Stock.		200,000
Paid-In Capital in Excess of Par Value—Common.		20,000
To record the issuance of 10,000 shares of stock for cash.		

Notice that the credit to the Common Stock account is the par value ($20) times the number of shares issued. The excess over par value ($20,000) is credited to Paid-In Capital in Excess of Par Value and is part of the paid-in capital contributed by the stockholders. Thus, **paid-in capital in excess of par (or stated) value** represents capital contributed to a corporation in addition to that assigned to the shares issued and recorded in capital stock accounts.

The paid-in capital section of the balance sheet appears as follows:

Paid-in capital:		
Common stock—par value, $20; 10,000 shares		
authorized, issued, and outstanding	$200,000	
Paid-in capital in excess of par value—common	20,000	
Total paid-in capital	$220,000	

Issuance of No-Par, Stated Value Stock for Cash

When no-par stock with a stated value is issued, the shares are carried in the capital stock account at the stated value. Any amounts received in excess of the stated value per share represent a part of the capital of the corporation and should be credited to Paid-In Capital in Excess of Stated Value. The legal capital of a corporation issuing no-par shares with a stated value is generally equal to the total stated value of the shares issued.

To illustrate, assume that the DeWitt Corporation, which is authorized to issue 10,000 shares of capital stock without par value, assigns a stated value of $20 per share to its stock. The 10,000 authorized shares are issued for cash at $22 per share. The entry to record this transaction is:

Cash 220,000
    Common Stock.   200,000
    Paid-In Capital in Excess of Stated Value—Common   20,000
To record issuance of 10,000 shares for cash.

The paid-in capital section of the balance sheet appears as follows:

Paid-in capital:
   Common stock—without par value; stated value, $20;
      10,000 shares authorized, issued, and outstanding $200,000
   Paid-in capital in excess of stated value—common   20,000
       Total paid-in capital $220,000

The $20,000 received over and above the stated value of $200,000 is carried permanently as paid-in capital because it is a part of the capital originally contributed by the stockholders. However, the legal capital of the DeWitt Corporation is $200,000.

Issuance of No-Par Stock without a Stated Value for Cash

If a corporation issues no-par stock without a stated value, the entire amount received is credited to the capital stock account. For instance, consider the above illustration of DeWitt Corporation involving the issuance of no-par stock. If no stated value had been assigned, the entry would have been as follows:

Cash 220,000
    Common Stock.   220,000
To record the issuance of 10,000 shares for cash.

Since shares may be issued at different times and at differing amounts, the credits to the capital stock account will not be at a uniform amount per share, in contrast to when par value shares or shares with a stated value are issued.

To continue our example, the paid-in capital section of the company's balance sheet would be as follows:

Paid-in capital:
   Common stock—without par or stated value; 10,000 shares
      authorized, issued, and outstanding $220,000
       Total paid-in capital $220,000

The actual capital contributed by stockholders is $220,000. In some states, the entire amount received for shares without par or stated value is the amount of legal capital. The legal capital in this example would then be equal to $220,000.

RECORDING CAPITAL STOCK ISSUED BY SUBSCRIPTION

Stock is often issued through subscriptions. A subscription is a contract to acquire a certain number of shares of stock at a specified price, with payment to be made at a specified date or dates. A subscriber is a person contracting to acquire the shares. Recording the issuance of capital stock by subscription involves three steps:

1. Receipt of subscriptions for the issuance of the capital stock.
2. Collection of the subscriptions receivable.

3. Issuance of the stock certificates when subscriptions have been collected in full.

When a corporation receives subscriptions, it debits an asset account, Subscriptions Receivable, and credits a stockholders' equity account, Common Stock Subscribed. Since stock certificates are not issued until a subscriber has paid in full, the stock subscribed account is used to show the amount of stock subscribed but not yet issued. If the subscriptions are received in excess of par or stated value of the stock, the excess is credited to the Paid-In Capital in Excess of Par (or Stated) Value account. After subscriptions have been collected in full, the stock certificates are issued, the Common Stock Subscribed account is debited, and the Common Stock account is credited.

To illustrate, assume that Lake Company receives subscriptions for 5,000 shares of $100 par value common stock at $120 per share on June 20, 1994. The entry to record the subscriptions is:

1994				
June	20	Subscriptions Receivable—Common		
		(5,000 shares × $120)	600,000	
		Common Stock Subscribed		
		(5,000 shares × $100)		500,000
		Paid-In Capital in Excess of Par Value—Common		100,000
		To record subscriptions to 5,000 shares of $100 par value common stock at $120 per share.		

On June 30, 1994, Lake Company collects 80% of the subscription price from each of the subscribers. The entry to record this collection is:

1994				
June	30	Cash	480,000	
		Subscriptions Receivable—Common		480,000
		Received 80% on each of the subscriptions of June 20, 1994.		

If the subscriptions had originally been accompanied by an 80% partial payment, the two entries shown above would be combined as follows:

1994				
June	20	Cash	480,000	
		Subscriptions Receivable—Common	120,000	
		Common Stock Subscribed		500,000
		Paid-In Capital in Excess of Par Value—Common		100,000
		To record subscriptions to 5,000 shares of $100 par value common stock at $120 per share and an 80% partial payment.		

When Lake Company collects the subscriptions in full on July 15, 1994, it issues certificates and makes the following entries:

1994				
July	15	Cash	120,000	
		Subscriptions Receivable—Common		120,000
		To record collection of the remaining subscriptions.		
	15	Common Stock Subscribed	500,000	
		Common Stock		500,000
		Certificates were issued for 5,000 shares paid in full.		

ILLUSTRATION 13.3

Partial Balance Sheet

LAKE COMPANY
Partial Balance Sheet
June 30, 1994

Assets

Current assets:

Subscriptions receivable—common . . . . $ 120,000

Stockholders' Equity

Paid-in capital:

Common stock—$100 par value per share;
100,000 shares authorized; issued and
outstanding, 20,000 shares $2,000,000

Subscribed but not issued, 5,000 shares (see
subscriptions receivable) 500,000 $2,500,000

Paid-in capital in excess of par value—common   100,000

Total paid-in capital. $2,600,000

When par value preferred stock instead of common stock is involved, the entries are the same except that the corresponding preferred stock account titles would be used.

Balance Sheet Presentation of Subscriptions Receivable and Stock Subscribed

Illustration 13.3 presents the June 30, 1994, partial balance sheet for Lake Company, assuming 5,000 shares of $100 par value common stock were subscribed at $120 per share and that subscriptions receivable of $120,000 were still due as of June 30, 1994. Two accounts, Subscriptions Receivable—Common and Common Stock Subscribed, are included because the subscriptions of June 20 have not been collected in full.

The Common Stock Subscribed account is considered a temporary capital stock account. The $500,000 balance of this account represents the par value of shares subscribed but not yet issued. The balance of the Common Stock Subscribed account is presented immediately below the Common Stock account. The reference in Illustration 13.3 to subscriptions receivable (following the caption "Subscribed but not issued, 5,000 shares") informs the reader that $120,000 remains to be paid in before the 5,000 subscribed shares will be issued.

Subscriptions receivable will normally be collected within a matter of days or weeks. Subscriptions receivable are, therefore, properly classified as a current asset in the balance sheet. The account should be displayed separately and not included in the total of trade accounts receivable. In some instances, the subscriptions will not be collected within the coming operating cycle. The account, Subscriptions Receivable, is then properly classified as a noncurrent asset and preferably shown under the caption "Other assets" near the bottom of the assets section of the balance sheet.

Defaulted Subscriptions

A defaulted subscription occurs when a subscriber to a stock subscription contract fails to make a required installment payment. Since these contracts often call for an immediate initial cash payment, with the balance payable in periodic installments, the defaulting subscriber may have paid part of the total subscription price. State incorporation laws generally govern the disposition of the amount paid in and the balance of the contract. Three usual courses of action are (1) the subscriber may receive as many shares as have been paid for in full, with the balance of the contract being canceled; (2) the amount paid in may be refunded (often after deducting any expenses and losses incurred in selling the shares to another party); or (3) the amount paid in may be declared forfeited to the corporation. In the third case, the amount retained should be credited to a Paid-In Capital from Defaulted Subscriptions account to indicate the source of the capital.

CAPITAL STOCK ISSUED FOR PROPERTY OR SERVICES

When capital stock is issued for property or services, the dollar amount of the exchange must be determined. Accountants generally record the transaction at the fair value of (1) the property or services received or (2) the stock issued, whichever is more clearly evident.

To illustrate, assume that the owners of a tract of land deeded the land to a corporation in exchange for 1,000 shares of $12 par value common stock. The fair market value of the land can only be estimated. At the time of the exchange, the stock has an established total market value of $14,000. The required entry is:

Land	14,000	
Common Stock.		12,000
Paid-In Capital in Excess of Par Value—Common.		2,000
To record the receipt of land for capital stock.		

As another example, assume 100 shares of common stock with a par value of $40 per share are issued in exchange for legal services received in organizing a corporation. No shares have been recently traded, so they do not have an established market value. The attorney previously agreed to a price of $5,000 for these legal services but decided to accept stock in lieu of cash. In this example, the correct entry is:

Organization Costs	5,000	
Common Stock.		4,000
Paid-In Capital in Excess of Par Value—Common.		1,000
To record the receipt of legal services for capital stock.		

The services should be valued at the price previously agreed on since that value is more clearly evident than the market value of the shares. An asset account should be debited because these services will benefit the corporation throughout its entire life. The amount by which the value of the services received exceeds the par value of the shares issued is credited to a Paid-In Capital in Excess of Par Value—Common account.

BALANCE SHEET PRESENTATION OF PAID-IN CAPITAL IN EXCESS OF PAR (OR STATED) VALUE—COMMON OR PREFERRED

As already noted, amounts received in excess of the par or stated value of shares issued should be credited to an account called Paid-In Capital in Excess of Par (or Stated) Value—Common (or Preferred). The amounts received in excess of par or stated value should be carried in separate accounts for each class of stock issued. Using the following assumed data, the stockholders' equity section of the balance sheet of a company with both preferred and common stock outstanding would appear as follows:

Stockholders' equity:			
Paid-in capital:			
Preferred stock—$100 par value, 6% cumulative; 1,000 shares authorized, issued, and outstanding.	$100,000		
Common stock—without par value, stated value $5; 100,000 shares authorized, 80,000 shares issued and outstanding	400,000	$500,000	
Paid-in capital in excess of par (or stated) value:			
From preferred stock issuances.	$ 5,000		
From common stock issuances.	20,000	25,000	
Total paid-in capital			$525,000
Retained earnings.			200,000
Total stockholders' equity			$725,000

BOOK VALUE

Objective 6

Determine book values of both preferred and common stock

The total book value of a corporation's outstanding shares is equal to the recorded net asset value of the corporation—that is, assets minus liabilities. Quite simply, **the amount of net assets is equal to stockholders' equity.** When **only** common stock is outstanding, book value per share is computed by dividing total stockholders' equity by the number of common shares outstanding plus common shares subscribed but not yet issued. In calculating book value, an assumption is made that (1) the corporation could be liquidated without incurring any further expenses, (2) the assets could be sold at their recorded amounts, and (3) the liabilities could be satisfied at their recorded amounts.

Assume the stockholders' equity of a corporation is as follows:

Stockholders' equity:		
Paid-in capital:		
Common stock—without par value, stated value $10; authorized, 20,000 shares; issued and outstanding, 15,000 shares	$150,000	
Paid-in capital in excess of stated value.	10,000	
Total paid-in capital.		$160,000
Retained earnings		50,000
Total stockholders' equity		$210,000

The book value per share of the stock is determined as follows:

Total stockholders' equity	$210,000
Total shares outstanding	÷15,000
Book value per share	$ 14

When two or more classes of capital stock are outstanding, the computation of book value per share is more complex. The book value for each share of stock depends on the rights of the preferred stockholders. Preferred stockholders typically are entitled to a specified liquidation value per share, plus cumulative dividends in arrears, if any, since most preferred stocks are preferred as to assets and are cumulative. In each case, the specific provisions in the preferred stock contract will govern.

To illustrate, the Celoron Corporation's stockholders' equity is as follows:

Stockholders' equity:		
Paid-in capital:		
Preferred stock—$100 par value, 6% cumulative; 5,000 shares authorized, issued, and outstanding.	$ 500,000	
Common stock—$10 par value, 200,000 shares authorized, issued, and outstanding	2,000,000	
Paid-in capital in excess of par value—preferred	200,000	
Total paid-in capital		$2,700,000
Retained earnings		400,000
Total stockholders' equity		$3,100,000

The preferred stock is 6%, cumulative, and nonparticipating. It is preferred as to dividends and as to assets in liquidation to the extent of the liquidation value of $100 per share, plus any cumulative dividends on the preferred stock. Dividends for four years are unpaid. Book values of each class of stock are calculated as follows:

		Total	Per Share
Total stockholders' equity		$3,100,000	
Book value of preferred stock (5,000 shares):			
Liquidation value (5,000 shares × $100)	$500,000		
Dividends (4 years at $30,000)	120,000	620,000	$124.00*
Book value of common stock (200,000 shares)		$2,480,000	12.40†

* $620,000 ÷ 5,000 shares.
† $2,480,000 ÷ 200,000 shares.

Notice that the paid-in capital in excess of par value—preferred did not get assigned to the preferred stock in determining the book values. Only the liquidation value and cumulative dividends on the preferred stock are assigned to the preferred stock.

Assume now that the features attached to the preferred stock in the above example are the same except that the preferred stockholders have the right to receive $103 per share in liquidation. The book values of each class of stock would be:

		Total	Per Share
Total stockholders' equity		$3,100,000	
Book value of preferred stock (5,000 shares):			
Liquidation value (5,000 shares × $103)	$515,000		
Dividends (4 years at $30,000)	120,000	635,000	$127.00
Book value of common stock (200,000 shares)		$2,465,000	12.33

Book value rarely equals market value of a stock because many of the assets have changed in value due to inflation. Thus, the shares of many corporations are traded regularly at market prices that are different from their book values.

ETHICS	Joe Morrison is the controller for Belex Corporation. He is involved in a discussion with other members of management concerning how to get rid of some potentially harmful toxic waste materials that are a by-product of the company's manufacturing process.
A CLOSER LOOK	

There are two alternative methods of disposing of the materials. The first alternative is to bury the waste in steel drums on a tract of land that is adjacent to the factory building. There is currently no legal prohibition against doing this. The cost of disposing of the materials in this way is estimated to be $50,000 per year. The best estimate is that the steel drums would not leak for at least 50 years, but probably would begin leaking after that time. The second alternative is to seal the materials in lead drums that would be disposed of at sea by a waste management company. The cost of this alternative is estimated to be $400,000 per year. This method of disposal has been certified as the preferred method of disposal by the federal government. The best estimate is that the lead drums would never rupture or leak.

Belex Corporation has seen some tough economic times. The company suffered losses until last year, when it showed a profit of $750,000 as a result of a new manufacturing project. So far, the waste materials from that project have been accumulating in two large vats on the company's land. However, these vats are almost full, so a decision must be made soon on how to dispose of the materials. One group of managers is arguing in favor of the first alternative because it is legally permissible and will result in annual profits of about $700,000. They point out that using the second alternative would reduce profits to about $350,000 per year and cut managers' bonuses in half. They also claim that some of their competitors are now using the first alternative, and to use the second alternative would place the company at a serious competitive disadvantage.

Another group of managers argues that the second alternative is the only safe alternative to pursue. They claim that when the steel drums start leaking they will contaminate the ground water and could cause serious health problems. When this contamination occurs, the company will lose public support and may even have to pay for the cleanup. The cost of that cleanup could run into the millions.

Required
- a. Which alternative would benefit the company and its management over the next several years?
- b. Which alternative would benefit society?
- c. If you were Joe, which side of the argument would you take?

Since the stock market is frequently referred to as an economic indicator, the knowledge you now have on corporate stock issuances should help you relate to stocks traded in the market. Chapter 14 continues the discussion of paid-in capital and also discusses treasury stock, retained earnings, and dividends.

UNDERSTANDING THE LEARNING OBJECTIVES:

1. State the advantages and disadvantages of the corporate form of business.
- ☐ Advantages:
  1. Easy transfer of ownership.
  2. Limited liability.
  3. Continuous existence of the entity.
  4. Easy capital generation.
  5. Professional management.
  6. Separation of owners and entity.

☐ Disadvantages:
1. Double taxation.
2. Government regulation.
3. Entrenched, inefficient management.
4. Limited ability to raise creditor capital.

2. List the values commonly associated with capital stock and give their definitions.
☐ Par value—an arbitrary amount assigned to each share of a given class of stock and printed on the stock certificate.
☐ Stated value—an arbitrary amount assigned by the board of directors to each share of a given class of no-par stock.
☐ Market value—the price at which shares of capital stock are bought and sold in the market.
☐ Book value—the amount per share that each stockholder would receive if the corporation were liquidated without incurring any further expenses and if assets were sold and liabilities liquidated at their recorded amounts.
☐ Liquidation value—the amount a stockholder would receive if a corporation discontinues operations, pays its liabilities, and distributes the remaining cash among the stockholders.
☐ Redemption value—the price per share at which a corporation may call in (redeem) its capital stock for retirement.

3. List the various kinds of stock and describe the differences between them.
☐ Capital stock authorized—the number of shares of stock that a corporation is entitled to issue as designated in its charter.
☐ Capital stock issued—the number of shares of stock that have been sold and issued to stockholders.
☐ Capital stock outstanding—the number of authorized shares of stock that have been issued and that are still currently held by stockholders.
☐ Two classes of capital stock:
1. Common stock—represents the residual equity.
2. Preferred stock—may be preferred as to dividends and/or assets. Also may be participating, cumulative, and/or callable.

4. Present in proper form the stockholders' equity section of a balance sheet.
☐ If the company has paid-in capital in excess of par value:

Stockholders' equity:
 Paid-in capital:
  Preferred stock—$100 par value, 6%
   cumulative; 1,000 shares authorized,
   issued, and outstanding $100,000
  Common stock—without par value, stated
   value $5; 100,000 shares authorized,
   80,000 shares issued and outstanding . . . 400,000 $500,000

  Paid-in capital in excess of par (or stated) value:
   From preferred stock issuances . . . . $ 5,000
   From common stock issuances   20,000   25,000

    Total paid-in capital $525,000
 Retained earnings   200,000

    Total stockholders' equity. $725,000

5. Account for the issuances of stock for cash, by subscription, and for other assets.

    The following examples illustrate the issuance for cash of (1) stock with a par value, (2) no-par value stock with a stated value, and (3) no-par value stock without a stated value.

    ☐ Issuance of par value stock for cash—10,000 shares of $20 par value common stock issued for $22 per share.

Cash	220,000	
Common Stock		200,000
Paid-In Capital in Excess of Par Value—Common		20,000

    ☐ Issuance of no-par, stated value stock for cash—10,000 shares (no-par value) with $20 per share stated value issued for $22 per share.

Cash	220,000	
Common Stock		200,000
Paid-In Capital in Excess of Stated Value—Common . . .		20,000

    ☐ Issuance of no-par stock without a stated value for cash—10,000 shares (no-par value) issued at $22 per share.

Cash	220,000	
Common Stock		220,000

6. Determine book values of both preferred and common stock.

    ☐ *Example:* A corporation has 200,000 shares of common stock and 5,000 shares of preferred stock outstanding. Preferred stock is 6% cumulative, and nonparticipating. It is preferred as to dividends and as to assets in liquidation to the extent of the liquidation value of $100 per share, plus any cumulative dividends on the preferred stock. Dividends for three years are unpaid. Total stockholders' equity is $4,100,000. Calculations are as follows:

		Total	**Per Share**
Total stockholders' equity.		$4,100,000	
Book value of preferred stock (5,000 shares):			
Liquidation value (5,000 × $100)	$500,000		
Dividends (3 years at $30,000)	90,000	590,000	$118.00
Book value of common stock (200,000 shares) . .		$3,510,000	17.55

DEMONSTRATION PROBLEM 13-A

Rose Company has paid all required preferred dividends through December 31, 1988. Its outstanding stock consists of 10,000 shares of $125 par value common stock and 4,000 shares of 6%, $125 par value preferred stock. During five successive years, the company's dividend declarations were as follows:

1989	$85,000
1990	52,500
1991	7,500
1992	15,000
1993	67,500

Required   Compute the amount of dividends that would have been paid to each class of stock in each of the last five years assuming the preferred stock is:

a.   Cumulative and nonparticipating.

b.   Noncumulative and nonparticipating.

SOLUTION TO DEMONSTRATION PROBLEM 13–A

ROSE COMPANY

		Assumptions	
Year	Dividends to	*(a)*	*(b)*
1989	Preferred	$30,000*	$30,000
	Common	55,000	55,000
1990	Preferred	30,000	30,000
	Common	22,500	22,500
1991	Preferred	7,500	7,500
	Common	–0–	–0–
1992	Preferred	15,000	15,000
	Common	–0–	–0–
1993	Preferred	67,500†	30,000‡
	Common	–0–	37,500

* 4,000 shares × $125 × 0.06 = $30,000.

† $30,000 + $22,500 preferred dividend missed in 1991 + $15,000 preferred dividend missed in 1992.

‡ Only the basic $30,000 dividend is paid because the stock is noncumulative.

DEMONSTRATION PROBLEM 13–B

Bulldog Company has been authorized to issue 100,000 shares of $6 par value common stock and 1,000 shares of 14%, cumulative, nonparticipating preferred stock with a par value of $12.

Required   a.   Prepare the entries for the following transactions that all took place in June 1993:

1.   50,000 shares of common stock are subscribed at $24 per share, with a down payment of 10% of the issue price.

2.   750 shares of preferred stock are issued for cash at $18 per share.

3.   1,000 shares of common stock are issued in exchange for legal services received in the incorporation process. The fair market value of the legal services is $9,000.

4.   The balance of the stock subscriptions is paid, and the stock is issued.

b.   Prepare the paid-in capital section of Bulldog's balance sheet as of June 30, 1993.

SOLUTION TO DEMONSTRATION PROBLEM 13–B

a.

1. Cash	120,000	
Subscriptions Receivable—Common	1,080,000	
Common Stock Subscribed		300,000
Paid-In Capital in Excess of Par Value—Common		900,000
To record subscriptions to 50,000 shares at $24 per share, with 10% down payment.		
2. Cash	13,500	
Preferred Stock		9,000
Paid-In Capital in Excess of Par Value—Preferred		4,500
To record the issuance of 750 shares for cash, at $18 per share.		
3. Organization Costs	9,000	
Common Stock		6,000
Paid-In Capital in Excess of Par Value—Common		3,000
To record issuance of 1,000 shares in exchange for legal services.		
4. Cash	1,080,000	
Subscriptions Receivable—Common		1,080,000
To record collection of balance due on subscriptions.		
Common Stock Subscribed	300,000	
Common Stock		300,000
To record issuance of certificates for 50,000 shares, fully paid.		

b.

BULLDOG COMPANY
Partial Balance Sheet
June 30, 1993

Paid-in capital:			
Preferred stock—$12 par value, 14% cumulative; 1,000 shares authorized; issued and outstanding, 750 shares		$ 9,000	
Common stock—$6 par value per share; 100,000 shares authorized; issued and outstanding, 51,000 shares		306,000	$ 315,000
Paid-in capital in excess of par value:			
From preferred stock issuances		$ 4,500	
From common stock issuances		903,000	907,500
Total paid-in capital			$1,222,500

NEW TERMS

Articles of incorporation The application for the corporation's charter. *610*

Board of directors Elected by the stockholders and is primarily responsible for formulating policies for the corporation. The board also authorizes contracts, declares dividends, establishes executive salaries, and grants authorization to borrow money. *612*

Book value per share Stockholders' equity per share; the amount per share each stockholder would receive if the corporation were liquidated without incurring any further expenses and if assets were sold and liabilities liquidated at their recorded amounts. *615, 627*

Bylaws A set of rules or regulations adopted by the board of directors of a corporation to govern the conduct of corporate affairs. The bylaws must be in agreement with the laws of the state and the policies and purposes in the corporate charter. *610*

Callable preferred stock If the stock is nonconvertible, it must be surrendered to the company when the holder is requested to do so. If the stock is convertible, it may be either surrendered or converted into common shares when called. *619*

Call premium (on preferred stock)   The difference between the amount at which a corporation calls its preferred stock for redemption and the par value of the stock. *619*

Capital stock   Transferable units of ownership in a corporation. *613*

Capital stock authorized   The number of shares of stock that a corporation is entitled to issue as designated in its charter. *615*

Capital stock issued   The number of shares of stock that have been sold and issued to stockholders. *615*

Capital stock outstanding   The number of shares of authorized stock that have been issued and that are currently held by stockholders. *615*

Common stock   Shares of stock representing the residual equity in the corporation. If only one class of stock is issued, it is known as *common stock*. All other claims rank ahead of common stockholders' claims. *616*

Convertible preferred stock   Preferred stock that is convertible into common stock of the issuing corporation. *619*

Corporate charter   The contract between the state and the incorporators of a corporation, and their successors, granting the corporation its legal existence. *610*

Corporation   An entity recognized by law as possessing an existence separate and distinct from its owners; that is, it is a separate legal entity. A corporation is granted many of the rights, and placed under many of the obligations, of a natural person. In any given state, all corporations organized under the laws of that state are **domestic corporations;** all others are **foreign corporations.** *608, 609*

Cumulative preferred stock   Preferred stock for which the right to receive a basic dividend accumulates if dividend has not been paid; unpaid cumulative preferred dividends must be paid before any dividends can be paid on the common stock. *617*

Defaulted subscription   Occurs when a subscriber to a stock subscription contract fails to make a required installment payment. *625*

Discount on capital stock   The amount by which the par value of shares issued exceeds their issue price. The original issuance of shares at a discount is illegal in most states. *614*

Dividend   A distribution of assets (usually cash) that represents a withdrawal of earnings by the owners. Dividends are similar in nature to withdrawals by sole proprietors and partners. *616*

Dividend on preferred stock   The amount paid to preferred stockholders as a return for the use of their money; usually a fixed or stated amount expressed in dollars per share or as a percentage of par value per share. *616*

Dividends in arrears   Cumulative unpaid dividends, including quarterly dividends not declared for the current year. *617*

Domestic corporation   See Corporation.

Foreign corporation   See Corporation.

Incorporators   Persons seeking to bring a corporation into existence. *609*

Legal capital (stated capital)   An amount prescribed by law (often par value or stated value of shares outstanding) below which a corporation may not reduce stockholders' equity through the declaration of dividends or other payments to stockholders. *614*

Liquidation value   The amount a stockholder will receive if a corporation discontinues operations and liquidates by selling its assets, paying its liabilities, and distributing the remaining cash among the stockholders. *615*

Market value   The price at which shares of capital stock are bought and sold in the market. *614*

Minutes book   The record book in which actions taken at stockholders' and board of directors' meetings are recorded; the written authorization for many actions taken by corporate officers. *613*

Noncumulative preferred stock   Preferred stock on which the right to receive a dividend expires if the dividend is not declared. *617*

Nonparticipating preferred stock   Preferred stock that is entitled to its cumulative stated dividend only, regardless of the size of the dividend paid on common stock. *618*

No-par stock   Capital stock without par value, to which a stated value may or may not be assigned. *614*

Organization costs   Costs of organizing a corporation, such as incorporation fees and legal fees applicable to incorporation. *610*

Paid-in capital   Amount of stockholders' equity that normally results from the cash or other assets invested by owners; it may also result from services provided for shares of stock and certain other transactions. *620*

Paid-in capital in excess of par (or stated) value—common or preferred   Capital contributed to a corporation in addition to that assigned to the shares issued and recorded in capital stock accounts. *622*

Participating preferred stock   Preferred stock that is entitled to receive dividends above the stated preference rate under certain conditions specified in the preferred stock contract. *618*

Par value   An arbitrary amount printed on each stock certificate that may be assigned to each share of a given class of stock, usually at the time of incorporation. *614, 615*

Preemptive right   The right of stockholders to buy additional shares in a proportion equal to the percentage of shares already owned. *611*

Preferred stock   Capital stock that carries certain

features or rights not carried by common stock. Preferred stock may be preferred as to dividends, preferred as to assets, or preferred as to both dividends and assets. Preferred stock may be callable and/or convertible and may be cumulative or noncumulative and participating or nonparticipating. *616*

Proxy A legal document signed by a stockholder, giving another person the authority to vote the stockholder's shares at a stockholders' meeting. *612*

Redemption value The price per share at which a corporation may call in (or redeem) its capital stock for retirement. *615*

Retained earnings The part of stockholders' equity resulting from accumulated net income, reduced by dividends and net losses. *620*

Shares of stock Units of ownership in a corporation. *608*

Stated value An arbitrary amount assigned by the board of directors to each share of a given class of no-par stock. *614*

Stock certificate A printed or engraved document serving as evidence that the holder owns a certain number of shares of capital stock. *613*

Stockholders' ledger Contains a group of subsidiary accounts showing the number of shares of stock currently held by each stockholder. *613*

Stock preferred as to assets Means that in liquidation, the preferred stockholders are entitled to receive the par value (or a larger stipulated liquidation value) per share before any assets may be distributed to common stockholders. *618*

Stock preferred as to dividends Means that the preferred stockholders are entitled to receive a specified dividend per share before any dividend on common stock is paid. *616*

Stock registrar Typically, a bank that maintains records of the shares outstanding for a company. *613*

Stock-transfer agent Typically, a bank or trust company employed by a corporation to transfer stock between buyers and sellers. *613*

Stock without par value See No-par stock.

Subscribers Persons who contract to acquire shares, usually in an original issuance of stock by a corporation. *623*

Subscription A contract to acquire a certain number of shares of stock, at a specified price, with payment to be made at a specified date or dates. *623*

Unissued shares Capital stock authorized but not yet issued. *615*

SELF-TEST

True-False

Indicate whether each of the following statements is true or false.

1. A person may favor the corporate form of organization for a risky business enterprise primarily because a corporation's shares can be easily transferred.

2. In the event of corporate liquidation, stockholders whose stock is preferred as to assets are entitled to receive the par value of their shares before any amounts are distributed to creditors or common stockholders.

3. The par value of a share of capital stock is no indication of the market value or book value of the share of stock.

4. When stock subscriptions are received for common stock at par value, the Common Stock account is credited.

5. When 10,000 shares of $10 par value common stock are issued in payment for a parcel of land with a fair market value of $150,000, the Common Stock account is credited for $100,000 and the Paid-In Capital in Excess of Par Value—Common account is credited for $50,000.

Multiple-Choice

Select the best answer for each of the following questions.

1. Which of the following is not an advantage of the corporate form of organization?
   a. Separate legal entity.
   b. Limited liability of stockholders.
   c. Double taxation.
   d. Easy transfer of ownership.

2. An arbitrary amount assigned to each share of a given class of stock and printed on the stock certificate is:
   a. Market value.
   b. Par value.
   c. Redemption value.
   d. Liquidation value.

3. Which of the following stock could have dividends in arrears?
   a. Common stock.
   b. Noncumulative preferred stock.
   c. Participating preferred stock.
   d. Cumulative preferred stock.

4. Eugene Corporation issued 5,000 shares of $20 par

value common stock at $35 per share. The amount that would be credited to Common Stock is:

a. $100,000.
b. $75,000.
c. $275,000.
d. $175,000.
e. None of the above.

5. You are given the following information: Capital Stock, $20,000 ($20 par), Paid-In Capital in Excess

of Par Value—Common, $50,000; and Retained Earnings, $100,000. Assuming only one class of stock, the book value per share is:

a. $170.
b. $70.
c. $20.
d. $100.
e. None of the above.

Now turn to page 646 to check your answers.

QUESTIONS

1. Cite the major advantages of the corporate form of business organization and indicate why each is considered an advantage.

2. What is meant by the statement that corporate income is subject to double taxation? Cite several other disadvantages of the corporate form of organization.

3. Why is Organization Expense not a good title for the account that records the costs of organizing a corporation? Could you justify leaving the balance of an Organization Costs account intact throughout the life of a corporation?

4. What are the basic rights associated with a share of capital stock if there is only one class of stock outstanding?

5. Explain the purpose or function of *(a)* the stockholders' ledger, *(b)* the minutes book, *(c)* the stock-transfer agent, and *(d)* the stock registrar.

6. What are the differences between par value stock and stock with no-par value?

7. Corporate capital stock is seldom issued for less than par value. Give two reasons why this statement is true.

8. Explain the terms *liquidation value* and *redemption value*.

9. What are the meanings of the terms *stock preferred as to dividends* and *stock preferred as to assets?*

10. What do the terms *(a) cumulative* and *noncumulative* and *(b) participating* and *nonparticipating* mean in regard to preferred stock?

11. What are dividends in arrears, and how should they be disclosed in the financial statements?

12. A corporation has 1,000 shares of 8%, $100 par value, cumulative, preferred stock outstanding. Dividends on this stock have not been declared for three years. Is the corporation legally liable to its preferred stockholders for these dividends? How should this fact be shown in the balance sheet, if at all?

13. Explain why a corporation might issue a preferred

stock that is both convertible into common stock and callable.

14. Explain the nature of the account entitled, Paid-In Capital in Excess of Par Value. Under what circumstances is this account credited?

15. Wright Corporation issued 5,000 shares of $50 par value common stock at $60 per share. What is the legal capital of Wright Corporation, and why is the amount of legal capital important?

16. Explain the nature of the Subscriptions Receivable account. How should it be classified in the balance sheet? On what occasions is it debited or credited?

17. What is meant by a defaulted subscription and what courses of action can be taken when subscriptions are defaulted?

18. What is the general approach of the accountant in determining the dollar amount at which to record the issuance of capital stock for services or property other than cash?

19. What assumptions are made in determining book value?

20. Assuming there is no preferred stock outstanding, how can the book value per share of common stock be determined? Of what significance is the book value per share? What is the relationship of book value per share to market value per share?

MAYTAG CORPORATION

21. *Real world question* Based on the financial statements of Maytag Corporation contained in Appendix E, what was the number of shares of common stock authorized?

THE LIMITED, INC.

22. *Real world question* Based on the financial statements of The Limited, Inc., contained in Appendix E, what was the 1989 ending paid-in capital?

HARLAND

23. *Real world question* Based on the financial statements of John H. Harland Company contained in Appendix E, what was the 1989 ending number of shares of common stock issued?

EXERCISES

Exercise 13–1
Determine dividends for common and preferred stock
(L.O. 3)

Tony Corporation has outstanding 1,000 shares of noncumulative, nonparticipating preferred stock and 2,000 shares of common stock. The preferred stock is entitled to an annual dividend of $40 per share before dividends are declared on common stock. What are the total dividends received by each class of stock if Tony Corporation distributes $112,000 in dividends in 1993?

Exercise 13–2
Determine dividends for common and preferred stock
(L.O. 3)

Mason Corporation has 2,000 shares outstanding of cumulative, nonparticipating preferred stock and 6,000 shares of common stock. The preferred stock is entitled to an annual dividend of $9 per share before dividends are declared on common stock. No preferred dividends were paid for last year and the current year. What are the total dividends received by each class of stock if Mason Corporation distributes $54,000 in dividends?

Exercise 13–3
Determine dividends for common and preferred stock for five-year period
(L.O. 3)

The preferred stock contract of Kopel Corporation specifies that the preferred shares will participate on an equal amount per share basis with the common shares after $4 has been distributed per share of preferred stock and common stock. There are 1,000 shares of noncumulative preferred stock outstanding and 9,000 shares of common stock outstanding. Determine the dividends that will be paid to each class for the following years:

Year	Total Dividend to Be Distributed
1993	$ 4,000
1994	20,000
1995	40,000
1996	50,000
1997	60,000

Exercise 13–4
Journalize stock issuance
(L.O. 5)

Haber Company issued 10,000 shares of common stock for $420,000 cash. The common stock has a par value of $40 per share. Give the journal entry for the stock issuance.

Exercise 13–5
Prepare entries for stock issuance
(L.O. 5)

Smith Company issued 30,000 shares of $40 par value common stock for $1,360,000. What is the journal entry for this transaction? What would the journal entry be if the common stock has no-par or stated value?

Exercise 13–6
Journalize stock subscriptions
(L.O. 5)

Davis Company has been authorized to issue 100,000 shares of $100 par value common stock, of which 20,000 shares are outstanding. On February 20, 1993, the company received subscriptions for 15,000 shares at $120 per share. What would be the journal entry on February 20, 1993?

Exercise 13–7
Journalize stock issuance for property
(L.O. 5)

One hundred shares of $100 par value common stock were issued to the incorporators of a corporation in exchange for land (which cost the incorporators $13,000 one year ago) needed by the corporation for use as a plant site. Experienced appraisers recently valued the land at $15,000. What journal entry would be appropriate to record the acquisition of the land?

Exercise 13–8
Journalize stock issuance to satisfy liability
(L.O. 5)

Sanders Corporation owes a trade creditor $12,000 on open account which the corporation does not have sufficient cash to pay. The trade creditor suggests that Sanders Corporation issue to him 750 shares of the $10 par value common stock, which is currently selling on the market at $16. Present the entry or entries that should be made on Sanders Corporation's books.

Exercise 13–9
Journalize stock issuance for legal services
(L.O. 5)

Why would a law firm ever consider accepting stock of a new corporation having a total par value of $60,000 as payment in full of a $90,000 bill for legal services rendered? If such a transaction occurred, give the journal entry the issuing company would make on its books.

Exercise 13–10

Compute the book value and average price of common stock
(L.O. 6)

The stockholders' equity section of Hollis Company's balance sheet is as follows:

Stockholders' equity:
Paid-in capital:
Common stock—without par value, $5 stated value;
authorized 100,000 shares; issued and
outstanding, 70,000 shares $350,000
Paid-in capital in excess of stated value.   136,000

Total paid-in capital $486,000
Retained earnings   54,000

Total stockholders' equity $540,000

Compute the average price at which the 70,000 issued shares of common stock were sold. Compute the book value per share of common stock.

PROBLEMS: SERIES A

Problem 13–1A

Determine dividends for common stock and cumulative and noncumulative preferred stock
(L.O. 3)

On January 1, 1989, the retained earnings of Nichols Company were $90,000. Net income for the succeeding five years was as follows:

1989	$60,000
1990	45,000
1991	1,000
1992	10,000
1993	55,000

The outstanding capital stock of the corporation consisted of 2,000 shares of preferred stock with a par value of $100 per share that pays a dividend of $4 per year and 8,000 shares of no-par common stock with a stated value of $50 per share. No dividends were in arrears as of January 1, 1989.

Required

Prepare schedules showing how the net income for the above five years was distributed to the two classes of stock if in each of the years the entire current net income was distributed as dividends and the preferred stock was:

a.   Cumulative and nonparticipating.

b.   Noncumulative and nonparticipating.

Problem 13–2A

Prepare partial balance sheet involving par value stock
(L.O. 4)

Certain post-closing account balances for Rivera Company as of December 31, 1993, were as follows:

RIVERA COMPANY
Post-Closing Account Balances
December 31, 1993

Common Stock Subscribed (4,000 shares)	$200,000
Preferred Stock (6%, $120 par, 2,000 shares authorized, issued, and outstanding).	240,000
Common Stock ($50 par, 10,000 shares authorized, 6,000 shares issued and outstanding)	300,000
Paid-In Capital in Excess of Par—Common	25,600
Subscriptions Receivable—Common	46,080
Paid-In Capital in Excess of Par—Preferred	12,000
Retained Earnings	47,680

Required   From the above list of account balances, present in proper form the stockholders' equity section of the December 31, 1993, balance sheet.

Problem 13–3A

Journalize stock subscriptions and issuances for cash and prepare resulting stockholders' equity section (L.O. 5)

Bendo Company had the following stockholders' equity and related accounts on January 1, 1993.

Subscriptions Receivable—Preferred Stock	$ 16,000
Preferred Stock (8%, $20 par, 20,000 shares authorized,	
10,000 shares issued and outstanding)	200,000
Preferred Stock Subscribed (2,500 shares)	50,000
Common Stock ($160 par, 10,000 shares authorized,	
7,500 shares issued and outstanding)	1,200,000
Paid-In Capital in Excess of Par Value—Common	120,000
Retained Earnings	500,000

The following transactions occurred during 1993:

Jan. 10   Received the balance due on preferred stock subscribed; issued stock certificates.

Mar. 1   Received subscriptions for 5,000 shares of preferred stock at $28 per share; 40% of the subscription price was paid in cash.

Aug. 3   Issued 2,000 shares of common stock for $184 cash per share.

Required   *a.*   Prepare journal entries for the transactions that occurred in 1993.

b.   Prepare the stockholders' equity section of the balance sheet as of August 3, 1993.

Problem 13–4A

Journalize stock subscriptions and issuance of stock for cash (L.O. 5)

On July 1, 1993, Grenwich Company was authorized to issue 20,000 shares of $60 par value common stock. On July 7, subscriptions for 1,500 shares at $72 per share were received. The subscription contract requires a 10% immediate payment, with the remainder due on July 31. No stock certificates are to be issued until the subscriptions are paid in full.

Required

a.   Prepare the entries to record all transactions during July 1993, assuming the subscriptions are collected when due.

b.   Prepare the July 1993 entries assuming the stock is no-par stock without a stated value.

c.   Prepare the entry for July 7, 1993, assuming the subscriptions for the no-par stock in part *(b)* are accompanied by cash payment in full and the stock is issued.

Problem 13–5A

Post transactions; prepare balance sheets for par value stock, stated value stock, and no-par or stated value stock (L.O. 2, 4, 5)

On July 3, 1993, North American Company was authorized to issue 15,000 shares of common stock; 3,000 shares were issued immediately to the incorporators of the company for cash at $40 per share. On July 5, an additional 300 shares were issued to the incorporators for services rendered in organizing the company.

On July 6, 1993, legal and printing costs of $1,500 were paid. These costs related to securing the corporate charter and the stock certificates.

On July 10, subscriptions were received from the general public for 4,500 shares at $36 per share, with 25% of the subscription price paid in cash immediately. The balance is due August 10, 1993.

Required   *a.*   Set up T-accounts, and post the above transactions. Then prepare the balance sheet of the North American Company as of the close of July 10, 1993, assuming the authorized stock has a $20 par value.

b.   Repeat *(a)* for the T-accounts involving stockholders' equity, assuming the stock is no-par stock with a $30 stated value. Prepare the stockholders' equity section of the balance sheet.

c.   Repeat *(a)* for the T-accounts involving stockholders' equity, assuming the stock is no-par stock with no stated value. Prepare the stockholders' equity section of the balance sheet.

Problem 13–6A

Journalize stock transactions, including conversions; prepare stockholders' equity section
(L.O. 3–5)

Nellis Company received its charter on April 1, 1993, authorizing it to issue: (1) 10,000 shares of $100 par value, $8 cumulative, convertible preferred stock; (2) 10,000 shares of $3 cumulative no-par preferred stock having a stated value of $5 per share and a liquidation value of $25 per share; and (3) 100,000 shares of no-par common stock without a stated value.

On April 2, incorporators of the corporation acquired 50,000 shares of the common stock for cash at $20 per share, and 200 shares were issued to an attorney for services rendered in organizing the corporation. On April 3, the company issued all of its authorized shares of $8 convertible preferred stock for land valued at $400,000 and a building valued at $1,200,000. The property was subject to a mortgage of $600,000.

On April 4, subscriptions for 5,000 shares of the $3 preferred stock were received at $52 per share, with one half of the subscription price paid in cash. On April 8, the remaining 5,000 shares of $3 preferred stock were issued to an inventor for a patent. A subscription for 1,000 shares of common stock at $20 per share was also received, with a cash payment of $2,000 accompanying the subscription.

On April 25, the balance due on the April 4 subscriptions was collected, and the shares were issued. By April 30, the subscriber to the 1,000 shares of common stock had failed to pay the balance of his subscription, which he had agreed to pay in 10 days. Shares were issued for his down payment, and the balance of the contract was canceled.

Required

a.   Prepare general journal entries for the above transactions.

b.   Prepare the stockholders' equity section of the April 30, 1993, balance sheet. Assume retained earnings were $40,000.

c.   Assume that each share of the $8 convertible preferred stock is convertible into six shares of common stock and that one-half of the preferred is converted on September 1, 1996. Give the required journal entry.

Problem 13–7A

Prepare stockholders' equity section; determine book values of stock; and determine dividends for each class of stock
(L.O. 3, 6)

Zorn Company issued all of its 2,500 shares of authorized preferred stock on January 1, 1992, at $103 per share. The preferred stock is no-par stock, has a stated value of $5 per share, is entitled to a cumulative basic preference dividend of $6 per share, is callable at $110 beginning in 1997, and is entitled to $100 per share in liquidation plus cumulative dividends. On this same date, Zorn also issued 5,000 authorized shares of no-par common stock with a $10 stated value at $50 per share.

On December 31, 1993, the end of its second year of operations, the company's retained earnings amounted to $80,000. No dividends have been declared or paid on either class of stock since the date of issue.

Required

a.   Prepare the stockholders' equity section of Zorn Company's December 31, 1993, balance sheet.

b.   Compute the book value in total and per share of each class of stock as of December 31, 1993, assuming the preferred stock is nonparticipating.

c.   If $55,000 of dividends are to be declared as of December 31, 1993, compute the amount payable to each class of stock assuming the preferred stock is nonparticipating.

Problem 13–8A

Determine book value for each class of stock
(L.O. 6)

The stockholders' equity sections from three different corporations' balance sheets follow.

1. Stockholders' equity:

Paid-in capital:		
Preferred stock—7% cumulative and nonparticipating, $150 par value, 500 shares authorized, issued, and outstanding	$ 75,000	
Common stock—$30 par value, 10,000 shares authorized, issued, and outstanding	300,000	
Total paid-in capital		$ 375,000
Retained earnings		264,000
Total stockholders' equity.		$ 639,000

(All dividends have been paid.)

2. Stockholders' equity:

Paid-in capital:

Preferred stock—6% cumulative and nonparticipating, $50 par value, 10,000 shares authorized, issued, and outstanding	$ 500,000	
Common stock—$150 par value, 30,000 shares authorized, issued, and outstanding	4,500,000	
Total paid-in capital		$ 5,000,000
Retained earnings		55,000
Total stockholders' equity.		$ 5,055,000

(The current year's dividends have not been paid.)

3. Stockholders' equity:

Paid-in capital:

Preferred stock—7% cumulative and nonparticipating, $300 par value, 10,000 shares authorized, issued, and outstanding	$3,000,000	
Common stock—$150 par value, 50,000 shares authorized, issued, and outstanding	7,500,000	
Total paid-in capital		$10,500,000
Retained earnings (deficit)		(1,170,000)
Total stockholders' equity.		$ 9,330,000

(Dividends have not been paid for 2 previous years or the current year.)

Required Compute the book values per share of the preferred and common stock of each corporation assuming that in a liquidation the preferred stock receives par value plus dividends in arrears.

Problem 13–9A

Compute book values of a stockholder's preferred and common stock
(L.O. 6)

Larson, Inc., is a corporation in which all of the outstanding preferred and common stock is held by the four Larson brothers. The brothers have an agreement stating that the remaining brothers will, upon the death of a brother, purchase from the estate his holdings of stock in the company at book value.

The stockholders' equity section of the balance sheet for the company on December 31, 1993, the date of the death of Edward Larson, shows:

Stockholders' equity:

Paid-in capital:

Preferred stock—6%; $400 par value; $400 liquidation value; 4,000 shares authorized, issued, and outstanding	$1,600,000	
Paid-in capital in excess of par—preferred	80,000	
Common stock—without par value, $20 stated value, 60,000 shares authorized, issued, and outstanding	1,200,000	
Paid-in capital in excess of par—common	1,200,000	
Total paid-in capital		$4,080,000
Retained earnings.		160,000
Total stockholders' equity		$4,240,000

No dividends have been paid for the last year on the preferred stock, which is cumulative and nonparticipating. At the time of his death, Edward Larson held 2,000 shares of preferred stock and 10,000 shares of common stock of the company.

Required *a.* Compute the book value of the preferred stock.

b. Compute the book value of the common stock.

c. Compute the amount the remaining brothers must pay to the estate of Edward Larson for the preferred and common stock that he held at the time of his death.

PROBLEMS: SERIES B

Problem 13–1B

Determine dividends for common stock and cumulative and noncumulative preferred stock
(L.O. 3)

The outstanding capital stock of Hayes Corporation consisted of 3,000 shares of 10% preferred stock, $200 par value, and 30,000 shares of no-par common stock with a stated value of $200. The preferred was issued at $329.60, the common at $384 per share. On January 1, 1989, the retained earnings of the company were $200,000. During the succeeding five years, net income was as follows:

1989	$614,000
1990	408,000
1991	38,400
1992	128,000
1993	530,000

No dividends were in arrears as of January 1, 1989, and during the five years 1989–93, the board of directors declared dividends in each year equal to net income of the year.

Required

Prepare a schedule showing the dividends declared each year on each class of stock assuming the preferred stock is:

a.   Cumulative and nonparticipating.

b.   Noncumulative and nonparticipating.

Problem 13–2B

Prepare partial balance sheet involving par value stock
(L.O. 4)

Certain post-closing account balances for Chapin, Inc., as of December 31, 1993, were as follows:

CHAPIN, INC.
Partial List of Post-Closing Account Balances
December 31, 1993

Paid-In Capital in Excess of Par Value—Preferred	$ 30,000
Common Stock Subscribed (2,000 shares)	200,000
Subscriptions Receivable—Common	240,000
Preferred Stock (8%, $200 par value, 3,000 shares authorized,	
issued, and outstanding)	600,000
Paid-In Capital in Excess of Par Value—Common	72,000
Common Stock ($100 par value, 30,000 shares authorized;	
8,000 shares issued and outstanding)	800,000
Retained Earnings	784,000

Required

From the above list of account balances, prepare the stockholders' equity section of the December 31, 1993, balance sheet in proper form.

Problem 13–3B

Journalize stock subscriptions and prepare resulting balance sheet
(L.O. 5)

In the charter granted January 2, 1993, Classic Corporation was authorized to issue 2,000 shares of no-par common stock. The stock is to be issued under subscription agreements that call for immediate payment of one fourth of each subscription, with the remainder due on the first day of the following month.

On January 5, subscriptions for 600 shares at $50 per share were received, and on May 1 an additional 400 shares were subscribed at $60 per share. All subscriptions were collected in accordance with the agreements.

Required

a.   Prepare the entries to record all the transactions of January through May 1993, assuming no stock was issued until the subscriptions were paid in full.

b.   Prepare the May 31, 1993, balance sheet assuming there were no transactions other than those described above.

Problem 13–4B

Journalize stock issuances for cash, services (organization costs), and property; prepare resulting balance sheet (L.O. 5)

On December 27, 1992, Danny Company was authorized to issue 250,000 shares of $10 par value common stock. It then completed the following transactions:

1993

Jan. 14 Issued 45,000 shares of common stock at $12 per share for cash.

29 Gave the promoters of the corporation 25,000 shares of common stock for their services in organizing the company. The board of directors valued these services at $310,000.

Feb. 19 Exchanged 50,000 shares of common stock for the following assets at the indicated fair market values:

Land	$ 90,000
Building	220,000
Machinery	300,000

Required

a. Prepare general journal entries to record the transactions.

b. Prepare the balance sheet of the company as of March 1, 1993.

Problem 13–5B

Post transactions; prepare balance sheets for par value stock, stated value stock, and no-par or stated value stock (L.O. 2, 4, 5)

In the corporate charter that it received on May 1, 1993, Chandler Company was authorized to issue 15,000 shares of common stock. The company issued 1,000 shares immediately to each of two of the promoters for $54 per share, cash.

On July 2, the company issued 100 shares of stock to a lawyer to satisfy a $5,600 bill for legal services rendered in organizing the corporation.

On July 3, subscriptions, accompanied by a 10% down payment, were received from the general public for 6,000 shares at $56 per share.

On July 5, the company issued 1,000 shares to the principal promoter of the corporation in exchange for a patent. Another 200 shares were issued to this same person for costs incurred and services rendered in bringing the corporation into existence.

Required

a. Set up T-accounts, and post the above transactions. Then prepare a balance sheet for the Chandler Company as of July 5, 1993, assuming the authorized stock has a par value of $50 per share.

b. Repeat part *(a)* for the stockholders' equity accounts, and prepare the stockholders' equity section of the July 5 balance sheet assuming the stock authorized has no par value but has a $20 per share stated value.

c. Repeat part *(a)* for the stockholders' equity accounts assuming the stock authorized has neither par nor stated value. Prepare the stockholders' equity section of the balance sheet.

Problem 13–6B

Journalize stock issuances for cash, property, and services; journalize stock subscriptions; and prepare resulting stockholders' equity section (L.O. 5)

On May 1, 1993, Allied Company received a charter that authorized it to issue:

1. 4,000 shares of no-par preferred stock to which a stated value of $12 per share is assigned. The stock is entitled to a cumulative dividend of $9.60, convertible into two shares of common stock, callable at $208, and entitled to $200 per share in liquidation.

2. 1,500 shares of $400 par value, $20 cumulative preferred stock, which is callable at $420 and entitled to $412 in liquidation.

3. 60,000 shares of no-par common stock to which a stated value of $40 is assigned.

Transactions

May 1 All of the $9.60 cumulative preferred was subscribed and issued at $204 per share, cash.

2 All of the $20 cumulative preferred was exchanged for inventory, land, and buildings valued at $128,000, $160,000, and $340,000, respectively.

2 Subscriptions were received for 50,000 shares of common at $80 per share, with 10% of the subscription price paid immediately in cash.

May 3 Cash of $12,000 was paid to reimburse promoters for costs incurred for accounting, legal, and printing services. In addition, 1,000 shares of common stock were
issued to the promoters for their services.

31 All of the subscriptions to the common stock were collected and the shares
issued.

Required *a.* Prepare journal entries for the above transactions.

b. Assume that retained earnings were $200,000. Prepare the stockholders' equity
section of the May 31, 1993, balance sheet.

Problem 13–7B

Prepare stockholders'
equity section; determine
book values of stock; and
determine dividends for
each class of stock
(L.O. 3, 6)

On January 2, 1992, the date Foster Company received its charter, it issued all of its
authorized 3,000 shares of no-par preferred stock at $52 and all of its 12,000 authorized
shares of no-par common stock at $20 per share. The preferred stock has a stated value of
$25 per share, is entitled to a basic cumulative preference dividend of $3 per share, is
callable at $53 beginning in 1994, and is entitled to $50 per share plus cumulative dividends
in the event of liquidation. The common stock has a stated value of $5 per share.

On December 31, 1993, the end of the second year of operations, retained earnings were
$45,000. No dividends have been declared or paid on either class of stock.

Required *a.* Prepare the stockholders' equity section of Foster Company's December 31,
1993, balance sheet.

b. Compute the book value of each class of stock assuming the preferred stock is
nonparticipating.

c. If $21,000 of dividends were declared as of December 31, 1993, compute the
amount paid to each class of stock assuming the preferred stock is
nonparticipating.

Problem 13–8B

Compute total market
value for common stock;
compute book value of
common and preferred
stock
(L.O. 6)

The common stock of Sanders Corporation is selling on a stock exchange for $37.50 per
share. The stockholders' equity of the corporation at December 31, 1993, consists of:

Stockholders' equity:
  Paid-in capital:
    Preferred stock—9% cumulative and nonparticipating,
      $50 par value, 3,000 shares authorized, issued,
      and outstanding $150,000
    Common stock—$30 par value, 30,000 shares authorized, issued,
      and outstanding   900,000
        Total paid-in capital $1,050,000
  Retained earnings   147,750
        Total stockholders' equity $1,197,750

Assume that in liquidation the preferred stock is entitled to par value plus cumulative
unpaid dividends.

Required *a.* What is the total market value of all of the corporation's common stock assuming
all shares are valued at the most recent price?

b. If all dividends have been paid on the preferred stock as of December 31, 1993,
what are the book values of the preferred stock and the common stock?

c. If two years' dividends were due on the preferred stock as of December 31, 1993,
what are the book values of the preferred stock and common stock?

Problem 13–9B

Compute book values of a
stockholder's preferred
and common stock
(L.O. 6)

Golden Corporation has an agreement with each of its 15 preferred and 30 common stockholders that in the event of the death of a stockholder, it will purchase at book value from
the stockholder's estate or heirs the shares of Golden Corporation stock held by the
deceased at the time of death. The book value is to be computed in accordance with
generally accepted accounting principles.

Following is the stockholders' equity section of the Golden Corporation's December 31,
1993, balance sheet.

Stockholders' equity:

Paid-in capital:

$12 no-par preferred stock—$40 stated value; 3,000 shares authorized, issued, and outstanding	$ 120,000
Common stock—$50 par value, 60,000 shares authorized, issued, and outstanding	3,000,000
Paid-in capital in excess of stated value—preferred	672,000
Paid-in capital in excess of par value—common	24,000

Total paid-in capital	$3,816,000
Retained earnings	1,440,000
Total stockholders' equity	$5,256,000

The preferred stock is cumulative and entitled to $240 per share plus cumulative dividends in liquidation. No dividends have been paid for 1½ years.

A stockholder who owned 100 shares of preferred stock and 1,000 shares of common stock died on December 31, 1993. You have been employed by the stockholder's executor to compute the book value of each class of stock and to determine the price to be paid for the stock held by her late husband.

Required   Prepare a schedule showing the computation of the amount to be paid for the deceased stockholder's preferred and common stock.

BUSINESS DECISION PROBLEMS

Decision Problem 13–1

Compute dividends on preferred stock and common stock and determine their relationship to stock prices (L.O. 3)

Eastern Company and Western Company are two companies that have extremely stable net income amounts of $6,000,000 and $4,000,000, respectively. Both companies distribute all their net income as dividends each year. Eastern Company has 100,000 shares of $100 par value, 6% preferred stock, and 500,000 shares of $10 par value common stock outstanding. Western Company has 50,000 shares of $50 par value, 8% preferred stock, and 400,000 shares of $10 par value common stock outstanding. Both preferred stocks are cumulative and nonparticipating.

Required   *a.*   Compute the annual dividend per share of preferred stock and per share of common stock for each company.

b.   Based solely on the above information, which common stock would you predict to have the higher market price per share? Why?

Decision Problem 13–2

Determine book values and their relationship to investment decisions (L.O. 6)

Frank Clayborn recently inherited $192,000 cash that he wishes to invest in one of the following securities: common stock of the Durden Corporation or common stock of the Simmons Corporation. Both corporations manufacture the same types of products and have been in existence for five years. The stockholders' equity sections of the two corporations' latest balance sheets are shown below:

DURDEN CORPORATION

Stockholders' equity:

Paid-in capital:
Common stock—$50 par value, 30,000 shares authorized,
issued, and outstanding $1,500,000
Retained earnings.   1,380,000

Total stockholders' equity $2,880,000

SIMMONS CORPORATION

Stockholders' equity:

Paid-in capital:
Preferred stock—8%, $200 par value, cumulative
and nonparticipating, 4,000 shares authorized, issued,
and outstanding. . . . . $ 800,000
Common stock—$50 par value, 40,000 shares authorized,
issued, and outstanding   2,000,000

Total paid-in capital $2,800,000
Retained earnings.   224,000

Total stockholders' equity $3,024,000

The Durden Corporation has paid a cash dividend of $2.40 per share each year since its creation; its common stock is currently selling for $236 per share. The Simmons Corporation's common stock is currently selling for $192 per share. The current year's dividend and three prior years' dividends on the preferred stock are in arrears. The preferred stock has a liquidation value of $240 per share.

Required   *a.*   What is the book value per share of the Durden Corporation common stock and the Simmons Corporation common stock? Is book value the major determinant of market value of the stock?

           b.   Based solely on the above information, which investment would you recommend? Why?

Decision Problem 13–3
Determine original
issuance price of common
stock
(L.O. 4)

From the shareholders' equity section of the consolidated balance sheet of The Coca-Cola Company located in Appendix E, determine the price paid per share of common stock upon original issuance.

Bear in mind that the preferred stock is presented at its liquidation value. Also, assume that the capital surplus represents additional paid-in capital and is *only* the additional paid-in capital from the issuance of common stock.

ANSWERS TO SELF-TEST

True-False

1. *False.* The primary reason a person may prefer the corporate form of business organization in a situation involving considerable risk is that stockholders can lose only the amount of capital they have invested in a corporation.

2. *False.* The claims of the creditors rank ahead of the claims of the stockholders, even those stockholders whose stock is preferred as to assets.

3. *True.* Par value is simply the amount per share that is credited to the Capital Stock account for each share issued and is no indication of the market value or the book value of the stock.

4. *False.* When stock subscriptions are received, a temporary account, Common (or Preferred) Stock Subscribed account, is credited unless the subscriptions are fully paid.

5. *True.* When capital stock is issued for property or services, the transaction is recorded at the fair value of (1) the property or services received or (2) the stock issued, whichever value is more clearly evident.

Multiple-Choice

1. *c*. This feature of corporations is one of the disadvantages of the corporate form of organization.

2. *b*. Par value is an arbitrary amount assigned to each share of a given class of stock and is printed on the stock certificate.

3. *d*. Dividends in arrears are cumulative unpaid dividends. Only cumulative preferred stock could have dividends in arrears.

4. *a*. The amount credited to the Common Stock account is computed as follows:

$$5{,}000 \text{ shares} \times \$20 = \$100{,}000$$

5. *a*. The book value of common stock is computed as follows:

Total book value of stockholders' equity ($20,000 + $50,000 + $100,000)	$170,000
Total shares	÷1,000
Book value per share	$ 170

14

CORPORATIONS: PAID-IN CAPITAL, RETAINED EARNINGS, DIVIDENDS, AND TREASURY STOCK

LEARNING OBJECTIVES

After studying this chapter, you should be able to:

1. Identify the different sources of paid-in capital and describe how they would be presented on a balance sheet.
2. Account for a cash dividend, a stock dividend, a stock split, and a retained earnings appropriation.
3. Account for the acquisition and reissuance of treasury stock.
4. Describe the proper accounting treatment of discontinued operations, extraordinary items, and changes in accounting principles.
5. Define prior period adjustments and show their proper presentation in the financial statements.
6. Compute earnings per share.

As owners of a corporation, stockholders provide much of the capital for its operation. On the balance sheet, the stockholders' interest in the corporation is shown as paid-in capital under stockholders' equity. Also included in stockholders' equity is the capital accumulated through the retention of corporate earnings (retained earnings). Paid-in capital is a relatively permanent portion of stockholders' equity; retained earnings are a relatively temporary portion of corporate capital and are the source of stockholders' dividends.

The preceding chapter discussed the paid-in capital obtained by issuing shares of stock for cash, property, or services. In this chapter, you will learn about additional sources of paid-in capital and items affecting retained earnings.

PAID-IN (OR CONTRIBUTED) CAPITAL

<table>
<tr>
<td>

Objective 1

Identify the different sources of paid-in capital and describe how they would be presented on a balance sheet

</td>
<td>

As you learned in the preceding chapter, paid-in capital, or contributed capital, refers to all of the contributed capital of a corporation, including that capital carried in the capital stock accounts. In the general ledger, no account titled "Paid-In Capital" is maintained. Instead, a separate account is established for each source of paid-in capital.

Illustration 14.1 summarizes several sources of stockholders' equity and gives examples of general ledger account titles used to record increases and decreases in capital from each of these sources. Chapter 13 discussed some of these general ledger accounts. This chapter will discuss other general ledger accounts used to record sources of stockholders' equity.

The stockholders' equity section of a balance sheet should show the different sources of the corporation's paid-in capital since these sources are important information. For example, these additional sources may be from stock dividends, treasury stock transactions, or donations.

</td>
</tr>
</table>

Paid-In Capital—Stock Dividends

When a corporation declares a stock dividend, the corporation distributes additional shares of stock (instead of cash) to its present stockholders. In a later section, this chapter discusses and illustrates how the issuance of a stock dividend results in a credit to a Paid-In Capital—Stock Dividends account.

Paid-In Capital—Treasury Stock Transactions

Another source of capital is treasury stock transactions. Treasury stock is the corporation's own stock, either preferred or common, that has been issued and then reacquired by the issuing corporation; it is legally available for reissuance. If a corporation reacquires shares of its own outstanding capital stock at one price and later reissues them at a higher price, corporate capital is increased by the difference between the two prices. If the reissue price is **less** than acquisition cost, corporate capital is decreased. Treasury stock transactions are discussed at length later in this chapter.

Paid-In Capital—Donations

Occasionally, a corporation receives gifts of assets, such as a gift of a $500,000 building. These donated gifts increase stockholders' equity and are called donated capital. The entry to record the gift of a $500,000 building is a debit to Buildings and a credit to Paid-In Capital—Donations. This entry should be made in the amount of the $500,000 fair market value of the gift when received.

ILLUSTRATION 14.1

Sources of Stockholders' Equity

Sources of Stockholders' Equity	Illustrative General Ledger Account Titles
I. Capital paid in (or contributed).	
A. For, or assigned to, shares:	
1. Issued to the extent of par or stated value or the amount received for shares without par or stated value.	Common Stock 5% Preferred Stock
2. Subscribed but not issued to the extent of par or stated value or the amount subscribed for shares without par or stated value.	Common (Preferred) Stock Subscribed
3. To be distributed as a stock dividend.	Stock Dividend Distributable—Common (Preferred)
4. In addition to par or stated value:	
a. In excess of par.	Paid-In Capital in Excess of Par Value—Common (Preferred)
b. In excess of stated value.	Paid-In Capital in Excess of Stated Value—Common (Preferred)
c. Resulting from declaration of stock dividends.	Paid-In Capital—Stock Dividends
d. Resulting from reissue of treasury stock at a price above its acquisition price.	Paid-In Capital—Common (Preferred) Treasury Stock Transactions
B. Other than for shares, whether from stockholders or from others.	Paid-In Capital—Donations
II. Capital accumulated by retention of earnings (retained earnings).	
A. Appropriated retained earnings.	Appropriation per Loan Agreement
B. Free and unappropriated retained earnings.	Retained Earnings (Unappropriated)

RETAINED EARNINGS

Objective 2

Account for a cash dividend, a stock dividend, a stock split, and a retained earnings appropriation

The retained earnings portion of stockholders' equity results from accumulated earnings, reduced by net losses and dividends. Like paid-in capital, retained earnings is a source of assets received by a corporation. Paid-in capital is the actual investment by the stockholders; retained earnings is the investment by the stockholders through earnings not yet withdrawn.

The balance in the corporation's Retained Earnings account is the corporation's net income, less net losses, from the date the corporation began to the present, less the sum of dividends paid during this period. Net income increases Retained Earnings, while net losses and dividends decrease Retained Earnings in any given year. Thus, the balance in Retained Earnings represents the corporation's accumulated net income not distributed to stockholders.

When the Retained Earnings account has a debit balance, a deficit exists. A deficit is shown as retained earnings with a negative amount in the stockholders' equity section of the balance sheet. The title of the general ledger account need not be changed even though it contains a debit balance. The most common credits and debits made to Retained Earnings are for income (or losses) and dividends. Occasionally, other entries are made to the Retained Earnings account. We will discuss some of these entries later in the chapter.

PAID-IN CAPITAL AND RETAINED EARNINGS ON THE BALANCE SHEET

The following stockholders' equity section of a balance sheet presents the various sources of capital in proper form:

Stockholders' equity:

Paid-in capital:		
Preferred stock—6%, $100 par value; authorized, issued, and outstanding, 4,000 shares	$ 400,000	
Common stock—no par value, $5 stated value; authorized, issued, and outstanding, 400,000 shares	2,000,000	$2,400,000
Paid-in capital—		
From preferred stock issuances*	$ 40,000	
From donations	10,000	50,000
Total paid-in capital		$2,450,000
Retained earnings		500,000
Total stockholders' equity		$2,950,000

* This label is not the exact account title but is representative of the descriptions used on balance sheets. The exact account title could be used, but shorter descriptions are often shown.

In highly condensed, published balance sheets, the details regarding the sources of the paid-in capital in excess of par or stated value are often omitted and replaced by a single item, such as:

Paid-in capital in excess of par (or stated) value $50,000

DIVIDENDS

Dividends are distributions of earnings by a corporation to its stockholders. Usually dividends are paid in cash, but additional shares of the corporation's own capital stock may also be distributed as dividends. Occasionally, dividends are paid in merchandise or other assets. Since dividends are the means whereby the owners of a corporation share in the earnings of the corporation, they are charged against retained earnings.

Before dividends can be paid, they must be declared by the board of directors and recorded in the corporation's minutes book. Three dividend dates are significant:

1. **Date of declaration.** This date indicates when the board of directors takes action in the form of a motion and declares that dividends should be paid. The board action creates the liability for dividends payable (or stock dividends distributable for stock dividends).

2. **Date of record.** The board of directors establishes this date; the date of record determines the stockholders who will receive the dividends. The corporation's records (the stockholders ledger) determine the corporation's stockholders as of the date of record.

3. **Date of payment.** This date indicates when the corporation will pay the dividend to the stockholders.

To illustrate how these three dates relate to an actual situation, assume the board of directors of the Allen Corporation declared a cash dividend on May 5, 1994 (date of declaration). The cash dividend declared is $1.25 per share to stockholders of record on July 1, 1994 (date of record), payable on July 10 (date of payment). Since financial transactions occur on both the date of declaration (a liability is incurred) and on the date of payment (cash is paid), journal entries will be required on both of these dates. No journal entry is required on the date of record.

Illustration 14.2 shows the frequencies of dividend payments made by a sample of 600 companies for the years 1986–89. Cash dividends are far more numerous than stock dividends or dividends in kind (paid in merchandise or other assets).

Cash Dividends

Cash dividends are cash distributions of net income by a corporation to its stockholders. To illustrate the entries for cash dividends, consider the following example. On January 21, 1994, a corporation's board of directors declared a 2% quarterly cash dividend on $100,000 of outstanding preferred stock. This dividend is one fourth of the annual dividend on 1,000 shares of $100 par value, 8% preferred stock. The dividend will be paid on March 1, 1994, to stockholders of record on February 5, 1994. The entries at the declaration and payment dates are as follows (**no entry is made on the date of record**):

1994					
Jan.	21	Retained Earnings		2,000	
		Dividends Payable			2,000
		Dividend declared: 2% on $100,000 of outstanding preferred stock, payable March 1, 1994, to stockholders of record on February 5, 1994.			
Mar.	1	Dividends Payable		2,000	
		Cash			2,000
		Paid the dividend declared on January 21, 1994.			

Often a cash dividend is stated as so many dollars per share. For instance, the quarterly dividend could have been stated as $2 per share. When a cash dividend is declared, some companies debit a Dividends account instead of Retained Earnings. (Both methods are acceptable.) The Dividends account is then closed to Retained Earnings at the end of the fiscal year. This closing entry is similar in nature to the closing of owner's drawings in Chapter 4.

Once a cash dividend is declared and notice of the dividend is given to stockholders, it generally cannot be rescinded unless all stockholders agree to such action.[1] Thus, the credit balance in the Dividends Payable account appears as a current liability on the balance sheet.

Stock Dividends

Stock dividends are payable in additional shares of the declaring corporation's capital stock. When stock dividends are declared, additional shares of the same class of stock as that held by the stockholders are issued to those stockholders.

Corporations usually account for stock dividends by transferring a sum from retained earnings to permanent paid-in capital. The amount transferred for stock dividends is usually the fair market value of the distributed shares. Most states permit corporations to debit Retained Earnings or any paid-in capital accounts other than those representing legal capital for stock dividends. In most circumstances, however, Retained Earnings will be debited for the declaration of a stock dividend.

[1] Stockholders might agree to rescind (cancel) a dividend that has already been declared if the company is in difficult financial circumstances and needs to retain the cash to pay bills or acquire assets that are needed to continue operations.

ILLUSTRATION 14.2

Types of Dividends

| | **Number of Companies** | | | |
	1989	1988	1987	1986
Cash dividends paid to common stock shareholders:				
Per share amount disclosed in retained earnings statement	301	310	324	335
Per share amount not disclosed in retained earnings statement	174	165	150	152
Total	475	475	474	487
Cash dividends paid to preferred stock shareholders:				
Per share amount disclosed in retained earnings statement	63	60	79	75
Per share amount not disclosed in retained earnings statement	87	80	81	81
Total	150	140	160	156
Dividends paid by pooled companies	—	3	3	2
Stock dividends	10	12	8	14
Dividends in kind	7	11	10	17
Stock purchase rights	54	78	44	117

Source: American Institute of Certified Public Accountants, *Accounting Trends & Techniques* (New York: AICPA, 1990), p. 303.

Stock dividends have no effect on the total amount of stockholders' equity or on net assets. They merely decrease retained earnings and increase paid-in capital by an equal amount. Immediately after the distribution of a stock dividend, each share of similar stock has a lower book value per share. This decrease occurs because more shares are outstanding with no increase in total stockholders' equity.

Stock dividends do not affect the individual stockholder's percentage of ownership in the corporation. For example, if a stockholder owns 1,000 shares in a corporation having 100,000 shares of stock outstanding, that stockholder owns 1% of the outstanding shares. After a 10% stock dividend, the stockholder will still own 1% of the outstanding shares—1,100 of the 110,000 outstanding shares.

A corporation might declare a stock dividend for several reasons:

1. Retained earnings may have become large relative to total stockholders' equity, or the corporation may simply desire a larger permanent capitalization.

2. The market price of the stock may have risen above a desirable trading range. A stock dividend will generally reduce the per share market value of the company's stock.

3. The corporation may wish to have more stockholders (who might then buy its products) and expects to eventually increase their number by increasing the number of shares outstanding. Some of the stockholders receiving the stock dividend are likely to sell the shares to other persons.

4. Stock dividends may be used to silence stockholders' demands for cash dividends from a corporation that does not have sufficient cash to pay cash dividends.

A stock dividend is categorized as a small stock dividend or a large stock dividend according to the percentage of shares issued as a stock dividend, and different accounting treatments are used for each.

Recording Small Stock Dividends A stock dividend of less than 20 to 25% of the outstanding shares is considered a **small stock dividend** and is assumed to have little effect on the market value (quoted market price) of the shares. Thus, the dividend is accounted for at the present market value of the outstanding shares.

Assume a corporation is authorized to issue 20,000 shares of $100 par value common stock, of which 8,000 shares are outstanding. Its board of directors declares a 10% stock dividend (800 shares). The quoted market price of the stock is $125 per share immediately before the stock dividend is announced. Since the distribution is less than 20 to 25% of the outstanding shares, the dividend is accounted for at market value. The entry for the declaration of the stock dividend on August 10, 1994, is:

Aug.	10	Retained Earnings (or Stock Dividends) (800 shares × $125) . . .	100,000	
		Stock Dividend Distributable—Common		
		(800 shares × $100)		80,000
		Paid-In Capital—Stock Dividends		
		(800 shares × $25)		20,000
		To record the declaration of a 10% stock dividend; shares to be distributed on September 20, 1994, to stockholders of record on August 31, 1994.		

The entry to record the issuance of the shares is:

Sept.	20	Stock Dividend Distributable—Common	80,000	
		Common Stock		80,000
		To record the distribution of 800 shares of common stock as authorized in stock dividend declared on August 10, 1994.		

The Stock Dividend Distributable—Common account is a stockholders' equity (paid-in capital) account credited for the par or stated value of the shares distributable when recording the declaration of a stock dividend. Since a stock dividend distributable is not to be paid with assets, it is not a liability. If a balance sheet is prepared between the date the 10% dividend is declared and the date the shares are issued, the proper statement presentation of the effects of the stock dividend is:

Stockholders' equity:		
Paid-in capital:		
Common stock—$100 par value; authorized, 20,000 shares; issued and outstanding, 8,000 shares	$800,000	
Stock dividend distributable on September 20, 1994, 800 shares at par value.	80,000	
Total par value of shares issued and to be issued	$880,000	
Paid-in capital from stock dividends.	20,000	
Total paid-in capital		$ 900,000
Retained earnings.		150,000
Total stockholders' equity		$1,050,000

Suppose, on the other hand, that the common stock in the above example is no-par stock and has a stated value of $50 per share. In this case, the entry to record the declaration of the stock dividend (when the market value is $125) is:

```
Retained Earnings (800 shares × $125) . . . . . . . . . . . . . .    100,000
    Stock Dividend Distributable—Common
        (800 shares × $50) . . . . . . . . . . . . . . .                        40,000
        Paid-In Capital—Stock Dividends (800 shares × $75) . . . . . . .        60,000
    To record the declaration of a stock dividend.
```

The entry to record the issuance of the stock dividend is:

```
Stock Dividend Distributable—Common . . . . . . . . . . . . . .     40,000
    Common Stock . . . . . . . . . . . . . . . . . . . . . . . .                40,000
    To record the issuance of the stock dividend.
```

Recording Large Stock Dividends   A stock dividend of more than 20 to 25% of the outstanding shares is considered a **large stock dividend.** Since one purpose of a large stock dividend is to reduce the market value of the stock so the shares can be traded more easily, the old market value of the stock should not be used in the entry. Such dividends are accounted for at their **par** or **stated** value rather than at their fair market value. Stocks without par or stated value are accounted for at the amounts established by the laws of the state of incorporation or by the board of directors.

To illustrate the treatment of a stock dividend of more than 20 to 25%, assume X Corporation has been authorized to issue 10,000 shares of $10 par value common stock, of which 5,000 shares are outstanding. X Corporation declared a 30% stock dividend (1,500 shares) on September 20, 1994, to be issued on October 15, 1994. The required entries are:

Sept.	20	Retained Earnings (or Stock Dividends) (1,500 shares × $10) . . .	15,000	
		Stock Dividend Distributable—Common		15,000
		To declare a 30% stock dividend.		
Oct.	15	Stock Dividend Distributable—Common	15,000	
		Common Stock		15,000
		To issue the 30% stock dividend.		

Note that in contrast to the small stock dividend that was accounted for at market value, the 30% stock dividend is accounted for at par value (1,500 shares × $10 = $15,000). Because of the differences in accounting for large and small stock dividends, the relative size of the stock dividend must be determined before making any journal entries.

Illustration 14.3 shows the effect of a small and large stock dividend on the stockholders' equity.

Stock Splits

A *stock split* is a distribution of 100% or more of additional shares of the issuing corporation's stock accompanied by a corresponding reduction in the par value per share. The corporation receives no assets in this transaction. The purpose of a stock split is to cause a large reduction in the market price per share of the outstanding stock. A two-for-one split doubles the number of shares outstanding,

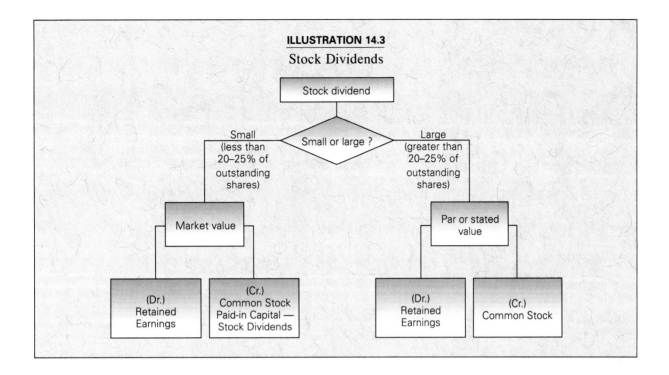

ILLUSTRATION 14.3
Stock Dividends

a three-for-one split triples the number of shares, and so on. The par value per share is reduced at the same time so that the total dollar amount credited to common stock remains the same. For instance, in a two-for-one split, the par value per share is halved.[2] If the corporation issues 100% more stock without a reduction in the par value per share, the transaction is considered a 100% stock dividend rather than a two-for-one stock split.

The entry to record a stock split depends on the particular circumstances. Usually, only the number of shares outstanding and the par or stated value need to be changed in the records. (The number of shares authorized may also change.) Thus, a two-for-one stock split in which the par value of the shares is decreased from $20 to $10 would be recorded as follows:

Common Stock—$20 par value	100,000	
Common Stock—$10 par value		100,000
To record a two-for-one stock split; 5,000 shares of $20 par value common stock were replaced by 10,000 shares of $10 par value common stock.		

Illustration 14.4 summarizes the effects of stock dividends and stock splits. Stock dividends and stock splits have no effect on the total amount of stockholders' equity. In addition, stock splits have no effect on the total amount of paid-in capital or retained earnings. They merely increase the number of shares outstanding and decrease the par value per share. Stock dividends increase paid-in capital and decrease retained earnings by equal amounts.

---

[2] If a corporation *reduces* the par value of its stock without issuing more shares, say, from $100 to $60 per share, then $40 per share must be removed from the appropriate capital stock account and credited to Paid-In Capital—Recapitalization. Further discussion of this process, called *recapitalization*, is beyond the scope of this text.

ILLUSTRATION 14.4

Summary of Effects of Stock Dividends and Stock Splits

	Total Stockholders' Equity	Common Stock	Paid-In Capital— Common	Retained Earnings	Number of Shares Outstanding	Par Value per Share
Stock dividends:						
Small	No effect	Increases	Increases	Decreases	Increases	No effect
Large	No effect	Increases	No effect	Decreases	Increases	No effect
Stock splits	No effect	No effect	No effect	No effect	Increases	Decreases

---

Legality of Dividends

In the preceding chapter, you learned that corporate laws differ as to their provisions regarding the legality of a dividend. The **legal** or **stated capital** of a corporation is established by state law as that portion of the stockholders' equity that must be maintained intact, unimpaired by dividend declarations or other distributions to stockholders. The legal capital is often established at an amount equal to the par or stated value of the shares issued or at an amount equal to a minimum price per share issued.

The objective of these state corporate laws is to protect the corporation's creditors, whose claims have priority over those of the corporation's stockholders. To illustrate the significance of the legal capital concept, assume that a corporation has severe financial difficulty and is about to go out of business. If there were no legal capital restrictions on dividends, the stockholders of a corporation in financial difficulty might attempt to pay themselves a cash dividend or have the corporation buy back their stock, leaving no funds available for the corporation's creditors.

The board of directors of a corporation possesses sole power to declare dividends. The legality of a dividend generally depends on the amount of retained earnings available for dividends—not on the net income of any one period. Dividends may be paid in periods in which losses are incurred, provided retained earnings and the cash position justify the dividend. And in some states, dividends may be declared from current earnings even though an accumulated deficit exists. The financial advisability of declaring a dividend depends on the cash position of the corporation.

Liquidating Dividends

Normally, dividends are reductions of retained earnings since they are distributions of the corporation's net income. However, dividends may be distributions of contributed capital. These dividends are called liquidating dividends.

Liquidating dividends are debited to a paid-in capital account. Corporations should disclose to stockholders the source of any dividends that are not distributions of net income by indicating which paid-in capital account was debited as a result of the dividend. The legality of paying liquidating dividends depends on the source of the paid-in capital and the laws of the state of incorporation.

RETAINED EARNINGS APPROPRIATIONS

The amount of a corporation's retained earnings that may be paid as cash dividends may be less than total retained earnings for several reasons, contractual or voluntary. These contractual or voluntary restrictions or limitations on retained earnings are called retained earnings appropriations. For example, a loan contract may state that part of a corporation's $100,000 of retained earnings is not available for cash dividends until the loan is paid, or a board of directors may decide that assets resulting from net income should be used for plant expansion rather than for cash dividends. An example of a voluntary restriction was described in General Electric's annual report. In that report, cash dividends were limited "to support enhanced productive capability and to provide adequate financial resources for internal and external growth opportunities."

Retained earnings appropriations may be formally recorded by transferring amounts from Retained Earnings to accounts such as "Appropriation for Loan Agreement" or "Retained Earnings Appropriated for Plant Expansion." Retained earnings appropriations are sometimes referred to as *retained earnings reserves*, but use of the term *reserves* is discouraged.

Appropriations of retained earnings may also be made for pending litigation, for debt retirement, for contingencies in general, and for other purposes. Such appropriations do not reduce total retained earnings. Their purpose is merely to disclose to balance sheet readers that a portion of retained earnings is not available for cash dividends. Thus, the recording of these appropriations simply guarantees that the corporation will limit its outflow of cash dividends while repaying a loan, expanding a plant, or taking on some other costly endeavor. Recording retained earnings appropriations does not involve the setting aside of cash for the indicated purpose. The establishment of a separate fund would require a specific directive from the board of directors. Thus, the only entry required to record the appropriation of $25,000 of retained earnings to fulfill the provisions in a loan agreement is:

Retained Earnings	25,000	
Appropriation per Loan Agreement		25,000
To record restriction on retained earnings.		

When the retained earnings appropriation has served its purpose of restricting dividends and the loan has been repaid, the board of directors may decide to return the appropriation intact to Retained Earnings. The entry to do this is:

Appropriation per Loan Agreement	25,000	
Retained Earnings		25,000
To return balance in Appropriation per Loan Agreement account to Retained Earnings.		

Retained Earnings Appropriations on the Balance Sheet

On the balance sheet, retained earnings appropriations should be shown in the stockholders' equity section as follows:

Stockholders' equity:		
Paid-in capital:		
Preferred stock—8%, $50 par value; 500 shares authorized, issued, and outstanding	$25,000	
Common stock—$5 par value; 10,000 shares authorized, issued, and outstanding	50,000	
Total paid-in capital		$ 75,000
Retained earnings:		
Appropriated:		
Per loan agreement	$25,000	
Unappropriated	20,000	
Total retained earnings		45,000
Total stockholders' equity		$120,000

Note that a retained earnings appropriation does not reduce stockholders' equity but merely earmarks (restricts) a portion of that equity for a specific reason.

The formal practice of recording and reporting retained earnings appropriations is decreasing and being replaced by footnote explanations such as the following:

Note 7. Retained earnings restrictions. According to the provisions in the loan agreement, retained earnings available for dividends are limited to $20,000.

Such footnotes appear after the formal financial statements in a section called "Notes to Financial Statements." The Retained Earnings account on the balance sheet would be referenced as follows: "Retained Earnings (see note 7) . . . $45,000."

Changes in the composition of retained earnings reveal important information about a corporation to financial statement users. A separate formal statement is issued to disclose such changes. This statement is called the *statement of retained earnings*.

STATEMENT OF RETAINED EARNINGS

A statement of retained earnings is a formal statement showing the items causing changes in unappropriated and appropriated retained earnings during a stated period of time. Changes in unappropriated retained earnings usually consist of the addition of net income (or deduction of net loss) and the deduction of dividends and appropriations. Changes in appropriated retained earnings consist of increases or decreases in appropriations.

Illustration 14.5 shows a statement of retained earnings. Ward Corporation's only new appropriation during 1994 was an additional $35,000 for plant expansion. This new $35,000 is added to the $25,000 beginning balance in that account and subtracted from unappropriated retained earnings. An alternative to the statement of retained earnings is the statement of stockholders' equity.

STATEMENT OF STOCKHOLDERS' EQUITY

Most corporations include four financial statements in their annual reports: a balance sheet, an income statement, a statement of stockholders' equity (in place of a statement of retained earnings), and a statement of cash flows (to be discussed in Chapter 18). A statement of stockholders' equity is a summary of the transactions affecting the accounts in the stockholders' equity section of the balance sheet during a stated period of time. These transactions include activities affecting both paid-in capital and retained earnings accounts. Thus, the statement of stockholders' equity includes the information contained in a statement of retained earnings plus some additional information. The columns in the statement of stockholders' equity reflect the major account titles within the stockholders' equity section: the types of stock issued and outstanding, paid-in capital in excess of par (or stated) value, retained earnings, and treasury stock. Each row indicates the effects of major transactions affecting one or more stockholders' equity accounts.

Illustration 14.6 shows a statement of stockholders' equity. The first row indicates the beginning balances of each account in the stockholders' equity section. This summary shows that Larkin Corporation issued 10,000 shares of common stock, declared a 5% stock dividend on common stock, repurchased 1,200 shares of treasury stock, earned net income of $185,000, and paid cash dividends on both its preferred and common stock. After the transactions' effects are indicated within each row, each column's components are added or subtracted to determine the ending balance in each stockholders' equity account.

ILLUSTRATION 14.5

Statement of Retained Earnings

WARD CORPORATION
Statement of Retained Earnings
For Year Ended December 31, 1994

Unappropriated retained earnings:

January 1, 1994, balance		$180,000
Add: Net income.		80,000
		$260,000
Less: Dividends	$15,000	
Appropriation for plant expansion	35,000	50,000
Unappropriated retained earnings, December 31, 1994		$210,000

Appropriated retained earnings:

Appropriation for plant expansion, January 1, 1994, balance	$25,000	
Add: Increase in 1994	35,000	$ 60,000
Appropriation for contract obligation, January 1, 1994, balance.		20,000
Appropriated retained earnings, December 31, 1994		$ 80,000
Total retained earnings, December 31, 1994.		$290,000

ILLUSTRATION 14.6

Statement of Stockholders' Equity

LARKIN CORPORATION
Statement of Stockholders' Equity
For the Year Ended December 31, 1994

	$50 Par Value, 6% Preferred Stock	$20 Par Value Common Stock	Paid-In Capital in Excess of Par Value	Retained Earnings	Treasury Stock	Total
Balance, January 1, 1994	$250,000	$300,000	$200,000	$500,000	$(42,000)	$1,208,000
Issuance of 10,000 shares of common stock		200,000	100,000			300,000
5% stock dividend on common stock, 1,250 shares.		25,000	27,500	(52,500)		–0–
Purchase of 1,200 shares of treasury stock					(48,000)	(48,000)
Net income				185,000		185,000
Cash dividends:						
Preferred stock				(15,000)		(15,000)
Common stock.				(25,000)		(25,000)
Balance, December 31, 1994	$250,000	$525,000	$327,500	$592,500	$(90,000)	$1,605,000

TREASURY STOCK

Objective 3

Account for the acquisition and reissuance of treasury stock

Treasury stock is the corporation's own capital stock that has been issued and then reacquired by the corporation; it has not been canceled and is legally available for later reissuance. Also, treasury stock is **not** classified as **unissued stock** because unissued stock is stock that has never been issued.

As you may recall, if a corporation has additional **authorized** but **unissued** shares of stock that are to be issued after the date of original issue, the preemptive right requires that additional authorized and unissued shares must, in most states, be offered first to existing stockholders on a pro rata basis. However, treasury stock may be reissued without violating the preemptive right provisions of state laws; that is, treasury stock does not have to be offered to current stockholders on a pro rata basis.

A corporation may reacquire its own capital stock as treasury stock to (1) cancel and retire the stock, (2) reissue the stock later at a higher price, (3) reduce the number of shares outstanding and thereby increase earnings per share, or (4) use the stock for issuance to employees. If the intent of reacquisition is cancellation and retirement, the treasury shares exist only until they are retired and canceled by a formal reduction of corporate capital.

For dividend or voting purposes, most state corporate laws consider treasury stock as issued but not outstanding, since the shares are no longer in the possession of stockholders. Also, treasury shares are not considered outstanding in calculating earnings per share. However, treasury shares usually are considered outstanding for purposes of determining legal capital, which would include outstanding shares plus treasury shares.

In states that consider treasury stock as part of legal capital, the cost of treasury stock may not exceed the amount of retained earnings at the date the shares are reacquired. This regulation protects creditors by preventing the corporation from using funds to purchase its own stock instead of paying its debts when the corporation is in financial difficulty. Thus, if a corporation is subject to such a law (as is assumed in this text), the retained earnings available for dividends are limited to the amount in excess of the cost of the treasury shares on hand.

Acquisition and Reissuance of Treasury Stock

When treasury stock is acquired, the stock is recorded at cost as a debit in a stockholders' equity account called **Treasury Stock**.[3] Reissuances are credited to the Treasury Stock account at the cost of acquisition. Any excess of the reissue price over cost is credited to Paid-In Capital—Treasury Stock Transactions because it represents additional paid-in capital.

To illustrate, assume that on February 18, 1994, the Hillside Corporation reacquired 100 shares of its outstanding common stock for $55 each. (The company's stockholders' equity consisted solely of common stock and retained earnings.) On April 18, 1994, the company reissued 30 shares for $58 each. The entries to record these events are:

1994				
Feb.	18	Treasury Stock—Common (100 shares × $55).	5,500	
		Cash		5,500
		Acquired 100 shares of treasury stock at $55.		
Apr.	18	Cash (30 shares × $58)	1,740	
		Treasury Stock—Common (30 shares × $55)		1,650
		Paid-In Capital—Common Treasury Stock Transactions		90
		Reissued 30 shares of treasury stock at $58; cost is $55 per share.		

---

[3] Another acceptable method of accounting for treasury stock transactions is called the par value method. Further discussion of the par value method is left to intermediate accounting texts.

When the reissue price of subsequent shares is **less** than the acquisition price, the difference between cost and reissue price is debited to Paid-In Capital—Common Treasury Stock Transactions. This account, however, is not permitted to develop a debit balance. By definition, no paid-in capital account can have a debit balance. If Hillside reissued an additional 20 shares at $52 per share on June 12, 1994, the entry would be:

June	12	Cash (20 shares × $52)	1,040	
		Paid-In Capital—Common Treasury Stock Transactions	60	
		Treasury Stock—Common (20 shares × $55)		1,100
		Reissued 20 shares of treasury stock at $52; cost is $55 per share.		

At this point, the credit balance in the Paid-In Capital—Common Treasury Stock Transactions account would be $30. If the remaining 50 shares are reissued on July 16, 1994, for $53 per share, the entry would be:

July	16	Cash (50 shares × $53)	2,650	
		Paid-In Capital—Common Treasury Stock Transactions	30	
		Retained Earnings	70	
		Treasury Stock—Common (50 shares × $55)		2,750
		Reissued 50 shares of treasury stock at $53; cost is $55 per share.		

Note that the Paid-In Capital—Common Treasury Stock Transactions account credit balance has been exhausted. If more than $30 is debited to that account, it would develop a debit balance. Thus, the remaining $70 of the excess of cost over reissue price is regarded as a special distribution to the stockholders involved and is debited to the Retained Earnings account.

When stockholders **donate** stock to a corporation, the treatment is slightly different. Since donated treasury shares have no cost, only a memo entry is made when they are received.[4] The only formal entry required is to debit Cash and credit the Paid-In Capital—Donations account when the stock is reissued. For example, if donated treasury stock is sold for $5,000, the entry would be:

Cash	5,000	
Paid-In Capital—Donations.		5,000
To record the sale of donated treasury stock.		

Treasury Stock on the Balance Sheet

When treasury stock is held on a balance sheet date, it is customarily shown on that statement at cost, as a deduction from the sum of total paid-in capital and retained earnings, as shown on page 665.

---

[4] The method illustrated here is called the *memo* method. Other acceptable methods of accounting for donated stock are the *cost* method and *par value* method. These latter two methods are discussed in intermediate accounting texts.

A BROADER PERSPECTIVE

GENERAL SIGNAL CORPORATION
Partial Balance Sheet
($000)

	December 1988	December 1987
Shareholders' equity (notes 6 through 9):		
Common stock, par value $1 per share; authorized 75,000,000 shares; issued 30,737,505 in 1988, 29,584,000 in 1987	$ 41,842	$ 40,692
Additional paid-in capital.	295,916	236,818
Retained earnings	705,226	731,000
Cumulative translation adjustments.	(2,062)	(12,662)
	$1,040,922	$995,848
Common stock in treasury, at cost; 11,677,913 shares in 1988, 2,112,379 shares in 1987 . . .	(579,876)	(88,697)
Total shareholders' equity	$ 461,046	$907,151

Notes to Consolidated Financial Statements

6 (In part): Capital Stock

Treasury Stock

Number of Shares	1988	1987	1986
Balance at beginning of year	2,112,379	732,202	600,322
Common stock reacquired*	9,585,274	1,380,578	132,296
Common stock issued under the company's incentive compensation plan . . .	(19,740)	(401)	(416)
Balance at end of year	11,677,913	2,112,379	732,202

* Includes the repurchase of 9,572,627 shares in December 1988 pursuant to the company's tender offer to shareholders, as well as the repurchase of 1,355,900 and 116,400 shares on the open market in 1987 and 1986, respectively, in connection with the company's share repurchase program. The remaining shares were reacquired in connection with the company's stock option plans.

Self-Tender Offer

On November 17, 1988, the company commenced a "Dutch Auction" self-tender offer to shareholders for the repurchase of nine million shares of its own common stock, subject to increase at the company's discretion. Under the terms of the offer, shareholders were invited to tender their shares by December 15, 1988, at prices ranging from $44 to $51 per share as specified by each shareholder.

At the conclusion of the offer, approximately 10.9 million shares had been tendered, of which the company repurchased 9,572,627 shares at $51 per share for a total cost of approximately $491 million, including legal and financial consulting fees. The total shares repurchased represent approximately one-third of the outstanding shares at that date.

The transaction was financed through existing cash balances and debt capacity.

Had the repurchase taken place as of January 1, 1987, the company's net earnings and earnings per share for the year ended December 31, 1987, would have been $44.3 million, or $2.37 per share. For the year ended December 31, 1988, the company would have realized a net loss of $1.8 million, or $.10 per share. If both the repurchase and the acquisition of GCA Corporation (as discussed in Note 3 of these financial statements) had taken place as of January 1, 1987, net earnings and earnings per share for the year ended December 31, 1987, would have been $30.5 million, or $1.55 per share. A net loss of $3.6 million, or $.19 per share, would have resulted for the year ended December 31, 1988. Net sales would not have changed as a result of the repurchase.

Source: Based on American Institute of Certified Public Accountants, *Accounting Trends & Techniques* (New York: AICPA, 1989), p. 220.

ILLUSTRATION 14.7

Stockholders' Equity Section of the Balance Sheet

HYPOTHETICAL CORPORATION
Partial Balance Sheet
December 31, 1994

Stockholders' equity:

Paid-in capital:

Preferred stock—8%, $100 par value; 2,000 shares authorized,
issued, and outstanding . . . . $ 200,000

Common stock—$10 par value; authorized, 100,000 shares,
issued, 80,000 shares of which 1,000 are held in
the treasury $800,000

Stock dividend distributable on common stock on January 15,
1995, 7,900 shares 79,000   879,000

Paid-in capital—

From common stock issuances. . . . . $ 40,000
From stock dividends 60,000
From treasury stock transactions 30,000
From donations. 50,000   180,000

Total paid-in capital $1,259,000

Retained earnings:
Appropriated:
Per loan agreement $250,000
Unappropriated (restricted to the extent of $20,000, the cost
of treasury shares held) 150,000

Total retained earnings   400,000

Total paid-in capital and retained earnings $1,659,000
Less: Treasury stock, common, 1,000 shares at cost   20,000

Total stockholders' equity $1,639,000

Stockholders' equity:

Paid-in capital:

Common stock—$10 par value; authorized and issued, 20,000 shares,
of which 2,000 shares are in the treasury $200,000

Retained earnings (including $22,000 restricted by acquisition of treasury
stock) 80,000

Total paid-in capital and retained earnings $280,000
Less: Treasury stock at cost, 2,000 shares   22,000

Total stockholders' equity $258,000

**Stockholders'
Equity on the
Balance Sheet**

Much of what has been discussed so far in Chapters 13 and 14 can be summarized through presentation of the stockholders' equity section of the balance sheet of a hypothetical corporation (Illustration 14.7). This partial balance sheet shows (1) the amount of capital assigned to shares outstanding; (2) the capital contributed for outstanding shares in addition to that assigned to the shares; (3) other forms of paid-in capital; and (4) retained earnings, appropriated and unappropriated.

NET INCOME INCLUSIONS AND EXCLUSIONS

Objective 4

Describe the proper accounting treatment of discontinued operations, extraordinary items, and changes in accounting principles

Accounting has long faced the problem of what to include in the net income reported for a period. Should net income include only the revenues and expenses related to normal operations? Or should it include the results of discontinued operations and unusual, nonrecurring gains and losses? And further, should the determination of net income for 1994, for example, include an item that can be clearly associated with a prior year, such as additional federal income taxes for 1993? Or should such items, including corrections of errors, be carried directly to retained earnings? How are the effects of making a change in accounting principle (like a change in depreciation methods) to be reported?

APB Opinion No. 9 (December 1966) sought to provide answers to some of these questions. The *Opinion* directed that unusual and nonrecurring items that have an earnings or loss effect should be classified as extraordinary items (reported in the income statement) or as prior period adjustments (reported in the statement of retained earnings). Extraordinary items were to be reported separately after net income from regular continuing activities.

Illustrations 14.8 (p. 667) and 14.10 (p. 670) show the reporting of discontinued operations, extraordinary items, changes in accounting principle, and prior period adjustments. For Illustrations 14.8 and 14.10, assume that the Anson Company has 1,000,000 shares of common stock outstanding and the company's earnings are taxed at 40%. Also, assume the following:

1. Anson sold its Cosmetics Division on August 1, 1994, at a loss of $500,000. The net operating loss of that division through July 31, 1994, was $2,000,000.

2. Anson had a taxable gain in 1994 of $40,000 from voluntary early retirement of debt (extraordinary item).

3. Anson changed depreciation methods in 1994 (change in accounting principle), and the cumulative effect of the changes was a $6,000 decrease in prior years' depreciation expense.

4. In 1994, it was discovered that the $200,000 cost of land acquired in 1993 had been expensed for both financial accounting and tax purposes. A prior period adjustment was made in 1994.

Now the effects of these assumptions will be explained in greater detail.

Discontinued Operations

A discontinued operation occurs when a segment (usually an unprofitable department or division) of a business is sold to another company or has been abandoned. When a company discontinues a segment, it shows the information relating to the segment in a special section of the income statement immediately after income from continuing operations and before extraordinary items. Two items of information are reported:

1. The income or loss (net of tax effect) from the segment's operations for the portion of the current year before it was discontinued.

2. The gain or loss (net of tax effect) on disposal of the segment.

To illustrate, Anson's sale of its Cosmetics Division on July 31 led to a before-tax loss of $500,000. The after-tax loss was $500,000 × 60% = $300,000. The operating loss before taxes through July 31 was $2,000,000. The after-tax operating loss for that period was $2,000,000 × 60% = $1,200,000. This information is included on the income statement, as shown in Illustration 14.8.

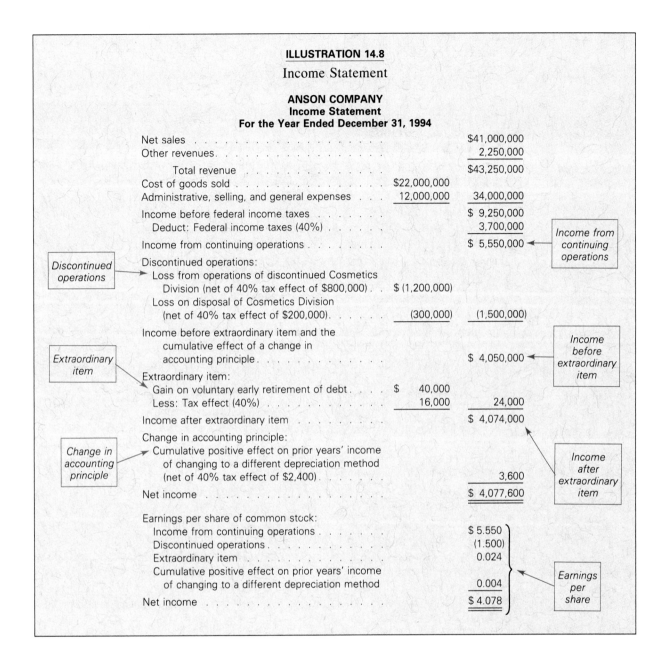

ILLUSTRATION 14.8

Income Statement

ANSON COMPANY
Income Statement
For the Year Ended December 31, 1994

Net sales		$41,000,000
Other revenues		2,250,000
Total revenue		$43,250,000
Cost of goods sold	$22,000,000	
Administrative, selling, and general expenses	12,000,000	34,000,000
Income before federal income taxes		$ 9,250,000
Deduct: Federal income taxes (40%)		3,700,000
Income from continuing operations		$ 5,550,000
Discontinued operations:		
Loss from operations of discontinued Cosmetics Division (net of 40% tax effect of $800,000)	$ (1,200,000)	
Loss on disposal of Cosmetics Division (net of 40% tax effect of $200,000)	(300,000)	(1,500,000)
Income before extraordinary item and the cumulative effect of a change in accounting principle		$ 4,050,000
Extraordinary item:		
Gain on voluntary early retirement of debt	$ 40,000	
Less: Tax effect (40%)	16,000	24,000
Income after extraordinary item		$ 4,074,000
Change in accounting principle:		
Cumulative positive effect on prior years' income of changing to a different depreciation method (net of 40% tax effect of $2,400)		3,600
Net income		$ 4,077,600
Earnings per share of common stock:		
Income from continuing operations		$ 5.550
Discontinued operations		(1.500)
Extraordinary item		0.024
Cumulative positive effect on prior years' income of changing to a different depreciation method		0.004
Net income		$ 4.078

Income from continuing operations → (pointing to $ 5,550,000)

Discontinued operations → (pointing to Discontinued operations section)

Extraordinary item → (pointing to Extraordinary item section)

Income before extraordinary item → (pointing to $ 4,050,000)

Change in accounting principle → (pointing to Change in accounting principle section)

Income after extraordinary item → (pointing to $ 4,074,000)

Earnings per share → (pointing to Earnings per share section)

Extraordinary Items   Prior to 1973, companies tended to report a gain or loss as an extraordinary item if it was **either** unusual in nature **or** occurred infrequently. As a result, companies were inconsistent in the financial reporting of certain gains and losses. This inconsistency led to the issuance of *APB Opinion No. 30* (September 1973). *Opinion No. 30* redefined extraordinary items as those that are unusual in nature **and** that occur infrequently. Note that both conditions must be met—unusual nature and infrequent occurrence. Whether an item is unusual and infrequent is to be determined in light of the environment in which the company operates. Examples of extraordinary items include gains or losses that are the direct result of a major casualty (a flood), a confiscation of property by a foreign government, or a prohibition under a newly enacted law. *FASB Statement No. 4* further directs that gains and losses from the voluntary early **extinguishment** (retirement) of debt are extraordinary items.

Extraordinary items are to be included in the determination of periodic net income, but disclosed separately (net of their tax effects, if any) in the income statement. As shown in the income statement presented in Illustration 14.8, income before extraordinary items must be reported, and then income after extraordinary items is reported. Income before extraordinary items is income from continuing operations less applicable income taxes plus or minus the gain or loss from discontinued operations.

Gains or losses related to ordinary business activities are not extraordinary items regardless of their size. For example, material write-downs of uncollectible receivables, obsolete inventories, and intangible assets are not extraordinary items. However, such items may be separately disclosed as part of income from continuing operations.

Illustration 14.9 shows that in a sample of 600 companies for the years 1986–89, both the number of companies reporting extraordinary items and the total number of extraordinary items decreased significantly in 1988 and 1989.

Changes in Accounting Principle

A company's reported net income and financial position can be altered materially by *changes in accounting principle*. Changes in accounting principle are changes in accounting methods pertaining to such items as inventory and depreciation. Examples of changes in accounting principle are a change in inventory valuation method from FIFO to LIFO or a change in depreciation method from accelerated to straight-line.

According to *APB Opinion No. 20*, a company should consistently apply the same accounting methods from one period to another. However, a company may make a change if the newly adopted method is preferable and if the change is adequately disclosed in the financial statements. In the period in which a company makes a change in principle, it must disclose on the financial statements the nature of the change, its justification, and its effect on net income. Also, the company must show on the income statement for the year of the change (Illustration 14.8) the cumulative effect of the change on prior years' income (net of tax).

As an example of a change in accounting principle, assume that Anson purchased a machine on January 2, 1992, for $30,000. The machine has a useful life of five years with no salvage value expected. Anson decided to depreciate the machine for financial reporting purposes using the sum-of-the-years'-digits method. At the beginning of 1994, the company decided to change to the straight-line method of depreciation. The cumulative effect of the change in accounting principle is computed as follows:

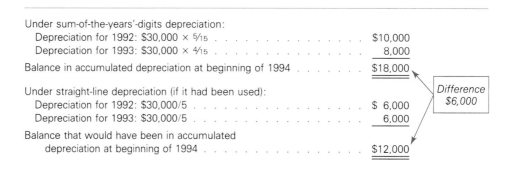

Under sum-of-the-years'-digits depreciation:
Depreciation for 1992: $30,000 × 5/15 . . . . $10,000
Depreciation for 1993: $30,000 × 4/15 8,000
Balance in accumulated depreciation at beginning of 1994 . . . . $18,000

Under straight-line depreciation (if it had been used):
Depreciation for 1992: $30,000/5 . . . . $ 6,000
Depreciation for 1993: $30,000/5 6,000
Balance that would have been in accumulated
   depreciation at beginning of 1994 . . . . $12,000

Difference $6,000

The accumulated depreciation account balance would have been $6,000 less under the straight-line method. Also, depreciation expense over the two years would have been $6,000 less. Assume that federal income tax would have been $2,400 more ($6,000 × 0.4). The net effect of the change is $6,000 − $2,400 = $3,600.

ILLUSTRATION 14.9

Extraordinary Items

	1989	1988	1987	1986
Nature:				
Debt extinguishments	16	26	53	54
Operating loss carryforwards	26	35	80	50
Litigation settlements	3	6	2	4
Other	9	6	9	19
Total extraordinary items	54	73	144	127
Number of companies:				
Presenting extraordinary items	49	67	127	107
Not presenting extraordinary items	551	533	473	493
Total companies	600	600	600	600

Source: Based on American Institute of Certified Public Accountants, *Accounting Trends & Techniques* (New York: AICPA, 1990), p. 291.

Therefore, Anson corrects the appropriate account balances by reducing (debiting) the accumulated depreciation account balance by $6,000, crediting an account entitled Cumulative Effect of Change in Accounting Principle for $3,600 (which will be closed to Retained Earnings during the normal closing process), and crediting Federal Income Taxes Payable for $2,400. The journal entry would be:

Accumulated Depreciation—Machinery	6,000	
Cumulative Effect of Change in Accounting Principle		3,600
Federal Income Taxes Payable		2,400
To record the effect of changing from sum-of-the-years'-digits depreciation to straight-line depreciation on machinery.		

The cumulative effect of changing to the straight-line depreciation method is reported in Illustration 14.8 at the after-tax amount of $3,600.

Prior Period Adjustments

Objective 5

Define prior period adjustments and show their proper presentation in the financial statements

According to *FASB Statement No. 16*, prior period adjustments consist almost entirely of corrections of errors in previously published financial statements. Corrections of abnormal, nonrecurring errors that may have been caused by the improper use of an accounting principle or by mathematical mistakes are considered to be prior period adjustments. Normal, recurring corrections and adjustments, which follow inevitably from the use of estimates in accounting practice, are not treated as prior period adjustments. Also, mistakes corrected in the same year they occur are not prior period adjustments. To illustrate a prior period adjustment, suppose that Anson purchased land in 1993 at a total cost of $200,000 and recorded this amount in an expense account instead of in the Land account. Discovery of the error on May 1, 1994, after publication of the 1993 financial statements, would require a prior period adjustment. The adjustment would be recorded directly in the Retained Earnings account. Assuming the error had resulted in an $80,000 underpayment of taxes in 1993, the entry to correct the error would be:

ILLUSTRATION 14.10

Statement of Retained Earnings

ANSON COMPANY
Statement of Retained Earnings
For the Year Ended December 31, 1994

Retained earnings, January 1, 1994	$5,000,000
Prior period adjustment:	
Correction of error of expensing land (net of tax effect of $80,000)	120,000
Retained earnings, January 1, 1994, as adjusted	$5,120,000
Add: Net income	4,077,600
	$9,197,600
Less: Dividends	500,000
Retained earnings, December 31, 1994	$8,697,600

Prior period adjustment →

May	1	Land	200,000	
		Federal Income Taxes Payable		80,000
		Retained Earnings (or Prior Period Adjustment— Land)		120,000
		To correct an accounting error expensing land.		

Prior period adjustments are not reported on the income statements but are shown in the current-year financial statements as adjustments to the opening balance of retained earnings on the statement of retained earnings (Illustration 14.10).

Accounting for Tax Effects

Most discontinued operations, extraordinary items, changes in accounting principle, and prior period adjustments affect the amount of income taxes a corporation must pay. A question arises as to how to report the income tax effect of these items. *FASB Statement No. 96*[5] requires that all of these items be reported **net of their tax effects,** as shown in Illustrations 14.8 and 14.10. Net-of-tax effect means that items are shown at the dollar amounts remaining after deducting the income tax effects. Thus, the total effect of a discontinued operation, an extraordinary item, a change in accounting principle, or a prior period adjustment is shown in one place in the appropriate financial statement. The reference to "Income from continuing operations" in the income statement represents the results of transactions (including income taxes) that are normal for the business and may be expected to recur. Note that the tax effect of an item may be shown separately, as it is for the gain on voluntary early retirement of debt in Illustration 14.8, or may be mentioned parenthetically with only the net amount shown (see loss from discontinued operations and change in accounting principle in Illustration 14.8 and correction of error in Illustration 14.10).

---

[5] FASB, *Statement of Financial Accounting Standards No. 96*, "Accounting for Income Taxes" (Stamford. Conn., 1987). Copyright © by the Financial Accounting Standards Board, High Ridge Park, Stamford, Connecticut 06905, U.S.A.

ETHICS ▬▬▬▬▬ **A CLOSER LOOK**	Ace Chemical Company is a small, privately held company that has been operating at a profit for years. The current balance in the Cash account is $8 million, and the balance in Retained Earnings is $4 million. The company's plant assets consist of special purpose equipment that can produce only certain chemicals. The company has long-term debt with a principal balance of $10 million. The officers of the company (all of whom are stockholders) are concerned about the future prospects of the company. Many similar companies have been sued by customers and employees claiming that toxic chemicals produced by the company caused their health problems. No such suits have yet been filed against Ace, but the officers fully expect them to be filed within the next two years.

The company's stock is not listed on a stock exchange, nor has it recently been traded. The officers hold 70% of the stock and estimate that their total stockholdings have a current market value of about $8 million (although its value would be much lower if all the facts were known). They are worried that if suits are filed and the company loses, there will not even be enough remaining assets to satisfy creditors' claims, and the officers' stock would be worthless. Private legal counsel has informed the officers that the company is likely to lose any suits that are filed.

One of the officers suggested that they could at least receive something for their stock by having the company buy half of the shares held by the officers at a total price of $4 million. Another officer asked if such a treasury stock transaction would be legal. The response was that the transaction would be legal because it did not "dip into" the present legal capital of the company. Retained earnings would be reduced to a zero balance, but would not develop a debit balance as a result of the transaction.

Required   *a.*   Is this transaction fair to the creditors?

b.   Why wouldn't the officers merely declare a $4 million cash dividend? Is the proposed treasury stock transaction fair to the other stockholders?

c.   If you were one of the officers, would you "feel right" about going ahead with this proposed treasury stock transaction?

EARNINGS PER SHARE

Objective 6

Compute earnings per share

A major item of interest to investors and potential investors is how much a company earned during the current year, both in total and for each share of stock outstanding. The earnings per share amount is calculated only for the common shares of ownership. Earnings per share (EPS) is computed as net income available to common stockholders in a period divided by the average number of common shares outstanding during that period. Income available to common stockholders is net income less any dividends on preferred stock. The regular preferred dividend on cumulative preferred stock (but *not* a dividend in arrears) is deducted, whether or not declared, but only declared dividends are deducted on noncumulative preferred stock.

To illustrate, assume that Hoffman Company had 5,000 shares of common stock outstanding with net income of $24,000 during 1994. EPS would be computed as follows:

$$\text{EPS} = \frac{\text{Net income available to common stockholders}}{\text{Average number of common shares outstanding}}$$

$$= \frac{\$24,000}{5,000 \text{ shares}}$$

$$= \$4.80 \text{ per share}$$

EPS is usually calculated and presented for each major category on the face of the income statement. In other words, an EPS calculation is made for income from continuing operations, discontinued operations, extraordinary items, changes in accounting principle, and net income. Note in Illustration 14.8 that the EPS amounts are reported at the bottom of the income statement.

Summary of Illustrative Financial Statements

Note especially the following facts in Illustrations 14.8 and 14.10:

1. Income from continuing operations of $5,550,000 is more representative of the continuing earning power of the company than is the net income figure of $4,077,600.

2. The special items shown below income from continuing operations are reported at their actual impact on the company—that is, net of their tax effect.

3. EPS is reported both before ($5.550) and after ($4.078) the discontinued operations, extraordinary item, and the cumulative effect of a change in accounting principle.

4. The correction of the $200,000 error adds only $120,000 to retained earnings. This result occurs because the mistake was included in the 1993 tax return and taxes were therefore underpaid by $80,000. In the 1994 return, the $80,000 of taxes would have to be paid.

This chapter completes the study of stockholders' equity. In Chapter 15, you will learn about bonds—another source of capital for companies and a vehicle for investment by investors.

UNDERSTANDING THE LEARNING OBJECTIVES

1. Identify the different sources of paid-in capital and describe how they would be presented on a balance sheet.
   - ☐ Paid-in capital is presented in the stockholders' equity section of the balance sheet. Each source of paid-in capital is listed separately.
   - ☐ Sources of paid-in capital are:
     1. Common stock.
     2. Preferred stock.
     3. In excess of par value or stated value (common and preferred).
     4. Stock dividends.
     5. Treasury stock transactions.
     6. Donations.

2. Account for a cash dividend, a stock dividend, a stock split, and a retained earnings appropriation.
   - ☐ Cash dividend of 3% on $100,000 of outstanding common stock: declared on July 1 and paid on September 15.

July	1	Retained Earnings	3,000	
		Dividends Payable		3,000
Sept	15	Dividends Payable	3,000	
		Cash		3,000

   - ☐ Ten percent stock dividend on 10,000 shares of common stock outstanding; par value, $100; market value at declaration, $125 per share.

Jan.	1	Retained Earnings (1,000 shares × $125)	125,000	
		Stock Dividend Distributable—Common		
		(1,000 shares × $100)		100,000
		Paid-In Capital—Stock Dividends		
		(1,000 shares × $25)		25,000
Feb.	1	Stock Dividend Distributable—Common	100,000	
		Common Stock		100,000

- ☐ Thirty percent stock dividend on 10,000 shares of common stock outstanding: declared on January 1 and payable on February 1; par value, $100.

Jan.	1	Retained Earnings (3,000 shares × $100)	300,000	
		Stock Dividend Distributable—Common		300,000
Feb.	1	Stock Dividend Distributable—Common	300,000	
		Common Stock		300,000

- ☐ Stock split: 1,000 shares of $50 par value common stock replaced by 2,000 shares of $25 par value common stock.

Common Stock—$50 par value	50,000	
Common Stock—$25 par value		50,000

- ☐ Retained earnings appropriation: $75,000 appropriated for plant expansion.

Retained Earnings	75,000	
Retained Earnings Appropriated for Plant		
Expansion.		75,000

3. Account for the acquisition and reissuance of treasury stock.

- ☐ Treasury stock transactions: 100 shares of common stock were reacquired at $100 each and reissued for $105 each.

Treasury Stock—Common (100 shares × $100)	10,000	
Cash		10,000
Cash (100 shares × $105)	10,500	
Treasury Stock—Common (100 shares × $100)		10,000
Paid-In Capital—Common Treasury Stock		
Transactions (100 shares × $5).		500

4. Describe the proper accounting treatment of discontinued operations, extraordinary items, and changes in accounting principles.

- ☐ The income or loss (net of tax effect) from the segment's operations for the portion of the current year before it was discontinued is reported on the income statement after "Income from continuing operations."
- ☐ The gain or loss (net of tax effect) on disposal of the segment is also reported in that same section of the income statement.
- ☐ Extraordinary items are those items that are both unusual in nature and infrequent in occurrence. Extraordinary items are shown on the income

statement (net of tax effects) after "Income from continuing operations."

☐ In the period in which a change in principle is made, the nature of the change, its justification, and its effect on net income must be disclosed in the financial statements. Also, the cumulative effect of the change on prior years' income (net of tax) must be shown on the income statement for the year of change after "Income from continuing operations."

5. Define prior period adjustments and show their proper presentation in the financial statements.

☐ Prior period adjustments consist of errors in previously published financial statements. Prior period adjustments are shown as a correction to the beginning retained earnings balance on the statement of retained earnings.

6. Compute earnings per share.

☐ Earnings per share is computed as net income available to common stockholders in a period divided by the average number of common stock shares outstanding during that period.

☐ EPS is usually calculated and presented for each major category on the face of the income statement.

DEMONSTRATION PROBLEM 14–A

Wake Corporation has outstanding 10,000 shares of $150 par value common stock.

Required   Prepare the entries to record:

a. The declaration of a cash dividend of $1.50 per share.

b. The declaration of a stock dividend of 10% at a time when the market value per share is $185.

c. The declaration of a stock dividend of 40% at a time when the market value per share is $195.

SOLUTION TO DEMONSTRATION PROBLEM 14–A

a.

Retained Earnings (or Dividends)	15,000	
Dividends Payable		15,000
To record declaration of a cash dividend.		

b.

Retained Earnings (or Stock Dividends)		
(1,000 shares × $185)	185,000	
Stock Dividend Distributable—Common		
(1,000 shares × $150)		150,000
Paid-In Capital—Stock Dividends		35,000
To record declaration of a small stock dividend (10%).		

c.

Retained Earnings (or Stock Dividends) (4,000 shares × $150)	600,000	
Stock Dividend Distributable—Common		600,000
To record declaration of a large stock dividend (40%).		

DEMONSTRATION PROBLEM 14–B

Following are selected transactions of Brace Company:

1. The company reacquired 200 shares of its own $100 par value common stock, previously issued at $105 per share, for $20,600.
2. Fifty of the treasury shares were reissued at $110 per share, cash.
3. Seventy of the treasury shares were reissued at $95 per share, cash.
4. Stockholders of the corporation donated 100 shares of their common stock to the company.
5. The 100 shares of treasury stock received by donation were reissued for $9,000.

Required   Prepare the necessary journal entries to record the above transactions.

SOLUTION TO DEMONSTRATION PROBLEM 14–B

1. Treasury Stock   20,600
        Cash   20,600
        Acquired 200 shares at $20,600 ($103 per share).

2. Cash (50 shares × $110)   5,500
        Treasury Stock—Common (50 shares × $103)   5,150
        Paid-In Capital—Common Treasury Stock Transactions   350
        Reissued 50 shares at $110 per share; cost is $5,150.

3. Cash (70 shares × $95)   6,650
    Paid-In Capital—Common Treasury Stock Transactions
        (50 shares × $7)   350
    Retained Earnings.   210
        Treasury Stock—Common (70 shares × $103)   7,210
        Reissued 70 shares at $95 per share; cost is $7,210.

4. Stockholders donated 100 shares of common stock to the company. (Only memo entry is made.)

5. Cash   9,000
        Paid-In Capital—Donations (100 shares × $90)   9,000
        Reissued donated shares at $90 per share.

DEMONSTRATION PROBLEM 14–C

Selected account balances of Nike Corporation at December 31, 1994, are:

Common Stock (no par value; 100,000 shares authorized,
  issued, and outstanding; stated value of $20 per share) $2,000,000
Retained Earnings   570,000
Dividends Payable (in cash, declared December 15 on preferred stock).   16,000
Preferred Stock (8%, par value $200; 1,000 shares authorized, issued,
  and outstanding)   200,000
Paid-In Capital from Donation of Plant Site   100,000
Paid-In Capital in Excess of Par Value—Preferred   8,000

Required   Present in good form the stockholders' equity section of the balance sheet.

SOLUTION TO DEMONSTRATION PROBLEM 14–C

ACE CORPORATION
Partial Balance Sheet
December 31, 1994

Stockholders' equity:

Paid-in capital:

Preferred stock—8%, par value $200; 1,000 shares authorized,
issued, and outstanding . . . . $ 200,000

Common stock—no par value, stated value of $20 per share;
100,000 shares authorized, issued, and outstanding 2,000,000

Paid-in capital from donation of plant site 100,000

Paid-in capital in excess of par value—preferred 8,000

Total paid-in capital $2,308,000

Retained earnings 570,000

Total stockholders' equity $2,878,000

NEW TERMS

Cash dividends Cash distributions of net income by a corporation to its stockholders. *653*

Changes in accounting principle Changes in accounting methods pertaining to such items as inventory and depreciation. *668*

Contributed capital See Paid-in capital.

Date of declaration (of dividends) The date the board of directors takes action in the form of a motion that dividends be paid. *652*

Date of payment (of dividends) The date of actual payment of a dividend, or issuance of additional shares in the case of a stock dividend. *652*

Date of record (of dividends) The date of record established by the board that determines the stockholders who will receive dividends. *652*

Deficit A debit balance in the Retained Earnings account. *651*

Discontinued operation When a segment of a business is sold to another company or is abandoned. *666*

Dividends Distribution of earnings by a corporation to its stockholders. *652*

Dividends (cash) See Cash dividends.

Dividends (stock) See Stock dividends.

Donated capital Results from donation of assets to the corporation, which increases stockholders' equity. *650*

Earnings per share (EPS) Earnings to the common stockholders on a per share basis, computed as net income available to common stockholders divided by the average number of common shares outstanding. *671*

Extraordinary items Items that are both unusual in nature and infrequent in occurrence; reported in the income statement net of their tax effects, if any. *667*

Income available to common stockholders Net income less any dividends on preferred stock. *671*

Income before extraordinary items Income from

operations less applicable income taxes, if any, plus or minus any gain or loss from discontinued operations. *668*

Liquidating dividends Dividends that are a return of contributed capital, not a distribution chargeable to retained earnings. *658*

Net-of-tax effect Used for discontinued operations, extraordinary items, changes in accounting principle, and prior period adjustments, whereby items are shown at the dollar amounts remaining after deducting the effects of such items on income taxes, if any, payable currently. *670*

Paid-in capital All of the contributed capital of a corporation, including that carried in capital stock accounts. When the words *paid-in capital* are included in the account title, the account contains capital contributed in addition to that assigned to the shares issued and recorded in the capital stock accounts. *650*

Paid-In Capital—Treasury Stock Transactions The account credited when treasury stock is reissued for more than its cost; this account is debited to the extent of its credit balance when such shares are reissued at less than cost. *662*

Prior period adjustments Consist almost entirely of corrections of errors in previously published financial statements. Prior period adjustments are reported in the statement of retained earnings net of their tax effects, if any. *669*

Retained earnings That part of stockholders' equity resulting from earnings; the account to which the results of corporate activity, including prior period adjustments, are carried and to which dividends and certain items resulting from capital transactions are charged. *651*

Retained earnings appropriations Contractual or voluntary restrictions or limitations on retained earnings that reduce the amount of dividends that may be declared. *658*

Statement of retained earnings A formal statement showing the items causing changes in unappropriated and appropriated retained earnings during a stated period of time. *660*

Statement of stockholders' equity A summary of the transactions affecting the accounts in the stockholders' equity section of the balance sheet during a stated period of time. *660*

Stock dividends Dividends that are payable in additional shares of the declaring corporation's capital stock. *653*

Stock Dividend Distributable—Common account The stockholders' equity (paid-in capital) account credited for the par or stated value of the shares distributable when recording the declaration of a stock dividend. *655*

Stock split A distribution of 100% or more of additional shares of the issuing corporation's stock accompanied by a corresponding reduction in the par value per share. The purpose of a stock split is to cause a large reduction in the market price per share of the outstanding stock. *656*

Treasury stock Shares of capital stock issued and reacquired by the issuing corporation; they have not been formally canceled and are available for reissuance. *650, 661*

SELF-TEST

True-False

Indicate whether each of the following statements is true or false.

1. The Retained Earnings account describes one source of paid-in capital of a corporation.

2. Since treasury stock has been issued once, it may be reissued without violating the preemptive right of the stockholders.

3. The payment of a cash dividend decreases a corporation's current liabilities.

4. The declaration of a stock dividend increases a corporation's current liabilities.

5. A retained earnings appropriation involves the setting aside of cash for the indicated purpose.

6. Damage suffered from destruction by an earthquake of a plant in Georgia would probably be an extraordinary item.

Multiple-Choice

Select the best answer for each of the following questions.

1. Which of the following is not included in paid-in capital?
   a. Common Stock Subscribed.
   b. Paid-In Capital—Donations.
   c. Stock Dividend Distributable.
   d. Appropriation per Loan Agreement.

2. White Company issued 20,000 shares of $10 par value common stock at $12 per share. White reacquired 2,000 shares of its own stock at a cost of $15 per share. The entry to record the reacquisition is:

   a. Premium on
      Treasury Stock 10,000
      Treasury Stock 20,000
          Cash   30,000

   b. Premium on
      Treasury Stock 6,000
      Treasury Stock 24,000
          Cash   30,000

   c. Treasury Stock 30,000
          Cash   30,000

   d. Treasury Stock 20,000
      Paid-In Capital—
      Treasury Stock
      Transactions 10,000
          Cash   30,000

3. If the company reissues 1,000 shares of the treasury stock for $18 per share in (2), the entry is:

   a. Cash 18,000
          Treasury Stock . . .   15,000
          Paid-In Capital—
          Treasury Stock
          Transactions . . .   3,000

   b. Cash 18,000
          Treasury Stock . . .   18,000

   c. Cash 18,000
          Treasury Stock . . .   15,000
          Retained Earnings . .   3,000

   d. Cash 18,000
          Treasury Stock . . .   10,000
          Retained Earnings . .   8,000

4. Treasury stock should be shown on the balance sheet as a:
   a. Reduction of the corporation's stockholders' equity.

    b. Current asset.

    c. Current liability.

    d. Investment asset.

5. An individual stockholder is entitled to receive any dividends declared on stock owned, provided the stock is held on the:

    a. Date of declaration.

    b. Date of record.

    c. Date of payment.

    d. Last day of a fiscal year.

6. ABC Corporation declared the regular quarterly dividend of $0.50 per share. ABC had issued 21,000 shares and subsequently reacquired 1,000 shares as treasury stock. What would be the total amount of the dividend?

    a. $12,000.

    b. $14,000.

    c. $10,000.

    d. $2,000.

7. Which of the following items is not reported as a separate line item below income from continuing operations, net of tax effects, in the income statement?

    a. Extraordinary items.

    b. Prior period adjustments.

    c. Discontinued operations.

    d. Changes in accounting principle.

Now turn to page 690 to check your answers.

QUESTIONS

1. Name several sources of paid-in capital. Would it suffice to maintain one account called Paid-In Capital for all sources of paid-in capital? Why or why not?

2. What are the main parts of the stockholders' equity in a corporation? Explain the difference between them.

3. Does accounting for treasury stock resemble accounting for an asset? Is treasury stock an asset? If not, where is it properly shown on a balance sheet?

4. What are some possible reasons for a corporation to reacquire its own capital stock as treasury stock?

5. What is the purpose underlying the statutes that provide for restriction of retained earnings in the amount of the cost of treasury stock? Are such statutes for the benefit of stockholders, management, or creditors?

6. What is the effect of each of the following on the total stockholders' equity of a corporation: *(a)* declaration of a cash dividend, *(b)* payment of a cash dividend already declared, *(c)* declaration of a stock dividend, and *(d)* issuance of a stock dividend already declared?

7. The following dates are associated with a cash dividend of $25,000: July 15, July 31, and August 15. Identify each of the three dates and describe the journal entry required on each, if any.

8. On May 10, Wilson sold his capital stock in Tango Corporation directly to Boris for $15,000, endorsing his stock certificate and giving it to Boris. Boris placed the stock certificate in his safe. On May 8, the board of directors of the Tango Corporation declared a dividend, payable on June 5 to stockholders of record on May 17. On May 30, Boris sent the certificate to the transfer agent of the Tango Corporation for transfer. Who received the dividend? Why?

9. How should a declared but unpaid cash dividend be shown on the balance sheet? A declared but unissued stock dividend?

10. What are the possible reasons for a corporation to declare a stock dividend?

11. Why is a dividend consisting of the distribution of additional shares of the common stock of the declaring corporation not considered income to the recipient stockholders?

12. What is the difference between a small stock dividend and a large stock dividend?

13. What are liquidating dividends?

14. What is the purpose of a retained earnings appropriation?

15. Discuss the format and elements contained in a statement of stockholders' equity.

16. Describe a discontinued operation.

17. What are extraordinary items? Where and how are they reported?

18. Give an example of a change in accounting principle. How is each reported?

19. What are prior period adjustments? Where and how are they reported?

20. Why are stockholders and potential investors interested in the amount of a corporation's earnings per share? What does the earnings per share amount reveal that total income does not?

The Coca-Cola Company

21. *Real world question* From the consolidated statements of shareholders' equity of The Coca-Cola Company in Appendix E, identify the 1989 total amount for each of the following items:

    a. Sales to employees exercising stock options.

    b. Purchase of common stock for treasury.

    c. Total cash dividends.

    d. Balance—December 31, 1989.

MAYTAG
CORPORATION

22. *Real world question* Based on the financial statements of Maytag Corporation contained in Appendix E, what was the 1989 number of shares of common stock in treasury?

THE LIMITED, INC.

23. *Real world question* Based on the balance sheet dated February 3, 1990, of The Limited, Inc. contained in Appendix E, what was the cost of treasury stock?

HARLAND

24. *Real world question* Based on the financial statements of John H. Harland Company contained in Appendix E, what was the 1989 ending number of shares in treasury?

EXERCISES

Exercise 14–1

Prepare stockholders' equity section of balance sheet
(L.O. 1)

The December 31, 1993, trial balance of Hoyle Corporation had the following account balances:

Common Stock (no-par value; 200,000 shares authorized, issued, and outstanding; stated value of $10 per share)	$2,000,000
Notes Payable (12% due May 1, 1994)	250,000
Retained Earnings, Unappropriated	1,250,000
Dividends Payable in Cash (declared December 15, on preferred stock)	6,000
Appropriation per Loan Agreement	240,000
Preferred Stock (6%, par value $100; 2,000 shares authorized, issued, and outstanding)	200,000
Paid-In Capital in Excess of Stated Value—Common	150,000
Paid-In Capital in Excess of Par Value—Preferred	20,000

Present in proper form the stockholders' equity section of the balance sheet.

Exercise 14–2

Prepare journal entries for reacquisition and reissuance of treasury stock
(L.O. 3)

Watts Company had outstanding 50,000 shares of $15 stated value common stock, all issued at $18 per share, and had retained earnings of $600,000. The company reacquired 2,000 shares of its stock for cash at book value from the widow of a deceased stockholder.

a. Give the entry to record the reacquisition of the stock.

b. Give the entry to record the subsequent reissuance of this stock at $37.50 per share.

c. Give the entry required if the stock is instead reissued at $22.50 per share and there were no prior treasury stock transactions.

Exercise 14–3

Prepare journal entry(ies) for reissuance of donated stock
(L.O. 3)

Payne Company received 200 shares of its $50 stated value common stock on December 1, 1993, as a donation from a stockholder. On December 15, 1993, it reissued the stock for $15,600 cash. Give the journal entry or entries necessary for these transactions.

Exercise 14–4

Prepare journal entries for cash dividend
(L.O. 2)

Bailey Company has issued all of its authorized 5,000 shares of $100 par value common stock. On February 1, 1993, the board of directors declared a dividend of $3 per share payable on March 15, 1993, to stockholders of record on March 1, 1993. Give the necessary journal entries.

Exercise 14–5

Prepare journal entries for cash dividend when treasury stock is held
(L.O. 2)

The stockholders' equity section of Wright Company's balance sheet on December 31, 1993, shows 100,000 shares of authorized and issued $40 stated value common stock, of which 9,000 shares are held in the treasury. On this date, the board of directors declared a cash dividend of $4 per share payable on January 21, 1994, to stockholders of record on January 10. Give dated journal entries for the above.

Exercise 14–6

Prepare journal entry for small stock dividend and discuss large stock dividend
(L.O. 2)

Bryan Company has outstanding 75,000 shares of common stock without par or stated value, which were issued at an average price of $36 per share, and retained earnings of $1,440,000. The current market price of the common stock is $54 per share. Total authorized stock consists of 500,000 shares.

a. Give the required entry to record the declaration of a 10% stock dividend.

b.   If, alternatively, the company declared a 30% stock dividend, what additional information would you need before making a journal entry to record the dividend?

Exercise 14–7

Prepare journal entries for stock split and small stock dividend

(L.O. 2)

Kross Corporation's stockholders' equity consisted of 60,000 authorized shares of $20 par value common stock, of which 30,000 shares had been issued at par, and retained earnings of $750,000. The company then split its stock, two for one, by changing the par value of the old shares and issuing new $10 par shares.

a.   Give the required journal entry to record the stock split.

b.   Suppose instead that the company declared and later issued a 10% stock dividend. Give the required journal entries, assuming that the market value on the date of declaration was $25 per share.

Exercise 14–8

Prepare journal entry for appropriation of retained earnings and explain

(L.O. 2)

The balance sheet of Bryan Company contains the following:

Appropriation per loan agreement	$375,000

a.   Give the journal entry made to create this account.

b.   Explain the reason for the appropriation's existence and its manner of presentation in the balance sheet.

Exercise 14–9

Prepare income statement and statement of retained earnings

(L.O. 2, 4)

Kelly Company has revenues of $40 million, expenses of $32 million, a tax-deductible earthquake loss (its first such loss) of $2 million, and a tax-deductible loss of $3 million resulting from the voluntary early extinguishment (retirement) of debt. The assumed income tax rate is 40%. The company's beginning-of-the-year retained earnings were $15 million, and a dividend of $1 million was declared.

a.   Prepare an income statement for the year.

b.   Prepare a statement of retained earnings for the year.

Exercise 14–10

Prepare statement of retained earnings

(L.O. 2, 5)

Mooney Company had retained earnings of $21,000 as of January 1, 1993. In 1993, Mooney Company had sales of $60,000, cost of goods sold of $36,000, and other operating expenses, excluding taxes, of $12,000. In 1993, Mooney Company discovered that it had, in error, depreciated land over the last three years resulting in a balance in the accumulated depreciation account of $12,000. The assumed tax rate for Mooney Company is 40%. Present in proper form a statement of retained earnings for the year ended December 31, 1993.

Exercise 14–11

Calculate EPS; present information in income statement format

(L.O. 6)

The following information relates to Wiseman Corporation for the year ended December 31, 1993:

Common stock outstanding.	75,000 shares
Income from continuing operations	$1,904,000
Loss on discontinued operations (net of tax)	300,000
Extraordinary gain (net of tax)	180,000

Calculate EPS for the year ended December 31, 1993. Present the information in the same format as would be used in the corporation's income statement.

Exercise 14–12

Calculate EPS; comment on resulting amounts

(L.O. 6)

Cassidy Company had an average number of shares of common stock outstanding of 200,000 in 1993 and 215,000 in 1994. Net income for these two years was as follows:

1993	$920,000
1994	960,000

a.   Calculate EPS for the years ended December 31, 1993, and 1994.

b.   What might the resulting figures tell a stockholder or a potential investor?

PROBLEMS: SERIES A

Problem 14–1A

Prepare stockholders' equity section of balance sheet
(L.O. 1)

The trial balance of Paul Corporation as of December 31, 1993, contains the following selected balances:

Notes Payable (17%, due May 1, 1995)	$2,000,000
Allowance for Uncollectible Accounts	30,000
Common Stock (without par value, $10 stated value; 300,000 shares authorized, issued, and outstanding)	3,000,000
Retained Earnings, Unappropriated	250,000
Dividends Payable (in cash, declared December 15 on preferred stock)	7,000
Appropriation for Pending Litigation	300,000
Preferred Stock (6%, $100 par value; 3,000 shares authorized, issued, and outstanding)	300,000
Paid-In Capital—Donations	200,000
Paid-In Capital in Excess of Par Value—Preferred	5,000

Required   Prepare the stockholders' equity section of the balance sheet as of December 31, 1993.

Problem 14–2A

Prepare journal entries for cash dividend and small stock dividend
(L.O. 2)

The stockholders' equity section of Wells Company's December 31, 1992, balance sheet follows:

Stockholders' equity:		
Paid-in-capital:		
Common stock—$30 par value; authorized, 2,000 shares; issued and outstanding, 1,000 shares	$30,000	
Paid-in capital in excess of par value	1,500	
Total paid-in capital		$31,500
Retained earnings		12,000
Total stockholders' equity		$43,500

On July 15, 1993, the board of directors declared a cash dividend of $3 per share, which was paid on August 1, 1993. On December 1, 1993, the board declared a stock dividend of 10%, and the shares were issued on December 15, 1993. Market value of the stock was $36 on December 1 and $42 on December 15.

Required   Prepare journal entries for the above dividend transactions.

Problem 14–3A

Prepare journal entries for appropriations of retained earnings
(L.O. 2)

The ledger of Larson Company includes the following account balances on September 30, 1993:

Appropriation for Contingencies	$ 42,000
Appropriation for Plant Expansion	78,400
Retained Earnings, Unappropriated	140,000

During October 1993, the company took action to:

1. Increase the appropriation for contingencies by $12,600.
2. Decrease the appropriation for plant expansion by $32,900.
3. Establish an appropriation per loan agreement, with an annual increase of $10,500.
4. Declare a cash dividend of $31,500.

Required   Prepare the journal entries to record the above transactions of Larson Company.

Problem 14–4A

Present statement of
retained earnings
(L.O. 2)

Using the information given in Problem 14-3A, prepare a statement of retained earnings for Larson Company for the period ended October 31, 1993.

Problem 14–5A

Prepare journal entries for
retained earnings
appropriation and small
stock dividend
(L.O. 2)

Following are selected transactions of Robin Corporation:

1988

Dec. 31   By action of the board of directors, $180,000 of retained earnings was appropriated to provide for future expansion of the company's main building. (On the last day of each of the four succeeding years, the same action was taken. You need not make entries for these years.)

1993

Jan.   3   Obtained, at a cost of $1,800, a building permit to construct a new wing on the main plant building.

July 30   Paid $720,000 to Able Construction Company for completion of the new wing.

Aug.   4   The board of directors authorized the release of the sum appropriated for expansion of the plant building.

       4   The board of directors declared a 10% common stock dividend on the 25,000 shares of $200 par value common stock outstanding. The market price on this date was $264 per share.

Required   Prepare journal entries to record all of the above transactions.

Problem 14–6A

Present statement of
retained earnings
(L.O. 2)

The following information relates to Edney Corporation for the year 1993:

Net income for the year	$ 350,000
Dividends declared on common stock	49,000
Dividends declared on preferred stock	28,000
Retained earnings, January 1, unappropriated	1,050,000
Appropriation for retirement of bonds	140,000
Balance in "Appropriation for possible loss of a lawsuit," no longer needed on December 31 because of a favorable court decision, is (by Directors' order) returned to unappropriated retained earnings	175,000

Required   Prepare a statement of retained earnings for the year ended December 31, 1993.

Problem 14–7A

Prepare journal entries for
treasury stock
transactions and for cash
dividends; present
stockholders' equity
section
(L.O. 2, 3)

The stockholders' equity of Stone Company as of December 31, 1992, consisted of 20,000 shares of authorized, issued, and outstanding $20 par value common stock, paid-in capital in excess of par of $96,000, and retained earnings of $160,000. Following are selected transactions for 1993:

May   1   Acquired 3,000 shares of its own common stock at $40 per share.
June 1   Reissued 500 shares at $48.
      30   Reissued 700 shares at $36.
Oct.   1   Declared a cash dividend of $2 per share.
      31   Paid the cash dividend declared on October 1.

Net income for the year was $32,000. No other transactions affecting retained earnings occurred during the year.

Required   a.   Prepare general journal entries for the above transactions.
            b.   Prepare the stockholders' equity section of the December 31, 1993, balance sheet.

Problem 14–8A

Prepare journal entries for stock transactions, cash dividend, small stock dividend, and retained earnings appropriation; prepare statement of retained earnings and stockholders' equity section of balance sheet (L.O. 2, 3)

The stockholders' equity section of Hays Company's December 31, 1992, balance sheet appears below:

Stockholders' equity:

Paid-in capital:		
Preferred stock—$50 par value, 5%; authorized, 5,000 shares; issued and outstanding, 2,500 shares.		$125,000
Common stock—without par or stated value; authorized, 50,000 shares; issued, 25,000 shares of which 500 are held in treasury . . .		187,500
Paid-in capital in excess of par—preferred.		2,500
Total paid-in capital		$315,000
Retained earnings:		
Appropriated:		
For plant expansion.	$ 12,500	
Unappropriated (restricted as to dividends to the extent of $5,000, the cost of the treasury stock held)	105,000	
Total retained earnings		117,500
Total paid-in capital and retained earnings		$432,500
Less: Treasury stock, common, at cost (500 shares)		5,000
Total stockholders' equity		$427,500

Following are selected transactions that occurred in 1993:

Jan. 13   Subscriptions were received for 550 shares of previously unissued common stock at $11.

Feb. 4   A plot of land was accepted as payment in full for 500 shares of common stock, and the stock was issued. Closing market price of the common stock on this date was $10 per share.

Mar. 24   All of the treasury stock was reissued at $12 per share.

June 22   All stock subscriptions were collected in full, and the shares were issued.

23   The regular semiannual dividend on the preferred stock was declared.

30   The preferred dividend was paid.

July 3   A 10% stock dividend was declared on the common stock. Market price on this date was $14.

18   The stock dividend shares were issued.

Oct. 4   The company reacquired 105 shares of its common stock at $12.

Dec. 18   The regular semiannual dividend on the preferred stock and a $0.20 per share dividend on the common stock were declared.

31   Both dividends were paid.

31   An additional appropriation of retained earnings of $2,500 for plant expansion was authorized.

Required   a.   Prepare journal entries to record the 1993 transactions.

b.   Prepare a statement of retained earnings for the year 1993, assuming net income for the year was $21,562.

c.   Prepare the stockholders' equity section of the December 31, 1993, balance sheet.

Problem 14–9A

Prepare income statement
and statement of retained
earnings
(L.O. 2, 4, 5)

Selected data of Dennis Company for the year ended December 31, 1993, are:

Sales, net.	$400,000
Interest expense.	36,000
Cash dividends on common stock	60,000
Selling and administrative expenses	98,000
Cash dividends on preferred stock.	28,000
Rent revenue	160,000
Cost of goods sold.	260,000
Flood loss (has never occurred before).	80,000
Interest revenue.	36,000
Other revenue.	60,000
Depreciation and maintenance on rental equipment	108,000
Stock dividend on common stock	120,000
Operating income on Plastics Division up to point of sale in 1993	20,000
Gain on disposal of Plastics Division	10,000
Litigation loss (has never occurred before)	160,000
Cumulative positive effect on prior years' income of changing to a different depreciation method	32,000

Assume the applicable federal income tax rate is 40%. All above items of expense, revenue, and loss are included in the computation of taxable income. The litigation loss resulted from a court award of damages for patent infringement on a product that the company produced and sold in 1989 and 1990, but was discontinued in 1990. In addition, the company discovered that in 1992 it had erroneously charged to expense the $100,000 cost of a tract of land purchased that year and had made the same error on its tax return for 1992. Retained earnings as of January 1, 1993, were $2,240,000. Assume there were 10,000 shares of common stock and 5,000 shares of preferred stock outstanding for the entire year.

Required   Prepare an income statement and a statement of retained earnings for 1993.

PROBLEMS: SERIES B

Problem 14–1B

Prepare stockholders'
equity section of balance
sheet
(L.O. 1)

Following are selected data and accounts of King, Inc., as of May 31, 1993:

Paid-In Capital in Excess of Par Value—Preferred	$ 4,200
Retained Earnings, Unappropriated.	72,000
Allowance for Uncollectible Accounts	24,000
Common Stock (without par value, stated value $30; 20,000 shares authorized, issued, and outstanding)	600,000
Appropriation for Retirement of Bonds.	90,000
Dividends Payable (cash)	3,600
Paid-In Capital in Excess of Stated Value—Common.	24,000
Notes Payable (17%, due April 1, 1999)	360,000
Preferred Stock (7%, par value $60; 2,000 shares authorized, issued, and outstanding).	120,000
Paid-In Capital—Donations	18,000

Required   Prepare the stockholders' equity section of the company's balance sheet as of May 31, 1993.

Problem 14–2B

Prepare journal entries for cash dividend and small stock dividend

(L.O. 2)

The only stockholders' equity items of Godwin Company at June 30, 1993, are:

Stockholders' equity:

Paid-in capital:

Common stock—$200 par value, 5,000 shares authorized, 3,000 shares issued and outstanding	$600,000	
Paid-in capital in excess of par value	240,000	
Total paid-in capital		$ 840,000
Retained earnings		240,000
Total stockholders' equity		$1,080,000

On August 4, 1993, a 4% cash dividend was declared, payable on September 3. On November 16, a 10% stock dividend was declared. The shares were issued on December 1. The market value of the common stock was $360 per share on November 16 and $354 per share on December 1.

Required   Prepare journal entries for the above dividend transactions.

Problem 14–3B

Prepare stockholders' equity section of balance sheet

(L.O. 3)

The bookkeeper of J. M. Beaver Company has prepared the following incorrect statement of stockholders' equity for the year ended December 31, 1993:

Stockholders' equity:

Paid-in capital:

Preferred stock—6%, cumulative (8,000 shares)	$209,000	
Common stock—50,000 shares	595,000	
Total paid-in capital		$ 804,000
Retained earnings		341,000
Total stockholders' equity		$1,145,000

The authorized stock consists of 12,000 shares of preferred stock with a $25 par value and 75,000 shares of common stock, $10 par value. The preferred stock was issued on two occasions: (1) 5,000 shares at par, and (2) 3,000 shares at $28 per share. The 50,000 shares of common stock were issued at $13 per share. Five thousand shares of treasury common stock were reacquired for $55,000; the bookkeeper deducted the cost of the treasury stock from the Common Stock account.

Required   Prepare the correct stockholders' equity section of the balance sheet at December 31, 1993.

Problem 14–4B

Prepare journal entries for stock dividend, treasury stock transactions, and retained earnings appropriation

(L.O. 2, 3)

The stockholders' equity of Bishop Company at January 1, 1993, is as follows:

Common stock—no-par value, stated value of $10; 100,000 shares authorized, 60,000 shares issued	$600,000
Paid-in capital in excess of stated value	100,000
Appropriation per loan agreement	37,600
Unappropriated retained earnings	212,000
Treasury stock (3,000 shares at cost)	(36,000)

During 1993, the following transactions occurred in the order listed:

1. Issued 10,000 shares of stock for $184,000.
2. Declared a 4% stock dividend when the market price was $24 per share.
3. Sold 1,000 shares of treasury stock for $21,600.

4. Issued stock certificates for the stock dividend declared in transaction (2).
5. Bought 2,000 shares of treasury stock for $33,600.
6. Increased the appropriation by $21,600 per loan agreement.

Required   Prepare journal entries as necessary for the above transactions.

Problem 14–5B

Prepare journal entries for retained earnings appropriation, asset acquisition, and stock dividend
(L.O. 2)

Following are selected transactions of Adrian Corporation:

1986
Dec. 31   The board of directors authorized the appropriation of $100,000 of retained earnings to provide for the future acquisition of a new plant site and the construction of a new building. (On the last day of the six succeeding years, the same action was taken. You need not make entries for these six years.)

1991
Jan. 2   Purchased a new plant site for cash, $200,000.
Mar. 29   Entered into a contract for construction of a new building, payment to be made within 30 days following completion.

1993
Feb. 10   Following final inspection and approval of the new building, Dome Construction Company was paid in full, $1,000,000.
Mar. 10   The board of directors authorized release of the retained earnings appropriated for the plant site and building.
Apr. 2   A 5% stock dividend on the 100,000 shares of $100 par value common stock outstanding was declared. The market price on this date was $110 per share.

Required   Prepare journal entries for all of the above transactions.

Problem 14–6B

Prepare statement of retained earnings
(L.O. 2)

Following are selected data of Oliver Corporation at December 31, 1993:

Net income for the year	$192,000
Dividends declared on preferred stock	27,000
Retained earnings appropriated during the year for future plant expansion	90,000
Dividends declared on common stock	24,000
Retained earnings, January 1, unappropriated	270,000
Directors ordered that the balance in the "Appropriation per loan agreement," related to a loan repaid on March 31, 1993, be returned to unappropriated retained earnings	180,000

Required   Prepare a statement of retained earnings for the year ended December 31, 1993.

Problem 14–7B

Prepare journal entries for treasury stock transactions and for cash dividend; prepare stockholders' equity section of balance sheet
(L.O. 2, 3)

The stockholders' equity of Grove Company on December 31, 1992, consisted of 1,000 authorized, issued, and outstanding shares of $18 cumulative preferred stock, stated value $60 per share, which were originally issued at $298 per share; 100,000 shares authorized, issued, and outstanding of no-par, $40 stated value common stock, which were originally issued at $40; and retained earnings of $280,000. Following are selected transactions and other data relating to 1993.

1. The company reacquired 2,000 shares of its common stock at $84.
2. One thousand of the treasury shares were reissued at $72.
3. Stockholders donated 1,000 shares of common stock to the company. These shares were immediately reissued at $64 to provide working capital.
4. The first quarter's dividend of $4.50 per share was declared and paid on the preferred stock. No other dividends were declared or paid during 1993.

The company suffered a net loss of $56,000 for the year 1993.

Required   a. Prepare journal entries for the numbered transactions above.
          b. Prepare the stockholders' equity section of the December 31, 1993, balance sheet.

Problem 14–8B

Prepare journal entries to close retained earnings appropriation and for treasury stock transactions and cash dividends; prepare statement of retained earnings and stockholders' equity section of balance sheet
(L.O. 2, 3)

The stockholders' equity section of Bunn Company's October 31, 1992, balance sheet appears below:

Stockholders' equity:
Paid-in capital:
 Preferred stock—$50 par value, 6%; 1,000 shares
  authorized; 350 shares issued and outstanding . . . . $ 17,500
 Common stock—$5 par value; 100,000 shares authorized;
  40,000 shares issued and outstanding 200,000
 Paid-in capital from donation of plant site 12,500

  Total paid-in capital . . . . . ' $230,000

Retained earnings:
 Appropriated:
  Appropriation for contingencies . . . . $ 10,000
 Unappropriated 27,750

  Total retained earnings 37,750

   Total stockholders' equity $267,750

During the ensuing fiscal year, the following transactions were entered into by Bunn Company:

1. The appropriation of $10,000 of retained earnings had been authorized in October 1992 because of the likelihood of an unfavorable court decision in a pending lawsuit. The suit was brought by a customer seeking damages for the company's alleged breach of a contract to supply the customer with certain products at stated prices in 1991. The suit was concluded on March 6, 1993; with a court order directing the company to pay $8,750 in damages. These damages were not deductible in determining the income tax liability. The board ordered the damages paid and the appropriation closed. The loss does not qualify as an extraordinary item.

2. The company acquired 1,000 shares of its own common stock at $7.50 in May 1993. On June 30, it reissued 500 of these shares at $6.

3. Dividends declared and paid during the year were 6% on preferred stock and 15 cents per share on common stock. Both dividends were declared on September 1 and paid on September 30, 1993.

For the fiscal year, the company had net income after income taxes of $9,500, excluding the loss of the lawsuit.

Required
a. Prepare journal entries for the numbered transactions above.
b. Prepare a statement of retained earnings for the year ended October 31, 1993.
c. Prepare the stockholders' equity section of the October 31, 1993, balance sheet.

Problem 14–9B

Present income statement and statement of retained earnings
(L.O. 2, 4, 5)

Selected data for Ross Company for 1993 are given below:

Common stock—$5 par value	$500,000
Sales, net	435,000
Selling and administrative expenses.	80,000
Cash dividends declared and paid.	30,000
Cost of goods sold	200,000
Depreciation expense	30,000
Interest revenue	5,000
Loss on write-down of obsolete inventory	10,000
Retained earnings (as of 12/31/92)	500,000
Operating loss on Candy Division up to point of sale in 1993	10,000
Loss on disposal of Candy Division	50,000
Earthquake loss.	24,000
Cumulative negative effect on prior years' income of changing from straight-line to an accelerated method of computing depreciation	16,000

Assume the applicable federal income tax rate is 40%. All of the items of expense, revenue, and loss are included in the computation of taxable income. The earthquake loss resulted from the first earthquake experienced at the company's location. In addition, the company discovered that in 1992 it had erroneously charged to expense the $40,000 cost of a tract of land purchased that year and had made the same error on its tax return for 1992.

Required

a.   Prepare an income statement for the year ended December 31, 1993.

b.   Prepare a statement of retained earnings for the year ended December 31, 1993.

BUSINESS DECISION PROBLEMS

Decision Problem 14–1

Determine amount of dividends received and effects on stock prices
(L.O. 2)

The stockholders' equity section of the Wade Corporation's balance sheet for June 30, 1993, is shown below:

Stockholders' equity:		
Paid-in capital:		
Common stock—$10 par value; authorized 200,000 shares; issued and outstanding 80,000 shares.	$800,000	
Paid-in capital in excess of par value	480,000	
Total paid-in capital		$1,280,000
Retained earnings.		760,000
Total stockholders' equity		$2,040,000

On July 1, 1993, the corporation's directors declared a 10% stock dividend distributable on August 2 to stockholders of record on July 16. On November 1, 1993, the directors voted a $1.20 per share annual cash dividend payable on December 2 to stockholders of record on November 16. For four years prior to 1993, the corporation had paid an annual cash dividend of $1.26.

As of July 1, 1993, Bill Hale owned 8,000 shares of Wade Corporation's common stock, which he had purchased four years earlier. The market value of his stock was $24 per share on July 1, 1993, and $21.82 per share on July 16, 1993.

Required

a.   What amount of cash dividends will Hale receive in 1993? How does this amount differ from the amount of cash dividends Hale received in each of the previous four years?

b.   For what logical reason did the price of the stock drop from $24 to $21.82 on July 16, 1993?

    c.   Is Hale better off as a result of the stock dividend and the $1.20 cash dividend than he would have been if he had just received the $1.26 cash dividend? Why?

Decision Problem 14–2

Analyze journal entries for impropriety and make subsequent corrections (L.O. 2, 3)

Shown below are some journal entries made by the bookkeeper for Swanson Corporation:

1.	Retained Earnings	3,000	
	Reserve for Uncollectible Accounts		3,000
	To record the adjusting entry for uncollectible accounts.		
2.	Retained Earnings	12,000	
	Reserve for Depreciation		12,000
	To record depreciation expense.		
3.	Retained Earnings	30,000	
	Reserve for Plant Expansion.		30,000
	To record retained earnings appropriation.		
4.	Retained Earnings	2,000	
	Stock Dividend Distributable—Common		2,000
	To record 10% stock dividend declaration (100 shares to be distributed—$20 par value, $30 market value).		
5.	Stock Dividend Distributable—Common	2,000	
	Common Stock		2,000
	To record distribution of stock dividend.		
6.	Treasury Stock.	8,000	
	Cash		8,000
	To record acquisition of 200 shares of $20 par value common stock at $40 per share.		
7.	Cash	4,400	
	Treasury Stock.		4,400
	To record sale of 100 treasury shares at $44 per share.		
8.	Cash	1,700	
	Treasury Stock.		1,700
	To record sale of 50 treasury shares at $34 per share.		
9.	Common Stock	4,000	
	Dividends Payable		4,000
	To record declaration of cash dividend.		
10.	Dividends Payable	4,000	
	Cash		4,000
	To record payment of cash dividend.		

Required

Analyze the above journal entries in connection with their explanations and decide whether each is correct or incorrect. The explanations are all correct. If a journal entry is incorrect, prepare the journal entry that should have been made.

Decision Problem 14–3

Determine the number of shares of common stock issued and cost of treasury stock (L.O. 3)

In the financial statements of General Signal Corporation located in "A Broader Perspective," footnote (6) discusses the treasury stock transactions that occurred during the 1988 fiscal period. Refer to the 1988 information provided in the partial balance sheet and the footnote.

Required

a.   Determine the number of common stock shares issued and outstanding.

b.   Determine the average cost of treasury stock shares on hand at the end of both 1987 and 1988 as shown in the balance sheet.

c.   For what reasons might General Signal acquire treasury stock?

ANSWERS TO SELF-TEST

True-False

1. *False*. The paid-in capital of a corporation only includes capital contributed by stockholders or others. The Retained Earnings account balance reflects the excess of the company's aggregate net income since its formation over all dividends distributed and aggregate net losses.

2. *True*. Treasury stock may be reissued without violating the preemptive right.

3. *True*. The payment of a cash dividend decreases the current liability, dividends payable, set up by the declaration of the cash dividend.

4. *False*. The declaration of a stock dividend does not increase current liabilities because the stock dividend is not to be paid with assets.

5. *False*. An appropriations of retained earnings merely indicates that a portion of retained earnings is not available for cash dividends. Thus, such appropriations have nothing to do with setting aside of cash.

6. *True*. Such losses are likely to be unusual in nature and nonrecurring.

Multiple-Choice

1. *d.* Appropriation per Loan Agreement is part of retained earnings.

2. *c.* When treasury stock is reacquired, the stock is recorded at cost in a debit-balance stockholders' equity account, Treasury Stock.

3. *a.* The excess of the reissue price over the cost of treasury stock is recorded in the Paid-In Capital—Treasury Stock Transactions account.

4. *a.* Treasury stock is customarily shown as a deduction from total stockholders' equity.

5. *b.* The date of record determines who is to receive the dividends.

6. *c.* The total amount of dividends is computed as follows:

Total outstanding shares at declaration:	
(21,000 − 1,000) shares	20,000
Dividend per share	× $0.50
Total dividend amount	$10,000

7. *b.* Prior period adjustments are shown as adjustments to the opening balance of retained earnings on the statement of retained earnings.

15

BONDS PAYABLE AND BOND INVESTMENTS

LEARNING OBJECTIVES

After studying this chapter, you should be able to:

1. Describe the features of bonds and tell how bonds differ from shares of stock.

2. List the advantages and disadvantages of financing with long-term debt and prepare examples showing how financial leverage is employed.

3. Prepare journal entries for bonds issued at face value.

4. Explain how interest rates affect bond prices and what causes a bond to sell at a premium or a discount.

5. Apply the concept of present value to compute the price of a bond.

6. Prepare journal entries for bonds issued at a discount or a premium.

7. Prepare journal entries for bond redemptions and bond conversions.

8. Prepare journal entries for bond investments.

9. Explain future value and present value concepts and make required calculations (Appendix).

In previous chapters, you learned that corporations obtain cash for recurring business operations from stock issuances, profitable operations, and short-term borrowing (current liabilities). However, when situations arise that require large amounts of cash, such as the purchase of a building, corporations also raise cash from long-term borrowing, that is, by issuing bonds. The issuing of bonds results in a Bonds Payable account. The first part of this chapter discusses the issuing of bonds and accounting for bonds payable from the issuer's point of view.

The second part of this chapter looks at bond transactions from the investors' point of view. Since corporations are legal entities, they, like individuals, can invest in stocks and bonds issued by other corporations that are regularly traded on national exchanges. These types of investments can offer a rate of return substantially greater than a savings account. Chapter 16 discusses stock investments.

BONDS PAYABLE

Objective 1

Describe the features of bonds and tell how bonds differ from shares of stock

A bond is a long-term debt, or liability, owed by its issuer. Physical evidence of the debt lies in a negotiable bond certificate. In contrast to long-term notes, which usually mature in 10 years or less, bond maturities often run for 20 years or more.

Generally, a bond issue consists of a large number of $1,000 bonds rather than one large bond. For example, a company seeking to borrow $100,000 would issue one hundred (100) $1,000 bonds rather than one (1) $100,000 bond. This practice enables investors with less cash to invest to purchase some of the bonds.

Bonds derive their value primarily from two promises made by the borrower to the lender or bondholder. The borrower promises to pay (1) the face value or **principal amount** of the bond on a specific maturity date in the future and (2) **periodic interest** at a specified rate on face value at stated dates, usually semiannually, until the maturity date.

Large companies often have numerous long-term notes and bond issues outstanding at any one time. The various issues generally have different stated interest rates and will mature at different points in the future. Companies present this information in the footnotes to their financial statements. Illustration 15.1 shows a portion of the long-term borrowings footnote from Du Pont's 1989 Annual Report. All of the items labeled "debentures" are bond issues outstanding.

Comparison with Stock

A bond differs from a share of stock in several ways:

1. A bond is a debt or liability of the issuer, while a share of stock is a unit of ownership.
2. A bond has a maturity date when it must be paid. A share of stock does not mature; stock remains outstanding indefinitely unless the company decides to retire it.
3. Most bonds require stated periodic interest payments by the company. In contrast, dividends to stockholders are payable only when declared; even preferred dividends need not be paid in a particular period if the board of directors so decides.
4. Bond interest is deductible by the issuer in computing both net income and taxable income, while dividends are not deductible in either computation.

Selling (Issuing) Bonds

A company seeking to borrow millions of dollars generally will not be able to borrow from a single lender. By selling (issuing) bonds to the public, the company is able to secure the necessary funds.

ILLUSTRATION 15.1

Du Pont's Long-Term Borrowings
(in thousands)

December 31	1989	1988
U.S. dollar:		
Industrial development bonds due 2001–2002	$ 223	$ 223
Zero coupon notes due 1990 ($300 face value, 13.99% yield to maturity)	—	258
Medium-term notes due 1990–1992[1]	446	300
12.88% notes due 1992	—	150
10.13% notes due 1992	252	—
7.50% notes due 1993	250	250
9.00% notes due 1994	255	—
11.25% notes due 1995	150	150
8.45% notes due 1996	300	—
8.70% notes due 1998	133	150
8.00% notes due 1998	46	49
9.13% debentures due 1999	102	110
7.50% debentures due 1999	54	58
8.88% debentures due 2001	160	170
6.00% debentures due 2001 ($660 face value, 13.95% yield to maturity)	358	349
8.25% notes due 2002	60	65
8.45% debentures due 2004	198	198
8.50% debentures due 2006	182	182
9.38% debentures due 2009	190	200
8.50% debentures due 2016	300	300
Other loans (various currencies) due 1990–2016	576[2]	172
Unamortized discount[3]	(155)	(176)
	$4,080	$3,158

[1] Average interest rates at December 31, 1989 and 1988, were 8.27 percent and 8.81 percent.

[2] Includes notes denominated as 100 million European Currency Units (ECUs) with a 9.0 percent interest rate. Concurrent with the issuance of these notes, the company entered into a currency swap agreement that effectively established U.S. dollar-denominated principal ($109) and interest (8.73 percent) obligations over the term of the ECU notes. Also includes notes denominated as 160 million Australian dollars with a 16.5 percent interest rate issued by the company's majority-owned Canadian subsidiary, which have been effectively converted to a 149 million Canadian dollar obligation with an imputed 12.43 percent annual cost through a series of currency swap agreements and forward exchange contracts.

[3] Unamortized discount results principally from revaluation of debt acquired from Conoco in 1981, based on an imputed rate of 15.63 percent. The face amount of such debt included above at December 31, 1989 and 1988, was $772 and $839.

Source: Du Pont 1989 Annual Report.

Usually companies sell their bond issues through an investment company or banker called an underwriter. The underwriter performs many tasks for the bond issuer, such as advertising, selling, and delivering the bonds to the purchasers. Often the underwriter guarantees the issuer a fixed price for the bonds, expecting to earn a profit by selling the bonds for more than the fixed price.

When a company sells bonds to the public, many purchasers buy the bonds. Rather than deal with each purchaser individually, the issuing company appoints a *trustee* to represent the bondholders. The trustee usually is a bank or trust company. The main duty of the trustee is to see that the borrower fulfills the provisions of the *bond indenture*. A bond indenture is the contract or loan agreement under which the bonds are issued. The indenture deals with matters such as the interest rate, maturity date and maturity amount, possible restrictions on dividends, repayment plans, and other provisions relating to the debt. If the issuing company does not adhere to the bond indenture provisions, the issuer is said to be in default. The trustee is expected to take action to force the issuer to comply with the indenture.

Characteristics of Bonds

As stated earlier, a bond is a long-term liability that derives its value from two promises made to the purchasers: (1) the issuing company will repay the principal at a specified later time, and (2) the issuing company will make periodic interest payments (usually every six months) until that time. Bonds may differ in other respects; they may be secured or unsecured bonds, registered or unregistered (bearer) bonds, and term or serial bonds. We discuss these differences and others below.

Certain bond features are matters of legal necessity, such as how a company pays interest and transfers ownership. Such features usually do not affect the issue price of the bonds. Other features, such as convertibility into common stock, are called *sweeteners* because they are designed to make the bonds more attractive to potential purchasers. These sweeteners may increase the issue price of a bond.

Secured Bonds   A secured bond is a bond for which a company has pledged specific property to ensure its payment. Mortgage bonds are the most common type of secured bonds. A mortgage is a legal claim (lien) on specific property that gives the bondholder the right to possess the pledged property if the company fails to make required payments.

Unsecured Bonds   An unsecured bond is called a debenture bond, or simply a debenture. A debenture is an unsecured bond backed only by the general creditworthiness of the issuer, not by a lien on any specific property. A financially sound company will be able to issue debentures more easily than a company experiencing financial difficulty.

Registered Bonds   A registered bond is a bond with the owner's name on the bond certificate and in the register of bond owners kept by the bond issuer or its agent, the registrar. Bonds may be registered as to principal (or face value of the bond) or as to both principal and interest. Most bonds in our economy are registered as to principal only. If a bond is registered as to both principal and interest, the bond interest is paid by check. Ownership of registered bonds is transferred by endorsing the bond and registering it in the new owner's name. Registered bonds are easily replaced if lost or stolen.

Unregistered (Bearer) Bonds   An unregistered (bearer) bond is assumed to be the property of its holder or bearer, since the owner's name does not appear on the bond certificate or in a separate record. Ownership is transferred by physical delivery of the bond.

Coupon Bonds   A coupon bond is a bond not registered as to interest. Coupon bonds carry detachable coupons for the interest they pay. At the end of each interest period, the coupon for the period is clipped and presented to a stated party, usually a bank, for collection.

Term Bonds and Serial Bonds   A term bond is a bond that matures on the same date as all other bonds in a given bond issue. Serial bonds are bonds in a given bond issue with maturities spread over several dates. For instance, one fourth of the bonds may mature on December 31, 1995, another one fourth on December 31, 1996, and so on.

Callable Bonds   A callable bond contains a provision that gives the issuer the right to call (buy back) the bond before its maturity date. The provision is similar to the call provision in some preferred stocks. A company might exercise this call right if outstanding bonds bear interest at a much higher rate than the company would have to pay if it issued new but similar bonds. The exercise of the call provision normally requires the company to pay the bondholder a call premium of about $30 to $70 per $1,000 bond. A call premium is the price paid in excess of face value that the issuer of bonds must pay to redeem (call) bonds before their maturity date.

Convertible Bonds   A convertible bond is a bond that may be exchanged for shares of stock of the issuing corporation at the bondholder's option. A convertible bond has a stipulated conversion rate of some number of shares for each $1,000 bond. Any type of bond may be convertible, but this feature usually is added to rather risky debenture bonds to make them more attractive to investors.

Bonds with Stock Warrants   A stock warrant allows the bondholder to purchase shares of common stock at a fixed price for a stated period of time. Warrants issued with long-term debt may be nondetachable or detachable. A bond with **nondetachable warrants** is virtually the same as a convertible bond; the holder must surrender the bond to acquire the common stock. **Detachable warrants** allow bondholders to keep their bonds and still purchase shares of stock through exercise of the warrants.

Junk Bonds   Junk bonds are high-interest rate, high-risk bonds that were issued in the 1980s to finance corporate restructurings. These restructurings took the form of management buyouts (called leveraged buyouts or LBOs), hostile takeovers of companies by outside parties, or friendly takeovers of companies by outside parties. As of the early 1990s, junk bonds were out of favor because many of the issuers had defaulted on their interest payments and some of the issuers had declared bankruptcy or sought relief from the bondholders by negotiating new debt terms.

Advantages of Issuing Debt

Objective 2

List the advantages and disadvantages of financing with long-term debt and prepare examples showing how financial leverage is employed

Several advantages come from raising cash by issuing bonds rather than stock. First, the current stockholders do not have to dilute or surrender their control of the company when funds are obtained by borrowing rather than issuing more shares of stocks. Second, it may also be less expensive to issue debt rather than additional stock because the interest payments made to bondholders are tax deductible while dividends are not. Finally, probably the most important reason to issue bonds is that the use of debt may increase the earnings of stockholders through favorable financial leverage.

Favorable Financial Leverage   A company has favorable financial leverage when it uses borrowed funds to increase earnings per share (EPS) of common stock. Increased EPS usually result from earning a higher rate of return than the rate of interest paid for the borrowed money. For example, suppose a company borrowed money at 10% and earned a 15% rate of return. The 5% difference increases earnings.

Illustration 15.2 provides a more comprehensive example of favorable financial leverage. The two companies in the illustration are identical in every respect

A BROADER PERSPECTIVE

EXCESSES OF '80s READY TO EXPLODE
For Many Debt-Heavy Companies, the
Question Is When and How Hard

The story has gotten to be a regular feature: "Debt-laden _____ Corp., on the brink of defaulting on millions in junk bonds/bank loans, said it would file for Chapter 11 bankruptcy protection unless bondholders/lenders agree to a restructuring."

Fill in the blank with any of a growing number of companies. Resorts International. Integrated Resources. Campeau. Jim Walter Corp. Southland. Two weeks ago, Circle K Corp. made precisely that statement before winning a seven-month reprieve to negotiate with bondholders. Wednesday, reports surfaced that West Point-Pepperell's acquirer, William Farley, plans to go the Resorts route. Resorts acquirer Merv Griffin surrendered his majority ownership to give stock to bondholders and avoid a forced Chapter 11 filing. Farley Inc. reportedly plans the same deal, though officials wouldn't comment.

Peering at these scenes from the $2.1 trillion mountain of corporate debt built in the 1980s is unsettling indeed. Not only did that debt pile up 2½ times as fast as the economy grew, it did so at higher and higher cost. Roughly 28% of it, or $600 million, is in high-interest junk bonds or high-interest bank loans. That's a big reason why U.S. corporations' net interest payments exceed their after-tax profits for the first time since 1934—and why corporate bankruptcy filings in key courts such as the Southern District of New York are growing at a 30% annual rate.

*   *   *   *   *

Source: David Craig and Beth Belton, *USA Today*, April 12, 1990, p. 1B.

except in the way they are financed. Company A issued only capital stock, while Company B issued equal amounts of 10% bonds and capital stock. Both companies have $20,000,000 of assets, and both earned $4,000,000 of income from operations. If we divide income from operations by assets ($4,000,000 ÷ $20,000,000), we see that both companies earned 20% on assets employed. Yet B's stockholders fared far better than A's. The ratio of net income to stockholders' equity is 18% for B, while it is only 12% for A.

Assume that both companies issued their stock at the beginning of 1994 at $10 per share. B's $1.80 EPS are 50% greater than A's $1.20 EPS. This EPS difference probably would cause B's shares to sell at a substantially higher market price than A's shares. B's larger EPS would also allow a larger dividend on B's shares.

Company B in Illustration 15.2 is employing financial leverage, or is said to be trading on the equity. The company is using its stockholders' equity as a basis for securing funds on which it pays a fixed return. Company B expects to earn more from the use of such funds than their fixed after-tax cost. As a result, Company B increases its rate of return on stockholders' equity and EPS.[1]

Disadvantages of Issuing Debt

Several disadvantages accompany the use of debt financing. First, the borrower has a fixed interest payment that must be met each period to avoid default. Second, use of debt also reduces a company's ability to withstand a major loss. For example, assume that instead of having net income, both Company A and Company B in Illustration 15.2 sustain a net loss in 1994 of $11,000,000. At the end

---

[1] Issuing bonds is only one method of using leverage. Other methods of using financial leverage include issuing preferred stock or long-term notes.

ILLUSTRATION 15.2

Favorable Financial Leverage

COMPANIES A AND B CONDENSED STATEMENTS
Balance Sheets
December 31, 1994

	Company A	Company B
Total assets	$20,000,000	$20,000,000
Bonds payable, 10%		$10,000,000
Stockholders' equity (capital stock).	$20,000,000	10,000,000
Total equities	$20,000,000	$20,000,000

Income Statements
For the Year Ended December 31, 1994

	Company A	Company B
Income from operations	$ 4,000,000	$ 4,000,000
Interest expense.		1,000,000
Income before federal income taxes	$ 4,000,000	$ 3,000,000
Deduct: Federal income taxes (40%).	1,600,000	1,200,000
Net income	$ 2,400,000	$ 1,800,000
Number of common shares outstanding	2,000,000	1,000,000
Earnings per share (EPS) (Net income ÷ Number of common shares outstanding)	$1.20	$1.80
Rate of return on assets employed (Income from operations ÷ Total assets; both companies $4,000,000/$20,000,000)	20%	20%
Rate of return on stockholders' equity (Net income ÷ Stockholders' equity):		
Company A ($2,400,000/$20,000,000)	12%	
Company B ($1,800,000/$10,000,000)		18%

---

of 1994, Company A will still have $9,000,000 of stockholders' equity and can continue operations with a chance of recovery, as shown below. Company B, on the other hand, would have negative stockholders' equity of $1,000,000 and the bondholders could force the company to liquidate if B could not make interest payments as they came due. The result of sustaining the loss by the two companies is as follows:

COMPANIES A AND B
Partial Balance Sheets
December 31, 1994

	Company A	Company B
Stockholders' equity:		
Paid-in capital:		
Common stock	$ 20,000,000	$ 10,000,000
Retained earnings	(11,000,000)	(11,000,000)
Total stockholders' equity.	$ 9,000,000	$ (1,000,000)

A third disadvantage of debt financing is that it also causes a company to experience unfavorable financial leverage when income from operations falls below a certain level. Unfavorable financial leverage results when the cost of borrowed funds exceeds the revenue they generate; it is the reverse of **favorable**

financial leverage. In the above example, if income from operations fell to $1,000,000, the rates of return on stockholders' equity would be 3% for A and zero for B, as shown in the schedule below:

COMPANIES A AND B
Income Statements
For the Year Ended December 31, 1994

	Company A	Company B
Income from operations.	$1,000,000	$1,000,000
Interest expense		1,000,000
Income before federal income taxes	$1,000,000	$ –0–
Deduct: Federal income taxes (40%)	400,000	–0–
Net income	$ 600,000	$ –0–
Rate of return on stockholders' equity:		
Company A ($600,000/$20,000,000)	3%	
Company B ($0/$10,000,000)		0%

The fourth disadvantage of issuing debt is that loan agreements often require the maintenance of a certain amount of working capital (Current assets − Current liabilities) and place limitations on dividends and additional borrowings.

Accounting for Bonds Issued at Face Value

Objective 3

Prepare journal entries for bonds issued at face value

When a company issues bonds, it incurs a long-term liability on which periodic interest payments must be made, usually twice a year. If interest dates fall on other than balance sheet dates, the company will need to accrue interest in the proper periods. The following examples illustrate the accounting for bonds issued at face value on an interest date and issued at face value between interest dates.

Bonds Issued at Face Value on an Interest Date   Valley Company's accounting year ends on December 31. On December 31, 1994, Valley issued 10-year, 12% bonds with a $100,000 face value, for $100,000. The bonds are dated December 31, 1994, call for semiannual interest payments on June 30 and December 31, and mature on December 31, 2004. Valley made the required interest and principal payments when due. The entries for the 10 years are summarized below.

On December 31, 1994, the date of issuance, the entry is:

1994				
Dec.	31	Cash	100,000	
		Bonds Payable		100,000
		To record bonds issued at face value.		

On each June 30 and December 31 for 10 years, beginning June 30, 1995 (ending June 30, 2004), the entry would be:

Each year June and	30			
Dec.	31	Bond Interest Expense ($100,000 × 0.12 × ½)	6,000	
		Cash		6,000
		To record periodic interest payment.		

On December 31, 2004, the maturity date, the entry would be:

2004				
Dec.	31	Bond Interest Expense	6,000	
		Bonds Payable	100,000	
		Cash		106,000
		To record final interest and bond redemption payment.		

Note that no adjusting entries are needed because the interest payment date falls on the last day of the accounting period. The income statement for each of the 10 years 1995–2004 would show Bond Interest Expense of $12,000 ($6,000 × 2); the balance sheet at the end of each of the years 1994–2002 would report bonds payable of $100,000 in long-term liabilities. At the end of 2003, the bonds would be reclassified as a current liability because they will be paid within the next year.

The real world is more complicated. For example, assume the Valley bonds were dated October 31, 1994, issued on that same date, and pay interest each April 30 and October 31. In this case, an adjusting entry is needed on December 31 to accrue interest for two months, November and December. That entry would be:

1994				
Dec.	31	Bond Interest Expense ($100,000 × 0.12 × $2/12$)	2,000	
		Bond Interest Payable.		2,000
		To accrue two months' interest expense.		

The April 30, 1995, entry would be:

1995				
Apr.	30	Bond Interest Expense ($100,000 × 0.12 × $4/12$)	4,000	
		Bond Interest Payable.	2,000	
		Cash		6,000
		To record semiannual interest payment.		

The October 31, 1995, entry would be:

1995				
Oct.	31	Bond Interest Expense	6,000	
		Cash		6,000
		To record semiannual interest payment.		

Each year similar entries would be made for the semiannual payments and the year-end accrued interest. The $2,000 Bond Interest Payable would be reported as a current liability on the December 31 balance sheet for each year.

Bonds Issued at Face Value between Interest Dates   Bonds are not always issued on the date they start to bear interest. Regardless of when the bonds are physically issued, interest starts to accrue from the **most recent** interest date. The bonds are reported to be selling at a stated price "plus accrued interest." The issuer of the bonds must pay holders of the bonds a full six months' interest at each interest date. Thus, investors purchasing bonds after the bonds begin to accrue interest must pay the seller for the unearned interest accrued since the preceding interest date. The bondholders will be reimbursed for this accrued interest when they receive their first six months' interest check.

Using the facts for the Valley bonds dated December 31, 1994, suppose Valley issued its bonds on May 31, 1995, instead of on December 31, 1994. The entry required is:

1995				
May	31	Cash	105,000	
		Bonds Payable		100,000
		Bond Interest Payable ($100,000 × 0.12 × 5/12)		5,000
		To record bonds issued at face value plus accrued interest.		

This entry records the $5,000 received for the accrued interest as a debit to Cash and a credit to Bond Interest Payable.

The entry required on June 30, 1995, when the full six months' interest is paid, is:

1995				
June	30	Bond Interest Expense ($100,000 × 0.12 × ½)	1,000	
		Bond Interest Payable.	5,000	
		Cash		6,000
		To record bond interest payment.		

This entry records $1,000 interest expense on the $100,000 of bonds that were outstanding for one month. The $5,000 is the amount previously collected from the bondholders on May 31 as accrued interest and is now being returned to them.

Bond Prices and Interest Rates

Objective 4

Explain how interest rates affect bond prices and what causes a bond to sell at a premium or discount

The price of a bond issue often differs from its face value. The amount a bond sells for above face value is called a premium. The amount a bond sells for below face value is called a discount. A difference between face value and issue price exists whenever the market rate of interest for similar bonds differs from the contract rate of interest on the bonds. The market interest rate (also called the effective rate or yield) is the minimum rate of interest that investors will accept on bonds of a particular risk category. The higher the risk category, the higher the minimum rate of interest that investors will accept. The contract rate of interest (also called the **stated, coupon,** or **nominal rate**) is stated in the bond indenture, is printed on the face of each bond, and is used to determine the amount of cash that will be paid each interest period. The market rate fluctuates from day to day, responding to factors such as the interest rate the Federal Reserve Board charges banks to borrow from it, government actions to finance the national debt, and the supply of, and demand for, money.

Market and contract rates of interest are likely to differ. The contract rate must be set before the bonds are actually sold to allow time for such activities as printing the bonds. Assume, for instance, that the contract rate for a bond issue is set at 12%. If the market rate is equal to the contract rate, the bonds will sell at their face value. However, by the time the bonds are sold, the market rate could be higher or lower than the contract rate. As shown in Illustration 15.3, if the market rate is lower than the contract rate, the bonds will sell for more than their face value. Thus, if the market rate is 10% and the contract rate is 12%, the bonds will sell at a premium. Investors will be attracted to bonds offering a contract rate

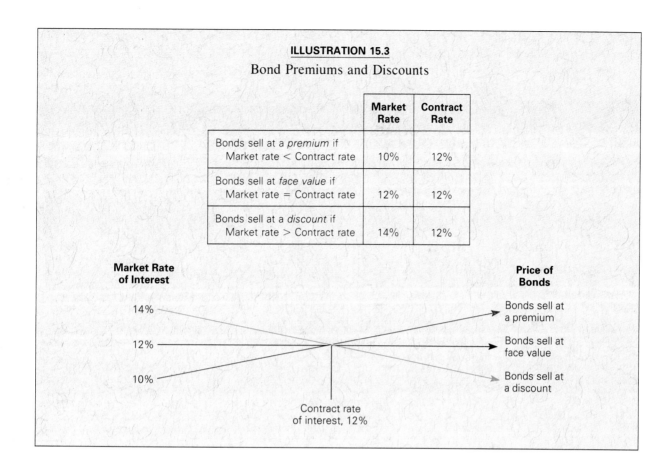

ILLUSTRATION 15.3

Bond Premiums and Discounts

	Market Rate	Contract Rate
Bonds sell at a *premium* if Market rate < Contract rate	10%	12%
Bonds sell at *face value* if Market rate = Contract rate	12%	12%
Bonds sell at a *discount* if Market rate > Contract rate	14%	12%

Market Rate of Interest

Price of Bonds

14% — Bonds sell at a premium

12% — Bonds sell at face value

10% — Bonds sell at a discount

Contract rate of interest, 12%

higher than the market rate and will bid up their price. If the market rate is higher than the contract rate, the bonds will sell for less than their face value. Thus, if the market rate is 14% and the contract rate is 12%, the bonds will sell at a discount. Investors will not be interested in bonds bearing a contract rate less than the market rate unless the price is reduced. The effect of selling bonds at a premium or a discount is to allow the purchasers of the bonds to earn the market rate of interest on their investment.

Computing Bond Prices

Objective 5

Apply the concept of present value to compute the price of a bond

Computing long-term bond prices involves finding **present values** using compound interest. The Appendix to this chapter explains the concepts of future value and present value. If you do not understand the present value concept, you should read the Appendix before continuing with this section.

Buyers and sellers negotiate a price that will yield the going rate of interest for bonds of a particular risk class. The price investors will pay for a given bond issue is equal to the present value of the bonds. Present value is computed by discounting the promised cash flows from the bonds—principal and interest—using the market, or effective, rate. Market rate is used because the bonds must yield at least this rate or investors will be attracted to alternative investments. The life of the bonds is stated in terms of interest (compounding) periods. The interest rate used is the effective rate **per interest period,** which is found by dividing the annual rate by the number of times interest is paid per year. For example, if the annual rate is 12%, the semiannual rate would be 6%.

Bond prices usually are quoted as percentages of face value—100 means 100% of face value, 97 means 97% of face value, and 103 means 103% of face value. For example, one hundred $1,000 face value bonds issued at 103 have a price of $103,000. Regardless of the issue price, at maturity the issuer of the bonds must pay back the investor(s) the face value of the bonds.

Bonds Issued at Face Value   The following example illustrates the specific steps involved in computing the price of bonds. Assume Carr Company issues 12% bonds with a $100,000 face value to yield 12%. The bonds are dated and issued on June 30, 1994, call for semiannual interest payments on June 30 and December 31, and mature on June 30, 1997.[2] The bonds will sell at face value because they offer 12% and investors seek 12%. Potential purchasers have no reason to offer a premium or demand a discount. One way to prove the bonds would be sold at face value is by showing that their present value is $100,000:

	Cash Flow	×	Present Value Factor	=	Present Value
Principal of $100,000 due in six interest periods multiplied by present value factor for 6% from Table G.3, Appendix G (end of text)	$100,000	×	0.70496	=	$ 70,496
Interest of $6,000 due at end of each of six interest periods multiplied by present value factor for 6% from Table G.4, Appendix G (end of text)	6,000	×	4.91732	=	29,504
Total price (present value)					$100,000

This schedule shows that if investors seek an effective rate of 6% per six-month period, they should pay $100,000 for these bonds. **Notice that the same number of interest periods and semiannual interest rates are used in discounting both the principal and interest payments to their present values.** The entry to record the sale of these bonds on June 30, 1994, debits Cash and credits Bonds Payable for $100,000.

Bonds Issued at a Discount   Assume the $100,000, 12% Carr bonds are sold to yield a current market rate of 14% annual interest, or 7% per semiannual period. The present value (selling price) of the bonds is computed as follows:

	Cash Flow	×	Present Value Factor	=	Present Value
Principal of $100,000 due in six interest periods multiplied by present value factor for 7% from Table G.3, Appendix G (end of text)	$100,000	×	0.66634	=	$66,634
Interest of $6,000 due at end of each of six interest periods multiplied by present value factor for 7% from Table G.4, Appendix G (end of text)	6,000	×	4.76654	=	28,599
Total price (present value)					$95,233

Note that in computing the present value of the bonds, the actual $6,000 cash interest payment that will be made each period is still used. **The amount of cash**

---

[2] Bonds do not normally mature in such a short time; we use a three-year life for illustrative purposes only.

the company pays as interest does not depend on the market interest rate. However, the market rate per semiannual period—7%—does change, and this new rate is used to find interest factors in the tables.

The journal entry to record issuance of the bonds is:

1994				
June	30	Cash	95,233	
		Discount on Bonds Payable	4,767	
		Bonds Payable		100,000
		To record bonds issued at a discount.		

In recording the bond issue, Bonds Payable is credited for the face value of the debt. The difference between face value and price received is debited to Discount on Bonds Payable, a contra account to Bonds Payable. Carr reports the bonds payable and discount on bonds payable in the balance sheet as follows:

Long-term liabilities:
    Bonds payable, 12%, due June 30, 1997 . . . . $100,000
        Less: Discount on bonds payable. 4,767 $95,233

The $95,233 is called the carrying value, or net liability, of the bonds. Carrying value is the face value of the bonds minus any unamortized discount or plus any unamortized premium. The next section discusses unamortized premium on bonds payable.

Bonds Issued at a Premium   Assume that Carr issued the $100,000 face value of 12% bonds to yield a current market rate of 10%. The bonds would sell at a premium calculated as follows:

	Cash Flow	×	Present Value Factor	=	Present Value
Principal of $100,000 due in six interest periods multiplied by present value factor for 5% from Table G.3, Appendix G (end of text)	$100,000	×	0.74622	=	$ 74,622
Interest of $6,000 due at end of each of six interest periods multiplied by present value factor for 5% from Table G.4, Appendix G (end of text)	6,000	×	5.07569	=	30,454
Total price (present value).					$105,076

The journal entry to record the issuance of the bonds is:

1994				
June	30	Cash	105,076	
		Bonds Payable		100,000
		Premium on Bonds Payable		5,076
		To record bonds issued at a premium.		

The carrying value of these bonds at issuance is $105,076, consisting of face value of $100,000 and premium of $5,076. The premium is an adjunct account shown on the balance sheet as an addition to bonds payable as follows:

Long-term liabilities:
  Bonds payable, 12%, due June 30, 1997 . . . . $100,000
      Add: Premium on bonds payable 5,076 $105,076

Discount/Premium Amortization

When a company issues bonds at a premium or discount, bond interest expense recorded each period differs from bond interest payments. A discount **increases** and a premium **decreases** the amount of interest expense. For example, if Carr issues bonds with a face value of $100,000 for $95,233, the total interest cost of borrowing would be $40,767: $36,000 (which is six payments of $6,000) plus the discount of $4,767. If the bonds had been issued at $105,076, the total interest cost of borrowing would be $30,924: $36,000 less the premium of $5,076. The $4,767 discount or $5,076 premium must be allocated or charged to the six periods that benefit from the use of borrowed money. Two methods are available for amortizing a discount or premium on bonds—the straight-line method and the effective interest rate method.

The straight-line method records interest expense at a **constant amount;** the effective interest rate method records interest expense at a **constant rate.** *APB Opinion No. 21* states that the straight-line method may be used **only when it does not differ materially from the effective interest rate method.** In many cases, the differences will not be material.

The Straight-Line Method   The straight-line method of amortization is a procedure that allocates an equal amount of discount or premium to each month the bonds are outstanding. The amount is calculated by dividing the discount or premium by the total number of months from the **date of issuance** to the maturity date. For example, if Carr sells its $100,000 face value bonds for $95,233, the $4,767 discount would be charged to interest expense at a rate of $132.42 per month (equal to $4,767/36). Total discount amortization for six months would be $794.52, computed as follows: $132.42 × 6. Interest expense for each six-month period then would be $6,794.52, calculated as follows: $6,000 + ($132.42 × 6). The entry to record the expense on December 31, 1994, would be:

1994				
Dec.	31	Bond Interest Expense.	6,794.52	
		Cash.		6,000.00
		Discount on Bonds Payable ($132.42 × 6)		794.52
		To record interest payment and discount amortization.		

By the maturity date, all of the discount will have been amortized.

To illustrate the straight-line method applied to a premium, recall earlier that Carr sold its $100,000 face value bonds for $105,076. Carr would amortize the $5,076 premium on these bonds at a rate of $141 ($5,076/36) per month. The entry for the first period's semiannual interest expense on bonds sold at a premium is:

```
1994
Dec. 31  Bond Interest Expense  . . . . . . . . . . . . . . . . . . . . .   5,154
         Premium on Bonds Payable ($141 × 6) . . . . . . . . . . . . .     846
               Cash  . . . . . . . . . . . . . . . . . . . . . . . . . .           6,000
         To record interest payment and premium amortization.
```

By the maturity date, all of the premium will have been amortized.

The Effective Interest Rate Method   *APB Opinion No. 21* recommends an amortization procedure called the effective interest rate method, or simply the interest method. Under the interest method, **interest expense for any interest period is equal to the effective (market) rate of interest on the date of issuance times the carrying value of the bonds at the beginning of that interest period.** Using the Carr example of 12% bonds with a face value of $100,000 sold to yield 14%, the carrying value at the beginning of the first interest period is the selling price of $95,233. The interest expense for the first semiannual period would be recorded as follows:

```
1994
Dec. 31  Bond Interest Expense ($95,233 × 0.14 × ½) . . . . . . . . . .   6,666
               Cash ($100,000 × 0.12 × ½)  . . . . . . . . . . . . . .             6,000
               Discount on Bonds Payable  . . . . . . . . . . . . . . .              666
         To record discount amortization and interest payment.
```

Note that interest expense is the carrying value times the **effective** interest rate. The cash payment is the face value times the **contract** rate. The discount amortized for the period is the difference between the two amounts.

After the above entry, the carrying value of the bonds is $95,899, or $95,233 + $666. The balance in the Discount on Bonds Payable account was reduced by $666 to $4,101, or $4,767 − $666. Assuming the accounting year ends on December 31, the entry to record the payment of interest for the second semiannual period on June 30, 1995, is:

```
1995
June 30  Bond Interest Expense ($95,899 × 0.14 × ½) . . . . . . . . . .   6,713
               Cash ($100,000 × 0.12 × ½)  . . . . . . . . . . . . . .             6,000
               Discount on Bonds Payable  . . . . . . . . . . . . . . .              713
         To record discount amortization and interest payment.
```

The effective interest rate method is also applied to premium amortization. If the Carr bonds had been issued at $105,076 to yield 10%, the premium would be $5,076. Interest expense would be calculated in the same manner as for bonds sold at a discount. However, the entry would differ somewhat, showing a debit to the premium account. The entry for the first interest period is:

```
1994
Dec. 31  Bond Interest Expense ($105,076 × 0.10 × ½) . . . . . . . . . .   5,254
         Premium on Bonds Payable  . . . . . . . . . . . . . . . . . .      746
               Cash ($100,000 × 0.12 × ½) . . . . . . . . . . . . . . .            6,000
         To record interest payment and premium amortization.
```

After the first entry, the carrying value of the bonds is $104,330, or $105,076 − $746. The premium account now carries a balance of $4,330, or $5,076 − $746. The entry for the second interest period is:

1995				
June	30	Bond Interest Expense ($104,330 × 0.10 × ½)	5,216*	
		Premium on Bonds Payable	784	
		Cash ($100,000 × 0.12 × ½)		6,000
		To record interest payment and premium amortization.		
		* Rounded down.		

Discount and Premium Amortization Schedules   A discount amortization schedule (Illustration 15.4) and a premium amortization schedule (Illustration 15.5) can be used to aid in preparing entries for interest expense. Usually, companies prepare such schedules when they first issue bonds, often using computer programs designed for this purpose. The companies then refer to the schedules whenever they make journal entries to record interest. Note that in each period the amount of interest expense changes; interest expense gets larger when a discount is involved and smaller when a premium is involved. This fluctuation occurs because the carrying value to which a constant interest rate is applied changes each interest payment date. With a discount, carrying value increases; with a premium, it decreases. However, the actual cash paid as interest is always a constant amount determined by multiplying the bond's face value by the contract rate.

Note that total interest expense of $40,767 for the discount situation in Illustration 15.4 is equal to $36,000 (which is six $6,000 payments) **plus** the $4,767 discount. This amount agrees with the earlier computation of total interest expense. In Illustration 15.5 total interest expense in the premium situation is $30,924, or $36,000 (which is six $6,000 payments) **less** the $5,076 premium. In both illustrations, at the maturity date the carrying value of the bonds is equal to the face value because the discount or premium has been fully amortized.

Adjusting Entry for Partial Period   Illustrations 15.4 and 15.5 can be used to obtain amounts needed if Carr must accrue interest for a partial period. Instead of a calendar-year accounting period, assume the fiscal year of the bond issuer ends on August 31. Using the information provided in the premium amortization schedule (Illustration 15.5), the adjusting entry needed on August 31, 1994, is:

1994				
Aug.	31	Bond Interest Expense ($5,254 × ⅖)	1,751	
		Premium on Bonds Payable ($746 × ⅖)	249	
		Bond Interest Payable ($6,000 × ⅖)		2,000
		To record two months' accrued interest.		

This entry records interest for two months, July and August, of the six-month interest period ending on December 31, 1994. The first line of Illustration 15.5 shows the interest expense and premium amortization for the six months. The above entry thus records two sixths (or one third) of the amounts for this six-month period. The remaining four months' interest is recorded when the first payment is made on December 31, 1994. That entry reads:

ILLUSTRATION 15.4

Discount Amortization Schedule for Bonds Payable

(A) Interest Payment Date	(B) Interest Expense Debit (E × 0.14 × ½)	(C) Cash Credit ($100,000 × 0.12 × ½)	(D) Discount on Bonds Payable Credit (B − C)	(E) Carrying Value of Bonds Payable (previous balance in E + D)
Issue price				$ 95,233
12/31/94	$ 6,666	$ 6,000	$ 666	95,899
6/30/95	6,713	6,000	713	96,612
12/31/95	6,763	6,000	763	97,375
6/30/96	6,816	6,000	816	98,191
12/31/96	6,873	6,000	873	99,064
6/30/97	6,936*	6,000	936	100,000
	$40,767	$36,000	$4,767	

* Includes rounding difference.

ILLUSTRATION 15.5

Premium Amortization Schedule for Bonds Payable

(A) Interest Payment Date	(B) Interest Expense Debit (E × 0.10 × ½)	(C) Cash Credit ($100,000 × 0.12 × ½)	(D) Premium on Bonds Payable Debit (C − B)	(E) Carrying Value of Bonds Payable (previous balance in E − D)
Issue price				$105,076
12/31/94	$ 5,254	$ 6,000	$ 746	104,330
6/30/95	5,216*	6,000	784	103,546
12/31/95	5,177	6,000	823	102,723
6/30/96	5,136	6,000	864	101,859
12/31/96	5,093	6,000	907	100,952
6/30/97	5,048	6,000	952	100,000
	$30,924	$36,000	$5,076	

* Rounded down.

1994				
Dec.	31	Bond Interest Payable.	2,000	
		Bond Interest Expense ($5,254 × 4/6)	3,503	
		Premium on Bonds Payable ($746 × 4/6)	497	
		Cash		6,000
		To record four months' interest expense and semiannual interest payment.		

Similar entries for August 31 and December 31 will be made in the remaining years in the life of the bonds. The amounts will differ, however, because the interest method of accounting for bond interest is being used. The entry for each June 30 would be as indicated in Illustration 15.5.

Redeeming Bonds Payable

Bonds may be (1) paid at maturity, (2) called, or (3) purchased in the market and retired. Each action is referred to as redemption of bonds or the extinguishment of debt. If a company pays its bonds at maturity, it would have already amortized any related discount or premium. The only entry required at maturity would debit Bonds Payable and credit Cash for the face amount of the bonds as follows:

1997				
June	30	Bonds Payable	100,000	
		Cash		100,000
		To pay bonds on maturity date.		

An issuer may redeem some or all of its outstanding bonds before maturity by calling them. Or bonds may be purchased in the market and retired. In either case, the accounting is the same. Assume that on January 1, 1996, Carr calls bonds totaling $10,000 of the $100,000 face value bonds in Illustration 15.5 at 103, or $10,300. Accrued interest, if any, will be added to the price. In this example, however, assume that the interest due on this date has been paid. A look at the last column on the line dated 12/31/95 in Illustration 15.5 reveals that the carrying value of the bonds is $102,723, which consists of Bonds Payable of $100,000 and Premium on Bonds Payable of $2,723. Since 10% of the bond issue is being redeemed, 10% must be removed from each of these two accounts. A loss is incurred for the excess of the price paid for the bonds, $10,300, over their carrying value, $10,272. The required entry is:

1996				
Jan.	1	Bonds Payable	10,000	
		Premium on Bonds Payable ($2,723 ÷ 10)	272	
		Loss on Bond Redemption ($10,272 − $10,300)	28	
		Cash		10,300
		To record bonds redeemed.		

According to *FASB Statement No. 4,* gains and losses from **voluntary early** retirement of bonds are extraordinary items, if material. Such gains and losses are reported in the income statement, net of their tax effects, as described in Chapter 15.

Serial Bonds

To avoid the burden of redeeming an entire bond issue at one time, **serial bonds** may be issued that mature over several dates. Assume that on June 30, 1989, Jasper Company issued $100,000 face value, 12% serial bonds at 100. Interest is payable each year on June 30 and December 31. A total of $20,000 of the bonds mature each year starting on June 30, 1994. Jasper has a calendar-year accounting period. Entries required for 1994 for interest expense and maturing debt are:

1994				
June	30	Bond Interest Expense ($100,000 × 0.12 × ½)	6,000	
		Cash		6,000
		To record interest payment.		
	30	Serial Bonds Payable	20,000	
		Cash		20,000
		To record retirement of serial debt.		
Dec.	31	Bond Interest Expense ($80,000 × 0.12 × ½)	4,800	
		Cash		4,800
		To record payment of semiannual interest expense.		

Note that interest expense for the last six months of 1994 is calculated only on the remaining outstanding debt ($100,000 original issue less the $20,000 that matured on June 30, 1994). Each year after the amount of bonds maturing that year is retired, interest expense decreases proportionately. The $20,000 amount maturing the next year is reported as a current liability on each year-end balance sheet. The remaining debt is a long-term liability.

Bond Redemption or Sinking Funds

Bond investors are naturally concerned about the safety of their investments. They fear the company may default on paying the entire principal at the maturity date. This concern has led to the inclusion of provisions in some bond indentures that require companies to make periodic payments to a bond redemption fund, often called a sinking fund. These payments are used by the fund trustee (usually a bank) to redeem a stated amount of bonds annually and pay the accrued bond interest. The trustee determines which bonds are to be called and uses the cash deposited in the fund only to redeem these bonds and pay their accrued interest.

To illustrate, assume Hand Company has 12% coupon bonds outstanding that pay interest on March 31 and September 30 and were issued at face value. The bond indenture requires that Hand pay a trustee the sum of $53,000 each September 30. The trustee is to use the funds to call $50,000 of Hand's bonds (assuming no call premium) and to pay $3,000 accrued interest on bonds called. The entry for the payment to the trustee is:

Sept.	30	Sinking Fund.	53,000	
		Cash		53,000
		To record payment to trustee of required deposit.		

The trustee calls $50,000 of bonds, pays for the bonds and accrued interest, and notifies Hand. The trustee also bills Hand for its fee and expenses incurred of $325. Assuming no interest has been recorded on these bonds for the period ended September 30, the entries are:

Sept.	30	Bonds Payable.	50,000	
		Bond Interest Expense	3,000	
		Sinking Fund.		53,000
		To record bond redemption and interest paid by trustee.		
	30	Sinking Fund Expense	325	
		Cash		325
		To record trustee fee and expenses.		

If a balance exists in the Sinking Fund account at year-end, it is included in a category labeled "Investments" or "Other Assets" on the balance sheet. The $50,000 of bonds that must be retired during the coming year usually is described as "Current maturity of long-term debt" and reported as a current liability on the balance sheet.

The existence of a sinking fund does not necessarily mean that the company has created a retained earnings appropriation entitled "Appropriation for Bonded Indebtedness." A sinking fund usually is contractual (required by the bond indenture), and an appropriation of retained earnings is simply an announcement by the board of directors that dividend payments will be limited over the term of the bonds. The former requires cash to be paid in to a trustee, and the latter is a restriction of retained earnings available for dividends to owners. Also, even if the indenture does not require a sinking fund, the corporation may decide to (1) pay into a sinking fund and not appropriate retained earnings, (2) appropriate retained earnings and not pay into a sinking fund, (3) do neither, or (4) do both.

Convertible Bonds

A company may add to the attractiveness of its bonds by giving the bondholders the option to **convert** the bonds to shares of the issuer's common stock. The conversions of convertible bonds are accounted for by treating the carrying value of bonds surrendered as the capital contributed for shares issued.

Suppose a company has $10,000 face value of bonds outstanding. Each $1,000 bond is convertible into 50 shares of the issuer's $10 par value common stock. On May 1, when the carrying value of the bonds was $9,800, all of the bonds were presented for conversion. The entry required is:

May	1	Bonds Payable	10,000	
		Discount on Bonds Payable		200
		Common Stock ($10,000 ÷ $1,000 = 10 bonds;		
		10 bonds × 50 shares × $10 par)		5,000
		Paid-In Capital in Excess of Par Value—Common		4,800
		To record bonds converted to common stock.		

The entry eliminates the $9,800 book value of the bonds from the accounts by debiting Bonds Payable for $10,000 and crediting Discount on Bonds Payable for $200. Common Stock is credited for the par value of the 500 shares issued (500 shares × $10 par). The excess amount ($4,800) is credited to Paid-In Capital in Excess of Par Value—Common.

BOND INVESTMENTS

Objective 8

Prepare journal entries for bond investments

Companies may purchase bonds as either short-term or long-term investments. Usually, companies make short-term investments in bonds to earn income on what might otherwise be idle cash. These investments may yield a higher return than other available alternatives. Long-term investments in bonds are usually made for reasons other than a return on idle cash. Sometimes companies invest on a long-term basis in other companies to guarantee needed raw materials; or, a company could become a dealer or distributor of another company's products. In any event, the most common reason for long-term investments is to establish a long-term relationship between two companies.

When short-term bond investments are marketable (readily salable), accountants consider them as a temporary use of cash available for operations and report them as current assets. Long-term investments are reported in the investments section of the balance sheet below current assets, whether they are marketable or not.

To aid in assessing the risk of various bond investments, the evaluations of bond rating services may be used. The two leading bond rating services are Moody's Investors Service and Standard & Poor's Corporation. The ratings used by these services are:

	Moody's	Standard & Poor's
Highest quality to upper medium	Aaa	AAA
	Aa	AA
	A	A
Medium to speculative	Baa	BBB
	Ba	BB
	B	B
Poor to lowest quality	Caa	CCC
	Ca	CC
	C	C
In default, value is questionable		DDD
		DD
		D

Junk bonds are normally rated at Ba (Moody's) and BB (Standard & Poor's) or below. As a company's prospects change over time, the ratings of its outstanding bonds will normally change because of the higher or lower probability that the company can pay the interest and principal on the bonds when due. A severe recession may cause many companies' bond ratings to decline.

Bond prices are quoted in certain newspapers. For instance, Citicorp's bonds were recently quoted as follows in *The Wall Street Journal:*

Issue (Rating: Moody's/S&P)	Coupon	Maturity	Price	Change	Yield	Change
Citicorp (Baa/A)	9.000	04/15/99	80.799	0.010	12.800	unch

The information indicates that the bonds are rated Baa by Moody's and A by Standard & Poor's. Thus, the two rating services differ slightly as to the risk of the bonds. The bonds carry a coupon rate of 9%. The bonds mature on April 15, 1999. The current price is $80.799 per hundred, or $807.99 for a $1,000 bond. The price the preceding day was $80.789, since the change was 0.010, or 80.799 compared to 80.789. The current price yields a return to investors of 12.8%, which is unchanged from the preceding day because the change in price was so small. As the market rate of interest changes from day to day, the market price of the bonds varies inversely. Thus, if the market rate of interest declines, the market price of bonds increases, and vice versa.

Short-Term Bond Investments

Short-term bond investments are recorded in a single account at cost, which includes the price paid for the bonds and often includes a broker's commission. These investments are listed among the current assets on the balance sheet. As explained earlier, if investors purchase bonds between interest dates, they pay the accrued interest and collect the amount paid later when they receive the semiannual interest. **Premiums and discounts on short-term bond investments are not amortized because the length of time the bonds will be held is not known.**

To illustrate, assume that on May 31, 1994, Bay Company purchased as a short-term investment $10,000 face value, 12% bonds of Ace Company at 102, plus $100 of accrued interest from April 30. A $70 broker's commission was also paid. The entry required is:

1994				
May	31	Temporary Investments (or Marketable Securities) ($10,200 + $70)	10,270	
		Bond Interest Receivable ($10,000 × 0.12 × 1/12)	100	
		Cash		10,370
		To record bonds purchased.		

On September 30, 1994, Bay sold the Ace bonds at 103.5, plus accrued interest of $500. A $70 broker's commission was charged on the sale. Before computing the gain or loss on the sale, the broker's commission is deducted from selling price to compute net proceeds to the seller ($10,350 − $70 = $10,280). The gain or loss is the difference between net proceeds and cost. In this example, the gain is $10, or $10,280 − $10,270. Note that accrued interest does not affect the amount of gain or loss because it is paid for by the purchaser. The entry to record the sale is:

1994				
Sept.	30	Cash ($10,350 + $500 − $70)	10,780	
		Temporary Investments		10,270
		Bond Interest Receivable (from above entry)		100
		Bond Interest Revenue ($10,000 × 0.12 × 4/12)		400
		Gain on Sale of Temporary Investments		10
		To record sale of temporary investments.		

The purchaser will receive the semiannual interest check from Ace to cover the $500 of accrued interest paid to Bay. Bay records only $400 of the $500 of interest received as interest revenue, since it held the bonds for only four months.

Long-Term Bond Investments

Long-term investments in bonds also are recorded in a single account at cost, which includes any premium or discount. These investments are listed in an "Investments" category among the assets on the balance sheet. A premium or discount on long-term bond investments is amortized, although it is not recorded in a separate account by the investing company as it is by the issuing company.

Bonds Purchased at a Discount   Assume that on June 30, 1994, Mann Company purchased as a long-term investment $100,000 face value of Carr Company's 12% bonds for $95,233 (including broker's commission), a price that yields 14%. These bonds are the same Carr Company bonds that were described in Illustration 15.4. The entry to record the purchase is:

1994				
June	30	Bond Investments	95,233	
		Cash		95,233
		To record bonds purchased at a discount.		

Note that the debit to the Bond Investments account included the broker's commission paid to acquire the bonds.

Since Mann intends to hold the bonds to maturity, the discount is amortized over the remaining life of the bonds. Although either the straight-line method or the interest method could be used to amortize the discount, we are using the interest method. Under this method, interest revenue on bonds purchased by

ILLUSTRATION 15.6

Discount Amortization Schedule for Bond Investments

(A) Interest Payment Date	(B) Cash Debit ($100,000 × 0.12 × ½)	(C) Bond Interest Revenue Credit (E × 0.14 × ½)	(D) Bond Invest- ments Debit (C − B)	(E) Carrying Value of Bond Investments (previous balance in E + D)
Purchase price				$ 95,233
12/31/94	$ 6,000	$ 6,666	$ 666	95,899
6/30/95	6,000	6,713	713	96,612
12/31/95	6,000	6,763	763	97,375
6/30/96	6,000	6,816	816	98,191
12/31/96	6,000	6,873	873	99,064
6/30/97	6,000	6,936*	936	100,000
	$36,000	$40,767	$4,767	

* Includes rounding difference.

Mann is computed in the same manner as the issuer's interest expense—the bond price is multiplied by the effective interest rate per period. To compute Mann's discount amortization, we can use a similar procedure to that used for Carr—compute the difference between interest revenue (expense) and cash received (paid). The first period's interest revenue is $6,666, or $95,233 × 0.14 × ½. The cash received is $6,000, or $100,000 × 0.12 × ½. The discount amortized is $666, or $6,666 − $6,000. If Mann has a calendar-year accounting period, the required entry is:

```
1994
Dec. 31  Cash . . . . . . . . . . . . . . . . . . . . . . . .      6,000
         Bond Investments . . . . . . . . . . . . . . . .        666
             Bond Interest Revenue . . . . . . . . . . . .                 6,666
         To record accrued bond interest revenue.
```

Note that in the entry, the amount added to the Bond Investments account is equal to the discount amortized on the issuer's books. The discount is amortized even though it is not set up in a separate account on the investor's books. The original discount is $4,767, and this amount must be included in bond interest revenue on Mann's books during the life of the bonds. Illustration 15.6 shows how the $4,767 is added to periodic interest revenue and to Bond Investments. The debits gradually increase the Bond Investments account balance to the face value of $100,000 by the maturity date.

Mann's December 31, 1994, balance sheet would show Bond Investments of $95,899. If Mann's fiscal year ended on November 30, the adjusting entry on that date would be the same as the December 31 entry, except all amounts would be five sixths of the December 31 amounts and Bond Interest Receivable instead of Cash would be debited.

If the straight-line method were used, discount amortization would be $795 per period, or $4,767/6. Bond interest revenue would be $6,795, or $6,000 + $795.

ILLUSTRATION 15.7

Premium Amortization Schedule for Bond Investments

(A) Interest Payment Date	(B) Cash Debit ($100,000 × 0.12 × ½)	(C) Bond Interest Revenue Credit (E × 0.10 × ½)	(D) Bond Investments Credit (B − C)	(E) Carrying Value of Bond Investments (previous balance in E − D)
Purchase price.				$105,076
12/31/94	$ 6,000	$ 5,254	$ 746	104,330
6/30/95	6,000	5,216*	784	103,546
12/31/95	6,000	5,177	823	102,723
6/30/96	6,000	5,136	864	101,859
12/31/96	6,000	5,093	907	100,952
6/30/97	6,000	5,048	952	100,000
	$36,000	$30,924	$5,076	

* Rounded down.

Bonds Purchased at a Premium   To illustrate accounting for bonds purchased at a premium, assume that on June 30, 1994, Ladd Company paid $105,076 for $100,000 face value of 12% bonds, a price that yields 10%. Ladd has a calendar-year accounting period. These bonds are the Carr Company bonds shown in Illustration 15.5. The entry to record the purchase would be:

1994 June	30	Bond Investments . . . . Cash . . . . To record bonds purchased at a premium.	105,076	105,076

Here again, interest revenue for the first interest period can be computed by multiplying the purchase price by the effective rate: $105,076 × 0.10 × ½ = $5,254. The entry to record the $5,254 is:

1994 Dec.	31	Cash . . . . Bond Investments . . . . Bond Interest Revenue . . . . To record bond interest revenue received.	6,000	746 5,254

The premium is amortized by crediting the Bond Investments account. If bonds are held to maturity, the balance in the Bond Investments account would be gradually decreased to the maturity value of $100,000, as shown in Illustration 15.7. Bond interest revenue for the second six months can be read from Illustration 15.6, or it can be computed: ($105,076 − $746) × 0.10 × ½ = $5,216.

ETHICS	The Rawlings brothers inherited 300,000 shares (30%) of the common stock of the

ETHICS

A CLOSER LOOK

The Rawlings brothers inherited 300,000 shares (30%) of the common stock of the Rawlings Furniture Company from their father, who had founded the company 55 years earlier. One brother served as president of the company, and the other two brothers served as vice presidents. The company, which produced a line of fine furniture that was sold nationwide, earned an average of $4 million per year. Located in Jamesville, New York, the company had provided steady employment for approximately 10% of the city's population. The city had benefited from the revenues the company attracted to the area and from the generous gifts provided by the father.

The remainder of the common stock was widely held and was traded in the over-the-counter market. No other stockholder held more than 4% of the stock. The stock had recently traded at $30 per share. The company has $10 million of 10% bonds outstanding, which mature in 15 years.

The brothers enjoyed the money they received from the company, but did not enjoy the work. They also were frustrated by the fact that they did not own a controlling interest (more than 50%) of the company. If they had a controlling interest, they could make important decisions without obtaining the agreement of the other stockholders.

With the assistance of a New York City brokerage house, the brothers decided to pursue a plan that could increase their wealth. The company would offer to buy back a certain number of shares of common stock at $40 per share. These shares would then be canceled, and the Rawlings brothers would have a controlling interest. The stock buyback would be financed by issuing 10-year, 18%, high-interest bonds (called junk bonds). The brokerage house had located some financial institutions that would be willing to buy the bonds. The interest payments on the junk bonds would be $3 million per year. The brothers thought the company could make these payments unless the country entered a recession. If need be, wage increases could be severely restricted or eliminated and the company's pension plan could be terminated. If the junk bonds could be paid at maturity, the brothers would own the controlling interest in what could be an extremely valuable company. If the interest payments could not be met or if the junk bonds were defaulted at maturity, the company could eventually be forced to liquidate. The risks are high, but so are the potential rewards.

If another buyer entered the picture at this point and bid an even higher amount for the stock, the brothers could sell their shares and exit the company. Two of the brothers hoped that another buyer might bid as much as $50 per share so they could sell their shares and pursue other interests. The changes a new buyer might make are unpredictable at this point.

Required

a. What motivates the brothers to pursue this new strategy?

b. Are the brothers the only ones assuming the risks?

c. How will workers, the city, the holders of the original bond issue, and the other present stockholders be affected if the junk bonds are issued and are then defaulted?

d. How might these parties (stakeholders) be affected if a new buyer outbids the management?

e. What ethical considerations are involved?

If we used the straight-line method, the periodic amortization of the premium would be $846, or $5,076/6. Interest revenue would be a constant semiannual amount of $5,154, or $6,000 − $846.

Sale of Bond Investments

When a company sells its bond investments, usually a gain or loss must be recorded. The difference between the price received and the carrying value of the bonds on the date they are sold determines whether the bonds are sold at a gain or a loss. Suppose that on June 30, 1996, Ladd Company sold all of its bonds, which had a carrying value of $101,859 (Illustration 15.7), for $102,500 less a $500 broker's commission. The required entry is:

1996					
June	30	Cash	102,000	
		Bond Investments		101,859
		Gain on Sale of Bond Investments		141
		To record sale of bond investments.		

Since the bond sale occurred on an interest payment date, the payment of interest had already been recorded, and no accrued interest existed. Ladd's gain (or loss, if one had occurred) on the sale is reported on the income statement as a nonoperating item, not as an extraordinary item.

Valuation of Bond Investments

Short-term bond investments are reported at cost (or sometimes at lower-of-cost-or-market). Long-term bond investments are carried and reported at amortized cost. Amortized cost is equal to acquisition cost plus discount amortized or less premium amortized. An exception exists when a substantial, permanent decline in market value occurs. Long-term bond investments are then written down by debiting an account called Loss on Market Decline of Bond Investments and crediting Bond Investments.

Once long-term bond investments have been written down, traditional accounting conservatism dictates that they may not be written up, not even to their original cost, if market price recovers. The written-down amount serves as the basis for computing gain or loss when the bonds are sold.

Chapter 16 discusses stock investments of corporations. Some of these investments are for a small percentage of the outstanding shares and some are for a "controlling interest" of more than 50% of the outstanding shares. In Chapter 16, you will learn new terms such as **parent company** and **subsidiary company.**

UNDERSTANDING THE LEARNING OBJECTIVES

1. Describe the features of bonds and tell how bonds differ from shares of stock.
   - A bond is a liability (with a maturity date) that bears interest that is deductible in computing both net income and taxable income.
   - A stock is a unit of ownership on which a dividend is paid only if declared, and dividends are not deductible in determining net income or taxable income.
   - Bonds may be secured or unsecured, registered or unregistered, callable, and/or convertible.

2. List the advantages and disadvantages of financing with long-term debt and prepare examples showing how financial leverage is employed.
   - Advantages include stockholders retaining control of the company, tax deductibility of interest, and possible creation of favorable financial leverage.
   - Disadvantages include having to make a fixed interest payment each period, reduction in a company's ability to withstand a major loss, possible limitations on dividends and future borrowings, and possible reduction in earnings per share caused by unfavorable financial leverage.

3. Prepare journal entries for bonds issued at face value.
   □ If bonds are issued at face value on an interest date, no accrued interest is recorded.
   □ If bonds are issued between interest dates, accrued interest must be recorded.

4. Explain how interest rates affect bond prices and what causes a bond to sell at a premium or discount.
   □ If the market rate is lower than the contract rate, the bonds will sell for more than their face value, and a premium will be recorded.
   □ If the market rate is higher than the contract rate, the bonds will sell for less than their face value, and a discount will be recorded.

5. Apply the concept of present value to compute the price of a bond.
   □ The present value of the principal plus the present value of the interest payments is equal to the price of the bond.
   □ The contract rate of interest is used to determine the amount of future cash interest payments.
   □ The effective rate of interest is used to discount the future payment of principal and of interest back to the present value.

6. Prepare journal entries for bonds issued at a discount or premium.
   □ When bonds are issued, Cash is debited, and Bonds Payable is credited. If the bonds were issued at a discount, Discount on Bonds Payable is also debited. If the bonds were issued at a premium, Premium on Bonds Payable is also credited. If the bonds are issued between interest dates, Bond Interest Payable is also credited.
   □ Any premium or discount must be amortized over the period the bonds are outstanding.
   □ Under the effective interest rate method, interest expense for any period is equal to the effective (market) rate of interest at date of issuance times the carrying value of the bond at the beginning of that interest period.
   □ Under the straight-line method of amortization, an equal amount of discount or premium is allocated to each month the bonds are outstanding.

7. Prepare journal entries for bond redemptions and bond conversions.
   □ When bonds are redeemed before they mature, a loss or gain (an extraordinary item, if material) on bond redemption may occur.
   □ A bond sinking fund might be required in the bond indenture.
   □ Bonds may be convertible into shares of stock. The carrying value of the bonds is considered to be the capital contributed for shares of stock issued.

8. Prepare journal entries for bond investments.
   □ When bonds are purchased as a long-term investment, Bond Investments is debited, and Cash is credited.
   □ Premiums and discounts on short-term bond investments are not amortized because the length of time the bonds will be held is not known.
   □ Premiums or discounts on bond investments are not recorded in a separate account. Instead, they affect the amount recorded in the Bond Investments account.

☐ Premiums and discounts on long-term bond investments are amortized in a manner similar to that used for bonds payable.

9. Explain future value and present value concepts and make the required calculations (Appendix).

☐ The future value of an investment is the amount to which a sum of money invested today will grow in a stated time period at a specified interest rate.

☐ Present value is the current worth of a future cash receipt and is the reciprocal of future value. To discount future receipts is to bring them back to their present values.

APPENDIX: FUTURE VALUE AND PRESENT VALUE

Objective 9

Explain future value and present value concepts and make required calculations

The concepts of interest, future value, and present value are widely applied in business decision making. Therefore, accountants need to understand these concepts to properly record certain business transactions.

THE TIME VALUE OF MONEY

The concept of the time value of money stems from the logical preference for a dollar today rather than a dollar at any future date. Most individuals would prefer having a dollar today rather than at some future date because (1) the risk exists that the future dollar will never be received; and (2) if the dollar is on hand now, it can be invested, resulting in an increase in total dollars possessed at that future date.

Most business decisons involve a comparison of cash flows in and out of the company. To be useful in decision making, such comparisons must be in terms of dollars of the same point in time. That is, the dollars held now must be accumulated or rolled forward, or future dollars must be discounted or brought back to the present before comparisons are valid. Such comparisons involve future value and present value concepts.

FUTURE VALUE

The future value or worth of any investment is the amount to which a sum of money invested today will grow in a stated time period at a specified interest rate. The interest involved may be simple interest or compound interest. Simple interest is interest on principal only. For example, $1,000 invested today for two years at 12% simple interest will grow to $1,240 since interest is $120 per year. The principal of $1,000, plus 2 × $120, is equal to $1,240. Compound interest is interest on principal **and** on interest of prior periods. For example, $1,000 invested for two years at 12% compounded annually will grow to $1,254.40 as shown below.

Principal or present value	$1,000.00
Interest, year 1 = $1,000 × 0.12 =	120.00
Value at end of year 1	$1,120.00
Interest, year 2 = $1,120 × 0.12 =	134.40
Value at end of year 2 (future value)	$1,254.40

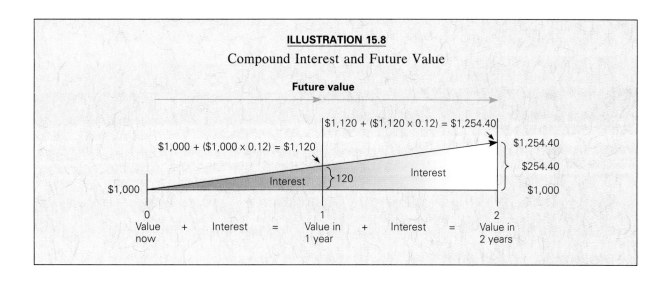

ILLUSTRATION 15.8

Compound Interest and Future Value

Illustration 15.8 graphically portrays these computations of future worth and shows how $1,000 grows to $1,254.40 with a 12% interest rate compounded annually. The effect of compounding is $14.40—the interest in the second year that was based on the interest computed for the first year, or $120 × 0.12 = $14.40.

The task of computing the future worth to which any invested amount will grow at a given rate for a stated period is aided by the use of interest tables. An example is Table G.1 in Appendix G at the end of this text. To use the Appendix G tables, first determine the number of compounding periods involved. A compounding period may be any length of time, such as a day, a month, a quarter, a half-year, or a year, but normally not more than a year. The number of compounding periods is equal to the number of years in the life of the investment times the number of compoundings per year. Five years compounded annually is five periods, five years compounded quarterly is 20 periods, and so on.

Next, determine the interest rate per compounding period. Interest rates are usually quoted in annual terms; in fact, federal law requires statement of the interest rate in annual terms in some situations. Divide the annual rate by the number of compounding periods per year to get the proper rate per period. Only with an annual compounding will the annual rate be the rate per period. All other cases involve a lower rate. For example, if the annual rate is 12% and interest is compounded monthly, the rate per period (one month) will be 1%.

To use the tables, find the number of periods involved in the Period column. Move across the table to the right, stopping in the column headed by the Interest Rate per Period, which yields a number called a **factor. The factor shows the amount to which an investment of $1 will grow for the periods and the rate involved.** To compute future worth of the investment, multiply the number of dollars in the given situation by this factor. For example, suppose your parents tell you that they will invest $8,000 at 12% for four years and give you the amount to which this investment grows if you graduate from college in four years. How much will you receive at the end of four years if the interest rate is 12% compounded annually? How much will you receive if the interest rate is 12% compounded quarterly?

To calculate these amounts, look at Appendix G, Table G.1. In the intersection of the 4 period row and the 12% column, you find the factor 1.57352. Multiplying this factor by $8,000 yields $12,588.16, the answer to the first question. To answer the second question, look at the intersection of the 16 period row and the 3%

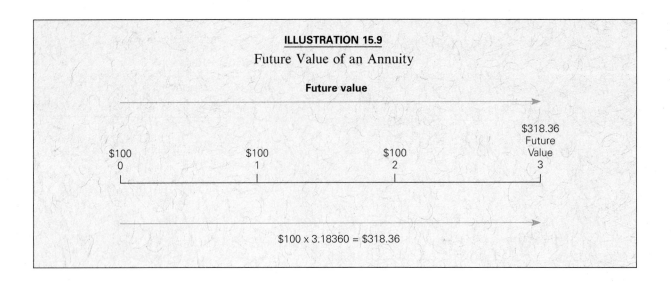

ILLUSTRATION 15.9

Future Value of an Annuity

Future value

$100
0

$100
1

$100
2

$318.36
Future
Value
3

$100 x 3.18360 = $318.36

column. The factor is 1.60471, and the value of your investment is $12,837.68. The more frequent compounding would add $12,837.68 − $12,588.16 = $249.52 to the value of your investment. The reason for this difference in amounts is that 12% compounded quarterly is a higher rate than 12% compounded annually.

Future Value of an Annuity

An annuity is a series of equal cash flows (often called **rents**) spaced equally in time. The semiannual interest payments received on a bond investment are a common example of an annuity. Assume that $100 will be received at the end of each of the next three semiannual periods. The interest rate is 6% per semiannual period. It is possible, using Appendix G, Table G.1, to find the future value of each of the $100 receipts as follows:

Future value (after three periods) of $100
   received at the **end** of the—
First period: 1.12360 × $100 = $112.36
Second period: 1.06000 × 100 = 106.00
Third period: 1.00000 × 100 = 100.00
Total future value $318.36

Such a procedure would become quite tedious if the annuity consisted of many receipts. Fortunately, tables are available to calculate the total future value directly. See Appendix G, Table G.2. For the annuity described above, one single factor can be identified by looking at the 3 period row and 6% column. The factor is 3.18360, and when multiplied by $100, yields $318.36, which is the same answer as above. Illustration 15.9 graphically presents the future value of an annuity.

PRESENT VALUE

Present value is the current worth of a future cash receipt and is the reciprocal of future value. In future value, a sum of money is possessed now, and its future value must be calculated. In present value, rights to future cash receipts are possessed now, and their current worth is to be calculated. Future cash receipts are discounted to find their present values. **To discount future receipts is to bring them back to their present values.**

Assume that you have the right to receive $1,000 in one year. If the appropriate interest rate is 12% compounded annually, what is the present value of this $1,000 future cash receipt? You know that the present value is less than $1,000 because $1,000 due in one year is not worth $1,000 today. You also know that the $1,000 due in one year is equal to some amount, P, plus interest on P at 12% for one year. Thus, $P + 0.12P = \$1,000$, or $1.12P = \$1,000$. Dividing $1,000 by 1.12, you get $892.86; this amount is the present value of your future $1,000. If the $1,000 was due in two years, you would find its present value by dividing $892.86 by 1.12, which equals $797.20. Portrayed graphically, present value looks similar to future value, except for the direction of the arrows (Illustration 15.10).

Table G.3 (Appendix G) contains present value factors for combinations of a number of periods and interest rates. Table G.3 is used in the same manner as Table G.1. For example, the present value of $1,000 due in four years at 16% compounded annually is $552.29, computed as $1,000 × 0.55229. The 0.55229 is the present value factor found in the intersection of the 4 period row and the 16% column.

As another example, suppose that you wish to have $4,000 in three years to pay for a vacation in Europe. If your investment will increase at a 20% rate compounded quarterly, how much should you invest now? To find the amount, you would use the present value factor found in Table G.3, 12 period row, 5% column. This factor is 0.55684, which means that an investment of about 55½ cents today would grow to $1 in 12 periods at 5% per period. To have $4,000 at the end of three years, you must invest 4,000 times this factor (0.55684), or $2,227.36.

Present Value of an Annuity

The semiannual interest payments on a bond are a common example of an annuity. An illustration will be used to show how to calculate the present value of an annuity. Assume that $100 will be received at the end of each of the next three semiannual periods. The interest rate is 6% per semiannual period. By using Table G.3 (Appendix G), you can find the present value of each of the three $100 payments as follows:

```
Present value of $100 due in:
  1 period:  0.94340 × $100 = $ 94.34
  2 periods: 0.89000 ×  100 =   89.00
  3 periods: 0.83962 ×  100 =   83.96
Total present value . . . . .  $267.30
```

Such a procedure could become quite tedious if the annuity consisted of a large number of payments. Fortunately, tables are also available showing the present values of an annuity of $1 per period for varying interest rates and periods. See Appendix G, Table G.4. For the annuity described above, a single factor can be obtained from the table to represent the present value of an annuity of $1 per period for three (semiannual) periods at 6% per (semiannual) period. This factor is 2.67301; it is equal to the sum of the present value factors for $1 due in one period, $1 in two periods, and $1 in three periods found in Appendix G, Table G.3. When this factor is multiplied by $100, the number of dollars in each payment, it yields the present value of the annuity, $267.30. Illustration 15.11 graphically presents the present value of this annuity and shows that we find the present value of the three $100 cash flows by multiplying the $100 by a present value of an annuity factor, 2.67301.

Suppose you won a prize in a lottery that awarded you your choice of receiving $10,000 at the end of each of the next five years or $35,000 cash today. You believe you can earn interest on invested cash at 15% per year. Which option

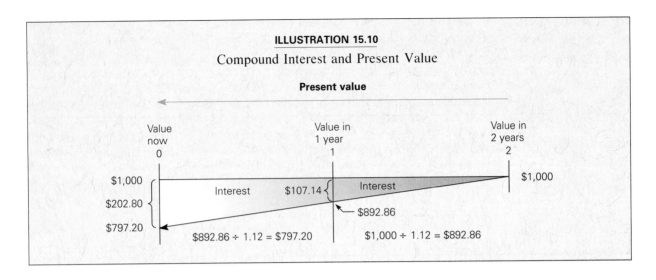

ILLUSTRATION 15.10

Compound Interest and Present Value

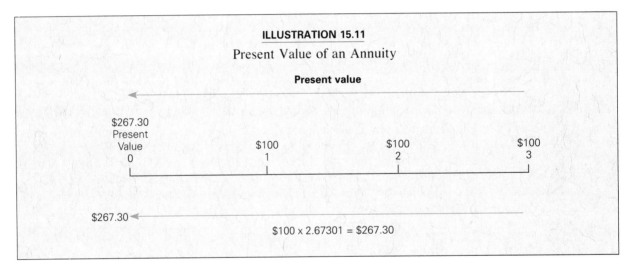

ILLUSTRATION 15.11

Present Value of an Annuity

should you choose? To answer the question, you should compute the present value of an annuity of $10,000 per period for five years at 15%. The present value is $33,521.60, or $10,000 × 3.35216. You should accept the immediate payment of $35,000 since it has the larger present value.

DEMONSTRATION PROBLEM 15–A

Jackson Company issued $100,000 face value of 15%, 20-year bonds on April 30, 1994. The bonds are dated April 30, 1994, call for semiannual interest payments on April 30 and October 31, and are issued to yield 16% (8% per period).

Required   *a.*   Compute the amount received for the bonds.

   b.   Prepare an amortization schedule. Enter data in the schedule for only the first two interest periods. Use the interest method.

   c.   Prepare journal entries to record issuance of the bonds, the first six months' interest expense on the bonds, the adjustment needed on December 31, 1994 (assuming Jackson's accounting year ends on that date), and the second six months' interest expense on April 30, 1995.

SOLUTION TO DEMONSTRATION PROBLEM 15–A

a.

Price received:
Present value of principal: $100,000 × 0.04603
  (see Appendix G, Table G.3, 40 period row, 8% column) . . . . $ 4,603
Present value of interest: $7,500 × 11.92461
  (see Appendix G, Table G.4, 40 period row, 8% column) 89,435
Total $94,038

b.

(A) Interest Payment Date	(B) Bond Interest Expense Debit (E × 0.16 × ½)	(C) Cash Credit ($100,000 × 0.15 × ½)	(D) Discount on Bonds Payable Credit (B − C)	(E) Carrying Value of Bonds Payable (previous balance in E + D)
Issue price				$94,038
10/31/94	$7,523	$7,500	$23	94,061
4/30/95	7,525	7,500	25	94,086

c.

JACKSON COMPANY
GENERAL JOURNAL

1994				
Apr.	30	Cash	94,038	
		Discount on Bonds Payable	5,962	
		Bonds Payable		100,000
		Issued $100,000 face value of 20-year, 15% bonds to yield 16%.		
Oct.	31	Bond Interest Expense	7,523	
		Discount on Bonds Payable		23
		Cash		7,500
		Paid semiannual bond interest expense.		
Dec.	31	Bond Interest Expense ($7,525 × ⅓)	2,508	
		Discount on Bonds Payable		8
		Bond Interest Payable ($7,500 × ⅓)		2,500
		To record accrual of two months' interest expense.		
1995				
Apr.	30	Bond Interest Payable.	2,500	
		Bond Interest Expense ($7,525 × ⅔)	5,017	
		Discount on Bonds Payable		17
		Cash		7,500
		Paid semiannual bond interest expense.		

DEMONSTRATION PROBLEM 15–B

On May 31, 1994, Martin Company purchased $10,000 face value of 8%, 10-year bonds issued by Shane Company. The bonds mature on May 31, 2004, call for semiannual interest payments on May 31 and November 30, and were issued for cash of $8,754, a price that yields an effective rate of 10%. The bonds are considered a long-term investment by Martin Company, which has a December 31 accounting year-end.

Required   Prepare journal entries to record the investment in the Shane bonds, to record the interest collected on November 30, 1994, and to adjust the accounts on December 31, 1994. Use the effective interest rate method.

SOLUTION TO DEMONSTRATION PROBLEM 15–B

MARTIN COMPANY
GENERAL JOURNAL

1994					
May	31	Bond Investments		8,754	
		Cash			8,754
		To record purchase of $10,000 face value of bonds.			
Nov.	30	Cash ($10,000 × 0.08 × ½)		400	
		Bond Investments		38	
		Bond Interest Revenue ($8,754 × 0.10 × ½)			438
		To record semiannual interest revenue.			
Dec.	31	Bond Interest Receivable ($10,000 × 0.08 × ¹⁄₁₂)		67	
		Bond Investments		6	
		Bond Interest Revenue [($8,754 + $38) × 0.10 × ¹⁄₁₂]			73
		To accrue one month's interest revenue.			

NEW TERMS

Annuity   A series of equal cash flows spaced in time. *720*

Bearer bond   See Unregistered bond.

Bond   A long-term debt, or liability, owed by its issuer. A **bond certificate** is a negotiable instrument and is the formal, physical evidence of the debt owed. *692*

Bond indenture   The contract or loan agreement under which bonds are issued. *693*

Bond redemption (or sinking) fund   A fund used to bring about gradual redemption of a bond issue. *709*

Callable bond   A bond that gives the issuer the right to call (buy back) the bond before its maturity date. *695*

Call premium   The price paid in excess of face value that the issuer of bonds must pay to redeem (call) bonds before their maturity date. *695*

Carrying value (of bonds)   The face value of bonds minus any unamortized discount or plus any unamortized premium. Sometimes referred to as **net liability** on the bonds when used for bonds payable. *703*

Compound interest   Interest calculated on the principal and on interest of prior periods. *718*

Contract rate of interest   The interest rate printed on the bond certificates and specified on the bond indenture; also called the **stated, coupon,** or **nominal rate.** *700*

Convertible bond   A bond that may be exchanged for shares of stock of the issuing corporation at the bondholders' option. *695, 710*

Coupon bond   A bond not registered as to interest; it carries detachable coupons that are to be clipped and presented for payment of interest due. *694*

Debenture bond   An unsecured bond backed only by the general creditworthiness of its issuer. *694*

Discount (on bonds)   Amount a bond sells for below face value. *700*

Effective interest rate method (interest method)   A procedure for calculating periodic interest expense (or revenue) in which the first period's interest is computed by multiplying the carrying value of bonds payable (bond investments) by the market rate at the issue date. The difference between computed interest expense (revenue) and the interest paid (received), based on the contract rate times face value, is the discount or premium amortized for the period. Computations for subsequent periods are based on carrying value at the beginning of the period. *705*

Face value   Principal amount, or maturity amount or value, of a bond. *692*

Favorable financial leverage   An increase in EPS and rate of return on stockholders' equity resulting from earning a higher rate of return on borrowed funds than the fixed cost of such funds. **Unfavorable financial leverage** results when the cost of borrowed funds exceeds the income they generate, resulting in decreased income to stockholders. *695, 697*

Future value or worth   The amount to which a sum of money invested today will grow in a stated time period at a specified interest rate. *718*

Interest method See Effective interest rate method. *705*

Junk bonds High-interest rate, high-risk bonds that were issued in the 1980s to finance corporate restructurings. *695*

Market interest rate The minimum rate of interest investors will accept on bonds of a particular risk category. Also called **effective rate** or **yield.** *700*

Mortgage A legal claim (lien) on specific property that gives the bondholder the right to possess the pledged property if the company fails to make required payments. A bond secured by a mortgage is called a **mortgage bond.** *694*

Premium (on bonds) Amount a bond sells for above face value. *700*

Present value The current worth of a future cash receipt(s); computed by discounting future receipts at a stipulated interest rate. *720*

Registered bond A bond with the owner's name on the bond certificate and in the register of bond owners kept by the bond issuer or its agent, the registrar. *694*

Secured bond A bond for which a company has pledged specific property to ensure its payment. *694*

Serial bonds Bonds in a given bond issue with maturities spread over several dates. *694, 708*

Simple interest Interest on principal only. *718*

Sinking fund See Bond redemption fund.

Stock warrant A right that allows the bondholder to purchase shares of common stock at a fixed price for a stated period of time. Warrants issued with long-term debt may be **detachable** or **nondetachable.** *695*

Straight-line method of amortization A procedure that, when applied to bond discount or premium, allocates an equal amount of discount or premium to each period in the life of a bond. *704*

Term bond A bond that matures on the same date as all other bonds in a given bond issue. *694*

Trading on the equity A company using its stockholders' equity as a basis for securing funds on which it pays a fixed return. *696*

Trustee Usually a bank or trust company appointed to represent the bondholders in a bond issue and to enforce the provisions of the bond indenture against the issuer. *693*

Underwriter An investment company that performs many tasks for the bond issuer in issuing bonds; may also guarantee the issuer a fixed price for the bonds. *693*

Unfavorable financial leverage Results when the cost of borrowed funds exceeds the revenue they generate; it is the reverse of **favorable financial leverage.** *697*

Unregistered (bearer) bond Ownership transfers by physical delivery. *694*

Unsecured bond A **debenture bond,** or simply a **debenture.** *694*

SELF-TEST

True-False

Indicate whether each of the following statements is true or false.

1. An unsecured bond is also called a debenture bond.

2. Callable bonds may be called at the option of the holder of the bonds.

3. Favorable financial leverage results when borrowed funds are used to increase earnings per share of common stock.

4. If the market rate of interest exceeds the contract rate, the bonds will be issued at a discount.

5. The straight-line method of amortization is the recommended method.

Multiple-Choice

Select the best answer for each of the following questions.

1. Harner Company issued $100,000 of 12% bonds on March 1, 1994. The bonds are dated January 1, 1994, and were issued at 96 plus accrued interest. The entry to record the issuance would be:

   a. Cash 98,000
       Discount on Bonds
         Payable 4,000
         Bonds Payable . .   100,000
         Bond Interest
           Payable   2,000

   b. Cash 102,000
       Bonds Payable . .   100,000
       Bond Interest
         Payable   2,000

   c. Cash 96,000
       Discount on Bonds
         Payable 4,000
         Bonds Payable . .   100,000

   d. None of the above.

2. If the bonds in (1) had been issued at 104, the entry to record the issuance would have been:

726 Part II Accounting for Assets, Liabilities, and Stockholders' Equity

a. Cash. 104,000

Bonds Payable . .   100,000

Payable   4,000

b. Cash. 102,000

Bonds Payable . .   100,000

Payable   2,000

c. Cash. 106,000

Bonds Payable . .   100,000

Payable   4,000

Expense   2,000

d. None of the above.

3. On January 1, 1994, the Alvarez Company issued $400,000 face value of 8%, 10-year bonds for cash of $328,298, a price to yield 11%. The bonds pay interest semiannually and mature on January 1, 2004. Using the effective interest rate method, the bond interest expense for the first six months of 1995 would be:

a. $36,113.

b. $18,056.

c. $32,000.

d. $16,000.

4. If the straight-line amortization method had been used in (3), the interest expense for the first six months would have been:

a. $39,170.

b. $32,000.

c. $18,000.

d. $19,585.

5. Assume that the Hanford Insurance Company bought 20% of the Alvarez bonds in (3). Assuming the discount is amortized at each interest date, the journal entry to record the receipt of the first six months of interest would be:

a. Cash. 3,200

    Bond Investments. . .   411

        Bond Interest

            Revenue   3,611

b. Cash. 3,200

        Bond Interest

            Revenue   3,200

c. Cash. 3,611

        Bond Interest

            Revenue   3,611

d. Cash. 4,022

    Bond Investments. . .   411

        Bond Interest

            Revenue   3,611

Now turn to page 733 to check your answers.

QUESTIONS

1. What are the advantages of obtaining long-term funds by the issuance of bonds rather than additional shares of capital stock? What are the disadvantages?

2. What is a bond indenture? What parties are usually associated with it? Explain why.

3. Explain what is meant by the terms *coupon, callable, convertible,* and *debenture.*

4. What is meant by the term *trading on the equity?*

5. When bonds are issued between interest dates, why should the issuing corporation receive cash equal to the amount of accrued interest (accrued since the preceding interest date) in addition to the issue price of the bonds?

6. Why might it be more accurate to describe a sinking fund as a bond redemption fund?

7. Indicate how each of the following items should be classified in a balance sheet on December 31, 1993.

    a. Cash balance in a sinking fund.

    b. Accrued interest on bonds payable.

    c. Debenture bonds payable due in 2003.

    d. Premium on bonds payable.

    e. First-mortgage bonds payable, due July 1, 1994.

    f. Discount on bonds payable.

    g. First National Bank—Interest account.

    h. Convertible bonds payable due in 1996.

8. Why is the effective interest rate method of computing periodic interest expense considered theoretically preferable to the straight-line method?

9. Why would an investor whose intent is to hold bonds to maturity pay more for the bonds than their face value?

10. Describe the amortization of a premium or discount on a short-term bond investment.

11. Describe the amortization of a premium or discount on a long-term bond investment.

12. Under what circumstances should bond investments be written down below their carrying value?

13. *Real world question* Refer to "A Broader Perspective" on page 696. Why are so many of the companies mentioned in trouble?

14. *Real world question* The 1989 annual report of Fuqua Industries contained the following paragraph in the notes to the financial statements:

    The 9⅞% Senior Subordinated Debentures are redeemable at the option of Fuqua at 103.635% of the principal amount plus accrued interest if redeemed prior to March 15, 1990, and at decreasing prices thereafter. Mandatory sinking fund payments of $3,000,000 (which Fuqua may increase to $6,000,000 annually) began in 1982 and are intended to retire, at par plus accrued interest, 75% of the issue prior to maturity.

Answer the following questions about this quote:
a. What does the term *debentures* mean?
b. How much is the call premium initially? Does this premium decrease over time?
c. Under what circumstances might Fuqua want to increase the sinking fund payments?

EXERCISES

Exercise 15–1
Record issuance of bonds, adjusting entry, and payment of interest
(L.O. 3)

On September 30, 1994, Chico Company issued $480,000 face value of 12%, 10-year bonds dated August 31, 1994, at 100, plus accrued interest. Interest is paid semiannually on February 28 and August 31. Chico's accounting year ends on December 31. Prepare journal entries to record the issuance of these bonds, the accrual of interest at year-end, and the payment of the first interest coupon.

Exercise 15–2
Record bond investments, adjusting entry, and collection of interest
(L.O. 8)

Benz Company, with an accounting year ending on December 31, bought $20,000 face value of the bonds in Exercise 15–1 on September 30. Prepare entries to record the purchase, the necessary year-end adjusting entry, and the receipt of the first six months' interest.

Exercise 15–3
Compute bond interest expense; show how bond price was determined
(L.O. 4–6)

On December 31, 1993, Stillwagon Company issued $400,000 face value of 8%, 10-year bonds for cash of $328,298, a price to yield 11%. The bonds pay interest semiannually and mature on December 31, 2003.

a. State which is higher, the market rate of interest or the contract rate.
b. Compute the bond interest expense for the first six months of 1993, using the interest method.
c. Show how the $328,298 price must have been determined.

Exercise 15–4
Record bond investment and first period's interest
(L.O. 8)

Lang Company purchased bonds with a face value of $80,000 issued by Stillwagon Company (Exercise 15–3) as a long-term investment on December 31, 1993. Prepare the journal entry to record the investment. Also, prepare the entry to record the receipt of interest on the bonds for the first six months of 1994, using the interest method.

Exercise 15–5
Calculate interest using straight-line amortization
(L.O. 6, 8)

Compute the annual interest expense on the bonds in Exercise 15–3 and the interest revenue on the bonds in Exercise 15–4, assuming the bond discount is amortized using the straight-line method.

Exercise 15–6
Prepare entry to record interest payment
(L.O. 6)

After recording the payment of the interest coupon due on June 30, 1994, the accounts of San Martin Company showed Bonds Payable of $400,000 and Premium on Bonds Payable of $14,096. Interest is payable semiannually on June 30 and December 31. The five-year, 12% bonds have a face value of $400,000 and were originally issued to yield 10%. Prepare the journal entry to record the payment of interest on December 31, 1994. Use the interest method.

Exercise 15–7
Record call of bonds and payment of interest
(L.O. 7)

On June 30, 1994 (a semiannual interest payment date), Brickland Company redeemed all of its $400,000 face value of 10% bonds outstanding by calling them at 106. The bonds were originally issued on June 30, 1990, at 100. Prepare the journal entry to record the payment of the interest and the redemption of the bonds on June 30, 1994.

Exercise 15–8
Record conversion of bonds
(L.O. 7)

After interest was paid on September 30, 1994, $38,000 face value of Coleman Company's $380,000 face value of outstanding bonds were converted into 4,000 shares of the company's $5 par value common stock. Prepare the journal entry to record the conversion, assuming the bonds were issued at 100.

Exercise 15–9
Record accrued interest, and purchase and retirement of bonds (L.O. 7)

On August 31, 1993, as part of the provisions of its bond indenture, O'Keefe Company acquired $120,000 of its outstanding bonds on the open market at 96 plus accrued interest. These bonds were originally issued at face value and carry a 12% interest rate, payable semiannually. The bonds are dated November 30, 1982, and pay semiannual interest on May 31 and November 30. Prepare the journal entries required to record the accrual of the interest to the acquisition date on the bonds acquired and the acquisition of the bonds.

Exercise 15–10
Record interest received for six-month period given adjusting entry previously made (L.O. 8)

On December 31, 1994, the end of its accounting year, Jagers Company prepared an adjusting entry to record $40,000 accrued interest revenue earned on 12% bonds with a $900,000 face value that were purchased on August 31, 1994, to yield 14%. The bonds are dated August 31, 1994, and call for semiannual interest payments on August 31 and February 28. Prepare the journal entry on February 28, 1995, to record the interest revenue, the discount amortization, and the collection of interest.

Exercise 15–11
Record sinking fund transactions (L.O. 7)

McLeod Company is required to make a deposit of $144,000 plus semiannual interest expense of $4,320 on October 31, 1993, to the trustee of its sinking fund so that the trustee can redeem $144,000 of McLeod's bonds on that date. The bonds were issued at 100. Prepare the journal entries required on October 31 to record the sinking fund deposit, the bond retirement, payment of interest (due on that date), and payment of trustee expenses, assuming the latter is $450.

Exercise 15–12
Prepare journal entries related to temporary investment in bonds (L.O. 8)

On June 30, 1993, Middleton Company purchased as a temporary investment $40,000 face value of Premo Company's 12% bonds at 101. In addition to the purchase price, Middleton paid $800 accrued interest from April 30 and a $140 broker's commission.

On September 30, 1993, Middleton sold the Premo bonds at 102.5, plus accrued interest of $2,000, and less a $140 broker commission.

Prepare journal entries on Middleton Company's books to record the purchase and sale of the Premo Company bonds.

Exercise 15–13
Determine present value of a lump-sum payment (based on Appendix) (L.O. 9)

What is the present value of a lump-sum payment of $44,000 due in five years if the market rate of interest is 10% per year (compounded annually) and the present value of $1 due in five periods at 10% is 0.62092?

Exercise 15–14
Determine present value of an annuity (based on Appendix) (L.O. 9)

What is the present value of a series of semiannual payments of $2,000 due at the end of each six months for the next five years if the market rate of interest is 10% per year and the present value of an annuity of $1 for 10 periods at 5% is 7.72173?

Exercise 15–15
Determine present value of an annuity (based on Appendix) (L.O. 9)

Sam Lopez bought a ticket in the New York State lottery for $1, hoping to strike it rich. To his amazement, he won $4,000,000. Payment was to be received in equal amounts at the end of each of the next 20 years. Sam heard from relatives and "friends" he had not heard from in years. They all wanted to renew their relationship with this "new millionaire." Federal and state income taxes were going to be about 40% (31% for federal and 9% for state) on each year's income from the lottery check. The discount rate to use in all present value calculations is 12%.

a. How much will Sam actually receive after taxes each year?
b. Is Sam a millionaire in terms of the present value of his cash inflow after taxes?
c. What is the present value of the net amount the state has to pay out? Remember that the state gets part of the money back in the form of taxes.

Exercise 15–16
Determine future value of an annuity (based on Appendix) (L.O. 9)

After Sam Lopez won $4,000,000 in the New York State lottery, he decided to purchase $20,000 of lottery tickets at the end of each year for the next 20 years. He was hoping to hit the lottery again, but he never did. If the state can earn 12% on ticket revenue received, how much will the annuity of $20,000 from Sam grow to by the end of 20 years?

PROBLEMS: SERIES A

Problem 15–1A

Compute two prices for bond issue and first period's interest (L.O. 5, 6)

Dalton Company is seeking to issue $400,000 face value of 10%, 15-year bonds. The bonds are dated June 30, 1993, call for semiannual interest payments, and mature on June 30, 2008.

Required

a. Compute the price investors should offer if they seek a yield of 8% on these bonds. Also, compute the first six months' interest, assuming the bonds are issued at this price. Use the interest method.

b. Repeat part *(a)*, assuming investors seek a yield of 12%.

Problem 15–2A

Record bond interest expense payment and accrual for partial period (L.O. 6)

On July 1, 1993, Badgett Corporation issued $600,000 face value of 10%, 10-year bonds. The bonds call for semiannual interest payments and mature on July 1, 2003. Badgett received cash of $531,180, a price that yields 12%.

Required

Assume that Badgett's fiscal year ends on March 31. Prepare journal entries to record the bond interest expense on January 1, 1994, and the adjustment needed on March 31, 1994, using the interest method.

Problem 15–3A

Record issuance of bonds and payment of interest; record purchase and accrual of interest on investor's books (L.O. 3, 8)

On June 1, 1993, Batross Corporation issued $180,000 of 10-year, 16% bonds dated April 1, 1993, at 100. Interest on bonds is payable semiannually on presentation of the appropriate coupon. All of the bonds are of $1,000 denomination. The company's accounting period ends on June 30, with semiannual statements prepared on December 31 and June 30. The interest payment dates are April 1 and October 1.

All of the first coupons on the bonds are presented to the company's bank and paid on October 2, 1993. All but one of the second coupons are similarly received and paid on April 1, 1994.

Required

a. Prepare all necessary journal entries for the above transactions through April 1, 1994, including the adjusting entry needed at June 30, 1993.

b. Huff Company purchased $60,000 of Batross Corporation's bonds on June 1, 1993, as a long-term investment. The company prepares financial statements on September 30. Prepare all journal entries for Huff Company relating to the bonds through September 30, 1993.

Problem 15–4A

Compute issue price of bonds; prepare amortization schedule; journalize bond issuance; accrue interest (L.O. 5, 6)

Heath Company issued $600,000 face value of 15%, 20-year bonds on October 1, 1993. The bonds are dated October 1, 1993, call for semiannual interest payments on April 1 and October 1, and are issued to yield 16% (8% per period).

Required

a. Compute the amount received for the bonds.

b. Prepare an amortization schedule similar to that shown in Illustration 15.4. Enter data in the schedule for only the first two interest periods. Use the interest method.

c. Prepare journal entries to record issuance of the bonds, the first six months' interest expense on the bonds, and the adjustment needed on May 31, 1994, assuming Heath's fiscal year ends on that date.

Problem 15–5A

Record bond investment, full and partial period's interest, and sale of bonds (L.O. 8)

Ferris Company purchased $30,000 face value of the Heath Company bonds (Problem 15–4A) when they were issued on October 1, 1993, as a long-term investment.

Required

a. Prepare journal entries to record purchase of the bonds, receipt of the first six months' interest, and the adjustment needed on June 30, 1994, assuming a fiscal year ended on that date. Use the interest method.

b. Assume that Ferris Company sold all of these bonds on October 1, 2003, for $29,850 cash, after detaching the interest coupon for payment due on this date.

The bonds have a carrying value, properly adjusted to date, of $28,542. Prepare the journal entry to record the sale.

Problem 15–6A

Compute price of bonds; prepare amortization schedule; journalize bond issuance, payment of first period's interest, and accrual of partial period's interest

(L.O. 5, 6)

Frishkoff Company issued $400,000 face value of 18%, 20-year bonds on October 1, 1993. The bonds are dated October 1, 1993, call for semiannual interest payments on April 1 and October 1, and are issued to yield 16% (8% per period).

Required

a.   Compute the amount received for the bonds.

b.   Prepare an amortization schedule similar to that shown in Illustration 15.5. Enter data in the schedule for only the first two interest periods. Use the interest method.

c.   Prepare entries to record the issuance of the bonds, the first six months' interest on the bonds, and the adjustment needed on June 30, 1994, assuming Frishkoff's fiscal year ends on that date.

Problem 15–7A

Record bond investment, collection of full period's interest, accrual of partial period's interest, and call of bonds

(L.O. 7, 8)

Turner Corporation purchased $120,000 face value of the Frishkoff Company bonds (Problem 15–6A) when they were issued on October 1, 1993, as a long-term investment.

Required

a.   Prepare journal entries to record the purchase of the bonds, the receipt of the first six months' interest, and the adjustment needed on June 30, 1994, assuming a fiscal year ending on that date. Use the interest method.

b.   Assume that on October 1, 2003, Frishkoff called all of the bonds at 105. Turner received a check for $136,800 [($120,000 face value of bonds × 105) + $10,800] as payment of the semiannual interest due on this date. Prepare the entry to record the receipt of the $136,800. The properly adjusted carrying value of the bonds on this date was $131,836.

Problem 15–8A

Record serial bond transactions, and show financial reporting

(L.O. 7)

Du Pree Company issued $300,000 of 16% serial bonds on July 1, 1993, at face value. The bonds are dated July 1, 1993; call for semiannual interest payments on July 1 and January 1; and mature at the rate of $60,000 per year, with the first maturity date falling on July 1, 1998. The company's accounting period ends on September 30.

Required

Prepare journal entries to record the interest payment of July 1, 1998; the maturing of $60,000 of bonds on July 1, 1998; and the adjusting entry needed on September 30, 1998. Also, show how the bonds will be presented in the company's balance sheet for September 30, 1998.

PROBLEMS: SERIES B

Problem 15–1B

Compute two prices on bond issue and first period's interest

(L.O. 5, 6)

Swanson Company is seeking to issue $400,000 face value of 10%, 20-year bonds. The bonds are dated June 30, 1993, call for semiannual interest payments, and mature on June 30, 2013.

Required

a.   Compute the price investors should offer if they seek a yield of 8% on these bonds. Also, compute the first six months' interest assuming the bonds are issued at that price. Use the interest method.

b.   Repeat part *(a)* assuming investors seek a yield of 12%.

Problem 15–2B

Record bond interest expense and accrual for partial period

(L.O. 6)

On July 1, 1993, Wardlaw Corporation issued $400,000 face value of 8%, 10-year bonds. These bonds call for semiannual interest payments and mature on July 1, 2003. Wardlaw received cash of $350,152, a price that yields 10%.

Required

Assume that Wardlaw's fiscal year ends on March 31. Prepare journal entries to record the bond interest expense on January 1, 1994, and the adjustment needed on March 31, 1994, using the interest method.

Problem 15–3B

Record issuance of bonds, payment of bonds, payment of interest, and partial period accrual; record purchase and receipt of interest on investor's books
(L.O. 3, 8)

On December 1, 1993, Rayburn Corporation issued $300,000 of 10-year, 9% bonds dated July 1, 1993, at 100. Interest on the bonds is payable semiannually on July 1 and January 1. All of the bonds are registered. The company's accounting period ends on March 31. Quarterly financial statements are prepared.

The company deposits a sum of money sufficient to pay the semiannual interest on the bonds in a special checking account in First National Bank and draws interest payment checks on this account. The deposit is made the day before the checks are drawn.

Required

a. Prepare journal entries to record the issuance of the bonds; the December 31 adjusting entry; the January 1, 1994, interest payment; and the adjusting entry needed on March 31, 1994, to prepare quarterly financial statements.

b. Hobbs Corporation bought $60,000 of the Rayburn Company bonds on December 1, 1993, as a long-term investment. The company's year-end is December 31. Prepare all journal entries for Hobbs Corporation for these bonds through December 31, 1993.

Problem 15–4B

Compute issue price of bonds; prepare amortization schedule; journalize bond issuance and interest payment
(L.O. 5, 6)

Grierson Company issued $400,000 face value of 16%, 20-year bonds on July 1, 1993. The bonds are dated July 1, 1993, call for semiannual interest payments on July 1 and January 1, and were issued to yield 12% (6% per period).

Required

a. Compute the amount received for the bonds.

b. Prepare an amortization schedule similar to that shown in Illustration 15.5. Enter data in the schedule for only the first two interest periods. Use the interest method.

c. Prepare journal entries to record issuance of the bonds, the first six months' interest expense on the bonds, and the adjustment needed on May 31, 1994, assuming Grierson's fiscal year ends on that date.

Problem 15–5B

Record bond investment, first two periods' interest, and sale of bonds
(L.O. 8)

Dodson Company purchased $80,000 face value of the Grierson Company bonds (Problem 15–4B) when they were issued on July 1, 1993, as a long-term investment.

Required

a. Prepare entries to record purchase of the bonds, receipt of the first six months' interest, and the adjustment needed on June 30, 1994, assuming a fiscal year ended on that date. Use the interest method.

b. Assume that Dodson Company sold all of these bonds on July 1, 2003, for cash of $96,000 after detaching the interest coupon for payment due on this date. The bonds have a carrying value, properly adjusted to date, of $98,352. Prepare the journal entry to record the sale.

Problem 15–6B

Compute price of bonds; prepare amortization schedule; journalize bond issuance; and record two interest payments
(L.O. 5, 6)

Gutman Company issued $400,000 face value of 10%, 20-year bonds on July 1, 1993. The bonds are dated July 1, 1993, call for semiannual interest payments on July 1 and January 1, and are issued to yield 12% (6% per period).

Required

a. Compute the amount received for the bonds.

b. Prepare an amortization schedule similar to that shown in Illustration 15.4. Enter data in the schedule for only the first two interest periods. Use the interest method.

c. Prepare entries to record the issuance of the bonds, the first six months' interest on the bonds, and the adjustment needed on June 30, 1994, assuming Gutman's fiscal year ends on that date.

Problem 15–7B

Record bond investment, first two interest checks, and call of bonds
(L.O. 7, 8)

Michel Corporation purchased $40,000 face value of the Gutman Company bonds (Problem 15–6B) when they were issued on July 1, 1993, as a long-term investment.

Required

a. Prepare journal entries to record the purchase of the bonds, the receipt of the first six months' interest, and the adjustment needed on June 30, 1994, assuming a fiscal year ending on that date. Use the interest method.

b. Assume that on July 1, 2003, Gutman called all of the bonds at 105. Michel received a check for $44,000 [($40,000 face value of bonds × 105) + $2,000] as payment of the semiannual interest coupons due on this date. Prepare the journal entry to record the receipt of the $44,000. The properly adjusted carrying value of the bonds on this date was $35,412.

Problem 15–8B

Record serial bond transactions, and show financial reporting (L.O. 7)

Gear Company issued $50,000 of 12% bonds on July 1, 1993, at face value. The bonds are dated July 1, 1993, call for semiannual payments on July 1 and January 1, and mature at the rate of $5,000 per year on July 1, beginning in 1998. The company's accounting period ends on September 30.

Required

a. Prepare journal entries to record the interest expense and payment for the six months ending July 1, 1998; the maturing of the bonds on July 1, 1998; and the adjusting entries needed on September 30, 1998.

b. Show how the bonds will be presented in the company's balance sheet for September 30, 1998.

BUSINESS DECISION PROBLEMS

Decision Problem 15–1

Analyze two financing proposals; decide whether investment should be made (L.O. 2)

A company is trying to decide whether to invest $4 million on plant expansion and $2 million to finance a related increase in inventories and accounts receivable. The $6 million expansion is expected to increase business volume substantially. Profit forecasts indicate that income from operations will rise from $3.2 million to $4.4 million. The income tax rate will be about 40%. Net income last year was $1,830,000. Interest expense on debt now outstanding is $140,000 per year. There are 200,000 shares of common stock currently outstanding.

The $6 million needed can be obtained in two alternative ways:

1. Finance entirely by issuing additional shares of common stock at an expected issue price of $150 per share.

2. Finance two thirds with bonds, one third with additional stock. The bonds would have a 20-year life, bear interest at 10%, and sell at face value. The issue price of the stock would be $160 per share.

Required

Should the investment be made? If so, which financing plan would you recommend? (Hint: Calculate earnings per share for last year and for future years under each of the alternatives.)

Decision Problem 15–2

Choose which of two bond issues to purchase (L.O. 5)

You are an investor in bonds of various companies. An account executive of a brokerage firm has brought the following bonds to your attention:

1. S Company bonds—remaining life, 12 years; interest rate, 6% payable semiannually. Price: $650 per $1,000 bond.

2. B Company bonds—remaining life, 13 years; interest rate, 15% payable semiannually. Price: $1,180 per $1,000 bond.

From a study of available alternatives, you reach the conclusion that either bond would be a suitable investment if the yield were 12%.

Required

In which of the above bonds should you invest, if either? Explain.

Decision Problem 15–3

Decide whether to convert or surrender bonds (real world problem) (L.O. 7)

The 1988 annual report of Emhart Corporation contained the following paragraph in its notes to the financial statements:

The 6¾% convertible subordinated debentures may be converted into shares of common stock at a price of $26.50 per share at any time prior to maturity. They are redeemable at prices decreasing from 105 percent of face amount currently to 100 percent in July 1993. At December 31, 1988, a total of 1,886,794 common shares were reserved for the conversion of the debentures.

Required   Answer the following questions about this quote:

   a.   If you held one $1,000 bond, how many shares of stock would you receive if you converted the bond into shares of stock? (Hint: You can use the principal amount of the bond to buy shares of stock at the stated price.)

   b.   Assume you held one $1,000 bond and the bond was called by the company at a price of 105% of the face amount. If the current market price per share of the stock was $29, would you convert the bond into shares of stock or would you surrender the bond?

ANSWERS TO SELF-TEST

True-False

1. *True.* These unsecured bonds are also called debenture bonds and are backed only by the general creditworthiness of the issuer.

2. *False.* Callable bonds may be called at the option of the issuer.

3. *True.* This statement is the definition of favorable financial leverage. However, unfavorable financial leverage can result when favorable financial leverage was planned. Unfavorable financial leverage will result if earnings before interest and taxes are much lower than anticipated. Then earnings per share for the common stockholders would be lower than they would have been without the borrowing.

4. *True.* Purchasers will not be willing to pay the face amount if the market rate of interest exceeds the contract rate. By paying less than the face value, purchasers can earn the market rate of interest on the bonds.

5. *False.* The interest method is the recommended method. The straight-line method may only be used when the results are not materially different from the interest method.

Multiple-Choice

1. *a.* The discount of $4,000 must be recorded. Also, the accrued interest must be recognized ($100,000 × 12% × $\frac{2}{12}$ = $2,000).

2. *c.* The premium is $4,000, and the accrued interest is $2,000. Both must be recognized.

3. *b.* The interest is ($328,298 × 0.11 × $\frac{1}{2}$) = $18,056.

4. *d.* The interest would have been ($400,000 × 0.04) + ($71,702/20) = $19,585.

5. *a.* The debit to Cash is ($80,000 × 0.04) = $3,200. The credit to Bond Interest Expense is $65,660 × 0.055 = $3,611. The debit to Bond Investments is $3,611 − $3,200 = $411.

16

STOCK INVESTMENTS— COST, EQUITY, AND CONSOLIDATIONS

After studying this chapter, you should be able to:

1. Report stock investments and distinguish between the cost and equity methods of accounting for stock investments.
2. Prepare journal entries to account for short-term stock investments and for long-term stock investments of less than 20%.
3. Prepare journal entries to account for long-term stock investments of 20%–50%.
4. Describe the nature of parent and subsidiary corporations.
5. Prepare consolidated financial statements through the use of a consolidated statement work sheet.
6. Identify the differences between purchase accounting and pooling of interests accounting.
7. Describe the uses and limitations of consolidated financial statements.

Often a large company attempts to "take over" a smaller company by acquiring a controlling interest (more than 50% of the outstanding shares) in that "target" company. Some of these takeover attempts are "friendly" (not resisted by the target company), and some are "unfriendly" (resisted by the target company). If the attempt is successful, the two companies become one business entity for accounting purposes, and consolidated financial statements are prepared. The company that takes over another company is called the *parent company;* the company acquired is called the *subsidiary company.* This chapter discusses accounting for parent and subsidiary companies.

When a corporation purchases the stock of another corporation, the method of accounting for the stock investment depends on the corporation's **motivation** for making the investment and the **relative size** of the investment. A corporation's motivation for purchasing the stock of another company may be as (1) a short-term investment of excess cash; (2) a long-term investment in a substantial percentage of another company's stock to ensure a supply of a required raw material (for example, when large oil companies invest heavily in, or purchase outright, "wildcat" oil drilling companies); or (3) a long-term investment for expansion (when a company purchases another profitable company rather than starting a new business operation). On the balance sheet, the first type of investment is classified as a current asset, and the last two types are classified as long-term (noncurrent) investments. As explained in the chapter, the purchaser's level of ownership of the investee company determines whether the investment is accounted for by the cost method or the equity method.

COST AND EQUITY METHODS

Objective 1

Report stock investments and distinguish between the cost and equity methods of accounting for stock investments

Investors in common stock can use two methods to account for their investments—the cost method or the equity method. Under both methods, the investment is initially recorded at cost (price paid at acquisition). Under the cost method, the investor company does not adjust the investment account balance subsequently. Instead, when the investor company receives dividends, they are credited to a Dividends Revenue account. Under the equity method, the investor company adjusts the investment account for the investor company's share of the investee's reported income, losses, and dividends.

The Accounting Principles Board has identified the circumstances under which each method must be used. This chapter illustrates each of those circumstances. The general rules for determining the appropriate method of accounting are summarized below.

Types of Common Stock Investment	Method of Accounting Required by Accounting Principles Board in Most Cases
All short-term investments	Cost
Long-term investments of:	
Less than 20%:	
If no significant influence	Cost
If significant influence	Equity
20%–50%	Equity
More than 50%	Cost or equity

ACCOUNTING FOR SHORT-TERM STOCK INVESTMENTS AND FOR LONG-TERM STOCK INVESTMENTS OF LESS THAN 20%

Objective 2

Prepare journal entries to account for short-term stock investments and for long-term stock investments of less than 20%

Accountants use the cost method to account for all short-term stock investments. When a company owns less than 50% of the outstanding stock of another company as a long-term investment, the percentage of ownership determines whether the cost method or the equity method is used. If the purchasing company owns less than 20% of the outstanding stock of the investee company and does not exercise significant influence over that company, the cost method is used. If the purchasing company owns from 20% to 50% of the outstanding stock of the investee company or owns less than 20% but still exercises significant influence over the investee company, the equity method is used. Thus, the cost method is used for all short-term stock investments and almost all long-term stock investments of less than 20%. For investments of more than 50%, either the cost or equity method can be used because the application of consolidation procedures yields the same result.

Cost Method for Short-Term Investments and for Long-Term Investments of Less than 20%

Under the cost method, stock investments are recorded at cost, which usually is the cash paid for the stock. Most stocks are purchased from other investors (not the issuing company) through brokers who execute "trades" in an organized market, such as the New York Stock Exchange. Thus, cost will usually consist of the price paid for the shares, plus a broker's commission.

For example, assume that Brewer Corporation purchased as a short-term investment 1,000 shares of Cowen Company's $10 par value common stock at 14⅛, plus a $175 broker's commission. Stock prices are quoted in dollars and fractions of one dollar; thus, 14⅛ means $14.125 per share. The entry needed by Brewer to record its investment is:

Current Marketable Equity Securities [(1,000 shares × $14.125) + $175 commission]	14,300	
Cash		14,300
Purchased 1,000 shares of Cowen common stock as a short-term investment at 14⅛, plus commission.		

If the stock had been purchased as a long-term investment, the account debited would have been Noncurrent Marketable Equity Securities. Note that the par value of Cowen's stock is not relevant to the investing corporation.

Accounting for Cash Dividends Received Investments in stock provide dividend revenue. As a general rule, cash dividends are debited to Cash and credited to Dividends Revenue when received by the investor. The only exception to this general rule is when a dividend declared in one accounting period is payable in the next. This exception allows a company to record the revenue in the proper accounting period. Assume that Cowen declared a $1 per share cash dividend on December 1, 1994, to stockholders of record as of December 20, payable on January 15, 1995. The following entry should be made by Brewer in 1994:

1994				
Dec.	1	Dividends Receivable	1,000	
		Dividends Revenue		1,000
		To record $1 per share cash dividend on Cowen common stock, payable January 15, 1995.		

When the dividend is collected on January 15, Cash is debited, and Dividends Receivable is credited:

1995				
Jan.	15	Cash	1,000	
		Dividends Receivable		1,000
		To record the receipt of a cash dividend on Cowen common stock.		

Stock Dividends and Stock Splits   As discussed in Chapter 14, a company might declare a stock dividend rather than a cash dividend. An investor does not recognize revenue upon receipt of the additional shares of stock from a stock dividend. The investor merely records the number of additional shares received and reduces the cost per share for each share held. For example, if Cowen distributed a 10% stock dividend in February 1995, Brewer, which held 1,000 shares at a cost of $14,300, would receive another 100 shares and would then hold 1,100 shares at a cost per share of $13 ($14,300/1,100 shares). Similarly, when a corporation declares a stock split, the investor would note the shares received and the reduction in the cost per share.

Sale of Stock Investments   When shares are sold, the gain or loss on the sale is the difference between the net proceeds received and the carrying value of the shares sold. Assume, for example, that on May 1, 1995, Brewer sold 500 of the Cowen shares at $17 per share, less a $200 broker's commission. (Remember that the cost per share was reduced to $13 after the stock dividend was received in February 1995.) The entry needed to record the sale of shares at a gain is:

1995				
May	1	Cash [(500 × $17) − $200]	8,300	
		Current Marketable Equity Securities (500 × $13)		6,500
		Realized Gain on Sale of Current Marketable Equity		
		Securities		1,800
		To record sale of 500 shares of Cowen common stock.		

The entries shown above are appropriate whenever less than 20% of the outstanding stock is held, regardless of whether the investment is temporary or long-term. The only difference is in the use of the current or noncurrent distinction in the investment account title. Investments are classified as current or noncurrent, depending on the management's intention to hold the investment for a short period (one year or less) or a long period (more than one year).

Generally, the cost of the above investments remains the carrying value until the investments are sold. The FASB has, however, required a year-end valuation procedure for such investments to provide better information to users of financial statements.

Subsequent Valuation of Stock Investments under the Cost Method

FASB Statement No. 12[1] (1975) governs the valuation of **marketable equity securities** that are being accounted for under the cost method. Marketable refers to the fact that the stocks are readily salable; equity securities are common and preferred stocks.

---

[1] FASB, *Statement of Financial Accounting Standards No. 12*, "Accounting for Certain Marketable Securities" (Stamford, Conn., 1975). Copyright © by the Financial Accounting Standards Board, High Ridge Park, Stamford, Connecticut 06905, U.S.A. Quoted (or excerpted) with permission. Copies of the complete document are available from the FASB.

The FASB *Statement* requires that at year-end, companies adjust the carrying value to the lower-of-cost-or-market (LCM) for portfolios (groups) of these investment securities. (The lower-of-cost-or-market method was applied to inventories in Chapter 6.) Current investments and noncurrent investments in marketable equity securities are considered to be two separate investment portfolios, and LCM is applied independently to each portfolio.[2]

Suppose that in a marketable equity securities portfolio, the market value is lower than the cost. The write-down to market is journalized through the use of a **valuation account** called *Allowance for Market Decline of Current (Noncurrent) Marketable Equity Securities*. A valuation account is used rather than a direct credit to the investment account because the LCM valuation is based on the **total** value of the securities held in each portfolio. When the valuation is based on the total value, stock investments that have increased in value can offset other investments that have decreased in value.

Current Marketable Equity Securities   To illustrate the application of the LCM method to **current marketable equity securities,** assume that Hanson Company has the securities shown in Illustration 16.1 in its current investment stock portfolio.

Applying the LCM method reveals that the portfolio should be written down by $1,000—from $20,000 to $19,000. The increases in the market value of Company A and Company B shares offset $3,000 of the $4,000 decrease in market value of the Company C shares, leaving only the net decrease of $1,000. The journal entry required at the end of 1994 is:

1994				
Dec.	31	Unrealized Loss on Current Marketable Equity Securities	1,000	
		Allowance for Market Decline of Current Marketable Equity Securities		1,000
		To record unrealized loss from market decline of current marketable equity securities.		

Note that the debit is to the Unrealized Loss on Current Marketable Equity Securities account. This loss is called *unrealized* because the securities have not been sold. However, **the loss is reported in the income statement as a deduction in arriving at net income.** The credit in the above entry is to the valuation account, Allowance for Market Decline of Current Marketable Equity Securities, which is a contra account to the Current Marketable Equity Securities account. (The valuation account is somewhat similar to the Allowance for Uncollectible Accounts account.) The securities and the contra account are reported on the balance sheet as follows:

HANSON COMPANY
Partial Balance Sheet
December 31, 1994

Current assets:

Marketable equity securities (cost of $20,000 less
  allowance for market decline of $1,000) $19,000

If Hanson sold all its short-term investments on January 1, 1995, the company would receive $19,000 (assuming no change in market values from the previous

---

[2] A portfolio is simply a group of stock investments that a company holds at a given time.

ILLUSTRATION 16.1

Stock Portfolio of Hanson Company

Company	No. of Shares	Cost per Share	Market Price per Share, 12/31/94	Total Cost	Total Market, 12/31/94	Increase/ (Decrease) in Market Value
A.	200	$35	$40	$ 7,000	$ 8,000	$ 1,000
B.	400	10	15	4,000	6,000	2,000
C.	100	90	50	9,000	5,000	(4,000)
				$20,000	$19,000	$(1,000)

day). The loss on the sale results from market changes in 1994 rather than in 1995; the LCM procedure placed that loss in the proper year.

Assume now that in 1995, Hanson sold the 400 shares of Company B for $6,000, a $2,000 gain over cost of the shares. The entry for the sale is:

Cash	6,000	
Current Marketable Equity Securities		4,000
Realized Gain on Sale of Current Marketable Equity Securities . . .		2,000
To record sale of the Company B securities.		

Note that the $2,000 gain on the sale of Company B stock is calculated without reference to the current balance in the allowance account. The $1,000 credit balance in the allowance account did not change the carrying value of any individual security. The securities are still being carried in the asset account at the actual cost paid for them. **Realized gains and losses are calculated by comparing the net proceeds from the sale with the actual cost of the securities sold.** No changes are made to the allowance account during the year when stock investments are bought or sold.

A subsequent recovery in the market value of the portfolio is recognized by reducing the allowance, which increases the carrying value of the portfolio. Remember, however, that a portfolio may never be carried at more than its original cost. Now assume that at the end of 1995, Hanson again determined the cost and market value of its portfolio as shown in Illustration 16.2. Since total cost is $16,000 and total market value is $15,600, an allowance of only $400 is needed to state the portfolio at LCM. Since the allowance has a $1,000 balance, the following entry is necessary to reduce the balance of the allowance to $400:

1995			
Dec.	31	Allowance for Market Decline of Current Marketable Equity Securities	600	
		Recovery of Unrealized Loss on Current Marketable Equity Securities		600
		To record gain from recovery of market value of current marketable equity securities.		

The account credited is a recovery of the previously recorded unrealized loss and **is reported in the income statement.** If the total market value had risen above $16,000, only $1,000 of the recovery could be recognized. This restriction prevents the stock from being carried at more than its original cost. The securities and the allowance are shown in the 1995 balance sheet as follows:

ILLUSTRATION 16.2

Stock Portfolio of Hanson Company

Company	No. of Shares	Cost per Share	Market Price per Share, 12/31/95	Total Cost	Total Market, 12/31/95	Increase/ (Decrease) in Market Value
A.	200	$35	$40	$ 7,000	$ 8,000	$ 1,000
C.	100	90	76	9,000	7,600	(1,400)
				$16,000	$15,600	$ (400)

HANSON COMPANY
Partial Balance Sheet
December 31, 1995

Current assets:

Marketable equity securities (cost of $16,000 less
allowance for market decline of $400) $15,600

Noncurrent Marketable Equity Securities   Assume a portfolio of noncurrent (or long-term) marketable equity securities has a cost of $32,000 and a current market value on December 31, 1994, of $31,000. The treatment of the loss depends on whether it results from a temporary decline in the market value of the **portfolio** or from a permanent decline in the value of an **individual security.** Assume first that the loss is related to a "temporary" decline in the portfolio. The required entry is:

1994				
Dec.	31	Unrealized Loss on Noncurrent Marketable Equity Securities . . .	1,000	
		Allowance for Market Decline of Noncurrent Marketable Equity Securities		1,000
		To record unrealized loss from market decline of noncurrent marketable equity securities.		

Information from both of the above accounts would appear on the balance sheet as follows:

HANSON COMPANY
Partial Balance Sheet
December 31, 1994

Investments:

Noncurrent marketable equity securities (cost of $32,000 less
allowance for market decline of $1,000). . . . . $ 31,000

Stockholders' equity:

Capital stock . . . . $xxx,xxx
Additional paid-in capital . . . . x,xxx

Total paid-in capital . . . . $xxx,xxx
Less: Unrealized loss on noncurrent marketable equity securities . . . 1,000

$xxx,xxx
Retained earnings . . . . xx,xxx
Total stockholders' equity . . . . $xxx,xxx

Note that the unrealized loss for noncurrent marketable equity securities appears in the balance sheet as a deduction from total paid-in capital rather than in the income statement (as it does for current marketable equity securities). Alternatively, the unrealized loss could be reported as a deduction from total stockholders' equity. The unrealized loss on noncurrent marketable equity securities is **not** included in the determination of net income because it is not expected to be realized in the near future. These securities are being held on a long-term basis and will probably not be sold soon. Losses on current securities are included in net income because, being related to a current asset, they are more likely to be realized by the company in the next period.

Later recoveries of market value up to the original cost of $32,000 are debited to the allowance and credited to the unrealized loss account. Thus, if the market value of the noncurrent portfolio increases by $1,700 by December 31, 1995, the adjusting entry is:

1995				
Dec.	31	Allowance for Market Decline of Noncurrent Marketable Equity Securities	1,000	
		Unrealized Loss on Noncurrent Marketable Equity Securities .		1,000
		To record recovery of market value of noncurrent marketable equity securities.		

We can record only $1,000 of the $1,700 increase in market value because recording the entire $1,700 would result in valuing the securities at **more** than their original cost. Generally accepted accounting principles do not permit recording such an increase in value, and the associated gain, until the securities are actually sold. However, the $1,000 increase may be recorded because it represents a recovery in the securities' market value up to their original cost.

If a loss on an individual noncurrent security is determined to be "permanent," it is recorded as a realized loss and deducted in determining net income. The entry to record a permanent loss of $1,400 reads:

Realized Loss on Noncurrent Marketable Equity Securities	1,400	
Noncurrent Marketable Equity Securities		1,400
To record loss in value of noncurrent marketable equity securities.		

No part of the $1,400 loss is subject to reversal if the market price of the stock recovers. **The stock's reduced value is now its "cost," and values in excess of cost are not recorded until a sale occurs.**

THE EQUITY METHOD FOR LONG-TERM INVESTMENTS OF BETWEEN 20% AND 50%

Objective 3

Prepare journal entries to account for long-term stock investments of 20%–50%

When a company (the investor) purchases between 20% and 50% of the outstanding stock of another company (the investee) as a long-term investment, the purchasing company is said to have significant influence over the investee company. In certain cases, a company may have significant influence even when the investment is less than 20%. In either situation, the investment must be accounted for under the equity method.

When the equity method is used in accounting for stock investments, the investor company must recognize its share of the investee company's income, regardless of whether or not dividends are received. The logic behind this treatment is that the investor company may exercise influence over the declaration of dividends and thereby manipulate its own income by influencing the investee's decision to declare (or not declare) dividends.

Thus, when the **investee** reports income or losses, the **investor** company must recognize its share of the investee's income or losses. For example, assume that Tone Company (the investor) owns 30% of Dutch Company (the investee) and Dutch reports $50,000 net income in the current year. Under the equity method, Tone will make the following entry as of the end of 1994:

Investment in Dutch Company	15,000	
Income from Dutch Company ($50,000 × 0.30)		15,000
To recognize 30% of Dutch Company's net income.		

The $15,000 income from Dutch would be reported on Tone's 1994 income statement. The investment account is also increased by $15,000.

If the investee incurs a loss, the investor company debits a loss account and credits the investment account for the investor's share of the loss. For example, assume Dutch incurs a loss of $10,000 in 1995. Since Tone still owns 30% of Dutch, Tone records its share of the loss as follows:

Loss from Dutch Company ($10,000 × 0.30)	3,000	
Investment in Dutch Company		3,000
To record 30% of Dutch Company's loss.		

The $3,000 loss would be reported on Tone's income statement for 1995. The $3,000 **credit reduces Tone's equity in the investee.**

Furthermore, because dividends are a distribution of income to the owners of the corporation, if Dutch declares and pays $20,000 in dividends, the following entry would also be required for Tone:

Cash	6,000	
Investment in Dutch Company ($20,000 × 0.30)		6,000
To record receipt of 30% of dividends paid by Dutch Company.		

Under the equity method illustrated above, the Investment in Dutch Company account will always reflect Tone's 30% interest in the net assets of Dutch.

REPORTING FOR STOCK INVESTMENTS OF MORE THAN 50%

Many companies have expanded in recent years by purchasing a major portion, or all, of another company's outstanding voting stock. The purpose of such acquisitions ranges from seeking to ensure a source of raw materials (such as oil), to desiring to enter into a new industry, or simply seeking to receive income on the investment. Both corporations still remain separate legal entities, regardless of the investment purpose. In this section, you will study how to account for business combinations.

Parent and Subsidiary Corporations

As stated in the introduction to this chapter, a corporation that owns more than 50% of the outstanding voting common stock of another corporation is called the parent company. The corporation acquired and controlled by the parent company is known as the subsidiary company.

Objective 4

Describe the nature of
parent and subsidiary
corporations

A parent company and its subsidiaries maintain their own accounting records and prepare their own financial statements. However, since a central management **controls** the parent and its subsidiaries and they are related to each other, the parent company is usually **required** to prepare one set of financial statements. These statements, called consolidated statements, consolidate the parent's financial statement amounts with those of its subsidiaries and show the parent and its subsidiaries as a single enterprise. In this section, you will learn how to prepare consolidated statements.

According to *FASB Statement No. 94,* consolidated statements **must be prepared** (1) when one company owns a majority (more than 50%) of the outstanding voting common stock of another company and (2) unless control is likely to be temporary or if it does not rest with the majority owner (e.g., company is in legal reorganization or bankruptcy).[3] Thus, almost all subsidiaries must be included in the consolidated financial statements under *FASB Statement No. 94.* Previously, subsidiaries that were in a markedly dissimilar business than that of the parent would not be included in the consolidated statements.

Eliminations

Financial transactions involving a parent and one of its subsidiaries or between two of its subsidiaries are called intercompany transactions. In preparing consolidated financial statements, the effects of intercompany transactions must be eliminated by making elimination entries. Elimination entries allow the presentation of all account balances as if the parent and its subsidiaries were a single economic enterprise. **Elimination entries are made only on a consolidated statement work sheet, not in the accounting records of the parent or subsidiaries.** After elimination entries are prepared, the amounts remaining for each account on the work sheet are totaled and used to prepare the consolidated financial statements.

To illustrate the need for elimination entries, assume Y Company organized the Z Company, receiving all of Z Company's $100,000 par value common stock for $100,000 cash. The parent records the following entry on its books:

Investment in Z Company	100,000	
Cash		100,000
To record an investment in Z Company. Purchased 100% of Z Company stock.		

Z Company, the subsidiary, records the following entry on its books:

Cash	100,000	
Common Stock		100,000
To record issuance of all of the common stock to Y Company.		

An elimination entry is needed to offset the parent company's subsidiary investment account against the stockholders' equity accounts of the subsidiary. When the consolidated balance sheet is prepared, the required elimination on the work sheet is:

---

[3] FASB, *Statement of Financial Accounting Standards No. 94,* "Consolidation of All Majority-Owned Subsidiaries" (Stamford, Conn., 1987), p. 5. Copyright © by the Financial Accounting Standards Board, High Ridge Park, Stamford, Connecticut 06905, U.S.A.

Common Stock—Z Company	100,000	
Investment in Z Company		100,000

This elimination is required because the parent company's investment in the stock of the subsidiary actually represents an equity interest in the net assets of the subsidiary. Unless the investment is eliminated, the same resources will appear twice on the consolidated balance sheet—first as the investment account of the parent and second as the assets of the subsidiary. The elimination of Z Company's common stock is necessary to avoid double counting stockholders' equity. Viewing the two companies as if they were one, the Z Company common stock is really not outstanding; it is held within the consolidated group.

Consolidated financial statements present financial data as though the companies were a single entity. Since no entity can owe an amount to itself or be due an amount from itself, intercompany receivables and payables (amounts owed to and due from companies within the consolidated group) are items that also must be eliminated during the preparation of consolidated financial statements. For example, assume a parent company purchases $5,000 of bonds issued by its subsidiary company. In this case, no debt is owed to or due from any entity outside the consolidated enterprise, so those balances would be eliminated by an entry like the following that offsets the Investment in Bonds against the Bonds Payable:

Bonds Payable (subsidiary company)	5,000	
Investment in Bonds (parent company)		5,000
To eliminate intercompany bonds and bond investment.		

Other intercompany balances would be similarly eliminated when consolidated statements are prepared.

CONSOLIDATED BALANCE SHEET AT TIME OF ACQUISITION

A parent company may acquire a subsidiary at the book value of the subsidiary or at a cost above or below book value. Also, the parent may acquire 100% of the outstanding voting common stock of the subsidiary or may acquire some lesser percentage exceeding 50%.

Acquisition of Subsidiary at Book Value

Objective 5

Prepare consolidated financial statements through the use of a consolidated statement work sheet

To consolidate assets and liabilities of a parent company and its subsidiaries, a consolidated statement work sheet similar to the one shown in Illustration 16.3 is prepared. A consolidated statement work sheet is an informal record in which elimination entries are made for the purpose of showing account balances as if the parent and its subsidiaries were a single economic enterprise. The first two columns of the work sheet show assets, liabilities, and stockholders' equity of the parent and subsidiary as they appear on each corporation's balance sheet. The pair of columns labeled Eliminations allows intercompany items to be offset and consequently eliminated from the consolidated statement. The final column shows the amounts that will appear on the consolidated balance sheet.

The work sheet shown in Illustration 16.3 consolidates the accounts of P Company and its subsidiary, S Company, on January 1, 1994. P Company acquired S Company on January 1, 1994, by purchasing all of its outstanding voting common stock for $106,000 cash, which was the **book value** of the stock. Book value is equal to stockholders' equity, or net assets (assets minus liabilities). Thus, com-

ILLUSTRATION 16.3

Consolidated Balance Sheet Work Sheet (stock acquired at book value)

P COMPANY AND SUBSIDIARY S COMPANY
Work Sheet for Consolidated Balance Sheet
January 1, 1994 (date of acquisition)

	P Company	S Company	Eliminations Debit	Eliminations Credit	Consolidated Amounts
Assets					
Cash	26,000	12,000			38,000
Notes receivable	5,000			(2) 5,000	
Accounts receivable, net	24,000	15,000			39,000
Merchandise inventory	35,000	30,000			65,000
Investment in S Company	106,000			(1) 106,000	
Equipment, net	41,000	15,000			56,000
Buildings, net	65,000	35,000			100,000
Land	20,000	10,000			30,000
	322,000	117,000			328,000
Liabilities and Stockholders' Equity					
Accounts payable	18,000	6,000			24,000
Notes payable		5,000	(2) 5,000		
Common stock	250,000	100,000	(1) 100,000		250,000
Paid-in capital in excess					
of par value—common		4,000	(1) 4,000		–0–
Retained earnings	54,000	2,000	(1) 2,000		54,000
	322,000	117,000	111,000	111,000	328,000

mon stock ($100,000), paid-in capital in excess of par value—common ($4,000), and retained earnings ($2,000) equal $106,000. When P Company acquired the S Company stock, P Company made the following entry:

Investment in S Company 106,000
    Cash   106,000
    To record investment in S Company.

The Investment in S Company account appears as an asset on P Company's balance sheet. By buying the subsidiary's stock, the parent acquired a 100% equity, or ownership, interest in the subsidiary's net assets. Thus, if both the investment account and the subsidiary's assets appear on the consolidated balance sheet, the same resources will be counted twice. The Common Stock and Retained Earnings accounts of the subsidiary also represent an equity interest in the subsidiary's assets. Therefore, P's investment in S Company must be offset against S Company's stockholders' equity accounts so that the subsidiary's assets and the ownership interest in these assets appear only once on the consolidated balance sheet. This elimination is accomplished by entry (1) under "Eliminations" on the work sheet. The entry debits S Company's Common Stock for

$100,000, Paid-In Capital in Excess of Par Value—Common for $4,000, and Retained Earnings for $2,000 and credits Investment in S Company for $106,000. In journal entry form, the elimination entry is:

Common Stock.	100,000	
Paid-In Capital in Excess of Par Value—Common.	4,000	
Retained Earnings	2,000	
Investment in S Company.		106,000
To eliminate investment account and subsidiary stockholders' equity.		

Entry *(2)* is required to eliminate the effect of an intercompany transaction (intercompany debt, in this case). On the date it acquired S Company, P Company loaned S Company $5,000. The loan is recorded as a $5,000 note receivable on P's books and a $5,000 note payable on S's books. If the elimination entry is not made on the work sheet, the consolidated balance sheet will show $5,000 owed to the consolidated enterprise **by itself.** From the viewpoint of the consolidated equity, neither an asset nor a liability exists. Therefore, entry *(2)* is made on the work sheet to eliminate both the asset and liability. The entry debits Notes Payable and credits Notes Receivable for $5,000. In general journal form, entry *(2)* is:

Notes Payable	5,000	
Notes Receivable.		5,000
To eliminate intercompany payable and receivable.		

In making elimination entries, it is important to understand that **the entries are made only on the consolidated statement work sheet; no elimination entries are made in the accounting records of either P Company or S Company.** The final work sheet column is then used to prepare the consolidated balance sheet.

Acquisition of Subsidiary at a Cost above or below Book Value

In the previous illustration, P Company acquired 100% of S Company at a cost **equal** to book value. In some cases, subsidiaries may be acquired at a cost **greater than** or **less than** book value. For example, assume P Company purchased 100% of S Company's outstanding voting common stock for $125,000 (instead of $106,000). The book value of this stock is $106,000. Cost exceeds book value by $19,000. P Company's management may have paid more than book value because (1) the subsidiary's earnings prospects justify paying a price greater than book value or (2) the total fair market value of the subsidiary's assets exceeds their total book value.

According to the Accounting Principles Board *(APB Opinion No. 16)*, in cases where cost exceeds book value because of expected above-average earnings, the excess should be labeled *goodwill* on the consolidated balance sheet. Goodwill is an intangible value attached to a business primarily due to above-average earnings prospects. (This concept was discussed in Chapter 11.) On the other hand, if the excess is attributable to the belief that assets of the subsidiary are undervalued, then the asset values on the consolidated balance sheet should be increased to the extent of the excess.[4] In Illustration 16.4, it is assumed that $4,000 is due to the undervaluation of land owned by the company, and the remaining $15,000 of the excess of cost over book value is attributable to expected above-average earnings. As a result, $4,000 of the $19,000 excess is added to Land, and the other $15,000 is identified as "Goodwill" on the work sheet (Illustration 16.4) and on the balance sheet (Illustration 16.5).

---

[4] *APB Accounting Principles* (Chicago: Commerce Clearing House, Inc., 1973), vol. II, p. 6655.

ILLUSTRATION 16.4

Consolidated Balance Sheet Work Sheet (stock acquired at more than book value)

P COMPANY AND SUBSIDIARY S COMPANY
Work Sheet for Consolidated Balance Sheet
January 1, 1994 (date of acquisition)

	P Company	S Company	Eliminations Debit	Eliminations Credit	Consolidated Amounts
Assets					
Cash	7,000	12,000			19,000
Notes receivable	5,000			(2) 5,000	
Accounts receivable, net	24,000	15,000			39,000
Merchandise inventory	35,000	30,000			65,000
Investment in S Company	125,000			(1) 125,000	
Equipment, net	41,000	15,000			56,000
Buildings, net	65,000	35,000			100,000
Land	20,000	10,000	(1) 4,000		34,000
Goodwill			(1) 15,000		15,000
	322,000	117,000			328,000
Liabilities and Stockholders' Equity					
Accounts payable	18,000	6,000			24,000
Notes payable		5,000	(2) 5,000		
Common stock	250,000	100,000	(1) 100,000		250,000
Paid-in capital in excess of par value—common		4,000	(1) 4,000		–0–
Retained earnings	54,000	2,000	(1) 2,000		54,000
	322,000	117,000	130,000	130,000	328,000

The goodwill is established as part of the first elimination entry. Elimination entry *(1)* in Illustration 16.4 involves debits to the subsidiary's Common Stock for $100,000, Paid-In Capital in Excess of Par Value—Common for $4,000, Retained Earnings for $2,000, Land for $4,000, and Goodwill for $15,000, and a credit to Investment in S Company for $125,000. In journal form, entry *(1)* is:

Common Stock.	100,000	
Paid-In Capital in Excess of Par Value—Common.	4,000	
Retained Earnings	2,000	
Land	4,000	
Goodwill.	15,000	
Investment in S Company		125,000

   To eliminate investment and subsidiary stockholders' equity and to establish increased value of land and goodwill.

Entry *(2)* is the same as elimination entry *(2)* in Illustration 16.3. Entry *(2)* eliminates the intercompany loan by debiting Notes Payable and crediting Notes Receivable for $5,000.

After these elimination entries are made, the remaining amounts are consolidated and extended to the Consolidated Amounts column. The amounts in this

---

ILLUSTRATION 16.5

Consolidated Balance Sheet

P COMPANY AND SUBSIDIARY S COMPANY
Consolidated Balance Sheet
January 1, 1994
Assets

Current assets:

Cash.	$ 19,000	
Accounts receivable, net.	39,000	
Merchandise inventory.	65,000	
Total current assets		$123,000

Property, plant, and equipment:

Equipment, net.	$ 56,000	
Buildings, net.	100,000	
Land.	34,000	
Total property, plant, and equipment		190,000
Goodwill.		15,000
Total assets		$328,000

Liabilities and Stockholders' Equity

Current liabilities:

Accounts payable.		$ 24,000

Stockholders' equity:

Common stock.	$250,000	
Retained earnings.	54,000	
Total stockholders' equity		304,000
Total liabilities and stockholders' equity		$328,000

---

column are then used to prepare the consolidated balance sheet shown in Illustration 16.5. Notice that the $15,000 debit to Goodwill is carried to the Consolidated Amounts column and appears as an asset in the consolidated balance sheet.

As noted earlier, a company may purchase all or part of another company at more than book value and create goodwill on the consolidated balance sheet. The Accounting Principles Board, in *APB Opinion No. 17*, requires that all goodwill be amortized over a period not to exceed 40 years. This amortization is necessary under both the cost and the equity methods, but a discussion of this topic will be left to a more advanced text.

Under some circumstances, a parent company may pay less than book value of the subsidiary's net assets. In such cases, it is highly unlikely that a "bargain" purchase has been made. The most logical explanation for the price paid is that some of the subsidiary's assets are overvalued. The Accounting Principles Board requires that the excess of book value over cost be used to reduce proportionately the value of the noncurrent assets acquired (except long-term investments in marketable securities). If noncurrent assets are reduced to zero, the remaining dollar amount should be classified as a deferred credit.[5]

Acquisition of Less than 100% of a Subsidiary

Sometimes a parent company acquires less than 100% of the outstanding voting common stock of a subsidiary. For example, assume P Company acquired 80% (instead of 100%) of S Company's outstanding voting common stock. P Company

---

[5] Ibid., p. 6655.

ILLUSTRATION 16.6

Consolidated Balance Sheet Work Sheet (80% of stock acquired at more than book value)

P COMPANY AND SUBSIDIARY S COMPANY
Work Sheet for Consolidated Balance Sheet
January 1, 1994 (date of acquisition)

	P Company	S Company	Eliminations Debit	Eliminations Credit	Consolidated Amounts
Assets					
Cash	42,000	12,000			54,000
Notes receivable	5,000			(2) 5,000	
Accounts receivable, net	24,000	15,000			39,000
Merchandise inventory	35,000	30,000			65,000
Investment in S Company	90,000			(1) 90,000	
Equipment, net	41,000	15,000			56,000
Buildings, net	65,000	35,000			100,000
Land	20,000	10,000			30,000
Goodwill			(1) 5,200		5,200
	322,000	117,000			349,200
Liabilities and Stockholders' Equity					
Accounts payable	18,000	6,000			24,000
Notes payable		5,000	(2) 5,000		
Common stock	250,000	100,000	(1) 100,000		250,000
Paid-in capital in excess of par value—common		4,000	(1) 4,000		–0–
Retained earnings	54,000	2,000	(1) 2,000		54,000
Minority interest				(1) 21,200	21,200
	322,000	117,000	116,200	116,200	349,200

is the majority stockholder, but another group of stockholders exists that owns the remaining 20% of the stock. Stockholders who own less than 50% of a subsidiary's outstanding voting common stock are called *minority stockholders*, and their claim or interest in the subsidiary is called the minority interest. **Minority stockholders** have an interest in the subsidiary's net assets and share the subsidiary's income or loss with the parent company.

Illustration 16.6 shows the elimination entries required when P Company purchases 80% of S Company's stock for $90,000. The book value of the stock acquired by P Company is $84,800 (80% of $106,000). Assuming no assets are undervalued, the excess of cost ($90,000) over book value ($84,800) of $5,200 can be attributed to S Company's above-average earnings prospects (goodwill).

Elimination entry *(1)* eliminates S Company's stockholders' equity by debiting Common Stock for $100,000, Paid-In Capital in Excess of Par Value—Common for $4,000, and Retained Earnings for $2,000. Minority interest is established by crediting a Minority Interest account for $21,200 (20% of $106,000). The investment account is eliminated by crediting Investment in S Company for $90,000. The debit required to make the debits equal the credits is $5,200. The $5,200 is debited to Goodwill. In journal form, the elimination entry *(1)* is:

ILLUSTRATION 16.7

Consolidated Balance Sheet

P COMPANY AND SUBSIDIARY S COMPANY
Consolidated Balance Sheet
January 1, 1994
Assets

Current assets:

Cash.	$ 54,000	
Accounts receivable, net.	39,000	
Merchandise inventory.	65,000	
Total current assets .		$158,000

Property, plant, and equipment:

Equipment, net .	$ 56,000	
Buildings, net.	100,000	
Land.	30,000	
Total property, plant, and equipment .		186,000
Goodwill .		5,200
Total assets .		$349,200

Liabilities and Stockholders' Equity

Liabilities:

Accounts payable .		$ 24,000
Minority interest .		21,200

Stockholders' equity:

Common stock .	$250,000	
Retained earnings .	54,000	
Total stockholders' equity .		304,000
Total liabilities and stockholders' equity .		$349,200

Common Stock.	100,000	
Paid-In Capital in Excess of Par Value—Common.	4,000	
Retained Earnings	2,000	
Goodwill.	5,200	
Investment in S Company .		90,000
Minority Interest .		21,200
To eliminate investment and subsidiary stockholders' equity and to establish minority interest and goodwill.		

Elimination entry *(2)* is the same as shown in Illustration 16.6. The entry eliminates intercompany debt by debiting Notes Payable and crediting Notes Receivable for $5,000.

On the consolidated balance sheet (Illustration 16.7), minority interest appears between the liabilities and stockholders' equity sections.

ACCOUNTING FOR INCOME, LOSSES, AND DIVIDENDS OF A SUBSIDIARY

If a subsidiary is operating profitably, its net assets and retained earnings increase. When the subsidiary pays dividends, both the parent company and minority stockholders share in the distribution. All transactions of the subsidiary are recorded in the accounting records of the subsidiary in a normal manner.

As noted earlier, two different methods used by an investor to account for investments in common stock are the **cost** and **equity methods.** A parent company may use either the cost or equity method of accounting for its investment in a consolidated subsidiary. This choice is allowed because the investment account is eliminated during the consolidation process; therefore, the results are identical after consolidation. To illustrate the consolidation process at a date after acquisition, we will assume the parent company uses the equity method.

CONSOLIDATED FINANCIAL STATEMENTS AT A DATE AFTER ACQUISITION

As described earlier, under the equity method, the investment account on the parent company's books increases and decreases as the parent records its share of the income, losses, and dividends reported by the subsidiary. Thus, the balance in the investment account differs after acquisition from its balance on the date of acquisition. Consequently, the amounts eliminated on the consolidated statement work sheet will differ from year to year. As an illustration, assume the following facts:

1. P Company acquired 100% of the outstanding voting common stock of S Company on January 1, 1994. P Company paid $121,000 for stockholders' equity totaling $106,000. The excess of cost over book value is attributable to *(a)* an undervaluation of land amounting to $4,000 and *(b)* the remainder to S Company's above-average earnings prospects.
2. During 1994, S Company earned $20,000 from operations.
3. On December 31, 1994, S Company paid a cash dividend of $8,000.
4. S Company owes P Company $5,000 on a note at December 31.
5. Including its share (100%) of S Company's income, P Company earned $31,000 during 1994.
6. P Company paid a cash dividend of $10,000 during December 1994.
7. P Company uses the equity method of accounting for its investment in S Company.

The financial statements for the two companies as of December 31, 1994, are given in the first two columns of Illustration 16.8.

The type of work sheet shown in Illustration 16.8 will be used to prepare a consolidated income statement, statement of retained earnings, and balance sheet. Notice that in Illustration 16.8, P Company has a balance of $20,000 in its Income of S Company account and a balance of $133,000 in its Investment in S Company account. These balances are the result of the following journal entries made by P Company in 1994:

1994				
Jan.	1	Investment in S Company	121,000	
		Cash		121,000
		To record 100% investment in subsidiary.		
Dec.	31	Investment in S Company	20,000	
		Income of S Company		20,000
		To record income of subsidiary.		
	31	Cash	8,000	
		Investment in S Company		8,000
		To record dividends received from subsidiary.		

ILLUSTRATION 16.8

Consolidated Work Sheet One Year after Acquisition

P COMPANY AND SUBSIDIARY S COMPANY
Work Sheet for Consolidated Financial Statements
December 31, 1994

	P Company	S Company	Eliminations Debit	Eliminations Credit	Consolidated Amounts
Income Statement					
Revenue from sales	397,000	303,000			700,000
Income of S Company	20,000		(1) 20,000		
Cost of goods sold	(250,000)	(180,000)			(430,000)
Expenses (excluding depreciation and taxes)	(100,000)	(80,000)			(180,000)
Depreciation expense	(7,400)	(5,000)			(12,400)
Federal income tax expense	(28,600)	(18,000)			(46,600)
Net income— carried forward	31,000	20,000			31,000*
Statement of Retained Earnings					
Retained earnings— January 1:					
P Company	54,000				54,000
S Company		6,000	(3) 6,000		
Net income— brought forward	31,000	20,000			31,000*
	85,000	26,000			85,000*
Dividends:					
P Company	(10,000)				(10,000)
S Company		(8,000)		(2) 8,000	
Retained earnings—Dec. 31—carries forward	75,000	18,000			75,000*
Balance Sheet **Assets**					
Cash	38,000	16,000			54,000
Notes receivable	5,000			(4) 5,000	
Accounts receivable, net	25,000	18,000			43,000
Merchandise inventory	40,000	36,000			76,000
Investment in S Company	133,000		(2) 8,000	(3) 121,000	
				(1) 20,000	
Equipment, net	36,900	12,000			48,900
Buildings, net	61,700	33,000			94,700
Land	20,000	10,000	(3) 4,000		34,000
Goodwill			(3) 11,000		11,000
	359,600	125,000			361,600*
Liabilities and Stockholders' Equity					
Accounts payable	19,600	2,000			21,600
Notes payable	15,000	5,000	(4) 5,000		15,000
Common stock	250,000	100,000	(3) 100,000		250,000
Retained earnings— brought forward	75,000	18,000			75,000*
	359,600	125,000	154,000	154,000	361,600*

* Totals are determined vertically, not horizontally.

ILLUSTRATION 16.9

Consolidated Income Statement

P COMPANY AND SUBSIDIARY S COMPANY
Consolidated Income Statement
For the Year Ended December 31, 1994

Revenue from sales.		$700,000
Cost of goods sold		430,000
Gross margin.		$270,000
Expenses (excluding depreciation and taxes)	$180,000	
Depreciation expense	12,400	
Federal income tax expense	46,600	239,000
Net income		$ 31,000

The elimination entries on the work sheet in Illustration 16.8 are explained below.

Entry (1): During the year, S Company earned $20,000. P Company increased its investment account balance by $20,000. The first entry *(1)* on the work sheet eliminates the subsidiary's income from the Investment in S Company account and the Income of S Company account ($20,000). This entry reverses the entry made on the books of P Company to recognize the parent's share of the subsidiary's income (the first December 31 entry above).

Entry (2): When S Company paid its cash dividend, P Company debited Cash and credited the investment account for $8,000 (the second December 31 entry above). The second entry *(2)* restores the investment account to its balance before the dividends from S Company were deducted. That is, P Company's investment account is debited and S Company's dividends account is credited for $8,000. On a consolidated basis, a company cannot pay a dividend to itself.

Entry (3): This entry eliminates the original investment account balance ($121,000) and the subsidiary's stockholders' equity accounts as of the date of acquisition (retained earnings of $6,000 and common stock of $100,000). The entry also establishes goodwill of $11,000 and increases land by $4,000 to account for the excess of acquisition cost over book value.

Entry (4): This entry eliminates the intercompany debt of $5,000.

After the first three entries have been made, the investment account contains a zero balance from the viewpoint of the consolidated entity.

After the eliminations have been made, the corresponding amounts are added together and placed in the Consolidated Amounts column. Notice that certain totals in the first two columns do not add across to the total shown in the Consolidated Amounts column. For instance, consolidated net income is $31,000, not $31,000 plus $20,000. The net income row in the Income Statement section is carried forward to the net income row in the Statement of Retained Earnings section. Likewise, the ending retained earnings row in the Statement of Retained Earnings section is carried forward to the retained earnings row in the Balance Sheet section. The final work sheet column is then used to prepare the consoli-

---

ILLUSTRATION 16.10

Consolidated Statement of Retained Earnings

P COMPANY AND SUBSIDIARY S COMPANY
Consolidated Statement of Retained Earnings
For the Year Ended December 31, 1994

Retained earnings, January 1, 1994	$54,000
Net income	31,000
Subtotal	$85,000
Dividends	10,000
Retained earnings, December 31, 1994	$75,000

ILLUSTRATION 16.11

Consolidated Balance Sheet

P COMPANY AND SUBSIDIARY S COMPANY
Consolidated Balance Sheet
December 31, 1994

Assets

Current assets:

Cash	$ 54,000	
Accounts receivable, net	43,000	
Merchandise inventory	76,000	
Total current assets		$173,000

Property, plant, and equipment:

Equipment, net	$ 48,900	
Buildings, net	94,700	
Land	34,000	
Total property, plant, and equipment		177,600
Goodwill		11,000
Total assets		$361,600

Liabilities and Stockholders' Equity

Current liabilities:

Accounts payable	$ 21,600	
Notes payable	15,000	
Total liabilities		$ 36,600

Stockholders' equity:

Common stock	$250,000	
Retained earnings	75,000	
Total stockholders' equity		325,000
Total liabilities and stockholders' equity		$361,600

---

dated income statement (Illustration 16.9), consolidated statement of retained earnings (Illustration 16.10), and consolidated balance sheet (Illustration 16.11).[6] As stated earlier, amortization of goodwill is ignored in the illustration.

---

[6] Appendix E at the end of the text shows consolidated financial statements for actual corporations.

A BROADER PERSPECTIVE

FASB SCANS CONSOLIDATION ISSUES

Norwalk, Conn.—When the Financial Accounting Standards Board issued Statement 94, *Consolidation of All Majority-Owned Subsidiaries,* it was just one part of a larger project that could introduce broad changes to this area of accounting.

Currently the Board is examining practical as well as theoretical issues relating to two types of consolidation policies—an economic unit concept and a parent company concept—that will form the basis for future accounting pronouncements.

* * * * *

The parent company concept comes much closer to current practice as it views consolidated statements as an extension of the parent company. Thus ownership becomes the major criterion.

Adoption of the economic unit concept would represent a significant departure from current practice in that its basic criterion for consolidation hinges on the parent company's control and equity in another organization.

"Some questions the Board is discussing," Morris [the FASB project manager] said, "are whether you can control another company through management contracts or voting trusts, or if you own a large minority interest when the rest of the company is widely held."

Morris added that Board members have expressed reservations that standards based on control might result in accountants having to make too many subjective judgments. "That you won't have consistent application is a concern," he said.

Corporate officials have expressed their desire that the FASB move cautiously if it intends to change the present majority-ownership requirement for consolidations.

"The good thing about the 50 percent rule is that it represents a bright line test," said Robert Matza, vp and controller for Shearson Lehman Hutton Inc. and a member of the FASB's advisory task force on the consolidations project.

However, Matza did concede that consolidation of entities with less than 50 percent ownership does sometimes seem appropriate depending on the parent corporation's degree of control.

"Maybe better disclosure of entities owned on an equity basis could cover these situations," he said.

Morris said the Board's dissatisfaction with present practice centers around complex financings that allow a parent to control an entity without the vestiges of ownership that would make it a subsidiary for consolidation purposes.

Despite these problems, Morris said the FASB is fully examining the ramifications of consolidation policies.

"The Board is concerned with issuing any standard that will radically change practice," he added. "The members aren't content to buy into a concept and let procedures fall where they may because it happens to be consistent with the overall concept."

A second aspect of the project that is currently underway concerns when a new basis of accounting is appropriate for use in the separate financial statements of an entity that is or has been a subsidiary.

"The Board has examined what circumstances would create a new reporting entity with new values," said FASB project manager Janice Schneider. "As a practical matter the same criterion that drives consolidation policy might very well be the same criterion that drives the new basis determination."

Source: *Accounting Today,* February 5, 1990, p. 30. Reprinted with permission.

PURCHASE VERSUS POOLING OF INTERESTS

Objective 6

Identify the differences between purchase accounting and pooling of interests accounting

In this chapter's illustrations, we have assumed that the parent company acquired the subsidiary's common stock in exchange for cash. The acquiring company could also have used assets other than cash in the exchange. This kind of transaction—the exchange of cash or other assets for the common stock of another company—is called a purchase. When assets other than cash are used, the cost of the acquired company's stock is the fair market value of the assets given up or of the stock received, whichever can be more clearly and objectively determined.

A company can also acquire the common stock of another company by issuing its own common stock in exchange for the other company's common stock. When

---

ILLUSTRATION 16.12

Business Combinations

	1989	1988	1987	1986
Pooling of interests method	18	14	21	22
Purchase method	219	216	194	239

Source: Based on American Institute of Certified Public Accountants, *Accounting Trends & Techniques* (New York: AICPA, 1990), p. 49.

---

such an exchange occurs, the stockholders of both companies maintain a joint ownership interest in the combined company. Such a business combination involving the issuance of common stock in exchange for common stock is classified as a pooling of interests if it meets all the criteria cited in *APB Opinion No. 16*. If a combination resulting from an exchange of stock does not qualify as a pooling of interests, it must be recorded as a purchase.

The purchase and pooling of interests methods are **not** alternatives that can be applied to the same situation. Given the circumstances surrounding a particular business combination, only one of the two methods—purchase or pooling of interests—is appropriate. *APB Opinion No. 16* specifies 12 conditions that must be met before a business combination can be classified as a pooling of interests. For example, two of these conditions are (1) the combination must be effected in one transaction or be completed within one year in accordance with a specific plan, and (2) one corporation must issue only its common stock (no cash or other assets) in exchange for 90% or more of the voting common stock of another company. **If all 12 conditions specified by the APB are met, the resulting business combination must be accounted for as a pooling of interests. Otherwise, the purchase method must be used to account for the combination.**

When the pooling of interests method is used, the parent company's investment is recorded at the **book value of the subsidiary's net assets** (assets minus liabilities). Since the investment is recorded at the book value of the subsidiary's net assets, **there can be no goodwill or changes in asset valuations** from consolidation. The subsidiary's retained earnings at the date of acquisition become a part of the consolidated retained earnings, whereas under the purchase method they do not. Also, under the pooling of interests method, all subsidiary income for the year of acquisition is included in the consolidated net income in the year of acquisition. Under the purchase method, only that portion of the subsidiary's income that arises after the date of acquisition is included in consolidated net income.

From the above discussion, it should be apparent that these two methods will lead to significant differences in financial statement amounts. For instance, under the purchase method, any excess of investment cost over the book value of the ownership interest acquired must be used to increase the value of any assets that are undervalued or must be recognized as goodwill from consolidation. Under the pooling of interests method, on the other hand, book value—rather than cost—is the amount of the investment. Thus, whenever cost exceeds book value, either more depreciation or more amortization will be recorded under the purchase method than under the pooling of interests method, and consolidated net income will be smaller under the purchase method than under the pooling of interests method.

Illustration 16.12 shows the number of business combinations involving the two methods that occurred in a sample of 600 companies for the years 1986–89. The purchase method was used much more extensively than the pooling of interests method.

ETHICS
━━━━━━━━
A CLOSER LOOK

Corporate Raider's Suit Forces Publisher to Revise Dividends—Texas billionaire Robert M. Bass has won a 20-month wrangle to increase the value of his investment in the company that owns the St. Petersburg Times.

Times Publishing, which also owns several magazines, including Congressional Quarterly and Georgia Trend, agreed Friday to redeem its preferred stock and "increase substantially" the dividends on its common stock. Mr. Bass owns 40 percent of the common stock.

The heart of the courtroom dispute was Mr. Bass's contention that preferred shareholders got a better deal on dividends than did common shareholders. The Poynter Institute for Media Studies holds virtually all the preferred shares.

* * * * *

. . . The disproportionate division of dividends between preferred and common stock was set up to assure a steady flow of income to the Poynter Institute.

Formerly debt-free Times Publishing is borrowing an undisclosed amount of money to complete the deal.

* * * * *

The settlement resolves a dispute that began 40 years ago between Nelson Poynter and his sister, Eleanor Poynter Jamison, over stock ownership.

The Bass group became involved when Mrs. Jamison's heirs sold her common stock to the group for $28 million after failing to get the price they wanted from the newspaper.

Required

a. What type of stockholder is Mr. Bass?

b. Was he receiving a fair return on his investment?

c. For what possible reasons were the dividends structured as they were? What feature of preferred dividends permitted most of the dividends to go to the preferred stockholders?

d. Did the court decide that the dividend distribution was equitable? What is your personal opinion of the court's decision?

Source: Melissa Turner, *The Atlanta Journal and Constitution*, August 18, 1990, p. B-2.

USES AND LIMITATIONS OF CONSOLIDATED STATEMENTS

Objective 7

Describe the uses and limitations of consolidated financial statements

Consolidated financial statements are of primary importance to stockholders, managers, and directors of the parent company. The parent company benefits from the income and other financial strengths of the subsidiary. Likewise, the parent company suffers from a subsidiary's losses.

On the other hand, consolidated financial statements are of limited use to the creditors and minority stockholders of the subsidiary. The subsidiary's creditors have a claim against the subsidiary alone; they cannot look to the parent company for payment. Minority stockholders in the subsidiary do not benefit or suffer from the parent company's operations. These minority stockholders benefit from the subsidiary's income and financial strengths; they suffer from the subsidiary's losses and financial weaknesses. Thus, the subsidiary's creditors and minority stockholders are more interested in the subsidiary's individual financial statements than in the consolidated statements. Because of these factors, annual reports **always** include the financial statements of the consolidated entity, and **sometimes** include the financial statements of certain subsidiary companies alone, but **never** include the parent company's financial statements alone.

UNDERSTANDING THE LEARNING OBJECTIVES

1. Report stock investments and distinguish between the cost and equity methods of accounting for stock investments.

   □ Under the cost method, the investor company records its investment at the price paid at acquisition and does **not** adjust the investment account balance subsequently. The cost method is used for all short-term investments, long-term investments of less than 20% where the purchasing company does not exercise significant influence over the investee company, and may be used for long-term investments of more than 50%.

   □ Under the equity method, the investment is also initially recorded at acquisition price, but is then adjusted periodically for the investor company's share of the investee's reported income, losses, and dividends. The equity method is used for all long-term investments of between 20% and 50% and may be used for investments of more than 50%. This method is also used for investments of less than 20% if the purchasing company exercises significant influence over the investee company.

2. Prepare journal entries to account for short-term stock investments and for long-term stock investments of less than 20%.

   □ Under the cost method, the initial investment is debited to either Current Marketable Equity Securities or Noncurrent Marketable Equitable Securities, depending on whether the investment is a short-term or long-term investment.

   □ At the end of each accounting period, the company must adjust the carrying value of the portfolio for each of the two groups—current investments and noncurrent investments. The lower-of-cost-or-market (LCM) method is applied independently to each of these portfolios.

   □ Under the cost method, dividends received are credited to Dividend Revenue.

   □ Under the equity method, the initial investment is debited to an Investment in (Company Name) account. Income, losses, and dividends result in increases or decreases to the investment account.

3. Prepare journal entries to account for long-term investments of 20%–50%.

   □ The equity method must be used.

   □ The initial investment is debited to an Investment in (Company Name) account. The purchasing company's share of the investee's income is debited to the investment account, and the purchaser's share of the investee's losses and dividends is credited to the investment account as they are reported by the investee.

4. Describe the nature of parent and subsidiary corporations.

   □ A corporation that owns more than 50% of the outstanding voting common stock of another corporation is called the *parent company*.

   □ The corporation acquired and controlled by the parent company is known as the *subsidiary company*.

   □ A parent company and its subsidiaries maintain their own accounting records and prepare their own financial statements, but the parent company must also prepare consolidated financial statements. The consolidated financial statements consolidate the financial results of the parent and subsidiaries as a single enterprise.

☐ Consolidated financial statements must be prepared (1) when one company owns more than 50% of the outstanding voting stock of another company and (2) unless control is likely to be temporary or if it does not rest with the majority owner.

☐ In preparing consolidated financial statements, the effects of intercompany transactions must be eliminated by making elimination entries. Elimination entries are made **only** on a consolidated statement work sheet, not in the accounting records of the parent or subsidiaries.

☐ One elimination entry is needed to offset the parent company's subsidiary investment account against the stockholders' equity accounts of the subsidiary. Intercompany receivables and payables also must be eliminated.

5. Prepare consolidated financial statements through the use of a consolidated statement work sheet.

☐ A consolidated financial statement work sheet is an informal record in which elimination entries are made for the purpose of showing account balances as if the parent and its subsidiaries were a single economic enterprise.

☐ A consolidated balance sheet work sheet is prepared at time of acquisition. The first two columns of the work sheet show assets, liabilities, and stockholders' equity of the parent and subsidiary as they appear on each corporation's individual balance sheet. The next pair of columns shows the eliminations. The final column shows the amounts that will appear on the consolidated balance sheet.

☐ A consolidated work sheet is prepared at various dates after acquisition. The first two columns show the income statements, statements of retained earnings, and balance sheets of the parent and subsidiary. The next pair of columns shows the eliminations. The final column shows the amounts that will appear in the consolidated financial statements.

6. Identify the differences between purchase accounting and pooling of interests accounting.

☐ The exchange of cash or other assets for the common stock of another company is called a *purchase*. Any other combination that does not qualify as a pooling of interests must be accounted for as a purchase.

☐ When a company exchanges some of its own common stock for all or some of the other company's common stock, the business combination is classified as a pooling of interests (if certain other criteria are met). If a combination results from an exchange of stock but does not qualify as a pooling of interests, it must be recorded as a purchase.

☐ When the purchase method is used, the parent company's investment is recorded at cost, which may be greater than or less than book value. When the pooling of interests method is used, the parent company's investment is recorded at the book value of the subsidiary's net assets.

7. Describe the uses and limitations of consolidated financial statements.

☐ Consolidated financial statements are of primary importance to stockholders, managers, and directors of the parent company. On the other hand, consolidated financial statements are of limited use to the creditors and minority stockholders of the subsidiary.

DEMONSTRATION PROBLEM 16–A

Following are selected transactions and other data for Shelley Company for 1994:

Mar. 21 Purchased 600 shares of Ty Company common stock at $48.75 per share, plus a $450 broker's commission. Also purchased 100 shares of Ron Company common stock at $225 per share, plus a $376 broker's commission. Both investments are expected to be temporary.

June 2 Received cash dividends of $1.50 per share on the Ty common shares and $3 per share on the Ron common shares.

Aug. 12 Received shares representing a 100% stock dividend on the Ron shares.

30 Sold 100 shares of Ron common stock at $120 per share, less a $360 broker's commission.

Sept. 15 Received shares representing a 10% stock dividend on the Ty common stock. Market price today was $52.50 per share.

Dec. 31 Per share market values for the two investments in common stock are Ty, $45.75, and Ron, $106.50. Both investments are considered temporary.

Required Prepare journal entries to record the above transactions and the necessary adjustments for a December 31 closing.

SOLUTION TO DEMONSTRATION PROBLEM 16–A

SHELLEY COMPANY
GENERAL JOURNAL

1994				
Mar.	21	Current Marketable Equity Securities	52,576	
		Cash		52,576
		To record purchase of 600 shares of Ty common stock for $29,700 and 100 shares of Ron common stock for $22,876.		
June	2	Cash	1,200	
		Dividend Revenue		1,200
		To record cash dividends: $900 Ty, and $300 Ron.		
Aug.	12	Received 100 shares of Ron common stock as a 100% stock dividend. The new cost per share is $22,876 ÷ 200 shares = $114.38.		
	30	Cash	11,640	
		Current Marketable Equity Securities		11,438
		Gain on Sale of Current Marketable Equity Securities		202
		To record sale of current marketable equity securities: proceeds = $12,000 − $360; cost = $114.38 × 100 shares.		
Sept.	15	Received 60 shares of Ty common stock as a 10% stock dividend. New cost per share is $29,700 ÷ 660 shares = $45.		
Dec.	31	Unrealized Loss on Current Marketable Equity Securities	293	
		Allowance for Market Decline of Current Marketable Equity Securities		293
		To write current marketable equity securities down to market value:		

	Cost	Market	Inc. (Dec.) in Market Value
Ty common stock.	$29,700	$30,195*	$ 495
Ron common stock	11,438	10,650†	(788)
Total	$41,138	$40,845	$(293)

* $45.75 × 660 shares = $30,195.
† $106.50 × 100 shares = $10,650.

DEMONSTRATION PROBLEM 16–B

Samford Company acquired all of the outstanding voting common stock of Massey Company on January 2, 1994, for $300,000 cash. After the close of business on the date of acquisition, the balance sheets for the two companies were as follows:

	Samford Company	Massey Company
Assets		
Cash	$ 75,000	$ 30,000
Accounts receivable, net.	90,000	37,500
Notes receivable	15,000	7,500
Merchandise inventory	112,500	45,000
Investment in Massey Company	300,000	
Investment in bonds		30,000
Plant and equipment, net	303,000	195,000
Total assets	$895,500	$345,000
Liabilities and Stockholders' Equity		
Accounts payable	$ 75,000	$ 45,000
Notes payable	22,500	15,000
Bonds payable	225,000	
Common stock—$7.50 par value	300,000	150,000
Paid-in capital in excess of par value—common		60,000
Retained earnings.	273,000	75,000
Total liabilities and stockholders' equity	$895,500	$345,000

On January 2, 1994, Massey Company borrowed $15,000 from Samford Company by giving a note. On that same day, Massey Company purchased $30,000 of Samford Company's bonds. The excess of cost over book value is attributable to Massey Company's above-average earnings prospects.

Required Prepare a work sheet for a consolidated balance sheet on the date of acquisition.

SOLUTION TO DEMONSTRATION PROBLEM 16–B

SAMFORD COMPANY AND SUBSIDIARY MASSEY COMPANY
Work Sheet for Consolidated Balance Sheet
January 2, 1994 (date of acquisition)

	Samford Company	Massey Company	Eliminations		Consolidated Amounts
			Debit	Credit	
Assets					
Cash	75,000	30,000			105,000
Accounts receiable, net	90,000	37,500			127,500
Notes receivable	15,000	7,500		(2) 15,000	7,500
Merchandise inventory	112,500	45,000			157,500
Investment in Massey Co.	300,000			(1) 300,000	
Investment in bonds		30,000		(3) 30,000	–0–
Plant and equipment, net	303,000	195,000			498,000
Goodwill			(1) 15,000		15,000
	895,500	345,000			910,500
Liabilities and Stockholders' Equity					
Accounts payable	75,000	45,000			120,000
Notes payable	22,500	15,000	(2) 15,000		22,500
Bonds payable	225,000		(3) 30,000		195,000
Common stock—$7.50 par	300,000	150,000	(1) 150,000		300,000
Paid-in capital in excess of par value—common		60,000	(1) 60,000		–0–
Retained earnings	273,000	75,000	(1) 75,000		273,000
	895,500	345,000	345,000	345,000	910,500

NEW TERMS

Consolidated statement work sheet An informal record on which elimination entries are made for the purpose of showing account balances as if the parent and its subsidiaries were a single economic enterprise. 745

Consolidated statements The financial statements that result from consolidating the parent's financial statement amounts with those of its subsidiaries (after certain eliminations have been made). The consolidated statements reflect the financial position and results of operations of a single economic enterprise. 744

Cost method A method of accounting for stock investments in which the investor company does not adjust the investment account balance after it is initially recorded at cost. Dividends received from the investee are credited to a Dividends Revenue account. 736

Elimination entries Entries made on a consolidated statement work sheet to remove certain intercompany items and transactions. Elimination entries allow the presentation of all account balances as if the parent and its subsidiaries were a single economic enterprise. 744

Equity method A method of accounting for stock investments where the investment account is adjusted

periodically for the investor company's share of the investee's income, losses, and dividends as they are reported by the investee. 736, 742

Goodwill An intangible value attached to a business primarily due to above-average earnings prospects. 747

Intercompany transactions Financial transactions involving a parent and one of its subsidiaries or between two of the subsidiaries. 744

Investee A company that has 20% to 50% of its stock purchased by another company (the investor) as a long-term investment. 742

Investor A company that purchases 20% to 50% of the stock of another company (the investee) as a long-term investment. 742

Marketable equity securities Readily salable common and preferred stocks of other companies. 738

Minority interest The claim or interest of the stockholders who own less than 50% of a subsidiary's outstanding voting common stock. The minority stockholders have an interest in the subsidiary's net assets and share the subsidiary's earnings with the parent company. 750

Parent company   A corporation that owns more than 50% of the outstanding voting common stock of another corporation. *743*

Pooling of interests   A business combination that meets certain criteria specified in *APB Opinion No. 16*, including the issuance of common stock in exchange for common stock. *757*

Purchase   A transaction in which one company issues cash or other assets to acquire common stock of another company. Also, any combination that does not qualify as a pooling of interests. *756*

Subsidiary company   A corporation acquired and controlled by a parent corporation; control is established by ownership of more than 50% of the subsidiary's outstanding voting common stock. *743*

SELF-TEST

True-False

Indicate whether each of the following statements is true or false.

1. Under the cost method, the investment account is adjusted when dividends are received.

2. The cost method should be used when a corporation makes a long-term investment of less than 20%, and there is no significant control.

3. In the case of a stock split, the investor does not recognize revenue, but rather reduces the cost per share of stock.

4. Current and noncurrent marketable equity securities should be separately grouped in applying the lower-of-cost-or-market rules.

5. When making elimination entries, the entries are made only on the consolidated work sheet and not on the accounting records of the parent and subsidiary.

Multiple-Choice

Select the best answer for each of the following questions.

1. In which of the following cases is the investor company limited to use of the equity method in accounting for its stock investments?
   a. Short-term investments.
   b. Long-term investments of less than 20%.
   c. Long-term investments of 20%–50%.
   d. Long-term investments of more than 50%.

2. Under the equity method, which of the following is true?
   a. Dividends received reduce the investment account.
   b. Dividends received increase the investment account.
   c. The investor's share of net income decreases the investment account.
   d. The investor's share of net loss increases the investment account.

3. When the lower-of-cost-or-market rules are followed, which of the following is true when the market value of the portfolio of current marketable equity securities falls below their cost?

   a. The Unrealized Losses on Current Marketable Equity Securities is credited.
   b. The Recovery of Market Value of Current Marketable Equity Securities is credited.
   c. The Allowance for Market Decline of Current Marketable Equity Securities is debited.
   d. The Unrealized Loss on Current Marketable Equity Securities is debited.

4. Under the equity method, the investment account will always reflect only the:
   a. Dividends paid by the investee corporation.
   b. Investor's interest in the net assets of the investee.
   c. Investor's share of net income.
   d. Historical cost of the investment.

5. The excess of cost over the book value of an investment that is due to expected above-average earnings is labeled on the consolidated balance sheet as:
   a. Goodwill.
   b. Common stock.
   c. Retained earnings.
   d. Loss on investment.

Now turn to page 776 to check your answers.

QUESTIONS

1. For what reasons do corporations purchase the stock of other corporations?

2. Under what circumstances is the equity method used to account for stock investments?

3. Of what significance is par value to the investing corporation?

4. What is the purpose of preparing consolidated financial statements?

5. Under what circumstances must consolidated financial statements be prepared?

6. Why is it necessary to make elimination entries on the consolidated statement work sheet? Are these elimination entries also posted to the accounts of the parent and subsidiary? Why or why not?

7. Why might a corporation pay an amount in excess of the book value for a subsidiary's stock? Why might it pay an amount less than the book value of the subsidiary's stock?

8. The item "Minority interest" often appears as one amount in the consolidated balance sheet. What does this item represent?

9. How do a subsidiary's income, losses, and dividends affect the investment account of the parent when the equity method of accounting is used?

10. Distinguish between a purchase and a pooling of interests.

11. When must each of the following methods be used to account for a business combination?
    a. Purchase.
    b. Pooling of interests.

12. List three differences that exist between the purchase and pooling of interests methods of accounting for business combinations.

13. Why are consolidated financial statements of limited usefulness to the creditors and minority stockholders of a subsidiary?

14. Why does a company make short-term investments?

15. When is an investment in stock considered short term?

16. What is the difference between a *realized loss* and an *unrealized loss*?

MAYTAG
CORPORATION

17. *Real world question*   Based on the financial statements of Maytag Corporation contained in Appendix E, what was the 1988 Investment in Chicago Pacific Corporation balance?

HARLAND

18. *Real world question*   Based on the financial statements of John H. Harland Company contained in Appendix E, what was the 1989 ending investments balance?

EXERCISES

Exercise 16–1
Prepare entries to record an investment
(L.O. 1, 3)

Hart Company acquired 100% of the outstanding voting common stock of Clark Company for $600,000. On the date of acquisition, Clark Company's stockholders' equity consisted of common stock, $400,000, and retained earnings, $120,000. What journal entry should be made by Hart Company to record the above transaction?

Exercise 16–2
Prepare elimination entry as of the date of acquisition
(L.O. 5)

Assume for the data in Exercise 16–1 that a consolidated statement work sheet is prepared on the date of acquisition. What elimination entry must be made? (The subsidiary's tangible assets are not overvalued or undervalued.)

Exercise 16–3
Prepare elimination entry as of the date of acquisition
(L.O. 5)

Boyce, Inc., acquired 100% ownership of Oaks Company for $720,000 after evaluating its assets and finding that its building is undervalued by $6,000 and it expects to earn above-average income. Boyce, Inc., management attaches a $40,000 value to these income prospects. Oaks Company's Common Stock account has a balance of $450,000, and its Retained Earnings account has a balance of $224,000. Boyce, Inc.'s Common Stock account has a balance of $640,000, and its Retained Earnings account balance is $250,000. Prepare the necessary elimination entry at the date of acquisition.

Exercise 16–4
Prepare elimination entry as of the date of acquisition
(L.O. 5)

If the following balances exist prior to the preparation of a consolidated balance sheet, what elimination entry is needed if the parent owns 100% of the subsidiary?

	Parent Company	Subsidiary Company
Common stock	$1,360,000	$200,000
Investment in S Company	300,000	
Retained earnings	720,000	100,000

Exercise 16–5

Prepare entries to record and eliminate an investment in subsidiary (L.O. 5)

On February 1, 1993, Miami Company acquired 100% of the outstanding voting common stock of Atlanta Company for $430,000 cash. The stockholders' equity of Atlanta Company consisted of common stock, $350,000, and retained earnings, $80,000. Prepare (a) the entry to record the investment in Atlanta Company and (b) the elimination entry that would be made on the consolidated statement work sheet for a balance sheet as of the date of acquisition.

Exercise 16–6

Prepare entries to record and eliminate an investment in subsidiary (L.O. 5)

Oglesby Corporation acquired, for cash, 80% of the outstanding voting common stock of Tint Company. On the date of its acquisition, Tint Company's stockholders' equity consisted of common stock, $1,400,000, and retained earnings, $520,000. The cost of the investment exceeded the book value by $72,000, attributable to above-average income prospects. Prepare (a) the entry to record the investment in Tint Company and (b) the entry to eliminate the investment for purposes of preparing consolidated financial statements as of the date of acquisition.

Exercise 16–7

Compute difference between cost and book value of common stock investments (L.O. 5)

On January 1, 1993, Company J acquired 85% of the outstanding voting common stock of Company Y. On that date, Company Y's stockholders' equity consisted of:

Common stock, $80 par; 20,000 shares authorized, issued, and outstanding	$1,600,000
Retained earnings	250,000
Total stockholders' equity	$1,850,000

Compute the difference between cost and book value in each of the following cases:

a. Company J pays $1,572,500 cash for its interest in Y.

b. Company J pays $1,850,000 cash for its interest in Y.

c. Company J pays $1,500,000 cash for its interest in Y.

Exercise 16–8

Compute balance in investment account and minority interest at year-end (L.O. 3, 5)

Paper Company purchased 90% of Metal Company's outstanding voting common stock on January 2, 1993. Paper Company paid $310,000 for its proportionate equity of $270,000: $180,000, common stock; and $90,000, retained earnings. The difference was due to undervalued land owned by Metal Company. Metal Company earned $36,000 during 1993 and paid cash dividends of $12,000.

a. Compute the balance in the investment account on December 31, 1993.

b. Compute the amount of the minority interest on (1) January 2, 1993, and (2) December 31, 1993.

Exercise 16–9

Prepare equity method entries for an investment (L.O. 1, 3)

Jennings Company owns 75% of Maine Company's outstanding common stock and uses the equity method of accounting. Maine Company reported net income of $272,000 for 1993. On December 31, 1993, Maine Company paid a cash dividend of $80,000. In 1994, Maine Company incurred a net loss of $50,000. Prepare entries to reflect these events on Jennings Company's books.

Exercise 16–10

Compute book value, difference between cost and book value, and minority interest of an investment (L.O. 5)

On January 1, 1993, the stockholders' equity section of Spencer Company's balance sheet was as follows:

Stockholders' equity:	
Paid-in capital:	
Common stock—$60 par value; authorized, 100,000 shares; issued and outstanding, 75,000 shares	$4,500,000
Paid-in capital in excess of par value	750,000
Total paid-in capital	$5,250,000
Retained earnings	450,000
Total stockholders' equity	$5,700,000

Ninety percent of Spencer Company's outstanding voting common stock was acquired by Thomas Company on January 1, 1993, for $5,010,000. Compute *(a)* the book value of the investment, *(b)* the difference between cost and book value, and *(c)* the minority interest.

Exercise 16–11

Prepare equity method entries for an investment (L.O. 1, 3)

Battey Company acquired 80% of the outstanding voting common stock of Lestor Company for $960,000 on January 2, 1993. During 1993, Lestor Company had net income of $150,000 and paid out $72,000 in dividends on common stock. What journal entries should be made by Battey Company to record the above events, assuming it uses the equity method?

Exercise 16–12

Prepare work sheet for consolidated balance sheet at acquisition (L.O. 5)

On January 1, 1993, Bellamy Company acquired 75% of the outstanding voting common stock of Kwik Company for $296,000. Also on January 1, 1993, Kwik Company borrowed $24,000 from Bellamy Company. The debt is evidenced by a note. Show how the consolidated statement work sheet shown below would be completed. The subsidiary's tangible assets are neither overvalued nor undervalued.

BELLAMY COMPANY AND SUBSIDIARY KWIK COMPANY
Work Sheet for Consolidated Balance Sheet
January 1, 1993

	Bellamy Company	Kwik Company	Eliminations		Consolidated Amounts
			Debit	Credit	
Assets					
Cash	92,000	36,000			
Notes receivable	24,000				
Accounts receivable, net	58,000	38,000			
Merchandise inventory	68,000	54,000			
Investment in Kwik Co.	296,000				
Equipment, net	94,000	100,000			
Buildings, net	166,000	148,000			
Land	56,000	44,000			
	854,000	420,000			
Liabilities and Stockholders' Equity					
Notes payable		24,000			
Accounts payable	72,000	20,000			
Common stock	500,000	220,000			
Retained earnings	282,000	156,000			
	854,000	420,000			

Exercise 16–13

Prepare journal entries for current marketable equity securities (L.O. 2)

Stephens Company made the following short-term investment in the capital stock of Comer and Colbert Corporations on September 13, 1993:

4,000 shares of Comer Corporation at $40 per share	$160,000
2,000 shares of Colbert Corporation at $60 per share.	120,000
Total cost of short-term investments	$280,000

On December 31, 1993, the per share market values of Comer and Colbert were $30 and $62, respectively. Stephens Company sold 1,000 shares of Colbert on June 1, 1994, for $56 per share. The market values of Comer and Colbert stock on December 31, 1994, were $38 and $50 per share, respectively. Prepare all necessary journal entries for Stephens Company to reflect the above information.

PROBLEMS: SERIES A

Problem 16–1A

Prepare equity method entries for an investment and eliminating entries for consolidated work sheet (L.O. 1, 3)

Diana Company acquired 90% of the outstanding voting common stock of Blanca Company on January 1, 1993, for $900,000 cash. Diana Company uses the equity method. During 1993, Blanca reported $180,000 net income and paid $60,000 in cash dividends. The stockholders' equity section of the December 31, 1992, balance sheet for Blanca was as follows:

Stockholders' equity:	
Common stock—$10 par	$ 800,000
Retained earnings	200,000
Total stockholders' equity	$1,000,000

Required

a. Prepare general journal entries to record the investment and the effect of Blanca Company's income and dividends on Diana Company's accounts.

b. Prepare the elimination entry that would be made on the consolidated statement work sheet for a balance sheet as of the date of acquisition.

Problem 16–2A

Prepare equity method entries for an investment, and compute the investment account balance (L.O. 1, 3)

Gas Company acquired 68% of the outstanding voting common stock of Power Company for $600,000 on January 1, 1992. The investment is accounted for under the equity method. During the years 1992–94, Power Company reported the following:

	Net Income (loss)	Dividends Paid
1992	$90,600	$49,500
1993	20,700	8,750
1994	(1,100)	4,400

Required

a. Prepare general journal entries to record the investment and the effect of the subsidiary's income, loss, and dividends on Gas Company's accounts.

b. Compute the investment account balance on December 31, 1994.

Problem 16–3A

Prepare work sheet for consolidated balance sheet at acquisition (L.O. 5)

Gary Company acquired all of the outstanding voting common stock of A. F. Company on January 3, 1993, for $504,000. On the date of acquisition, the balance sheets for the two companies were as follows:

	Gary Company	A. F. Company
Assets		
Cash	$ 84,000	$ 72,000
Accounts receivable	162,000	150,000
Notes receivable	90,000	24,000
Merchandise inventory	234,000	108,000
Investment in A. F. Company	504,000	
Equipment, net	432,000	198,000
Total assets	$1,506,000	$552,000
Liabilities and Stockholders' Equity		
Accounts payable	$ 156,000	$ 48,000
Common stock—$20 par	720,000	348,000
Retained earnings	630,000	156,000
Total liabilities and stockholders' equity	$1,506,000	$552,000

Required   Prepare a work sheet for a consolidated balance sheet on the date of acquisition.

Problem 16–4A

Prepare work sheet and
consolidated balance
sheet at acquisition
(L.O. 5)

Times Company acquired all of the outstanding voting common stock of Golf Company on
January 1, 1993, for $180,000. At the end of business on the date of acquisition, the balance
sheets for the two companies were as follows:

	Times Company	Golf Company
Assets		
Cash.	$ 37,500	$ 11,250
Accounts receivable.	18,000	15,000
Notes receivable	7,500	4,500
Merchandise inventory.	57,000	36,000
Investment in Golf Company	180,000	
Equipment, net	51,000	30,750
Buildings, net.	138,750	69,000
Land.	58,500	18,750
Total assets	$548,250	$185,250
Liabilities and Stockholders' Equity		
Accounts payable	$ 33,000	$ 15,000
Notes payable	9,000	10,500
Common stock—$40 par	397,500	148,500
Retained earnings.	108,750	11,250
Total liabilities and stockholders' equity	$548,250	$185,250

The management of Times Company thinks Golf Company's land is undervalued by
$6,750. The remainder of cost over book value is due to superior income potential.

On the date of acquisition, Golf Company borrowed $7,500 from Times Company by
giving a note.

Required

a. Prepare a work sheet for a consolidated balance sheet on the date of acquisition.

b. Prepare a consolidated balance sheet for January 1, 1993.

Problem 16–5A

Prepare work sheet for
consolidated financial
statements
(L.O. 5)

Refer back to Problem 16–4A and assume that Times Company uses the equity method.
Assume the following are the adjusted trial balances for Times Company and Golf Company on December 31, 1993.

	Times Company	Golf Company
Cash	$ 36,000	$ 15,178
Accounts receivable	23,064	17,250
Notes receivable.	14,250	3,750
Merchandise inventory, December 31	63,750	42,000
Investment in Golf Company	188,306	
Equipment, net	47,814	28,828
Buildings, net	131,812	65,550
Land	58,500	18,750
Cost of goods sold.	336,000	90,000
Expenses (excluding depreciation and taxes)	90,000	33,752
Depreciation expense	10,124	5,372
Income tax expense	23,736	5,146
Dividends.	19,874	7,424
Total debits	$1,043,230	$333,000
Accounts payable	$ 30,000	$ 15,750
Notes payable.	11,250	7,500
Common stock—$40 par	397,500	148,500
Retained earnings	108,750	11,250
Income of Golf Company	15,730	
Revenue from sales	480,000	150,000
Total credits.	$1,043,230	$333,000

There is no intercompany debt at the end of the year.

Required   Prepare a work sheet for consolidated financial statements on December 31, 1993.

Problem 16–6A

Prepare consolidated
income statement,
statement of retained
earnings, and balance
sheet (L.O. 5)

Using the work sheet prepared for Problem 16–5A, prepare the following items:

a.   Consolidated income statement for the year ended December 31, 1993.

b.   Consolidated statement of retained earnings for the year ended December 31, 1993.

c.   Consolidated balance sheet for December 31, 1993.

Problem 16–7A

Prepare journal entries for
current marketable equity
securities
(L.O. 2, 3)

Roger Fulton is the financial manager for Nelson Industries, Inc. The company has been doing extremely well in the last two years and is currently holding a significant amount of idle cash, which Roger has decided to invest in various marketable securities. On May 25, 1993, Roger purchased the following stocks for Nelson to hold in its short-term investment portfolio:

1,500 shares of Dale Companies @ $20 per share	$30,000
1,250 shares of Trans Motor Transports @ $4 per share. . . .	5,000
500 shares of Corto Industries @ $10 per share	5,000
500 shares of Texas, Inc., @ $50 per share	25,000
	$65,000

Listed below are transactions that occurred in regard to the marketable securities portfolio of Nelson Industries during the remainder of 1993 and the years 1994 and 1995.

1993

June 15   Sold 750 shares of Trans Motor Transports stock at $8 per share.

Oct. 27   Received a $2 per share dividend on the Dale Companies' stock and a $1 per share dividend on the Corto Industries' stock.

Nov. 15   Purchased 250 shares of Jet Air Service, Inc., at $6 per share.

Dec. 20   Sold all the Corto Industries stock at $8 per share.

     31   The following market quotations were available for each of the securities owned by Nelson:

Dale Companies	$14 per share
Trans Motor Transports	6 per share
Texas, Inc.	54 per share
Jet Air Service, Inc.	2 per share

1994

Jan. 14   Sold the remaining Trans Motor Transports stock at $12 per share.

Feb. 4   Purchased 1,000 shares of Georgia Airlines stock at $9 per share.

June 10   Received a $4 per share dividend on the 500 shares of Texas, Inc.

Sept. 7   Sold the Jet Air Service stock at $9.50 per share.

Dec. 12   Purchased 125 shares of Freightways, Ltd. at $4 per share.

     31   The following market quotations were available for each of the securities owned by Nelson:

Dale Companies	$14 per share
Texas, Inc.	50 per share
Georgia Airlines	10 per share
Freightways, Ltd.	2 per share

1995

Jan. 28   Sold half of the Dale Companies' stock at $24 per share.

Mar.   6   Purchased 250 shares of Selleck Enterprises at $30 per share.

Apr.   9   Received a $10 per share dividend on the Texas, Inc., stock.

Sept. 5   Sold 375 shares of the Georgia Airlines stock at $16 per share.

Nov. 17   Sold all the Freightways, Ltd. stock for $3 per share.

Dec. 31   The following market quotations were available for each of the securities owned by Nelson:

Dale Companies	$20 per share
Texas, Inc.	54 per share
Georgia Airlines	18 per share
Selleck Enterprises	22 per share

Required   Journalize all of the above transactions for Nelson Industries regarding its portfolio of current marketable equity securities.

PROBLEMS: SERIES B

Problem 16–1B

Prepare equity method entries for an investment and eliminating entries for consolidated work sheet (L.O. 1, 3)

On January 1, 1993, Reilly Company acquired 80% of the outstanding voting common stock of Shelby Company for $180,000 cash. Reilly Company uses the equity method. During 1993, Shelby reported $30,000 net income and paid $15,000 in dividends. The stockholders' equity section of the December 31, 1992, balance sheet for Shelby was as follows:

Stockholders' equity:	
Common stock—$10 par	$187,500
Retained earnings	37,500
Total stockholders' equity	$225,000

Required   *a.*   Prepare general journal entries to record the investment and the effect of Shelby Company's income and dividends on Reilly Company's accounts.

             b.   Prepare the elimination entry that would be made on the consolidated statement work sheet for a balance sheet as of the date of acquisition.

Problem 16–2B

Prepare equity method entries for an investment, and compute the investment account balance (L.O. 1, 3)

Bell Company acquired 75% of the outstanding voting common stock of Maddox Company for $976,000 cash on January 1, 1992. The investment is accounted for under the equity method. During 1992, 1993, and 1994, Maddox Company reported the following:

	Net Income (loss)	Dividends Paid
1992	$300,800	$236,800
1993	(83,200)	–0–
1994	63,200	28,800

Required   *a.*   Prepare general journal entries to record the investment and the effect of the subsidiary's income, loss, and dividends on Bell Company's accounts.

             b.   Compute the investment account balance on December 31, 1994.

Problem 16–3B

Prepare work sheet for consolidated balance sheet at acquisition (L.O. 5)

Southern Company acquired 100% of the outstanding voting common stock of Verde Company on January 1, 1993, for $190,000 cash. At the end of business on the date of acquisition, the balance sheets for the two companies were as follows:

	Southern Company	Verde Company
Assets		
Cash.	$ 15,000	$ 35,000
Accounts receivable	35,000	45,000
Notes receivable	25,000	15,000
Merchandise inventory.	62,500	37,500
Investment in Verde Company	190,000	
Equipment, net.	55,000	70,000
Total assets	$382,500	$202,500
Liabilities and Stockholders' Equity		
Accounts payable.	$ 40,000	$ 12,500
Notes payable	30,000	–0–
Common stock—$40 par	250,000	150,000
Retained earnings.	62,500	40,000
Total liabilities and stockholders' equity	$382,500	$202,500

Also on January 1, 1993, Southern Company borrowed $15,000 from Verde Company by giving a note.

Required   Prepare a work sheet for a consolidated balance sheet on the date of acquisition.

Problem 16–4B

Prepare work sheet and consolidated balance sheet; prepare consolidated balance sheet (L.O. 5)

Stepp Company acquired 100% of the outstanding voting common stock of the Coyne Company on January 2, 1993, for $900,000 cash. At the end of business on the date of acquisition, the balance sheets for the two companies were as follows:

	Stepp Company	Coyne Company
Assets		
Cash.	$ 105,000	$ 60,000
Accounts receivable.	78,000	48,000
Notes receivable	120,000	30,000
Merchandise inventory.	165,000	78,000
Investment in Coyne Company	900,000	
Equipment, net.	216,000	150,000
Buildings, net.	630,000	330,000
Land.	255,000	135,000
Total assets	$2,469,000	$831,000
Liabilities and Stockholders' Equity		
Accounts payable.	$ 39,000	$ 45,000
Notes payable	30,000	36,000
Common stock—$30 par	1,800,000	600,000
Retained earnings.	600,000	150,000
Total liabilities and stockholders' equity	$2,469,000	$831,000

The excess of cost over book value is attributable to the above-average income prospects of Coyne Company. On the date of acquisition, Coyne Company borrowed $24,000 from Stepp Company by giving a note.

Required   *a.*   Prepare a work sheet for a consolidated balance sheet as of the date of acquisition.

           b.   Prepare a consolidated balance sheet for January 2, 1993.

Problem 16–5B

Prepare work sheet for consolidated financial statements
(L.O. 5)

Refer back to Problem 16–4B and assume that Stepp Company uses the equity method. Assume the following are the adjusted trial balances for Stepp Company and Coyne Company on December 31, 1993:

	Stepp Company	Coyne Company
Cash	$ 117,000	$ 105,000
Accounts receivable	126,000	60,000
Notes receivable	105,000	15,000
Merchandise inventory, December 31	165,000	95,700
Investment in Coyne Company	930,000	
Equipment, net	205,200	142,500
Buildings, net	604,800	316,800
Land	255,000	135,000
Cost of goods sold	600,000	210,000
Expenses (excluding depreciation and taxes)	240,000	90,300
Depreciation expense	36,000	20,700
Income tax expense	195,000	63,000
Dividends	180,000	36,000
Total debits	$3,759,000	$1,290,000
Accounts payable	$ 45,000	$ 60,000
Notes payable	48,000	30,000
Common stock—$30 par	1,800,000	600,000
Retained earnings—Jan. 1	600,000	150,000
Revenue from sales	1,200,000	450,000
Income of Coyne Company	66,000	
Total credits	$3,759,000	$1,290,000

There is no intercompany debt at the end of the year.

Required   Prepare a work sheet for consolidated financial statements on December 31, 1993.

Problem 16–6B

Prepare consolidated income statement, statement of retained earnings, and balance sheet
(L.O. 5)

Using the work sheet prepared for Problem 16–5B, prepare the following items:

a.   Consolidated income statement for the year ended December 31, 1993.

b.   Consolidated statement of retained earnings for the year ended December 31, 1993.

c.   Consolidated balance sheet for December 31, 1993.

Problem 16–7B

Prepare journal entries for current marketable equity securities
(L.O. 2, 3)

Bland Company purchased the following securities on November 18, 1993, for short-term investment purposes:

2,500 shares of Rax Corporation @ $24	$60,000
1,000 shares of Alaska, Ltd. stock @ $16	16,000
500 shares of Carrier Systems stock @ $6	3,000
	$79,000

On December 19, Bland received a dividend for $2 per share on the Rax Corporation stock. On December 30, Bland sold the 500 shares of Carrier Systems stock for $2 per share. On December 31, the market values of the Rax Corporation stock and the Alaska, Ltd. stock were $26 and $8 per share, respectively.

During 1994, the following transactions occurred relative to Bland's portfolio of marketable equity securities: On February 19, Bland bought 250 shares of Grading stock at $14 per share as a short-term investment. On October 30, Bland sold 1,500 shares of Rax stock for $38 per share. On December 31, the market values of the securities held by Bland were as follows:

Rax Corporation stock	$30 per share
Alaska, Ltd. stock	10 per share
Grading stock	4 per share

On January 15, 1995, Bland sold the Grading stock for $11 per share. On April 16, Bland received a $4 per share cash dividend from Alaska, Ltd. Bland purchased 2,000 shares of First Bank and Trust stock on May 7, 1995, for $20 per share as a short-term investment. The Rax Corporation stock was sold on June 15, 1995, for $50 per share. The market values for the shares of stock held by Bland Corporation on December 31, 1994, were:

Alaska, Ltd. stock	$12
First Bank and Trust stock	36

Required   Prepare all journal entries for Bland Corporation relative to investments in marketable securities for the years 1993, 1994, and 1995.

BUSINESS DECISION PROBLEMS

Decision Problem 16–1
Prepare a consolidated balance sheet
(L.O. 5)

On January 2, 1993, Vanilla Company acquired 60% of the voting common stock of Strawberry Corporation for $400,000 cash. The excess of cost over book value was due to above-average earnings prospects. Vanilla and Strawberry are engaged in similar lines of business. Vanilla has hired you to help it prepare consolidated financial statements. Vanilla has already collected the following information for both companies as of January 2, 1993:

	Vanilla Company	Strawberry Corporation
Assets		
Cash.	$ 40,000	$ 30,000
Accounts receivable	60,000	70,000
Merchandise inventory.	160,000	120,000
Investment in Strawberry Corporation	400,000	
Plant and equipment, net	520,000	410,000
Total assets	$1,180,000	$630,000
Liabilities and Stockholders' Equity		
Accounts payable	$ 80,000	$ 30,000
Common stock—$40 par	800,000	400,000
Retained earnings.	300,000	200,000
Total liabilities and stockholders' equity	$1,180,000	$630,000

Required   *a.*   Vanilla believes consolidated financial statements can be prepared simply by adding together the amounts in the two individual columns. Is Vanilla correct? If not, why not?

b.   Prepare a consolidated balance sheet for the date of acquisition.

Decision Problem 16–2

Determine method of accounting used, amount of equity income included by parent, and total income of subsidiary (L.O. 1)

In the footnotes of The Coca-Cola Company financial statements located in Appendix E, footnote (3) discloses the August 1989 purchase of Coca-Cola Amatil Limited; the balance sheet lists the carrying value of that investment at $524,931,000.

Required

Based on the information in footnote (3), determine the method of accounting used (cost, equity, purchase, or pooling-of-interests) and the amount of equity income included by The Coca-Cola Company in its 1989 annual report. Then, assume that Coca-Cola Amatil Limited ends its fiscal year on December 31, 1989, and estimate the total net income earned by Coca-Cola Amatil Limited.

ANSWERS TO SELF-TEST

True-False

1. *False.* Under the cost method of accounting for stock investments, the Dividend Revenue account rather than the investment account is adjusted.

2. *True.* For long-term investments of less than 20%, the cost method should be used.

3. *True.* Revenue is not recognized when there is a stock split. The new number of shares is recorded, and the cost per share is reduced.

4. *True.* Current investments should be considered separately from noncurrent investments in applying lower of cost or market.

5. *True.* Eliminating entries are not made on the accounting records of the parent and subsidiary. Only the work sheet is affected by elimination entries made during consolidation.

Multiple-Choice

1. *c.* The Accounting Principles Board has said that investors must use the equity method when accounting for long-term investments of 20%–50%.

2. *a.* Under the equity method, dividends received reduce the investment account; the other choices are not true.

3. *d.* If the market value of securities falls below their cost, an unrealized loss account is debited.

4. *b.* Under the equity method, the investment account will always reflect the investor's interest in the net assets of the investee.

5. *a.* If cost is greater than the book value of an investment because of expected above-average earnings, *APB Opinion No. 16* tells us that the excess cost should be labeled goodwill.

The purpose of issuing financial statements is to provide useful information to decision makers. One of the newest and most useful financial statements is the statement of cash flows, which shows the sources of cash inflows and cash outflows.

Those interested in the financial statements of a corporation include investors, creditors, suppliers, customers, government agencies, labor unions, employees, and the general public. These people study the relationships between amounts in financial statements to help them analyze the statements. They may ask questions such as: Are current assets large enough to pay current liabilities? Does this corporation generate enough cash from its operations to keep paying dividends at the current level?

To understand financial statements, readers should be aware of the current business environment. This information can be found in *The Wall Street Journal, Business Week, Nation's Business,* and other business literature.

III

ANALYSIS OF FINANCIAL STATEMENTS AND CASH FLOWS

17

ANALYSIS AND INTERPRETATION OF FINANCIAL STATEMENTS

LEARNING OBJECTIVES

After studying this chapter, you should be able to:

1. Describe and explain the objectives of financial statement analysis.

2. Calculate and explain changes in financial statements using horizontal analysis, vertical analysis, and trend analysis.

3. Perform ratio analysis on financial statements using liquidity ratios, long-term solvency ratios, profitability tests, and market tests.

4. Describe the considerations used in financial statement analysis.

As you may recall, the two primary objectives of every business are solvency and profitability. Solvency is the ability of a company to pay debts as they come due; it is reflected on the company's balance sheet. Profitability is the ability of a company to generate income; it is reflected on the company's income statement. Generally, all those interested in the affairs of a company are especially interested in its solvency and profitability.

This chapter discusses several common methods used to analyze and relate to one another the data in financial statements and, as a result, gain a clear picture of the solvency and profitability of a company. A company's financial statements are analyzed internally by management and externally by investors and creditors.

Management's analysis of financial statements primarily relates to **parts** of the company. This approach enables management to plan, evaluate, and control operations within the company. Investors and creditors generally focus their analysis of financial statements on the company as a **whole.** This analysis helps them decide whether to invest in or extend credit to the company. In this chapter, we discuss financial statement analysis as conducted by outside parties, such as investors and creditors, who rely primarily on a company's financial statements for their information.

OBJECTIVES OF FINANCIAL STATEMENT ANALYSIS

Objective 1

Describe and explain the objectives of financial statement analysis

Financial statement analysis consists of applying analytical tools and techniques to financial statements and other relevant data to obtain useful information. This information is shown as significant relationships between data and trends in those data that assess the company's **past performance** and **current financial position.** The information shows the results or consequences of prior management decisions. In addition, the information is used to **make predictions** that may have a direct effect on decisions made by users of financial statements.

Present investors and potential investors are both interested in the future ability of a company to earn profits—its profitability. These investors wish to predict future dividends and changes in the market price of the company's common stock. Since both dividends and price changes are likely to be influenced by earnings, investors may seek to predict earnings. The company's past earnings record is the logical starting point in predicting future earnings.

Sometimes outside parties, such as creditors, are interested in predicting a company's solvency rather than its profitability. The liquidity of the company affects its short-term solvency. The company's liquidity is its state of possessing liquid assets, such as (1) cash and (2) other assets that will soon be converted to cash. Since companies must pay short-term debts soon, liquid assets must be available for their payment. For example, a bank that is asked to extend a 90-day loan to a company would want to know the company's projected short-term liquidity. Of course, the company's predicted ability to repay the 90-day loan is likely to be based at least partially on proven past ability to pay off debts.

Long-term creditors are interested in a company's long-term solvency, which is usually determined by the relationship of a company's assets to its liabilities. Generally, a company is considered solvent when its assets exceed its liabilities so that the company has a positive stockholders' equity. The larger the assets are in relation to the liabilities, the greater the long-term solvency of the company, since the company's assets could shrink significantly before its liabilities would exceed its assets and destroy the company's solvency.

FINANCIAL STATEMENT ANALYSIS

Several types of analyses can be performed on a company's financial statements. All of these analyses rely on comparisons or relationships of data because comparisons and relationships enhance the utility or practical value of accounting information. For example, knowing that a company's net income last year was $100,000 may or may not, by itself, be useful information. Some usefulness is added when we know that the prior year's net income was $25,000. And even more useful information is gained if we know the amounts of sales and assets of the company. Such comparisons or relationships may be expressed as:

1. Absolute increases and decreases for an item from one period to the next.
2. Percentage increases and decreases for an item from one period to the next.
3. Trend percentages.
4. Percentages of single items to an aggregate total.
5. Ratios.

Items 1 and 2 make use of comparative financial statements. Comparative financial statements present the same company's financial statements for two or more successive periods in side-by-side columns. Illustrations 17.1 and 17.2 show comparative financial statements of Knight Corporation for the years ended December 31, 1994, and 1993. The calculation of dollar changes (column 3 of Illustration 17.1 and column 9 of Illustration 17.2) or percentage changes (column 4 of Illustration 17.1 and column 10 of Illustration 17.2) in the statement items or totals is known as horizontal analysis. This type of analysis helps detect changes in a company's performance and highlights trends.

Trend percentages (item 3) are similar to horizontal analysis except that a base year or period is selected, and comparisons are made to the base year or period. Trend percentages are useful for comparing financial statements over **several years** because they disclose changes and trends occurring through time.

Information about a company can also be gained by the vertical analysis of the composition of a single financial statement, such as an income statement. Vertical analysis (item 4) consists of the study of a single financial statement in which each item is expressed as a **percentage of a significant total.** The use of vertical analysis is especially helpful in analyzing income statement data such as the percentage of cost of goods sold to sales. For example, columns 11 and 12 of Illustration 17.2 show that in 1993, cost of goods sold was 65.4% of sales and decreased to 63.2% of sales in 1994. Vertical analysis is a useful tool in analyzing intracompany data.

Financial statements that show only percentages and no absolute dollar amounts are called common-size statements. All percentage figures in a common-size balance sheet are expressed as percentages of total assets (columns 5 and 6 of Illustration 17.1), while all the items in a common-size income statement are expressed as percentages of net sales (columns 11 and 12 of Illustration 17.2). The use of common-size statements facilitates vertical analysis of a company's financial statements. For instance, looking at columns 11 and 12 of Illustration 17.2 gives you a better idea of the relationship of each item to sales than looking at columns 7 and 8.

Ratios (item 5) are expressions of logical relationships between certain items in the financial statements. The financial statements of a single period are generally used. Many ratios can be computed from the same set of financial statements. A ratio can show a relationship between two items on the same financial statement or between two items on different financial statements (e.g., balance sheet and

ILLUSTRATION 17.1

Comparative Balance Sheets

KNIGHT CORPORATION
Comparative Balance Sheets
December 31, 1994, and 1993

Exhibit A

	December 31		Increase or (Decrease) 1994 over 1993		Percent of Total Assets December 31	
	(1) 1994	(2) 1993	(3) Dollars*	(4) Percent*	(5) 1994	(6) 1993
Assets						
Current assets:						
Cash	$ 80,200	$ 55,000	$25,200	45.8	12.6	10.0
Accounts receivable, net	124,200	132,600	(8,400)	(6.3)	19.6	24.1
Notes receivable	55,000	50,000	5,000	10.0	8.7	9.1
Merchandise inventory	110,800	94,500	16,300	17.2	17.4	17.1
Prepaid expenses	3,600	4,700	(1,100)	(23.4)	0.6	0.9
Total current assets	$373,800	$336,800	$37,000	11.0	58.8†	61.1†
Property, plant, and equipment:						
Land	$ 21,000	$ 21,000	$ –0–	–0–	3.3	3.8
Building	205,000	160,000	45,000	28.1	32.3	29.0
Less: Accumulated depreciation	(27,000)	(22,400)	(4,600)	20.5	(4.3)	(4.1)
Furniture and fixtures	83,200	69,800	13,400	19.2	13.1	12.7
Less: Accumulated depreciation	(20,800)	(14,100)	(6,700)	47.5	(3.3)	(2.6)
Total property, plant, and equipment	$261,400	$214,300	$47,100	22.0	41.2†	38.9†
Total assets	$635,200	$551,100	$84,100	15.3	100.0	100.0
Liabilities and Stockholders' Equity						
Current liabilities:						
Accounts payable	$ 70,300	$ 64,600	$ 5,700	8.8	11.1	11.7
Notes payable	20,000	15,100	4,900	32.5	3.1	2.7
Taxes accrued	36,800	30,200	6,600	21.9	5.8	5.5
Total current liabilities	$127,100	$109,900	$17,200	15.7	20.0	20.0†
Long-term liabilities:						
Mortgage notes payable, land and building, 12%, 1996	43,600	60,800	(17,200)	(28.3)	6.9	11.0
Total liabilities	$170,700	$170,700	$ –0–	0.0	26.9	31.0
Stockholders' equity:						
Common stock, par value $10 per share	$240,000	$200,000	$40,000	20.0	37.8	36.3
Retained earnings	224,500	180,400	44,100	24.4	35.3	32.7
Total stockholders' equity	$464,500	$380,400	$84,100	22.1	73.1	69.0
Total liabilities and stockholders' equity	$635,200	$551,100	$84,100	15.3	100.0	100.0

* Dollars = (1) − (2); percent = (3) ÷ (2).
† Rounding difference.

income statement). The choice of ratios to be prepared is limited only by the requirement that the items used to construct a ratio have a logical relationship to one another.

Sources of Information

External financial analysts obtain their information from various sources. The annual reports and quarterly reports issued by publicly held companies are the major sources of information. Also, publicly held companies must file detailed

ILLUSTRATION 17.2

Comparative Statements of Income and Retained Earnings

KNIGHT CORPORATION
Comparative Statements of Income and Retained Earnings
For the Years Ended December 31, 1994, and 1993   **Exhibit B**

	Year Ended December 31		Increase or (Decrease) 1994 over 1993		Percent of Net Sales	
	(7) 1994	(8) 1993	(9) Dollars*	(10) Percent*	(11) 1994	(12) 1993
Net sales	$986,400	$765,500	$220,900	28.9	100.0	100.0
Cost of goods sold	623,200	500,900	122,300	24.4	63.2	65.4
Gross margin	$363,200	$264,600	$ 98,600	37.3	36.8	34.6
Operating expenses:						
Selling expenses	$132,500	$ 84,900	$ 47,600	56.1	13.4	11.1
Administrative expenses	120,300	98,600	21,700	22.0	12.2	12.9
Total operating expenses	$252,800	$183,500	$ 69,300	37.8	25.6	24.0
Net operating income	$110,400	$ 81,100	$ 29,300	36.1	11.2	10.6
Other expenses	3,000	2,800	200	7.1	0.3	0.4
Income before federal income taxes	$107,400	$ 78,300	$ 29,100	37.2	10.9	10.2
Deduct: Federal income taxes	48,300	31,700	16,600	52.4	4.9	4.1
Net income	$ 59,100	$ 46,600	$ 12,500	26.8	6.0	6.1
Retained earnings, January 1	180,400	146,300	34,100	23.3		
	$239,500	$192,900	$ 46,600	24.2		
Dividends declared	15,000	12,500	2,500	20.0		
Retained earnings, December 31	$224,500	$180,400	$ 44,100	24.4		

* Dollars = (7) − (8); percent = (9) ÷ (8).

annual reports (Form 10-K) and quarterly reports (Form 10-Q) with the Securities and Exchange Commission. These reports are available to the public for a small charge.

Business publications, such as *The Wall Street Journal, Forbes,* and others, report industry financial news. Some credit agencies, such as Dun & Bradstreet, Moody's, and Standard and Poor's, offer useful information about industry averages and credit ratings. Robert Morris Associates publishes Annual Statement Studies, which present ratios and other information for 223 different industries.

HORIZONTAL ANALYSIS AND VERTICAL ANALYSIS: AN ILLUSTRATION

Objective 2

Calculate and explain changes in financial statements using horizontal analysis, vertical analysis, and trend analysis

Illustrations 17.1 and 17.2 will serve as a basis for a more complete illustration of horizontal analysis and vertical analysis of a balance sheet and a statement of income and retained earnings. Recall that horizontal analysis calculates changes in comparative statement items or totals, whereas vertical analysis consists of a comparison of items on a single financial statement.

Analysis of a Balance Sheet

Imagine that you are a prospective investor of Knight and have acquired the comparative financial statements shown in Illustrations 17.1 and 17.2. Columns 1, 2, and 3 in Illustration 17.1 show the absolute dollar amounts for each item for

December 31, 1993, and December 31, 1994, and the change for the year. If the change between the two dates is an increase from 1993 to 1994, the change is shown as a positive figure. The percentage change is calculated by dividing the dollar change by the dollar balance of the earlier year. If the change is a decrease, it is shown in parentheses. A few of the observations you could make from your horizontal analysis of Illustration 17.1 are:

1. Total current assets have increased $37,000, consisting largely of a $25,200 increase in cash, while total current liabilities have increased only $17,200.

2. Total assets have increased $84,100, while total liabilities have remained unchanged.

3. The increase in total assets has been financed by the sale of common stock, $40,000, and by the retention of earnings, $44,100.

Next, you study column 4 in Illustration 17.1, which expresses as a percentage the dollar change in column 3. Frequently, these percentage increases and decreases are more informative than absolute amounts, as is illustrated by the current asset and current liability changes. Although the absolute amount of current assets has increased more than twice the amount of current liabilities, the percentages reveal that current assets increased 11%, while current liabilities increased 15.7%. Thus, current liabilities are increasing at a rate faster than the current assets that will be used to pay them. However, in view of the substantial amount of cash possessed, the company is not likely to fail to pay its debts as they come due.

The percentages in column 4 lead you, the analyst, to several other observations. For one thing, the 28.3% decrease in mortgage notes payable indicates that interest charges will be lower; thus, this decrease will tend to increase net income in the future. The 24.4% increase in retained earnings and the 45.8% increase in cash may indicate that higher dividends can be paid in the future.

The vertical analysis of Knight's balance sheet discloses each account's significance relative to total assets or equities. This comparison aids in assessing the importance of the changes in each account. Columns 5 and 6 in Illustration 17.1 express the dollar amounts of each item in columns 1 and 2 as a percentage of total assets or equities. For example, although prepaid expenses declined $1,100 in 1994, a decrease of 23.4%, the account represents less than 1% of total assets and, therefore, probably does not have great significance. The vertical analysis also shows that total debt financing decreased by 4.1 percentage points, from 31% of total equities (liabilities and stockholders' equity) in 1993, to 26.9% in 1994. At the same time, the percentage of stockholder financing to total assets of the company increased from 69.0% to 73.1%.

Analysis of Statement of Income and Retained Earnings

Illustration 17.2 provides the information needed to analyze Knight's comparative statements of income and retained earnings. Such a statement merely combines the income statement and the statement of retained earnings. Columns 7 and 8 in Illustration 17.2 show the dollar amounts for the years 1994 and 1993, respectively. Columns 9 and 10 show the absolute and percentage increase and decrease in each item from 1993 to 1994. The amounts and percentages in columns 11 and 12 are computed by dividing each item by net sales. Examination of the comparative statements of income and retained earnings shows the following:

1. Net sales increased 28.9% in 1994.

2. Gross margin increased 37.3% in 1994.

3. Selling expenses increased 56.1% in 1994.
4. Federal income taxes rose by 52.4% in 1994.
5. Net income increased 26.8% in 1994, while dividends increased 20.0%.
6. Net income per dollar of net sales remained virtually constant over the two years (6.1% in 1993 and 6.0% in 1994).

Considering both horizontal analysis and vertical analysis information, you would conclude that an increase in the gross margin rate from 34.6% to 36.8%, coupled with a 28.9% increase in net sales, resulted in a 37.3% increase in gross margin in 1994. The increase in net income was held to 26.8% because selling expenses increased 56.1% and federal income taxes increased 52.4%. Predicting net income for 1995 would be made easier if you, the analyst, knew whether this increase in selling expenses is expected to recur. Other expenses remained basically the same, on a percentage-of-sales basis, over the two-year period.

Having completed the horizontal analysis and vertical analysis of Knight's balance sheet and statement of income and retained earnings, you are ready to study trend percentages and ratio analysis. The last section in this chapter discusses some final considerations in financial statement analysis. Professional financial statement analysts use several tools and techniques to determine the solvency and profitability of companies.

TREND PERCENTAGES

Trend percentages are also referred to as index numbers and are used for the comparison of financial information over time to a base year or period. Trend percentages are calculated by:

1. Selecting a base year or period.
2. Assigning a weight of 100% to the amounts appearing on the base-year financial statements.
3. Expressing the corresponding amounts shown on the other years' financial statements as a percentage of base-year or period amounts. The percentages are computed by dividing nonbase-year amounts by the corresponding base-year amounts and then multiplying the result by 100.

The following information is given to illustrate the calculation of trend percentages:

	1993	1994	1995	1996
Sales	$350,000	$367,500	$441,000	$485,000
Cost of goods sold	200,000	196,000	230,000	285,000
Gross margin	$150,000	$171,500	$211,000	$200,000
Operating expenses	145,000	169,000	200,000	192,000
Income before income taxes	$ 5,000	$ 2,500	$ 11,000	$ 8,000

If 1993 is the base year, trend percentages are calculated for each year by dividing sales by $350,000; cost of goods sold by $200,000; gross margin by $150,000; operating expenses by $145,000; and income before income taxes by $5,000. After all divisions have been made, each result is multiplied by 100, and the resulting percentages that reflect trends appear as follows:

	1993	1994	1995	1996
Sales	100%	105%	126%	139%
Cost of goods sold	100	98	115	143
Gross margin	100	114	141	133
Operating expenses	100	117	138	132
Income before income taxes	100	50	220	160

Such trend percentages indicate changes that are taking place in an organization and highlight the direction of these changes. For instance, the percentage of sales is increasing each year or period (compared to the base year or period). Income before income taxes, however, does not show the same steady increase because cost of goods sold and operating expenses have an uneven rate and direction of change. Percentages can provide clues to a user as to which items need further investigation or analysis. In reviewing trend percentages, a financial statement user should pay close attention to the trends in related items, such as the cost of goods sold in relation to sales. Trend analysis that shows a constantly declining gross margin rate may be a signal that future net income will decrease.

As useful as trend percentages are, they have one drawback. Expressing changes as percentages is usually straightforward as long as the amount in the base year or period is positive—that is, not zero or negative. A $30,000 increase in notes receivable cannot be expressed in percentages if the increase is from zero last year to $30,000 this year. Also, an increase from a loss last year of $10,000 to income this year of $20,000 cannot be expressed in percentage terms.

Proper analysis does not stop with the calculation of increases and decreases in amounts or percentages over several years. Such changes generally indicate areas worthy of further investigation and are merely clues that may lead to significant findings. Accurate predictions depend on many factors, including economic and political conditions; management's plans regarding new products, plant expansion, and promotional outlays; and the expected activities of competitors. Consideration of these factors in conjunction with horizontal analysis, vertical analysis, and trend analysis should provide a reasonable basis for predicting future performance.

RATIO ANALYSIS

Objective 3

Perform ratio analysis on financial statements using liquidity ratios, long-term solvency ratios, profitability tests, and market tests

Logical relationships exist between certain accounts or items in a company's financial statements. These accounts may appear on the same statement or they may appear on two different statements. The dollar amounts of the related accounts or items are set up in fraction form and called *ratios*. These ratios can be broadly classified as (1) liquidity ratios; (2) equity, or long-term solvency, ratios; (3) profitability tests; and (4) market tests.

Liquidity Ratios

Liquidity ratios are used to indicate a company's short-term debt-paying ability. Thus, these ratios are designed to show interested parties the company's capacity to meet maturing current liabilities.

Current, or Working Capital, Ratio   Working capital is the excess of current assets over current liabilities. The ratio that relates current assets to current liabilities is known as the current, or working capital, ratio. The current ratio indicates the ability of a company to pay its current liabilities from current assets and, thus, shows the strength of the company's working capital position.

The current ratio is computed by dividing current assets by current liabilities:

$$\text{Current ratio} = \frac{\text{Current assets}}{\text{Current liabilities}}$$

The ratio is usually stated in terms of the number of dollars of current assets to one dollar of current liabilities (although the dollar signs usually are omitted). Thus, if current assets total $150,000 and current liabilities total $100,000, the ratio is expressed as 1.5 : 1, meaning that the company has $1.50 of current assets for each $1 of current liabilities.

The current ratio provides a better index of a company's ability to pay current debts than does the absolute amount of working capital. To illustrate, assume that Company A and Company B have current assets and current liabilities on December 31, 1993, as follows:

	Company A	Company B
Current assets *(a)*	$11,000,000	$200,000
Current liabilities *(b)*	10,000,000	100,000
Working capital *(a − b)*	$ 1,000,000	$100,000
Current ratio *(a ÷ b)*	1.1 : 1	2 : 1

Company A has 10 times as much working capital as Company B. Company B, however, has a superior debt-paying ability, since it has $2 of current assets for each $1 of current liabilities. Company A has only $1.10 of current assets for each $1 of current liabilities.

Short-term creditors are particularly interested in the current ratio since the conversion of inventories and accounts receivable into cash is the primary source from which the company obtains the cash to pay short-term creditors. Long-term creditors are also interested in the current ratio because a company that is unable to pay short-term debts may be forced into bankruptcy. For this reason, many bond indentures, or contracts, contain a provision requiring that the borrower maintain at least a certain minimum current ratio. A company can increase its current ratio by issuing long-term debt or capital stock or by selling noncurrent assets.

A company must also guard against a current ratio that is too high, especially if caused by idle cash, slow-paying customers, and/or slow-moving inventory. Decreased net income can result when too much capital that could be used profitably elsewhere is tied up in current assets.

Refer back to the Knight Corporation data in column 4 of Illustration 17.1 which indicate that current liabilities are increasing more rapidly than current assets. Such an observation also can be made directly using changes in the current ratio. Knight's current ratios for 1993 and 1994 follow:

	December 31		Amount of Increase
	1994	**1993**	
Current assets *(a)*	$373,800	$336,800	$37,000
Current liabilities *(b)*	127,100	109,900	17,200
Working capital *(a − b)*	$246,700	$226,900	$19,800
Current ratio *(a ÷ b)*	2.94 : 1	3.06 : 1	

Although Knight's working capital increased by $19,800, or 8.7%, its current ratio fell from 3.06 to 2.94, reflecting that its current liabilities increased faster than its current assets.

Acid-Test (Quick) Ratio   The current ratio is not the only measure of a company's short-term debt-paying ability. Another measure, called the acid-test (quick) ratio, is the ratio of quick assets (cash, marketable securities, and net receivables) to current liabilities. Inventories and prepaid expenses are excluded from current assets to compute quick assets because they might not be readily convertible into cash.

The formula for the acid-test ratio is:

$$\text{Acid-test ratio} = \frac{\text{Quick assets}}{\text{Current liabilities}}$$

Short-term creditors are interested particularly in this ratio, since it relates the "pool" of cash and immediate cash inflows to immediate cash outflows.

The acid-test ratios for 1993 and 1994 for Knight are:

| | December 31 | | Amount of Increase |
	1994	1993	
Quick assets (a)	$259,400	$237,600	$21,800
Current liabilities (b)	127,100	109,900	17,200
Net quick assets (a − b)	$132,300	$127,700	$ 4,600
Acid-test ratio (a ÷ b)	2.04 : 1	2.16 : 1	

In deciding whether the acid-test ratio is satisfactory, you must consider the **quality** of the marketable securities and receivables. An accumulation of poor-quality marketable securities or receivables, or both, could cause an acid-test ratio to appear deceptively favorable. When referring to marketable securities, poor quality means securities that are likely to generate losses when sold. Poor-quality receivables are those that may be uncollectible or not collectible until long past due. The quality of receivables depends primarily on their age, which can be assessed by preparing an aging schedule or by calculating the accounts receivable turnover. (Refer to Chapter 9 for a discussion of an accounts receivable aging schedule.)

Accounts Receivable Turnover   Turnover is the relationship between the amount of an asset and some measure of its use. Accounts receivable turnover is the number of times per year that the average amount of receivables is collected. The ratio is calculated by dividing net credit sales by average net accounts receivable, that is, accounts receivable after deducting the allowance for uncollectible accounts:

$$\frac{\text{Accounts receivable}}{\text{turnover}} = \frac{\text{Net credit sales (or net sales)}}{\text{Average net accounts receivable}}$$

When a ratio compares an income statement item (like net credit sales) with a balance sheet item (like accounts receivable), the balance sheet item should be an average. Ideally, average net accounts receivable should be computed by averaging the end-of-month balances or end-of-week balances of net accounts receivable outstanding during the period. The greater the number of observations used, the more accurate the resulting average. Often, only the beginning-of-year and end-of-year balances are averaged because this information is easily obtainable from comparative financial statements. Sometimes a formula calls for the use of an average balance, but only the year-end amount is available. Then the analyst must use the year-end amount.[1]

In theory, only net credit sales should be used in the numerator of the accounts receivable turnover ratio because those are the only sales that generate accounts receivable. However, if cash sales are relatively small or their proportion to total sales remains fairly constant, reliable results can be obtained by using total net sales. In most cases, the analyst may have to use total net sales because the separate amounts of cash sales and credit sales are not reported on the income statement.

Knight's accounts receivable turnover ratios for 1993 and 1994 are shown below. Since beginning-of-year data for 1993 are not provided in Illustration 17.1, assume net accounts receivable on January 1, 1993, totaled $121,200.

	1994	1993	Amount of Increase or (Decrease)
Net sales (a)	$986,400	$765,500	$220,900
Net accounts receivable:			
January 1	$132,600	$121,200	$ 11,400
December 31	124,200	132,600	(8,400)
Total (b)	$256,800	$253,800	$ 3,000
Average net accounts receivable (c) (b ÷ 2 = c)	$128,400	$126,900	
Turnover of accounts receivable (a ÷ c)	7.68	6.03	

The turnover ratio provides an indication of how quickly the receivables are being collected. For Knight in 1994, the turnover ratio indicates that accounts receivable were collected, or "turned over," slightly more than seven times per year. The ratio may be better understood and more easily compared with a company's credit terms if it is converted into a number of days, as is illustrated in the next ratio.

Number of Days' Sales in Accounts Receivable The number of days' sales in accounts receivable ratio, which also is called the **average collection period for accounts receivable,** is calculated as follows:

$$\text{Number of days' sales in accounts receivable (average collection period for accounts receivable)} = \frac{\text{Number of days in year (365)}}{\text{Accounts receivable turnover}}$$

The turnover ratios for Knight given above can be used to show that the number of days' sales in accounts receivable decreased from about 61 days (365/6.03) in 1993 to 48 days (365/7.68) in 1994. The change means that the average collection period for the corporation's accounts receivable decreased from 61 to 48 days. Thus, the ratio measures the average liquidity of accounts receivable and gives an indication of their quality. Generally, the shorter the collection period, the higher the quality of receivables. However, the average collection period will vary by industry; for example, collection periods will be short in utility companies and much longer in some retailing companies. A comparison of the average collection period with the credit terms extended customers by the company will provide

---

[1] These general comments about the use of averages in a ratio apply to the other ratios involving averages discussed in this chapter.

further insight into the quality of the accounts receivable. For example, receivables arising under terms of 2/10, n/30 that have an average collection period of 75 days need to be investigated further. It is important to determine why customers are paying their accounts much later than expected.

Inventory Turnover   A company's inventory turnover ratio shows the number of times its average inventory is sold during a period. Inventory turnover is calculated as follows:

$$\text{Inventory turnover} = \frac{\text{Cost of goods sold}}{\text{Average inventory}}$$

In comparing an income statement item and a balance sheet item, both should be measured in comparable dollars. Notice that both the numerator and denominator are measured in terms of cost rather than sales dollars. (Earlier, when calculating accounts receivable turnover, both numerator and denominator were measured in sales dollars.) Inventory turnover relates a measure of sales volume to the average amount of goods on hand to produce this sales volume.

Assume that Knight's inventory on January 1, 1993, was $85,100. The following schedule shows that the inventory turnover increased slightly from 5.58 times per year in 1993 to 6.07 times per year in 1994. These turnover ratios can be converted to the number of days it takes a company to sell its entire stock of inventory; this conversion is made by dividing 365 by the inventory turnover. For Knight, the average inventory was sold in about 60 days (365/6.07) in 1994 as contrasted to about 65 days (365/5.58) in 1993.

	1994	1993	Amount of Increase
Cost of goods sold (a)	$623,200	$500,900	$122,300
Merchandise inventory:			
January 1	$ 94,500	$ 85,100	$ 9,400
December 31	110,800	94,500	16,300
Total (b).	$205,300	$179,600	$ 25,700
Average inventory (c) (b ÷ 2 = c)	$102,650	$ 89,800	
Turnover of inventory (a ÷ c)	6.07	5.58	

Other things being equal, a manager who is able to maintain the highest inventory turnover ratio is considered the most efficient. Yet, other things are not always equal. For example, a company that achieves a high inventory turnover ratio by keeping extremely small inventories on hand may incur larger ordering costs, lose quantity discounts, and lose sales due to lack of adequate inventory. In attempting to earn satisfactory income, management must balance the costs of inventory storage and obsolescence and the cost of tying up funds in inventory against possible losses of sales and other costs associated with keeping too little inventory on hand.

Total Assets Turnover   Total assets turnover shows the relationship between the dollar volume of sales and average total assets used in the business and is calculated as follows:

$$\text{Total assets turnover} = \frac{\text{Net sales}}{\text{Average total assets}}$$

This ratio measures the efficiency with which a company uses its assets to generate sales. The larger the total assets turnover, the larger will be the income on each dollar invested in the assets of the business.

For Knight, the total assets turnover ratios for 1993 and 1994 are shown below. Assume that total assets as of January 1, 1993, were $510,200.

	1994	1993	Amount of Increase
Net sales *(a)*	$ 986,400	$ 765,500	$220,900
Total assets:			
January 1	$ 551,100	$ 510,200	$ 40,900
December 31	635,200	551,100	84,100
Total *(b)*	$1,186,300	$1,061,300	$125,000
Average total assets *(c) (b ÷ 2 = c)*	$ 593,150	$ 530,650	
Turnover of total assets *(a ÷ c)*	1.66 : 1	1.44 : 1	

In 1993, each dollar of total assets produced $1.44 of sales; and in 1994 each dollar of assets produced $1.66 of sales. In other words, between 1993 and 1994, Knight had an increase of $0.22 of sales per dollar of investment in assets.

Equity, or Long-Term Solvency, Ratios

Equity, or long-term solvency, ratios show the relationship between debt and equity financing in a company.

Equity (Stockholders' Equity) Ratio   The two basic sources of assets in a business are owners (stockholders) and creditors, and the combined interests of the two groups are referred to as *total equities*. In ratio analysis, however, the term *equity* generally refers only to stockholders' equity. Thus, the equity (stockholders' equity) ratio indicates the proportion of total assets (or total equities) provided by stockholders (owners) on any given date. The formula for the equity ratio is:

$$\text{Equity ratio} = \frac{\text{Stockholders' equity}}{\text{Total assets (or total equities)}}$$

Knight's liabilities and stockholders' equity, taken from Illustration 17.1, are given below. Knight's equity ratio increased from 69.0% in 1993 to 73.1% in 1994. The schedule below shows that the company's stockholders increased their proportionate equity in the company's assets by making additional investments in the company's common stock and by retaining income earned during the year.

	December 31, 1994		December 31, 1993	
	Amount	Percent	Amount	Percent
Current liabilities	$127,100	20.0	$109,900	20.0
Long-term liabilities	43,600	6.9	60,800	11.0
Total liabilities	$170,700	26.9	$170,700	31.0
Common stock	$240,000	37.8	$200,000	36.3
Retained earnings	224,500	35.3	180,400	32.7
Total stockholders' equity	$464,500	73.1	$380,400	69.0
Total equity (equal to total assets)	$635,200	100.0	$551,100	100.0

The equity ratio must be interpreted carefully. From a creditor's point of view, a high proportion of stockholders' equity is desirable. A high equity ratio indicates the existence of a large protective buffer for creditors in the event a company suffers a loss. However, from an owner's point of view, a high proportion of stockholders' equity may or may not be desirable. If borrowed funds can be used by the business to generate income in excess of the net after-tax cost of the interest on such borrowed funds, a lower percentage of stockholders' equity may be desirable.

To illustrate the effect of higher leveraging (i.e., a larger proportion of debt), assume that Knight could have financed its present operations with $40,000 of 12% bonds instead of 4,000 shares of common stock. The effect on income for 1994 would be as follows, assuming a federal income tax rate of 40%:

Net income as presently stated (Illustration 17.2)	$59,100
Deduct additional interest on debt (0.12 × $40,000)	4,800
	$54,300
Add reduced tax due to interest deduction (0.4 × $4,800)	1,920
Adjusted net income	$56,220

As shown, net income is reduced when leverage is increased by issuing bonds instead of common stock. However, there are also fewer shares of common stock outstanding. Assume that the company has 24,000 shares of common stock outstanding. Earnings per share (EPS) increase from $2.46 (or $59,100/24,000 shares) to $2.81 (or $56,220/20,000 shares). Since investors place heavy emphasis on EPS amounts, many companies in recent years have introduced large portions of debt into their capital structures to increase EPS.

It should be pointed out, however, that too low a percentage of stockholders' equity (too much debt) has its dangers. Financial leverage magnifies losses per share as well as EPS since there are fewer shares of stock over which to spread the losses. A period of business recession may result in operating losses and shrinkage in the value of assets, such as receivables and inventory, which in turn may lead to an inability to meet fixed payments for interest and principal on the debt. As a result, the company may be forced into liquidation, and the stockholders could lose their entire investments.

Stockholders' Equity to Debt (Debt to Equity) Ratio   The relative equities of owners and creditors may be expressed in several ways. To say that creditors hold a 26.9% interest in the assets of Knight on December 31, 1994, is equivalent to saying stockholders hold a 73.1% interest. In many cases, this relationship is expressed as a ratio—**stockholders' equity to debt ratio.**

$$\frac{\text{Stockholders' equity}}{\text{to debt ratio}} = \frac{\text{Stockholders' equity}}{\text{Total debt}}$$

Such a ratio for Knight would be 2.23 : 1 (or $380,400/$170,700) on December 31, 1993, and 2.72 : 1 (or $464,500/$170,700) on December 31, 1994. This ratio is often inverted and called the **debt to equity ratio.** Some analysts use only long-term debt rather than total debt in calculating these ratios. These analysts do not consider short-term debt to be part of the capital structure since it will be paid within one year.

Profitability Tests   Profitability is an important measure of a company's operating success. Generally, we are concerned with two areas when judging profitability: (1) relationships on the income statement that indicate a company's ability to recover costs and expenses, and (2) relationships of income to various balance sheet measures that indicate the company's relative ability to earn income on assets employed. Each of the following ratios utilizes one of these relationships.

Rate of Return on Operating Assets The best measure of earnings performance without regard to the sources of assets is the relationship of net operating income to operating assets, which is known as the rate of return on operating assets. This ratio is designed to show the earning power of the company as a bundle of assets. By disregarding both nonoperating assets and nonoperating income elements, the rate of return on operating assets measures the profitability of the company in carrying out its primary business functions. The ratio can be broken down into two elements—the operating margin and the turnover of operating assets.

Operating margin reflects the percentage of each dollar of net sales that becomes net operating income. Net operating income excludes nonoperating income elements such as extraordinary items, nonoperating revenues such as interest revenue, and nonoperating expenses such as interest expense. The formula for operating margin is:

$$\text{Operating margin} = \frac{\text{Net operating income}}{\text{Net sales}}$$

Turnover of operating assets shows the amount of sales dollars generated for each dollar invested in operating assets. Operating assets are all assets actively used in producing operating revenues. Year-end operating assets are typically used, even though in theory an average would be better. Nonoperating assets are assets owned by a company, but not used in producing operating revenues, such as land held for future use, a factory building rented to another company, and long-term bond investments.

These nonoperating assets are not used in evaluating earnings performance. Total assets also should not be used because they include nonoperating assets that do not contribute to the generation of sales. The formula for the turnover of operating assets is:

$$\text{Turnover of operating assets} = \frac{\text{Net sales}}{\text{Operating assets}}$$

The rate of return on operating assets of a company is equal to its operating margin multiplied by turnover of operating assets. The more a company earns per dollar of sales and the more sales it makes per dollar invested in operating assets, the higher will be the return per dollar invested. Rate of return on operating assets is expressed by the following formulas:

$$\frac{\text{Rate of return}}{\text{on operating assets}} = \frac{\text{Operating}}{\text{margin}} \times \frac{\text{Turnover of}}{\text{operating assets}}$$

or

$$\frac{\text{Rate of return}}{\text{on operating assets}} = \frac{\text{Net operating income}}{\text{Net sales}} \times \frac{\text{Net sales}}{\text{Operating assets}}$$

Since net sales appears in both ratios (once as a numerator and once as a denominator), we can cancel it out, and the formula for rate of return on operating assets becomes:

$$\frac{\text{Rate of return on}}{\text{operating assets}} = \frac{\text{Net operating income}}{\text{Operating assets}}$$

For analytical purposes, the formula should remain in the form that shows margin and turnover separately, since it provides more information.

The rates of return on operating assets for Knight Corporation for 1993 and 1994 are calculated below.

	1994	1993	Amount of Increase
Net operating income *(a)*	$110,400	$ 81,100	$ 29,300
Net sales *(b)*	$986,400	$765,500	$220,900
Operating assets* *(c)*	$635,200	$551,100	$ 84,100
Operating margin *(a ÷ b)*	11.19%	10.59%	
Turnover of operating assets *(b ÷ c)*	1.55 : 1	1.39 : 1	
Rate of return on operating assets *(a ÷ c)*	17.38%	14.72%	

* Knight Corporation had no nonoperating assets, so total assets are used in the calculation.

Securing Desired Rate of Return on Operating Assets   Companies that are to survive in the economy must attain some minimum rate of return on operating assets. However, this minimum rate of return can be attained in many different ways. To illustrate, consider a grocery store and a jewelry store, each with a rate of return of 8% on operating assets. The grocery store normally would attain this rate of return with a low margin and a high turnover, while the jewelry store would have a high margin and a low turnover, as shown below.

	Margin × Turnover =		Rate of Return on Operating Assets
Grocery store	1%	× 8.0 times =	8%
Jewelry store	20	× 0.4 =	8

Net Income to Net Sales (Return on Sales) Ratio   Another measure of a company's profitability is the **net income to net sales** ratio, calculated as follows:

$$\text{Net income to net sales} = \frac{\text{Net income}}{\text{Net sales}}$$

This ratio measures the proportion of the sales dollar that remains after the deduction of all expenses. The computations for Knight are:

	1994	1993	Amount of Increase
Net income *(a)*	$ 59,100	$ 46,600	$ 12,500
Net sales *(b)*	$986,400	$765,500	$220,900
Ratio of net income to net sales *(a ÷ b)*	5.99%	6.09%	

Although the ratio of net income to net sales indicates the net amount of profit on each sales dollar, care must be exercised in the use and interpretation of this ratio. The amount of net income includes all types of nonoperating items that may occur in a particular period; therefore, net income includes the effects of such things as extraordinary items and interest charges. Thus, a period that contains the effects of an extraordinary item will not be comparable to a period that contains no extraordinary items. Also, since interest expense is deductible in the determination of net income while dividends are not, net income is affected by the methods used to finance a company's assets.

Net Income to Average Common Stockholders' Equity   From the stockholders' point of view, an important measure of the income-producing ability of a company is the relationship of net income to average common stockholders' equity, also called **rate of return on average common stockholders' equity,** or simply the return on equity (ROE). Although stockholders are interested in the ratio of operating income to operating assets as a measure of management's efficient use of assets, they are even more interested in the return the company earns on each dollar of stockholders' equity. The formula for net income to average common stockholders' equity is:

$$\text{Net income to average common stockholders' equity} = \frac{\text{Net income}}{\text{Average common stockholders' equity}}$$

The ratios for Knight are shown below. Assume that total common stockholders' equity on January 1, 1993, was $321,500.

	1994	1993	Amount of Increase
Net income (a)	$ 59,100	$ 46,600	$ 12,500
Total common stockholders' equity:			
January 1	$380,400	$321,500	$ 58,900
December 31	464,500	380,400	84,100
Total (b)	$844,900	$701,900	$143,000
Average common stockholders' equity (c) (b ÷ 2 = c)	$422,450	$350,950	
Ratio of net income to common stockholders' equity (a ÷ c)	13.99%	13.28%	

The increase in the ratio from 13.28% to 13.99% would be regarded favorably by stockholders. This ratio indicates that for each dollar of capital invested by a stockholder, the company earned nearly 14 cents in 1994.

Trading on the Equity   Sometimes, two companies will have the same return on assets but will have different returns on stockholders' equity, as shown in the example below.

	Company 1	Company 2
Return on assets	12.0%	12.0%
Return on stockholders' equity	6.4	8.0

The difference of 1.6% in Company 2's favor is the result of Company 2's use of borrowed funds, particularly long-term debt, in its capital structure. Use of these funds (or preferred stock with a fixed return) is called **trading on the equity.** When a company is trading profitably on the equity, it is generating a higher rate of return on its borrowed funds than it is paying for the use of the funds. The excess, in this case 1.6%, is accruing to the benefit of the common stockholders, because their earnings are being increased.

Magnifying the gains from this type of activity for the stockholders is sometimes called the use of **leverage.** Using leverage is a risky process because losses also can be magnified, to the disadvantage of the common stockholders. Trading on the equity and leverage were discussed in Chapter 15.

Earnings per Share of Common Stock   Probably the measure used most widely to appraise a company's operations is earnings per share (EPS) of common stock. EPS is equal to earnings available to common stockholders divided by the weighted-average number of shares of common stock outstanding. The financial press regularly publishes actual and forecasted EPS amounts for publicly traded corporations, together with period-to-period comparisons. The Accounting Principles Board noted the significance attached to EPS by requiring that such amounts be reported on the face of the income statement.[2] (Chapter 14 illustrated how earnings per share should be presented on the income statement.)

The calculation of EPS may be fairly simple or highly complex depending on a corporation's capital structure. A company has a simple capital structure if it has no outstanding securities (e.g., convertible bonds, convertible preferred stocks, warrants, or options) that can be exchanged for common stock. If a company has such securities outstanding, it has a complex capital structure.

A company with a simple capital structure reports a single EPS amount, calculated as follows:

$$\text{EPS of common stock} = \frac{\text{Earnings available to common stockholders}}{\text{Weighted-average number of common shares outstanding}}$$

The amount of earnings available to common stockholders is equal to net income minus the current year's preferred dividends, whether such dividends have been declared or not.

Determining the Weighted-Average Number of Shares   The denominator in the EPS fraction is the weighted-average number of common shares outstanding for the period. If the number of shares outstanding did not change during the period, the weighted-average number of shares outstanding would, of course, be the number of shares outstanding at the end of the period. The balance in the Common Stock account of Knight (Illustration 17.1) was $200,000 on December 31, 1993. The common stock has a $10 par value. Assuming that no shares were issued or redeemed during 1993, the weighted-average number of shares outstanding would be 20,000 (or $200,000/$10 per share).

If the number of shares changed during the period, such a change increases or decreases the capital invested in the company and should affect earnings available to stockholders. To compute the weighted-average number of shares outstanding, the change in the number of shares is weighted by the portion of the year that those shares were outstanding. Shares are only considered outstanding during those periods that the related capital investment is available to produce income.

To illustrate, note that Knight's Common Stock balance increased by $40,000 (4,000 shares) during 1994. Assume that 3,000 of these shares were issued on April 1, 1994, and the other 1,000 shares were issued on October 1, 1994. The computation of the weighted-average shares outstanding would be as follows:

---

[2] Accounting Principles Board, *Opinion No. 15,* "Reporting Earnings per Share" (New York: AICPA, 1969), par. 12.

20,000 shares × 1 year.	20,000
3,000 shares × ¾ year (April–December)	2,250
1,000 shares × ¼ year (October–December)	250
Weighted-average number of shares outstanding	22,500

An alternate method looks at the total number of shares outstanding, weighted by the portion of the year that the number of shares was outstanding, as follows:

20,000 shares × ¼ year (January–March)	5,000
23,000 shares × ½ year (April–September).	11,500
24,000 shares × ¼ year (October–December)	6,000
Weighted-average number of shares outstanding	22,500

Another alternative method is as follows:

20,000 shares ×	3 months =	60,000	share-months
23,000 shares ×	6 months =	138,000	share-months
24,000 shares ×	3 months =	72,000	share-months
	12 months =	270,000	share-months

270,000 share-months/12 months = 22,500 shares

Note that all three methods give the same result.

Since Knight had no preferred stock outstanding in either 1993 or 1994, EPS of common stock is computed as follows:

	1994	1993	Amount of Increase
Net income (a)	$59,100	$46,600	$12,500
Average number of shares of common stock outstanding (b)	22,500	20,000	2,500
EPS of common stock (a ÷ b)	$2.63	$2.33	

The increase of approximately 13% in EPS from $2.33 to $2.63 would probably be viewed quite favorably by Knight's stockholders.

EPS and Stock Dividends or Splits   Increases in shares outstanding as a result of a stock dividend or split do not require weighting for fractional periods. Such shares do not increase the capital invested in the business and therefore do not affect income. All that is required is to restate all prior calculations of EPS using the increased number of shares. For example, assume a company reported EPS for 1993 as $1 (or $100,000/100,000 shares) and earned $150,000 in 1994. The only change in common stock over the two years was a two-for-one stock split on December 1, 1994, which doubled the shares outstanding to 200,000. EPS for 1993 would be restated as $0.50 (or $100,000/200,000 shares) and would be $0.75 ($150,000/200,000 shares) for 1994.

Primary EPS and Fully Diluted EPS   In the merger wave of the 1960s, corporations often issued securities to finance their acquisitions of other companies. Many of the securities issued were *calls on common* or possessed *equity kickers*. These terms mean that the securities were convertible to, or exchangeable for, shares of their issuers' common stock. As a result, many complex problems arose in computing EPS. *APB Opinion No. 15* provides guidelines for solving these problems. A company with a complex capital structure must present at least two EPS calculations, primary EPS and fully diluted EPS. Because of the complexities involved in the calculations, further discussion of these two EPS amounts is reserved for an intermediate accounting text.

Times Interest Earned Ratio   Creditors, especially long-term creditors, want to know whether a borrower can meet its required interest payments when those payments come due. The times interest earned ratio, or **interest coverage ratio,** is an indication of such an ability. It is computed as follows:

$$\frac{\text{Times interest}}{\text{earned ratio}} = \frac{\text{Income before interest and taxes (IBIT)}}{\text{Interest expense}}$$

The ratio is a rough comparison of cash inflows from operations with cash outflows for interest expense. **Income before interest and taxes (IBIT)** is used in the numerator since there would be no income taxes if interest expense is equal to or greater than IBIT. (To find income before interest and taxes, take net income and add back the interest and taxes.) Analysts disagree on whether the denominator should be only interest on long-term debt or total interest expense. We prefer the use of total interest expense since failure to make any required interest payment is a serious matter.

Assume that a company has IBIT of $100,000 and that the interest expense for the same period is $10,000. The times interest earned ratio is 10:1. The company earned enough during the period to pay its interest expense 10 times over. Low or negative interest coverage ratios suggest that the borrower could default on required interest payments. A company is not likely to be able to continue interest payments over many periods if it fails to earn enough income to cover them. On the other hand, interest coverage of 10 to 20 times suggests that the company is not likely to default on interest payments.

Times Preferred Dividends Earned Ratio   Preferred stockholders, like bondholders, must usually be satisfied with a fixed-dollar return on their investments. They are interested in the company's ability to make preferred dividend payments each year. This ability can be measured by computing the times preferred dividends earned ratio, which is computed as follows:

$$\frac{\text{Times preferred dividends}}{\text{earned ratio}} = \frac{\text{Net income}}{\text{Annual preferred dividends}}$$

Suppose a company has net income of $48,000 and has $100,000 ($100 par value) of 8% preferred stock outstanding. The number of times the annual preferred dividends are earned would be:

$$\frac{\$48,000}{\$8,000} = 6:1, \text{ or 6 times}$$

The higher this rate, the higher is the probability that the preferred stockholders will receive their dividends each year.

Market Tests   Certain ratios are computed using information from the financial statements and information about market price of the company's stock. These tests help investors and potential investors assess the relative merits of the various stocks in the marketplace.

The yield on a stock investment refers to either an earnings yield or a dividends yield.

Earnings Yield on Common Stock   A company's earnings yield per share of common stock is calculated as follows:

$$\text{Earnings yield on common stock} = \frac{\text{EPS}}{\text{Current market price per share of common stock}}$$

Suppose, for example, that a company has common stock with an EPS of $2 and that the quoted market price of the stock on the New York Stock Exchange is $30. The earnings yield on common stock would be:

$$\frac{\$2}{\$30} = 6\tfrac{2}{3}\%$$

Price-Earnings Ratio   When inverted, the earnings yield on common stock is called the price-earnings ratio. In the case cited above, the price-earnings ratio is:

$$\text{Price-earnings ratio} = \frac{\text{Current market price per share of common stock}}{\text{EPS}} = \frac{\$30}{\$2} = 15:1$$

Investors would say that this stock is selling at 15 times earnings, or at a multiple of 15. These investors might have a specific multiple in mind as being the one that should be used to judge whether the stock is underpriced or overpriced. Different investors may have different estimates of the proper price-earnings ratio for a given stock and also different estimates of the future earnings prospects of the company. These different estimates may be factors that cause one investor to sell stock at a particular price and another investor to buy at that price.

Dividend Yield on Common Stock   The dividend paid per share of common stock is also of much interest to common stockholders. When the current annual dividend per share of common stock is divided by the current market price per share, the result is called the dividend yield on common stock. If the company whose stock sells at $30 per share paid a $1.50 per share dividend, the dividend yield would be:

$$\text{Dividend yield on common stock} = \frac{\text{Dividend per share of common stock}}{\text{Current market price per share of common stock}} = \frac{\$1.50}{\$30.00} = 5\%$$

Payout Ratio on Common Stock   Using dividend yield, investors can compute the payout ratio on a stock. Payout ratio on common stock is computed as the dividend per share of common stock divided by EPS. The payout ratio for the above stock is:

$$\text{Payout ratio on common stock} = \frac{\text{Dividend per share of common stock}}{\text{EPS}} = \frac{\$1.50}{\$2.00} = 75\%$$

A payout ratio of 75% means that the company paid out 75% of its earnings in the form of dividends. Some investors are attracted by the stock of companies that pay out a large percentage of their earnings. Other investors are attracted by the stock of companies that retain and reinvest a large percentage of their earnings.

ILLUSTRATION 17.3

Cash Flow per Share of Common Stock

(In thousands except per share data)	Fiscal Year		
	1987	1986	1985
Net Operating Revenues	$3,329,134	$1,951,008	$1,271,959
Cost of sales (includes purchases from The Coca-Cola Company of approximately $652,800 in 1987, $392,400 in 1986, and $265,400 in 1985)	1,916,724	1,137,720	755,709
Gross Profit	$1,412,410	$ 813,288	$ 516,250
Selling, administrative and general expenses	1,075,290	645,218	431,747
Operating Income	$ 337,120	$ 168,070	$ 84,503
Interest income	11,566	6,327	4,587
Interest expense	(171,466)	(82,526)	(31,945)
Other income (deductions)	(4,445)	(7,101)	6,483
Income Before Income Taxes	$ 172,775	$ 84,770	$ 63,628
Income taxes	84,403	56,978	27,721
Net Income	$ 88,372	$ 27,792	$ 35,907
Net Income Per Share	$ .63	$ .36	$ .52
Dividends Per Share	$ .05	$ —	$ —
Average Shares Outstanding	140,036	76,705	68,600
Operating Cash Flow Data:			
Operating income	$ 337,120	$ 168,070	$ 84,503
Depreciation	122,900	68,203	50,698
Amortization	71,633	24,095	4,785
Operating Cash Flow	$ 531,653	$ 260,368	$ 139,986
Cash flow per share	$ 3.80	$ 3.39	$ 2.04

Source: Coca-Cola Enterprises, Inc., *1987 Annual Report.* Selected Financial Data and Consolidated Statements of Income. Coca-Cola Enterprises, Inc., Atlanta, Georgia, 1987. (At the time of publication of the information in this illustration, the FASB had not yet prohibited publication of cash flow per share data.)

The tax status of the investor has a great deal to do with this preference. Investors in high tax brackets often prefer to have the company reinvest the earnings with the expectation that this reinvestment will result in share price appreciation.

Dividend Yield on Preferred Stock Preferred stockholders, as well as common stockholders, are interested in dividend yields. The computation of the dividend yield on preferred stock is similar to the common stock dividend yield computation. Suppose a company has 2,000 shares of $100 par value, 8% preferred stock outstanding with a current market price of $110 per share. The dividend yield on preferred stock is computed as follows:

$$\text{Dividend yield on preferred stock} = \frac{\text{Dividend per share of preferred stock}}{\text{Current market price per share of preferred stock}} = \frac{\$8}{\$110} = 7.27\%$$

Through the use of dividend yield rates, different preferred stocks having different annual dividends and different market prices can be compared.

Cash Flow per Share of Common Stock   The cash flow per share of common stock ratio is calculated by:

$$\text{Cash flow per share of common stock} = \frac{\text{Operating cash flow}}{\text{Average number of shares of common stock outstanding}}$$

Currently, FASB *Statement No. 95* does not permit use of this ratio for external reporting purposes. However, some companies, like mortgage and investment banking firms, do use this ratio to judge the company's ability to pay dividends and pay liabilities. An example of the cash flow per share of common stock ratio is shown in Illustration 17.3.

FINAL CONSIDERATIONS IN FINANCIAL STATEMENT ANALYSIS

Objective 4

Describe the considerations used in financial statement analysis

Standing alone, a single financial ratio may not be informative. Greater insight can be obtained by computing and analyzing several related ratios for a company. Illustration 17.4 summarizes the ratios presented in this chapter.

Financial analysis relies heavily on informed judgment. Percentages and ratios are guides to aid comparison and are useful in uncovering potential strengths and weaknesses. However, the financial analyst should seek the basic causes behind changes and established trends.

Need for Comparable Data

Analysts must be sure that their comparisons are valid—especially when the comparisons are of items for different periods or different companies. Consistent accounting practices must be followed if valid interperiod comparisons are to be made. Comparable intercompany comparisons are more difficult to secure. Accountants cannot do much more than disclose the fact that one company is using FIFO and another is using LIFO for inventory and cost of goods sold computations. Such a disclosure alerts analysts that intercompany comparisons of inventory turnover ratios, for example, may not be comparable.

Also, when comparing a company's ratios to industry averages provided by an external source such as Dun & Bradstreet, the analyst must calculate the company's ratios in the same manner as the reporting service. Thus, if Dun & Bradstreet uses net sales (rather than cost of goods sold) to compute inventory turnover, so should the analyst. Net sales is used because all companies do not compute and report cost of goods sold amounts in the same manner. Ratios based on net sales may lead to different conclusions from those obtained using cost of goods sold because gross margin rates may differ. For example, Company A and Company B may both have $100 sales and $10 average inventory for an identical inventory turnover of 10 (or $100/$10) based on sales. However, if Company A's gross margin rate is 40%, its inventory turnover based on cost of goods sold is 6 [or ($100 − $40)/$10]. If Company B's gross margin rate is 30%, its cost of goods sold is $70, and its inventory turnover is 7 [or ($100 − $30)/$10].

Influence of External Factors

Facts and conditions not disclosed by the financial statements may, however, affect their interpretation. A single important event may have been largely responsible for a given relationship. For example, a new product may have been unexpectedly put on the market by competitors, making it necessary for the company under study to sell at lower prices a product suddenly rendered obsolete. Such an event would severely affect the percentage of gross margin to net sales. Yet there may be little or no chance that such an event will happen again.

A BROADER PERSPECTIVE

GENERAL ELECTRIC COMPANY

Results of the 1980s

General Electric Company and consolidated affiliates

Earnings Per Share
Averaged 10.9% annual growth

Operating Margin
Improved to 11.3% of sales

Market Value
Went from 11th to 2nd

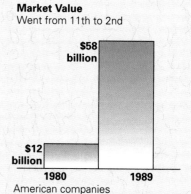

American companies

Dividends Per Share
Averaged 9.5% annual growth

Total Cost Productivity
More than tripled

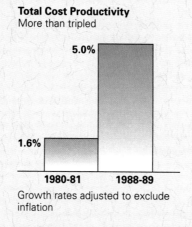

Growth rates adjusted to exclude inflation

Average Annual Yield
Outperformed peer groups

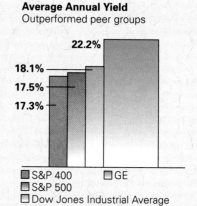

With dividend reinvestment assumed

Financial Highlights

(Dollar amounts in millions; per-share amounts in dollars)	1989	1988	Percent Increase
Revenues	$54,574	$50,089	9%
Net earnings	3,939	3,386	16
Dividends declared	1,537	1,314	17
Per share			
Net earnings	4.36	3.75	16
Dividends declared	1.70	1.46	16
Earned on average share owners' equity	20.0%	19.4%	

ILLUSTRATION 17.4

Summary of Ratios

Ratio	Formula	Significance
Current, or working capital, ratio	Current assets ÷ Current liabilities	Test of debt-paying ability
Acid-test (quick) ratio	Quick assets (Cash + Marketable securities + Net receivables) ÷ Current liabilities	Test of immediate debt-paying ability
Accounts receivable turnover	Net credit sales (or net sales) ÷ Average net accounts receivable	Test of quality of accounts receivable
Number of days' sales in accounts receivable (average collection period of accounts receivable)	Number of days in year (365) ÷ Accounts receivable turnover	Test of quality of accounts receivable
Inventory turnover	Cost of goods sold ÷ Average inventory	Test of whether or not a sufficient volume of business is being generated relative to inventory
Total assets turnover	Net sales ÷ Average total assets	Test of whether or not the volume of business generated is adequate relative to amount of capital invested in business
Equity (stockholders' equity) ratio	Stockholders' equity ÷ Total assets (or total equities)	Index of long-run solvency and safety
Stockholders' equity to debt (debt to equity) ratio	Stockholders' equity ÷ Total debt	Measure of the relative proportion of stockholders' and of creditors' equities
Rate of return on operating assets	Net operating income ÷ Operating assets or Operating margin × Turnover of operating assets	Measure of managerial effectiveness
Net income to net sales (return on sales ratio)	Net income ÷ Net sales	Indicator of the amount of net profit on each dollar of sales
Net income to average common stockholders' equity	Net income ÷ Average common stockholders' equity	Measure of what a given company earned for its stockholders from all sources as a percentage of the stockholders' investment
EPS of common stock	Earnings available to common stockholders ÷ Weighted-average number of common shares outstanding	Influence on the market price per share
Times interest earned ratio	Income before interest and taxes ÷ Interest expense	Test of likelihood that creditors will continue to receive their interest payments
Times preferred dividends earned ratio	Net income ÷ Annual preferred dividends	Test of likelihood that preferred stockholders will receive their dividend each year
Earnings yield on common stock	EPS ÷ Current market price per share of common stock	Comparison with other common stocks
Price-earnings ratio	Current market price per share of common stock ÷ EPS	Index of whether a stock is relatively cheap or expensive based on ratio
Dividend yield on common stock	Dividend per share of common stock ÷ Current market price per share	Comparison with other common stocks
Payout ratio on common stock	Dividend per share of common stock ÷ EPS	Index of whether company pays out a large percentage of earnings as dividends or reinvests most of its earnings
Dividend yield on preferred stock	Dividend per share of preferred stock ÷ Current market price per share of preferred stock	Comparison with other preferred stocks
Cash flow per share of common stock	Operating cash flow ÷ Average number of shares of common stock outstanding	Test of ability to pay dividends and liabilities

General business conditions within the business or industry of the company under study must be considered. A corporation's downward trend in earnings, for example, is less alarming if the industry trend or the general economic trend is also downward.

Consideration should be given to the seasonal nature of some businesses. If the balance sheet date represents the seasonal peak in the volume of business, for example, the ratio of current assets to current liabilities may acceptably be much lower than if the balance sheet date is in a season of low activity.

Potential investors should consider the market risk associated with the prospective investment. Market risk is determined by comparing the changes in the price of a stock in relation to the changes in the average price of all stocks. For instance, when the average price went up by 8%, Company X's price increased 20% while Company Y's increased 5%. Company X's stock has a greater potential for gain than Company Y's. It also has a greater risk of loss if the average price goes down. In addition, the potential investor should realize that acquiring the ability to make informed judgments is a long process and does not occur overnight. Using ratios and percentages without considering the underlying causes may lead to incorrect conclusions.

Impact of Inflation

The usefulness of conventional financial statements has been questioned. The primary reason for this uncertainty is that financial statements fail to reveal the impact of inflation on the reporting entity. A primary rule to follow in making comparisons is to be sure that the items being compared are comparable. The old adage is that you should not add apples and oranges and call the total either apples or oranges. Yet, the accountant does exactly this when dollars of different real worth are added or subtracted as if they were the same. The worth of a dollar declines during periods of inflation.

Considerable debate has existed over the proper response by accountants to inflation. Some argue that we should change our unit of measure from the nominal, unadjusted dollar to a dollar of a constant purchasing power. Others maintain that only by adopting current cost as the attribute measured will the real effect of inflation on an entity be revealed. How each of these alternative approaches could be implemented and what they are likely to reveal are discussed in Appendix C at the end of the text.

Need for Standards of Comparison

Relationships between financial statement items become more meaningful when standards are available for comparison. Comparisons with standards provide a starting point for the analyst's thinking and lead to further investigation and, ultimately, to conclusions and business decisions. Such standards consist of (1) those in the analyst's own mind as a result of experience and observations, (2) those provided by the records of past performance and financial position of the business under study, and (3) those provided about other enterprises. Examples of this last type of standard are data available through trade associations, universities, research organizations (such as Dun & Bradstreet and Robert Morris Associates), and governmental units (such as the Federal Trade Commission).

In financial statement analysis, you must remember that standards for comparison vary by industry, and financial analysis must be carried out with knowledge of specific industry characteristics. For example, a wholesale grocery company would have large inventories available to be shipped to retailers and a relatively small investment in property, plant, and equipment, while an electric utility company would have no merchandise inventory (except for repair parts) and a large investment in property, plant, and equipment.

ETHICS	Tom Knisley is Baxter Company's new chief accountant. He had been fired from his $250,000 position as controller with XYZ Corporation when it was taken over in a hostile takeover by the Denning Corporation. Tom is 57 years old and finally found this new position with a salary of $70,000 per year after searching for a position for two years. During his search he had become very disillusioned and was about to conclude that nobody wants you if you are over 55. Tom had grown tired of playing golf every day and was very pleased to have this new position with Baxter Company.
A CLOSER LOOK	

Baxter Company has $2 million of bonds payable outstanding. Tom noticed that the agreement with the bondholders states that if the current ratio falls below 2:1 at any time during the life of the bonds, two unfavorable events could occur. First, the bondholders would be entitled to appoint two members to the board of directors of the company, and, second, the bondholders would be entitled to decide that the entire principal of $2 million is due and payable immediately.

In preparing the financial statements at year-end, Tom noticed that current assets were $7 million and current liabilities were $3 million. He was relieved to see that the current ratio was in excess of the 2:1 requirement. On closer investigation, Tom discovered that a $2 million investment in the stock of Bidwell Company is being carried in the Current Marketable Equity Securities account and included in current assets. He checked the financial statements from previous years, and this investment had been given the same treatment. When he asked about the matter, the reply was, ''We invested in that stock to assure ourselves of a source of supply for some of our raw materials. Although we do not intend to sell this stock, we could sell it at any time. Therefore, we consider the stock a current asset and carry it in the Current Marketable Equity Securities account.''

Tom realizes that in the situation described, this investment should be carried in the Noncurrent Marketable Equity Securities account and included among noncurrent assets as a long-term investment. Apparently the company's auditor, Sam Jenks, CPA, had never taken issue with the classification as a current asset. Tom wondered whether he should do likewise to avoid being considered a ''troublemaker.''

Required

a. What would be the consequences of Tom reclassifying this item as a long-term investment?

b. Why has the auditor probably not taken issue with the classification of this item as a current asset?

c. What would you do if you were Tom?

Even within an industry, variations may exist. Acceptable current ratios, gross margin percentages, debt to equity ratios, and other relationships vary widely depending on unique conditions within an industry. Therefore, it is important to know the industry to make comparisons that have real meaning.

This chapter discussed the analysis and interpretation of financial statements. In Chapter 18, the statement of cash flows will be discussed.

UNDERSTANDING THE LEARNING OBJECTIVES

1. Describe and explain the objectives of financial statement analysis.

- ☐ Financial statement analysis consists of applying analytical tools and techniques to financial statements and other relevant data to obtain useful information.

- ☐ This information is shown as significant relationships between data and trends in those data assessing the company's **past performance** and **current financial position.**

□ The information is also used to **make predictions** that may have a direct effect on decisions made by many users of financial statements.

□ Present and potential company investors use this information to assess the profitability of the firm.

□ Outside parties and long-term creditors sometimes are interested in a company's solvency, and thus use the information in predicting the company's solvency.

2. Calculate and explain changes in financial statements using horizontal analysis, vertical analysis, and trend analysis.

□ Horizontal analysis is the calculation of dollar changes or percentage changes in comparative statement items or totals. Use of this analysis helps detect changes in a company's performance and highlights trends.

□ Vertical analysis consists of a study of a single financial statement in which each item is expressed as a percentage of a significant total. Use of this analysis is especially helpful in analyzing income statement data such as the percentage of cost of goods sold to sales or the percentage of gross margin to sales.

□ Trend analysis is used to compare financial information over time to a base year. The analysis is calculated by:

1. Selecting a base year or period.

2. Assigning a weight of 100% to the amounts appearing on the base-year financial statements.

3. Expressing the corresponding amounts shown on the other years' financial statements as a percentage of base-year or period amounts. The percentages are computed by dividing nonbase-year amounts by the corresponding base-year amounts and then multiplying the results by 100.

Trend analysis indicates changes that are taking place in an organization and highlights the direction of these changes.

3. Perform ratio analysis on financial statements using liquidity ratios, long-term solvency ratios, profitability tests, and market tests.

□ **Liquidity ratios** are used to indicate a company's short-term debt-paying ability. These ratios include (1) current, or working capital, ratio; (2) acid-test (quick) ratio; (3) accounts receivable turnover; (4) number of days' sales in accounts receivable; (5) inventory turnover; and (6) total assets turnover.

□ **Equity, or long-term solvency, ratios** show the relationship between debt and equity financing in a company. These ratios include (1) equity (stockholders' equity) ratio and (2) stockholders' equity to debt ratio.

□ **Profitability tests** are an important measure of a company's operating success. These tests include (1) rate of return on operating assets, (2) net income to net sales, (3) net income to average common stockholders' equity, (4) earnings per share of common stock, (5) times interest earned ratio, and (6) times preferred dividends earned ratio.

□ **Market tests** help investors and potential investors assess the relative merits of the various stocks in the marketplace. These tests include (1) earnings yield on common stock, (2) price-earnings ratio, (3) dividend yield on common stock, (4) payout ratio on common stock, (5) dividend yield on preferred stock, and (6) cash flow per share of common stock.

4. Describe the considerations used in financial statement analysis.

☐ **Need for comparative data:** Analysts must be sure that their comparisons are valid—especially when the comparisons are of items for different periods or different companies.

☐ **Influence of external factors:** A single important event, such as the unexpected placing of a product on the market by a competitor, may affect the interpretation of the financial statements. Also, the general business conditions and the possible seasonal nature of the business must be taken into consideration, since these factors could have an impact on the statements.

☐ **Impact of inflation:** Since financial statements fail to reveal the impact of inflation on the reporting entity, one must make sure that the items being compared are all comparable; that is, the impact of inflation has been taken into consideration.

☐ **Need for comparative standards:** It is important in financial statement analysis to remember that standards for comparison vary by industry, and financial analysis must be carried out with knowledge of specific industry characteristics.

DEMONSTRATION PROBLEM 17–A

Comparative financial statements of Abel Company for 1994 and 1993 follow:

ABEL COMPANY
Comparative Income Statements
For the Years Ended December 31, 1994, and 1993
(in thousands)

	1994	1993
Net sales	$1,100	$950
Cost of goods sold	705	598
Gross margin	$ 395	$352
Operating expenses	291	257
Income before income taxes	$ 104	$ 95
Income taxes	45	40
Net income	$ 59	$ 55

ABEL COMPANY
Comparative Balance Sheets
December 31, 1994, and 1993
(in thousands)

	1994	1993
Assets		
Cash	$ 29	$ 30
Accounts receivable, net	67	74
Merchandise inventory	113	91
Plant assets, net	236	237
Total assets	$445	$432
Liabilities and Stockholders' Equity		
Current liabilities	$ 78	$ 70
Long-term liabilities	94	94
Common stock	240	240
Retained earnings	33	28
Total liabilities and stockholders' equity	$445	$432

Required *a.* Prepare comparative common-size income statements for 1994 and 1993.
   b. Perform a horizontal analysis of the comparative balance sheets.
   c. Comment on the results of *(a)* and *(b)*.

SOLUTION TO DEMONSTRATION PROBLEM 17–A

a.

ABEL COMPANY
Common-Size Comparative Income Statements
For the Years Ended December 31, 1994, and 1993

	Percent	
	1994	1993
Net sales	100.00	100.00
Cost of goods sold	64.09	62.95
Gross margin	35.91	37.05
Operating expenses	26.45	27.05
Income before income taxes	9.46*	10.00
Income taxes	4.09	4.21
Net income	5.37*	5.79

* Rounding difference.

b.

ABEL COMPANY
Comparative Balance Sheets
December 31, 1994, and 1993
(in thousands)

	1994	1993	Increase or Decrease 1994 over 1993 Amount	Percent
Assets				
Cash	$ 29	$ 30	$ (1)	(3.33)
Accounts receivable, net	67	74	(7)	(9.46)
Merchandise inventory	113	91	22	24.18
Plant assets, net	236	237	(1)	(0.42)
Total assets	$445	$432	$13	3.01
Liabilities and Stockholders' Equity				
Current liabilities	$ 78	$ 70	$ 8	11.43
Long-term liabilities	94	94	–0–	–0–
Common stock	240	240	–0–	–0–
Retained earnings	33	28	5	17.86
Total liabilities and stockholders' equity	$445	$432	$13	3.01

c. The $150,000 increase in sales yielded only a $43,000 increase in gross margin because the gross margin rate decreased from 37.05% to 35.91%. Although operating expenses increased from $257,000 to $291,000, they declined relatively from 27.05% to 26.45% of sales. This change together with the change in gross margin combined to hold net income to an increase of $4,000, which represents a decline of 0.42% in the rate of net income to sales. The significant change in the balance sheet was the 24.18% increase in merchandise inventory that was financed by decreases in cash and accounts receivable and by increases in current liabilities and in retained earnings. The company is in a less liquid position at the end of 1994 than at the end of 1993.

DEMONSTRATION PROBLEM 17–B

The balance sheet and supplementary data for Carey Corporation are shown below.

CAREY CORPORATION
Balance Sheet
December 31, 1993

Assets

Cash		$ 50,000
Marketable securities.		30,000
Accounts receivable, net		70,000
Merchandise inventory		150,000
Building.	$400,000	
Less: Accumulated depreciation	100,000	300,000
Total assets		$600,000

Liabilities and Stockholders' Equity

Accounts payable	$ 30,000
Bank loans payable.	10,000
Mortgage notes payable, due in 1996	40,000
Bonds payable, 10%, due December 31, 1998	100,000
Common stock, $100 par value	300,000
Retained earnings	120,000
Total liabilities and stockholders' equity.	$600,000

Supplementary data

1. 1993 net income, $60,000.
2. 1993 cost of goods sold, $540,000.
3. 1993 net sales, $900,000.
4. Merchandise inventory, January 1, 1993, $100,000.
5. Net interest expense, $15,000.
6. 1993 net income before interest and taxes, $130,000.
7. Net accounts receivable on January 1, 1993, $50,000.
8. Total assets on January 1, 1993, $540,000.

Required Compute the following ratios:

a. Current ratio.
b. Acid-test ratio.
c. Accounts receivable turnover.
d. Inventory turnover.
e. Total assets turnover.
f. Equity ratio.
g. EPS of common stock.
h. Times interest earned ratio.

SOLUTION TO DEMONSTRATION PROBLEM 17–B

a. Current ratio:

$$\frac{\text{Current assets}}{\text{Current liabilities}} = \frac{\$300,000}{\$40,000} = 7.5:1$$

b. Acid-test ratio:

$$\frac{\text{Quick assets}}{\text{Current liabilities}} = \frac{\$150,000}{\$40,000} = 3.75:1$$

c. Accounts receivable turnover:

$$\frac{\text{Net sales}}{\text{Average net accounts receivable}} = \frac{\$900,000}{\$60,000} = 15 \text{ times}$$

d. Inventory turnover:

$$\frac{\text{Cost of goods sold}}{\text{Average inventory}} = \frac{\$540,000}{\$125,000} = 4.32 \text{ times}$$

e. Total assets turnover:

$$\frac{\text{Net sales}}{\text{Average total assets}} = \frac{\$900,000}{\$570,000} = 1.58 \text{ times}$$

f. Equity ratio:

$$\frac{\text{Stockholders' equity}}{\text{Total assets}} = \frac{\$420,000}{\$600,000} = 70\%$$

g. EPS of common stock:

$$\frac{\text{Earnings available to common stockholders}}{\text{Weighted-average number of common shares outstanding}} = \frac{\$60,000}{3,000} = \$20$$

h. Times interest earned ratio:

$$\frac{\text{Income before interest and taxes}}{\text{Interest expense}} = \frac{\$130,000}{\$15,000} = 8.67:1, \text{ or } 8.67 \text{ times}$$

NEW TERMS

Accounts receivable turnover Net credit sales divided by average net accounts receivable. *790*

Acid-test (quick) ratio Ratio of quick assets (cash, marketable securities, net receivables) to current liabilities. *790*

Cash flow per share of common stock Operating cash flow divided by the average number of shares of common stock outstanding. *803*

Common-size statements Show only percentages and no absolute dollar amounts. *783*

Comparative financial statements Present the same company's financial statements for two or more successive periods in side-by-side columns. *783*

Current ratio Current assets divided by current liabilities. *788*

Debt to equity ratio Total debt divided by stockholders' equity. *794*

Dividend yield on common stock Dividend per share of common stock divided by current market price per share of common stock. *801*

Dividend yield on preferred stock Dividend per share of preferred stock divided by current market price per share of preferred stock. *802*

Earnings per share (EPS) The amount of earnings available to common stockholders (which equals net income less preferred dividends) divided by weighted-average number of shares of common stock outstanding. *798*

Earnings yield on common stock Ratio of current EPS to current market price per share of common stock. *801*

Equity (stockholders' equity) ratio The ratio of stockholders' equity to total assets (or total equities). *793*

Horizontal analysis Analysis of a company's financial statements for two or more successive periods showing percentage and/or absolute changes from prior year. This type of analysis helps detect changes in a company's performance and highlights trends. *783*

Inventory turnover Cost of goods sold divided by average inventory. *792*

Liquidity Company's state of possessing liquid assets, such as (1) cash and (2) other assets that will soon be converted to cash. *782*

Net income to average common stockholders' equity Net income divided by average common stockholders' equity; often called **rate of return on average common stockholders' equity,** or simply **return on equity (ROE).** *797*

Net income to net sales Net income divided by net sales. *796*

Nonoperating assets Assets owned by a company but not used in producing operating revenues. *795*

Nonoperating income elements Elements that are excluded from net operating income because they are not directly related to operations; includes such elements as extraordinary items, interest revenue, and interest expense. *795*

Number of days' sales in accounts receivable The number of days in a year (365) divided by the accounts receivable turnover. Also called the **average collection period for accounts receivable.** *791*

Operating assets All assets actively used in producing operating revenues. *795*

Operating margin Net operating income divided by net sales. *795*

Payout ratio on common stock The ratio of dividends per share of common stock divided by EPS. *801*

Price-earnings ratio The ratio of current market price per share of common stock divided by the EPS of the stock. *801*

Quick ratio Same as acid-test ratio.

Rate of return on operating assets (Net operating income ÷ Net sales) × (Net sales ÷ Operating assets). Result is equal to net operating income divided by operating assets. *795*

Return on equity (ROE) Net income divided by average common stockholders' equity. *797*

Stockholders' equity to debt ratio Stockholders' equity divided by total debt; often used in inverted form and called the **debt to equity ratio.** *794*

Times interest earned ratio A ratio computed by dividing income before interest and taxes by interest expense (also called **interest coverage ratio**). *800*

Times preferred dividends earned ratio Net income divided by annual preferred dividends. *800*

Total assets turnover Net sales divided by average total assets. *792*

Trend percentages Similar to horizontal analysis except that a base year or period is selected, and comparisons are made to the base year or period. *783*

Turnover The relationship between the amount of an asset and some measure of its use. See Accounts receivable turnover, Inventory turnover, and Total assets turnover. *790*

Turnover of operating assets Net sales divided by operating assets. *795*

Vertical analysis The study of a single financial statement in which each item is expressed as a percentage of a significant total; for example, percentages of sales calculations. *783*

Working capital ratio Same as current ratio.

Yield (on stock) The yield on a stock investment refers to either an earnings yield or a dividend yield. *801* Also see Earnings yield on common stock and Dividend yield on common stock and preferred stock.

SELF-TEST

True-False

Indicate whether each of the following statements is true or false.

1. An objective of financial statement analysis is to provide information about the company's past performance and current financial position.

2. Vertical analysis helps detect changes in a company's performance over several periods and highlights trends.

3. Common-size statements provide information about changes in dollar amounts relative to the previous periods.

4. Liquidity ratios show a company's capacity to pay maturing current liabilities.

5. A company that is quite profitable may find it difficult to pay its accounts payable.

6. Financial statement analysts must be sure that comparable data are used among companies to make the comparisons valid.

Multiple-Choice

Select the best answer for each of the following questions.

The following data were abstracted from the December 31, 1994, balance sheet of Cox Company:

Cash	$ 68,000
Marketable securities	32,000
Accounts and notes receivable, net	92,000
Merchandise inventory	122,000
Prepaid expenses	6,000
Accounts and notes payable, short term	128,000
Accrued liabilities	32,000
Bonds payable, long term	200,000

1. The current ratio is:
   a. 1:2.
   b. 2:1.
   c. 1.2:1.
   d. 3:1.

2. The acid-test ratio is:
   a. 1:2.
   b. 2:1.
   c. 1.2:1.
   d. 3:1.

Boehmer Company shows the following data on its 1994 financial statements.

Accounts receivable, January 1	$ 360,000
Accounts receivable, December 31	480,000
Merchandise inventory, January 1	450,000
Merchandise inventory, December 31	510,000
Gross sales	2,400,000
Sales returns and allowances	90,000
Net sales	2,310,000
Cost of goods sold	1,680,000
Income before interest and taxes	360,000
Interest on bonds	96,000
Net income	192,000

3. The accounts receivable turnover is:
   a. 5.5 times per year.
   b. 5.714 times per year.
   c. 5 times per year.
   d. 6.667 times per year.

4. The inventory turnover is:
   a. 5 times per year.
   b. 4.8125 times per year.
   c. 3.5 times per year.
   d. 4 times per year.

5. The times interest earned ratio is:
   a. 4.75 times per year.
   b. 3.75 times per year.
   c. 2 times per year.
   d. 3 times per year.

Now turn to page 828 to check your answers.

QUESTIONS

1. Distinguish between horizontal and vertical analysis of financial statements.

2. What are common-size financial statements? What item is assigned a value of 100% in the common-size income statement, and what item is assigned a value of 100% in the common-size balance sheet?

3. How do trend percentages differ from comparative financial statements?

4. What are the changes, absolute and percentage, if net income of $60,000 earned in 1994 is compared to a net loss sustained in 1993 of $15,000? What are the changes if the net loss was sustained in 1994 after earning net income in 1993?

5. Explain the meaning of the statement: "With 1984 equal to 100, net sales increased from 225 in 1993 to 260 in 1994."

6. Think of a situation where the current ratio is misleading as an indicator of short-term debt-paying ability. Does the acid-test ratio offer a remedy to the situation you have described? Describe a situation where the acid-test ratio will not suffice either.

7. A provision in a bond indenture requires the borrower to maintain positive working capital. Explain what this requirement means and why such a provision is included in an indenture.

8. What do turnover ratios express and what do they measure?

9. What can be interpreted from the accounts receivable turnover ratio?

10. The higher the accounts receivable turnover rate, the better off the company. Do you agree? Why?

11. What does the inventory turnover ratio show?

12. Through the use of turnover ratios, explain why a company might seek to increase the volume of its sales even though such an increase can be secured only at reduced prices.

13. Of what significance is the equity ratio? What are the alternative ways of conveying the same information?

14. Before Ruby Company issued $15,000 of long-term notes (due more than a year from the date of issue) in exchange for a like amount of accounts payable, its acid-test ratio was 2:1. Will this

transaction increase, decrease, or have no effect on (a) the current ratio and (b) the equity ratio?

15. How is rate of return on operating assets determined? Can two companies with "operating margins" of 5% and 1%, respectively, both have rates of return of 20% on operating assets? How?

16. Indicate which of the relationships illustrated in this chapter would be used to judge:
    a. The short-term debt-paying ability of the company.
    b. The overall efficiency of the company without regard to the sources of assets.
    c. The return to owners of a corporation.
    d. The safety of bondholders' interest.
    e. The safety of preferred stockholders' dividends.

17. Indicate how each of the following ratios or measures is calculated:
    a. Payout.
    b. EPS of common stock.
    c. Price-earnings.
    d. Dividend yield on common stock.
    e. Dividend yield on preferred stock.
    f. Times interest earned.

g. Times preferred dividends earned.
h. Return on common stockholders' equity.

18. Explain why the EPS for 1993 and 1994 must be adjusted in a three-year summary of earnings data presented in 1995, assuming there was a 20% stock dividend distributed in June 1995.

19. Cite some deficiencies in accounting information that would limit its usefulness for analyzing a particular company over a 10-year period.

The Coca-Cola Company

20. *Real world question* From the financial highlights of The Coca-Cola Company in Appendix E, determine the percentage change in operating income from 1988 to 1989.

The Coca-Cola Company

21. *Real world question* From the financial highlights of The Coca-Cola Company in Appendix E, determine the 1989 net income per common share.

The Coca-Cola Company

22. *Real world question* From the financial highlights of The Coca-Cola Company in Appendix E, determine the 1989 cash dividends per common share.

EXERCISES*

Exercise 17–1

Perform horizontal and vertical analysis
(L.O. 2)

Income statement data for Knox Company for 1994 and 1993 are:

	1994	1993
Net sales	$1,051,200	$811,800
Cost of goods sold	759,300	554,550
Selling expenses	144,000	130,050
Administrative expenses	95,700	81,300
Income taxes	21,000	19,500

Prepare a horizontal and vertical analysis of the above income data in a form similar to that in Illustration 17.2. Comment on the results of this analysis.

Exercise 17–2

Determine effects of various transactions on the current ratio
(L.O. 3)

Under each of the three conditions listed below, compute the current ratio after each of the transactions described. Current assets are now $225,000. (Consider each transaction independently.) The current ratio before the transactions is:

a. 1 : 1.
b. 2 : 1.
c. 0.5 : 1.

Transactions
1. Purchased $225,000 of merchandise on account.
2. Purchased $112,500 of machinery for cash.
3. Issued stock for $112,500 cash.

---

* By using the ratio module in the General Ledger Applications Software (GLAS) package, you can work any of the exercises or problems in Chapter 17 that deal with ratios.

Exercise 17–3

Compute average number of days receivables are outstanding; determine effect of increase in turnover

(L.O. 3)

A company has sales of $1,003,750 per year. Its average accounts receivable balance is $200,750.

a.   What is the average number of days an account receivable is outstanding?

b.   Assuming released funds can be invested at 10%, how much could the company earn by reducing the collection period of the accounts receivable to 50 days?

c.   What assumption must you make in order for this income calculation to be correct?

Exercise 17–4

Compute inventory turnover

(L.O. 3)

From the following partial income statement calculate the inventory turnover for the period.

Net sales		$625,740
Cost of goods sold:		
Beginning inventory	$ 60,000	
Purchases	444,000	
Cost of goods available for sale	$504,000	
Less: Ending inventory	69,600	
Cost of goods sold		434,400
Gross margin		$191,340
Operating expenses		90,000
Net operating income.		$101,340

Exercise 17–5

Compute EPS

(L.O. 3)

Apple Company had 20,000 shares of common stock outstanding on January 1, 1993. On April 1, 1993, it issued 5,000 additional shares for cash. The income available for common stockholders for 1993 was $200,000. What amount of EPS of common stock should the company report?

Exercise 17–6

Compute times interest earned

(L.O. 3)

A company paid interest of $16,000, incurred federal income taxes of $44,000, and had net income (after taxes) of $84,000. How many times was the interest earned?

Exercise 17–7

Compute times dividends earned and dividend yield

(L.O. 3)

Exchange Company had 6,000 shares of $100 par value, 5% preferred stock outstanding. Net income after taxes was $180,000. The market price per share was $120.

a.   How many times were the preferred dividends earned?

b.   What was the yield on the preferred stock, assuming the regular preferred dividends were declared and paid?

Exercise 17–8

Compute price-earnings ratio

(L.O. 3)

A company had 11,250 shares of $50 par value common stock outstanding. Net income was $75,000. Current market price per share is $100. Compute the price-earnings ratio.

Exercise 17–9

Compute rate of return on operating assets

(L.O. 3)

Celebration's, Inc., had net sales of $1,180,000, gross margin of $630,000, and operating expenses of $455,000. Total assets (all operating) were $1,035,000. Compute Kelly's rate of return on operating assets.

Exercise 17–10

Compute weighted-average number of shares outstanding

(L.O. 3)

New Company began the year 1993 with 75,000 shares of common stock outstanding. On March 31, it issued 12,000 shares for cash; and on September 30, it purchased 6,000 treasury shares for cash. Compute the weighted-average number of common shares outstanding for the year.

Exercise 17–11

Compute rate of return on
stockholders' equity
(L.O. 3)

Coupon Company started 1994 with total stockholders' equity of $675,000. Its net income for 1994 was $180,000, and $30,000 of dividends were declared. Compute the rate of return on average stockholders' equity for 1994.

Exercise 17–12

Compute EPS for current
and prior year
(L.O. 3)

A company reported EPS of $4 (or $400,000/100,000 shares) for 1993, ending the year with 100,000 shares outstanding. In 1994, the company earned net income of $660,000, issued 40,000 shares of common stock for cash on September 30; and distributed a 100% stock dividend on December 31. Compute EPS for 1994 and compute the adjusted EPS for 1993 that would be shown in the 1994 annual report.

PROBLEMS: SERIES A

Problem 17–1A

Perform horizontal and
vertical analysis and
comment on the results
(L.O. 2)

Presented below are Action Company's comparative balance sheets at the end of 1994 and 1993. The comparative statements of income and retained earnings for the years ended December 31, 1994, and 1993, are also given.

ACTION COMPANY
Comparative Balance Sheets
December 31, 1994, and 1993

	1994	1993
Assets		
Current assets:		
Cash.	$ 71,400	$ 38,850
Accounts receivable, net.	203,350	197,750
Merchandise inventory.	505,750	525,350
Total current assets	$ 780,500	$ 761,950
Plant assets, net	658,000	626,500
Total assets	$1,438,500	$1,388,450
Liabilities and Stockholders' Equity		
Current liabilities:		
Accounts payable and accruals	$ 199,500	$ 425,950
Notes payable	140,000	350,000
Total current liabilities	$ 339,500	$ 775,950
Long-term liabilities:		
Bonds payable	420,000	–0–
Total liabilities.	$ 759,500	$ 775,950
Stockholders' equity:		
Common stock	$ 350,000	$ 350,000
Retained earnings	329,000	262,500
Total stockholders' equity	$ 679,000	$ 612,500
Total liabilities and stockholders' equity	$1,438,500	$1,388,450

ACTION COMPANY
Comparative Statements of Income and Retained Earnings
For the Years Ended December 31, 1994, and 1993

	1994	1993
Net sales.	$2,885,750	$2,749,950
Cost of goods sold	1,830,850	1,753,850
Gross margin.	$1,054,900	$ 996,100
Operating expenses:		
Selling	$ 423,850	$ 449,750
Administrative	392,700	363,650
Total operating expenses.	$ 816,550	$ 813,400
Net operating income	$ 238,350	$ 182,700
Interest expense	64,400	42,000
Income before income taxes	$ 173,950	$ 140,700
Income taxes.	70,000	56,000
Net income.	$ 103,950	$ 84,700
Retained earnings, January 1	262,500	212,800
	$ 366,450	$ 297,500
Dividends	37,450	35,000
Retained earnings, December 31	$ 329,000	$ 262,500

Required *a.* Perform a horizontal and vertical analysis of the above financial statements in a manner similar to that shown in Illustrations 17.1 and 17.2.

b. Comment on the results of the analysis in part *(a)*.

Problem 17–2A

Perform trend analysis and comment on the results
(L.O. 2)

You are given the following data for a company:

	1993	1994	1995	1996
Sales.	$540,000	$618,000	$720,000	$1,020,000
Cost of goods sold	360,000	390,000	540,000	780,000
Gross margin	$180,000	$228,000	$180,000	$ 240,000
Operating expenses	144,000	153,600	176,400	211,200
Net operating income	$ 36,000	$ 74,400	$ 3,600	$ 28,800

Required *a.* Prepare a statement showing the trend percentages for each of the above items, using 1993 as the base year.

b. Comment on the trends noted.

Problem 17–3A

Compute working capital, current ratio, and acid-test ratio and comment on the results
(L.O. 3)

The following account balances are taken from the ledger of Lense Company:

	December 31	
	1994	1993
Allowance for Uncollectible Accounts	$ 76,800	$ 60,000
Prepaid Expenses	36,000	48,000
Accrued Liabilities	168,000	148,800
Cash in Bank A	876,000	780,000
Bank Overdraft in Bank B (credit balance)	–0–	102,000
Accounts Payable	571,200	468,000
Merchandise Inventory.	1,428,000	1,579,200
Bonds Payable (due in 1997)	492,000	475,200
Marketable Securities	174,000	117,600
Notes Payable (due in six months).	362,400	218,400
Accounts Receivable.	1,126,800	1,039,200

Required   *a.*   Compute the amount of working capital as of both year-end dates.

         b.   Compute the current ratio as of both year-end dates.

         c.   Compute the acid-test ratio as of both year-end dates.

         d.   Comment briefly on the company's short-term financial position.

Problem 17–4A

Determine effects of various transactions on working capital and current ratio (L.O. 3)

On December 31, 1993, Sandman Company's current ratio was 3:1. Assume that the following transactions were completed on that date and indicate *(a)* whether the amount of working capital would have been increased, decreased, or unaffected by each transaction; and *(b)* whether the current ratio would have been increased, decreased, or unaffected by each transaction. (Consider each transaction independently.)

1. Purchased merchandise on account.
2. Paid a cash dividend declared on November 15, 1993.
3. Sold equipment for cash.
4. Temporarily invested cash in marketable securities.
5. Sold obsolete merchandise for cash (at a loss).
6. Issued 10-year bonds for cash.
7. Amortized goodwill.
8. Paid cash for inventory.
9. Purchased land for cash.
10. Returned merchandise that had not been paid for.
11. Wrote off an account receivable as uncollectible. Uncollectible amount is less than the balance of the Allowance for Uncollectible Accounts.
12. Accepted a 90-day note from a customer in settlement of customer's account receivable.
13. Declared a stock dividend on common stock.

Problem 17–5A

Prepare comparative financial statements in percentages; compute current, acid-test, and equity ratios for two years (L.O. 2, 3)

Builders Company provides you with the following data:

BUILDERS COMPANY
Comparative Balance Sheets
December 31, 1994, and 1993

	1994	1993
Assets		
Cash	$100,000	$ 64,000
Accounts receivable, net	180,000	92,000
Merchandise inventory	140,000	112,000
Plant assets, net	144,000	108,000
Total assets	$564,000	$376,000
Liabilities and Stockholders' Equity		
Accounts payable	$ 76,000	$ 52,000
Notes payable	100,000	56,000
Common stock	260,000	184,000
Retained earnings	128,000	84,000
Total liabilities and stockholders' equity	$564,000	$376,000
Other data:		
Sales	$760,000	$580,000
Gross margin	460,000	380,000
Selling and administrative expenses	240,000	212,000
Interest expense	8,000	2,800

Cash dividends of $168,000 were paid in 1994. In 1994, plant assets were increased by giving a note of $18,000 for machinery. The note matures October 1, 1997. All other notes are short term.

Required   *a.*   Prepare comparative income statements that show each item's percentage of net sales.

       b.   Prepare comparative balance sheets that show each item's percentage of total assets.

       c.   Compute the current ratios as of both dates.

       d.   Compute the acid-test ratios as of both dates.

       e.   Compute the percentage of stockholders' equity to total assets and debt to equity ratios as of both dates.

Problem 17–6A

Compute numerous standard ratios (L.O. 3)

The following balance sheet and supplementary data are for Decor Corporation for 1994:

DECOR CORPORATION
Balance Sheet
December 31, 1994

Assets

Current assets:

Cash	$ 225,000	
Marketable securities	120,000	
Accounts receivable, net	195,000	
Merchandise inventory	165,000	$ 705,000

Property, plant, and equipment:

Plant assets	$2,550,000	
Less: Accumulated depreciation	187,500	2,362,500
Total assets		$3,067,500

Liabilities and Stockholders' Equity

Current liabilities:

Accounts payable	$ 127,500	
Bank loans payable	52,500	$ 180,000

Long-term liabilities:

Mortgage notes payable, due in 2004	$ 67,500	
Bonds payable, 6%, due December 31, 2004	322,500	390,000
Total liabilities		$ 570,000

Stockholders' equity:

Common stock, par value $50 per share	$1,650,000	
Appropriation for bond sinking fund	60,000	
Retained earnings	787,500	2,497,500
Total liabilities and stockholders' equity		$3,067,500

Supplementary data

1. 1994 net income amounted to $225,000.

2. 1994 income before interest and taxes was $450,000.

3. 1994 cost of goods sold was $600,000.

4. 1994 net sales amounted to $1,125,000.

5. Merchandise inventory on December 31, 1993, was $112,500.

6. Interest expense for the year was $22,500. (Some long-term liabilities were paid during the year.)

7. Beginning-of-the-year data was as follows:

Accounts receivable	$ 197,500
Stockholders' equity	2,271,200
Total assets	2,576,000

Required   Calculate the following ratios. Where you would normally use the average amount for an item in a ratio, but the information is not available to do so, use the year-end balance. Show computations.

a.   Current.

b.   Percentage of net income to stockholders' equity.

c.   Turnover of inventory.

d.   Average collection period of accounts receivable (there are 365 days in 1994).

e.   EPS of common stock.

f.   Number of times interest was earned.

g.   Stockholders' equity.

h.   Percentage of net income to total assets.

i.   Turnover of total assets.

j.   Acid-test.

Problem 17–7A

Compute rate of return on operating assets, and demonstrate effects of various transactions on this rate of return (L.O. 3)

Commercial Company has net operating income of $120,000 and operating assets of $600,000. Its net sales are $1,200,000.

The accountant for the company computes the rate of return on operating assets after first computing the operating margin and the turnover of operating assets.

Required

a.   Show the computations the accountant made.

b.   Indicate whether the operating margin and turnover will increase or decrease and then determine what the actual rate of return on operating assets would be after each of the following changes. The events are not interrelated; consider each separately, starting from the original rate of return on operating assets position. No other changes occurred.

1.   Sales were increased by $30,000. The amount of operating income and operating assets did not change.

2.   Management found some cost savings in the manufacturing process and was able to reduce operating expenses by $7,500. The savings resulted from the use of fewer materials to manufacture the same quantity of goods. As a result, average inventory was $3,000 lower than it otherwise would have been. Operating revenue was not affected by the reduction in inventory.

3.   The company invested $15,000 of cash (received on accounts receivable) in a plot of land it plans to use in the future (a nonoperating asset); income was not affected.

4.   The federal income tax rate on amounts of taxable income over $75,000 was increased from 17% to 20%. The taxes have not yet been paid.

5.   The company issued bonds and used the proceeds to buy $75,000 of machinery to be used in the business. Interest payments are $3,750 per year. Operating income increased by $15,000 (net sales did not change).

Problem 17–8A

Compute EPS, rate of return on sales and on stockholders' equity, and number of times interest earned for two years (L.O. 3)

The following information is available for Heavy-D Company:

	1994	1993
Net sales	$819,000	$507,000
Income before interest and taxes	214,500	165,750
Net income	108,225	122,850
Interest expense	17,550	15,600
Stockholders' equity, December 31 (on December 31, 1992, $390,000)	594,750	458,250
Common stock, par value $75, December 31	507,000	448,500

Additional shares of common stock were issued on January 1, 1994.

Required   Compute the following for both 1993 and 1994:

a. EPS of common stock.

b. Percentage of net income to net sales.

c. Rate of return on average stockholders' equity.

d. Number of times interest was earned.

Compare and comment.

PROBLEMS: SERIES B

Problem 17–1B

Perform horizontal and
vertical analysis and
comment on the results
(L.O. 2)

Ernst Company's comparative balance sheets as of December 31, 1994, and 1993 are presented below. Also illustrated are the company's comparative statements of income and retained earnings for the years ended December 31, 1994, and 1993.

ERNST COMPANY
Comparative Balance Sheets
December 31, 1994, and 1993

	1994	1993
Assets		
Current assets:		
Cash.	$ 5,000	$ 7,600
Accounts receivable, net.	12,000	11,200
Merchandise inventory.	28,900	29,000
Total current assets	$45,900	$47,800
Plant assets, net	41,550	35,800
Total assets	$87,450	$83,600
Liabilities and Stockholders' Equity		
Current liabilities:		
Accounts payable and accruals	$20,000	$21,500
Notes payable	–0–	11,000
Total current liabilities	$20,000	$32,500
Long-term liabilities:		
Bonds payable	15,000	–0–
Total liabilities.	$35,000	$32,500
Stockholders' equity:		
Common stock	$50,000	$50,000
Retained earnings.	2,450	1,100
Total stockholders' equity	$52,450	$51,100
Total liabilities and stockholders' equity	$87,450	$83,600

ERNST COMPANY
Comparative Statements of Income and Retained Earnings
For the Years Ended December 31, 1994, and 1993

	1994	1993
Net sales.	$172,250	$149,000
Cost of goods sold	104,250	92,400
Gross margin	$68,000	$56,600
Operating expenses:		
Selling expenses	$32,500	$26,700
Administrative expenses	24,000	22,800
Total operating expenses.	$ 56,500	$ 49,500
Net operating income	$ 11,500	$ 7,100
Interest expense	9,000	6,000
Income before federal income taxes.	$ 2,500	$ 1,100
Federal income taxes	1,000	400
Net income.	$ 1,500	$ 700
Retained earnings, January 1	1,100	500
	$ 2,600	$ 1,200
Dividends	150	100
Retained earnings, December 31	$ 2,450	$ 1,100

Required *a.* Perform a horizontal and vertical analysis of the above financial statements in a manner similar to that shown in Illustrations 17.1 and 17.2.

b. Comment on the results of the analysis in part *(a)*.

Problem 17–2B

Perform trend analysis and comment on the results
(L.O. 2)

You are given the following data for a company:

	1993	1994	1995	1996
Sales	$525,000	$581,250	$682,500	$862,500
Cost of goods sold	337,500	356,250	397,500	562,500
Gross margin	$187,500	$225,000	$285,000	$300,000
Operating expenses	168,750	195,000	225,000	258,750
Net operating income	$ 18,750	$ 30,000	$ 60,000	$ 41,250

Required *a.* Prepare a statement showing the trend percentages for each item above, using 1993 as the base year.

b. Comment on the trends noted.

Problem 17–3B

Compute working capital, current ratio, and acid-test ratio and comment on the results
(L.O. 3)

From the following data for Storage Company compute the *(a)* working capital; *(b)* current ratio; and *(c)* acid-test ratio, all as of both dates; and *(d)* comment briefly on the company's short-term financial position.

	December 31	
	1994	1993
Notes payable (due in 90 days)	$112,800	$ 92,400
Merchandise inventory	480,000	422,880
Cash	151,944	188,040
Marketable securities	74,400	45,000
Accrued liabilities	28,800	33,120
Accounts receivable.	282,000	276,000
Accounts payable	166,560	108,720
Allowance for uncollectible accounts	35,520	23,040
Bonds payable (due 1998)	222,000	235,200
Prepaid expenses.	9,720	11,160

Problem 17–4B

Determine effects of
various transactions on
working capital and
current ratio
(L.O. 3)

Factory Products, Inc., has a current ratio on December 31, 1993, of 2 : 1. If the following transactions were completed on that date, indicate *(a)* whether the amount of working capital would have been increased, decreased, or unaffected by each transaction; and *(b)* whether the current ratio would have been increased, decreased, or unaffected by each transaction (consider each independently).

1. Sold building for cash.
2. Exchanged old equipment for new equipment. (No cash was involved.)
3. Declared a cash dividend on preferred stock.
4. Sold merchandise on account (at a profit).
5. Retired mortgage notes that would have matured in 2007.
6. Issued stock dividend to common stockholders.
7. Paid cash for a patent.
8. Temporarily invested cash in government bonds.
9. Purchased inventory for cash.
10. Wrote off an account receivable as uncollectible. Uncollectible amount is less than the balance in the Allowance for Uncollectible Accounts.
11. Paid the cash dividend on preferred stock.
12. Purchased a computer and gave a two-year promissory note.
13. Collected accounts receivable.
14. Borrowed cash from a bank on a 120-day promissory note.
15. Discounted a customer's note. Interest expense was involved.

Problem 17–5B

Prepare comparative
financial statements in
percentages; compute
current, acid-test, and
equity ratios for two years
(L.O. 2, 3)

The following are comparative balance sheets of the Iron Corporation on December 31, 1994, and 1993:

IRON CORPORATION
Comparative Balance Sheets
December 31, 1994, and 1993

	1994	1993
Assets		
Cash	$ 187,500	$ 212,500
Accounts receivable, net	162,500	187,500
Merchandise inventory	112,500	137,500
Plant assets, net	250,000	112,500
Total assets	$ 712,500	$ 650,000
Liabilities and Stockholders' Equity		
Accounts payable	$ 100,000	$ 62,500
Notes payable	87,500	107,500
Common stock	275,000	275,000
Retained earnings	250,000	205,000
Total liabilities and stockholders' equity	$ 712,500	$ 650,000
Other data:		
Sales	$1,150,000	$1,000,000
Gross margin	475,000	425,000
Selling and administrative expenses	300,000	275,000
Interest expense	10,000	5,000

During 1994, a note in the amount of $62,500 was given for equipment purchased at that price. Unlike the company's other notes, which are short term, the $62,500 note matures in 1998. Cash dividends were $37,500 for 1993 and $95,000 for 1994.

Required   *a.* Prepare comparative income statements that show each item's percentage of net sales.

    b.   Prepare comparative balance sheets that show each item's percentage of total assets.

    c.   Compute the current ratios as of both dates.

    d.   Compute the acid-test ratios as of both dates.

    e.   Compute the percentage of stockholders' equity to total assets and debt to equity ratios as of both dates.

Problem 17–6B

Compute numerous standard ratios (L.O. 3)

The following condensed balance sheet and supplementary data are for Lumpkin Company for 1994:

LUMPKIN COMPANY
Balance Sheet
December 31, 1994

Assets

Current assets:

Cash.	$ 400,000	
Marketable securities	250,000	
Accounts receivable, net.	650,000	
Merchandise inventory.	420,000	$1,720,000

Property, plant, and equipment:

Plant assets	$3,000,000	
Less: Accumulated depreciation	550,000	2,450,000
Total assets		$4,170,000

Liabilities and Stockholders' Equity

Current liabilities:

Accounts payable	$ 300,000	
Bank loans payable (due in six months)	80,000	$ 380,000

Long-term liabilities:

Mortgage notes payable due in 2000	$ 175,000	
Bonds payable, 8%, due December 31, 2002.	800,000	975,000

Stockholders' equity:

Common stock, par value $100 per share	$2,300,000	
Appropriation for bond sinking fund	115,000	
Retained earnings.	400,000	2,815,000
Total liabilities and stockholders' equity		$4,170,000

Supplementary data

1. 1994 interest expense: $80,000. (Some long-term liabilities were paid during the year.)

2. 1994 net sales: $3,000,000.

3. 1994 cost of goods sold: $2,100,000.

4. 1994 net income: $200,000.

5. 1994 income before interest and taxes: $400,000.

6. Merchandise inventory, December 31, 1993: $625,000.

Required   Calculate the following ratios. Where you would normally use the average amount for an item in a ratio, but the information is not available to do so, use the year-end balance. Show computations.

    a.   Current ratio.

    b.   Percentage of net income to stockholders' equity.

    c.   Inventory turnover.

    d.   Average collection period of accounts receivable (there are 365 days in 1994).

e.   EPS of common stock.

f.   Number of times interest was earned.

g.   Stockholders' equity.

h.   Percentage of net income to total assets.

i.   Turnover of total assets.

j.   Acid-test.

Problem 17–7B

Compute rate of return on operating assets, and demonstrate effects of various transactions on this rate of return (L.O. 3)

The following information is available about three companies:

	Operating Assets	Net Operating Income	Net Sales
Red Company	$ 300,000	$ 40,000	$ 440,000
White Company	1,800,000	130,000	4,000,000
Blue Company	8,000,000	1,050,000	7,500,000

Required

a.   Determine the operating margin, turnover of operating assets, and rate of return on operating assets for each company.

b.   In the subsequent year, the following changes took place (no other changes occurred):

Red Company bought some new machinery at a cost of $50,000. Net operating income increased by $4,000 as a result of an increase in sales of $80,000.

White Company sold some equipment it was using that was relatively unproductive. The book value of the equipment sold was $200,000. As a result of the sale of the equipment, sales declined by $100,000, and operating income declined by $2,000.

Blue Company purchased some new retail outlets at a cost of $2,000,000. As a result, sales increased by $3,000,000, and operating income increased by $160,000.

1.   Which company has the largest absolute change in—
   a.   Operating margin?
   b.   Turnover of operating assets?
   c.   Rate of return on operating assets?
2.   Which one realized the largest dollar change in operating income? Explain this change in view of the rate of return on operating asset changes.

Problem 17–8B

Compute EPS, rate of return on sales and stockholders' equity, and number of times interest earned for two years (L.O. 3)

You have managed to determine the following data about a company:

	1994	1993
Net sales	$1,980,000	$1,530,000
Income before interest and taxes	324,000	108,000
Net income	162,000	54,000
Interest expense.	54,000	25,200
Stockholders' equity, January 1	1,350,000	1,080,000
Stockholders' equity, December 31	1,620,000	1,350,000
Common stock, par value $30, December 31	1,080,000	648,000

Additional shares of common stock were issued on January 1, 1994.

Required

Compute the following for both 1993 and 1994:

a.   EPS of common stock.

b.   Percentage of net income to net sales.

c.   Rate of return on stockholders' equity.

d.   Number of times interest was earned.

Compare and comment.

BUSINESS DECISION PROBLEMS

Decision Problem 17–1

Compute net income, identify reason for cash increase, state main sources of financing, and indicate further analyses needed
(L.O. 2, 3)

Shown below are the comparative balance sheets of Center Corporation for December 31, 1994, and 1993.

CENTER CORPORATION
Comparative Balance Sheets
December 31, 1994, and 1993

	1994	1993
Assets		
Cash	$280,000	$ 56,000
Accounts receivable, net	50,400	67,200
Merchandise inventory	224,000	235,200
Plant and equipment, net	156,800	168,000
Total assets	$711,200	$526,400
Liabilities and Stockholders' Equity		
Accounts payable	$ 56,000	$ 56,000
Common stock	392,000	392,000
Retained earnings	263,200	78,400
Total liabilities and stockholders' equity	$711,200	$526,400

Required

a. What was the net income for 1994, assuming no dividend payments?

b. What was the primary source of the large increase in the cash balance from 1993 to 1994?

c. What are the two main sources of assets for Center Corporation?

d. What other comparisons and procedures would you use to complete the analysis of the balance sheet started above?

Decision Problem 17–2

Compute turnover ratios for four years and number of days' sales in accounts receivable; evaluate effectiveness of company's credit policy
(L.O. 3)

The information below was obtained from the annual reports of Filtration Manufacturing Company.

	1991	1992	1993	1994
Accounts receivable, net	$ 270,000	$ 540,000	$ 720,000	$ 990,000
Net sales	2,400,000	3,300,000	3,750,000	4,800,000

Required

a. If cash sales account for 30% of all sales and credit terms are always 1/10. n/60. determine all turnover ratios possible and the number of days' sales in accounts receivable at all possible dates. (The number of days' sales in accounts receivable should be based on average accounts receivable and net credit sales.)

b. How effective is the company's credit policy?

Decision Problem 17–3

Analyze investment alternatives
(L.O. 2, 3)

Michael Herndon is interested in investing in one of three companies (X. Y. or Z) by buying its common stock. The companies' shares are selling at about the same price. The long-term capital structures of the companies are as follows:

	Company X	Company Y	Company Z
Bonds with a 10% interest rate.	$ –0–	$ –0–	$ 800,000
Preferred stock with an 8% dividend rate	–0–	800,000	–0–
Common stock, $20 par	1,600,000	800,000	800,000
Retained earnings	128,000	128,000	128,000
Total long-term equity	$1,728,000	$1,728,000	$1,728,000
Number of common shares outstanding	80,000	40,000	40,000

Mr. Herndon has consulted two investment advisers. One adviser believes that each of the companies will earn $128,000 per year before interest and taxes. The other adviser believes that each company will earn about $400,000 per year before interest and taxes.

Required   *a.*   Compute each of the following, assuming first the estimate made by the first adviser is used and then the one made by the second adviser is used:
1.   Income available for common stockholders, assuming a 40% tax rate.
2.   EPS of common stock.
3.   Rate of return on total stockholders' equity.

b.   Which stock should Mr. Herndon select if he believes the first adviser?

c.   Are the stockholders as a group (common and preferred) better off with or without the use of long-term debt in the above companies?

Decision Problem 17–4

Analyze management's objectives and performance from the viewpoints of a creditor and an investor (real world problem) (L.O. 2, 3)

The following selected financial data excerpted from the 1989 annual report of Maytag Corporation represents the summary information that management presented for interested parties to review.

MAYTAG CORPORATION
Selected Financial Data
Thousands of Dollars Except Per Share Data

	1989*	1988	1987	1986	1985
Net sales.	$3,088,753	$1,885,641	$1,822,106	$1,632,924	$1,571,032
Cost of sales	2,312,645	1,413,627	1,318,122	1,183,377	1,141,119
Income taxes	75,500	79,700	105,300	97,500	99,300
Income from continuing operations	131,472	135,522	147,678	114,739	119,318
Percent of income from continuing operations to net sales	4.3%	7.2%	8.1%	7.0%	7.6%
Income from continuing operations per share	$ 1.27	$ 1.77	$ 1.84	$ 1.32	$ 1.38
Dividends paid per share.	0.950	0.950	0.950	0.850	0.825
Average shares outstanding (in thousands).	103,694	76,563	80,151	86,619	86,502
Working capital	$ 650,905	$ 317,145	$ 286,124	$ 330,116	$ 393,967
Depreciation of property, plant, and equipment	68,077	34,454	35,277	32,659	33,765
Additions to property, plant, and equipment	127,838	101,756	42,564	45,619	41,066
Total assets	2,436,319	1,330,069	854,925	882,576	893,608
Long-term debt	876,836	518,165	140,765	46,189	98,570
Total debt to capitalization	50.6%	51.5%	28.1%	11.0%	16.9%
Shareowners' equity per share	$ 8.89	$ 6.55	$ 5.43	$ 6.53	$ 6.48

* These amounts reflect the acquisition of Hoover on January 26, 1989.

Required   *a.*   As a creditor, what do you believe management's objectives should be? What information above would assist a creditor in judging management's performance?

b.   As an investor, what do you believe management's objectives should be? What information above would assist an investor in judging management's performance?

c.   What other information might be considered useful?

ANSWERS TO SELF-TEST

True-False

1. *True.* Financial statement analysis consists of applying analytical tools and techniques to financial statements and other relevant data to obtain useful information.

2. *False.* Horizontal analysis provides useful information about the changes in a company's performance over several periods by analyzing comparative financial statements of the same company for two or more successive periods.

3. *False.* Common-size statements show only percentage figures, such as percentages of total assets and percentages of net sales.

4. *True.* Liquidity ratios such as the current ratio and acid-test ratio indicate a company's short-term debt-paying ability.

5. *True.* The accrual net income shown on the income statement is not cash basis income and does not indicate cash flows.

6. *True.* Analysts must use comparable data when making comparisons of items for different periods or different companies.

Multiple-Choice

1. *b.* Current assets:

    $68,000 + $32,000 + $92,000

    + $122,000 + $6,000 = $320,000

    Current liabilities:

    $128,000 + $32,000 = $160,000

    Current ratio:

    $320,000/$160,000 = 2 : 1

2. *c.* Quick assets:

    $68,000 + $32,000 + $92,000 = $192,000

    Current liabilities:

    $128,000 + $32,000 = $160,000

    Acid-test ratio:

    $192,000/$160,000 = 1.2 : 1

3. *a.* Net sales:

    $2,310,000

Average accounts receivable:

    ($360,000 + $480,000)/2 = $420,000

Accounts receivable turnover:

    $2,310,000/$420,000 = 5.5

4. *c.* Cost of goods sold:

    $1,680,000.

Average inventory:

    ($450,000 + $510,000)/2 = $480,000

Inventory turnover:

    $1,680,000/$480,000 = 3.5

5. *b.*

Income before interest and taxes	$360,000
Interest on bonds	96,000

Times interest earned ratio:

    $360,000/$96,000 = 3.75 times

18

STATEMENT OF CASH FLOWS

After studying this chapter, you should be able to:

1. Explain the purposes and uses of the statement of cash flows.
2. Describe the content of the statement of cash flows and where certain items would appear on the statement.
3. Describe how to calculate cash flows from operating activities under both the direct and indirect methods.
4. Prepare a statement of cash flows under both the direct and indirect methods showing cash flows from operating activities, investing activities, and financing activities.
5. Describe the historical development from a statement of changes in financial position to a statement of cash flows.

In your study of the statement of income and retained earnings (as separate statements or combined) and the balance sheet, you may have realized that these financial statements do not answer all the questions raised by users of financial statements. Such questions include: How much cash was generated by the company's operations? How can the Cash account be overdrawn when my accountant said the business was profitable? Why is such a profitable company only able to pay such small dividends? How much was spent for new plant and equipment, and where did the company get the cash for the expenditures? How was the company able to pay a dividend when it incurred a net loss for the year?

Through 1987, a statement called the statement of changes in financial position answered these questions. In July 1988, the statement of cash flows replaced the statement of changes in financial position.

In this chapter, you will learn about the statement of cash flows. The statement of cash flows is another major required financial statement and shows important information that is not shown directly in the other financial statements.

PURPOSES OF THE STATEMENT OF CASH FLOWS

Objective 1

Explain the purposes and uses of the statement of cash flows

In November 1987, the Financial Accounting Standards Board issued *Statement of Financial Accounting Standards No. 95,* "Statement of Cash Flows."[1] The *Statement* became effective for annual financial statements for fiscal years ending after July 15, 1988. Thus, the statement of cash flows is now one of the major financial statements issued by a company.

The main purpose of the statement of cash flows is to report on the cash receipts and cash disbursements of an entity during an accounting period. Cash is broadly defined to include both cash and "cash equivalents," such as short-term investments in Treasury bills, commercial paper, and money market funds. A secondary purpose is to report on the entity's investing and financing activities for the period. As shown in Illustration 18.1, the statement of cash flows reports the effects on cash during a period of a company's operating, investing, and financing activities. The effects of investing and financing activities that do not affect cash are shown in a schedule separate from the statement of cash flows.

USES OF THE STATEMENT OF CASH FLOWS

The statement of cash flows summarizes the effects on cash of the operating, investing, and financing activities of a company during an accounting period; it reports on past management decisions on such matters as issuance of capital stock or sale of long-term bonds. This information is available only in bits and pieces from the other financial statements. Since cash flows are vital to a company's financial health, the statement of cash flows provides useful information to management, investors, creditors, and other interested parties.

Management Uses

Since the statement of cash flows presents the effects on cash of all significant operating, investing, and financing activities, by reviewing the statement, management can see the effects of its past major policy decisions in quantitative form. The statement may show a flow of cash from operating activities large enough to finance all projected capital needs internally rather than having to incur long-term

[1] FASB, *Statement of Financial Accounting Standards No. 95,* "Statement of Cash Flows" (Stamford, Conn., 1987). Copyright by the Financial Accounting Standards Board, High Ridge Park, Stamford, Connecticut 06905. U.S.A. Quoted (or excerpted) with permission. Copies of the complete document are available from the FASB.

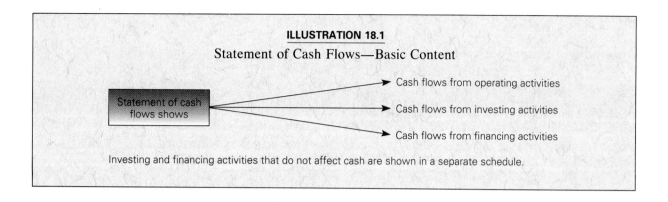

ILLUSTRATION 18.1

Statement of Cash Flows—Basic Content

Statement of cash flows shows

→ Cash flows from operating activities

→ Cash flows from investing activities

→ Cash flows from financing activities

Investing and financing activities that do not affect cash are shown in a separate schedule.

debt or issue additional stock. Or, if the company has been experiencing cash shortages, management can use the statement to determine why such shortages are occurring. Management may also use the statement to recommend to the board of directors a reduction in dividends to conserve cash.

Investor and Creditor Uses

The information in a statement of cash flows should help investors, creditors, and others to assess the following:

1. Enterprise's ability to generate positive future net cash flows.
2. Enterprise's ability to meet its obligations.
3. Enterprise's ability to pay dividends.
4. Enterprise's need for external financing.
5. Reasons for differences between net income and associated cash receipts and payments.
6. Effects on an enterprise's financial position of both its cash and noncash investing and financing transactions during the period (disclosed in a separate schedule).

INFORMATION IN THE STATEMENT OF CASH FLOWS

Objective 2

Describe the content of the statement of cash flows and where certain items would appear on the statement

The statement of cash flows classifies cash receipts and disbursements as operating, investing, and financing cash flows. Both inflows and outflows are included within each category. Illustration 18.2 shows how activities can be classified for purposes of preparing a statement of cash flows.

Operating activities **generally include the cash effects (inflows and outflows) of transactions and other events that enter into the determination of net income. Cash inflows** from operating activities affect items that appear on the income statement and include (1) cash receipts from sales of goods or services; (2) interest received from making loans; (3) dividends received from investments in equity securities; and (4) other cash receipts that do not arise from transactions defined as investing or financing activities, such as amounts received to settle lawsuits, proceeds of certain insurance settlements, and refunds from suppliers.

Cash outflows for operating activities affect items that appear on the income statement and include payments (1) to acquire inventory; (2) to other suppliers and employees for other goods or services; (3) to lenders and other creditors for interest; and (4) all other cash payments that do not arise from transactions defined as investing or financing activities, such as taxes and payments to settle lawsuits, cash contributions to charities, and cash refunds to customers.

Investing activities **generally include transactions involving the acquisition or disposal of noncurrent assets.** Thus, **cash inflows** from investing activities include

---

ILLUSTRATION 18.2

Rules for Classifying Activities in the Statement of Cash Flows

Operating activities   Cash effects of transactions and other events that enter into the determination of net income

Cash inflows from:
   Sales of goods or services
   Interest
   Dividends
   Other sources not related to investing or
      financing activities (e.g., insurance
      settlements)

Cash outflows for:
   Merchandise inventory
   Salaries and wages
   Interest
   Other expenses
   Other items not related to investing or
      financing activities (e.g., contributions to
      charities)

Investing activities   Transactions involving the acquisition or disposal of noncurrent assets

Cash inflows from:
   Sale of property, plant, and equipment
   Sale of marketable securities
   Collection of loans

Cash outflows for:
   Purchase of property, plant, and equipment
   Purchase of marketable securities
   Making of loans

Financing activities   Transactions with creditors and owners

Cash inflows from:
   Issuing capital stock
   Issuing debt (bonds, mortgages, notes, and
      other short- or long-term borrowing of
      cash)

Cash outflows for:
   Purchase of treasury stock
   Payment of debt
   Cash dividends

---

cash received from the sale of property, plant, and equipment; cash received from the sale of marketable securities; and cash received from the collection of loans made to others. **Cash outflows** for investing activities include cash paid to purchase property, plant, and equipment; cash paid to purchase marketable securities; and cash paid to make loans to others.

Financing activities **generally include the cash effects (inflows and outflows) of transactions and other events involving creditors and owners. Cash inflows** from financing activities include cash received from issuing capital stock and bonds, mortgages, and notes, and from other short- or long-term borrowing. **Cash outflows** for financing activities include payments of cash dividends or other distributions to owners (including cash paid to purchase treasury stock) and repayments of amounts borrowed. Payment of interest is not included because interest expense appears on the income statement and is therefore included in operating activities. Paying cash to settle accounts payable, wages payable, and income taxes payable are not financing activities. These payments are operating activities.

CASH FLOWS FROM OPERATING ACTIVITIES

Objective 3

Describe how to calculate cash flows from operating activities under both the direct and indirect methods

Cash flows from operating activities show the net amount of cash received or disbursed during a given period for items that normally appear on the income statement. These cash flows can be calculated using the direct or indirect method. The direct method deducts from cash sales only those operating expenses that **consumed cash.** Under this method, each item on the income statement is *directly* converted to a cash basis. Alternatively, the indirect (addback) method starts with accrual basis net income and *indirectly* adjusts net income for items that affected reported net income but **did not involve cash.**

The FASB **encourages** use of the direct method but **permits** use of the indirect method. The indirect method is used more frequently, as shown in the table below. Whenever accountants have been given a choice between the indirect and direct methods in similar situations, the indirect method has been used almost exclusively. We will discuss and illustrate both methods.

Method of Reporting Cash Flows from Operating Activities

	Number of Companies	
	1989	**1988**
Indirect method	583	526
Direct method	17	16
Total	600	542

Source: American Institute of Certified Public Accountants, *Accounting Trends & Techniques* (New York: AICPA, 1990), p. 350.

Under the direct method, each item on the income statement must be converted to a cash basis. Thus, the name *direct method* is used. For instance, assume that sales are stated at $100,000 on an accrual basis. If accounts receivable increased by $5,000, cash collections from customers would be $95,000, calculated at $100,000 − $5,000. All remaining items on the income statement are also converted to a cash basis. This process will be illustrated later.

Under the indirect method, net income is adjusted (rather than adjusting individual items in the income statement) for (1) changes in current assets (other than cash) and current liabilities, and (2) items that were included in net income but did not affect cash. Thus, the name *indirect method* is used.

The most common example of an operating expense that does not affect cash is depreciation expense. The journal entry to record depreciation debits an expense account and credits an accumulated depreciation account. This transaction has no effect on cash and therefore should not be included when measuring cash from operations. Because depreciation is deducted in arriving at net income, net income understates cash from operations. Under the indirect method, since net income is used as a starting point in measuring cash flows from operating activities, depreciation expense must be added back to net income.

Consider the following example. Company A had net income for the year of $20,000 after deducting depreciation of $10,000, yielding $30,000 of positive cash flows. Thus, Company A had $30,000 positive cash flows from operating activities. Company B had a net loss for the year of $4,000 after deducting $10,000 of depreciation. Although Company B experienced a loss, the company had $6,000 of positive cash flows from operating activities, as shown below:

	Company A	Company B
Net income (loss).	$20,000	$(4,000)
Add depreciation expense (which did not require use of cash).	10,000	10,000
Positive cash flows from operating activities	$30,000	$ 6,000

836 Part III Analysis of Financial Statements and Cash Flows

Company B's loss would have had to exceed $10,000 for the company to have negative cash flows from operating activities.

Companies have other expenses and losses that are added back to net income because they do not actually use the company's cash; these addbacks are often called noncash charges or expenses. Besides depreciation, the items added back include amounts of depletion that were expensed, amortization of intangible assets such as patents and goodwill, amortization of discount on bonds payable, and losses from disposals of noncurrent assets.

To illustrate the addback of the losses from disposal of noncurrent assets, assume that Quick Company sold a piece of equipment for $6,000. The equipment had cost $10,000 and had accumulated depreciation of $3,000. The journal entry to record the sale was:

Cash	6,000	
Accumulated Depreciation	3,000	
Loss on Sale of Equipment	1,000	
Equipment		10,000
To record disposal of equipment at a loss.		

Quick would show the $6,000 inflow from the sale of the equipment as a cash inflow from investing activities on its statement of cash flows. Although Quick deducted the loss of $1,000 in calculating net income, the total $6,000 effect on cash (which reflects the $1,000 loss) has already been recognized as resulting from an investing activity. Thus, Quick must add the loss back to net income in converting net income to cash flows from operating activities to avoid double-counting the loss.

Certain revenues and gains included in arriving at net income do not provide cash; these items are called noncash credits or revenues. These revenues and gains must be deducted from net income to compute cash flows from operating activities. Such items include gains from disposals of noncurrent assets, income from investments carried under the equity method, and amortization of premium on bonds payable.

To illustrate why the gain on the disposal of a noncurrent asset must be deducted from net income, assume that Quick sold the equipment mentioned above for $9,000. The journal entry to record the sale is:

Cash	9,000	
Accumulated Depreciation	3,000	
Equipment		10,000
Gain on Sale of Equipment		2,000
To record disposal of equipment at a gain.		

Quick shows the $9,000 inflow from the sale of equipment on its statement of cash flows as a cash inflow from investing activities. Thus, the total $9,000 effect on cash (including the $2,000 gain) has already been recognized as resulting from an investing activity. Since the $2,000 gain is also included in calculating net income, Quick must deduct the gain in converting net income to cash flows from operating activities to avoid double-counting the gain.

STEPS IN PREPARING STATEMENT OF CASH FLOWS

Objective 4

Prepare a statement of cash flows under both the direct and indirect methods showing cash flows from operating activities, investing activities, and financing activities

This section discusses the procedures accountants follow to prepare a statement of cash flows. These procedures are illustrated using the financial statements and additional data for Welby Company given in Illustration 18.3.

After determining the change in cash, the first step in preparing the statement of cash flows is to calculate the cash flows from operating activities, using either the direct or indirect method. The second step is to analyze all of the noncurrent accounts for changes resulting from investing and financing activities. The third step is to arrange the information gathered in steps 1 and 2 into the proper format for the statement of cash flows.

Step 1: Determining Cash Flows from Operating Activities—Direct Method

Under the direct method, the income statement must be converted from the accrual basis to the cash basis. Changes in balance sheet accounts that are related to items on the income statement must be considered. The accounts involved are all current assets or current liabilities. The following schedule shows which balance sheet accounts are related to the items on the income statement in the Welby example:

Income Statement Items	Related Balance Sheet Accounts	Cash Flows from Operating Activities
Sales	Accounts Receivable	Cash received from customers
Cost of goods sold	Accounts Payable and Merchandise Inventory	Cash paid for merchandise
Operating expenses and taxes	Accrued Liabilities and Prepaid Expenses	Cash paid for operating expenses

For other income statement items, the relationship is often obvious. For instance, salaries payable relates to salaries expense, federal income tax payable relates to federal income tax expense, prepaid rent relates to rent expense, and so on.

The balance sheet accounts affect the income statement items as follows:

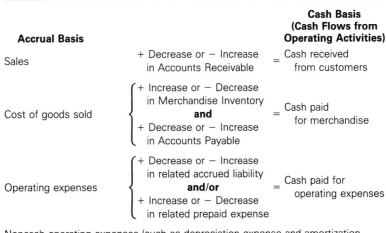

Noncash operating expenses (such as depreciation expense and amortization expense), revenues, gains, and losses are reduced to zero in the cash basis income statement.

ILLUSTRATION 18.3

Financial Statements and Other Data

WELBY COMPANY
Comparative Balance Sheets
December 31, 1994, and 1993

	1994	1993	Increase/ (Decrease)
Assets			
Cash	$ 21,000	$ 10,000	$11,000
Accounts receivable, net.	30,000	20,000	10,000
Merchandise inventory	26,000	30,000	(4,000)
Plant assets	70,000	50,000	20,000
Accumulated depreciation	(10,000)	(5,000)	(5,000)
Total assets	$137,000	$105,000	$32,000
Liabilities and Stockholders' Equity			
Accounts payable.	$ 9,000	$ 15,000	$ (6,000)
Accrued liabilities payable	2,000	–0–	2,000
Common stock ($10 par value)	90,000	60,000	30,000
Retained earnings.	36,000	30,000	6,000
Total liabilities and stockholders' equity	$137,000	$105,000	$32,000

WELBY COMPANY
Income Statement
For the Year Ended December 31, 1994

Sales		$140,000
Cost of goods sold		100,000
Gross margin		$ 40,000
Operating expenses (other than depreciation)	$25,000	
Depreciation expense	5,000	30,000
Net income.		$ 10,000

Additional data
1. Plant assets purchased for cash during 1994 amounted to $20,000.
2. Common stock with a par value of $30,000 was issued at par for cash.
3. Cash dividends declared and paid in 1994 totaled $4,000.

As a general rule, an increase in a current asset (other than cash) decreases cash inflow or increases cash outflow. Thus, when accounts receivable increases, sales revenue on a cash basis decreases (some customers who bought merchandise have not yet paid for it). When inventory increases, cost of goods sold on a cash basis increases (increasing cash outflow). When a prepaid expense increases, the related operating expense on a cash basis increases. (For example, a company not only paid for insurance expense but also paid cash to increase prepaid insurance.) The effect on cash flows is just the opposite for decreases in these other current assets.

An increase in a current liability increases cash inflow or decreases cash outflow. Thus, when accounts payable increases, cost of goods sold on a cash basis decreases (instead of paying cash, the purchase was made on credit). When an accrued liability (such as salaries payable) increases, the related operating expense (salaries expense) on a cash basis decreases. (For example, the company incurred more salaries than it paid.) Decreases in current liabilities have just the opposite effects on cash flows.

ILLUSTRATION 18.4

Working Paper to Convert Income Statement from Accrual Basis to
Cash Basis

WELBY COMPANY
Income Statement
For the Year Ended December 31, 1994

	Accrual Basis		Add	Deduct	Cash Basis (Cash Flows from Operating Activities)
Sales		$140,000		$10,000[1]	$130,000
Cost of goods sold	$100,000		$6,000[2]	4,000[3]	$102,000
Operating expenses . . .	25,000			2,000[4]	23,000
Depreciation expense . . .	5,000			5,000	–0–
		130,000			125,000
Net income		$ 10,000			$ 5,000

[1] Increase in Accounts Receivable.
[2] Decrease in Accounts Payable.
[3] Decrease in Merchandise Inventory.
[4] Increase in Accrued Liabilities Payable.

In the Welby example, there are no prepaid expenses. The current assets and current liabilities affecting the income statement items changed as follows:

	Increase	Decrease
Accounts receivable.	$10,000	
Merchandise inventory		$4,000
Accounts payable.		6,000
Accrued liabilities payable	2,000	

Thus, the income statement for Welby can be converted to a cash basis as shown in Illustration 18.4.

Alternate Step 1: Determining Cash Flows from Operating Activities—Indirect Method

Under the indirect method, certain adjustments are necessary to convert net income to cash flows from operating activities. First, changes that occurred in current accounts other than cash must be analyzed for their effects on cash. Then, noncash items such as depreciation that affected net income but not cash must be taken into account. Welby had only one such item—depreciation expense of $5,000. Applying these adjustments to Welby's financial statements and other data in Illustration 18.3 yields the following schedule:

Cash flows from operating activities:		
Net income.	$ 10,000	
Adjustments to reconcile net income to net cash provided by operating activities:		
Increase in accounts receivable.	(10,000)	
Decrease in merchandise inventory	4,000	
Decrease in accounts payable	(6,000)	
Increase in accrued liabilities payable	2,000	
Depreciation expense	5,000	
Net cash provided by operating activities		$5,000

Notice that both the direct and indirect methods result in $5,000 net cash provided by operating activities.

The following table can be used to make the adjustments to net income for the changes in current assets and current liabilities:

For changes in these current assets and current liabilities:	Make these adjustments to convert accrual basis net income to cash basis net income:	
	Add	**Deduct**
Accounts receivable. . . .	Decrease	Increase
Merchandise inventory . .	Decrease	Increase
Prepaid expenses	Decrease	Increase
Accounts payable	Increase	Decrease
Accrued liabilities payable .	Increase	Decrease

Notice in the above summary that all changes in current asset accounts are handled in a similar manner. Also, all changes in current liability accounts are handled in a similar manner, but in the opposite manner from that of the current asset changes. A more condensed table to use in making these adjustments is:

For Changes in—	Add the Changes to Net Income	Deduct the Changes from Net Income
Current assets	Decreases	Increases
Current liabilities	Increases	Decreases

In applying the rules given in the above table, a decrease in a current asset is added to net income; an increase in a current asset is deducted from net income. For current liabilities, increases are added to net income, and decreases are deducted from net income.

The complete adjustment or conversion procedure used in the comprehensive example beginning on page 841 is summarized below:

Accrual basis net income
     + or − Changes in noncash current asset and current liability accounts
     + Expenses and losses not affecting cash
     − Revenues and gains not affecting cash
     = Cash flows from operating activities

Step 2: Analyzing the Noncurrent Accounts

Now that the changes in current accounts have been analyzed for their effect on cash, we will examine the noncurrent accounts. Remember that a change in a noncurrent account usually comes about because cash is received or disbursed.

In the Welby example, we must analyze four noncurrent accounts: Retained Earnings, Plant Assets, Accumulated Depreciation, and Common Stock.

1. The analysis of the noncurrent accounts can begin with any of the noncurrent accounts, but we will begin by reviewing the Retained Earnings account. Retained Earnings is the account to which net income or loss for the period was closed. The $6,000 increase in this account consists of $10,000 of net income less $4,000 of dividends paid. The net income amount can be found in the income statement. Both net income and dividends must be entered on the statement of cash flows in Illustration 18.5, Part B. The $10,000 net income is used as the starting figure in determin-

ing cash flows from operating activities. Thus, net income of $10,000 is entered on the statement in the cash flows from operating activities section.

2. The Plant Assets account increased by $20,000 during the year. The additional data indicate that plant assets of $20,000 were purchased during the period. A purchase of plant assets is shown as a deduction in the cash flows from investing activities section.

3. The $5,000 increase in the Accumulated Depreciation account equals the amount of depreciation expense shown in the income statement for the period. As shown earlier, because depreciation does not affect cash, under the addback method it must be added back to net income on the statement of cash flows to convert accrual net income to a cash basis.

4. The $30,000 increase in common stock resulted from the issuance of stock at par value, as disclosed in the additional data (item 2) given in Illustration 18.3. An issuance of stock is shown in the statement of cash flows as a positive amount in the cash flows from financing activities section.

Step 3: Arranging Information in the Statement of Cash Flows

After we have analyzed the noncurrent accounts, we can prepare the statement of cash flows from the information generated. Part A of Illustration 18.5 presents the statement of cash flows for Welby using the direct method. Part B shows the statement of cash flows for Welby using the indirect method.

The statement of cash flows has three major sections: cash flows from operating activities, cash flows from investing activities, and cash flows from financing activities. The format in the operating activities section differs for the direct and indirect methods. The direct method adjusts each item in the income statement to a cash basis. The indirect method makes these same adjustments but to net income rather than to each item in the income statement. Both methods eliminate the effects of noncash items, such as depreciation, and also eliminate gains and losses on sales of plant assets.

The only item shown in the cash flows from investing activities section is the cash outflow of $20,000 for the purchase of plant assets. In a more complex situation, other items could be included in this category.

Two items are shown under the cash flows from financing activities section. The issuance of common stock resulted in a cash inflow of $30,000. The payment of dividends resulted in a cash outflow of $4,000.

The last line of the statement is the $11,000 increase in cash for the year. Other examples could have a decrease in cash for the year.

COMPREHENSIVE ILLUSTRATION

This section presents a more complete example of the procedures followed to prepare a statement of cash flows. A working paper (shown later in Illustration 18.8) is an aid in preparing the statement for both the direct and indirect methods. For the direct method, the information regarding cash flows from operations is used to show the reconciliation of that figure with net income. An additional working paper is used to convert the income statement to a cash basis for use in the statement of cash flows.

The basic data for the example are found in Illustrations 18.6 and 18.7, which present the United States Corporation's statement of income and retained earnings (combined) for the year ended December 31, 1994, and comparative balance sheets for the years 1994 and 1993.

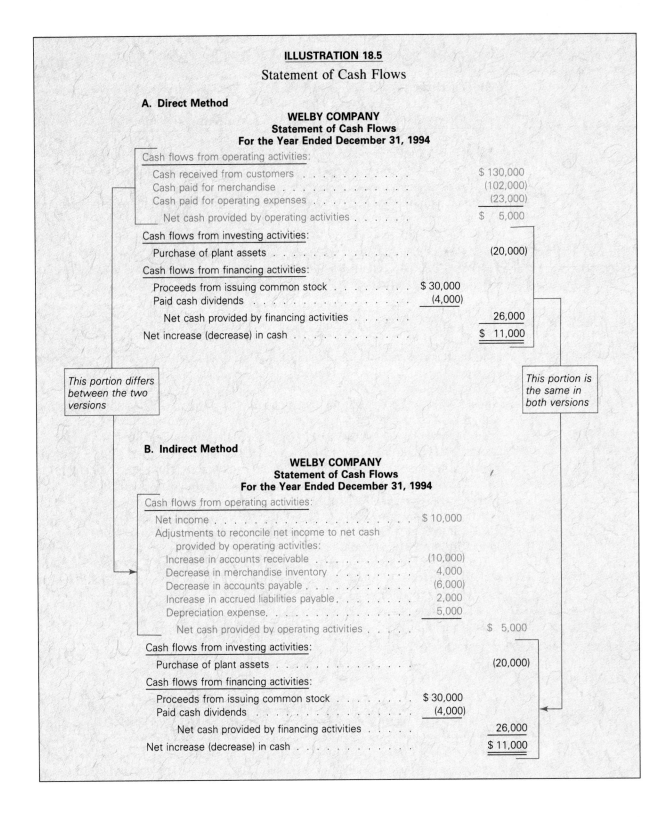

ILLUSTRATION 18.5

Statement of Cash Flows

A. Direct Method

WELBY COMPANY
Statement of Cash Flows
For the Year Ended December 31, 1994

Cash flows from operating activities:

Cash received from customers		$ 130,000
Cash paid for merchandise		(102,000)
Cash paid for operating expenses		(23,000)
Net cash provided by operating activities		$ 5,000

Cash flows from investing activities:

Purchase of plant assets		(20,000)

Cash flows from financing activities:

Proceeds from issuing common stock	$ 30,000	
Paid cash dividends	(4,000)	
Net cash provided by financing activities		26,000
Net increase (decrease) in cash		$ 11,000

This portion differs between the two versions

This portion is the same in both versions

B. Indirect Method

WELBY COMPANY
Statement of Cash Flows
For the Year Ended December 31, 1994

Cash flows from operating activities:

Net income		$ 10,000
Adjustments to reconcile net income to net cash provided by operating activities:		
Increase in accounts receivable	(10,000)	
Decrease in merchandise inventory	4,000	
Decrease in accounts payable	(6,000)	
Increase in accrued liabilities payable	2,000	
Depreciation expense	5,000	
Net cash provided by operating activities		$ 5,000

Cash flows from investing activities:

Purchase of plant assets		(20,000)

Cash flows from financing activities:

Proceeds from issuing common stock	$ 30,000	
Paid cash dividends	(4,000)	
Net cash provided by financing activities		26,000
Net increase (decrease) in cash		$ 11,000

Assume the following information about the noncurrent accounts of the United States Corporation is available:

1. No investments were made during the year. Investments that cost $8,000 were sold for $9,700.

ILLUSTRATION 18.6

Statement of Income and Retained Earnings

UNITED STATES CORPORATION
Statement of Income and Retained Earnings
For the Year Ended December 31, 1994

Net sales		$1,464,200
Cost of goods sold		871,150
Gross margin		$ 593,050
Operating expenses:		
Salaries expense	$215,000	
Depreciation expense ($3,250, buildings; $31,050, equipment)	34,300	
Supplies expense	7,320	
Advertising expense	90,000	
Taxes expense, payroll, and property	26,000	
General and administrative expenses	123,780	
Total operating expenses		496,400
Income from operations		$ 96,650
Other revenues:		
Interest revenue	$ 1,950	
Gain on sale of long-term investments	1,700	3,650
		$ 100,300
Other expenses:		
Interest expense	$ 3,800	
Loss on sale of equipment	900	4,700
Income before federal income taxes		$ 95,600
Deduct: Federal income taxes		45,250
Net income		$ 50,350
Retained earnings, January 1, 1994		84,100
Subtotal		$ 134,450
Deduct: Dividends declared and paid		18,000
Retained earnings, December 31, 1994		$ 116,450

2. Land and buildings with a cost of $65,000 ($45,000 for the buildings and $20,000 for the land) were acquired, subject to a mortgage note of $35,000.

3. During the year, the corporation sold equipment for $2,600 that had an original cost of $20,000 and accumulated depreciation of $16,500.

4. The common stock was issued for cash.

The working paper in Illustration 18.8 for United States Corporation is used to analyze the transactions and prepare the statement of cash flows. The following discussion describes the items and traces their effects in the entries made on the working paper.

The steps in preparing the working paper are described below:

1. Enter the beginning account balances of all balance sheet accounts in the first column and the ending account balances in the fourth column. Notice that the debit items are listed first, followed by the credit items.

2. Total the debits and credits in the first and fourth columns to make sure that debits equal credits in each column.

ILLUSTRATION 18.7

Comparative Balance Sheets

UNITED STATES CORPORATION
Comparative Balance Sheets
December 31, 1994, and 1993

	1994	1993	Increase/ (Decrease)
Assets			
Current assets:			
Cash	$ 46,300	$ 40,900	$ 5,400
Accounts receivable, net	112,160	101,000	11,160
Merchandise inventory	130,600	115,300	15,300
Prepaid advertising	3,100	4,700	(1,600)
Total current assets	$292,160	$261,900	$30,260
Investments	$ 17,000	$ 25,000	$ (8,000)
Property, plant, and equipment:			
Land	$100,000	$ 80,000	$20,000
Buildings	175,000	130,000	45,000
Accumulated depreciation—buildings	(29,750)	(26,500)	(3,250)
Equipment	198,000	175,000	23,000
Accumulated depreciation—equipment	(57,650)	(43,100)	(14,550)
Total property, plant, and equipment	$385,600	$315,400	$70,200
Total assets	$694,760	$602,300	$92,460
Liabilities and Stockholders' Equity			
Current liabilities:			
Accounts payable	$ 91,420	$ 86,870	$ 4,550
Salaries payable	9,890	12,230	(2,340)
Federal income taxes payable	12,000	14,100	(2,100)
Total current liabilities	$113,310	$113,200	$ 110
Long-term liabilities:			
Mortgage note payable, 10% (on land and buildings)	$ 35,000	$ –0–	$35,000
Bonds payable, 8%, due 1997	40,000	40,000	–0–
Total long-term liabilities	$ 75,000	$ 40,000	$35,000
Total liabilities	$188,310	$153,200	$35,110
Stockholders' equity:			
Common stock, stated value, $50 per share	$390,000	$365,000	$25,000
Retained earnings	116,450	84,100	32,350
Total stockholders' equity	$506,450	$449,100	$57,350
Total liabilities and stockholders' equity	$694,760	$602,300	$92,460

3. Write "Cash Flows from Operating Activities" immediately below the total of the credit items. Skip sufficient lines for recording adjustments to convert accrual net income to cash flows from operating activities. Then write "Cash Flows from Investing Activities" and allow enough space for those items. Finally, write "Cash Flows from Financing Activities" and allow enough space for those items.

4. Enter entries for analyzing transactions in the second and third columns. The entries serve two functions: (a) they explain the change in each ac-

ILLUSTRATION 18.8

Working Paper for Statement of Cash Flows

UNITED STATES CORPORATION
Working Paper for Statement of Cash Flows
For the Year Ended December 31, 1994

	Account Balances 12/31/93	Analysis of Transactions for 1994		Account Balances 12/31/94
		Debit	Credit	
Debits				
Cash	40,900	(0) 5,400		46,300
Accounts Receivable	101,000	(2) 11,160		112,160
Merchandise Inventory	115,300	(3) 15,300		130,600
Prepaid Advertising	4,700		(4) 1,600	3,100
Investments	25,000		(8) 8,000	17,000
Land	80,000	(9) 20,000		100,000
Buildings	130,000	(9) 45,000		175,000
Equipment	175,000	(11) 43,000	(10) 20,000	198,000
Totals	671,900			782,160
Credits				
Accumulated Depreciation—Buildings	26,500		(13) 3,250	29,750
Accumulated Depreciation—Equipment	43,100	(10) 16,500	(13) 31,050	57,650
Accounts Payable	86,870		(5) 4,550	91,420
Salaries Payable	12,230	(6) 2,340		9,890
Federal Income Taxes Payable	14,100	(7) 2,100		12,000
Mortgage Note Payable	–0–		(9) 35,000	35,000
Bonds Payable	40,000			40,000
Common Stock	365,000		(12) 25,000	390,000
Retained Earnings	84,100	(14) 18,000	(1) 50,350	116,450
Totals	671,900	178,800	178,800	782,160
Cash Flows from Operating Activities:				
Net Income		(1) 50,350		
Increase in Accounts Receivable			(2) 11,160	
Increase in Merchandise Inventory			(3) 15,300	
Decrease in Prepaid Advertising		(4) 1,600		
Increase in Accounts Payable		(5) 4,550		
Decrease in Salaries Payable			(6) 2,340	
Decrease in Federal Income Taxes Payable			(7) 2,100	
Gain on Sale of Investments			(8) 1,700	
Loss on Sale of Equipment		(10) 900		
Depreciation Expense—Buildings		(13) 3,250		
Depreciation Expense—Equipment		(13) 31,050		
Cash Flows from Investing Activities:				
Proceeds from Sale of Investments		(8) 9,700		
Purchase of Land and Buildings (cash portion)			(9) 30,000	
Proceeds from Sale of Equipment		(10) 2,600		
Purchase of Equipment			(11) 43,000	
Cash Flows from Financing Activities:				
Proceeds from Issuing Common Stock		(12) 25,000		
Payment of Cash Dividends			(14) 18,000	
Increase in Cash for Year			(0) 5,400	
Noncash Investing and Financing Activities:				
Mortgage Note Issued to Acquire Land and Buildings		(9) 35,000	(9) 35,000	
Totals		164,000	164,000	

count and *(b)* they classify the changes into operating, investing, and financing activities. These entries will be discussed individually in the next section.

5. Total the debits and credits in the second and third columns; they should be equal. You will have one pair of totals for the balance sheet items and another pair for the bottom portion of the working paper. The bottom portion of the working paper is used to prepare the statement of cash flows.

Completing the Working Paper

To complete the working paper in Illustration 18.8, we must analyze the change in each noncash balance sheet account. Remember that the focus of this working paper is on cash and that every change in cash is accompanied by a change in a noncash balance sheet account. After entries have been properly made to analyze all changes in noncash balance sheet accounts, the working paper will show all activities affecting cash flows. The explanations below are keyed to numbers of the entries on the working paper.

Entry (0). The beginning and ending cash balances are compared to determine the change in the Cash account during the year, which is a $5,400 increase. An entry is made on the working paper debiting Cash for $5,400 and crediting Increase in Cash for Year near the bottom of the schedule. This entry is labeled *(0)* because it does not explain the change in cash but is the "target" of the analysis. The entry sets out the change in cash that the statement seeks to explain. No further attention need be paid to cash in completing the working paper.

Attention is now directed toward changes in other balance sheet accounts. These accounts can be dealt with in any order, but first we will record the net income for the period and then analyze the current assets (other than cash) and the current liabilities. Then, we will analyze the changes in the noncurrent accounts.

Entry (1). The combined statement of income and retained earnings reveals that net income for 1994 was $50,350. Entry *(1)* records the $50,350 as the starting point in measuring cash flows from operating activities and credits Retained Earnings as a partial explanation of the change in that account.

The next task is to analyze changes in current accounts other than Cash. The current accounts of United States Corporation are closely related to operations, and their changes are included in converting net income to cash flows from operating activities. The changes in the current accounts are analyzed in the manner previously discussed (pages 839–40).

Entry (2). The $11,160 increase in accounts receivable must be deducted from net income when converting it to cash flows from operating activities. If accounts receivable increased, sales to customers exceeded cash received from customers. To convert net income to a cash basis, the $11,160 must be deducted.

The working paper technique makes the recording of these effects almost mechanical. Accounts Receivable must be debited for $11,160 to increase it from $101,000 to $112,160. If Accounts Receivable is debited, a credit must be entered for an item that can be entitled "Increase in Accounts Receivable." The increase is deducted from net income in converting it to cash flows from operating activities.

Entry (3) is virtually a duplicate of entry *(2)*, except it involves merchandise inventory rather than receivables.

Entry (4) is similar to the above two entries, except it has the opposite effect because prepaid advertising decreased.

Entry (5) records the effect of an increase in accounts payable on net income in converting it to cash flows from operating activities.

Entries (6) and (7) record the effects of decreases in two other current liability accounts (Salaries Payable and Federal Income Taxes Payable) in converting net income to cash flows from operating activities.

Next, we analyze the changes in the noncurrent balance sheet accounts.

Entry (8). Investments is the first noncurrent account. The additional information discloses that investments were sold at a gain. The transaction was recorded in the following manner:

Cash	9,700	
Investments		8,000
Gain on Sale of Investments		1,700

The $9,700 cash resulting from the sale of investments is reported in the "Cash Flows from Investing Activities" section (entry 8) in the lower part of Illustration 18.8. Entry (8) also removes the $1,700 gain on sale of investments from cash flows from operating activities because this amount is already included as part of the cash resulting from the sale of investments. If the $9,700 cash received from the sale is reported in the "Cash Flows from Investing Activities" section and the gain is not removed from cash flows from operating activities, the $1,700 gain will be counted twice. Note that the entry on the working paper is identical to the original journal entry for the sale, except for the $9,700 debit. Instead of debiting Cash, a properly described investing activity "Proceeds from Sale of Investments" is debited. The $8,000 credit accounts fully for the decrease in the Investments account balance; if this credit had not fully accounted for the change, there would have to be other transactions involving the Investments account to analyze and report.

Entry (9). The changes in the Land and Buildings accounts resulted from the following entry:

Land	20,000	
Buildings.	45,000	
Cash		30,000
Mortgage Note Payable		35,000

This transaction requires two entries on the working paper. First, Land and Buildings are debited for $20,000 and $45,000, respectively, and an item described as "Purchase of Land and Buildings" is credited for $30,000 in the investing activity section for the cash portion. Second, an entry labeled "Mortgage Note Issued to Acquire Land and Buildings" is entered at the bottom of the work sheet in both the debit and credit columns for the $35,000 noncash portion of the transaction. This item is listed on the work sheet so you will not forget to include it in a separate schedule. This transaction is an example of a significant financing and investing activity that must be included in a separate schedule even though part of it did not affect cash.

Entry (10). The Equipment account shows a net increase of $23,000 resulting from two transactions: a $43,000 purchase (shown in entry *11* below) and a $20,000 retirement. The net change in the account must be analyzed to show both transactions.

Data relating to the $20,000 retirement were included in the additional information provided. The computation of the loss on sale can be summarized as follows using data provided in the additional information:

Cost of equipment sold (given)	$20,000[1]
Less: Accumulated depreciation (given)	16,500[2]
Book value of equipment sold	$ 3,500
Less: Cash received (given)	2,600[3]
Loss on sale (as shown in income statement)	$ 900[4]

[1] Shown as a credit to Equipment on the working paper.
[2] Shown as a debit to Accumulated Depreciation—Equipment on the working paper.
[3] Shown as proceeds from sale of equipment under "Cash Flows from Investing Activities."
[4] Shown as an addition to net income under "Cash Flows from Operating Activities."

The working paper shows cash resulting from the sale of equipment under the investing activities section and explains part of the changes in the Equipment and the Accumulated Depreciation—Equipment accounts. The loss is added back to net income because it is a noncash item that was deducted in arriving at net income. The loss has exactly the same effect as depreciation expense.

Entry (11). This entry debits the Equipment account and credits "Purchase of Equipment" in the investing activities section for the $43,000 cash spent to acquire new equipment. The $43,000 debit to Equipment along with the $20,000 credit to Equipment in entry (10) fully accounts for the $23,000 increase in the account balance as shown below.

Equipment

Beg. bal.	175,000		
(11)	43,000	(10)	20,000
End. bal.	198,000		

Entry (12). This entry shows the $25,000 cash received from sale of common stock as a "financing activity." The entry also explains the change in the Common Stock account. If stock had been sold for more than its stated value of $50 per share, the excess would be recorded in a separate Paid-In Capital in Excess of Stated Value account. However, the total amount of cash received from the issuance of common stock would have been reported as a single figure on the statement of cash flows. Only this total amount received is significant to creditors and other users of the financial statements trying to judge the solvency of the company.

Entry (13). This entry adds $3,250 building depreciation and $31,050 equipment depreciation back to net income and credits the respective accumulated depreciation accounts. The depreciation expense can be found (1) on the statement of income and retained earnings, or (2) by solving for the credit needed to balance the accumulated depreciation accounts on the balance sheet. The $31,050 credit to the accumulated depreciation account for equipment less the $16,500 debit to this account in entry (10) explains fully the increase in this account from $43,100 to $57,650 as shown below.

Accumulated Depreciation—Equipment

		Beg. bal.	43,100
(10)	16,500	(13)	31,050
		End. bal.	57,650

Entry *(14)*. This entry debits Retained Earnings and credits Payment of Cash Dividends for the $18,000 dividends declared and paid. The entry also completes the explanation of the change in Retained Earnings as shown below. Notice that on the statement of cash flows, the dividends must be **paid** to be included as a cash outflow from financing activities.

Retained Earnings

		Beg. bal.	84,100
(14)	18,000	*(1)*	50,350
		End. bal.	116,450

If Retained Earnings had changed for reasons other than net income or cash dividends, the causes of the changes must be determined to decide whether they should be reported in the statement of cash flows. **Transactions such as stock dividends and stock splits would not be reported on the statement of cash flows or in a separate schedule because they lack significance from an analytical viewpoint and do not affect cash.** However, an entry must be made on the working paper to explain the changes caused by a stock dividend or split, even if cash were not affected. All changes in all noncash accounts must be explained to show that a change affecting cash was not overlooked.

The analysis of the noncash accounts is now complete. To be sure that a change has not been overlooked, the debits and credits in the middle two columns opposite the 1993 balances are added to or subtracted from those balances, line by line. If the working paper has been properly prepared, the results will be the 1994 balances listed in the fourth column. For the balance sheet accounts, every line must foot (total) across. For example, the $43,000 debit is added to the beginning balance for Equipment, and the $20,000 credit is deducted to get an ending balance of $198,000.

Next, the debits and credits for the balance sheet account entries and for the statement of cash flows are added to make sure that they are equal in both sections. Note that entries made in the working paper are used only to derive cash flows into and out of the company. These entries are not entered in the company's accounting system because the transactions that caused the cash flows have already been recorded.

Preparing the Statement of Cash Flows

The data in the lower section of the working paper are now used to prepare the statement of cash flows under the indirect method shown in Illustration 18.9. Information about all material investing and financing activities of an enterprise that do not result in cash receipts or disbursements in the period are to be reported in a separate schedule, rather than in the statement of cash flows. The disclosure may be in narrative form. United States Corporation had one such transaction, the issuance of a mortgage note to acquire land and buildings. A separate schedule might appear as follows:

Schedule of noncash financing and investing activities:

Mortgage note issued to acquire land and buildings $35,000

ILLUSTRATION 18.9

Statement of Cash Flows—Indirect Method

UNITED STATES CORPORATION
Statement of Cash Flows
For the Year Ended December 31, 1994

Cash flows from operating activities:

Net income		$ 50,350
Adjustments to reconcile net income to net cash provided by operating activities:		
Increase in accounts receivable	(11,160)	
Increase in merchandise inventory	(15,300)	
Decrease in prepaid advertising	1,600	
Increase in accounts payable	4,550	
Decrease in salaries payable	(2,340)	
Decrease in federal income taxes payable	(2,100)	
Gain on sale of investment	(1,700)	
Loss on sale of equipment	900	
Depreciation expense—buildings	3,250	
Depreciation expense—equipment	31,050	
Net cash provided by operating activities		$ 59,100

Cash flows from investing activities:

Proceeds from sale of investments	$ 9,700	
Purchase of land and buildings (cash portion)	(30,000)	
Proceeds from sale of equipment	2,600	
Payment for purchase of equipment	(43,000)	
Net cash used in investing activities		(60,700)

Cash flows from financing activities:

Proceeds from issuing common stock	$ 25,000	
Paid cash dividends	(18,000)	
Net cash provided by financing activities		7,000
Net increase in cash		$ 5,400

If the direct method is used, the information relating to the indirect method of calculating cash flows from operating activities in the bottom part of the working paper (Illustration 18.8) and in the top part of Illustration 18.9 would appear in a separate supporting schedule rather than in the statement of cash flows. Also, an additional working paper is needed if the direct method is used. This working paper converts the items on the income statement to a cash basis, as shown in Illustration 18.10.

Notice that depreciation is eliminated when converting to a cash basis since it does not involve an outflow of cash in the current period. Also, the gain from sale of long-term investments and the loss on sale of equipment are eliminated since the proceeds of these transactions are reported in the cash flows from investing activities section in the statement of cash flows.

Illustration 18.11 shows the statement of cash flows under the direct method. Notice that the only difference between the direct and indirect methods is in the cash flows from operating activities section.

ILLUSTRATION 18.10

Working Paper to Convert Income Statement from Accrual Basis to Cash Basis

UNITED STATES CORPORATION
Income Statement
For the Year Ended December 31, 1994

	Accrual Basis	Add	Deduct	Cash Basis (Cash Flows from Operating Activities)
Net sales.	$1,464,200		$11,160[1]	$1,453,040
Cost of goods sold	871,150	$15,300[2]	4,550[3]	881,900
Gross margin	$ 593,050			$ 571,140
Operating expenses:				
Salaries expense	$215,000	2,340[4]		$217,340
Depreciation expense	34,300		34,300	–0–
Supplies expense	7,320			7,320
Advertising expense.	90,000		1,600[5]	88,400
Taxes expense, payroll and property. . .	26,000			26,000
General administrative expenses	123,780			123,780
Total operating expenses	496,400			462,840
Income from operations	$ 96,650			$ 108,300
Other revenues:				
Interest revenue	$ 1,950			$ 1,950
Gain on sale of long-term investment . .	1,700		1,700	–0–
	3,650			1,950
	$ 100,300			$ 110,250
Other expenses:				
Interest expense	$ 3,800			$ 3,800
Loss on sale of equipment	900		900	–0–
	4,700			3,800
Income before federal income taxes . . .	$ 95,600			$ 106,450
Deduct: Federal income taxes	45,250	2,100[6]		47,350
Net income.	$ 50,350			$ 59,100

[1] Increase in Accounts Receivable.
[2] Increase in Merchandise Inventory.
[3] Increase in Accounts Payable.
[4] Decrease in Salaries Payable.
[5] Decrease in Prepaid Advertising.
[6] Decrease in Federal Income Taxes Payable.

WORKING CAPITAL OR CASH FLOWS

Objective 5

Describe the historical development from a statement of changes in financial position to a statement of cash flows

Through the middle of 1988, a statement of changes in financial position was required to report on funds flows. This statement showed the sources and uses of funds as the two main categories rather than categorizing according to operating activities, investing activities, and financing activities. *Funds* were generally defined as either working capital or cash. Working capital is equal to current assets minus current liabilities. The common practice before 1983 was to define *funds* as working capital.

Accountants prepared statements based on working capital for several reasons. Accurate information was needed about the flows of liquid assets (working capi-

ILLUSTRATION 18.11

Statement of Cash Flows—Direct Method

UNITED STATES CORPORATION
Statement of Cash Flows
For the Year Ended December 31, 1994

Cash flows from operating activities:

Cash received from customers	$1,453,040	
Cash paid for merchandise for resale	(881,900)	
Cash paid to employees	(217,340)	
Cash paid for supplies	(7,320)	
Cash paid for advertising	(88,400)	
Taxes paid, payroll and property	(26,000)	
General administrative expenses paid	(123,780)	
Interest received	1,950	
Interest paid	(3,800)	
Federal income taxes paid	(47,350)	
Net cash provided by operating activities		$ 59,100

Cash flows from investing activities:

Proceeds from sale of investments	$ 9,700	
Purchase of land and buildings (cash portion)	(30,000)	
Proceeds from sale of equipment	2,600	
Payment for purchase of equipment	(43,000)	
Net cash used in investing activities		(60,700)

Cash flows from financing activities:

Proceeds from issuing common stock	$ 25,000	
Payment of cash dividends	(18,000)	
Net cash provided by financing activities		7,000
Net increase in cash		$ 5,400

tal) through a company because such flows are the lifeblood of a business. Yet constant changes in accounting principles yielded net income amounts that often were not good measures of such liquid asset flows from operations. In addition, attention focused on the total amount of working capital rather than the composition of working capital, including how much of it was cash.

The Shift toward Cash Flows

Beginning in 1983, more than half of a sample of 600 companies voluntarily used the cash definition of funds. There were several reasons for this shift toward the cash definition of funds. Many companies experienced severe cash flow problems, not working capital problems. The FASB noted the importance of cash flows in the Conceptual Framework Project, stating that "the reporting of meaningful components of future cash flows is generally more useful than reporting changes in working capital."[2] Shortly after publication of this statement, the Financial Executives Institute (FEI) recommended that its members adopt the cash basis in

_____

[2] FASB, *Proposed Statement of Financial Accounting Concepts*, "Reporting Income, Cash Flows, and Financial Position of Business Enterprises," Exposure Draft (Stamford, Conn., 1981), p. xi.

A BROADER PERSPECTIVE

CASH FLOW STATEMENT ISSUED BY GASB FOR '90

Norwalk, Conn.—The Governmental Accounting Standards Board has issued a statement that will require governmental business-type entities to provide a cash-flow statement as part of a full set of financials.

GASB Statement 9 takes effect for fiscal years beginning after Dec. 15, 1989. Thus, the standard will affect 1990 calendar-year reporting.

Under Statement 9, an entity's statement of cash flows would replace the currently required statement of changes in financial position.

All proprietary and nonexpendable trust funds and governmental entities that use proprietary fund accounting would be subject to the provisions of Statement 9.

Public employee retirement systems and pension trust funds are exempted from the provisions of Statement 9 and are not currently required to provide a statement of changes in financial position. However, the GASB will address that disclosure issue in its pension plan accounting project.

According to GASB chairman James F. Antonio, Statement 9 is based on the provisions of Statement 95 of the Financial Accounting Standards Board. That document contains standards for cash flow statements issued by private-sector entities.

Antonio noted, however, that Statement 9 "takes into account the differences in environment between the public and private sectors and is therefore somewhat different from FASB Statement 95."

The new GASB standard requires that a statement of cash flows classify cash receipts and payments according to the activities they stem from—whether operations, noncapital financing, capital and related financing, or investments.

"The Board," Antonio pointed out, "is encouraging governmental entities to report cash flows from operating activities by the direct method, which shows major classes of operating cash receipts and payments. However, that statement does permit the use of the indirect, or reconciliation, method."

Antonio added that although Statement 9 applies only to proprietary and nonexpendable trust funds of government entities, there may be a need in the future for cash-flow information in governmental funds.

"Cash-flow information for all types of funds," he said, "will be addressed in the Board's project on the financial reporting model."

Source: *Accounting Today,* October 9, 1989, p. 30. Reprinted with permission.

preparing a statement of changes in financial position.[3] The FEI represents approximately 95% of the companies with securities traded on the New York Stock Exchange and the American Stock Exchange.

The shifting of attention from working capital flows to cash flows is also supported by developments in modern finance. The investment decision is seen more clearly as one in which cash outlays are compared with expected cash returns, appropriately discounted for time and risk. Management, investors, and creditors are all alike in that each "invests" cash to get future cash returns. Thus, users need information to enable them to make predictions of the amounts, timing, and uncertainty surrounding expected cash receipts. Users also need information to provide feedback on prior assessments of cash flows.

Information on prior **cash** flows provides a better basis for making predictions of future cash flows than does information on prior **working capital** flows. Cash flows often differ sharply from working capital flows. For example, a rapidly expanding business that increases its working capital by expanding inventories

---

[3] Financial Executives Institute, *Alert,* December 14, 1981.

ETHICS

A CLOSER LOOK

Americus Company is a small computer software company with about 20 stockholders. Bill Jackson, president of the company, is under some pressure by the board of directors to run the business in such a way as to allow the "normal" dividend of $500,000 to be paid each year. At the board meetings, several directors seem to focus on the statement of cash flows to see if cash flows from operating activities are high enough to allow for the $500,000 dividend to be paid. Since dividends are viewed as a distribution of profits, these board members believe that the source of dividends should be cash flow from operations rather than cash flow from financing or investing activities.

The accountant, Jim Pettry, calculated the amounts that would appear in this year's statement of cash flows and showed them to Bill. Cash flows from operating activities were only $450,000. Bill expressed some disappointment and said, "A few of those board members are going to be very unhappy that we did not generate at least $500,000 from operations. We may have to cut the dividend this year." Jim said that these figures were only preliminary and he would recalculate the amounts to make sure they were right.

When Jim recalculated the amounts he noticed that there was an item "Proceeds from loan, $100,000" listed under "Cash flows from financing activities." He concluded that it would really be quite harmless to report that item as "Increase in notes payable, $100,000" under "Cash flows from operating activities." The loan had a maturity date of three years in the future. Jim concluded that everyone concerned would be happier if this "innocent mistake" were to be made in the final version of the statement of cash flows, so he prepared the statement in this way.

Required

a. What amount should be shown as "net cash provided by operating activities"?
b. Are the board members likely to discover the mistake?
c. Is the mistake really harmless from a financial point of view? Why?
d. What do you think of the ethics of the action that Jim took?

and accounts receivable may not have enough cash to meet current bills. Cash flow analysis, rather than working capital analysis, is required to reveal such potential problems.

The adoption of the statement of cash flows completed the shift from a working capital emphasis to a cash emphasis. The statement of cash flows seems to provide information on cash flows in a more useful and understandable format than did the old statement of changes in financial position.

EPILOGUE

You have now completed the last chapter in this text. The appendixes at the end of the book contain information that you may want to study on your own even if it is not assigned. Appendix A describes accounting for single proprietorships and partnerships. Appendix B discusses payroll accounting and federal income taxes. Appendix C covers accounting for the effects of inflation. Inflation accounting at one time was mandatory, but now it is optional. Appendix D gives a brief introduction to accounting for governmental units and other not-for-profit organizations. Appendix E shows excerpts from the annual reports of The Coca-Cola Company, Maytag Corporation, The Limited, Inc., and John H. Harland Company. These annual reports illustrate many of the concepts and financial statements presented in the text.

Appendix F presents the codes of ethics for two important accounting groups—the American Institute of Certified Public Accountants (AICPA) and the Institute of Management Accountants (IMA). Studying these codes of ethics gives you an understanding of the high ethical standards that are expected of accountants. Appendix G contains compound interest and annuity tables, which you used when you covered the chapter on bonds.

UNDERSTANDING THE LEARNING OBJECTIVES

1. Explain the purposes and uses of the statement of cash flows.
   - □ The statement of cash flows summarizes the effects on cash of the operating, financing, and investing activities of a company during an accounting period.
   - □ Management can see the effects of its past major policy decisions in quantitative form.
   - □ Investors and creditors can assess the entity's ability to generate positive future net cash flows, to meet its obligations, and to pay dividends, and can assess the need for external financing.

2. Describe the content of the statement of cash flows and where certain items would appear on the statement.
   - □ Operating activities generally include the cash effects (inflows and outflows) of transactions and other events that enter into the determination of net income. The cash flows from operating activities can be measured in two ways. The direct method deducts from cash sales only those operating expenses that consumed cash. The indirect method starts with net income and adjusts net income for items that affected reported net income but did not involve cash.
   - □ Investing activities generally include transactions involving the acquisition or disposal of noncurrent assets.
   - □ Financing activities generally include the cash effects (inflows and outflows) of transactions and other events involving creditors and owners.

3. Describe how to calculate cash flows from operating activities under both the direct and indirect methods.
   - □ The direct method deducts from cash sales only those operating expenses that consumed cash.
   - □ The indirect method starts with accrual basis net income and indirectly adjusts net income for items that affected reported net income but did not involve cash.

4. Prepare a statement of cash flows under both the direct and indirect methods showing cash flows from operating activities, investing activities, and financing activities.
   - □ The first step is to determine the cash flows from operating activities. Either the direct or indirect method may be used.
   - □ The second step is to analyze all the noncurrent accounts for changes in cash resulting from investing and financing activities.
   - □ The third step is to arrange the information gathered in steps 1 and 2 into the format required for the statement of cash flows.

5. Describe the historical development from a statement of changes in financial position to a statement of cash flows.
   - □ Until July 1988, a statement of changes in financial position was required to report on funds flows. This statement showed the sources and

uses of funds as the two main categories. Funds generally meant working capital (current assets minus current liabilities).

☐ In late 1987, the Financial Accounting Standards Board issued a standard requiring the substitution of a statement of cash flows for the statement of changes in financial position effective for annual financial statements for fiscal years ending after July 15, 1988.

DEMONSTRATION PROBLEM

Given below are comparative balance sheets of Dells Corporation as of June 30, 1994, and June 30, 1993. The income statement for the year ended June 30, 1994, and certain additional data are also provided.

DELLS CORPORATION
Comparative Balance Sheets
June 30, 1994, and 1993

	1994	1993	Increase (Decrease)
Assets			
Current assets:			
Cash	$ 30,000	$ 80,000	$ (50,000)
Accounts receivable, net.	160,000	100,000	60,000
Merchandise inventory	100,000	70,000	30,000
Prepaid rent	20,000	10,000	10,000
Total current assets	$310,000	$260,000	$ 50,000
Property, plant, and equipment:			
Equipment	$400,000	$200,000	$200,000
Accumulated depreciation—equipment	(60,000)	(50,000)	(10,000)
Total property, plant, and equipment	$340,000	$150,000	$190,000
Total assets	$650,000	$410,000	$240,000
Liabilities and Stockholders' Equity			
Current liabilities:			
Accounts payable.	$ 50,000	$ 40,000	$ 10,000
Notes payable—bank	–0–	50,000	(50,000)
Salaries payable	10,000	20,000	(10,000)
Federal income taxes payable	30,000	20,000	10,000
Total current liabilities	$ 90,000	$130,000	$ (40,000)
Stockholders' equity:			
Common stock, $10 par.	$300,000	$100,000	$200,000
Paid-in capital in excess of par	50,000	–0–	50,000
Retained earnings.	210,000	180,000	30,000
Total stockholders' equity	$560,000	$280,000	$280,000
Total liabilities and stockholders' equity	$650,000	$410,000	$240,000

DELLS CORPORATION
Statement of Income and Retained Earnings
For the Year Ended June 30, 1994

Sales		$1,000,000
Cost of goods sold	$600,000	
Salaries and wages expense.	200,000	
Rent expense	40,000	
Depreciation expense.	20,000	
Interest expense	3,000	
Loss on sale of equipment	7,000	870,000
Income before federal income taxes		$ 130,000
Deduct: Federal income taxes		60,000
Net income		$ 70,000
Retained earnings, July 1, 1993		180,000
		$ 250,000
Deduct: Dividends		40,000
Retained earnings, June 30, 1994		$ 210,000

Additional data

1. Equipment with a cost of $20,000, on which $10,000 of depreciation had been recorded, was sold for cash. Additional equipment was purchased.

2. Stock was issued for cash.

Required   Using the data given for Dells Corporation:

a. Prepare a working paper for a statement of cash flows.

b. Prepare a statement of cash flows—indirect method.

c. Prepare a working paper to convert net income from an accrual basis to a cash basis. Then prepare a partial statement of cash flows—direct method, showing only the cash flows from operating activities section.

SOLUTION TO DEMONSTRATION PROBLEM

a.

DELLS CORPORATION
Working Paper for Statement of Cash Flows
For the Year Ended June 30, 1994

	Account Balances 6/30/93	Analysis of Transactions for 1994		Account Balances 6/30/94
		Debit	Credit	
Debits				
Cash	80,000		(0) 50,000	30,000
Accounts Receivable	100,000	(2) 60,000		160,000
Merchandise Inventory	70,000	(3) 30,000		100,000
Prepaid Rent	10,000	(4) 10,000		20,000
Equipment	200,000	(10) 220,000	(9) 20,000	400,000
	460,000			710,000
Credits				
Accumulated Depreciation	50,000	(9) 10,000	(11) 20,000	60,000
Accounts Payable	40,000		(5) 10,000	50,000
Notes Payable—Bank	50,000	(6) 50,000		–0–
Salaries Payable	20,000	(7) 10,000		10,000
Federal Income Taxes Payable	20,000		(8) 10,000	30,000
Common Stock, $10 Par	100,000		(12) 200,000	300,000
Paid-In Capital in Excess of Par	–0–		(12) 50,000	50,000
Retained Earnings	180,000	(13) 40,000	(1) 70,000	210,000
Totals	460,000	430,000	430,000	710,000
Cash Flows from Operating Activities:				
Net Income		(1) 70,000		
Increase in Accounts Receivable			(2) 60,000	
Increase in Merchandise Inventory			(3) 30,000	
Increase in Prepaid Rent			(4) 10,000	
Increase in Accounts Payable		(5) 10,000		
Decrease in Salaries Payable			(7) 10,000	
Increase in Federal Income Taxes Payable		(8) 10,000		
Loss on Sale of Equipment		(9) 7,000		
Depreciation Expense		(11) 20,000		
Cash Flows from Investing Activities:				
Proceeds from Sale of Equipment		(9) 3,000		
Purchases of Property, Plant, and Equipment			(10) 220,000	
Cash Flows from Financing Activities:				
Repayment of Bank Note			(6) 50,000	
Proceeds from Issuing Common Stock		(12) 250,000		
Payment of Cash Dividends			(13) 40,000	
Decrease in Cash		(0) 50,000		
Totals		420,000	420,000	

b.

DELLS CORPORATION
Statement of Cash Flows—Indirect Method
For the Year Ended June 30, 1994

Cash flows from operating activities:

Net income		$ 70,000
Adjustments to reconcile net income to net cash provided by operating activities:		
Increase in accounts receivable	(60,000)	
Increase in merchandise inventory	(30,000)	
Increase in prepaid rent.	(10,000)	
Increase in accounts payable	10,000	
Decrease in salaries payable.	(10,000)	
Increase in federal income taxes payable	10,000	
Loss on sale of equipment	7,000	
Depreciation expense.	20,000	
Net cash provided by operating activities		$ 7,000

Cash flows from investing activities:

Proceeds from sale of equipment	$ 3,000	
Purchases of property, plant, and equipment	(220,000)	
Net cash used by investing activities		(217,000)

Cash flows from financing activities:

Proceeds from issuing common stock	$ 250,000	
Repayment of bank note	(50,000)	
Dividends paid.	(40,000)	
Net cash provided by financing activities		160,000
Net increase (decrease) in cash		$ (50,000)

---

c.

DELLS CORPORATION
Working Paper to Convert Income Statement
from Accrual Basis to Cash Basis
For the Year Ended June 30, 1994

	Accrual Basis		Add	Deduct	Cash Basis (Cash Flows from Operating Activities)
Sales		$1,000,000		$60,000[a]	$940,000
Cost of goods sold	$600,000		$30,000[b]	10,000[c]	$620,000
Salaries and wages expense	200,000		10,000[d]		210,000
Rent expense	40,000		10,000[e]		50,000
Depreciation expense. . . .	20,000			20,000	–0–
Interest expense	3,000				3,000
Loss on sale of equipment .	7,000			7,000	–0–
Federal income taxes. . . .	60,000			10,000[f]	50,000
		930,000			933,000
Net income		$ 70,000			$ 7,000

[a] Increase in Accounts Receivable.
[b] Increase in Merchandise Inventory.
[c] Increase in Accounts Payable.
[d] Decrease in Salaries Payable.
[e] Increase in Prepaid Rent.
[f] Increase in Federal Income Taxes Payable.

DELLS CORPORATION
Partial Statement of Cash Flows—Direct Method
For the Year Ended June 30, 1994

Cash flows from operating activities:

Cash received from customers.	$ 940,000
Cash paid for merchandise	(620,000)
Salaries and wages paid.	(210,000)
Rent paid	(50,000)
Interest paid	(3,000)
Federal income taxes paid.	(50,000)
Net cash provided by operating activities	$7,000

NEW TERMS

Cash flows from operating activities The net amount of cash received or disbursed during a given period on items that normally appear on the income statement. *834*

Direct method Deducts from cash sales only those operating expenses that consumed cash. *834*

Financing activities Generally include the cash effects of transactions and other events involving creditors and owners. Cash payments made to settle current liabilities such as accounts payable, wages payable, and income taxes payable are not financing activities. These payments are operating activities. *834*

Indirect method A method of determining cash flows from operating activities that starts with net income and indirectly adjusts net income for items that do not involve cash. Also called the **addback** method. *834*

Investing activities Generally include transactions involving the acquisition or disposal of noncurrent assets. Examples include cash received or paid from the sale or purchase of property, plant, and equipment; marketable securities; and loans made to others. *833*

Noncash charges or expenses Expenses and losses that are added back to net income because they do not actually use cash of the company. The items added back include amounts of depreciation on plant assets, depletion that was expensed, amortization of intangible

assets such as patents and goodwill, amortization of discount on bonds payable, and losses from disposals of noncurrent assets. *836*

Noncash credits or revenues Revenues and gains included in arriving at net income that do not provide cash; examples include gains from disposals of noncurrent assets, income from investments carried under the equity method, and amortization of premium on bonds payable. *836*

Operating activities Generally include the cash effects of transactions and other events that enter into the determination of net income. *833*

Statement of cash flows A statement that summarizes the effects on cash of the operating, investing, and financing activities of a company during an accounting period. Both inflows and outflows are included in each category. The statement of cash flows must be prepared each time an income statement is prepared. *832*

Statement of changes in financial position A statement formerly required that reported the flows of cash or working capital into and out of a business in a given time period; it also showed significant financing and investing activities that did not involve cash or working capital flows. *851*

Working capital Equal to current assets minus current liabilities. *851*

SELF-TEST

True-False

Indicate whether each of the following statements is true or false.

1. The requirement for a statement of cash flows was preceded by the requirement for the statement of changes in financial position.

2. The statement of cash flows is one of the major financial statements.

3. Investing activities are transactions with creditors and owners.

4. The direct method of calculating cash flows from operations is encouraged by the FASB and is the predominant method used.

5. Issuance of capital stock and the subsequent reacquisition of some of those shares would both be financing activities.

Multiple-Choice

Select the best answer for each of the following questions.

1. Which of the following statement is true?
    a. The direct method of calculating cash flows from operations starts with net income and adjusts for noncash revenues and expenses and changes in current assets and current liabilities.
    b. The indirect method of calculating cash flows from operations adjusts each item in the income statement to a cash basis.
    c. The description in *(a)* and *(b)* should be reversed.
    d. The direct method is easier to use than the indirect method.

2. Investing activities include all of the following except:
    a. Payment of debt.
    b. Collection of loans.
    c. Making of loans.
    d. Sale of marketable securities.

3. If sales on an accrual basis are $500,000 and accounts receivable increased by $30,000, the cash received from customers would be:
    a. $500,000.
    b. $470,000.
    c. $530,000.
    d. Cannot be determined.

4. Assume cost of goods sold on an accrual basis is $300,000, accounts payable increased by $20,000, and inventory increased by $50,000. Cash paid for merchandise is:
    a. $370,000.
    b. $230,000.
    c. $270,000.
    d. $330,000.

5. Assume net income was $200,000, depreciation expense was $10,000, accounts receivable increased by $15,000, and accounts payable increased by $5,000. The amount of cash flows from operating activities is:
    a. $200,000.
    b. $180,000.
    c. $210,000.
    d. $190,000.

Now turn to page 876 to check your answers.

QUESTIONS

1. What are the purposes of the statement of cash flows?

2. What are some of the uses of the statement of cash flows?

3. What information is contained in the statement of cash flows?

4. Which activities are generally included in operating activities?

5. Which activities are included in investing activities?

6. Which activities are included in financing activities?

7. Where should investing and financing activities that do not involve cash flows be reported?

8. Explain the difference between the direct and indirect methods for computing cash flows from operating activities.

9. What are noncash expenses? How are they treated in computing cash flows from operating activities?

10. Describe the treatment of a gain on the sale of equipment in preparing a statement of cash flows under the indirect method.

11. Depreciation is sometimes referred to as a source of cash. Is it a source of cash? Explain.

12. Why is it unlikely that cash flows from operating activities will be equal to net income for the same period?

13. If the net income for a given period is $25,000, does this mean there is an increase in cash of the same amount? Why or why not?

14. Why might a company have positive cash flows from operating activities even though operating at a net loss?

15. Give two reasons why analysts seem to prefer cash flow statements to statements that report working capital flows.

16. Indicate the type of activity each of the following transactions represents (operating, investing, or financing) and whether it is an inflow or an outflow.
    a. Sold goods.
    b. Purchased building.
    c. Issued capital stock.
    d. Received cash dividends.
    e. Paid cash dividends.
    f. Purchased treasury stock.
    g. Sold marketable securities.
    h. Made a loan.
    i. Paid interest on loan.
    j. Paid bond principal.
    k. Received proceeds of insurance settlement.
    i. Made contribution to charity.

17. *Real world question* Refer to "A Broader Perspective" on page 853. What major categories (activities) will be included in the statement of

cash flows for governmental business-type entities? Are the rules and recommendations regarding the direct or indirect methods for reporting cash flows from operating activities similar to or different from those contained in *FASB Statement No. 95?*

18. *Real world question* Refer to Appendix E at the end of this text. Of the four companies represented, which use the direct method of reporting cash flows from operating activities and which use the indirect method?

EXERCISES

Exercise 18–1

Report specific items on statement of cash flows (L.O. 2, 4)

Indicate how the following data should be reported in a statement of cash flows. A company paid $120,000 cash for land. A building was acquired for $240,000 by assuming a mortgage on the building.

Exercise 18–2

Report specific items on statement of cash flows (L.O. 2, 4)

The following data are from the Automobile and the Accumulated Depreciation—Automobile accounts of a certain company:

	Automobile			
Date		**Debit**	**Credit**	**Balance**
Jan. 1	Balance brought forward.			32,000
July 1	Traded for new auto.		32,000	–0–
	New auto	35,200		35,200
	Accumulated Depreciation—Automobile			
Jan. 1	Balance brought forward.			24,000
July 1	One-half year's depreciation		4,000	28,000
	Auto traded.	28,000		–0–
Dec. 31	One-half year's depreciation		4,400	4,400

The old auto was traded for a new one, with the difference in values paid in cash. The income statement for the year shows a loss on the exchange of autos of $2,400.

Indicate the dollar amounts, the descriptions of these amounts, and their exact locations in a statement of cash flows—indirect method.

Exercise 18–3

Compute cash used to purchase plant assets (L.O. 2, 4)

Following are balance sheet data for Luoma Corporation.

	December 31	
	1995	**1994**
Cash	$ 23,500	$ 13,000
Accounts receivable, net	70,500	67,000
Merchandise inventory	41,500	51,000
Prepaid expenses.	4,500	5,500
Plant assets (net of accumulated depreciation)	117,500	115,000
Accounts payable.	61,000	63,500
Accrued liabilities payable	20,000	20,500
Capital stock	150,000	150,000
Retained earnings	26,500	17,500

Assume that the depreciation recorded in 1995 was $7,500. Compute the cash spent to purchase plant assets, assuming no assets were sold or scrapped in 1995.

Exercise 18–4

Prepare statements of cash flows (L.O. 4)

Use the data in Exercise 18–3. Assume the net income for 1995 was $12,000, depreciation was $7,500, and dividends declared and paid were $3,000. Prepare a statement of cash flows—indirect method.

Exercise 18–5
Calculate the amount of cash paid for merchandise
(L.O. 3)

Cost of goods sold in the income statement for the year ended 1994 was $314,000. The balances in Merchandise Inventory and Accounts Payable were:

	January 1, 1994	December 31, 1994
Merchandise Inventory	$160,000	$170,000
Accounts Payable.	44,000	36,000

Calculate the amount of cash paid for merchandise for 1994.

Exercise 18–6
Compute cash flows from operating activities
(L.O. 3)

The income statement of a company shows net income of $75,000; merchandise inventory on January 1 was $76,500 and on December 31 was $94,500; accounts payable for merchandise purchases were $57,000 on January 1 and $63,000 on December 31. Compute the cash flows from operating activities.

Exercise 18–7
Compute cash flows from operating activities
(L.O. 3)

The operating expenses and taxes (including $60,000 of depreciation) of a company for a given year were $600,000. Net income was $300,000. Prepaid insurance decreased from $18,000 to $12,000 during the year, while wages payable increased from $24,000 to $36,000 during the year. Compute the cash flows from operating activities under the indirect method.

Exercise 18–8
Indicate treatment of dividend
(L.O. 2, 4)

Dividends payable increased by $6,000 during a year in which total dividends declared were $120,000. What amount appears for dividends paid in the statement of cash flows?

Exercise 18–9
Show effects of conversion from accrual to cash basis income
(L.O. 3)

Fill in the following chart, showing how increases and decreases in these accounts affect the conversion of accrual basis income to cash basis income.

	Add	Deduct
Accounts Receivable		
Merchandise Inventory		
Prepaid Expenses		
Accounts Payable		
Accrued Liabilities Payable		

PROBLEMS: SERIES A

Problem 18–1A
Prepare working paper to convert income statement to cash basis; prepare cash flows from operating activities under both methods
(L.O. 2, 3)

The income statement and other data of the Hartgraves Corporation are given below.

HARTGRAVES CORPORATION
Income Statement
For the Year Ended December 31, 1994

Sales		$700,000
Cost of goods sold		250,000
Gross margin		$450,000
Operating expenses (other than depreciation)	$120,000	
Depreciation expense	40,000	160,000
Net income		$290,000

Changes in current assets (other than cash) and current liabilities during the year were:

	Increase	Decrease
Accounts receivable	$20,000	
Merchandise inventory.		$40,000
Prepaid insurance	16,000	
Accounts payable		30,000
Accrued liabilities payable	8,000	

Depreciation was the only noncash item affecting net income.

Required *a.* Prepare a working paper to calculate cash flows from operating activities under the direct method.

b. Prepare the cash flows from operating activities section of the statement of cash flows under the *direct method*.

c. Prove that the same cash flows amount will be obtained under the indirect method by preparing the cash flows from operating activities section of the statement of cash flows under the *indirect method*. You need not prepare a working paper.

Problem 18–2A

Prepare statement of cash flows under the indirect method (L.O. 4)

Given below are comparative balance sheets and other data of Comisky Corporation:

COMISKY CORPORATION
Comparative Balance Sheets
December 31, 1995, and 1994

	1995	1994
Assets		
Cash	$ 28,070	$ 14,000
Accounts receivable, net	40,050	39,500
Supplies on hand.	1,500	1,700
Prepaid rent	600	800
Land	180,000	200,000
Equipment	120,000	95,000
Accumulated depreciation—equipment	(50,000)	(45,000)
Total assets	$320,220	$306,000
Liabilities and Stockholders' Equity		
Accounts payable	$ 5,220	$ 30,200
Accrued liabilities payable	9,000	7,500
Bonds payable (in 2001).	100,000	100,000
Common stock ($20 par)	130,000	110,000
Paid-in capital in excess of par	15,000	–0–
Retained earnings	61,000	58,300
Total liabilities and stockholders' equity	$320,220	$306,000

Additional data

1. Land was sold for a gain of $2,000.

2. No equipment was sold. Additional equipment was purchased for cash.

3. Stock was issued for cash.

4. Dividends declared and paid during 1995 totaled $35,500.

Required Prepare a statement of cash flows under the indirect method. Try to do so without preparing a working paper.

Problem 18–3A

Prepare working paper and statement of cash flows under the indirect method (L.O. 4)

The information given below is related to Martin Corporation.

MARTIN CORPORATION
Comparative Balance Sheets
December 31, 1995, and 1994

	1995	1994
Assets		
Cash.	$ 22,500	$ 30,000
Accounts receivable, net	59,000	60,000
Merchandise inventory.	175,000	120,000
Equipment	412,500	315,000
Accumulated depreciation—equipment	(120,000)	(105,000)
Investments	75,000	15,000
Total assets	$624,000	$435,000
Liabilities and Stockholders' Equity		
Accounts payable	$ 21,750	$ 18,750
Accrued liabilities payable	2,250	3,750
Capital stock—common—$10 par.	375,000	300,000
Paid-in capital in excess of par	150,000	75,000
Retained earnings.	75,000	37,500
Total liabilities and stockholders' equity	$624,000	$435,000

Additional data

1. Net income was $67,500 for the year.
2. Fully depreciated equipment costing $15,000 was sold for $3,750 and equipment costing $112,500 was purchased for cash.
3. Depreciation expense for the year was $30,000.
4. Investments were purchased, $60,000.
5. An additional 7,500 shares of common stock were issued for cash at $20 per share.
6. Cash dividends of $30,000 were declared and paid.

Required *a.* Prepare a working paper for a statement of cash flows.

b. Prepare a statement of cash flows under the indirect method.

Problem 18–4A

Prepare working paper and statement of cash flows under the indirect method
(L.O. 4)

The following information is from the accounting records of Taylor Corporation for the fiscal years 1995 and 1994.

TAYLOR CORPORATION
Comparative Balance Sheets
June 30, 1995, and 1994

	1995	1994
Assets		
Cash.	$ 26,250	$ 21,000
Accounts receivable, net	84,000	42,000
Merchandise inventory.	42,000	47,250
Prepaid expenses	7,875	13,125
Investment in stock of affiliated company	94,500	78,750
Buildings.	199,500	147,000
Accumulated depreciation—buildings	(31,500)	(26,250)
Equipment	257,250	210,000
Accumulated depreciation—equipment	(78,750)	(63,000)
Total assets	$601,125	$469,875
Liabilities and Stockholders' Equity		
Accounts payable	$ 73,500	$ 47,250
Accrued liabilities payable	10,500	15,750
Five-year note payable	52,500	–0–
Capital stock—$50 par.	420,000	367,500
Retained earnings	44,625	39,375
Total liabilities and stockholders' equity	$601,125	$469,875

Additional data

1. Net income for year ended June 30, 1995, was $26,250.
2. Additional shares of stock of the affiliated company were acquired for cash.
3. No equipment or building retirements occurred during the year.
4. Equipment was purchased for cash.
5. The five-year note was issued to pay for a building erected on land leased by the company.
6. Stock was issued at par for cash.
7. Dividends declared and paid were $21,000.

Required   a. Prepare a working paper for a statement of cash flows.

b. Prepare a statement of cash flows under the indirect method. Prepare a separate schedule of noncash investing and financing activities.

Problem 18–5A
Prepare working paper
and statement of cash
flows under both methods
(L.O. 4)

The Wallace Corporation comparative balance sheets at December 31, 1995, and 1994, and the statement of income and retained earnings for 1995 are presented below.

WALLACE CORPORATION
Comparative Balance Sheets
December 31, 1995, and 1994

	1995	1994
Assets		
Current assets:		
Cash.	$ 9,750	$ 13,000
Accounts receivable, net.	82,550	63,700
Merchandise inventory.	79,300	72,800
Prepaid insurance	1,950	2,600
Total current assets	$173,550	$152,100
Property, plant, and equipment:		
Land.	$ 32,500	$ 19,500
Buildings.	130,000	65,000
Accumulated depreciation—buildings	(16,250)	(13,000)
Equipment	149,500	139,750
Accumulated depreciation—equipment	(81,250)	(65,000)
Total property, plant, and equipment	$214,500	$146,250
Total assets	$388,050	$298,350
Liabilities and Stockholders' Equity		
Current liabilities:		
Accounts payable	$ 61,100	$ 58,500
Federal income taxes payable	23,400	19,500
Salaries and wages payable	2,600	1,950
Accrued liabilities payable	3,900	2,600
Total current liabilities	$ 91,000	$ 82,550
Long-term liabilities:		
Bonds, payable, 9%	65,000	65,000
Total liabilities	$156,000	$147,550
Stockholders' equity:		
Capital stock—common	$195,000	$130,000
Paid-in capital in excess of par	9,750	–0–
Retained earnings.	27,300	20,800
Total stockholders' equity	232,050	150,800
Total liabilities and stockholders' equity	$388,050	$298,350

WALLACE CORPORATION
Income Statement and Statement of Retained Earnings
For the Year Ended December 31, 1995

Sales, net		$585,000
Cost of goods sold		390,000
Gross margin.		$195,000
Salaries and wages expense	$97,500	
Depreciation expense	24,050	
Insurance expense	1,300	
Other expenses (including interest)	32,500	
Loss on sale of equipment.	650	156,000
Income before federal income taxes		$ 39,000
Deduct: Federal income taxes		16,900
Net income		$ 22,100
Retained earnings, December 31, 1994		20,800
		$ 42,900
Less: Dividends (declared and paid).		15,600
Retained earnings, December 31, 1995		$ 27,300

Additional data

1. $3,250 of cash and all of the additional capital stock issued during the year were exchanged for land and a building.

2. Equipment having an original cost of $6,500 and on which $4,550 of depreciation was recorded was sold at a loss of $650. Equipment additions were for cash.

Required　*a.* Prepare a working paper for a statement of cash flows.

b. Prepare a statement of cash flows under the indirect method. Prepare a separate schedule of noncash investing and financing activities.

c. Prepare a working paper to convert the income statement to a cash basis.

d. Prepare a statement of cash flows under the direct method.

PROBLEMS: SERIES B

Problem 18–1B

Prepare working paper to convert income statement to cash basis; prepare cash flows from operating activities under both methods
(L.O. 2, 3)

The income statement and other data of Garcia Corporation are given below.

GARCIA CORPORATION
Income Statement
For the Year Ended December 3, 1994

Sales		$360,000
Cost of goods sold		190,000
Gross margin		$170,000
Operating expenses (other than depreciation)	$70,000	
Depreciation expense	20,000	90,000
Net income		$ 80,000

Changes in current assets (other than cash) and current liabilities during the year were:

	Increase	Decrease
Accounts receivable.		$10,000
Merchandise inventory.	$ 6,000	
Prepaid insurance	4,000	
Accounts payable	12,000	
Accrued liabilities payable	2,000	

Depreciation was the only noncash item affecting net income.

Required a. Prepare a working paper to calculate cash flows from operating activities under the *direct method*.

b. Prepare the cash flows from operating activities section of the statement of cash flows under the *direct method*.

c. Prove that the same cash flows amount will be obtained under the indirect method by preparing the cash flows from operating activities section of the statement of cash flows under the *indirect method*. You need not prepare a working paper.

Problem 18–2B
Prepare statement of cash flows under the indirect method (L.O. 4)

Following are Kinney Company's comparative balance sheets at May 31, 1995, and 1994, and a statement of retained earnings for the year ended May 31, 1995:

KINNEY COMPANY
Comparative Balance Sheets
May 31, 1995, and 1994

	1995	1994
Assets		
Cash	$ 69,750	$ 60,000
Accounts receivable, net	94,500	108,000
Merchandise inventory	90,000	75,000
Investment in subsidiary	71,250	60,000
Land	52,500	37,500
Equipment	324,750	285,000
Accumulated depreciation—equipment	(58,500)	(45,000)
Patents	8,250	12,000
Total assets	$652,500	$592,500
Liabilities and Stockholders' Equity		
Accounts payable	$ 72,500	$ 48,000
Taxes payable	7,000	9,000
Bonds payable.	150,000	150,000
Common stock—$100 par.	300,000	300,000
Retained earnings	123,000	85,500
Total liabilities and stockholders' equity	$652,500	$592,500

KINNEY COMPANY
Statement of Retained Earnings
For the Year Ended May 31, 1994

Balance, May 31, 1994.	$ 85,500
Net income.	75,000
	$160,500
Dividends declared and paid	37,500
Balance, May 31, 1995.	$123,000

Additional data

1. A tract of land adjacent to land owned was purchased for cash during the year.

2. New equipment with a cost of $48,750 was purchased for cash during the year, while fully depreciated equipment with a cost of $9,000 was discarded.

3. Depreciation of $22,500 and patent amortization of $3,750 were charged to expense during the year.

4. Additional shares of stock of the subsidiary company were acquired for cash.

Required   Prepare a statement of cash flows under the indirect method. Try to do so without preparing a working paper.

Problem 18–3B

Prepare working paper and statement of cash flows under the indirect method
(L.O. 4)

Given below are comparative balance sheets and other data of Castillo, Inc.:

CASTILLO, INC.
Comparative Balance Sheets
December 31, 1995, and 1994

	1995	1994
Assets		
Cash.	$ 46,105	$ 21,000
Accounts receivable, net.	26,075	24,250
Merchandise inventory.	30,000	35,000
Supplies on hand	1,750	2,550
Prepaid insurance .	1,400	1,200
Land.	180,000	142,500
Equipment .	270,000	300,000
Accumulated depreciation—equipment	(75,000)	(67,500)
Total assets .	$480,330	$459,000
Liabilities and Stockholders' Equity		
Accounts payable .	$ 15,330	$ 46,300
Salaries payable.	4,000	2,000
Accrued liabilities payable	2,000	8,250
Long-term note payable	150,000	150,000
Common stock ($5 par)	185,000	165,000
Paid-in capital in excess of par	32,500	–0–
Retained earnings.	91,500	87,450
Total liabilities and stockholders' equity	$480,330	$459,000

Additional data

1. Land was bought for cash.

2. Equipment costing $50,000 with accumulated depreciation of $30,000 was sold for a gain of $3,500, and equipment costing $20,000 was purchased for cash.

3. Depreciation expense for the year was $37,500.

4. Common stock was issued for cash.

5. Dividends declared and paid in 1995 totaled $52,950.

Required   *a.*   Prepare a working paper for a statement of cash flows.
         b.   Prepare a statement of cash flows under the indirect method.

Problem 18-4B

Prepare working paper and statement of cash flows under the indirect method (L.O. 4)

Given below are comparative balance sheets and other data of Bartlett Corporation.

BARTLETT CORPORATION
Comparative Balance Sheets
June 30, 1995, and 1994

	1995	1994
Assets		
Cash.	$ 241,800	$ 132,600
Accounts receivable, net	750,750	432,900
Merchandise inventory.	819,000	850,200
Prepaid insurance	3,900	5,850
Land.	312,000	351,000
Buildings	2,184,000	1,209,000
Machinery and tools	858,000	468,000
Accumulated depreciation—machinery and tools . .	(809,250)	(510,900)
Total assets	$4,360,200	$2,938,650
Liabilities and Stockholders' Equity		
Accounts payable	$ 126,750	$ 175,500
Accrued liabilities payable	85,800	11,700
Bank loans (due in 1997)	56,550	66,300
Mortgage bonds payable	382,200	185,250
Common stock—$100 par	1,755,000	585,000
Paid-in capital in excess of par	58,500	–0–
Retained earnings	1,895,400	1,914,900
Total liabilities and stockholders' equity	$4,360,200	$2,938,650

Additional data

1. Net income for year was $78,000.
2. Depreciation for the year was $356,850.
3. There was a gain of $7,800 on the sale of land.
4. The additional mortgage bonds were issued at face value as partial payment for a building valued at $975,000.
5. Machinery and tools were purchased for $448,500 cash.
6. Fully depreciated machinery with a cost of $58,500 was scrapped and written off.
7. Additional common stock was issued at $105 per share.
8. Dividends declared and paid were $97,500.

Required   *a.* Prepare a working paper for a statement of cash flows.

b. Prepare a statement of cash flows under the indirect method. Prepare a separate schedule of noncash investing and financing activities.

Problem 18-5B

Prepare working paper and statement of cash flows under both methods (L.O. 4)

The income statement for Raffa Company for the year ended December 31, 1995, shows:

Net sales		$448,000
Cost of goods sold	$262,500	
Operating expenses.	70,000*	
Major repairs.	35,000	
Interest expense	10,500	
Loss on sale of equipment.	5,600	383,600
Income before federal income taxes		$ 64,400
Deduct: Federal income taxes		33,600
Net income		$ 30,800

* Including $14,000 of depreciation expense.

Comparative balance sheets for the company show:

RAFFA COMPANY
Comparative Balance Sheets
December 31, 1995, and 1994

	1995	1994
Assets		
Current assets:		
Cash.	$ 33,600	$ 28,000
Accounts receivable, net.	67,900	53,200
Merchandise inventory.	147,000	126,000
Prepaid expenses	11,200	4,200
Total current assets	$259,700	$211,400
Property, plant, and equipment:		
Buildings	$ 70,000	$ 70,000
Accumulated depreciation—buildings	(38,500)	(35,000)
Equipment	129,500	91,000
Accumulated depreciation—equipment	(44,100)	(42,000)
Total property, plant, and equipment	$116,900	$ 84,000
Total assets	$376,600	$295,400
Liabilities and Stockholders' Equity		
Current liabilities:		
Accounts payable	$ 39,550	$ 57,750
Accrued liabilities payable	11,550	10,150
Federal income taxes payable	33,600	31,500
Total current liabilities	$ 84,700	$ 99,400
Long-term liabilities:		
Bonds, payable, 15%	70,000	70,000
Total liabilities	$154,700	$169,400
Stockholders' equity:		
Capital stock—common, $100 par	$175,000	$105,000
Paid-in capital in excess of par	17,500	–0–
Retained earnings.	29,400	21,000
Total stockholders' equity	$221,900	$126,000
Total liabilities and stockholders' equity	$376,600	$295,400

Additional data

1. Equipment sold had an original cost of $21,000. Depreciation on equipment for the year amounted to $10,500.
2. Dividends declared and paid during the year totaled $22,400.
3. Accrued expenses payable and prepaid expenses relate solely to operating expenses.
4. Capital stock was issued for cash.

Required   a.   Prepare a working paper for a statement of cash flows.

            b.   Prepare a statement of cash flows under the indirect method.

            c.   Prepare a working paper to convert the income statement to a cash basis.

            d.   Prepare a statement of cash flows under the direct method.

BUSINESS DECISION PROBLEMS

Decision Problem 18–1

Prepare a statement of cash flows using the indirect method and answer owner's questions (L.O. 1, 2, 4)

Hudson, Inc., is a sports equipment center owned and operated by William Hudson. During 1995, the company replaced $18,000 of the center's fully depreciated equipment with new equipment costing $23,000. Although a midyear dividend of $5,000 was paid, William found it necessary to borrow $5,000 from his bank on a two-year note. He feels further borrowing may be needed since the Cash account is dangerously low at year-end.

Given below are the income statement and "cash flow statement," as William's accountant calls it, for 1995.

HUDSON, INC.
Income Statement
For the Year Ended December 31, 1995

Sales.		$200,000
Cost of goods sold	$140,000	
Operating expenses and taxes	49,700	189,700
Net income.		$ 10,300

HUDSON, INC.
Cash Flow Statement
For the Year Ended December 31, 1995

Cash received:		
From operations:		
Net income.		$10,300
Depreciation		5,000
Total cash from operations		$15,300
Note issued to bank		5,000
Mortgage note issued		16,000
Total funds provided		$36,300
Cash paid:		
New equipment.	$23,000	
Dividends.	5,000	28,000
Increase in cash.		$ 8,300

William is very concerned about what he sees in the above statements and how it relates to what he knows has actually happened. He turns to you for help. Specifically, he wants to know why the cash flow statement shows an increase in cash when he knows the cash balance decreased from $11,000 to $1,500 during the year. Also, why is depreciation shown as providing cash?

You believe you can answer William's questions. You ask for and receive the following condensed balance sheet data:

HUDSON, INC.
Comparative Balance Sheets
December 31, 1995, and 1994

	December 31	
	1995	1994
Assets		
Current assets:		
Cash.	$ 1,500	$ 11,000
Accounts receivable, net.	17,800	13,200
Merchandise inventory.	28,500	17,500
Prepaid expenses	700	300
Total current assets	$ 48,500	$ 42,000
Property, plant, and equipment:		
Equipment	$ 40,000	$ 35,000
Accumulated depreciation—equipment	(11,000)	(24,000)
Total property, plant, and equipment	$ 29,000	$ 11,000
Total assets	$ 77,500	$ 53,000
Liabilities and Stockholders' Equity		
Current liabilities:		
Accounts payable	$ 8,700	$ 10,000
Accrued liabilities payable	600	1,100
Total current liabilities	$ 9,300	$ 11,100
Long-term liabilities:		
Notes payable	5,000	–0–
Mortgage note payable	16,000	–0–
Total liabilities	$ 30,300	$ 11,100
Stockholders' equity:		
Common stock	$ 40,000	$ 40,000
Retained earnings.	7,200	1,900
Total stockholders' equity	47,200	41,900
Total liabilities and stockholders' equity	$ 77,500	$ 53,000

Required Prepare a correct statement of cash flows using the indirect method that will show why Hudson, Inc., is having such a difficult time keeping sufficient cash on hand. Also, answer William's questions.

Decision Problem 18–2

Prepare a schedule showing cash flows from operating activities under the indirect method and decide whether certain goals can be met
(L.O. 4)

Following are comparative balance sheets for Dunlap Company:

DUNLAP COMPANY
Comparative Balance Sheets
December 31, 1995, and 1994

	1995	1994
Assets		
Cash.	$ 60,000	$ 37,500
Accounts receivable, net	60,000	45,000
Merchandise inventory.	90,000	52,500
Land.	67,500	60,000
Buildings	90,000	90,000
Accumulated depreciation—buildings	(30,000)	(27,000)
Equipment	285,000	225,000
Accumulated depreciation—equipment	(52,500)	(48,000)
Goodwill	120,000	150,000
Total assets	$690,000	$585,000
Liabilities and Stockholders' Equity		
Accounts payable	$ 75,000	$ 45,000
Accrued liabilities payable	30,000	22,500
Capital stock	315,000	300,000
Paid-in capital—stock dividends.	75,000	67,500
Paid-in capital—land donations	15,000	–0–
Retained earnings	180,000	150,000
Total liabilities and stockholders' equity	$690,000	$585,000

An analysis of the Retained Earnings account for the year reveals the following:

Balance, January 1, 1995		$150,000
Add: Net income for the year		97,500
		$247,500
Less: Cash dividends	$45,000	
Stock dividends.	22,500	67,500
Balance, December 31, 1995		$180,000

Additional data

a. Equipment with a cost of $30,000 on which $27,000 of depreciation had been accumulated was sold during the year at a loss of $1,500. Included in net income is a gain on the sale of land of $9,000.

b. The president of Dunlap Company has set two goals for 1996: (1) increase cash by $40,000 and (2) increase cash dividends by $45,000. The company's activities in 1996 are expected to be quite similar to those of 1995, and no new fixed assets will be acquired.

Required Prepare a schedule showing cash flows from operating activities under the indirect method for 1995. Can the company meet its president's goals for 1996? Explain.

Decision Problem 18–3

Decide whether four real companies can maintain their current dividends (real world problem)
(L.O. 1)

Refer to Appendix E at the end of the text. Evaluate the ease with which each of the four companies represented will be able to maintain their dividend payments in the future at 1989 amounts. (Hint: Compare current dividend amounts with cash flows from operating activities.) Rank the companies in terms of their ability to maintain their dividend payments by dividing their cash flows from operating activities by their dividends paid.

ANSWERS TO SELF-TEST

True-False

1. *True*. Before July 1988, the statement of changes in financial position was required. This statement usually emphasized changes in working capital rather than changes in cash.

2. *True*. The statement of cash flows must be published every time an income statement is published.

3. *False*. Investing activities are transactions involving the acquisition or disposal of noncurrent assets. Transactions with creditors and owners are financing activities.

4. *False*. While the direct method is the method encouraged by the FASB, it is not the predominant method in use. In a recent study, only about 3% of the companies surveyed used the direct method.

5. *True*. Both of these transactions are with owners and therefore would be financing activities.

Multiple-Choice

1. *c*. The descriptions in *(a)* and *(b)* would be correct if they were reversed. The indirect method is easier to use, and this characteristic is probably the main reason why it is used by most companies.

2. *a*. Payment of debt is a financing activity because it is a transaction with creditors. All of the others are investing activities because they are transactions involving the acquisition or disposal of noncurrent assets.

3. *b*. Sales of $500,000 minus the increase in accounts receivable of $30,000 = $470,000.

4. *d*. Cost of goods sold of $300,000, less increase in accounts payable of $20,000, plus increase in inventory of $50,000 = $330,000.

5. *a*. Net income of $200,000, plus depreciation of $10,000, less increase in accounts receivable of $15,000, plus increase in accounts payable of $5,000 = $200,000.

A

SINGLE PROPRIETORSHIPS AND PARTNERSHIPS

INTRODUCTION

As you probably recall from Chapter 1, the three common forms of business entities in the United States are single proprietorships, partnerships, and corporations. This appendix discusses accounting for single proprietorships and partnerships. Single proprietorships and partnerships are more numerous than corporations, but corporations hold more assets and generate substantially more revenues than unincorporated businesses.

The major difference between a single proprietorship and a partnership is the number of owners. The Uniform Partnership Act defines a **partnership** as "an association of two or more persons to carry on as co-owners a business for profit." This "association of persons" must establish the basis on which the partnership will operate—the partnership agreement. As an "association of persons," partnerships have certain characteristics and advantages and disadvantages. However, you will note in studying this appendix that the basic accounting process and accounting principles are the same for both single proprietorships and partnerships.

OWNER'S EQUITY ACCOUNTS

The owner's equity accounts of a single proprietorship consist of a capital account and a drawing account for the owner, as follows:

Kent Holding, Capital
Kent Holding, Drawing

Drawings are cash or other assets taken out of a single proprietorship or partnership by an owner for personal use.

The owners' equity accounts of a partnership consist of a capital account and a drawing account for each partner, as follows:

Sue Camp, Capital
Sue Camp, Drawing

Tom Gilbert, Capital
Tom Gilbert, Drawing

Capital accounts are credited with capital investments (contributions) made by the owners, and drawing accounts are debited for withdrawals of cash or other assets made by the owners. For example, assume that Sam Rachels invested $31,000 in a sporting goods store on January 2, 1994. The following entry was made:

1994				
Jan.	2	Cash	31,000	
		Sam Rachels, Capital		31,000
		To record owner's investment in the business.		

When Mr. Rachels withdrew $1,400 from the business on March 8, 1994, the following entry was made:

1994				
Mar.	8	Sam Rachels, Drawing	1,400	
		Cash		1,400
		To record owner's withdrawal of funds.		

SINGLE PROPRIETORSHIPS

A single proprietorship is a business owned by an individual and often managed by that same individual. The characteristics of the capital and drawing accounts of a single proprietorship are set forth below, based on the trial balance shown in Illustration A.1. Note that the trial balance has no inventory account; the company began its operations this year with a beginning inventory of $0. The ending inventory for Sam Rachels' business at December 31, 1994, was $16,200. When the trial balance was taken at December 31, 1994, the capital and drawing accounts of Rachels were as follows:

Sam Rachels, Capital

Date		Explanation	Post. Ref.	Debit	Credit	Balance
1994 Jan.	2	Cash investment			3 1 0 0 0	3 1 0 0 0

Sam Rachels, Drawing

Date		Explanation	Post. Ref.	Debit	Credit	Balance
1994 Mar.	8	Cash		1 4 0 0		1 4 0 0
June	17	Cash		2 8 0 0		4 2 0 0
Sept.	9	Cash		2 6 0 0		6 8 0 0
Dec.	16	Cash		3 2 0 0		1 0 0 0 0

The ending inventory is set up, and the expense and revenue accounts are closed to Income Summary. The Income Summary account appears as follows:

Income Summary

Date		Explanation	Post. Ref.	Debit	Credit	Balance
1994 Dec.	31	To close sales			1 1 7 0 0 0	1 1 7 0 0 0
	31	To close sales returns and expenses		1 0 1 2 0 0		1 5 8 0 0

The balance of the Income Summary account, $15,800 (representing the net income for the year), is now closed to the Sam Rachels, Capital account:

ILLUSTRATION A.1

Trial Balance of a Single Proprietorship

RACHELS' SPORTING GOODS
Trial Balance
December 31, 1994

	Debits	Credits
Cash	$ 17,600	
Accounts Receivable	21,000	
Accounts Payable		$ 18,000
Sam Rachels, Capital		31,000
Sam Rachels, Drawing	10,000	
Sales		117,000
Sales Returns	5,000	
Purchases	84,000	
Rent Expense	5,200	
Delivery Expense	6,700	
Store Expense	16,500	
	$166,000	$166,000

1994					
Dec.	31	Income Summary		15,800	
		Sam Rachels, Capital			15,800
		To close the Income Summary account.			

Finally, the balance of the drawing account is closed to the capital account:

1994					
Dec.	31	Sam Rachels, Capital		10,000	
		Sam Rachels, Drawing			10,000
		To close the drawing account.			

FINANCIAL STATEMENTS FOR A SINGLE PROPRIETORSHIP

The balance sheet of Rachels' Sporting Goods is shown in Illustration A.2. As the illustration shows, the balance sheet of a single proprietorship differs from that of a corporation only in the owner's equity section. The stockholders' equity section on the balance sheet of a corporation keeps separate accounts for contributed capital and retained earnings, whereas the owner's equity section of the proprietorship commingles both contributed capital and retained earnings in the capital account.

The income statement of a single proprietorship (Illustration A.3) is similar to that of any other type of business organization, except the income of the business is not taxed to the business. All income is taxable to the owner whether withdrawn or not.

A single proprietorship may also prepare a statement of owner's capital, which reflects the changes in the owner's capital account for the year. Such a statement

---

ILLUSTRATION A.2

Balance Sheet of a Single Proprietorship

RACHELS' SPORTING GOODS
Balance Sheet
December 31, 1994

Assets		Liabilities and Owner's Equity	
Current assets:		Current liabilities:	
Cash	$17,600	Accounts payable.	$18,000
Accounts receivable	21,000	Owner's equity:	
Merchandise inventory	16,200	Sam Rachels, capital	36,800
		Total liabilities and owner's	
Total assets	$54,800	equity.	$54,800

ILLUSTRATION A.3

Income Statement of a Single Proprietorship

RACHELS' SPORTING GOODS
Income Statement
For the Year Ended December 31, 1994

Gross sales		$117,000
Less: Sales returns		5,000
Net sales		$112,000
Cost of goods sold:		
Purchases	$84,000	
Deduct: Merchandise Inventory, December 31, 1994	16,200	
Cost of goods sold		67,800
Gross margin		$ 44,200
Deduct operating expenses:		
Rent expense	$ 5,200	
Delivery expense	6,700	
Store expense	16,500	28,400
Net income		$ 15,800

would show the beginning capital balance, add (deduct) net income (loss), add any additional investments, and deduct drawings to arrive at the ending capital balance. The ending capital balance appears on the balance sheet of the single proprietorship under "Owner's equity."

PARTNERSHIPS AND THE PARTNERSHIP AGREEMENT

A partnership is based on a partnership agreement or contract known as the articles of copartnership. The partnership agreement serves as a basis for the formation, operation, and liquidation of a partnership and should be in writing to avoid any misunderstanding or disagreements. Partnerships, however, can be formed without a written agreement.

A partnership agreement should specify the nature of the business, the capital contributions and duties of each partner, and the rights of each partner in the event of dissolution of the partnership. The agreement should also state the manner in which income and losses are to be divided among the partners.

When partners originally draw up their partnership agreement, they cannot anticipate all future events. If an issue relating to the formation, operation, and termination of a partnership arises that is not covered by the agreement, the provisions of the **Uniform Partnership Act** govern in those states that have adopted this act. Otherwise, common law as found in prior court decisions will determine the outcome of the disputed issue.

The Uniform Partnership Act has 45 sections presented in eight major parts. Three of these major parts pertain to:

1. Relations of partners to persons dealing with the partnership.
2. Relations of partners to one another.
3. Dissolution and winding up of a partnership.

Attention will be drawn to some of these sections in the discussion that follows.

CHARACTERISTICS OF A PARTNERSHIP

A partnership has several characteristics that distinguish it from a corporation. These characteristics include voluntary association, mutual agency, limited life, unlimited liability, and co-ownership of property. Each characteristic is discussed below.

Voluntary Association

Any person who has the right to enter into legal contracts may enter into a partnership with other persons. However, a person may not be forced into a partnership against that person's will. Each partner is an owner and member of management, and unless otherwise specified in the partnership agreement, each has an equal voice or vote in the partnership's activities.

Mutual Agency

Each partner is an **agent** of the partnership. This **mutual agency** of partners means each partner has the power to bind the remaining partners to any contract within the apparent scope of the partnership's business. For example, a partner could bind a partnership composed of physicians to a contract for medical supplies, but not to a contract to deliver an airplane. The individual partners must act in the best interests of the partnership and not their personal interests when dealing in partnership matters.

Limited Life

A partnership can be terminated at any time since it is a voluntary association. The **termination (dissolution)** of a partnership may be caused by the withdrawal, retirement, insanity, death, or bankruptcy of any one of the partners. Thus, a partnership is said to have a limited life. If any of the events that may cause dissolution occur, the remaining partners may continue the business, but a new partnership entity is created. A partnership may also end because the period for which it was formed has expired or the specific purpose for which it was organized has been achieved.

Unlimited Liability

Each partner may be held liable for all debts of the partnership—a potential peril known as **unlimited liability** of each partner. If a partnership cannot pay its debts, creditors may satisfy their claims by attaching (seizing) the partners' personal assets.

Each partner's personal creditors have first claim on that partner's personal assets, but any remaining personal assets may be used to satisfy partnership creditors. For example, assume that partner A has personal assets of $10,000 and personal liabilities of $8,000, and the partnership is now unable to pay its creditors. The partnership's creditors could require partner A to pay the $2,000 excess of personal assets over personal debts to satisfy their claims on the partnership. The partnership creditors do not have to divide the debts among all partners; the creditors could seize the assets of only **one** partner to satisfy their claims. A partner who pays all of the partnership's debts acquires the right to be reimbursed by the other partners for their shares of the debts. Persons thinking of entering into a partnership agreement must carefully consider this unlimited liability feature of partnerships.

Co-ownership of Property

When individual partners contribute property, they give up the right to their exclusive use of the property, and the property is owned jointly by all partners. Unless an agreement to the contrary exists, each partner has an equal right to the partnership property.

ADVANTAGES OF A PARTNERSHIP

Forming a partnership has several advantages. A partnership is (1) sufficiently flexible to permit reasonable accumulations of capital and talent, (2) easier and less expensive to organize than a corporation, (3) not required to observe as many laws and regulations as a corporation, and (4) not subject to separate corporation taxation because each partner reports his or her share of partnership income and is individually taxed. Individuals may find it advantageous to form a partnership when (1) business capital requirements exceed the amount that may be raised by a single proprietor or (2) a variety of talent and knowledge from other persons who are willing to share the risks and rewards of ownership may result in a more profitable business.

DISADVANTAGES OF A PARTNERSHIP

Perhaps the greatest disadvantage of a partnership lies in the unlimited liability feature, or the fact that each partner may be held liable for all partnership debts. In this respect, corporations have an advantage over partnerships. A corporation's stockholders are not personally liable for the corporation's debts, and stockholders' losses usually cannot exceed the amount invested in the corporation.

Another disadvantage is the feature of mutual agency. Since one partner may bind the partnership to a contract, a partner who fails to exercise good judgment can cause the loss of partnership assets and, possibly, the loss of personal assets of other partners.

As a functioning organization, a partnership generally becomes unwieldy when it has many partners. And by virtue of the limited life feature, a partnership is subject to possible termination due to many uncontrollable circumstances, such as the death of a partner.

Since partners are co-owners of a partnership's net assets, the transfer of ownership from a partner to another person may be difficult to accomplish. When a partner withdraws from a partnership, the remaining partners will either have to purchase the withdrawing partner's interest or approve of the person to whom that interest is sold. Since a partnership is a **voluntary** association of persons, the remaining partners do not have to accept the buyer of an interest in a partnership as a partner. If a buyer acceptable as a partner cannot be found, the partners may have to terminate the partnership.

UNIQUE FEATURES OF PARTNERSHIP ACCOUNTING

Because a division of interests exists in a partnership that does not exist in a single proprietorship, the accounting records for a partnership differ somewhat from those of a single proprietorship. The unique accounting features in a partnership relate specifically to the partners' capital and drawing accounts, division of business income or loss, and changes in ownership of the partnership.

**The Partners'
Capital Accounts**

A capital account is maintained for each partner. The total balance in a partner's capital account after year-end closing entries represents that partner's ownership equity in the business. Each partner's capital account is:

1. Credited with the original investment.
2. Credited with subsequent investments.
3. Credited with the agreed share of net income.
4. Debited with the agreed share of net loss.
5. Debited with permanent capital reductions.
6. Debited with the balance of the partner's drawing account at the end of each fiscal period.

To illustrate the use of the capital accounts, assume that James Law and Todd Hart, who have each been in business as single proprietors, decide to form a partnership. The formation of a partnership creates a new accounting entity. Since assets of a business should be accounted for at fair market value when they are acquired, the assets contributed by each partner will be recorded at their fair market values. These values may differ from the historical cost amounts shown in the separate accounting records of the individual proprietorships. Shown below are the fair market values of the assets contributed to the partnership and the liabilities assumed by the partnership.

Law		**Hart**	
Cash	$ 5,600	Cash	$ 6,600
Accounts receivable	6,800	Merchandise inventory	3,400
Merchandise inventory	12,000	Land	8,000
Trucks	3,000	Buildings	20,000
Accounts payable	(3,200)	Accounts payable	(2,200)

The journal entries on January 1, 1994, to record the investment of each partner are as follows:

Cash	5,600	
Accounts Receivable	6,800	
Merchandise Inventory	12,000	
Trucks	3,000	
Accounts Payable		3,200
James Law, Capital		24,200
To record the investment of Law in the partnership of Law and Hart.		
Cash	6,600	
Merchandise Inventory	3,400	
Land	8,000	
Buildings	20,000	
Accounts Payable		2,200
Todd Hart, Capital		35,800
To record the investment of Hart in the partnership of Law and Hart.		

On August 1, 1994, the partners made the following additional cash investments that were credited to their capital accounts. The required journal entry is:

Cash	5,800	
James Law, Capital		2,400
Todd Hart, Capital		3,400
To record additional cash investments.		

On December 31, 1994, before closing the books, the capital accounts of the partners would appear as follows (the journal page numbers appearing in the Post. Ref. column throughout this section are assumed page numbers):

James Law, Capital

Date		Explanation	Post. Ref.	Debit	Credit	Balance
1994						
Jan.	1	Original investment	J1		24,200	24,200
Aug.	1	Additional cash investment	J15		2,400	26,600

Todd Hart, Capital

Date		Explanation	Post. Ref.	Debit	Credit	Balance
1994						
Jan.	1	Original investment	J1		35,800	35,800
Aug.	1	Additional cash investment	J15		3,400	39,200

During the accounting period, partners sometimes withdraw cash or merchandise from the partnership for personal use. A drawing account is maintained for each partner to record the partner's withdrawals. The next section discusses withdrawals by partners.

Partners' Drawing Accounts

Partners may withdraw either cash or merchandise from the business. **Withdrawals of cash** are charged to the partners' drawing accounts and credited to Cash. The partnership agreement should specify whether **withdrawals of merchandise** are to be valued at **cost** or **selling price.** If merchandise is valued at cost, the withdrawal is debited to the partner's drawing account and credited to Purchases. If merchandise is valued at selling price, the withdrawal is debited to the partner's drawing account and credited to Sales. As a matter of equity between parties, it would be preferable to charge such merchandise withdrawals at selling price if the withdrawals of one partner will be many times that of the other(s). If all partners withdraw about the same amount, either method will have about the same results.

To illustrate drawing accounts, assume that Hart and Law made withdrawals as indicated below.

James Law, Drawing

Date		Explanation	Post. Ref.	Debit	Credit	Balance
1994						
Feb.	7	Cash	J3	1,600		1,600
Apr.	8	Merchandise (at cost)	J7	1,700		3,300
July	31	Cash	J14	1,750		5,050
Dec.	1	Cash	J23	1,650		6,700

Todd Hart, Drawing

Date		Explanation	Post. Ref.	Debit	Credit	Balance
1994						
Mar.	1	Cash	J5	1,900		1,900
June	7	Cash	J11	1,700		3,600
Sept.	18	Cash	J18	2,000		5,600
Dec.	4	Merchandise (at cost)	J23	1,600		7,200

As a rule, partners may not withdraw any part of their original investment without the consent of all partners. Whether partners may withdraw against any future investments to their capital accounts depends on the partnership agreement. **Withdrawals of investments** should be debited directly to the capital account rather than to the drawing account unless stated otherwise in the agreement. Since withdrawals of investments are not considered normal withdrawals, they are not entered in the drawing account.

End-of-Period Entries

At the end of the fiscal period, adjusting entries are made, and all expense and revenue accounts are closed to Income Summary in the same manner as was illustrated for a single proprietorship. The Income Summary account is closed to the partners' capital accounts (as it was to the owner's capital account in a single proprietorship). The amount of net income or loss allocated to each partner is based on methods outlined in the partnership agreement. Each partner's drawing account is then closed to that partner's capital account. The drawing accounts are not closed to the Income Summary account because they are not an expense of the business but merely temporary owners' equity accounts used to accumulate each partner's withdrawals during a period.

To illustrate, assume that the partnership of Law and Hart has net income of $30,000 for the year ended December 31, 1994, and that the partners had decided to divide income equally. The journal entry to close net income to the capital accounts is:

Income Summary.	30,000	
James Law, Capital		15,000
Todd Hart, Capital		15,000
To close net income to the capital accounts.		

The next step is to close the balances of the partners' drawing accounts (shown in the ledger accounts above) to their capital accounts by the following journal entries:

James Law, Capital	6,700	
James Law, Drawing		6,700
To close the December 31, 1994, drawing account.		
Todd Hart, Capital	7,200	
Todd Hart, Drawing		7,200
To close the December 31, 1994, drawing account.		

After the entries are posted, the drawing and capital accounts of Law and Hart appear as follows:

James Law, Drawing

Date		Explanation	Post. Ref.	Debit	Credit	Balance
1994						
Feb.	7	Cash	J3	1,600		1,600
Apr.	8	Merchandise (at cost)	J7	1,700		3,300
July	31	Cash	J14	1,750		5,050
Dec.	1	Cash	J23	1,650		6,700
	31	To capital	J24		6,700	–0–

James Law, Capital

Date		Explanation	Post. Ref.	Debit	Credit	Balance
1994						
Jan.	1	Original investment	J1		24,200	24,200
Aug.	1	Additional cash investment	J15		2,400	26,600
Dec.	31	Net income	J24		15,000	41,600
	31	From drawing	J24	6,700		34,900

Todd Hart, Drawing

Date		Explanation	Post. Ref.	Debit	Credit	Balance
1994						
Mar.	1	Cash	J5	1,900		1,900
June	7	Cash	J11	1,700		3,600
Sept.	18	Cash	J18	2,000		5,600
Dec.	4	Merchandise (at cost)	J23	1,600		7,200
	31	To capital	J24		7,200	–0–

Todd Hart, Capital

Date		Explanation	Post. Ref.	Debit	Credit	Balance
1994						
Jan.	1	Original investment	J1		35,800	35,800
Aug.	1	Additional cash investment	J15		3,400	39,200
Dec.	31	Net income	J24		15,000	54,200
	31	From drawing	J24	7,200		47,000

DIVISION OF PARTNERSHIP INCOME OR LOSS

Partnership income and losses are divided in accordance with provisions in the partnership agreements. The agreed way that a partnership's income and losses are to be shared is called the income and loss ratio (profit and loss ratio or earnings and loss ratio). **If the agreement is silent with respect to the division of income and losses, income and losses are divided equally among the partners.** If an agreement exists as to income distribution but not losses, losses are divided in the same manner as income. However, a partnership agreement will often specify the means by which both income and losses are to be distributed to the partners.

The method of distribution of income and losses may be based on many factors. If each partner invests an equal amount, has approximately equal ability, devotes the same amount of time to the business, and has the same wealth at risk, then net income or net losses should probably be divided equally. If variations in the foregoing factors exist between partners, a method of income or loss distribution should be devised to reflect such differences. For example, a partner who manages the business all week may be allocated a salary out of net income before an equal distribution of the remainder to all partners. This salary is part of the income sharing agreement and is **not** an expense of the partnership, nor is it a cash outflow of the business.

For example, A and B have a partnership in which partner A manages the store during the week and both partners share the work load equally on the weekends. The partnership agreement states that in sharing income and losses, A is to be given credit for a "salary" of $10,000, and the remaining net income is to be shared equally by the two partners. Net income for the year is $50,000. When the Income Summary account is closed, A's capital account will be credited with $30,000, and B's capital account will be credited with $20,000, as shown below.

	A	B	Total	Net Income to Be Distributed
Net income				$50,000
Salary to A	$10,000		$10,000	40,000
Remainder divided equally	20,000	$20,000	40,000	–0–
Distribution	$30,000	$20,000	$50,000	

In some partnerships, one partner may invest a larger amount of capital than another. When this situation occurs, the partner with the larger capital investment may insist that interest be allowed on capital balances in the division of income, with the remainder to be divided equally among the partners. This **interest** would simply be a means of equitable compensation to the partner with the larger investment. As in the salary example, this interest factor is **not** an expense in income determination.

Common methods of dividing income are listed below. Illustrations of each method follow.

1. Net income divided in a set ratio such as:
   a. Equally.
   b. Agreed ratio other than equal.
   c. Ratio of partners' capital account balances at the beginning of fiscal period.
   d. Ratio of average capital investment.
2. Net income divided by allowing interest on the capital investments, or salaries, or both, with remaining net income divided in an agreed ratio.

Examples showing the division of net income (or net loss) are given in the next section.

Illustrations of Distributions of Partnership Income

The illustrations that follow relate to the partnerships of Anders and Budd. Net income for the year ended December 31, 1994, was $60,000. During 1994, Anders' drawings were $14,000, and Budd's drawings were $22,000. The capital account balances of the partners on December 31, 1994, before closing were Anders, $85,000, and Budd, $134,000.

Case 1.   Net Income Divided by a Set Ratio   The division of income or losses may be based on only one factor, as is shown in each of the following situations.

a. Net Income Divided Equally   In this instance, the income and loss ratio is 1 : 1, or 50% and 50%. The capital accounts of Anders and Budd would each be credited with $30,000 of net income ($60,000/2).

Income Summary.	60,000	
Anders, Capital		30,000
Budd, Capital.		30,000
To record distribution of net income to partners.		

b. Net Income Divided by an Agreed Ratio Other than Equal   Assume that the agreed ratio is 3 : 2 to Anders and Budd, respectively. According to this ratio, 60% would go to Anders and 40% to Budd. Such an income and loss sharing ratio may reflect an attempt to take into consideration such factors as work load or special talent. In this example, Anders would be credited with $36,000 and Budd with $24,000 ($60,000 × 0.60 = $36,000; $60,000 × 0.40 = $24,000).

Income Summary.	60,000	
Anders, Capital		36,000
Budd, Capital.		24,000
To record distribution of net income to partners.		

c. Net Income Divided by Ratio of Partners' Capital Account Balances at the Beginning of the Fiscal Period   Assume that Anders' and Budd's capital balances on January 1, 1994, were $40,000 and $80,000, respectively. Total capital of the partnership at the beginning of the year was $120,000. Assuming a net income of $60,000, Anders had one third ($40,000/$120,000) of the total capital and Budd, two thirds ($80,000/$120,000). Net income is allocated $20,000 (one third of $60,000) to Anders and $40,000 (two thirds of $60,000) to Budd.

Income Summary.	60,000	
Anders, Capital		20,000
Budd, Capital.		40,000
To record distribution of net income to partners.		

d. Net Income Divided by Ratio of Average Capital Investment   Under this method of dividing net income, details must be provided showing the timing of the investment by each partner. Illustration A.4 contains assumed data on Anders' and

ILLUSTRATION A.4
Computation of Average Capital

Anders, Capital

Date	Debits	Credits	Balance	Months Unchanged	Month-Dollars (weighted equivalent)
Jan. 1			$ 40,000	6	$ 240,000
July 1		$15,000	55,000	5	275,000
Dec. 1		30,000	85,000	1	85,000
				12	$ 600,000

Average capital of Anders: $600,000 ÷ 12 = $50,000.

Budd, Capital

Date	Debits	Credits	Balance	Months Unchanged	Month-Dollars (weighted equivalent)
Jan. 1			$ 80,000	7	$ 560,000
Aug. 1		$ 4,000	84,000	3	252,000
Nov. 1		50,000	134,000	2	268,000
				12	$1,080,000

Average capital of Budd: $1,080,000 ÷ 12 = $90,000.

Budd's capital account balances. The "month-dollars" amounts for Anders and Budd are determined by multiplying their balance by the number of months for which this balance remained unchanged. The average capital is found by dividing the total month-dollars by 12.

The ratio of average capital investment is computed by dividing each partner's average capital by the total average capital of $140,000 ($50,000 for Anders and $90,000 for Budd). This ratio is then used to compute the distribution of net income. Thus, Anders' capital account is credited with $21,429 ($50,000/$140,000 × $60,000) of net income; Budd's capital account is credited with $38,571 ($90,000/$140,000 × $60,000).

Income Summary.	60,000	
Anders, Capital		21,429
Budd, Capital.		38,571
To record distribution of net income to partners.		

Case 2. Net Income Divided by Allowing Salaries, or Interest on Capital Investments, or Both, with Remaining Net Income Divided by an Agreed Ratio   Salary and interest allowances may be specified in the partnership agreement to compensate partners for differences in investment, time spent with the business, and other factors.

a. Continuing the example of the Anders and Budd partnership, assume that salaries allowed are Anders, $16,000; and Budd, $10,000. The partners are also to be allowed 6% interest on their beginning capital balances. January 1 capital balances were Anders, $40,000; and Budd, $80,000. The remaining income is to be divided equally. The $60,000 net income for the current year is distributed as follows:

	Anders	Budd	Total	Income to Be Distributed
Net income				$60,000
Salary	$16,000	$10,000	$26,000	34,000
Interest (6% on beginning				
capital balance)	2,400	4,800	7,200	26,800
Remainder divided equally	13,400	13,400	26,800	–0–
Distribution	$31,800	$28,200	$60,000	

The entry to divide net income is:

Income Summary.	60,000	
Anders, Capital		31,800
Budd, Capital.		28,200
To record net income between the partners.		

b. **Even if the allowances for salaries and interest exceed net income, or if the period has a net loss, the partners still are given credit for their full amounts of interest and salary.** For example, in the situation above, if there was a loss of $20,000 instead of net income of $60,000 for the year, the division would be as follows:

	Anders	Budd	Total	Loss to Be Distributed
Net loss				$(20,000)
Salary	$ 16,000	$ 10,000	$ 26,000	(46,000)
Interest (6% on beginning				
capital balance)	2,400	4,800	7,200	(53,200)
Remainder divided equally	(26,600)	(26,600)	(53,200)	–0–
Distribution	$ (8,200)	$(11,800)	$(20,000)	

The entry to divide the net loss would be:

Anders, Capital	8,200	
Budd, Capital.	11,800	
Income Summary.		20,000
To divide net loss between the partners.		

c. The sharing of income may result in a credit to one partner's capital account and a debit to another partner's capital account. For example, assume that the partnership earned $3,200 of net income for the current year. The $3,200 would be distributed as follows:

	Anders	Budd	Total	Income to Be Distributed
Net income				$ 3,200
Salary	$ 16,000	$ 10,000	$ 26,000	(22,800)
Interest (6% on beginning				
capital balance)	2,400	4,800	7,200	(30,000)
Remainder divided equally	(15,000)	(15,000)	(30,000)	–0–
Distribution	$ 3,400	$ (200)	$ 3,200	

The entry to close the Income Summary account would be:

```
Income Summary.  .  .  .  .  .  .  .  .  .  .  .  .  .  .  .  .  .  .  .  .  .  .  .  .    3,200
Budd, Capital.  .  .  .  .  .  .  .  .  .  .  .  .  .  .  .  .  .  .  .  .  .  .  .  .  .      200
      Anders, Capital.  .  .  .  .  .  .  .  .  .  .  .  .  .  .  .  .  .  .  .  .  .  .                 3,400
   To divide net income between the partners.
```

Partnership Agreement Governs   This section has illustrated some factors that partners might consider when drawing up the income or sharing provisions in the partnership agreement. However, income may be shared in **any** manner the partners decide. Once the partners agree on how income is to be shared, the accountant's task is simply to apply the agreed provisions as literally as possible.

FINANCIAL STATEMENTS OF A PARTNERSHIP

Since a partnership is very similar to a single proprietorship, the accounting and financial reporting for these forms of organization are basically the same. As shown above, a partnership has as many capital accounts as it has partners, and any income or losses must be distributed to these accounts. This section details the preparation of financial statements for a partnership.

Partnership Income Statement

A partnership's income statement may differ slightly from that of a single proprietorship. Since partners are co-owners of the business, the income statement may contain a schedule showing the distribution of the period's net income or net loss to each partner. Illustration A.5 shows this feature for the Anders and Budd partnership using the data given in Case 2(a) on pages 890–91.

Statement of Partners' Capital

At the close of each period, a statement of partners' capital is prepared. This statement (1) is prepared from the capital accounts in the general ledger, (2) summarizes the effects of transactions of the capital account balance of each partner and in total for all partners for the period, and (3) serves the same purpose as the statement of owner's capital in a single proprietorship.

The statement of partners' capital presents details not readily shown on the balance sheet. The balance sheet contains only the final balance of each partner's capital account when it is accompanied by a statement of partners' capital.

The statement of partners' capital for the Anders and Budd partnership is presented in Illustration A.6. The statement is prepared by using the information on additional investments given in Illustration A.4 and information on drawings given on page 889.

ILLUSTRATION A.5

Partnership Income Statement

ANDERS AND BUDD
Income Statement
For the Year Ended December 31, 1994

Sales		$600,000
Cost of goods sold		360,400
Gross margin		$239,600
Operating expenses:		
Miscellaneous selling	$100,000	
Miscellaneous administrative	80,000	180,000
Net operating income		$ 59,600
Nonoperating revenue: Interest		400
Net income		$ 60,000

Distribution of Net Income

	Anders	Budd	Total
Salary	$16,000	$10,000	$26,000
Interest	2,400	4,800	7,200
Remainder equally	13,400	13,400	26,800
Net income	$31,800	$28,200	$60,000

ILLUSTRATION A.6

Statement of Partners' Capital

ANDERS AND BUDD
Statement of Partners' Capital
For the Year Ended December 31, 1994

	Anders	Budd	Total
Capital account balances, January 1, 1994	$ 40,000	$ 80,000	$120,000
Add: Additional investments	45,000	54,000	99,000
Capital account balances, December 31, 1994, before 1994 income distribution	$ 85,000	$134,000	$219,000
Net income per income statement	31,800	28,200	60,000
Capital account balances before drawings are deducted	$116,800	$162,200	$279,000
Deduct: Drawings	14,000	22,000	36,000
Capital account balances, December 31, 1994	$102,800	$140,200	$243,000

Partnership Balance Sheet

The only distinctive feature of a partnership balance sheet is the presentation of the capital accounts in the owners' equity section, as shown in Illustration A.7. Instead of a single capital account, the owners' equity section contains a separate capital account for each partner. However, if a partnership has many partners, the balance sheet may show only the total amount, called *Partners' capital*. Then, each partner's name and capital balance would be reported in a supporting schedule. Accountants use supporting schedules to provide detailed information concerning individual items on the primary financial statements.

ILLUSTRATION A.7

Partnership Balance Sheet

ANDERS AND BUDD
Balance Sheet
December 31, 1994

Assets		Liabilities and Owners' Equity		
Cash	$ xxx	Liabilities:		
Accounts receivable	xxx	Accounts payable . .	$ xxx	
Merchandise inventory	xxx	Notes payable	xxx	
Land	xxx	Total liabilities . . .	$ xxx	
		Owners' equity:		
		Anders, capital	$102,800	
		Budd, capital	140,200	243,000
		Total liabilities and		
Total assets	$ xxx	owners' equity		$ xxx

Note: No amounts are provided for items other than owners' equity because these amounts were not given in the illustrative data.

Because partnerships are voluntary associations among people, the possibility of changes in ownership exists. In the next section, we discuss some of the changes in partnership composition and how these changes are recorded in the accounts of a partnership.

CHANGES IN PARTNERSHIP COMPOSITION

A partnership is legally terminated when a new partner is admitted or an existing partner withdraws, retires, or dies. Usually, the old partnership is succeeded without interruption by the new partnership that differs from the old partnership only to the extent of the change in partners. Then, the partnership termination is only technical, and the business operations and accounting continue. Such a technical termination of a partnership, which we discuss next, differs substantially from liquidation of a partnership, which we discuss later in this appendix.

Admission of a New Partner

A new partner can gain admission to a partnership either by purchasing an interest from one or more existing partners or by investing assets in the partnership. Illustration A.8 shows each of these options.

Purchase of an Interest in a Personal Transaction between Individuals   When a new partner purchases an interest directly from an existing partner, the partnership's assets and liabilities remain unchanged. The exchange of cash and other assets for the equity interest is a personal transaction between two individuals, occurring outside the partnership. **The entry on the partnership's books simply transfers a portion of the partnership capital from the outgoing partner to the incoming partner.**

To illustrate, assume that Smith and Jones are partners with capital account balances of $15,000 and $13,000, respectively. Farr purchases from Jones an $8,000 interest in the partnership capital. The journal entry on the partnership's books is:

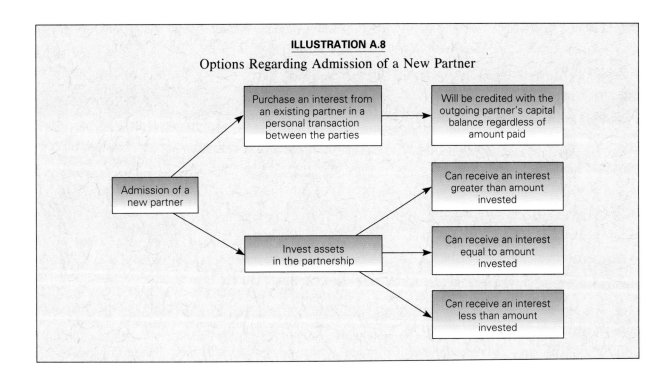

ILLUSTRATION A.8

Options Regarding Admission of a New Partner

Jones, Capital	8,000	
Farr, Capital		8,000
To transfer $8,000 of Jones' interest in the partnership assets to Farr.		

The price that Farr paid Jones might be more or less than $8,000, but this difference is not reflected on the books of the partnership since there was no flow of assets to or from the partnership. The journal entry merely reflects the transfer of the $8,000 interest in the partnership from the old partner to the new partner.

Investment in the Partnership When a new partner acquires an interest in a partnership by investing assets (such as cash, inventory, or buildings) in the business, both partnership assets and total owners' equity increase. The journal entry for such an investment must record these increases. Three examples of a new partner's investment in a partnership follow.

Case 1. New Partner Receives an Interest Equal to Amount Invested To illustrate, assume that the partnership of Crowe and Lang has the following assets and equities:

Assets		Equities	
Cash	$15,000	Crowe, capital	$35,000
Other assets	55,000	Lang, capital	35,000
Total assets	$70,000	Total equities	$70,000

Crowe and Lang agree to admit Potter as a partner with a 50% interest in the partnership in return for an investment of $70,000 cash. The entry to record Potter's investment is:

Cash	70,000	
Potter, Capital		70,000
To record Potter's investment in the partnership.		

After the above transaction, the partnership will have the following assets and equities:

Assets		Equities	
Cash	$ 85,000	Crowe, capital	$ 35,000
Other assets.	55,000	Lang, capital	35,000
		Potter, capital	70,000
Total assets	$140,000	Total equities	$140,000

The one-half interest in the equity of the partnership credited to Potter does not automatically entitle Potter to receive one half of the future income or loss of the partnership. Income and loss distribution is a separate matter on which the three partners must agree. If the new partnership agreement does not specify how income and losses are to be shared, the law assumes that the new partners intend to share income and losses equally, which means Crowe, Lang, and Potter would each receive one third of the income or loss.

Case 2. New Partner Receives an Interest Less than Amount Invested If an existing partnership consistently earns above-average income, the existing partners may require a new partner to pay a bonus for admission to the partnership. For example, Marsh and Will operate a partnership that has had above-average net income for the past 10 years. The two partners share income and losses in a ratio of 2:1—that is, Marsh receives two thirds and Will receives one third. The partners' capital account balances show $55,000 for Marsh and $75,000 for Will. Marsh and Will agree to admit Gray as a partner with a one-fourth interest in both capital and income in exchange for $50,000. Gray's equity in the partnership is $45,000, computed as follows:

Equities of old partners ($55,000 + $75,000)	$130,000
Investment of new partner	50,000
Total equities of new partnership.	$180,000
Gray's one-fourth equity ($180,000 × ¼)	$ 45,000

The entry to record Gray's investment in the partnership is:

Cash	50,000	
Gray, Capital		45,000
Marsh, Capital (⅔ of $5,000).		3,333
Will, Capital (⅓ of $5,000)		1,667
To record Gray's investment in partnership.		

Notice that Gray paid $50,000 for an equity of only $45,000. The $5,000 difference is a bonus to the existing partners, which they share according to their income and loss ratio 2 : 1.

Case 3.   New Partner Receives an Interest Greater than Amount Invested   Sometimes an incoming partner may be able to provide cash that is desperately needed by the business, or may have extraordinary abilities or business contacts that can help increase the partnership's income. In such cases, the existing partners may be willing to give the new partner a bonus—that is, an equity in the partnership greater than the new partner's investment. For example, assume Bentz and Hahn are partners with capital balances of $100,000 and $60,000, respectively. They share income and losses in a 3 : 2 ratio. The partnership desperately needs cash, so the partners are willing to give Kirby a one-fourth equity interest in the partnership for an investment of only $40,000 cash. Kirby agrees, invests $40,000, and receives an equity interest computed as follows:

Equities of old partners ($100,000 + $60,000)	$160,000
Investment of new partner	40,000
Total equities of new partnership	$200,000
Kirby's one-fourth equity ($200,000 × ¼)	$ 50,000

The entry to record Kirby's investment in the partnership is:

Cash	40,000	
Bentz, Capital (⅗ of $10,000)	6,000	
Hahn, Capital (⅖ of $10,000)	4,000	
Kirby, Capital		50,000
To record Kirby's investment in partnership.		

Notice that the $10,000 bonus is contributed by the old partners in their income and loss sharing ratio of 3 : 2. After Kirby is admitted to the partnership, the partners should agree on new income sharing provisions.

Alternative methods could be used to record the admission of a new partner, but these methods are left for an advanced text. Next, we consider changes in partnership ownership brought about by the retirement or withdrawal of a partner.

Retirement or Withdrawal of a Partner

When partners decide to retire, two options exist: they can sell their partnership interest, or they can withdraw assets from the partnership. Partners can sell their interest to existing partners or to a new partner. Illustration A.9 summarizes the options available to a retiring partner. Each option requires the consent of the existing partners.

Sale of an Interest in a Personal Transaction between Individuals   When a retiring partner sells his or her interest to the existing partners or to a new partner, the entry made on the partnership books transfers the retiring partner's capital balance to the purchaser(s). To illustrate, assume that Harris, a partner in the Harris, Brown, and Wilson partnership, sells his $100,000 interest in the partnership to Brown and Wilson (equally) for $125,000. The entry would be:

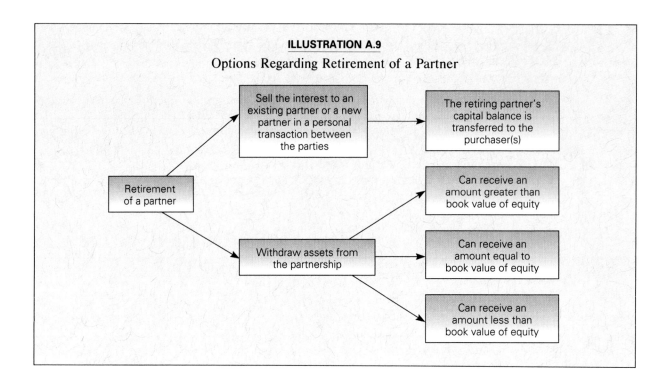

ILLUSTRATION A.9

Options Regarding Retirement of a Partner

Harris, Capital 100,000	
Brown, Capital	50,000
Wilson, Capital	50,000
To transfer Harris' capital balance to Brown and Wilson.	

The amount paid is not recorded on the partnership books because the transaction was between individuals and involved no flow of assets to or from the partnership.

If Harris sells his equity interest to a new partner, Roberts, for $85,000, the entry would be:

Harris, Capital 100,000	
Roberts, Capital	100,000
To transfer Harris' capital balance to Roberts.	

Again, regardless of the amount exchanged between the individuals, the only entry is one transferring the retiring partner's capital balance to the purchaser.

Withdrawal of Assets from Partnership A partnership agreement should contain the procedures to be followed when a partner retires. Specifically, these procedures should indicate how to compute the price the partnership should pay for the retiring partner's equity interest.

To compute this price, the first step is usually to have the partnership accounts audited to ensure their accuracy. Then, the fair market values of the assets are determined. When the assets are revalued at their fair market values, the partners' capital accounts should reflect the gains and losses from this revaluation. This revaluation is necessary because (1) after the withdrawal of a partner, a new entity is created that should record its assets at their fair values at the time of reorganization; and (2) the retiring partner will be credited or charged for a share of previously unrecorded gains or losses that must be considered in computing the retiring partner's share of the partnership's net assets at time of withdrawal. The retiring partner is typically paid an amount equal to the new balance in that partner's capital account.

Sometimes asset revaluations are not recorded when a partner retires, and the retiring partner is paid an amount that differs from the partner's capital account balance. Such asset revaluations might not be reflected because (1) too much effort may be required to change recorded book values, (2) the partners may not want to pay for an audit of the books and records, and (3) the partners may underestimate the effect that the difference between book values and fair market values would have on their capital balances.

Next, we give three examples illustrating the withdrawal of assets from the partnership by a retiring partner. In these examples, the retiring partner receives (1) adjusted book value of equity, (2) more than the adjusted book value of equity, and (3) less than the book value of equity.

Case 1. Retiring Partner Receives Adjusted Book Value of Equity Assume that Green, South, and Rock are partners sharing income and losses in a 3 : 1 : 1 ratio. Rock decides to retire when the partnership books show the following recorded values:

Assets			Equities	
Cash		$ 30,000	Green, capital	$ 50,000
Accounts receivable . .		10,000	South, capital	30,000
Merchandise inventory		40,000	Rock, capital	20,000
Equipment	$50,000			
Less: Accumulated				
depreciation	30,000	20,000		
Total assets		$100,000	Total equities	$100,000

The partnership books are audited. Certain accounts receivable, recorded at $500, are found to be uncollectible and are written off. Since changes in replacement costs occurred, merchandise inventory is revalued at $45,500, and plant and equipment are revalued at $54,000. Accumulated depreciation is increased to $32,000. The journal entries to record this information are:

Green, Capital	300	
South, Capital	100	
Rock, Capital	100	
Accounts Receivable		500
To write off uncollectible accounts receivable.		
Merchandise Inventory	5,500	
Green, Capital		3,300
South, Capital		1,100
Rock, Capital		1,100
To revalue inventory.		
Equipment	4,000	
Accumulated Depreciation—Equipment		2,000
Green, Capital		1,200
South, Capital		400
Rock, Capital		400
To revalue plant and equipment.		

Assuming that the gains and losses computed from asset revaluations eventually would have been realized and reflected in net income, the partners would share these gains and losses according to their income and loss ratio. Thus, after the above entries have been posted, the restated amounts of the partnership's assets and equities would be:

Assets			Equities		
Cash		$ 30,000	Green, capital		$ 54,200
Accounts receivable . .		9,500	South, capital		31,400
Merchandise inventory .		45,500	Rock, capital		21,400
Equipment	$54,000				
Less: Accumulated					
depreciation	32,000	22,000			
Total assets		$107,000	Total equities		$107,000

With assets revalued and capital accounts adjusted, Rock has a $21,400 interest in partnership assets. Assuming that Rock is paid cash, the entry to record Rock's retirement is:

Rock, Capital	21,400	
Cash		21,400
To record Rock's withdrawal from the partnership.		

Instead of cash, Rock could have received any combination of assets (such as some inventory and a car owned by the partnership) totaling $21,400 to which the partners agreed. Or Rock could have accepted a note payable by the new partnership of Green and South. In any case, Green and South must now agree on a new income and loss sharing provision because a new partnership entity exists.

Case 2.   *Retiring Partner Receives More than the Book Value of Equity*   Sometimes the partners may not revalue assets or adjust the accounts when a partner withdraws. Instead, the partners may agree that the assets are undervalued and the withdrawing partner should receive assets worth **more** than the book value of that partner's equity; or the remaining partners may be so anxious for the partner to withdraw that they are willing to give up assets worth **more** than the book value of that partner's equity. In both cases, the retiring partner, in effect, withdraws assets equal to the book value of that partner's own equity plus part of the book value of the remaining partners' equities.

To illustrate, assume that North, East, and West are partners who share income and losses in a 3 : 2 : 1 ratio. East withdraws from the partnership at a time when it has the following assets and equities:

Assets		Equities	
Cash	$30,000	North, capital	$50,000
Merchandise inventory	40,000	East, capital	25,000
Equipment, net	20,000	West, capital	15,000
Total assets	$90,000	Total equities	$90,000

The partners agree that the assets are undervalued by $3,000, but they do not wish to adjust the accounts to current market values. If the accounts had been revalued, East's capital account would have been increased by $1,000, or two sixths of the $3,000 adjustment. East is therefore allowed to withdraw $26,000 cash from the partnership for his equity interest. The entry to record East's withdrawal is:

East, Capital	25,000	
North, Capital	750	
West, Capital.	250	
Cash		26,000
To record East's withdrawal from the partnership.		

East withdrew $1,000 more than the book value of his equity. Instead of revaluing the assets and adjusting the accounts (as shown in Case 1), the excess amount of $1,000 is charged to North's and West's capital accounts on the basis of their income and loss ratio of 3 : 1 (¾ × $1,000 = $750 to North; and ¼ × $1,000 = $250 to West).

Case 3.   *Retiring Partner Receives Less than the Book Value of Equity*

Sometimes the partners may agree that the assets are overvalued in the books, but do not want to adjust the accounts when one partner retires. The partners may then agree that the withdrawing partner should receive assets worth **less** than the book value of his or her equity. Or a partner may be so anxious to withdraw from a partnership that the partner is willing to accept assets worth **less** than the book value of his or her equity. In both cases, the undrawn equity is divided between the remaining partners in their income and loss ratio and credited to their capital accounts.

To illustrate, assume that Alda, Fonda, and Moore are partners who share income and losses in an 8 : 7 : 5 ratio. The partnership's assets and equities follow:

Assets		**Equities**	
Cash	$21,000	Alda, capital	$25,000
Merchandise inventory	24,000	Fonda, capital	22,000
Equipment, net	20,000	Moore, capital	18,000
Total assets	$65,000	Total equities	$65,000

Moore is anxious to withdraw from the partnership and willing to accept $16,000 as an equity settlement. Alda and Fonda agree to the settlement. The entry to record Moore's withdrawal is:

Moore, Capital	18,000	
Cash		16,000
Alda, Capital		1,067
Fonda, Capital		933
To record Moore's withdrawal from the partnership.		

Moore withdrew $2,000 less than the book value of her equity. The undrawn $2,000 is credited to the capital accounts of Alda and Fonda in their income and loss sharing ratio of 8 : 7, that is, ⁸⁄₁₅ × $2,000 and ⁷⁄₁₅ × $2,000.

The illustrations above involved technical terminations or dissolutions of partnerships. One partnership was terminated but was succeeded immediately by another partnership that carried on substantially the same business operations. In the next section, attention is given to circumstances in which business operations cease, and the partnership is legally terminated.

LIQUIDATION OF A PARTNERSHIP

The **liquidation of a partnership** means that business operations have ended, assets have been sold for cash, cash has been paid to creditors and partners, and the partnership has been legally terminated.

Partnerships may be liquidated for a number of reasons. Some common reasons for liquidation include:

1. The objective sought in forming the partnership has been achieved.
2. The time period for which the partnership was formed has expired.
3. Newly enacted legislation has made the partnership's activities illegal.
4. The partnership or one of its partners is bankrupt.

Liquidation may take place rapidly or over an extended period. If liquidation is rapid, a single cash distribution may be made to the partners after all assets are sold and the liabilities paid. If liquidation is prolonged, more than one cash distribution may be made to the partners. Only those liquidations that involve a single payment to partners are discussed below.

Partnership Liquidation Illustrated

In the following illustrations, we assume that all noncash assets are sold, the resulting gain or loss is distributed to the partners' capital accounts, all liabilities are paid, and a single distribution is made to partners to complete the liquidation process.

The partnership of Ring, Scott, and Terry is liquidated on August 1, 1994. The income and loss ratio is Ring, 40%; Scott, 35%; and Terry, 25%. A condensed trial balance prepared just before liquidation is shown in Illustration A.10. The three cases that follow are based on the Ring, Scott, and Terry partnership.

Case 1. Assets Sold at a Gain   The noncash assets are sold for $95,000, and the $5,000 gain on the sale is distributed to the partners in their income and loss ratio. The liabilities are paid in full. **The remaining cash is distributed to the partners in accordance with the balances of their capital accounts, not in the income and loss ratio.**

The journal entries to record the foregoing facts and the liquidation of the partnership on August 1, 1994, follow:

Cash	95,000	
Other Assets.		90,000
Gain on Disposal of Plant Assets		5,000
To record disposal of plant assets..		
Gain on Disposal of Plant Assets	5,000	
Ring, Capital ($5,000 × 0.40).		2,000
Scott, Capital ($5,000 × 0.35)		1,750
Terry, Capital ($5,000 × 0.25)		1,250
To distribute gain on disposal of plant assets.		
Other Liabilities.	10,000	
Cash		10,000
To record the settlement of partnership liabilities.		

After the above entries are posted, the partners' capital accounts show:

Ring, Capital		Scott, Capital		Terry, Capital	
	Beg. bal. 30,000		Beg. bal. 30,000		Beg. bal. 30,000
	Gain from disposal of plant assets 2,000		Gain from disposal of plant assets 1,750		Gain from disposal of plant assets 1,250
	End. bal. 32,000		End. bal. 31,750		End. bal. 31,250

The Cash account now shows a balance of $95,000 (or $10,000 + $95,000 − $10,000). The entry to record the cash distributed to partners is:

Ring, Capital	32,000	
Scott, Capital	31,750	
Terry, Capital	31,250	
Cash		95,000
To distribute remaining cash to partners based on balances of their capital accounts.		

Case 2. Assets Sold at a Loss The noncash assets of Ring, Scott, and Terry are sold for $70,000, and the $20,000 loss on the sale is distributed to the partners' capital accounts according to the income and loss ratio. The liabilities are paid in full. The remaining cash is distributed to the partners in accordance with the balances of their capital accounts.

The journal entries are:

Cash	70,000	
Loss from Disposal of Plant Assets	20,000	
Other Assets		90,000
To record disposal of plant assets.		
Ring, Capital (20,000 × 0.40)	8,000	
Scott, Capital (20,000 × 0.35)	7,000	
Terry, Capital (20,000 × 0.25)	5,000	
Loss from Disposal of Plant Assets		20,000
To distribute the loss from disposal of plant assets.		
Other Liabilities	10,000	
Cash		10,000
To record the settlement of partnership liabilities.		

After the above entries have been posted, the accounts show Cash, $70,000; Ring, Capital, $22,000; Scott, Capital, $23,000; and Terry, Capital, $25,000. The entry to record the cash distributed to partners is:

Ring, Capital	22,000	
Scott, Capital	23,000	
Terry, Capital	25,000	
Cash		70,000
To distribute cash to partners.		

Case 3. Assets Sold at a Loss When One Partner's Share of the Loss Is Greater than the Balance of that Partner's Capital Account In Case 2, the loss charged to the capital account of each partner is smaller than that partner's capital account

ILLUSTRATION A.10

Condensed Trial Balance

RING, SCOTT, AND TERRY
Trial Balance
August 1, 1994

	Debits	Credits
Cash	$ 10,000	
Other Assets	90,000	
Other Liabilities		$ 10,000
Ring, Capital.		30,000
Scott, Capital		30,000
Terry, Capital		30,000
	$100,000	$100,000

balance. However, a partner's share of the loss may be greater than that partner's capital account balance. When a loss is charged to a partner and a debit balance is created in that partner's capital account, the debit balance represents an amount owed by that partner to the partnership. The cash available for distribution will be insufficient to pay the other partners in full until the partner with the debit balance pays in the amount owed to the partnership. If the partner with the debit balance is unable to pay, the remaining partners must bear this loss according to the income and loss ratio existing between them.

To illustrate, assume that the noncash assets of Ring, Scott, and Terry are sold for only $10,200. Entries to record the foregoing facts and the liquidation of the partnership follow:

Cash	10,200	
Loss from Disposal of Plant Assets	79,800	
Other Assets		90,000
To record disposal of plant assets.		
Ring, Capital (79,800 × 0.40)	31,920	
Scott, Capital (79,800 × 0.35)	27,930	
Terry, Capital (79,800 × 0.25)	19,950	
Loss from Disposal of Plant Assets		79,800
To distribute loss from disposal of plant assets.		
Other Liabilities.	10,000	
Cash		10,000
To record the settlement of partnership liabilities.		

At this stage of the liquidation, the partner's capital accounts have the following balances:

Ring, Capital		Scott, Capital		Terry, Capital	
	Beg. bal. 30,000		Beg. bal. 30,000		Beg. bal. 30,000
Loss from disposal of plant assets 31,920		Loss from disposal of plant assets 27,930		Loss from disposal of plant assets 19,950	
End. bal. 1,920		End. bal. 2,070		End. bal. 10,050	

ILLUSTRATION A.11

Liquidation Work Sheet

	Ring	Scott	Terry	Total
Income and loss ratio	40%	35%	25%	100%
Original capital account balance	$ 30,000	$ 30,000	$ 30,000	$ 90,000
Apportionment of loss on sale of assets	(31,920)	(27,930)	(19,950)	(79,800)
Capital balances after loss apportionment	$ (1,920)	$ 2,070	$ 10,050	$ 10,200
Ring's cash contribution	1,920			1,920
Ending capital account balances	$ –0–	$ 2,070	$ 10,050	$ 12,120
Liquidating distribution		(2,070)	(10,050)	(12,120)
Balance	$ –0–	$ –0–	$ –0–	$ –0–

Note: ( ) = debit.

Only $10,200 (or $10,000 + $10,200 − $10,000) of cash is available for distribution to Scott and Terry, while the combined balance of their capital accounts is $12,120. To pay Scott and Terry the amounts owed, the partnership needs $1,920 more cash, which is the amount owed the partnership by Ring who is unable to pay. The $1,920 is thus a loss that must be shared by Scott and Terry in their income and loss sharing ratio of 35 : 25. Thus, Scott's share of the loss is $1,120 (or $35/60 \times \$1,920$), and Terry's share is $800 (or $25/60 \times \$1,920$).

The debit balance in Ring's capital account is closed and the loss absorbed by Scott and Terry, as shown in the following entry:

Scott, Capital.	1,120	
Terry, Capital.	800	
Ring, Capital		1,920
To charge Scott and Terry with Ring's capital deficiency.		

The only accounts left on the books now are the Cash account and Scott's and Terry's capital accounts. The remaining cash is distributed to Scott and Terry in the amounts now shown in their capital accounts:

Scott, Capital.	950	
Terry, Capital.	9,250	
Cash		10,200
To record final cash distribution to partners.		

With this entry, all accounts of the partnership now have zero balances, and the partnership has ended. As individuals, Scott and Terry have the legal right to collect the $1,920 Ring owes them. However, the partnership is now liquidated; no further entries will be made on its books.

Suppose that in the example above, Ring was able to pay the $1,920 owed the partnership prior to closing the accounts. The following entries would be needed:

Cash		1,920	
Ring, Capital			1,920
To record payment of capital deficiency by Ring.			
Scott, Capital		2,070	
Terry, Capital		10,050	
Cash			12,120
To record final cash distribution to partners in liquidation.			

Notice that Ring does not receive any cash in the final settlement. He had to pay cash to the partnership to bring his capital account to a zero balance.

Assuming that Ring pays the amount owed the partnership, the analysis of the partnership liquidation may be aided by the preparation of a liquidation work sheet as shown in Illustration A.11.

The liquidation work sheet brings together all the necessary calculations and illustrates the amounts involved in a partnership liquidation. This work sheet can be helpful to the accountant, the partners, and other interested parties.

DEMONSTRATION PROBLEM

The Rowle and Davis partnership had the following income and loss sharing agreement:

1. Rowle receives an annual salary of $24,000.
2. Rowle and Davis each receive interest of 10% on their capital balances at the beginning of the year.
3. The remainder is divided by Rowle and Davis in a 2 : 1 ratio.

On January 1, 1994, the partners' capital account balances were Rowle, $60,000; and Davis, $80,000. On December 31, 1994, the partners' drawing account balances were Rowle, $20,000; and Davis, $16,000. Net income for the year ended December 31, 1994, was $40,000.

Required   *a.*   Prepare a schedule showing the distribution of net income to the partners.

            b.   Prepare journal entries to close the Income Summary account and the drawing accounts.

            c.   Assume that on January 1, 1995, Rowle and Davis admitted Becky to a 25% interest in capital for an investment of $64,000 cash. Prepare the entry to admit Becky.

SOLUTION TO DEMONSTRATION PROBLEM

a.

	Rowle	Davis	Total	Amount to Be Distributed
Net income				$40,000
Salaries	$24,000	$–0–	$24,000	16,000
Interest on beginning capital balances:				
Rowle (10% of $60,000)	6,000			
Davis (10% of $80,000)		8,000	14,000	2,000
Remainder (2 : 1)	1,334	666	2,000	–0–
Distribution	$31,334	$8,666	$40,000	

b.

1994 Dec.	31	Income Summary	40,000	
		Rowle, Capital.		31,334
		Davis, Capital		8,666
		To divide net income between the partners.		
	31	Rowle, Capital.	20,000	
		Davis, Capital	16,000	
		Rowle, Drawing		20,000
		Davis, Drawing		16,000
		To close drawing accounts.		

c.

1994 Jan.	1	Cash	64,000	
		Becky, Capital.		52,000
		Rowle, Capital.		8,000
		Davis, Capital		4,000
		To record admission of Becky to the partnership.		

Computations are:

Equities of old partners on January 1, 1994 ($60,000 + $80,000)	$140,000
Net income for 1994	40,000
Drawings in 1994	(36,000)
Equities of old partners, January 1, 1995	$144,000
Capital contributed by Becky	64,000
Total capital after admission of Becky . . .	$208,000
Becky's share ($208,000 × 25%)	$ 52,000
Bonus to the old partners: $64,000 − $52,000	$ 12,000
Rowle: $12,000 × ⅔ = ...	$ 8,000
Davis: $12,000 × ⅓ = ...	4,000

NEW TERMS

Agent One who has the authority to act for another (the partnership) or in the place of another. See Mutual agency. *882*

Articles of copartnership See Partnership agreement. *881*

Drawings Cash or other assets taken out of a single proprietorship or partnership by an owner for personal use. *878*

Income and loss ratio The agreed way that a partnership's income or losses are shared. Often called the **profit and loss ratio** or the **earnings and loss ratio**. *888*

Interest (on capital invested) A means often used in the sharing of income to give weight to the relative amounts of capital invested by the partners. The interest is sometimes based on the beginning-of-year balances in the capital accounts and sometimes on the average balances in the capital accounts. The interest is **not** an expense to be deducted in arriving at net income, nor is it a cash outflow of the business. *888*

Liquidation of a partnership Means that business operations have ended, assets have been sold for cash, cash has been paid to creditors and partners, and the partnership has been legally terminated. *902*

Mutual agency The power possessed by a partner to bind a partnership to any contract within the apparent scope of the partnership's business. *882*

Partnership "An association of two or more persons to carry on as co-owners a business for profit." *878*

Partnership agreement Also known as articles of copartnership (when in written form); the conditions or provisions accepted by all of the partners to serve as the basis for the formation, operation, and liquidation of the partnership. *881*

Salary (granted to partners) A means often used in the sharing of income to reward certain partners for spending more time than other partners in running the affairs of the business. This salary is **not** an expense of the partnership in determining net income, nor is it a cash outflow of the business. *888*

Single proprietorship   A business owned by an individual and often managed by that same individual. *879*

Statement of owner's capital   A financial statement that summarizes the transactions affecting the capital balance of the sole proprietor for a period of time. *880*

Statement of partners' capital   A financial statement that (1) is prepared from the capital accounts in the general ledger, (2) summarizes the effects of transactions on the capital balance of each partner and in total for all partners, and (3) serves the same purpose as the statement of owner's capital in a single proprietorship. *892*

Termination (dissolution)   The legal dissolution of a partnership brought on by a change in partners. *882*

Uniform Partnership Act   A written law adopted in many states that provides the general framework of law relating to the formation, operation, and termination of a partnership. *882*

Unlimited liability   A characteristic of partnerships under which owners are liable for more than merely the amounts invested in the business, since their personal assets may also be taken to satisfy the claims of business creditors. *882*

QUESTIONS

1. Chris Ross is currently operating a small machine shop. He is considering forming a partnership with an employee, Homer Medley, whom he considers an excellent worker and supervisor and with whom he gets along well. Prepare a brief list of the advantages and disadvantages to Ross of the potential partnership.

2. Many matters are usually covered in the typical partnership agreement. Some of them are of little significance to the accountant, while others are quite crucial. What are some crucial provisions as far as the accountant is concerned?

3. Pierce and McCoch are partners in a local grocery store. Both take home sufficient merchandise to feed their families. Would you suggest that the merchandise taken home be recorded at selling price or cost? Why?

4. Can you think of a set of circumstances in which you might be willing to enter into a partnership with another person, do all of the work needed to run the business, provide all of the capital, and yet be willing to allow the other person a substantial share of the net income?

5. What is meant by the term *mutual agency,* as it refers to partnerships?

6. Why should a partnership agreement be quite specific regarding the treatment of withdrawals by partners insofar as the sharing of income and losses is concerned?

7. What are three reasons for the formation of partnerships?

8. How are losses divided among partners in a partnership when the agreement is silent as to losses?

9. What is a statement of partners' capital?

10. Describe two different ways in which a new partner can be admitted to a partnership.

11. Why might a newly admitted partner's capital account balance differ from the amount actually invested?

12. Why might a withdrawing partner receive assets worth more or less than the book value of his or her equity?

13. In what ways may a partnership be legally terminated?

14. What are four acts or conditions that will lead to the liquidation of a partnership?

15. What procedures are followed in liquidating a partnership?

EXERCISES

Exercise A–1

Compute investment, withdrawals, and net income

Terry Early opened a flower shop on March 1, 1994, with an investment of $40,000. On December 31, 1994, her capital account showed a balance (after closing) of $70,000. Compute the missing amount in each of the following cases:

	Additional Investment	Withdrawals	Net Income (loss)
a.	$20,000	$ 8,000	?
b.	4,000	14,000	?
c.	–0–	?	$50,000
d.	?	6,000	20,000
e.	50,000	16,000	?

Exercise A–2 Determine each partner's share of income	Stoner, Nail, and Grissom are partners. In 1994, net income of their partnership is $480,000. How much will be credited to each partner in the income distribution if: *a.*　Nothing is said in the partnership agreement concerning the division of income? *b.*　The income and loss sharing ratio is 50 : 30 : 20, respectively?
Exercise A–3 Record income distribution, and close drawing accounts	Give the entry to record the division of income in *(b)* of Exercise A–2. Also give the entry to record the closing of the drawing accounts, assuming drawings were $60,000, $80,000, and $40,000, respectively.
Exercise A–4 Determine distribution of a net loss	Given an income and loss ratio of 5 : 3 : 2, how would the three partners in Exercise A–2 share a loss of $300,000? Give the journal entry.
Exercise A–5 Determine partner's share of net income	Partner M was credited with a salary of $24,000 and interest of $12,000 on his capital account and was charged with $2,000 as his share of the balance in the Income Summary account, after taking partners' salaries and interest on partners' capital balances into account. He withdrew $28,000 during the year. What amount will he report to the Internal Revenue Service as his share of the partnership's income?
Exercise A–6 Determine each partner's share of income	The capital account balances of A and B stood at $100,000 and $320,000 throughout the entire year. A withdrew $36,000, and B withdrew $60,000; and these drawings were normal withdrawals rather than withdrawals of investment. 　　Net income for the year was $110,000. If salaries are to be allowed A and B in the amounts of $36,000 and $60,000 and the balance of the income is distributed equally, what will be each partner's total share of the income for the year?
Exercise A–7 Compute average capital investment	Given the following capital account, compute the average capital investment for the year:

Penn, Capital

Mar. 1	36,000	Jan. 1	192,000
Aug. 1	8,000	May 1	96,000
Dec. 1	20,000	June 1	12,000

Exercise A–8 Prepare schedule showing distribution of income	E and Y are partners. They agree that each partner can withdraw $3,000 in cash at the end of each month, with such withdrawals debited to each partner's drawing account. In sharing income, 10% interest is to be allowed on average capital investment, taking into consideration withdrawals in excess of the allowed $3,000 per month. Each partner is to be credited with a salary of $30,000 per year. The remainder of the income or loss is to be shared equally by E and Y. 　　E's capital account at January 1 was $250,000. He withdrew $16,000 on July 1, in addition to the allowed $3,000 monthly cash withdrawals. 　　Y's capital account balance at January 1 was $350,000. He withdrew $20,000 on April 1 and $28,000 on October 1. He also withdrew the allowed $3,000 cash per month. 　　Prepare a short schedule showing the distribution of $180,000 net income for the current year.
Exercise A–9 Record acquisition of interest of existing partners	J, K, and L are partners with capital account balances of $90,000, $110,000, and $80,000, respectively. Q now acquires one third of J's interest and one half of L's interest for $63,000 in personal transactions between the individuals. Prepare the entry to record Q's acquisition of an interest in the partnership.
Exercise A–10 Determine incoming partner's equity, and record admission	Ronnie, Ricky, and Mike are partners with capital account balances of $80,000, $120,000, and $200,000, respectively. The partners agree to admit Johnny to a one-fourth interest in both capital and income for an $80,000 cash investment in the partnership. Determine Johnny's equity in the new partnership, and prepare the journal entry to record the admission of Johnny. (Assume that the original partners shared income and losses in the ratio of 3 : 3 : 4.)

Exercise A–11

Record asset revaluation and retirement of a partner

Ed, Fred, and Ted are partners with capital account balances of $600,000, $400,000, and $300,000, respectively. They share income and losses in a 4:3:2 ratio. Fred decides to withdraw. The partnership revalues its assets from $1,300,000 to $1,480,000. Fred then receives cash equal to the recorded amount of his equity after assets have been adjusted to current market value. These adjustments involved an increase in inventory of $100,000 and an increase in plant and equipment of $80,000. Prepare journal entries to adjust the partnership accounts and to record the withdrawal of Fred.

Exercise A–12

Record partner's withdrawal from the partnership

Spangler, Conkle, and Hirsch are partners with capital balances of $100,000, $80,000, and $60,000, respectively. They share income and losses in a 5:3:2 ratio. Hirsch withdraws and is paid $70,000 for his equity interest by the partnership. Give the journal entry to record the withdrawal of Hirsch.

Exercise A–13

Record partner's withdrawal from the partnership

Ames, Anthony, and Bibb are partners with capital accounts of $35,000, $60,000, and $45,000, respectively. They share income and losses in a 2:3:4 ratio. Although Bibb believes assets of the partnership are fairly valued, she is so anxious to retire that she accepts a $40,000 cash payment in full for her equity. Prepare the journal entry to record Bibb's withdrawal.

Exercise A–14

Record partnership liquidation

Uno, Dos, and Tres are partners with capital balances of $650,000, $440,000, and $280,000, respectively. They share income and losses in a 4:4:2 ratio. Total net assets (Assets − Liabilities) are $1,370,000, consisting of $1,570,000 of noncash assets and $200,000 of liabilities. The partnership is liquidated by selling the assets for $1,280,000, paying the liabilities, and distributing the remaining cash to the partners. Prepare the necessary journal entries.

Exercise A–15

Record partnership liquidation

The liability and capital accounts of the firm of Jones and Matthews are as follows:

Accounts Payable	$120,000
Jones, Capital	180,000
Matthews, Capital	360,000
Total	$660,000

All of the firm's assets (all noncash) are sold for $588,000, and that amount of cash is on hand even though the entry to record sale of the assets has not been recorded. Income and losses are shared 3:2 by Jones and Matthews. Prepare entries to record sale of the assets, distribution of the loss, and payment of the $588,000 to creditors and the partners.

Exercise A–16

Record partnership liquidation

The trial balance of the J-M partnership is as follows:

	Debits	Credits
Assets	$800,000	
Accounts Payable		$ 80,000
J, Capital		480,000
M, Capital		240,000
	$800,000	$800,000

The partners decide to liquidate. The assets are sold for $360,000, and the cash is paid out. Prepare the necessary journal entries, assuming an equal share of income and losses.

Exercise A–17

Close Income Summary account; record partnership liquidation

Lisa, Eva, and Mary are partners. Certain data for their firm are:

	Lisa	Eva	Mary	Total
Capital balances prior to entering effects of 1994 operations	$294,000	$82,000	$194,000	$570,000
Loss for year ended December 31, 1994				60,000
Income and loss ratio	20%	50%	30%	100%

The partners decide to liquidate. There are no liabilities. All of the assets are noncash assets and are sold for $300,000 cash.

a. Prepare the journal entry to close the 1994 loss.

b. Prepare journal entries for the sale of the assets and the distribution of cash to partners. The partners had invested all of their personal assets in the firm prior to liquidation and will not be able to pay any deficiency in their capital accounts.

PROBLEMS

Problem A–1

Record formation of partnership from two single proprietorships

Dave Parkman and Tracie Hearn, who were in business as sole proprietors, decided to combine all of their business assets and liabilities in a new partnership in which they share income and losses equally. Balance sheets of the two individuals on the date of the formation of the partnership were as shown:

DAVE PARKMAN
Balance Sheet
September 4, 1994
Assets

Cash	$ 32,000
Accounts receivable, net	120,000
Merchandise inventory	72,000
Equipment, net.	160,000
Total assets	$384,000

Liabilities and Owner's Equity

Accounts payable.	$184,000
Dave Parkman, capital.	200,000
Total liabilities and owner's equity	$384,000

TRACIE HEARN
Balance Sheet
September 4, 1994
Assets

Cash	$112,000
Accounts receivable, net	136,000
Merchandise inventory	160,000
Total	$408,000

Liabilities and Owner's Equity

Accounts payable.	$176,000
Tracie Hearn, capital	232,000
Total liabilities and owner's equity	$408,000

An appraisal of the assets showed market values for the assets of Parkman as follows: accounts receivable, $112,000; merchandise inventory, $96,000; and equipment, $120,000. A similar appraisal placed the following market values on Hearn's assets: accounts receivable, $136,000; and merchandise inventory, $104,000.

Required   Prepare journal entries to record the capital contributions of Parkman and Hearn to their newly formed partnership.

Problem A-2

Determine and journalize division of income under alternative provisions

An analysis of the capital accounts for 1994 of Harry and Sandra, partners, showed:

Harry

Jan. 1	Balance	$240,000
June 1	Capital withdrawal	60,000
Nov. 1	Additional investment	60,000

Sandra

Jan. 1	Balance	$ 60,000
July 1	Additional investment	140,000

The balance in the Income Summary account showed net income of $100,000 for 1994.

Required

Prepare a schedule showing the distribution of the net income under each of the following assumptions with regard to income distribution. Also prepare the entries to distribute the income and to close the drawing accounts. (Note: In each instance, assume drawings were equal to salaries allowed for each partner.)

a. Harry and Sandra are allowed annual salaries of $30,000 and $36,000, respectively; 8% interest is allowed on average capital balances; and the balance of the income is shared equally.

b. Equal annual salaries of $40,000 are allowed to each partner; interest at 10% is allowed on capital balances at the beginning of the year; and the balance is shared in a 3 : 2 ratio between Harry and Sandra, respectively.

Problem A-3

Determine division of income; prepare entries to distribute income and close drawing accounts; prepare schedule of changes in partners' capital accounts

The C and P partnership agreement contained the following provisions relative to the sharing of income and losses: (1) C is to be allowed interest at 10% on her capital account balance as of the beginning of the year; (2) P is to be allowed a salary of $2,700 per month; and (3) any remaining balance of income or loss is to be shared equally. The net income for 1994 was $81,000.

Required

a. Assuming that C's and P's capital account balances on January 1, 1994, were $270,000 and $67,500, respectively, prepare a schedule showing the distribution of net income and the entry required to record it.

b. Prepare the entry needed to close the partners' drawing accounts, which had the following balances (before closing) on December 31, 1994: C, zero; and P, $32,400.

c. Present a statement of partners' capital showing the changes occurring in 1994 in the capital account of each partner.

Problem A-4

Prepare schedules showing division of income under alternative provisions

The capital account balances (unchanged during the year) on December 31, 1994, for Joe and Jan, partners, are $160,000 for Joe and $80,000 for Jan. Joe withdrew $26,000, and Jan withdrew $40,000 during the year, with all withdrawals charged to their respective drawing accounts. Net loss for the year amounted to $28,000.

Required

Prepare schedules showing the distribution of income to each partner for the year 1994 under each of the following assumed provisions in the partnership agreement relating to the sharing of income:

a. Salaries of $22,000 and $48,000 are allowed to Joe and Jan, respectively; the remaining income is divided according to capital account balances at the beginning of the year.

b. Salaries of $16,000 and $24,000 are allowed to Joe and Jan, respectively; interest is allowed on capital account balances at the beginning of the year at 10%; no further provisions relating to income sharing are included in the partnership agreement.

Problem A-5

Prepare schedules showing division of income at various amounts of income and loss

Pat and Charles are partners in a retail hardware store. Their partnership agreement calls for salaries to Pat of $124,800 and to Charles of $249,600, and interest at 10% on average capital for the year. Any remaining balance is to be shared equally.

During 1994, each partner drew his allowed salary; no withdrawals in excess of allowed salaries were made. The capital accounts of the two partners remained unchanged during the year at $624,000 for Pat and $936,000 for Charles.

Required   Present schedules showing the distribution of net income (loss), assuming that the income statement for 1994 showed:

a. $748,800 of net income.

b. $312,000 of net income.

c.   A loss of $124,800.

Problem A–6

Prepare adjusting and closing entries, income statement, statement of partners' capital, and balance sheet

Robert and Frank are partners operating a retail store having a fiscal year ending on June 30. Their partnership agreement calls for annual salaries of $24,000 to Robert and $32,000 to Frank, interest at 8% on average capital account balances throughout the year, and the balance of the income to be shared equally. The June 30, 1994, trial balance follows.

	Debits	Credits
Cash	$ 80,800	
Accounts Receivable	128,000	
Merchandise Inventory, July 1, 1993	57,600	
Accounts Payable		$ 81,600
Notes Payable		40,000
Robert, Capital		56,000
Frank, Capital		40,000
Robert, Drawing	16,000	
Frank, Drawing	20,000	
Sales		856,000
Purchases	544,000	
Purchase Returns		8,000
Employee Salaries and Wages	24,000	
Rent Expense	104,000	
Delivery Expense	33,600	
Store Expense	73,600	
	$1,081,600	$1,081,600

The $40,000 note payable is a 120-day note dated April 1, 1994, and calls for interest at 10% per year. The inventory at June 30, 1994, is $66,400. The only change in the capital accounts during the year was an additional $16,000 investment by Robert on January 1. The drawing account balances and annual salaries are independent of each other.

Required   Prepare the following for the partnership:

a.   The necessary adjusting and closing entries.

b.   An income statement for the year ended June 30, 1994. Include the distribution of net income.

c.   A statement of partners' capital for the year ended June 30, 1994.

d.   A balance sheet for June 30, 1994.

Problem A–7

Record admission of new partner

Jill, George, and Carla are partners who share income and losses in a 3 : 2 : 1 ratio. They decided to admit Jeff to the partnership at a time when their capital account balances were:

Jill, Capital	$380,000
George, Capital	170,000
Carla, Capital	170,000

Required   Prepare journal entries to record Jeff's admission to the partnership under each of the following, unrelated conditions:

a.   Jeff acquired 40% of George's interest for $110,000 paid to George.

b.   Jeff acquired all of Carla's interest for $150,000 paid to Carla.

c.   Jeff invested $520,000 in the firm for a one-half interest in capital.

d.   Jeff was admitted to a one-fifth interest in capital for an investment of $120,000.

Problem A–8
Record admission of new partner

X and Y are partners with capital account balances of $171,600 and $93,600, respectively. Income and losses are shared in a 3:2 ratio.

Required
Prepare the journal entries to record the admission of Z to the partnership in each of the following independent situations.

a.   Z paid $52,000 to Y for one half of Y's interest.
b.   Z invested sufficient cash in the firm to acquire a one-fourth interest in capital of the new firm.
c.   Z invested $98,800 for a one-fifth interest in capital.
d.   Z invested $67,600 for a one-fourth interest.

Problem A–9
Record withdrawal of partner

On December 31, Scott Brown, a member of the firm of Brown and Grey, decided to retire. The partners have shared income and losses equally. On this date their capital account credit balances were:

Scott Brown.	$250,000
Leslie Brown	160,000
Ted Grey	160,000

Required

Prepare entries to record the withdrawal of Scott Brown under each of the following, unrelated assumptions. All payments are to be in cash, and assets are not to be revalued.

a.   Scott Brown was paid $250,000.
b.   Scott Brown was paid $300,000.
c.   Scott Brown was paid $230,000.

Problem A–10
Record withdrawal of partner

Hendrix, Waters, and Conlon are partners in HWC Associates. Ledger account balances on January 1, 1994, are:

	Debits	Credits
Cash.	$ 28,000	
Accounts Receivable.	48,000	
Allowance for Uncollectible Accounts		$ 4,000
Merchandise Inventory.	100,000	
Equipment	24,000	
Accumulated Depreciation—Equipment		8,000
Accounts Payable		32,000
Hendrix, Capital		80,000
Waters, Capital		60,000
Conlon, Capital		16,000
	$200,000	$200,000

The partners share income and losses in a 5:3:2 ratio.

Required

Assume that Conlon retires from the firm and receives a check for $20,000. Prepare entries to record Conlon's retirement, assuming:

a.   The assets were not revalued.
b.   Inventory was revalued at $124,000, and equipment was revalued to a net value of $12,000.

Problem A–11
Record partnership liquidation

Use the data in Problem A–10 above but ignore the revaluation of assets in part (b). Assume that the partners decided to liquidate. All of the noncash assets were sold for $60,000. After the assets were sold, the liabilities were paid, the remaining cash was distributed to the partners, and the books were closed.

Required Prepare journal entries to record liquidation of the partnership. Assume that none of the partners has other assets to cover possible debit balances in his capital account.

Problem A–12
Record partnership liquidation

Given below is the balance sheet of the ABC Partnership on April 30, 1994, the date the partners decided to liquidate their firm.

ABC PARTNERSHIP
Balance Sheet
April 30, 1994

Assets

Cash	$ 80,000
Accounts receivable	160,000
Merchandise inventory	400,000
Plant and equipment, net	800,000
Total assets	$1,440,000

Liabilities and Owners' Equity

Accounts payable.	$ 760,000
A, capital	280,000
B, capital	200,000
C, capital	200,000
Total liabilities and owners' equity	$1,440,000

On May 1, the noncash assets were sold for $712,000. A, B, and C share income and losses in a 5:3:2 ratio.

Required Prepare all necessary journal entries to record the sale of the assets and the distribution of cash to creditors and partners. Assume that all partners who had debit balances in their capital accounts after loss distributions immediately paid cash to the firm equal to the debit balances.

BUSINESS DECISION PROBLEMS

Decision Problem A–1
Analyze effects of proposed change in income and loss sharing provisions

David Roberts and Tiny Manley have owned and operated a sporting goods store as a partnership. Their capital account balances as of December 31, 1994, were Roberts, $640,000; and Manley, $216,000. Income and losses are shared equally after allowing salaries of $64,000 to Roberts and $56,000 to Manley. Applying these provisions to the net income of $240,000 in 1993 resulted in a distribution of $124,000 to Roberts and $116,000 to Manley. Roberts considers this sharing quite unfair. He notes that he devotes full time to the store, while Manley has other interests that occupy about half of his time. Roberts also notes that his equity is substantially more than Manley's in the partnership because he has not drawn all of his income. He proposes that the partnership agreement be changed to call for salaries of $80,000 to himself and $40,000 to Manley, that interest at 10% per year be allowed on beginning-of-year capital account balances, and that any remaining income be shared equally.

Manley agrees that some modification seems necessary because of changed circumstances. But before agreeing to Roberts' proposed changes, he wants to know the effects of such changes.

Required Assume that the capital account balances as of January 1, 1994, were Roberts, $560,000; and Manley, $200,000.

a. Prepare a schedule showing how the income for 1994 would have been shared if Roberts' suggested provisions had been in effect for the year.

b. Prepare a schedule showing how much each partner's share of the 1994 income would have increased or decreased if Roberts' proposed revisions of the partnership agreement had been in effect for 1994.

c.   Is Manley more or less likely to accept Roberts' proposals if future net income is substantially greater or less than $240,000 per year?

Decision Problem A–2

Determine proper amount for partner to receive in liquidation settlement

Bill Pendley and Rubis Gadell are partners sharing income and losses equally in a business that has been very successful for all 25 years of its existence. The partners have been studying what they consider a very tempting offer to buy their business, thus allowing them to retire. Shortly after receiving this offer, Pendley was hospitalized as a result of an auto accident. The partners agreed that they should sell, and Gadell was authorized to negotiate the sale of the business.

Sometime later, Gadell appeared at the hospital and gave Pendley a check for $240,000 as his share of the cash available to the partners on liquidation of the partnership. He also gave Pendley a balance sheet for the partnership as of the day before the date of the sale. Summarized, this balance sheet showed:

Cash	$ 30,000
Other assets	390,000
Total	$420,000
Liabilities	$ 90,000
Pendley, capital	180,000
Gadell, capital	150,000
Total	$420,000

Gadell explained that he had sold all of the other assets and the firm name for $540,000—a price he considered excellent. Pendley agreed the price was excellent but was unsure about whether the check Gadell gave him was in the correct amount.

Required

a.   Show the computations Gadell made to arrive at a $240,000 check for Pendley.

b.   Is $240,000 the correct amount? If not, compute the correct amount.

B

PAYROLL ACCOUNTING AND FEDERAL INCOME TAXES

INTRODUCTION

Most of you have had either a part-time or full-time job and have been paid weekly, semimonthly, or monthly. You probably were disappointed when you received your first paycheck because the deductions were greater than you expected. Payroll accounting includes the record-keeping necessary to account for employees' paychecks and deductions. Since a company's payroll costs are one of the largest expenses a company incurs, payroll accounting is an important function.

This appendix discusses the objectives of payroll accounting and the methods used to achieve these objectives. Computations of gross and net earnings and the major documents and forms used in payroll accounting are explained. Even though many businesses today use computerized payroll systems, the objectives and methods used to compute amounts and deductions are the same as for manual systems. The rates and bases used are those in effect for 1991.

The appendix also describes various federal income tax provisions that affect business corporations. This discussion includes differences between net income before taxes and taxable income, tax rates, and accounting methods used for tax purposes. (The tax concepts and procedures in this appendix are current up through the 1990 Revenue Reconciliation Act, but they will probably change because of further actions taken by Congress.)

PAYROLL ACCOUNTING

In most business organizations, accounting for payroll is particularly important because (1) payrolls often represent the largest expense that a company incurs, (2) both federal and state governments require that detailed payroll records be maintained, and (3) companies must file regular payroll reports with both state and federal governments and make remittances of amounts withheld or otherwise due. Thus, the general objectives of payroll accounting are to process such data as hours worked, pay rates, and payroll deductions so that the company can:

1. Establish internal control over payroll and protect against fraud in payroll transactions.
2. Prepare and record a payroll, including gross earnings, payroll taxes and deductions, employee earnings record, and the payroll journal.
3. Pay the payroll using the payroll checking account. Also provide accurate and timely paychecks, as well as an explanation of payroll data.
4. Record employer payroll taxes, including FICA (social security) taxes, federal unemployment taxes, and state unemployment taxes.
5. Remit taxes withheld, unemployment taxes, and other deductions to the proper government agency or other organization.
6. Prepare adjusting entries for end-of-period accruals, including wages, payroll taxes, and vacation pay.

This section discusses the objectives of payroll accounting and the methods of achieving these objectives. You should be aware that even though many businesses today use more efficient computerized payroll systems, the objectives and methods used to compute amounts and deductions are the same as for manual systems.

ESTABLISHING INTERNAL CONTROL OVER PAYROLL

In small companies, the owner-manager may provide adequate internal control over payroll transactions by actually computing and preparing the payroll. Larger companies obtain internal control through application of the general principles of internal control and the more specific guides to controls over cash disbursements, as described in Chapter 8. Separation of duties is a crucial aspect of internal control over payroll transactions. Ideally, timekeeping, payroll preparation, payroll record-keeping, and payroll distribution functions should be performed by different employees.

If an employee's compensation is based on hours worked, the company must maintain an accurate record of each employee's time. In small companies, the owner may simply make notations in a notebook stating when employees report to work and leave work. Larger companies often use a time clock for hourly employees. Each day when employees report to work, every employee inserts a timecard into the clock, which prints the date and time on the card. Employees follow the same procedure when leaving work. Companies must safeguard against one employee punching in or out for another employee; for example, the company could station someone at the time clock to supervise the check-in and check-out procedures.

In small companies, the owner usually knows the hours each employee works. The owner, or a bookkeeper, may keep the company payroll records and compute the employees' earnings and deductions, as well as prepare, sign, and distribute the paychecks. Most large companies use the following procedure to prepare paychecks: At a regular interval before payday, the payroll department collects and verifies each employee's pay rate and hours worked to compute total (gross) pay. At this point, all legally required and authorized deductions are subtracted from the total (gross) pay, individual payroll records are updated, and payroll checks are prepared. Checks are then sent to the treasurer's office for signature. Supporting documents, such as employees' earnings statements showing earnings and deductions to date, may accompany the checks. Each check should be delivered to the employee in person or deposited directly by the employer into the employee's bank account.

Payroll Fraud

Whenever cash is disbursed, the potential for fraud exists. Some payroll fraud schemes used successfully in the past are listed below.

1. A payroll department employee pays another employee more than that employee has actually earned, and then the payroll department employee receives a kickback of part of the overpayment.
2. A payroll department employee makes out a payroll check payable to a former or fictitious employee and then cashes the check.
3. A payroll department employee prepares and cashes duplicate payroll checks.

Because of these and other schemes, companies must exercise great care to ensure payroll accuracy. Separation of duties is one way to help ensure accuracy. Fraudulent transactions are difficult to arrange and cover up when one employee's work serves as a check on another's. For example, if a payroll department employee falsifies the hours worked by a plant employee in an attempt to overpay the employee, the changed hours on the payroll record will not agree with the timecard record. Collusion by two payroll department employees would be required to commit such a fraud unless the same employee has access to timecards, other payroll records, and payroll checks.

Maintenance of accurate employment and payroll records is also crucial. As soon as possible, payroll department personnel must be informed of the hiring and termination of employees so that they know which employees currently work for the company. This information helps prevent the writing of fictitious checks. Also, current copies of documents authorizing payroll deductions should be on hand. Payroll fraud can be reduced by keeping accurate, detailed records for each employee. Companies must be alert to the possibility of payroll fraud and take steps to prevent it.

PREPARING AND RECORDING A PAYROLL

To prepare and record a payroll, you must begin by determining an employee's gross earnings. Since gross earnings are generally not the amount the employee receives, the next step is to compute the employee's payroll taxes and other payroll deductions. Using examples, the paragraphs that follow explain this phase of payroll accounting.

Computing Gross Earnings

Although the terms *wages* and *salaries* are often used interchangeably, they are not the same. The term *wages* generally refers to gross earnings of employees who are paid by the hour for only the actual hours worked. The term *salaries,* on the other hand, usually refers to gross earnings of employees who are paid a flat amount per week or month regardless of the number of hours worked in a period.

An employee's gross earnings are the employee's total pay or compensation, including regular pay and overtime premium. The computation of gross earnings for wage employees and salaried employees differs. Computing gross earnings for wage employees usually consists of simply multiplying the number of hours the employee worked by the employee's hourly wage rate. For example, 40 hours times $10 per hour gives gross earnings of $400 for the week. Since the gross earnings for salaried employees are usually a specified yearly amount, the annual salary is divided by the number of pay periods in the year. For example, assuming an employee is paid monthly and earns $36,000 a year, you would divide $36,000 by 12 months to determine the monthly gross earnings of $3,000. In some instances, however, the calculation of gross earnings is a little more detailed due to legal or contractual requirements.

The federal Wages and Hours Law (also called the Fair Labor Standards Act) requires that (1) most employees who are paid by the hour be paid a minimum of 1½ times their normal rate for hours worked in excess of 40 per week and (2) employees be paid at least the minimum wage. The minimum wage rate is set by the federal government and changes from time to time. In addition to this federal law, some union contracts also call for premium pay rates for certain hours worked, such as double time for work on Sunday. You should be aware that executive, administrative, and some professional employees are salaried and exempt from both the minimum wage and overtime pay provisions. However, lower-level nonprofessional, salaried employees are generally subject to the minimum wage and overtime pay provisions.

The payroll department must maintain detailed time records to ensure that legal and contractual requirements are being met. In the absence of valid records, assessments for overtime pay may later be made against the employer.

Three situations follow that illustrate how to compute gross earnings that include overtime premiums.

1. Mary Kennedy's basic wage rate is $9 per hour. Her overtime premium, then, is one half of $9, or $4.50 per hour. Mary's gross pay for a week in which she worked 48 hours is $468. The $468 is computed as $(48 \times \$9) + (8 \times \$4.50)$, or $(\$432 + \$36) = \$468$. (An alternative calculation is [40 hours $\times$ $9] + [8 hours $\times$ $13.50] = $468.)

2. Grace Early's basic $18,200 annual salary is paid over 52 weeks at a guaranteed weekly minimum of $350 (40 $\times$ $8.75 per hour), even though she often only works 37.5 hours per week. She is entitled to overtime pay for hours worked in excess of 40 per week. Her gross earnings for working 42 hours in a week are computed as $350 + (2 $\times$ 1.5 $\times$ $8.75) = $376.25.

3. Dan Brown is paid $0.50 for each unit of product machined. In the current week, he worked 48 hours and completed 960 units. His gross pay before

ILLUSTRATION B.1
Employee's Withholding Allowance Certificate (Form W-4)

Form **W-4** Department of the Treasury Internal Revenue Service	**Employee's Withholding Allowance Certificate** ▶ For Privacy Act and Paperwork Reduction Act Notice, see reverse.	OMB No. 1545-0010 **19̲91**

1 Type or print your first name and middle initial: John R.   Last name: Hanson   **2** Your social security number: 253-13-2807

Home address (number and street or rural route): 325 St. George Drive

3 Marital status: ☐ Single ☒ Married ☐ Married, but withhold at higher Single rate. Note: *If married, but legally separated, or spouse is a nonresident alien, check the Single box.*

City or town, state, and ZIP code: Athens, GA 30605

4 Total number of allowances you are claiming (from line G above or from the Worksheets on back if they apply) . . . **4** | 3

5 Additional amount, if any, you want deducted from each pay . . . . **5** $

6 I claim exemption from withholding and I certify that I meet **ALL** of the following conditions for exemption:
- Last year I had a right to a refund of **ALL** Federal income tax withheld because I had **NO** tax liability; **AND**
- This year I expect a refund of **ALL** Federal income tax withheld because I expect to have **NO** tax liability; **AND**
- This year if my income exceeds $550 and includes nonwage income, another person cannot claim me as a dependent.

If you meet all of the above conditions, enter the year effective and "EXEMPT" here . . . . . ▶ **6** | 19

7 Are you a full-time student? (**Note:** *Full-time students are not automatically exempt.*) . . . . **7** ☐ Yes ☒ No

Under penalties of perjury, I certify that I am entitled to the number of withholding allowances claimed on this certificate or entitled to claim exempt status

Employee's signature ▶   Date ▶   , 19

8 Employer's name and address (**Employer:** Complete 8 and 10 **only if sending to IRS**): Doug's Ace Hardware, 1290 Atlanta Highway, Athens, GA 30605 **9** Office code (optional) **10** Employer identification number: 15-249363

overtime premium is $480 (960 × $0.50). The $480 is divided by 48 hours to get $10 as his regular hourly rate for the week. Therefore, Dan's overtime premium is $5 per hour, and his total overtime pay is $40 (8 × $5). His gross earnings for the week are $480 + $40, or $520.

Computing Payroll Taxes and Deductions

Required deductions from gross earnings include withholdings for federal income taxes, state income taxes, and FICA (social security) taxes. Employees may choose to have various other deductions taken from their checks.

Federal and State Income Taxes Wage earners in the United States are under a pay-as-you-go federal income tax system. This concept means that most employees must pay federal income taxes on wages as they are earned during the year. Employers withhold **federal income tax** when the employee's earnings are paid, and the amount of federal income tax withheld is noted on the employee's check stub. These federal taxes are remitted (sent) periodically by the employer to federally specified banks or to the Internal Revenue Service (IRS). Companies located in states with state income taxes also must withhold **state income tax** from employees' paychecks and remit these amounts to the revenue authority in those states. Amounts paid to independent contractors, such as outside consultants, are not subject to withholding for federal income tax and FICA tax.

The amount of income tax withheld from each employee's pay depends on the (1) amount of earnings, (2) frequency of the payroll period, and (3) the number of withholding allowances claimed by the employee. Withholding allowances are claimed by the employee on an Employee's Withholding Allowance Certificate (Form W-4) filed with the employer, usually the first day on the job. Illustration B.1 shows the W-4 form of John Hanson, who claims three withholding allowances, which usually means that he will claim three exemptions on his federal income tax return—one for himself, one for his wife, and one for his child. An exemption is a fixed amount of income ($2,050 in 1990, and an estimated $2,150 in 1991) that is not subject to taxation.

A wage bracket withholding table (Illustration B.2) is a table provided by the Internal Revenue Service to help employers determine the amount of federal income tax to withhold from employees' paychecks. This particular table is to be used for married persons who are paid weekly. When the federal income tax laws are revised, the table amounts change. Such tables are provided for both married and single persons for various pay periods, such as weekly, biweekly, and monthly. The amount of income taxes withheld changes with the number of withholding allowances claimed.

On or before January 31, after the end of each calendar year, an employer is required to prepare for each employee a four-copy (or more) Wage and Tax Statement (Form W-2) for the previous calendar-year earnings. An example of a W-2 that was used in a recent year is shown in Illustration B.3. This form provides wage and tax data needed to prepare the employee's personal federal and state income tax returns. One copy is sent by the employer to the Social Security Administration, which then transmits data contained on the form to the Internal Revenue Service. The other three copies of the W-2 are given to the employee. Of these three, one copy is filed with the employee's federal income tax return, one is filed with the state income tax return (if the employee lives in a state that has a state income tax), and one is retained by the employee as a personal record. The IRS uses data from the form to determine whether the employee has reported the proper amount of earned income and taxes withheld on the tax return.

FICA (Social Security) Taxes   The FICA (social security) tax was created by passage of the Federal Insurance Contributions Act in 1935. Persons who are currently working in jobs covered by the act must pay a certain percentage of their earnings (up to a maximum specified amount) into special trust funds. Employee contributions are matched by equal payments by employers. Money paid into the trust is used to finance retirement benefits and medical benefits (medicare) paid to persons and their families who are currently retired or disabled and who qualify for such benefits under the act. Full retirement benefits are available to workers who reach age 65; reduced benefits can be applied for at age 62. Additional voluntary medical insurance is available to persons age 65 and over.

The amount of FICA tax withheld for each employee was 7.65% of the first $52,000 of wages in 1990 and 7.65% of the first $53,400 of wages in 1991. Of this 7.65 cents per dollar, 1.45 cents is for Medicare Hospital Insurance, and 6.2 cents is for old-age, survivors, and disability insurance. The $53,400 limit only applies to the old-age, survivors, and disability portion of FICA taxes. The 1.45 cents per dollar for Medicare Hospital Insurance is deducted on all wages and self-employment income up to $125,000. Thus, the FICA rate is 7.65% on the first $53,400 and 1.45% on amounts over $53,400 up to $125,000 of earned income. The rates and bases scheduled to go into effect after 1991 continue to incorporate an inflation factor based on the change in the average covered wage in the United States during the preceding calendar year.

Other Payroll Deductions   Besides payroll deductions for taxes, companies may make other deductions from an employee's gross earnings. Some union contracts require companies to deduct union dues from gross pay as a convenience to employees and the union. The union then receives from the employer the dues withheld from the employees. Medical insurance and life insurance premiums may also be deducted from gross pay. These deductions are made most often when a company offers group life insurance plans to its employees. The amounts de-

ILLUSTRATION B.2
Federal Wage Bracket Withholding Table

WEEKLY Payroll Period — Employee MARRIED — Effective January 1, 1991

And the wages are-		And the number of withholding allowances claimed is—										
At least	But less than	0	1	2	3	4	5	6	7	8	9	10 or more
		The amount of income tax to be withheld shall be—										
$0	$70	$0	$0	$0	$0	$0	$0	$0	$0	$0	$0	$0
70	75	1	0	0	0	0	0	0	0	0	0	0
75	80	1	0	0	0	0	0	0	0	0	0	0
80	85	2	0	0	0	0	0	0	0	0	0	0
85	90	3	0	0	0	0	0	0	0	0	0	0
90	95	4	0	0	0	0	0	0	0	0	0	0
95	100	4	0	0	0	0	0	0	0	0	0	0
100	105	5	0	0	0	0	0	0	0	0	0	0
105	110	6	0	0	0	0	0	0	0	0	0	0
110	115	7	0	0	0	0	0	0	0	0	0	0
115	120	7	1	0	0	0	0	0	0	0	0	0
120	125	8	2	0	0	0	0	0	0	0	0	0
125	130	9	3	0	0	0	0	0	0	0	0	0
130	135	10	3	0	0	0	0	0	0	0	0	0
135	140	10	4	0	0	0	0	0	0	0	0	0
140	145	11	5	0	0	0	0	0	0	0	0	0
145	150	12	6	0	0	0	0	0	0	0	0	0
150	155	13	6	0	0	0	0	0	0	0	0	0
155	160	13	7	1	0	0	0	0	0	0	0	0
160	165	14	8	2	0	0	0	0	0	0	0	0
165	170	15	9	2	0	0	0	0	0	0	0	0
170	175	16	9	3	0	0	0	0	0	0	0	0
175	180	16	10	4	0	0	0	0	0	0	0	0
180	185	17	11	5	0	0	0	0	0	0	0	0
185	190	18	12	5	0	0	0	0	0	0	0	0
190	195	19	12	6	0	0	0	0	0	0	0	0
195	200	19	13	7	1	0	0	0	0	0	0	0
200	210	21	14	8	2	0	0	0	0	0	0	0
210	220	22	16	10	3	0	0	0	0	0	0	0
220	230	24	17	11	5	0	0	0	0	0	0	0
230	240	25	19	13	6	0	0	0	0	0	0	0
240	250	27	20	14	8	2	0	0	0	0	0	0
250	260	28	22	16	9	3	0	0	0	0	0	0
260	270	30	23	17	11	5	0	0	0	0	0	0
270	280	31	25	19	12	6	0	0	0	0	0	0

At least	But less than	0	1	2	3	4	5	6	7	8	9	10 or more
280	290	33	26	20	14	8	2	0	0	0	0	0
290	300	34	28	22	15	9	3	0	0	0	0	0
300	310	36	29	23	17	11	5	0	0	0	0	0
310	320	37	31	25	18	12	6	0	0	0	0	0
320	330	39	32	26	20	14	8	1	0	0	0	0
330	340	40	34	28	21	15	9	3	0	0	0	0
340	350	42	35	29	23	17	11	4	0	0	0	0
350	360	43	37	31	24	18	12	6	0	0	0	0
360	370	45	38	32	26	20	14	7	1	0	0	0
370	380	46	40	34	27	21	15	9	3	0	0	0
380	390	48	41	35	29	23	17	10	4	0	0	0
390	400	49	43	37	30	24	18	12	6	0	0	0
400	410	51	44	38	32	26	20	13	7	1	0	0
410	420	52	46	40	33	27	21	15	9	2	0	0
420	430	54	47	41	35	29	23	16	10	4	0	0
430	440	55	49	43	36	30	24	18	12	5	0	0
440	450	57	50	44	38	32	26	19	13	7	1	0
450	460	58	52	46	39	33	27	21	15	8	2	0
460	470	60	53	47	41	35	29	22	16	10	4	0
470	480	61	55	49	42	36	30	24	18	11	5	0
480	490	63	56	50	44	38	32	25	19	13	7	0
490	500	64	58	52	45	39	33	27	21	14	8	2
500	510	66	59	53	47	41	35	28	22	16	10	3
510	520	67	61	55	48	42	36	30	24	17	11	5
520	530	69	62	56	50	44	38	31	25	19	13	6
530	540	70	64	58	51	45	39	33	27	20	14	8
540	550	72	65	59	53	47	41	34	28	22	16	9
550	560	73	67	61	54	48	42	36	30	23	17	11
560	570	75	68	62	56	50	44	37	31	25	19	12
570	580	76	70	64	57	51	45	39	33	26	20	14
580	590	78	71	65	59	53	47	40	34	28	22	15
590	600	79	73	67	60	54	48	42	36	29	23	17
600	610	81	74	68	62	56	50	43	37	31	25	18
610	620	82	76	70	63	57	51	45	39	32	26	20
620	630	84	77	71	65	59	53	46	40	34	28	21

ILLUSTRATION B.2

(concluded)

WEEKLY Payroll Period — Employee MARRIED — Effective January 1, 1991

And the wages are-		And the number of withholding allowances claimed is—										
At least	But less than	0	1	2	3	4	5	6	7	8	9	10 or more
		The amount of income tax to be withheld shall be—										
$630	$640	$85	$79	$73	$66	$60	$54	$48	$42	$35	$29	$23
640	650	87	80	74	68	62	56	49	43	37	31	24
650	660	88	82	76	69	63	57	51	45	38	32	26
660	670	90	83	77	71	65	59	52	46	40	34	27
670	680	91	85	79	72	66	60	54	48	41	35	29
680	690	93	86	80	74	68	62	55	49	43	37	30
690	700	94	88	82	75	69	63	57	51	44	38	32
700	710	96	89	83	77	71	65	58	52	46	40	33
710	720	97	91	85	78	72	66	60	54	47	41	35
720	730	99	92	86	80	74	68	61	55	49	43	36
730	740	102	94	88	81	75	69	63	57	50	44	38
740	750	104	95	89	83	77	71	64	58	52	46	39
750	760	107	97	91	84	78	72	66	60	53	47	41
760	770	110	99	92	86	80	74	67	61	55	49	42
770	780	113	101	94	87	81	75	69	63	56	50	44
780	790	116	104	95	89	83	77	70	64	58	52	45
790	800	118	107	97	90	84	78	72	66	59	53	47
800	810	121	110	98	92	86	80	73	67	61	55	48
810	820	124	113	101	93	87	81	75	69	62	56	50
820	830	127	115	104	95	89	83	76	70	64	58	51
830	840	130	118	107	96	90	84	78	72	65	59	53
840	850	132	121	109	98	92	86	79	73	67	61	54
850	860	135	124	112	101	93	87	81	75	68	62	56
860	870	138	127	115	103	95	89	82	76	70	64	57
870	880	141	129	118	106	96	90	84	78	71	65	59
880	890	144	132	121	109	98	92	85	79	73	67	60
890	900	146	135	123	112	100	93	87	81	74	68	62
900	910	149	138	126	115	103	95	88	82	76	70	63
910	920	152	141	129	117	106	96	90	84	77	71	65
920	930	155	143	132	120	109	98	91	85	79	73	66
930	940	158	146	135	123	111	100	93	87	80	74	68
940	950	160	149	137	126	114	103	94	88	82	76	69
950	960	163	152	140	129	117	105	96	90	83	77	71
960	970	166	155	143	131	120	108	97	91	85	79	72
970	980	169	157	146	134	123	111	99	93	86	80	74
At least	But less than	0	1	2	3	4	5	6	7	8	9	10 or more
980	990	172	160	149	137	125	114	102	94	88	82	75
990	1,000	174	163	151	140	128	117	105	96	89	83	77
1,000	1,010	177	166	154	143	131	119	108	97	91	85	78
1,010	1,020	180	169	157	145	134	122	111	99	92	86	80
1,020	1,030	183	171	160	148	137	125	113	102	94	88	81
1,030	1,040	186	174	163	151	139	128	116	105	95	89	83
1,040	1,050	188	177	165	154	142	131	119	107	97	91	84
1,050	1,060	191	180	168	157	145	133	122	110	99	92	86
1,060	1,070	194	183	171	159	148	136	125	113	101	94	87
1,070	1,080	197	185	174	162	151	139	127	116	104	95	89
1,080	1,090	200	188	177	165	153	142	130	119	107	97	90
1,090	1,100	202	191	179	168	156	145	133	121	110	98	92
1,100	1,110	205	194	182	171	159	147	136	124	113	101	93
1,110	1,120	208	197	185	173	162	150	139	127	115	104	95
1,120	1,130	211	199	188	176	165	153	141	130	118	107	96
1,130	1,140	214	202	191	179	167	156	144	133	121	109	98
1,140	1,150	216	205	193	182	170	159	147	135	124	112	101
1,150	1,160	219	208	196	185	173	161	150	138	127	115	104
1,160	1,170	222	211	199	187	176	164	153	141	129	118	106
1,170	1,180	225	213	202	190	179	167	155	144	132	121	109
1,180	1,190	228	216	205	193	181	170	158	147	135	123	112
1,190	1,200	230	219	207	196	184	173	161	149	138	126	115
1,200	1,210	233	222	210	199	187	175	164	152	141	129	118
1,210	1,220	236	225	213	201	190	178	167	155	143	132	120
1,220	1,230	239	227	216	204	193	181	169	158	146	135	123
1,230	1,240	242	230	219	207	195	184	172	161	149	137	126
1,240	1,250	244	233	221	210	198	187	175	163	152	140	129
1,250	1,260	247	236	224	213	201	189	178	166	155	143	132
1,260	1,270	250	239	227	215	204	192	181	169	157	146	134
1,270	1,280	253	241	230	218	207	195	183	172	160	149	137

$1,280 and over   Use Table 1(b) for a **MARRIED person** on [page 33].   Also see the instructions on [page 3].

ILLUSTRATION B.3

Wage and Tax Statement (Form W-2)

2 Employer's name, address, and ZIP code		16-0331690	Form W-2 Wage and Tax Statement 1990
Doug's Ace Hardware 1290 Atlanta Highway Athens, GA 30605		17	18 Other

3 Employer's identification number 15-249363	4 Employer's state I.D. number 33048	5 Employee's social security numbr y 253-13-2807	
6 Deceased Pension plan	Legal rep Deferred compensation	7 Allocated tips	19 Employee's name, address and ZIP code
8 Advance EIC payment	9 Federal income tax withheld $1,968	10 Wages, tips, other compensation $20,000	John R. Hanson 325 St. George Drive Athens, GA 30605
11 Social security tax withheld $1,530	12 Social security wages $20,000	13 Social security tips	
14 Nonqualified plans	15 Dependent care benefits	16 Fringe benefits incl. in Box 10	

24 State income tax $296.44	25 State wages,tips,etc. $20,000	26 Name of state Georgia	27 Local income tax	28 Local wages,tips,etc.	29 Name of locality

ILLUSTRATION B.4

Employee Earnings Record

Name: John R. Hanson
Address: 325 St. George Drive
Athens, Ga. 30605
Date of birth: June 20, 1950
Date employed: March 12, 1972

Social Security No. 253 13 2807
Sex: Male (x) Female ( )
Single ( ) Married (x)
Withholding allowances ___3___
Date terminated _____

Employee No. ___5___
Position: Sales
Hourly pay rate $13.00
Spouse: Susan
Telephone No. 394-1776

1991* Period Ended	Total Hours	Earnings			Deductions					Payment		Cumu- lative Gross Earnings
		Regular	Overtime	Gross	Federal Income Tax	FICA Tax	State Income Tax	Medical Insur- ance	Other	Net Pay	Check No.	
Feb. 5	40	520.00		520.00	50.00	39.78	6.78	24.00		399.44	673	520.00
12	40	520.00		520.00	50.00	39.78	6.78	24.00		399.44	807	1,040.00
19	45	520.00	97.50	617.50	63.00	47.24	8.06	24.00		475.20	913	1,657.50

* 1991 dates are used throughout this appendix because the tax rates used are as of 1991.

ducted are paid directly by the employer to the insurance companies. Employees may also authorize payroll deductions for loan repayments to, or savings in, the employees' credit union. Employee pledges to charities, such as the United Way Fund, are often collected through payroll deductions.

Other less common deductions are for pension or retirement plans, where the employee is obligated to pay at least a portion of the cost of the plan. Some businesses may allow payroll deductions to pay for merchandise purchased by the employee. Employees may purchase U.S. Savings Bonds through payroll deductions. The number and types of optional payroll deductions are determined by the company, the employment contract, and the employee.

Maintaining Employee Earnings Record

Federal law requires employers to maintain an adequate payroll record for each employee. This record is called an employee earnings record. As shown in Illustration B.4, an employee earnings record shows information such as name, social

ILLUSTRATION B.5

Payroll Journal (or Register)

PAYROLL JOURNAL (OR REGISTER)

Date Week Ended 1991	Employee	Gross Pay			Deductions				Salaries Payable (Net Pay) Cr.	Check No.
		Sales Salaries Expense Dr.	Delivery Salaries Expense Dr.	Office Salaries Expense Dr.	Employees' Federal Income Taxes Payable Cr.	FICA Taxes Payable Cr.	Employees' State Income Taxes Payable Cr.	Employees' Medical Insurance Premiums Payable Cr.		
Feb. 5	John Hanson	520.00			50.00	39.78	6.78	24.00	399.44	673
	Robert Lash		510.00		68.00	39.02	4.18	10.00	388.80	674
	Mike Miller	750.00			82.00	57.38	7.29	20.00	583.33	675
	Bill Norman	640.00			77.00	48.96	5.83	15.00	493.21	676
	Allison Wheeler	590.00			69.00	45.14	5.17	15.00	455.69	677
	Cathy Yorb			520.00	64.00	39.78	4.24	10.00	401.98	678
		2,500.00	510.00	520.00	410.00	270.06	33.49	94.00	2,722.45	

security number, address, phone number, date employed, date of birth, marital status, number of withholding allowances claimed, pay rate, and present job within the company. For each pay period, the record also shows the number of hours worked, gross pay, deductions, and net pay. Cumulative gross pay during the year is included to indicate when the maximum amounts have been reached for FICA tax withholdings and unemployment taxes (which will be discussed later in the chapter). The amounts shown in Illustration B.4 for federal withholding may differ from current amounts and are used for illustrative purposes only.

Preparing Payroll Journal

A business may use a payroll journal (Illustration B.5) to reduce the work involved in recording payroll. A payroll journal contains a debit column for each category of salary expense, such as sales, delivery, and office. Credit columns are included for withholdings made for various taxes and other deductions and Salaries Payable. These amounts all represent liabilities that must be paid either to agencies on the employee's behalf or to the employees. Note that a Check No. column is included to show which check was used to pay the Salaries Payable liability amounts. Postings can be made directly from the payroll journal to the ledger. Alternatively, a payroll register can be used merely to collect the information so a journal entry can be made in the general journal. If the payroll shown in Illustration B.5 were recorded in the general journal, the entry would be as follows:

1991 Feb.	5	Sales Salaries Expense.	2,500.00	
		Delivery Salaries Expense	510.00	
		Office Salaries Expense	520.00	
		Employees' Federal Income Taxes Payable.		410.00
		FICA Taxes Payable		270.06
		Employees' State Income Taxes Payable.		33.49
		Employees' Medical Insurance Premiums Payable.		94.00
		Salaries Payable.		2,722.45
		To record the payroll for the week ending February 5.		

All accounts credited in the February 5 entry are current liabilities and will be reported on the balance sheet if not paid prior to the preparation of financial statements. When the payroll is actually paid, the payment will be recorded in the cash disbursements journal as a debit to Salaries Payable and a credit to Cash of $2,722.45.

PAYING THE PAYROLL—PAYROLL CHECKING ACCOUNT

The use of a payroll checking account—a separate checking account maintained by the business only to pay salaries and wages—is common among companies with many employees who are paid by check. In general, a payroll checking account is used as follows: The payroll checking account is established by depositing a small amount in the account and debiting Payroll Checking and crediting Cash. Before each payday, the payroll is prepared and recorded in a routine manner. One check is drawn on the company's regular checking account for the net payroll amount. This check is deposited in the payroll checking account. The accountant debits Salaries Payable and credits Cash. Payroll checks are then drawn on the payroll checking account and issued to employees. As the payroll checks are cashed by employees and clear the bank, the payroll checking account balance approaches zero.

The use of a payroll checking account has several advantages:

1. A distinctive payroll check form may be used, with spaces provided on an attachment for gross earnings, various payroll deductions, and net cash paid. See Illustration B.6.

2. Payroll checks, identifiable as such, are easily cashed by employees.

3. The work of reconciling the bank balances can be divided among employees. Only one check is drawn on the general bank account. The hundreds or thousands of payroll checks issued each payday are drawn on the payroll bank account. Occasionally, payroll checks will be negotiated many times or lost before clearing the bank. Including these items in the payroll reconciliation simplifies the reconciliation of the general Cash account.

4. Only one authorization is prepared, calling for one check drawn on the general bank account; therefore, payroll checks are issued without separately prepared and signed authorizations.

5. Individual payroll checks need not be entered in the regular cash disbursements record; payroll check numbers are inserted in the payroll journal, and repetition of the entering of checks is avoided.

6. The chance of fraud is reduced in a small business. Since the monthly payroll is not likely to be large, a large bogus payroll check could not clear the bank.

RECORDING EMPLOYER PAYROLL TAXES

An employer is generally obligated to pay three taxes levied on payrolls. The entry to record these taxes results in three liabilities: FICA Taxes Payable, State Unemployment Taxes Payable, and Federal Unemployment Taxes Payable.

FICA (Social Security) Taxes

An employer is required to match the amount of FICA tax withheld from each employee's pay. For example, total FICA tax in 1991 amounted to 15.3% of the first $53,400 of each employee's earnings; half (7.65%) was paid by the employee, and half (7.65%) by the employer. An additional 1.45% must be paid on amounts over $53,400 up to $125,000 of earned income.

ILLUSTRATION B.6

Payroll Check and Supporting Employee's Earnings Statement

Employee	Hours Worked	Rate per Hour	Regular Earn- ings	Extra for Overtime	Gross Earn- ings	Fed. Inc. Tax W/H	FICA	State Inc. Tax W/H	Hosp. Ins.	Net Pay
John R. Hanson	40	13.00	520.00	0	520.00	50.00	39.78	6.78	24.00	399.44

Retain this stub for your records - Detach before cashing check

---

ACE HARDWARE

DOUG'S ACE HARDWARE
1290 Atlanta Highway
ATHENS, GEORGIA 30605

673

February 8 ___ 19__91__ 64-1240/611

PAY TO THE ORDER OF John R. Hanson $ 399.44

Three hundred ninety-nine and $^{44}/100's_ ———————— DOLLARS

The CITIZENS and SOUTHERN BANK
NORTH SPRINGS OFFICE
ATLANTA, GEORGIA

FOR_____   _George C. Beacham_

⑈000673⑈ ⑉0611⑈1240⑇ 038 82 131⑈

Federal Unemployment Tax

The Federal Unemployment Tax Act (FUTA) requires employers to pay a federal unemployment tax based on employee salaries and wages. This tax helps finance a cooperative federal-state system of unemployment compensation. Unemployment benefits are paid to qualified unemployed persons by each of the states and territorial governments. State unemployment laws vary only in minor respects; the Federal Unemployment Tax Act sets forth certain minimum standards that must be met by each state.

The federal unemployment tax rate generally has varied based on the actions of Congress. In 1991, the rate was 6.2% of the first $7,000 of wages paid to each employee. This rate will be used for illustrative purposes. The Federal Unemployment Tax Act provides that employers may have a maximum credit of 5.4% against their federal unemployment tax for amounts that were paid to the state. This credit, in effect, makes the federal unemployment tax rate (6.2% − 5.4%) = 0.8% on the first $7,000 of individual employee wages.

State Unemployment Tax

The state unemployment tax generally is 5.4% of the first $7,000 of gross earnings per employee. This rate and base will be used for illustrative purposes in this appendix. A merit rate can be gained by employers to reduce the state rate to as little as 0.5% in some states and even to zero in other states. A reduced rate is earned by employers with low turnover and few layoffs. Employers with lower merit rates can still deduct a credit of 5.4% against their federal unemployment tax rate.

Payroll Tax Entry

Employer payroll taxes are usually recorded at the same time as the payroll to which they relate. For example, the employer's payroll taxes (at 1991 rates) on the amount of the February 5 payroll in Illustration B.5 are recorded as follows:

Feb.	5	Payroll Taxes Expense	488.92	
		FICA Taxes Payable		270.06
		State Unemployment Taxes Payable.		190.62
		Federal Unemployment Taxes Payable		28.24
		To record employer's payroll taxes.		

Remember that these amounts are in addition to amounts withheld from employees. This journal entry debits Payroll Taxes Expense for the total of the employer's three payroll taxes. The credit to FICA Taxes Payable is equal to the amount deducted from the employees' gross pay. Both the employer's and employees' FICA taxes can be credited to the same liability account, since both are payable at the same time to the same agency. The credits to the state and federal unemployment accounts are for 5.4% and 0.8%, respectively, of the $3,530 of gross pay for this payroll period. We assumed that no employee had been paid more than $7,000 in the current year. Any earnings in excess of $7,000 would have been excluded from the computation of unemployment taxes, since those taxes are levied only on the first $7,000 of annual income per employee.

REMITTING TAXES WITHHELD, UNEMPLOYMENT TAXES, AND OTHER DEDUCTIONS

Generally, within one month after the end of each calendar quarter, an employer must file an **Employer's Quarterly Federal Tax Return (Form 941)** with the Internal Revenue Service. This form reports the amount of FICA and income taxes withheld for the preceding quarter. The employer reports (1) total wages subject to withholding, (2) federal income taxes withheld, (3) total wages subject to FICA tax, (4) amount of FICA taxes due (from both employer and employees), and (5) combined amount of income tax withheld and FICA taxes due. A similar form is required by states with state income tax laws.

Taxes Withheld

For remittance purposes, federal income taxes withheld and both the employees' and employer's FICA taxes are combined. Generally, employers are required to deposit such taxes in a Federal Reserve Bank or an authorized commercial bank called a **federal depository bank.** When deposited, these amounts are credited by the bank to an Internal Revenue Service account. Deposit requirements are quite detailed and depend on the amount of taxes collected relative to the time elapsed since the last deposit. The more dollars of taxes that are collected, the more rapidly deposits must be made. Taxes properly deposited are considered paid.

Assuming the amount of federal income taxes withheld is $3,687 and the amount of combined FICA taxes is $2,500, the entry to record this deposit is:

Employees' Federal Income Taxes Payable	3,687.00	
FICA Taxes Payable	2,500.00	
Cash		6,187.00
To record deposit of taxes withheld and employer FICA taxes.		

State and city income taxes must be withheld by employers in most states and in many cities. The procedures for withholding and the required remittances are usually modeled after federal income tax regulations. The entry for employers to record payment of these taxes debits Employees' State (City) Income Taxes Payable and credits Cash.

ILLUSTRATION B.7

Summary of Payroll Taxes

Type of Tax	Who Pays for It	Amount of Tax
FICA (social security)	Both employer and employee pay at current rate	7.65% of first $53,400, and 1.45% on amounts over $53,400 up to $125,000, that each employee earns annually*
Income	Employee	Varies with earnings and exemptions
State unemployment	Employer (usually)	5.4% of first $7,000 each employee earns annually†
Federal unemployment	Employer	0.8% of first $7,000 each employee earns annually‡

* This rate and base are for 1991.

† Some states have a higher rate and/or base than this. Also, most states allow reduction from the basic rate to firms with low labor turnover.

‡ The federal rate varies, but in this appendix it is assumed to be 6.2%. An allowance of 5.4% is granted for amounts paid to the state, thus reducing the effective rate to 0.8%.

Unemployment Taxes

The amount of federal unemployment taxes to be deposited is determined quarterly. When a certain amount is reached, these taxes must be deposited in a federal depository bank. Assuming the amount of federal unemployment taxes is $400, the entry to record the deposit is:

Federal Unemployment Taxes Payable	400.00	
Cash		400.00
To record deposit of federal unemployment taxes.		

Remittance requirements for state unemployment taxes vary from state to state. Quarterly reports and payments are usually required by the end of the month following the quarter's end. The entry to record the payment is a debit to State Unemployment Taxes Payable and a credit to Cash.

Other Payroll Deductions

The remittance of other types of payroll deductions varies based on the agency or organization to which payment is to be made. Monthly payment is likely for union dues, medical insurance premiums, charitable contributions, and pension contributions.

A summary of the various payroll taxes appears in Illustration B.7.

PREPARING END-OF-PERIOD ACCRUALS

Adjusting entries are usually needed at year-end to accrue wages, employer's payroll taxes, and vacation pay.

Wages and Payroll Taxes

The matching principle requires accrued wages and employer payroll taxes on these wages to be recorded at the end of every period. To illustrate, assume that Doug's Hardware Company accrues the following salaries and payroll taxes on December 31, 1991: sales salaries, $900; delivery salaries, $160; office salaries, $210; and employer's FICA tax expense, $97.16. The required entries are:

Dec.	31	Sales Salaries Expense.	900.00	
		Delivery Salaries Expense	160.00	
		Office Salaries Expense	210.00	
		Salaries Payable.		1,270.00
		To accrue salaries.		
	31	Payroll Taxes Expense	97.16	
		FICA Taxes Payable		97.16
		To accrue payroll taxes.		

Note in the first entry that credits are not entered in separate liability accounts for payroll deductions. These deductions will be recorded when the payroll is paid since they are not actually withheld from the employees until then. The second entry recorded the employer's FICA taxes on $1,270 of salaries. We assumed that no employee had reached the maximum FICA limit; therefore, all accrued salaries would be subject to FICA taxation. Accrued federal and state unemployment taxes were not included in this example because by year-end all employees' earnings should have surpassed the $7,000 maximum amount subject to taxation.

Some companies do not accrue employer's payroll taxes at year-end. The following reasons are given for this violation of the matching principle: (1) no legal liability for such taxes exists until the wages are paid, (2) such taxes do not vary much in amount from year to year, and (3) the amounts of such taxes are likely to be immaterial. A policy of not accruing payroll taxes is acceptable under these circumstances.

Vacation Pay

Most employees in this country are entitled to annual vacations of from one to four weeks at full regular pay. The compensation received while on vacation is called vacation pay. Thus, the employer annually pays an employee for 52 weeks but receives services for a fewer number of weeks.

How to account for vacation pay raises an important question: Should vacation pay be expensed when paid, or should it be accrued over the period in which the employee works to earn the vacation? *FASB Statement No. 43,* "Accounting for Compensated Absences," requires the accrual of a liability for vacation pay if the following conditions are met:

1. The employer is obligated to pay as a result of services already received.
2. The employee's right to vacation pay does not depend on continued performance of services.
3. It is probable the vacation pay will be paid.
4. The amount of vacation pay can be reasonably estimated.

Assume Davis Company estimates that out of every 25 workdays employees will earn 1 day of vacation pay. As a result, vacation pay is to be accrued at a rate of 4% (1 day/25 days) of gross pay. The entry to accrue vacation pay on a $3,200 payroll is:

Vacation Pay Expense ($3,200 × 0.04).	128.00	
Estimated Vacation Pay Payable.		128.00
To accrue vacation pay.		

Accruing vacation pay in this manner records the expense over the period in which it was earned rather than when it was paid, which method results in a better matching of expenses and revenues. A liability is also recorded for the vacation pay currently owed by the employer to employees. Often employees must forfeit vacation pay earned if they leave the company before some minimum length of time, such as one year. If turnover of these employees is expected, the amount of the entry to accrue vacation pay should be reduced accordingly.

When vacation pay is paid, the estimated liability account is debited, and various accounts are credited for taxes, other deductions, and cash payment. For example, an employee earning $400 per week is to be paid for two weeks' vacation. A payroll check is drawn for the net pay due and entered in the payroll journal. Using assumed deductions, the entry in general journal form would be:

Estimated Vacation Pay Payable.	800.00	
Employees' Federal Income Taxes Payable.		141.00
FICA Taxes Payable .		61.20
Medical Insurance Premiums Payable .		50.00
Employees' State Income Taxes Payable.		11.00
Cash.		536.80
To record payment of vacation pay.		

CONSIDERING MORE EFFICIENT METHODS OF PAYROLL ACCOUNTING

The payroll deductions described in this appendix are used effectively by many small companies. However, some of these companies use a manual system called a pegboard system of payroll accounting to increase efficiency. Such a system aligns the payroll check, the individual earnings record, and the payroll journal in such a way that all three are completed with one writing. Instead of having to record gross pay, deductions, and net pay three different times for each employee, the recording is done only once by using a pegboard system of payroll accounting. Of course, the forms must be designed so that they are compatible. Use of such a system can reduce clerical time dramatically. Also, many microcomputer accounting software packages used by small companies have payroll modules that can easily handle all the payroll functions described in this appendix.

In larger companies, minicomputers or mainframe computers often are used to perform the payroll function. Also, many banks and service bureaus offer computerized payroll processing services.

CORPORATE FEDERAL INCOME TAXATION

Most corporations organized for profit must file a federal income tax return and pay corporate income tax on their net income. Not-for-profit organizations, specifically exempted by law, do not file an income tax return but must file an annual return of information.

INCOME BEFORE TAXES VERSUS TAXABLE INCOME

Income before federal income taxes (as shown on the income statement) and taxable income (as shown in the corporation's tax return) need not necessarily agree. Some of the reasons why they might differ are:

1. Certain items of revenue and expense included in the computation of business income are excluded from the computation of taxable income. For instance, interest earned on certain state, county, or municipal bonds is not subject to tax although this interest is a component of business in-

come. Additionally, the general rule is that only "ordinary" and "necessary" business expenses and "reasonable" amounts of salaries can be deducted for tax purposes. Life insurance premiums are not deductible if the corporation is the beneficiary; however, proceeds received from life insurance policies are not taxed. Costs of attempting to influence legislation are not deductible. A corporation may deduct from taxable income 80% of any dividends received from other domestic corporations. Goodwill may not be amortized for tax purposes even though it must be for accounting purposes.

2. The timing of recognition of items of revenue and expense often varies for tax purposes from the timing used in determining business income. Interpretations of the tax code have generally held that revenue received in advance is taxable when received and that current expenses based on estimates of future costs (such as costs of performance under service contracts) are not deductible until actually incurred. Thus, taxable income is determined at least partially on a cash basis, while business income is determined on an accrual basis. The installment sales method could formerly be used for tax purposes but only rarely for accounting purposes. Under this method, revenue was recognized for tax purposes only when collections were received. Also, certain elective accounting methods may be used for tax purposes that are different from those methods used for financial statements. For instance, often a corporation may use straight-line depreciation for book purposes and a different depreciation method for tax purposes.

For a given corporation, the reconciliation between net income before taxes and taxable income may appear as follows:

Net income before taxes per income statement		$111,000
Add:		
Life insurance premiums paid	$1,050	
Service revenue received in advance	7,500	
Estimated expenses under service contracts	1,500	10,050
		$121,050
Deduct:		
Interest on New York State bonds	$4,500	
Difference in depreciation for tax purposes ($9,000)		
and for book purposes ($6,000)	3,000	7,500
Taxable income		$113,550

Tax Rates

Once taxable income is determined, a tax rate is applied to find the amount of tax liability. As of this writing, the graduated tax rates applicable to corporations are as shown in Illustration B.8.

To illustrate, using these corporate tax rates, a corporation with taxable income of $110,000 will have a tax liability of $26,150, computed as follows:

Tax on first $50,000 (at 15%)	$ 7,500
Tax on next $25,000 (at 25%)	6,250
Tax on next $25,000 (at 34%)	8,500
Tax on remaining $10,000 (at 39%)	3,900
	$26,150

ILLUSTRATION B.8

Corporate Tax Rates

Corporate Taxable Income	Tax Rate
$0–$ 50,000.	15%
$ 50,001–$ 75,000.	25
$ 75,001–$100,000.	34
$100,000–$335,000.	39

A corporation with taxable income over $335,000 will pay a flat tax rate of 34% on all taxable income.

Likewise, a corporation with taxable income of $500,000 will have a tax liability of $170,000 ($500,000 × 34%).

The tax law requires an alternative minimum tax to be calculated and paid by the corporation if the minimum tax is higher than the ordinary tax. The tax will be calculated at 20% of taxable income adjusted by adding back a number of the tax breaks allowed to arrive at taxable income and reduced, in some cases, by an exemption of up to $40,000.

Loss Carryback and Carryforward

A provision of the tax law allows corporations to carry losses incurred in the current year back 3 years and forward 15 years to offset past or future taxes. (Alternatively, the corporation may elect to only carry the loss forward for 15 years.) A loss carryback is a current loss that has been applied against taxable income of prior periods, thereby resulting in a tax refund in the current period. In applying a loss carryback, the company must apply the loss to the oldest year first, then the next oldest, and so on until the loss has been completely "used up" by offsetting it against ordinary taxable income of these years. The corporation recomputes its taxes for those previous years using the rates then in effect.

To illustrate this provision, assume the amounts of taxable income (or loss) shown below (1991 rates were used to compute taxes paid):

Year	Taxable Income (or loss)	Taxes Paid	Taxes Recovered
1990	$ 7,500	$1,125	$1,125
1991	10,000	1,500	1,500
1992	2,500·	375	375
1993	(50,000)	–0–	–0–
1994	20,000	–0–	–0–
1995	5,000	–0–	–0–
1996	15,000	1,500	–0–
1997	25,000	3,750	–0–
1998	30,000	4,500	–0–

The loss of $50,000 in 1993 would first be offset against the $7,500 of taxable income in 1990, then the $10,000 in 1991, and next the $2,500 in 1992. The company would recover the taxes previously paid in those years, which total $3,000.

At this point, the company would have a loss carryforward of $30,000. A loss carryforward is a current loss that will be applied against taxable income in future periods, thereby reducing the taxes payable of future periods. In the above example, the company would apply $20,000 of this $30,000 toward taxable income in 1994 and therefore would pay no taxes in that year. At this point, $10,000 of the carryforward remains: $5,000 of this amount would be used to offset taxable income in the next year (1995), and the other $5,000 would be applied against 1996 taxable income.

Accounting Methods Used for Tax Purposes

Accrual Method The method of accounting used determines when revenues and expenses are recognized. Most corporations and large businesses use the accrual method. Under this method, revenues are generally recognized when earned. The earning of revenue normally occurs when services are rendered or when goods are delivered. When payment has been received before the revenue has been earned, an exception may require recognition of income at the time payment is received.

Expenses are generally recognized when liabilities are incurred for goods or services received. Costs of assets are deferred and charged to expense in the period in which the assets are used or consumed.

Modified Cash Method Sole proprietorships, partnerships, and certain small corporations may use a modified cash method. This method is described as a "modified" (rather than a "pure") cash method because long-term assets cannot be charged to expense when purchased, nor can all prepaid expenses (such as a three-year insurance premium) be deducted when paid. Also, revenues must be reported when constructively received even though the cash is not yet in the possession of the business. For instance, a check received at the end of the year is considered revenue even though it has not been cashed. If inventories are a substantial factor in producing income, the company must use the accrual basis for recognizing sales, cost of goods sold, and related asset (inventory and accounts receivable) and liability (accounts payable) accounts.

Accounting for Inventories Accountants use several different methods to account for inventories. Each method assumes a different flow of costs and thus results in a different taxable income if used for tax purposes. In recent years many firms have adopted LIFO (last-in, first-out), in which the last goods purchased are assumed to be the first ones sold. Under this method, during periods of rising prices, the most recent **higher** costs are charged against revenues and the asset, inventory, is shown at lower earlier costs. The result is lower net income and lower taxes. The tax law generally permits a company to use the LIFO method for tax purposes only if it uses LIFO for financial statement purposes.

Depreciation Methods Used for Tax Purposes Tax depreciation is substantially different than depreciation used for accounting purposes. In accounting, depreciation methods are designed to match the expense of a capital investment against the revenue the investment produces. The depreciable period or useful life used for tax purposes is based on law and has no relationship to the actual useful life of the related asset; thus, no attempt is made to match revenues and expenses.

Prior to 1981, several depreciation methods were available for tax purposes, including the sum-of-the-years'-digits method and the uniform-rate-on-declining-balance method. The Economic Recovery Tax Act of 1981 introduced a new depreciation system known as the Accelerated Cost Recovery System (ACRS). However, generally effective January 1, 1987, the Tax Reform Act of 1986 substantially modified the ACRS rules. For purposes of this text, we shall refer to these rules as modified ACRS.

ILLUSTRATION B.9

Modified ACRS

Class of Investment	Kinds of Assets
3 years	Investments in some short-lived assets.
5 years	Automobiles, light-duty trucks, and machinery and equipment used in research and development.
7 years	All other machinery and equipment, such as dies, drills, or presses, furniture, and fixtures.
10 years	Some longer-lived equipment.
15 years	Sewage treatment plants and telephone distribution plants.
20 years	Sewer pipes and very long-lived equipment.
27.5 years	Residential rental property.
31.5 years	Nonresidential real estate.

Capital assets are grouped into one of eight different classes (Illustration B.9). Each class has an assigned life over which costs of the assets (not reduced by salvage) are depreciated.

Capital assets in the 3-, 5-, 7-, and 10-year classes may be depreciated by using the 200% declining-balance method. Assets in the 15- and 20-year classes may be depreciated by using the 150% declining-balance method. Assets in the 27.5- and 31.5-year classes must be depreciated by using straight-line depreciation. The declining-balance methods result in faster write-offs in the first few years of an investment's life. Cash saved from reduced taxes in the early years of life of the assets can be invested in new productive assets or can be applied to the replacement of the old assets when they become obsolete or worn out.

Once the asset has been classified, the depreciation schedule for the life of the asset can be completed. To illustrate a depreciation schedule, assume that Bigwig Company acquired and placed in service a depreciable asset on January 1, 1991, for $10,000. The asset falls into the five-year class. The depreciation schedule for the asset would be as follows:

Year	Recovery Percentage*	×	Original Cost	=	Depreciation Expense	Total Accumulated Depreciation	Book Value
1991	20	×	$10,000	=	$ 2,000	$ 2,000	$ 8,000
1992	32	×	10,000	=	3,200	5,200	4,800
1993	19	×	10,000	=	1,900	7,100	2,900
1994	15	×	10,000	=	1,500	8,600	1,400
1995	14	×	10,000	=	1,400	10,000	–0–

* These percentages are calculated by the authors using the 200% declining-balance procedure with one-half year depreciation taken in the year the asset is placed in service and switching to the straight-line method in 1994 in order to maximize depreciation. Percentages were rounded to whole numbers.

Tax depreciation is very desirable from the corporation's viewpoint since it decreases taxable income and hence the corporation's tax liability. However, when revenues are expected to be low in the early years and high in later years, it may be beneficial for taxpayers to spread the depreciation more evenly over the entire life of the asset rather than taking most of it in the earlier years of an asset's life. For this reason, the law provides an alternative. The taxpayer may elect to use the straight-line method rather than the accelerated (table) method.

INCOME TAX ALLOCATION

Taxable income and income before federal income taxes (for simplicity, pre-tax income) for a corporation may differ sharply for a number of reasons. In fact, the tax return may show a loss, while the income statement shows positive pre-tax income. This difference raises a question about the amount of income taxes to be shown on the income statement. The answer lies in the nature of the items causing the difference between taxable income and pre-tax income. Some items create permanent differences, while others create temporary (or timing) differences. Both kinds of differences are discussed below.

Permanent Differences

Certain types of revenues and expenses included in the computation of net income for book purposes are excluded from the computation of taxable income. **Permanent differences** between taxable income and financial statement pre-tax income are caused by tax law provisions that exclude certain items of expense, revenue, gain, or loss as elements of taxable income. For instance, interest earned on certain state, county, or municipal bonds is included in book net income but is not subject to tax and therefore is not included in determining taxable income. The same is true for life insurance proceeds received by a corporation. Other items that are expensed for book purposes are not deductible for tax purposes, such as premiums paid for officers' life insurance, costs of attempting to influence legislation, and amortization of goodwill. These are only a few of the numerous items for which the tax treatment is completely different from the accounting treatment. These differences in treatment **never** change or reverse themselves. Therefore, they are called **permanent differences.** Such differences cause no accounting problem—the estimated actual amount of income tax expense for the year is shown on the income statement even if this method results in reporting only $1,000 of income tax expense on $100,000 of pre-tax income.

Temporary Differences

Other items of revenue and expense are often recognized at different times for tax purposes and for financial reporting purposes. A **temporary difference** is a difference between taxable income and financial statement pre-tax income caused by items that affect both taxable income and pre-tax income, but in different periods. For example, interpretations of the tax code generally have held that revenue received in advance is taxable when received and that current expenses based on estimates of future costs (such as costs of performance under service contracts) are not deductible until incurred. Temporary differences can also result from using accounting methods for tax purposes that are different than the ones used for financial reporting purposes. For example, a corporation may use straight-line depreciation for book purposes and modified ACRS depreciation for tax purposes. Eventually these revenues and expenses are recognized in computing both accounting income and taxable income. Therefore, these variations between taxable income and pre-tax net income are called temporary differences.

For a given corporation, the reconciliation between (1) income before income taxes per the income statement and (2) taxable income per the tax return appears below:

Income before income taxes per income statement		$74,000
Add:		
Life insurance premium paid	$ 700	
Service revenue received in advance	5,000	
Estimated expenses under service contracts	1,000	6,700
		$80,700
Deduct:		
Interest on New York State bonds.	$3,000	
Difference in depreciation for tax purposes ($8,000)		
and for book purposes ($6,000)	2,000	5,000
Taxable income		$75,700

As discussed above, temporary differences include items that will be included in both taxable income and in pre-tax income, but in different periods. The items involved thus will have a tax effect. When temporary differences exist, generally accepted accounting principles require application of tax allocation procedures. Under interperiod income tax allocation, the tax effect of an element of expense or revenue, or loss or gain, that will affect taxable income is allocated to the period in which the item is recognized for accounting purposes, regardless of the period in which the element is recognized for tax purposes.

In the preceding reconciliation between net income before taxes and taxable income, the life insurance premiums paid (for which the corporation is beneficiary of the policy) are **never deductible** for income tax purposes, and the interest on New York State bonds is **never taxable.** These are permanent differences and therefore involve no interperiod income tax allocation. The other reconciling items are temporary differences for which interperiod income tax allocation procedures are required.

Income Tax Allocation Illustrated To illustrate the tax allocation procedure required for temporary differences, assume that:

1. A firm acquired a depreciable asset on January 1, 1991, for $10,000 that has an estimated useful life of five years with no expected scrap value.

2. The firm uses the straight-line depreciation method for financial reporting purposes and the modified ACRS method for tax purposes (the related asset falls into the five-year class for which depreciation has been previously calculated).

3. Net income before depreciation and income taxes is $10,000 for each year of the asset's life.

4. No other items cause differences between pre-tax income and taxable income.

5. The tax rate is 15% (to simplify the illustration).

The tax liability for each year would be as shown in Illustration B.10.

Income tax expense for each year for financial reporting purposes would be as shown in Illustration B.11.

Note that for 1992, tax depreciation ($3,200, Illustration B.10) exceeds the book expense for depreciation ($2,000, Illustration B.11) by $1,200, but that effect is reversed during 1993 through 1995 so that depreciation at the end of 1995 is the same ($10,000) in both cases. Since the effects reverse over time, they constitute temporary differences for which deferred income taxes are provided in the books. Because tax and book depreciation happen to be the same for 1991, no deferred

ILLUSTRATION B.10

Calculation of Tax Liability

	1991	1992	1993	1994	1995	Total
Income before depreciation and income taxes.	$10,000	$10,000	$10,000	$10,000	$10,000	$50,000
Depreciation for tax purposes	2,000	3,200	1,900	1,500	1,400	10,000
Taxable income.	$ 8,000	$ 6,800	$ 8,100	$ 8,500	$ 8,600	$40,000
Income taxes payable (15% of taxable income).	$ 1,200	$ 1,020	$ 1,215	$ 1,275	$ 1,290	$ 6,000

ILLUSTRATION B.11

Evaluation of Tax Expense

	1991	1992	1993	1994	1995	Total
Income before depreciation and income taxes.	$10,000	$10,000	$10,000	$10,000	$10,000	$50,000
Depreciation (straight-line method) .	2,000	2,000	2,000	2,000	2,000	10,000
Pre-tax income .	$ 8,000	$ 8,000	$ 8,000	$ 8,000	$ 8,000	$40,000
Income tax expense (15% of pre-tax income).	1,200	1,200	1,200	1,200	1,200	6,000
Net income	$ 6,800	$ 6,800	$ 6,800	$ 6,800	$ 6,800	$34,000

income tax is needed for that year. The required entries for 1991 and 1992 to record income taxes and to set up deferred income taxes for the temporary difference for the excess of tax depreciation over financial depreciation are:

	1991		1992	
Federal Income Tax Expense .	1,200		1,200	
Federal Income Tax Payable .		1,200		1,020
Deferred Federal Income Tax Payable .		–0–		180
To record income tax expense.				

The required entries for 1993 through 1995 to record income taxes and to reduce the deferred income taxes as the temporary difference reverses (i.e., financial depreciation exceeds tax depreciation) are:

	1993		1994		1995	
Federal Income Tax Expense .	1,200		1,200		1,200	
Deferred Federal Income Tax Payable .	15		75		90	
Federal Income Tax Payable .		1,215		1,275		1,290
To record income tax expense.						

Note again that the amount of tax expense recognized remains constant at $1,200 even though the tax liability varies from $1,020 for 1992 to $1,290 for 1995. The normalizing of the tax expense for each year is accomplished by making entries in the Deferred Federal Income Tax Payable account. The tables clearly show that the tax expense for the five years is $6,000 and that the tax payments for the five years also sum to $6,000. The only difference is that the tax expense charged to each year is not the same amount as the actual liability for the year.

In this simplified example, the Deferred Federal Income Tax Payable account has a zero balance at the end of five years. However, actual business experience has shown that once a Deferred Federal Income Tax Payable account is established, it is seldom decreased or reduced to zero. The reason is that most businesses acquire new depreciable assets, usually at higher prices. The result is that depreciation for tax purposes continues to be greater than depreciation for financial reporting purposes, and the balance in the Deferred Federal Income Tax Payable account also continues to grow. For this reason, many accountants seriously question the validity of tax allocation in circumstances such as those described above. Also, some accountants question whether a company can have a liability at a reporting date for income taxes for tax years that have not yet started. Discussion of these controversial issues must be left to more advanced texts. In the above example, the Deferred Federal Income Tax Payable account would be reported as a long-term liability on the balance sheet because the asset causing its existence is classified as a long-term asset.

THE NEED FOR TAX PLANNING

Numerous examples could be given for showing that business decisions are influenced greatly by their tax effects. With the advent of relatively high tax rates, tax planning has become an essential function of management.

The tax laws are extremely complicated and are changing constantly. Those persons who desire to stay current with the status of the law, and with the interpretations of the law made by courts, must specialize in this area.

PERSONAL FEDERAL INCOME TAXES

One of the deductions from employees' gross wages mentioned in the appendix was for federal income taxes. The purpose of this section is to give an introductory understanding of personal income taxes.

WHO MUST FILE A RETURN

In general, all U.S. citizens and resident aliens must file a federal income tax return. More specifically, the determination of who must file a return depends on filing status and income level. The income level changes frequently, so you should check the latest requirements.

Filing Status

Four basic filing statuses may be used in filing an income tax return. These are single, married filing jointly, married filing separately, and head of household. All of these statuses are self-explanatory except head of household, which typically is an unmarried or legally separated person who maintains a residence for a person qualifying as a dependent of the taxpayer.

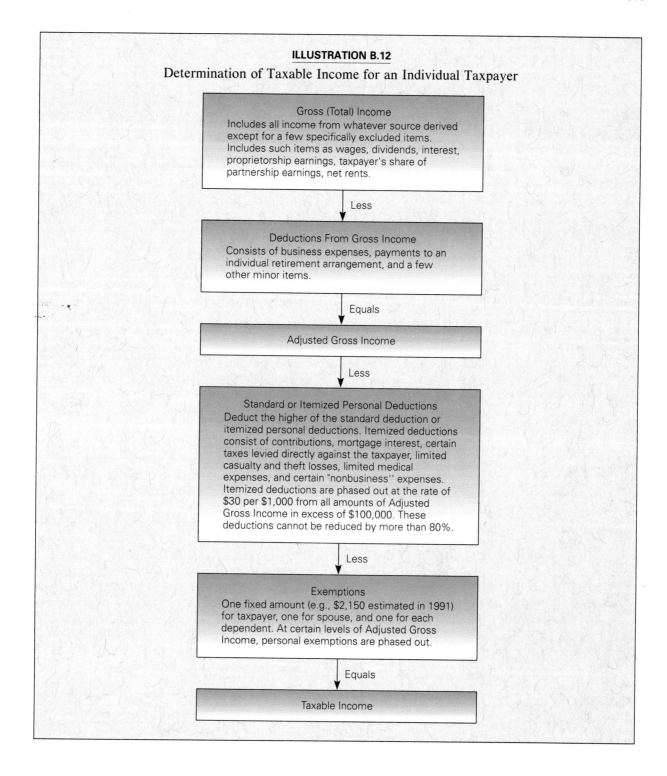

ILLUSTRATION B.12

Determination of Taxable Income for an Individual Taxpayer

Gross (Total) Income
Includes all income from whatever source derived
except for a few specifically excluded items.
Includes such items as wages, dividends, interest,
proprietorship earnings, taxpayer's share of
partnership earnings, net rents.

Less

Deductions From Gross Income
Consists of business expenses, payments to an
individual retirement arrangement, and a few
other minor items.

Equals

Adjusted Gross Income

Less

Standard or Itemized Personal Deductions
Deduct the higher of the standard deduction or
itemized personal deductions. Itemized deductions
consist of contributions, mortgage interest, certain
taxes levied directly against the taxpayer, limited
casualty and theft losses, limited medical
expenses, and certain "nonbusiness" expenses.
Itemized deductions are phased out at the rate of
$30 per $1,000 from all amounts of Adjusted
Gross Income in excess of $100,000. These
deductions cannot be reduced by more than 80%.

Less

Exemptions
One fixed amount (e.g., $2,150 estimated in 1991)
for taxpayer, one for spouse, and one for each
dependent. At certain levels of Adjusted Gross
Income, personal exemptions are phased out.

Equals

Taxable Income

GROSS INCOME

Illustration B.12 contains a general model of the determination of taxable income. The model starts with gross (total) income. Gross income includes all income from whatever source derived, except income specifically exempted, such as social security benefits. Gross income includes wages, interest, dividends, tips, bonuses, gambling winnings, gains from property sales, and prizes (including noncash prizes). Even income generated illegally, such as by theft, must be included in gross income. The general rule is that every income item, unless specifically exempted by law, must be included in gross income.

Exclusions from Gross Income

Income items specifically excluded are interest on certain state and municipal bonds, social security benefits, workers' compensation insurance benefits, and several employee "fringe" benefits, such as employer-paid health insurance premiums. Also, gifts, inheritances, certain disability benefits, scholarships, and the proceeds from life insurance policies are excluded.

ADJUSTED GROSS INCOME

Taxpayers are allowed to deduct certain items from gross income in arriving at adjusted gross income. Deductions for adjusted gross income include business expenses (certain limitations apply), payments by certain individuals to individual retirement accounts (IRAs) or payments to Keogh retirement plans, and alimony paid to a former spouse.

Employees may also deduct from gross income contributions to an individual retirement account (IRA) if neither the taxpayer nor the taxpayer's spouse is an active participant in an employer-sponsored retirement plan, including tax-sheltered annuities, government plans, and Keogh plans. An IRA is a retirement savings account usually set up in a bank, savings and loan association, insurance company, mutual fund, or brokerage firm. The annual deduction is limited to the lesser of 100% of earnings or $2,000 for an individual, $4,000 for a married couple if both spouses have jobs, and $2,250 for a married couple if only one spouse has earned income. Deductions can only be based on earned income, not "passive" income, such as interest and dividends. The maximum amount is phased out, however, where adjusted gross income (before the IRA deduction) is over $40,000 on a joint return or $25,000 for an unmarried individual. The deduction is eliminated when adjusted gross income reaches $50,000 on a joint return or $35,000 for an unmarried person.

Because self-employed individuals are not covered by company-established retirement plans, they are allowed to establish their own retirement plan called a Keogh plan (pronounced Key-oh). Keogh plans are available only to self-employed individuals. A self-employed individual (e.g., a consultant) may contribute annually the lesser of $30,000 or about 13% of self-employment income (20% for money-purchase arrangements) to a profit-sharing Keogh plan. Additional details concerning IRAs and Keogh plans are left to more advanced textbooks.

TAXABLE INCOME

Taxpayers are allowed certain additional deductions and exemptions in arriving at taxable income. The deductions from adjusted gross income are specified by law and consist of two categories: (1) the standard deduction or (2) itemized or personal deductions. Individuals may use either the standard deduction amount or the itemized deductions, whichever amount is higher. The standard deduction amount set by Congress for each type of taxpayer changes frequently. A taxpayer will itemize deductions only if such deductions exceed the standard deduction amount.

To the extent that adjusted gross income exceeds $100,000 for married persons filing jointly or single persons and $50,000 for married persons filing separately, itemized deductions are phased out. For example, a taxpayer (married filing jointly or single) with an adjusted gross income of $150,000 will lose ($150,000–$100,000) × 3% = $1,500 of itemized deductions. These deductions cannot be reduced by more than 80%.

Itemized Deductions

The more common itemized deductions include:

1. Taxes. Real estate taxes, personal property taxes, and state and local income taxes are deductible. License fees, state sales taxes, and federal excise taxes are not deductible.

2. Interest. Interest paid on mortgages on the principal residence and the second residence is generally deductible. The interest must be attributable to loans not exceeding the original purchase price plus the cost of any house improvements (unless the excess mortgage is incurred for educational or medical expenses).

3. Charitable contributions. Gifts to educational, religious, scientific, and charitable organizations are deductible to the extent they do not exceed 50% of adjusted gross income. Donations to individuals, labor unions, and organizations that seek to influence legislation are not deductible.

4. Medical expenses. Within certain limits, unreimbursed hospital, medical, and dental expenses incurred by taxpayers and their dependents are deductible. Only that amount of medical costs that exceeds 7.5% of adjusted gross income is deductible. The entire cost of prescription drugs and insulin can be included in medical costs. The cost of other drugs and medicines cannot be included.

To clarify the treatment of medical expenses, assume that in 1991, a taxpayer with an adjusted gross income of $20,000 paid $550 of health insurance premiums, incurred other medical expenses of $700, and incurred prescription drug costs of $400. The medical deduction is:

Health insurance premiums	$ 550
Other unreimbursed medical expenses	700
Medicine costs	400
	$1,650
Less: 7.5% of adjusted gross income (0.075 × $20,000)	1,500
Medical deduction	$ 150

5. Casualty losses. Casualty losses are sudden and unexpected losses resulting from theft, accidents, storms, fires, and similar events. They are deductible to the extent that **each** casualty loss exceeds $100, **and** that the total of all unreimbursed casualty losses for the year exceeds 10% of adjusted gross income. Thus, to compute the deduction, subtract $100 from the dollar amount of **each** loss (ignore losses of less than $100) to obtain an adjusted casualty loss. Then, from the sum of the adjusted casualty losses, subtract 10% of adjusted gross income. The positive difference is the casualty loss deduction. To illustrate, assume a taxpayer had adjusted gross income of $50,000 and suffered two casualty losses during the year—a fire loss of $9,000 and a theft loss of $12,000. The casualty loss deduction is computed as follows:

Adjusted fire loss ($9,000 − $100)	$ 8,900
Adjusted theft loss ($12,000 − $100)	11,900
Total	$20,800
Less: 10% of adjusted gross income	5,000
Casualty loss deduction	$15,800

6. Other deductions. In general, this category consists of expenses related to the taxpayer's business or profession that are not deductible from gross income. Included are the costs of professional publications and dues, union dues, safe-deposit box rentals, income tax preparer's fees, business entertainment, and job-related clothing and tools. These miscellaneous deductions are only deductible to the extent that they exceed 2% of adjusted gross income.

EXEMPTIONS

The final step to determine taxable income is to deduct exemptions. The dollar amount of exemptions is determined by multiplying the number of exemptions allowed the taxpayer by $2,150 (estimated) in 1991. The exemption allowance will increase in the future because of indexing for inflation. Thus, if a taxpayer has two exemptions in 1991, the dollar amount would be $4,300 ($2,150 × 2). Married persons filing jointly are both considered taxpayers and are allowed one exemption each even though only one spouse has income. An additional exemption may be taken for each dependent.

A dependent for tax purposes is a person who (1) is closely related to the taxpayer or who lived as a member of the taxpayer's family for the entire year; (2) had an income of less than $2,150; (3) received more than half of his or her support from the taxpayer; and (4) who, if married, did not file a joint return with a spouse for the taxable year. An individual eligible to be claimed as a dependent on another taxpayer's return may not deduct any amount as a personal exemption.

Personal exemptions are phased out for certain high-income taxpayers. The phase out begins at different levels of adjusted gross income, depending on the taxpayer's status. For married individuals filing a joint return this level is $150,000, for heads of households it is $100,000, and for married persons filing separately it is $75,000. The reduction is 2% for each $2,500 or fraction thereof in excess of the threshold amount.

COMPUTING TAX LIABILITY

Once taxable income has been determined, the tax liability can be computed using the rates given in Illustration B.13. The tax rates in effect for 1991 will be used unless otherwise stated.

To illustrate the use of these rates, assume Mr. and Mrs. Olson file a joint return showing taxable income of $36,280. Their tax liability is computed as follows:

$$\text{Tax} = \$5,100 + [28\% \times (\$36,280 - \$34,000)]$$
$$= \$5,100 + \$638.40$$
$$= \$5,738.40$$

Marginal and Effective Tax Rates

A quick look at the tax rate schedules in Illustration B.13 shows clearly that the rates are progressive. Progressive tax rates increase with successively higher amounts of taxable income. For example, the taxable income of a single taxpayer between $20,350 and $49,300 is taxed at a 28% rate. These percentages are called marginal tax rates. A marginal tax rate is the rate applied to the next dollar of taxable income or each incremental amount of income. Such rates are important in decision making because they show the marginal effect of a decision. For example, assume that Joe Hardy, a single taxpayer in the 28% tax bracket, could earn $400 on a plumbing job if he would work on Sunday. But being in the 28% bracket means that Joe would have to pay $112 ($400 × 0.28) more income taxes if he takes the job, which means that he would net only $288 from the job. Joe may

---

ILLUSTRATION B.13

Estimated Tax Rate Schedule for 1991

Schedule X—Single Individuals

If taxable income is:		The tax is:	of the amount
Over—	but not over—		over—
$ 0	$20,350	15%	$ 0
20,350	49,300	$ 3,052 plus 28%	20,350
49,300		11,158.50 plus 31%	49,300

Schedule Y-1—Married Persons, Joint Returns

If taxable income is:		The tax is:	of the amount
Over—	but not over—		over—
$ 0	$34,000	15%	$ 0
34,000	82,150	$ 5,100 plus 28%	34,000
82,150		18,582 plus 31%	82,150

Schedule Y-2—Married Persons, Separate Returns

If taxable income is:		The tax is:	of the amount
Over—	but not over—		over—
$ 0	$17,000	15%	$ 0
17,000	41,075	$ 2,550 plus 28%	17,000
41,075		9,291 plus 31%	41,075

Schedule Z—Head of Household

If taxable income is:		The tax is:	of the amount
Over—	but not over—		over—
$ 0	$27,300	15%	$ 0
27,300	70,450	$ 4,095 plus 28%	27,300
70,450		16,177 plus 31%	70,450

Note: These tax schedules were estimated by Commerce Clearing House before the IRS had issued the official figures. They include the estimated inflation adjustment for 1991.

---

decide he would rather watch a football game or go fishing. This type of analysis illustrates the correct use of the marginal tax rate.

The effective tax rate rather than the marginal rate should be used as a measure of total taxes to be paid. The effective tax rate is the average rate of taxation of a given amount of taxable income. For example, if Joe Hardy earns $34,600 for the year, he is in the 28% marginal tax rate bracket. However, he does not pay $9,688 ($34,600 × 0.28) per year in taxes. Joe actually pays taxes at a 20.4% rate computed as follows:

$$\frac{\text{Effective}}{\text{(average) tax rate}} = \frac{\text{Total taxes paid}}{\text{Total taxable income}}$$

$$= \frac{(\$3,052 + [28\% \times (\$34,600 - \$20,350)])^*}{\$34,600}$$

$$= \frac{\$7,042}{\$34,600} = 20.4\%$$

* These rates were taken from Illustration B.13 for a single taxpayer.

CAPITAL GAINS AND LOSSES

Capital assets are all items of property other than inventories, receivables, copyrights, certain governmental obligations, and real and depreciable property used in a trade or business. Investments in capital stocks and bonds are examples of capital assets. A gain is an excess of selling price over cost.

Taxation of Capital Gains

Some capital gains escape taxation. For example, a taxpayer, age 55 or older, may exclude from gross income up to $125,000 ($62,500 on a separate return) of any gain on sale of the taxpayer's home.

All other capital gains are taxed at the same rates as ordinary income, but not to exceed 28%.

The tax law relative to net capital losses is more complex, containing certain limitations. Discussion of these losses is left for a more advanced text.

TAX CREDITS

A tax credit is a direct deduction from the amount of taxes to be paid, resulting largely from certain expenditures made by the taxpayer. Since tax credits reduce the amount of taxes to be paid dollar for dollar, they are much more valuable to the taxpayer than deductions. A tax credit of $100 saves $100 of cash; a $100 deduction, on the other hand, is worth only $100 times the taxpayer's marginal tax rate. The maximum value, then, of any deduction in 1991 is 31% of the amount of the deduction since the highest tax rate is 31%.

Tax credits are available for persons with low earned income levels, for the elderly, for child and dependent care expenses, for income taxes paid to foreign countries, and for wages paid in work incentive programs.

FILING THE TAX RETURN

Personal tax returns generally must be filed on or by April 15 of the year following the tax year. Extensions may be filed, but payment of any tax liability is still due by April 15. Most taxpayers are also employees; therefore, taxes are withheld by employers under our pay-as-you-go tax system. Also, taxpayers having income above a prescribed amount that is not subject to withholding must pay an estimated tax. This estimated tax must be paid in four installments. Underpayments may be subject to penalties and interest charges. The taxes withheld and the estimated taxes paid are entered as offsets to the total tax liability on the tax return. Any remaining unpaid taxes are paid to the Internal Revenue Service when the return is filed. In some cases, tax withholdings and estimated taxes paid may have exceeded tax liability, and the taxpayer can claim a refund.

COMPREHENSIVE ILLUSTRATION—PERSONAL INCOME TAXES

An actual tax return consists of a number of preprinted forms that are filled out by the taxpayer. Taxpayers will file either Form 1040 EZ (the easy form), Form 1040A (often called the short form), or Form 1040 (the long form). A taxpayer who intends to itemize deductions or who has taxable income of $50,000 or more may not file either Form 1040 EZ or Form 1040A. A taxpayer who uses the long form generally must attach various schedules to it. Two common schedules included in

---

ILLUSTRATION B.14

Joint Tax Return Computations

Salary . . . . :		$58,000
Interest income		4,000
Dividend income		6,000
Capital gain ($10,000) less capital loss ($1,000).		9,000
Adjusted gross income		$77,000
Itemized deductions:		
Medical expense ($5,925 − $5,775; total medical costs less 7.5% of adjusted gross income). . .	$ 150	
Charitable contributions	2,240	
Taxes (real estate on home, state income).	5,670	
Casualty loss ($8,250 − $7,700; total adjusted casualty losses less 10% of adjusted gross		
income)	550	
Miscellaneous (professional dues, subscriptions, etc.) [$1,980 − ($77,000 × 0.02)].	440	
	$ 9,050	
Standard deduction amount*	$ 5,450	
Higher of itemized deductions versus standard deduction		9,050
		$67,950
Exemptions (4 × $2,150)		8,600
Taxable income.		$59,350
Income tax ($5,100 + [28% × ($59,350 − $34,000)])		$12,198
Less: Applicable tax credits		–0–
Total tax liability		$12,198
Income taxes withheld	$12,400	
Estimated taxes paid	800	13,200
Income taxes refund due		$ 1,002

* This amount was correct for 1990. The amount for 1991 was not available as of this writing.

---

the long form are Schedule A and Schedule B. Schedule A shows the itemized deductions, while Schedule B lists all dividends and interest income when dividend and interest income exceeds a certain amount. As mentioned earlier in this appendix, one copy of the taxpayer's Form W-2 is attached to the tax return. The W-2 is issued by the employer and shows wages earned and taxes withheld during the period on these wages.

Illustration B.14 shows a brief summary schedule of the tax return items for Lee and Dora Bowman, for 1991, who are married and file a joint return. Lee is chief engineer for a manufacturing company; Dora is a full-time homemaker. Both taxpayers are under age 65; they have two dependent children, ages 13 and 15. Dora owns a number of bonds and shares of stock, some of which she sold during the year, realizing $10,000 of capital gains and $1,000 of capital losses. Total income taxes withheld during the year amounted to $12,400. In addition, Lee and Dora paid estimated taxes of $800. Other information needed to compute the Bowmans' tax liability and tax payment are shown in the illustration. The income tax of $12,198 is computed using the tax rate schedule in Illustration B.13.

DEMONSTRATION PROBLEM B–1

Johnson Company employs four persons as salespersons (all are married) and pays them weekly salaries as shown below. The number of exemptions and weekly deductions for hospital insurance for each employee are also given.

	Weekly Salary	Exemptions	Hospital Insurance
Jenny Cain	$420	2	$20
Susan Davis	500	4	25
Ellen Griffin	400	3	25
David Oakes	310	1	10

Each employee has 4% withheld for state income tax and 6% withheld for the retirement plan. Use the wage bracket withholding table in Illustration B.2 to determine the federal income taxes to be withheld.

Required   *a.*   Prepare the payroll journal for the week ending January 8, 1991, using headings that will accomplish the purpose. (The check numbers are 701–4.) Use 7.65% as the rate for FICA taxes (social security).

b.   Assuming that the payroll journal is a memorandum record only, prepare the general journal entry to record the payroll.

c.   Prepare the entry to transfer funds from general cash to the special payroll checking account.

d.   Prepare the entry to record the employer's payroll taxes using the rates given in this chapter. (In actual practice, this entry often is made only at the end of the month.)

e.   Prepare the entry to record the payment on January 11 of the federal income taxes and FICA taxes due to be paid to the federal government. (In actual practice, this entry often is made only at the end of the month or quarter, depending on the amounts involved.)

SOLUTION TO DEMONSTRATION PROBLEM B–1

a.

PAYROLL JOURNAL

Date Week Ended 1991	Employee	Gross Pay— Sales Salaries Expense Dr.	Employees' Federal Income Taxes Payable Cr.	FICA Taxes Payable Cr.	Employees' State Income Taxes Payable Cr.	Employees' Medical Insurance Premiums Payable Cr.	Employees' Retirement Plan Premiums Payable Cr.	Salaries Payable (Net Pay) Cr.	Check No.
Jan. 8	Jenny Cain	420.00	41.00	32.13	16.80	20.00	25.20	284.87	701
	Susan Davis	500.00	41.00	38.25	20.00	25.00	30.00	345.75	702
	Ellen Griffin	400.00	32.00	30.60	16.00	25.00	24.00	272.40	703
	David Oakes	310.00	31.00	23.72	12.40	10.00	18.60	214.28	704
		1,630.00	145.00	124.70	65.20	80.00	97.80	1,117.30	

b.

	1991				
	Jan.	8	Sales Salaries Expense	1,630.00	
			Employees' Federal Income Taxes Payable		145.00
			FICA Taxes Payable		124.70
			Employees' State Income Taxes Payable		65.20
			Employees' Medical Insurance Premiums Payable . . .		80.00
			Employees' Retirement Plan Premiums Payable		97.80
			Salaries Payable		1,117.30
			To record the payroll for the week ending January 8.		

c.

	1991				
	Jan.	8	Salaries Payable	1,117.30	
			Cash		1,117.30
			To record the transfer of funds to cover the January 8 payroll.		

d.

	1991				
	Jan.	8	Payroll Taxes Expenses	225.76	
			FICA Taxes Payable		124.70
			State Unemployment Taxes Payable		88.02
			Federal Unemployment Taxes Payable		13.04
			To record payroll taxes on the January 8 payroll.		

e.

	Jan.	11	Employees' Federal Income Taxes Payable	145.00	
			FICA Taxes Payable	249.40	
			Cash		394.40
			To record payment of federal income taxes payable and FICA taxes payable from the January 8 payroll.		

DEMONSTRATION PROBLEM B-2

The records of Mark Corporation show the following for the calendar year just ended:

Sales	$187,500
Interest earned on—	
State of New Jersey bonds	1,500
City of Miami bonds	750
Essex County, Ohio, School District No. 2 bonds	375
Cost of goods sold and other expenses	157,500
Allowable extra depreciation deduction under modified ACRS	2,250
Dividends declared	7,500
Revenue received in advance, considered taxable income of this year	1,500
Contribution made to influence legislation (included in the $157,500 listed above)	150

Required   *a.*   Prepare a schedule showing the computation of taxable income.

              b.   Compute the amount of the corporation's tax that was payable for the current year. (Use the rates mentioned in this appendix.)

c. Prepare the adjusting entry necessary to recognize federal income taxes expense, assuming income tax allocation procedures are followed. The only permanent differences are the contribution to influence legislation and the nontaxable interest.

SOLUTION TO DEMONSTRATION PROBLEM B–2

a.

MARK CORPORATION
Computation of Taxable Income
Current Year

Sales		$187,500
Cost of goods sold and other expenses		157,500
Operating income.		$ 30,000
Other income: Interest		2,625
Book income before taxes		$ 32,625
Adjustments for permanent differences:		
Interest (all governmental; nontaxable)	$(2,625)	
Contribution (not deductible)	150	(2,475)
Income on which to compute tax expense.		$ 30,150
Adjustments for temporary differences:		
Revenue received in advance	$ 1,500	
Additional depreciation	(2,250)	(750)
Taxable income.		$ 29,400

b.   Computation of tax: $0.15 \times \$29{,}400.00 = \$4{,}410$

c.

Federal Income Taxes Expense	4,522.50*	
Federal Income Taxes Payable		4,410.00
Deferred Federal Income Taxes Payable.		112.50

* Federal Income Taxes Expense is computed as follows:

Computation of taxes:
15% × $30,150 = $4,522.50
Tax expense = $4,522.50
Tax payable from *(b)* = $4,410

NEW TERMS

Accelerated Cost Recovery System (ACRS)   A tax method of depreciation that assigns depreciable assets to particular classes that have specified lives for depreciation purposes. *935*

Adjusted gross income   Gross income minus business expenses and several other items. *942*

Capital assets   All items of property **other than** inventories, receivables, copyrights, certain governmental obligations, and real or depreciable property used in a trade or business. Examples include investments in capital stocks and bonds. *946*

Deductions (itemized)   Deducted from adjusted gross income for items such as contributions, interest on mortgage, certain taxes, limited casualty losses, limited

medical expenses, and limited "nonbusiness" expenses. *943*

Deductions for adjusted gross income   Most business expenses, payments to individual retirement plans, and certain other minor items. *942*

Deductions from adjusted gross income   Specified by law; either standard deduction amount or itemized deductions. *942*

Deductions from gross earnings   Required payroll deductions, such as federal and state income taxes withheld, FICA taxes withheld, and other deductions, such as medical insurance premiums and union dues. *921*

Effective tax rate   The average rate of taxation on a given amount of taxable income. *945*

Employee earnings record A record maintained by an employer for each employee (see Illustration B.4) showing such details as hours worked, pay rate, gross pay, deductions, net pay, and personal biographical data. *925*

Employee's Withholding Allowance Certificate (Form W-4) The form (see Illustration B.1) on which an employee indicates the number of exemptions to be used in calculating federal (and state) income tax withheld. *921*

Employer's Quarterly Federal Tax Return (Form 941) A form used to report the amount of FICA and withholding taxes for a quarter. *929*

Estimated tax A tax that must be paid in four installments by persons having amounts of income above a certain level that are not subject to withholding. *946*

Exemption A fixed amount ($2,150 in 1991) the taxpayer may deduct from adjusted gross income for the taxpayer, the spouse, and each dependent. *944*

Fair Labor Standards Act See Wages and Hours Law.

Federal depository bank A bank authorized to accept deposits of taxes by employers for credit to the Internal Revenue Service. *929*

Federal (state) income tax withheld The amount withheld for federal (state) income taxes deducted from employee earnings by the employer and remitted to the appropriate governmental agency under the pay-as-you-go system of government financing. *921*

Federal unemployment tax A tax of 6.2% levied on the first $7,928 of wages paid per employee to help finance the joint federal-state system of unemployment compensation. A credit of up to 5.4% may be taken for amounts paid to a state unemployment fund, thus reducing the rate to 0.8%. *928*

FICA (social security) tax The amount deducted from an employee's wages and paid into a special fund used to pay retirement and other benefits. In 1991, the rate was 7.65% on the first $53,400 of wages paid. An additional 1.45% is due on amounts over $53,400, up to $125,000. *922*

Gross earnings Total pay or compensation of an employee's regular pay and overtime premium. *920*

Gross income Includes all income from whatever source derived, except for a few specifically excluded items. *941*

Head of household An unmarried or legally separated person (and one married to a nonresident alien) who maintains a residence for a relative or a dependent. *940*

Interperiod income tax allocation A procedure whereby the tax effects of an element of expense or revenue, or loss or gain, that will affect taxable income are allocated to the period in which the item is recognized for accounting purposes, regardless of the period in which it is recognized for tax purposes. *938*

Itemized deductions See Deductions (itemized).

Loss carryback A current loss that has been applied against taxable income of prior periods, thereby resulting in a tax refund in the current period. *934*

Loss carryforward A current loss that will be applied against taxable income in future years, thereby reducing the taxes payable in future periods. *935*

Marginal tax rate The rate applied to the next dollar of taxable income or each incremental amount of income. *944*

Merit rate A reduction in the state unemployment tax rate below 5.4% as a reward for low turnover and few layoffs. *928*

Minimum wage Lowest hourly compensation an employer may pay an employee as required by the Wages and Hours Law. *920*

Modified ACRS A tax method of depreciation that assigns assets to particular groups that have specified lives for depreciation purposes. The 1986 Tax Reform Act modified the existing accelerated cost recovery system. *935*

Payroll checking account A separate checking account used only for payroll checks. Each payday, funds are transferred from the general Cash account to cover the amount of the payroll checks. One of the purposes is to keep the "clutter" of outstanding payroll checks from making more complex the reconciliation of the general Cash account. *927*

Payroll journal A formal record showing the details of each payroll, including gross pay, deductions, net pay, and check number for each employee (see Illustration B.5). It may be used as a book of original entry (in which case postings to accounts would be made from it) or it may be only a memorandum record. *926*

Pegboard system of payroll accounting A system that aligns the payroll check, the earnings record, and the payroll journal in such a way that all three are completed simultaneously with one writing. *932*

Permanent differences Differences between taxable income and pre-tax income caused by tax provisions that exclude an item of expense, revenue, gain, or loss as an element of taxable income. *937*

Social security tax See FICA tax.

Standard deduction amount The standard deduction amount may be taken in lieu of itemized deductions. *942*

State unemployment tax A tax of 5.4% (typically) on the first $7,000 of gross earnings per employee per year to finance unemployment benefits. A **merit rate** for not laying off employees may reduce the percent below 5.4%. *928*

Tax credit A direct reduction of the amount of taxes payable. *946*

Taxable income Adjusted gross income minus deductions, minus exemptions; the amount of income on which taxes payable is computed. *942*

Temporary (or timing) differences Differences

between taxable income and financial statement pre-tax income caused by items that affect both taxable income and pre-tax income, but in different periods. *937*

Timecard   A form used to maintain a record of when an employee reports to and leaves work; it is used as a source document for calculating gross pay. *919*

Vacation pay   Compensation received by employees while on vacation; it is actually earned by employees in the periods worked prior to the vacation. *931*

Wage and Tax Statement (Form W-2)   A form that the employer must furnish to each employee after the end of the year showing gross wages, amounts withheld, and net pay (see Illustration B.3). It is used by the

employee in preparing his or her personal federal income tax return. *922*

Wage bracket withholding table   A table supplied by the IRS (see Illustration B.2) that shows the amount of federal income tax to be withheld given the wage paid and the number of withholding allowances claimed. *922*

Wages and Hours Law (Fair Labor Standards Act)   Requires that most employees be paid at least 1½ times their normal rate for hours worked in excess of 40 hours per week. It also requires that at least the minimum wage be paid. *920*

Withholding allowances   A means of adjusting income taxes withheld from employee periodic earnings for exemptions that will be claimed on the income tax return. *921*

QUESTIONS

1. Describe some of the purposes of a payroll accounting system.

2. List the various functions regarding payroll and give a method for establishing internal control over these functions.

3. Describe how the system of internal control relating to payroll works. (Begin with the recording of time and end with the issuance of the paycheck.)

4. Identify some schemes involving payroll that have been used to defraud a company.

5. Why should a distinction be made between employees and independent contractors? Give an example of each.

6. What requirements does the Wages and Hours Law place on employers? Why should accurate records be maintained as to hours worked by employees?

7. List the common deductions from gross pay.

8. What is the purpose of the Employee's Withholding Allowance Certificate (Form W-4)?

9. What purposes does the Wage and Tax Statement (Form W-2) serve?

10. Against which parties are FICA taxes levied and in what amounts?

11. What is the purpose of the Employer's Quarterly Federal Tax Return (Form 941)?

12. What are the federal and state rates for unemployment tax? What is a merit rate and what effect does it have on the credit granted by the federal government for amounts paid to the state?

13. Why should an employer maintain an individual earnings record for each employee?

14. Describe two ways in which the payroll journal might be utilized in the payroll accounting system.

15. Under what conditions would the use of a special payroll checking account be desirable? How does such an account operate?

16. What are the arguments for and against accruing employer's payroll taxes at the end of the accounting period?

17. What payroll procedures might be employed that would be more efficient than the system described in the chapter? Why are these other methods not always used in a given system?

18. A classmate states: "Why all the fuss about deferring revenues and recognizing expenses sooner for tax purposes? All net taxable income is taxed eventually anyway. It is only a matter of putting off the payment. I don't think these manipulations are worth the effort." Comment.

19. What factors might cause net income on a corporation's income statement to differ from its taxable income?

20. Classified among the long-term liabilities of A Corporation is an account entitled Deferred Federal Income Taxes Payable. Explain the nature of this account.

21. Define the term *adjusted gross income* as it is used for personal income tax purposes.

22. For what kinds of expenditures may personal deductions be taken on one's personal federal income tax return?

23. What are exemptions, and by how much does each one reduce taxable income?

EXERCISES

Note: Unless directed otherwise, use 1991 federal income tax rates for exercises involving individuals.

Exercise B–1

Determine withholding amounts for employees

Gomez Company employs four persons whose weekly wages and exemptions are as follows:

	Wage	Exemptions
John Sampson.	$430	4
Thomas McPherson	310	2
John Lauber.	380	3
Robert Conrad	540	5

Assume these employees are married. Using Illustration B.2, determine the correct amount to withhold for federal income tax per week.

Exercise B–2

Compute maximum weeks of unemployment taxes

Using the data in Exercise B-1, calculate how many weeks it would take before the employer would no longer incur federal or state unemployment taxes on each individual.

Exercise B–3

Compute FICA taxes

Using the data in Exercise B-1 and assuming a rate of 7.65% and a maximum base of $53,400, how much would the employer withhold for FICA tax from each employee for the entire year? How much would the employer's FICA tax expense be for the year?

Exercise B–4

Prepare journal entry to record payroll

The January 15, 1991, gross payroll for salaries of West Corporation is $4,800. The total federal income tax withheld is $1,050. The employees' share of FICA taxes withheld is $367.20. What is the correct entry at the time of payment, assuming no prior recording of salaries? (Ignore federal and state unemployment taxes.)

Exercise B–5

Compute difference in payroll taxes under two alternatives

Sandra Bixby is trying to decide whether to hire four workers to perform a particular job at $36,000 each per year, or 12 workers to perform a particular job on a part-time basis at $12,000 each per year. Using the rates given in this appendix, calculate the difference in the employer's payroll tax expense under the two alternatives.

Exercise B–6

Prepare journal entry to record unemployment taxes

Hilliard Company is in a state that has a state unemployment rate of 5.4%. Due to a record of stable employment, the company has earned a merit rate of 4.8%. Total wages on which it incurred federal and state unemployment taxes for March were $15,000. Prepare an entry to record federal and state unemployment taxes for March.

Exercise B–7

Prepare journal entries to record accrued wages and payroll taxes

At the end of December, Busbee Company had accrued wages of $1,000 ($500 for sales salaries, $300 for office salaries, and $200 for maintenance wages). The company makes the accrual for payroll taxes on accrued wages. Assume that no employee has earned over $53,400 (including the above wages) and that unemployment taxes still accrue only on the maintenance wages. Prepare the necessary adjusting entry to accrue the wages and payroll taxes.

Exercise B–8

Prepare journal entry to record unaccrued payroll taxes

Using the data in Exercise B-7, what entry would the company make if it did not follow the practice of accruing payroll taxes on accrued wages?

Exercise B–9

Compute corporate tax liability

a. Drexler Corporation has taxable income of $20,000, $50,000, and $70,000 in its first three years of operations. Determine the amount of federal income taxes Drexler will incur each year.

b. Assume that in the fourth year of operations, Drexler Corporation suffered a loss of $95,000. How much could it recover in back taxes?

Exercise B–10

Prepare journal entry to record income tax chargeable and tax liability for year

The before-tax income reported on the income statement of Mosley Corporation for a given year amounts to $200,000, while its taxable income is only $160,000. The difference is attributable entirely to additional modified ACRS depreciation taken for tax purposes. If the current income tax rate is assumed to be 40%, give the entry to record the income tax expense for the year and the taxes payable for the year.

Exercise B–11

Determine number of exemptions allowed

Paul Trent is 68 years old, and his wife is 65 years old and blind. They have three sons, ages 22, 24, and 29. The son who is 22 is a full-time student in college and does not claim himself as an exemption. His parents contribute $4,000 per year toward his living expenses, which is more than one half of his support. The other two sons are self-supporting. How many exemptions are Paul and his wife entitled to on their joint return?

Exercise B–12

Compute tax liability

John Benton has gross income of $40,000, deductions from gross income of $2,000, itemized deductions of $1,500, and six full exemptions (two personal and four dependent). He is filing a joint return with his wife, who has no income. How much is their tax liability? (Use the 1991 rates, $2,150 per exemption, and assume a $5,000 standard deduction amount.)

PROBLEMS

Problem B–1

Compute FICA taxes, unemployment taxes, and total employer tax expense

Carter Company has 18 employees and an annual payroll of $350,000; 4 employees earn $63,000 each per year; and 14 employees earn $7,000 each per year.

Required

a. What is the annual FICA tax (1) for the employer and (2) for the employees? (Use rates shown for 1991.)

b. What is the amount of federal and state unemployment tax per year, assuming a federal rate of 6.2% and a state rate of 5.4% for this employer?

c. Which of the preceding items would constitute expenses on the records of Carter Company?

Problem B–2

Prepare journal entries to record payroll, FICA taxes, unemployment taxes, and payment of taxes

Ace Company pays its employees once each month. The payroll data for October are as follows:

Gross payroll	$41,200	(One employee is above the $7,000 limit. Prior to October, the employee's gross salary was $37,000, and the employee's gross October salary was $3,000.)
Federal income tax withheld	4,400	
FICA tax	?	
State income tax	3% of gross salary	

Required Prepare entries to record:

a. The October payroll.

b. The employer's FICA tax for October (use 1991 rates).

c. The employer's federal and state unemployment taxes, assuming that the federal rate is 6.2% and the state rate is 5.4%.

d. Payment of the various taxes.

Problem B–3

Prepare payroll journal, record payroll, record employer's payroll taxes, and record transfer of funds to payroll checking account

Sanchez Company employs six persons in its fast-food franchise operation. The names of the employees, weekly wages, and number of exemptions are as follows:

Employee	Weekly Wage	Number of Exemptions
Bikram Garcha	$600	4
Norman Harbaugh	350	2
Fred Massey	340	3
Becky Rogers	450	1
Marc Schaefer	370	2
Paula Stephan	330	5

State income tax is withheld from employees at the rate of 5% on all wages paid. All of the employees are married.

Required   *a.*   Prepare a payroll journal with the following headings: Date Week Ended, Employee, Gross Pay—Salaries Expense Dr., Employees' Federal Income Taxes Payable Cr., FICA Taxes Payable Cr., Employees' State Income Taxes Payable Cr., Salaries Payable (Net Pay) Cr., and Check No.

                 b.   Using the withholding table and rates given in this appendix (including 7.65% for FICA taxes using 1991 rates, 6.2% for federal unemployment, and 5.4% for state unemployment), enter the payroll data in the payroll journal for the week ending January 8, 1991. Check numbers used were 405–10.

                 c.   Assuming the payroll journal is used as a memorandum record, prepare an entry as it would appear in the general journal to record the payroll.

                 d.   Prepare the entry to record the employer's payroll taxes for FICA and unemployment.

                 e.   Prepare the entry to record the transfer of funds to the special payroll checking account on January 8.

Problem B–4

Prepare journal entries to account for accrued payroll

At the end of the year (1991), Santos Company has $30,000 of accrued wages ($15,000 sales salaries; $9,000 delivery wages; and $6,000 office salaries). Of this total, $25,000 are subject to FICA tax, and $8,000 are subject to unemployment taxes.

Required

a.   Describe the two alternatives the company may follow in making the adjusting entry and explain why these alternatives exist.

b.   Prepare the adjusting entry under the two alternatives. (Use the 7.65% rate mentioned in this appendix for FICA, 6.2% for federal unemployment, and 5.4% for state unemployment.)

Problem B–5

Prepare schedule showing computation of taxable income; compute the tax liability

The records of Bell Corporation show the following for the calendar year just ended:

Sales.	$375,000
Nontaxable interest earned on—	
State of New York bonds.	3,000
City of Detroit bonds.	1,500
Howard County, Ohio, School District No. 1 bonds	375
Cost of goods sold and other expenses	315,000
Loss on sale of asset	3,000
Gain on sale of asset acquired two years ago.	7,500
Allowable extra depreciation deduction for tax purposes	4,500
Dividends declared.	15,000
Revenue received in advance, considered taxable income of this year	3,000
Contribution made to influence legislation (included in the $315,000 listed above). . . .	300

Required   *a.*   Present a schedule showing the computation of taxable income.

                 b.   Compute the corporation's tax for the current year. (Use the tax rates mentioned in this appendix.)

Problem B–6

Prepare schedule showing computation of tax liability; calculate yearly allocation of tax expense; prepare journal entries; prepare T-accounts

Moore Company expects to have income before depreciation and income taxes of $300,000 each year for the period 1991–94. The company acquires an asset for $360,000, which is expected to last four years and have no scrap value at the end of that period. For financial accounting purposes, the company uses the straight-line depreciation method; and for tax purposes, the property is three-year modified ACRS property. Assume that the recovery percentages are 25%, 37.5%, 18.75%, and 18.75% for each of the four years, respectively. Assume the tax rate is 40% (for the sake of simplicity) and no other items exist that cause differences between income before taxes on the income statement and taxable income.

Required   *a.*   Prepare a schedule showing the actual tax liability for each year.

                 b.   Calculate the income tax expense that should be shown each year, assuming income tax allocation procedures are to be used.

                 c.   Prepare journal entries to record the income tax expense and income tax liability for each year.

   d.   Show how the entries prepared in part *(c)* would be summarized in T-accounts. How would the amounts appearing in these accounts eventually be cleared from the accounts?

Problem B–7

Calculate taxable income

Todd Carlson was about to calculate his taxable income for 1991. He gathered together the following information:

Gross wages	$25,000
Interest received on savings account	1,200
Capital gain	13,000
Contribution to individual retirement account (not participant in employer pension plan)	2,250
Property taxes on residence	2,850
State income tax	3,600
Mortgage interest paid	6,300
Contributions to church	2,700

     Mr. Carlson is married and files a joint return. He has two young children who live with him and his wife. Assume a standard deduction of $5,000.

Required

Calculate the amount of taxable income for 1991 for Mr. and Mrs. Carlson.

BUSINESS DECISION PROBLEMS

Decision Problem B–1

Recommend procedures to strengthen internal control over payroll

John Watson operates a fine restaurant and employs 15 employees. He is interested in food preparation, supervision of servers, and customer relations. He has little aptitude for record-keeping. As a result, he hired Fred Rogers to do all of the paperwork for the business. Fred's duties include preparing the payroll, keeping payroll records, signing the payroll checks, distributing the payroll checks, and reconciling the bank account. The payroll checks are written on the general Cash account rather than on a special payroll checking account.

     Business seems good, but the cash position keeps getting tighter. Wages expense seems somewhat higher than Mr. Watson believes it should be. Mr. Rogers assures Mr. Watson that all is well regarding payroll. Mr. Watson suspects something is wrong regarding the payroll function.

Required

   a.   What could be wrong?

   b.   What would you recommend to Mr. Watson to correct the situation?

Decision Problem B–2

Determine which payroll system to use with alternative number of employees

Pat Wilson owns and runs a motel and has 10 employees. She has one opportunity to acquire a chain of five other motels (with an additional 50 employees). A second opportunity exists to acquire a second chain of 20 other motels (with an additional 200 employees). She will only consider acquiring the second chain if she acquires the first chain.

     Ms. Wilson is wondering about which type of payroll system to use, given the fact that she may have 10, 60, or 260 employees. Estimated costs of three alternative payroll systems are as follows:

	Clerical Cost per Employee/Week	Cost of Forms per Employee/Week	Service Charge per Week
Manual system	$1.50	$0.20	$ 0
Pegboard system	0.50	0.30	10*
Computer Service Bureau	0.25	0.10	100

* An initial charge for pegboard equipment expressed as a weekly charge.

Required

Calculate the cost per week of using each system for 10, 60, and 260 employees, respectively. Which is the least costly alternative number of employees?

C

INFLATION ACCOUNTING

INTRODUCTION

Until recent years, no attempt had been made to include the impact of inflation on the results of operations and financial position of the reporting company. A serious problem faced by accountants—how to account for and report financial data in periods of inflation—is discussed in this appendix.

INFLATION—A SERIOUS REPORTING PROBLEM

A period of inflation is a time during which prices in general are rising, while a period of deflation occurs when prices in general are falling. Only in periods of high inflation, like in the 1970s, has the historical cost approach to recording accounting data been severely criticized. During times of inflation, the historical cost approach often reports a positive net income when the economic value of the owner's investment has not even been maintained.

There are two widely recommended accounting approaches to the problem of inflation. One approach is current cost accounting. The current cost accounting approach shows the current cost or value of items in the financial statements. The other approach is constant dollar accounting, also known as general price-level adjusted accounting. The constant dollar accounting approach shows financial statement historical cost figures as adjusted for changes in the general price level.

The Nature and Measurement of Inflation

In a period of inflation, the "real value" of the dollar—its ability to purchase goods and services—falls. In a period of deflation, the real value of the dollar rises.

Changes in the general level of prices are measured by means of a general price index, such as the consumer price index (CPI). A price index is a weighted average of prices for various goods and services. A base year is chosen and assigned a value of 100 for comparative purposes. If the index stands at 108 a year later, this means that prices in general rose 8% during the year. An index of 200 would mean that prices on the average doubled. Since the index is an average, prices of individual types of items may change at different rates and may, in some cases, actually decline. For example, the CPI shows that prices for a "basket" of selected consumer goods doubled in the decade of the 1970s. However, during that same decade, gasoline prices quadrupled, while the price of electronic handheld calculators declined very sharply.

The real value or purchasing power of the dollar relative to that of the base year is shown by the reciprocal of the price index; the ratio is simply inverted. For example, if the index for 1994 is 200 and for 1984 is 100, the price index is 200/100, meaning that prices have doubled since 1984. Alternatively, the reciprocal of the price index is 100/200, meaning that the value of the dollar in 1994 has dropped to one half, or 50%, of its purchasing power in 1984.

Because accounting measurements consist largely of dollars of historical cost, financial reports are inadequate in periods of inflation. Historical cost accounting measures accounting transactions in terms of the actual dollars expended or received. Such a measurement system has worked well in periods of stable prices. However, the system does not work well when the dollar, in terms of its purchasing power, is a sharply changing unit of measure.

To illustrate, assume that a tract of land was purchased for $2,000 and held several years before being sold for $2,500. While the land was held, a general price index rose from 100 to 140. Historical cost accounting would report recovery of the $2,000 cost and income of $500 as a gain on sale of the land. However, if we measure this transaction in terms of dollars of constant purchasing power, a far different result is obtained. To get back the purchasing power originally invested in the land, the land would have to be sold for $2,800 ($2,000 × 140/100). Since only $2,500 was received, no real income has been earned because the cost has not been recovered. In fact, a loss of $300 of current purchasing power was incurred.

Consequences of Ignoring Effects of Inflation

As shown in the example above, transactions and, therefore, financial statements that have not been adjusted for the effects of inflation may yield misleading information. Such information may make comparisons between companies difficult. Suppose Company A acquired a tract of land for $100,000 several years ago. Now Company B acquires a virtually identical tract of land for $150,000, paying the higher price because prices in general have risen 50% since Company A bought its land. Immediately, both companies sell their land for $150,000 each. Company A would appear to have the more efficient management because it was able to earn $50,000 on the sale of the land, while Company B earned nothing. In reality, the two companies are in the same position relative to the sale of the land because they have the same number of dollars of current purchasing power. The financial statement difference is caused by recording and continuing to carry the land at its historical cost.

As another example of the consequences of ignoring the effects of inflation, assume the above land was instead a depreciable asset, such as a building. Company A and Company B earn exactly the same number of dollars of revenues and, except for depreciation, have exactly the same number of dollars of expenses. If both companies had assumed a 10-year useful life on the asset and apply straight-line depreciation to the building, A will have a larger net income than B simply due to the fact that the historical cost of Company A's asset is lower and, therefore, its recorded depreciation expense is lower than the recorded depreciation expense for B.

Failure to adjust for the impact of inflation may lead to invalid conclusions. A five-year summary of sales may show that sales dollars have increased 50% over the period. If sales prices have increased 60% over the five years, physical sales volume has actually declined.

Other consequences flow from a failure to adjust financial reports for the effects of inflation. Companies are paying taxes on "income" when in reality, costs may not have been covered. Also, financial reports that fail to reflect the impact of inflation may be misleading to individual decision makers, causing them to make decisions that are not in their best interests.

Accounting Responses to Changing Prices

Specific price-level changes relate to changes in the price of a particular good or service, such as calculators or computers. General price-level changes relate to the changes in the economy as a whole, such as those reflected by the consumer price index. A specific price-level change may change in the same, or opposite, direction as the general price level, and at the same or a different rate. Because of this, there are two types of price changes (specific and general) and two recommended approaches to accounting for changing prices. These recommended approaches are:

1. Change the basis of measurement from historical cost to current cost or value; this approach is called current cost accounting.

2. Change the basis of measurement from the actual historical (nominal) dollar to a dollar of constant purchasing power; this approach is referred to as constant dollar accounting (or general price-level accounting).

An example of these two approaches is necessary before turning to a more detailed illustration. Assume the following facts regarding the purchase and resale of 1,000 units of a product.

Date	Transaction	Amount	Price-Level Index
January 1, 1994	Purchased 1,000 units	$3,000	100
December 31, 1994	Sold 1,000 units	5,000	120

The current cost of the units on December 31, 1994, was $3,900. The company incurred $800 of expenses to sell the units.

Under conventional (historical cost) accounting, net income from operations for 1994 would be:

Sales		$5,000
Cost of goods sold	$3,000	
Other expenses	800	3,800
Income from continuing operations*		$1,200

* Income from continuing operations in most cases is the same as income from operations. The technical difference between these terms is covered in intermediate accounting.

The $1,200 of income results from deducting the historical cost of the goods sold as well as the other expenses from sales revenue. The company appears to be better off after the transactions because it has not only recovered the original dollar investment in the goods, together with the expenses incurred, but also has an additional $1,200. The fact that the current replacement cost of the goods sold exceeds their historical cost by $900 ($3,900 − $3,000) is ignored. Also, no attention is paid to the fact that the dollars recovered do not have the same purchasing power as those originally invested.

Using the preceding example, Illustration C.1 compares net income from continuing operations under historical cost and each of the two inflation accounting methods.

The second set of columns in Illustration C.1 shows the income from continuing operations using the current cost method. The current cost of an asset is the amount that would have to be paid currently to acquire the asset. In the columns headed "Current Cost Accounting," net income from continuing operations is computed by deducting the current cost of replacing the goods sold and the other expenses from current revenues. No adjustments are made for **general** price-level changes. Calculating net income from continuing operations in this manner is supported on the grounds that the sale of an inventory item leads directly to a further action—replenishment of the inventory—if the company is to remain a going concern. A better picture of a company's ability to compete in its markets may also be provided by comparing current revenues with current costs rather than with outdated historical costs. In addition, we can say that only the $300 represents "disposable" income. Only $300 or less can be distributed to owners without reducing the scale of operations since the remainder of the funds is necessary to replace inventory sold and to maintain productive facilities at their present level.

In Illustration C.1, in the columns headed "Constant Dollar Accounting," cost of goods sold is restated in end-of-1994 dollars by use of a ratio of the current price index to the old price index: $3,000 × 120/100 = $3,600. The $3,600 is the amount of purchasing power invested in the goods expressed in the end-of-1994 dollars. Thus, the $3,600 is restated into the same dollars in which the sales revenue is expressed. The $800 of other expenses is assumed to be selling expenses incurred at point of sale (such as sales commissions), which are already stated in end-of-

ILLUSTRATION C.1

Alternative Reporting Approaches—Statement of Income from Continuing Operations

	Historical Cost Accounting		Current Cost Accounting		Constant Dollar Accounting	
Sales		$5,000		$5,000		$5,000
Cost of goods sold	$3,000		$3,900		$3,600	
Other expenses	800		800		800	
Total expenses.		$3,800		$4,700		$4,400
Income from continuing operations		$1,200		$ 300		$ 600

1994 dollars. All dollar amounts are now expressed in comparable terms—end-of-1994 dollars. The company is better off because it has increased its purchasing power by $600. Under constant dollar accounting, net income is a measurement of increased purchasing power—the entity's increased ability to acquire goods and services.

The next two sections illustrate the current cost and constant dollar accounting methods applied to the income statement of a hypothetical company—Carol Company.

CURRENT COST ACCOUNTING

In the past, inflation-adjusted statements have generally been recommended, not required, as supplementary information to conventional financial statements. In 1979, the FASB issued a standard that **required** certain large, publicly held corporations to present certain supplementary information about the effects of inflation.[1]

To illustrate a statement from continuing operations prepared on a current cost basis, we use the data from the historical cost income statement of Carol Company in Illustration C.2.

Management has determined that the cost of goods sold in terms of current cost is $146,000, and the current cost of the plant assets was $160,000 on December 31, 1993, and $180,000 on December 31, 1994. No additions or retirements of plant assets occurred in 1994. Carol depreciates its plant assets over a 20-year life, or an annual rate of 5% on a straight-line basis.

Current cost depreciation for 1994 can be computed by multiplying the average current cost of the plant assets for the year by the annual depreciation rate of 5%. The amount is:

$$\frac{\$160,000 + \$180,000}{2} \times 5\% = \$8,500$$

The $146,000 current cost of goods sold and $8,500 current cost depreciation are shown in an income statement prepared under current cost accounting. Sales and

[1] FASB, *Statement of Financial Accounting Standards No. 33,* "Financial Reporting and Changing Prices" (Stamford, Conn., 1979). Copyright © by Financial Accounting Standards Board, High Ridge Park, Stamford, Connecticut 06905, U.S.A. Quoted (or excerpted) with permission. Copies of the complete document are available from the FASB.

ILLUSTRATION C.2

Statement of Income from Continuing Operations—
Historical Cost Basis

CAROL COMPANY
Statement of Income from Continuing Operations
For the Year Ended December 31, 1994

Sales		$200,000
Cost of goods sold:		
Merchandise inventory, January 1, 1994	$ 20,000	
Purchases	160,000	
Goods available for sale	$180,000	
Merchandise inventory, December 31, 1994	40,000	
Cost of goods sold		140,000
Gross margin		$ 60,000
Depreciation	$ 4,000	
Other expenses	46,000	50,000
Income from continuing operations		$ 10,000

ILLUSTRATION C.3

Comparison of Historical Cost and Current Cost Income Statements

CAROL COMPANY
Statements of Income from Continuing Operations
For the Year Ended December 31, 1994

	Historical Cost	Current Cost
Sales	$200,000	$200,000
Cost of goods sold	$140,000	$146,000
Depreciation expense	4,000	8,500
Other expenses	46,000	46,000
Total	$190,000	$200,500
Income (loss) from continuing operations	$ 10,000	$ (500)

---

other expenses do not need to be adjusted, since they are already expressed at current cost for the year.

Illustration C.3 shows the amounts that would be reported in the historical cost and current cost income statements shown for Carol Company.

Current Cost Accounting—Pros and Cons

The advantages of current cost accounting include:

1. Specific current costs incurred by a company are shown.
2. Current costs, rather than historical costs, are deducted from current revenues to calculate net income, which allows a more meaningful matching of effort and accomplishment.
3. If dividends are limited to an amount equal to or less than current cost income from continuing operations, the economic capital of the company is maintained.

The disadvantages of current cost include:

1. Current costs may be subjective.
2. Current costs may be difficult and costly to determine.

CONSTANT DOLLAR ACCOUNTING

As already discussed briefly, historical dollar amounts in an income statement may be converted or restated into a number of constant dollars that have an equivalent amount of purchasing power. When adjusted for inflation, conventional financial statements are called constant dollar or general price-level adjusted financial statements.

To illustrate an income statement prepared on a constant dollar basis, we again refer to Illustration C.2 for Carol Company.

To convert historical dollars into constant end-of-year dollars, the formula is:

$$\text{Historical dollars} \times \frac{\text{Price index at end of current period}}{\text{Price index at date of historical transaction}} = \text{Constant dollars}$$

To convert the income statement of Carol to a constant dollar basis, certain assumptions must be made from information provided. These data follow:

1. The general price-level index stood at 100 on December 31, 1993, and at 108 on December 31, 1994.
2. Sales, purchases, other expenses, and taxes were incurred uniformly throughout the year; thus, on the average, these items were incurred when the price index was 104.
3. Inventories are costed on a FIFO basis. The beginning inventory was acquired when the price index was 98, and the ending inventory was acquired when the index stood at 106.
4. The price index was 54 when the plant assets were acquired.

The procedure for converting the Carol income statement in Illustration C.2 to constant dollars is as follows: First, all revenues, purchases, and expenses were assumed to occur uniformly throughout the year; therefore, these items are converted by multiplying their historical amounts by a ratio of 108/104. Beginning inventory is converted using a ratio of 108/98, while ending inventory is converted using a 108/106 ratio. Since depreciation is calculated on the historical costs of the related assets that were acquired when the index stood at 54, depreciation expense is converted using a ratio of 108/54. Illustration C.4 shows Carol's restated income statement. Purchasing power gains and losses are discussed in the next section.

Purchasing Power Gains and Losses Purchasing power gains and losses result from holding monetary assets and liabilities during inflation or deflation. Monetary items are cash and other assets and liabilities that represent fixed claims to cash, such as accounts and notes receivable and payable. Nonmonetary items include all items on the balance sheet other than monetary items. A purchasing power gain results from holding monetary liabilities during inflation or monetary assets during deflation. A purchasing power loss results from holding monetary assets during inflation or monetary liabilities during deflation.

Assume that Bill Allen holds $1,000 of cash during a year in which prices in general rose 25%. Even though Bill has his $1,000 at year-end, he has less pur-

---

ILLUSTRATION C.4

Income Statement—Constant Dollar Basis (end-of-year dollars)

CAROL COMPANY
Restated Income for the Year Ended December 31, 1994
(in constant end-of-year 1994 dollars)

	Historical Dollars	× Conversion Ratio	= Constant Dollars
Sales	$200,000 ×	108/104	= $207,692
Cost of goods sold:			
Merchandise inventory, January 1, 1994	$ 20,000 ×	108/98	= $ 22,041
Purchases	160,000 ×	108/104	= 166,154
Goods available for sale	$180,000		$188,195
Merchandise inventory, December 31, 1994	40,000 ×	108/106	= 40,755
Cost of goods sold	$140,000		$147,440
Gross margin	$ 60,000		$ 60,252
Expenses:			
Depreciation	$ 4,000 ×	108/54	= $ 8,000
Other expenses	46,000 ×	108/104	= 47,769
Total expenses	$ 50,000		$ 55,769
Income from continuing operations	$ 10,000		$ 4,483
Purchasing power gain on monetary items			2,625
Net income	$ 10,000		$ 7,108

---

chasing power than he did at the beginning of the year. Bill needs to have $1,250 ($1,000 × 125/100) at year-end to be as well off as he was at the start of the year. Therefore, during the year, Bill has sustained a purchasing power loss of $250.

Conversely, a gain results from being in debt during inflation. Assume that Kathy Rice owes $600 during a year in which prices rise 40%. The original debt has a year-end purchasing power equivalent of $840 ($600 × 140/100). Kathy can satisfy the debt by paying $600 currently. Thus, she has experienced a purchasing power gain of $240.

Assume that Carol Company, in Illustration C.4, experienced a purchasing power gain of $2,625 during 1994. This amount would be added to net income from continuing operations on the restated income statement. Carol Company has net income on a constant dollar basis of $7,108, which is nearly 30% less than the net income shown on the conventional (historical cost) income statement.

Constant Dollar Accounting—Pros and Cons

The advantages of constant dollar accounting include the following:

1. Measurement of the impact of inflation on a company is objective because adjustments made to convert the statements to a constant dollar basis are based on historical cost.
2. Comparability of the financial statements between companies is improved because of the use of the same procedures and the same index numbers for each firm.
3. There is greater comparability of the financial statements of a single company through time since effects of price-level changes are removed by stating all amounts in dollars of the same purchasing power.

ILLUSTRATION C.5

Inflation Impact Disclosures

CAROL COMPANY
Statement of Income Adjusted for Changing Prices
For the Year Ended December 31, 1994

	Historical Cost	Current Cost	Constant Dollar (end-of-year dollars)
Sales.	$200,000	$200,000	$207,692
Cost of goods sold	$140,000	$146,000	$147,440
Expenses:			
Depreciation expense	4,000	8,500	8,000
Other expenses	46,000	46,000	47,769
Total	$190,000	$200,500	$203,209
Income (loss) from continuing operations	$ 10,000	$ (500)	$ 4,483
Purchasing power gain on monetary items			2,625
Net income	$ 10,000	$ (500)	$ 7,108

The disadvantages of constant dollar accounting include:

1. Benefits resulting from the use of such statements have not been shown to exceed the costs of preparing these statements.

2. The assumption that the impact of inflation affects all companies equally is not true.

3. Only one deficiency—the changing value of the measuring unit—is corrected; the effects of specific price changes are ignored. This deficiency is undoubtedly the most significant limitation of constant dollar accounting.

Illustration C.5 shows a comparison of all three income statements for Carol Company.

Which method of adjusting for inflation is correct? There is no simple answer. Each method is correct if one accepts the definitions of cost and income assumed under that particular method. A much more important question is: Which method is more useful to users of the financial reports? The answer to this question has been of considerable concern to many people, including members of the FASB and the staff of the SEC.

THE FASB REQUIREMENTS

FASB Statement No. 33 called for disclosure by companies in their annual reports both of the impact of specific price changes and of general inflation on earnings and other selected items. The *Statement* did not require full, completely adjusted financial statements, nor did it affect the way the basic (primary) financial statements are prepared, since all required disclosures appeared as supplementary information. The *Statement* applied only to publicly held companies (1) with total assets in excess of $1 billion (after deducting accumulated depreciation) or (2) having $125 million (before deducting accumulated depreciation) of inventories and property, plant, and equipment. Thus, about 1,200 to 1,400 large, publicly held companies were directly affected. The FASB also encouraged all companies to report the effects of inflation by applying the methods described in *FASB Statement No. 33*.

For fiscal years ended on or after December 25, 1979, affected companies initially had to report as supplementary information:

a. Net income on a current cost basis.

b. Net income on a constant dollar basis (historical cost adjusted for the effects of general inflation).

c. Purchasing power gain or loss on monetary items.[2]

Other disclosure requirements, including a five-year summary of selected financial data, also existed.

Uncertainty over whether constant dollar information or current cost information is preferable caused the FASB to initially require both types. This uncertainty was shown in responses sent to the FASB by various users when the proposed statement was circulated. Some knowledgeable persons preferred current cost information, while others preferred constant dollar information.

Since *FASB Statement No. 33* was released in 1979, companies and financial statement users have had several years of experience with both approaches. In 1984, the FASB indicated its preference for current cost information over constant dollar information. In *FASB Statement No. 82*, the FASB eliminated the requirement for reporting constant dollar information in supplemental financial statements to reduce the cost incurred in preparing financial statements.[3] Under *FASB Statement No. 82*, the reporting of current cost information was still required. However, a company could substitute constant dollar information for current cost information. In 1986, the FASB issued *FASB Statement No. 89*, which *encourages*, but *does not require*, companies to disclose supplementary information on the effects of changing prices.[4] Because reporting the effects of inflation is now optional and the inflation rate is low, many companies no longer include this supplemental information in their annual reports.

DEMONSTRATION PROBLEM

Duncan Book Company's financial statements included the following partial income statement:

DUNCAN BOOK COMPANY
Partial Income Statement
For the Year Ended December 31, 1994

Sales		$250,000
Cost of goods sold	$180,000	
Depreciation	3,000	
Other expenses	15,000	198,000
Income from continuing operations		$ 52,000

Sales were made uniformly throughout the year. The cost of goods sold consisted of books acquired when the general price index stood at 105. This same

---

[2] *FASB Statement No. 33*, pars. 29–35.

[3] FASB, *Statement of Financial Accounting Standards No. 82*, "Financial Reporting and Changing Prices: Elimination of Certain Disclosures" (Stamford, Conn., 1984). Copyright © by Financial Accounting Standards Board, High Ridge Park, Stamford, Connecticut, 06905, USA.

[4] FASB, *Statement of Financial Accounting Standards No. 89*, "Financial Reporting and Changing Prices" (Stamford, Conn., 1987). Copyright © by Financial Accounting Standards Board, High Ridge Park, Stamford, Connecticut, 06905, USA.

index ended the year at 120 and averaged 110 for the year. The current cost of the goods sold was $200,000.

The $3,000 depreciation reported is on a delivery truck that cost $12,000 when the general price index stood at 100. The truck had a current cost of $14,000 at the beginning of 1994 and a current cost of $16,000 at the end of 1994. The other expenses were incurred uniformly throughout the year, were paid in cash, and are substantially equal to their current cost at time of incurrence.

Assume that Duncan experienced a purchasing power gain of $1,500 during 1994.

Required *a.* Prepare a statement showing current cost income from continuing operations for the year ended December 31, 1994.

b. Prepare a statement showing constant dollar income in December 31, 1994, dollars for the year then ended.

SOLUTION TO DEMONSTRATION PROBLEM

a.

DUNCAN BOOK COMPANY
Statement of Current Cost Income from Continuing Operations
For the Year Ended December 31, 1994

Sales		$250,000
Cost of goods sold	$200,000	
Depreciation ($14,000 + $16,000)/2 × 0.25	3,750	
Other expenses	15,000	218,750
Income from continuing operations.		$ 31,250

b.

DUNCAN BOOK COMPANY
Statement of Constant Dollar Income
In End-of-Year Dollars
For the Year Ended December 31, 1994

Sales ($250,000 × 120/110)		$272,727
Cost of goods sold ($180,000 × 120/105)	$205,714	
Depreciation ($3,000 × 120/100)	3,600	
Other expenses ($15,000 × 120/110)	16,364	225,678
Income from continuing operations		$ 47,049
Purchasing power gain on monetary items		1,500
Net income		$ 48,549

NEW TERMS

Constant dollar accounting A recommended approach to deal with the problem of accounting for inflation by changing the unit of measure from the actual historical (nominal) dollar to a dollar of constant purchasing power. *959*

Current cost The amount that would have to be paid currently to acquire an asset. *960*

Current cost accounting A recommended approach to deal with the problem of accounting for inflation by

showing current cost or value of items in the financial statements. *959*

Deflation (period of) Exists when prices in general are falling. *958*

General price-level accounting See Constant dollar accounting.

Historical cost accounting Conventional accounting in which accounting measurements are in terms of the actual dollars expended or received. *958*

Inflation (period of)   Exists when prices in general are rising. *958*

Monetary items   Cash and other assets and liabilities that represent fixed claims to cash, such as accounts and notes receivable and payable. *963*

Nonmonetary items   All items on the balance sheet other than monetary items; examples are inventories, plant assets, capital stock, and stockholders' equity. *963*

Price index   A weighted average of prices for various goods and services. A base year is chosen and assigned a value of 100 for comparative purposes. *958*

Purchasing power gain   The gain that results from holding monetary liabilities during inflation or monetary assets during deflation. *963*

Purchasing power loss   The loss that results from holding monetary assets during inflation or monetary liabilities during deflation. *963*

QUESTIONS

1. How might a tax supposedly on income be really a tax on capital?

2. What two basic approaches might be used to reveal the impact of inflation on financial statements?

3. When items in a set of financial statements are all converted into constant dollars, what do they have in common?

4. If an index of the general level of prices rose 15% in a period, what is the effect on the value or real worth of the dollar?

5. How is the dollar amount for land adjusted under constant dollar accounting?

6. Explain the typical adjustment of sales and most expenses under constant dollar accounting.

7. Identify whether each of the following items is a monetary or nonmonetary item:

   a. Cash.
   b. Equipment.
   c. Notes receivable.
   d. Merchandise inventory.
   e. Accounts receivable.
   f. Patents.
   g. Common stock.
   h. Land.
   i. Accounts payable.
   j. Buildings.

8. What are purchasing power gains and losses? When do purchasing power gains occur? When do purchasing power losses occur?

9. If supplementary disclosures are made, how are the effects of inflation shown?

10. What is the major deficiency in constant dollar accounting?

EXERCISES

Exercise C–1

Compute income under historical cost accounting, current cost accounting, and constant dollar accounting

Assume the following facts regarding the purchase and sale of 100 units of a product:

Date	Transaction	Amount	Price-Level Index
January 1, 1994	Purchased 100 units	$36,000	100
December 31, 1994	Sold 100 units	60,000	110

The company incurred $7,200 of expenses to sell the units. The replacement cost of the units on December 31, 1994, was $42,000. Prepare a schedule showing net income from continuing operations under historical cost accounting, current cost accounting, and constant dollar accounting.

Exercise C–2

Convert cost of goods sold section of income statement to constant dollar amounts

The cost of goods sold section of the conventional (historical cost) income statement for Thurgood Company appears below:

Cost of goods sold:	
Merchandise inventory, January 1, 1994.	$ 72,000
Purchases	216,000
Goods available for sale	$288,000
Merchandise inventory, December 31, 1994.	36,000
Cost of goods sold	$252,000

The general price-level index was 100 on December 31, 1993, and 110 on December 31, 1994. The FIFO inventories were acquired when the index stood at 96 for the beginning inventory and 108 for the ending inventory. Purchases were incurred uniformly throughout the year. Convert the cost of goods sold section of the income statement to end-of-year constant dollar amounts.

Exercise C–3

Compute current cost depreciation

R Company's plant assets at December 31, 1993, had a historical cost of $100,000 and accumulated depreciation of $40,000 (10% annual depreciation rate). No additions or retirements occurred in 1994. The current cost of the plant assets on December 31, 1993, was $130,000 and on December 31, 1994 was $150,000. Compute the current cost depreciation for 1994.

Exercise C–4

Determine purchasing power gain or loss

In each of the situations given, determine the amount of purchasing power gain or loss:

a. You hold cash of $20,000 during a year in which prices in general rose 10%.

b. You are in debt $10,000 during a year in which prices in general rose 8%.

PROBLEMS

Problem C–1

Compute income on both current cost and constant dollar basis

A partial income statement for Bluebird Company for the year ended December 31, 1994, in terms of historical dollars follows:

BLUEBIRD COMPANY		
Partial Income Statement		
For the Year Ended December 31, 1994		
Sales		$880,000
Cost of goods sold	$504,000	
Depreciation	48,000	
Other expenses	96,800	648,800
Income from continuing operations		$231,200

The sales were made uniformly throughout the year. The cost of goods sold consisted of goods acquired when the general price index stood at 105. This same index ended the year at 120 and averaged 110 for the year. The current cost of the goods sold was $600,000.

The $48,000 of depreciation reported is on a machine that cost $240,000 when the general price index stood at 90. The machine is being depreciated over a five-year period with no expected salvage value. The machine had a current cost of $400,000 at the beginning of 1994 and a current cost of $480,000 at the end of 1994.

Required

a. Prepare a statement showing current cost income from continuing operations for the year ended December 31, 1994.

b. Prepare a statement showing income from continuing operations in constant end-of-year 1994 dollars for the year ended December 31, 1994.

Problem C–2

Prepare income statement in constant dollars

Finkler Company began business on January 2, 1994, with $384,000 of inventory and $192,000 of equipment. An index of the general level of prices stood at 100 on January 2, 1994. This index rose uniformly throughout the year, averaging 125 for the year, and ending at 150. Finkler's income statement for the year in historical dollars is given below.

FINKLER COMPANY
Income Statement
For the Year Ended December 31, 1994

Sales		$480,000
Cost of goods sold		240,000
Gross margin		$240,000
Depreciation	$48,000	
Other expenses	96,000	144,000
Net income		$ 96,000

In 1994, Finkler sold goods out of the beginning inventory with a cost of $240,000 for $480,000 cash. Expenses in the amount of $96,000 were incurred uniformly throughout the year and were paid in cash. No new equipment was purchased during the year.

Required   Prepare an income statement for 1994 with all amounts expressed in constant end-of-year 1994 dollars. The purchasing power loss on net monetary items was $4,800.

Problem C–3

Compute income on both current cost and constant dollar basis

Following is a partial income statement for McMannus Home Furnishings for the year ended December 31, 1994:

McMANNUS HOME FURNISHINGS
Partial Income Statement
For the Year Ended December 31, 1994

Sales		$840,000
Cost of goods sold	$540,800	
Depreciation	32,000	
Other expenses	168,000	740,800
Income from continuing operations		$ 99,200

Sales were made uniformly throughout the year. Other expenses were also incurred rather uniformly throughout the year and largely on a cash basis. Thus, their historical cost is substantially equal to their current cost. The depreciation reported relates to a machine acquired at a cost of $320,000 that is being depreciated over a 10-year life on a straight-line basis.

The current cost of the goods sold was $600,000 at the time of sale. The current (gross) cost of the machine was $520,000 at the beginning of 1994 and $600,000 at the end of the year. An index of the general level of prices stood at 80 when the machine was acquired, stood at 100 at the beginning of 1994, averaged 105 for 1994, and ended the year at 110. The index stood at 104 when the goods sold were acquired.

Required   *a.*   Prepare a statement showing current cost income from continuing operations for the year ended December 31, 1994.

           b.   Prepare a statement showing constant dollar income from continuing operations in end-of-year dollars for the year ended December 31, 1994.

D

AN INTRODUCTION TO GOVERNMENTAL AND NONPROFIT ACCOUNTING

INTRODUCTION

Much attention is paid to accounting for profit-seeking, business entities. But almost half of the gross national product (a measure of the market value of goods and services produced in any year) is expended by governmental and nonprofit entities. *Governmental agencies* include local, state, and national governments and all of their subentities (such as the Bureau of Licenses or the Internal Revenue Service). *Nonprofit entities* include colleges and universities, voluntary health and welfare agencies, churches, civic organizations, labor unions, political parties, private schools, country clubs, hospitals, and museums. All of us either contribute to such organizations by paying dues or taxes or by making donations, and many of us are benefited by their activities.

External users of the financial reports of these nonbusiness entities are not owners of the entity. They do not expect to make a return *on* their "contribution" and, in most cases, do not expect a return *of* their contribution. Thus, performance of the entity is not measured by net income. Rather, performance measurement is in terms of how well the entity met its stated objectives and by the changes in its resources.

We feel a need to know whether the funds received by these organizations are spent for their intended purposes. For instance, assume you had contributed a substantial sum to a charity that claimed the funds would be used to benefit victims of a particular illness. You later discover that 90% of the funds received by this organization had been spent on fund raising and administrative salaries, and only 10% had been spent on programs for those with the illness. The next time the organization approaches you for a contribution, you probably will decide to give elsewhere.

One thing we cannot avoid in life is taxes. Since taxes must be paid, we are interested in how the funds are controlled and spent. We are upset when we learn that funds were spent on projects we do not support and are also upset to learn of graft and corruption involving funds we have entrusted to governmental officials. Sound accounting and reporting practices can help avoid these abuses.

BACKGROUND OF GOVERNMENTAL AND NONPROFIT ACCOUNTING

In 1934, the Municipal Finance Officers Association (later named the Government Financial Officers Association) was instrumental in the formation of the National Committee on Municipal Accounting. This committee worked periodically through the years to upgrade accounting and reporting standards for governmental accounting and to address current problems. In 1949, the committee's name was changed to the National Committee on Government Accounting so that its activities might address all governmental entities except the federal government and its agencies. In the late 1970s, the FASB was urged by some to take sole responsibility for government accounting issues. But this move was opposed by some government accounting groups.

Instead, the Governmental Accounting Standards Board (GASB) was established in 1984 to set accounting and financial reporting standards for state and local governments. The standards set by the GASB are not mandatory for governmental units, but they represent "good" accounting practices that are highly recommended and likely to be used.

Certain standards established by other organizations remain in effect until the GASB sets standards in a given topic area. The GASB is the successor to the National Council on Governmental Accounting (NCGA), which set governmental accounting standards for many years. All NCGA pronouncements in effect on a given topic as of 1984 remain in effect until the GASB issues a pronouncement in that topic area. Also, entities in the public sector, such as universities, hospitals, and utilities, must follow generally accepted accounting principles established by the FASB unless the GASB has issued a pronouncement applicable to that type of entity.

The GASB is a parallel organization to the Financial Accounting Standards Board (FASB), which establishes financial and reporting standards in the private sector. Both organizations are under the guidance of the Financial Accounting Foundation.

FUND ACCOUNTING

All governmental units and most nonprofit entities receive financial resources that can only be used for special purposes. For instance, a university may receive cash that can only be spent by the School of Accountancy to provide scholarships to deserving students. The university may also have a separate fund that can only be used for research on human behavior. Such special funds must be kept separate and accounted for separately so the moneys will be spent for their intended purpose. Each such fund has its own set of self-balancing accounts that show assets, liabilities, and fund equity.

The National Council on Governmental Accounting (NCGA) defined a *fund* as follows:

A fund is defined as a fiscal and accounting entity with a self-balancing set of accounts recording cash and other financial resources, together with all related liabilities and residual equities, or balances, and changes therein, which are segregated for the purpose of carrying on specific activities or attaining certain objectives in accordance with special regulations, restrictions, or limitations.[1]

Types of Funds

The three major types of funds are governmental, proprietary, and fiduciary. Governmental funds are established in accordance with some law authorizing the fund to receive certain revenues and make certain types of expenditures. Proprietary funds are established to provide services to users on a cost-reimbursement basis. Revenues and expenses are recorded in a manner similar to those of business entities, and net income may result. Fiduciary funds account for assets held by the entity as a trustee or agent. Some fiduciary funds are accounted for in the same way as governmental funds (revenues and expenditures), and some are accounted for in the same way as proprietary funds (matching of revenues and expenses).

Governmental Funds Governmental funds consist of four different types. The descriptions of these funds are paraphrased from the ones given in a document published by the National Council on Governmental Accounting.[2]

1. *General Fund*—account for all financial resources not required to be accounted for in some other fund.
2. *Special Revenue Funds*—account for proceeds from specific revenue sources, such as gasoline taxes. Expenditures are legally limited to certain specified purposes, such as highway construction and repairs.
3. *Capital Projects Funds*—account for financial resources accumulated for the acquisition or construction of major capital facilities, such as an airport.
4. *Debt Service Funds*—account for the accumulation of financial resources to pay off the principal and interest on long-term debt, such as school construction bonds.

Until 1987, *special assessment funds* accounted for the financing of public improvements or services designed to benefit the properties against which the

---

[1] *Codification of Governmental Accounting and Financial Reporting Standards* (Stamford, Conn.: Governmental Accounting Standards Board, 1987), sec. 1100.102.

[2] GASB Cod., sec. 1300.104, as amended by *Government Accounting Standards Board Statement No. 6,* "Accounting and Financial Reporting for Special Assessments" (Stamford, Conn.: Government Accounting Standards Board, 1987).

special assessments were levied. An example was when a city government assessed homeowners for future hook-ups to the city water system. The GASB, in *Statement No. 6* issued in 1987, eliminated the special assessment type fund from governmental reports. These transactions are now accounted for in the general fund, a special revenue fund, or an enterprise fund, whichever type best fits their nature.

Proprietary Funds Proprietary funds are of two types—enterprise and internal service. Descriptions of these funds are as follows:

1. *Enterprise Funds*—account for operations financed and operated like a private business entity, such as a golf course operated by a city. Also may be used in other situations where the governing body decides that an operation should be accounted for in a manner similar to a business (revenues, expenses, and net income) for some reason, such as management control, ensuring that physical capital is maintained, or public policy.

2. *Internal Service Funds*—account for the financing of goods or services, on a cost-reimbursement basis, provided by one agency or department of a governmental entity to another department or agency of that same entity or to some other governmental entity. For example, the department of public works of a city provides snow removal services for the city's Bureau of Licenses after a major snow storm.

Fiduciary Funds Only one type of fiduciary fund exists—trust and agency funds. This fund is described as follows:

> *Trust and Agency Funds*—account for assets held by a governmental entity as a trustee or agent for another party. For example, a state might hold in trust the pension funds of its employees.

A governmental entity should maintain only the number of funds needed to satisfy the law and provide sound financial information. If only one fund is needed, only one fund should be used.

Besides the special types of funds, two *account groups* account for fixed assets and long-term liabilities. The two account groups are as follows:

1. *General Fixed Assets Account Group*—accounts for all fixed assets of a governmental entity except those accounted for in a specific proprietary fund or trust fund. No depreciation is recorded on these assets. Depreciation is recorded on assets accounted for in proprietary funds and some trust funds.

2. *General Long-Term Debt Group*—accounts for all long-term liabilities associated with the financing of capital acquisitions.

BASES OF ACCOUNTING USED

Proprietary funds and certain fiduciary funds use full accrual accounting just as business entities do. All other funds use a "modified cash basis," or a combination of the accrual and cash bases. The modified cash basis is described as follows:

Revenues should be recognized in the accounting period in which they become available and measurable. Expenditures should be recognized in the accounting period in which the fund liability is incurred, if measurable, except for unmatured interest on general long-term debt, which should be recognized when due.[3]

---

[3] GASB Cod., sec. 1100.108 (as amended by *GASB Statement No. 6*).

In business accrual accounting, revenues are recognized when they are "earned." This same rule cannot be used in governmental and fund accounting because revenues are not earned. Thus, revenues are recognized when they are "available" and "measurable." Revenues are considered available when they are "collectible within the current period or soon enough thereafter to be used to pay liabilities of the current period."[4]

Expenditures are generally recognized in the period to which they relate because the liability is incurred in that same period. This rule is quite similar to business accrual accounting, which states that expenses are recognized when they are incurred.

A SAMPLE OF ENTRIES MADE IN FUND ACCOUNTING

Some of the entries made in fund accounting may seem strange at first. But when you understand why they are made, they make more sense.

First of all, the budget for certain types of funds is entered in the general ledger by making an entry as follows:

Estimated Revenues	50,000,000	
Appropriations		47,000,000
Budgetary Fund Balance		3,000,000
To record the annual operating budget.		

Actual revenues are recorded as they become available and measurable. A comparison can be made between actual revenues and budgeted revenues at all times. If actual revenues are expected to fall short of budgeted revenues, reductions in planned expenditures can be made. (At the end of the year, after the budgeted amounts in the general ledger have served their control function, the entry made above is reversed during the closing process.)

Government entities normally issue purchase orders for goods and supplies they desire to purchase. These purchase orders are commitments for future expenditures. A record must be kept of outstanding purchase orders so that the entity will not commit to spend more than it has available to spend. Thus, a purchase order issued to purchase goods is charged to an Encumbrances account as follows:

Encumbrances	20,000	
Fund Balance Reserved for Encumbrances		20,000
To record encumbrances for purchase orders issued.		

When the goods actually arrive, the above entry is reversed and the expenditure is recorded. Assume the cost of the goods is $19,500. The entries are as follows:

Fund Balance Reserved for Encumbrances	20,000	
Encumbrances		20,000
To reverse encumbrances of $20,000 on delivery of goods costing $19,500.		

Expenditures	19,500	
Cash (or Vouchers Payable)		19,500
To record an expenditure for goods purchased.		

[4] GASB Cod., sec. 1600.106.

ILLUSTRATION D.1

NAME OF GOVERNMENT UNIT
Combined Balance Sheet—All Fund Types and Account Groups
December 31, 19x2

	Government Fund Types				
Assets	**General**	**Special Revenue**	**Debt Service**	**Capital Projects**	**Special Assessment***
Cash	$258,500	$101,385	$ 43,834	$ 431,600	$232,185
Cash with fiscal agent	—	—	102,000	—	—
Investments at cost or amortized cost	65,000	37,200	160,990	—	—
Receivables (net of allowances for uncollectibles):					
Taxes	58,300	2,500	3,829	—	—
Accounts	8,300	3,300	—	100	—
Special assessments	—	—	—	—	646,035
Notes	—	—	—	—	—
Loans	—	—	—	—	—
Accrued interest	50	25	1,557	—	350
Due from other funds	2,000	—	—	—	—
Due from other governments	30,000	75,260	—	640,000	—
Advances to Internal Service Funds	65,000	—	—	—	—
Inventory of supplies, at cost	7,200	5,190	—	—	—
Prepaid expenses	—	—	—	—	—
Restricted assets:					
Cash	—	—	—	—	—
Investments, at cost or amortized cost	—	—	—	—	—
Land	—	—	—	—	—
Buildings	—	—	—	—	—
Accumulated depreciation	—	—	—	—	—
Improvements other than buildings	—	—	—	—	—
Accumulated depreciation	—	—	—	—	—
Machinery and equipment	—	—	—	—	—
Accumulated depreciation	—	—	—	—	—
Construction in progress	—	—	—	—	—
Amount available in Debt Service Funds	—	—	—	—	—
Amount to be provided for retirement of general long-term debt	—	—	—	—	—
Total Assets	$494,350	$224,860	$312,210	$1,071,700	$878,570

* *GASB Statement No. 6* eliminated this type of fund as of June 1987.
Source: NCGA *Statement No. 1*, pp. 30–31.

The encumbrance system keeps the entity from spending more than it may legally spend. The total of expenditures and encumbrances shows how much has been spent and committed at any point in time.

FINANCIAL STATEMENTS ISSUED BY GOVERNMENTAL ENTITIES

Illustration D.1 shows a sample combined balance sheet for all fund types and account groups. You may not understand every item on the balance sheet, but at least you will gain some understanding of what the balance sheet for a governmental entity might look like.

Proprietary Fund Types		Fiduciary Fund Type	Account Groups		Totals (memorandum only)	
Enterprise	Internal Service	Trust and Agency	General Fixed Assets	General Long-Term Debt	December 31, 19x2	December 31, 19x1
$ 257,036	$ 29,700	$ 216,701	$ —	$ —	$ 1,570,941	$ 1,258,909
—	—	—	—	—	102,000	—
—	—	1,239,260	—	—	1,502,450	1,974,354
—	—	580,000	—	—	644,629	255,400
29,130	—	—	—	—	40,830	32,600
—	—	—	—	—	646,035	462,035
2,350	—	—	—	—	2,350	1,250
—	—	35,000	—	—	35,000	40,000
650	—	2,666	—	—	5,298	3,340
2,000	12,000	11,189	—	—	27,189	17,499
—	—	—	—	—	745,260	101,400
—	—	—	—	—	65,000	75,000
23,030	40,000	—	—	—	75,420	70,900
1,200	—	—	—	—	1,200	900
113,559	—	—	—	—	113,559	272,968
176,800	—	—	—	—	176,800	143,800
211,100	20,000	—	1,259,500	—	1,490,600	1,456,100
447,700	60,000	—	2,855,500	—	3,363,200	2,836,700
(90,718)	(4,500)	—	—	—	(95,218)	(83,500)
3,887,901	15,000	—	1,036,750	—	4,939,651	3,922,200
(348,944)	(3,000)	—	—	—	(351,944)	(283,750)
1,841,145	25,000	—	452,500	—	2,318,645	1,924,100
(201,138)	(9,400)	—	—	—	(210,538)	(141,900)
22,713	—	—	1,722,250	—	1,744,963	1,359,606
—	—	—	—	210,210	210,210	284,813
—	—	—	—	1,889,790	1,889,790	1,075,187
$6,375,514	$184,800	$2,084,816	$7,326,500	$2,100,000	$21,053,320	$17,059,911

Other types of financial statements prepared by governmental entities include:

Combined statement of revenues, expenditures, and changes in fund balances (all fund types).

Combined statement of revenues, expenditures, and changes in fund balances—budget and actual (general and special revenue fund types).

Combined statement of revenues, expenses, and changes in retained earnings (all proprietary types).

Combined statement of cash flows (all proprietary funds).

Notes to the financial statements are an important part of the statements. These notes further explain the amounts included in the statements.

ILLUSTRATION D.1

(concluded)

NAME OF GOVERNMENT UNIT
Combined Balance Sheet—All Fund Types and Account Groups, Continued
December 31, 19x2

		Government Fund Types			
Liabilities and Fund Equity	**General**	**Special Revenue**	**Debt Service**	**Capital Projects**	**Special Assessment***
Liabilities:					
Vouchers payable	$118,261	$ 33,850	$ —	$ 29,000	$ 20,600
Contracts payable	57,600	18,300	—	69,000	50,000
Judgments payable	—	2,000	—	22,600	11,200
Accrued liabilities	—	—	—	—	10,700
Payable from restricted assets:					
Construction contracts	—	—	—	—	—
Fiscal agent	—	—	—	—	—
Accrued interest	—	—	—	—	—
Revenue bonds	—	—	—	—	—
Deposits	—	—	—	—	—
Due to other taxing units	—	—	—	—	—
Due to other funds	24,189	2,000		1,000	
Due to student groups	—	—	—	—	—
Deferred revenue	15,000	—	—	—	—
Advance from General Fund	—	—	—	—	—
Matured bonds payable	—	—	100,000	—	—
Matured interest payable	—	—	2,000	—	—
General obligation bonds payable	—	—	—	—	—
Revenue bonds payable	—	—	—	—	—
Special assessment bonds payable	—	—	—	—	555,000
Total liabilities	215,050	56,150	102,000	121,600	647,500
Fund equity:					
Contributed capital	—	—	—	—	—
Investment in general fixed assets	—	—	—	—	—
Retained earnings:					
Reserved for revenue bond retirement	—	—	—	—	—
Unreserved	—	—	—	—	—
Fund balances:					
Reserved for encumbrances	38,000	46,500	—	941,500	185,000
Reserved for inventory of supplies	7,200	5,190	—	—	—
Reserved for advance to Internal Service Funds	65,000	—	—	—	—
Reserved for loans	—	—	—	—	—
Reserved for endowments	—	—	—	—	—
Reserved for employees' retirement system	—	—	—	—	—
Unreserved:					
Designated for debt service	—	—	210,210	—	46,070
Designated for subsequent years' expenditures	50,000	—	—	—	—
Undesignated	119,100	117,020	—	8,600	—
Total fund equity	279,300	168,710	210,210	950,100	231,070
Total liabilities and fund equity	$494,350	$224,860	$312,210	$1,071,700	$878,570

The notes to the financial statements are an integral part of this statement.

Source: NCGA *Statement 1*, pp. 30–31.

	Proprietary Fund Types		Fiduciary Fund Type	Account Groups		Totals (memorandum only)	
	Enterprise	Internal Service	Trust and Agency	General Fixed Assets	General Long-Term Debt	December 31, 19x2	December 31, 19x1
	$ 131,071	$ 15,000	$ 3,350	$ —	$ —	$ 351,132	$ 223,412
	8,347	—	—	—	—	203,247	1,326,511
	—	—	—	—	—	35,800	32,400
	16,870	—	4,700	—	—	32,270	27,417
	17,760	—	—	—	—	17,760	—
	139	—	—	—	—	139	—
	32,305	—	—	—	—	32,305	67,150
	48,000	—	—	—	—	48,000	52,000
	63,000	—	—	—	—	63,000	55,000
	—	—	680,800	—	—	680,800	200,000
	—	—	—	—	—	27,189	17,499
	—	—	1,850	—	—	1,850	1,600
	—	—	—	—	—	15,000	3,000
	—	65,000	—	—	—	65,000	75,000
	—	—	—	—	—	100,000	—
	—	—	—	—	—	2,000	—
	700,000	—	—	—	2,100,000	2,800,000	2,110,000
	1,798,000	—	—	—	—	1,798,000	1,846,000
	—	—	—	—	—	555,000	420,000
	2,815,492	80,000	690,700	—	2,100,000	6,828,492	6,456,989
	1,392,666	95,000	—	—	—	1,487,666	815,000
	—	—	—	7,326,500	—	7,326,500	5,299,600
	129,155	—	—	—	—	129,155	96,975
	2,038,201	9,800	—	—	—	2,048,001	1,998,119
	—	—	—	—	—	1,211,000	410,050
	—	—	—	—	—	12,390	10,890
	—	—	—	—	—	65,000	75,000
	—	—	50,050	—	—	50,050	45,100
	—	—	134,000	—	—	134,000	94,000
	—	—	1,426,201	—	—	1,426,201	1,276,150
	—	—	—	—	—	256,280	325,888
	—	—	—	—	—	50,000	50,000
	—	—	(216,135)	—	—	28,585	106,150
	3,560,022	104,800	1,394,116	7,326,500	—	14,224,828	10,602,922
	$6,375,514	$184,800	$2,084,816	$7,326,500	$2,100,000	$21,053,320	$17,059,911

NONPROFIT ENTITIES

Many nongovernmental, nonprofit entities also use fund accounting approximately in the form described above. The use of fund accounting results in financial resources being accounted for and reported according to restrictions imposed by external parties or by the governing board of the nonprofit entity.

Six fund groups are commonly used by nonprofit entities (the actual titles used for these funds by any given entity may vary). These fund groups are:

1. *Current Funds*—used to support current operations.
2. *Plant Funds*—used to acquire new fixed assets, renew and replace old fixed assets, and retire indebtedness associated with fixed assets.
3. *Endowment and Similar Funds*—used for a specific purpose. For instance, in a university an endowment fund is invested, and the income it earns is used to supplement the salary of a "chaired" professor and pay his or her travel expenses.
4. *Agency Funds*—used for financial resources being held for another party. An example is where a university, acting as an agent, holds cash and other assets for the employees' credit union.
5. *Annuity of Life Income Funds*—used in a situation where a donor contributes a certain sum to the nonprofit entity with the condition that he or she will receive the income from that investment while living. After the donor dies, the principle reverts to the Current Fund Group to be used at the discretion of the governing board.
6. *Loan Funds*—used to provide loans to certain individuals. An example is a student loan fund operated by a university.

Nonprofit entities using funds such as those described include colleges and universities, hospitals, voluntary health and welfare organizations, country clubs, political parties, libraries, labor unions, private schools, and churches. Again, such entities should only use the minimum number of funds required to account for their operations.

RECENT DEVELOPMENTS IN GOVERNMENTAL AND NONPROFIT ACCOUNTING

The GASB issued its first "concepts" statement, titled "Objectives of Financial Reporting," in May 1987. GASB concepts statements do not establish standards but provide the framework within which standards can be developed. The three general objectives described in the statement are:

☐ Financial reporting should assist in fulfilling government's duty to be publicly accountable and should enable users to assess that accountability.
☐ Financial reporting should assist users in evaluating the operating results of the governmental entity for the year.
☐ Financial reporting should assist users in assessing the level of services that can be provided by the entity and its ability to meet its obligations when due.

Since that time, the GASB has issued several standards on various accounting matters. The GASB also has several projects under way that might affect depreciation practices now followed. As described earlier, no depreciation is currently recorded on fixed assets in many of the funds.

A BROADER PERSPECTIVE

WHITE FLAG SAVES GASB

Norwalk, Conn.—Faced with the almost certain demise of the Governmental Accounting Standards Board, its parent, the Financial Accounting Foundation has retreated from a showdown with 10 dissident groups over who should shape the future of government accounting.

Reversing the strong stance it had taken only two weeks earlier, the Foundation's board of trustees on Nov. 16 said it would support a proposal that leaves accounting for hospitals, utilities, colleges and other "special entities" under GASB control.

The trustees had cited the need to compare the financial statements of publicly and privately-owned institutions within these groups as the reason for an Oct. 30 vote to assign jurisdiction over the special entities to the private sector's standards-setter, the Financial Accounting Standards Board.

Infringement on the GASB's authority prompted the 10 groups that represent financial officers in government to take immediate steps to boycott the GASB and to attempt to form a separate standard-setting body.

Such a move would have meant the loss of key financial support for the Foundation, which serves as parent organization to both the GASB and FASB. However, the Foundation also appeared resolved to settling a jurisdictional battle that has been raging since the GASB was formed in 1984.

"With all the negotiating that's gone on and everything that's been said, the thought that this has been settled so quickly is really hard to believe," said Relmond Van Daniker, executive director of the National Association of State Auditors, Comptrollers and Treasurers.

NASACT was one of the 10 organizations threatening to leave the GASB. Its executive committee has already informed the Foundation that it supports the new proposal. Like the other government groups, it is now awaiting a formal vote by the trustees to adopt the measure.

A possible explanation for the dramatic change of events may have been a Nov. 15 letter to Foundation president John F. Ruffle from Freda S. Johnson, executive vp and director of the public finance department of Moody's Investors Service.

The bond rating agency said it found the Foundation's reasons for putting the special entities under FASB jurisdiction "disturbing" because further efforts toward comparability were unnecessary.

Moody's said financial analysts were able to adjust for any differences that may exist in the few situations where public and private sector financials are actually compared. Moody's also cautioned the Foundation that its decision "may, in fact, lead to situations where analysis is impaired rather than assisted."

Ruffle said that the Moody's letter did not play a major role in persuading the Foundation to put forth the new proposal. Instead, he said the Foundation's decision resulted from its willingness to continue working on ways to settle the jurisdiction issue even after the Oct. 30 vote.

"The much larger question was were we going to revert back to the chaos that existed prior to 1984 [when the GASB was founded] and have accounting for all state and local governments fall into disrepute over this issue," said Ruffle. "Or were we going to stand back and say, 'On balance does that make sense?'"

For his part, Van Daniker said he thought the Foundation was influenced by the speed in which the government groups moved to disassociate themselves from the GASB and set up their own standards-setting body.

"For the first time they might have realized that we were going forward with what we had been saying all along," he said.

One group disappointed with the Foundation's change of mind is the National Association of College and University Business Officers, which has been pushing for uniformity among its public and private sector members.

"We'll have a very militant faction that will say the standards-setting process is a big farce," said Robin Jenkins, an official with the Washington-based group.

Source: Stephen M. Cowherd, *Accounting Today*, December 4, 1989, pp. 1 and 32.

You have been given a brief introduction to governmental and nonprofit accounting in this appendix. For more information, see Leon E. Hay and Earl R. Wilson, *Accounting for Governmental and Nonprofit Entities*, 9th ed. (Homewood, Ill.: Richard D. Irwin, Inc., 1991).

E

CONSOLIDATED FINANCIAL STATEMENTS (ANNUAL REPORTS)

APPENDIX OUTLINE

Excerpts from the following 1989 annual reports are reproduced in this appendix:

1. The Coca-Cola Company and Subsidiaries: Financial Highlights, Selected Financial Data, Consolidated Balance Sheets, Consolidated Statements of Income, Consolidated Statements of Shareholders' Equity, Consolidated Statements of Cash Flows, Notes to Consolidated Financial Statements, and Report of Independent Auditors.

2. Maytag Corporation: Statements of Consolidated Income, Statements of Consolidated Financial Condition, and Statements of Consolidated Cash Flows.

3. The Limited, Inc.: Consolidated Statements of Income, Consolidated Balance Sheets, and Consolidated Statements of Cash Flows.

4. John H. Harland Company and Subsidiaries: Statements of Consolidated Income, Consolidated Balance Sheets, and Statements of Consolidated Cash Flows.

Financial Highlights
(In millions except per share data)

THE COCA-COLA COMPANY AND SUBSIDIARIES

Year Ended December 31,	1989	1988	Percent Change
Net operating revenues	$8,965.8	$8,337.8	7.5%
Operating income	$1,725.8	$1,598.3	8.0%
Income from continuing operations before income taxes	$1,764.3	$1,626.4	8.5%
Income from continuing operations	$1,192.8	$1,089.0	9.5%
Net income	$1,723.8	$1,044.7	65.0%
Preferred stock dividends	$ 21.4	$ 6.4	234.4%
Net income available to common shareholders	$1,702.4*	$1,038.3	64.0%*
Income per common share from continuing operations	$ 3.39	$ 2.97	14.1%
Net income per common share	$ 4.92*	$ 2.85	72.6%*
Cash dividends per common share	$ 1.36	$ 1.20	13.3%
Average common shares outstanding	346.0	364.6	(5.1%)
Common shareholders' equity at year-end	$3,185.5	$3,045.3	4.6%
Income from continuing operations available to common shareholders to average common shareholders' equity	37.6%	34.7%	
Closing market price per common share	$ 77.25	$ 44.63	73.1%

*Net income available to common shareholders in 1989 includes an after-tax gain of $509 million ($1.47 per common share) from the sale of the Company's equity interest in Columbia Pictures Entertainment, Inc. (CPE) in November and an after-tax gain of $36 million ($.10 per common share) from the sale of the Company's bottled water business in August. Excluding these gains, net income available to common shareholders was $1,157 million, an increase of 11.5 percent from the prior year, while net income per common share was $3.35, an increase of 17.5 percent from the prior year.

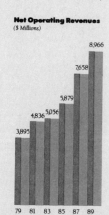

Net Operating Revenues
($ Millions)

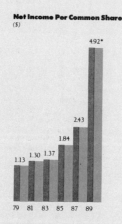

Net Income Per Common Share
($)

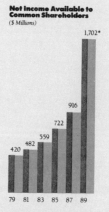

Net Income Available to Common Shareholders
($ Millions)

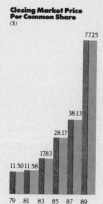

Closing Market Price Per Common Share
($)

Selected Financial Data

(In millions except per share data)

Year Ended December 31,	1989	1988	1987
Summary of Operations (a) (b)			
Net operating revenues	$8,966	$8,338	$7,658
Cost of goods sold	3,892	3,702	3,633
Gross profit	5,074	4,636	4,025
Selling, administrative and general expenses	3,348	3,038	2,665
Provisions for restructured operations and disinvestment	–	–	36
Operating income	1,726	1,598	1,324
Interest income	205	199	232
Interest expense	308	230	297
Equity income	75	92	64
Other	66	(33)	40
Income from continuing operations before income taxes	1,764	1,626	1,363
Income taxes	571	537	496
Income from continuing operations	$1,193	$1,089	$ 867
Net income	$1,724	$1,045	$ 916
Preferred stock dividends	22	7	–
Net income available to common shareholders	$1,702(c)	$1,038	$ 916
Per Common Share Data (a) (d)			
Income from continuing operations	$ 3.39	$ 2.97	$ 2.30
Net income	4.92(c)	2.85	2.43
Cash dividends	1.36	1.20	1.12
Year-End Position			
Cash, cash equivalents and marketable securities	$1,182	$1,231	$1,489
Property, plant and equipment – net	2,021	1,759	1,602
Total assets	8,283	7,451	8,606
Long-term debt	549	761	909
Total debt	1,981	2,124	2,995
Shareholders' equity	3,485	3,345	3,187
Total capital (e)	5,466	5,469	6,182
Financial Ratios			
Income from continuing operations available to common shareholders to average common shareholders' equity	37.6%	34.7%	26.0%
Income from continuing operations before interest expense to average total capital	25.6%	21.3%	18.3%
Total-debt-to-total-capital	36.2%	38.8%	48.4%
Net-debt-to-net-capital (f)	17.7%	24.3%	21.1%
Common stock dividend cash payout	27.6%(g)	42.1%	46.1%
Other Data			
Average common shares outstanding (d)	346	365	377
Capital expenditures	$ 462	$ 387	$ 304
Depreciation	181	167	152
Market price per common share at December 31 (d)	77.25	44.63	38.13

(a) Operating results have been restated to report the Company's equity income (loss) from CPE, which was sold in November 1989, as a discontinued operation.

(b) In 1982, the Company adopted SFAS No. 52, "Foreign Currency Translation."

(c) Net income available to common shareholders in 1989 includes an after-tax gain of $509 million ($1.47 per common share) from the sale of the Company's equity interest in CPE and an after-tax gain of $36 million ($.10 per common share) from the sale of the Company's bottled water business. Excluding these gains, net income available to common shareholders was $1,157 million, while net income per common share was $3.35.

THE COCA-COLA COMPANY AND SUBSIDIARIES

1986	1985	1984	1983	1982	1981	1980	1979
$6,977	$5,879	$5,442	$5,056	$4,760	$4,836	$4,640	$3,895
3,454	2,909	2,738	2,580	2,472	2,675	2,594	2,101
3,523	2,970	2,704	2,476	2,288	2,161	2,046	1,794
2,446	2,163	1,855	1,648	1,515	1,441	1,366	1,150
180	–	–	–	–	–	–	–
897	807	849	828	773	720	680	644
154	151	133	90	119	85	56	46
208	196	128	77	76	34	30	10
45	52	42	35	25	20	14	18
410	69	13	2	11	(20)	(13)	(7)
1,298	883	909	878	852	771	707	691
471	314	360	374	379	339	313	305
$ 827	$ 569	$ 549	$ 504	$ 473	$ 432	$ 394	$ 386
$ 934	$ 722	$ 629	$ 559	$ 512	$ 482	$ 422	$ 420
–	–	–	–	–	–	–	–
$ 934	$ 722	$ 629	$ 559	$ 512	$ 482	$ 422	$ 420
$ 2.14	$ 1.45	$ 1.38	$ 1.23	$ 1.21	$ 1.17	$ 1.06	$ 1.04
2.42	1.84	1.59	1.37	1.32	1.30	1.14	1.13
1.04	.99	.92	.89	.83	.77	.72	.65
$ 895	$ 843	$ 768	$ 559	$ 254	$ 344	$ 235	$ 153
1,538	1,483	1,284	1,247	1,233	1,160	1,045	976
7,675	6,341	5,241	4,540	4,212	3,373	3,152	2,710
996	801	631	428	423	132	121	22
1,848	1,280	1,310	520	493	227	213	130
3,479	2,948	2,751	2,912	2,779	2,271	2,075	1,919
5,327	4,228	4,061	3,432	3,272	2,498	2,288	2,049
25.7%	20.0%	19.4%	17.7%	18.7%	19.9%	19.7%	21.1%
20.1%	16.8%	16.7%	16.4%	17.9%	18.8%	18.9%	20.3%
34.7%	30.3%	32.3%	15.2%	15.1%	9.1%	9.3%	6.3%
15.5%	18.7%	20.8%	5.6%	13.6%	2.9%	7.7%	6.3%
43.0%	53.8%	57.9%	65.0%	62.9%	59.2%	63.2%	57.5%
387	393	396	408	390	372	372	372
$ 346	$ 412	$ 300	$ 324	$ 273	$ 279	$ 241	$ 309
151	130	119	111	104	94	87	77
37.75	28.17	20.79	17.83	17.33	11.58	11.13	11.50

(d) Adjusted for a three-for-one stock split in 1986.
(e) Shareholders' equity plus total debt.
(f) Net debt and net capital exclude temporary investments and excess cash, cash equivalents and marketable securities in excess of
    minimum operating requirements.
(g) The dividend payout ratio in 1989, excluding the after-tax effects of the gain on sale of CPE and Belmont Springs, was 41 percent.

Consolidated Balance Sheets
(In thousands except share data)

December 31,	**1989**	1988
Assets		
Current		
Cash and cash equivalents	**$1,096,020**	$1,145,346
Marketable securities, at cost (approximates market)	**85,671**	85,844
	1,181,691	1,231,190
Trade accounts receivable, less allowances of $14,347		
in 1989 and $14,616 in 1988	**768,335**	627,248
Finance subsidiary – receivables	**52,093**	156,728
Inventories	**789,077**	778,816
Prepaid expenses and other assets	**812,304**	451,450
Total Current Assets	**3,603,500**	3,245,432
Investments and Other Assets		
Investments in affiliates		
Coca-Cola Enterprises Inc.	**695,195**	733,295
Coca-Cola Amatil Limited	**524,931**	–
Other, principally bottling companies	**710,297**	580,619
Columbia Pictures Entertainment, Inc.	**–**	598,059
Finance subsidiary – receivables and investments	**140,520**	167,689
Long-term receivables and other assets	**354,881**	309,897
	2,425,824	2,389,559
Property, Plant and Equipment		
Land	**146,482**	116,726
Buildings and improvements	**950,251**	853,252
Machinery and equipment	**1,890,960**	1,645,652
Containers	**307,012**	293,277
	3,294,705	2,908,907
Less allowances for depreciation	**1,273,486**	1,149,832
	2,021,219	1,759,075
Goodwill and Other Intangible Assets	**231,993**	56,546
	$8,282,536	$7,450,612

THE COCA-COLA COMPANY AND SUBSIDIARIES

December 31,	1989	1988
Liabilities and Shareholders' Equity		
Current		
Accounts payable and accrued expenses	**$1,386,516**	$1,080,970
Loans and notes payable		
Finance subsidiary	**184,691**	253,628
Other	**1,234,617**	1,000,896
Current maturities of long-term debt	**12,858**	108,915
Accrued taxes – including income taxes	**839,248**	424,488
Total Current Liabilities	**3,657,930**	2,868,897
Long-Term Debt		
Finance subsidiary	**–**	41,584
Other	**548,708**	719,475
	548,708	761,059
Other Liabilities	**294,358**	205,702
Deferred Income Taxes	**296,055**	269,652
Shareholders' Equity		
Preferred stock, $1 par value –		
Authorized: 100,000,000 shares; 3,000 shares of Cumulative		
Money Market Preferred Stock issued and outstanding,		
stated at aggregate liquidation preference	**300,000**	300,000
Common stock, $1 par value –		
Authorized: 700,000,000 shares;		
Issued: 418,909,789 shares in 1989;		
417,394,567 shares in 1988	**418,910**	417,395
Capital surplus	**437,324**	380,264
Reinvested earnings	**5,618,312**	4,385,142
Unearned restricted stock issued for future services	**(45,892)**	(51,467)
Foreign currency translation adjustment	**(7,206)**	(17,010)
	6,721,448	5,414,324
Less treasury stock, at cost (81,894,886 common		
shares in 1989; 62,606,056 common shares in 1988)	**3,235,963**	2,069,022
	3,485,485	3,345,302
	$8,282,536	$7,450,612

See Notes to Consolidated Financial Statements.

Consolidated Statements of Income
(In thousands except per share data)

THE COCA-COLA COMPANY AND SUBSIDIARIES

Year Ended December 31,	1989	1988	1987
Net Operating Revenues	$8,965,786	$8,337,831	$7,658,341
Cost of goods sold	3,892,069	3,701,472	3,633,159
Gross Profit	5,073,717	4,636,359	4,025,182
Selling, administrative and general expenses	3,347,932	3,038,058	2,665,022
Provisions for restructured operations	–	–	36,370
Operating Income	1,725,785	1,598,301	1,323,790
Interest income	205,035	199,333	232,032
Interest expense	308,034	230,513	296,772
Equity income	75,490	92,542	64,393
Other income (deductions)–net	4,847	(33,243)	531
Gain on sale of Belmont Springs Water Co., Inc.	61,187	–	–
Gain on sale of stock by T.C.C. Beverages Ltd.	–	–	39,654
Income from Continuing Operations Before Income Taxes	1,764,310	1,626,420	1,363,628
Income taxes	571,471	537,434	496,348
Income from Continuing Operations	1,192,839	1,088,986	867,280
Equity income (loss) from discontinued operation	21,537	(44,283)	48,856
Gain on sale of discontinued operation (net of income taxes of $421,021)	509,449	–	–
Net Income	1,723,825	1,044,703	916,136
Preferred stock dividends	21,392	6,426	–
Net Income Available to Common Shareholders	$1,702,433	$1,038,277	$ 916,136
Income (Loss) Per Common Share			
Continuing operations	$ 3.39	$ 2.97	$ 2.30
Discontinued operation	1.53	(0.12)	0.13
Net Income Per Common Share	$ 4.92	$ 2.85	$ 2.43
Average Common Shares Outstanding	345,981	364,612	377,372

See Notes to Consolidated Financial Statements.

Consolidated Statements of Shareholders' Equity
(In thousands except per share data)

THE COCA-COLA COMPANY AND SUBSIDIARIES

Three Years Ended *December 31, 1989*	Preferred Stock	Common Stock	Capital Surplus	Reinvested Earnings	Unearned Restricted Stock	Foreign Currency Translation	Treasury Stock
Balance December 31, 1986		$414,492	$299,345	$3,624,046	$(35,888)	$(118,087)	$(704,817)
Sales to employees exercising stock options		1,307	23,364	–	–	–	566
Tax benefit from employees' stock option plans		–	8,207	–	–	–	–
Translation adjustments (net of income taxes of $3,394)		–	–	–	–	113,840	–
Stock issued under Restricted Stock Award Plan, less amortization of $6,330		178	7,678	–	(1,526)	–	–
Purchase of common stock for treasury		–	–	–	–	–	(605,110)
Net income		–	–	916,136	–	–	–
Cash dividends							
Common (per share – $1.12)		–	–	(421,540)	–	–	–
In-kind dividends (per common share – $.90)		–	–	(335,017)	–	–	–
Balance December 31, 1987		415,977	338,594	3,783,625	(37,414)	(4,247)	(1,309,361)
Sales to employees exercising stock options		906	18,880	–	–	–	(1,459)
Tax benefit from employees' stock option plans		–	5,491	–	–	–	–
Translation adjustments (net of income taxes of $19)		–	–	–	–	(12,763)	–
Stock issued under Restricted Stock Award Plan, less amortization of $7,884		512	21,424	–	(14,053)	–	–
Purchase of common stock for treasury		–	–	–	–	–	(758,202)
Preferred stock issued	$300,000	–	(4,125)	–	–	–	–
Net income		–	–	1,044,703	–	–	–
Cash dividends							
Preferred	–	–	–	(6,426)	–	–	–
Common (per share – $1.20)	–	–	–	(436,760)	–	–	–
Balance December 31, 1988	300,000	417,395	380,264	4,385,142	(51,467)	(17,010)	(2,069,022)
Sales to employees exercising stock options	–	1,481	39,914	–	–	–	(3,804)
Tax benefit from employees' stock option and restricted stock plans	–	–	14,811	–	–	–	–
Translation adjustments (net of income taxes of $900)	–	–	–	–	–	9,804	–
Stock issued under Restricted Stock Award Plan, less amortization of $7,944	–	34	2,335	–	5,575	–	–
Purchase of common stock for treasury	–	–	–	–	–	–	(1,163,137)
Net income	–	–	–	1,723,825	–	–	–
Cash dividends							
Preferred	–	–	–	(21,392)	–	–	–
Common (per share – $1.36)	–	–	–	(469,263)	–	–	–
Balance December 31, 1989	$300,000	$418,910	$437,324	$5,618,312	$(45,892)	$ (7,206)	$(3,235,963)

See Notes to Consolidated Financial Statements.

Consolidated Statements of Cash Flows
(In thousands)

THE COCA-COLA COMPANY AND SUBSIDIARIES

Year Ended December 31,	1989	1988	1987
Operating Activities			
Net income	$1,723,825	$1,044,703	$ 916,136
Depreciation and amortization	183,765	169,768	154,525
Deferred income taxes	37,036	43,915	(27,005)
Equity income, net of dividends	(76,088)	(35,758)	(79,667)
Net unrealized loss (gain) on exchange	(31,043)	27,945	(12,958)
Gain on sale of businesses before income taxes	(1,006,664)	–	–
Gain on sale of stock by T.C.C. Beverages Ltd.	–	–	(39,654)
Provisions for restructured operations	–	–	36,370
Net change in operating assets and liabilities	279,382	(83,736)	263,941
Net cash provided by operating activities	1,110,213	1,166,837	1,211,688
Investing Activities			
Additions to finance subsidiary receivables and investments	(57,006)	(172,866)	(131,665)
Collections of finance subsidiary receivables and investments	188,810	145,358	71,492
Purchases of investments and other assets	(858,510)	(128,526)	(339,248)
Proceeds from disposals of investments and other assets	126,850	77,049	53,559
Proceeds from sale of businesses	1,680,073	–	–
Decrease (increase) in marketable securities	(3,889)	19,702	32,455
Purchases of property, plant and equipment	(462,466)	(386,757)	(303,545)
Proceeds from disposals of property, plant and equipment	60,665	43,332	124,504
Decrease (increase) in temporary investments and other	(120,649)	207,721	303,435
Collection of notes receivable – Columbia Pictures			
Entertainment, Inc.	–	544,889	–
Net cash provided by (used in) investing activities	553,878	349,902	(189,013)
Net cash provided by operations after reinvestment	1,664,091	1,516,739	1,022,675
Financing Activities			
Due to Columbia Pictures Entertainment, Inc.	–	–	(576,741)
Issuances of debt	336,370	140,929	1,074,269
Payments of debt	(410,690)	(992,527)	(4,628)
Preferred stock issued	–	300,000	–
Common stock issued (includes treasury)	41,395	29,035	39,774
Purchase of common stock for treasury	(1,166,941)	(759,661)	(605,110)
Cash dividends (common and preferred)	(490,655)	(443,186)	(421,540)
Net cash used in financing activities	(1,690,521)	(1,725,410)	(493,976)
Effect of Exchange Rate Changes on Cash	(22,896)	(29,543)	93,087
Cash and Cash Equivalents			
Net increase (decrease) during the year	(49,326)	(238,214)	621,786
Balance at beginning of year	1,145,346	1,383,560	761,774
Balance at end of year	$1,096,020	$1,145,346	$1,383,560

See Notes to Consolidated Financial Statements.

Notes to Consolidated Financial Statements

THE COCA-COLA COMPANY AND SUBSIDIARIES

1. Accounting Policies. The major accounting policies and practices followed by the Company and its subsidiaries are as follows:

Consolidation: The consolidated financial statements include the accounts of the Company and all subsidiaries where control is not temporary. The Company's investments in companies in which it has the ability to exercise significant influence over operating and financial policies are accounted for on the equity method. Accordingly, the Company's share of the earnings of these companies is included in consolidated net income. The Company's investments in other companies, including investments where control is temporary, are carried at cost. All significant intercompany accounts and transactions are eliminated in consolidation.

Certain amounts in the 1988 and 1987 financial statements have been reclassified to conform to the current year presentation.

Net Income Per Common Share: Net income per common share is computed by dividing net income less dividends on preferred stock by the weighted average number of common shares outstanding.

Cash Equivalents: Marketable securities that are highly liquid and have maturities of three months or less at the date of purchase are classified as cash equivalents.

Inventories: Inventories are valued at the lower of cost or market. In general, inventories are valued on the basis of average cost or first-in, first-out (FIFO) methods. However, certain soft drink and citrus inventories are valued on the last-in, first-out (LIFO) method. The excess of current costs over LIFO stated values amounted to approximately $34 million and $30 million at December 31, 1989 and 1988, respectively.

Property, Plant and Equipment: Property, plant and equipment is stated at cost, less allowance for depreciation. Depreciation expense is determined principally by the straight-line method. The annual rates of depreciation are 2 percent to 10 percent for buildings and improvements and 7 percent to 34 percent for machinery, equipment and containers.

Goodwill and Other Intangible Assets: Goodwill and other intangible assets are stated on the basis of cost and, if acquired subsequent to October 31, 1970, are being amortized, principally on a straight-line basis, over the estimated future periods to be benefited (not exceeding 40 years). Accumulated amortization was approximately $3 million at December 31, 1989 and 1988.

Income Taxes: All income tax amounts and balances have been computed in accordance with APB Opinion No. 11, "Accounting for Income Taxes."

2. Inventories consist of the following (in thousands):

December 31,	1989	1988
Finished goods	$304,150	$297,850
Work in process	22,240	7,113
Raw materials and supplies	462,687	473,853
	$789,077	$778,816

3. Investments in and Advances to Affiliated Companies.

Coca-Cola Enterprises Inc. (CCE) is the largest bottler of Company products in the United States. The Company owns approximately 49 percent of the outstanding common stock of CCE and accordingly, accounts for its investment under the equity method of accounting. A summary of financial information for CCE is as follows (in thousands):

	December 29, 1989	December 30, 1988
Current assets	$ 493,387	$ 488,462
Noncurrent assets	4,238,559	4,180,745
Total assets	$4,731,946	$4,669,207
Current liabilities	$ 996,122	$ 550,121
Noncurrent liabilities	2,055,687	2,310,709
Total liabilities	$3,051,809	$2,860,830
Net assets	$1,680,137	$1,808,377
Company equity investment	$ 695,195	$ 733,295

Year Ended	December 29, 1989	December 30, 1988	January 1, 1988
Net operating revenues	$3,881,947	$3,874,445	$3,329,134
Cost of goods sold	2,313,032	2,268,038	1,916,724
Gross profit	$1,568,915	$1,606,407	$1,412,410
Income before income taxes	$ 137,931	$ 267,721	$ 172,775
Net income available to common shareholders	$ 53,507	$ 142,719	$ 88,372
Company equity income	$ 26,218	$ 63,757	$ 43,302

Notes to Consolidated Financial Statements

Net syrup/concentrate and sweetener sales to CCE were $764 million in 1989, $714 million in 1988 and $606 million in 1987. The Company also provides certain administrative and other services to CCE under negotiated fee arrangements. The Company engages in a wide range of marketing programs, media advertising and other similar arrangements to promote the sale of Company products in territories in which CCE operates. The Company's direct support for certain CCE marketing activities and participation with CCE in cooperative advertising and other marketing programs, net of fees charged for services provided, amounted to approximately $178 million in 1989, $163 million in 1988 and $133 million in 1987.

In December 1988, CCE sold one of its bottling subsidiaries and recorded a pre-tax gain of approximately $104 million. The purchaser was a bottling company that is 22 percent-owned by the Company. In October 1988, CCE initiated a share repurchase program for up to 25 million shares of its common stock. The Company is participating in this repurchase program and has entered into an agreement with CCE whereby the Company will sell a sufficient number of its CCE shares such that its continuing ownership interest will remain at approximately 49 percent. In connection with this agreement, the Company sold 3 million shares to CCE in 1989 for aggregate proceeds of approximately $49 million. In 1988, the Company received $77 million for the sale of 5.3 million shares to CCE. When CCE completed the purchase of 5.3 million shares from public shareholders in 1989, an adjusting payment was received from CCE for approximately $13 million. This amount represented the difference between the aggregate proceeds paid to the Company and the aggregate proceeds paid to the public shareholders, net of commissions paid by CCE, in accordance with the repurchase agreement.

Based on the closing price on the New York Stock Exchange, the market value of the Company's investment in CCE at December 31, 1989, was approximately $965 million.

Other Equity Investments: In August 1989, through a reorganization and tender, the Company acquired 59.5 percent of the outstanding common stock of Coca-Cola Amatil Limited (Amatil), formerly AMATIL Limited, for an aggregate purchase price of approximately $491 million including certain acquisition-related costs. Amatil is an Australian-based bottler of Company products with businesses in snack foods, communications and packaging. Amatil operates in Australia, New Zealand, Asia and Europe. The Company intends to reduce its ownership interest in Amatil below 50 percent and accordingly, the investment has been accounted for under the equity method of accounting. The excess of the Company's investment over its equity in the underlying net assets of Amatil was approximately $407 million, which is being amortized primarily over 40 years.

In January 1989, the Company received $2 million and 1.1 million shares of common stock of Coca-Cola Bottling Co. Consolidated (Consolidated) in exchange for 100 percent of the common stock of a bottling company which had been accounted for as a temporary investment. Such shares, with a carrying value of approximately $43 million, increased the Company's ownership interest in Consolidated from 20 percent to approximately 30 percent. In June 1987, the Company acquired approximately 1.6 million common shares of previously unissued common stock of Consolidated, a 20 percent ownership interest, for approximately $63 million.

In September 1987, T.C.C. Beverages Ltd. (TCC), a Canadian bottling company composed of substantially all of the Company-owned bottling operations in Canada, completed an initial public offering of 51 percent of its stock. The Company recognized a non-cash gain of approximately $40 million as a result of this transaction. TCC is carrying on business as Coca-Cola Beverages.

In June 1987, the Company purchased 2,219 shares of previously unissued common shares of Johnston Coca-Cola Bottling Group, Inc. (Johnston) for approximately $54 million, which increased the Company's ownership interest to approximately 22 percent.

In January 1987, the Company contributed its Great Britain bottling and canning assets to a corporate joint venture in which the Company owns a 49 percent common equity interest.

Operating results include the Company's equity income from affiliated companies since dates of investment. A summary of financial information for the Company's equity investments in bottling companies mentioned above and other equity investees, none of which are individually significant, follows (in thousands):

December 31,	1989	1988
Current assets	$1,504,051	$ 926,829
Noncurrent assets	3,441,552	1,953,703
Total assets	$4,945,603	$2,880,532
Current liabilities	$1,666,205	$ 857,606
Noncurrent liabilities	1,947,918	1,166,597
Total liabilities	$3,614,123	$2,024,203
Net assets	$1,331,480	$ 856,329
Company equity investments	$1,157,363	$ 484,698

Year Ended December 31,	**1989**	1988	1987
Net operating revenues	**$5,598,946**	$3,673,640	$1,810,244
Cost of goods sold	**3,633,647**	2,412,869	1,110,568
Gross profit	**$1,965,299**	$1,260,771	$ 699,676
Income before income taxes	**$ 199,255**	$ 114,599	$ 27,240
Net income	**$ 123,752**	$ 66,445	$ 17,712
Company equity income	**$ 49,272**	$ 28,785	$ 13,506

The market value of the Company's equity investments in publicly traded bottling companies, excluding CCE, exceeded the Company's carrying value at December 31, 1989, by approximately $47 million.

The balance sheet caption "Other, principally bottling companies" also includes various investments that are carried at cost.

4. Finance Subsidiary. Coca-Cola Financial Corporation (CCFC) provides loans and other forms of financing to Coca-Cola bottlers and customers for the acquisition of sales-related equipment and for other business purposes. The approximate contractual maturities of finance receivables for the five years succeeding December 31, 1989, are as follows (in thousands):

1990	$52,093
1991	31,936
1992	25,957
1993	14,190
1994	7,157

These amounts do not reflect possible prepayments or renewals. Finance receivables include amounts due from Johnston of $59 million and $167 million at December 31, 1989 and 1988, respectively. Johnston is an equity investment of the Company.

5. Short-term Borrowings and Credit Arrangements. Loans and notes payable consist of commercial paper and notes payable to banks and other financial institutions.

Under lines of credit and other credit facilities for short-term debt with various financial institutions, the Company may borrow up to $925 million. These lines of credit are subject to normal banking terms and conditions. At December 31, 1989, the unused portion of the credit lines was $837 million, of which $605 million was available to support commercial paper borrowings. Some of the financial arrangements require compensating balances which are not material.

6. Accrued Taxes are composed of the following amounts (in thousands):

December 31,	**1989**	1988
Income taxes	**$750,753**	$357,614
Sales, payroll and miscellaneous taxes	**88,495**	66,874
	$839,248	$424,488

7. Long-term Debt consists of the following amounts (in thousands):

December 31,	**1989**	1988
11⅜% notes due November 28, 1991	**$ 85,675**	$ 85,675
9⅞% series B notes due November 26, 1992	**31,034**	–
5¾% notes due April 24, 1996	**212,623**	240,641
5¾% notes due March 25, 1998	**148,854**	140,929
12¾% notes due August 1, 1989	–	98,786
9⅞% notes redeemed on August 1, 1989	–	87,907
9⅞% series A notes redeemed on November 26, 1989	–	100,000
Coca-Cola Financial Corporation	–	41,584
Other	**83,380**	74,452
	561,566	869,974
Less current portion	**12,858**	108,915
	$548,708	$761,059

Notes outstanding at December 31, 1989, were issued outside the United States and are redeemable at the Company's option under certain conditions related to U.S. and foreign tax laws. The 9⅞ percent series A notes redeemed on November 26, 1989, were issued with detachable warrants that granted the holder the right to receive additional notes bearing the same interest rate and maturing in 1992. The 9⅞ percent series B notes due November 26, 1992, were issued upon the exercise of the warrants. The 5¾ percent notes due April 24, 1996, of which $123 million has been designated as a hedge against the Company's net investment in Coca-Cola (Japan) Company, Ltd. at December 31, 1989, are denominated in Japanese yen. The 5¾ percent notes due March 25, 1998, are denominated in deutsche marks. Portions of such notes have been swapped for Swiss and Belgian franc denominated liabilities. The Company has designated such borrowings as hedges against its net investments in those respective countries.

Notes to Consolidated Financial Statements

Other long-term debt consists of various mortgages and notes with maturity dates ranging from 1990 to 2013. Interest on a portion of this debt varies with the changes in the prime rate, and the weighted average interest rate applicable to the remainder is approximately 12.7 percent.

Maturities of long-term debt for the five years succeeding December 31, 1989, are as follows (in thousands):

1990	$12,858
1991	96,673
1992	46,839
1993	11,581
1994	11,827

The above notes include various restrictions, none of which are presently significant to the Company.

The Company is contingently liable for guarantees of indebtedness owed by some of its independent bottling licensees ($96 million), and others, totaling approximately $115 million at December 31, 1989. In addition, the Company has guaranteed the collection of certain accounts receivable and contract rights sold by CPE with recourse that had uncollected balances of approximately $25 million at December 31, 1989; CPE has agreed to indemnify the Company against losses, if any, which could arise from such guarantees.

8. Preferred Stock. On September 7, 1988, the Company issued four series of non-voting Cumulative Money Market Preferred Stock (MMP), consisting of 750 shares each. All shares were issued at a price of $100,000 per share. Dividends, which are cumulative, are generally determined every 49 days through auction procedures. Weighted average dividend rates (per annum) were as follows:

Series	Weighted Average Dividend Rate Year Ended December 31,	
	1989	1988
A	**7.10%**	6.52%
B	**7.08%**	6.51%
C	**7.03%**	6.77%
D	**6.98%**	6.81%

The shares of MMP of each series are redeemable on the second business day preceding any dividend payment date at the option of the Company, as a whole or in part, at $100,000 per share plus accrued dividends.

9. Common Stock. The number of common stock shares outstanding and related changes for the three years ended December 31, 1989, are as follows (in thousands):

	1989	1988	1987
Stock outstanding at January 1,	**354,789**	372,356	385,011
Stock issued to employees exercising stock options	**1,481**	906	1,339
Stock issued under Restricted Stock Award Plan	**34**	512	178
Purchase of common stock for treasury	**(19,289)**	(18,985)	(14,172)
Stock outstanding at December 31,	**337,015**	354,789	372,356

10. Stock Options and Other Stock Plans. The 1989 and amended 1983 Restricted Stock Award Plans provide that 5,000,000 and 3,000,000 shares of restricted common stock, respectively, may be granted to certain officers and key employees of the Company. Shares issued under the 1983 plan are subject to forfeiture if the employee leaves the Company for reasons other than death, disability or retirement prior to a change of control in the Company and may not be transferred by the employee prior to the occurrence of one of these events. The employee receives dividends on the shares and may vote the shares. Within 60 days of the date of death, disability or retirement of the employee and immediately upon a change of control in the Company, the Company will pay the employee an amount equal to the federal, state and local taxes incurred by the employee as a result of the stock award. Shares granted were 34,000 shares, 511,500 shares and 178,500 shares in 1989, 1988 and 1987, respectively. At December 31, 1989, 5,000,000 and 401,000 shares were available to be granted under the 1989 and amended 1983 Restricted Stock Award Plans, respectively.

The Company's 1987 Stock Option Plan covers 8,000,000 shares of the Company's common stock. The Plan provides for the granting of stock appreciation rights and stock options to certain officers and employees. The stock appreciation rights permit the holder, upon surrendering all or part of the related stock option, to receive cash, common stock or a combination thereof, in an amount up to 100 percent of the difference between the market price and the option price. Included in options outstanding at December 31, 1989, were various options granted under previous plans and other options granted not as a part of an option plan.

Further information relating to options is as follows:

	1989	1988	1987
Options outstanding at January 1,	8,657,790	5,610,347	6,065,924
Options granted in the year	15,900	4,182,950	1,111,850
Options exercised in the year	(1,481,228)	(905,598)	(1,339,584)
Options cancelled in the year	(440,436)	(229,909)	(227,843)
Options outstanding at December 31,	6,752,026	8,657,790	5,610,347
Options exercisable at December 31,	4,280,423	3,413,083	3,168,149
Shares available at December 31, for options which may be granted	3,321,308	3,258,451	7,539,184
Option prices per share Exercised in the year	$10-$45	$10-$39	$10-$39
Unexercised at December 31,	$10-$47	$10-$45	$10-$45

In 1988, the Company entered into Incentive Unit Agreements, whereby certain officers will be granted cash awards based on the market value of 300,000 shares of the Company's common stock at the measurement dates. In 1985, the Company entered into Performance Unit Agreements, whereby certain officers will be granted cash awards based on the difference in the market value of 555,000 shares of the Company's common stock at the measurement dates and the base price of $20.63, the market value as of January 2, 1985.

11. Pension Plans. The Company and its subsidiaries sponsor and/or contribute to various pension plans covering substantially all U.S. employees and certain employees in non-U.S. locations. The benefits are based on years of service and the employee's compensation in certain periods in the last years of employment. Pension costs are generally funded currently, subject to regulatory funding limitations. In 1987, the Company adopted Statement of Financial Accounting Standards No. 87 (SFAS 87), "Employers' Accounting for Pensions," which became effective for U.S. plans in 1987 and for non-U.S. plans in 1989. SFAS 87 caused a decrease in 1987 pension expense of approximately $13 million. The impact on 1989 pension expense was insignificant.

Total pension expense amounted to approximately $23 million in 1989, $24 million in 1988 and $21 million in 1987. Net pension cost for the Company's defined benefit plans subject to SFAS 87 requirements in 1989, 1988 and 1987 included the following components (in thousands):

	Non-U.S. Plans	U.S. Plans		
	1989	1989	1988	1987
Service cost—benefits earned during the period	$12,133	$ 9,830	$11,762	$11,175
Interest cost on projected benefit obligation	12,539	35,393	35,233	32,873
Actual return on plan assets	(16,108)	(95,254)	(62,357)	(33,439)
Net amortization and deferral	2,240	56,548	25,785	(2,395)
Net periodic pension cost	$10,804	$ 6,517	$10,423	$ 8,214

The following table sets forth the funded status for the Company's defined benefit plans at December 31, 1989 and 1988 (in thousands):

	Non-U.S. Plans		U.S. Plans			
	December 31, 1989		**December 31, 1989**		December 31, 1988	
	Assets Exceed Accumulated Benefits	Accumulated Benefits Exceed Assets	Assets Exceed Accumulated Benefits	Accumulated Benefits Exceed Assets	Assets Exceed Accumulated Benefits	Accumulated Benefits Exceed Assets
Actuarial present value of benefit obligation						
Vested benefit obligation	**$137,005**	**$ 2,991**	**$284,986**	**$ 40,985**	$278,066	$ 38,001
Accumulated benefit obligation	**$141,920**	**$ 4,995**	**$305,853**	**$ 43,391**	$307,643	$ 39,494
Projected benefit obligation	**$201,107**	**$ 6,375**	**$364,328**	**$ 49,619**	$366,692	$ 46,475
Plan assets at fair value (primarily listed stocks, bonds and government securities)	207,806	1,961	529,067	–	495,709	–
Plan assets in excess of (or less than) projected benefit obligation	6,699	(4,414)	164,739	(49,619)	129,017	(46,475)
Unrecognized net (asset) liability at transition	9,949	1,064	(42,299)	23,669	(54,672)	24,642
Unrecognized net (gain) loss	(10,926)	540	(117,237)	(1,533)	(68,377)	620
Adjustment required to recognize minimum liability	–	(56)	–	(15,908)	–	–
Accrued pension asset (liability) included in the consolidated balance sheet	$ 5,722	$(2,866)	$ 5,203	$(43,391)	$ 5,968	$(21,213)

The assumptions used in computing the above information are presented below:

	Non-U.S. Plans	U.S. Plans		
	1989	1989	1988	1987
Weighted average discount rates	7%	9%	9%	8%
Rates of increase in compensation levels	4%	6%	6%	6%
Expected long-term rates of return on assets	8%	9%	8%	8%

In the fourth quarter of 1989, approximately $40 million in assets and approximately $29 million representing the present value of accumulated benefit obligations were transferred to a successor plan to cover active and terminated vested participants of CCE. This transfer included a pro rata portion of surplus assets in the plan.

Prior to the adoption of SFAS No. 87, locations outside of the United States were not required to report the actuarial present value of accumulated plan benefits or net assets available for benefits. For such plans, the value of the pension funds and balance sheet accruals exceeded the estimated value of benefits as of January 1, 1988, as determined by consulting actuaries.

The Company also has a plan that provides post-retirement health care and life insurance benefits to virtually all domestic employees who retire with a minimum of five years of service; the annual cash cost of these benefits is not significant.

12. Income Taxes. The components of income before income taxes for both continuing and discontinued operations consist of the following (in thousands):

Year Ended December 31,	1989	1988	1987
United States	$1,459,213	$ 439,149	$ 358,755
Foreign	1,257,104	1,142,988	1,053,729
	$2,716,317	$1,582,137	$1,412,484

Income taxes for continuing and discontinued operations consist of the following amounts (in thousands):

Year Ended December 31,	United States	State & Local	Foreign	Total
1989				
Current	$478,004	$84,072	$393,380	$955,456
Deferred	(8,025)	160	44,901	37,036
1988				
Current	$ 53,084	$14,329	$426,106	$493,519
Deferred	14,857	4,641	24,417	43,915
1987				
Current	$ 49,282	$16,004	$458,067	$523,353
Deferred	(32,466)	(4,615)	10,076	(27,005)

The Company made income tax payments of approximately $537 million, $517 million and $411 million in 1989, 1988 and 1987, respectively.

A reconciliation of the statutory U.S. federal rates and effective rates for continuing operations is as follows:

Year Ended December 31,	1989	1988	1987
Statutory rate	34.0%	34.0%	40.0%
State income taxes—net of federal benefit	1.0	.8	.5
Earnings in jurisdictions taxed at rates different from the U.S. federal rate	(1.6)	(.8)	(3.7)
Equity income	(1.5)	(2.0)	(1.9)
Other—net	.5	1.0	1.5
	32.4%	33.0%	36.4%

Deferred taxes are provided principally for depreciation, certain employee compensation-related expenses and certain capital transactions that are recognized in different years for financial statement and income tax purposes. The Company has manufacturing facilities in Puerto Rico that operate under a Puerto Rican tax exemption that expires December 31, 2009.

Appropriate U.S. and foreign income taxes have been provided for earnings of subsidiary companies that are expected to be remitted to the parent company in the near future. Accumulated unremitted earnings of foreign subsidiaries that are expected to be required for use in the foreign operations were approximately $143 million at December 31, 1989, exclusive of amounts, which if remitted, would result in little or no tax.

13. Acquisitions. In August 1989, the Company acquired all of the Coca-Cola bottling operations of Pernod Ricard for an aggregate purchase price of approximately $140 million. The fair value of assets acquired was $285 million and liabilities assumed were $145 million. Pernod Ricard operated the Coca-Cola bottling, canning and distribution business in six major territories in France. The acquisition was accounted for by the purchase method.

In August 1988, the Company acquired the citrus food-service assets of H.P. Hood Inc. for approximately $45 million. This acquisition was accounted for by the purchase method.

The operating results of the above companies have been included in the consolidated statements of income from their respective dates of acquisition and did not have a significant effect on operating results.

In August 1989, the Company entered into a joint venture with C-C Bottlers Ltd., an Australian Coca-Cola bottler, to acquire the largest soft drink company and licensed bottler of Coca-Cola products in New Zealand. The Company made an investment of approximately $38 million and guaranteed certain indebtedness of the joint venture. In December 1989, the Company entered into an agreement to sell its interest in the joint venture to Amatil, subject to certain conditions. In July 1989, the Company acquired the outstanding stock of Frank Lyon Company, the sole shareholder of Coca-Cola Bottling Company of Arkansas (CCBC of Arkansas), for approximately $232 million, including assumed debt. The investment in CCBC of Arkansas is considered temporary and accordingly, is recorded at cost.

See Note 3 for discussion of the equity investment in Amatil in August 1989.

Notes to Consolidated Financial Statements

14. Discontinued Operation and Divestitures. In November 1989, the Company sold its entire equity interest in Columbia Pictures Entertainment, Inc. (CPE) for approximately $1.55 billion in cash. The equity interest consisted of approximately 49 percent of the outstanding common shares of CPE and 1,000 shares of preferred stock. The sale resulted in a gain before income taxes of approximately $930 million. On an after-tax basis, the gain was approximately $509 million or $1.47 per common share. The effective tax rate of 45 percent on the gain on the sale of CPE differs from the statutory U.S. federal rate of 34 percent due primarily to differences between the book basis and tax basis of the Company's investment in CPE.

CPE has been reported as a discontinued operation and accordingly, the gain from the sale of CPE and the Company's equity income (loss) from CPE has been reported separately from continuing operations. The Company had accounted for its investment in CPE under the equity method of accounting on a one month lag basis due to different fiscal year ends for the respective companies. Included in the Company's equity income (loss) from discontinued operation for fiscal years 1989, 1988 and 1987 is the Company's proportionate share of CPE's operating results for the period from December 1, 1988 to October 31, 1989, the period from December 18, 1987 to November 30, 1988, and the period from January 1 to December 17, 1987, respectively.

In August 1989, the Company sold Belmont Springs Water Co., Inc., a bottled water operation, which resulted in a gain before income taxes of approximately $61 million.

In January 1988, the Company purchased The Coca-Cola Bottling Company of Memphis, Tenn., which was subsequently sold along with substantially all of the bottling operations of The Coca-Cola Bottling Company of Southern Florida, Inc. to CCE for approximately $500 million in cash plus the assumption of indebtedness, the total of which approximated the Company's carrying value.

In July 1987, the Company sold a significant portion of the Rainwater Bottlers to CCE for approximately $174 million. The remaining operations of Rainwater Bottlers were sold in August 1987 for approximately $40 million. The total proceeds from the 1987 sales approximated the Company's carrying value.

15. Provisions for Restructured Operations. In 1987, the Company recorded a $36 million charge related to restructuring activities in its Foods Business Sector. This charge relates to transitional matters associated with the change in industry environment and a revised operating strategy concurrent with a change in senior management.

16. Interest. The Company capitalizes interest costs incurred as part of the acquisition or construction of major assets. All other interest is expensed as incurred. The components of net interest expense are summarized in the following table (in thousands):

	1989	1988	1987
Total interest incurred	$314,592	$238,666	$302,545
Less—capitalized interest	6,558	8,153	5,773
Interest expense	308,034	230,513	296,772
Interest income	(205,035)	(199,333)	(232,032)
Net interest expense	$102,999	$ 31,180	$ 64,740

Interest paid was approximately $319 million, $250 million and $275 million in 1989, 1988 and 1987, respectively.

17. Net Change in Operating Assets and Liabilities. The changes in operating assets and liabilities, net of effects of acquisitions and divestitures of businesses, are as follows (in thousands):

	1989	1988	1987
Decrease (increase) in trade accounts receivable	$ (99,496)	$33,887	$ (11,182)
Increase in inventories	(34,709)	(25,744)	(29,372)
Decrease (increase) in prepaid expenses and other assets	(204,222)	(35,496)	49,659
Increase (decrease) in accounts payable and accrued expenses	88,940	(36,139)	121,414
Increase (decrease) in accrued taxes	456,544	(17,618)	105,117
Increase (decrease) in other liabilities	72,325	(2,626)	28,305
	$279,382	$(83,736)	$263,941

THE COCA-COLA COMPANY AND SUBSIDIARIES

18. Lines of Business. Information concerning operations in different lines of business at December 31, 1989, 1988 and 1987 and for the years then ended is presented below (in millions). The Company operates principally in the soft drink industry. Citrus, fruit drinks and other products are included in the Foods Business Sector. Intercompany transfers between sectors are not material.

1989	Soft Drinks		Foods	Corporate	Consolidated
	USA	International			
Net Operating Revenues	$2,565.7	$4,759.2	$1,583.3	$ 57.6	$8,965.8
Operating Income	390.6	1,517.6	87.4	(269.8)	1,725.8
Identifiable Operating Assets	1,814.4	2,806.0	695.3	1,036.4(a)	6,352.1
Equity Income				75.5(b)	75.5
Investments in Affiliates				1,930.4(c)	1,930.4
Capital Expenditures	136.3	215.6	61.6	49.0	462.5
Depreciation and Amortization	73.9	48.4	30.7	30.8	183.8

1988	Soft Drinks		Foods	Corporate	Consolidated
	USA	International			
Net Operating Revenues	$2,284.4	$4,503.8	$1,512.1	$ 37.5	$8,337.8
Operating Income	351.9	1,338.8	89.3	(181.7)	1,598.3
Identifiable Operating Assets	1,711.9	2,097.1	694.1	1,035.5(a)	5,538.6
Equity Income				92.5(b)	92.5
Investments in Affiliates				1,912.0(c)	1,912.0
Capital Expenditures	80.2	159.2	82.0	65.4	386.8
Depreciation and Amortization	66.9	42.8	32.0	28.1	169.8

1987	Soft Drinks		Foods	Corporate	Consolidated
	USA	International			
Net Operating Revenues	$2,120.1	$4,109.2	$1,414.3	$ 14.7	$7,658.3
Operating Income	323.6	1,108.9	66.6(d)	(175.3)	1,323.8
Identifiable Operating Assets	2,047.4	2,126.7	627.3	1,586.0(a)	6,387.4
Equity Income				64.4(b)	64.4
Investments in Affiliates				2,218.1(c)	2,218.1
Capital Expenditures	78.0	92.3	55.4	77.8	303.5
Depreciation and Amortization	60.3	43.0	28.9	22.3	154.5

(a) General corporate identifiable operating assets are composed principally of marketable securities and fixed assets.

(b) Equity income has been restated to exclude the Company's equity income (loss) from CPE, which has been reported as a discontinued operation.

(c) Includes investments in soft drink bottling companies and joint ventures for all periods and CPE for 1988 and 1987. The Company's investment in CPE, which was sold in November 1989, approximated $598.1 million and $989.4 million at December 31, 1988 and 1987, respectively.

(d) Includes provisions for restructured operations aggregating $36 million.

Notes to Consolidated Financial Statements   THE COCA-COLA COMPANY AND SUBSIDIARIES

19. Operations in Geographic Areas. Information about the Company's operations in different geographic areas at December 31, 1989, 1988 and 1987 and for the years then ended is presented below (in millions). Intercompany transfers between geographic areas are not material.

1989	United States	Latin America	European Community	Northeast Europe and Africa	Pacific and Canada	Corporate	Consolidated
Net Operating Revenues	$4,022.2	$646.2	$1,855.1	$425.2	$1,959.5	$ 57.6	$8,965.8
Operating Income	468.2	226.7	540.6	147.3	612.8	(269.8)	1,725.8
Identifiable Operating Assets	2,476.0	515.4	1,342.8	328.8	652.7	1,036.4(a)	6,352.1
Equity Income						75.5(b)	75.5
Investments in Affiliates						1,930.4(c)	1,930.4

1988	United States	Latin America	European Community	Northeast Europe and Africa	Pacific and Canada	Corporate	Consolidated
Net Operating Revenues	$3,683.6	$583.2	$1,618.3	$385.2	$2,030.0	$ 37.5	$8,337.8
Operating Income	433.9	179.5	465.7	130.4	570.5	(181.7)	1,598.3
Identifiable Operating Assets	2,353.4	431.8	754.8	279.4	683.7	1,035.5(a)	5,538.6
Equity Income						92.5(b)	92.5
Investments in Affiliates						1,912.0(c)	1,912.0

1987	United States	Latin America	European Community	Northeast Europe and Africa	Pacific and Canada	Corporate	Consolidated
Net Operating Revenues	$3,459.1	$558.0	$1,383.4	$326.1	$1,917.0	$ 14.7	$7,658.3
Operating Income	384.5(d)	153.2	393.2	114.9	453.3	(175.3)	1,323.8
Identifiable Operating Assets	2,625.9	368.3	751.0	289.8	766.4	1,586.0(a)	6,387.4
Equity Income						64.4(b)	64.4
Investments in Affiliates						2,218.1(c)	2,218.1

Identifiable Liabilities of Operations Outside the United States amounted to approximately $1,082.8 million, $946.2 million and $949.6 million at December 31, 1989, 1988 and 1987, respectively.

(a) General corporate identifiable operating assets are composed principally of marketable securities and fixed assets.

(b) Equity income has been restated to exclude the Company's equity income (loss) from CPE, which has been reported as a discontinued operation.

(c) Includes investments in soft drink bottling companies and joint ventures for all periods and CPE for 1988 and 1987. The Company's investment in CPE, which was sold in November 1989, approximated $598.1 million and $989.4 million at December 31, 1988 and 1987, respectively.

(d) Includes provisions for restructured operations aggregating $36 million.

Net Operating Revenues
(Millions)

United States	$4,022
Pacific and Canada	$1,960
European Community	$1,855
Latin America	$ 646
N.E. Europe and Africa	$ 425

Operating Income
(Millions)

United States	$468
Pacific and Canada	$613
European Community	$541
Latin America	$227
N.E. Europe and Africa	$147

Report of Independent Auditors   THE COCA-COLA COMPANY AND SUBSIDIARIES

Board of Directors and Shareholders
The Coca-Cola Company
Atlanta, Georgia

We have audited the accompanying consolidated balance sheets of The Coca-Cola Company and subsidiaries as of December 31, 1989 and 1988, and the related consolidated statements of income, shareholders' equity and cash flows for each of the three years in the period ended December 31, 1989. These financial statements are the responsibility of the Company's management. Our responsibility is to express an opinion on these financial statements based on our audits.

We conducted our audits in accordance with generally accepted auditing standards. Those standards require that we plan and perform the audit to obtain reasonable assurance about whether the financial statements are free of material misstatement. An audit includes examining, on a test basis, evidence supporting the amounts and disclosures in the financial statements. An audit also includes assessing the accounting principles used and significant estimates made by management, as well as evaluating the overall financial statement presentation. We believe that our audits provide a reasonable basis for our opinion.

In our opinion, the financial statements referred to above present fairly, in all material respects, the consolidated financial position of The Coca-Cola Company and subsidiaries at December 31, 1989 and 1988, and the consolidated results of their operations and their cash flows for each of the three years in the period ended December 31, 1989, in conformity with generally accepted accounting principles.

Ernst & Young

Atlanta, Georgia
January 26, 1990

MAYTAG CORPORATION

STATEMENTS OF CONSOLIDATED INCOME
Thousands of Dollars Except Per Share Data

	Year Ended December 31		
	1989	1988	1987
Net sales	**$3,088,753**	$1,885,641	$1,822,106
Cost of sales	**2,312,645**	1,413,627	1,318,122
Gross profit	**776,108**	472,014	503,984
Selling, general and administrative expenses	**496,165**	245,807	248,611
Operating income	**279,943**	226,207	255,373
Interest expense	**(83,398)**	(19,738)	(10,788)
Other–net	**10,427**	8,753	8,393
Income from continuing operations			
before income taxes	**206,972**	215,222	252,978
Income taxes	**75,500**	79,700	105,300
Income from continuing operations	**131,472**	135,522	147,678
Discontinued operations			
Income from discontinued operations, less applicable income taxes			
(1988–$12,800; 1987–$3,700) including 1988 gain			
from sale of $17,972		23,040	5,025
Net Income	**$ 131,472**	$ 158,562	$ 152,703
Income per average share of Common stock			
Income from continuing operations	**$1.27**	$1.77	$1.84
Net Income	**1.27**	2.07	1.91

See notes to consolidated financial statements.

Reproduced with permission of Maytag Corporation.

MAYTAG CORPORATION

STATEMENTS OF CONSOLIDATED FINANCIAL CONDITION
Thousands of Dollars

	December 31	
ASSETS	**1989**	1988
Current Assets		
Cash and cash equivalents	$ **39,261**	$ 10,503
Accounts receivable, less allowance–(1989–$8,730; 1988–$3,820)	**502,992**	250,299
Inventories	**546,917**	262,705
Deferred income taxes	**34,594**	33,876
Other current assets	**15,938**	6,251
Total current assets	**1,139,702**	563,634
Other Assets		
Marketable securities	**9,488**	11,045
Pension investments	**185,693**	26,020
Investment in Chicago Pacific Corporation		384,561
Intangibles, less allowance for amortization–($9,737)	**356,309**	
Miscellaneous	**38,794**	29,640
Total other assets	**590,284**	451,266
Property, Plant and Equipment		
Land	**51,941**	7,737
Buildings and improvements	**256,727**	143,576
Machinery and equipment	**713,688**	399,050
Construction in progress	**47,921**	71,803
	1,070,277	622,166
Less allowances for depreciation	**363,944**	306,997
Total property, plant and equipment	**706,333**	315,169
Total Assets	**$2,436,319**	$1,330,069

See notes to consolidated financial statements.

	December 31	
LIABILITIES AND SHAREOWNERS' EQUITY	**1989**	1988
Current Liabilities		
Notes payable	**$ 68,713**	$ 7,700
Accounts payable	**179,496**	101,379
Compensation to employees	**60,312**	31,649
Accrued liabilities	**158,198**	77,621
Income taxes payable	**5,486**	21,491
Current maturities of long-term debt	**16,592**	6,649
Total current liabilities	**488,797**	246,489
Deferred Income Taxes	**60,434**	52,260
Long-Term Debt	**876,836**	518,165
Other Noncurrent Liabilities	**72,055**	11,677
Shareowners' Equity		
Common stock		
Authorized–200,000,000 shares (par value $1.25)		
Issued–1989–117,150,593 shares; 1988–89,674,506 shares,		
including shares in treasury	**146,438**	112,093
Additional paid-in capital	**488,137**	41,022
Retained earnings	**672,359**	640,819
	1,306,934	793,934
Less:		
Cost of Common stock in treasury		
(1989–11,586,073 shares; 1988–13,094,035 shares)	**258,356**	291,115
Employee stock plans	**67,117**	1,341
Foreign currency translation	**43,264**	
Total shareowners' equity	**938,197**	501,478
Total Liabilities and Shareowners' Equity	**$2,436,319**	$1,330,069

MAYTAG CORPORATION

STATEMENTS OF CONSOLIDATED CASH FLOWS
Thousands of Dollars

	Year Ended December 31		
	1989	1988	1987
Operating Activities			
Income from continuing operations	**$131,472**	$135,522	$147,678
Adjustments to reconcile income to net cash			
provided by (used in) operating activities:			
Depreciation and amortization	**76,994**	34,454	35,277
Deferred income taxes	**7,400**	1,200	800
Changes in selected working capital items:			
Inventories	**(79,401)**	(11,973)	(21,371)
Receivables and other current assets	**(35,829)**	(53,676)	(6,297)
Current liabilities	**(94,037)**	24,131	14,654
Prepaid pension contributions	**(7,566)**	(3,751)	3,707
Other–net	**(4,518)**	(1,603)	(6,291)
	(5,485)	124,304	168,157
Discontinued operations including change in net assets		(23,527)	6,638
Net cash provided by (used in) operations	**(5,485)**	100,777	174,795
Investing Activities			
Proceeds from sale of furniture companies	**196,780**		
Proceeds from reversion of excess pension investments	**17,875**		
Investment in Chicago Pacific Corporation		(384,691)	
Marketable securities	**1,557**	4,128	1,955
Capital expenditures–net	**(110,563)**	(98,143)	(40,405)
Cash of acquired company	**23,515**		
Proceeds from sale of discontinued operations		75,272	31,985
Total investing activities	**129,164**	(403,434)	(6,465)
Financing Activities			
Treasury stock purchases	**(64,161)**		(216,320)
Proceeds from credit agreements and long-term borrowings	**317,500**	384,000	100,000
Reduction in long-term debt and notes payable	**(264,101)**	(13,652)	(5,878)
Stock options exercised and other Common stock transactions	**19,495**	544	3,665
Dividends	**(99,932)**	(72,712)	(75,603)
Total financing activities	**(91,199)**	298,180	(194,136)
Effect of exchange rates on cash	**(3,722)**		
Increase (decrease) in cash and cash equivalents	**28,758**	(4,477)	(25,806)
Cash and cash equivalents at beginning of year	**10,503**	14,980	40,786
Cash and Cash Equivalents at End of Year	**$ 39,261**	$ 10,503	$ 14,980

See notes to consolidated financial statements.

CONSOLIDATED STATEMENTS OF INCOME

(thousands except per share amounts)

	1989	1988	1987
Net Sales	**$4,647,916**	$4,070,777	$3,527,941
Costs of Goods Sold, Occupancy and Buying Costs	**3,201,281**	2,856,074	2,535,166
Gross Income	**1,446,635**	1,214,703	992,775
General, Administrative and Store Operating Expenses	**821,381**	747,285	583,903
Operating Income	**625,254**	467,418	408,872
Interest Expense	**(58,059)**	(63,418)	(40,322)
Other Income (Expense), net	**6,731**	(7,864)	9,638
Income Before Income Taxes	**573,926**	396,136	378,188
Provision for Income Taxes	**227,000**	151,000	143,000
Net Income	**$ 346,926**	$ 245,136	$ 235,188
Net Income Per Share	**$ 1.92**	$ 1.36	$ 1.25

The accompanying Notes are an integral part of these Consolidated Financial Statements.

NET INCOME

(in millions)

CAGR 48% (Compound Annual
Growth Rate, last ten years.)

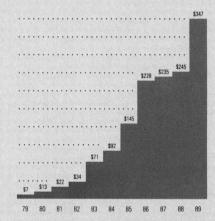

NET INCOME PER SHARE

CAGR 44%

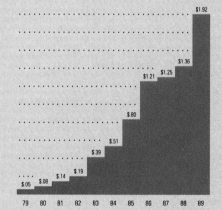

Reproduced with permission of The Limited, Inc.

CONSOLIDATED BALANCE SHEETS
(thousands)

Assets	Feb 3, 1990	Jan 28, 1989
Current Assets		
Cash and Equivalents	$ 21,734	$ 15,276
Accounts Receivable	596,171	531,461
Inventories	482,136	407,006
Other	63,703	69,851
Total Current Assets	1,163,744	1,023,594
Property and Equipment, net	1,172,688	1,066,646
Other Assets	82,054	55,266
Total Assets	$2,418,486	$2,145,506
Liabilities and Shareholders' Equity		
Current Liabilities		
Accounts Payable	$ 175,319	$ 189,184
Accrued Expenses	239,921	189,579
Income Taxes	62,980	77,192
Total Current Liabilities	478,220	455,955
Long-Term Debt	445,674	517,952
Deferred Income Taxes	214,858	198,893
Other Long-Term Liabilities	39,280	26,499
Shareholders' Equity		
Common Stock	94,863	94,863
Paid-in Capital	196,232	203,693
Retained Earnings	1,168,842	879,386
	1,459,937	1,177,942
Less Treasury Stock, at cost	(219,483)	(231,735)
Total Shareholders' Equity	1,240,454	946,207
Total Liabilities and Shareholders' Equity	$2,418,486	$2,145,506

The accompanying Notes are an integral part of these Consolidated Financial Statements.

CONSOLIDATED STATEMENTS OF CASH FLOWS

(thousands)

	1989	1988	1987
Cash Flows from Operating Activities:			
Net income	$346,926	$245,136	$235,188
Impact of other operating activities on cash flows:			
Depreciation and amortization	164,713	142,469	109,353
Change in assets and liabilities:			
Accounts receivable	(65,742)	(16,930)	13,735
Inventories	(101,580)	(44,072)	7,796
Accounts payable and accrued expenses	59,764	91,570	(18,266)
Income taxes	(14,212)	53,136	19,572
Other assets and liabilities	14,370	21,570	2,390
Net Cash Provided from Operating Activities	404,239	492,879	369,768
Investing Activities:			
Capital expenditures	(318,427)	(288,972)	(283,590)
Disposition of Lerner Woman	34,098	—	—
Acquisition of Abercrombie & Fitch	—	(45,206)	—
Other	11,505	7,989	(25,721)
Net Cash Used for Investing Activities	(272,824)	(326,189)	(309,311)
Financing Activities:			
Net (repayments) borrowings under long-term debt agreements	(322,278)	(163,048)	263,580
Proceeds from issuance of unsecured notes	250,000	—	—
Purchase of treasury stock	—	—	(240,007)
Dividends paid	(57,470)	(42,982)	(44,724)
Stock options and other	4,791	6,663	5,391
Net Cash Used for Financing Activities	(124,957)	(199,367)	(15,760)
Net Increase (Decrease) in Cash and Equivalents	6,458	(32,677)	44,697
Cash and equivalents, beginning of year	15,276	47,953	3,256
Cash and Equivalents, End of Year	$ 21,734	$ 15,276	$ 47,953

The accompanying Notes are an integral part of these Consolidated Financial Statements.

JOHN H. HARLAND COMPANY AND SUBSIDIARIES

Statements Of Consolidated Income

	Year Ended December 31		
	1989	1988	1987
NET SALES	$344,734,268	$333,315,000	$318,141,433
COST AND EXPENSES:			
Cost of Sales	172,385,708	171,122,146	161,870,397
Selling, general, and administrative expenses	78,110,425	77,307,391	76,052,641
Employees' profit sharing	7,977,680	7,831,547	7,161,586
Total	258,473,813	256,261,084	245,084,624
INCOME FROM OPERATIONS	86,260,455	77,053,916	73,056,809
INTEREST AND OTHER INCOME — NET	5,517,840	4,205,609	4,990,533
INCOME BEFORE INCOME TAXES	91,778,295	81,259,525	78,047,342
INCOME TAXES	33,726,786	27,936,190	30,532,955
NET INCOME	$ 58,051,509	$ 53,323,335	$ 47,514,387
NET INCOME PER COMMON SHARE	$ 1.54	$ 1.41	$ 1.26

See Significant Accounting Policies and Notes to Financial Statements.

Reproduced with permission of John H. Harland Company.

JOHN H. HARLAND COMPANY AND SUBSIDIARIES

Consolidated Balance Sheets

| | December 31 | |
	1989	1988
ASSETS		
CURRENT ASSETS:		
Cash and cash equivalents	$ 60,947,664	$ 49,526,054
Short-term investments, at cost which approximates market	17,907,720	8,250,163
Accounts receivable from customers, less allowance		
for doubtful accounts of $688,403 and $740,480	53,816,200	52,471,766
Inventories	21,809,224	19,536,268
Other	8,296,268	7,985,897
Total current assets	162,777,076	137,770,148
INVESTMENTS AND OTHER ASSETS:		
Investments	12,729,569	22,128,543
Other	2,133,207	2,031,400
Total investments and other assets	14,862,776	24,159,943
PROPERTY, PLANT, AND EQUIPMENT:	234,162,498	211,150,194
Less accumulated depreciation and amortization	90,720,909	77,715,911
Property, plant, and equipment − net	143,441,589	133,434,283
TOTAL	$ 321,081,441	$ 295,364,374

See Significant Accounting Policies and Notes to Financial Statements.

| | December 31 | |
	1989	1988
LIABILITIES AND SHAREHOLDERS' EQUITY		
CURRENT LIABILITIES:		
Accounts payable — trade	$ 5,353,130	$ 6,153,101
Industrial revenue bond — demand	4,000,000	4,000,000
Accrued liabilities:		
Salaries, wages, and employee benefits	9,163,729	10,192,642
Taxes	1,275,792	4,746,405
Other	4,223,153	4,572,456
Total current liabilities	24,015,804	29,664,604
LONG-TERM LIABILITIES:		
Long-term debt	11,276,093	11,231,517
Deferred income taxes	9,757,061	6,181,249
Deferred compensation	3,436,927	3,920,497
Total long-term liabilities	24,470,081	21,333,263
Total liabilities	48,485,885	50,997,867
SHAREHOLDERS' EQUITY:		
Common stock, authorized 144,000,000 shares of $1.00 par value, 37,907,591 and 37,907,552 shares issued	37,907,591	37,907,552
Additional paid-in capital	6,656,216	7,845,500
Foreign currency translation adjustment	137,000	465,154
Retained earnings	235,568,337	203,144,969
Total shareholders' equity	280,269,144	249,363,175
Less 335,905 and 225,592 shares in treasury, at cost	7,673,588	4,996,668
Shareholders' equity - net	272,595,556	244,366,507
TOTAL	$321,081,441	$295,364,374

JOHN H. HARLAND COMPANY AND SUBSIDIARIES

Statements Of Consolidated Cash Flows

	Year Ended December 31		
	1989	1988	1987
OPERATING ACTIVITIES:			
Net Income	$ 58,051,509	$ 53,323,335	$ 47,514,387
Adjustments to reconcile net income to			
net cash provided by operating activities:			
Depreciation and amortization	18,041,528	16,379,816	13,962,415
Provision for losses on accounts receivable	225,140	304,875	202,872
Deferred income taxes	3,575,812	2,099,172	2,356,889
Deferred compensation	286,337	274,041	837,154
(Gain) loss on sale of equipment	360,266	(713,253)	97,807
Change in assets and liabilities:			
Accounts receivable	(1,569,574)	(8,456,242)	(1,099,560)
Inventories and other current assets	(2,583,327)	537,827	(7,380,904)
Accounts payable and accrued expenses	(5,648,800)	(4,391,825)	(797,097)
Short-term investments	(9,657,557)	13,513,743	16,196,676
Other — net	(950,253)	(29)	(443,981)
Net cash provided by operating activities	60,131,081	72,871,460	71,446,658
INVESTING ACTIVITIES:			
Purchases of property, plant, and equipment	(28,707,383)	(32,612,756)	(39,903,984)
Proceeds from sale of equipment	376,821	2,403,166	799,502
Long-term investments	9,398,974	(6,351,183)	(7,379,718)
Net cash used in investing activities	(18,931,588)	(36,560,773)	(46,484,200)
FINANCING ACTIVITIES:			
Sale of common stock	4,812,027	5,632,553	3,706,937
Dividends paid	(25,628,141)	(20,970,852)	(14,467,982)
Repurchase of stock	(9,412,729)	(8,012,116)	(5,693,874)
Other	450,960	261,382	538,683
Net cash used in financing activities	(29,777,883)	(23,089,033)	(15,916,236)
Increase in cash and cash equivalents	11,421,610	13,221,654	9,046,222
Cash and cash equivalents at beginning of year	49,526,054	36,304,400	27,258,178
Cash and cash equivalents at end of year	$ 60,947,664	$ 49,526,054	$ 36,304,400
Cash paid during the year for:			
Interest	$ 1,963,756	$ 1,248,719	$ 1,208,955
Income taxes	31,534,504	29,536,724	28,185,381

See Significant Accounting Policies and Notes to Financial Statements.

F

AICPA CODE OF PROFESSIONAL CONDUCT AND IMA STANDARDS OF ETHICAL BEHAVIOR FOR MANAGEMENT ACCOUNTANTS

INTRODUCTION

This appendix contains the codes of ethics for members of two important accounting organizations—the American Institute of Certified Public Accountants (AICPA) and the Institute of Management Accountants (IMA). By reading these codes, you can begin to understand the high standards of conduct that are expected of accountants. Being subjected to a code of ethics will not necessarily cause a dishonest person to behave honestly. However, an honest person will learn what behavior is expected and is likely to abide by the code.

American Institute of Certified Public Accountants
CODE OF PROFESSIONAL CONDUCT
as of June 1, 1990

COMPOSITION, APPLICABILITY, AND COMPLIANCE

The Code of Professional Conduct of the American Institute of Certified Public Accountants consists of two sections—(1) the Principles and (2) the Rules. The Principles provide the framework for the Rules, which govern the performance of professional services by members. The Council of the American Institute of Certified Public Accountants is authorized to designate bodies to promulgate technical standards under the Rules, and the bylaws require adherence to those Rules and standards.

The Code of Professional Conduct was adopted by the membership to provide guidance and rules to all members—those in public practice, in industry, in government, and in education—in the performance of their professional responsibilities.

Compliance with the Code of Professional Conduct, as with all standards in an open society, depends primarily on members' understanding and voluntary actions, secondarily on reinforcement by peers and public opinion, and ultimately on disciplinary proceedings, when necessary, against members who fail to comply with the Rules.

SECTION I—PRINCIPLES

Preamble

Membership in the American Institute of Certified Public Accountants is voluntary. By accepting membership, a certified public accountant assumes an obligation of self-discipline above and beyond the requirements of laws and regulations.

These Principles of the Code of Professional Conduct of the American Institute of Certified Public Accountants express the profession's recognition of its responsibilities to the public, to clients, and to colleagues. They guide members in the performance of their professional responsibilities and express the basic tenets of ethical and professional conduct. The Principles call for an unswerving commitment to honorable behavior, even at the sacrifice of personal advantage.

Article I
Responsibilities

In carrying out their responsibilities as professionals, members should exercise sensitive professional and moral judgments in all their activities.

As professionals, certified public accountants perform an essential role in society. Consistent with that role, members of the American Institute of Certified Public Accountants have responsibilities to all those who use their professional services. Members also have a continuing responsibility to cooperate with each other to improve the art of accounting, maintain the public's confidence, and carry out the profession's special responsibilities for self-governance. The collective efforts of all members are required to maintain and enhance the traditions of the profession.

Article II
The Public Interest

Members should accept the obligation to act in a way that will serve the public interest, honor the public trust, and demonstrate commitment to professionalism.

A distinguishing mark of a profession is acceptance of its responsibility to the public. The accounting profession's public consists of clients, credit grantors, governments, employers, investors, the business and financial community, and others who rely on the objectivity and integrity of certified public accountants to maintain the orderly functioning of commerce. This reliance imposes a public interest responsibility on certified public accountants. The public interest is defined as the collective well-being of the community of people and institutions the profession serves.

In discharging their professional responsibilities, members may encounter conflicting pressures from among each of those groups. In resolving those conflicts, members should act with integrity, guided by the precept that when members fulfill their responsibility to the public, clients' and employers' interests are best served.

Those who rely on certified public accountants expect them to discharge their responsibilities with integrity, objectivity, due professional care, and a genuine interest in serving the public. They are expected to provide quality services, enter into fee arrangements, and offer a range of services—all in a manner that demonstrates a level of professionalism consistent with these Principles of the Code of Professional Conduct.

All who accept membership in the American Institute of Certified Public Accountants commit themselves to honor the public trust. In return for the faith that the public reposes in them, members should seek continually to demonstrate their dedication to professional excellence.

Article III
Integrity

To maintain and broaden public confidence, members should perform all professional responsibilities with the highest sense of integrity.

Integrity is an element of character fundamental to professional recognition. It is the quality from which the public trust derives and the benchmark against which a member must ultimately test all decisions.

Integrity requires a member to be, among other things, honest and candid within the constraints of client confidentiality. Service and the public trust should not be subordinated to personal gain and advantage. Integrity can accommodate the inadvertent error and the honest difference of opinion; it cannot accommodate deceit or subordination of principle.

Integrity is measured in terms of what is right and just. In the absence of specific rules, standards, or guidance, or in the face of conflicting opinions, a member should test decisions and deeds by asking: "Am I doing what a person of integrity would do? Have I retained my integrity?" Integrity requires a member to observe both the form and the spirit of technical and ethical standards; circumvention of those standards constitutes subordination of judgment.

Integrity also requires a member to observe the principles of objectivity and independence and of due care.

Article IV
Objectivity and Independence

A member should maintain objectivity and be free of conflicts of interest in discharging professional responsibilities. A member in public practice should be independent in fact and appearance when providing auditing and other attestation services.

Objectivity is a state of mind, a quality that lends value to a member's services. It is a distinguishing feature of the profession. The principle of objectivity imposes the obligation to be impartial, intellectually honest, and free of conflicts of interest. Independence precludes relationships that may appear to impair a member's objectivity in rendering attestation services.

Members often serve multiple interests in many different capacities and must demonstrate their objectivity in varying circumstances. Members in public practice render attest, tax, and management advisory services. Other members prepare financial statements in the employment of others, perform internal auditing services, and serve in financial and management capacities in industry, education, and government. They also educate and train those who aspire to admission into the profession. Regardless of service or capacity, members should protect the integrity of their work, maintain objectivity, and avoid any subordination of their judgment.

For a member in public practice, the maintenance of objectivity and independence requires a continuing assessment of client relationships and public responsibility. Such a member who provides auditing and other attestation services should be independent in fact and appearance. In providing all other services, a member should maintain objectivity and avoid conflicts of interest.

Although members not in public practice cannot maintain the appearance of independence, they nevertheless have the responsibility to maintain objectivity in rendering professional services. Members employed by others to prepare financial statements or to perform auditing, tax, or consulting services are charged with the same responsibility for objectivity as members in public practice and must be scrupulous in their application of generally accepted accounting principles and candid in all their dealings with members in public practice.

Article V
Due Care

A member should observe the profession's technical and ethical standards, strive continually to improve competence and the quality of services, and discharge professional responsibility to the best of the member's ability.

The quest for excellence is the essence of due care. Due care requires a member to discharge professional responsibilities with competence and diligence. It imposes the obligation to perform professional services to the best of a member's ability with concern for the best interest of those for whom the services are performed and consistent with the profession's responsibility to the public.

Competence is derived from a synthesis of education and experience. It begins with a mastery of the common body of knowledge required for designation as a certified public accountant. The maintenance of competence requires a commitment to learning and professional improvement that must continue throughout a member's professional life. It is a member's individual responsibility. In all engagements and in all responsibilities, each member should undertake to achieve a level of competence that will assure that the quality of the member's services meets the high level of professionalism required by these Principles.

Competence represents the attainment and maintenance of a level of understanding and knowledge that enables a member to render services with facility and acumen. It also establishes the limitations of a member's capabilities by dictating that consultation or referral may be required when a professional engagement exceeds the personal competence of a member or a member's firm. Each member is responsible for assessing his or her own competence—of evaluating whether education, experience, and judgment are adequate for the responsibility to be assumed.

Members should be diligent in discharging responsibilities to clients, employers, and the public. Diligence imposes the responsibility to render services promptly and carefully, to be thorough, and to observe applicable technical and ethical standards.

Due care requires a member to plan and supervise adequately any professional activity for which he or she is responsible.

Article VI
Scope and Nature
of Services

A member in public practice should observe the Principles of the Code of Professional Conduct in determining the scope and nature of services to be provided.

The public interest aspect of certified public accountants' services requires that such services be consistent with acceptable professional behavior for certified public accountants. Integrity requires that service and the public trust not be subordinated to personal gain and advantage. Objectivity and independence require that members be free from conflicts of interest in discharging professional responsibilities. Due care requires that services be provided with competence and diligence.

Each of these Principles should be considered by members in determining whether or not to provide specific services in individual circumstances. In some instances, they may represent an overall constraint on the nonaudit services that might be offered to a specific client. No hard-and-fast rules can be developed to help members reach these judgments, but they must be satisfied that they are meeting the spirit of the Principles in this regard.

In order to accomplish this, members should

☐ Practice in firms that have in place internal quality-control procedures to ensure that services are competently delivered and adequately supervised.

☐ Determine, in their individual judgments, whether the scope and nature of other services provided to an audit client would create a conflict of interest in the performance of the audit function for that client.

☐ Assess, in their individual judgments, whether an activity is consistent with their role as professionals (for example, is such activity a reasonable extension or variation of existing services offered by the member or others in the profession?).

SECTION II—RULES

Applicability
The bylaws of the American Institute of Certified Public Accountants require that members adhere to the Rules of the Code of Professional Conduct. Members must be prepared to justify departures from these Rules.

Interpretation Addressing the Applicability of the AICPA Code of Professional Conduct

For purposes of the Applicability Section of the Code, a "member" is a member or international associate of the American Institute of CPAs.

1. The Rules of Conduct that follow apply to all professional services performed except (a) where the wording of the rule indicates otherwise and (b) that a member who is practicing outside the United States will not be subject to discipline for departing from any of the rules stated herein as long as the member's conduct is in accord with the rules of the organized accounting profession in the country in which he or she is practicing. However, where a member's name is associated with financial statements under circumstances that would entitle the reader to assume that United States practices were followed, the member must comply with the requirements of Rules 202 and 203.

2. A member may be held responsible for compliance with the rules by all persons associated with him or her in the practice of public accounting who are either under the member's supervision or are the member's partners or shareholders in the practice.

3. A member shall not permit others to carry out on his or her behalf, either with or without compensation, acts, which if carried out by the member, would place the member in violation of the rules.

Client

A client is any person or entity, other than the member's employer, that engages a member or a member's firm to perform professional services or a person or entity with respect to which professional services are performed. The term "employer" for these purposes does not include those entities engaged in the practice of public accounting.

Council

The Council of the American Institute of Certified Public Accountants.

Enterprise

For purposes of the Code, the term "enterprise" is synonymous with the term "client."

Financial Statements

Statements and footnotes related thereto that purport to show financial position which relates to a point in time or changes in financial position which relate to a period of time, and statements which use a cash or other incomplete basis of accounting. Balance sheets, statements of income, statements of retained earnings, statements of changes in financial position [now called statements of cash flows], and statements of changes in owners' equity are financial statements.

Incidental financial data included in management advisory services reports to support recommendations to a client and tax returns and supporting schedules do not, for this purpose, constitute financial statements; and the statement, affidavit, or signature of preparers required on tax returns neither constitutes an opinion on financial statements nor requires a disclaimer of such opinion.

Firm

A proprietorship, partnership, or professional corporation or association engaged in the practice of public accounting, including individual partners or shareholders thereof.

Institute

The American Institute of Certified Public Accountants.

Interpretation of Rules of Conduct

Pronouncements issued by the division of professional ethics to provide guidelines concerning the scope and application of the rules of conduct.

Member

A member, associate member, or international associate of the American Institute of Certified Public Accountants.

Practice of Public Accounting

The practice of public accounting consists of the performance for a client, by a member or a member's firm, while holding out as CPA(s), of the professional services of accounting, tax, personal financial planning, litigation support services, and those professional services for which standards are promulgated by bodies designated by Council, such as Statements of Financial Accounting Standards, Statements on Auditing Standards, Statements on Standards for Accounting and Review Services, Statements on Standards for Management Advisory

Services, Statements of Governmental Accounting Standards, Statement on Standards for Attestation Engagements, and Statement on Standards for Accountants' Services on Prospective Financial Information.

However, a member or a member's firm, while holding out as CPA(s), is not considered to be in the practice of public accounting if the member or the member's firm does not perform, for any client, any of the professional services described in the preceding paragraph.

Professional Services

Professional services include all services performed by a member while holding out as a CPA.

Holding Out

In general, any action initiated by a member that informs others of his or her status as a CPA or AICPA-accredited specialist constitutes holding out as a CPA. This would include, for example, any oral or written representation to another regarding CPA status, use of the CPA designation on business cards or letterhead, the display of a certificate evidencing a member's CPA designation, or listing as a CPA in local telephone directories.

Rules

Rule 101 Independence

A member in public practice shall be independent in the performance of professional services as required by standards promulgated by bodies designated by Council.

Interpretation of Rule 101

Interpretation 101-1. Independence shall be considered to be impaired if, for example, a member had any of the following transactions, interests, or relationships:

A. During the period of a professional engagement or at the time of expressing an opinion, a member or a member's firm
1. Had or was committed to acquire any direct or material indirect financial interest in the enterprise.
2. Was a trustee of any trust or executor or administrator of any estate if such trust or estate had or was committed to acquire any direct or material indirect financial interest in the enterprise.
3. Had any joint, closely held business investment with the enterprise or with any officer, director, or principal stockholders thereof that was material in relation to the member's net worth or to the net worth of the member's firm.
4. Had any loan to or from the enterprise or any officer, director, or principal stockholder of the enterprise. This proscription does not apply to the following loans from a financial institution when made under normal lending procedures, terms, and requirements:
    a. Loans obtained by a member or a member's firm that are not material in relation to the net worth of such borrower.
    b. Home mortgages.
    c. Other secured loans, except loans guaranteed by a member's firm which are otherwise unsecured.
B. During the period covered by the financial statements, during the period of the professional engagement, or at the time of expressing an opinion, a member or a member's firm
1. Was connected with the enterprise as a promoter, underwriter or voting trustee, as a director or officer, or in any capacity equivalent to that of a member of management or of an employee.
2. Was a trustee for any pension or profit-sharing trust of the enterprise.

The above examples are not intended to be all-inclusive.

Rule 102 Integrity and Objectivity

In the performance of any professional service, a member shall maintain objectivity and integrity, shall be free of conflicts of interest, and shall not knowingly misrepresent facts or subordinate his or her judgment to others.

Rule 201 General Standards

A member shall comply with the following standards and with any interpretations thereof by bodies designated by Council.

A. *Professional Competence.* Undertake only those professional services that the member or the member's firm can reasonably expect to be completed with professional competence.

B. *Due Professional Care.* Exercise due professional care in the performance of professional services.

C. *Planning and Supervision.* Adequately plan and supervise the performance of professional services.

D. *Sufficient Relevant Data.* Obtain sufficient relevant data to afford a reasonable basis for conclusions or recommendations in relation to any professional services performed.

Rule 202 Compliance With Standards

A member who performs auditing, review, compilation, management advisory, tax, or other professional services shall comply with standards promulgated by bodies designated by Council.

Rule 203 Accounting Principles

A member shall not (1) express an opinion or state affirmatively that the financial statements or other financial data of any entity are presented in conformity with generally accepted accounting principles or (2) state that he or she is not aware of any material modifications that should be made to such statements or data in order for them to be in conformity with generally accepted accounting principles, if such statements or data contain any departure from an accounting principle promulgated by bodies designated by Council to establish such principles that has a material effect on the statements or data taken as a whole. If, however, the statements or data contain such a departure and the member can demonstrate that due to unusual circumstances the financial statements or data would otherwise have been misleading, the member can comply with the rule by describing the departure, its approximate effects, if practicable, and the reasons why compliance with the principle would result in a misleading statement.

Rule 301 Confidential Client Information

A member in public practice shall not disclose any confidential client information without the specific consent of the client.

This rule shall not be construed (1) to relieve a member of his or her professional obligations under rules 202 and 203, (2) to affect in any way the member's obligation to comply with a validly issued and enforceable subpoena or summons, (3) to prohibit review of a member's professional practice under AICPA or state CPA society authorization, or (4) to preclude a member from initiating a complaint with or responding to any inquiry made by a recognized investigative or disciplinary body.

Members of a recognized investigative or disciplinary body and professional practice reviewers shall not use to their own advantage or disclose any member's confidential client information that comes to their attention in carrying out their official responsibilities. However, this prohibition shall not restrict the exchange of information with a recognized investigative or disciplinary body or affect, in any way, compliance with a validly issued and enforceable subpoena or summons.

Rule 302 Contingent Fees

A member in public practice shall not perform for a contingent fee any professional services for, or receive such a fee from, a client for whom the member or member's firm also performs:

(a) an audit or review of a financial statement; or

(b) A compilation of a financial statement when the member expects, or reasonably might expect, that a third party will use the financial statement and the member's compilation report does not disclose a lack of independence; or

(c) an examination of prospective financial information.

This prohibition applies during the period in which the member or the member's firm is engaged to perform any of the services listed above and the period covered by any historical financial statements involved in any such listed services.

For purposes of this rule, a contigent fee is a fee established for the performance of any service pursuant to an arrangement in which no fee will be charged unless a specified finding or result is attained, or in which the amount of the fee is otherwise dependent upon the finding or result of such service.

A member's fees may vary depending, for example, on the complexity of services rendered. Fees are not regarded as being contingent if fixed by courts or other public authorities, or, in tax matters, if determined based on the results of judicial proceedings or the findings of governmental agencies.

Rule 401 [There are currently no rules in the 400 series.]

Rule 501 Acts Discreditable

A member shall not commit an act discreditable to the profession

Rule 502 Advertising and Other Forms of Solicitation

A member in public practice shall not seek to obtain clients by advertising or other forms of solicitation in a manner that is false, misleading, or deceptive. Solicitation by the use of coercion, over-reaching, or harassing conduct is prohibited.

Rule 503 Commissions and Referral Fees

A. Prohibited commissions

A member in public practice shall not for a commission recommend or refer to a client any product or service, or for a commission recommend or refer any product or service to be supplied by a client, or receive a commission, when the member or the member's firm also performs for that client:

(a) an audit or review of a financial statement; or

(b) a compilation of a financial statement when the member expects, or reasonably might expect, that a third party will use the financial statement and the member's compilation report does not disclose a lack of independence; or

(c) an examination of prospective financial information.

This prohibition applies during the period in which the member is engaged to perform any of the services listed above and the period covered by any historical financial statements involved in such listed services.

B. Disclosure of permitted commissions

A member in public practice who is not prohibited by this rule from performing services for or receiving a commission and who is paid or expects to be paid a commission shall disclose that fact to any person or entity to whom the member recommends or refers a product or service to which the commission relates.

C.   Referral fees

Any member who accepts a referral fee for recommending or referring any service of a CPA to any person or entity or who pays a referral fee to obtain a client shall disclose such acceptance or payment to the client.

Rule 504 [*There is currently no rule 504.*]

Rule 505 Form of Practice and Name

A member may practice public accounting only in the form of a proprietorship, a partnership, or a professional corporation whose characteristics conform to resolutions of Council.

A member shall not practice public accounting under a firm name that is misleading. Names of one or more past partners or shareholders may be included in the firm name of a successor partnership or corporation. Also, a partner or shareholder surviving the death or withdrawal of all other partners or shareholders may continue to practice under such name which includes the name of past partners or shareholders for up to two years after becoming a sole practitioner.

A firm may not designate itself as "Members of the American Institute of Certified Public Accountants" unless all of its partners or shareholders are members of the Institute.

Institute of Management Accountants
STANDARDS OF ETHICAL CONDUCT FOR MANAGEMENT ACCOUNTANTS

Management accountants have an obligation to the organizations they serve, their profession, the public, and themselves to maintain the highest standards of ethical conduct. In recognition of this obligation, the National Association of Accountants has promulgated the following standards of ethical conduct for management accountants. Adherence to these standards is integral to achieving the *Objectives of Management Accounting*.[1] Management accountants shall not commit acts contrary to these standards nor shall they condone the commission of such acts by others within their organizations.

COMPETENCE

Management accountants have a responsibility to:

☐ Maintain an appropriate level of professional competence by ongoing development of their knowledge and skills.

☐ Perform their professional duties in accordance with relevant laws, regulations, and technical standards.

☐ Prepare complete and clear reports and recommendations after appropriate analyses of relevant and reliable information.

CONFIDENTIALITY

Management accountants have a responsibility to:

☐ Refrain from disclosing confidential information acquired in the course of their work except when authorized, unless legally obligated to do so.

☐ Inform subordinates as appropriate regarding the confidentiality of information acquired in the course of their work and monitor their activities to assure the maintenance of that confidentiality.

☐ Refrain from using or appearing to use confidential information acquired in the course of their work for unethical or illegal advantage either personally or through third parties.

INTEGRITY

Management accountants have a responsibility to:

☐ Avoid actual or apparent conflicts of interest and advise all appropriate parties of any potential conflict.

☐ Refrain from engaging in any activity that would prejudice their ability to carry out their duties ethically.

☐ Refuse any gift, favor, or hospitality that would influence or would appear to influence their actions.

☐ Refrain from either actively or passively subverting the attainment of the organization's legitimate and ethical objectives.

☐ Recognize and communicate professional limitations or other constraints that

---

[1] National Association of Accountants, *Statements on Management Accounting: Objectives of Management Accounting*, Statement No. 1C New York, N.Y., June 1, 1983.

would preclude responsible judgment or successful performance of an activity.

☐ Communicate unfavorable as well as favorable information and professional judgments or opinions.

☐ Refrain from engaging in or supporting any activity that would discredit the profession.

OBJECTIVITY

Management accountants have a responsibility to:

☐ Communicate information fairly and objectively.

☐ Disclose fully all relevant information that could reasonably be expected to influence an intended user's understanding of the reports, comments, and recommendations presented.

RESOLUTION OF ETHICAL CONFLICT

In applying the standards of ethical conduct, management accountants may encounter problems in identifying unethical behavior or in resolving an ethical conflict. When faced with significant ethical issues, management accountants should follow the established policies of the organization bearing on the resolution of such conflict. If these policies do not resolve the ethical conflict, management accountants should consider the following courses of action:

☐ Discuss such problems with the immediate superior except when it appears that the superior is involved, in which case the problem should be presented initially to the next higher managerial level. If satisfactory resolution cannot be achieved when the problem is initially presented, submit the issues to the next higher managerial level.

   If the immediate superior is the chief executive officer, or equivalent, the acceptable reviewing authority may be a group such as the audit committee, executive committee, board of directors, board of trustees, or owners. Contact with levels above the immediate superior should be initiated only with the superior's knowledge, assuming the superior is not involved.

☐ Clarify relevant concepts by confidential discussion with an objective advisor to obtain an understanding of possible courses of action.

☐ If the ethical conflict still exists after exhausting all levels of internal review, the management accountant may have no other recourse on significant matters than to resign from the organization and to submit an informative memorandum to an appropriate representative of the organization.

Except where legally prescribed, communication of such problems to authorities or individuals not employed or engaged by the organization is not considered appropriate.

G

COMPOUND INTEREST AND ANNUITY TABLES

APPENDIX OUTLINE

The following tables are included in this Appendix:

TABLE G.1

Future Value of \$1 at Compound Interest: 0.5%–10%

$$F_{in} = (1 + i)^n$$

Period	.5%	1%	1.5%	2%	2.5%	3%	3.5%	4%	4.5%	5%
1	1.00500	1.01000	1.01500	1.02000	1.02500	1.03000	1.03500	1.04000	1.04500	1.05000
2	1.01003	1.02010	1.03023	1.04040	1.05063	1.06090	1.07123	1.08160	1.09203	1.10250
3	1.01508	1.03030	1.04568	1.06121	1.07689	1.09273	1.10872	1.12486	1.14117	1.15762
4	1.02015	1.04060	1.06136	1.08243	1.10381	1.12551	1.14752	1.16986	1.19252	1.21551
5	1.02525	1.05101	1.07728	1.10408	1.13141	1.15927	1.18769	1.21665	1.24618	1.27628
6	1.03038	1.06152	1.09344	1.12616	1.15969	1.19405	1.22926	1.26532	1.30226	1.34010
7	1.03553	1.07214	1.10984	1.14869	1.18869	1.22987	1.27228	1.31593	1.36086	1.40710
8	1.04071	1.08286	1.12649	1.17166	1.21840	1.26677	1.31681	1.36857	1.42210	1.47746
9	1.04591	1.09369	1.14339	1.19509	1.24886	1.30477	1.36290	1.42331	1.48610	1.55133
10	1.05114	1.10462	1.16054	1.21899	1.28008	1.34392	1.41060	1.48024	1.55297	1.62889
11	1.05640	1.11567	1.17795	1.24337	1.31209	1.38423	1.45997	1.53945	1.62285	1.71034
12	1.06168	1.12683	1.19562	1.26824	1.34489	1.42576	1.51107	1.60103	1.69588	1.79586
13	1.06699	1.13809	1.21355	1.29361	1.37851	1.46853	1.56396	1.66507	1.77220	1.88565
14	1.07232	1.14947	1.23176	1.31948	1.41297	1.51259	1.61869	1.73168	1.85194	1.97993
15	1.07768	1.16097	1.25023	1.34587	1.44830	1.55797	1.67535	1.80094	1.93528	2.07893
16	1.08307	1.17258	1.26899	1.37279	1.48451	1.60471	1.73399	1.87298	2.02237	2.18287
17	1.08849	1.18430	1.28802	1.40024	1.52162	1.65285	1.79468	1.94790	2.11338	2.29202
18	1.09393	1.19615	1.30734	1.42825	1.55966	1.70243	1.85749	2.02582	2.20848	2.40662
19	1.09940	1.20811	1.32695	1.45681	1.59865	1.75351	1.92250	2.10685	2.30786	2.52695
20	1.10490	1.22019	1.34686	1.48595	1.63862	1.80611	1.98979	2.19112	2.41171	2.65330
21	1.11042	1.23239	1.36706	1.51567	1.67958	1.86029	2.05943	2.27877	2.52024	2.78596
22	1.11597	1.24472	1.38756	1.54598	1.72157	1.91610	2.13151	2.36992	2.63365	2.92526
23	1.12155	1.25716	1.40838	1.57690	1.76461	1.97359	2.20611	2.46472	2.75217	3.07152
24	1.12716	1.26973	1.42950	1.60844	1.80873	2.03279	2.28333	2.56330	2.87601	3.22510
25	1.13280	1.28243	1.45095	1.64061	1.85394	2.09378	2.36324	2.66584	3.00543	3.38635
26	1.13846	1.29526	1.47271	1.67342	1.90029	2.15659	2.44596	2.77247	3.14068	3.55567
27	1.14415	1.30821	1.49480	1.70689	1.94780	2.22129	2.53157	2.88337	3.28201	3.73346
28	1.14987	1.32129	1.51722	1.74102	1.99650	2.28793	2.62017	2.99870	3.42970	3.92013
29	1.15562	1.33450	1.53998	1.77584	2.04641	2.35657	2.71188	3.11865	3.58404	4.11614
30	1.16140	1.34785	1.56308	1.81136	2.09757	2.42726	2.80679	3.24340	3.74532	4.32194

5.5%	6%	6.5%	7%	7.5%	8%	8.5%	9%	9.5%	10%
1.05500	1.06000	1.06500	1.07000	1.07500	1.08000	1.08500	1.09000	1.09500	1.10000
1.11303	1.12360	1.13423	1.14490	1.15563	1.16640	1.17723	1.18810	1.19903	1.21000
1.17424	1.19102	1.20795	1.22504	1.24230	1.25971	1.27729	1.29503	1.31293	1.33100
1.23882	1.26248	1.28647	1.31080	1.33547	1.36049	1.38586	1.41158	1.43766	1.46410
1.30696	1.33823	1.37009	1.40255	1.43563	1.46933	1.50366	1.53862	1.57424	1.61051
1.37884	1.41852	1.45914	1.50073	1.54330	1.58687	1.63147	1.67710	1.72379	1.77156
1.45468	1.50363	1.55399	1.60578	1.65905	1.71382	1.77014	1.82804	1.88755	1.94872
1.53469	1.59385	1.65500	1.71819	1.78348	1.85093	1.92060	1.99256	2.06687	2.14359
1.61909	1.68948	1.76257	1.83846	1.91724	1.99900	2.08386	2.17189	2.26322	2.35795
1.70814	1.79085	1.87714	1.96715	2.06103	2.15892	2.26098	2.36736	2.47823	2.59374
1.80209	1.89830	1.99915	2.10485	2.21561	2.33164	2.45317	2.58043	2.71366	2.85312
1.90121	2.01220	2.12910	2.25219	2.38178	2.51817	2.66169	2.81266	2.97146	3.13843
2.00577	2.13293	2.26749	2.40985	2.56041	2.71962	2.88793	3.06580	3.25375	3.45227
2.11609	2.26090	2.41487	2.57853	2.75244	2.93719	3.13340	3.34173	3.56285	3.79750
2.23248	2.39656	2.57184	2.75903	2.95888	3.17217	3.39974	3.64248	3.90132	4.17725
2.35526	2.54035	2.73901	2.95216	3.18079	3.42594	3.68872	3.97031	4.27195	4.59497
2.48480	2.69277	2.91705	3.15882	3.41935	3.70002	4.00226	4.32763	4.67778	5.05447
2.62147	2.85434	3.10665	3.37993	3.67580	3.99602	4.34245	4.71712	5.12217	5.55992
2.76565	3.02560	3.30859	3.61653	3.95149	4.31570	4.71156	5.14166	5.60878	6.11591
2.91776	3.20714	3.52365	3.86968	4.24785	4.66096	5.11205	5.60441	6.14161	6.72750
3.07823	3.39956	3.75268	4.14056	4.56644	5.03383	5.54657	6.10881	6.72507	7.40025
3.24754	3.60354	3.99661	4.43040	4.90892	5.43654	6.01803	6.65860	7.36395	8.14027
3.42615	3.81975	4.25639	4.74053	5.27709	5.87146	6.52956	7.25787	8.06352	8.95430
3.61459	4.04893	4.53305	5.07237	5.67287	6.34118	7.08457	7.91108	8.82956	9.84973
3.81339	4.29187	4.82770	5.42743	6.09834	6.84848	7.68676	8.62308	9.66836	10.83471
4.02313	4.54938	5.14150	5.80735	6.55572	7.39635	8.34014	9.39916	10.58686	11.91818
4.24440	4.82235	5.47570	6.21387	7.04739	7.98806	9.04905	10.24508	11.59261	13.10999
4.47784	5.11169	5.83162	6.64884	7.57595	8.62711	9.81822	11.16714	12.69391	14.42099
4.72412	5.41839	6.21067	7.11426	8.14414	9.31727	10.65277	12.17218	13.89983	15.86309
4.98395	5.74349	6.61437	7.61226	8.75496	10.06266	11.55825	13.26768	15.22031	17.44940

TABLE G.1

(concluded)

Future Value of $1 at Compound Interest: 10.5%–20%

Period	10.5%	11%	11.5%	12%	12.5%	13%	13.5%	14%	14.5%	15%
1	1.10500	1.11000	1.11500	1.12000	1.12500	1.13000	1.13500	1.14000	1.14500	1.15000
2	1.22103	1.23210	1.24323	1.25440	1.26563	1.27690	1.28822	1.29960	1.31102	1.32250
3	1.34923	1.36763	1.38620	1.40493	1.42383	1.44290	1.46214	1.48154	1.50112	1.52088
4	1.49090	1.51807	1.54561	1.57352	1.60181	1.63047	1.65952	1.68896	1.71879	1.74901
5	1.64745	1.68506	1.72335	1.76234	1.80203	1.84244	1.88356	1.92541	1.96801	2.01136
6	1.82043	1.87041	1.92154	1.97382	2.02729	2.08195	2.13784	2.19497	2.25337	2.31306
7	2.01157	2.07616	2.14252	2.21068	2.28070	2.35261	2.42645	2.50227	2.58011	2.66002
8	2.22279	2.30454	2.38891	2.47596	2.56578	2.65844	2.75402	2.85259	2.95423	3.05902
9	2.45618	2.55804	2.66363	2.77308	2.88651	3.00404	3.12581	3.25195	3.38259	3.51788
10	2.71408	2.83942	2.96995	3.10585	3.24732	3.39457	3.54780	3.70722	3.87307	4.04556
11	2.99906	3.15176	3.31149	3.47855	3.65324	3.83586	4.02675	4.22623	4.43466	4.65239
12	3.31396	3.49845	3.69231	3.89598	4.10989	4.33452	4.57036	4.81790	5.07769	5.35025
13	3.66193	3.88328	4.11693	4.36349	4.62363	4.89801	5.18736	5.49241	5.81395	6.15279
14	4.04643	4.31044	4.59037	4.88711	5.20158	5.53475	5.88765	6.26135	6.65697	7.07571
15	4.47130	4.78459	5.11827	5.47357	5.85178	6.25427	6.68248	7.13794	7.62223	8.13706
16	4.94079	5.31089	5.70687	6.13039	6.58325	7.06733	7.58462	8.13725	8.72746	9.35762
17	5.45957	5.89509	6.36316	6.86604	7.40616	7.98608	8.60854	9.27646	9.99294	10.76126
18	6.03283	6.54355	7.09492	7.68997	8.33193	9.02427	9.77070	10.57517	11.44192	12.37545
19	6.66628	7.26334	7.91084	8.61276	9.37342	10.19742	11.08974	12.05569	13.10039	14.23177
20	7.36623	8.06231	8.82058	9.64629	10.54509	11.52309	12.58686	13.74349	15.00064	16.36654
21	8.13969	8.94917	9.83495	10.80385	11.86323	13.02109	14.28608	15.66758	17.17573	18.82152
22	8.99436	9.93357	10.96597	12.10031	13.34613	14.71383	16.21470	17.86104	19.66621	21.64475
23	9.93876	11.02627	12.22706	13.55235	15.01440	16.62663	18.40369	20.36158	22.51781	24.89146
24	10.98233	12.23916	13.63317	15.17863	16.89120	18.78809	20.88818	23.21221	25.78290	28.62518
25	12.13548	13.58546	15.20098	17.00006	19.00260	21.23054	23.70809	26.46192	29.52141	32.91895
26	13.40971	15.07986	16.94910	19.04007	21.37793	23.99051	26.90868	30.16658	33.80202	37.85680
27	14.81772	16.73865	18.89824	21.32488	24.05017	27.10928	30.54135	34.38991	38.70331	43.53531
28	16.37359	18.57990	21.07154	23.88387	27.05644	30.63349	34.66443	39.20449	44.31529	50.06561
29	18.09281	20.62369	23.49477	26.74993	30.43849	34.61584	39.34413	44.69312	50.74101	57.57545
30	19.99256	22.89230	26.19667	29.95992	34.24330	39.11590	44.65559	50.95016	58.09846	66.21177

15.5%	16%	16.5%	17%	17.5%	18%	18.5%	19%	19.5%	20%
1.15500	1.16000	1.16500	1.17000	1.17500	1.18000	1.18500	1.19000	1.19500	1.20000
1.33402	1.34560	1.35722	1.36890	1.38063	1.39240	1.40422	1.41610	1.42802	1.44000
1.54080	1.56090	1.58117	1.60161	1.62223	1.64303	1.66401	1.68516	1.70649	1.72800
1.77962	1.81064	1.84206	1.87389	1.90613	1.93878	1.97185	2.00534	2.03926	2.07360
2.05546	2.10034	2.14600	2.19245	2.23970	2.28776	2.33664	2.38635	2.43691	2.48832
2.37406	2.43640	2.50009	2.56516	2.63164	2.69955	2.76892	2.83976	2.91211	2.98598
2.74204	2.82622	2.91260	3.00124	3.09218	3.18547	3.28117	3.37932	3.47997	3.58318
3.16706	3.27841	3.39318	3.51145	3.63331	3.75886	3.88818	4.02139	4.15856	4.29982
3.65795	3.80296	3.95306	4.10840	4.26914	4.43545	4.60750	4.78545	4.96948	5.15978
4.22493	4.41144	4.60531	4.80683	5.01624	5.23384	5.45989	5.69468	5.93853	6.19174
4.87980	5.11726	5.36519	5.62399	5.89409	6.17593	6.46996	6.77667	7.09654	7.43008
5.63617	5.93603	6.25045	6.58007	6.92555	7.28759	7.66691	8.06424	8.48037	8.91610
6.50977	6.88579	7.28177	7.69868	8.13752	8.59936	9.08528	9.59645	10.13404	10.69932
7.51879	7.98752	8.48326	9.00745	9.56159	10.14724	10.76606	11.41977	12.11018	12.83918
8.68420	9.26552	9.88300	10.53872	11.23487	11.97375	12.75778	13.58953	14.47167	15.40702
10.03025	10.74800	11.51370	12.33030	13.20097	14.12902	15.11797	16.17154	17.29364	18.48843
11.58494	12.46768	13.41346	14.42646	15.51114	16.67225	17.91480	19.24413	20.66590	22.18611
13.38060	14.46251	15.62668	16.87895	18.22559	19.67325	21.22904	22.90052	24.69575	26.62333
15.45460	16.77652	18.20508	19.74838	21.41507	23.21444	25.15641	27.25162	29.51143	31.94800
17.85006	19.46076	21.20892	23.10560	25.16271	27.39303	29.81035	32.42942	35.26615	38.33760
20.61682	22.57448	24.70839	27.03355	29.56618	32.32378	35.32526	38.59101	42.14305	46.00512
23.81243	26.18640	28.78527	31.62925	34.74026	38.14206	41.86043	45.92331	50.36095	55.20614
27.50335	30.37622	33.53484	37.00623	40.81981	45.00763	49.60461	54.64873	60.18134	66.24737
31.76637	35.23642	39.06809	43.29729	47.96327	53.10901	58.78147	65.03199	71.91670	79.49685
36.69016	40.87424	45.51433	50.65783	56.35684	62.66863	69.65604	77.38807	85.94045	95.39622
42.37713	47.41412	53.02419	59.26966	66.21929	73.94898	82.54240	92.09181	102.69884	114.47546
48.94559	55.00038	61.77318	69.34550	77.80767	87.25980	97.81275	109.58925	122.72511	137.37055
56.53216	63.80044	71.96576	81.13423	91.42401	102.96656	115.90811	130.41121	146.65651	164.84466
65.29464	74.00851	83.84011	94.92705	107.42321	121.50054	137.35111	155.18934	175.25453	197.81359
75.41531	85.84988	97.67373	111.06465	126.22227	143.37064	162.76106	184.67531	209.42916	237.37631

TABLE G.2

Future Value of an Ordinary Annuity of $1 per Period: 0.5%–10%

$$F_{A_{in}} = \frac{(1 + i)^n - 1}{i}$$

Period	.5%	1%	1.5%	2%	2.5%	3%	3.5%	4%	4.5%	5%
1	1.00000	1.00000	1.00000	1.00000	1.00000	1.00000	1.00000	1.00000	1.00000	1.00000
2	2.00500	2.01000	2.01500	2.02000	2.02500	2.03000	2.03500	2.04000	2.04500	2.05000
3	3.01502	3.03010	3.04522	3.06040	3.07562	3.09090	3.10622	3.12160	3.13702	3.15250
4	4.03010	4.06040	4.09090	4.12161	4.15252	4.18363	4.21494	4.24646	4.27819	4.31012
5	5.05025	5.10101	5.15227	5.20404	5.25633	5.30914	5.36247	5.41632	5.47071	5.52563
6	6.07550	6.15202	6.22955	6.30812	6.38774	6.46841	6.55015	6.63298	6.71689	6.80191
7	7.10588	7.21354	7.32299	7.43428	7.54743	7.66246	7.77941	7.89829	8.01915	8.14201
8	8.14141	8.28567	8.43284	8.58297	8.73612	8.89234	9.05169	9.21423	9.38001	9.54911
9	9.18212	9.36853	9.55933	9.75463	9.95452	10.15911	10.36850	10.58280	10.80211	11.02656
10	10.22803	10.46221	10.70272	10.94972	11.20338	11.46388	11.73139	12.00611	12.28821	12.57789
11	11.27917	11.56683	11.86326	12.16872	12.48347	12.80780	13.14199	13.48635	13.84118	14.20679
12	12.33556	12.68250	13.04121	13.41209	13.79555	14.19203	14.60196	15.02581	15.46403	15.91713
13	13.39724	13.80933	14.23683	14.68033	15.14044	15.61779	16.11303	16.62684	17.15991	17.71298
14	14.46423	14.94742	15.45038	15.97394	16.51895	17.08632	17.67699	18.29191	18.93211	19.59863
15	15.53655	16.09690	16.68214	17.29342	17.93193	18.59891	19.29568	20.02359	20.78405	21.57856
16	16.61423	17.25786	17.93237	18.63929	19.38022	20.15688	20.97103	21.82453	22.71934	23.65749
17	17.69730	18.43044	19.20136	20.01207	20.86473	21.76159	22.70502	23.69751	24.74171	25.84037
18	18.78579	19.61475	20.48938	21.41231	22.38635	23.41444	24.49969	25.64541	26.85508	28.13238
19	19.87972	20.81090	21.79672	22.84056	23.94601	25.11687	26.35718	27.67123	29.06356	30.53900
20	20.97912	22.01900	23.12367	24.29737	25.54466	26.87037	28.27968	29.77808	31.37142	33.06595
21	22.08401	23.23919	24.47052	25.78332	27.18327	28.67649	30.26947	31.96920	33.78314	35.71925
22	23.19443	24.47159	25.83758	27.29898	28.86286	30.53678	32.32890	34.24797	36.30338	38.50521
23	24.31040	25.71630	27.22514	28.84496	30.58443	32.45288	34.46041	36.61789	38.93703	41.43048
24	25.43196	26.97346	28.63352	30.42186	32.34904	34.42647	36.66653	39.08260	41.68920	44.50200
25	26.55912	28.24320	30.06302	32.03030	34.15776	36.45926	38.94986	41.64591	44.56521	47.72710
26	27.69191	29.52563	31.51397	33.67091	36.01171	38.55304	41.31310	44.31174	47.57064	51.11345
27	28.83037	30.82089	32.98668	35.34432	37.91200	40.70963	43.75906	47.08421	50.71132	54.66913
28	29.97452	32.12910	34.48148	37.05121	39.85980	42.93092	46.29063	49.96758	53.99333	58.40258
29	31.12439	33.45039	35.99870	38.79223	41.85630	45.21885	48.91080	52.96629	57.42303	62.32271
30	32.28002	34.78489	37.53868	40.56808	43.90270	47.57542	51.62268	56.08494	61.00707	66.43885

5.5%	6%	6.5%	7%	7.5%	8%	8.5%	9%	9.5%	10%
1.00000	1.00000	1.00000	1.00000	1.00000	1.00000	1.00000	1.00000	1.00000	1.00000
2.05500	2.06000	2.06500	2.07000	2.07500	2.08000	2.08500	2.09000	2.09500	2.10000
3.16802	3.18360	3.19922	3.21490	3.23062	3.24640	3.26222	3.27810	3.29402	3.31000
4.34227	4.37462	4.40717	4.43994	4.47292	4.50611	4.53951	4.57313	4.60696	4.64100
5.58109	5.63709	5.69364	5.75074	5.80839	5.86660	5.92537	5.98471	6.04462	6.10510
6.88805	6.97532	7.06373	7.15329	7.24402	7.33593	7.42903	7.52333	7.61886	7.71561
8.26689	8.39384	8.52287	8.65402	8.78732	8.92280	9.06050	9.20043	9.34265	9.48717
9.72157	9.89747	10.07686	10.25980	10.44637	10.63663	10.83064	11.02847	11.23020	11.43589
11.25626	11.49132	11.73185	11.97799	12.22985	12.48756	12.75124	13.02104	13.29707	13.57948
12.87535	13.18079	13.49442	13.81645	14.14709	14.48656	14.83510	15.19293	15.56029	15.93742
14.58350	14.97164	15.37156	15.78360	16.20812	16.64549	17.09608	17.56029	18.03852	18.53117
16.38559	16.86994	17.37071	17.88845	18.42373	18.97713	19.54925	20.14072	20.75218	21.38428
18.28680	18.88214	19.49981	20.14064	20.80551	21.49530	22.21094	22.95338	23.72363	24.52271
20.29257	21.01507	21.76730	22.55049	23.36592	24.21492	25.09887	26.01919	26.97738	27.97498
22.40866	23.27597	24.18217	25.12902	26.11836	27.15211	28.23227	29.36092	30.54023	31.77248
24.64114	25.67253	26.75401	27.88805	29.07724	30.32428	31.63201	33.00340	34.44155	35.94973
26.99640	28.21288	29.49302	30.84022	32.25804	33.75023	35.32073	36.97370	38.71350	40.54470
29.48120	30.90565	32.41007	33.99903	35.67739	37.45024	39.32300	41.30134	43.39128	45.59917
32.10267	33.75999	35.51672	37.37896	39.35319	41.44626	43.66545	46.01846	48.51345	51.15909
34.86832	36.78559	38.82531	40.99549	43.30468	45.76196	48.37701	51.16012	54.12223	57.27500
37.78608	39.99273	42.34895	44.86518	47.55253	50.42292	53.48906	56.76453	60.26384	64.00250
40.86431	43.39229	46.10164	49.00574	52.11897	55.45676	59.03563	62.87334	66.98891	71.40275
44.11185	46.99583	50.09824	53.43614	57.02790	60.89330	65.05366	69.53194	74.35286	79.54302
47.53800	50.81558	54.35463	58.17667	62.30499	66.76476	71.58322	76.78981	82.41638	88.49733
51.15259	54.86451	58.88768	63.24904	67.97786	73.10594	78.66779	84.70090	91.24593	98.34706
54.96598	59.15638	63.71538	68.67647	74.07620	79.95442	86.35455	93.32398	100.91430	109.18177
58.98911	63.70577	68.85688	74.48382	80.63192	87.35077	94.69469	102.72313	111.50116	121.09994
63.23351	68.52811	74.33257	80.69769	87.67931	95.33883	103.74374	112.96822	123.09377	134.20994
67.71135	73.63980	80.16419	87.34653	95.25526	103.96594	113.56196	124.13536	135.78767	148.63093
72.43548	79.05819	86.37486	94.46079	103.39940	113.28321	124.21473	136.30754	149.68750	164.49402

TABLE G.2

(concluded)

Future Value of an Ordinary Annuity of $1 per Period: 10.5%–20%

Period	10.5%	11%	11.5%	12%	12.5%	13%	13.5%	14%	14.5%	15%
1 ...	1.00000	1.00000	1.00000	1.00000	1.00000	1.00000	1.00000	1.00000	1.00000	1.00000
2 ...	2.10500	2.11000	2.11500	2.12000	2.12500	2.13000	2.13500	2.14000	2.14500	2.15000
3 ...	3.32602	3.34210	3.35822	3.37440	3.39062	3.40690	3.42322	3.43960	3.45602	3.47250
4 ...	4.67526	4.70973	4.74442	4.77933	4.81445	4.84980	4.88536	4.92114	4.95715	4.99337
5 ...	6.16616	6.22780	6.29003	6.35285	6.41626	6.48027	6.54488	6.61010	6.67594	6.74238
6 ...	7.81361	7.91286	8.01338	8.11519	8.21829	8.32271	8.42844	8.53552	8.64395	8.75374
7 ...	9.63404	9.78327	9.93492	10.08901	10.24558	10.40466	10.56628	10.73049	10.89732	11.06680
8 ...	11.64561	11.85943	12.07744	12.29969	12.52628	12.75726	12.99273	13.23276	13.47743	13.72682
9 ...	13.86840	14.16397	14.46634	14.77566	15.09206	15.41571	15.74675	16.08535	16.43166	16.78584
10 ...	16.32458	16.72201	17.12997	17.54874	17.97857	18.41975	18.87256	19.33730	19.81425	20.30372
11 ...	19.03866	19.56143	20.09992	20.65458	21.22589	21.81432	22.42036	23.04452	23.68731	24.34928
12 ...	22.03772	22.71319	23.41141	24.13313	24.87913	25.65018	26.44711	27.27075	28.12197	29.00167
13 ...	25.35168	26.21164	27.10372	28.02911	28.98902	29.98470	31.01746	32.08865	33.19966	34.35192
14 ...	29.01361	30.09492	31.22065	32.39260	33.61264	34.88271	36.20482	37.58107	39.01361	40.50471
15 ...	33.06004	34.40536	35.81102	37.27971	38.81422	40.41746	42.09247	43.84241	45.67058	47.58041
16 ...	37.53134	39.18995	40.92929	42.75328	44.66600	46.67173	48.77496	50.98035	53.29282	55.71747
17 ...	42.47213	44.50084	46.63616	48.88367	51.24925	53.73906	56.35958	59.11760	62.02027	65.07509
18 ...	47.93170	50.39594	52.99932	55.74971	58.65541	61.72514	64.96812	68.39407	72.01321	75.83636
19 ...	53.96453	56.93949	60.09424	63.43968	66.98733	70.74941	74.73882	78.96923	83.45513	88.21181
20 ...	60.63081	64.20283	68.00508	72.05244	76.36075	80.94683	85.82856	91.02493	96.55612	102.44358
21 ...	67.99704	72.26514	76.82566	81.69874	86.90584	92.46992	98.41541	104.76842	111.55676	118.81012
22 ...	76.13673	81.21431	86.66062	92.50258	98.76908	105.49101	112.70149	120.43600	128.73249	137.63164
23 ...	85.13109	91.14788	97.62659	104.60289	112.11521	120.20484	128.91619	138.29704	148.39871	159.27638
24 ...	95.06985	102.17415	109.85364	118.15524	127.12961	136.83147	147.31988	158.65862	170.91652	184.16784
25 ...	106.05219	114.41331	123.48681	133.33387	144.02081	155.61956	168.20806	181.87083	196.69941	212.79302
26 ...	118.18767	127.99877	138.68780	150.33393	163.02341	176.85010	191.91615	208.33274	226.22083	245.71197
27 ...	131.59737	143.07864	155.63689	169.37401	184.40134	200.84061	218.82483	238.49933	260.02285	283.56877
28 ...	146.41510	159.81729	174.53513	190.69889	208.45151	227.94989	249.36618	272.88923	298.72616	327.10408
29 ...	162.78868	178.39719	195.60668	214.58275	235.50795	258.58338	284.03062	312.09373	343.04145	377.16969
30 ...	180.88149	199.02088	219.10144	241.33268	265.94644	293.19922	323.37475	356.78685	393.78246	434.74515

15.5%	16%	16.5%	17%	17.5%	18%	18.5%	19%	19.5%	20%
1.00000	1.00000	1.00000	1.00000	1.00000	1.00000	1.00000	1.00000	1.00000	1.00000
2.15500	2.16000	2.16500	2.17000	2.17500	2.18000	2.18500	2.19000	2.19500	2.20000
3.48902	3.50560	3.52222	3.53890	3.55562	3.57240	3.58922	3.60610	3.62302	3.64000
5.02982	5.06650	5.10339	5.14051	5.17786	5.21543	5.25323	5.29126	5.32951	5.36800
6.80945	6.87714	6.94545	7.01440	7.08398	7.15421	7.22508	7.29660	7.36877	7.44160
8.86491	8.97748	9.09145	9.20685	9.32368	9.44197	9.56172	9.68295	9.80568	9.92992
11.23897	11.41387	11.59154	11.77201	11.95533	12.14152	12.33064	12.52271	12.71779	12.91590
13.98101	14.24009	14.50415	14.77325	15.04751	15.32700	15.61181	15.90203	16.19776	16.49908
17.14807	17.51851	17.89733	18.28471	18.68082	19.08585	19.49999	19.92341	20.35632	20.79890
20.80602	21.32147	21.85039	22.39311	22.94997	23.52131	24.10749	24.70886	25.32580	25.95868
25.03095	25.73290	26.45570	27.19994	27.96621	28.75514	29.56737	30.40355	31.26433	32.15042
29.91075	30.85017	31.82089	32.82393	33.86030	34.93107	36.03734	37.18022	38.36088	39.58050
35.54692	36.78620	38.07134	39.40399	40.78585	42.21866	43.70424	45.24446	46.84125	48.49660
42.05669	43.67199	45.35311	47.10267	48.92337	50.81802	52.78953	54.84091	56.97529	59.19592
49.57548	51.65951	53.83638	56.11013	58.48496	60.96527	63.55559	66.26068	69.08547	72.03511
58.25968	60.92503	63.71938	66.64885	69.71983	72.93901	76.31338	79.85021	83.55714	87.44213
68.28993	71.67303	75.23307	78.97915	82.92080	87.06804	91.43135	96.02175	100.85079	105.93056
79.87486	84.14072	88.64653	93.40561	98.43194	103.74028	109.34615	115.26588	121.51669	128.11667
93.25547	98.60323	104.27321	110.28456	116.65753	123.41353	130.57519	138.16640	146.21244	154.74000
108.71007	115.37975	122.47829	130.03294	138.07260	146.62797	155.73160	165.41802	175.72387	186.68800
126.56013	134.84051	143.68721	153.13854	163.23531	174.02100	185.54194	197.84744	210.99002	225.02560
147.17695	157.41499	168.39560	180.17209	192.80149	206.34479	220.86720	236.43846	253.13308	271.03072
170.98937	183.60138	197.18087	211.80134	227.54175	244.48685	262.72763	282.36176	303.49403	326.23686
198.49272	213.97761	230.71571	248.80757	268.36155	289.49448	312.33225	337.01050	363.67536	392.48424
230.25910	249.21402	269.78381	292.10486	316.32482	342.60349	371.11371	402.04249	435.59206	471.98108
266.94926	290.08827	315.29813	342.76268	372.68167	405.27211	440.76975	479.43056	521.53251	567.37730
309.32639	337.50239	368.32233	402.03234	438.90096	479.22109	523.31215	571.52237	624.23135	681.85276
358.27198	392.50277	430.09551	471.37783	516.70863	566.48089	621.12490	681.11162	746.95647	819.22331
414.80414	456.30322	502.06127	552.51207	608.13264	669.44745	737.03300	811.52283	893.61298	984.06797
480.09878	530.31173	585.90138	647.43912	715.55585	790.94799	874.38411	966.71217	1068.86751	1181.88157

TABLE G.3

Present Value of $1 at Compound Interest: 0.5–7%

$$P_{i,n} = \frac{1}{(1 + i)^n}$$

Period	.5%	1%	1.5%	2%	2.5%	3%	3.5%	4%	4.5%	5%	5.5%	6%	6.5%	7%
1 ...	0.99502	0.99010	0.98522	0.98039	0.97561	0.97087	0.96618	0.96154	0.95694	0.95238	0.94787	0.94340	0.93897	0.93458
2 ...	0.99007	0.98030	0.97066	0.96117	0.95181	0.94260	0.93351	0.92456	0.91573	0.90703	0.89845	0.89000	0.88166	0.87344
3 ...	0.98515	0.97059	0.95632	0.94232	0.92860	0.91514	0.90194	0.88900	0.87630	0.86384	0.85161	0.83962	0.82785	0.81630
4 ...	0.98025	0.96098	0.94218	0.92385	0.90595	0.88849	0.87144	0.85480	0.83856	0.82270	0.80722	0.79209	0.77732	0.76290
5 ...	0.97537	0.95147	0.92826	0.90573	0.88385	0.86261	0.84197	0.82193	0.80245	0.78353	0.76513	0.74726	0.72988	0.71299
6 ...	0.97052	0.94205	0.91454	0.88797	0.86230	0.83748	0.81350	0.79031	0.76790	0.74622	0.72525	0.70496	0.68533	0.66634
7 ...	0.96569	0.93272	0.90103	0.87056	0.84127	0.81309	0.78599	0.75992	0.73483	0.71068	0.68744	0.66506	0.64351	0.62275
8 ...	0.96089	0.92348	0.88771	0.85349	0.82075	0.78941	0.75941	0.73069	0.70319	0.67684	0.65160	0.62741	0.60423	0.58201
9 ...	0.95610	0.91434	0.87459	0.83676	0.80073	0.76642	0.73373	0.70259	0.67290	0.64461	0.61763	0.59190	0.56735	0.54393
10 ...	0.95135	0.90529	0.86167	0.82035	0.78120	0.74409	0.70892	0.67556	0.64393	0.61391	0.58543	0.55839	0.53273	0.50835
11 ...	0.94661	0.89632	0.84893	0.80426	0.76214	0.72242	0.68495	0.64958	0.61620	0.58468	0.55491	0.52679	0.50021	0.47509
12 ...	0.94191	0.88745	0.83639	0.78849	0.74356	0.70138	0.66178	0.62460	0.58966	0.55684	0.52598	0.49697	0.46968	0.44401
13 ...	0.93722	0.87866	0.82403	0.77303	0.72542	0.68095	0.63940	0.60057	0.56427	0.53032	0.49856	0.46884	0.44102	0.41496
14 ...	0.93256	0.86996	0.81185	0.75788	0.70773	0.66112	0.61778	0.57748	0.53997	0.50507	0.47257	0.44230	0.41410	0.38782
15 ...	0.92792	0.86135	0.79985	0.74301	0.69047	0.64186	0.59689	0.55526	0.51672	0.48102	0.44793	0.41727	0.38883	0.36245
16 ...	0.92330	0.85282	0.78803	0.72845	0.67362	0.62317	0.57671	0.53391	0.49447	0.45811	0.42458	0.39365	0.36510	0.33873
17 ...	0.91871	0.84438	0.77639	0.71416	0.65720	0.60502	0.55720	0.51337	0.47318	0.43630	0.40245	0.37136	0.34281	0.31657
18 ...	0.91414	0.83602	0.76491	0.70016	0.64117	0.58739	0.53836	0.49363	0.45280	0.41552	0.38147	0.35034	0.32189	0.29586
19 ...	0.90959	0.82774	0.75361	0.68643	0.62553	0.57029	0.52016	0.47464	0.43330	0.39573	0.36158	0.33051	0.30224	0.27651
20 ...	0.90506	0.81954	0.74247	0.67297	0.61027	0.55368	0.50257	0.45639	0.41464	0.37689	0.34273	0.31180	0.28380	0.25842
21 ...	0.90056	0.81143	0.73150	0.65978	0.59539	0.53755	0.48557	0.43883	0.39679	0.35894	0.32486	0.29416	0.26648	0.24151
22 ...	0.89608	0.80340	0.72069	0.64684	0.58086	0.52189	0.46915	0.42196	0.37970	0.34185	0.30793	0.27751	0.25021	0.22571
23 ...	0.89162	0.79544	0.71004	0.63416	0.56670	0.50669	0.45329	0.40573	0.36335	0.32557	0.29187	0.26180	0.23494	0.21095
24 ...	0.88719	0.78757	0.69954	0.62172	0.55288	0.49193	0.43796	0.39012	0.34770	0.31007	0.27666	0.24698	0.22060	0.19715
25 ...	0.88277	0.77977	0.68921	0.60953	0.53939	0.47761	0.42315	0.37512	0.33273	0.29530	0.26223	0.23300	0.20714	0.18425
26 ...	0.87838	0.77205	0.67902	0.59758	0.52623	0.46369	0.40884	0.36069	0.31840	0.28124	0.24856	0.21981	0.19450	0.17220
27 ...	0.87401	0.76440	0.66899	0.58586	0.51340	0.45019	0.39501	0.34682	0.30469	0.26785	0.23560	0.20737	0.18263	0.16093
28 ...	0.86966	0.75684	0.65910	0.57437	0.50088	0.43708	0.38165	0.33348	0.29157	0.25509	0.22332	0.19563	0.17148	0.15040
29 ...	0.86533	0.74934	0.64936	0.56311	0.48866	0.42435	0.36875	0.32065	0.27902	0.24295	0.21168	0.18456	0.16101	0.14056
30 ...	0.86103	0.74192	0.63976	0.55207	0.47674	0.41199	0.35628	0.30832	0.26700	0.23138	0.20064	0.17411	0.15119	0.13137
31 ...	0.85675	0.73458	0.63031	0.54125	0.46511	0.39999	0.34423	0.29646	0.25550	0.22036	0.19018	0.16425	0.14196	0.12277
32 ...	0.85248	0.72730	0.62099	0.53063	0.45377	0.38834	0.33259	0.28506	0.24450	0.20987	0.18027	0.15496	0.13329	0.11474
33 ...	0.84824	0.72010	0.61182	0.52023	0.44270	0.37703	0.32134	0.27409	0.23397	0.19987	0.17087	0.14619	0.12516	0.10723
34 ...	0.84402	0.71297	0.60277	0.51003	0.43191	0.36604	0.31048	0.26355	0.22390	0.19035	0.16196	0.13791	0.11752	0.10022
35 ...	0.83982	0.70591	0.59387	0.50003	0.42137	0.35538	0.29998	0.25342	0.21425	0.18129	0.15352	0.13011	0.11035	0.09366
36 ...	0.83564	0.69892	0.58509	0.49022	0.41109	0.34503	0.28983	0.24367	0.20503	0.17266	0.14552	0.12274	0.10361	0.08754
37 ...	0.83149	0.69200	0.57644	0.48061	0.40107	0.33498	0.28003	0.23430	0.19620	0.16444	0.13793	0.11579	0.09729	0.08181
38 ...	0.82735	0.68515	0.56792	0.47119	0.39128	0.32523	0.27056	0.22529	0.18775	0.15661	0.13074	0.10924	0.09135	0.07646
39 ...	0.82323	0.67837	0.55953	0.46195	0.38174	0.31575	0.26141	0.21662	0.17967	0.14915	0.12392	0.10306	0.08578	0.07146
40 ...	0.81914	0.67165	0.55126	0.45289	0.37243	0.30656	0.25257	0.20829	0.17193	0.14205	0.11746	0.09722	0.08054	0.06678
41 ...	0.81506	0.66500	0.54312	0.44401	0.36335	0.29763	0.24403	0.20028	0.16453	0.13528	0.11134	0.09172	0.07563	0.06241
42 ...	0.81101	0.65842	0.53509	0.43530	0.35448	0.28896	0.23578	0.19257	0.15744	0.12884	0.10554	0.08653	0.07101	0.05833
43 ...	0.80697	0.65190	0.52718	0.42677	0.34584	0.28054	0.22781	0.18517	0.15066	0.12270	0.10003	0.08163	0.06668	0.05451
44 ...	0.80296	0.64545	0.51939	0.41840	0.33740	0.27237	0.22010	0.17805	0.14417	0.11686	0.09482	0.07701	0.06261	0.05095
45 ...	0.79896	0.63905	0.51171	0.41020	0.32917	0.26444	0.21266	0.17120	0.13796	0.11130	0.08988	0.07265	0.05879	0.04761
46 ...	0.79499	0.63273	0.50415	0.40215	0.32115	0.25674	0.20547	0.16461	0.13202	0.10600	0.08519	0.06854	0.05520	0.04450
47 ...	0.79103	0.62646	0.49670	0.39427	0.31331	0.24926	0.19852	0.15828	0.12634	0.10095	0.08075	0.06466	0.05183	0.04159
48 ...	0.78710	0.62026	0.48936	0.38654	0.30567	0.24200	0.19181	0.15219	0.12090	0.09614	0.07654	0.06100	0.04867	0.03887
49 ...	0.78318	0.61412	0.48213	0.37896	0.29822	0.23495	0.18532	0.14634	0.11569	0.09156	0.07255	0.05755	0.04570	0.03632
50 ...	0.77929	0.60804	0.47500	0.37153	0.29094	0.22811	0.17905	0.14071	0.11071	0.08720	0.06877	0.05429	0.04291	0.03395
51 ...	0.77541	0.60202	0.46798	0.36424	0.28385	0.22146	0.17300	0.13530	0.10594	0.08305	0.06518	0.05122	0.04029	0.03173
52 ...	0.77155	0.59606	0.46107	0.35710	0.27692	0.21501	0.16715	0.13010	0.10138	0.07910	0.06178	0.04832	0.03783	0.02965
53 ...	0.76771	0.59016	0.45426	0.35010	0.27017	0.20875	0.16150	0.12509	0.09701	0.07533	0.05856	0.04558	0.03552	0.02771
54 ...	0.76389	0.58431	0.44754	0.34323	0.26358	0.20267	0.15603	0.12028	0.09284	0.07174	0.05551	0.04300	0.03335	0.02590
55 ...	0.76009	0.57853	0.44093	0.33650	0.25715	0.19677	0.15076	0.11566	0.08884	0.06833	0.05262	0.04057	0.03132	0.02420
56 ...	0.75631	0.57280	0.43441	0.32991	0.25088	0.19104	0.14566	0.11121	0.08501	0.06507	0.04987	0.03827	0.02941	0.02262
57 ...	0.75255	0.56713	0.42799	0.32344	0.24476	0.18547	0.14073	0.10693	0.08135	0.06197	0.04727	0.03610	0.02761	0.02114
58 ...	0.74880	0.56151	0.42167	0.31710	0.23879	0.18007	0.13598	0.10282	0.07785	0.05902	0.04481	0.03406	0.02593	0.01976
59 ...	0.74508	0.55595	0.41544	0.31088	0.23297	0.17483	0.13138	0.09886	0.07450	0.05621	0.04247	0.03213	0.02434	0.01847
60 ...	0.74137	0.55045	0.40930	0.30478	0.22728	0.16973	0.12693	0.09506	0.07129	0.05354	0.04026	0.03031	0.02286	0.01726

Period	.5%	1%	1.5%	2%	2.5%	3%	3.5%	4%	4.5%	5%	5.5%	6%	6.5%	7%
61 ..	0.73768	0.54500	0.40325	0.29881	0.22174	0.16479	0.12264	0.09140	0.06822	0.05099	0.03816	0.02860	0.02146	0.01613
62 ..	0.73401	0.53960	0.39729	0.29295	0.21633	0.15999	0.11849	0.08789	0.06528	0.04856	0.03617	0.02698	0.02015	0.01507
63 ..	0.73036	0.53426	0.39142	0.28720	0.21106	0.15533	0.11449	0.08451	0.06247	0.04625	0.03428	0.02545	0.01892	0.01409
64 ..	0.72673	0.52897	0.38563	0.28157	0.20591	0.15081	0.11062	0.08126	0.05978	0.04404	0.03250	0.02401	0.01777	0.01317
65 ..	0.72311	0.52373	0.37993	0.27605	0.20089	0.14641	0.10688	0.07813	0.05721	0.04195	0.03080	0.02265	0.01668	0.01230
66 ..	0.71952	0.51855	0.37432	0.27064	0.19599	0.14215	0.10326	0.07513	0.05474	0.03995	0.02920	0.02137	0.01566	0.01150
67 ..	0.71594	0.51341	0.36879	0.26533	0.19121	0.13801	0.09977	0.07224	0.05239	0.03805	0.02767	0.02016	0.01471	0.01075
68 ..	0.71237	0.50833	0.36334	0.26013	0.18654	0.13399	0.09640	0.06946	0.05013	0.03623	0.02623	0.01902	0.01381	0.01004
69 ..	0.70883	0.50330	0.35797	0.25503	0.18199	0.13009	0.09314	0.06679	0.04797	0.03451	0.02486	0.01794	0.01297	0.00939
70 ..	0.70530	0.49831	0.35268	0.25003	0.17755	0.12630	0.08999	0.06422	0.04590	0.03287	0.02357	0.01693	0.01218	0.00877
71 ..	0.70179	0.49338	0.34746	0.24513	0.17322	0.12262	0.08694	0.06175	0.04393	0.03130	0.02234	0.01597	0.01143	0.00820
72 ..	0.69830	0.48850	0.34233	0.24032	0.16900	0.11905	0.08400	0.05937	0.04204	0.02981	0.02117	0.01507	0.01074	0.00766
73 ..	0.69483	0.48366	0.33727	0.23561	0.16488	0.11558	0.08116	0.05709	0.04023	0.02839	0.02007	0.01421	0.01008	0.00716
74 ..	0.69137	0.47887	0.33229	0.23099	0.16085	0.11221	0.07842	0.05490	0.03849	0.02704	0.01902	0.01341	0.00947	0.00669
75 ..	0.68793	0.47413	0.32738	0.22646	0.15693	0.10895	0.07577	0.05278	0.03684	0.02575	0.01803	0.01265	0.00889	0.00625
76 ..	0.68451	0.46944	0.32254	0.22202	0.15310	0.10577	0.07320	0.05075	0.03525	0.02453	0.01709	0.01193	0.00835	0.00585
77 ..	0.68110	0.46479	0.31777	0.21766	0.14937	0.10269	0.07073	0.04880	0.03373	0.02336	0.01620	0.01126	0.00784	0.00546
78 ..	0.67772	0.46019	0.31308	0.21340	0.14573	0.09970	0.06834	0.04692	0.03228	0.02225	0.01536	0.01062	0.00736	0.00511
79 ..	0.67434	0.45563	0.30845	0.20921	0.14217	0.09680	0.06603	0.04512	0.03089	0.02119	0.01456	0.01002	0.00691	0.00477
80 ..	0.67099	0.45112	0.30389	0.20511	0.13870	0.09398	0.06379	0.04338	0.02956	0.02018	0.01380	0.00945	0.00649	0.00446
81 ..	0.66765	0.44665	0.29940	0.20109	0.13532	0.09124	0.06164	0.04172	0.02829	0.01922	0.01308	0.00892	0.00609	0.00417
82 ..	0.66433	0.44223	0.29497	0.19715	0.13202	0.08858	0.05955	0.04011	0.02707	0.01830	0.01240	0.00841	0.00572	0.00390
83 ..	0.66102	0.43785	0.29062	0.19328	0.12880	0.08600	0.05754	0.03857	0.02590	0.01743	0.01175	0.00794	0.00537	0.00364
84 ..	0.65773	0.43352	0.28632	0.18949	0.12566	0.08350	0.05559	0.03709	0.02479	0.01660	0.01114	0.00749	0.00504	0.00340
85 ..	0.65446	0.42922	0.28209	0.18577	0.12259	0.08107	0.05371	0.03566	0.02372	0.01581	0.01056	0.00706	0.00473	0.00318
86 ..	0.65121	0.42497	0.27792	0.18213	0.11960	0.07870	0.05190	0.03429	0.02270	0.01506	0.01001	0.00666	0.00445	0.00297
87 ..	0.64797	0.42077	0.27381	0.17856	0.11669	0.07641	0.05014	0.03297	0.02172	0.01434	0.00948	0.00629	0.00417	0.00278
88 ..	0.64474	0.41660	0.26977	0.17506	0.11384	0.07419	0.04845	0.03170	0.02079	0.01366	0.00899	0.00593	0.00392	0.00260
89 ..	0.64154	0.41248	0.26578	0.17163	0.11106	0.07203	0.04681	0.03048	0.01989	0.01301	0.00852	0.00559	0.00368	0.00243
90 ..	0.63834	0.40839	0.26185	0.16826	0.10836	0.06993	0.04522	0.02931	0.01903	0.01239	0.00808	0.00528	0.00346	0.00227
91 ..	0.63517	0.40435	0.25798	0.16496	0.10571	0.06789	0.04369	0.02818	0.01821	0.01180	0.00766	0.00498	0.00324	0.00212
92 ..	0.63201	0.40034	0.25417	0.16173	0.10313	0.06591	0.04222	0.02710	0.01743	0.01124	0.00726	0.00470	0.00305	0.00198
93 ..	0.62886	0.39638	0.25041	0.15856	0.10062	0.06399	0.04079	0.02606	0.01668	0.01070	0.00688	0.00443	0.00286	0.00185
94 ..	0.62573	0.39246	0.24671	0.15545	0.09816	0.06213	0.03941	0.02505	0.01596	0.01019	0.00652	0.00418	0.00269	0.00173
95 ..	0.62262	0.38857	0.24307	0.15240	0.09577	0.06032	0.03808	0.02409	0.01527	0.00971	0.00618	0.00394	0.00252	0.00162
96 ..	0.61952	0.38472	0.23947	0.14941	0.09343	0.05856	0.03679	0.02316	0.01462	0.00924	0.00586	0.00372	0.00237	0.00151
97 ..	0.61644	0.38091	0.23594	0.14648	0.09116	0.05686	0.03555	0.02227	0.01399	0.00880	0.00555	0.00351	0.00222	0.00141
98 ..	0.61337	0.37714	0.23245	0.14361	0.08893	0.05520	0.03434	0.02142	0.01338	0.00838	0.00526	0.00331	0.00209	0.00132
99 ..	0.61032	0.37341	0.22901	0.14079	0.08676	0.05359	0.03318	0.02059	0.01281	0.00798	0.00499	0.00312	0.00196	0.00123
100 ..	0.60729	0.36971	0.22563	0.13803	0.08465	0.05203	0.03026	0.01980	0.01226	0.00760	0.00473	0.00295	0.00184	0.00115
101 ..	0.60427	0.36605	0.22230	0.13533	0.08258	0.05052	0.03098	0.01904	0.01173	0.00724	0.00448	0.00278	0.00173	0.00108
102 ..	0.60126	0.36243	0.21901	0.13267	0.08057	0.04905	0.02993	0.01831	0.01122	0.00690	0.00425	0.00262	0.00162	0.00101
103 ..	0.59827	0.35884	0.21577	0.13007	0.07860	0.04762	0.02892	0.01760	0.01074	0.00657	0.00403	0.00247	0.00152	0.00094
104 ..	0.59529	0.35529	0.21258	0.12752	0.07669	0.04623	0.02794	0.01693	0.01028	0.00626	0.00382	0.00233	0.00143	0.00088
105 ..	0.59233	0.35177	0.20944	0.12502	0.07482	0.04488	0.02699	0.01627	0.00984	0.00596	0.00362	0.00220	0.00134	0.00082
106 ..	0.58938	0.34828	0.20635	0.12257	0.07299	0.04358	0.02608	0.01565	0.00941	0.00567	0.00343	0.00208	0.00126	0.00077
107 ..	0.58645	0.34484	0.20330	0.12017	0.07121	0.04231	0.02520	0.01505	0.00901	0.00540	0.00325	0.00196	0.00118	0.00072
108 ..	0.58353	0.34142	0.20029	0.11781	0.06947	0.04108	0.02435	0.01447	0.00862	0.00515	0.00308	0.00185	0.00111	0.00067
109 ..	0.58063	0.33804	0.19733	0.11550	0.06778	0.03988	0.02352	0.01391	0.00825	0.00490	0.00292	0.00174	0.00104	0.00063
110 ..	0.57774	0.33469	0.19442	0.11324	0.06613	0.03872	0.02273	0.01338	0.00789	0.00467	0.00277	0.00165	0.00098	0.00059
111 ..	0.57487	0.33138	0.19154	0.11101	0.06451	0.03759	0.02196	0.01286	0.00755	0.00445	0.00262	0.00155	0.00092	0.00055
112 ..	0.57201	0.32810	0.18871	0.10884	0.06294	0.03649	0.02122	0.01237	0.00723	0.00423	0.00249	0.00146	0.00086	0.00051
113 ..	0.56916	0.32485	0.18592	0.10670	0.06140	0.03543	0.02050	0.01189	0.00692	0.00403	0.00236	0.00138	0.00081	0.00048
114 ..	0.56633	0.32164	0.18318	0.10461	0.05991	0.03440	0.01981	0.01143	0.00662	0.00384	0.00223	0.00130	0.00076	0.00045
115 ..	0.56351	0.31845	0.18047	0.10256	0.05845	0.03340	0.01914	0.01099	0.00633	0.00366	0.00212	0.00123	0.00072	0.00042
116 ..	0.56071	0.31530	0.17780	0.10055	0.05702	0.03243	0.01849	0.01057	0.00606	0.00348	0.00201	0.00116	0.00067	0.00039
117 ..	0.55792	0.31218	0.17518	0.09858	0.05563	0.03148	0.01786	0.01016	0.00580	0.00332	0.00190	0.00109	0.00063	0.00036
118 ..	0.55514	0.30908	0.17259	0.09665	0.05427	0.03056	0.01726	0.00977	0.00555	0.00316	0.00180	0.00103	0.00059	0.00034
119 ..	0.55238	0.30602	0.17004	0.09475	0.05295	0.02967	0.01668	0.00940	0.00531	0.00301	0.00171	0.00097	0.00056	0.00032
120 ..	0.54963	0.30299	0.16752	0.09289	0.05166	0.02881	0.01611	0.00904	0.00508	0.00287	0.00162	0.00092	0.00052	0.00030

TABLE G.3

(continued)

Present Value of $1 at Compound Interest: 7.5%–14%

Period	7.5%	8%	8.5%	9%	9.5%	10%	10.5%	11%	11.5%	12%	12.5%	13%	13.5%	14%
1 ...	0.93023	0.92593	0.92166	0.91743	0.91324	0.90909	0.90498	0.90090	0.89686	0.89286	0.88889	0.88496	0.88106	0.87719
2 ...	0.86533	0.85734	0.84946	0.84168	0.83401	0.82645	0.81898	0.81162	0.80436	0.79719	0.79012	0.78315	0.77626	0.76947
3 ...	0.80496	0.79383	0.78291	0.77218	0.76165	0.75131	0.74116	0.73119	0.72140	0.71178	0.70233	0.69305	0.68393	0.67497
4 ...	0.74880	0.73503	0.72157	0.70843	0.69557	0.68301	0.67073	0.65873	0.64699	0.63553	0.62430	0.61332	0.60258	0.59208
5 ...	0.69656	0.68058	0.66505	0.64993	0.63523	0.62092	0.60700	0.59345	0.58026	0.56743	0.55493	0.54276	0.53091	0.51937
6 ...	0.64796	0.63017	0.61295	0.59627	0.58012	0.56447	0.54932	0.53464	0.52042	0.50663	0.49327	0.48032	0.46776	0.45559
7 ...	0.60275	0.58349	0.56493	0.54703	0.52979	0.51316	0.49712	0.48166	0.46674	0.45235	0.43846	0.42506	0.41213	0.39964
8 ...	0.56070	0.54027	0.52067	0.50187	0.48382	0.46651	0.44989	0.43393	0.41860	0.40388	0.38974	0.37616	0.36311	0.35056
9 ...	0.52158	0.50025	0.47988	0.46043	0.44185	0.42410	0.40714	0.39092	0.37543	0.36061	0.34644	0.33288	0.31992	0.30751
10 ...	0.48519	0.46319	0.44229	0.42241	0.40351	0.38554	0.36845	0.35218	0.33671	0.32197	0.30795	0.29459	0.28187	0.26974
11 ...	0.45134	0.42888	0.40764	0.38753	0.36851	0.35049	0.33344	0.31728	0.30198	0.28748	0.27373	0.26070	0.24834	0.23662
12 ...	0.41985	0.39711	0.37570	0.35553	0.33654	0.31863	0.30175	0.28584	0.27083	0.25668	0.24332	0.23071	0.21880	0.20756
13 ...	0.39056	0.36770	0.34627	0.32618	0.30734	0.28966	0.27308	0.25751	0.24290	0.22917	0.21628	0.20416	0.19278	0.18207
14 ...	0.36331	0.34046	0.31914	0.29925	0.28067	0.26333	0.24713	0.23199	0.21785	0.20462	0.19225	0.18068	0.16985	0.15971
15 ...	0.33797	0.31524	0.29414	0.27454	0.25632	0.23939	0.22365	0.20900	0.19538	0.18270	0.17089	0.15989	0.14964	0.14010
16 ...	0.31439	0.29189	0.27110	0.25187	0.23409	0.21763	0.20240	0.18829	0.17523	0.16312	0.15190	0.14150	0.13185	0.12289
17 ...	0.29245	0.27027	0.24986	0.23107	0.21378	0.19784	0.18316	0.16963	0.15715	0.14564	0.13502	0.12522	0.11616	0.10780
18 ...	0.27205	0.25025	0.23028	0.21199	0.19523	0.17986	0.16576	0.15282	0.14095	0.13004	0.12002	0.11081	0.10235	0.09456
19 ...	0.25307	0.23171	0.21224	0.19449	0.17829	0.16351	0.15001	0.13768	0.12641	0.11611	0.10668	0.09806	0.09017	0.08295
20 ...	0.23541	0.21455	0.19562	0.17843	0.16282	0.14864	0.13575	0.12403	0.11337	0.10367	0.09483	0.08678	0.07945	0.07276
21 ...	0.21899	0.19866	0.18029	0.16370	0.14870	0.13513	0.12285	0.11174	0.10168	0.09256	0.08429	0.07680	0.07000	0.06383
22 ...	0.20371	0.18394	0.16617	0.15018	0.13580	0.12285	0.11118	0.10067	0.09119	0.08264	0.07493	0.06796	0.06167	0.05599
23 ...	0.18950	0.17032	0.15315	0.13778	0.12402	0.11168	0.10062	0.09069	0.08179	0.07379	0.06660	0.06014	0.05434	0.04911
24 ...	0.17628	0.15770	0.14115	0.12640	0.11326	0.10153	0.09106	0.08170	0.07335	0.06588	0.05920	0.05323	0.04787	0.04308
25 ...	0.16398	0.14602	0.13009	0.11597	0.10343	0.09230	0.08240	0.07361	0.06579	0.05882	0.05262	0.04710	0.04218	0.03779
26 ...	0.15254	0.13520	0.11990	0.10639	0.09446	0.08391	0.07457	0.06631	0.05900	0.05252	0.04678	0.04168	0.03716	0.03315
27 ...	0.14190	0.12519	0.11051	0.09761	0.08626	0.07628	0.06749	0.05974	0.05291	0.04689	0.04158	0.03689	0.03274	0.02908
28 ...	0.13200	0.11591	0.10185	0.08955	0.07878	0.06934	0.06107	0.05382	0.04746	0.04187	0.03696	0.03264	0.02885	0.02551
29 ...	0.12279	0.10733	0.09387	0.08215	0.07194	0.06304	0.05527	0.04849	0.04256	0.03738	0.03285	0.02889	0.02542	0.02237
30 ...	0.11422	0.09938	0.08652	0.07537	0.06570	0.05731	0.05002	0.04368	0.03817	0.03338	0.02920	0.02557	0.02239	0.01963
31 ...	0.10625	0.09202	0.07974	0.06915	0.06000	0.05210	0.04527	0.03935	0.03424	0.02980	0.02596	0.02262	0.01973	0.01722
32 ...	0.09884	0.08520	0.07349	0.06344	0.05480	0.04736	0.04096	0.03545	0.03070	0.02661	0.02307	0.02002	0.01738	0.01510
33 ...	0.09194	0.07889	0.06774	0.05820	0.05004	0.04306	0.03707	0.03194	0.02754	0.02376	0.02051	0.01772	0.01532	0.01325
34 ...	0.08553	0.07305	0.06243	0.05339	0.04570	0.03914	0.03355	0.02878	0.02470	0.02121	0.01823	0.01568	0.01349	0.01162
35 ...	0.07956	0.06763	0.05754	0.04899	0.04174	0.03558	0.03036	0.02592	0.02215	0.01894	0.01621	0.01388	0.01189	0.01019
36 ...	0.07401	0.06262	0.05303	0.04494	0.03811	0.03235	0.02748	0.02335	0.01987	0.01691	0.01440	0.01228	0.01047	0.00894
37 ...	0.06885	0.05799	0.04888	0.04123	0.03481	0.02941	0.02487	0.02104	0.01782	0.01510	0.01280	0.01087	0.00923	0.00784
38 ...	0.06404	0.05369	0.04505	0.03783	0.03179	0.02673	0.02250	0.01896	0.01598	0.01348	0.01138	0.00962	0.00813	0.00688
39 ...	0.05958	0.04971	0.04152	0.03470	0.02903	0.02430	0.02036	0.01708	0.01433	0.01204	0.01012	0.00851	0.00716	0.00604
40 ...	0.05542	0.04603	0.03827	0.03184	0.02651	0.02209	0.01843	0.01538	0.01285	0.01075	0.00899	0.00753	0.00631	0.00529
41 ...	0.05155	0.04262	0.03527	0.02921	0.02421	0.02009	0.01668	0.01386	0.01153	0.00960	0.00799	0.00666	0.00556	0.00464
42 ...	0.04796	0.03946	0.03251	0.02680	0.02211	0.01826	0.01509	0.01249	0.01034	0.00857	0.00711	0.00590	0.00490	0.00407
43 ...	0.04461	0.03654	0.02996	0.02458	0.02019	0.01660	0.01366	0.01125	0.00927	0.00765	0.00632	0.00522	0.00432	0.00357
44 ...	0.04150	0.03383	0.02761	0.02255	0.01844	0.01509	0.01236	0.01013	0.00832	0.00683	0.00561	0.00462	0.00380	0.00313
45 ...	0.03860	0.03133	0.02545	0.02069	0.01684	0.01372	0.01119	0.00913	0.00746	0.00610	0.00499	0.00409	0.00335	0.00275
46 ...	0.03591	0.02901	0.02345	0.01898	0.01538	0.01247	0.01012	0.00823	0.00669	0.00544	0.00444	0.00362	0.00295	0.00241
47 ...	0.03340	0.02686	0.02162	0.01742	0.01405	0.01134	0.00916	0.00741	0.00600	0.00486	0.00394	0.00320	0.00260	0.00212
48 ...	0.03107	0.02487	0.01992	0.01598	0.01283	0.01031	0.00829	0.00668	0.00538	0.00434	0.00350	0.00283	0.00229	0.00186
49 ...	0.02891	0.02303	0.01836	0.01466	0.01171	0.00937	0.00750	0.00601	0.00483	0.00388	0.00312	0.00251	0.00202	0.00163
50 ...	0.02689	0.02132	0.01692	0.01345	0.01070	0.00852	0.00679	0.00542	0.00433	0.00346	0.00277	0.00222	0.00178	0.00143
51 ...	0.02501	0.01974	0.01560	0.01234	0.00977	0.00774	0.00615	0.00488	0.00388	0.00309	0.00246	0.00196	0.00157	0.00125
52 ...	0.02327	0.01828	0.01438	0.01132	0.00892	0.00704	0.00556	0.00440	0.00348	0.00276	0.00219	0.00174	0.00138	0.00110
53 ...	0.02164	0.01693	0.01325	0.01038	0.00815	0.00640	0.00503	0.00396	0.00312	0.00246	0.00194	0.00154	0.00122	0.00096
54 ...	0.02013	0.01567	0.01221	0.00953	0.00744	0.00582	0.00455	0.00357	0.00280	0.00220	0.00173	0.00136	0.00107	0.00085
55 ...	0.01873	0.01451	0.01126	0.00874	0.00680	0.00529	0.00412	0.00322	0.00251	0.00196	0.00154	0.00120	0.00094	0.00074
56 ...	0.01742	0.01344	0.01037	0.00802	0.00621	0.00481	0.00373	0.00290	0.00225	0.00175	0.00137	0.00107	0.00083	0.00065
57 ...	0.01621	0.01244	0.00956	0.00736	0.00567	0.00437	0.00338	0.00261	0.00202	0.00157	0.00121	0.00094	0.00073	0.00057
58 ...	0.01508	0.01152	0.00881	0.00675	0.00518	0.00397	0.00305	0.00235	0.00181	0.00140	0.00108	0.00083	0.00065	0.00050
59 ...	0.01402	0.01067	0.00812	0.00619	0.00473	0.00361	0.00276	0.00212	0.00162	0.00125	0.00096	0.00074	0.00057	0.00044
60 ...	0.01305	0.00988	0.00749	0.00568	0.00432	0.00328	0.00250	0.00191	0.00146	0.00111	0.00085	0.00065	0.00050	0.00039

Period	7.5%	8%	8.5%	9%	9.5%	10%	10.5%	11%	11.5%	12%	12.5%	13%	13.5%	14%
61 ..	0.01214	0.00914	0.00690	0.00521	0.00394	0.00299	0.00226	0.00172	0.00131	0.00099	0.00076	0.00058	0.00044	0.00034
62 ..	0.01129	0.00847	0.00636	0.00478	0.00360	0.00271	0.00205	0.00155	0.00117	0.00089	0.00067	0.00051	0.00039	0.00030
63 ..	0.01050	0.00784	0.00586	0.00439	0.00329	0.00247	0.00185	0.00140	0.00105	0.00079	0.00060	0.00045	0.00034	0.00026
64 ..	0.00977	0.00726	0.00540	0.00402	0.00300	0.00224	0.00168	0.00126	0.00094	0.00071	0.00053	0.00040	0.00030	0.00023
65 ..	0.00909	0.00672	0.00498	0.00369	0.00274	0.00204	0.00152	0.00113	0.00085	0.00063	0.00047	0.00035	0.00027	0.00020
66 ..	0.00845	0.00622	0.00459	0.00339	0.00250	0.00185	0.00137	0.00102	0.00076	0.00056	0.00042	0.00031	0.00023	0.00018
67 ..	0.00786	0.00576	0.00423	0.00311	0.00229	0.00169	0.00124	0.00092	0.00068	0.00050	0.00037	0.00028	0.00021	0.00015
68 ..	0.00732	0.00534	0.00390	0.00285	0.00209	0.00153	0.00113	0.00083	0.00061	0.00045	0.00033	0.00025	0.00018	0.00014
69 ..	0.00680	0.00494	0.00359	0.00262	0.00191	0.00139	0.00102	0.00075	0.00055	0.00040	0.00030	0.00022	0.00016	0.00012
70 ..	0.00633	0.00457	0.00331	0.00240	0.00174	0.00127	0.00092	0.00067	0.00049	0.00036	0.00026	0.00019	0.00014	0.00010
71 ..	0.00589	0.00424	0.00305	0.00220	0.00159	0.00115	0.00083	0.00061	0.00044	0.00032	0.00023	0.00017	0.00012	0.00009
72 ..	0.00548	0.00392	0.00281	0.00202	0.00145	0.00105	0.00075	0.00055	0.00039	0.00029	0.00021	0.00015	0.00011	0.00008
73 ..	0.00510	0.00363	0.00259	0.00185	0.00133	0.00095	0.00068	0.00049	0.00035	0.00026	0.00018	0.00013	0.00010	0.00007
74 ..	0.00474	0.00336	0.00239	0.00170	0.00121	0.00086	0.00062	0.00044	0.00032	0.00023	0.00016	0.00012	0.00009	0.00006
75 ..	0.00441	0.00311	0.00220	0.00156	0.00111	0.00079	0.00056	0.00040	0.00028	0.00020	0.00015	0.00010	0.00008	0.00005
76 ..	0.00410	0.00288	0.00203	0.00143	0.00101	0.00071	0.00051	0.00036'	0.00026	0.00018	0.00013	0.00009	0.00007	0.00005
77 ..	0.00382	0.00267	0.00187	0.00131	0.00092	0.00065	0.00046	0.00032	0.00023	0.00016	0.00012	0.00008	0.00006	0.00004
78 ..	0.00355	0.00247	0.00172	0.00120	0.00084	0.00059	0.00041	0.00029	0.00021	0.00014	0.00010	0.00007	0.00005	0.00004
79 ..	0.00330	0.00229	0.00159	0.00110	0.00077	0.00054	0.00038	0.00026	0.00018	0.00013	0.00009	0.00006	0.00005	0.00003
80 ..	0.00307	0.00212	0.00146	0.00101	0.00070	0.00049	0.00034	0.00024	0.00017	0.00012	0.00008	0.00006	0.00004	0.00003
81 ..	0.00286	0.00196	0.00135	0.00093	0.00064	0.00044	0.00031	0.00021	0.00015	0.00010	0.00007	0.00005	0.00004	0.00002
82 ..	0.00266	0.00182	0.00124	0.00085	0.00059	0.00040	0.00028	0.00019	0.00013	0.00009	0.00006	0.00004	0.00003	0.00002
83 ..	0.00247	0.00168	0.00115	0.00078	0.00054	0.00037	0.00025	0.00017	0.00012	0.00008	0.00006	0.00004	0.00003	0.00002
84 ..	0.00230	0.00156	0.00106	0.00072	0.00049	0.00033	0.00023	0.00016	0.00011	0.00007	0.00005	0.00003	0.00002	0.00002
85 ..	0.00214	0.00144	0.00097	0.00066	0.00045	0.00030	0.00021	0.00014	0.00010	0.00007	0.00004	0.00003	0.00002	0.00001
86 ..	0.00199	0.00134	0.00090	0.00060	0.00041	0.00028	0.00019	0.00013	0.00009	0.00006	0.00004	0.00003	0.00002	0.00001
87 ..	0.00185	0.00124	0.00083	0.00055	0.00037	0.00025	0.00017	0.00011	0.00008	0.00005	0.00004	0.00002	0.00002	0.00001
88 ..	0.00172	0.00114	0.00076	0.00051	0.00034	0.00023	0.00015	0.00010	0.00007	0.00005	0.00003	0.00002	0.00001	0.00001
89 ..	0.00160	0.00106	0.00070	0.00047	0.00031	0.00021	0.00014	0.00009	0.00006	0.00004	0.00003	0.00002	0.00001	0.00001
90 ..	0.00149	0.00098	0.00065	0.00043	0.00028	0.00019	0.00013	0.00008	0.00006	0.00004	0.00002	0.00002	0.00001	0.00001
91 ..	0.00139	0.00091	0.00060	0.00039	0.00026	0.00017	0.00011	0.00008	0.00005	0.00003	0.00002	0.00001	0.00001	0.00001
92 ..	0.00129	0.00084	0.00055	0.00036	0.00024	0.00016	0.00010	0.00007	0.00004	0.00003	0.00002	0.00001	0.00001	0.00001
93 ..	0.00120	0.00078	0.00051	0.00033	0.00022	0.00014	0.00009	0.00006	0.00004	0.00003	0.00002	0.00001	0.00001	0.00001
94 ..	0.00112	0.00072	0.00047	0.00030	0.00020	0.00013	0.00008	0.00005	0.00004	0.00002	0.00002	0.00001	0.00001	0.00000
95 ..	0.00104	0.00067	0.00043	0.00028	0.00018	0.00012	0.00008	0.00005	0.00003	0.00002	0.00001	0.00001	0.00001	0.00000
96 ..	0.00097	0.00062	0.00040	0.00026	0.00016	0.00011	0.00007	0.00004	0.00003	0.00002	0.00001	0.00001	0.00001	0.00000
97 ..	0.00090	0.00057	0.00037	0.00023	0.00015	0.00010	0.00006	0.00004	0.00003	0.00002	0.00001	0.00001	0.00000	0.00000
98 ..	0.00084	0.00053	0.00034	0.00021	0.00014	0.00009	0.00006	0.00004	0.00002	0.00002	0.00001	0.00001	0.00000	0.00000
99 ..	0.00078	0.00049	0.00031	0.00020	0.00013	0.00008	0.00005	0.00003	0.00002	0.00001	0.00001	0.00001	0.00000	0.00000
100 ..	0.00072	0.00045	0.00029	0.00018	0.00011	0.00007	0.00005	0.00003	0.00002	0.00001	0.00001	0.00000	0.00000	0.00000
101 ..	0.00067	0.00042	0.00026	0.00017	0.00010	0.00007	0.00004	0.00003	0.00002	0.00001	0.00001	0.00000	0.00000	0.00000
102 ..	0.00063	0.00039	0.00024	0.00015	0.00010	0.00006	0.00004	0.00002	0.00002	0.00001	0.00001	0.00000	0.00000	0.00000
103 ..	0.00058	0.00036	0.00022	0.00014	0.00009	0.00005	0.00003	0.00002	0.00001	0.00001	0.00001	0.00000	0.00000	0.00000
104 ..	0.00054	0.00033	0.00021	0.00013	0.00008	0.00005	0.00003	0.00002	0.00001	0.00001	0.00000	0.00000	0.00000	0.00000
105 ..	0.00050	0.00031	0.00019	0.00012	0.00007	0.00005	0.00003	0.00002	0.00001	0.00001	0.00000	0.00000	0.00000	0.00000
106 ..	0.00047	0.00029	0.00018	0.00011	0.00007	0.00004	0.00003	0.00002	0.00001	0.00001	0.00000	0.00000	0.00000	0.00000
107 ..	0.00044	0.00027	0.00016	0.00010	0.00006	0.00004	0.00002	0.00001	0.00001	0.00001	0.00000	0.00000	0.00000	0.00000
108 ..	0.00041	0.00025	0.00015	0.00009	0.00006	0.00003	0.00002	0.00001	0.00001	0.00000	0.00000	0.00000	0.00000	0.00000
109 ..	0.00038	0.00023	0.00014	0.00008	0.00005	0.00003	0.00002	0.00001	0.00001	0.00000	0.00000	0.00000	0.00000	0.00000
110 ..	0.00035	0.00021	0.00013	0.00008	0.00005	0.00003	0.00002	0.00001	0.00001	0.00000	0.00000	0.00000	0.00000	0.00000
111 ..	0.00033	0.00019	0.00012	0.00007	0.00004	0.00003	0.00002	0.00001	0.00001	0.00000	0.00000	0.00000	0.00000	0.00000
112 ..	0.00030	0.00018	0.00011	0.00006	0.00004	0.00002	0.00001	0.00001	0.00001	0.00000	0.00000	0.00000	0.00000	0.00000
113 ..	0.00028	0.00017	0.00010	0.00006	0.00004	0.00002	0.00001	0.00001	0.00000	0.00000	0.00000	0.00000	0.00000	0.00000
114 ..	0.00026	0.00015	0.00009	0.00005	0.00003	0.00002	0.00001	0.00001	0.00000	0.00000	0.00000	0.00000	0.00000	0.00000
115 ..	0.00024	0.00014	0.00008	0.00005	0.00003	0.00002	0.00001	0.00001	0.00000	0.00000	0.00000	0.00000	0.00000	0.00000
116 ..	0.00023	0.00013	0.00008	0.00005	0.00003	0.00002	0.00001	0.00001	0.00000	0.00000	0.00000	0.00000	0.00000	0.00000
117 ..	0.00021	0.00012	0.00007	0.00004	0.00002	0.00001	0.00001	0.00000	0.00000	0.00000	0.00000	0.00000	0.00000	0.00000
118 ..	0.00020	0.00011	0.00007	0.00004	0.00002	0.00001	0.00001	0.00000	0.00000	0.00000	0.00000	0.00000	0.00000	0.00000
119 ..	0.00018	0.00011	0.00006	0.00004	0.00002	0.00001	0.00001	0.00000	0.00000	0.00000	0.00000	0.00000	0.00000	0.00000
120 ..	0.00017	0.00010	0.00006	0.00003	0.00002	0.00001	0.00001	0.00000	0.00000	0.00000	0.00000	0.00000	0.00000	0.00000

TABLE G.3

(concluded)

Present Value of $1: 14.5%–20%

Period	14.5%	15%	15.5%	16%	16.5%	17%	17.5%	18%	18.5%	19%	19.5%	20%
1	0.87336	0.86957	0.86580	0.86207	0.85837	0.85470	0.85106	0.84746	0.84388	0.84034	0.83682	0.83333
2	0.76276	0.75614	0.74961	0.74316	0.73680	0.73051	0.72431	0.71818	0.71214	0.70616	0.70027	0.69444
3	0.66617	0.65752	0.64901	0.64066	0.63244	0.62437	0.61643	0.60863	0.60096	0.59342	0.58600	0.57870
4	0.58181	0.57175	0.56192	0.55229	0.54287	0.53365	0.52462	0.51579	0.50714	0.49867	0.49038	0.48225
5	0.50813	0.49718	0.48651	0.47611	0.46598	0.45611	0.44649	0.43711	0.42796	0.41905	0.41036	0.40188
6	0.44378	0.43233	0.42122	0.41044	0.39999	0.38984	0.37999	0.37043	0.36115	0.35214	0.34339	0.33490
7	0.38758	0.37594	0.36469	0.35383	0.34334	0.33320	0.32340	0.31393	0.30477	0.29592	0.28736	0.27908
8	0.33850	0.32690	0.31575	0.30503	0.29471	0.28478	0.27523	0.26604	0.25719	0.24867	0.24047	0.23257
9	0.29563	0.28426	0.27338	0.26295	0.25297	0.24340	0.23424	0.22546	0.21704	0.20897	0.20123	0.19381
10	0.25819	0.24718	0.23669	0.22668	0.21714	0.20804	0.19935	0.19106	0.18315	0.17560	0.16839	0.16151
11	0.22550	0.21494	0.20493	0.19542	0.18639	0.17781	0.16966	0.16192	0.15456	0.14757	0.14091	0.13459
12	0.19694	0.18691	0.17743	0.16846	0.15999	0.15197	0.14439	0.13722	0.13043	0.12400	0.11792	0.11216
13	0.17200	0.16253	0.15362	0.14523	0.13733	0.12989	0.12289	0.11629	0.11007	0.10421	0.09868	0.09346
14	0.15022	0.14133	0.13300	0.12520	0.11788	0.11102	0.10459	0.09855	0.09288	0.08757	0.08258	0.07789
15	0.13120	0.12289	0.11515	0.10793	0.10118	0.09489	0.08901	0.08352	0.07838	0.07359	0.06910	0.06491
16	0.11458	0.10686	0.09970	0.09304	0.08685	0.08110	0.07575	0.07078	0.06615	0.06184	0.05782	0.05409
17	0.10007	0.09293	0.08632	0.08021	0.07455	0.06932	0.06447	0.05998	0.05582	0.05196	0.04839	0.04507
18	0.08740	0.04081	0.07474	0.06914	0.06399	0.05925	0.05487	0.05083	0.04711	0.04367	0.04049	0.03756
19	0.07633	0.07027	0.06471	0.05961	0.05493	0.05064	0.04670	0.04308	0.03975	0.03670	0.03389	0.03130
20	0.06666	0.06110	0.05602	0.05139	0.04715	0.04328	0.03974	0.03651	0.03355	0.03084	0.02836	0.02608
21	0.05822	0.05313	0.04850	0.04430	0.04047	0.03699	0.03382	0.03094	0.02831	0.02591	0.02373	0.02174
22	0.05085	0.04620	0.04199	0.03819	0.03474	0.03162	0.02879	0.02622	0.02389	0.02178	0.01986	0.01811
23	0.04441	0.04017	0.03636	0.03292	0.02982	0.02702	0.02450	0.02222	0.02016	0.01830	0.01662	0.01509
24	0.03879	0.03493	0.03148	0.02838	0.02560	0.02310	0.02085	0.01883	0.01701	0.01538	0.01390	0.01258
25	0.03387	0.03038	0.02726	0.02447	0.02197	0.01974	0.01774	0.01596	0.01436	0.01292	0.01164	0.01048
26	0.02958	0.02642	0.02360	0.02109	0.01886	0.01687	0.01510	0.01352	0.01211	0.01086	0.00974	0.00874
27	0.02584	0.02297	0.02043	0.01818	0.01619	0.01442	0.01285	0.01146	0.01022	0.00912	0.00815	0.00728
28	0.02257	0.01997	0.01769	0.01567	0.01390	0.01233	0.01094	0.00971	0.00863	0.00767	0.00682	0.00607
29	0.01971	0.01737	0.01532	0.01351	0.01193	0.01053	0.00931	0.00823	0.00728	0.00644	0.00571	0.00506
30	0.01721	0.01510	0.01326	0.01165	0.01024	0.00900	0.00792	0.00697	0.00614	0.00541	0.00477	0.00421
31	0.01503	0.01313	0.01148	0.01004	0.00879	0.00770	0.00674	0.00591	0.00518	0.00455	0.00400	0.00351
32	0.01313	0.01142	0.00994	0.00866	0.00754	0.00658	0.00574	0.00501	0.00438	0.00382	0.00334	0.00293
33	0.01147	0.00993	0.00861	0.00746	0.00648	0.00562	0.00488	0.00425	0.00369	0.00321	0.00280	0.00244
34	0.01001	0.00864	0.00745	0.00643	0.00556	0.00480	0.00416	0.00360	0.00312	0.00270	0.00234	0.00203
35	0.00875	0.00751	0.00645	0.00555	0.00477	0.00411	0.00354	0.00305	0.00263	0.00227	0.00196	0.00169
36	0.00764	0.00653	0.00559	0.00478	0.00410	0.00351	0.00301	0.00258	0.00222	0.00191	0.00164	0.00141
37	0.00667	0.00568	0.00484	0.00412	0.00352	0.00300	0.00256	0.00219	0.00187	0.00160	0.00137	0.00118
38	0.00583	0.00494	0.00419	0.00355	0.00302	0.00256	0.00218	0.00186	0.00158	0.00135	0.00115	0.00098
39	0.00509	0.00429	0.00362	0.00306	0.00259	0.00219	0.00186	0.00157	0.00133	0.00113	0.00096	0.00082
40	0.00444	0.00373	0.00314	0.00264	0.00222	0.00187	0.00158	0.00133	0.00113	0.00095	0.00080	0.00068
41	0.00388	0.00325	0.00272	0.00228	0.00191	0.00160	0.00134	0.00113	0.00095	0.00080	0.00067	0.00057
42	0.00339	0.00282	0.00235	0.00196	0.00164	0.00137	0.00114	0.00096	0.00080	0.00067	0.00056	0.00047
43	0.00296	0.00245	0.00204	0.00169	0.00141	0.00117	0.00097	0.00081	0.00068	0.00056	0.00047	0.00039
44	0.00259	0.00213	0.00176	0.00146	0.00121	0.00100	0.00083	0.00069	0.00057	0.00047	0.00039	0.00033
45	0.00226	0.00186	0.00153	0.00126	0.00104	0.00085	0.00071	0.00058	0.00048	0.00040	0.00033	0.00027
46	0.00197	0.00161	0.00132	0.00108	0.00089	0.00073	0.00060	0.00049	0.00041	0.00033	0.00028	0.00023
47	0.00172	0.00140	0.00114	0.00093	0.00076	0.00062	0.00051	0.00042	0.00034	0.00028	0.00023	0.00019
48	0.00150	0.00122	0.00099	0.00081	0.00066	0.00053	0.00043	0.00035	0.00029	0.00024	0.00019	0.00016
49	0.00131	0.00106	0.00086	0.00069	0.00056	0.00046	0.00037	0.00030	0.00024	0.00020	0.00016	0.00013
50	0.00115	0.00092	0.00074	0.00060	0.00048	0.00039	0.00031	0.00025	0.00021	0.00017	0.00014	0.00011
51	0.00100	0.00080	0.00064	0.00052	0.00041	0.00033	0.00027	0.00022	0.00017	0.00014	0.00011	0.00009
52	0.00088	0.00070	0.00056	0.00044	0.00036	0.00028	0.00023	0.00018	0.00015	0.00012	0.00009	0.00008
53	0.00076	0.00061	0.00048	0.00038	0.00031	0.00024	0.00019	0.00015	0.00012	0.00010	0.00008	0.00006
54	0.00067	0.00053	0.00042	0.00033	0.00026	0.00021	0.00017	0.00013	0.00010	0.00008	0.00007	0.00005
55	0.00058	0.00046	0.00036	0.00028	0.00022	0.00018	0.00014	0.00011	0.00009	0.00007	0.00006	0.00004
56	0.00051	0.00040	0.00031	0.00025	0.00019	0.00015	0.00012	0.00009	0.00007	0.00006	0.00005	0.00004
57	0.00044	0.00035	0.00027	0.00021	0.00017	0.00013	0.00010	0.00008	0.00006	0.00005	0.00004	0.00003
58	0.00039	0.00030	0.00023	0.00018	0.00014	0.00011	0.00009	0.00007	0.00005	0.00004	0.00003	0.00003
59	0.00034	0.00026	0.00020	0.00016	0.00012	0.00009	0.00007	0.00006	0.00004	0.00003	0.00003	0.00002
60	0.00030	0.00023	0.00018	0.00014	0.00010	0.00008	0.00006	0.00005	0.00004	0.00003	0.00002	0.00002

Period	14.5%	15%	15.5%	16%	16.5%	17%	17.5%	18%	18.5%	19%	19.5%	20%
61	0.00026	0.00020	0.00015	0.00012	0.00009	0.00007	0.00005	0.00004	0.00003	0.00002	0.00002	0.00001
62	0.00023	0.00017	0.00013	0.00010	0.00008	0.00006	0.00005	0.00003	0.00003	0.00002	0.00002	0.00001
63	0.00020	0.00015	0.00011	0.00009	0.00007	0.00005	0.00004	0.00003	0.00002	0.00002	0.00001	0.00001
64	0.00017	0.00013	0.00010	0.00007	0.00006	0.00004	0.00003	0.00003	0.00002	0.00001	0.00001	0.00001
65	0.00015	0.00011	0.00009	0.00006	0.00005	0.00004	0.00003	0.00002	0.00002	0.00001	0.00001	0.00001
66	0.00013	0.00010	0.00007	0.00006	0.00004	0.00003	0.00002	0.00002	0.00001	0.00001	0.00001	0.00001
67	0.00011	0.00009	0.00006	0.00005	0.00004	0.00003	0.00002	0.00002	0.00001	0.00001	0.00001	0.00000
68	0.00010	0.00007	0.00006	0.00004	0.00003	0.00002	0.00002	0.00001	0.00001	0.00001	0.00001	0.00000
69	0.00009	0.00006	0.00005	0.00004	0.00003	0.00002	0.00001	0.00001	0.00001	0.00001	0.00000	0.00000
70	0.00008	0.00006	0.00004	0.00003	0.00002	0.00002	0.00001	0.00001	0.00001	0.00001	0.00000	0.00000
71	0.00007	0.00005	0.00004	0.00003	0.00002	0.00001	0.00001	0.00001	0.00001	0.00000	0.00000	0.00000
72	0.00006	0.00004	0.00003	0.00002	0.00002	0.00001	0.00001	0.00001	0.00000	0.00000	0.00000	0.00000
73	0.00005	0.00004	0.00003	0.00002	0.00001	0.00001	0.00001	0.00001	0.00000	0.00000	0.00000	0.00000
74	0.00004	0.00003	0.00002	0.00002	0.00001	0.00001	0.00001	0.00001	0.00000	0.00000	0.00000	0.00000
75	0.00004	0.00003	0.00002	0.00001	0.00001	0.00001	0.00001	0.00001	0.00000	0.00000	0.00000	0.00000
76	0.00003	0.00002	0.00002	0.00001	0.00001	0.00001	0.00000	0.00000	0.00000	0.00000	0.00000	0.00000
77	0.00003	0.00002	0.00002	0.00001	0.00001	0.00001	0.00000	0.00000	0.00000	0.00000	0.00000	0.00000
78	0.00003	0.00002	0.00001	0.00001	0.00001	0.00000	0.00000	0.00000	0.00000	0.00000	0.00000	0.00000
79	0.00002	0.00002	0.00001	0.00001	0.00001	0.00000	0.00000	0.00000	0.00000	0.00000	0.00000	0.00000
80	0.00002	0.00001	0.00001	0.00001	0.00000	0.00000	0.00000	0.00000	0.00000	0.00000	0.00000	0.00000
81	0.00002	0.00001	0.00001	0.00001	0.00000	0.00000	0.00000	0.00000	0.00000	0.00000	0.00000	0.00000
82	0.00002	0.00001	0.00001	0.00001	0.00000	0.00000	0.00000	0.00000	0.00000	0.00000	0.00000	0.00000
83	0.00001	0.00001	0.00001	0.00000	0.00000	0.00000	0.00000	0.00000	0.00000	0.00000	0.00000	0.00000
84	0.00001	0.00001	0.00001	0.00000	0.00000	0.00000	0.00000	0.00000	0.00000	0.00000	0.00000	0.00000
85	0.00001	0.00001	0.00000	0.00000	0.00000	0.00000	0.00000	0.00000	0.00000	0.00000	0.00000	0.00000
86	0.00001	0.00001	0.00000	0.00000	0.00000	0.00000	0.00000	0.00000	0.00000	0.00000	0.00000	0.00000
87	0.00001	0.00001	0.00000	0.00000	0.00000	0.00000	0.00000	0.00000	0.00000	0.00000	0.00000	0.00000
88	0.00001	0.00000	0.00000	0.00000	0.00000	0.00000	0.00000	0.00000	0.00000	0.00000	0.00000	0.00000
89	0.00001	0.00000	0.00000	0.00000	0.00000	0.00000	0.00000	0.00000	0.00000	0.00000	0.00000	0.00000
90	0.00001	0.00000	0.00000	0.00000	0.00000	0.00000	0.00000	0.00000	0.00000	0.00000	0.00000	0.00000
91	0.00000	0.00000	0.00000	0.00000	0.00000	0.00000	0.00000	0.00000	0.00000	0.00000	0.00000	0.00000
92	0.00000	0.00000	0.00000	0.00000	0.00000	0.00000	0.00000	0.00000	0.00000	0.00000	0.00000	0.00000
93	0.00000	0.00000	0.00000	0.00000	0.00000	0.00000	0.00000	0.00000	0.00000	0.00000	0.00000	0.00000
94	0.00000	0.00000	0.00000	0.00000	0.00000	0.00000	0.00000	0.00000	0.00000	0.00000	0.00000	0.00000
95	0.00000	0.00000	0.00000	0.00000	0.00000	0.00000	0.00000	0.00000	0.00000	0.00000	0.00000	0.00000
96	0.00000	0.00000	0.00000	0.00000	0.00000	0.00000	0.00000	0.00000	0.00000	0.00000	0.00000	0.00000
97	0.00000	0.00000	0.00000	0.00000	0.00000	0.00000	0.00000	0.00000	0.00000	0.00000	0.00000	0.00000
98	0.00000	0.00000	0.00000	0.00000	0.00000	0.00000	0.00000	0.00000	0.00000	0.00000	0.00000	0.00000
99	0.00000	0.00000	0.00000	0.00000	0.00000	0.00000	0.00000	0.00000	0.00000	0.00000	0.00000	0.00000
100	0.00000	0.00000	0.00000	0.00000	0.00000	0.00000	0.00000	0.00000	0.00000	0.00000	0.00000	0.00000
101	0.00000	0.00000	0.00000	0.00000	0.00000	0.00000	0.00000	0.00000	0.00000	0.00000	0.00000	0.00000
102	0.00000	0.00000	0.00000	0.00000	0.00000	0.00000	0.00000	0.00000	0.00000	0.00000	0.00000	0.00000
103	0.00000	0.00000	0.00000	0.00000	0.00000	0.00000	0.00000	0.00000	0.00000	0.00000	0.00000	0.00000
104	0.00000	0.00000	0.00000	0.00000	0.00000	0.00000	0.00000	0.00000	0.00000	0.00000	0.00000	0.00000
105	0.00000	0.00000	0.00000	0.00000	0.00000	0.00000	0.00000	0.00000	0.00000	0.00000	0.00000	0.00000
106	0.00000	0.00000	0.00000	0.00000	0.00000	0.00000	0.00000	0.00000	0.00000	0.00000	0.00000	0.00000
107	0.00000	0.00000	0.00000	0.00000	0.00000	0.00000	0.00000	0.00000	0.00000	0.00000	0.00000	0.00000
108	0.00000	0.00000	0.00000	0.00000	0.00000	0.00000	0.00000	0.00000	0.00000	0.00000	0.00000	0.00000
109	0.00000	0.00000	0.00000	0.00000	0.00000	0.00000	0.00000	0.00000	0.00000	0.00000	0.00000	0.00000
110	0.00000	0.00000	0.00000	0.00000	0.00000	0.00000	0.00000	0.00000	0.00000	0.00000	0.00000	0.00000
111	0.00000	0.00000	0.00000	0.00000	0.00000	0.00000	0.00000	0.00000	0.00000	0.00000	0.00000	0.00000
112	0.00000	0.00000	0.00000	0.00000	0.00000	0.00000	0.00000	0.00000	0.00000	0.00000	0.00000	0.00000
113	0.00000	0.00000	0.00000	0.00000	0.00000	0.00000	0.00000	0.00000	0.00000	0.00000	0.00000	0.00000
114	0.00000	0.00000	0.00000	0.00000	0.00000	0.00000	0.00000	0.00000	0.00000	0.00000	0.00000	0.00000
115	0.00000	0.00000	0.00000	0.00000	0.00000	0.00000	0.00000	0.00000	0.00000	0.00000	0.00000	0.00000
116	0.00000	0.00000	0.00000	0.00000	0.00000	0.00000	0.00000	0.00000	0.00000	0.00000	0.00000	0.00000
117	0.00000	0.00000	0.00000	0.00000	0.00000	0.00000	0.00000	0.00000	0.00000	0.00000	0.00000	0.00000
118	0.00000	0.00000	0.00000	0.00000	0.00000	0.00000	0.00000	0.00000	0.00000	0.00000	0.00000	0.00000
119	0.00000	0.00000	0.00000	0.00000	0.00000	0.00000	0.00000	0.00000	0.00000	0.00000	0.00000	0.00000
120	0.00000	0.00000	0.00000	0.00000	0.00000	0.00000	0.00000	0.00000	0.00000	0.00000	0.00000	0.00000

TABLE G.4

Present Value of an Ordinary Annuity of $1 per Period: 0.5%–7%

$$P_{A_{i,n}} = \frac{1 - \dfrac{1}{(1 + i)^n}}{i}$$

Period	.5%	1%	1.5%	2%	2.5%	3%	3.5%	4%	4.5%	5%	5.5%	6%	6.5%	7%
1	0.99502	0.99010	0.98522	0.98039	0.97561	0.97087	0.96618	0.96154	0.95694	0.95238	0.94787	0.94340	0.93897	0.93458
2	1.98510	1.97040	1.95588	1.94156	1.92742	1.91347	1.89969	1.88609	1.87267	1.85941	1.84632	1.83339	1.82063	1.80802
3	2.97025	2.94099	2.91220	2.88388	2.85602	2.82861	2.80164	2.77509	2.74896	2.72325	2.69793	2.67301	2.64848	2.62432
4	3.95050	3.90197	3.85438	3.80773	3.76197	3.71710	3.67308	3.62990	3.58753	3.54595	3.50515	3.46511	3.42580	3.38721
5	4.92587	4.85343	4.78264	4.71346	4.64583	4.57971	4.51505	4.45182	4.38998	4.32948	4.27028	4.21236	4.15568	4.10020
6	5.89638	5.79548	5.69719	5.60143	5.50813	5.41719	5.32855	5.24214	5.15787	5.07569	4.99553	4.91732	4.84101	4.76654
7	6.86207	6.72819	6.59821	6.47199	6.34939	6.23028	6.11454	6.00205	5.89270	5.78637	5.68297	5.58238	5.48452	5.38929
8	7.82296	7.65168	7.48593	7.32548	7.17014	7.01969	6.87396	6.73274	6.59589	6.46321	6.33457	6.20979	6.08875	5.97130
9	8.77906	8.56602	8.36052	8.16224	7.97087	7.78611	7.60769	7.43533	7.26879	7.10782	6.95220	6.80169	6.65610	6.51523
10	9.73041	9.47130	9.22218	8.98259	8.75206	8.53020	8.31661	8.11090	7.91272	7.72173	7.53763	7.36009	7.18883	7.02358
11	10.67703	10.36763	10.07112	9.78685	9.51421	9.25262	9.00155	8.76048	8.52892	8.30641	8.09254	7.88687	7.68904	7.49867
12	11.61893	11.25508	10.90751	10.57534	10.25776	9.95400	9.66333	9.38507	9.11858	8.86325	8.61852	8.38384	8.15873	7.94269
13	12.55615	12.13374	11.73153	11.34837	10.98318	10.63496	10.30274	9.98565	9.68285	9.39357	9.11708	8.85268	8.59974	8.35765
14	13.48871	13.00370	12.54338	12.10625	11.69091	11.29607	10.92052	10.56312	10.22283	9.89864	9.58965	9.29498	9.01384	8.74547
15	14.41662	13.86505	13.34323	12.84926	12.38138	11.93794	11.51741	11.11839	10.73955	10.37966	10.03758	9.71225	9.40267	9.10791
16	15.33993	14.71787	14.13126	13.57771	13.05500	12.56110	12.09412	11.65230	11.23402	10.83777	10.46216	10.10590	9.76776	9.44665
17	16.25863	15.56225	14.90765	14.29187	13.71220	13.16612	12.65132	12.16567	11.70719	11.27407	10.86461	10.47726	10.11058	9.76322
18	17.17277	16.39827	15.67256	14.99203	14.35336	13.75351	13.18968	12.65930	12.15999	11.68959	11.24607	10.82760	10.43247	10.05909
19	18.08236	17.22601	16.42617	15.67846	14.97889	14.32380	13.70984	13.13394	12.59329	12.08532	11.60765	11.15812	10.73471	10.33560
20	18.98742	18.04555	17.16864	16.35143	15.58916	14.87747	14.21240	13.59033	13.00794	12.46221	11.95038	11.46992	11.01851	10.59401
21	19.88798	18.85698	17.90014	17.01121	16.18455	15.41502	14.69797	14.02916	13.40472	12.82115	12.27524	11.76408	11.28498	10.83553
22	20.78406	19.66038	18.62082	17.65805	16.76541	15.93692	15.16712	14.45112	13.78442	13.16300	12.58317	12.04158	11.53520	11.06124
23	21.67568	20.45582	19.33086	18.29220	17.33211	16.44361	15.62041	14.85684	14.14777	13.48857	12.87504	12.30338	11.77014	11.27219
24	22.56287	21.24339	20.03041	18.91393	17.88499	16.93554	16.05837	15.24696	14.49548	13.79864	13.15170	12.55036	11.99074	11.46933
25	23.44554	22.02316	20.71961	19.52346	18.42438	17.41315	16.48151	15.62208	14.82821	14.09394	13.41393	12.78336	12.19788	11.65358
26	24.32402	22.79520	21.39863	20.12104	18.95061	17.87684	16.89035	15.98277	15.14661	14.37519	13.66250	13.00317	12.39237	11.82578
27	25.19803	23.55961	22.06762	20.70690	19.46401	18.32703	17.28536	16.32959	15.45130	14.64303	13.89810	13.21053	12.57500	11.98671
28	26.06769	24.31644	22.72672	21.28127	19.96489	18.76411	17.66702	16.66306	15.74287	14.89813	14.12142	13.40616	12.74648	12.13711
29	26.93302	25.06579	23.37608	21.84438	20.45355	19.18845	18.03577	16.98371	16.02189	15.14107	14.33310	13.59072	12.90749	12.27767
30	27.79405	25.80771	24.01584	22.39646	20.93029	19.60044	18.39205	17.29203	16.28889	15.37245	14.53375	13.76483	13.05868	12.40904
31	28.65080	26.54229	24.64615	22.93770	21.39541	20.00043	18.73628	17.58849	16.54439	15.59281	14.72393	13.92909	13.20063	12.53181
32	29.50328	27.26959	25.26714	23.46833	21.84918	20.38877	19.06887	17.87355	16.78889	15.80268	14.90420	14.08404	13.33393	12.64656
33	30.35153	27.98969	25.87895	23.98856	22.29188	20.76579	19.39021	18.14765	17.02286	16.00255	15.07507	14.23023	13.45909	12.75379
34	31.19555	28.70267	26.48173	24.49859	22.72379	21.13184	19.70068	18.41120	17.24676	16.19290	15.23703	14.36814	13.57661	12.85401
35	32.03537	29.40858	27.07559	24.99862	23.14516	21.48722	20.00066	18.66461	17.46101	16.37419	15.39055	14.49825	13.68696	12.94767
36	32.87102	30.10751	27.66068	25.48884	23.55625	21.83225	20.29049	18.90828	17.66604	16.54685	15.53607	14.62099	13.79057	13.03521
37	33.70250	30.79951	28.23713	25.96945	23.95732	22.16724	20.57053	19.14258	17.86224	16.71129	15.67400	14.73678	13.88786	13.11702
38	34.52985	31.48466	28.80505	26.44064	24.34860	22.49246	20.84109	19.36786	18.04999	16.86789	15.80474	14.84602	13.97921	13.19347
39	35.35309	32.16303	29.36458	26.90259	24.73034	22.80822	21.10250	19.58448	18.22966	17.01704	15.92866	14.94907	14.06499	13.26493
40	36.17223	32.83469	29.91585	27.35548	25.10278	23.11477	21.35507	19.79277	18.40158	17.15909	16.04630	15.04630	14.14553	13.33171
41	36.98729	33.49969	30.45896	27.79949	25.46612	23.41240	21.59910	19.99305	18.56611	17.29437	16.15746	15.13802	14.22115	13.39412
42	37.79830	34.15811	30.99405	28.23419	25.82061	23.70136	21.83488	20.18563	18.72355	17.42321	16.26300	15.22454	14.29216	13.45245
43	38.60527	34.81001	31.52123	28.66156	26.16645	23.98190	22.06269	20.37079	18.87421	17.54591	16.36303	15.30617	14.35884	13.50696
44	39.40823	35.45545	32.04062	29.07996	26.50385	24.25427	22.28279	20.54884	19.01838	17.66277	16.45785	15.38318	14.42144	13.55791
45	40.20720	36.09451	32.55234	29.49016	26.83302	24.51871	22.49545	20.72004	19.15635	17.77407	16.54773	15.45583	14.48023	13.60552
46	41.00219	36.72724	33.05649	29.89231	27.15417	24.77545	22.70092	20.88465	19.28837	17.88007	16.63292	15.52437	14.53543	13.65002
47	41.79322	37.35370	33.55319	30.28658	27.46748	25.02471	22.89944	21.04294	19.41471	17.98102	16.71366	15.58903	14.58725	13.69161
48	42.58032	37.97396	34.04255	30.67312	27.77315	25.26671	23.09124	21.19513	19.53561	18.07716	16.79020	15.65003	14.63592	13.73047
49	43.36350	38.58808	34.52468	31.05208	28.07137	25.50166	23.27656	21.34147	19.65130	18.16872	16.86275	15.70757	14.68161	13.76680
50	44.14279	39.19612	34.99969	31.42361	28.36231	25.72976	23.45562	21.48218	19.76201	18.25593	16.93152	15.76186	14.72452	13.80075
51	44.91820	39.79814	35.46767	31.78785	28.64616	25.95123	23.62862	21.61749	19.86795	18.33898	16.99670	15.81308	14.76481	13.83247
52	45.68975	40.39419	35.92874	32.14495	28.92308	26.16624	23.79576	21.74758	19.96933	18.41807	17.05848	15.86139	14.80264	13.86212
53	46.45746	40.98435	36.38300	32.49505	29.19325	26.37499	23.95726	21.87267	20.06634	18.49340	17.11705	15.90697	14.83816	13.88984
54	47.22135	41.56866	36.83054	32.83828	29.45683	26.57766	24.11330	21.99296	20.15918	18.56515	17.17255	15.94998	14.87151	13.91573
55	47.98145	42.14719	37.27147	33.17479	29.71398	26.77443	24.26405	22.10861	20.24802	18.63347	17.22517	15.99054	14.90282	13.93994
56	48.73776	42.71999	37.70588	33.50469	29.96486	26.96544	24.40971	22.21982	20.33303	18.69854	17.27504	16.02881	14.93223	13.96256
57	49.49031	43.28712	38.13387	33.82813	30.20962	27.15094	24.55045	22.32675	20.41439	18.76052	17.32232	16.06492	14.95984	13.98370
58	50.23911	43.84863	38.55554	34.14523	30.44841	27.33101	24.68642	22.42957	20.49224	18.81954	17.36712	16.09898	14.98577	14.00346
59	50.98419	44.40459	38.97097	34.45610	30.68137	27.50583	24.81780	22.52843	20.56673	18.87575	17.40960	16.13111	15.01011	14.02192
60	51.72556	44.95504	39.38027	34.76089	30.90866	27.67556	24.94473	22.62349	20.63802	18.92929	17.44985	16.16143	15.03297	14.03918

Period	.5%	1%	1.5%	2%	2.5%	3%	3.5%	4%	4.5%	5%	5.5%	6%	6.5%	7%
61 ...	52.46324	45.50004	39.78352	35.05969	31.13040	27.84035	25.06738	22.71489	20.70624	18.98028	17.48801	16.19003	15.05443	14.05531
62 ...	53.19726	46.03964	40.18080	35.35264	31.34673	28.00034	25.18587	22.80278	20.77152	19.02883	17.52418	16.21701	15.07458	14.07038
63 ...	53.92762	46.57390	40.57222	35.63984	31.55778	28.15567	25.30036	22.88729	20.83399	19.07508	17.55847	16.24246	15.09350	14.08447
64 ...	54.65435	47.10287	40.95785	35.92141	31.76369	28.30648	25.41097	22.96855	20.89377	19.11912	17.59096	16.26647	15.11127	14.09764
65 ...	55.37746	47.62661	41.33779	36.19747	31.96458	28.45289	25.51785	23.04668	20.95098	19.16107	17.62177	16.28912	15.12795	14.10994
66 ...	56.09698	48.14516	41.71210	36.46810	32.16056	28.59504	25.62111	23.12181	21.00572	19.20102	17.65096	16.31049	15.14362	14.12144
67 ...	56.81291	48.65857	42.08089	36.73343	32.35177	28.73305	25.72088	23.19405	21.05811	19.23907	17.67864	16.33065	15.15833	14.13219
68 ...	57.52529	49.16690	42.44423	36.99356	32.53831	28.86704	25.81727	23.26351	21.10824	19.27530	17.70487	16.34967	15.17214	14.14223
69 ...	58.23411	49.67020	42.80219	37.24859	32.72030	28.99712	25.91041	23.33030	21.15621	19.30981	17.72974	16.36762	15.18511	14.15162
70 ...	58.93942	50.16851	43.15487	37.49862	32.89786	29.12342	26.00040	23.39451	21.20211	19.34268	17.75330	16.38454	15.19728	14.16039
71 ...	59.64121	50.66190	43.50234	37.74374	33.07108	29.24604	26.08734	23.45626	21.24604	19.37398	17.77564	16.40051	15.20872	14.16859
72 ...	60.33951	51.15039	43.84467	37.98406	33.24008	29.36509	26.17134	23.51564	21.28808	19.40379	17.79682	16.41558	15.21945	14.17625
73 ...	61.03434	51.63405	44.18194	38.21967	33.40495	29.48067	26.25251	23.57273	21.32830	19.43218	17.81689	16.42979	15.22953	14.18341
74 ...	61.72571	52.11292	44.51422	38.45066	33.56581	29.59288	26.33092	23.62762	21.36680	19.45922	17.83591	16.44320	15.23900	14.19010
75 ...	62.41365	52.58705	44.84160	38.67711	33.72274	29.70183	26.40669	23.68041	21.40363	19.48497	17.85395	16.45585	15.24788	14.19636
76 ...	63.09815	53.05649	45.16414	38.89913	33.87584	29.80760	26.47989	23.73116	21.43888	19.50950	17.87104	16.46778	15.25623	14.20220
77 ...	63.77926	53.52127	45.48191	39.11680	34.02521	29.91029	26.55062	23.77996	21.47262	19.53285	17.88724	16.47904	15.26407	14.20767
78 ...	64.45697	53.98146	45.79498	39.33019	34.17094	30.00999	26.61896	23.82689	21.50490	19.55510	17.90260	16.48966	15.27142	14.21277
79 ...	65.13132	54.43709	46.10343	39.53940	34.31311	30.10679	26.68498	23.87201	21.53579	19.57628	17.91716	16.49968	15.27833	14.21755
80 ...	65.80231	54.88821	46.40732	39.74451	34.45182	30.20076	26.74878	23.91539	21.56534	19.59646	17.93095	16.50913	15.28482	14.22201
81 ...	66.46996	55.33486	46.70672	39.94560	34.58714	30.29200	26.81041	23.95711	21.59363	19.61568	17.94403	16.51805	15.29091	14.22617
82 ...	67.13428	55.77709	47.00170	40.14275	34.71916	30.38059	26.86996	23.99722	21.62070	19.63398	17.95643	16.52646	15.29663	14.23007
83 ...	67.79531	56.21494	47.29231	40.33603	34.84796	30.46659	26.92750	24.03579	21.64660	19.65141	17.96818	16.53440	15.30200	14.23371
84 ...	68.45304	56.64845	47.57863	40.52552	34.97362	30.55009	26.98309	24.07287	21.67139	19.66801	17.97932	16.54188	15.30704	14.23711
85 ...	69.10750	57.07768	47.86072	40.71129	35.09621	30.63115	27.03680	24.10853	21.69511	19.68382	17.98987	16.54895	15.31178	14.24029
86 ...	69.75871	57.50265	48.13864	40.89342	35.21582	30.70986	27.08870	24.14282	21.71781	19.69887	17.99988	16.55561	15.31622	14.24326
87 ...	70.40668	57.92342	48.41246	41.07198	35.33251	30.78627	27.13884	24.17579	21.73953	19.71321	18.00936	16.56190	15.32040	14.24604
88 ...	71.05142	58.34002	48.68222	41.24704	35.44635	30.86045	27.18728	24.20749	21.76032	19.72687	18.01835	16.56783	15.32431	14.24864
89 ...	71.69296	58.75249	48.94800	41.41867	35.55741	30.93248	27.23409	24.23797	21.78021	19.73987	18.02688	16.57342	15.32800	14.25106
90 ...	72.33130	59.16088	49.20985	41.58693	35.66577	31.00241	27.27932	24.26728	21.79924	19.75226	18.03495	16.57870	15.33145	14.25333
91 ...	72.96647	59.56523	49.46784	41.75189	35.77148	31.07030	27.32301	24.29546	21.81746	19.76406	18.04261	16.58368	15.33470	14.25545
92 ...	73.59847	59.96557	49.72201	41.91362	35.87462	31.13621	27.36523	24.32256	21.83489	19.77529	18.04987	16.58838	15.33774	14.25743
93 ...	74.22734	60.36195	49.97242	42.07218	35.97524	31.20021	27.40602	24.34861	21.85156	19.78599	18.05675	16.59281	15.34060	14.25928
94 ...	74.85307	60.75441	50.21913	42.22762	36.07340	31.26234	27.44543	24.37367	21.86753	19.79619	18.06327	16.59699	15.34329	14.26101
95 ...	75.47569	61.14298	50.46220	42.38002	36.16917	31.32266	27.48350	24.39776	21.88280	19.80589	18.06945	16.60093	15.34581	14.26262
96 ...	76.09522	61.52770	50.70168	42.52943	36.26261	31.38122	27.52029	24.42092	21.89742	19.81513	18.07531	16.60465	15.34818	14.26413
97 ...	76.71166	61.90862	50.93761	42.67592	36.35376	31.43808	27.55584	24.44319	21.91140	19.82394	18.08086	16.60816	15.35040	14.26555
98 ...	77.32503	62.28576	51.17006	42.81953	36.44269	31.49328	27.59018	24.46461	21.92479	19.83232	18.08612	16.61147	15.35249	14.26687
99 ...	77.93536	62.65917	51.39907	42.96032	36.52946	31.54687	27.62337	24.48520	21.93760	19.84031	18.09111	16.61460	15.35445	14.26810
100 ...	78.54264	63.02888	51.62470	43.09835	36.61411	31.59891	27.65543	24.50500	21.94985	19.84791	18.09584	16.61755	15.35629	14.26925
101 ...	79.14691	63.39493	51.84700	43.23368	36.69669	31.64942	27.68640	24.52404	21.96158	19.85515	18.10032	16.62033	15.35802	14.27033
102 ...	79.74817	63.75736	52.06601	43.36635	36.77726	31.69847	27.71633	24.54234	21.97281	19.86205	18.10457	16.62295	15.35964	14.27133
103 ...	80.34644	64.11619	52.28178	43.49642	36.85586	31.74609	27.74525	24.55995	21.98355	19.86862	18.10860	16.62542	15.36117	14.27228
104 ...	80.94173	64.47148	52.49437	43.62394	36.93255	31.79232	27.77318	24.57687	21.99382	19.87488	18.11241	16.62776	15.36260	14.27315
105 ...	81.53406	64.82325	52.70381	43.74896	37.00736	31.83720	27.80018	24.59315	22.00366	19.88083	18.11603	16.62996	15.36394	14.27398
106 ...	82.12344	65.17153	52.91016	43.87153	37.08035	31.88078	27.82626	24.60879	22.01307	19.88651	18.11946	16.63204	15.36521	14.27474
107 ...	82.70989	65.51637	53.11346	43.99170	37.15156	31.92308	27.85146	24.62384	22.02208	19.89191	18.12271	16.63400	15.36639	14.27546
108 ...	83.29342	65.85779	53.31375	44.10951	37.22104	31.96416	27.87581	24.63831	22.03070	19.89706	18.12579	16.63585	15.36750	14.27613
109 ...	83.87405	66.19583	53.51108	44.22501	37.28882	32.00404	27.89933	24.65222	22.03894	19.90196	18.12872	16.63759	15.36855	14.27676
110 ...	84.45180	66.53053	53.70550	44.33824	37.35494	32.04276	27.92206	24.66560	22.04684	19.90663	18.13148	16.63924	15.36953	14.27735
111 ...	85.02666	66.86191	53.89704	44.44926	37.41946	32.08035	27.94402	24.67846	22.05439	19.91108	18.13411	16.64079	15.37045	14.27789
112 ...	85.59867	67.19001	54.08576	44.55810	37.48240	32.11684	27.96523	24.69082	22.06162	19.91531	18.13659	16.64226	15.37131	14.27840
113 ...	86.16783	67.51486	54.27168	44.66480	37.54380	32.15227	27.98573	24.70272	22.06853	19.91934	18.13895	16.64364	15.37212	14.27888
114 ...	86.73416	67.83649	54.45486	44.76941	37.60371	32.18667	28.00554	24.71415	22.07515	19.92318	18.14119	16.64494	15.37289	14.27933
115 ...	87.29767	68.15494	54.63533	44.87197	37.66216	32.22007	28.02467	24.72514	22.08148	19.92684	18.14331	16.64617	15.37360	14.27975
116 ...	87.85838	68.47024	54.81313	44.97252	37.71918	32.25250	28.04316	24.73571	22.08754	19.93033	18.14531	16.64733	15.37428	14.28014
117 ...	88.41630	68.78242	54.98831	45.07110	37.77481	32.28398	28.06103	24.74588	22.09334	19.93364	18.14722	16.64843	15.37491	14.28050
118 ...	88.97144	69.09150	55.16089	45.16775	37.82908	32.31454	28.07829	24.75565	22.09889	19.93680	18.14902	16.64946	15.37550	14.28084
119 ...	89.52382	69.39753	55.33093	45.26250	37.88203	32.34421	28.09496	24.76505	22.10420	19.93981	18.15073	16.65043	15.37606	14.28116
120 ...	90.07345	69.70052	55.49845	45.35539	37.93369	32.37302	28.11108	24.77409	22.10929	19.94268	18.15235	16.65135	15.37658	14.28146

TABLE G.4

(continued)

Present Value of an Ordinary Annuity of $1 per Period: 7.5%–14%

Period	7.5%	8%	8.5%	9%	9.5%	10%	10.5%	11%	11.5%	12%	12.5%	13%	13.5%	14%
1	0.93023	0.92593	0.92166	0.91743	0.91324	0.90909	0.90498	0.90090	0.89686	0.89286	0.88889	0.88496	0.88106	0.87719
2	1.79557	1.78326	1.77111	1.75911	1.74725	1.73554	1.72396	1.71252	1.70122	1.69005	1.67901	1.66810	1.65732	1.64666
3	2.60053	2.57710	2.55402	2.53129	2.50891	2.48685	2.46512	2.44371	2.42262	2.40183	2.38134	2.36115	2.34125	2.32163
4	3.34933	3.31213	3.27560	3.23972	3.20448	3.16987	3.13586	3.10245	3.06961	3.03735	3.00564	2.97447	2.94383	2.91371
5	4.04588	3.99271	3.94064	3.88965	3.83971	3.79079	3.74286	3.69590	3.64988	3.60478	3.56057	3.51723	3.47474	3.43308
6	4.69385	4.62288	4.55359	4.48592	4.41983	4.35526	4.29218	4.23054	4.17029	4.11141	4.05384	3.99755	3.94250	3.88867
7	5.29660	5.20637	5.11851	5.03295	4.94961	4.86842	4.78930	4.71220	4.63704	4.56376	4.49230	4.42261	4.35463	4.28830
8	5.85730	5.74664	5.63918	5.53482	5.43344	5.33493	5.23919	5.14612	5.05564	4.96764	4.88205	4.79877	4.71774	4.63886
9	6.37889	6.24689	6.11906	5.99525	5.87528	5.75902	5.64632	5.53705	5.43106	5.32825	5.22848	5.13166	5.03765	4.94637
10	6.86408	6.71008	6.56135	6.41766	6.27880	6.14457	6.01477	5.88923	5.76777	5.65022	5.53643	5.42624	5.31952	5.21612
11	7.31542	7.13896	6.96898	6.80519	6.64730	6.49506	6.34821	6.20652	6.06975	5.93770	5.81016	5.68694	5.56786	5.45273
12	7.73528	7.53608	7.34469	7.16073	6.98384	6.81369	6.64996	6.49236	6.34058	6.19437	6.05348	5.91765	5.78666	5.66029
13	8.12584	7.90378	7.69095	7.48690	7.29118	7.10336	6.92304	6.74987	6.58348	6.42355	6.26976	6.12181	5.97943	5.84236
14	8.48915	8.24424	8.01010	7.78615	7.57185	7.36669	7.17018	6.98187	6.80133	6.62817	6.46201	6.30249	6.14928	6.00207
15	8.82712	8.55948	8.30424	8.06069	7.82818	7.60608	7.39382	7.19087	6.99671	6.81086	6.63289	6.46238	6.29893	6.14217
16	9.14151	8.85137	8.57533	8.31256	8.06226	7.82371	7.59622	7.37916	7.17194	6.97399	6.78479	6.60388	6.43077	6.26506
17	9.43396	9.12164	8.82519	8.54363	8.27604	8.02155	7.77939	7.54879	7.32909	7.11963	6.91982	6.72909	6.54694	6.37286
18	9.70601	9.37189	9.05548	8.75563	8.47127	8.20141	7.94515	7.70162	7.47004	7.24967	7.03984	6.83991	6.64928	6.46742
19	9.95908	9.60360	9.26772	8.95011	8.64956	8.36492	8.09515	7.83929	7.59644	7.36578	7.14652	6.93797	6.73946	6.55037
20	10.19449	9.81815	9.46334	9.12855	8.81238	8.51356	8.23091	7.96333	7.70982	7.46944	7.24135	7.02475	6.81890	6.62313
21	10.41348	10.01680	9.64363	9.29224	8.96108	8.64869	8.35376	8.07507	7.81149	7.56200	7.32565	7.10155	6.88890	6.68696
22	10.61719	10.20074	9.80980	9.44243	9.09688	8.77154	8.46494	8.17574	7.90269	7.64465	7.40058	7.16951	6.95057	6.74294
23	10.80669	10.37106	9.96295	9.58021	9.22089	8.88322	8.56556	8.26643	7.98447	7.71843	7.46718	7.22966	7.00491	6.79206
24	10.98297	10.52876	10.10410	9.70661	9.33415	8.98474	8.65662	8.34814	8.05782	7.78432	7.52638	7.28288	7.05279	6.83514
25	11.14695	10.67478	10.23419	9.82258	9.43758	9.07704	8.73902	8.42174	8.12361	7.84314	7.57901	7.32998	7.09497	6.87293
26	11.29948	10.80998	10.35409	9.92897	9.53203	9.16095	8.81359	8.48806	8.18261	7.89566	7.62578	7.37167	7.13213	6.90608
27	11.44138	10.93516	10.46460	10.02658	9.61830	9.23722	8.88108	8.54780	8.23552	7.94255	7.66736	7.40856	7.16487	6.93515
28	11.57338	11.05108	10.56645	10.11613	9.69707	9.30657	8.94215	8.60162	8.28298	7.98442	7.70432	7.44120	7.19372	6.96066
29	11.69617	11.15841	10.66033	10.19828	9.76902	9.36961	8.99742	8.65011	8.32554	8.02181	7.73717	7.47009	7.21914	6.98304
30	11.81039	11.25778	10.74684	10.27365	9.83472	9.42691	9.04744	8.69379	8.36371	8.05518	7.76638	7.49565	7.24153	7.00266
31	11.91664	11.34980	10.82658	10.34280	9.89472	9.47901	9.09271	8.73315	8.39795	8.08499	7.79234	7.51828	7.26126	7.01988
32	12.01548	11.43500	10.90008	10.40624	9.94952	9.52638	9.13367	8.76860	8.42866	8.11159	7.81541	7.53830	7.27864	7.03498
33	12.10742	11.51389	10.96781	10.46444	9.99956	9.56943	9.17074	8.80054	8.45619	8.13535	7.83592	7.55602	7.29396	7.04823
34	12.19295	11.58693	11.03024	10.51784	10.04526	9.60857	9.20429	8.82932	8.48089	8.15656	7.85415	7.57170	7.30745	7.05985
35	12.27251	11.65457	11.08778	10.56682	10.08699	9.64416	9.23465	8.85524	8.50304	8.17550	7.87036	7.58557	7.31934	7.07005
36	12.34652	11.71719	11.14081	10.61176	10.12511	9.67651	9.26213	8.87859	8.52291	8.19241	7.88476	7.59785	7.32982	7.07899
37	12.41537	11.77518	11.18969	10.65299	10.15992	9.70592	9.28700	8.89963	8.54072	8.20751	7.89757	7.60872	7.33904	7.08683
38	12.47941	11.82887	11.23474	10.69082	10.19171	9.73265	9.30950	8.91859	8.55670	8.22099	7.90895	7.61833	7.34718	7.09371
39	12.53899	11.87858	11.27625	10.72552	10.22074	9.75696	9.32986	8.93567	8.57103	8.23303	7.91906	7.62684	7.35434	7.09975
40	12.59441	11.92461	11.31452	10.75736	10.24725	9.77905	9.34829	8.95105	8.58389	8.24378	7.92806	7.63438	7.36065	7.10504
41	12.64596	11.96723	11.34979	10.78657	10.27146	9.79914	9.36497	8.96491	8.59541	8.25337	7.93605	7.64104	7.36621	7.10969
42	12.69392	12.00670	11.38229	10.81337	10.29357	9.81740	9.38006	8.97740	8.60575	8.26194	7.94316	7.64694	7.37111	7.11376
43	12.73853	12.04324	11.41225	10.83795	10.31376	9.83400	9.39372	8.98865	8.61502	8.26959	7.94947	7.65216	7.37543	7.11733
44	12.78003	12.07707	11.43986	10.86051	10.33220	9.84909	9.40608	8.99878	8.62334	8.27642	7.95509	7.65678	7.37923	7.12047
45	12.81863	12.10840	11.46531	10.88120	10.34904	9.86281	9.41727	9.00791	8.63080	8.28252	7.96008	7.66086	7.38258	7.12322
46	12.85454	12.13741	11.48877	10.90018	10.36442	9.87528	9.42729	9.01614	8.63749	8.28796	7.96451	7.66448	7.38554	7.12563
47	12.88794	12.16427	11.51038	10.91760	10.37847	9.88662	9.43656	9.02355	8.64349	8.29282	7.96846	7.66768	7.38814	7.12774
48	12.91902	12.18914	11.53031	10.93358	10.39130	9.89693	9.44485	9.03022	8.64887	8.29716	7.97196	7.67052	7.39043	7.12960
49	12.94792	12.21216	11.54867	10.94823	10.40301	9.90630	9.45235	9.03624	8.65369	8.30104	7.97508	7.67302	7.39245	7.13123
50	12.97481	12.23348	11.56560	10.96168	10.41371	9.91481	9.45914	9.04165	8.65802	8.30450	7.97785	7.67524	7.39423	7.13266
51	12.99982	12.25323	11.58119	10.97402	10.42348	9.92256	9.46529	9.04653	8.66190	8.30759	7.98031	7.67720	7.39580	7.13391
52	13.02309	12.27151	11.59557	10.98534	10.43240	9.92960	9.47085	9.05093	8.66538	8.31035	7.98250	7.67894	7.39718	7.13501
53	13.04474	12.28843	11.60882	10.99573	10.44055	9.93600	9.47588	9.05489	8.66850	8.31281	7.98444	7.68048	7.39839	7.13597
54	13.06487	12.30410	11.62103	11.00525	10.44799	9.94182	9.48043	9.05846	8.67130	8.31501	7.98617	7.68184	7.39947	7.13682
55	13.08360	12.31861	11.63229	11.01399	10.45478	9.94711	9.48456	9.06168	8.67382	8.31697	7.98771	7.68304	7.40041	7.13756
56	13.10103	12.33205	11.64266	11.02201	10.46099	9.95191	9.48829	9.06457	8.67607	8.31872	7.98907	7.68411	7.40124	7.13821
57	13.11723	12.34449	11.65222	11.02937	10.46666	9.95629	9.49166	9.06718	8.67809	8.32029	7.99029	7.68505	7.40198	7.13878
58	13.13231	12.35601	11.66104	11.03612	10.47183	9.96026	9.49472	9.06954	8.67990	8.32169	7.99137	7.68589	7.40262	7.13928
59	13.14633	12.36668	11.66916	11.04231	10.47656	9.96387	9.49748	9.07165	8.68152	8.32294	7.99232	7.68663	7.40319	7.13972
60	13.15938	12.37655	11.67664	11.04799	10.48088	9.96716	9.49998	9.07356	8.68298	8.32405	7.99318	7.68728	7.40369	7.14011

Period	7.5%	8%	8.5%	9%	9.5%	10%	10.5%	11%	11.5%	12%	12.5%	13%	13.5%	14%
61	13.17152	12.38570	11.68354	11.05320	10.48482	9.97014	9.50225	9.07528	8.68429	8.32504	7.99394	7.68786	7.40413	7.14044
62	13.18281	12.39416	11.68990	11.05798	10.48842	9.97286	9.50430	9.07683	8.68546	8.32593	7.99461	7.68837	7.40452	7.14074
63	13.19331	12.40200	11.69576	11.06237	10.49171	9.97532	9.50615	9.07822	8.68651	8.32673	7.99521	7.68882	7.40487	7.14100
64	13.20308	12.40926	11.70116	11.06640	10.49471	9.97757	9.50783	9.07948	8.68745	8.32743	7.99574	7.68922	7.40517	7.14123
65	13.21217	12.41598	11.70614	11.07009	10.49745	9.97961	9.50935	9.08061	8.68830	8.32807	7.99621	7.68958	7.40544	7.14143
66	13.22062	12.42221	11.71073	11.07347	10.49996	9.98146	9.51072	9.08163	8.68906	8.32863	7.99663	7.68989	7.40567	7.14160
67	13.22848	12.42797	11.71496	11.07658	10.50224	9.98315	9.51196	9.08255	8.68974	8.32913	7.99701	7.69017	7.40588	7.14176
68	13.23580	12.43330	11.71885	11.07943	10.50433	9.98468	9.51309	9.08338	8.69035	8.32958	7.99734	7.69042	7.40606	7.14189
69	13.24260	12.43825	11.72245	11.08205	10.50624	9.98607	9.51411	9.08413	8.69090	8.32999	7.99764	7.69063	7.40622	7.14201
70	13.24893	12.44282	11.72576	11.08445	10.50798	9.98734	9.51503	9.08480	8.69139	8.33034	7.99790	7.69083	7.40636	7.14211
71	13.25482	12.44706	11.72881	11.08665	10.50957	9.98849	9.51586	9.08541	8.69183	8.33066	7.99813	7.69100	7.40648	7.14221
72	13.26030	12.45098	11.73162	11.08867	10.51102	9.98954	9.51662	9.08595	8.69222	8.33095	7.99834	7.69115	7.40659	7.14229
73	13.26539	12.45461	11.73421	11.09052	10.51235	9.99049	9.51730	9.08644	8.69257	8.33121	7.99852	7.69128	7.40669	7.14236
74	13.27013	12.45797	11.73660	11.09222	10.51356	9.99135	9.51792	9.08688	8.69289	8.33143	7.99869	7.69140	7.40678	7.14242
75	13.27454	12.46108	11.73880	11.09378	10.51467	9.99214	9.51848	9.08728	8.69318	8.33164	7.99883	7.69150	7.40685	7.14247
76	13.27864	12.46397	11.74083	11.09521	10.51568	9.99285	9.51899	9.08764	8.69343	8.33182	7.99896	7.69160	7.40692	7.14252
77	13.28246	12.46664	11.74270	11.09653	10.51660	9.99350	9.51945	9.08797	8.69366	8.33198	7.99908	7.69168	7.40698	7.14256
78	13.28601	12.46911	11.74443	11.09773	10.51744	9.99409	9.51986	9.08826	8.69387	8.33213	7.99918	7.69175	7.40703	7.14260
79	13.28931	12.47140	11.74601	11.09883	10.51821	9.99463	9.52024	9.08852	8.69405	8.33226	7.99927	7.69181	7.40707	7.14263
80	13.29238	12.47351	11.74748	11.09985	10.51892	9.99512	9.52057	9.08876	8.69422	8.33237	7.99935	7.69187	7.40711	7.14266
81	13.29524	12.47548	11.74883	11.10078	10.51956	9.99556	9.52088	9.08897	8.69436	8.33247	7.99942	7.69192	7.40715	7.14268
82	13.29790	12.47729	11.75007	11.10163	10.52015	9.99597	9.52116	9.08916	8.69450	8.33257	7.99949	7.69197	7.40718	7.14270
83	13.30037	12.47897	11.75122	11.10241	10.52068	9.99633	9.52141	9.08934	8.69462	8.33265	7.99955	7.69201	7.40721	7.14272
84	13.30267	12.48053	11.75228	11.10313	10.52117	9.99667	9.52164	9.08949	8.69472	8.33272	7.99960	7.69204	7.40723	7.14274
85	13.30481	12.48197	11.75325	11.10379	10.52162	9.99697	9.52185	9.08963	8.69482	8.33279	7.99964	7.69207	7.40725	7.14275
86	13.30680	12.48331	11.75415	11.10440	10.52202	9.99724	9.52203	9.08976	8.69490	8.33285	7.99968	7.69210	7.40727	7.14277
87	13.30865	12.48455	11.75497	11.10495	10.52240	9.99749	9.52220	9.08987	8.69498	8.33290	7.99972	7.69212	7.40729	7.14278
88	13.31037	12.48569	11.75574	11.10546	10.52274	9.99772	9.52235	9.08998	8.69505	8.33294	7.99975	7.69214	7.40730	7.14279
89	13.31197	12.48675	11.75644	11.10593	10.52305	9.99793	9.52249	9.09007	8.69511	8.33299	7.99978	7.69216	7.40731	7.14280
90	13.31346	12.48773	11.75709	11.10635	10.52333	9.99812	9.52262	9.09015	8.69517	8.33302	7.99980	7.69218	7.40732	7.14280
91	13.31485	12.48864	11.75768	11.10675	10.52359	9.99829	9.52273	9.09023	8.69522	8.33306	7.99982	7.69219	7.40733	7.14281
92	13.31614	12.48948	11.75823	11.10711	10.52383	9.99844	9.52283	9.09029	8.69526	8.33309	7.99984	7.69221	7.40734	7.14282
93	13.31734	12.49026	11.75874	11.10744	10.52404	9.99859	9.52293	9.09036	8.69530	8.33311	7.99986	7.69222	7.40735	7.14282
94	13.31846	12.49098	11.75921	11.10774	10.52424	9.99871	9.52301	9.09041	8.69534	8.33314	7.99988	7.69223	7.40736	7.14283
95	13.31949	12.49165	11.75964	11.10802	10.52442	9.99883	9.52309	9.09046	8.69537	8.33316	7.99989	7.69224	7.40736	7.14283
96	13.32046	12.49227	11.76004	11.10827	10.52458	9.99893	9.52315	9.09050	8.69540	8.33318	7.99990	7.69225	7.40737	7.14283
97	13.32136	12.49284	11.76040	11.10851	10.52473	9.99903	9.52322	9.09054	8.69543	8.33319	7.99991	7.69225	7.40737	7.14284
98	13.32219	12.49337	11.76074	11.10872	10.52487	9.99912	9.52327	9.09058	8.69545	8.33321	7.99992	7.69226	7.40738	7.14284
99	13.32297	12.49386	11.76105	11.10892	10.52500	9.99920	9.52332	9.09061	8.69547	8.33322	7.99993	7.69226	7.40738	7.14284
100	13.32369	12.49432	11.76134	11.10910	10.52511	9.99927	9.52337	9.09064	8.69549	8.33323	7.99994	7.69227	7.40738	7.14284
101	13.32437	12.49474	11.76160	11.10927	10.52522	9.99934	9.52341	9.09067	8.69551	8.33324	7.99995	7.69227	7.40739	7.14284
102	13.32499	12.49513	11.76184	11.10942	10.52531	9.99940	9.52345	9.09069	8.69552	8.33325	7.99995	7.69228	7.40739	7.14285
103	13.32557	12.49549	11.76207	11.10956	10.52540	9.99945	9.52348	9.09071	8.69553	8.33326	7.99996	7.69228	7.40739	7.14285
104	13.32611	12.49582	11.76227	11.10969	10.52548	9.99950	9.52351	9.09073	8.69555	8.33327	7.99996	7.69228	7.40739	7.14285
105	13.32662	12.49613	11.76246	11.10981	10.52555	9.99955	9.52354	9.09075	8.69556	8.33328	7.99997	7.69229	7.40739	7.14285
106	13.32709	12.49642	11.76264	11.10991	10.52562	9.99959	9.52357	9.09077	8.69557	8.33328	7.99997	7.69229	7.40740	7.14285
107	13.32752	12.49668	11.76280	11.11001	10.52568	9.99963	9.52359	9.09078	8.69558	8.33329	7.99997	7.69229	7.40740	7.14285
108	13.32793	12.49693	11.76295	11.11010	10.52573	9.99966	9.52361	9.09079	8.69558	8.33329	7.99998	7.69229	7.40740	7.14285
109	13.32831	12.49716	11.76309	11.11019	10.52578	9.99969	9.52363	9.09080	8.69559	8.33330	7.99998	7.69230	7.40740	7.14285
110	13.32866	12.49737	11.76322	11.11026	10.52583	9.99972	9.52365	9.09082	8.69560	8.33330	7.99998	7.69230	7.40740	7.14285
111	13.32898	12.49756	11.76333	11.11033	10.52587	9.99975	9.52366	9.09082	8.69560	8.33330	7.99998	7.69230	7.40740	7.14285
112	13.32929	12.49774	11.76344	11.11040	10.52591	9.99977	9.52368	9.09083	8.69561	8.33331	7.99999	7.69230	7.40740	7.14285
113	13.32957	12.49791	11.76354	11.11046	10.52595	9.99979	9.52369	9.09084	8.69561	8.33331	7.99999	7.69230	7.40740	7.14285
114	13.32983	12.49807	11.76363	11.11051	10.52598	9.99981	9.52370	9.09085	8.69562	8.33331	7.99999	7.69230	7.40740	7.14285
115	13.33008	12.49821	11.76371	11.11056	10.52601	9.99983	9.52371	9.09085	8.69562	8.33332	7.99999	7.69230	7.40740	7.14286
116	13.33030	12.49834	11.76379	11.11060	10.52603	9.99984	9.52372	9.09086	8.69562	8.33332	7.99999	7.69230	7.40740	7.14286
117	13.33051	12.49846	11.76386	11.11065	10.52606	9.99986	9.52373	9.09086	8.69563	8.33332	7.99999	7.69230	7.40740	7.14286
118	13.33071	12.49858	11.76393	11.11069	10.52608	9.99987	9.52374	9.09087	8.69563	8.33332	7.99999	7.69230	7.40741	7.14286
119	13.33089	12.49868	11.76399	11.11072	10.52610	9.99988	9.52374	9.09087	8.69563	8.33332	7.99999	7.69230	7.40741	7.14286
120	13.33106	12.49878	11.76405	11.11075	10.52612	9.99989	9.52375	9.09088	8.69563	8.33332	7.99999	7.69230	7.40741	7.14286

TABLE G.4

(concluded)

Present Value of an Ordinary Annuity of $1 per Period: 14.5%–20%

Period	14.5%	15%	15.5%	16%	16.5%	17%	17.5%	18%	18.5%	19%	19.5%	20%
1	0.87336	0.86957	0.86580	0.86207	0.85837	0.85470	0.85106	0.84746	0.84388	0.84034	0.83682	0.83333
2	1.63612	1.62571	1.61541	1.60523	1.59517	1.58521	1.57537	1.56564	1.55602	1.54650	1.53709	1.52778
3	2.30229	2.28323	2.26443	2.24589	2.22761	2.20958	2.19181	2.17427	2.15698	2.13992	2.12309	2.10648
4	2.88410	2.85498	2.82634	2.79818	2.77048	2.74324	2.71643	2.69006	2.66412	2.63859	2.61346	2.58873
5	3.39223	3.35216	3.31285	3.27429	3.23646	3.19935	3.16292	3.12717	3.09208	3.05763	3.02382	2.99061
6	3.83600	3.78448	3.73407	3.68474	3.63645	3.58918	3.54291	3.49760	3.45323	3.40978	3.36721	3.32551
7	4.22358	4.16042	4.09876	4.03857	3.97979	3.92238	3.86631	3.81153	3.75800	3.70570	3.65457	3.60459
8	4.56208	4.48732	4.41451	4.34359	4.27449	4.20716	4.14154	4.07757	4.01519	3.95437	3.89504	3.83716
9	4.85771	4.77158	4.68789	4.60654	4.52746	4.45057	4.37578	3.30302	4.23223	4.16333	4.09627	4.03097
10	5.11591	5.01877	4.92458	4.83323	4.74460	4.65860	4.57513	4.49409	4.41538	4.33893	4.26466	4.19247
11	5.34140	5.23371	5.12951	5.02864	4.93099	4.83641	4.74479	4.65601	4.56994	4.48650	4.40557	4.32706
12	5.53834	5.42062	5.30693	5.19711	5.09098	4.98839	4.88918	4.79322	4.70037	4.61050	4.52349	4.43922
13	5.71034	5.58315	5.46055	5.34233	5.22831	5.11828	5.01207	4.90951	4.81044	4.71471	4.62217	4.53268
14	5.86056	5.72448	5.59355	5.46753	5.34619	5.22930	5.11666	5.00806	4.90333	4.80228	4.70474	4.61057
15	5.99176	5.84737	5.70870	5.57546	5.44747	5.32419	5.20567	5.09158	4.98171	4.87586	4.77384	4.67547
16	6.10634	5.95423	5.80840	5.66850	5.53422	5.40529	5.28142	5.16235	5.04786	4.93770	4.83167	4.72956
17	6.20641	6.04716	5.89472	5.74870	5.60878	5.47461	5.34589	5.22233	5.10368	4.98966	4.88006	4.77463
18	6.29381	6.12797	5.96945	5.81785	5.67277	5.53385	5.40075	5.27316	5.15078	5.03331	4.92055	4.81219
19	6.37014	6.19823	6.03416	5.87746	5.72770	5.58449	5.44745	5.31624	5.19053	5.07003	4.95443	4.84350
20	6.43680	6.25933	6.09018	5.92884	5.77485	5.62777	5.48719	5.35275	5.22408	5.10086	4.98279	4.86958
21	6.49502	6.31246	6.13868	5.97314	5.81532	5.66476	5.52101	5.38368	5.25239	5.12677	5.00652	4.89132
22	6.54587	6.35866	6.18068	6.01133	5.85006	5.69637	5.54980	5.40990	5.27628	5.14855	5.02638	4.90943
23	6.59028	6.39884	6.21704	6.04425	5.87988	5.72340	5.57430	5.43212	5.29644	5.16685	5.04299	4.92453
24	6.62907	6.43377	6.24852	6.07263	5.90548	5.74649	5.59515	5.45095	5.31345	5.18223	5.05690	4.93710
25	6.66294	6.46415	6.27577	6.09709	5.92745	5.76623	5.61289	5.46691	5.32780	5.19515	5.06853	4.94759
26	6.69252	6.49056	6.29937	6.11818	5.94631	5.78311	5.62799	5.48043	5.33992	5.20601	5.07827	4.95632
27	6.71836	6.51353	6.31980	6.13636	5.96250	5.79753	5.64084	5.49189	5.35014	5.21513	5.08642	4.96360
28	6.74093	6.53351	6.33749	6.15204	5.97639	5.80985	5.65178	5.50160	5.35877	5.22280	5.09324	4.96967
29	6.76064	6.55088	6.35281	6.16555	5.98832	5.82039	5.66109	5.50983	5.36605	5.22924	5.09894	4.97472
30	6.77785	6.56598	6.36607	6.17720	5.99856	5.82939	5.66901	5.51681	5.37219	5.23466	5.10372	4.97894
31	6.79288	6.57911	6.37755	6.18724	6.00734	5.83709	5.67576	5.52272	5.37738	5.23921	5.10771	4.98245
32	6.80601	6.59053	6.38749	6.19590	6.01489	5.84366	5.68150	5.52773	5.38175	5.24303	5.11106	4.98537
33	6.81747	6.60046	6.39609	6.20336	6.02136	5.84928	5.68638	5.53197	5.38545	5.24625	5.11386	4.98781
34	6.82749	6.60910	6.40354	6.20979	6.02692	5.85409	5.69054	5.53557	5.38856	5.24895	5.11620	4.98984
35	6.83623	6.61661	6.40999	6.21534	6.03169	5.85820	5.69407	5.53862	5.39119	5.25122	5.11816	4.99154
36	6.84387	6.62314	6.41558	6.22012	6.03579	5.86171	5.69708	5.54120	5.39341	5.25312	5.11980	4.99295
37	6.85054	6.62881	6.42041	6.22424	6.03930	5.86471	5.69965	5.54339	5.39528	5.25472	5.12117	4.99412
38	6.85637	6.63375	6.42460	6.22779	6.04232	5.86727	5.70183	5.54525	5.39686	5.25607	5.12232	4.99510
39	6.86146	6.63805	6.42823	6.23086	6.04491	5.86946	5.70368	5.54682	5.39820	5.25720	5.12328	4.99592
40	6.86590	6.64178	6.43136	6.23350	6.04713	5.87133	5.70526	5.54815	5.39932	5.25815	5.12408	4.99660
41	6.86978	6.64502	6.43408	6.23577	6.04904	5.87294	5.70660	5.54928	5.40027	5.25895	5.12475	4.99717
42	6.87317	6.64785	6.43643	6.23774	6.05068	5.87430	5.70775	5.55024	5.40107	5.25962	5.12532	4.99764
43	6.87613	6.65030	6.43847	6.23943	6.05208	5.87547	5.70872	5.55105	5.40175	5.26019	5.12579	4.99803
44	6.87872	6.65244	6.44024	6.24089	6.05329	5.87647	5.70955	5.55174	5.40232	5.26066	5.12618	4.99836
45	6.88098	6.65429	6.44176	6.24214	6.05433	5.87733	5.71026	5.55232	5.40280	5.26106	5.12651	4.99863
46	6.88295	6.65591	6.44308	6.24323	6.05522	5.87806	5.71086	5.55281	5.40321	5.26140	5.12679	4.99886
47	6.88467	6.65731	6.44423	6.24416	6.05598	5.87868	5.71137	5.55323	5.40355	5.26168	5.12702	4.99905
48	6.88618	6.65853	6.44522	6.24497	6.05664	5.87922	5.71180	5.55359	5.40384	5.26191	5.12721	4.99921
49	6.88749	6.65959	6.44608	6.24566	6.05720	5.87967	5.71217	5.55389	5.40409	5.26211	5.12738	4.99934
50	6.88864	6.66051	6.44682	6.24626	6.05768	5.88006	5.71249	5.55414	5.40429	5.26228	5.12751	4.99945
51	6.88964	6.66132	6.44746	6.24678	6.05809	5.88039	5.71275	5.55436	5.40447	5.26242	5.12762	4.99954
52	6.89052	6.66201	6.44802	6.24722	6.05845	5.88068	5.71298	5.55454	5.40461	5.26254	5.12772	4.99962
53	6.89128	6.66262	6.44850	6.24760	6.05876	5.88092	5.71318	5.55469	5.40474	5.26264	5.12780	4.99968
54	6.89195	6.66315	6.44892	6.24793	6.05902	5.88113	5.71334	5.55483	5.40484	5.26272	5.12786	4.99974
55	6.89253	6.66361	6.44928	6.24822	6.05924	5.88131	5.71348	5.55494	5.40493	5.26279	5.12792	4.99978
56	6.89304	6.66401	6.44959	6.24846	6.05944	5.88146	5.71360	5.55503	5.40500	5.26285	5.12797	4.99982
57	6.89348	6.66435	6.44987	6.24868	6.05960	5.88159	5.71370	5.55511	5.40507	5.26290	5.12801	4.99985
58	6.89387	6.66466	6.45010	6.24886	6.05974	5.88170	5.71379	5.55518	5.40512	5.26294	5.12804	4.99987
59	6.89421	6.66492	6.45030	6.24902	6.05987	5.88180	5.71386	5.55524	5.40516	5.26297	5.12807	4.99989
60	6.89451	6.66515	6.45048	6.24915	6.05997	5.88188	5.71393	5.55529	5.40520	5.26300	5.12809	4.99991

Period	14.5%	15%	15.5%	16%	16.5%	17%	17.5%	18%	18.5%	19%	19.5%	20%
61	6.89477	6.66534	6.45063	6.24927	6.06006	5.88195	5.71398	5.55533	5.40523	5.26303	5.12811	4.99993
62	6.89499	6.66552	6.45076	6.24937	6.06014	5.88200	5.71403	5.55536	5.40526	5.26305	5.12812	4.99994
63	6.89519	6.66567	6.45088	6.24946	6.06020	5.88206	5.71406	5.55539	5.40528	5.26307	5.12814	4.99995
64	6.89536	6.66580	6.45098	6.24953	6.06026	5.88210	5.71413	5.55542	5.40530	5.26308	5.12815	4.99996
65	6.89551	6.66591	6.45106	6.24960	6.06031	5.88214	5.71415	5.55544	5.40532	5.26309	5.12816	4.99996
66	6.89565	6.66601	6.45114	6.24965	6.06035	5.88217	5.71415	5.55546	5.40533	5.26310	5.12816	4.99997
67	6.89576	6.66609	6.45120	6.24970	6.06039	5.88219	5.71417	5.55547	5.40534	5.26311	5.12817	4.99998
68	6.89586	6.66617	6.45125	6.24974	6.06042	5.88222	5.71419	5.55548	5.40535	5.26312	5.12818	4.99998
69	6.89595	6.66623	6.45130	6.24978	6.06045	5.88224	5.71420	5.55549	5.40536	5.26313	5.12818	4.99998
70	6.89602	6.66629	6.45134	6.24981	6.06047	5.88225	5.71421	5.55550	5.40537	5.26313	5.12819	4.99999
71	6.89609	6.66634	6.45138	6.24983	6.06049	5.88227	5.71422	5.55551	5.40537	5.26314	5.12819	4.99999
72	6.89615	6.66638	6.45141	6.24986	6.06050	5.88228	5.71423	5.55552	5.40538	5.26314	5.12819	4.99999
73	6.89620	6.66642	6.45144	6.24988	6.06052	5.88229	5.71424	5.55552	5.40538	5.26314	5.12820	4.99999
74	6.89624	6.66645	6.45146	6.24989	6.06053	5.88230	5.71425	5.55553	5.40539	5.26314	5.12820	4.99999
75	6.89628	6.66648	6.45148	6.24991	6.06054	5.88231	5.71425	5.55553	5.40539	5.26315	5.12820	4.99999
76	6.89632	6.66650	6.45150	6.24992	6.06055	5.88231	5.71426	5.55554	5.40539	5.26315	5.12820	5.00000
77	6.89635	6.66653	6.45151	6.24993	6.06056	5.88232	5.71426	5.55554	5.40540	5.26315	5.12820	5.00000
78	6.89637	6.66654	6.45153	6.24994	6.06057	5.88232	5.71427	5.55554	5.40540	5.26315	5.12820	5.00000
79	6.89640	6.66656	6.45154	6.24995	6.06057	5.88233	5.71427	5.55555	5.40540	5.26315	5.12820	5.00000
80	6.89642	6.66657	6.45155	6.24996	6.06058	5.88233	5.71427	5.55555	5.40540	5.26315	5.12820	5.00000
81	6.89643	6.66659	6.45156	6.24996	6.06058	5.88234	5.71427	5.55555	5.40540	5.26315	5.12820	5.00000
82	6.89645	6.66660	6.45157	6.24997	6.06058	5.88234	5.71428	5.55555	5.40540	5.26315	5.12820	5.00000
83	6.89646	6.66661	6.45157	6.24997	6.06059	5.88234	5.71428	5.55555	5.40540	5.26316	5.12820	5.00000
84	6.89647	6.66661	6.45158	6.24998	6.06059	5.88234	5.71428	5.55555	5.40540	5.26316	5.12820	5.00000
85	6.89648	6.66662	6.45158	6.24998	6.06059	5.88234	5.71428	5.55555	5.40540	5.26316	5.12820	5.00000
86	6.89649	6.66663	6.45159	6.24998	6.06059	5.88234	5.71428	5.55555	5.40540	5.26316	5.12820	5.00000
87	6.89650	6.66663	6.45159	6.24998	6.06060	5.88235	5.71428	5.55555	5.40540	5.26316	5.12820	5.00000
88	6.89651	6.66664	6.45159	6.24999	6.06060	5.88235	5.71428	5.55555	5.40540	5.26316	5.12820	5.00000
89	6.89651	6.66664	6.45160	6.24999	6.06060	5.88235	5.71428	5.55555	5.40540	5.26316	5.12820	5.00000
90	6.89652	6.66664	6.45160	6.24999	6.06060	5.88235	5.71428	5.55555	5.40540	5.26316	5.12820	5.00000
91	6.89652	6.66665	6.45160	6.24999	6.06060	5.88235	5.71428	5.55555	5.40540	5.26316	5.12820	5.00000
92	6.89652	6.66665	6.45160	6.24999	6.06060	5.88235	5.71428	5.55555	5.40540	5.26316	5.12820	5.00000
93	6.89653	6.66665	6.45160	6.24999	6.06060	5.88235	5.71428	5.55555	5.40540	5.26316	5.12820	5.00000
94	6.89653	6.66665	6.45160	6.24999	6.06060	5.88235	5.71428	5.55555	5.40540	5.26316	5.12820	5.00000
95	6.89653	6.66666	6.45161	6.25000	6.06060	5.88235	5.71428	5.55555	5.40540	5.26316	5.12820	5.00000
96	6.89654	6.66666	6.45161	6.25000	6.06060	5.88235	5.71428	5.55555	5.40540	5.26316	5.12820	5.00000
97	6.89654	6.66666	6.45161	6.25000	6.06060	5.88235	5.71428	5.55555	5.40541	5.26316	5.12820	5.00000
98	6.89654	6.66666	6.45161	6.25000	6.06060	5.88235	5.71428	5.55556	5.40541	5.26316	5.12820	5.00000
99	6.89654	6.66666	6.45161	6.25000	6.06060	5.88235	5.71429	5.55556	5.40541	5.26316	5.12821	5.00000
100	6.89654	6.66666	6.45161	6.25000	6.06060	5.88235	5.71429	5.55556	5.40541	5.26316	5.12821	5.00000
101	6.89654	6.66666	6.45161	6.25000	6.06060	5.88235	5.71429	5.55556	5.40541	5.26316	5.12821	5.00000
102	6.89654	6.66666	6.45161	6.25000	6.06061	5.88235	5.71429	5.55556	5.40541	5.26316	5.12821	5.00000
103	6.89655	6.66666	6.45161	6.25000	6.06061	5.88235	5.71429	5.55556	5.40541	5.26316	5.12821	5.00000
104	6.89655	6.66666	6.45161	6.25000	6.06061	5.88235	5.71429	5.55556	5.40541	5.26316	5.12821	5.00000
105	6.89655	6.66666	6.45161	6.25000	6.06061	5.88235	5.71429	5.55556	5.40541	5.26316	5.12821	5.00000
106	6.89655	6.66666	6.45161	6.25000	6.06061	5.88235	5.71429	5.55556	5.40541	5.26316	5.12821	5.00000
107	6.89655	6.66666	6.45161	6.25000	6.06061	5.88235	5.71429	5.55556	5.40541	5.26316	5.12821	5.00000
108	6.89655	6.66666	6.45161	6.25000	6.06061	5.88235	5.71429	5.55556	5.40541	5.26316	5.12821	5.00000
109	6.89655	6.66667	6.45161	6.25000	6.06061	5.88235	5.71429	5.55556	5.40541	5.26316	5.12821	5.00000
110	6.89655	6.66667	6.45161	6.25000	6.06061	5.88235	5.71429	5.55556	5.40541	5.26316	5.12821	5.00000
111	6.89655	6.66667	6.45161	6.25000	6.06061	5.88235	5.71429	5.55556	5.40541	5.26316	5.12821	5.00000
112	6.89655	6.66667	6.45161	6.25000	6.06061	5.88235	5.71429	5.55556	5.40541	5.26316	5.12821	5.00000
113	6.89655	6.66667	6.45161	6.25000	6.06061	5.88235	5.71429	5.55556	5.40541	5.26316	5.12821	5.00000
114	6.89655	6.66667	6.45161	6.25000	6.06061	5.88235	5.71429	5.55556	5.40541	5.26316	5.12821	5.00000
115	6.89655	6.66667	6.45161	6.25000	6.06061	5.88235	5.71429	5.55556	5.40541	5.26316	5.12821	5.00000
116	6.89655	6.66667	6.45161	6.25000	6.06061	5.88235	5.71429	5.55556	5.40541	5.26316	5.12821	5.00000
117	6.89655	6.66667	6.45161	6.25000	6.06061	5.88235	5.71429	5.55556	5.40541	5.26316	5.12821	5.00000
118	6.89655	6.66667	6.45161	6.25000	6.06061	5.88235	5.71429	5.55556	5.40541	5.26316	5.12821	5.00000
119	6.89655	6.66667	6.45161	6.25000	6.06061	5.88235	5.71429	5.55556	5.40541	5.26316	5.12821	5.00000
120	6.89655	6.66667	6.45161	6.25000	6.06061	5.88235	5.71429	5.55556	5.40541	5.26316	5.12821	5.00000

NEW TERMS INDEX

SUBJECT INDEX

Chart of Accounts Used Consistently in the
First Eleven Chapters of This Text (concluded)

Account Number	Account Title

Revenue and Gain Accounts (concluded)

408	Commissions Revenue
409	Legal Fees Revenue
410	Sales
411	Sales Discounts
412	Sales Returns and Allowances
413	Membership and Lesson Revenue
414	Management Fee Revenue
415	Subscriptions Revenue
418	Interest Revenue
420	Miscellaneous Revenue
421	Gain on Disposal of Plant Assets
422	Other Revenue

Cost of Goods Sold, Operating Expense, and Loss Accounts

500	Purchases
501	Purchase Discounts
502	Purchase Returns and Allowances
503	Transportation-In
504	Cost of Goods Sold
505	Advertising Expense
506	Gas and Oil Expense
507	Salaries Expense (or Wages Expense)
508	Sales Salaries Expense
509	Office Salaries Expense
510	Officers' Salaries Expense
511	Utilities Expense
512	Insurance Expense
513	Feed Expense
515	Rent Expense
516	Store Supplies Expense
518	Supplies Expense
519	Delivery Expense
520	Depreciation Expense — Buildings
521	Depreciation Expense — Trucks
522	Depreciation Expense — Automobiles
523	Depreciation Expense — Office Furniture
524	Depreciation Expense — Equipment
525	Depreciation Expense — Office Equipment
526	Depreciation Expense — Store Fixtures
527	Depreciation Expense — Machinery
528	Depreciation Expense — Land Improvements
529	Depreciation Expense — Furniture and Fixtures
530	Repairs Expense
531	Entertainment Expense
532	Travel Expense
533	Property Tax Expense